Psychology

Modules for Active Learning

Custom 13th Edition

Dennis Coon | John O. Mitterer

CENGAGE
Learning·

Australia • Brazil • Japan • Korea • Mexico • Singapore • Spain • United Kingdom • United States

CENGAGE
Learning®

Psychology: Modules for Active Learning: Custom 13th Edition

Source:

Psychology: Modules for Active Learning, 13th Edition
Dennis Coon | John O. Mitterer
© 2015, 2012 Cengage Learning. All rights reserved.

Senior Manager, Student Engagement:

Linda deStefano

Janey Moeller

Manager, Student Engagement:

Julie Dierig

Marketing Manager:

Rachael Kloos

Manager, Production Editorial:

Kim Fry

Manager, Intellectual Property Project Manager:

Brian Methe

Senior Manager, Production and Manufacturing:

Donna M. Brown

Manager, Production:

Terri Daley

For product information and technology assistance, contact us at
Cengage Learning Customer & Sales Support, 1-800-354-9706

For permission to use material from this text or product,
submit all requests online at **cengage.com/permissions**
Further permissions questions can be emailed to
permissionrequest@cengage.com

This book contains select works from existing Cengage Learning resources and was produced by Cengage Learning Custom Solutions for collegiate use. As such, those adopting and/or contributing to this work are responsible for editorial content accuracy, continuity and completeness.

Compilation © 2014 Cengage Learning

ISBN-13: 978-1-305-04525-5

ISBN-10: 1-305-04525-4

WCN: 01-100-101

Cengage Learning

5191 Natorp Boulevard
Mason, Ohio 45040
USA

Cengage Learning is a leading provider of customized learning solutions with office locations around the globe, including Singapore, the United Kingdom, Australia, Mexico, Brazil, and Japan. Locate your local office at:
international.cengage.com/region.

Cengage Learning products are represented in Canada by Nelson Education, Ltd.

For your lifelong learning solutions, visit **www.cengage.com/custom.**

Visit our corporate website at **www.cengage.com.**

Printed in the United States of America

Brief Contents

How to Study Psychology
Well, Hello There!

As your authors, we are delighted to welcome you to the "manual" for this textbook. No! Don't skip this, please. Read on.

Few of us prefer to start a new adventure by reading a manual. We just want to step off the airplane and begin our vacation, get right into that new computer game, or start using our new camera or smartphone. Please be patient. Successfully learning psychology depends on how *reflective* you are as you read your textbook, listen during your classes, study for exams, and then write them.

Students who get good grades tend to work more reflectively, or smarter, not just longer or harder. They also tend to understand and remember more of what they've learned long after their exams are over. Psychology is for their lives, not just for their exams. In this module, we explore a variety of ways to become more reflective learners.

© Blend Images/Alamy

SURVEY QUESTIONS

1.1 What is reflective learning?

1.2 What is the best way to read a textbook?

1.3 How can learning in class be improved?

1.4 What is the best way to study?

1.5 What are some ways to be a more effective test-taker?

1.6 How can procrastination be overcome?

1.7 Can digital media help with reflective processing?

Reflective Learning— Academic All-Stars

SURVEY QUESTION 1.1: What is reflective learning?

You have undoubtedly spent the occasional evening vegging out in front of the television. It probably was fun, but you may have noticed that you didn't think too much about what you were watching and that your subsequent memories are not detailed. You were engaging in **experiential processing**, more or less passively, effortlessly, and automatically soaking up the experience (Kahneman, 2011; Norman, 1994). There is usually nothing wrong with experiential processing; we humans rely on it frequently. As we will see in later modules of this book, most perception, as well as some learning, intuition, and creativity, depends in part on experiential processing.

Experiential processing is appropriate for entertainment, but it doesn't work well if your goal is to learn course material. To see why this might be the case, think back to, say, a recent job interview. It is highly unlikely that you got through the interview by relying on experiential processing alone (and even less likely that you landed the job if you did). Instead, you actively and carefully listened to the questions and put some serious effort into thinking through the implications of answering in different ways before responding. No drifting off here; you were focused and controlled until you left the interview, when you likely breathed a much-deserved sigh of relief.

By reacting mindfully (Siegel, 2007), you engaged in **reflective processing** (Kahneman, 2011; Norman, 1994). Rather than just having an experience, you *actively thought* about it. Reflective processing is involved whenever experiential processing is not enough and you must actively and effortfully control your thoughts to focus on the matter at hand.

"I'm too busy going to college to study."

Reflective learning occurs when you engage in deliberately reflective and active self-guided study (Hofer & Yu, 2003; Kaplan, 2008). Simply put, you will learn more from a textbook, a lecture, or a website if you mindfully reflect on what you are experiencing. You will also remember it better. (In memory terms, the result of reflective learning is called *elaborative processing*, which you can learn more about in Module 32.) Here, in general, is how you can change passive studying into reflective learning:

1. *Set specific, objective learning goals.* Begin each learning session with specific goals in mind. What knowledge or skills are you trying to master? What do you hope to accomplish (Burka & Yuen, 2008)?

2. *Plan a learning strategy.* How will you accomplish your goals? Make daily, weekly, and monthly plans for learning. Then put them into action.

3. *Be your own teacher.* Effective learners silently give themselves guidance and ask themselves questions. For example, as you are learning, you might ask yourself, "What are the important ideas here? What do I remember? What don't I understand? What do I need to review? What should I do next?"

4. *Monitor your progress.* Reflective learning depends on self-monitoring. Exceptional learners keep records of their progress toward learning goals (pages read, hours of studying, assignments completed, and so forth). They quiz themselves, use study guides, and find other ways to check their understanding while learning.

5. *Reward yourself.* When you meet your daily, weekly, or monthly goals, reward your efforts in some way, such as going to a movie or downloading some new music. Be aware that self-praise also rewards learning. Being able to say "Hey, I did it!" can be rewarding. In the long run, success, self-improvement, and personal satisfaction are the real payoffs for learning.

6. *Evaluate your progress and goals.* It is a good idea to frequently evaluate your performance records and goals. Do any specific areas of your work need improvement? If you are not making good progress toward long-range goals, do you need to revise your short-term targets?

7. *Take corrective action.* If you fall short of your goals, you may need to adjust how you budget your time. You may also need to change your learning environment to deal with distractions such as browsing the web, daydreaming, talking to friends, or testing the limits of your hearing with your iPod.

If you discover that you lack certain knowledge or skills, ask for help, take advantage of tutoring programs, or look for information beyond your courses and textbooks. Knowing how to reflectively control learning can be a key to life-long enrichment and personal empowerment (Van Blerkom, 2012).

Reflective Reading—How to Tame a Textbook

SURVEY QUESTION 1.2: What is the best way to read a textbook?

How can I be more reflective while reading? One powerful way to be more reflective is through **self-reference**. As you read, relate new facts, terms, and concepts to your own experiences and information you already know well. Doing this will make new ideas more personally meaningful and easier to remember. **Critical thinking** is another powerful way to be more reflective. Critical thinkers pause to evaluate, compare, analyze, critique, and synthesize what they are reading (Chaffee, 2012). You should, too. In Module 2, we will learn how to think critically about psychology.

🔴 **Figure 1.1**

The reflective SQ4R method promotes active learning and information processing. You begin with a survey of the module, or module section, depending on how much you plan to read. You then proceed through cycles of questioning, reading, reciting, and reflecting and conclude with a review of the section or the entire module.

These ways to improve learning can be combined into the **reflective SQ4R method**. SQ4R stands for *survey, question, read, recite, reflect,* and *review*, which are six steps that can help you get more out of your reading:

S = *Survey.* Skim through a module before you begin reading it. Start by looking at topic headings, figure captions, and summaries. Try to get an overall picture of what lies ahead. Because this book is organized into short modules, you can survey just one module at a time if you prefer.

Q = *Question.* As you read, reword each topic heading into one or more questions. For example, when you read the heading "Stages of Sleep," you might ask: "Is there more than one stage of sleep?" "What are the stages of sleep?" "How do they differ?" Asking questions prepares you to read with a purpose.

R1 = *Read.* The first R in SQ4R stands for *read.* As you read, look for answers to the questions you asked. Read in short bites, from one topic heading to the next, and then stop. For difficult material, you may want to read only a paragraph or two at a time.

R2 = *Recite.* After reading a small amount, you should pause and recite or rehearse. Try to mentally answer your questions. Also, make brief notes to summarize what you just read. Making notes will reveal what you do and don't know, so you can fill in gaps in your knowledge (Peverly et al., 2003).

If you can't summarize the main ideas, skim over each section again. Until you can understand and remember what you just read, there's little point to reading more. After you've studied a short bite of text, turn the next topic heading into questions. Then read to the following heading. Remember to look for answers as you read and to recite or take notes before moving on. Ask yourself repeatedly, "What is the main idea here?"

Repeat the question–read–recite cycle until you've finished an entire module (or just a part of a module if you want to read shorter units).

R3 = *Reflect.* As you read, reflect on what you are reading. As stated earlier, two powerful ways to do this are self-reference and critical thinking. This is the most important step in the reflective SQ4R method. The more mindfulness and genuine interest you can bring

to your reading, the more you will learn (Hartlep & Forsyth, 2000; Wong, 2012).

R4 = *Review.* When you're done reading, skim back over a module or read your notes. Then check your memory by reciting and quizzing yourself again. Try to make frequent, active review a standard part of your study habits (see 🔴 **Figure 1.1**).

Does this really work? You bet! Using a reflective reading strategy improves learning and course grades (Taraban, Rynearson, & Kerr, 2000). It also results in enhanced long-term understanding. Simply reading straight through a textbook can give you intellectual indigestion. That's why it's better to stop often to survey, question, recite, reflect, review, and digest information as you read.

How to Use *Psychology: Modules for Active Learning*

You can apply the reflective SQ4R method to any text. However, we have specifically designed this textbook to help you actively learn psychology. Consider trying out the following suggestions as you work through this module:

Survey Each module opens with a survey that includes a short introduction to what will be covered as well as a list of *Survey Questions.* You can use these features to identify important ideas as you begin reading. The introduction should help interest you in the topics you will be reading about, and the

Experiential processing *Thought that is passive, effortless, and automatic.*

Reflective processing *Thought that is active, effortful, and controlled.*

Reflective learning *Deliberately reflective and active self-guided study.*

Self-reference *The practice of relating new information to prior life experience.*

Critical thinking *An ability to evaluate, compare, analyze, critique, and synthesize information.*

Reflective SQ4R method *An active study–reading technique based on these steps: survey, question, read, recite, reflect, and review.*

Survey Questions are a good guide to the kinds of information you should look for as you read. In fact, answers to the Survey Questions are a good summary of the core concepts in each module. If, years from now, you still remember those core concepts, your authors will be happy indeed.

After you've studied these features, take a few minutes to do your own survey of the module, including the figure captions and module-ending material. Doing so will help you build a mental map of upcoming topics.

Question *How can I use the reflective SQ4R method to make reading more interesting and effective?* Try to actively interact with your textbooks as you read. Perhaps the most effective way to do this is to ask yourself a lot of questions as you read. For example, as noted earlier, modules and major module sections begin with headings; try turning them into questions. One Module 2 heading is Critical Thinking—Take It with a Grain of Salt. Turn this into a question that occurs to you, such as "Why should I be skeptical of what I read?" If you read with an aim toward answering your questions, you will be much more likely to get the key points in what you are reading. *Dialogue Questions* like the one that began this paragraph will also help you focus on seeking information as you read. These questions are much like those running through the minds of students like you as they read this book. Similarly, the *Survey Questions* are repeated throughout each module to help you recognize key topics. Try to anticipate these questions. Even better, be sure to ask your own questions.

Read As an aid to reading, important terms are printed in boldface type and defined when they first appear. (Some are followed by pronunciations—capital letters show which syllables are accented.) You'll also find a *running glossary* in the lower corner of pages you are reading, so you never have to guess about the meaning of technical terms. If you want to look up a term from a lecture or another module, check the main *Subject Index/Glossary*. This minidictionary is located near the end of the book. In addition, figures and tables will help you quickly grasp important concepts.

Recite and Reflect To help you study in smaller "bites," each module in this textbook ends with a study guide called a *Knowledge Builder.* By answering the *Recite* questions in the Knowledge Builders, you can check how well you remember what you just read. In addition, *Think Critically* questions invite you to reflect more deeply about the hows and whys of what you have just read, and *Self-Reflect* questions invite self-reference to help you connect new ideas to your own life. (Don't forget to take notes and recite and reflect on your own.)

This book also provides other opportunities for you to reflect on what you are reading. Every few modules, you will encounter a *Psychology in Action* module. These discussions are filled with practical ideas you can relate to your own life. In many modules, *Discovering Psychology* boxes also invite you to relate psychology to your own behavior. *Critical Thinking* boxes present intriguing questions you can use to sharpen your critical thinking skills. In addition, *Human Diversity* boxes encourage you to reflect on the rich variability of human experience; *Brainwaves* boxes show how the brain relates to psychology; and *The Clinical File* boxes show how psychology can be applied to treat clinical problems.

Review Each module concludes with a point-by-point *Summary* to help you identify psychology's big ideas and enduring principles. These summaries are organized around the same Survey Questions you read at the beginning of the module. You can also return to the glossary items throughout each module for further review.

● Table 1.1 summarizes how this text helps you apply the reflective SQ4R method. Even with all this help, there is still much more you can do on your own.

TABLE 1.1	Using the Reflective SQ4R Method
Survey	• Module-Opening Introduction • Survey Questions • Figure Captions • Module Summaries
Question	• Topic Headings • Survey Questions • In-Text Dialogue Questions
Read	• Boldface Terms • Running Glossary (in margin) • Figures and Tables
Recite	• Recite Questions (in Knowledge Builders) • Practice Quizzes (online) • Notes (make them while reading)
Reflect	• Reflect Questions, including Think Critically and Self-Reflect questions (in Knowledge Builders) • Psychology in Action Modules (throughout the text) • Boxed Features (throughout the text)
Review	• Module Summaries • Boldface Terms • Running Glossary (in margin) • Figures and Tables • Practice Quizzes (online)

Reflective Note-Taking— LISAN Up!

SURVEY QUESTION 1.3: How can learning in class be improved?

Just as studying a textbook is best done reflectively, so, too, is learning in class (Norman, 1994). Like effective reading, good notes come from actively seeking information. A **reflective listener** avoids distractions and skillfully gathers ideas. Here's a listening/note-taking plan that works for many students. The letters LISAN, pronounced like the word *listen,* will help you remember the steps:

L = *Lead. Don't follow.* Read assigned materials before coming to class. Try to anticipate what your teacher will say by asking yourself questions. If your teacher provides course notes or PowerPoint® overheads before lectures, survey them before coming to class. Reflective questions can come from those materials or from study guides, reading assignments, or your own curiosity.

I = *Ideas.* Every lecture is based on a core of ideas. Usually, an idea is followed by examples or explanations. Ask yourself often, "What is the main idea now? What ideas support it?"

S = *Signal words.* Listen for words that tell you what direction the instructor is taking. For instance, here are some signal words:

There are three reasons . . .	Here come ideas
Most important is . . .	Main idea
On the contrary . . .	Opposite idea
As an example . . .	Support for main idea
Therefore . . .	Conclusion

A = *Actively listen.* Sit where you can get involved and ask questions. Bring questions you want answered from the last lecture or from your text. Raise your hand at the beginning of class or approach your professor before the lecture. Do anything that helps you stay active, alert, and engaged.

N = *Note-taking.* Students who take accurate lecture notes tend to do well on tests (Williams & Eggert, 2002). However, don't try to be a tape recorder. Listen to everything, but be selective and write down only key points. If you are too busy writing, you may not grasp what your professor is saying. When you're taking notes, it might help to think of yourself as a reporter who is trying to get a good story (Ryan, 2001; Wong, 2012).

Most students take reasonably good notes—and then don't use them! Many students wait until just before exams to review. By then, their notes have lost much of their meaning. If you don't want your notes to seem like chicken scratches, it pays to review them daily (Ellis, 2013).

Using and Reviewing Your Notes

When you review, you will learn more if you take these extra steps (Burka & Yuen, 2008; Ellis, 2013; Santrock & Halonen, 2013):

- As soon as you can, reflect on your notes to fill in gaps, complete thoughts, and look for connections among ideas.
- Remember to link new ideas to what you already know.
- Summarize your notes. Boil them down and organize them.
- After each class session, write down several major ideas, definitions, or details that are likely to become test questions. Then, make up questions from your notes and be sure you can answer them.

Summary The letters LISAN are a guide to active listening, but listening and good note-taking are not enough. You must also review, organize, reflect, extend, and think about new ideas. Use active listening to get involved in your classes and you will undoubtedly learn more (Van Blerkom, 2012).

Reflective Study Strategies— Making a Habit of Success

SURVEY QUESTION 1.4: What is the best way to study?

Grades depend as much on effort as they do on intelligence. However, don't forget that good students work more efficiently, not just harder. Many study practices are notoriously unreflective, such as recopying lecture notes, studying class notes but not the textbook (or the textbook but not class notes), outlining modules, answering study questions with the book open, and "group study" (which often becomes a party). The best students emphasize quality: They study their books and notes in depth and attend classes regularly. It's a mistake to blame poor grades on events "beyond your control."

Reflective listener *A person who knows how to maintain attention, avoid distractions, and actively gather information from lectures.*

Students who are motivated to succeed usually get better grades (Perry et al., 2001). Let's consider a few more things you can do to improve your study habits.

Study in a Specific Place

Ideally, you should study in a quiet, well-lit area free of distractions. If possible, you should also have one place only for studying. Do nothing else there: Keep magazines, MP3 players, friends, cell phones, pets, Twitter®, video games, puzzles, food, lovers, sports cars, elephants, pianos, televisions, Facebook®, and other distractions out of the area. In this way, the habit of studying will become strongly linked with one specific place. Then, rather than trying to force yourself to study, all you have to do is go to your study area. Once there, you'll find it is relatively easy to get started.

Use Spaced Study Sessions

It is reasonable to review intensely before an exam. However, you're taking a big risk if you are only cramming (learning new information at the last minute). Spaced practice is much more efficient (Anderson, 2010a). **Spaced practice** consists of a large number of relatively short study sessions. Long, uninterrupted study sessions are called **massed practice**. (If you "massed up" your studying, you probably messed it up, too.)

Cramming places a big burden on memory. Usually, you shouldn't try to learn anything new about a subject during the last day before a test. It is far better to learn small amounts every day and review frequently.

Try Mnemonics

Learning has to start somewhere, and memorizing is often the first step. Many of the best ways to improve memory are covered in Modules 35 and 36. Let's consider just one type of technique here.

A **mnemonic** (nuh-MON-ik) is a memory aid. Mnemonics can be created in several ways. Most mnemonics link new information to ideas or images that are easy to remember. For example, what if you want to remember that the Spanish word for duck is *pato* (pronounced POT-oh)? To use a mnemonic, you could picture a duck in a pot or a duck wearing a pot for a hat. Likewise, to remember that the cerebellum controls coordination, you might picture someone named "Sarah Bellum" who is very coordinated. For best results, make your mnemonic images exaggerated or bizarre, vivid, and interactive (Macklin & McDaniel, 2005; Radvansky, 2011).

Mnemonics help make new information more familiar and memorable. Forming an image of a duck wearing a pot for a hat might help you remember that *pato* (pronounced POT-oh) is the Spanish word for duck.

Test Yourself

A great way to improve grades is to take practice tests before the real one (Karpicke & Blunt, 2011). In other words, reflective studying should include **self-testing**, in which you pose questions to yourself. You can use flash cards, Knowledge Builder Recite, Think Critically, and Self-Reflect questions, online quizzes, a study guide, or other means. As you study, ask yourself several questions and be sure you can answer them. Studying without self-testing is like practicing for a basketball game without shooting any baskets.

For more convenient self-testing, your professor may make a *Study Guide* or a separate booklet of *Practice Quizzes* available. You can use either to review for tests. Practice quizzes are also available on the *Psychology CourseMate* website, as described later. However, don't use practice quizzes as a substitute for studying your textbook and lecture notes. Trying to learn from quizzes alone will probably *lower* your grades. It is best to use quizzes to find out what topics you need to study in more depth (Brothen & Wambach, 2001).

Overlearn

Many students underprepare for exams, and most overestimate how well they will do. A solution to both problems is **overlearning**, in which you continue studying beyond your initial mastery of a topic. In other words, plan to do extra study and review after you think you are prepared for a test. One way to overlearn is to approach all tests as if they will be essays. That way, you will learn more completely, so you really know your stuff.

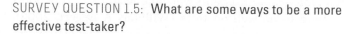

Reflective Test Taking— Are You Test Wise?

SURVEY QUESTION 1.5: What are some ways to be a more effective test-taker?

If I read, listen, and study effectively, is there anything else I can do to improve my grades? You must also be able to show what you know on tests. Here are some ways to improve your test-taking skills:

General Test-Taking Skills

You'll do better on all types of tests if you observe the following guidelines (Van Blerkom, 2012; Wood & Willoughby, 1995):

1. Read all directions and questions carefully. They may give you good advice or clues.
2. Survey the test quickly before you begin.
3. Answer easy questions before spending time on more difficult ones.
4. Be sure to answer all questions.
5. Use your time wisely.
6. Ask for clarification when necessary.

Objective Tests Several additional strategies can help you do better on objective tests. Objective tests (multiple-choice and true-false items) require you to recognize a correct answer among wrong ones or a true statement versus a false one. Here are some strategies for taking objective tests:

1. Relate the question to what you know about the topic. Then, read the alternatives. Does one match the answer you expected to find? If none match, reexamine the choices and look for a partial match.
2. Read all the choices for each question before you make a decision. Here's why: If you immediately think that *a* is correct and stop reading, you might miss seeing a better answer like both *a* and *d*.
3. Read rapidly and skip items you are unsure about. You may find free information in later questions that will help you answer difficult items.
4. Eliminate certain alternatives. With a four-choice multiple-choice test, you have one chance in four of guessing right. If you can eliminate two alternatives, your guessing odds improve to 50-50.
5. Be sure to answer any skipped items, unless there is a penalty for guessing. Even if you are not sure of the answer, you may be right. If you leave a question blank, it is automatically wrong. When you are forced to guess, don't choose the longest answer or the letter you've used the least. Both strategies lower scores more than random guessing does.
6. Following this bit of folk wisdom is a mistake: "Don't change your answers on a multiple-choice test. Your first choice is usually right." This is wrong. If you change answers, you are more likely to *gain* points than to lose them. This is especially true if you are uncertain of your first choice or it was a hunch and if your second choice is more reflective (Higham & Gerrard, 2005).
7. Search for the one best answer to each question. Some answers may be partly true, yet flawed in some way. If you are uncertain, try rating each multiple-choice alternative on a 1 to 10 scale. The answer with the highest rating is the one you are looking for.
8. Remember that few circumstances are always or never present. Answers that include superlatives such as *most, least, best, worst, largest,* or *smallest* are often false.

Essay Tests Essay questions are a weak spot for students who lack organization, don't support their ideas, or don't directly answer the question (Van Blerkom, 2012). When you take an essay exam, try the following:

1. Read the question carefully. Be sure to note key words, such as *compare, contrast, discuss, evaluate, analyze,* and *describe.* These words all demand a certain emphasis in your answer.
2. Answer the question. If the question asks for a definition and an example, make sure you provide both. Providing just a definition or just an example will get you half marks.
3. Reflect on your answer for a few minutes and list the main points you want to make. Just write them as they come to mind. Then rearrange the ideas in a logical order and begin writing. Elaborate plans or outlines are not necessary.
4. Don't beat around the bush or pad your answer. Be direct. Make a point and support it. Get your list of ideas into words.
5. Look over your essay for errors in spelling and grammar. Save this for last. Your ideas are more important. You can work on spelling and grammar separately if they affect your grades.

Short-Answer Tests Tests that ask you to fill in a blank, define a term, or list specific items can be difficult. Usually, the questions themselves contain little information. If you don't know the answer, you won't get much help from the questions.

Spaced practice *Practice spread over many relatively short study sessions.*
Massed practice *Practice done in a long, uninterrupted study session.*
Mnemonic *A memory aid or strategy.*
Self-testing *Evaluating learning by posing questions to yourself.*
Overlearning *Continuing to study and learn after you think you've mastered a topic.*

The best way to prepare for short-answer tests is to over-learn the details of the course. As you study, pay special attention to lists of related terms.

Again, it is best to start with the questions whose answers you're sure you know. Follow that by completing the questions whose answers you think you probably know. Questions whose answers you have no idea about can be left blank.

See ● **Figure 1.2** for a summary of study skills.

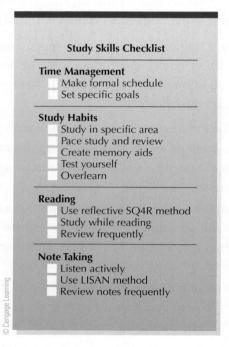

Study Skills Checklist

Time Management
- [ ] Make formal schedule
- [ ] Set specific goals

Study Habits
- [ ] Study in specific area
- [ ] Pace study and review
- [ ] Create memory aids
- [ ] Test yourself
- [ ] Overlearn

Reading
- [ ] Use reflective SQ4R method
- [ ] Study while reading
- [ ] Review frequently

Note Taking
- [ ] Listen actively
- [ ] Use LISAN method
- [ ] Review notes frequently

© Cengage Learning

● **Figure 1.2**

Procrastination— Avoid the Last-Minute Blues

SURVEY QUESTION 1.6: How can procrastination be overcome?

All these reflective techniques are fine. But what can I do about procrastination? A tendency to procrastinate is almost universal. Even when procrastination doesn't lead to failure, it can cause much suffering (Sirois & Tosti, 2012; Wohl, Pychyl, & Bennett, 2010). Procrastinators work only under pressure, skip classes, give false reasons for late work, and feel ashamed of their last-minute efforts. They also tend to feel frustrated, bored, and guilty more often (Blunt & Pychyl, 2005).

Why do so many students procrastinate? Many students equate grades with their *personal worth*—that is, they act as if grades tell whether they are good, smart people who will succeed in life. By procrastinating, they can blame poor work on a late start, rather than a lack of ability (Beck, Koons, & Milgrim, 2000). After all, it wasn't their best effort, was it?

Perfectionism is a related problem. If you expect the impossible, it's hard to start an assignment. Students with high standards often end up with all-or-nothing work habits (Onwuegbuzie, 2000).

Time Management

Most procrastinators must eventually face the self-worth issue. Nevertheless, most can improve by learning study skills and better time management. We have already discussed general study skills, so let's consider time management in a little more detail.

A **weekly time schedule** is a written plan that allocates time for study, work, and leisure activities. To prepare your schedule, make a chart showing all the hours in each day of the week. Then fill in times that are already committed: sleep, meals, classes, work, team practices, lessons, appointments, and so forth. Next, fill in times when you will study for various classes. Finally, label the remaining hours as open or free times.

Each day, you can use your schedule as a checklist. That way you'll know at a glance which tasks are done and which still need attention (Burka & Yuen, 2008).

You may also find it valuable to make a **term schedule** that lists the dates of all quizzes, tests, reports, papers, and other major assignments for each class.

Be sure to treat your study times as serious commitments, but respect your free times, too. And remember, students who study hard and practice time management *do* get better grades (Rau & Durand, 2000).

Goal Setting

As mentioned earlier, students who are reflective, active learners set **specific goals** for studying. Such goals should be clear-cut and measurable (Burka & Yuen, 2008). If you find it hard to stay motivated, try setting goals for the semester, the week, the day, and even for single study sessions. Also, be aware that more effort early in a course can greatly reduce the stress you might experience later. If your professors don't give frequent assignments, set your own day-by-day goals. That way, you can turn big assignments into a series of smaller tasks that you can complete (Ariely & Wertenbroch, 2002). An example would be reading, studying, and reviewing eight pages a day to complete a forty-page chapter in five days. For this textbook, reading one module every day or two might be a good pace. Remember, many small steps can add up to an impressive journey.

Make Learning an Adventure

A final point to remember is that you are most likely to procrastinate if you think a task will be unpleasant (Pychyl et al., 2000). Learning can be hard work. Nevertheless, many students find ways to make schoolwork interesting and enjoyable. Try to approach your schoolwork as if it were a game, a sport, an adventure, or simply a way to become a better person. The best educational experiences are challenging, yet fun (Ferrari & Scher, 2000; Santrock & Halonen, 2013).

Virtually every topic is interesting to someone, somewhere. You may not be particularly interested in the sex life of South American tree frogs. However, a biologist might be fascinated. (Another tree frog might be, too.) If you wait for teachers to make their courses interesting, you are missing the point. Interest is a matter of your attitude (Sirois & Tosti, 2012).

Using Digital Media—Netting New Knowledge

SURVEY QUESTION 1.7: Can digital media help with reflective processing?

Digital media offer another way to be more reflective. Search the Internet for any psychological term, from *amnesia* to *zoophobia*, and you will find a vast array of information. Websites range from the authoritative, like the one provided by the American Psychological Association, to Wikipedia entries and personal blogs. However, be aware that information on the Internet is not always accurate. It is wise to approach most websites with a healthy dose of skepticism.

MindTap

How would I find information about psychology on the Internet? Your first stop should be MindTap for Psychology: Modules for Active Learning. MindTap's highly personalized, fully online learning platform integrates all of the authoritative content, assignments, and services that accompany this book in one place. It guides you through a presentation of the course curriculum via an innovative learning path that can be tailored by your instructor to include video and other interactive activities. You will complete reading assignments, annotate your readings, complete homework, get detailed instant feedback on Guided Practice Activities and engage with quizzes and assessments. MindTap includes a variety of web-apps known as "MindApps"—allowing functionality like having the text read aloud to you as well as synchronizing your notes with your personal Evernote account. MindApps are woven into the MindTap platform and enhance your learning experience.

Aplia Guided Practice Activities

Aplia is an online homework solution that offers interactive chapter assignments, tutorials, and other multimedia features. As you complete online assignments, you receive immediate grades and feedback on each problem set. Aplia assignments are automatically graded and entered into your instructor's Aplia gradebook. Aplia's My Practice Reviews are randomized questions made up of question types on which you originally scored 80% or less. This adaptive learning feature helps you to study efficiently and effectively. A basic version of Aplia is available as a MindApp and provides the Guided Practice activities in the MindTap learning path.

Psychology Websites

For more psychology on the Internet, check out some of these interesting, high-quality websites.

PsycINFO Psychological knowledge can also be found through specialized online databases. One of the best is PsycINFO, offered by the American Psychological Association (APA). PsycINFO provides summaries of the scientific and scholarly literature in psychology. Each record in PsycINFO consists of an abstract (short summary), plus notes about the author, title, source, and other details. All entries are indexed using key terms. Thus, you can search for various topics by entering words such as *drug abuse, postpartum depression,* or *creativity.*

Weekly time schedule *A written plan that allocates time for study, work, and leisure activities during a one-week period.*
Term schedule *A written plan that lists the dates of all major assignments for each of your classes for an entire term.*
Specific goals *Goals with clearly defined and measurable outcomes.*
PsycINFO *A searchable, online database that provides brief summaries of the scientific and scholarly literature in psychology.*

Almost every college and university subscribes to PsycINFO. You can usually search PsycINFO from a terminal in your college library or computer center—for free. PsycINFO can also be directly accessed (for a fee) through the Internet via APA's PsycINFO Direct service. For more information on how to gain access to PsycINFO, check out this website: **www.apa.org/pubs/databases/psycinfo/index.aspx**.

The APA and APS Websites The APA and APS (Association for Psychological Science) maintain online libraries of general-interest articles on many topics. They are well worth consulting when you have questions about psychological issues. You'll find them at **www.apa.org** and **www.psychologicalscience.org**. For links to recent articles in newspapers and magazines, check the APA's PsycPORT page at **www.apa.org/news/psycport/index.aspx**.

A Final Word

There is a distinction in Zen between *live* words and *dead* words. Live words come from personal experience; dead words are about a subject. This book will be only a collection of dead words unless you accept the challenge of taking an intellectual journey. You will find many helpful, useful, and exciting ideas in the pages that follow. To make them yours, you must set out to actively and reflectively learn as much as you can. The ideas presented here should get you off to a good start. Good luck!

For more information, consult any of the following books:

Chaffee, J. (2012). *Thinking critically* (10th ed.). Belmont, CA: Cengage Learning/Wadsworth.

Ellis, D. (2013). *Becoming a master student: Concise* (14th ed.). Belmont, CA: Cengage Learning/Wadsworth.

Santrock, J. W., & Halonen, J. S. (2013). *Your guide to college success: Strategies for achieving your goals* (7th ed.). Belmont, CA: Cengage Learning/Wadsworth.

Van Blerkom, D. L. (2012). *College study skills: Becoming a strategic learner* (7th ed.). Belmont, CA: Cengage Learning/Wadsworth.

Wong, W. (2012). *Essential study skills* (7th ed.). Belmont, CA: Cengage Learning/Wadsworth.

Module 1: Summary

1.1 What is reflective learning?
- **1.1.1** Reflective learning is deliberately reflective and active self-guided study.

1.2 What is the best way to read a textbook?
- **1.2.1** Reflective reading, which involves actively thinking about what is being read, is better than passive reading.
- **1.2.2** One way to be a more active reader is to follow the six steps of the reflective SQ4R method: survey, question, read, recite, reflect, and review.

1.3 How can learning in class be improved?
- **1.3.1** Reflective learning in class involves active listening.
- **1.3.2** One way to be a more active listener in class is to follow the five steps of the LISAN method: lead, don't follow; ideas; signal words; actively listen; note-taking.

1.4 What is the best way to study?
- **1.4.1** More reflective studying involves studying in a specific place, using spaced study sessions, trying mnemonics, testing yourself, and overlearning.

1.5 What are some ways to be a more effective test-taker?
- **1.5.1** A variety of guidelines are available for improving general test-taking skills.
- **1.5.2** More specialized strategies are available for objective tests, essay tests, and short-answer tests.

1.6 How can procrastination be overcome?
- **1.6.1** Procrastination can be overcome through time management, setting goals, and making learning an adventure.

1.7 Can digital media help with reflective processing?
- **1.7.1** Digital media offer another way to be more reflective, as long as care is taken to approach all websites with a healthy dose of skepticism.

Module 1: Knowledge Builder

Recite

1. Setting learning goals and monitoring your progress are important parts of _____ learning.

2. The four Rs in reflective SQ4R stand for read, recite, reflect, and review. *T or F?*

3. When using the LISAN method, students try to write down as much of a lecture as possible so that their notes are complete. *T or F?*

4. Spaced study sessions are usually superior to massed practice. *T or F?*

5. According to research, you should almost always stick with your first answer on multiple-choice tests. *T or F?*

6. To use the technique known as overlearning, you should continue to study after you feel you have mastered a topic. *T or F?*

7. Procrastination is related to seeking perfection and equating self-worth with grades. *T or F?*

Reflect

Think Critically

8. How are the reflective SQ4R method and the LISAN method related?

Self-Reflect

Which study skills do you think would help you the most? Which techniques do you already use? Which do you think you should try? To what extent do you already engage in self-regulated learning? What steps could you take to become a more active, goal-oriented learner?

ANSWERS

1. reflective 2. T 3. F 4. T 5. F 6. T 7. T 8. Both encourage people to be reflective and to actively seek information as a way of learning more effectively.

CENGAGE **brain**.com

Go to **cengagebrain.com** to access **MindTap for Coon/Mitterer** *Psychology Modules for Active Learning* and other online learning tools. MindTap is a fully online learning experience that combines all the tools you need—readings, multimedia, activities, and assessments—into a singular personalized Learning Path that guides you through the course.

Introducing Psychology:
Psychology, Critical Thinking, and Science

Why?

What's 24 miles to a dreamer? In October 2012, Felix Baumgartner jumped out of a balloon-powered capsule from that far above the earth. The ultimate skydiver, he then plummeted toward the earth at speeds exceeding 800 miles an hour before opening his parachutes to glide in for a safe landing.

What could Felix possibly have been thinking, you might wonder. But you might equally wonder why people get married, join the navy, run triathlons, grow roses, become suicide bombers, go to college, or live out their lives in monasteries. You might even wonder, at least sometimes, why *you* do the things you do. In other words, the odds are that you are curious about human behavior (just like your authors, we should point out). That may even be a part of the reason you are taking a course in psychology and reading this book.

How, in general, do psychologists set out to look for answers to questions about human behavior, for example, "Why, Felix, why?" Let's find out.

Jay Nemeth/ZUMAPRESS/Newscom

SURVEY QUESTIONS

2.1 What is psychology and what are its goals?

2.2 What is critical thinking?

2.3 How does psychology differ from false explanations of behavior?

2.4 How is the scientific method applied in psychological research?

Psychology—Behave!

SURVEY QUESTION 2.1: What is psychology and what are its goals?

Those of us who wonder about Felix's extreme skydiving are not the first humans to be curious about human behavior. Even the word *psychology* is thousands of years old, coming from the ancient Greek roots *psyche*, meaning mind, and *logos*, meaning knowledge or study. However, have you ever seen or touched a mind? The mind can't be studied directly, so **psychology** is defined as the scientific study of overt behavior and mental processes (covert behavior).

To what does behavior refer in the definition of psychology? Any directly observable action or response—eating, hanging out, sleeping, talking, or sneezing—is an *overt behavior*. So are studying, gambling, watching television, tying your shoes, giving someone a gift, learning Spanish, reading this book, and, yes, extreme skydiving. But psychologists haven't left out the mind; they also study *covert behaviors*. These are private mental events, such as thinking, dreaming, remembering, and other mental processes (Jackson, 2012).

The modern field of psychology is an ever-changing vista of people and ideas that can help you better understand yourself and others. Psychology is about love, stress, therapy, persuasion, hypnosis, perception, memory, death, conformity, creativity, learning, personality, aging, intelligence, sexuality, emotion, happiness, wisdom, and much more. Although we might envy those who skydive from the edge of space, perform on Broadway, explore the ocean's depths, or walk on the moon, the ultimate frontier lies much closer to home. Every life is a journey, and every day is its own adventure.

© Louie Psihoyos/Science Faction/Corbis

Psychologists are highly trained professionals who have specialized skills in counseling and therapy, measurement and testing, research and experimentation, statistics, diagnosis, treatment, and many other areas. Here psychologist Steven LaBerge wears goggles designed to alert him that he is dreaming to increase his chances of having a lucid dream (Hobson, 2009).

Today, psychology is both a science and a profession. As scientists, some psychologists do research to discover new knowledge. Others apply psychology to solve problems in fields such as mental health, business, education, sports, law, medicine, and the design of machines (Davey, 2011). Still others are teachers who share their knowledge with students. Later, we return to the profession of psychology. For now, let's focus on how psychologists create knowledge. Whether they work in a lab, a clinic, or a classroom, all psychologists rely on critical thinking and especially information gained from scientific research.

Seeking Knowledge in Psychology

Isn't psychology really just a matter of using your common sense? Many people regard themselves as expert people watchers and form their own commonsense theories of behavior. However, you may be surprised to learn how often self-appointed authorities and long-held commonsense beliefs about human behavior are wrong. For example, have you ever heard that some people are left-brained and some are right-brained? Or that subliminal advertising really works? Or that men and women communicate differently? It turns out that these widely held beliefs, and many others, are wrong (Lilienfeld et al., 2010).

But how could common sense be wrong so often? One problem is that much of what passes for common sense is vague and inconsistent. For example, it is frequently said that you should "strike while the iron is hot." With this in mind, you make a snap decision to buy a cellphone because the offer is time-limited. Later, when you complain to a friend about getting locked into an expensive data plan, she scolds you that everybody knows "haste makes waste."

Further, commonsense statements like these work best after the fact. If your cellphone had worked out, the iron would have, indeed, been "hot." After your purchase turned out to be a bust, it took no insight at all for your friend to point it out.

Another problem with common sense is that it often depends on limited personal observation. For example, has someone ever told you he heard that people in New York City (or Mexico, or Canada, or Paris, or wherever) are rude? This often means no more than that someone had a bad encounter on one visit. It may well say nothing about those people in general.

Unlike such casual observation, psychologists rely on **scientific observation**. Although both are based on gathering *empirical evidence* (information gained from direct observation), unlike everyday personal experiences, scientific observation is *systematic*, or carefully planned. Scientific observations also are *intersubjective*, which means that more than one observer can confirm them.

Sometimes, commonsense answers go unchallenged for lack of a suitable **research method**—a systematic scientific approach to answering particular questions. In the past, it was commonsense to take the word of people who say they never dream. Then the EEG (electroencephalograph, or brainwave machine) was invented. Certain EEG patterns, and the presence of eye movements, can reveal whether a person is dreaming. People who never dream, it turns out, dream frequently. If they are awakened during a dream, they vividly remember it. Thus, the EEG helped make the study of dreaming more scientific.

Basically, the scientific approach says, "Let's take a more objective look" (Stanovich, 2013). Psychologists study behavior

Psychology   *The scientific study of overt behavior and mental processes (covert behavior).*
Scientific observation   *An empirical investigation structured to answer questions about the world in a systematic and intersubjective fashion (observations can be reliably confirmed by multiple observers).*
Research method   *A systematic approach to answering scientific questions.*

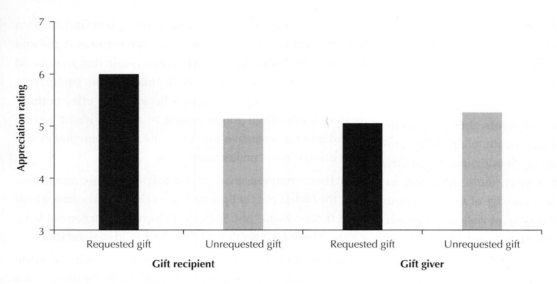

● **Figure 2.1**
Results of an empirical study. The graph shows that the recipients of gifts appreciate gifts they have requested more than gifts the giver chooses. Gift givers were slightly more likely to believe that recipients would prefer receiving an unrequested gift (although the difference was not statistically significant.) (Data adapted from Gino & Flynn, 2011.)

directly by systematically collecting data (observed facts) so they can draw valid conclusions. Would you say it's true, for instance, that "the clothes make the man"? Do you believe that "you can't judge a book by its cover"? Why argue about it? As psychologists, we simply get some people who are well dressed and some who are not and, through scientific observation, find out who makes out better in a variety of situations!

Here's an example of gathering empirical evidence: Have you ever wondered if, when it comes to giving gifts, it really is "the thought that counts"? Francesca Gino and Francis Flynn (2011) decided to find out. They asked gift recipients to rate how much they would appreciate getting a gift they requested as opposed to one chosen by the gift giver. It turns out people prefer gifts they specifically request over gifts the giver *thinks* might be appreciated. In contrast, gift givers believed that

recipients would be just as appreciative of a gift they chose for them (see ● **Figure 2.1**).

Isn't the outcome of this study fairly predictable? It isn't if you started out believing otherwise. Sometimes the results of studies match our personal observations or commonsense beliefs and sometimes they come as a surprise. In this instance, you may have guessed the outcome. Your suspicions were confirmed by scientific observation. However, it could easily have turned out differently.

How about getting money for a gift; does that make a difference? Gino and Flynn (2011) checked that out as well. They found that gift recipients preferred getting money even more than getting a gift they requested, even though gift givers thought exactly the opposite. Apparently, we struggle more with the idea of thoughtful gifts when we are the givers than when we are the recipients.

Psychology's Goals

What do psychologists hope to achieve? As scientists, our ultimate goal is to benefit humanity (O'Neill, 2005). More specifically, the goals of psychology are to *describe, understand, predict,* and *control* behavior. What do psychology's goals mean in practice? Let's see.

Description Answering psychological questions often begins with a careful description of behavior. **Description**, or naming and classifying, is typically based on making a detailed record of scientific observations.

But a description doesn't explain anything, does it? No. Useful knowledge begins with accurate description, but descriptions fail to answer the important "why" questions. *Why* do more

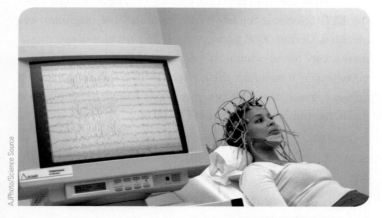

The scientific study of dreaming was made possible by use of the EEG, a device that records the tiny electrical signals the brain generates as a person sleeps. The EEG converts these electrical signals into a written record of brain activity. Certain shifts in brain activity, coupled with the presence of rapid eye movements, are strongly related to dreaming.

AJPhoto/Science Source

women attempt suicide, and *why* do more men complete it? *Why* are people more aggressive when they are uncomfortable? *Why* are bystanders often unwilling to help in an emergency? (And *why* did Felix start extreme skydiving?)

Understanding We have met psychology's second goal when we can explain an event. That is, **understanding** usually means we can state the causes of a behavior. For example, research on bystander apathy reveals that people often fail to help when *other* possible helpers are nearby. Why? A diffusion of responsibility occurs. Basically, no one person feels personally obligated to pitch in. As a result, the more potential helpers there are, the less likely it is that anyone will help (Aronson, Wilson, & Akert, 2013; Darley, 2000). Now we can explain a perplexing problem.

Prediction Psychology's third goal, **prediction**, is the ability to forecast behavior accurately. Notice that our explanation of bystander apathy makes a prediction about the chances of getting help. If you've ever been stranded on a busy freeway with car trouble, you'll recognize the accuracy of this prediction: Having many potential helpers nearby is no guarantee that anyone will stop to help.

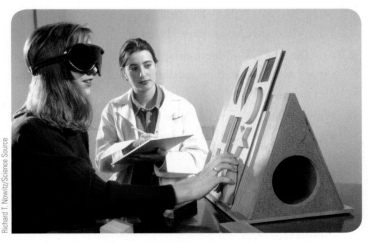

Richard T. Nowitz/Science Source

Some psychologists specialize in administering, scoring, and interpreting psychological tests, such as tests of intelligence, creativity, personality, or aptitude. This specialty, which is called psychometrics, is an example of using psychology to predict future behavior.

Control *Description, explanation, and prediction seem reasonable, but is control a valid goal?* Control may seem like a threat to personal freedom. However, to a psychologist, **control** simply refers to the ability to alter the conditions that affect behavior. If a clinical psychologist helps a person overcome a terrible fear of heights, control is involved. If you suggest changes in a classroom that help students learn better,

you have exerted control. Control is also involved in designing cars to keep drivers from making fatal errors. Clearly, psychological control must be used wisely and humanely.

In summary, psychology's goals are a natural outgrowth of our desire to understand behavior. Basically, they boil down to asking the following questions:

What is the nature of this behavior? (description)

Why does it occur? (understanding and explanation)

Can we forecast when it will occur? (prediction)

What conditions affect it? (control)

To achieve their goals of describing, understanding, predicting, and controlling behavior, psychologists rely on critical thinking and the scientific method. Critical thinking in psychology most often takes the form of collecting empirical evidence to evaluate theories, as guided by the scientific method. It would be impossible to answer most questions about human behavior without the aid of scientific research methods.

Critical Thinking—Take It with a Grain of Salt

SURVEY QUESTION 2.2: What is critical thinking?

How does critical thinking play a role in psychology? Most of us would be skeptical if offered a genuine Rolex watch or expensive designer sunglasses for just a few dollars on eBay. And most of us easily accept our ignorance of subatomic physics. But because we deal with human behavior every day, we sometimes think we already know what is true in psychology. All too often, we are tempted to buy commonsense beliefs, urban legends, and even outrageous claims about the powers of healing crystals, miraculous herbal remedies, astrology, psychics describing people's personalities and predicting their future, and so forth.

Description *In scientific research, the process of naming and classifying.*
Understanding *In psychology, understanding is achieved when the causes of a behavior can be stated.*
Prediction *In psychology, an ability to accurately forecast behavior.*
Control *In psychology, altering conditions that influence behavior.*

For this and many more reasons, learning to think critically is one of the lasting benefits of a college education. **Critical thinking** in psychology is a type of reflection (you *did* read Module 1, *How to Study Psychology*, right?) that involves asking whether a particular belief can be supported by scientific theory and observation (Yanchar, Slife, & Warne, 2008). Critical thinkers are willing to challenge conventional wisdom by asking hard questions (Jackson & Newberry, 2012).

For example, when it comes to achieving our goals, is it better to focus on how far we still have to go before we reach a goal, or should we focus on what we have already accomplished? Critical thinkers might immediately ask: "Is there any theory to support stressing either a goal focus or an accomplishment focus? Is there any empirical evidence either way? What could we do to find out for ourselves?" (Be on the lookout later in this module for some evidence concerning this question.)

Critical Thinking Principles

The heart of critical thinking is a willingness to actively *reflect* on ideas. Critical thinkers evaluate ideas by probing for weaknesses in their reasoning and analyzing the evidence supporting their beliefs. They question assumptions and look for alternate conclusions. True knowledge, they recognize, comes from constantly revising our understanding of the world. Critical thinking relies on the following basic principles (Elder, 2006; Jackson & Newberry, 2012; Kida, 2006):

1. *Few truths transcend the need for logical analysis and empirical testing.* Whereas religious beliefs and personal values may be held as matters of faith, most other ideas can and should be evaluated by applying the rules of logic, evidence, and the scientific method.

2. *Critical thinkers often wonder what it would take to show that a truth is false.* Critical thinkers actively seek to *falsify* beliefs, including their own. They are willing to admit when they are wrong. As Susan Blackmore (2000, p. 55) said when her studies caused her to abandon some long-held beliefs, "Admitting you are wrong is always hard—even though it's a skill that every psychologist has to learn." As a consequence, critical thinkers can be more confident in beliefs that have survived their attempts at falsification.

3. *Authority or claimed expertise does not automatically make an idea true or false.* Just because a teacher, guru, celebrity, or authority is convinced or sincere doesn't mean you should automatically believe or disbelieve that person. Naïvely accepting (or denying) the word of an expert is unscientific and self-demeaning unless you ask, "Is this a well-supported explanation, or is there a better one? What evidence convinced her or him?"

4. *Judging the quality of evidence is crucial.* Imagine you are a juror in a courtroom, judging claims made by two battling lawyers. To decide correctly, you can't just weigh the *amount* of evidence. You must also critically evaluate the *quality* of the evidence. Then you can give greater weight to the most credible facts.

5. *Critical thinking requires an open mind.* Be prepared to consider daring departures and go wherever the evidence leads. However, don't become so open-minded that you are simply gullible. Astronomer Carl Sagan once noted, "It seems to me that what is called for is an exquisite balance between two conflicting needs: the most skeptical scrutiny of all hypotheses that are served up to us and at the same time a great openness to new ideas" (Kida, 2006, p. 51).

To put these principles into action, here are some questions to ask as you evaluate new information (Browne & Keeley, 2010; Jackson & Newberry, 2012):

1. What claims are being made? What are their implications?

2. Are the claims understandable? Do they make logical sense? Is there another possible explanation? Is it a simpler explanation?

3. What empirical tests of these claims have been made (if any)? What was the nature and quality of the tests? Can they be repeated? Who did the tests? How reliable and trustworthy were the investigators? Do they have conflicts of interest? Do their findings appear to be objective? Has any other independent researcher duplicated the findings?

4. How good is the evidence? (In general, scientific observations provide the highest-quality evidence.)

5. Finally, how much credibility can the claim be given? High, medium, low, provisional?

A course in psychology naturally enriches thinking skills. In this book, all upcoming modules include *Think Critically* questions based on the ones you have seen here. Take the time to tackle these questions. The effort will sharpen your thinking abilities and make learning livelier. For an immediate thinking challenge, let's take a critical look at several nonscientific systems that claim to explain behavior.

Pseudopsychologies—Palms, Planets, and Personality

SURVEY QUESTION 2.3: How does psychology differ from false explanations of behavior?

A **pseudopsychology** (SUE-doe-psychology) is any unfounded system that resembles psychology. Many pseudopsychologies give the appearance of being scientific but are actually false. (*Pseudo* means false.) Pseudopsychologies are a type of **superstition**, an unfounded belief held without evidence or in the face of falsifying evidence.

Unlike real psychology, pseudopsychologies change little over time because followers seek evidence that confirms their beliefs and avoid evidence that falsifies them. Critical thinkers, scientists, and psychologists, in contrast, are skeptical of their own theories (Schick & Vaughn, 2014). They actively look for contradictions as a way to advance knowledge.

What are some examples of false psychologies? One pseudopsychology, known as *phrenology*, was popularized in the nineteenth century by Franz Gall, a German anatomy teacher. Phrenology claimed that the shape of the skull reveals personality traits. Psychological research has long since shown that bumps on the head have nothing to do with talents or abilities. The phrenologists were so far off that they listed the part of the brain that controls hearing as a center for combativeness! *Palmistry* is a similar false system that claims lines on the hand reveal personality traits and predict the future. Despite the overwhelming evidence against phrenology and palmistry, these pseudopsychologies are still practiced. Palmists, in particular, continue to separate the gullible from their money in many cities.

At first glance, a pseudopsychology called *graphology* might seem more

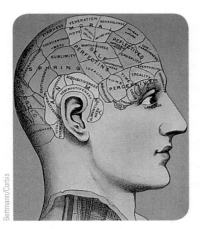

Phrenology was an attempt to assess personality characteristics by examining various areas of the skull. Phrenologists used charts such as the one shown here as guides. Like other pseudopsychologists, phrenologists made no attempt to empirically verify their concepts.

reasonable. Some graphologists claim that personality traits are revealed by handwriting. Based on such claims, some companies use graphologists to select job candidates (Bangerter et al., 2009). This is troubling because graphologists score close to zero on tests of accuracy in rating personality (Dazzi & Pedrabissi, 2009). Graphologists do no better than untrained college students in rating personality and job performance (Neter & Ben-Shakhar, 1989). Even a graphological society recommends that handwriting analysis should not be used to select people for jobs (Simner & Goffin, 2003). (By the way, graphology's failure at revealing personality should be separated from its value for detecting forgeries.)

Would you hire this man? Here's a sample of your author's handwriting. What do you think it reveals? Your interpretations are likely to be as accurate (or inaccurate) as those of a graphologist.

© Cengage Learning

Graphology seems harmless enough until you imagine being denied a job because a graphologist didn't like your handwriting. This false system has been used to determine who is hired, given bank credit, or selected for juries. In these and similar situations, pseudopsychologies do, in fact, harm people.

If pseudopsychologies have no scientific basis, how do they survive and why are they popular? Several reasons explain their survival and popularity, all of which can be illustrated by a critique of astrology.

Problems in the Stars

Arguably the most popular pseudopsychology, astrology holds that the positions of the stars and planets at the time of one's birth determine personality traits and affect behavior.

Critical thinking *In psychology, a type of reflection involving the support of beliefs through scientific explanation and observation.*
Pseudopsychology *Any false and unscientific system of beliefs and practices that is offered as an explanation of behavior.*
Superstition *Unfounded belief held without evidence or in spite of falsifying evidence.*

Like other pseudopsychologies, astrology has repeatedly been shown to have no scientific validity, either theoretically or empirically (Kelly, 1999; Rogers & Soule, 2009), for two reasons:

1. **The theory of astrology is unconvincing.** Astrology is based on a zodiac map invented several thousand years ago in the ancient civilization of Babylon. Unlike scientific theories, which are regularly falsified and rejected or revised accordingly, the basic underpinnings of astrology have remained relatively unchanged. To date, no astrologer has offered a convincing explanation of *how* the positions of the planets at a person's birth affect his or her future. Astrologers have also failed to explain *why* the moment of birth should be more important than, say, the moment of conception. (Perhaps it is because it is relatively easy to figure out the moment of birth and much trickier to determine the moment of conception.) Besides, the zodiac has shifted in the sky by one full constellation since astrology was first set up. (In other words, if astrology calls you a Scorpio, you are really a Libra, and so forth.) However, most astrologers simply ignore this shift (Martens & Trachet, 1998).

2. **The evidence against astrology *is* convincing.** One classic study of more than 3,000 predictions by famous astrologers found that only a small percentage was accurate. These successful predictions tended to be vague ("There will be a tragedy somewhere in the east in the spring") or easily guessed from current events (Culver & Ianna, 1988). Similarly, when astrologers are asked to match people with their horoscopes, they do no better than would be expected by chance. In one famous test, astrologers could not even use horoscopes to distinguish murderers from law-abiding people (Gauquelin, 1970). In fact, no connection exists between people's astrological signs and their intelligence or personality traits (Hartmann, Reuter, & Nyborg, 2006). There also is no connection between the compatibility of couples' astrological signs and their marriage and divorce rates or between astrological signs and leadership, physical characteristics, or career choices (Martens & Trachet, 1998).

In short, astrology doesn't work.

Then why does astrology often seem to work? Even the daily horoscopes printed in newspapers can seem uncannily accurate. For many people, this apparent accuracy can only mean that astrology is valid. Unfortunately, such *uncritical acceptance* overlooks a much simpler psychological explanation (see, for example, Rogers & Soule, 2009). The following discussion explains why astrology seems to work.

Uncritical Acceptance Perceptions of the accuracy of horoscopes are typically based on **uncritical acceptance**—the tendency to believe claims because they seem true or it would be nice if they were true. Horoscopes generally contain mostly flattering traits. Naturally, when your personality is described in *desirable* terms, it is hard to deny that the description has the ring of truth. How much acceptance would astrology receive if a birth sign read like this:

Virgo: You are the logical type and hate disorder. Your nitpicking is unbearable to your friends. You are cold, unemotional, and usually fall asleep while making love. Virgos make good doorstops.

Confirmation Bias Even when an astrological description contains a mixture of good and bad traits, it may seem accurate. To find out why, read the following personality description:

Your Personality Profile

You have many personality strengths, with some weaknesses to which you can usually adjust. You tend to be accepting of yourself. You are comfortable with some structure in your life but do enjoy diverse experiences from time to time. Although on the inside you might be a bit unsure of yourself, you appear under control to others. You are sexually well adjusted, although you do have some questions. Your life goals are more or less realistic. Occasionally, you question your decisions and actions because you're unsure that they are correct. You want to be liked and admired by other people. You are not using your potential to its full extent. You like to think for yourself and don't always take other people's word without thinking it through. You are not generally willing to disclose to others because it might lead to problems. You are a natural introvert, cautious, and careful around others, although there are times when you can be an extrovert who is the life of the party.

Does this describe your personality? A psychologist read a similar summary individually to college students who had taken a personality test. Only a few students felt that the description was inaccurate. Another classic study found that people rated the personality profile as more accurate than their actual horoscopes (French et al., 1991).

Reread the description and you will see that it contains both sides of several personality dimensions ("You are a natural introvert . . . although there are times when you can be an extrovert . . . ."). Its apparent accuracy is an illusion based on **confirmation bias**, in which we remember or notice things that confirm our expectations and forget the rest (Lilienfeld, Ammirati, & Landfield, 2009). The pseudopsychologies thrive on this effect. For example, you can always find Aquarius characteristics in an Aquarius. If you looked, however, you could also find Gemini, Scorpio, or whatever characteristics. Perhaps this explains why, in an amusing twist, 94 percent of those sent the full 10-page horoscope of a famous mass murderer accepted it as their own (Gauquelin, 1970).

Psychic mediums who claim that they can communicate with deceased friends and relatives of audience members also rely on confirmation bias. An analysis shows that the number of hits (correct statements) these people make tends to be low. Nevertheless, many viewers are impressed because of our natural tendency to remember apparent hits and ignore misses. Of course, particularly embarrassing misses are often edited out before such shows appear on television (Nickell, 2001).

The Barnum Effect Pseudopsychologies also take advantage of the **Barnum effect**, which is a tendency to consider personal descriptions accurate if they are stated in general terms (Kida, 2006). P. T. Barnum, the famed circus showman, had a formula for success: "Always have a little something for everybody." Like the all-purpose personality profile, palm readings, fortunes, horoscopes, and other techniques of pseudopsychology are stated in such general terms that they always have "a little something for everybody." To observe the Barnum effect, read all 12 of the daily horoscopes found in newspapers for several days. You will find that predictions for other signs fit events as well as those for your own sign. Try giving a friend the wrong horoscope sometime. Your friend may be quite impressed with the accuracy of the horoscope.

Astrology's popularity shows that many people have difficulty separating valid psychology from systems that seem valid but are not. The goal of this discussion has been to make you a more critical observer of human behavior and to clarify what is, and what is not, psychology. Here is what the "stars" say about your future:

> Emphasis is now on education and personal improvement. A learning experience of lasting value awaits you. Take care of scholastic responsibilities before engaging in recreation. The word *psychology* figures prominently in your future.

Remember, pseudopsychologies may seem like no more than a nuisance, but they can do real harm. For instance, people seeking treatment for psychological disorders may become the victims of self-appointed "experts" who offer ineffective, pseudoscientific therapies (Kida, 2006; Lilienfeld, Ruscio, & Lynn, 2008). Valid psychological principles are based on scientific theory and evidence, not fads, opinions, or wishful thinking.

Scientific Research—How to Think Like a Psychologist

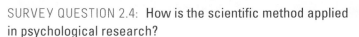

SURVEY QUESTION 2.4: How is the scientific method applied in psychological research?

Thinking critically about psychology begins with the careful recording of facts and events, the heart of all sciences. To be *scientific*, our observations must be *systematic*, so that they reveal something reliable about behavior (Stanovich, 2013). To use an earlier example, if you are interested in whether gift recipients prefer gifts they requested or gifts that were chosen for them, you will learn little by making haphazard observations of gift-giving at family birthday parties. To be of value, your observations must be planned and systematic.

The Scientific Method

The **scientific method** is a form of critical thinking based on careful collection of evidence, accurate description and measurement, precise definition, controlled observation, and repeatable results (Jackson, 2012; Yanchar, Slife, & Warne, 2008). In its ideal form, the scientific method has six elements:

1. Making observations
2. Defining a problem
3. Proposing a hypothesis
4. Gathering evidence/testing the hypothesis
5. Building a theory
6. Publishing results

Uncritical acceptance *The tendency to believe generally positive or flattering descriptions of oneself.*
Confirmation bias *The tendency to remember or notice information that fits one's expectations, while forgetting discrepancies.*
Barnum effect *The tendency to consider a personal description accurate if it is stated in general terms.*
Scientific method *A form of critical thinking based on careful measurement and controlled observation.*

Applying the scientific method to the study of behavior requires careful observation. Here, two psychologists observe and record a session in which a child's eating behavior is being tested.

Let's take a closer look at some elements of the scientific method. Earlier, we considered the question of whether goals are more attainable if people maintain a goal focus (stressing how much remains to be done to achieve the goal) or an achievement focus (stressing how much has already been achieved). All the basic elements of the scientific method are found in the following example, from Florida State University psychologist Kyle Conlon and his colleagues (2011).

Making Observations The researchers reviewed previously published studies, noting that both goal-focused and achievement-focused approaches are popular. If the goal is weight loss, for example, one goal-focused approach is to count down the pounds (only 10 pounds to go!), while one achievement-focused approach is to celebrate milestones. (Congratulations on losing the first 10 pounds!)

Defining a Problem The researchers also noted that maintaining a goal focus seems to inspire more goal-oriented behaviors. Thus, they defined their main problem as, "Will people lose more weight if they maintain a goal focus or if they maintain an achievement focus?"

Proposing a Hypothesis *What exactly is a "hypothesis"?* A **hypothesis** (hi-POTH-eh-sis) is a tentative statement about, or explanation of, an event or relationship. In common terms, a hypothesis is a *testable* hunch or educated guess about behavior. For example, you might hypothesize the following: "Frustration encourages aggression." How could you test this hypothesis? First, you have to decide how you are going to frustrate people. (This part might be fun.) Then you need to find a way to measure whether they become more aggressive.

(Not so much fun if you plan to be nearby.) Your observations would provide evidence to confirm or refute your hypothesis.

Because we cannot see or touch frustration, we must define it operationally. An **operational definition** states the exact procedures used to represent a concept. Operational definitions allow unobservable ideas, such as covert behaviors, to be tested in real-world terms (see ● **Figure 2.2**). For example, because you can't measure frustration directly, you might define *frustration* as "interrupting an adult before he or she can finish a puzzle and win an iPad." And *aggression* might be defined as "the number of times a frustrated individual insults the person who prevented work on the puzzle." In other words, covert behaviors are operationally defined in terms of overt behavior so they can be observed and studied scientifically.

Gathering Evidence/Testing the Hypothesis Now let's return to the question of whether weight loss is easier when you maintain a goal focus. To gather data, the researchers assigned participants to one of three weight-loss groups: goal-focused, achievement-focused, and no-focus control. Each group met for 12 weekly meetings and had access to a special website. As predicted, goal-focused individuals lost more weight than did either achievement-focused or control individuals. They also reported being more committed to reaching their goal weights.

Building a Theory *How do theories fit in?* A **theory** is a system of ideas designed to interrelate concepts and facts in a way that summarizes existing data and predicts future observations.

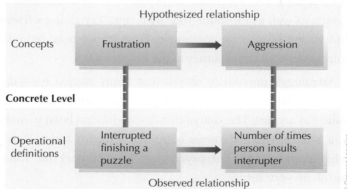

● **Figure 2.2**

Operational definitions are used to link concepts with concrete observations. Do you think the examples given are reasonable operational definitions of frustration and aggression? Operational definitions vary in how well they represent concepts. For this reason, many different experiments may be necessary to draw clear conclusions about hypothesized relationships in psychology.

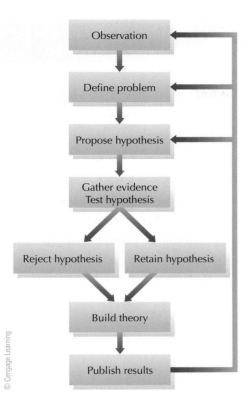

Figure 2.3

Psychologists use the logic of science to answer questions about behavior. Specific hypotheses can be tested in a variety of ways, including naturalistic observation, correlational studies, controlled experiments, clinical studies, and the survey method. Psychologists revise their theories to reflect the evidence they gather. New or revised theories then lead to new observations, problems, and hypotheses.

TABLE 2.1	Outline of a Research Report
Abstract	Research reports begin with a brief summary of the study and its findings. The abstract lets you get an overview without reading the entire article.
Introduction	The introduction describes the question to be investigated. It also provides background information by reviewing prior studies on the same or related topics.
Method	This section tells how and why observations were made. It also describes the specific procedures used to gather data. That way, other researchers can repeat the study to see if they get the same results.
Results	The outcome of the investigation is presented. Data may be graphed, summarized in tables, or statistically analyzed.
Discussion	The results of the study are discussed in relation to the original question. Implications of the study are explored, and further studies may be proposed.

Good theories summarize observations, explain them, allow prediction, and guide further research (● **Figure 2.3**). Without theories of forgetting, personality, stress, mental illness, and the like, psychologists would drown in a sea of disconnected facts (Stanovich, 2013).

Conlon and his colleagues interpreted their results as consistent with theories of motivation that stress the importance of being aware of how much work remains to be done to achieve a goal. The results were also portrayed as extending these theories into the field of health psychology and as being relevant to the design of health-intervention programs.

Publishing Results Because scientific information must always be *publicly available*, the results of psychological studies are usually published in professional journals (see ● **Table 2.1**). That way, other researchers can read about the results and make their own observations if they doubt the study's findings (Jackson, 2012). If others are able to *replicate* (repeat) the results of a study, those results become more credible.

In a scholarly article published in the *Journal of Experimental Social Psychology*, Conlon and his colleagues (2011) describe the question they investigated, the methods they used, and the results of their study comparing goal-focused and achievement-focused dieters.

Research Ethics

Aren't there rules about how scientists must treat the people they study? Psychology experiments sometimes raise *ethical* questions. Stanley Milgram's obedience studies are a classic example (see Module 71). Participants were ordered to give what they thought were painful electric shocks to another person (no shocks were actually given) (Milgram, 1963). Believing that they had hurt someone, many people left the experiment shaken and upset. A few suffered guilt and distress for some time afterward. Such experiments raise serious ethical

Hypothesis *The predicted outcome of an experiment or an educated guess about the relationship between variables.*
Operational definition *Defining a scientific concept by stating the specific actions or procedures used to measure it. For example, hunger might be defined as the number of hours of food deprivation.*
Theory *A system of ideas designed to interrelate concepts and facts in a way that summarizes existing data and predicts future observations.*

questions. Did the information gained justify the emotional costs? Was deception really necessary?

As a reply to such questions, American Psychological Association guidelines state: "Psychologists must carry out investigations with respect for the people who participate and with concern for their dignity and welfare" (American Psychological Association, 2010a; see ● Table 2.2). Ethical guidelines also apply to animals, where investigators are expected to "... ensure the welfare of animals and treat them humanely." To assure that ethical guidelines are properly applied, most university and college psychology departments have ethics committees that oversee research. Nevertheless, no easy answers exist for the ethical questions raised by psychology, and debate about specific experiments is likely to continue.

TABLE 2.2	Basic Ethical Guidelines for Psychological Researchers

Do no harm.

Accurately describe risks to potential participants.

Ensure that participation is voluntary.

Minimize any discomfort to participants.

Maintain confidentiality.

Do not unnecessarily invade privacy.

Use deception only when absolutely necessary.

Remove any misconceptions caused by deception (debrief).

Provide results and interpretations to participants.

Treat participants with dignity and respect.

© Cengage Learning

Module 2: Summary

2.1 What is psychology and what are its goals?

- **2.1.1** Psychology is the science of (overt) behavior and (covert) mental processes.
- **2.1.2** Psychologists are professionals who create and apply psychological knowledge.
- **2.1.3** Psychologists engage in critical thinking as they systematically gather and analyze empirical evidence to answer questions about behavior.
- **2.1.4** Psychologists gather scientific data in order to describe, understand, predict, and control behavior.

2.2 What is critical thinking?

- **2.2.1** Critical thinking is central to the scientific method, to psychology, and to the everyday understanding of behavior.
- **2.2.2** Critical thinking in psychology is a type of open-minded reflection involving the support of beliefs with scientific explanation and observation.
- **2.2.3** The validity of beliefs can be judged through logical analysis, evaluating evidence *for* and *against* the claim, and evaluating the *quality* of the evidence.
- **2.2.4** Critical thinkers seek to falsify claims by making up their own minds rather than automatically taking the word of experts.

2.3 How does psychology differ from false explanations of behavior?

- **2.3.1** Pseudopsychologies are unfounded systems that are frequently confused with valid psychology.

- **2.3.2** Unlike psychology, pseudopsychologies change little over time because followers seek evidence that appears to confirm their beliefs and avoid evidence that contradicts their beliefs.
- **2.3.3** Belief in pseudopsychologies is based in part on uncritical acceptance, confirmation bias, and the Barnum effect.

2.4 How is the scientific method applied in psychological research?

- **2.4.1** In the scientific method, systematic observation is used to test hypotheses about behavior and mental events. A powerful way to observe the natural world and draw valid conclusions, scientific research provides the highest-quality information about behavior and mental events.
- **2.4.2** Psychological research begins by defining problems and proposing hypotheses. Concepts must be defined operationally before they can be studied empirically.
- **2.4.3** Next, researchers gather evidence to test hypotheses. The results of scientific studies are made public so that others can evaluate them, learn from them, and use them to suggest new hypotheses, which lead to further research.
- **2.4.4** Psychological research must be done ethically to protect the rights, dignity, and welfare of participants.

Module 2: Knowledge Builder

Recite

1. Psychology is the _____ study of _____ and _____ processes.

2. Commonsense beliefs are often
   a. vague
   b. inconsistent
   c. based on limited observations
   d. all of the above

3. Which of the following questions relates most directly to the goal of *understanding* behavior?
   a. Do the scores of men and women differ on tests of thinking abilities?
   b. Why does a blow to the head cause memory loss?
   c. Will productivity in a business office increase if room temperature is raised or lowered?
   d. What percentage of college students suffer from test anxiety?

4. Personality descriptions provided by pseudopsychologies are stated in general terms, which provide "a little something for everybody." This fact is the basis of the
   a. palmist's fallacy
   b. uncritical acceptance pattern
   c. confirmation bias
   d. Barnum effect

5. A psychologist does a study to see whether exercising increases a sense of well-being. In the study, she will be testing a(n)
   a. hypothesis
   b. operational definition
   c. empirical definition
   d. anthropomorphic theory

6. _____ behaviors are operationally defined in terms of _____ behavior.
   a. Overt, covert
   b. Observable, overt
   c. Covert, overt
   d. Covert, abstract

Reflect

Think Critically

7. All sciences are interested in controlling the phenomena they study. True or false?

8. Try constructing a few Barnum statements, personality statements that are so general that almost everyone thinks they apply to themselves. Can you string them together to make a Barnum profile? Can you adapt the same statements to construct a Barnum horoscope?

Self-Reflect

At first, many students think that psychology is primarily about abnormal behavior and psychotherapy. Did you? How would you describe the field now?

How stringently do you evaluate your own beliefs and the claims made by others?

How might you scientifically test the old saw that you can't teach an old dog new tricks?

Follow the steps of the scientific method to propose a testable hypothesis and decide how you would gather evidence. (Well, OK, you don't have to publish your results.)

ANSWERS

1. scientific, (overt) behavioral, (covert) mental 2. d 3. b 4. d 5. a 6. c 7. False. Astronomy and archaeology are examples of sciences that do not share psychology's fourth goal. Think about it for a moment: No one can *control* the stars or the past. 8. The term *Barnum statement* comes from Levy (2003; but see also Rogers & Soule, 2009), who offers the following examples: You are afraid of being hurt. You are trying to find a balance between autonomy and closeness. You don't like being overly dependent. You just want to be understood.

Introducing Psychology: Psychology Then and Now

The Whole of Psychology

Throughout psychology's history, various viewpoints have helped us understand and interpret human behavior. For example, this design is made up entirely of broken circles. However, as the Gestalt psychologists of 100 years ago discovered, our perceptions have a powerful tendency to form meaningful patterns. Because of this, you probably see a triangle in this design, even though it is only an illusion. Your whole perceptual experience exceeds the sum of its parts. While the Gestalt "school" of psychology no longer exists, its key insights have been incorporated into many fields of contemporary psychology, from the study of perception to the practice of therapy.

Today, little more than 130 years after psychology became a recognized discipline, three complementary perspectives, the biological perspective, the psychological perspective, and the sociocultural perspective, guide research and theorizing in psychology. Also, psychologists around the world are now researching, teaching, and helping people in a wide range of

© Cengage Learning

specialties. In this module, we survey the whole of psychology from its beginnings until now.

SURVEY QUESTIONS

3.1 How did the field of psychology emerge?

3.2 What are the contemporary perspectives in psychology?

3.3 What are the major specialties in psychology?

A Brief History of Psychology— Psychology's Family Album

SURVEY QUESTION 3.1: How did the field of psychology emerge?

As we noted previously, people have been informally observing human behavior and philosophizing about it for thousands of years. In contrast, psychology's history as a science dates back a little more than 130 years to Leipzig, Germany. There, in 1879, Wilhelm Wundt (VILL-helm Voont), the father of psychology, set up a laboratory to study conscious experience.

How, Wundt wondered, do we experience sensations, images, and feelings? To find out, he systematically observed and measured stimuli of various kinds (lights, sounds, weights). A **stimulus** is any physical energy that affects a person and evokes a response (stimulus: singular; stimuli [STIM-you-lie]: plural). Wundt then used **introspection**, or looking inward, to probe his reactions to various stimuli. (Stop reading, close your eyes, and carefully examine your covert thoughts, feelings, and sensations: You are introspecting.) Over the years, Wundt studied vision, hearing, taste, touch, memory, time

Wilhelm Wundt, 1832–1920. Wundt is credited with making psychology an independent science, separate from philosophy. Wundt's original training was in medicine, but he became deeply interested in psychology. In his laboratory, Wundt investigated how sensations, images, and feelings combine to make up personal experience.

William James, 1842–1910. William James was the son of philosopher Henry James, Sr., and the brother of novelist Henry James. During his long academic career, James taught anatomy, physiology, psychology, and philosophy at Harvard University. James believed strongly that ideas should be judged in terms of their practical consequences for human conduct.

perception, and many other topics. By insisting on systematic observation and measurement, he asked some interesting questions and got psychology off to a good start (Schultz & Schultz, 2012).

Structuralism

Edward Titchener (TICH-in-er) brought Wundt's ideas to the United States. He called Wundt's ideas **structuralism** and tried to analyze the structure of mental life into basic elements, or building blocks.

How could he do that? You can't analyze experience like a chemical compound, can you? Perhaps not, but the structuralists tried mental chemistry, mostly by using introspection. For instance, an observer might hold an apple and decide that she had experienced the elements hue (color), roundness, and weight. Another question a structuralist might have asked is, "What basic tastes mix together to create complex flavors as different as broccoli, lime, bacon, and strawberry cheesecake?"

Introspection proved to be a poor way to answer most questions (Benjafield, 2012). Why? Because no matter how systematic the observations, the structuralists frequently *disagreed*. When they did, there was no way to settle intersubjective differences. Think about it. If you and a friend both introspect on your perceptions of an apple and end up listing different basic elements, who would be right? Despite such limitations, looking inward is still used as one source of insight in studies of hypnosis, meditation, problem solving, moods, and many other topics.

Functionalism

American scholar William James broadened psychology to include animal behavior, religious experience, abnormal

behavior, and other interesting topics. James's brilliant first book, *Principles of Psychology* (1890), helped establish the field as a separate discipline (Hergenhahn, 2009).

The term **functionalism** comes from James's interest in how the mind functions to help us adapt to the environment. James regarded consciousness as an ever-changing *stream* or *flow* of images and sensations—not a set of lifeless building blocks, as the structuralists claimed.

The functionalists admired Charles Darwin, who deduced that creatures evolve in ways that favor survival. According to Darwin's principle of **natural selection**, physical features that help animals adapt to their environments are retained in evolution. Similarly, the functionalists wanted to find out how the mind, perception, habits, and emotions help us adapt and survive.

What effect did functionalism have on modern psychology? Functionalism brought the study of animals into psychology. It also promoted *educational psychology* (the study of learning, teaching, classroom dynamics, and related topics). Learning makes us more adaptable, so the functionalists tried to find ways to improve education. For similar reasons, functionalism spurred the rise of *industrial psychology*, the study of people at work (see Module 75).

Stimulus *Any physical energy an organism senses.*
Introspection *To look within; to examine one's own thoughts, feelings, or sensations.*
Structuralism *The school of thought concerned with analyzing sensations and personal experience into basic elements.*
Functionalism *The school of psychology concerned with how behavior and mental abilities help people adapt to their environments.*
Natural selection *Darwin's theory that evolution favors those plants and animals best suited to their living conditions.*

Behaviorism

Functionalism and structuralism were soon challenged by **behaviorism**, the study of observable behavior. Behaviorist John B. Watson objected strongly to the study of the "mind" or conscious experience. He believed that introspection is unscientific precisely because there is no objective way to settle disagreements between observers. Watson realized that he could study the overt behavior of animals even though he couldn't ask animals questions or know what they were thinking (Benjafield, 2012). He simply observed the relationship between any *stimuli* (events in the environment) and an animal's **response** (any muscular action, glandular activity, or other identifiable aspect of behavior). These observations were objective because they did not involve introspecting on subjective experience. Why not, he asked, apply the same objectivity to study human behavior?

Watson soon adopted Russian physiologist Ivan Pavlov's (ee-VAHN PAV-lahv) concept of *conditioning* to explain most behavior. (A *conditioned response* is a learned reaction to a particular stimulus.) Watson claimed, "Give me a dozen healthy infants, well-formed, and my own special world to bring them up in and I'll guarantee to take any one at random and train him to become any type of specialist I might select—doctor, lawyer, artist, merchant-chief, and yes, beggarman and thief" (Watson, 1913/1994).

Would most psychologists agree with Watson's claim? No. The early behaviorists believed that all responses are *determined* by stimuli. Today, this is regarded as an overstatement. Just the same, by stressing the study of observable behavior, behaviorism helped make psychology a natural science, rather than a branch of philosophy.

Radical Behaviorism The best-known behaviorist, B. F. Skinner (1904–1990), believed that our actions are controlled by rewards and punishments. To study learning, Skinner created his famous conditioning chamber, or Skinner box. With it, he could present stimuli to animals and record their responses. Many of Skinner's ideas about learning grew out of work with rats and pigeons. Nevertheless, he believed that the same laws of behavior apply to humans. As a radical behaviorist, Skinner also believed that covert mental events, such as thinking, are not needed to explain behavior (Schultz & Schultz, 2012).

Behaviorists deserve credit for much of what we know about learning, conditioning, and the proper use of reward and punishment. Skinner was convinced that a designed culture based on positive reinforcement could encourage desirable behavior. (Skinner opposed the use of punishment because it doesn't teach correct responses.) Too often, he believed, misguided rewards lead to destructive actions that create problems such as overpopulation, pollution, and war.

Archives of the History of American Psychology, The Center for the History of Psychology, The University of Akron.

John B. Watson, 1878–1958. Watson's intense interest in observable behavior began with his doctoral studies in biology and neurology. Watson became a psychology professor at Johns Hopkins University in 1908 and advanced his theory of behaviorism. He remained at Johns Hopkins until 1920 when he left for a career in the advertising industry.

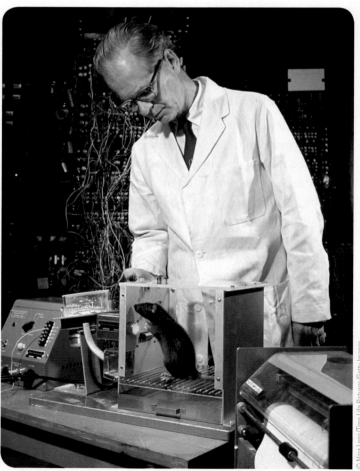

© Nina Leen/Time Life Pictures/Getty Images

B. F. Skinner, 1904–1990. Skinner studied simple behaviors under carefully controlled conditions. The Skinner Box you see here has been widely used to study learning in simplified animal experiments. In addition to advancing psychology, Skinner hoped that his radical brand of behaviorism would improve human life.

Cognitive Behaviorism Radical behaviorists have been criticized for ignoring the role that thinking plays in our lives. One critic even charged that Skinnerian psychology had "lost consciousness." However, many criticisms have been answered by **cognitive behaviorism**, a view that combines conditioning and cognition (thinking) to explain behavior (Zentall, 2002). As an example, let's say you frequently visit a particular website because it offers free streaming videos. A behaviorist would say that you visit the site because you are rewarded by the pleasure of watching interesting videos each time you go there. A cognitive behaviorist would add that, in addition, you *expect* to find free videos at the site. This is the cognitive part of your behavior.

Behaviorists deserve credit for much of what we know about learning, conditioning, and the proper use of reward and punishment. Behaviorism also is the source of behavior therapy, which uses learning principles to change problem behaviors such as overeating, unrealistic fears, or temper tantrums (see Modules 67 and 69 for more information).

Gestalt Psychology

Imagine that you just played "Happy Birthday" on a flute. Next, you play it on a guitar. The guitar duplicates none of the flute's sounds. Yet we notice something interesting: The melody is still recognizable—as long as the *relationship* between notes remains the same.

What would happen if you played the notes of "Happy Birthday" in the correct order but at a rate of one per hour? What would you have? Nothing! The separate notes would no longer be a melody. Perceptually, the melody is more than the individual notes that define it.

Observations like these launched the Gestalt school of thought. German psychologist Max Wertheimer (VERT-hi-mer) was the first to advance the Gestalt viewpoint. It is inaccurate, he said, to analyze psychological events into pieces, or elements, as the structuralists did. Accordingly, **Gestalt psychology** studied thinking, learning, and perception as whole units, not by analyzing experiences into parts. Their slogan was, "The whole is greater than the sum of its parts." In fact, the German word *Gestalt* means form, pattern, or whole.

Like a melody, many experiences cannot be broken into smaller units, as the structuralists proposed. For this reason, studies of perception and personality have been especially influenced by the Gestalt viewpoint. Gestalt psychology also inspired a type of psychotherapy (see Module 66).

Max Wertheimer, 1880–1941. Wertheimer first proposed the Gestalt viewpoint to help explain perceptual illusions. He later promoted Gestalt psychology as a way to understand not only perception, problem solving, thinking, and social behavior, but also art, logic, philosophy, and politics.

Archives of the History of American Psychology, The Center for the History of Psychology, The University of Akron.

Psychoanalytic Psychology

As American psychology grew more scientific, an Austrian doctor named Sigmund Freud was developing radically different ideas that opened new horizons in art, literature, and history, as well as psychology (Barratt, 2013; Chessick, 2010). Freud believed that mental life is like an iceberg: Only a small part is exposed to view. He called the area of the mind that lies outside of personal awareness the **unconscious**. According to Freud, our behavior is deeply influenced by unconscious thoughts, impulses, and desires—especially those concerning sex and aggression.

Sigmund Freud, 1856–1939. For more than 50 years, Freud probed the unconscious mind. In doing so, he altered modern views of human nature. His early experimentation with a "talking cure" for hysteria is regarded as the beginning of psychoanalysis. Through psychoanalysis, Freud added psychological treatment methods to psychiatry.

Imagno/Hulton Archive/Getty Images

Behaviorism *The school of psychology that emphasizes the study of overt, observable behavior.*

Response *Any muscular action, glandular activity, or other identifiable aspect of behavior.*

Cognitive behaviorism *An approach that combines behavioral principles with cognition (e.g. perception, thinking, anticipation) to explain behavior.*

Gestalt psychology *A school of psychology emphasizing the study of thinking, learning, and perception in whole units, not by analysis into parts.*

Unconscious *Contents of the mind that are beyond awareness, especially impulses and desires not directly known to a person.*

Freud theorized that many unconscious thoughts are *repressed*, or held out of awareness, because they are threatening. But sometimes, he said, they are revealed by dreams, emotions, or slips of the tongue. (Freudian slips are often humorous, as when a student who is late for class says, "I'm sorry I couldn't get here any later.")

Like the behaviorists, Freud believed that all thoughts, emotions, and actions are *determined*. In other words, nothing is an accident: If we probe deeply enough, we will find the causes of every thought or action. Unlike the behaviorists, he believed that unconscious processes (not external stimuli) were responsible.

Freud also was among the first to appreciate that childhood affects adult personality ("the child is father to the man"). Most of all, perhaps, Freud is known for creating **psychoanalysis**, the first fully developed psychotherapy, or "talking cure." Freudian psychotherapy explores unconscious conflicts and emotional problems (see Module 65).

It wasn't long before some of Freud's students modified Freud's ideas. Known as **neo-Freudians** (*neo* means new or recent), they accept much of Freud's theory but revise parts of it. Many, for instance, place less emphasis on sex and aggression and more on social motives and relationships. Some well-known neo-Freudians are Alfred Adler, Anna Freud (Freud's daughter), Karen Horney (HORN-eye), Carl Jung (yoong), Otto Rank (rahnk), and Erik Erikson. Today, Freud's ideas have been altered so much that few strictly psychoanalytic psychologists are left. However, his legacy is still evident in any **psychodynamic theory**, which continues to emphasize internal motives, conflicts, and unconscious forces (Moran, 2010).

Humanistic Psychology

Humanism is a view that focuses on subjective human experience. Humanistic psychologists are interested in human potentials, ideals, and problems.

How is the humanistic approach different from others? Carl Rogers, Abraham Maslow, and other humanists rejected the Freudian idea that we are ruled by unconscious forces. They also were uncomfortable with the behaviorist emphasis on conditioning. Both views have a strong undercurrent of **determinism**—the idea that behavior is determined by forces beyond our control. In contrast, the humanists stress **free will**, our ability to make voluntary choices. Of course, past experiences do affect us. Nevertheless, humanists believe that people can freely *choose* to live more creative, meaningful, and satisfying lives.

Abraham Maslow, 1908–1970. As a founder of humanistic psychology, Maslow was interested in studying people of exceptional mental health. Such self-actualized people, he believed, make full use of their talents and abilities. Maslow offered his positive view of human potential as an alternative to the perspectives of behaviorism and psychoanalysis.

Bettmann/Corbis

TABLE 3.1		The Early Development of Psychology
Perspective	**Date**	**Notable Events**
Experimental psychology	1875	• First psychology course offered by William James
	1878	• First American PhD in psychology awarded
	1879	• Wilhelm Wundt opens first psychology laboratory in Germany
	1883	• First American psychology lab founded at Johns Hopkins University
	1886	• First American psychology textbook written by John Dewey
Structuralism	1898	• Edward Titchener advances psychology based on introspection
Functionalism	1890	• William James publishes *Principles of Psychology*
	1892	• American Psychological Association founded
Psychodynamic psychology	1895	• Sigmund Freud publishes first studies
	1900	• Freud publishes *The Interpretation of Dreams*
Behaviorism	1906	• Ivan Pavlov reports his research on conditioned reflexes
	1913	• John Watson presents behaviorist view
Gestalt psychology	1912	• Max Wertheimer and others advance Gestalt viewpoint
Humanistic psychology	1942	• Carl Rogers publishes *Counseling and Psychotherapy*
	1943	• Abraham Maslow publishes "A Theory of Human Motivation."

© Cengage Learning

Humanists are interested in psychological needs for love, self-esteem, belonging, self-expression, creativity, and spirituality. Such needs, they believe, are as important as our biological urges for food and water. For example, newborn infants deprived of human love may die just as surely as they would if deprived of food.

How scientific is the humanistic approach? Initially, humanists were less interested in treating psychology as a science. They stressed subjective factors, such as one's self-image, self-evaluation, and frame of reference. (*Self-image* is your perception of your own body, personality, and capabilities. *Self-evaluation* refers to appraising yourself as good or bad. A *frame of reference* is a mental perspective used to interpret events.) Today, humanists still try to understand how we perceive ourselves and experience the world. However, most now do research to test their ideas, just as other psychologists do (Schneider, Bugental, & Pierson, 2001).

Maslow's concept of self-actualization is a key feature of humanism. **Self-actualization** refers to developing one's potential fully and becoming the best person possible. According to humanists, everyone has this potential. Humanists seek ways to help it emerge.

● Table 3.1 presents a summary of psychology's early development.

The Role of Diversity in Psychology's Early Days

Were all the early psychologists Caucasian men? Although women and ethnic minorities were long underrepresented among psychologists, there

Margaret Washburn, 1871–1939. In 1908, Washburn published *The Animal Mind*, an influential textbook on animal behavior.

were pioneers (Minton, 2000). In 1894, Margaret Washburn became the first woman to be awarded a PhD in psychology. By 1906 in America, about one psychologist in ten was a woman. In 1920, Francis Cecil Sumner became the first African-American man to earn a doctoral degree in psychology. Inez Beverly Prosser, the first African-American female psychologist, was awarded her PhD in 1933.

Francis Cecil Sumner, 1895–1954. Sumner served as chair of the Psychology Department at Howard University and wrote articles critical of the under-representation of African Americans in American colleges and universities.

Inez Beverly Prosser, ca. 1895–1934. Prosser was one of the early leaders in the debate about how to best educate African-American children.

The predominance of early Caucasian male psychologists is worrisome because it inadvertently introduced a narrowness into psychological theory and research. Biases concerning the race, ethnicity, age, and sexual orientation of researchers and participants in psychological research have definitely limited our understanding (Carroll, 2013; Guthrie, 2004). Far too many conclusions have been created by and/or based on small groups of people who do not represent the rich tapestry of humanity.

Since 2000, however, more than 70 percent of all undergraduate and graduate degrees in psychology have been awarded to women. Similarly, 25 percent of all undergraduate degrees and 16 percent of doctorates in psychology were awarded to persons of color (American Psychological Association, 2003a). Increasingly, psychology is coming to better reflect human diversity (American Psychological Association, 2012; Hyde, 2013).

Psychoanalysis *A Freudian approach to psychotherapy that emphasizes exploring unconscious conflicts.*
Neo-Freudian *A psychologist who accepts the broad features of Freud's theory but has revised the theory to fit his or her own concepts.*
Psychodynamic theory *Any theory of behavior that emphasizes internal conflicts, motives, and unconscious forces.*
Humanism *An approach to psychology that focuses on human experience, problems, potentials, and ideals.*
Determinism *The idea that all behavior has prior causes that would completely explain one's choices and actions if all such causes were known.*
Free will *The idea that human beings are capable of freely making choices or decisions.*
Self-actualization *The ongoing process of fully developing one's personal potential.*

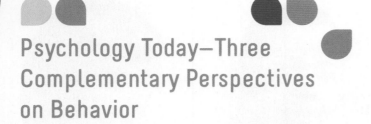

Psychology Today—Three Complementary Perspectives on Behavior

SURVEY QUESTION 3.2: What are the contemporary perspectives in psychology?

Key insights from the early schools of thought played an important role in the development of the three broad views

that shape modern psychology: the *biological, psychological,* and *sociocultural* perspectives (● Table 3.2).

The Biological Perspective

The **biological perspective** seeks to explain behavior in terms of biological principles such as brain processes, evolution, and genetics. By using new techniques, *biopsychologists* are producing exciting insights about how the brain relates to thinking, feelings, perception, abnormal behavior, and other topics. Biopsychologists and others who study the brain and nervous system, such as biologists and biochemists, together

TABLE 3.2	Contemporary Ways to Look at Behavior

Biological Perspective

Biopsychological View

Key Idea: *Human and animal behavior is the result of internal physical, chemical, and biological processes.*
Seeks to explain behavior through activity of the brain and nervous system, physiology, genetics, the endocrine system, and biochemistry; neutral, reductionistic, mechanistic view of human nature

Evolutionary View

Key Idea: *Human and animal behavior is the result of the process of evolution.*
Seeks to explain behavior through evolutionary principles based on natural selection; neutral, reductionistic, mechanistic view of human nature

Psychological Perspective

Behaviorist View

Key Idea: *Behavior is shaped and controlled by one's environment.*
Emphasizes the study of observable behavior and the effects of learning; stresses the influence of external rewards and punishments; neutral, scientific, somewhat mechanistic view of human nature

Cognitive View

Key Idea: *Much human behavior can be understood in terms of the mental processing of information.*
Concerned with thinking, knowing, perception, understanding, memory, decision making, and judgment; explains behavior in terms of information processing; neutral, somewhat computer-like view of human nature

Psychodynamic View

Key Idea: *Behavior is directed by forces within one's personality that are often hidden or unconscious.*
Emphasizes internal impulses, desires, and conflicts—especially those that are unconscious; views behavior as the result of clashing forces within personality; somewhat negative, pessimistic view of human nature

Humanistic View

Key Idea: *Behavior is guided by one's self-image, by subjective perceptions of the world, and by needs for personal growth.*
Focuses on subjective, conscious experience, human problems, potentials, and ideals; emphasizes self-image and self-actualization to explain behavior; positive, philosophical view of human nature.

Sociocultural Perspective

Sociocultural View

Key Idea: *Behavior is influenced by one's social and cultural context.*
Emphasizes that behavior is related to the social and cultural environment within which a person is born, grows up, and lives from day to day; neutral, interactionist view of human nature

explore the broader field of **neuroscience**. **Evolutionary psychology** looks at how human evolution and genetics might explain our current behavior.

The Psychological Perspective

The **psychological perspective** views behavior as the result of psychological processes within each person. This view continues to emphasize scientific observation, just as the early behaviorists did. However, the psychological perspective now includes *cognitive psychology*, which seeks to explain how mental processes, such as thoughts and feelings, influence our behavior (Reed, 2013). Cognitive psychology has gained prominence in recent years as researchers have devised research methods to objectively study covert behaviors, such as thinking, memory, language, perception, problem solving, consciousness, and creativity. With a renewed interest in thinking, it can be said that psychology has finally "regained consciousness" (Robins, Gosling, & Craik, 1998).

Freudian psychoanalysis continues to evolve into the broader *psychodynamic view*. Although many of Freud's ideas have been challenged or refuted, psychodynamic psychologists continue to trace our behavior to unconscious mental activity. They also seek to develop therapies to help people lead happier, fuller lives. The same is true of humanistic psychologists, although they stress subjective, conscious experience and the positive side of human nature, rather than unconscious processes.

Positive Psychology Psychologists have always paid attention to the negative side of human behavior. This is easy to understand because of the pressing need to solve human problems. However, more and more psychologists, some of them inspired by the humanists, have begun to ask, "What do we know about love, happiness, creativity, well-being, self-confidence, and achievement?" Together, such topics make up **positive psychology**, the study of human strengths, virtues, and optimal behavior (Compton & Hoffman, 2013). Many topics from positive psychology can be found in this book. Ideally, they will help your own life become more positive and fulfilling (Snyder, Lopez, & Pedrotti, 2011).

The Sociocultural Perspective

As you can see, it is helpful to view human behavior from more than one perspective. This is also true in another sense. The **sociocultural perspective** stresses the impact that social and cultural contexts have on our behavior. We are rapidly

Chris Parypa/Alamy

As illustrated by this photo from the second inauguration of President Barack Obama in 2013, America is becoming more diverse. To fully understand human behavior, personal differences based on age, race, culture, ethnicity, gender, and sexual orientation must be taken into account.

becoming a multicultural society. Over 100 million Americans are now African American, Hispanic, Asian American, Native American, or Pacific Islander (Humes, Jones, & Ramirez, 2010). In some large cities, such as Detroit and Baltimore, minority groups have become the majority.

How has this affected psychology? In the past, psychology was based mostly on the cultures of North America and Europe. Now, we must ask, do the principles of Western psychology apply to people in all cultures? Are some psychological concepts invalid in other cultures? Are any universal? As psychologists have probed such questions, one thing has become clear: Most of what we think, feel, and do is influenced, in one way or another, by the social and cultural worlds in which we live (Baumeister & Bushman, 2014; Henrich, Heine, Norenzayan, 2010).

Cultural Relativity Imagine that you are a clinical psychologist. Your client, Linda, who is a Native American, tells you

Biological perspective *The attempt to explain behavior in terms of underlying biological principles.*
Neuroscience *The broader field of biopsychologists and others who study the brain and nervous system, such as biologists and biochemists.*
Evolutionary psychology *The study of how human evolution and genetics might explain our current behavior.*
Psychological perspective *The traditional view that behavior is shaped by psychological processes occurring at the level of the individual.*
Positive psychology *The study of human strengths, virtues, and effective functioning.*
Sociocultural perspective *The focus on the importance of social and cultural contexts in influencing the behavior of individuals.*

that spirits live in the trees near her home. Is Linda suffering from a delusion? Is she abnormal? Cases like Linda's teach us to be wary of using narrow standards when judging others or comparing groups. Obviously, you will misjudge Linda's mental health if you fail to take her cultural beliefs into account. **Cultural relativity**—the idea that behavior must be judged relative to the values of the culture in which it occurs—can greatly affect our understanding of "other people," including the diagnosis and treatment of mental disorders (Lum, 2011). To be effective, psychologists must be sensitive to people who are ethnically and culturally different from themselves (Lowman, 2013).

A Broader View of Diversity In addition to cultural differences, the behavior of people is influenced by differences in age, ethnicity, gender, religion, disability, and sexual orientation, which all affect the **social norms** that guide behavior. Social norms are rules that define acceptable and expected behavior for members of various groups. Too often, the unstated standard for determining what is average, normal, or correct has been the behavior of middle-aged, white, heterosexual, middle-class Western males (Henrich, Heine, & Norenzayan, 2010). An appreciation of the fuller spectrum of human diversity can enrich your life as well as your understanding of psychology (Helgeson, 2012).

The Whole Human Today, many psychologists realize that a single perspective is unlikely to fully explain complex human behavior. As a result, they are *eclectic* (ek-LEK-tik) and draw insights from a variety of perspectives. As we will see throughout this book, insights from one perspective often complement insights from the others as we seek to better understand the whole human.

Psychologists—Guaranteed Not to Shrink

SURVEY QUESTION 3.3: What are the major specialties in psychology?

Do all psychologists do therapy and treat abnormal behavior? Less than 60 percent of psychologists are clinical and counseling psychologists. Regardless, every **psychologist** is highly trained in the methods, knowledge, and theories of psychology. Psychologists usually have earned a master's degree or a doctorate, typically requiring several years of postgraduate training. Twenty-nine percent are employed full-time at colleges or universities, where they teach and do research, consulting, or therapy. The remainder give psychological tests, do research in other settings, or serve as consultants to business, industry, government, or the military (see ● **Figure 3.1**).

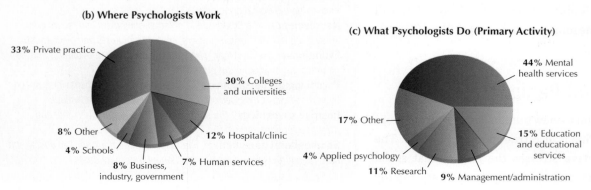

● **Figure 3.1**

(a) Specialties in psychology (APA Center for Workforce Studies, 2012). Percentages are approximate. (b) Where psychologists work (Cheal et al., 2009). (c) This chart shows the main activities psychologists do at work. Any one psychologist might participate in several of these activities during a work week. As you can see, most psychologists specialize in applied areas and work in applied settings (Cheal et al., 2009).

At present, the American Psychological Association (APA) consists of more than 50 divisions, each reflecting special skills or areas of interest. No matter where they are employed or what their area of specialization, many psychologists do research. Some do *basic research*, in which they seek knowledge for its own sake. For example, a psychologist might study memory simply to understand how it works. Others do *applied research* to solve immediate practical problems, such as finding ways to improve athletic performance (Davey, 2011). Some do both types of research. Some of the major specialties are listed in ● **Table 3.3**.

Have you ever wondered what it takes to become a psychologist? See "Is a Career in Psychology Right for You?"

Discovering Psychology

Is a Career in Psychology Right for You?

As you read these modules, we encourage you to frequently reflect on new ideas by relating them to your own life so you can better understand and remember them. Discovering Psychology features are designed to help you be more reflective about how psychology relates to your own life. Answer the following questions to explore whether you would enjoy becoming a psychologist:

1. I have a strong interest in human behavior. True or False?
2. I am good at recognizing patterns, evaluating evidence, and drawing conclusions. True or False?
3. I am emotionally stable. True or False?
4. I have good communication skills. True or False?
5. I find theories and ideas challenging and stimulating. True or False?
6. My friends regard me as especially sensitive to the feelings of others. True or False?
7. I enjoy planning and carrying out complex projects and activities. True or False?
8. Programs and popular books about psychology interest me. True or False?
9. I enjoy working with other people. True or False?
10. Clear thinking, objectivity, and keen observation appeal to me. True or False?

If you answered True to most of these questions, a career in psychology might be a good choice. Remember that many psychology majors also succeed in occupations such as management, public affairs, social services, business, sales, and education (Kuther & Morgan, 2013).

Animals and Psychology *Research involving animals was mentioned in some of the psychology specialties listed in Table 3.3. Why is that?* You may be surprised to learn that psychologists are interested in the behavior of *any* living creature—from flatworms to humans. Indeed, some comparative psychologists spend their entire careers studying rats, cats, dogs, parrots, or chimpanzees.

Killer whales living along the Pacific coast near the border of the United States and Canada are listed as endangered. Studies of their social behavior are enhancing efforts to conserve these magnificent creatures (Foster et al., 2012).

Although only a small percentage of psychological studies involve animals, they include many different types of research (Baker & Serdikoff, 2013). Some psychologists use an **animal model** to discover principles that apply to humans. For instance, animal studies have helped us understand stress, learning, obesity, aging, sleep, and many other topics. Psychology also can benefit animals. Behavioral studies can help us better care for domestic animals and those in zoos as well as conserve endangered species in the wild.

Cultural relativity *The idea that behavior must be judged relative to the values of the culture in which it occurs.*
Social norms *Rules that define acceptable and expected behavior for members of a group.*
Psychologist *A person highly trained in the methods, factual knowledge, and theories of psychology.*
Animal model *In research, an animal whose behavior is studied to derive principles that may apply to human behavior.*

TABLE 3.3 Types of Psychologists and What They Do

Specialty		Typical Activities	Sample Research Topic
Biopsychology	B*	Researches the brain, nervous system, and other physical origins of behavior	"I've been doing some exciting research on how the brain controls hunger."
Clinical	A	Does psychotherapy; investigates clinical problems; develops methods of treatment	"I'm curious about the relationship between early childhood trauma and adult relationships so I can help adults be more successful in their marriages."
Cognitive	B	Studies human thinking and information processing abilities	"I want to know how reasoning, problem solving, memory, and other mental processes relate to computer game playing."
Community	A	Promotes community-wide mental health through research, prevention, education, and consultation	"How can we prevent the spread of sexually transmitted diseases more effectively? That's what I want to better understand."
Comparative	B	Studies and compares the behavior of different species, especially animals	"Personally, I'm fascinated by the communication abilities of porpoises."
Consumer	A	Researches packaging, advertising, marketing methods, and characteristics of consumers	"My job is to improve the marketing of products that are environment-friendly.
Counseling	A	Does psychotherapy and personal counseling; researches emotional disturbances and counseling methods	"I am focused on better understanding why people become hoarders and how to help them stop."
Cultural	B	Studies the ways in which culture, subculture, and ethnic group membership affect behavior	"I am interested in how culture affects human eating behavior, especially the foods we eat and whether we eat with a spoon, chopsticks, or our fingers."
Developmental	A, B	Conducts research on infant, child, adolescent, and adult development; does clinical work with disturbed children; acts as consultant to parents and schools	"I'm focusing on transitions from the teenage years to early adulthood."
Educational	A	Investigates classroom dynamics, teaching styles, and learning; develops educational tests, evaluates educational programs	"My passion is to figure out how to help people with different learning styles be effective learners."
Engineering	A	Does applied research on the design of machinery, computers, airlines, automobiles, and so on for business, industry, and the military	"I'm studying how people use movement-based computer interfaces, like Xbox Kinect."
Environmental	A, B	Studies the effects of urban noise, crowding, attitudes toward the environment, and human use of space; acts as a consultant on environmental issues	"I am concerned about global warming and want to understand what impact rising temperatures have on human culture."
Evolutionary	B	Studies how behavior is guided by patterns that evolved during the long history of humankind	"I am studying some interesting trends in male and female mating choices."
Forensic	A	Studies problems of crime and crime prevention, rehabilitation programs, prisons, courtroom dynamics; selects candidates for police work	"I am interested in improving the reliability of eyewitness testimony during trials."
Gender	B	Researches differences between males and females, the acquisition of gender identity, and the role of gender throughout life	"I want to understand how young boys and girls are influenced by gender stereotypes."
Health	A, B	Studies the relationship between behavior and health; uses psychological principles to promote health and prevent illness	"How to better help people overcome drug addictions is my field of study."
Industrial-organizational	A	Selects job applicants; does skills analysis; evaluates on-the-job training; improves work environments and human relations in organizations and work settings	"Which plays a greater role in successful management styles, intelligence or emotion? That is my question."

TABLE 3.3		Types of Psychologists and What They Do, *continued*	
Specialty		**Typical Activities**	**Sample Research Topic**
Learning	B	Studies how and why learning occurs; develops theories of learning	"Right now, I'm investigating how patterns of reinforcement affect learning. I am especially interested in superstitious conditioning."
Medical	A	Applies psychology to manage medical problems, such as the emotional impact of illness, self-screening for cancer, compliance in taking medicine	"I want to know how to help people take charge of their own health."
Personality	B	Studies personality traits and dynamics; develops theories of personality and tests for assessing personality traits	"I am especially interested in the personality profiles of people willing to take extreme risks."
School	A	Does psychological testing, referrals, emotional and vocational counseling of students; detects and treats learning disabilities; improves classroom learning	"My focus is finding out how to keep students in school instead of having them drop out."
Sensation and perception	B	Studies the sense organs and the process of perception; investigates the mechanisms of sensation; develops theories about how perception occurs	"I am using a perceptual theory to study how we are able to recognize faces in a crowd."
Social	B	Investigates human social behavior, including attitudes, conformity, persuasion, prejudice, friendship, aggression, helping, and so forth	"My interest is interpersonal attraction. I place two strangers in a room and analyze how strongly they are attracted to each other."

Research in this area is typically applied (A), basic (B), or both (A, B).

© Cengage Learning

Helping People

Although most psychologists help people in one way or another, those interested in emotional problems usually specialize in clinical or counseling psychology (see Table 3.3). A **clinical psychologist** treats psychological problems or does research on therapies and mental disorders. In contrast, a **counseling psychologist** treats milder problems, such as troubles at work or school. However, such differences are fading, and many counseling psychologists now work full-time as therapists.

To become a clinical psychologist, it is best to have a doctorate (PhD, PsyD, or EdD). Most clinical psychologists have a PhD degree and follow a scientist-as-practitioner model—that is, they are trained to do either research or therapy. Many do both. Other clinicians earn the PsyD (Doctor of Psychology) degree, which emphasizes therapy skills rather than research (Stricker, 2011).

Does a psychologist need a license to offer therapy? At one time, it was possible in many states for anyone to hang out a shingle as a psychologist. Now psychologists not only must meet rigorous educational requirements but they must also meet stringent legal requirements. To work as a clinical or counseling psychologist, you must have a license issued by a state examining board. However, the law does not prevent you from calling yourself anything else you choose—therapist, rebirther, primal feeling facilitator, cosmic aura balancer, or life skills coach—or from selling your services to anyone willing to pay. Beware of people with self-proclaimed titles. Even if their intentions are honorable, they may have little training. A licensed psychologist who chooses to use a particular type of therapy is not the same as someone trained solely in that technique.

Psychologists are often inaccurately portrayed in the media as incompetent therapists. Some films have featured psychologists who are more disturbed than their patients (such as Jack Nicholson's character in *Anger Management*) or psychologists who are bumbling buffoons (such as Billy Crystal's character in *Analyze This*). In the Internet series *Web Therapy*,

Clinical psychologist *A psychologist who specializes in the treatment of psychological and behavioral disturbances or who does research on such disturbances.*

Counseling psychologist *A psychologist who specializes in the treatment of milder emotional and behavioral disturbances.*

Friends star Lisa Kudrow plays a hapless therapist who thinks real therapy can happen over the web in three minutes. Such characters may be dramatic and entertaining, but they seriously distort public perceptions of responsible and hardworking psychologists (Schultz, 2004).

Real clinical and counseling psychologists follow an ethical code that stresses (1) high levels of competence, integrity, and responsibility, (2) respect for people's rights to privacy, dignity, confidentiality, and personal freedom, and, above all, (3) protection of the client's welfare (American Psychological Association, 2010a; Barnett et al., 2007). Psychologists also are expected to use their knowledge to contribute to society. Many volunteer in the communities in which they live.

Other Mental Health Professionals

Clinical psychologists are not the only people who work in the field of mental health. Often, they coordinate their efforts with other specially trained professionals. What are the differences among psychologists, psychiatrists, psychoanalysts, counselors, and other mental health professionals? Each has a specific blend of training and skills.

Psychologists are all shrinks, right? Nope. A *shrink* (a slang term derived from head shrinkers) is a **psychiatrist**, a medical doctor who treats mental disorders, often by doing psychotherapy. Psychiatrists also can prescribe drugs, which is something psychologists usually cannot do. However, this is changing. Psychologists in New Mexico and Louisiana can now legally prescribe drugs, as can psychologists in the U.S. military. It will be interesting to see whether other states grant similar privileges (McGrath & Moore, 2010).

To be a psychoanalyst, you must have a moustache and goatee, spectacles, a German accent, and a well-padded couch—or so the media stereotype goes. In reality, to become a **psychoanalyst**, you must have an MD or PhD degree plus further training in Freudian psychoanalysis. In other words, either a physician or a psychologist may become a psychoanalyst by learning a specific type of psychotherapy.

In many states, counselors also do mental health work. A **counselor** is an adviser who helps solve problems with marriage, career, school, work, or the like. To be a licensed counselor (such as a marriage and family counselor, a child counselor, or a school counselor) typically requires a master's degree plus one or two years of full-time supervised counseling experience. Counselors learn practical helping skills and do not treat serious mental disorders.

A **psychiatric social worker** plays an important role in many mental health programs by applying social science principles to help patients in clinics and hospitals. Most psychiatric social workers hold an MSW (Master of Social Work) degree. Often, they assist psychologists and psychiatrists as part of a team. Their typical duties include evaluating patients and families, conducting group therapy, or visiting a patient's home, school, or job to alleviate problems.

Psychiatrist *A medical doctor with additional training in the diagnosis and treatment of mental and emotional disorders.*
Psychoanalyst *A mental health professional (usually a medical doctor) trained to practice psychoanalysis.*
Counselor *A mental health professional who specializes in helping people with problems that do not involve serious mental disorders; for example, marriage counselors, career counselors, or school counselors.*
Psychiatric social worker *A mental health professional trained to apply social science principles to help patients in clinics and hospitals.*

Module 3: Summary

3.1 How did the field of psychology emerge?

▪ **3.1.1** The field of psychology emerged over 130 years ago when researchers began to directly study and observe psychological events.

▪ **3.1.2** The first psychological laboratory was established in Germany in 1879 by Wilhelm Wundt, who studied conscious experience.

▪ **3.1.3** The first school of thought in psychology was structuralism, a kind of mental chemistry based on introspection.

▪ **3.1.4** Structuralism was followed by functionalism, behaviorism, and Gestalt psychology.

▪ **3.1.5** Psychodynamic approaches, such as Freud's psychoanalytic theory, emphasize the unconscious origins of behavior.

▪ **3.1.6** Humanistic psychology accentuates subjective experience, human potentials, and personal growth.

▪ **3.1.7** Because most early psychologists were Caucasian men, bias was inadvertently introduced into psychological research. Today, more women and minorities are becoming psychologists and being studied as research participants.

3.2 What are the contemporary perspectives in psychology?

▪ **3.2.1** Three complementary streams of thought in modern psychology are the biological perspective, including biopsychology and evolutionary psychology; the psychological perspective, including behaviorism, cognitive psychology, the psychodynamic approach, and humanism; and the sociocultural perspective.

▪ **3.2.2** Psychologists have recently begun to formally study positive aspects of human behavior, or positive psychology.

▪ **3.2.3** Most of what we think, feel, and do is influenced by the social and cultural worlds in which we live.

▪ **3.2.4** Today, many viewpoints within psychology have contributed to what is now an eclectic blend.

3.3 What are the major specialties in psychology?

▪ **3.3.1** The field of psychology now has dozens of specialties.

▪ **3.3.2** Psychological research can be basic or applied.

▪ **3.3.3** Psychologists may be directly interested in animal behavior, or they may study animals as models of human behavior.

▪ **3.3.4** Although psychologists, psychiatrists, psychoanalysts, counselors, and psychiatric social workers all work in the field of mental health, their training and methods differ considerably.

Module 3: Knowledge Builder

Recite

1. A psychotherapist is working with a person from an ethnic group other than her own. She should be aware of how cultural relativity and _____ affect behavior.

   a. the anthropomorphic error   *c.* biased sampling

   b. operational definitions   *d.* social norms

Match the following research areas with the topics they cover.

_____ 2. Developmental psychology   **A.** Attitudes, groups, leadership

_____ 3. Learning   **B.** Behavior as related to the legal system

_____ 4. Personality   **C.** Brain and nervous system

_____ 5. Sensation and perception   **D.** Child psychology

_____ 6. Biopsychology   **E.** Individual differences, motivation

_____ 7. Social psychology   **F.** Processing sensory information

_____ 8. Forensic psychology   **G.** Conditioning, memory

9. A psychologist who specializes in treating human emotional difficulties is called a _____ psychologist.

Reflect

Think Critically

10. Modern sciences like psychology are built on intersubjective observations, those that can be verified by two or more independent observers. Did structuralism meet this standard? Why or why not?

Self-Reflect

Which contemporary perspective most closely matches your own view of behavior? Can you explain why so many psychologists are eclectic?

Which specialty in psychology is most interesting to you? What is it about that specialty that most attracts you?

ANSWERS

thing that no other person can observe.
downfall was that each observer examined the contents of his or her own mind—which is some-
1. d **2.** D **3.** G **4.** E **5.** F **6.** C **7.** A **8.** B **9.** clinical or counseling **10.** No, it did not. Structuralism's

Introducing Psychology: The Psychology Experiment

Get Causality Right

Would she feel weird in a pair of those new wearable computer glasses? Sally worried people would stop to gawk. To find out, she borrowed a pair from someone who worked for the company that created them. After wearing them to work for a few days, she realized that they didn't make much difference, compared to her regular glasses. Sally resolved to get a pair as soon as possible.

Like Sally, we all conduct little experiments to detect cause-and-effect connections. In a more formal way, that is exactly what psychologists do when *they* want to explain *why* we act the way we do. Many different research strategies may be used to investigate human behavior. However, we must usually conduct an experiment to discover the *causes* of behavior. Experiments allow psychologists to carefully control conditions and bring cause-and-effect relationships into sharp focus. Hence, they are generally accepted as the most powerful scientific research tool. Let's see why.

AP Photo/Seth Wenig

SURVEY QUESTIONS

4.1 How is an experiment performed?

4.2 What is a double-blind experiment?

The Psychology Experiment— Where Cause Meets Effect

SURVEY QUESTION 4.1: How is an experiment performed?

The most powerful psychological research tool is the **experiment**—a formal trial undertaken to confirm or disconfirm a hypothesis about the causes of behavior. Psychologists carefully control conditions in experiments to identify cause-and-effect relationships. To perform an experiment, you would do the following:

1. Directly vary a condition you think might affect behavior.

2. Create two or more groups of subjects. These groups should be alike in all ways *except* the condition you are varying.

3. Record whether varying the condition has any effect on behavior.

Suppose you want to find out if using cell phones while driving affects the likelihood of having an accident. First, you would form two groups of people. Then you could give the members of one group a test of driving ability while they are using a cell phone. The second group would take the same test without using a cell phone. By comparing average driving ability scores for the two groups, you could tell if cell phone use affects driving ability.

As you can see, the simplest psychological experiment is based on two groups of **experimental subjects**—animals or people whose behavior is investigated. Human subjects also are called **participants**. One group is called the *experimental group*; the other becomes the *control group*. The experimental group and the control group are treated exactly alike except for the condition (or *variable*) you intentionally vary.

Variables and Groups

What are the different kinds of variables? A **variable** is any condition that can change and that might affect the outcome of the experiment. Identifying causes and effects in an experiment involves three types of variables:

1. An **independent variable** is a condition altered or varied by the experimenter, who sets its size, amount, or value. Independent variables are suspected *causes* for differences in behavior.

2. A **dependent variable** measures the result of the experiment—that is, dependent variables reveal the *effects* that independent variables have on *behavior*. Such effects are often revealed by measures of performance, such as test scores.

3. An **extraneous variable** is a condition that a researcher wants to prevent from affecting the outcome of the experiment.

We can apply these terms to our cell phone/driving experiment in this way: Cell phone use is the independent variable: We want to know if cell phone use affects driving ability. Driving ability (defined by scores achieved on a test of driving ability) is the dependent variable: We want to know if the ability to drive well depends on whether a person is using a cell phone. All other variables that could affect driving ability are extraneous. Examples of extraneous variables are the number of hours slept the night before the test, driving experience, and familiarity with the vehicle used in the experiment.

By the way, psychologist Davis Strayer and his colleagues have confirmed that almost all drivers talking on cell phones drive no better than people who are legally drunk, and texters are even worse drivers (Drews et al., 2009; Strayer, Drews, & Crouch, 2006; Watson & Strayer, 2010).

As you can see, an **experimental group** consists of participants exposed to the independent variable (cell phone use in the preceding example). Members of the **control group** are exposed to all other variables except the independent variable (cell phone use in the preceding example).

Let's examine another simple experiment. Suppose you notice that you seem to study better while listening to your iPod. This suggests the hypothesis that listening to music improves learning. We could test this idea by forming an experimental group that studies with music. A control group would study without music. Then we could compare their scores on a test.

Is a control group really needed? Can't people just study while listening to their iPods to see if they do better? Better than what? The control group provides a *point of reference* for comparison with the scores in the experimental group. Without a control group, it would be impossible to tell whether music had any effect on learning. If the average test score of the experimental group is higher than the average of the control group, we can conclude that music improves learning. If there is no difference, it's obvious that the independent variable had no effect on learning.

In this experiment, the amount learned (indicated by scores on the test) is the *dependent variable*. We are asking, Does the independent variable *affect* the dependent variable? (Does listening to music affect or influence learning?)

Experimental Control *How do we know that the people in one group aren't more intelligent than those in the other group?* It's true that personal differences in intelligence might affect the experiment. However, they can be controlled by randomly assigning people to groups. **Random assignment** means that a participant has an equal chance of being in either the experimental group or the control group. Randomization balances personal differences in the two groups. In our musical experiment, this could be done by simply flipping a coin for each participant: Heads, and the participant is in the experimental group; tails, it's the control group. This would result in few average differences in the number of people in each group who are women or men, geniuses or dunces, hungry, hungover, tall, music lovers, or whatever.

Experiment *A formal trial undertaken to confirm or disconfirm a hypothesis about cause and effect.*

Experimental subjects *Humans (also referred to as participants) or animals whose behavior is investigated in an experiment.*

Participants *Humans whose behavior is investigated in an experiment.*

Variable *Any condition that changes or can be made to change; a measure, event, or state that may vary.*

Independent variable *In an experiment, the condition being investigated as a possible cause of some change in behavior. The experimenter chooses the values that this variable takes.*

Dependent variable *In an experiment, the condition (usually a behavior) that is affected by the independent variable.*

Extraneous variable *Condition or factor excluded from influencing the outcome of an experiment.*

Experimental group *In a controlled experiment, the group of subjects exposed to the independent variable or experimental condition.*

Control group *In a controlled experiment, the group of subjects exposed to all experimental conditions or variables except the independent variable.*

Random assignment *The use of chance (for example, flipping a coin) to assign subjects to experimental and control groups.*

Other *extraneous,* or outside, variables—such as the amount of study time, the temperature in the room, the time of day, the amount of light, and so forth—also must be prevented from affecting the outcome of an experiment. How? Usually, this is done by making all conditions (except the independent variable) *exactly* alike for both groups. When all conditions are the same for both groups—*except* the presence or absence of music—then any difference in the amount learned *must* be caused by the music (● **Figure 4.1**).

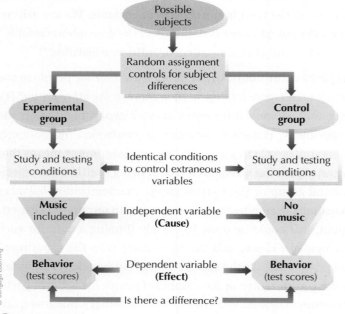

● **Figure 4.1**

Elements of a simple psychological experiment to assess the effects of music during study on test scores.

Cause and Effect Now let's summarize. In an experiment, two or more groups of subjects are treated differently with respect to the independent variable. In all other ways, they are treated the same—that is, extraneous variables are equalized for all groups. The effect of the independent variable (or variables) on some behavior (the dependent variable) is then measured. In a carefully controlled experiment, the independent variable is the only possible *cause* for any *effect* noted in the dependent variable. This allows clear cause-and-effect connections to be identified (● **Figure 4.2**).

Evaluating Results *How can we tell if the independent variable really made a difference?* This problem is handled statistically (see Module 79 for more information). Reports in psychology journals almost always include the statement, "Results

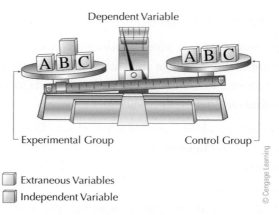

● **Figure 4.2**

Experimental control is achieved by balancing extraneous variables for the experimental group and the control group. For example, both groups could be formed so that the average age (A), education (B), and intelligence (C) of group members is the same. Then, the independent variable can be applied to the experimental group. If their behavior (the dependent variable) changes (in comparison with the control group), the independent variable must be causing the change.

were **statistically significant.**" This means that the obtained results would occur rarely by chance alone. To be statistically significant, a difference must be large enough that it would occur by chance in fewer than 5 experiments out of 100. Of course, findings also become more convincing when they can be *replicated* (repeated) by other researchers.

Double Blind—On Placebos and Self-Fulfilling Prophecies

SURVEY QUESTION 4.2: What is a double-blind experiment?

Suppose a researcher hypothesizes that the drug amphetamine (a stimulant) improves learning. She explains her hypothesis to her participants and gives experimental group participants an amphetamine pill before they begin studying. Control group members get nothing. Later, she assesses how much each participant learned. Does this experiment seem valid? It isn't. It is seriously flawed for several reasons.

Why is it flawed? The experimental group took the drug and the control group didn't. Differences in the amount they learned must have been caused by the drug, right? No. The drug wasn't the only difference between the groups. To start, because of what they were told, participants in the experimental group likely *expected* to learn more. Any observed differences between groups then might reflect differences in expectation, not the actual effect of the drug.

Research Participant Bias

In a well-designed experiment, you must be careful about what you tell participants. Small bits of information might create **research participant bias**, or changes in participants' behavior caused by the influence of their expectations. Notice also that experimental group participants swallowed a pill, and control participants did not. This is another form of research participant bias. It could be that those who swallowed a pill unconsciously *expected* to do better. After all, pills are medicine, aren't they? This alone might have created a **placebo effect**—changes in behavior caused by belief that one has taken a drug or received some other treatment. Suppose the researcher had not given the experimental group an amphetamine pill and instead had given them a **placebo** (plah-SEE-bo), or fake drug. Inactive substances such as sugar pills and

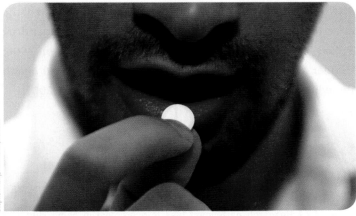

Stephen Kelly/PA Photos/Landov

The placebo effect is a major factor in medical treatments. Would you also expect the placebo effect to occur in psychotherapy? It does, which complicates studies on the effectiveness of new psychotherapies, but likely also enhances the effectiveness of psychotherapy (Justman, 2011).

saline (saltwater) injections are commonly used as placebos. If a placebo has any effect, it must be based on suggestion, rather than chemistry (White & McBurney, 2013).

Placebo effects can be quite powerful and usually account for at least one-third of the apparent effectiveness of the official treatment. For instance, a saline injection is 70 percent as effective as morphine in reducing pain. That's why doctors sometimes prescribe placebos—especially for complaints that seem to have no physical basis. Placebos have been shown to affect pain, anxiety, depression, alertness, tension, sexual

arousal, cravings for alcohol, and many other processes (Justman, 2011; Wampold et al., 2005). (See Module 55 for more information on placebos.)

How could an inert substance have any effect? Placebos alter our expectations, both conscious and unconscious, about our own emotional and physical reactions. Because we associate taking medicine with feeling better, we expect placebos to make us feel better, too (Benedetti, 2009; Czerniak & Davidson, 2012). After a person takes a placebo, brain activity linked with pain is reduced, so the effect is not imaginary (Wager et al., 2004).

Controlling Research Participant Bias *How can you avoid research participant bias?* To control for research participant bias, you could use a **single-blind experiment**. In this case, participants do not know whether they are in the experimental or the control group or whether they are receiving a real drug or a placebo. All participants are given the same instructions and everyone gets a pill or injection. People in the experimental group get a real drug, and those in the control group get a placebo. Because participants are *blind* as to the hypothesis under investigation and whether they received the drug, their expectations (conscious *and* unconscious) are the same. Any difference in their behavior must be caused by the drug. However, even this arrangement is not enough because researchers themselves sometimes affect experiments by influencing participants. Let's see how this occurs.

Researcher Bias

How could a researcher influence participants? As we noted earlier, when the experimenter explained her hypothesis to the participants, she likely biased the results of the study. But even if a researcher uses a single-blind procedure to avoid deliberately biasing participants, **researcher bias**—changes in

Statistically significant *Experimental results that would rarely occur by chance alone.*
Research participant bias *Changes in the behavior of research participants caused by the unintended influence of their own expectations.*
Placebo effect *Changes in behavior due to participants' expectations that a drug (or other treatment) will have some effect.*
Placebo *An inactive substance given in the place of a drug in psychological research or by physicians who want to treat a complaint by suggestion.*
Single-blind experiment *An arrangement in which participants remain unaware of whether they are in the experimental group or the control group.*
Researcher bias *Changes in participants' behavior caused by the unintended influence of a researcher's actions.*

behavior caused by the unintended influence of a researcher—remains a problem. Experimenters run the risk of finding what they expect to find because humans are sensitive to hints about what is expected of them (Rosenthal, 1994).

Researcher bias even applies outside the laboratory. Psychologist Robert Rosenthal (1973) reported a classic example of how expectations influence people: At the U.S. Air Force Academy Preparatory School, 100 airmen were randomly assigned to five different math classes. Their teachers did not know about this random placement. Instead, each teacher was told that his or her students had unusually high or low ability. Students in the classes labeled high ability improved much more in math scores than those in low-ability classes. Yet, initially, all the classes had students of equal ability.

Although the teachers were not conscious of any bias, apparently they subtly communicated their expectations to students. Most likely, they did this through tone of voice, body language, and by giving encouragement or criticism. Their hints, in turn, created a self-fulfilling prophecy that affected the students. A **self-fulfilling prophecy** is a prediction that prompts people to act in ways that make the prediction come true. For instance, many teachers underestimate the abilities of ethnic minority children, which hurts the students' chances for success (Jussim & Harber, 2005). In short, people sometimes become what we prophesy for them. It is wise to remember that others tend to live *up* or *down* to our expectations for them (Madon et al., 2011).

The Double-Blind Experiment Because of research participant bias and researcher bias, it is common to keep both participants and researchers *blind*. In a **double-blind experiment**, neither participants nor researchers know who is in the experimental group or the control group, including who received a drug and who took a placebo. This not only controls for research participant bias but it also keeps researchers from unconsciously influencing participants.

How can the researchers be blind; it's their experiment, isn't it? The researchers who designed the experiment, including preparing the pills or injections, typically hire research assistants to collect data from the participants. Even the research assistants are blinded in that they do not know which pill or injection is drug or placebo or whether any particular participant is in the experimental or control group.

Double-blind testing has shown that at least 50 percent of the effectiveness of antidepressant drugs, such as the wonder drug Prozac, is due to the placebo effect (Kirsch & Sapirstein, 1998; Rihmer et al., 2012). Much of the popularity of herbal health remedies also is based on the placebo effect (Seidman, 2001).

Module 4: Summary

4.1 How is an experiment performed?

- **4.1.1** Experiments involve two or more groups of subjects that differ only regarding the independent variable. Effects on the dependent variable are then measured. All other conditions (extraneous variables) are held constant.
- **4.1.2** Because the independent variable is the only difference between the experimental group and the control group, it is the only possible cause of a change in the dependent variable.
- **4.1.3** The design of experiments allows cause-and-effect connections to be clearly identified.

4.2 What is a double-blind experiment?

- **4.2.1** Research participant bias is a problem in some studies; the placebo effect is a source of research participant bias in experiments involving drugs.
- **4.2.2** Researcher bias is a related problem. Researcher expectations can create a self-fulfilling prophecy, in which a participant changes in the direction of the expectation.
- **4.2.3** In a double-blind experiment, neither the research participants nor the researchers collecting data know who was in the experimental group or the control group, allowing valid conclusions to be drawn.

Self-fulfilling prophecy *A prediction that prompts people to act in ways that make the prediction come true.*
Double-blind experiment *An arrangement in which both participants and experimenters are unaware of whether participants are in the experimental group or the control group, including who might have been administered a drug or a placebo.*

Module 4: Knowledge Builder

Recite

1. To understand cause and effect, a simple psychological experiment is based on creating two groups: the _____ group and the _____ group.

2. Three types of variables must be considered in an experiment: _____ variables (which are manipulated by the experimenter); _____ variables (which measure the outcome of the experiment); and _____ variables (factors to be excluded in a particular experiment).

3. A researcher performs an experiment to learn whether room temperature affects the amount of aggression displayed by college students under crowded conditions in a simulated prison environment. In this experiment, the independent variable is which of the following?
    - **a.** room temperature
    - **b.** the amount of aggression
    - **c.** crowding
    - **d.** the simulated prison environment

4. A procedure used to control both research participant bias and researcher bias in psychological experiments is the
    - **a.** correlation method
    - **b.** controlled experiment
    - **c.** double-blind experiment
    - **d.** random assignment of participants

Reflect

Think Critically

5. The following statement has a loophole: "I've been taking vitamin C tablets, and I haven't had a cold all year. Vitamin C is great!" What is the loophole?

Self-Reflect

We all conduct little experiments to detect cause-and-effect connections. If you enjoy music, for example, you might try listening with different types of headphones. The question then becomes, "Does the use of ear buds versus sound-cancelling headphones (the independent variable) affect the enjoyment of music (the dependent variable)?" Can you think of an informal experiment you've run in the last month? What were the variables? What was the outcome?

ANSWERS

1. experimental, control 2. independent, dependent, extraneous 3. a 4. c 5. The statement implies that vitamin C prevented colds. However, not getting a cold could be a coincidence. A controlled experiment with a group given vitamin C and a control group not taking vitamin C is needed to learn whether vitamin C has any effect on susceptibility to colds.

CENGAGE **brain**.com

Go to **cengagebrain.com** to access **MindTap for Coon/Mitterer** *Psychology Modules for Active Learning* and other online learning tools. MindTap is a fully online learning experience that combines all the tools you need—readings, multimedia, activities, and assessments—into a singular personalized Learning Path that guides you through the course.

Introducing Psychology: Nonexperimental Research Methods

Get Out the Crow Cam

Because it is not always possible to conduct experiments, psychologists gather evidence and test hypotheses in many other ways (Jackson, 2012). For example, psychologists who want to study behavior in natural settings use *naturalistic observation*. Using this technique, New Caledonian crows wearing tiny crow cams have been recorded using twigs to forage for food. Psychologists who are looking for interesting relationships between events often rely on the *correlational method*.

It also can be difficult or impossible to study rare events or unique individuals with the experimental method. When more detail about, say, mental disorders, such as depression or psychosis, is required, the *case study method* may be preferred. Likewise, the *survey method* allows questions about the behavior of large groups of people to be answered by conducting polls. Let's see how each of these nonexperimental methods is used to advance psychological knowledge.

© Jolyon Troscianko 2006

Naturalistic Observation

SURVEY QUESTION 5.1: Why do psychologists rely on naturalistic observation?

Psychologists sometimes rely on **naturalistic observation**, the observation of behavior in a *natural setting* (the typical environment in which a person or animal lives). For example, in 1960, Jane Goodall first observed a wild chimpanzee in Tanzania use a grass stem as a tool to remove termites from a termite mound (Van Lawick-Goodall, 1971). Notice that naturalistic observation provides only *descriptions* of behavior. To *explain* observations, we may need information from other research methods. Just the same, Goodall's discovery

showed that humans are not the only tool-making animals (Rutz et al., 2010).

Chimpanzees in zoos use objects as tools. Doesn't that demonstrate the same thing? Not necessarily. Naturalistic observation allows us to study behavior that hasn't been tampered with or altered by outside influences. Only by observing chimps in their natural environment can we tell whether they use tools without human interference.

Limitations

Doesn't the presence of human observers affect the animals' behavior? Yes. The observer effect is a major problem. The **observer effect** refers to changes in a subject's behavior caused by an awareness of being observed. Naturalists must be careful to keep their distance and avoid making friends with the animals they are watching. Likewise, if you are interested in why automobile drivers have traffic accidents, you can't simply get in people's cars and start taking notes. As a stranger, your presence would likely change the drivers' behaviors.

When possible, the observer effect can be minimized by concealing the observer. Another solution is to use hidden recorders. One naturalistic study of traffic accidents was done with video cameras installed in 100 cars (Dingus et al., 2006). It turns out that most accidents are caused by failing to look at the traffic in front of the car (eyes forward!). Hidden stationary video cameras have also provided valuable observations of many animal species.

As recording devices have become miniaturized, it has even become possible to attach critter cams directly to many species, allowing observations to be made across their natural ranges. As mentioned previously, zoologist Christian Rutz and his colleagues outfitted shy New Caledonian crows with crow cams to better understand their use of tools to forage for food (Rutz et al., 2007, 2010). Not only can these clever crows use twigs to reach food but they also can use a shorter twig to get a longer twig to get food (Wimpenny et al., 2009). Apparently, humans and other primates are not the only tool-using species.

Observer bias is a related problem in which observers see what they expect to see or record only selected details (Jackson, 2012). For instance, teachers in one classic study were told to watch normal elementary school children who had been labeled (for the study) as learning disabled, mentally challenged, emotionally disturbed, or normal. Sadly, teachers gave the children widely different ratings, depending on the labels used (Foster & Ysseldyke, 1976). In some situations, observer bias can have serious consequences (Spano, 2005). For example, a police officer who expects criminal behavior might shoot someone he assumes is reaching for a gun, but the person was simply reaching for his wallet.

A special mistake to avoid when observing animals is the **anthropomorphic error** (AN-thro-po-MORE-fik). This is the error of attributing human thoughts, feelings, or motives to animals—especially as a way to explain their behavior (Waytz, Epley, & Cacioppo, 2010). The temptation to assume that an animal is angry, jealous, bored, or guilty can be strong. If you have pets at home, you probably know difficult it is to avoid anthropomorphizing, but it can lead to false conclusions. For example, if your dog growls at your date, you might assume the dog doesn't like your companion. But it's possible your date is wearing a cologne or perfume that irritates the dog's nose.

Psychologists doing naturalistic studies make a special effort to minimize bias by keeping an **observational record**, or detailed summary of data and observations. As suggested by the study of traffic accidents and the use of critter cams, video recording often provides the most objective record of all. Despite its problems, naturalistic observation can supply a wealth of information and raise many interesting questions. In most scientific research, it is an excellent starting point.

Correlational Studies

SURVEY QUESTION 5.2: What is a correlational study?

Let's say a psychologist notes an association between the IQs of parents and their children, or between beauty and social popularity, or between anxiety and test performance. A **correlation** exists when two observations or events are linked together in an orderly way. In a **correlational study**, two factors are measured. Then a statistical technique is used to find their degree of correlation. (See Module 79 for more information.) For example, John Simister and Cary Cooper (2005) decided to find out if there is a correlation between crime and the weather. They obtained data on temperatures and criminal activity in Los Angeles over a four-year period. When they graphed air temperature and the frequency of aggravated assaults, a clear relationship emerged. Assaults and temperatures rise and fall more or less in parallel (so there may be something to the phrase *hot under the collar*). Knowing the temperature in Los Angeles now allows us to predict whether the number of aggravated assaults will increase.

Naturalistic observation *Observing behavior as it unfolds in natural settings.*

Observer effect *Changes in an organism's behavior brought about by an awareness of being observed.*

Observer bias *The tendency of an observer to distort observations or perceptions to match his or her expectations.*

Anthropomorphic error *The error of attributing human thoughts, feelings, or motives to animals, especially as a way to explain their behavior.*

Observational record *A detailed summary of observed events or a videotape of observed behavior.*

Correlation *The existence of a consistent, systematic relationship between two events, measures, or variables.*

Correlational study *A nonexperimental study designed to measure the degree of relationship (if any) between two or more events, measures, or variables.*

Correlation Coefficients

How is the degree of correlation expressed? The strength and direction of a relationship can be expressed as a **coefficient of correlation**. This can be calculated as a number falling somewhere between +1.00 and −1.00 (see Module 79). Drawing graphs of relationships can also help clarify their nature (see ● **Figure 5.1**). If the number is zero or close to zero, the association between two measures is weak or nonexistent (see Figure 5.1c). For example, the correlation between shoe size and intelligence is zero. (Sorry, size-12 readers.) If the correlation is +1.00, a perfect positive relationship exists (see Figure 5.1e); if it is −1.00, a perfect negative relationship has been discovered (see Figure 5.1a).

Correlations in psychology are rarely perfect. But the closer the coefficient is to +1.00 or −1.00, the stronger the relationship. For example, identical twins tend to have almost identical IQs. In contrast, the IQs of parents and their children are only generally similar. The correlation between the IQs of parents and children is .35; between identical twins it's .86.

What do the terms positive *and* negative correlation *mean?* In a *positive correlation*, higher scores in one measure are matched by higher scores in the other. For example, a moderate positive correlation exists between high school grades and college grades; students who do well in high school tend to do well in college (and the reverse) (see Figure 5.1d). In a *negative correlation*, higher scores on one measure are associated with lower scores on the other. We might observe, for instance, a moderate negative correlation between the number of hours that students play computer games and their grades—that is, more play is associated with lower grades (Figure 5.1b). (This is the well-known computer-game-zombie effect.)

Wouldn't that show that playing computer games too much causes lower grades? It might seem so, but as we noted previously, the best way to be confident that a cause-and-effect relationship exists is to perform a controlled experiment.

Correlation and Causation Correlational studies help us discover relationships and make predictions. However, correlation *does not* demonstrate **causation** (a cause–effect relationship) (Jackson & Newberry, 2012). It could be, for instance, that students who aren't interested in their classes have more time for computer games. If so, then their lack of study and lower grades is the result of disinterest, not excessive game playing (which is another result of disinterest in classes). Just because one thing *appears* to be directly related to another does not mean that a cause-and-effect connection exists.

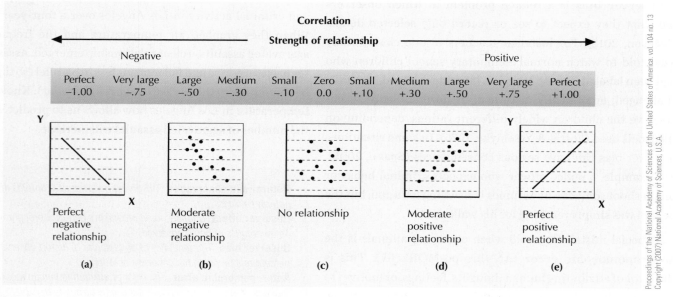

Proceedings of the National Academy of Sciences of the United States of America. vol. 104 no. 13
Copyright (2007) National Academy of Sciences, U.S.A.

● **Figure 5.1**

The correlation coefficient tells how strongly two measures are related. These graphs show a range of relationships between two measures, X and Y. If a correlation is negative (a), increases in one measure are associated with decreases in the other. (As Y gets larger, X gets smaller.) In a positive correlation (e), increases in one measure are associated with increases in the other. (As Y gets larger, X gets larger.) The center-left graph (b, moderate negative relationship) might result from comparing time spent playing computer games (Y) with grades (X): More time spent playing computer games is associated with lower grades. The center graph (c, no relationship) would result from plotting a person's shoe size (Y) and his or her IQ (X). The center-right graph (d, moderate positive relationship) could be a plot of grades in high school (Y) and grades in college (X) for a group of students: Higher grades in high school are associated with higher grades in college.

Here is another example of mistaking correlation for causation: What if a psychologist discovers a correlation between parents who smoke cigarettes and juvenile delinquency in their children? Does this show that parental smoking *causes* juvenile delinquency? Perhaps, but juvenile delinquents might drive their parents to take up smoking. Better yet, maybe both parental smoking and juvenile delinquency are related to some third factor, such as socioeconomic status. Poorer parents are more likely to be smokers, and poorer juveniles are more likely to become delinquents. To reiterate, just because one thing *appears* to cause another does not *confirm* that it does. The best way to be confident that a cause-and-effect relationship exists is to perform a controlled experiment.

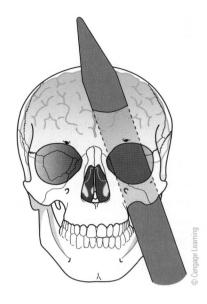

● Figure 5.2

Some of the earliest information on the effects of damage to frontal areas of the brain came from a case study of the accidental injury of Phineas Gage.

© Cengage Learning

Case Studies

SURVEY QUESTION 5.3: What benefits arise from case studies?

It may be impractical, unethical, or impossible to use the experimental method to study rare events, such as unusual mental disorders, childhood geniuses, or rampage school shootings (Harding, Fox, & Mehta, 2002). In such instances, a **case study**—an in-depth focus on a single participant—may be the best source of information. Clinical psychologists rely heavily on case studies, especially to investigate mental disorders such as depression or psychosis. Also, case studies of psychotherapy have provided many useful ideas about how to treat emotional problems (Wedding & Corsini, 2011).

Case studies may sometimes be thought of as *natural clinical tests* (accidents or other natural events that provide psychological data). Gunshot wounds, brain tumors, accidental poisonings, and similar disasters have provided much information about the human brain. One remarkable case from the history of psychology was reported by Dr. J. M. Harlow (1868). Phineas Gage, a young foreman on a work crew, was impaled by a 13-pound steel rod in the front of his brain as a result of a dynamite explosion (● Figure 5.2). Amazingly, he survived the accident. Within two months, Gage could walk, talk, and move normally, but the injury forever changed his personality. Instead of the honest and dependable worker he had been before, Gage became a surly, foul-mouthed liar. Dr. Harlow carefully recorded all details of what was perhaps the first in-depth case study of an accidental frontal lobotomy (the destruction of front brain matter).

When a Los Angeles carpenter named Michael Melnick suffered a similar injury in 1981, he recovered completely, with no lasting ill effects. Melnick's different reaction to a similar injury shows why psychologists prefer controlled experiments and often use lab animals for studies of the brain. Case studies lack formal control groups. This, of course, limits the conclusions that can be drawn from clinical observations.

Nevertheless, case studies can provide special opportunities to answer interesting questions. For instance, a classic case study in psychology concerns identical quadruplets, known as the Genain sisters. In addition to having identical genes, all four women became schizophrenic before age 25 (Rosenthal & Quinn, 1977). The chances of identical quadruplets all becoming schizophrenic are about 1 in 1.5 billion.

The Genains, who have been studied for more than 40 years, were in and out of mental hospitals most of their lives. The fact that they share identical genes suggests that heredity influences mental disorders. The fact that some of the sisters are more disturbed than others suggests that environmental conditions also affect mental illness. Myra, the least ill of the four, was the only sister who was able to avoid her father, an alcoholic who terrorized, spied on, and sexually molested the girls. Thus, cases like theirs provide insights that can't be obtained by any other means (Mirsky et al., 2000).

Coefficient of correlation *A statistical index ranging from −1.00 to +1.00 that indicates the direction and degree of correlation.*
Causation *The act of causing some effect.*
Case study *An in-depth focus on all aspects of a single person.*

Survey Method

SURVEY QUESTION 5.4: What is a survey?

Sometimes psychologists would like to ask everyone in the world a few well-chosen questions: "What form of discipline did your parents use when you were a child?" "What is the most dishonest thing you've done?" "Why do you think you run extreme marathons?" Honest answers to such questions can reveal much about people's behavior. It is impossible to question everyone, so doing a survey is often more practical.

In a **survey**, public polling techniques are often used to answer psychological questions (Babbie, 2013; Thrift, 2010). Typically, people in a representative sample are asked a series of carefully worded questions. A **representative sample** is a small group that accurately reflects a larger population. A good sample must include the same proportion of men, women, young, old, professionals, blue-collar workers, Republicans, Democrats, whites, African Americans, Native Americans, Latinos, Asians, and so on as found in the population as a whole.

A **population** is an entire group of animals or people belonging to a particular category (for example, all college students or all single women). Ultimately, we are interested in entire populations. By selecting a smaller sample, however, we can draw conclusions about the larger group without polling every person. Representative samples are often obtained by *randomly* selecting who will be included (● **Figure 5.3**). (Notice that this is similar to randomly assigning participants to groups in an experiment.)

How accurate is the survey method? Modern surveys like the Gallup and Harris polls can be quite accurate. However, if a survey is based on a biased sample, it could paint a false picture. A *biased sample* does not accurately reflect the population from which it was drawn. Surveys done by magazines, websites, and online information services can be quite biased. Surveys on gun-control laws done by *O: The Oprah Magazine* and *Guns and Ammo* magazine would probably produce different results—neither of which would represent the general population. That's why psychologists using the survey method go to great lengths to ensure that their samples are representative. Fortunately, people can often be polled by telephone or the Internet, which makes it easier to obtain large samples. Even if one person out of three refuses to answer survey questions, the results are still likely to be valid (Hutchinson, 2004).

For many years, the vast majority of human participants in psychology experiments have been recruited from introductory psychology courses. Further, most of these participants have been white members of the middle class, and most of the researchers have been Caucasian males (Guthrie, 2004). None of this automatically invalidates the results of psychology experiments. However, it may place some limitations on their meanings. The distinguished psychologist Edward Tolman once noted that much of psychology is based on two sets of subjects: rats and college sophomores. Tolman urged scientists to remember that rats are certainly not people and that some college sophomores may not be, either!

Internet Surveys Psychologists rely on the Internet to do online surveys and experiments. Web-based research can be a cost-effective way to reach large groups of people, especially those who are not easy to survey any other way (Smyth et al.,

● **Figure 5.3**

If you were conducting a survey in which a person's height might be an important variable, the upper, nonrandom sample would not be representative. The lower sample, selected using a table of random numbers, better represents the group as a whole.

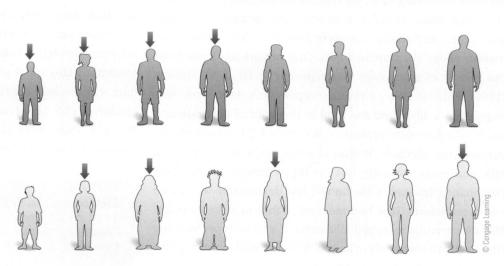

2010). Internet studies have provided interesting information about topics such as anger, decision making, racial prejudice, what disgusts people, religion, sexual attitudes, and much more. Biased samples can limit web-based research (it isn't easy to control who answers your online questionnaire), but psychologists are getting better at gathering valid information online (Lewis, Watson, & White, 2009).

Social Desirability Even well-designed surveys may be limited by another problem. If a psychologist were to ask you detailed questions about your sexual history and current sexual behavior, how accurate would your replies be? Would you exaggerate? Would you be embarrassed? Replies to survey questions are not always accurate or truthful. Many people show a distinct *courtesy bias* (a tendency to give polite or socially desirable answers). For example, answers to questions concerning sex, drinking or drug use, income, and church attendance tend to be less than truthful. Likewise, the week after an election, more people will say they voted than actually did (Babbie, 2013).

Summary Despite their limitations, surveys frequently produce valuable information. For instance, one survey explored the vulnerability of U.S. retail malls to terrorism with the goal of improving our capacity to prevent and respond to an attack (Rigakos et al., 2009). To sum up, the survey method can be a powerful research tool. Like other methods, it has limitations, but new techniques and strategies are providing valuable information about our behavior.

Is so much emphasis on science necessary in psychology? In a word, yes. Science is a powerful way of asking questions about the world and getting trustworthy answers. (● Table 5.1 summarizes many of the important ideas we have covered.)

TABLE 5.1	Comparison of Psychological Research Methods	
	Advantages	**Disadvantages**
Experimental Method	Clear cause-and-effect relationships can be identified; powerful controlled observations can be staged; no need to wait for natural event	May be somewhat artificial; some natural behavior not easily studied in laboratory (field experiments may avoid these objections)
Naturalistic Observation	Behavior is observed in a natural setting; much information is obtained, and hypotheses and questions for additional research can be formed	Little or no control is possible; observed behavior may be altered by the presence of the observer; observations may be biased; causes cannot be conclusively identified
Correlational Method	Demonstrates the existence of relationships; allows prediction; can be used in lab, clinic, or natural setting	Little or no control is possible; relationships may be coincidental; cause-and-effect relationships cannot be confirmed
Clinical Method	Takes advantage of natural clinical trials and allows investigation of rare or unusual problems or events	Little or no control is possible; does not provide a control group for comparison; subjective interpretation is often necessary; a single case may be misleading or unrepresentative
Survey Method	Allows information about large numbers of people to be gathered; can address questions not answered by other approaches	Obtaining a representative sample is critical and can be difficult to do; answers may be inaccurate; people may not do what they say or say what they do

© Cengage Learning

Survey *In psychology, a public polling technique used to answer psychological questions.*
Representative sample *A small, randomly selected part of a larger population that accurately reflects characteristics of the whole population.*
Population *An entire group of animals or people belonging to a particular category (for example, all college students or all married women).*

Module 5: Summary

5.1 Why do psychologists rely on naturalistic observation?

- **5.1.1** Unlike controlled experiments, nonexperimental methods usually cannot demonstrate cause-and-effect relationships.
- **5.1.2** Naturalistic observation is a starting place in many investigations. Two problems with naturalistic observation are the effects of the observer on the observed and observer bias.

5.2 What is a correlational study?

- **5.2.1** In the correlational method, relationships between two traits, responses, or events are measured and a correlation coefficient is computed to gauge the strength of the relationship.

Relationships in psychology may be positive or negative. Correlations allow prediction but do not demonstrate cause-and-effect.

5.3 What benefits arise from case studies?

- **5.3.1** Case studies provide insights into human behavior that can't be gained by other methods.

5.4 What is a survey?

- **5.4.1** In the survey method, people in a representative sample are asked a series of carefully worded questions. Obtaining a representative sample of people is crucial when the survey method is used to study large populations.

Module 5: Knowledge Builder

Recite

1. Two major problems in naturalistic observation are the effects of the observer and observer bias. **T or F?**

2. The _____ fallacy involves attributing human feelings and motives to animals.

3. Correlation typically does not demonstrate causation. **T or F?**

4. Which correlation coefficient represents the strongest relationship?
   - **a.** −0.86
   - **b.** +0.66
   - **c.** +0.10
   - **d.** +0.09

5. Case studies can often be thought of as natural tests and are frequently used by clinical psychologists. **T or F?**

6. For the survey method to be valid, a representative sample of people must be polled. **T or F?**

7. A problem with the survey method is that answers to questions may not always be _____ or _____.

Reflect

Think Critically

8. A psychologist conducting a survey at a shopping mall (The Gallery of Wretched Excess) flips a coin before stopping passersby. If the coin shows heads, he interviews the person; if it shows tails, he skips that person. Has the psychologist obtained a random sample?

9. Attributing mischievous motives to a car that is not working properly is a thinking error similar to anthropomorphizing. **T or F?**

Self-Reflect

Google "Critter cam" and find one you can watch. What species did you watch? What behaviors might you observe and record?

See if you can identify at least one positive correlation and one negative correlation that involve human behavior.

Have you ever known someone who suffered a brain injury or disease? How did his or her behavior change?

Have you ever been asked to complete a survey? If you agreed, were you honest about your answers? What would it say about accuracy if many people did not answer accurately?

ANSWERS

1. T 2. anthropomorphic 3. T 4. a 5. T 6. T 7. accurate, truthful 8. The psychologist's coin flips *might* produce a reasonably good sample of people *at the mall*. The problem is that people who go to the mall may be mostly from one part of town, from upper-income groups, or from some other nonrepresentative group. The psychologist's sample is likely to be seriously flawed. 9. Yes. It appears to be difficult for humans to resist thinking of other species and even machines in human terms.

Psychology in Action:
Thinking Critically about the Media

Klingon Speaker Needed

Have you ever played the game called "telephone" or "pass it down"? One person whispers a sentence to someone else who, in turn, whispers it down the line. Usually, when the person at the end of the line repeats the message, it has been humorously distorted. Similarly, modern media—especially the Internet—functions as a giant echo chamber awash with rumors, hoaxes, half-truths, and urban legends like the one about giant alligators living in New York sewers.

To help you get the most out of psychology, some modules in this book are named Psychology in Action. These modules offer ideas you can use now or in the future. No collection of practical information about psychology would be complete without a look at how to think critically about the giant game of "pass it down" that is the modern media.

Henning Kaiser/AFP/Getty Images

SURVEY QUESTION

6.1 How reliable is the psychological information found in the popular media?

Psychology in the Media— Are You Fluent in Klingon?

SURVEY QUESTION 6.1: How reliable is the psychological information found in the popular media?

Psychology is a popular topic in contemporary media. Unfortunately, much of what you will encounter is based on entertainment value rather than critical thinking or science. Here are some suggestions for separating high-quality information from misleading fiction.

Suggestion 1: Be skeptical. One of our all-time-favorite urban legends is a story about the health department in Oregon seeking a Klingon interpreter for mental health patients who spoke only in the fictional language used on the *Star Trek* television series. This tale started when a newspaper reported that Klingon was on a list of languages that some psychiatric patients claimed they could speak. The article specifically noted that, "In reality, no patient has yet tried to communicate in Klingon." Nevertheless, as the story echoed around the web, the idea that Oregon was looking for someone fluent in Klingon had become a "fact" (O'Neill, 2003).

Reports in the popular media tend to be made uncritically and with a definite bias toward reporting astonishing findings and telling interesting stories. When you say, "That's incredible," it often means, "That's not believable"—which is often true (Hughes, 2008; Stanovich, 2013).

Suggestion 2: Consider the source of information. It should be no surprise that information used to sell a product often reflects a desire for profit rather than the objective truth. Here is a typical advertising claim: "Government tests prove that no sleep medicine is stronger or more effective than Coma." A statement like this usually means that there was *no difference* between Coma and the other products tested. No other sleep aid was stronger or more effective. But none was weaker, either.

Remember that psychological services may be merchandised as well. Keep the source in mind when reading the claims of makers of home biofeedback machines, sleep-learning devices, subliminal CDs, and the like. Be wary of expensive courses that promise instant mental health and happiness, increased efficiency, memory, extrasensory perception (ESP) or psychic ability, control of the unconscious mind, an end to smoking, and so on. Usually, they are promoted with a few testimonials and many unsupported claims (Lilienfeld, Ruscio, & Lynn, 2008).

Psychic claims should be viewed with special caution. Google magician James Randi's Million Dollar Paranormal Challenge. Randi has long offered $1,000,000 to anyone demonstrating such abilities under controlled conditions. No one has even passed the preliminary tests.

Stage mentalists make a living by deceiving the public. Understandably, they are highly interested in promoting belief in their nonexistent powers. The same is true of the so-called psychic advisers promoted in television commercials. These charlatans use the Barnum effect (the tendency to consider personal descriptions accurate if they are stated in general terms; see Module 2) to create an illusion that they know private information about the people who call them (Nickell, 2001).

Suggestion 3: Beware of oversimplifications, especially those motivated by monetary gain. Courses or programs that offer a new personality in three sessions, six steps to love and fulfillment in marriage, or some newly discovered secret for unlocking the powers of the mind and the universe should be immediately suspect.

An excellent example of oversimplification is provided by websites devoted to a video that promises to reveal "the secret to unlimited joy, health, money, relationships, love, youth: everything you have ever wanted." According to these sites, all you need to do is put your desires out to the universe and the universe must respond by granting your wishes. And all it will cost you is the price of ordering the video. (It's no secret that the promoters are the real winners in this game.)

Suggestion 4: Remember, "for example" is no proof. After reading the preceding modules, you should be sensitive to the danger of selecting single examples. If you read, "Law student passes state bar exam using sleep-learning device," don't rush out to buy one. Systematic research showed long ago that these devices are of little or no value (Druckman & Bjork, 1994). A corollary to this suggestion is to ask: Are the reported observations important or widely applicable? Similarly, in 2002, baseball pitcher Randy Johnson began wearing a particular metal-impregnated twisted rope necklace designed to "stabilize the electricity flow through the body." By the 2010 World Series, hundreds of players were superstitiously wearing one, all without any scientific explanation of, or evidence for, their efficacy (Carroll, 2011).

Examples, anecdotes, single cases, and testimonials are all potentially deceptive. According to numerous testimonials, believers in the power of the secret described earlier have been showered with money, success, and happiness immediately after viewing the video. Someone is bound to win the lottery by sheer luck. Unfortunately, such *individual cases* (or even several) tell us nothing about what is true *in general* (Stanovich, 2013). How many people *didn't* win the lottery after buying the video? How many people bought the magic necklace to no avail? Similarly, studies of large groups of people show that smoking increases the likelihood of lung cancer. It is less relevant if you know a lifelong heavy smoker who is 95 years old. The general finding is the one to remember.

Suggestion 5: Ask yourself if there was a control group. The key importance of a control group in any experiment is frequently overlooked by the unsophisticated—an error to which you are no longer susceptible! The popular media are full of reports of experiments performed without control groups: "Talking to Plants Speeds Growth"; "Special Diet Controls Hyperactivity in Children"; "Graduates of Firewalking Seminar Risk Their Soles."

Firewalking is based on simple physics, not on supernatural psychological control. The temperature of the coals may be as high as 1,200°F. However, coals are like the air in a hot oven: They are inefficient at transferring heat during brief contact.

Consider the last example. Expensive commercial courses have long been promoted to teach people to walk barefoot on hot coals. (Why anyone would want to do this is an interesting question.) Firewalkers supposedly protect their feet with a technique called neurolinguistic programming. Many people have paid good money to learn the technique, and most do manage a quick walk on the coals. But is the technique necessary? And is anything remarkable happening? We need a comparison group.

Fortunately, physicist Bernard Leikind has provided one. Leikind showed with volunteers that anyone (with reasonably callused feet) can walk over a bed of coals without being burned. This is because the coals, which are light, fluffy carbon, transmit little heat when touched. The principle involved is similar to briefly putting your hand in a hot oven. If you touch a pan, you will be burned because metal transfers heat efficiently. But if your hand stays in the heated air, you'll be fine because air transmits little heat (Kida, 2006; Mitchell, 1987). Mystery solved.

Suggestion 6: Look for errors in distinguishing between correlation and causation. As you now know, it is dangerous to presume that one thing *caused* another just because they are correlated. In spite of this, you will see many claims based on questionable correlations. Here's an example of mistaking correlation for causation: Jeanne Dixon, a well-known astrologer, once answered a group of prominent scientists—who had declared that there is no scientific

foundation for astrology—by saying, "They would do well to check the records at their local police stations, where they will learn that the rate of violent crime rises and falls with lunar cycles." Dixon, of course, believes that the moon affects human behavior.

If it is true that violent crime is more frequent at certain times of the month, doesn't that prove her point? Far from it. Increased crime could be due to darker nights, the fact that we expect others to act crazier during a full moon, or any number of similar factors. Besides, direct studies of the alleged lunar effect have shown that it doesn't occur (Dowling, 2005). Moonstruck criminals, influenced by a bad moon rising, are a fiction (Iosif & Ballon, 2005).

Suggestion 7: Be sure to distinguish between observation and inference. If you see a person crying, is it correct to assume that she or he is sad? It seems reasonable to make this assumption, but it could easily be wrong. We can observe objectively that the person is crying, but to *infer* sadness may be an error. It could be that the individual has just peeled five pounds of onions. Maybe he or she just won a million-dollar lottery or is trying contact lenses for the first time.

Psychologists, politicians, physicians, scientists, and other experts often go far beyond the available facts in their claims. This does not mean that their inferences, opinions, and interpretations have no value; the opinion of an expert on the causes of mental illness, criminal behavior, learning problems, or whatever can be revealing. But be careful to distinguish between fact and opinion.

Summary We are all bombarded daily with such a mass of new information that it is difficult to absorb it. The available knowledge in an area like psychology, biology, or medicine is so vast that no single person can completely know and comprehend it. With this reality in mind, it becomes increasingly important that you become a critical, selective, and informed consumer of information (Lilienfeld et al., 2010). In fairness to the media, it also is worth pointing out that programs like the Discovery Channel's *MythBusters* and websites like Snopes.com are attempting to set the record straight. (No alligators lurk in the New York sewers, but do watch out for pythons in Florida's Everglades!)

Module 6: Summary

6.1   How reliable is the psychological information found in the popular media?

- **6.1.1** Information in the mass media varies greatly in quality and accuracy and should be approached with skepticism and caution.
- **6.1.2** It is essential to critically evaluate information from popular sources (or from any source, for that matter) to separate facts from fallacies.

- **6.1.3** Problems in media reports are often related to biased or unreliable sources of information, uncontrolled observation, misleading correlations, false inferences, oversimplification, use of single examples, and unrepeatable results.

Module 6: Knowledge Builder

Recite

1. Popular media reports usually stress objective accuracy. *T or F?*

2. Stage mentalists and psychics often use deception in their acts. *T or F?*

3. Blaming the lunar cycle for variations in the rate of violent crime is an example of mistaking correlation for causation. *T or F?*

4. If a psychology student uses a sleep-learning device to pass a midterm exam, it proves that the device works. *T or F?*

Reflect
Think Critically

5. Mystics have shown that fresh eggs can be balanced on their large ends during the vernal equinox when the sun is directly over the equator, day and night are equal in length, and the world is in perfect balance. What is wrong with their observation?

Self-Reflect

How actively do you evaluate and question claims made by an authority or found in the media? Could you be a more critical consumer of information? *Should* you be a more critical consumer of information?

_____

ANSWERS

1. F 2. T 3. T 4. F 5. Eggs can be balanced at any time you choose. The lack of a control group gives the illusion that something amazing is happening, but the equinox has nothing to do with egg balancing (Halpern, 2003).

CENGAGE brain.com

Go to **cengagebrain.com** to access **MindTap for Coon/Mitterer** *Psychology Modules for Active Learning* and other online learning tools. MindTap is a fully online learning experience that combines all the tools you need—readings, multimedia, activities, and assessments—into a singular personalized Learning Path that guides you through the course.

Brain and Behavior:
Neurons and the Nervous System

Punch-Drunk

He died of a self-inflicted gunshot wound to the stomach in February 2011. Not to his head, mind you, because he wanted to leave his brain to science. Two-time Super Bowl winner Dave Duerson blamed his post-football troubles, including memory loss, difficulty spelling words, depression, and moodiness, on the repeated concussions he suffered on the playing field. Sure enough, an autopsy revealed the same signs of chronic traumatic brain injury that have been found in dozens of other retired NFL players, as well as in athletes from many other violent sports, such as hockey and boxing. The boxers even have a name for it: punch-drunk.

We don't normally notice the key role the nervous system, and especially the brain, plays in all that makes us human. But an injury to this vital system, like the one Dave Duerson suffered, can dramatically change a person forever. How does it all work? Let's explore this fascinating realm.

© Flirt/Super Stock

SURVEY QUESTIONS

7.1 What are the major divisions of the nervous system?

7.2 How do neurons operate and communicate with each other?

7.3 Can the nervous system grow and heal itself?

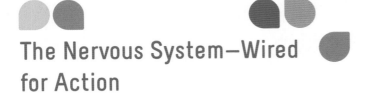

The Nervous System—Wired for Action

SURVEY QUESTION 7.1: What are the major divisions of the nervous system?

Who you are can be traced to electrical impulses flashing through your nervous system. What would happen if, say, you suffered a stroke? (A stroke occurs when an artery carrying blood in the brain bleeds or becomes blocked, causing some brain tissue to die.) Almost instantly, victims realize that something is wrong. You would, too, if you suddenly found that you couldn't move, feel parts of your body, see, or speak. However, some brain injuries are not so obvious. Many involve less dramatic, but equally disabling, changes in personality, thinking, judgment, or emotions. Some, like Dave Duerson's, can take years to become apparent (Banich & Compton, 2011).

Let's begin to better understand our nervous system, both when it is healthy and when it is not, by following Mike and Molly, who are out in the park, playing Frisbee. Although this may appear simple, a blaze of activity lights up many of the billions of **neurons** (NOOR-ons)—individual nerve cells—making up their nervous systems. To catch Mike's latest toss, a huge amount of information must be collected by Molly's eyes (where's that Frisbee going?), muscles (are my hands in place to catch it?), and other senses (what's that sound behind me?), and sent to the brain to be interpreted. Messages must then be sent back to direct countless muscle fibers (move my body and hands to catch that Frisbee while avoiding that couple chatting on the lawn behind me). This must happen over and over again, in real time, for as long as they keep playing. Before we dive into the details, let's get an overview of the wiring diagram that makes their game of catch possible (Freberg, 2010).

As you can see in ● **Figure 7.1**, the **central nervous system (CNS)** consists of the brain and spinal cord. The brain carries out most of the "computing" in the nervous system and communicates with the rest of the body through the large bundle of nerves called the spinal cord. The **peripheral nervous system (PNS)** is the intricate network of nerves that carries information between the CNS and the rest of the body. Thirty-one pairs of **spinal nerves** carry sensory and motor messages to and from the spinal cord. In addition, 12 pairs of **cranial nerves** leave the brain directly without passing through the spinal cord. Together, these nerves keep your entire body in communication with your brain.

Are nerves the same as neurons? No. Neurons are tiny. You need a microscope to see one. **Nerves** are large bundles of many neuron fibers (called *axons*). You can easily see nerves without magnification.

The Peripheral Nervous System

The peripheral nervous system can be divided into two major parts. The **somatic nervous system (SNS)** carries messages to and from the sense organs and skeletal muscles. In general, it controls voluntary behavior, such as when Mike does his victory dance whenever he catches the Frisbee. In contrast, the **autonomic nervous system (ANS)** serves the internal organs and glands. The word *autonomic* means self-governing. Activities the autonomic nervous system governs are mostly vegetative or automatic, such as heart rate, digestion, and perspiration. Thus, messages carried by the somatic system can make your hand move, but they cannot make your eyes dilate. Likewise, messages the ANS carries can stimulate digestion, but they cannot help you carry out a voluntary action, such as writing a letter. If Mike feels a flash of anger when he misses a catch, or a surge of love for Molly when she smiles,

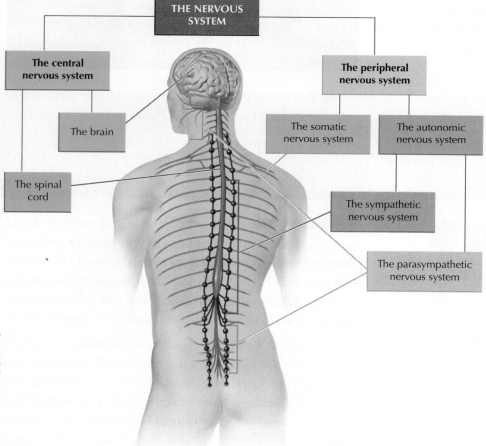

THE NERVOUS SYSTEM

The central nervous system
- The brain
- The spinal cord

The peripheral nervous system
- The somatic nervous system
- The autonomic nervous system
  - The sympathetic nervous system
  - The parasympathetic nervous system

● **Figure 7.1**

The nervous system can be divided into the central nervous system, made up of the brain and spinal cord, and the peripheral nervous system, composed of the nerves connecting the body to the central nervous system.

a brief burst of activity will spread through his autonomic nervous system.

The SNS and ANS work together to coordinate the body's internal reactions to events in the world outside the body. For example, if a snarling dog lunges at Molly, her SNS controls her leg muscles so that she can run. At the same time, her ANS raises her blood pressure, quickens her heartbeat, and so forth. The ANS can be divided into the *sympathetic* and *parasympathetic* branches.

How do the branches of the autonomic system differ? Both the sympathetic and the parasympathetic branches are related to emotional responses, such as crying, sweating, heart rate, and other involuntary behavior (● Figure 7.2). However, the **sympathetic branch** is an emergency system. It prepares the body for "fight or flight" during times of danger or high emotion. In essence, it arouses the body for action. In contrast, the **parasympathetic branch** quiets the body and returns it to a lower level of arousal. It is most active soon after an emotional event. The parasympathetic branch also helps keep vital processes such as heart rate, breathing, and digestion at moderate levels. Of course, both branches of the ANS are always active. At any given moment, their combined activity determines if your body is more or less relaxed or aroused.

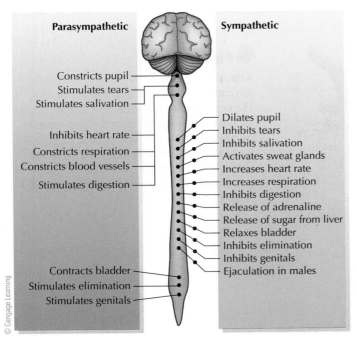

● Figure 7.2

Sympathetic and parasympathetic branches of the autonomic nervous system. Both branches control involuntary actions. The sympathetic system activates the body and the parasympathetic system quiets it. The sympathetic branch relays its messages through clusters of neurons outside the spinal cord.

How do neurons process information throughout the brain and the rest of the nervous system? Let's find out.

Neurons—Building a Biocomputer

SURVEY QUESTION 7.2: How do neurons operate and communicate with each other?

Viewed under a microscope, the nervous system is a large network of about 100 billion interlinked neurons—or nerve cells (Banich & Compton, 2011). Sustained by at least 10 times as many *glial cells* (cells that support neurons in a variety of ways, especially in the brain), neurons carry input from the senses to the brain, where other neurons process that input. Neurons also carry output from the brain in order to activate muscles and glands. Your command center, the brain, contains most of those neurons and does most of the "computing."

Oddly enough, a single neuron is not very smart—it takes many just to make you blink. But each neuron receives messages from many others and sends its own message to many others. Billions of neurons and connections may be involved when a rapper like Nicki Minaj performs. Especially in your brain, each neuron is linked to thousands of other neurons. The vast resulting network of 100 trillion or so connections allows you to process immense amounts of information, producing intelligence and consciousness (Toates, 2011). Undeniably, the human nervous system is the most amazing of all computers. Let's see how neurons operate and how they are "wired" together into the nervous system.

Neuron *An individual nerve cell.*
Central nervous system (CNS) *The brain and spinal cord.*
Peripheral nervous system (PNS) *All parts of the nervous system outside the brain and spinal cord.*
Spinal nerves *Major nerves that carry sensory and motor messages in and out of the spinal cord.*
Cranial nerves *Major nerves that leave the brain without passing through the spinal cord.*
Nerve *A bundle of neuron axons.*
Somatic nervous system (SNS) *The system of nerves linking the spinal cord with the body and sense organs.*
Autonomic nervous system (ANS) *The system of nerves carrying information to and from the internal organs and glands.*
Sympathetic branch *The branch of the ANS that arouses the body.*
Parasympathetic branch *The branch of the ANS that quiets the body.*

Parts of a Neuron

What does a neuron look like? What are its main parts? No two neurons are exactly alike, but most have four basic parts (● Figure 7.3). The dendrites (DEN-drytes), which look like tree roots, are neuron fibers that receive messages from other neurons. The soma (SOH-mah, or cell body) does the same. In addition, the soma sends its own messages (via nerve impulses) down a thin fiber called the axon (AK-sahn).

Although some axons are only 0.1 millimeter long (about the width of a human hair or a pencil line), others stretch up to a meter through the nervous system (from the base of your spine to your big toe, for instance). Like miniature cables, axons carry messages through the brain and nervous system. Large bundles of axons comprise most of the spinal cord and the nerves of the peripheral nervous system. Altogether, your brain contains about 3 million miles of axons (Breedlove, Watson, & Rosenzweig, 2010). Axons branch out into smaller fibers ending in bulb-shaped axon terminals. By forming connections with the dendrites and somas of other neurons, axon terminals allow information to pass from neuron to neuron.

Let's summarize with a metaphor. Imagine that you are standing in a long line of people who are holding hands. A person on the far-left end of the line wants to silently send a message to the person on the right end. She does this by pressing the hand of the person to her right, who presses the hand of the person to his right, and so on. The message arrives at your left hand (your dendrites). You decide whether to pass it on. (You are the soma.) The message goes out through your right arm (the axon). With your right hand (the axon terminals), you squeeze the hand of the person to your right, and the message moves on.

The Nerve Impulse

Electrically charged molecules called *ions* (EYE-ons) are found inside each neuron. Other ions lie outside the neuron. Some ions have a positive electrical charge, whereas others have a negative charge. When a neuron is inactive (or resting), more of these plus, or positive, charges exist outside the neuron and more minus, or negative, charges exist inside. As a result, the inside of each resting neuron in your brain has an electrical charge of about -60 to -70 millivolts at the axon. (A millivolt is one-thousandth of a volt.) That means every neuron in your brain acts like a tiny biological battery.

The electrical charge of an inactive neuron is called its resting potential. But neurons seldom get much rest: Messages arriving from other neurons constantly raise and lower the resting potential. If the electrical charge rises to

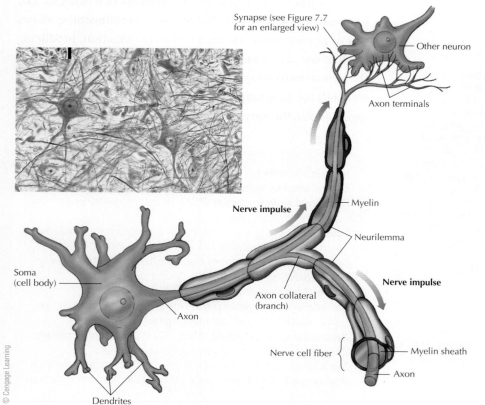

Synapse (see Figure 7.7 for an enlarged view)

Other neuron

Axon terminals

Nerve impulse

Myelin

Neurilemma

Nerve impulse

Soma (cell body)

Axon

Axon collateral (branch)

Nerve cell fiber {

Myelin sheath

Axon

Dendrites

● **Figure 7.3**

A neuron, or nerve cell. In the right foreground, you can see a nerve cell fiber in cross section. The upper-left photo gives a more realistic picture of the shape of neurons. Nerve impulses usually travel from the dendrites and soma to the branching ends of the axon. The nerve cell shown here is a motor neuron. The axons of motor neurons stretch from the brain and spinal cord to muscles or glands of the body.

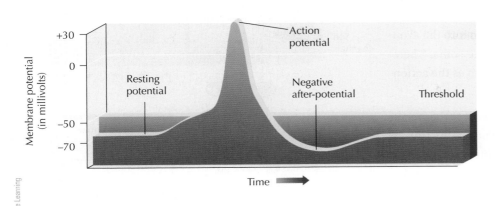
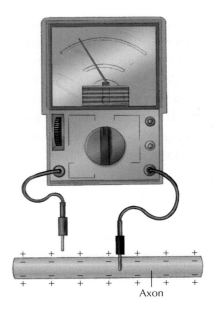

© Cengage Learning

Figure 7.4

Electrical probes placed inside and outside an axon measure its activity. (The scale is exaggerated here. Such measurements require ultrasmall electrodes.) The inside of an axon at rest is about −60 to −70 millivolts, compared with the outside. Electrochemical changes in a neuron generate an action potential. When sodium ions (Na+) that have a positive charge rush into the cell, its interior briefly becomes positive. This is the action potential. After the action potential, positive potassium ions (K+) flow out of the axon and restore its negative charge. (See Figure 7.5 for further explanation.)

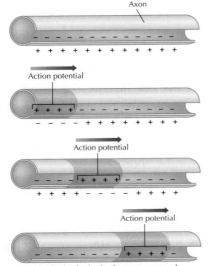

1. In its resting state, the axon has a negatively charged interior.

2. During an action potential, positively charged atoms (ions) rush into the axon. This briefly changes the electrical charge inside the axon from negative to positive. Simultaneously, the charge outside the axon becomes negative.

3. The action potential advances as positive and negative charges reverse in a moving zone of electrical activity that sweeps down the axon.

4. After an action potential passes, positive ions rapidly flow out of the axon to quickly restore its negative charge. An outward flow of additional positive ions returns the axon to its resting state.

© Cengage Learning

Figure 7.5

The inside of an axon normally has a negative electrical charge. The fluid surrounding an axon is normally positive. As an action potential passes along the axon, these charges reverse so that the interior of the axon briefly becomes positive. This process is described in more detail in Figure 7.6.

about −50 millivolts, the neuron will reach its *threshold*, or trigger point for firing (see ● **Figure 7.4**). It's as if the neuron says, "Ah-ha! It's time to send a message to my neighbors." When a neuron reaches its threshold, an **action potential**, or nerve impulse, sweeps down the axon at up to 200 miles per hour (● **Figure 7.5**). That may seem fast, but it still takes at least a split second to react. That's one reason it is so difficult to hit a 100-mile-per-hour professional baseball pitch.

Dendrites *Neuron fibers that receive incoming messages.*
Soma *The main body of a neuron or other cell.*
Axon *Fiber that carries information away from the cell body of a neuron.*
Axon terminals *Bulb-shaped structures at the ends of axons that form synapses with the dendrites and somas of other neurons.*
Resting potential *The electrical charge of an inactive neuron.*
Action potential *A nerve impulse.*

What happens during an action potential? Tiny tunnels or holes called **ion channels** pierce the axon membrane. Normally, these tiny openings are blocked by molecules that act like gates or doors. During an action potential, the gates pop open. This allows sodium ions (Na⁺) to rush into the axon (Toates, 2011). The channels first open near the soma. Then, gate after gate opens down the length of the axon as the action potential zips along (● Figure 7.6).

Each action potential is an *all-or-nothing event* (the nerve impulse occurs completely or not at all). You might find it helpful to picture the axon as a row of dominoes set on end. Tipping over the dominoes is an all-or-nothing act. Once the first domino drops, a wave of falling blocks zips rapidly to the end of the line. Similarly, when a nerve impulse is triggered near the soma, a wave of activity (the action potential) travels down the length of the axon. This is what happens in long chains of neurons as a dancer's brain tells her feet what to do next, beat after beat.

After each nerve impulse, the cell briefly dips below its resting level and becomes less willing or ready to fire. This **negative after-potential** occurs because potassium ions (K⁺) flow out of the neuron while the membrane gates are open (Figure 7.6). After a nerve impulse, ions flow both into and out of the axon, recharging it for more action. In our model, it takes an instant for the row of dominoes to be set up again. Soon, however, the axon is ready for another wave of activity.

Saltatory Conduction The axons of some neurons (such as the one pictured in Figure 7.3) are coated with a fatty layer called **myelin** (MY-eh-lin). Small gaps in the myelin help nerve impulses move faster. Instead of passing down the entire length of the axon, the action potential leaps from gap to gap, a process called **saltatory conduction**. (The Latin word *saltare* means to jump or leap.) Without the added speed of saltatory action potentials, it would probably be impossible to brake in time to avoid many automobile accidents. When the myelin layer is damaged, a person may suffer from numbness, weakness, or paralysis. That is what happens in *multiple sclerosis*, a disease that occurs when the immune system attacks and destroys the myelin in a person's body (Khan, Tselis, & Lisak, 2010).

Synapses and Neurotransmitters

How does information move from one neuron to another? The nerve impulse is primarily electrical. That's why electrically stimulating the brain affects behavior. To prove this point, researcher José Delgado once entered a bullring with a cape

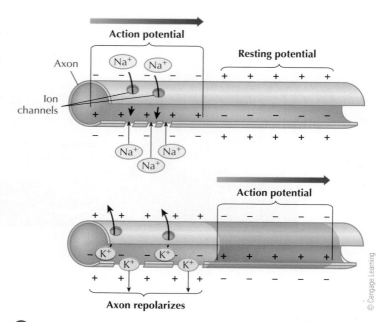

● **Figure 7.6**

The interior of an axon. The right end of the top axon is at rest. Thus, it has a negative charge inside. An action potential begins when ion channels open and sodium ions (Na⁺) rush into the axon. In this drawing, the action potential would travel from left to right along the axon. In the lower axon, the action potential has moved to the right. After it passes, potassium ions (K⁺) flow out of the axon. This quickly renews the negative charge inside the axon, so that it can fire again. Sodium ions that enter the axon during an action potential are pumped out more slowly. Removing them restores the original resting potential.

and a radio transmitter. The bull charged. Delgado retreated. At the last instant, the speeding bull stopped short. Why? Delgado had placed radio-activated electrodes (metal wires) deep within the bull's brain. These, in turn, stimulated control centers that brought the bull to a halt (Blackwell, 2012; Horgan, 2005).

In contrast to nerve impulses, communication between neurons is chemical. The microscopic space between two neurons, over which messages pass, is called a **synapse** (SIN-aps) (● Figure 7.7). When an action potential reaches the tips of the axon terminals, **neurotransmitters** (NOOR-oh-TRANS-mit-ers) are released into the synaptic gap. Neurotransmitters are chemicals that alter activity in neurons.

Let's return to our metaphor of people standing in a line. To be more accurate, you and the others shouldn't be holding hands. Instead, each person should have a squirt gun in his or her right hand. To pass along a message, you would squirt the left hand of the person to your right. When that person notices this "message," he or she would squirt the left hand of the person to the right, and so on.

TABLE 7.1	Major Neurotransmitters		
Neurotransmitter	**Main Mode of Action**	**Function in the Brain**	**Effects of Imbalance**
Acetylcholine	Excitatory neurotransmitter	Participates in movement, autonomic function, learning, and memory	Deficiency may play a role in Alzheimer's disease
Dopamine	Excitatory neurotransmitter	Participates in motivation, reward, planning of behavior	Deficiency may lead to Parkinson's disease, reduced feelings of pleasure; excess may lead to schizophrenia
GABA	Inhibitory neurotransmitter	Major inhibitory effect in the central nervous system; participates in moods	Deficiency may lead to anxiety
Glutamate	Excitatory neurotransmitter	Major excitatory effect in the central nervous system; participates in learning and memory	Excess may lead to neuron death and autism; deficiency may lead to tiredness
Norepinephrine	Excitatory neurotransmitter	Participates in arousal, vigilance, and mood	Excess may lead to anxiety
Serotonin	Inhibitory neurotransmitter	Participates in mood, appetite, and sleep	Deficiency may lead to depression and/or anxiety

Adapted from Freberg, 2010; Kalat, 2013.

When chemical molecules cross over a synapse, they attach to special receiving areas on the next neuron (see Figure 7.7). These tiny **receptor sites** on the cell membrane are sensitive to neurotransmitters. The sites are found in large numbers on neuron bodies and dendrites. Muscles and glands have receptor sites, too.

Do neurotransmitters always trigger an action potential in the next neuron? No, but they do change the likelihood of an action potential in the next neuron. Some neurotransmitters *excite* the next neuron (move it closer to firing). Others *inhibit* it (make firing less likely).

More than 100 neurotransmitter chemicals are found in the brain. Some examples are acetylcholine, dopamine, GABA, glutamate, norepinephrine, and serotonin (● Table 7.1).

Why are there so many neurotransmitters? Some neurotransmitters are used by specific pathways that interlink regions of the brain. It is as if different pathways *speak* different languages. Perhaps this helps prevent confusing crosstalk or intermixing of messages. For example, the brain has a reward

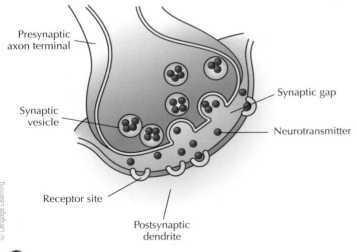

© Cengage Learning

● **Figure 7.7**

A highly magnified view of a synapse. Neurotransmitters are stored in tiny sacs called *synaptic vesicles* (VES-ih-kels). When a nerve impulse reaches the end of an axon, the vesicles move to the surface and release neurotransmitters. These molecules cross the synaptic gap to affect the next neuron. The size of the gap is exaggerated here; it is only about one millionth of an inch. Some transmitter molecules excite the next neuron and some inhibit its activity.

Ion channels *Tiny openings through the axon membrane.*
Negative after-potential *A drop in electrical charge below the resting potential.*
Myelin *A fatty layer coating some axons.*
Saltatory conduction *The process by which nerve impulses conducted down the axons of neurons coated with myelin jump from gap to gap in the myelin layer.*
Synapse *The microscopic space between two neurons, over which messages pass.*
Neurotransmitter *Any chemical released by a neuron that alters activity in other neurons.*
Receptor sites *Areas on the surface of neurons and other cells that are sensitive to neurotransmitters or hormones.*

or pleasure system that mainly *speaks* dopamine (although other neurotransmitters also are found in the system) (Mark et al., 2011; Opland, Leinninger, & Myers, 2010).

Slight variations in neurotransmitter function may be related to temperament differences in infancy and personality differences in adulthood (Ashton, 2007). Outright disturbances of any neurotransmitter can have serious consequences. For example, too much dopamine may cause schizophrenia (Kendler & Schaffner, 2011), whereas too little serotonin may underlie depression (Torrente, Gelenberg, & Vrana, 2012).

Many drugs mimic, duplicate, or block neurotransmitters. For example, the chemical structure of cocaine is similar to that of dopamine. In the short run, cocaine can trigger an increase in dopamine in the reward system resulting in a drug high (España et al., 2010). In the long run, the overuse of recreational drugs like cocaine overstimulates the reward system and disturbs dopamine function, resulting in drug addiction (Taber et al., 2012).

As another example, the drug curare (cue-RAH-ree) causes paralysis. Acetylcholine (ah-SEET-ul-KOH-leen) normally activates muscles. By attaching to receptor sites on muscles, curare blocks acetylcholine, preventing the activation of muscle cells. As a result, a person or animal given curare cannot move—a fact known to South American Indians of the Amazon River Basin, who use curare as an arrow poison for hunting. Without acetylcholine, a golfer couldn't even move, much less swing a club.

Neural Regulators More subtle brain activities are affected by chemicals called **neuropeptides** (NOOR-oh-PEP-tides). Neuropeptides do not carry messages directly. Instead, they *regulate* the activity of other neurons. By doing so, they affect memory, pain, emotion, pleasure, moods, hunger, sexual behavior, and other basic processes. For example, when you touch something hot, you jerk your hand away. The messages for this action are carried by neurotransmitters. At the same time, pain may cause the brain to release neuropeptides called *enkephalins* (en-KEF-ah-lins). These opiate-like neural regulators relieve pain and stress. Related neuropeptide chemicals called *endorphins* (en-DORF-ins) are released by the pituitary gland. Together, these chemicals reduce the pain so that it is not too disabling (Bruehl et al., 2012).

We now can explain the painkilling effect of placebos (fake pills or injections); they raise endorphin levels (Price, Finniss, & Benedetti, 2008). A release of endorphins also seems to underlie runner's high, masochism, acupuncture, and the euphoria sometimes associated with childbirth, painful initiation rites, and even sport parachuting (Janssen & Arntz, 2001). In each case, pain and stress cause the release of endorphins. In turn, these endorphins induce feelings of pleasure or euphoria similar to being high on morphine. People who say they are "addicted" to running may be closer to the truth than they realize. Ultimately, neural regulators may help explain depression, schizophrenia, drug addiction, and other puzzling topics.

Neural Networks

Let's put together what we now know about the nerve impulse and synaptic transmission to see how **neural networks**, interlinked collections of neurons, process information in our nervous systems (Zimmer, 2010). The simplest network, a **reflex arc**, occurs when a stimulus provokes an automatic response. Such reflexes arise within the spinal cord, without any help from the brain (● **Figure 7.8**). Imagine that Molly steps on a thorn. (Yes, they're still playing Frisbee.) Pain is detected in her foot by a *sensory neuron*—a neuron that carries messages from the senses toward the CNS. Instantly, the sensory neuron fires off a message to Molly's spinal cord.

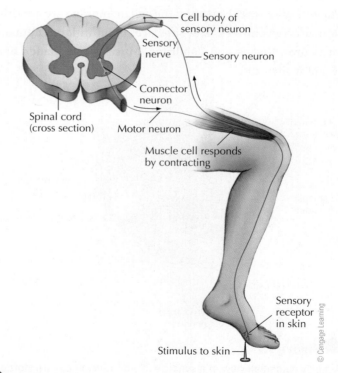

● Figure 7.8

A sensory-motor arc, or reflex, is set in motion by a stimulus to the skin (or other part of the body). The nerve impulse travels to the spinal cord and then back out to a muscle, which contracts. Such reflexes provide automatic protective devices for the body.

Inside the spinal cord, the sensory neuron synapses with a *connector neuron* (a neuron that links two others). The connector neuron activates a *motor neuron* (a neuron that carries commands from the CNS to muscles and glands). The muscle fibers are made up of *effector cells* (cells capable of producing a response). The muscle cells contract and cause Molly's foot to withdraw. Notice that no brain activity is required for a reflex arc to occur. Molly's body reacts automatically to protect itself.

In reality, even a simple reflex usually triggers more complex activity. For example, muscles of Molly's other leg must contract to support her as she shifts her weight. Even this can be done by the spinal cord, but it involves a bigger network of cells and several spinal nerves. Also, the spinal cord normally informs the brain of its actions. As her foot pulls away from the thorn, Molly will feel the pain and think, "Ouch! What was that?"

Perhaps you have realized how adaptive it is to have a spinal cord capable of responding on its own. Such automatic responses leave the brains of our Frisbee stars free to deal with more important information—such as the location of trees, lampposts, and chatting picnickers—as they take turns making grandstand catches.

Neural networks in the brain perform much more complex calculations. ● **Figure 7.9** shows a small neural network involved in making a decision. Five neurons synapse with a single neuron that, in turn, connects with three more neurons. At the time depicted in the diagram, the single neuron is receiving one stronger and two weaker excitatory messages (+) as well as two inhibitory ones (−). Does it fire an impulse? It depends: If enough exciting messages arrive close in time, the neuron will reach its threshold and fire—but only if it doesn't get too many inhibiting messages that push it *away* from its trigger point. In this way, messages are *combined* before a neuron "decides" to fire its all-or-nothing action potential.

Let's try another metaphor. You are out shopping with five friends and find a pair of jeans you want to buy. Three of them think you should buy the jeans; your best friend is especially positive (+); and two think you shouldn't (−). Because, on balance, the input is positive, you go ahead and buy the jeans. Maybe you even tell some other friends they should buy those jeans. Similarly, any single neuron in a neural network "listens" to the neurons that synapse with it and combines that input into an output. At any instant, a single neuron may weigh hundreds or thousands of inputs to produce an outgoing message. After the neuron recovers from the resulting action potential, it again combines the inputs, which may have changed in the meantime, into another output, and another, and another.

In this way, each neuron in your brain functions as a tiny computer. Compared with the average laptop computer, a neuron is terribly simple and slow. But multiply these events by billions of neurons and trillions of synapses, all operating at the same time, and you have an amazing computer—one that could easily fit inside a shoebox.

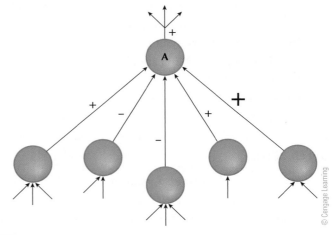

© Cengage Learning

● **Figure 7.9**

A small neural network. The actual network involved in processing decisions like these is much more complicated than illustrated. But the basic idea remains the same. Neuron A receives inputs from two weaker and one stronger excitatory connections (+) and two inhibitory connections (−) and combines the inputs into a "decision" to launch an action potential, which may help trigger further synaptic transmissions in other neurons.

Neuropeptides *Brain chemicals, such as enkephalins and endorphins, that regulate the activity of neurons.*
Neural networks *Interlinked collections of neurons that process information in the brain.*
Reflex arc *The simplest behavior, in which a stimulus provokes an automatic response.*

Neuroplasticity and Neurogenesis—Nervous System, Heal Thyself

SURVEY QUESTION 7.3: Can the nervous system grow and heal itself?

Our brains change in response to experience, a capacity termed **neuroplasticity**. Synaptic connections may grow stronger and new ones may form. (Figure 7.9 shows one particularly strong synapse—the large +.) In general, the repeated activation of synapses between two neurons strengthens the connection between them. This is known as *Hebb's rule* (Hebb, 1949). Inactive synaptic connections may weaken and even die.

Consequently, every new experience you have is reflected in changes to your brain. For example, rats raised in a complex environment have more synapses and longer dendrites in their brains than rats raised in a simpler environment (Kolb, Gibb, & Gorny, 2003). Or consider Nico and Brooke, teenagers who had a large portion of their brains removed as infants. Today, they are functioning well; over the years, their brains have compensated for their losses (Immordino-Yang, 2008; Kolb et al., 2011).

Are adult human brains also neuroplastic? Could Dave Duerson's brain have healed itself? Although adult brains are less neuroplastic, they can still be changed with patience and persistence. See "You Can Change Your Mind, But Can You Change Your Brain?" Unfortunately for people like Dave Duerson, who suffer from *chronic traumatic encephalopathy*, the prospects for recovery are not good because the brain damage suffered from head traumas can be extensive and often triggers a subsequent disease process that continues to damage the brain long after the original traumas have ended (Baugh et al., 2012).

The nervous system is "plastic" for another reason. It has long been known that nerves in the peripheral nervous system can regrow if they are damaged. The axons of most neurons in nerves outside the brain and spinal cord are covered by a thin layer of cells called the *neurilemma* (NOOR-rih-LEM-ah). (Return to Figure 7.3.) The neurilemma forms a tunnel that damaged fibers can follow as they repair themselves. Because of this, patients can expect to regain some control over severed limbs once they have been reattached.

In contrast, a serious injury to the spinal cord was long thought to be permanent. However, scientists are starting to make progress repairing damaged neurons in the spinal cord (Rossignol & Frigon, 2011). For instance, they have partially repaired cut spinal cords in rats by establishing cellular bridges to close the gap. Strategies include coaxing severed nerve fibers to grow across the gap (Cheng, Cao, & Olson, 1996), grafting nerve fibers to fill the gap (Féron et al., 2005), and injecting stem cells (immature cells that can mature into a variety of specialized cells, such as neurons) into the gap (Watson & Yeung, 2011). Research with mice and rats has already been followed up with some human trials. Imagine what that could mean to a person confined to a wheelchair. Although it is unwise to raise false hopes, solutions to such problems are beginning to emerge.

Can brain damage also be repaired? Until a few years ago, it was widely believed that we are born with all the brain cells we will ever have (Ben Abdallah et al., 2010). This led to the depressing idea that we all slowly go downhill because the

Think Critically

You Can Change Your Mind, But Can You Change Your Brain?

You can always change your mind. But does that have anything to do with your brain? According to scientists who study the brain, the answer must be "yes" because they believe that every mental event involves a brain event.

In one study, people suffering from an intense fear of spiders (arachnophobia) could touch spiders after undergoing cognitive behavior therapy. Images of their brains revealed reduced activity in brain areas related to the phobia (Paquette et al., 2003). Not only did they change their minds about spiders but they also changed their brains.

Another study focused on taxi drivers in London, England, who must learn the names and locations of tens of thousands of streets in order to earn their licenses. Not only do experienced cabbies have superior memory for street information but the parts of their brains responsible for processing this learning also are enlarged (Woollett & Maguire, 2011). Again, a learning experience changed their brains.

Just think: Every time you learn something, you are reshaping your living brain (Begley, 2006). There is even a fancy phrase to describe what you are doing: *self-directed neuroplasticity*. So as you study this psychology textbook, you are changing your mind—and your brain—about psychology.

brain loses thousands of neurons every day. Rather than facing a steady decline, we now know that a healthy 75-year-old brain has just as many neurons as it did when it was careening through life in the body of a 25-year-old.

Although it is true that the brain loses cells daily, it simultaneously grows new neurons to replace them. This process is called **neurogenesis** (noor-oh-JEN-uh-sis), the production of new brain cells (Lee, Clemenson, & Gage, 2011). Each day, thousands of new cells originate deep within the brain, move to the surface, and link up with other neurons to become part of the brain's circuitry. This was stunning news to brain scientists, who must now figure out what the new cells do. Most likely, they are involved in learning, memory, and our ability to adapt to changing circumstances (Canales, 2010).

The discovery of neurogenesis in adult brains is leading to new treatments for some types of brain damage (Ekonomou et al., 2011; Lagace, 2011). Imagine that a patient named Bobby has suffered a stroke, damaging some of the neurons responsible for controlling his left arm. What could be done to help Bobby recover from the resulting partial paralysis? One approach, called *constraint-induced movement therapy*, involves restraining Bobby's good right arm, forcing his impaired left arm to be more active. By using his left arm, Bobby could increase

neurogenesis in the damaged part of his brain (Taub, 2004). In another approach, drugs that speed up neurogenesis could be injected into the damaged area of Bobby's brain (Zhang, Zhang, & Chopp, 2005). Such techniques are beginning to offer new hope for people suffering from a variety of other disabilities, such as depression, addiction, and schizophrenia (Chambers, 2012; Fournier & Duman, 2012).

But don't these treatments assume that Bobby's brain is still capable of neurogenesis? What if it isn't? Brilliant! Although a stroke most likely doesn't damage the brain's ability to repair itself, it is quite possible that other brain disorders arise from impaired neurogenesis (Thompson et al., 2008). In fact, that is exactly the theory proposed by neuroscientists Carla Toro and Bill Deakin to explain schizophrenia, a serious mental disorder (Toro & Deakin, 2007). (For more on schizophrenia, see Module 61.) The brains of people who have schizophrenia are usually smaller than normal, indicating that they have fewer neurons. Toro and Deakin's idea is that the schizophrenic brain may be unable to continually create new neurons to replace old ones that have died. If they are right, new therapies to promote neurogenesis may hold the key to treating schizophrenia, one of the most devastating mental illnesses (Inta, Meyer-Lindenberg, & Gass, 2011).

Neuroplasticity *The capacity of the brain to change in response to experience.*
Neurogenesis *The production of new brain cells.*

Module 7: Summary

7.1 What are the major divisions of the nervous system?

- **7.1.1** Sensations, thoughts, feelings, motives, actions, memories, and all other human capacities are associated with nervous system activities and structures.
- **7.1.2** The nervous system can be divided into the central nervous system (CNS) and the peripheral nervous system (PNS).
- **7.1.3** The CNS is made up of the brain, which carries out most of the "computing" in the nervous system, and the spinal cord, which connects the brain to the PNS.
- **7.1.4** The PNS includes the somatic nervous system (SNS), which carries sensory information to the brain and motor commands to the body, and the autonomic nervous system (ANS), which controls vegetative and automatic bodily processes. The ANS has a sympathetic branch and a parasympathetic branch.

7.2 How do neurons operate and communicate with each other?

- **7.2.1** The dendrite and soma of a neuron combine neural input and send it down the axon to the axon terminals for output across the synapse to other neurons.

- **7.2.2** The firing of an action potential (nerve impulse) is basically an electrical event.
- **7.2.3** Communication between neurons is chemical: Neurotransmitters cross the synapse, attach to receptor sites, and excite or inhibit the receiving cell.
- **7.2.4** Chemicals called neuropeptides regulate activity in the brain.
- **7.2.5** All behavior can be traced to networks of neurons. The spinal cord can process simple reflex arcs.

7.3 Can the nervous system grow and heal itself?

- **7.3.1** The brain's circuitry is not static. The brain can rewire itself and even grow new nerve cells in response to changing environmental conditions.
- **7.3.2** Neurons and nerves in the peripheral nervous system can often regenerate. At present, damage in the central nervous system is usually permanent, although scientists are working on ways to repair damaged neural tissue.

Module 7: Knowledge Builder

Recite

1. The somatic and autonomic systems are part of the _____ nervous system.

2. The parasympathetic nervous system is most active during times of high emotion. ***T or F?***

3. The _____ and _____ are the receiving areas of a neuron where information from other neurons is accepted.

4. Nerve impulses are carried down the _____ to the _____.

5. The _____ potential becomes a(n) _____ potential when a neuron passes the threshold for firing.

6. Neuropeptides are transmitter substances that help regulate the activity of neurons. ***T or F?***

7. The simplest behavior sequence is a _____ _____.

Reflect

Think Critically

8. What effect would you expect a drug to have if it blocked passage of neurotransmitters across the synapse?

9. Where in all the brain's "hardware" do you think the mind is found? What is the relationship between mind and brain?

Self-Reflect

To remember the functions of major branches of the nervous system, think about what you *couldn't* do if each part were missing.

How does a neural network differ from the central processing unit of a computer?

ANSWERS

1. peripheral **2.** F **3.** dendrites, soma **4.** axon, axon terminals **5.** resting, action **6.** T **7.** reflex arc **8.** Such a drug could have wide-ranging effects, depending on which neurotransmitter(s) it blocked. If the drug blocked excitatory synapses, it would depress brain activity. If it blocked inhibitory messages, it would act as a powerful stimulant. **9.** These questions, known as the mind–body problem, have challenged thinkers for centuries. One recent view is that mental states are emergent properties of brain activity—that is, brain activity forms complex patterns that are, in a sense, more than the sum of their parts. Or, to use a rough analogy, if the brain were a musical instrument, then mental life would be like music played on that instrument.

Brain and Behavior: Brain Research

How to Look Under the Hood

Your 3-pound brain is wrinkled like a walnut, the size of a grapefruit, and the texture of tofu. How could such a squishy little blob of tissue enable us to become neuroscientists? To make music of exquisite beauty? To seek a cure for cancer? To fall in love? Or to read a book like this one? *Biopsychology* is the study of how biological processes, especially those occurring in the nervous system, relate to behavior.

In their research, many biopsychologists try to learn which parts of the brain control particular mental or behavioral functions, such as being able to recognize faces or move your hands. That is, they try to learn where functions are localized (located) in the brain. Many techniques have been developed to help identify brain structures and the functions they control. For example, the brain in this CT scan was damaged (shown in red) by a stroke, which occurs when an artery carrying blood in the brain bleeds or becomes blocked, causing some brain tissue to die. The location of the stroke determines what mental or behavioral functions are disrupted.

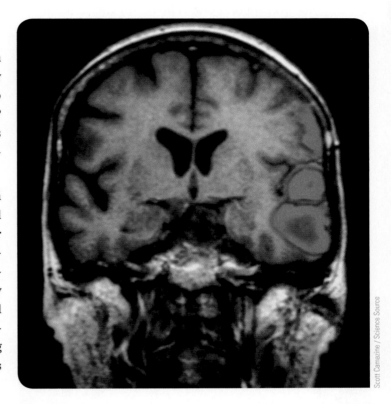

Scott Camazine / Science Source

SURVEY QUESTIONS

8.1 How are different parts of the brain identified?

8.2 What do the different parts of the brain do?

Mapping Brain Structure—Pieces of the Puzzle

SURVEY QUESTION 8.1: How are different parts of the brain identified?

Anatomists have learned much about brain structure by cutting apart (*dissecting*) autopsied human and animal brains and examining them under a microscope. Dissection reveals that the brain is made up of many anatomically distinct areas or parts. Less invasive newer methods, such as the *CT scan* and the *MRI scan*, can be used to map brain structures in living brains (Kalat, 2013).

CT Scan

Computerized scanning equipment has revolutionized the study of brain structures and made it easier to identify brain diseases and injuries. At best, conventional X-rays produce only shadowy images of the brain. A **computed tomographic (CT) scan** is a specialized X-ray that does a much better job of making the brain visible. In a CT scan, X-rays taken from a number of different angles are collected by a computer and formed into an image of the brain. A CT scan can reveal brain structure as well as the location of strokes (as in the image at the beginning of this module), injuries, tumors, and other brain disorders.

MRI Scan

Magnetic resonance imaging (MRI) uses a strong magnetic field, rather than X-rays, to produce an image of the body's interior. During an MRI scan, a person's body is placed inside a magnetic field. Processing by a computer then creates a three-dimensional model of the brain or body. Any two-dimensional plane, or slice, of the body can be selected and displayed as an image on a computer screen. MRI scans produce more detailed images than are possible with CT scans, allowing us to peer into the living brain almost as if it were transparent (●**Figure 8.1**).

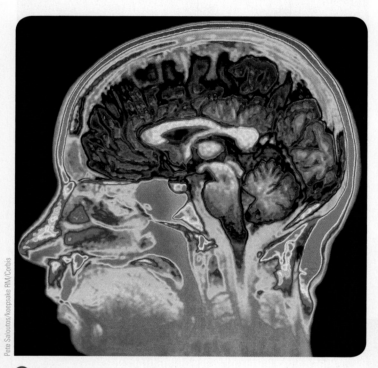

Pete Saloutos/keepsake RM/Corbis

● **Figure 8.1**

A colored MRI scan of the brain reveals many details. Can you identify any brain regions?

Mapping Brain Function— What Do the Parts Do?

SURVEY QUESTION 8.2: What do the different parts of the brain do?

Imagine a mechanic handing you a car part. Even though you can clearly see the *structure* of the part (it's about an inch long, with a round knob on one end, and a little prong . . .), you probably won't, just by looking at it, be able to figure out its *function* (. . . but is it part of the steering system, the brakes, or what?). Similarly, while it is valuable to be able to examine images of different brain structures, such as those made possible by CT scans and MRIs, it is another matter entirely to understand what role those structures play in normal brain function.

What parts of the brain allow us to think, feel, perceive, or act? To answer questions like this, we must **localize function** by linking psychological or behavioral capacities with particular brain structures. In many instances, this has been done through a **clinical case study**. Such a study examines changes in personality, behavior, or sensory capacity caused by brain diseases or injuries. If damage to a particular part of the brain consistently leads to a particular loss of function, then we say the function is *localized* in that structure. Presumably, that part of the brain controls the same function in all of us.

Although major brain injuries are easy enough to spot, psychologists also look for more subtle signs that the brain is not working properly. **Neurological soft signs**, as they are called, include clumsiness, an awkward gait, poor hand–eye coordination, and other problems with perception or fine muscle control (Raymond & Noggle, 2013). These telltale signs are "soft" in the sense that they aren't direct tests of the brain, like a CT or MRI scan. Long-term brain damage is usually first diagnosed with soft signs. Likewise, soft signs help psychologists diagnose problems ranging from childhood learning disorders to full-blown psychosis (Banich & Compton, 2011).

Instead of relying on clinical studies, researchers have learned much from **electrical stimulation of the brain (ESB)** (● **Figure 8.2**). For example, the surface of the brain can be "turned on" by stimulating it with a mild electrical current delivered through a thin insulated wire called an **electrode**. When this is done during brain surgery, the patient can describe the effect of the stimulation. (The brain has no pain receptors, so surgery can be done while a patient is awake. Only local painkillers are used for the scalp and skull. Any volunteers?) Even structures below the surface of the brain can be activated by lowering a stimulating electrode, insulated except at the tip, into a target area inside the brain. ESB can call forth behavior with astonishing power. Instantly, it can bring about aggression, alertness, escape, eating, drinking, sleeping, movement, euphoria, memories, speech, tears, and more.

Could ESB be used to control a person against his or her will? It might seem that ESB could be used to control a person like

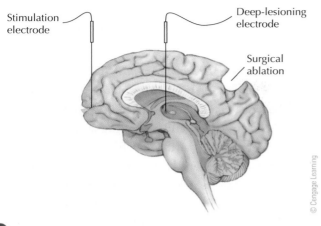

Stimulation electrode

Deep-lesioning electrode

Surgical ablation

© Cengage Learning

Figure 8.2

The functions of brain structures are explored by selectively activating or removing them. Brain research is often based on electrical stimulation, but chemical stimulation also is used at times.

a robot. But the details of emotions and behaviors elicited by ESB are modified by personality and circumstances. Sci-fi movies to the contrary, it would be impossible for a ruthless dictator to enslave people by "radio controlling" their brains.

An alternative approach is **ablation** (ab-LAY-shun), or surgical removal of parts of the brain (see Figure 8.2). When ablation causes changes in behavior or sensory capacity, we also gain insight into the purpose of the missing part. By using a technique called **deep lesioning** (LEE-zhun-ing), structures below the surface of the brain also can be removed. In this case, an electrode is lowered into a target area inside the brain and a strong electric current is used to destroy a small amount of brain tissue (see Figure 8.2). Again, changes in behavior give clues about the function of the affected area.

To find out what individual neurons are doing, we need to do a microelectrode recording. A *microelectrode* is an extremely thin glass tube filled with a salty fluid. The tip of a microelectrode is small enough to detect the electrical activity of a *single* neuron. Watching the action potentials of just one neuron provides a fascinating glimpse into the true origins of behavior. (The action potential shown in Module 7, Figure 7.4, was recorded with a microelectrode.)

Are any less invasive techniques available for studying brain function? Whereas CT scans and MRIs cannot tell us what different parts of the brain *do*, several other techniques allow us to observe the activity of parts of the brain without doing any damage at all. These include the EEG, PET scan, and fMRI (Kalat, 2013).

EEG

Electroencephalography (ee-LEK-tro-in-SEF-ah-LOG-ruh-fee) measures the waves of electrical activity produced near the surface of the brain. Small electrodes (disk-shaped metal plates) are placed on a person's scalp. Electrical impulses from the brain are detected and sent to an **electroencephalograph (EEG)**. The EEG amplifies these weak signals (brain waves) and records them on a moving sheet of paper or a computer screen (**Figure 8.3**). Various brain-wave patterns can identify the presence of tumors, epilepsy, and other diseases. The EEG also reveals changes in brain activity during sleep, daydreaming, hypnosis, and other mental states.

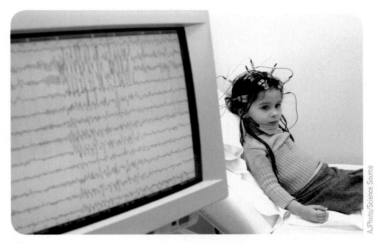

AJPhoto/Science Source

Figure 8.3

An EEG recording.

Computed tomographic (CT) scan *A computer-enhanced X-ray image of the brain or body.*
Magnetic resonance imaging (MRI) *An imaging technique that results in a three-dimensional image of the brain or body, based on its response to a magnetic field.*
Localization of function *The research strategy of linking specific structures in the brain with specific psychological or behavioral functions.*
Clinical case study *A detailed investigation of a single person, especially one suffering from some injury or disease.*
Neurological soft signs *Subtle behavioral signs of nervous system dysfunction, including clumsiness, an awkward gait, poor hand–eye coordination, and other perceptual and motor problems.*
Electrical stimulation of the brain (ESB) *Direct electrical stimulation and activation of brain tissue.*
Electrode *Any device (such as a wire, needle, or metal plate) used to electrically stimulate or destroy nerve tissue or to record its activity.*
Ablation *Surgical removal of tissue.*
Deep lesioning *Removal of tissue within the brain by use of an electrode.*
Electroencephalograph (EEG) *A device that detects, amplifies, and records electrical activity in the brain.*

PET Scan

A newer technology, called **positron emission tomography (PET)**, provides much more detailed images of activity both *near* the surface and *below* the surface of the brain. A PET scan detects positrons (subatomic particles) emitted by weakly radioactive glucose (sugar) as it is consumed by the brain. Because the brain runs on glucose, a PET scan shows which areas are using more energy. Higher energy use corresponds with higher activity. Thus, by placing positron detectors around the head and sending data to a computer, it is possible to create a moving, color picture of changes in brain activity. As you can see in ● **Figure 8.4**, PET scans reveal that specific brain areas are active when you see, hear, speak, or think.

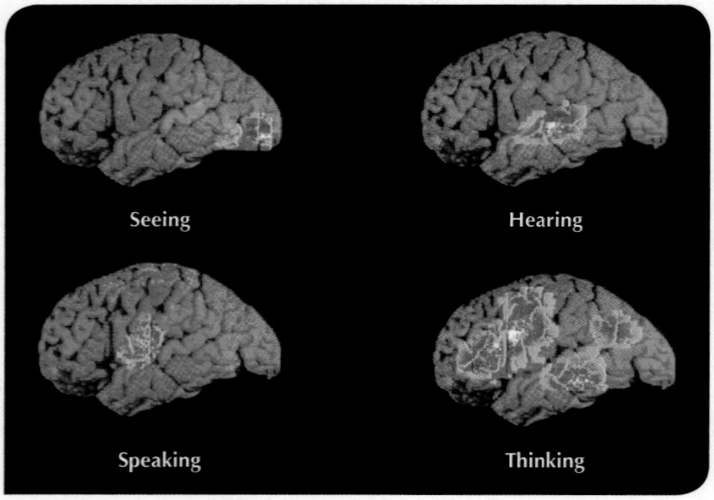

More active brains are good, right? Although we might assume that hardworking brains are smart brains, the reverse appears to be true (Neubauer & Fink, 2009). Using PET scans, psychologist Richard Haier and his colleagues first found that the brains of people who perform well on a difficult reasoning test consume less energy than those of poor performers (● **Figure 8.5**). Haier believes this shows that intelligence is related to brain efficiency: Less efficient brains work harder and still accomplish less (Haier, White, & Alkire, 2003). We've all had days like that!

Is it true that most people use only 10 percent of their brain capacity? This is one of the lasting myths about the brain. Brain scans show that all parts of the brain are active during waking hours. Obviously, some people make better use of their innate brainpower than others. Nevertheless, a normally functioning brain has no great hidden or untapped reserves of mental capacity.

fMRI

A **functional MRI (fMRI)** uses MRI technology to make brain activity visible. Like PET scans, fMRIs also provide images of activity throughout the brain. For example, if we scanned your brain while you are reading this textbook, areas of your brain involved in understanding what you read would be highlighted in an fMRI image. (In contrast, if we used MRI, rather than fMRI, we would get a beautiful image of your brain structure

WDCN/Univ. College London/Science Source

● **Figure 8.4**

Colored PET scans reveal different patterns of brain activation when we engage in different tasks.

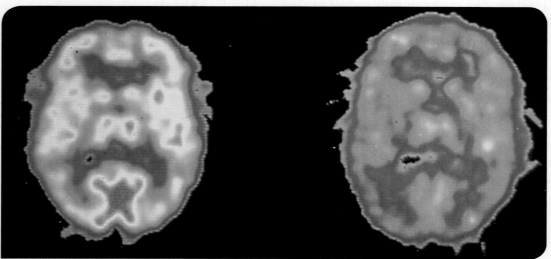

Courtesy of Richard Haier, University of California, Irvine

● **Figure 8.5**

In the images you see here, red, orange, and yellow indicate high consumption of glucose; green, blue, and pink show areas of low glucose use. The PET scan of the brain on the left shows that a man who solved 11 out of 36 reasoning problems burned more glucose than the man on the right, who solved 33.

without any clues as to which parts of your brain were more or less active.)

Psychiatrist Daniel Langleben and his colleagues (Langleben & Moriarty, 2012) have even used fMRI images to tell whether a person is lying. As ● **Figure 8.6** shows, the front of the brain is more active when a person is lying, rather than telling the truth. This may occur because it takes extra effort to lie, and the resulting extra brain activity is detected with fMRI (Langleben, 2008). Eventually, fMRI may help us distinguish between lies, false statements made with the intention to deceive, and *confabulations*, which are false claims believed to be true (Hirstein, 2005; Langleben, Dattilio, & Gutheil, 2006).

As they learn more about the human brain, researchers are creating digital three-dimensional brain maps. These "atlases" show brain structures and even their accompanying psychological functions. They promise to be valuable guides for medical treatment as well as for exploring the brain (Jellinger, 2009; Majka et al., 2012). Clearly, it is just a matter of time until even brighter beacons are flashed into the shadowy inner world of thought.

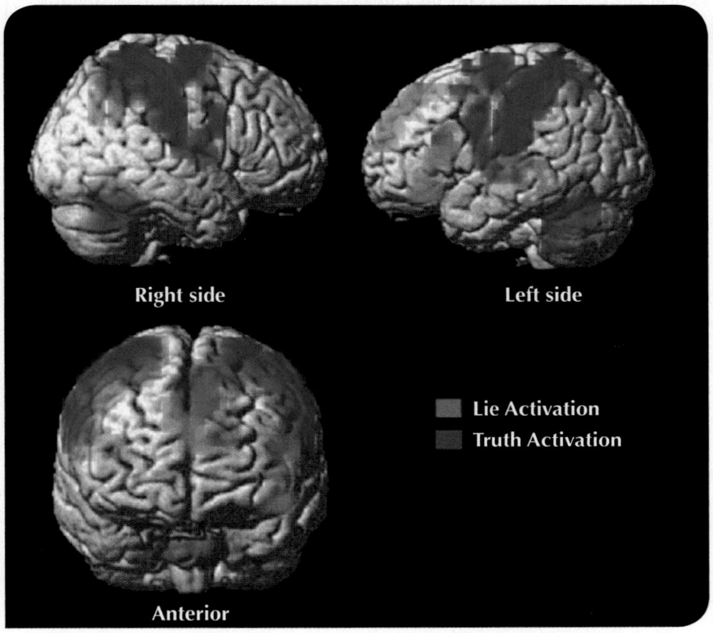

● **Figure 8.6**

Participants were asked to tell the truth or to lie while fMRI images of their brains were taken. When compared with telling the truth (*shown in blue*), areas toward the front of the brain were active during lying (*shown in red*). (Adapted from Langleben et al., 2005.)

Courtesy of Daniel Langleben, University of Pennsylvania.

Right side · Left side

Lie Activation
Truth Activation

Anterior

Module 8: Summary

8.1 How are different parts of the brain identified?
- **8.1.1** Brain structure is investigated though dissection and less intrusive CT scans and MRI scans.

8.2 What do the different parts of the brain do?
- **8.2.1** A major brain research strategy involves localization of function to link specific structures in the brain with specific psychological or behavioral functions.

- **8.2.2** Brain function is investigated through clinical case studies, electrical stimulation, ablation, deep lesioning, electrical recording, and microelectrode recording as well as less intrusive EEG recording, PET scans, and fMRI scans.

Positron emission tomography (PET) *An imaging technique that results in a computer-generated image of brain activity, based on glucose consumption in the brain.*
Functional MRI (fMRI) *MRI technique that records brain activity.*

Module 8: Knowledge Builder

Recite

1. Which of the following research techniques has the most in common with clinical studies of the effects of brain injuries?
   a. EEG recording
   b. deep lesioning
   c. microelectrode recording
   d. PET scan

2. CT scans cannot determine which part of your brain plays a role in speech because CT scans
   a. use X-rays
   b. reveal brain structure, not brain activity
   c. reveal brain activity, not brain structure
   d. use magnetic fields

3. _____ links brain structures to brain functions.

4. People only use 10 percent of their brain capacity. *T or F?*

Reflect

Think Critically

5. Deep lesioning is used to ablate an area in the hypothalamus of a rat. After the operation, the rat loses interest in food and eating. Why would it be a mistake to automatically conclude that the ablated area is a hunger center?

Self-Reflect

You suspect that a certain part of the brain is related to risk-taking. How could you use clinical studies, ablation, deep lesioning, and ESB to study the structure?

You want to know which areas of the brain's surface are most active when a person sees a face. What methods will you use?

ANSWERS

1. b 2. b 3. Localization of function 4. F 5. Other factors might explain the apparent loss of appetite. For example, the taste or smell of food might be affected, or the rat might simply have difficulty swallowing. It also is possible that hunger originates elsewhere in the brain and the ablated area merely relays messages that cause the rat to eat.

CENGAGE brain.com

Go to **cengagebrain.com** to access **MindTap for Coon/Mitterer** *Psychology Modules for Active Learning* and other online learning tools. MindTap is a fully online learning experience that combines all the tools you need—readings, multimedia, activities, and assessments—into a singular personalized Learning Path that guides you through the course.

Brain and Behavior:
Hemispheres and Lobes of the Cortex

Bigger Is Not Better

Bigger muscles usually mean more strength. Similarly, it is tempting to assume that bigger brains are smarter. If this were true, then geniuses should have huge brains. But they don't. For example, Albert Einstein's brain, shown here, is a normal size.

Compared with other creatures, our human intelligence is specifically related to the fact that our brains have a much larger cerebral cortex. Einstein's brain may reflect his genius in just this way. The parts of his cerebral cortex necessary for spatial reasoning (see arrows in b and c) have a unique anatomy and are larger than in most other brains.

The cortex can be divided into two hemispheres, which differ in what abilities they control, and smaller areas known as lobes. Parts of various lobes are responsible for the ability to see, hear, move, think, and speak. Thus, a map of the cerebral cortex is in some ways like a map of human behavior, as we shall see.

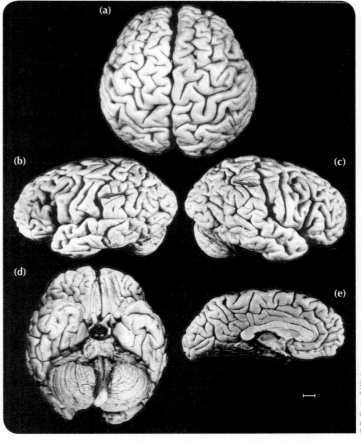

© Dr. Sandra F. Witelson

SURVEY QUESTIONS

9.1 How do the left and right hemispheres differ?

9.2 What are the different functions of the lobes of the cerebral cortex?

The Cerebral Cortex—My, What a Wrinkled Brain You Have!

SURVEY QUESTION 9.1: How do the left and right hemispheres differ?

In many ways, we humans are pretty unimpressive creatures. Other animals surpass us in almost every category of strength, speed, and sensory sensitivity. However, we do excel in intelligence.

Does that mean humans have the largest brains? No, that honor goes to whales, whose brains tip the scales at around 19 pounds. At 3 pounds, the human brain seems puny—until we compare brain weight to body weight. We then find that a sperm whale's brain is 1/10,000 of its weight. The ratio for humans is 1/60. And yet the ratio for tree shrews (small squirrel-like insect-eating mammals) is about 1/30. So our human brains are not noteworthy in terms of either absolute or relative weight (Coolidge & Wynn, 2009).

Although a small positive correlation exists between intelligence and brain size, overall size alone does not determine human intelligence (Johnson et al., 2008; Kievit et al., 2012).

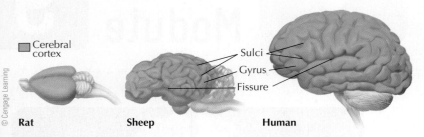

Cerebral cortex

Sulci
Gyrus
Fissure

Rat   Sheep   Human

© Cengage Learning

Figure 9.1

A more wrinkled cortex has greater cognitive capacity. Extensive corticalization is the key to human intelligence.

In fact, many parts of your brain are surprisingly similar to corresponding brain areas in other animals, such as lizards. It is your larger **cerebral cortex** (seh-REE-brel or ser-EH-brel) that sets you apart.

The cerebral cortex, which looks a little like a giant, wrinkled walnut, consists of the two large hemispheres that cover the upper part of the brain. The two hemispheres are divided into smaller areas known as *lobes*. The cerebral cortex covers most of the brain with a mantle of *gray matter* (spongy tissue made up mostly of cell bodies). Although the cortex is only 3 millimeters thick (one-tenth of an inch), it contains 70 percent of the neurons in the central nervous system. It is largely responsible for our ability to use language, make tools, acquire complex skills, and live in complex social groups (Coolidge & Wynn, 2009). In humans, the cortex is twisted and folded, and it is the largest brain structure. In lower animals, it is smooth and small (● **Figure 9.1**). The fact that humans are more intelligent than other animals is related to this **corticalization** (KORE-tih-kal-ih-ZAY-shun), or increase in the size and wrinkling of the cortex. Without the cortex, we humans wouldn't be much smarter than toads.

Cerebral Hemispheres

The cortex is composed of two sides, or *cerebral hemispheres* (half-globes), connected by a thick band of axon fibers called the *corpus callosum* (KORE-pus kah-LOH-sum) (● **Figure 9.2**). The left side of the brain mainly controls the right side of the body. Likewise, the right side of the brain mainly controls

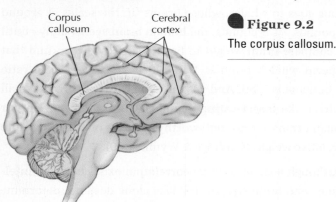

Corpus callosum

Cerebral cortex

© Cengage Learning

Figure 9.2

The corpus callosum.

left-body areas. If a stroke had damaged Einstein's brain, causing him to lose the ability to move his left arm or leg, the brain damage would have been to his right hemisphere.

Damage to one hemisphere may also cause a curious problem called *spatial neglect* (Silveri, Ciccarelli, & Cappa, 2011). A spatial neglect patient may pay no attention to one side of visual space (● **Figure 9.3**). Patients with right hemisphere damage may not eat food on the left side of a plate. Some even refuse to acknowledge a paralyzed left arm as their own (Hirstein, 2005). If you point to the "alien" arm, the patient is likely to say, "Oh, that's not my arm. It must belong to someone else."

Hemispheric Specialization

In 1981, Roger Sperry (1914–1994) won a Nobel Prize for his remarkable discovery that the right and left brain hemispheres perform differently on tests of language, perception, music, and other capabilities (Corballis, 2010b).

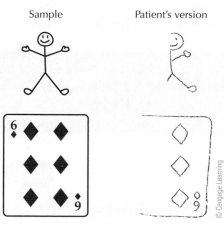

Sample   Patient's version

© Cengage Learning

Figure 9.3

Spatial neglect. A patient with right-hemisphere damage asked to copy images will likely neglect the left-hand side when drawing them. Shown images of a human-like stick figure or a playing card, such a patient might produce versions like those shown here. Similar instances of neglect occur in many patients with right-hemisphere damage (Silveri, Ciccarelli, & Cappa, 2011). Of course, a patient with left-hemisphere damage would neglect the right side of these images.

How is it possible to test only one side of the brain? One way is to work with people who've had a **split-brain operation**. In this rare surgery, the corpus callosum is cut to control severe epilepsy. The result is essentially a person with two brains in one body (Schechter, 2012). After the surgery, it is possible to send information to one hemisphere or the other (● **Figure 9.4**). However, after the right and left brain are separated, each hemisphere has its own separate perceptions, concepts, and impulses to act.

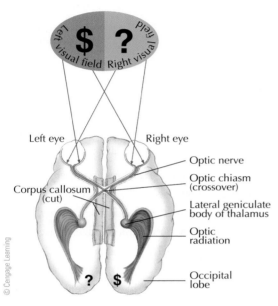

● **Figure 9.4**

Basic nerve pathways of vision. Notice that the left portion of each eye connects only to the left half of the brain; likewise, the right portion of each eye connects only to the right brain. When the corpus callosum is cut, a split brain results. Then, visual information can be sent to just one hemisphere by flashing it in the right or left visual field as the person stares straight ahead.

How does a split-brain person act after the operation? Having two "brains" in one body can create some interesting dilemmas. One split-brain patient, Karen, has to endure an out-of-control left hand. As Karen put it, "I'd light a cigarette, balance it on an ashtray, and then my left hand would reach forward and stub it out. It would take things out of my handbag and I wouldn't realize so I would walk away. I lost a lot of things before I realized what was going on" (Mosley, 2011). However, such conflicts are actually rare. That's because both halves of the brain normally have about the same experience at the same time. Also, if a conflict arises, one hemisphere usually overrides the other.

Split-brain effects are easiest to see in specialized testing. For example, we could flash a dollar sign to the right brain

and a question mark to the left brain of a patient named Tom (Figure 9.4 shows how this is possible.) Next, Tom is asked to draw what he saw, using his left hand, out of sight. Tom's left hand draws a dollar sign. If Tom is then asked to point with his right hand to a picture of what his hidden left hand drew, he will point to a question mark (Sperry, 1968). In short, for the split-brain person, one hemisphere may not know what is happening in the other. This has to be the ultimate case of the "right hand not knowing what the left hand is doing"! ● **Figure 9.5** provides another example of split-brain testing.

Right Brain/Left Brain *Earlier, it was stated that the hemispheres differ in abilities. In what ways are they different?* The brain divides its work in interesting ways. Roughly 95 percent of us use our left brain for language (speaking, writing, and understanding). In addition, the left hemisphere is superior at math, judging time and rhythm, and coordinating the order of complex movements, such as those needed for speech (Kell et al., 2011; Pinel & Dehaene, 2010).

Left Brain
- Language
- Speech
- Writing
- Calculation
- Time sense
- Rhythm
- Ordering of complex movements

Right Brain
- Nonverbal
- Perceptual skills
- Visualization
- Recognition of patterns, faces, melodies
- Recognition and expression of emotion
- Spatial skills
- Simple language comprehension

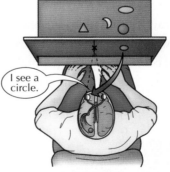 

Left Hemisphere　　　　**Right Hemisphere**

● **Figure 9.5**

A circle is flashed to the left brain of a split-brain patient and he is asked what he saw. He easily replies, "A circle." He also can pick out the circle by merely touching shapes with his right hand, which is out of sight behind a screen. However, his left hand can't identify the circle. If a triangle is flashed to the patient's right brain, he can't say what he saw (speech is controlled by the left hemisphere). He also can't identify the triangle by touch with the right hand. Now, however, the left hand has no difficulty picking out the triangle. In other tests, the hemispheres reveal distinct skills, as listed above the drawing.

Cerebral cortex　*The outer layer of the brain.*
Corticalization　*An increase in the relative size of the cerebral cortex.*
Split-brain operation　*Cutting the corpus callosum.*

In contrast, the right hemisphere can produce only the simplest language and numbers. Working with the right brain is like talking to a child who can say only a dozen words or so. To answer questions, the right hemisphere must use nonverbal responses, such as pointing at objects (see Figure 9.5).

Although it is poor at producing language, the right brain is especially good at perceptual skills, such as recognizing patterns, faces, and melodies; putting together a puzzle; or drawing a picture. It also helps you express emotions and detect the emotions that other people are feeling (Borod et al., 2002; Castro-Schilo & Kee, 2010).

Even though the right hemisphere is nearly "speechless," it is superior at some aspects of understanding language. If the right side of the brain is damaged, people lose their ability to understand jokes, irony, sarcasm, implications, and other nuances of language. Basically, the right hemisphere helps us see the overall context in which something is said (Beeman & Chiarello, 1998; Dyukova et al., 2010).

One Brain, Two Styles In general, the left hemisphere is involved mainly with *analysis* (breaking information into parts). It also processes information *sequentially* (in order, one item after the next). The right hemisphere appears to process information *holistically* (all at once) and *simultaneously*.

To summarize further, you could say that the right hemisphere is better at assembling pieces of the world into a coherent picture; it sees overall patterns and general connections. The left brain focuses on small details (● **Figure 9.6**). The right brain sees the

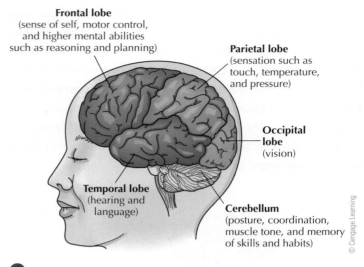

© Cengage Learning

● **Figure 9.7**

Lobes of the cerebral cortex.

wide-angle view; the left zooms in on specifics. The focus of the left brain is local; the right is global (Hübner & Volberg, 2005).

Are there left-brained and right-brained people? Numerous books and websites have been devoted to how to use the left brain or the right brain to manage, teach, draw, ride horses, learn, and even make love. But this is a drastic oversimplification because people normally use both sides of their brain at all times. It's true that some tasks may make *more* use of one hemisphere or the other. But in most real-world activities, the hemispheres share the work. Each does the parts it does best and shares information with the other side.

A smart brain is one that grasps both the details and the overall picture at the same time. For instance, during a concert, a guitarist will use her left brain to judge time and rhythm and coordinate the order of her hand movements. At the same time, she will use her right brain to recognize and organize melodies.

Lobes of the Cerebral Cortex—Hey, You, Four Lobes!

SURVEY QUESTION 9.2: What are the different functions of the lobes of the cerebral cortex?

Each of the two hemispheres of the cerebral cortex can be divided into several smaller lobes. Some of the lobes of the cerebral cortex are defined by larger fissures on the surface of the cortex. Others are regarded as separate areas because their functions are quite different (● **Figure 9.7**).

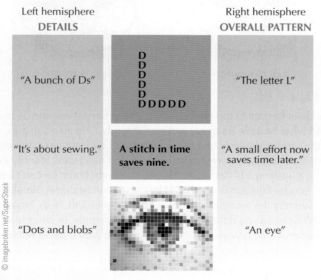

© imagebroker.net/SuperStock

● **Figure 9.6**

The left and right brain have different information-processing styles. The right brain gets the big pattern; the left focuses on small details.

The Frontal Lobes

The **frontal lobes** are associated with higher mental abilities and play a role in your sense of self. This area is also responsible for the control of movement. Specifically, an arch of tissue at the rear of the frontal lobes, called the **primary motor area (cortex)**, directs the body's muscles. If this area is stimulated with an electrical current, various parts of the body will twitch or move. The drawing wrapped around the motor cortex in ● **Figure 9.8** is out of proportion because it reflects the *dexterity* of body areas, not their size. The hands, for example, get more area than the feet. If you've ever wondered why your hands are more skilled or agile than your feet, it's partly because more motor cortex is devoted to the hands. Incidentally, due to neuroplasticity, learning and experience can alter these motor maps. For instance, violin, viola, and cello players have larger hand maps in the cortex (Hashimoto et al., 2004).

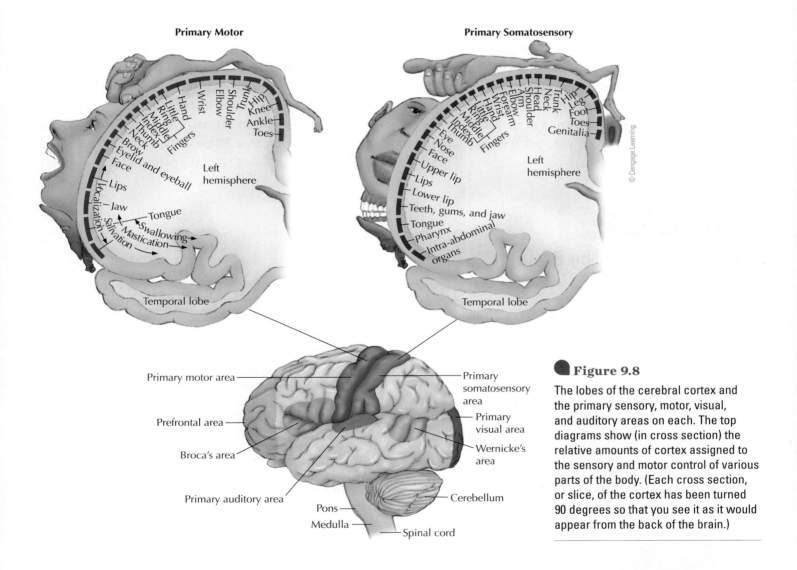

© Cengage Learning

● **Figure 9.8**

The lobes of the cerebral cortex and the primary sensory, motor, visual, and auditory areas on each. The top diagrams show (in cross section) the relative amounts of cortex assigned to the sensory and motor control of various parts of the body. (Each cross section, or slice, of the cortex has been turned 90 degrees so that you see it as it would appear from the back of the brain.)

Lobes of the cerebral cortex *Areas on the left and right cortex bordered by major fissures or defined by their functions.*
Frontal lobes *Areas of the cortex associated with movement, the sense of self, and higher mental functions.*
Primary motor area (cortex) *A brain area associated with control of movement.*

Motor cortex is one brain area that contains **mirror neurons**. These neurons become active when we perform an action *and* when we merely observe someone else carrying out the same action. (For more information about mirror neurons, see "Mirror, Mirror in the Brain.")

The rest of the frontal lobes are often referred to as *frontal association areas*. Only a small portion of the cerebral cortex (the primary areas) directly controls the body or receives information from the senses. All the surrounding areas, which are called **association areas (or association cortex)**, combine and process information. For example, if you see a rose, association areas help you connect your primary sensory impressions with memories, so that you can recognize the rose and name it. Some association areas also contribute to higher mental abilities, such as language. For example, a person with damage to association areas in the left hemisphere may suffer **aphasia** (ah-FAZE-yah), an impaired ability to use language.

One type of aphasia is related to **Broca's area** (BRO-cahs), a speech center that is part of the left frontal association area (for 5 percent of all people, the area is part of the right frontal association area). Damage to Broca's area causes *motor* (or *expressive*) *aphasia*, a great difficulty in speaking or writing (Grodzinsky & Santi, 2008). Generally, the person knows what she or he wants to say but can't seem to fluently utter the words (Burns & Fahy, 2010). Typically, a patient's grammar and pronunciation are poor and speech is slow and labored. For example, the person may say "bife" for bike, "seep" for sleep, or "zokaid" for zodiac.

The very front of the frontal association region is known as the **prefrontal area (or prefrontal cortex)**. This part of the brain is related to more complex behaviors (Banich & Compton, 2011). If the frontal lobes are damaged, a patient's personality and emotional life may change dramatically. Did you happen to read about Phineas Gage, the railroad foreman described in Module 5? He's the person who accidentally

Critical Thinking

Mirror, Mirror in the Brain

Italian researchers had just recorded an increase in the activity of a single neuron in the motor cortex of a monkey as it reached for food. A few seconds later, one of the researchers happened to reach for a snack of his own. The same neuron obligingly responded as if the monkey had reached for the food itself. Unexpectedly, a neuron involved in controlling a particular motor movement also was activated when the monkey merely observed that same motor movement in someone else. Just like that, the Italians discovered *mirror neurons* (Rizzolatti, Fogassi, & Gallese, 2006). Because they *mirror* actions performed by others, such neurons may explain how we can intuitively understand other people's behavior. They also may underlie our ability to learn new skills by imitation (Meini & Paternoster, 2012; Pineda, 2009).

Can this chimpanzee imitate researcher Jane Goodall by relying on mirror neurons?

The discovery of mirror neurons has triggered a flood of interest. Recently, researchers confirmed that mirror neurons are found in various areas of the brain and appear to exist in the human brain as well (Molenberghs, Cunnington, & Mattingley, 2012). In addition, neuroscientists speculate that newborn humans (and monkeys) are able to imitate others because networks of mirror neurons are activated when an infant watches someone perform an action. Then, the same mirror network can be used to perform that action (Lepage & Théret, 2007). Similarly, human empathy (the ability to identify with another person's experiences and feelings) may arise from activation of mirror neurons (Baird, Scheffer, & Wilson, 2011).

Mirror neurons may even partially explain *autism spectrum disorders*. In early childhood, children with autism begin to suffer from an impaired ability to interact and communicate with other people. Restricted and repetitive behavior such as head banging also is common. According to the *broken mirrors* hypothesis, autism may arise in infants whose mirror neuron system has been damaged by genetic defects or environmental risk factors (Gallese, Rochat, & Berchio, 2013). This explanation is attractive because autism's primary features of impaired communication and social interaction appear to be related to the role that mirror neurons play in reflecting the actions and words of others.

To date, these are just hypotheses that await empirical confirmation. More important, such possibilities are only just now leading to proposals for new therapies for autism (Wan et al., 2010). Nevertheless, the possibilities are exciting.

Attila Kisbenedek/AFP/Getty Images

destroyed much of his frontal cortex (Harlow, 1868). It's likely that Gage's personality changed after he suffered brain damage because the prefrontal cortex generates our sense of self, including an awareness of our current emotional state (Jenkins & Mitchell, 2011).

Reasoning or planning also may be affected (Roca et al., 2010). Patients with damage to the frontal lobes often get stuck on mental tasks and repeat the same wrong answers over and over (Stuss & Knight, 2002). PET scans suggest that much of what we call intelligence is related to increased activity in the frontal areas of the cortex (Duncan, 2005). Reduced frontal lobe function also leads to greater impulsivity, including increased risk for drug addiction (Crews & Boettiger, 2009). In turn, drug abuse can further damage this important area of the brain (Perry et al., 2011).

The Parietal Lobes

Bodily sensations register in the **parietal lobes** (puh-RYE-ih-tal), located just above the occipital lobes. Touch, temperature, pressure, and other somatic sensations flow into the **primary somatosensory area (cortex)** (SO-mat-oh-SEN-so-ree) of the parietal lobes. Again, we find that the map of bodily sensations is distorted. In the case of somatosensory cortex, the drawing in Figure 9.8 reflects the *sensitivity* of body areas, not their size. For example, the lips are large in the drawing because of their great sensitivity, whereas the back and trunk, which are less sensitive, are much smaller. Notice that the hands are also large in the map of body sensitivity—which is obviously an aid to musicians, typists, watchmakers, massage therapists, lovers, and brain surgeons.

The Temporal Lobes

The **temporal lobes** are located on each side of the brain. Auditory information is sent via the auditory nerve directly to the **primary auditory area (cortex)**. If we did a PET scan of your brain while you listened to your favorite song, your primary auditory area would be the first to light up, followed by association areas in your temporal lobes. Likewise, if we could electrically stimulate the primary auditory area of your temporal lobe, you would "hear" a series of sound sensations.

A left temporal lobe association area called **Wernicke's area** (VER-nick-ees) also functions as a language site (see Figure 9.8; again, for 5 percent of all people, the area is on the right temporal lobe). If it is damaged, the result is a *receptive* (or *fluent*) *aphasia*. Although the person can hear speech, he or she has difficulty understanding the meaning of words. Thus, when shown a picture of a chair, someone with Broca's aphasia might say "tssair." In contrast, a Wernicke's patient might *fluently*, but incorrectly, identify the photo as "truck" (Robson, Sage, & Ralph, 2012).

The Occipital Lobes

At the back of the brain, we find the **occipital lobes** (awk-SIP-ih-tal), the area of cortex concerned with vision. Patients with tumors (cell growths that interfere with brain activity) in the **primary visual area (cortex)**, the part of the cortex to first receive input from the eyes, experience blind spots in their vision.

Do the primary visual areas of the cortex correspond directly to what is seen? Images are mapped onto the cortex, but the map is greatly stretched and distorted (Toates, 2011). That's why it's important to avoid thinking of the visual area as a little television screen in the brain. Visual information creates complex patterns of activity in neurons; it does *not* make a television-like image.

One of the most fascinating results of brain injury is **visual agnosia** (ag-KNOW-zyah), an inability to identify seen objects. Visual agnosia is often caused by damage to the association areas on the occipital lobes (Farah, 2004). This condition

Mirror neurons *Neurons that become active when a motor action is carried out and when another organism is observed carrying out the same action.*

Association areas (association cortex) *All areas of the cerebral cortex that are not primarily sensory or motor in function.*

Aphasia *A speech disturbance resulting from brain damage.*

Broca's area *A language area related to grammar and pronunciation.*

Prefrontal area (prefrontal cortex) *The very front of the frontal lobes; involved in sense of self, reasoning, and planning.*

Parietal lobes *Areas of the cortex that include the sites in which body sensations register.*

Primary somatosensory area (cortex) *A receiving area for body sensations.*

Temporal lobes *Areas of the cortex that include the sites where hearing registers in the brain.*

Primary auditory area (cortex) *Part of the temporal lobe in which auditory information is first registered.*

Wernicke's area *A temporal lobe brain area related to language comprehension.*

Occipital lobes *Portion of the cerebral cortex in which vision registers in the brain.*

Primary visual area (cortex) *The part of the occipital lobe that first receives input from the eyes.*

Visual agnosia *An inability to identify seen objects.*

Human Diversity

His and Her Brains?

Many physical differences between male and female brains have been found, although their implications remain to be better understood (Cahill, 2006). One generalization that may stand the test of time is that men's and women's brains may well be specialized in different ways to arrive at the same capabilities (Tomasi & Volkow, 2012; Zaidi, 2010).

For example, in one classic series of studies, researchers observed brain activity as people did language tasks. Both men and women showed increased activity in Broca's area, on the left side of the brain, exactly as expected. Surprisingly, however, the left *and* the right brain were activated in more than half the women tested (see ● **Figure 9.9**). Despite this difference, the two sexes performed equally well on a task that involved sounding out words (Shaywitz et al., 1995).

Another study, this time focused on intelligence, also found that women are more likely than men to use both sides of their brains (Tang et al., 2010). In a different study, brain images of men and women with similar IQ scores revealed major differences in brain areas involved in intelligence (Haier et al., 2004). In general, the men had more gray matter (neuron cell bodies), whereas the women had more white matter (axons coated in myelin). Further, the women had more gray and white matter concentrated in their frontal lobes than the men. The men's gray matter was split between their frontal and parietal lobes, whereas their white matter was mostly in the temporal lobes.

Using both sides of the brain for language and other forms of intelligence may be a big advantage. For example, when Broca's area is

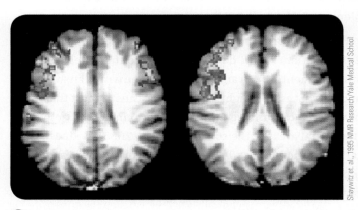

● **Figure 9.9**

Language tasks activate both sides of the brain in many women but only the left side in men.

damaged, some women can use the right side of their brains to compensate for the loss, which allows them to resume speaking (Sommer, 2010). A man with similar damage might be permanently impaired. Thus, when a man says, "I have half a mind to tell you what I think," he may be stating a curious truth. Regardless, it seems that nature has given the brains of men and women different routes to the same abilities (Burgaleta et al., 2012).

---

is sometimes referred to as *mindblindness*. For example, if we show Alice, an agnosia patient, a candle, she can see it and can describe it as "a long narrow object that tapers at the top." Alice can even draw the candle accurately, but she cannot name it. However, if she is allowed to feel the candle, she will name it immediately. In short, Alice can still see color, size, and shape. She just can't form the associations necessary to perceive the meanings of objects.

Are agnosias limited to objects? No. A fascinating form of mindblindness is **facial agnosia**, an inability to perceive familiar faces (Farah, 2006; Sacks, 2010). One patient with facial agnosia couldn't recognize her husband or mother when they visited her in the hospital, and she was unable to identify pictures of her children. However, as soon as visitors spoke, she knew them immediately by their voices.

Areas devoted to recognizing faces and the emotions they convey lie in association areas in the occipital and frontal lobes (Prochnow et al., 2013). These areas appear to be highly specialized. Why would parts of the brain be set aside solely for

processing faces? From an evolutionary standpoint, it is not really so surprising. After all, we are social animals for whom facial recognition is very important. This specialization is just one example of what a marvelous organ of consciousness we possess.

How about men's and women's brains? Are they specialized in different ways? Yes, they are. "His and Her Brains?" explains how.

In summary, the bulk of our daily experience and all of our understanding of the world can be traced to the different areas of the cortex. The human brain may be the most advanced and sophisticated of the brain-bearing species on earth. This, of course, is no guarantee that our marvelous biocomputer will be put to full use. Still, we must stand in awe of the potential it represents.

Facial agnosia *An inability to perceive familiar faces.*

Module 9: Summary

9.1 How do the left and right hemispheres differ?

- **9.1.1** The human brain is marked not by overall size but by advanced corticalization, or enlargement of the cerebral cortex.
- **9.1.2** Split brains can be created by cutting the corpus callosum. The split-brain individual shows a remarkable degree of independence between the right and left hemispheres.
- **9.1.3** The left hemisphere is good at analysis, and it processes small details sequentially. It contains speech or language centers in most people. It also specializes in writing, calculating, judging time and rhythm, and ordering complex movements.
- **9.1.4** The right hemisphere detects overall patterns; it processes information simultaneously and holistically. It is largely nonverbal and excels at spatial and perceptual skills, visualization, and recognition of patterns, faces, and melodies.

9.2 What are the different functions of the lobes of the cerebral cortex?

- **9.2.1** The frontal lobes contain the primary motor area (which includes many mirror neurons) and many association areas, which combine and process information. Damage to Broca's area results in motor aphasia, a difficulty in speaking or writing. The prefrontal cortex is related to abstract thought and one's sense of self.
- **9.2.2** The parietal lobes contain the primary sensory area, which processes bodily sensations.
- **9.2.3** The temporal lobes contain the primary auditory area and are responsible for hearing and language. Damage to Wernicke's area results in fluent aphasia, a difficulty understanding the meanings of words.
- **9.2.4** The occipital lobes contain the primary visual area that is responsible for vision.
- **9.2.5** Men's and women's brains are specialized in different ways.

Module 9: Knowledge Builder

Recite

See if you can match the following.

1. _____ Corpus callosum	**A.**	Visual area	
2. _____ Occipital lobes	**B.**	Language, speech, writing	
	C.	Motor cortex and abstract thinking	
3. _____ Parietal lobes	**D.**	Spatial skills, visualization, pattern recognition	
4. _____ Temporal lobes			
5. _____ Frontal lobes	**E.**	Speech disturbances	
6. _____ Association cortex	**F.**	Hearing	
	G.	Increased ratio of cortex in brain	
7. _____ Aphasias	**H.**	Bodily sensations	
8. _____ Corticalization	**I.**	Treatment for severe epilepsy	
9. _____ Left hemisphere	**J.**	Inability to identify seen objects	
10. _____ Right hemisphere	**K.**	Fibers connecting the cerebral hemispheres	
11. _____ Split brain	**L.**	Cortex that is not sensory or motor in function	
12. _____ Agnosia			

Reflect

Think Critically

13. If your brain were removed, replaced by another, and moved to a new body, which would you consider to be yourself, your old body with the new brain, or your new body with the old brain?

Self-Reflect

Learning the functions of the brain lobes is like learning areas on a map. Try drawing a map of the cortex. Can you label all the different "countries" (lobes)? Can you name their functions? Where is the primary motor area? The primary somatosensory area? Broca's area? Keep redrawing the map until it becomes more detailed and you can do it easily.

ANSWERS

1. K 2. A 3. H 4. F 5. C 6. L 7. E 8. G 9. B 10. D 11. I 12. J 13. Although there is no "correct" answer to this question, your personality, knowledge, personal memories, and self-concept all derive from brain activity—which makes a strong case for your old body being more nearly the "real you."

Brain and Behavior: The Subcortex and Endocrine System

Our Animal Brain

Although our cerebral cortex makes us uniquely human, it is important to recognize the critical role of our more primitive subcortex and its links to the endocrine system. For example, the cerebral cortex is surprisingly unnecessary for physical survival. You, or at least your body, would continue to live even if you lost large portions of your cerebral cortex. Not so with the subcortex, the brain structures immediately below the cerebral cortex. Serious damage to the subcortex, or lower brain, can result in coma and even death. Hunger, thirst, sleep, attention, sex, breathing, and many other vital functions are controlled by parts of the subcortex.

Similarly, our behavior is not solely a product of the nervous system. The endocrine glands form a second, more primitive, communication system in the body. Hormones can affect everything from personality and emotions to hunger and reactions to stress. Let's check out our animal brain.

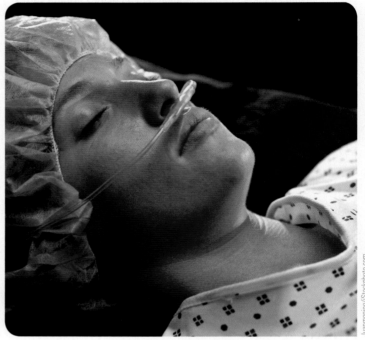

Juanmonino/iStockphoto.com

SURVEY QUESTIONS

10.1 What are the major parts of the subcortex?

10.2 How does the glandular system affect behavior?

The Subcortex—At the Core of the (Brain) Matter

SURVEY QUESTION 10.1: What are the major parts of the subcortex?

The subcortex lies immediately below the cerebral hemispheres. This area can be divided into the *brainstem* (or *hindbrain*), the *midbrain*, and the *forebrain*. (The forebrain also includes the cerebral cortex, which we discussed separately in Module 9, because of its size and importance.) For our purposes, the midbrain can be viewed as a link between the forebrain and the brainstem. Therefore, let's focus on the rest of the subcortex (● **Figure 10.1**).

The Hindbrain

Why are the lower brain areas so important? As the spinal cord joins the brain, it widens into the brainstem. The **brainstem** consists mainly of the medulla (meh-DUL-ah) and the cerebellum (ser-ah-BEL-uhm). The **medulla** contains centers important for the reflex control of vital life functions, including heart rate, breathing, swallowing, and the like. Various drugs, diseases, and injuries can disrupt the medulla and end or endanger life. You can also be left *locked-in* (see "Trapped!").

The **pons**, which looks like a small bump on the brainstem, acts as a bridge between the medulla and other brain areas. In addition to connecting with many other locations, including the cerebellum, the pons influences sleep and arousal.

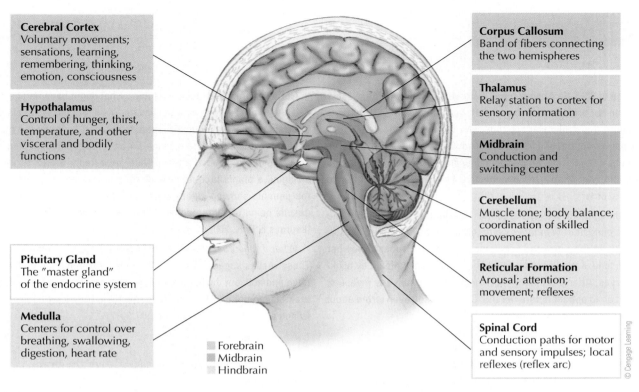

Cerebral Cortex
Voluntary movements; sensations, learning, remembering, thinking, emotion, consciousness

Hypothalamus
Control of hunger, thirst, temperature, and other visceral and bodily functions

Pituitary Gland
The "master gland" of the endocrine system

Medulla
Centers for control over breathing, swallowing, digestion, heart rate

Corpus Callosum
Band of fibers connecting the two hemispheres

Thalamus
Relay station to cortex for sensory information

Midbrain
Conduction and switching center

Cerebellum
Muscle tone; body balance; coordination of skilled movement

Reticular Formation
Arousal; attention; movement; reflexes

Spinal Cord
Conduction paths for motor and sensory impulses; local reflexes (reflex arc)

■ Forebrain
■ Midbrain
■ Hindbrain

© Cengage Learning

● **Figure 10.1**

This simplified drawing shows the main structures of the human brain and describes some of their most important features. (You can use the color code in the foreground to identify which areas are part of the forebrain, midbrain, and hindbrain.)

The cerebellum, which looks like a miniature cerebral cortex, lies at the base of the brain. Although there is growing evidence of a role in cognition and emotion (Schmahmann, 2010), the **cerebellum** primarily regulates posture, muscle tone, and muscular coordination. The cerebellum also stores memories related to skills and habits (Christian & Thompson, 2005). Again, we see that experience shapes the brain: Musicians, who practice special motor skills throughout their lives, have larger than average cerebellums (Hutchinson et al., 2003).

What happens if the cerebellum is injured? Without the cerebellum, tasks like walking, running, or playing catch become impossible. The first symptoms of a crippling disease called *spinocerebellar degeneration* are tremor, dizziness, and muscular weakness. Eventually, victims have difficulty merely standing, walking, or feeding themselves.

Reticular Formation A network of fibers and cell bodies called the **reticular formation (RF)** (reh-TICK-you-ler) lies inside the medulla and brainstem. As messages flow into the brain, the RF gives priority to some while turning others aside (Kalat, 2013). By doing so, the RF influences *attention*. The RF doesn't fully mature until adolescence, which may be why children have such short attention spans. The RF also modifies outgoing commands to the body. In this way, the RF affects muscle tone, posture, and movements of the eyes, face, head, body, and limbs. At the same time, the RF controls reflexes involved in breathing, sneezing, coughing, and vomiting.

The RF also keeps us vigilant, alert, and awake. Incoming messages from the sense organs branch into a part of the RF called the **reticular activating system (RAS)**. The RAS bombards the cortex with stimulation, keeping it active and alert. For instance, let's say a sleepy driver rounds a bend

Subcortex *All brain structures below the cerebral cortex.*
Brainstem *The lowest portions of the brain, including the cerebellum, medulla, pons, and reticular formation.*
Medulla *The structure that connects the brain with the spinal cord and controls vital life functions.*
Pons *An area on the brainstem that acts as a bridge between the medulla and other structures.*
Cerebellum *A brain structure that controls posture, muscle tone, and coordination.*
Reticular formation (RF) *A network within the medulla and brainstem; associated with attention, alertness, and some reflexes.*
Reticular activating system (RAS) *A part of the reticular formation that activates the cerebral cortex.*

The Clinical File

Trapped!

At the age of 33, Kate Adamson had a stroke that caused catastrophic damage to her brainstem. This event left her with *locked-in syndrome*: Just before the stroke she was fine, and the next moment, she was totally paralyzed, trapped in her own body and barely able to breathe (Cruse et al., 2011). Unable to move a muscle, but still fully awake and aware, she was unable to communicate her simplest thoughts and feelings to others.

Kate thought she was going to die. Her doctors, who thought she was in a *persistent vegetative state* (brain dead), did not administer painkillers as they inserted breathing and feeding tubes down her throat. In time, Kate discovered that she could communicate by blinking her eyes. After a recovery that was miraculous by any measure, she went on to appear before the U.S. Congress and even wrote about her experiences (Adamson, 2004).

Not everyone is so lucky. Just think what might have befallen Kate had she not even been able to blink her eyes (Schnakers et al., 2009). In one chilling study, coma researcher Steven Laureys and his colleagues used fMRI to reexamine 54 patients previously diagnosed as being brain dead. Patients were repeatedly asked to imagine swinging a tennis racquet or walking down a familiar street. Five of the patients showed clearly different brain activity to the two tasks despite being unable to communicate with doctors in any other way (Laureys & Boly, 2007).

What if they could "will" a computer to speak for them? Right on! These results suggest that not all totally locked-in patients are brain dead and hold out the hope that we may eventually be able to develop brain–computer interfaces to help free them from their bodily prisons (Monti et al., 2010; Shih & Krusienski, 2012).

---

and encounters a deer standing in the road. The driver snaps to attention and applies the brakes. She can thank her RAS for arousing the rest of her brain and averting an accident. If you're getting sleepy while reading this module, try pinching your ear—a little pain will cause the RAS to momentarily arouse your cortex.

The Forebrain

Like buried treasure, two of the most important parts of your body lie deep within your brain. The *thalamus* (THAL-uh-mus) and an area just below it called the *hypothalamus* (HI-po-THAL-uh-mus) are key parts of the forebrain (see Figure 10.1).

How could these be any more important than other areas already described? The **thalamus** acts as a final "switching station" for sensory messages on their way to the cortex. Vision, hearing, taste, and touch all pass through this small, football-shaped structure. Thus, injury to even small areas of the thalamus can cause deafness, blindness, or loss of any other sense, except smell.

The human hypothalamus is about the size of a small grape. Small as it may be, the **hypothalamus** is a kind of master control center for emotion and many basic motives (Toates, 2011). The hypothalamus affects behaviors as diverse as sex, rage, temperature control, hormone release, eating and drinking, sleep, waking, and emotion. The hypothalamus is basically a crossroads that connects many areas of the brain. It also is the final pathway for many kinds of behavior. That is, the hypothalamus is the last place where many behaviors are organized

or "decided on" before messages leave the brain, causing the body to react.

The Limbic System As a group, the hypothalamus, parts of the thalamus, the amygdala, the hippocampus, and other structures make up the limbic system (● Figure 10.2). The **limbic system** has a major role in producing emotion and

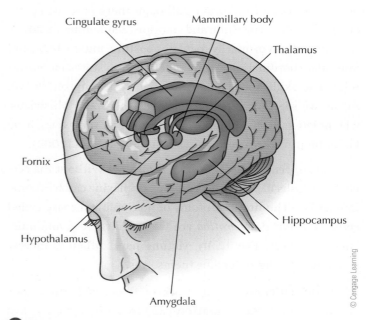

● **Figure 10.2**

Parts of the limbic system. Although only one side is shown here, the hippocampus and the amygdala extend into the temporal lobes at each side of the brain. The limbic system is a sort of primitive core of the brain strongly associated with emotion.

motivated behavior (LeDoux, 2012). Rage, fear, sexual response, and intense arousal can be localized to various points in the limbic system. Laughter, a delightful part of human social life, also has its origins in the limbic system (Wild et al., 2003).

During evolution, the limbic system was the earliest layer of the forebrain to develop. In lower animals, the limbic system helps organize basic survival responses: feeding, fleeing, fighting, and reproduction. In humans, a clear link to emotion remains. The amygdala (ah-MIG-dah-luh), in particular, is strongly related to fear (Amano et al., 2011).

The amygdala provides a primitive, quick pathway to the cortex. Like lower animals, we can be startled and, as such, are able to react to dangerous stimuli before we fully know what is going on (LeDoux, 2012). In situations in which true danger exists, such as in military combat, the amygdala's rapid response may aid survival. However, disorders of the brain's fear system can be very disruptive. An example is the war veteran who involuntarily dives into the bushes when he hears a car backfire. The role of the amygdala in emotion also may explain why people who suffer from phobias and disabling anxiety often feel afraid without knowing why (Lamprecht et al., 2009; Schlund & Cataldo, 2010).

Some parts of the limbic system have taken on additional, higher-level functions. A part called the hippocampus (HIP-oh-CAMP-us) is important for forming lasting memories (Jurd, 2011). The hippocampus lies inside the temporal lobes, which is why stimulating the temporal lobes can produce memory-like or dream-like experiences. The hippocampus also helps us navigate the space around us. The right side of your hippocampus will become more active, for instance, if you mentally plan a drive across town (Aradillas, Libon, & Schwartzman, 2011).

Psychologists have discovered that animals will learn to press a lever to deliver a dose of electrical stimulation to the limbic system. The animals act like the stimulation is satisfying or pleasurable. Indeed, several areas of the limbic system act as reward, or "pleasure," pathways (see Module 25). Many are found in the hypothalamus, where they overlap with areas that control thirst, sex, and hunger. As we mentioned in Module 7, many commonly abused drugs, such as cocaine, amphetamine, heroin, nicotine, marijuana, and alcohol, activate many of the same pleasure pathways. This appears to be part of the reason these drugs feel so rewarding (Niehaus, Cruz-Bermúdez, & Kauer, 2009).

You also might be interested to know that music you would describe as "thrilling" activates pleasure systems in your brain. This may explain some of the appeal of music that can send shivers down your spine (Salimpoor et al., 2011). (It also may explain why people pay so much for concert tickets!)

Punishment, or aversive, areas also have been found in the limbic system. When these locations are activated, animals show discomfort and work hard to turn off the stimulation. Because much of our behavior is based on seeking pleasure and avoiding pain, these discoveries continue to fascinate psychologists.

The Whole Person

We have seen that the human brain is an impressive assembly of billions of sensitive cells and nerve fibers. The brain controls vital bodily functions, keeps track of the external world, issues commands to the muscles and glands, responds to current needs, regulates its own behavior, and even creates the mind and the magic of consciousness—*all* at the same time.

Two final notes of caution are now in order. First, for the sake of simplicity, we have assigned functions to each part of the brain as if it were a computer. This is only partially true. In reality, the brain is a vast information-processing system. Incoming information scatters all over the brain and converges again as it goes out through the spinal cord to muscles and glands. The overall system is much more complicated than our discussion of separate parts implies. Second, we have stressed how the brain underlies all human experience. Again, this is only partially true. As we mentioned in Module 7, human experience also shapes the brain's circuits (Kolb & Whishaw, 2013). For example, practicing skills, such as cab driving, mathematics, or music, not only will improve performance, it also will result in a changed brain (Woollett & Maguire, 2011).

Thalamus *A brain structure that relays sensory information to the cerebral cortex.*

Hypothalamus *A small area of the brain that regulates emotional behaviors and motives.*

Limbic system *A system in the forebrain that is closely linked with emotional response.*

Amygdala *A part of the limbic system associated with fear responses.*

Hippocampus *A part of the limbic system associated with storing memories.*

The Endocrine System— My Hormones Made Me Do It

SURVEY QUESTION 10.2: How does the glandular system affect behavior?

Our behavior is not solely a product of the nervous system (Kalat, 2013). The endocrine (EN-duh-krin) glands form an equally important parallel communication system in the body. The **endocrine system** is made up of glands that secrete chemicals directly into the bloodstream or lymph system (●**Figure 10.3**). These chemicals, called **hormones**, are carried throughout the body, where they affect both internal activities and visible behavior. Hormones are related to neurotransmitters. Like other transmitter chemicals, hormones activate cells in the body. To respond, the cells must have receptor sites for the hormone. Hormones affect puberty, personality, dwarfism, jet lag, and much more.

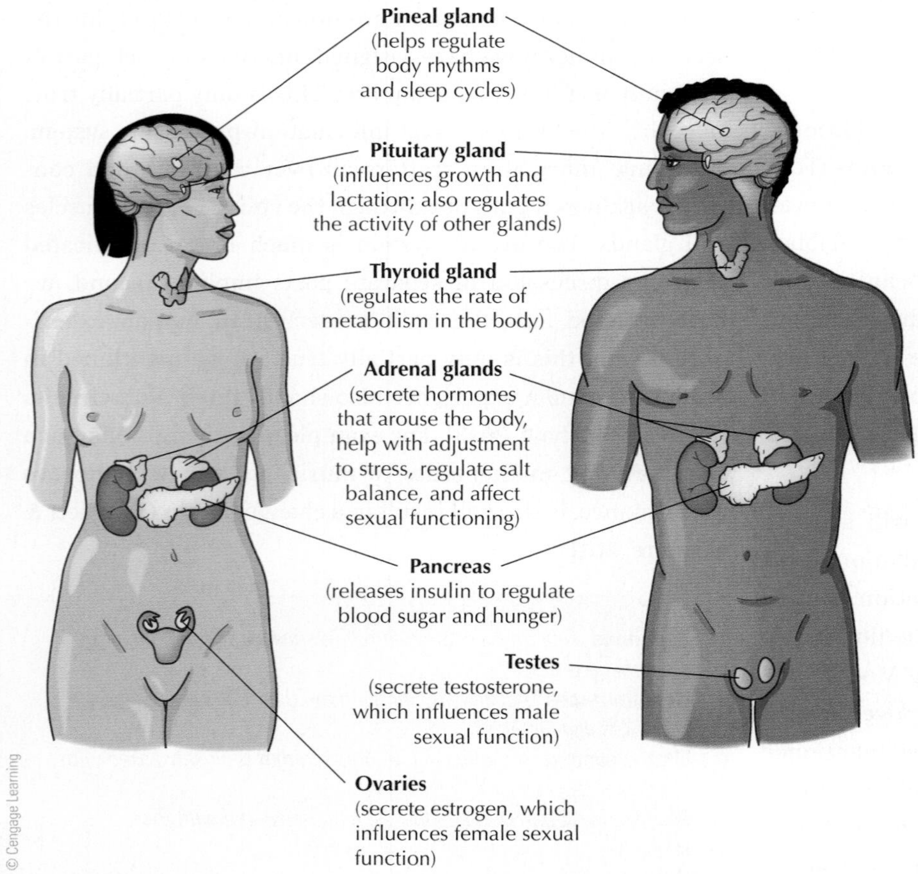

How do hormones affect behavior? Although we seldom are directly aware of them, hormones affect us in many ways (Toates, 2011). Here is a brief sample: Hormone output from the adrenal glands rises during stressful situations; androgens ("male" hormones) are related to the sex drive in both males and females; hormones secreted during times of high emotion intensify memory formation; at least some of the emotional turmoil of adolescence is due to elevated hormone levels; and different hormones prevail when you are angry rather than fearful. Pregnancy and motherhood cause the release of hormones that lead to the changes involved in maternal behavior (Henry & Sherwin, 2012). Even disturbing personality patterns may be linked to hormonal irregularities (Evardone, Alexander, & Morey, 2007). Because these are just samples, let's consider some additional effects hormones have on the body and behavior.

The **pituitary gland** is a pea-sized globe hanging from the base of the brain (see Figure 10.1). One of the pituitary's more important roles is to regulate growth (Beans, 2009). During childhood, the pituitary secretes a hormone that speeds body development. If too little **growth hormone** is released, a person may remain far smaller than average. If this condition is not treated, a child may be 6 to 12 inches shorter than age-mates. As adults, some will have *hypopituitary* (HI-po-pih-TU-ih-ter-ee) *dwarfism*. Such individuals are perfectly proportioned, but tiny. Regular injections of growth hormone can raise a hypopituitary child's height by several inches, usually to the short side of average.

Too much growth hormone produces *gigantism* (excessive bodily growth). Secretion of too much growth hormone late in the growth period causes *acromegaly* (AK-row-MEG-uh-lee), a condition in which the arms, hands, feet, and facial bones become enlarged. Acromegaly produces prominent facial features, which some people have used as a basis for careers as character actors, wrestlers, and the like.

Oxytocin, another important hormone released by the pituitary, plays a broad role in regulating many behaviors generally involved in happiness (Viero et al., 2010). These include pregnancy, parenthood, sexual activity,

Pineal gland
(helps regulate body rhythms and sleep cycles)

Pituitary gland
(influences growth and lactation; also regulates the activity of other glands)

Thyroid gland
(regulates the rate of metabolism in the body)

Adrenal glands
(secrete hormones that arouse the body, help with adjustment to stress, regulate salt balance, and affect sexual functioning)

Pancreas
(releases insulin to regulate blood sugar and hunger)

Testes
(secrete testosterone, which influences male sexual function)

Ovaries
(secrete estrogen, which influences female sexual function)

© Cengage Learning

● **Figure 10.3**
The endocrine system.

Not all little people have underactive pituitary glands. Peter Dinklage, who has won Emmy and Golden Globe awards for his brilliant role as the scheming Tyrion Lannister in the television series *Game of Thrones,* was born with *achondroplasia.* The most common cause of dwarfism, achondroplasia is a genetic disorder of bone development resulting in disproportionately short limbs.

social bonding, trust, and even reducing stress reactions (Gordon et al., 2010; Kingsley & Lambert, 2006; Stallen et al., 2012).

The pituitary is often called the "master gland" because it influences other endocrine glands (especially the thyroid, adrenal glands, and ovaries or testes). These glands in turn regulate such body processes as metabolism, responses to stress, and reproduction. But the master has a master: The pituitary is directed by the hypothalamus, which lies directly above it. In this way, the hypothalamus can affect glands throughout the body. This, then, is the major link between the brain and hormones (Kalat, 2013).

The **pineal gland** (pin-EE-ul) was once considered a useless remnant of evolution. In certain fishes, frogs, and lizards, the gland is associated with a well-developed light-sensitive organ, or so-called *third eye.* In humans, the function of the pineal gland is just now coming to light (so to speak). The pineal gland releases a hormone called **melatonin** (mel-ah-TONE-in) in response to daily variations in light. Melatonin levels in the bloodstream rise at dusk, peak around midnight, and fall again as morning approaches. As far as the brain is concerned, it's bedtime when melatonin levels rise (Norman, 2009).

The **thyroid gland**, located in the neck, regulates metabolism. As you may remember from a biology course, *metabolism* is the rate at which energy is produced and expended in the body. By altering metabolism, the thyroid can have a sizable effect on personality. A person suffering from *hyperthyroidism* (an overactive thyroid) tends to be thin, tense, excitable, and nervous. An underactive thyroid (*hypothyroidism*) in an adult can cause inactivity, sleepiness, slowness, obesity, and depression (Joffe, 2006). In infancy, hypothyroidism limits development of the nervous system, leading to severe intellectual disability.

When you are frightened or angry, some important reactions prepare your body for action: Your heart rate and blood pressure rise; stored sugar is released into the bloodstream for quick energy; your muscles tense and receive more blood; and your blood is prepared to clot more quickly in case of injury. As we discussed earlier, these changes are controlled by the autonomic nervous system. Specifically, the sympathetic branch of the ANS causes the adrenal glands to release the hormones *epinephrine* and *norepinephrine.* (Epinephrine also is known as adrenaline, which may be more familiar to you.) **Epinephrine** (ep-eh-NEF-rin), which is associated with fear, tends to arouse the body. **Norepinephrine**, which also functions as a neurotransmitter in the brain, also tends to arouse the body, but it is linked with anger.

The **adrenal glands** are located just under the back of the rib cage, atop the kidneys. The *adrenal medulla,* or inner core of the adrenal glands, is the source of epinephrine and norepinephrine. The *adrenal cortex,* or outer "bark" of the adrenal glands, produces a set of hormones called corticoids (KOR-tih-coids). One of their jobs is to regulate salt balance in the body. A deficiency of certain corticoids can evoke a powerful craving for the taste of salt in humans. The corticoids also help the body adjust to stress, and they are a secondary source of sex hormones.

An oversecretion of the adrenal sex hormones can cause *virilism* (exaggerated male characteristics). For instance, a

Endocrine system *Glands whose secretions pass directly into the bloodstream or lymph system.*

Hormones *Glandular secretions that affect bodily functions or behavior.*

Pituitary gland *The master gland at the base of the brain whose hormones influence other endocrine glands.*

Growth hormone *A hormone, secreted by the pituitary gland, that promotes body growth.*

Oxytocin *A hormone, released by the pituitary gland, that plays a broad role in regulating pregnancy, parenthood, sexual activity, social bonding, trust, and even reducing stress reactions.*

Pineal gland *Gland in the brain that helps regulate body rhythms and sleep cycles.*

Melatonin *Hormone released by the pineal gland in response to daily cycles of light and dark.*

Thyroid gland *Endocrine gland that helps regulate the rate of metabolism.*

Epinephrine *An adrenal hormone that tends to arouse the body; epinephrine is associated with fear. (Also known as adrenaline.)*

Norepinephrine *Both a brain neurotransmitter and an adrenal hormone that tends to arouse the body; norepinephrine is associated with anger. (Also known as noradrenaline.)*

Adrenal glands *Endocrine glands that arouse the body, regulate salt balance, adjust the body to stress, and affect sexual functioning.*

woman may grow a beard or a man's voice may become so low it is difficult to understand. Oversecretion early in life can cause *premature puberty* (full sexual development during childhood). One of the most remarkable cases on record is that of a 5-year-old Peruvian girl who gave birth to a son (Strange, 1965).

Because we are on the topic of sex hormones, a related issue is worth mentioning. One of the principal androgens, or male hormones, is testosterone, which is supplied in small amounts by the adrenal glands. (The testes are the main source of testosterone in males.) Perhaps you have heard about the use of anabolic steroids by athletes who want to bulk up or promote muscle growth. Most of these drugs are synthetic versions of testosterone.

Although there is some disagreement about whether steroids actually improve athletic performance, it is widely accepted that they may cause serious side effects (Kanayama et al., 2012; Sjöqvist, Garle, & Rane, 2008). Problems include voice deepening or baldness in women and shrinkage of the testicles, sexual impotence, or breast enlargement in men (Millman & Ross, 2003). Dangerous increases in hostility and aggression ("roid rage") also have been linked with steroid use (Lumia & McGinnis, 2010). Increased risk of heart attack and stroke, liver damage, and stunted growth also are common when younger adolescents use steroids. Understandably, almost all major sports organizations ban the use of anabolic steroids.

In this brief discussion of the endocrine system, we have considered only a few of the more important glands. Nevertheless, this should give you an appreciation of how completely behavior and personality are tied to the ebb and flow of hormones in the body.

Module 10: Summary

10.1 What are the major parts of the subcortex?

- **10.1.1** The brain can be subdivided into the forebrain, midbrain, and hindbrain. The subcortex includes hindbrain and midbrain brain structures as well as the lower parts of the forebrain, below the cortex.
- **10.1.2** The medulla contains centers essential for reflex control of heart rate, breathing, and other vegetative functions.
- **10.1.3** The pons links the medulla with other brain areas.
- **10.1.4** The cerebellum maintains coordination, posture, and muscle tone.
- **10.1.5** The reticular formation directs sensory and motor messages, and part of it, known as the RAS, acts as an activating system for the cerebral cortex.
- **10.1.6** The thalamus carries sensory information to the cortex.
- **10.1.7** The hypothalamus exerts powerful control over eating, drinking, sleep cycles, body temperature, and other basic motives and behaviors.

- **10.1.8** The limbic system is strongly related to emotion. It also contains distinct reward and punishment areas and an area known as the hippocampus that is important for forming memories.

10.2 How does the glandular system affect behavior?

- **10.2.1** Endocrine glands serve as a chemical communication system within the body. The ebb and flow of hormones from the endocrine glands entering the bloodstream affect behavior, moods, and personality.
- **10.2.2** Many of the endocrine glands are influenced by the pituitary (the master gland), which is in turn influenced by the hypothalamus. Thus, the brain controls the body through both the fast nervous system and the slower endocrine system.

Module 10: Knowledge Builder

Recite

1. Three major divisions of the brain are the brainstem or _____, the _____, and the _____.

2. Reflex centers for heartbeat and respiration are found in the
   - **a.** cerebellum
   - **b.** thalamus
   - **c.** medulla
   - **d.** RF

3. A portion of the reticular formation, known as the RAS, serves as an _____ system in the brain.
   - **a.** activating
   - **b.** adrenal
   - **c.** adjustment
   - **d.** aversive

4. The _____ is a final relay, or switching station, for sensory information on its way to the cortex.

5. Reward and punishment areas are found throughout the _____ system, which also is related to emotion.

6. The body's ability to resist stress is related to the action of the adrenal _____.

Reflect

Think Critically

7. Subcortical structures in humans are quite similar to corresponding lower brain areas in animals. Why would knowing this allow you to predict, in general terms, what functions the subcortex controls?

Self-Reflect

What are the major subcortical structures and what functions do they control? Why is it especially important to understand the limbic system and the role it plays in your emotional life?

ANSWERS

1. hindbrain, midbrain, forebrain 2. c 3. a 4. thalamus 5. limbic 6. cortex 7. Because the subcortex must be related to basic functions common to all higher animals: motives, emotions, sleep, attention, and vegetative functions such as heartbeat, breathing, and temperature regulation. The subcortex also routes and processes incoming information from the senses and outgoing commands to the muscles.

CENGAGEbrain.com

Go to **cengagebrain.com** to access **MindTap for Coon/Mitterer** *Psychology Modules for Active Learning* and other online learning tools. MindTap is a fully online learning experience that combines all the tools you need—readings, multimedia, activities, and assessments—into a singular personalized Learning Path that guides you through the course.

Psychology in Action:
Handedness

Tennis Anyone?

Throughout history, left-handedness has been frowned upon. Lefties have often been characterized as clumsy, awkward, unlucky, or insincere. The Latin word for left is actually *sinister*! In contrast, right-handedness is the paragon of virtue. The Latin word for right is *dexter*, and righties are more likely to be referred to as dexterous, coordinated, skillful, and just. But is there any basis in fact for these attitudes?

Not always. For example, left-handers, such as 2012 French Open tennis champion Rafael Nadal, shown here, have an advantage in sports such as fencing and tennis. Most likely, their movements are less familiar to opponents, who usually face right-handers. Why are there more right-handed than left-handed people? How do left-handed and right-handed people differ? Does being left-handed create any problems—or benefits? The answers to these questions lead us back to the brain, where handedness begins. Let's see what research has revealed about handedness, the brain, and you.

Christopher Lee/Getty Images for Ricoh

SURVEY QUESTION

11.1 In what ways do right- and left-handed individuals differ?

Handedness—Are You Sinister or Dexterous?

SURVEY QUESTION 11.1: In what ways do right- and left-handed individuals differ?

Are you left- or right-handed? In other words, what is your **handedness**? To find out, write your name on a sheet of paper, first using your right hand and then your left. You were probably much more comfortable writing with your dominant hand. This is interesting because the hands themselves have no real differences in strength or dexterity. The agility of your dominant hand is an outward expression of superior motor control on one side of the brain. If you are right-handed, there is more area on the left side of your brain devoted to controlling your right hand. If you are left-handed, the reverse applies.

The preceding exercise implies that you are either entirely right- or left-handed. But handedness is a matter of degree. To better assess your handedness, complete a few questions adapted from the Waterloo Handedness Questionnaire (Brown et al., 2006) by putting a check mark in the Right, Left, or Either column for each question. The more Rights you check, the more right-handed you are.

ARE YOU RIGHT- OR LEFT-HANDED?

	Right	Left	Either
With which hand would you hold a paintbrush to paint a wall?	_____	_____	_____
Which hand would you use to pick up a book?	_____	_____	_____
Which hand would you use to hold a spoon to eat soup?	_____	_____	_____
Which hand would you use to flip pancakes?	_____	_____	_____
Which hand would you use to pick up a piece of paper?	_____	_____	_____
Which hand would you use to draw a picture?	_____	_____	_____
Which hand would you use to insert and turn a key in a lock?	_____	_____	_____
Which hand would you use to throw a ball?	_____	_____	_____

About 90 percent of all humans are right-handed; 10 percent are left-handed. Most people (about 75 percent) are strongly right- or left-handed (McManus et al., 2010). The rest show some inconsistency in hand preference. Which are you?

Is there such a thing as being left-footed? Excellent question. Do you have "two left feet"? **Sidedness** is often measured by assessing hand, foot, eye, and ear preference (Greenwood et al., 2006). We also generally prefer breathing through one nostril over the other and even have a preference for which direction we lean our head when kissing (van der Kamp & Cañal-Bruland, 2011). (Do you kiss "right"?) Nevertheless, handedness remains the single most important behavioral indicator of sidedness.

If a person is strongly left-handed, does that mean the right hemisphere is dominant? Not necessarily. It's true that the right hemisphere controls the left hand, but a left-handed person's language-producing, **dominant hemisphere** may be on the opposite side of the brain.

Brain Dominance

About 95 percent of right-handers process speech in the left hemisphere and are left-brain dominant. A good 70 percent of left-handers produce speech from the left hemisphere, just as right-handed people do. About 19 percent of all lefties and 3 percent of righties use their right brain for language. Some left-handers (approximately 12 percent) use both sides of the brain for language processing. All told, more than 90 percent of the population uses the left brain for language (Szaflarski et al., 2011).

Is there any way for a person to tell which of his or her hemispheres is dominant? One classic clue is the way you write. Right-handed individuals who write with a straight hand and lefties who write with a hooked hand are more likely left-brain dominant for language. Left-handed people who write with their hand below the line, and righties who use a hooked position, are more likely right-brain dominant. Another hint is provided by hand gestures. If you gesture mostly with your right hand as you talk, you probably process language in your left hemisphere. Gesturing with your left hand is associated with right-brain language processing (Hellige, 1993). Writing position and gestures are not foolproof, however; the only sure way to check brain dominance is to do medical tests that involve assessing one cerebral hemisphere at a time (Jones, Mahmoud, & Phillips, 2011).

Causes of Handedness

Is handedness inherited from parents? Yes, at least partly (Corballis, 2010a). Clear hand preferences are apparent before birth (● **Figure 11.1**) and persist for at least 10 years after birth (Hepper, Wells, & Lynch, 2005). This suggests that handedness cannot be dictated. Parents should not try to force a left-handed child to use his or her right hand. To do so may create speech or reading problems (Klöppel et al., 2010).

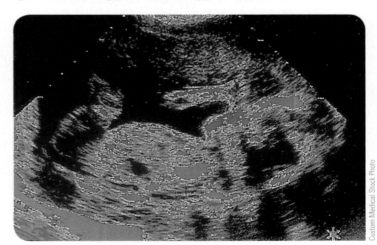

Custom Medical Stock Photo

● **Figure 11.1**

In this ultrasound image, a 4-month-old fetus sucks her right thumb. Research suggests that she will continue to prefer her right hand long after she is born and that she will be right-handed as an adult.

Handedness *A preference for the right or left hand in most activities.*
Sidedness *A combination of preference for hand, foot, eye, and ear.*
Dominant hemisphere *A term usually applied to the side of a person's brain that produces language.*

Studies of identical twins show that hand preferences are not directly inherited like eye color or skin color, however (Ooki, 2005; Reiss et al., 1999). Yet, two left-handed parents are more likely to have a left-handed child than two right-handed parents (McKeever, 2000). The best evidence to date shows that left-handedness is more common in males and is influenced by a single gene on the X (female) chromosome (Papadatou-Pastou et al., 2008).

On the other hand, environmental factors such as learning, birth traumas, and social pressure to use the right hand also can affect which hand you end up favoring (Bailey & McKeever, 2004; Domellöf, Johansson, & Rönnqvist, 2011). In the past, many left-handed children were forced to use their right hand for writing, eating, and other skills. This is especially true in collectivist cultures like India and Japan, where left-handedness is viewed as especially negative. It is no surprise that the proportion of left-handers in these societies is only about half that found in individualist cultures such as the United States and Canada (Ida & Mandal, 2003).

Advantage Right *Are there any drawbacks to being left-handed?* A small minority of lefties owe their hand preference to birth traumas (such as prematurity, low birth weight, and breech birth). These individuals have higher rates of allergies, learning disorders, and other problems (Betancur et al., 1990). Similarly, people with mixed handedness (as opposed to consistent left-handers) may be at risk for more immune-related diseases (Bryden, Bruyn, & Fletcher, 2005). (Mixed handedness means doing some things better with one hand and other things better with the other.)

Is it true that right-handed people live longer than left-handed people? It is true that there is a shortage of old lefties. One possible explanation lies in the widespread finding that left-handers are more accident-prone (Dutta & Mandal, 2005). However, the supposed clumsiness of lefties may well be a result of living in a right-handed world. One study showed that left-handed locomotive engineers have higher accident rates and suggested that the cause was the design of locomotive controls (Bhushan & Khan, 2006). If it can be gripped, turned, or pulled, it's probably designed for the right hand. Even toilet handles are on the right side.

On the other hand, the shortage of very old lefties may just reflect the fact that, in the past, more left-handed children were forced to become right-handed. That makes it look like many lefties don't survive to old age. In reality, they do, but many of them are masquerading as righties (Martin & Freitas, 2002).

Advantage Left *Are there any advantages to being left-handed?* Being left-handed has some clear advantages (Faurie et al., 2008). Throughout history, a notable number of artists have been lefties, from Leonardo da Vinci and Michelangelo to Pablo Picasso and M. C. Escher. It is interesting that five of the last seven U.S. presidents also have been lefties (Smits, 2011). Conceivably, because the right hemisphere is superior at imagery and visual abilities, there is some advantage to using the left hand for drawing or painting (Wilkinson et al., 2009). At the least, lefties are definitely better at visualizing three-dimensional objects. This may be why there are more left-handed architects, artists, and chess players than would be expected (Shimoda, Takeda, & Kato, 2012). Similarly, being right-handed does not guarantee sports superiority. Left-handers have done well in a variety of professional sports, including boxing, fencing, handball, and tennis (Dane & Erzurumluoglu, 2003; Gursoy et al., 2012; Holtzen, 2000).

Lateralization refers to specialization in the abilities of the brain hemispheres. One striking feature of lefties is that they are generally less lateralized than the right-handed. In fact, even the physical size and shape of their cerebral hemispheres are more alike. If you are a lefty, you can take pride in the fact that your brain is less lopsided than most! In general, left-handers are more symmetrical on almost everything, including eye dominance, fingerprints—even foot size (Bourne, 2008).

In some situations, less lateralization may be a real advantage. For instance, individuals who are moderately left-handed or are ambidextrous (can do things equally well with both hands) seem to have better than average pitch memory, which is a basic musical skill. Correspondingly, more musicians are ambidextrous than would normally be expected (Springer & Deutsch, 1998).

Math abilities also may benefit from fuller use of the right hemisphere. Students who are extremely gifted in math are much more likely to be left-handed or ambidextrous (Benbow, 1986). Even when ordinary arithmetic skills are concerned, lefties seem to excel (Annett, 2002; Annett & Manning, 1990).

The clearest advantage of being left-handed shows up when there is a brain injury. Because of their milder lateralization, left-handed individuals typically experience less language loss after damage to either brain hemisphere, and they recover more easily (Geschwind, 1979). Maybe having two left feet isn't so bad after all.

Lateralization *Differences between the two sides of the body; especially, differences in the abilities of the brain hemispheres.*

Module 11: Summary

11.1 In what ways do right- and left-handed individuals differ?

- **11.1.1** The vast majority of people are right-handed and, therefore, left-brain dominant for motor skills. More than 90 percent of right-handed persons and about 70 percent of the left-handed also produce speech from the left hemisphere.

- **11.1.2** Brain dominance and brain activity determine whether you are right-handed, left-handed, or ambidextrous.

- **11.1.3** Most people are strongly right-handed. A minority are strongly left-handed. A few have moderate or mixed hand preferences or they are ambidextrous. Thus, handedness is not a simple either/or trait.

- **11.1.4** Left-handed people tend to be less strongly lateralized than right-handed people (their brain hemispheres are not as specialized).

Module 11: Knowledge Builder

Recite

1. About 95 percent of left-handed people process language on the left side of the brain, the same as right-handed people. **T or F?**

2. Left-handed individuals who write with their hand below the writing line are likely to be right-brain dominant. **T or F?**

3. People basically learn to be right- or left-handed. **T or F?**

4. In general, left-handed individuals show less lateralization in the brain and throughout the body. **T or F?**

Reflect

Think Critically

5. News reports that left-handed people tend to die younger have been flawed in an important way: The average age of people in the left-handed group was younger than that of participants in the right-handed group. Why would this make a difference in the conclusions drawn?

Self-Reflect

Think for a moment about what you knew about handedness and left-handed people before you read this module. Which of your beliefs were correct? How has your knowledge about handedness changed?

ANSWERS

1. F 2. T 3. F 4. T 5. We can't tell if handedness or average age accounts for the difference in death rates. For example, if we start with a group of 20- to 30-year-old people, in which some die, the average age of death has to be between 20 and 30. If we start with a group of 30- to 40-year-old people, in which some die, the average age of death has to be between 30 and 40. Thus, the left-handed group might have an earlier average age at death simply because members of the group were younger to start with.

CENGAGEbrain.com

Go to **cengagebrain.com** to access **MindTap for Coon/Mitterer** *Psychology Modules for Active Learning* and other online learning tools. MindTap is a fully online learning experience that combines all the tools you need—readings, multimedia, activities, and assessments—into a singular personalized Learning Path that guides you through the course.

Human Development: Heredity and Environment

It's a Boy!

With those words, Gloria first glimpsed her amazing newborn baby, Joseph. Like parents everywhere, Gloria and her husband, Jay, wondered: How will Joseph's life unfold? What kind of a person will he be? Will he be a happy teenager, marry, become a father, find an interesting career, live a full and satisfying life?

Research tells a fascinating story about human growth and development, from birth and infancy to maturing, aging, and death. Understanding your development might well help you answer two important questions: "How did I become the person I am today?" and "Who will I become tomorrow?"

Like Joseph, our heredity and our environment will influence every stage of our lives. How does our genetic inheritance combine with our life experiences to shape who we are and who we will become? Let's look at this dance in more detail.

© Denys Kurbatov/Shutterstock

SURVEY QUESTION

12.1 How do heredity and environment affect development?

Nature and Nurture—It Takes Two to Tango

SURVEY QUESTION 12.1: How do heredity and environment affect development?

When we think of development, we naturally think of children growing up into adults. But even as adults, we never really stop changing. **Developmental psychology**, the study of progressive changes in behavior and abilities, involves every stage of life from conception to death, or womb to tomb (Kail & Cavanaugh, 2013). Heredity (our "nature") and environment (our "nurture") also affect us throughout our lifetimes. Some events, such as when Joseph reaches sexual maturity, are governed mostly by heredity. Others, such as when Joseph learns to swim, read, or drive a car, are matters primarily of environment.

But which is more important, heredity or environment? Neither. Biopsychologist Donald Hebb once offered a useful analogy: What is more important to define the area of a rectangle, height or width? Of course, both dimensions are essential. Without height *and* width, there is no rectangle. Similarly, if Joseph grows up to become a prominent civil rights lawyer, his success will be due to both heredity and environment.

Although heredity gives each of us a variety of potentials and limitations, these are, in turn, affected by environmental influences, such as learning, nutrition, disease, and culture. Ultimately, the person you are today reflects a continuous *interaction*, or interplay, between the forces of nature and nurture (Kalat, 2013).

Heredity

Heredity ("nature") refers to the genetic transmission of physical and psychological characteristics from parents to their children. An incredible number of personal features are set at conception, when a sperm cell and an egg cell (ovum) unite.

How does heredity operate? The nucleus of every human cell contains **DNA (deoxyribonucleic acid)** (dee-OX-see-RYE-bo-new-KLEE-ik). DNA is a long, ladder-like chain of pairs of chemical molecules (● **Figure 12.1**). The order of these molecules, or organic bases, acts as a code for genetic information. The DNA in each cell contains a record of all the instructions needed to make a human—with room left over to spare. A major scientific milestone was reached when the Human Genome Project completed sequencing all 3 billion chemical base pairs in human DNA (U.S. Department of Energy Office of Science, 2012).

© asiaselects/Corbis

Twins who share identical genes (identical twins) demonstrate the powerful influence of heredity. Even when they are reared apart, identical twins are strikingly alike in motor skills, physical development, and appearance. At the same time, twins are less alike as adults than they were as children, which shows environmental influences are at work (Freberg, 2010; Larsson, Larsson, & Lichtenstein, 2004).

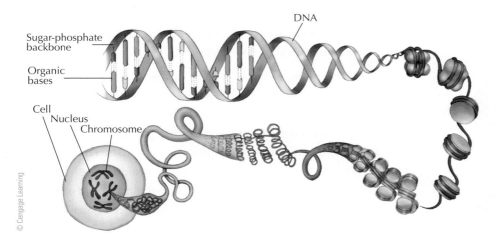

Sugar-phosphate backbone

Organic bases

Cell

Nucleus

Chromosome

DNA

© Cengage Learning

● Figure 12.1

(Top left) Linked molecules (organic bases) make up the rungs on DNA's twisted molecular ladder. The order of these molecules serves as a code for genetic information. The code provides a genetic blueprint that is unique for each individual (except identical twins). The drawing shows only a small section of a DNA strand. An entire strand of DNA is composed of billions of smaller molecules. *(Bottom left)* The nucleus of each cell in the body contains chromosomes made up of tightly wound coils of DNA. (Don't be misled by the drawing: Chromosomes are microscopic, and the chemical molecules that make up DNA are even smaller.)

Human DNA is organized into 46 **chromosomes**. (The word *chromosome* means colored body.) These thread-like structures hold the coded instructions of heredity (● **Figure 12.2**). Notable exceptions are sperm cells and ova, which contain only 23 chromosomes. Thus, Joseph received 23 chromosomes from Gloria and 23 from Jay. This is his genetic heritage.

Developmental psychology *The study of progressive changes in behavior and abilities from conception to death.*
Heredity ("nature") *The transmission of physical and psychological characteristics from parents to offspring through genes.*
DNA (deoxyribonucleic acid) *Deoxyribonucleic acid, a molecular structure that contains coded genetic information.*
Chromosomes *Thread-like colored bodies in the nucleus of each cell that are made up of DNA.*

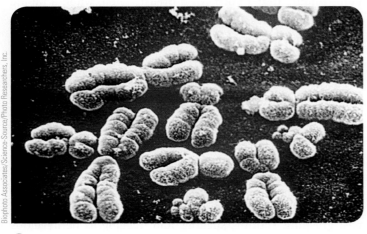

Biophoto Associates/Science-Source/Photo Researchers, Inc.

● Figure 12.2

This image, made with a scanning electron microscope, shows several pairs of human chromosomes. (Colors are artificial.)

Genes are small segments of DNA that affect a particular process or personal characteristic. Sometimes, a single gene is responsible for an inherited feature, such as Joseph's eye color. Genes may be dominant or recessive. A feature a **dominant gene** controls will appear every time the gene is present. A **recessive gene** must be paired with a second recessive gene before its effect will be expressed. For example, if Joseph got a blue-eye gene from Jay and a brown-eye gene from Gloria, Joseph will be brown eyed, because brown-eye genes are dominant.

If brown-eye genes are dominant, why do two brown-eyed parents sometimes have a blue-eyed child? If one or both parents have two brown-eye genes, the couple's children can only be brown eyed. But what if each parent has one brown-eye gene and one blue-eye gene? In that case, both parents would have brown eyes. Yet, there is one chance in four that their children will get two blue-eye genes and have blue eyes (● Figure 12.3).

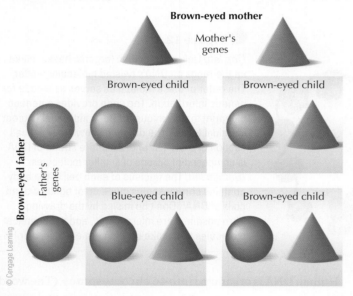

Brown-eyed mother

Mother's genes

Brown-eyed child

Brown-eyed child

Brown-eyed father

Father's genes

Blue-eyed child

Brown-eyed child

© Cengage Learning

● **Figure 12.3**

Gene patterns for children of brown-eyed parents, where each parent has one brown-eye gene and one blue-eye gene. Because the brown-eye gene is dominant, one child in four will be blue-eyed. Thus, there is a significant chance that two brown-eyed parents will have a blue-eyed child.

In actuality, few of our characteristics are controlled by single genes. Instead, most are **polygenic characteristics** (pol-ih-JEN-ik), controlled by many genes working in combination. So, for example, there is no one tall or short gene; in fact, almost *two hundred* genes have already been shown to play a role in determining height (Allen et al., 2010). Through the expression of genes, heredity determines eye color, height,

skin color, and susceptibility to some diseases. Also, genes can switch on (or off) at certain ages or developmental stages. In this way, heredity continues to exert a powerful influence throughout **maturation**, the physical growth and development of the body, brain, and nervous system (Cummings, 2011). As the *human growth sequence* unfolds, genetic instructions influence body size and shape, height, intelligence, athletic potential, personality traits, sexual orientation, and a host of other details (● Table 12.1).

Maturation in the Newborn

Newborn babies have physical and mental capacities that continue to surprise researchers and delight parents. The emergence of many of these capacities is closely related to maturation of the brain, nervous system, and body.

So human babies have already been maturing while in the womb? Don't be fooled. Even though human *neonates* (NEE-oh-NATE: newborn infant) will die if not cared for by adults, cannot lift their heads, turn over, or feed themselves, they are born with some basic survival skills and the capacity to continue to mature at breakneck speed.

For example, at birth, Joseph has several adaptive infant reflexes (Siegler, DeLoache, & Eisenberg, 2011). To elicit the *grasping reflex*, press an object in a neonate's palm and he will grasp it with surprising strength. Many infants, in fact, can hang from a raised bar, like little trapeze artists. The grasping reflex aids survival by helping infants avoid falling. You can observe the *rooting reflex* (reflexive head turning and nursing) by touching Joseph's cheek. Immediately, he will turn toward your finger, as if searching for something. The rooting reflex helps infants find a bottle or a breast. Then, when a nipple touches the infant's mouth, the *sucking reflex* (rhythmic nursing) helps her obtain needed food. Like other reflexes, this is a genetically programmed action.

The *Moro reflex* also is interesting. If Joseph's position is changed abruptly or if he is startled by a loud noise, he will make a hugging motion. This reaction has been compared to the movements baby monkeys use to cling to their mothers. (We leave it to the reader's imagination to decide whether there is any connection.)

Motor Development in Infancy Joseph will rapidly mature past grasping, rooting, sucking, and hugging as he develops more and more motor skills, such as sitting, crawling, standing, and walking. Of course, the *rate* of maturation varies from child to child. Nevertheless, the *order* of maturation is almost

TABLE 12.1	Human Growth Sequence	
Period	**Duration**	**Descriptive Name**
Prenatal Period	From conception to birth	
Germinal period	First 2 weeks after conception	Zygote
Embryonic period	2–8 weeks after conception	Embryo
Fetal period	From 8 weeks after conception to birth	Fetus
Neonatal Period	From birth to a few weeks after birth	Neonate
Infancy	From a few weeks after birth until child is walking securely; some children walk securely at less than a year, while others may not be able to until age 17–18 months	Infant
Early Childhood	From about 15–18 months until about 2–2½ years	Toddler
	From age 2–3 to about age 6	Preschool child
Middle Childhood	From about age 6 to 12	School-age child
Pubescence	Period of about 2 years before puberty	
Puberty	Point of development at which biological changes of pubescence reach a climax marked by sexual maturity	
Adolescence	From the beginning of pubescence until full social maturity is reached (difficult to fix duration of this period)	Adolescent
Adulthood Young adulthood (19–25) Adulthood (26–40) Maturity (41 plus)	From adolescence to death; sometimes subdivided into other periods as shown at left	Adult
Senescence	No defined limit that would apply to all people; extremely variable; characterized by marked physiological and psychological deterioration	Adult (senile), "old age"

Note: Various growth periods have no exact beginning or ending point. The ages are approximate, and each period may be thought of as blending into the next. (Table courtesy of Tom Bond.)

universal. For instance, Joseph was able to sit without support from Jay before he matured enough to stand. Indeed, infants around the world typically sit before they crawl, crawl before they stand, and stand before they walk (● **Figure 12.4**).

Oddly enough, Joseph never crawled. Like Joseph, a few children move directly from sitting to standing to walking. Even so, their motor development is orderly. In general, muscular control spreads in a pattern that is *cephalocaudal* (SEF-eh-lo-KOD-ul: from head to toe) and *proximodistal* (PROK-seh-moe-DIS-tul: from the center of the body to the extremities).

Although maturation has a big impact, motor skills don't simply emerge. Joseph must learn to control his actions. When babies are beginning to crawl or walk, they actively

try new movements and select those that work. Joseph's first efforts may be flawed—wobbly sitting or some shaky first steps. However, with practice, babies tune their movements to be smoother and more effective. Such learning is evident

Genes *Specific areas on a strand of DNA that carry hereditary information.*
Dominant gene *A gene whose influence will be expressed each time the gene is present.*
Recessive gene *A gene whose influence will be expressed only when it is paired with a second recessive gene.*
Polygenic characteristics *Personal traits or physical properties that are influenced by many genes working in combination.*
Maturation *The physical growth and development of the body and nervous system.*

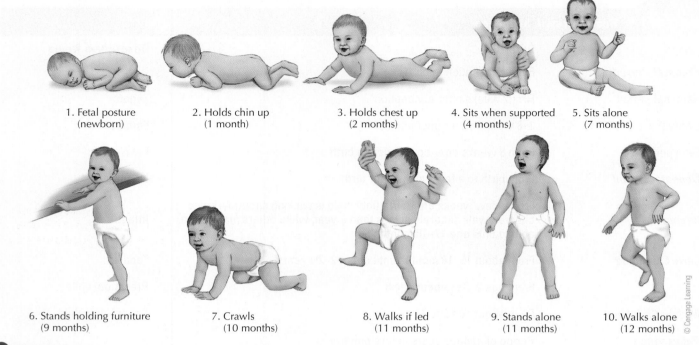

1. Fetal posture (newborn)
2. Holds chin up (1 month)
3. Holds chest up (2 months)
4. Sits when supported (4 months)
5. Sits alone (7 months)
6. Stands holding furniture (9 months)
7. Crawls (10 months)
8. Walks if led (11 months)
9. Stands alone (11 months)
10. Walks alone (12 months)

© Cengage Learning

Figure 12.4

Motor development. Most infants follow an orderly pattern of motor development. Although the order in which children progress is similar, there are large individual differences in the ages at which each ability appears. The ages listed are averages for American children. It is not unusual for many of the skills to appear one or two months earlier than average or several months later (Adolph & Berger, 2011). Parents should not be alarmed if a child's behavior differs some from the average.

from the very first months of life (Adolph & Berger, 2011; see **Figure 12.5**).

Sensory Development in Infancy Contrary to common belief, newborn babies are not oblivious to their surroundings. Neonates can see, hear, smell, taste, and respond to pain and touch. Although their senses are less acute, babies are very responsive. From birth, Joseph could follow a moving object with his eyes and turn in the direction of sounds.

An interesting glimpse into the world of infants comes from testing their vision. However, such testing is a challenge because infants cannot talk. Robert Fantz invented a device called a *looking chamber* to find out what infants can see and what holds their attention (**Figure 12.6a**). Imagine that Joseph is placed on his back inside the chamber, facing a lighted area above him. Next, two objects are placed in the chamber. By observing the movements of Joseph's eyes and the images they reflect, we can tell what he is looking at.

Such tests show that neonate vision is not as sharp as that of adults; they can most clearly see objects about a foot away from them. It is as if they are best prepared to see the people who love and care for them (Leppänen, 2011). Perhaps that's why babies have a special fascination with human faces.

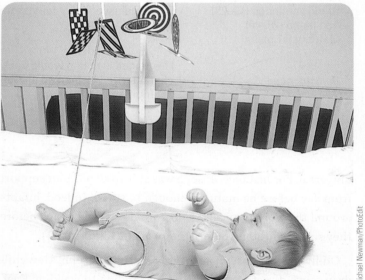

Michael Newman/PhotoEdit

Figure 12.5

Psychologist Gloriayn Rovee-Collier has shown that babies as young as 3 months old can learn to control their movements. In her experiments, babies lie on their backs under a colorful crib mobile. A ribbon is tied around the baby's ankle and connected to the mobile. Whenever babies spontaneously kick their legs, the mobile jiggles and rattles. Within a few minutes, infants learn to kick faster. Their reward for kicking is a chance to see the mobile move (Hayne & Rovee-Collier, 1995).

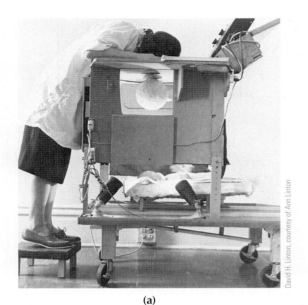

(a)

(b)

Figure 12.6

(a) Eye movements and fixation points of infants are observed in Fantz's looking chamber (Fantz, 1961). *(b)* When they are just days old, infants pay more attention to the faces of people who are gazing directly at them.

Just *hours* after they are born, babies prefer seeing their mother's face rather than a stranger's. When babies are only 2 to 5 days old, they will pay more attention to a person who is gazing directly at them rather than one who is looking away (Farroni et al., 2004) (**Figure 12.6b**).

Fantz also found that 3-day-old babies prefer complex patterns, such as checkerboards and bullseyes, to simpler colored rectangles. When Joseph is 6 months old, he will be able to recognize categories of objects that differ in shape or color. By 9 months of age, he will be able to tell the difference between dogs and birds or other groups of animals. By 1 year of age, he will see as well as his parents (Sigelman & Rider, 2012). So, a person really is inside that little body!

Readiness At what ages will Joseph be ready to feed himself, to walk alone, or to say goodbye to diapers? Such milestones tend to be governed by a child's **readiness** for rapid learning—that is, a minimum level of maturation must occur before many skills can be learned. Parents are asking for failure when they try to force a child to learn skills too early or too late (Joinson et al., 2009).

It is more difficult, for instance, to teach children to use a toilet before they have matured enough to control their bodies. Current guidelines suggest that toilet training goes most smoothly when it begins between 18 and 24 months of age. Consider the overeager parents who toilet trained a 14-month-old child in 12 trying weeks of false alarms and accidents. If they had waited until the child was 20 months old, they might have succeeded in just 3 weeks. Parents may control when toilet training starts, but maturation tends to dictate when it will be completed (Au & Stavinoha, 2008).

Newborn babies display a special interest in the human face. A preference for seeing their mother's face develops rapidly and encourages social interactions between mother and baby.

Readiness *A condition that exists when maturation has advanced enough to allow the rapid acquisition of a particular skill.*

On the other hand, parents who significantly delay the onset of toilet training may fare no better. The older a child is before toilet training begins, the more likely he or she is to fail to develop full bladder control and become a daytime wetter (Joinson et al., 2009). So why fight nature?

Environment

Our environment also exerts a profound influence on our development. **Environment ("nurture")** refers to the sum of all external conditions that affect a person. For example, the brain of a newborn baby has fewer *dendrites* (nerve cell branches) and *synapses* (connections between nerve cells) than an adult brain. However, the newborn brain is highly *plastic* (capable of being altered by experience). During the first three years of life, millions of new connections form in the brain every day. At the same time, unused connections disappear. As a result, early learning environments literally shape the developing brain, through "blooming and pruning" of synapses (Nelson, 1999; Walker et al., 2011).

Although human culture is accelerating the rate at which human DNA is evolving, modern humans are still genetically quite similar to cave dwellers who lived 30,000 years ago (Cochran & Harpending, 2009; Hawks et al., 2007). Nevertheless, a bright baby born today could learn to become almost anything—a ballet dancer, an engineer, a gangsta rapper, or a biochemist who likes to paint in watercolors. But a Stone Age baby could have become only a hunter or food gatherer.

Prenatal Influences Environmental factors actually start influencing development before birth. Although the *intra-uterine* (interior of the womb) environment is highly protected, environmental conditions can nevertheless affect the developing child. For example, during the last few months of Gloria's pregnancy, Joseph's fetal heart rate changed whenever he heard his mother's voice (Kisilevsky & Hains, 2011).

Had Gloria experienced excess stress during her pregnancy, Joseph might have been a smaller, weaker baby at birth (Schetter, 2011). If Gloria's health or nutrition had been poor or if she had had German measles, syphilis, or HIV, had used alcohol or drugs, or had been exposed to X-rays or radiation, Joseph's growth sequence might also have been harmed. In such cases, babies can suffer from **congenital problems**, or birth defects. These environmental problems affect the developing fetus and become apparent at birth. In contrast, **genetic disorders** are inherited from parents. Examples are sickle-cell anemia, hemophilia, cystic fibrosis, muscular dystrophy, albinism, and some types of intellectual disability.

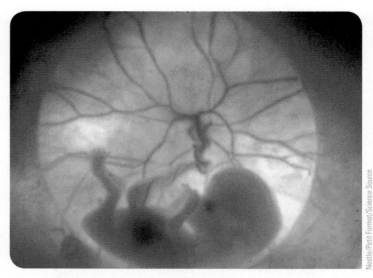

An 11-week-old fetus. Because of the rapid growth of basic structures, the developing fetus is sensitive to a variety of diseases, drugs, and sources of radiation. This is especially true during the first trimester (three months) of gestation (pregnancy).

How is it possible for the embryo or the fetus to be harmed? No direct intermixing of blood takes place between a mother and her unborn child. Yet some substances—especially drugs—do reach the fetus. Anything capable of disturbing normal development in the womb is called a **teratogen** (teh-RAT-uh-jen). Sometimes women are exposed to powerful teratogens, such as radiation, lead, pesticides, or polychlorinated biphenyls (PCBs), without knowing it. But pregnant women do have direct control over many teratogens. For example, a woman who takes cocaine runs a serious risk of injuring her fetus (Dow-Edwards, 2011). In short, when a pregnant woman takes drugs, her unborn child does, too.

Unfortunately, in the United States, alcohol and drugs are the greatest risk factors facing unborn children (Keegan et al., 2010). In fact, repeated heavy drinking during pregnancy is the most common cause of birth defects in the United States (Liles & Packman, 2009). Affected infants have *fetal alcohol syndrome (FAS)*, which includes low birth weight, a small head, bodily defects, and facial malformations. Many also suffer from emotional, behavioral, and mental disabilities (Hepper, Dornan & Lynch, 2012; Jones & Streissguth, 2010).

If a mother is addicted to morphine, heroin, or methadone, her baby may be born with an addiction. Tobacco use also is harmful. Smoking during pregnancy greatly reduces oxygen to the fetus. Heavy smokers risk miscarrying or having premature, underweight babies who are more likely to die soon after birth. Children of smoking mothers score lower on tests of language and mental ability (Clifford, Lang, & Chen, 2012).

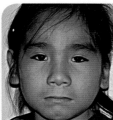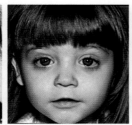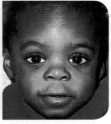

Some of the typical features of children suffering from fetal alcohol syndrome (FAS) include a small nonsymmetrical head, a short nose, a flattened area between the eyes, oddly shaped eyes, and a thin upper lip. Many of these features become less noticeable by adolescence. However, intellectual disabilities and other problems commonly follow the FAS child into adulthood. The children shown here represent moderate examples of FAS.

In other words, an unborn child's future can go "up in smoke." That goes for smoking marijuana as well (Goldschmidt et al., 2011).

Sensitive Periods Early experiences can have particularly lasting effects. For example, children who are abused may suffer lifelong emotional problems (Shin, Miller, & Teicher, 2013). At the same time, extra care can sometimes reverse the effects of a poor start in life (Walker et al., 2011). In short, environmental forces guide human development, for better or worse, throughout life.

Why do some experiences have more lasting effects than others? Part of the answer lies in the idea of a **sensitive period**. This is a time when children are more susceptible to particular types of environmental influences. Events that occur during a sensitive period can permanently alter the course of development (Bedny et al., 2012). For example, forming a loving bond with a caregiver early in life seems to be crucial for optimal development. Likewise, language abilities may become impaired when babies don't hear normal speech during their first year (Gheitury, Sahraee, & Hoseini, 2012; Thompson & Nelson, 2001).

Deprivation and Enrichment Some environments can be described as *deprived* or *enriched*. **Deprivation** refers to a lack of normal nutrition, stimulation, comfort, or love. **Enrichment** exists when an environment is deliberately made more stimulating, loving, and so forth.

What happens when children suffer severe deprivation? Tragically, a few mistreated children have spent their first years in closets, attics, and other restricted environments. When first discovered, these children are usually mute, intellectually disabled, and emotionally damaged (Wilson, 2003). Fortunately, such extreme deprivation is unusual.

Nevertheless, milder perceptual, intellectual, or emotional deprivation occurs in many families, especially those that must cope with poverty (Matthews & Gallo, 2011). Poverty can affect the development of children in at least two ways (Huston & Bentley, 2010; Sobolewski & Amato, 2005). First, poor parents may not be able to give their children necessities and resources such as nutritious meals, health care, or learning materials.

Children who grow up in poverty run a high risk of experiencing many forms of deprivation. There is evidence that lasting damage to social, emotional, and cognitive development occurs when children must cope with severe early deprivation.

Environment ("nurture") *The sum of all external conditions affecting development, including especially the effects of learning.*
Congenital problems *Problems or defects that originate during prenatal development in the womb.*
Genetic disorders *Problems caused by defects in the genes or by inherited characteristics.*
Teratogen *Anything capable of altering fetal development in nonheritable ways that cause birth defects.*
Sensitive period *During development, a period of increased sensitivity to environmental influences. It also is a time during which certain events must take place for normal development to occur.*
Deprivation *In development, the loss or withholding of normal stimulation, nutrition, comfort, love, and so forth; a condition of lack.*
Enrichment *In development, deliberately making an environment more stimulating, nutritional, comforting, loving, and so forth.*

As a result, impoverished children tend to be sick more often, their mental development lags, and they do poorly at school. Second, the stresses of poverty also can be hard on parents, leading to marriage problems, less positive parenting, and poorer parent–child relationships. The resulting emotional turmoil can damage a child's socioemotional development. In the extreme, it may increase the risk of delinquent behavior and mental illness.

Adults who grew up in poverty often remain trapped in a vicious cycle of continued poverty. Because over 46,000,000 Americans fell below the poverty line in 2011, this grim reality plays itself out in millions of American homes every day (U.S. Census Bureau, 2012).

Can an improved environment enhance development? To answer this question, psychologists have created *enriched environments* that are especially novel, complex, and stimulating. Enriched environments may be the soil from which brighter children grow. To illustrate, let's consider the effects of raising rats in a sort of "rat wonderland." The walls of their cages were decorated with colorful patterns, and each cage was filled with platforms, ladders, and cubbyholes. As adults, these rats were superior at learning mazes. In addition, they had larger, heavier brains, with a thicker cortex (Benloucif, Bennett, & Rosenzweig, 1995). Of course, it's a long leap from rats to people, but an actual increase in brain size is impressive. If extra stimulation can enhance the intelligence of a lowly rat, it's likely that human infants also benefit from enrichment. Many studies have shown that enriched environments improve abilities or enhance development (Phillips & Lowenstein, 2011). It would be wise for Jay and Gloria to make a point of nourishing Joseph's mind as well as his body (Monahan, Beeber, & Harden, 2012).

What can parents do to enrich a child's environment? They can encourage exploration and stimulating play by paying attention to what holds the baby's interest. It is better to childproof a house than to strictly limit what a child can touch. Actively enriching sensory experiences also are valuable. Infants are not vegetables. It makes perfect sense to take them outside, to hang mobiles over their cribs, to place mirrors nearby, to play music for them, or to rearrange their rooms now and then. Children progress most rapidly when they have responsive parents and stimulating play materials at home (Beeber et al., 2007). In light of this, it is wise to view all of childhood as a *relatively sensitive period* (Nelson, 1999; Walker et al., 2011).

The Whole Human

Nurture often affects the expression of hereditary tendencies through ongoing reciprocal influences. A good example of such influences is the fact that growing infants influence their parents' behavior at the same time they are changed by it.

Newborn babies differ noticeably in temperament. This is the inherited, physical core of personality. It includes sensitivity, irritability, distractibility, and typical mood (Shiner et al., 2012). According to one highly influential theory, about 40 percent of all newborns are *easy children* who are relaxed and agreeable. Ten percent are *difficult children* who are moody, intense, and easily angered. *Slow-to-warm-up children* (about 15 percent) are restrained, unexpressive, or shy. The remaining children do not fit neatly into a single category (Chess & Thomas, 1986).

Because of differences in temperament, some babies are more likely than others to smile, cry, vocalize, reach out, or pay attention. As a result, babies rapidly become active participants in their own development. For example, Joseph is an easy baby who smiles frequently and is easily fed. This encourages Gloria to touch, feed, and sing to Joseph. Gloria's affection rewards Joseph, causing him to smile more. Soon, a dynamic relationship blossoms between mother and child. Similarly, good parenting can reciprocally influence a shy child who, in turn, might become progressively less shy.

The reverse also occurs: Difficult children may make parents unhappy and elicit more negative parenting (Parke, 2004). Alternatively, negative parenting can turn a moderately shy child into a very shy one. This suggests that inherited temperaments are dynamically modified by a child's experiences (Bridgett et al., 2009; Kiff, Lengua, & Bush, 2011).

A person's developmental level is his or her current state of physical, emotional, and intellectual development. To summarize, three factors combine to determine your developmental level at any stage of life: *heredity, environment,* and your *own behavior,* each tightly interwoven with the others (Easterbrooks et al., 2013).

Temperament *The physical core of personality, including emotional and perceptual sensitivity, energy levels, typical mood, and so forth.*
Developmental level *An individual's current state of physical, emotional, and intellectual development.*

Module 12: Summary

12.1 How do heredity and environment affect development?

- **12.1.1** Heredity (nature) and environment (nurture) are interacting forces that are both necessary for human development. However, caregivers can only influence environment.
- **12.1.2** The chromosomes and genes in each cell of the body carry hereditary instructions. Most characteristics are polygenic and reflect the combined effects of dominant and recessive genes.
- **12.1.3** Maturation of the body and nervous system underlies the orderly development of motor and perceptual skills, cognitive abilities, emotions, and language. The rate of maturation varies from person to person.
- **12.1.4** The human neonate has several adaptive reflexes, including the grasping, rooting, sucking, and Moro reflexes.

- **12.1.5** Testing with a looking chamber reveals that neonates prefer complex patterns to simple ones; they also prefer human face patterns, especially familiar faces.
- **12.1.6** Many early skills are subject to the principle of readiness.
- **12.1.7** Prenatal development is influenced by environmental factors, such as various teratogens, including diseases, drugs, and radiation, as well as the mother's diet, health, and emotions.
- **12.1.8** During sensitive periods in development, infants are more sensitive to specific environmental influences.
- **12.1.9** Early perceptual, intellectual, or emotional deprivation seriously slows development, whereas deliberate enrichment of the environment has a beneficial effect on infants.
- **12.1.10** Temperament is hereditary. Most infants fall into one of three temperament categories: easy children, difficult children, and slow-to-warm-up children.
- **12.1.11** A child's developmental level reflects heredity, environment, and the effects of the child's own behavior.

Module 12: Knowledge Builder

Recite

1. Areas of the DNA molecule called genes are made up of dominant and recessive chromosomes. *T or F?*

2. Most inherited characteristics can be described as polygenic. *T or F?*

3. If one parent has one dominant brown-eye gene and one recessive blue-eye gene and the other parent has two dominant brown-eye genes, what is the chance that their child will have blue eyes?
   - **a.** 25 percent
   - **b.** 50 percent
   - **c.** 0 percent
   - **d.** 75 percent

4. The orderly sequence observed in the unfolding of many basic responses can be attributed to _____.

5. A _____ is a time of increased sensitivity to environmental influences.

6. Slow-to-warm-up children can be described as restrained, unexpressive, or shy. *T or F?*

7. As a child develops, a continuous _____ takes place between the forces of heredity and environment.

Reflect

Think Critically

8. Environmental influences can interact with genetic programming in an exceedingly direct way. Can you guess what it is?

Self-Reflect

Can you think of clear examples of some ways in which heredity and environmental forces have combined to affect your development?

How would maturation affect the chances of teaching an infant to eat with a spoon?

What kind of temperament did you have as an infant? How did it affect your relationship with your parents or caregivers?

ANSWERS

1. F 2. T 3. c 4. maturation 5. sensitive period 6. T 7. Interaction or interplay 8. Environmental conditions sometimes turn specific genes on or off, thus directly affecting the expression of genetic tendencies.

Human Development:
Emotional and Social Development in Childhood

Let's Be Close

Human infants mature from helpless babies to independent little people with dazzling speed. At no other time except infancy does development proceed as rapidly. By their third year, babies are usually able to stand, walk, talk, and explore. During the same period, a baby's early emotional life and relationships with other people also unfold on a timetable that is largely controlled by maturation.

Social development is rooted in emotional attachment and the need for physical contact as infants first form an emotional bond with an adult. One sign of attachment is the storm of crying that sometimes occurs when babies are left alone at bedtime. As many parents know, it is often eased by the presence of security objects, such as a stuffed animal or favorite blanket. While parents are the most important influences in early social development, later development is enhanced when play with other children begins to extend a child's social life beyond the family. Let's trace our early emotional and social development.

Michael Newman/PhotoEdit

SURVEY QUESTIONS

13.1 In what order do the emotions develop during infancy?

13.2 What is the significance of a child's emotional bond with adults?

13.3 How important are parenting styles?

Emotional Development in Infancy—Curious, Baby?

SURVEY QUESTION 13.1: In what order do the emotions develop during infancy?

Although experts do not yet agree on exactly how quickly emotions unfold (Oster, 2005), early emotional development also follows a pattern closely tied to maturation (Music, 2011; Panksepp & Pasqualini, 2005). Even the basic emotions of *anger, fear*, and *joy*—which appear to be unlearned—take time to develop. General *excitement* is the only emotion newborn infants clearly express. However, as Jay and Gloria can tell you, a baby's emotional life blossoms rapidly. One researcher (Bridges, 1932) observed that all the basic human emotions appear before age 2. Bridges found that emotions appear in a consistent order and that the first basic split is between pleasant and unpleasant emotions (● **Figure 13.1**).

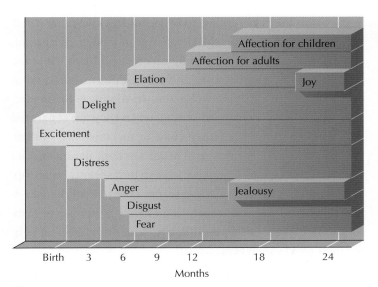

● Figure 13.1

The traditional view of infancy holds that emotions are rapidly differentiated from an initial capacity for excitement. (After K. M. B. Bridges, 1932. Reprinted by permission of the Society for Research in Child Development, Inc.)

Psychologist Carroll Izard thinks that infants can express several basic emotions as early as 10 weeks of age. When Izard looks carefully at the faces of babies, he sees abundant signs of emotion (Izard, Woodburn, & Finlon, 2010). The most common infant expression, he found, is not excitement, it's *interest*— followed by *joy, anger,* and *sadness* (Izard et al., 1995).

If Izard is right, then emotions are hardwired by heredity and related to evolution. Perhaps that's why smiling is one of a baby's most common reactions. Smiling probably helps babies survive by inviting parents to care for them.

At first, a baby's smiling is haphazard. By the age of 8 to 12 months, however, infants smile more frequently when another person is nearby (Jones & Hong, 2001; Mcquaid, Bibok, & Carpendale, 2009). This social smile is especially rewarding to parents. Infants can even use their social smile to communicate interest in an object, like the time Joseph gazed at favorite teddy bear and then smiled at his mother (Parlade et al., 2009). On the other hand, when new parents see and hear a crying baby, they feel annoyed, irritated, disturbed, or unhappy. Babies the world over, it seems, rapidly become capable of letting others know what they like and dislike. (Prove this to yourself sometime by driving a baby buggy.)

Social Development—Baby, I'm Stuck on You

SURVEY QUESTION 13.2: What is the significance of a child's emotional bond with adults?

A baby's **affectional needs** (needs for love and affection) are every bit as important as more obvious needs for food, water, and physical care.

In part to meet their affectional needs, infants rapidly begin to form **emotional attachments**, or close emotional bonds, with their primary caregivers (Music, 2011). As infants form their first emotional bond with an adult, usually a parent, they also begin to develop self-awareness and to become aware of others (Easterbrooks et al., 2013). This early **social development** lays a foundation for subsequent relationships with parents, siblings, friends, and relatives (Shaffer & Kipp, 2014).

To investigate mother-infant relationships, Harry Harlow separated baby rhesus monkeys from their mothers at birth. The real mothers were replaced with **surrogate mothers** (substitutes). Some were made of cold, unyielding wire. Others were covered with soft terry cloth (● **Figure 13.2**).

When the infants were given a choice between the two mothers, they spent most of their time clinging to the cuddly terry-cloth mother. This was true even when the wire mother held a bottle, making it the source of food. The "love" and attachment displayed toward the cloth replicas was identical to that shown toward natural mothers. For example, when frightened by rubber snakes, wind-up toys, and other "fear stimuli," the infant monkeys ran to their cloth mothers and clung to them for security. These classic studies suggest that attachment begins with **contact comfort**, the pleasant, reassuring feeling

Social smile *Smiling elicited by social stimuli, such as seeing a parent's face.*
Affectional needs *Emotional needs for love and affection.*
Emotional attachments *Especially close emotional bonds that infants form with their parents, caregivers, or others.*
Social development *The development of self-awareness, attachment to parents or caregivers, and relationships with other children and adults.*
Surrogate mother *A substitute mother (often an inanimate object or dummy in animal research).*
Contact comfort *A pleasant and reassuring feeling human and animal infants get from touching or clinging to something soft and warm, usually their mother.*

Nina Leen/Time & Life Pictures/Getty Images

Figure 13.2

An infant monkey clings to a cloth-covered surrogate mother. Baby monkeys become attached to the cloth "contact-comfort" mother but not to a similar wire mother. This is true even when the wire mother provides food. Contact comfort also may underlie the tendency of children to become attached to inanimate objects, such as blankets or stuffed toys.

infants get from touching something soft and warm, especially their mother.

There is a sensitive period (roughly the first year of life) during which this must occur for optimal development. Joseph's attachment during this period kept him close to his mother, Gloria, who provided safety, stimulation, and a secure "home base" from which Joseph could go exploring.

Mothers usually begin to feel attached to their babies before birth. For their part, as babies mature, they become more and more capable of bonding with their mothers. For the first few months, babies respond more or less equally to everyone. By two or three months, most babies prefer their mothers to strangers. By around seven months, babies generally become truly attached to their mothers, crawling after them if they can. Shortly thereafter, they begin to form attachments to other people as well, such as their father, grandparents, or siblings (Sigelman & Rider, 2012).

A direct sign that an emotional bond has formed appears around 8 to 12 months of age. At that time, Joseph will display **separation anxiety** (crying and signs of fear) when he is left alone or with a stranger. Mild separation anxiety is normal. When it is more intense, it may reveal a problem. At some point in their lives, about one in twenty children suffer from *separation anxiety disorder* (Herren, In-Albon, & Schneider, 2013). These children are miserable when they are separated from their parents, who they cling to or constantly follow. Some fear they will get lost and never see their parents again. Many refuse to go to school, which can be a serious handicap. Children tend to outgrow the disorder (Dick-Niederhauser & Silverman, 2006), but if separation anxiety is intense or lasts for more than a month, parents should seek professional help for their child (Allen et al., 2010).

All things considered, creating a bond of trust and affection between the infant and at least one other person is a key event during the first year of life. Parents are sometimes afraid of "spoiling" babies with too much attention, but for the first year or two, this is nearly impossible. In fact, a later capacity to experience warm and loving relationships may depend on it.

Attachment Quality According to psychologist Mary Ainsworth (1913–1999), the quality of attachment is revealed by how babies act when their mothers return after a brief separation (Ainsworth, 1989). Infants who develop a **secure attachment** have a stable and positive emotional bond. They are upset by the mother's (or caregiver's) absence and seek to be near her when she returns. Infants with an **insecure-avoidant attachment** have an anxious emotional bond. They tend to turn away from the mother (or caregiver) when she returns. **Insecure-ambivalent attachment** also is an anxious emotional bond. In this case, babies have mixed feelings: They both seek to be near the returning mother (or caregiver) and angrily resist contact with her (● **Figure 13.3**).

Attachment Category

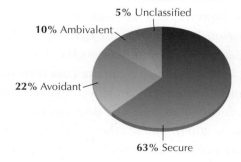

5% Unclassified
10% Ambivalent
22% Avoidant
63% Secure

Figure 13.3

In the United States, about two-thirds of all children from middle-class families are securely attached. About one child in three is insecurely attached. (Percentages are approximate.) (From Kaplan, 1998.)

Discovering Psychology

What's Your Attachment Style?

Do our first attachments continue to affect us as adults? Some psychologists believe they do, by influencing how we relate to friends and lovers (Bohlin & Hagekull, 2009; Vrtička & Vuilleumier, 2012). Read the following statements and see which best describes your adult relationships.

Secure Attachment Style

In general, I think most other people are well intentioned and trustworthy.

I find it relatively easy to get close to others.

I am comfortable relying on others and having others depend on me.

I don't worry much about being abandoned by others.

I am comfortable when other people want to get close to me emotionally.

Avoidant Attachment Style

I tend to pull back when things don't go well in a relationship.

I am somewhat skeptical about the idea of true love.

I have difficulty trusting my partner in a romantic relationship.

Other people tend to be too eager to seek commitment from me.

I get a little nervous if anyone gets too close emotionally.

Ambivalent Attachment Style

I have often felt misunderstood and unappreciated in my romantic relationships.

My friends and lovers have been somewhat unreliable.

I love my romantic partner but I worry that she or he doesn't really love me.

I would like to be closer to my romantic partner, but I'm not sure I trust her or him.

Do any of the preceding statements sound familiar? If so, they may describe your adult attachment style (Welch & Houser, 2010). Most adults have a secure attachment style that is marked by caring, supportiveness, and understanding. However, it's not unusual to have an avoidant attachment style that reflects a tendency to resist intimacy and commitment to others (Collins et al., 2002). An ambivalent attachment style is marked by mixed feelings about love and friendship (DeWall et al., 2011). Do you see any similarities between your present relationships and your attachment experiences as a child?

Attachment can have lasting effects (Bohlin & Hagekull, 2009; Morley & Moran, 2011). Infants who are securely attached during infancy later show resiliency, curiosity, problem-solving ability, and social skills in preschool. In contrast, attachment failures can be quite damaging (Santelices et al., 2011). Consider, for example, the plight of children raised in severely overcrowded orphanages (Rutter et al., 2009). These children get almost no attention from adults for the first year or two of their lives. Once adopted, many are poorly attached to their new parents. Some, for instance, will wander off with strangers, are anxious and remote, and don't like to be touched or to make eye contact with others (O'Conner et al., 2003). In short, for some children, a lack of affectionate care early in life leaves a lasting emotional impact well into adulthood. (See "What's Your Attachment Style?")

Promoting Secure Attachment One key to secure attachment is a mother who is accepting and sensitive to her baby's signals and rhythms. Poor attachment occurs when a mother's actions are inappropriate, inadequate, intrusive, overstimulating, or rejecting. An example is a mother who tries to play with a drowsy infant or who ignores a baby who is looking at her and vocalizing. The link between sensitive caregiving and secure attachment appears to apply to all cultures (Santelices et al., 2011).

What about attachment to fathers? Fathers of securely attached infants tend to be outgoing, agreeable, and happy in their marriage. In general, a warm family atmosphere—one that includes sensitive mothering *and* fathering—produces secure children (Gomez & McLaren, 2007; Mattanah, Lopez, & Govern, 2011).

Day Care

Does commercial day care interfere with the quality of attachment? It depends on the quality of day care. Overall, *high-quality* day care does not adversely affect attachment to parents. In fact, high-quality day care can improve children's social and mental skills (National Institute of Child Health and Human Development, 2010a). Children in high-quality day care tend to have better relationships with their mothers

Separation anxiety *Distress displayed by infants when they are separated from their parents or principal caregivers.*
Secure attachment *A stable and positive emotional bond.*
Insecure-avoidant attachment *An anxious emotional bond marked by a tendency to avoid reunion with a parent or caregiver.*
Insecure-ambivalent attachment *An anxious emotional bond marked by both a desire to be with a parent or caregiver and some resistance to being reunited.*

(or caregivers) and fewer behavior problems. They also have better cognitive skills and language abilities (Li et al., 2012).

However, all the positive effects just noted are *reversed* for low-quality day care. Low-quality day care *is* risky and *may* weaken attachment (Phillips & Lowenstein, 2011). Poor-quality day care can even create behavior problems that didn't exist beforehand (Pierrehumbert et al., 2002). Parents are wise to carefully evaluate and monitor the quality of day care their children receive.

What should parents look for when they evaluate the quality of day care? Parents seeking quality day care should look for responsive and sensitive care providers who offer plenty of attention and verbal and cognitive stimulation (Phillips & Lowenstein, 2011). This is more likely to occur in day-care centers with *at least* the following: (1) a small number of children per caregiver, (2) small overall group size (12 to 15), (3) trained care providers, (4) minimal staff turnover, and (5) stable, consistent care. (Also, avoid any day-care center with the words *zoo, menagerie,* or *stockade* in its name.)

Parental Influences—Life with Mom and Dad

SURVEY QUESTION 13.3: How important are parenting styles?

From the first few years of life, when caregivers are the center of a child's world, through to adulthood, the style and quality of mothering and fathering are very important.

Parenting Styles

Psychologist Diana Baumrind (1991, 2005) has studied the effects of three major **parental styles**, which are identifiable patterns of parental caretaking and interaction with children. See if you recognize the styles she describes.

Authoritarian parents enforce rigid rules and demand strict obedience to authority. Typically, they view children as having few rights but adult-like responsibilities. The child is expected to stay out of trouble and to accept, without question, what parents regard as right or wrong ("Do it because I say so"). Authoritarian parents tend to discipline their children through **power assertion**—physical punishment or a show of force, such as taking away toys or privileges. Power-oriented

"Your father and I have come to believe that incarceration is sometimes the only appropriate punishment."

techniques—particularly harsh or severe physical punishment—are associated with fear, hatred of parents, and a lack of spontaneity and warmth (Olson & Hergenhahn, 2013).

As an alternative, authoritarian parents may use **withdrawal of love**, or withholding affection, by refusing to speak to a child, threatening to leave, rejecting the child, or otherwise acting as if the child is temporarily unlovable. The children of authoritarian parents are usually obedient and self-controlled. But they also tend to be emotionally stiff, withdrawn, apprehensive, lacking in curiosity, and dependent on adults for approval. They also can develop low *self-esteem*. If you regard yourself as a worthwhile person, you have **self-esteem**. Low self-esteem is related to physical punishment and the withholding of love. And why not? What messages do children receive if a parent beats them or tells them they are not worthy of love?

Overly permissive parents give little guidance, allow too much freedom, or don't hold children accountable for their actions. Typically, the child has rights similar to an adult's but few responsibilities. Rules are not enforced, and the child usually gets his or her way ("Do whatever you want"). Permissive parents tend to produce dependent, immature children who misbehave frequently. Such children are aimless and likely to "run amok."

Some overly permissive parents genuinely wish to empower their children by imposing few limits on their behavior, making them feel special, and giving them everything they want (Mamen, 2004). But such good intentions can backfire, leaving parents with children who have developed an artificially high level of self-esteem and a sense of entitlement. Overly empowered offspring are often spoiled, self-indulgent, and lack self-control (Crocker, Moeller, & Burson, 2010).

Baumrind describes **authoritative parents** as those who supply firm and consistent guidance, combined with love and affection. Such parents balance their own rights with those of their children. They control their children's behavior through **management techniques**, which combine praise, recognition, approval, rules, reasoning, and the like to encourage desirable behavior. Effective parents are firm and consistent, not harsh or rigid. In general, they encourage the child to act responsibly, to think, and to make good decisions. This style produces children who are *resilient* (good at bouncing back after bad experiences) and who develop the strengths they need

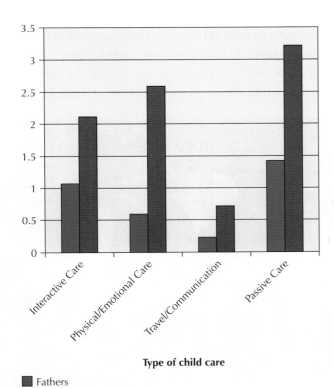

Type of child care

■ Fathers
■ Mothers

● **Figure 13.4**

Mother–child and father–child interactions. This graph shows what occurred on routine days in a sample of more than 1,400 Australian homes. Mothers spend about twice as long each day on child care, compared with fathers. Further, mothers spend more time on physical and emotional care (e.g., feeding, bathing, soothing) than on interactive care (e.g., playing, reading, activities); fathers show the reverse pattern. Finally, mothers spend more time on travel (e.g., driving children to sports or music lessons), communication (e.g., talking to teachers about their children), and passive care (e.g., supervising children while they play).
(Adapted from Craig, 2006.)

to thrive even in difficult circumstances (Bahr & Hoffmann, 2010; Kim-Cohen et al., 2004). The children of authoritative parents are competent, self-controlled, independent, assertive, and inquiring. They know how to manage their emotions and use positive coping skills (Eisenberg et al., 2003; Lynch, Geller, & Schmidt, 2004).

Maternal and Paternal Influences

Don't mothers and fathers parent differently? Yes. Although **maternal influences**—all the effects a mother has on her child—have a greater impact, fathers also make a unique contribution to parenting (Bjorklund & Hernández Blasi, 2012). Although fathers are spending more time with their children, mothers still do most of the nurturing and caretaking, especially of young children (Craig, 2006).

Studies of **paternal influences**—the sum of all effects a father has on his child—reveal that fathers are more likely to play with their children and tell them stories. In contrast, mothers are typically responsible for the physical and emotional care of their children (● **Figure 13.4**).

It might seem that the father's role as a playmate makes him less important. Not so. Joseph's playtime with Jay is quite valuable. From birth onward, fathers pay more visual attention to children than mothers. Fathers are much more tactile (lifting, tickling, and handling the baby), more physically arousing (engaging in rough-and-tumble play), and more likely to engage in unusual play (imitating the baby, for example). In comparison, mothers speak to infants more, play more

Parental styles *Identifiable patterns of parental caretaking and interaction with children.*
Authoritarian parents *Parents who enforce rigid rules and demand strict obedience to authority.*
Power assertion *The use of physical punishment or coercion to enforce child discipline.*
Withdrawal of love *Withholding affection to enforce child discipline.*
Self-esteem *Regarding oneself as a worthwhile person; a positive evaluation of oneself.*
Overly permissive parents *Parents who give little guidance, allow too much freedom, or do not require the child to take responsibility.*
Authoritative parents *Parents who supply firm and consistent guidance combined with love and affection.*
Management techniques *Combining praise, recognition, approval, rules, and reasoning to enforce child discipline.*
Maternal influences *The aggregate of all psychological effects mothers have on their children.*
Paternal influences *The aggregate of all psychological effects fathers have on their children.*

Fathering typically makes a contribution to early development that differs in emphasis from mothering.

conventional games (such as peekaboo), and, as noted, spend much more time in caregiving. Young children who spend a lot of time playing with their fathers tend to be more competent in many ways (Paquette, 2004; Tamis-LeMonda, et al., 2004).

Overall, fathers can be as affectionate, sensitive, and responsive as mothers. Nevertheless, infants and children tend to get very different views of males and females. Females, who offer comfort, nurturance, and verbal stimulation, tend to be close at hand. Males come and go, and when they are present, action, exploration, and risk-taking prevail. It's no wonder, then, that the parental styles of mothers and fathers have a major impact on children's gender role development (Holmes & Huston, 2010; Malmberg & Flouri, 2011).

Ethnic Differences: Four Flavors of Parenting

Do ethnic differences in parenting affect children in distinctive ways? Diana Baumrind's work provides a good overall summary of the effects of parenting. However, her conclusions are probably most valid for families whose roots lie in Europe. Child rearing in other ethnic groups often reflects different customs and beliefs. Cultural differences are especially apparent with respect to the meaning attached to a child's behavior. Is a particular behavior "good" or "bad"? Should it be encouraged or discouraged? The answer depends on parents' cultural values (Sorkhabi, 2012).

Making generalizations about groups of people is always risky. Nevertheless, some typical differences in child-rearing patterns have been observed in North American ethnic communities, as we discuss here (Parke, 2004).

African-American Families Traditional African-American values emphasize loyalty and interdependence among family members, security, developing a positive racial identity, and not giving up in the face of adversity (Rowley et al., 2012). African-American parents typically stress obedience and respect for elders (Dixon, Graber, & Brooks-Gunn, 2008). Child discipline tends to be fairly strict (Parke, 2004), but many African-American parents see this as a necessity, especially if they live in urban areas where safety is a concern. Self-reliance, resourcefulness, and an ability to take care of oneself in difficult situations also are qualities that African-American parents seek to promote in their children.

Hispanic Families Like African-American parents, Hispanic parents tend to have relatively strict standards of discipline (Dixon, Graber, & Brooks-Gunn, 2008). They also place a high value on *familismo*: the centrality of the family, with a corresponding stress on family values, family pride, and

In other ethnic communities, norms for effective parenting often differ in subtle ways from parenting styles in Euro-American culture.

loyalty (Glass & Owen, 2010). Hispanic families are typically affectionate and indulgent toward younger children. However, as children grow older, they are expected to learn social skills and to be calm, obedient, courteous, and respectful (Calzada, Fernandez, & Cortes, 2010). In fact, such social skills may be valued more than cognitive skills (Delgado & Ford, 1998). In addition, Hispanic parents tend to stress cooperation more than competition. Such values can put Hispanic children at a disadvantage in highly competitive, European-American culture.

Asian-American Families Asian cultures tend to be group oriented, and they emphasize interdependence among individuals. In contrast, Western cultures value individual effort and independence. This difference is often reflected in Asian-American child-rearing practices (Park et al., 2010). Asian-American children are often taught that their behavior can bring either pride or shame to the family. Therefore, they are obliged to set aside their own desires when the greater good of the family is at stake (Parke, 2004). Parents tend to act as home-based teachers who encourage hard work, moral behavior, and achievement. For the first few years, parenting is lenient and permissive. However, after about age 5, Asian-American parents begin to expect respect, obedience, self-control, and self-discipline from their children.

Arab-American Families In Middle Eastern cultures, children are expected to be polite, obedient, disciplined, and conforming (Erickson & Al-Timimi, 2001). Punishment may consist of spankings, teasing, or shaming in front of others. Arab-American fathers tend to be strong authority figures who demand obedience so that the family will not be shamed by a child's bad behavior. Success, generosity, and hospitality are highly valued in Arab-American culture. The pursuit of family honor encourages hard work, thrift, conservatism, and educational achievement. The welfare of the family is emphasized over individual identity. Thus, Arab-American children are raised to respect their parents, members of their extended family, and other adults (Medhus, 2001).

Implications Children are reared in a remarkable variety of ways around the world. In fact, many of the things we do in North America, such as making young children sleep alone, would be considered odd or wrong in other cultures. In the final analysis, parenting can be judged only if we know what culture or ethnic community a child is being prepared to enter (Sorkhabi, 2012).

Module 13: Summary

13.1   In what order do the emotions develop during infancy?

- **13.1.1** Emotions develop in a consistent order, starting with generalized excitement in newborn babies. Three of the basic emotions—fear, anger, and joy—may be unlearned.

13.2   What is the significance of a child's emotional bond with adults?

- **13.2.1** Meeting a baby's affectional needs is as important as meeting needs for physical care. Emotional attachment of human infants is a critical early event.
- **13.2.2** Infant attachment is reflected by separation anxiety. The quality of attachment can be classified as secure, insecure-avoidant, or insecure-ambivalent.

- **13.2.3** High-quality day care does not appear to harm children. Low-quality day care can be risky.

13.3   How important are parenting styles?

- **13.3.1** Studies suggest that parental styles have a substantial impact on emotional and intellectual development.
- **13.3.2** Three major parental styles are authoritarian, permissive, and authoritative (effective). Authoritative parenting, relying more on management techniques rather than power assertion or withdrawal of love, appears to benefit children the most.
- **13.3.3** Whereas mothers typically emphasize caregiving, fathers tend to function as playmates for infants.
- **13.3.4** Parental styles vary across cultures.

Module 13: Knowledge Builder

Recite

1. General excitement or interest is the clearest emotional response present in newborn infants, but meaningful expressions of delight and distress appear soon after. *T or F?*

2. Neonates display a social smile as early as 10 days after birth. *T or F?*

3. The development of separation anxiety in an infant corresponds to the formation of an attachment to parents. *T or F?*

4. High-quality day care can improve children's social and mental skills. *T or F?*

5. Fathers are more likely to act as playmates for their children, rather than as caregivers. *T or F?*

6. According to Diana Baumrind's research, effective parents are authoritarian in their approach to their children's behavior. *T or F?*

7. Asian-American parents tend to be more individually oriented than parents whose ethnic roots are European. *T or F?*

Reflect

Think Critically

8. Can emotional bonding begin before birth?

9. Which parenting style do you think would be most likely to lead to eating disorders in children?

Self-Reflect

Do you think that your experiences as a child, such as your early attachment pattern, affect your life as an adult? Can you think of any examples from your own life?

Do you know any parents who have young children and who are authoritarian, permissive, or authoritative? What are their children like?

Do you think parenting depends on ethnicity? If so, why? If not, why not?

ANSWERS

1. T 2. F 3. T 4. T 5. T 6. F 7. F 8. It certainly can for parents. When a pregnant woman begins to feel fetal movements, she becomes aware that a baby is coming to life inside her. Likewise, prospective parents who hear a fetal heartbeat at the doctor's office or see an ultrasound image of the fetus begin to become emotionally attached to the unborn child (Santrock, 2011). 9. Authoritarian parents who are too controlling about what their children eat as well as permissive parents who are too willing to withdraw from conflicts over eating can create problems for their children (Haycraft & Blissett, 2010).

CENGAGE**brain**.com

Go to **cengagebrain.com** to access **MindTap for Coon/Mitterer** *Psychology Modules for Active Learning* and other online learning tools. MindTap is a fully online learning experience that combines all the tools you need—readings, multimedia, activities, and assessments—into a singular personalized Learning Path that guides you through the course.

Human Development:
Language and Cognitive Development in Childhood

Make It Warmer, Daddy

There's something almost miraculous about a baby's early language and thought, which often leaves parents scratching their heads. For example, when Joseph was 3, he thought his bath was too hot and said to Jay, "Make it warmer, Daddy." At first, Jay was confused. The bath was already fairly hot. He grinned as he realized that Joseph meant, "Bring the water closer to the temperature we call *warm*." It makes perfect sense if you look at it that way.

As infants, how did we manage to leap into the world of language and thought? Although maturation (nature) provides the foundation for language learning and cognitive development, social development (nurture) plays a critical role, too. For example, parents use a distinctive style, called *motherese* or *parentese*, when speaking to an infant. In what other ways do nature and nurture work together to foster language and cognitive development in young children? Let's find out.

Gary Conner/Photolibrary/Getty Images

SURVEY QUESTIONS

14.1 How do children acquire language?

14.2 How do children learn to think?

Language Development—
Who Talks Baby Talk?

SURVEY QUESTION 14.1: How do children acquire language?

Language development is closely tied to maturation (Gleason & Ratner, 2013). As every parent knows, babies can cry from birth on. By 1 month of age, they use crying to gain attention. Typically, parents can tell whether an infant is hungry, angry, or in pain from the tone of the crying (Nakayama, 2010). Around 6 to 8 weeks of age, babies begin *cooing* (the repetition of vowel sounds such as "oo" and "ah").

By 7 months of age, Joseph's nervous system will be mature enough to allow him to grasp objects, smile, laugh, sit up, and *babble*. In the babbling stage, the consonants *b*, *d*, *m*, and *g* are combined with the vowel sounds to produce meaningless language sounds: *dadadadada* or *bababa*. At first, babbling is the same around the world. But soon, the language spoken by parents begins to have an influence (Goldstein & Schwade, 2008)—that is, Japanese babies start to babble in a way that sounds like Japanese, Mexican babies babble in Spanish-like sounds, and so on (Kuhl, 2004).

At about 1 year of age, children respond to real words such as *no* or *hi*. Soon afterward, the first connection between words and objects forms, and children may address their parents as "Mama" or "Dada." By age 18 months to 2 years, Joseph's vocabulary may include a hundred words or more. First comes the *single-word stage,* during which children use one word at a time, such as "go," "juice," or "up." Soon after, words are arranged in simple two-word sentences called *telegraphic speech:* "Want-Teddy"; "Mama-gone."

Language and the Terrible Twos

At about the same time that children begin to put two or three words together, they become much more independent. Two-year-olds understand some of the commands parents make, but they are not always willing to carry them out. A child like Joseph may assert his independence by saying, "No drink," "Me do it," "My cup, my cup," and the like. It can be worse, of course. A 2-year-old may look at you intently, make eye contact, listen as you shout "No, no!", and still pour her juice on the cat.

During their second year, children become increasingly capable of mischief and temper tantrums. Thus, calling this time "the terrible twos" is not entirely inappropriate. One-year-olds can do plenty of things parents don't want them to do. However, it's usually 2-year-olds who do things *because* you don't want them to (Gopnik, Meltzoff, & Kuhl, 2000). Perhaps parents can take some comfort in knowing that a stubborn, negative 2-year-old is simply becoming more independent. When Joseph is 2 years old, Gloria and Jay would be wise to remember that "This, too, shall pass."

After age 2, the child's comprehension and use of words take a dramatic leap forward. From this point on, vocabulary and language skills grow at a phenomenal rate (Fernald, Perfors, & Marchman, 2006). By first grade, Joseph will be able to understand around 8,000 words and use about 4,000. He will have truly entered the world of language.

The Roots of Language

What accounts for this explosion of language development? Linguist Noam Chomsky (1975, 1986) has long claimed that humans have a **biological predisposition**, or hereditary readiness to develop language. According to Chomsky, language patterns are inborn, much like a child's ability to coordinate walking. If such inborn language recognition does exist, it may explain why children around the world use a limited number of patterns in their first sentences. Typical patterns include (Mussen et al., 1979) the following:

Identification:	"See kitty."
Nonexistence:	"All gone milk."
Possession:	"My doll."
Agent-Action:	"Mama give."
Negation:	"Not ball."
Question:	"Where doggie?"

Does Chomsky's theory explain why language develops so rapidly? It is certainly part of the story (Saxton, 2010). But many psychologists feel that Chomsky underestimates the importance of learning and the social contexts that shape language development (Behne et al., 2012; Hoff, 2014). *Psycholinguists* (specialists in the psychology of language) have shown that imitation of adults and rewards for correctly using words (as when a child asks for a cookie) are an important part of language learning. Also, babies actively participate in language learning by asking questions, such as "What dis?" (Domingo & Goldstein-Alpern, 1999).

When a child makes a language error, parents typically repeat the child's sentence, with needed corrections, or ask a clarifying question to draw the child's attention to the error (Hoff, 2014). More important is the fact that parents and children begin to communicate long before the child can speak. A readiness to interact *socially* with parents may be as important as innate language recognition. The next section explains why.

Early Communication *How do parents communicate with infants before they can talk?* Parents go to a great deal of trouble to get babies to smile and vocalize. In doing so, they quickly learn to change their actions to keep the infant's attention, arousal, and activity at optimal levels. A familiar example is the "I'm-Going-to-Get-You game." In it, the adult says, "I'm gonna getcha . . . . I'm gonna getcha . . . . I'm gonna getcha . . . . Gotcha!" Through such games, adults and babies come to share similar rhythms and expectations (Carroll, 2008). Soon a system of shared **signals** is created, including touching, vocalizing, gazing, and smiling. These help lay a foundation for later language use (Tamis-LeMonda, Bornstein, & Baumwell, 2001). Specifically, signals establish a pattern of "conversational" *turn-taking* (alternate sending and receiving of messages).

Gloria	Joseph
	(smiles)
"Oh what a nice little smile!"	
"Yes, isn't that nice?"	(burps)
"Well, pardon you!"	
"Yes, that's better, Yes."	(vocalizes)
"Yes."	(smiles)
"What's so funny?"	

From the outside, such exchanges may look meaningless. In reality, they represent real communication (Behne et al., 2012). One study found that 6-week-old babies change their gaze at an adult's face when the adult's speech changes (Crown et al., 2002). Infants as young as 4 months engage in vocal turn-taking with adults (Jaffe et al., 2001). The more children interact with parents, the faster they learn to talk and the faster they learn thinking abilities (Hoff & Tian, 2005). Unmistakably, social relationships contribute to early language learning (Hoff, 2014; Vernon-Feagans et al., 2011).

Parentese When they talk to infants, parents use an exaggerated pattern of speaking called **motherese (parentese)**. Typically, they raise their tone of voice, use short, simple sentences, repeat themselves, and use frequent gestures (Gogate, Bahrick, & Watson, 2000). They also slow their rate of speaking and use exaggerated voice inflections: "Did Joseph eat it A-L-L UP?"

What is the purpose of such changes? Parents are apparently trying to help their children learn language (Soderstrom, 2007). When a baby is still babbling, parents tend to use long, adult-style sentences. But as soon as the baby says its first word, they switch to parentese. By the time babies are 4 months old, they prefer parentese over normal speech (Cooper et al., 1997).

In addition to being simpler, parentese has a distinct "musical" quality (Trainor & Desjardins, 2002). No matter what language mothers speak, the melodies, pauses, and inflections they use to comfort, praise, or give warning are universal. Psychologist Anne Fernald has found that mothers of all nations talk to their babies with similar changes in pitch. For instance, we praise babies with a rising, then falling pitch ("BRA-vo!" "GOOD girl!"). Warnings are delivered in a short, sharp rhythm ("Nein! Nein!" "Basta! Basta!" "No! Dude!"). To give comfort, parents use low, smooth, drawn-out tones ("Oooh poor baaa-by." "Oooh pobrecito."). A high-pitched, rising melody is used to call attention to objects ("See the pretty BIRDIE?") (Fernald, 1989).

Parentese helps parents get babies' attention, communicate with them, and teach them language (Thiessen, Hill, & Saffran, 2005). Later, as a child's speaking improves, parents tend to adjust their speech to the child's language ability. Especially from 18 months to 4 years of age, parents seek to clarify what a child says and prompt the child to say more.

In summary, some elements of language are innate. Nevertheless, our inherited tendency to learn language does not determine whether we will speak English or Vietnamese, Spanish or Russian. Environmental forces also influence whether a person develops simple or sophisticated language skills. The first 7 years of life are a sensitive period in language learning (Hoff, 2014). Clearly, a full flowering of speech requires careful cultivation.

Cognitive Development— Think Like a Child

SURVEY QUESTION 14.2: How do children learn to think?

Now that we have Joseph talking, let's move on to a broader view of intellectual development. Babies are smarter than many people think. While early on they don't have learned knowledge and skills *(crystallized intelligence)*, they do have a remarkable capability for rapid learning *(fluid intelligence)*. From an evolutionary perspective, a baby's mind is designed to soak up information, which it does at an amazing pace (Bjorklund, 2012). Although baby Joseph was a "sponge," soaking up new experiences, by the time he is 83, he will find it is much harder to learn new skills (such as becoming fluent in a second language) and will find himself relying much more on what he already knows.

From the earliest days of life, babies are learning how the world works. They immediately begin to look, touch, taste, and otherwise explore their surroundings. In the first months of life, babies are increasingly able to think, to learn from what they see, to make predictions, and to search for explanations. For example, Jerome Bruner (1983) observed that 3- to 8-week-old babies seem to understand that a person's voice and body should be connected. If a baby hears his mother's voice coming from where she is standing, the baby will remain calm. If her voice comes from a loudspeaker several feet away, the baby will become agitated and begin to cry.

Biological predisposition *The presumed hereditary readiness of humans to learn certain skills, such as how to use language, or a readiness to behave in particular ways.*
Signals *In early language development, behaviors, such as touching, vocalizing, gazing, or smiling, that allow nonverbal interaction and turn-taking between parent and child.*
Motherese (or parentese) *A pattern of speech used when talking to infants, marked by a higher-pitched voice; short, simple sentences; repetition, slower speech; and exaggerated voice inflections.*

As another example, psychologist Andrew Meltzoff has found that babies are born mimics. ● **Figure 14.1** shows Meltzoff as he sticks out his tongue, opens his mouth, and purses his lips at a 20-day-old girl. Will she imitate him? Videos of babies confirm that they imitate adult facial gestures while they can see them (mirror neurons, anyone?). As early as 9 months of age, infants can remember and imitate actions a day after seeing them (Heimann & Meltzoff, 1996; Meltzoff, 2005). Such mimicry obviously aids rapid learning in infancy.

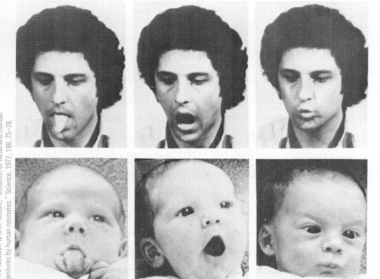

A.N. Meltzoff & M.K. Moore, "Imitation of facial and manual gestures by human neonates," Science, 1977, 198, 75–78.

● **Figure 14.1**

Infant imitation. In the top row of photos, Andrew Meltzoff makes facial gestures at an infant. The bottom row records the infant's responses. Videotapes of Meltzoff and of tested infants helped ensure objectivity.

Swiss psychologist and philosopher Jean Piaget (Jahn pea-ah-ZHAY) (1896–1980) provided some of the first great insights into how children develop thinking abilities when he proposed that children's cognitive skills progress through a series of maturational stages. Also, many psychologists have become interested in how children learn the intellectual skills valued by their culture. Typically, children do this with guidance from skilled "tutors" (parents and others).

Piaget's Theory of Cognitive Development

Piaget's ideas have deeply affected our view of children (Miller, 2011). According to Piaget (1951, 1952), children's thinking is, generally speaking, less abstract than that of adults. They tend to base their understanding on particular examples and objects they can see or touch. Also, children use fewer generalizations, categories, and principles. Piaget also believed that all children mature through a series of distinct stages in intellectual development. Many of his ideas came from observing his own children as they solved various thought problems. (It is tempting to imagine that Piaget's illustrious career was launched one day when his wife said to him, "Watch the children for a while, will you, Jean?")

Farrell Grehan/ Historical/Corbis

Jean Piaget (1896–1980)—philosopher, psychologist, and keen observer of children.

Mental Processes Piaget was convinced that intellect grows through processes he called assimilation and accommodation. **Assimilation** refers to using existing mental patterns in new situations. Let's say that little Sally is taken for a drive in the country. She sees her first live horse in a field, points, and calls out, "Horse!" She has already seen horses on television and even has a stuffed toy horse. In this case, she adds this new experience to her existing concept of *horse*. Piaget would say it has been *assimilated* to an existing knowledge structure.

In **accommodation**, existing ideas are modified to fit new requirements. For instance, suppose that a month later, Sally goes to the zoo, where she sees her first zebra. Proudly, she again exclaims, "Horse!" This time, her mother replies, "No dear, that's a zebra." Little Sally has *failed to assimilate* the zebra to her horse concept. She must now *accommodate* by creating a new concept, *zebra,* and modifying her concept of horse (*not* black and white stripes).

Sensorimotor Stage (0–2 Years) Look up from this book until your attention is attracted to something else in the room. Now close your eyes. Is the book still there? How do you know? As an adult, you can keep an image of the object in your "mind's eye." According to Piaget, newborns cannot create *internal representations* such as mental images. As a result, they lack **object permanence**, an understanding that objects continue to exist when they are out of sight.

For this reason, in the first two years of life, Joseph's intellectual development will be largely nonintellectual and nonverbal. He will be concerned mainly with learning to coordinate information from his senses with his motor movements. But sometime during their first year, babies begin to actively pursue disappearing objects. By age 2, they can anticipate the movement of an object behind a screen. For example, when watching a toy train, Joseph will look ahead to the end of a tunnel, rather than stare at the spot where the train disappeared.

In general, developments in this stage indicate that the child's conceptions are becoming more *stable*. Objects cease to appear and disappear magically, and a more orderly and predictable world replaces the confusing and disconnected sensations of infancy.

Preoperational Stage (2–7 Years)

Close your eyes again. Imagine the room you sleep in. What would it look like if you were perched on the ceiling and your bed were missing? You have now mentally operated on your image by *transforming* it. According to Piaget, even though preoperational children can form mental images or ideas, they are preoperational because they cannot easily use **transformations** to manipulate those images or ideas in their minds.

Difficulty in using transformations is why although children begin to think *symbolically* and use language before the age of 6 or 7, they still engage in concrete, **intuitive thought**—it makes little use of reasoning and logic. (Do you remember as a child thinking that the sun and the moon followed you when you took a walk?) Such thinking is also often labeled *superstitious*, especially when it persists into later childhood and adulthood (Wargo, 2008).

Let's visit Joseph at age 5: If you show him a short, wide glass full of milk and a taller, narrow glass full of milk, he most likely will tell you that the taller glass contains more milk (even if it doesn't). Joseph will tell you this even if he watches you pour milk from the short glass into an empty taller glass. Older children can easily mentally transform the pouring of the milk by mentally *reversing* it, to see that the shape of the container is irrelevant to the volume of milk it contains. But Joseph is preoperational; he cannot engage in the mental operation of transforming the tall, narrow glass of milk back into a short, wide glass. Thus, he is not bothered by the fact that the milk appears to be transformed from a smaller to a larger amount. Instead, he responds only to the fact that *taller* seems to mean *more* (● **Figure 14.2**).

After about age 7, children are no longer fooled by this situation. Perhaps that's why age 7 has been called the "age of reason." From age 7 on, we see a definite trend toward more logical, adult-like thought.

Tony Freeman/PhotoEdit

● **Figure 14.2**

Children under age 7 intuitively assume that a volume of liquid increases when it is poured from a short, wide container into a taller, thinner one. This boy thinks the tall container holds more than the short one. In reality, each holds the same amount of liquid. Children make such judgments based on the height of the liquid, not its volume.

During the preoperational stage, the child engages in **egocentric thought** and is unable to take the viewpoint of other people. The child's ego seems to stand at the center of his or her world. To illustrate, show a preoperational child a two-sided mirror. Then hold it between you and her, so she can see herself in it. If you ask her what she thinks *you* can see, she imagines that you see *her* face reflected in the mirror, instead

Assimilation *In Piaget's theory, the application of existing mental patterns to new situations (that is, the new situation is assimilated to existing mental schemes).*

Accommodation *In Piaget's theory, the modification of existing mental patterns to fit new demands (that is, mental schemes are changed to accommodate new information or experiences).*

Sensorimotor stage *Stage of intellectual development during which sensory input and motor responses become coordinated.*

Object permanence *Concept, gained in infancy, in which objects continue to exist even when they are hidden from view.*

Preoperational stage *Period of intellectual development during which children begin to use language and think symbolically, yet remain intuitive and egocentric in their thought.*

Transformation *The mental ability to change the shape or form of a substance (such as clay or water) and to perceive that its volume remains the same.*

Intuitive thought *Thinking that makes little or no use of reasoning and logic.*

Egocentric thought *Thought that is self-centered and fails to consider the viewpoints of others.*

of your own. She cannot mentally transform the view she sees into the view you must be seeing.

Such egocentrism explains why children can seem exasperatingly selfish or uncooperative at times. If Sally blocks your view by standing in front of the television, she assumes that you can see it if she can. If you ask her to move so you can see better, she may move so that *she* can see better! Sally is not being selfish in the ordinary sense. She just doesn't realize that your view differs from hers.

Crossing a busy street can be dangerous for the preoperational child. Because their thinking is still egocentric, younger children cannot understand why the driver of a car can't see them if they can see the car. Children under the age of 7 also cannot consistently judge speeds and distances of oncoming cars. Adults can easily overestimate the "street smarts" of younger children. It is advisable to teach children to cross with a light, in crosswalks, or with assistance.

In addition, the child's use of language is not as sophisticated as it might seem. Children have a tendency to confuse words with the objects they represent. If Sally calls a toy block a "car" and you use the block to make a "house," she may be upset. To children, the name of an object is as much a part of the object as its size, shape, and color.

Concrete Operational Stage (7–11 Years)

The hallmark of this stage is the ability to carry out mental operations such as *reversing* thoughts. A 4-year-old boy in the preoperational stage might have a conversation like the following (showing how a child's thinking *lacks* reversibility):

> "Do you have a brother?"
>
> "Yes."
>
> "What's his name?"
>
> "Billy."
>
> "Does Billy have a brother?"
>
> "No."

Reversibility of thought allows children in the concrete operational stage to recognize that if $4 \times 2 = 8$, then 2×4 does, too. Younger children must memorize each relationship separately. Thus, a preoperational child may know that $4 \times 9 = 36$, without being able to tell you what 9×4 equals.

The development of mental operations allows mastery of **conservation** (the concept that mass, weight, and volume remain unchanged when the shape of objects changes). Children have learned conservation when they understand that rolling a ball of clay into a "snake" does not increase the amount of clay. Likewise, pouring liquid from a tall, narrow glass into a shallow dish does not reduce the amount of liquid. In each case, the volume remains the same despite changes in shape or appearance. The original amount is *conserved* (see Figure 14.2).

During the concrete operational stage, children begin to use concepts of time, space, and number. The child can think logically about concrete objects or situations, categories, and principles. Such abilities help explain why children stop believing in Santa Claus when they reach this stage. Because they can *conserve* volume, they realize that Santa's sack couldn't possibly hold enough toys for millions of girls and boys.

Formal Operational Stage (11 Years and Up)

After about the age of 11, children begin to break away from concrete objects and specific examples. Thinking is based more on abstract principles, such as democracy, honor, or correlation. Children who reach this stage become self-reflective about their thoughts, and they become less egocentric. Older children and young adolescents also gradually become able to consider hypothetical possibilities (suppositions, guesses, or projections). For example, if you ask a younger child, "What do you think would happen if it suddenly became possible for people to fly?" the child might respond, "People can't fly." Older children are better able to consider such possibilities.

Full adult intellectual ability is attained during the stage of formal operations. Older adolescents are capable of inductive and deductive reasoning, and they can comprehend math, physics, philosophy, psychology, and other abstract systems. They can learn to test hypotheses in a scientific manner. Of course, not everyone reaches this level of thinking. Also, many adults can think formally about some topics, but their thinking becomes concrete when the topic is unfamiliar. This implies that formal thinking may be more a result of culture and learning than maturation. In any case, after late adolescence, improvements in intellect are based on gaining specific knowledge, experience, and wisdom, rather than on any leaps in basic thinking capacity.

How can parents apply Piaget's ideas? Piaget's theory suggests that the ideal way to guide intellectual development is to provide experiences that are only slightly novel, unusual, or challenging. Remember, a child's intellect develops mainly through accommodation. It is usually best to follow a *one-step-ahead strategy,* in which your teaching efforts are aimed just beyond a child's current level of comprehension (Brainerd, 2003).

Parents should avoid *forced teaching,* or "hothousing," which is like trying to force plants to bloom prematurely. Forcing children to learn reading, math, gymnastics, swimming, or music at an accelerated pace can bore or oppress them. True intellectual enrichment respects the child's interests. It does not make the child feel pressured to perform.

Piaget Today

Today, Piaget's theory remains a valuable road map for understanding how children think. On a broad scale, many of Piaget's ideas have held up well. However, there has been disagreement about specific details. For example, according to learning theorists, children continuously gain specific knowledge; they do not undergo stage-like leaps in general mental ability (Miller, 2011; Siegler, 2005). On the other hand, the growth in connections between brain cells occurs in waves that parallel some of Piaget's stages (see ● **Figure 14.3**). Thus, the truth may lie somewhere between Piaget's stage theory and modern learning theory.

In addition, it is now widely accepted that children develop cognitive skills somewhat earlier than Piaget originally thought (Bjorklund, 2012). For example, Piaget believed that

"Young man, go to your room and stay there until your cerebral cortex matures."

infants under the age of 1 year cannot think (use internal representations). Such abilities, he believed, emerge only after a long period of sensorimotor development. Babies, he said, have no memory of people and objects that are out of sight. Yet, we now know that infants begin forming representations of the world very early in life. For example, babies as young as 3 months of age appear to know that objects are solid and do not disappear when out of view (Baillargeon, 2004).

Why did Piaget fail to detect the thinking skills of infants? Most likely, he mistook babies' limited *physical* skills for *mental* incompetence. Piaget's tests required babies to search for objects or reach out and touch them. Newer, more sensitive methods are uncovering abilities Piaget missed. One such method takes advantage of the fact that babies, like adults, act surprised when they see something "impossible" or unexpected occur. To use this effect, psychologist Renee Baillargeon (1991, 2004) puts on little "magic shows" for infants. In her "theater," babies watch as possible and impossible events occur with toys or other objects. Some 3-month-old infants act surprised and gaze longer at impossible events, for example, seeing two solid objects appear to pass through each other. By the time they

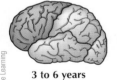 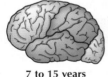 

3 to 6 years **7 to 15 years** **16 to 20 years**

Growth Pruning

© Cengage Learning

● **Figure 14.3**

Between the ages of 3 and 6, a tremendous wave of growth occurs in connections among neurons in the frontal areas of the brain. This corresponds to the time when children make rapid progress in their ability to think symbolically. Between the ages of 7 and 15, peak synaptic growth shifts to the temporal and parietal lobes. During this period, children become increasingly adept at using language, a specialty of the temporal lobes. In the late teens, the brain actively destroys unneeded connections, especially in the frontal lobes. This pruning of synapses sharpens the brain's capacity for abstract thinking (Restak, 2001).

Concrete operational stage *Period of intellectual development during which children become able to use the concepts of time, space, volume, and number but in ways that remain simplified and concrete, rather than abstract.*
Conservation *In Piaget's theory, mastery of the concept that the weight, mass, and volume of matter remain unchanged (are conserved) even when the shape or appearance of objects changes.*
Formal operational stage *Period of intellectual development characterized by thinking that includes abstract, theoretical, and hypothetical ideas.*

Before   After

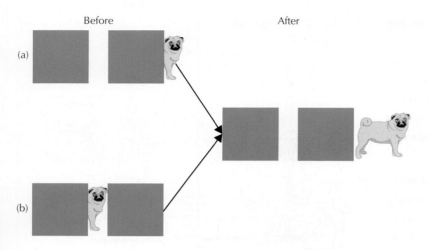

Figure 14.4

An infant watches as a toy is placed behind the right of two screens (*a*). After a delay of 70 seconds, a possible event occurs as the toy is brought back into view from behind the right screen. Alternately, the infant watches as the toy is placed behind the left of two screens (*b*). Now an impossible event occurs as the toy is again retrieved from behind the right screen. (A duplicate toy was hidden there before testing.) Eight-month-old infants react with surprise when they see the impossible event staged for them. Their reaction implies that they remember where the toy was hidden. Infants appear to have a capacity for memory and thinking that greatly exceeds what Piaget claimed is possible during the sensorimotor period. (Adapted from Baillargeon, De Vos, & Graber, 1989.)

are 8 months old, babies can remember where objects are (or should be) for at least one minute (● **Figure 14.4**).

Similarly, Piaget thought that children remain egocentric during the preoperational stage and become aware of perspectives other than their own only at age 7. Researchers have since begun to refer to this development as **theory of mind**, the understanding that people have mental states, such as thoughts, beliefs, and intentions, and that other people's mental states can be different from one's own. Psychologists currently believe that children as young as age 4 can understand that other people's mental states differ from their own (Doherty, 2009). (To read more about this fascinating development, see "Theory of Mind: I'm a Me! . . . and You're a You!")

Another criticism of Piaget is that he underestimated the impact of culture on mental development. The next section tells how Joseph will master the intellectual tools his culture values.

Critical Thinking

Theory of Mind: I'm a *Me*! . . . and You're a *You*!

A major step in human development is becoming aware of oneself as a person. When you look in a mirror, you recognize the image staring back as your own—except, perhaps, early on Monday mornings. Like many such events, initial self-awareness depends on maturation of the nervous system. In a typical test of self-recognition, infants are shown images of themselves on a television. Most infants are 18 months old before they recognize themselves (Nielsen & Dissanayake, 2004).

But just because a 2-year-old knows he is a *me* doesn't mean he knows you are a *you* (Samson & Apperly, 2010). At age 3, Eric once put his hands over his eyes and exclaimed to his friend, Laurence, "You can't see me now!" He knew he had a point of view but did not know his friend's point of view could be different from his own. Earlier, we saw that Piaget used the term *egocentrism* to refer to this endearing feature of young children and proposed that young children remain egocentric until they enter the concrete operational stage at about age 7. More recent evidence suggests that children become less egocentric beginning at about age 4 (Doherty, 2009). As noted earlier, this developing capacity is called *theory of mind* (Gopnik, 2009).

One way to assess whether a child understands that other people have their own mental states is the false-belief (or Sally-Anne) task. A child is shown two dolls, Sally and Anne. Sally has a basket and Anne has a box. Sally puts a coin in her basket and goes out to play. In the meantime, Anne takes the coin from Sally's basket and puts it into her box. Sally comes back and looks for the coin. To assess theory of mind, the child is asked where Sally will look for her coin. Although the child knows the coin is in Anne's box, the correct answer is that Sally will look in her basket. To answer correctly, the child must understand that Sally's point of view did not include what the child saw.

Theory of mind develops over time. It takes further development to appreciate that other people may lie, be sarcastic, make jokes, or use figures of speech. Some adults are not good at this. In fact, the available evidence suggests that children with autism spectrum disorders are particularly poor at this task (O'Hare et al., 2009).

A sense of self, or self-awareness, develops at about age 18 months. Before children develop self-awareness, they do not recognize their own image in a mirror. Typically, they think they are looking at another child. Some children hug the child in the mirror or go behind it looking for the child they see there (Lewis, 1995).

Ursula Markus/Science Source

Vygotsky's Sociocultural Theory

While Piaget stressed the role of maturation in cognitive development, Russian scholar Lev Vygotsky (1896–1934) focused on the impact of sociocultural factors. Many psychologists are convinced that Piaget gave too little credit to the effects of the learning environment. For example, children who grow up in villages where pottery is made can correctly answer questions about the conservation of clay at an earlier age than Piaget would have predicted. Vygotsky's (1962, 1978) key insight is that children's thinking develops through dialogues with more-capable persons.

How does that relate to intellectual growth? So far, no one has published *A Child's Guide to Life on Earth*. Instead, children must learn about life from various "tutors," such as parents, teachers, and older siblings. Even if *A Child's Guide to Life on Earth* did exist, we would need a separate version for every culture. It is not enough for children to learn how to think. They also must learn specific intellectual skills valued by their culture.

Like Piaget, Vygotsky believed that children actively seek to discover new principles. However, Vygotsky emphasized that many of a child's most important "discoveries" are guided by skillful tutors. Psychologists Jay Shaffer and Katherine Kipp (2014) offer the following example:

Tanya, a 4-year-old, has just received her first jigsaw puzzle as a birthday present. She attempts to work the puzzle but gets nowhere until her father comes along, sits down beside her, and gives her some tips. He suggests that it would be a good idea to put together the corners first, points to the pink area at the edge of one corner piece, and says, "Let's look for another pink piece." When Tanya seems frustrated, he places two interlocking pieces near each other so that she will notice them, and when Tanya succeeds, he offers words of encouragement. As Tanya gradually gets the hang of it, he steps back and lets her work more and more independently (p. 233).

Interactions like this are most helpful when they take place within a child's **zone of proximal development**.

What did Vygotsky mean by that? The word *proximal* means close or nearby. Vygotsky realized that, at any given time, some tasks are just beyond a child's reach. The child is close to having the mental skills needed to do the task, but it is a little too complex to be mastered alone. However, children working within this zone can make rapid progress if they receive sensitive guidance from a skilled partner (Morrissey & Brown,

2009). (Notice that this is similar to the one-step-ahead strategy described earlier.)

Vygotsky also emphasized a process he called **scaffolding**. A scaffold is a framework or temporary support. Vygotsky believed that adults help children learn how to think by "scaffolding," or supporting, their attempts to solve problems or discover principles (Daniels, 2005). To be most effective, scaffolding must be responsive to a child's needs. For example, as Tanya's father helped her with the puzzle, he tailored his hints and guidance to match her evolving abilities. The two of them worked together, step by step, so that Tanya could better understand how to assemble a puzzle. In a sense, Tanya's father set up a series of temporary bridges that helped her move into new mental territory. As predicted by Vygotsky's theory, the reading skills of 8- to 10-year-old children are closely related to the amount of verbal scaffolding their mothers provided at ages 3 and 4 (Dieterich et al., 2006).

During their collaborations with others, children learn important cultural beliefs and values. For example, imagine that a boy wants to know how many baseball cards he has. His mother helps him stack and count the cards, moving each card to a new stack as they count it. She then shows him how to write the number on a slip of paper so he can remember it. This teaches the child not only about counting but also that writing is valued in our culture. In other parts of the world, a child learning to count might be shown how to make notches on a stick or tie knots in a cord.

Implications Vygotsky saw that grown-ups play a crucial role in what children know. As they try to decipher the world, children rely on adults to help them understand how things work. Vygotsky further noticed that adults unconsciously adjust their behavior to give children the information they need to solve problems that interest the child. In this way, children use adults to learn about their culture and society (Gredler & Shields, 2008; Morrissey & Brown, 2009).

Theory of mind *The understanding that people have mental states, such as thoughts, beliefs, and intentions and that other people's mental states can be different from one's own.*

Zone of proximal development *Refers to the range of tasks a child cannot yet master alone but that she or he can accomplish with the guidance of a more capable partner.*

Scaffolding *The process of adjusting instruction so that it is responsive to a beginner's behavior and supports the beginner's efforts to understand a problem or gain a mental skill.*

Module 14: Summary

14.1 How do children acquire language?

- **14.1.1** Language development proceeds from crying to cooing, then babbling, to the use of single words, and then to telegraphic speech.
- **14.1.2** The underlying patterns of telegraphic speech suggest a biological predisposition to acquire language. This innate tendency is augmented by learning.
- **14.1.3** Prelanguage communication between parent and child involves shared rhythms, nonverbal signals, and turn-taking.
- **14.1.4** Motherese or parentese is a simplified, musical style of speaking that parents use to help their children learn language.

14.2 How do children learn to think?

- **14.2.1** Neonates begin to learn immediately and appear to be aware of the effects of their actions.
- **14.2.2** A child's intellect is less abstract than that of an adult. Jean Piaget theorized that intellectual growth occurs through a combination of assimilation and accommodation.

- **14.2.3** Piaget also held that children go through a fixed series of cognitive stages. The stages and their approximate age ranges are sensorimotor (0–2), preoperational (2–7), concrete operational (7–11), and formal operations (11–adult).
- **14.2.4** Caregivers should offer learning opportunities that are appropriate for a child's level of cognitive development.
- **14.2.5** Learning principles provide an alternate explanation that assumes that cognitive development is continuous; it does not occur in stages.
- **14.2.6** Studies of infants under the age of 1 year suggest that they are capable of thought well beyond that observed by Piaget. Similarly, children begin to outgrow egocentrism as early as age 4.
- **14.2.7** Lev Vygotsky's sociocultural theory emphasizes that a child's mental abilities are advanced by interactions with more-competent partners. Mental growth takes place in a child's zone of proximal development, where a more skillful person may scaffold the child's progress.

Module 14: Knowledge Builder

1. Simple two-word sentences are characteristic of _____ speech.

2. Noam _____ advanced the idea that language acquisition is built on innate patterns.

3. Pre-language turn-taking and social interactions are of special interest to a psycholinguist. *T or F?*

Recite

Match each item with one of the following stages.

- **a.** Sensorimotor
- **b.** Preoperational
- **c.** Concrete operational
- **d.** Formal operations

4. _____ egocentric thought
5. _____ abstract or hypothetical
6. _____ purposeful movement
7. _____ intuitive thought
8. _____ conservation
9. _____ reversibility thought
10. _____ object permanence
11. _____ nonverbal development
12. Vygotsky called the process of providing a temporary framework of supports for learning new mental abilities _____.

Reflect
Think Critically

13. In Western cultures, children as young as age 4 can understand that other people have mental states that differ from their own. In other words, they have developed a *theory of mind*. Is this ability uniquely Western, or might children from other cultures also develop a theory of mind?

Self Reflect

See if you can name and imitate the language abilities you had as you progressed from birth to age 2 years in order of occurrence.

You are going to make cookies with children of various ages. See if you can name each of Piaget's stages and give an example of what a child in that stage might be expected to do.

You have been asked to help a child learn to use a calculator to do simple addition. How would you identify the child's zone of proximal development for this task? How would you scaffold the child's learning?

ANSWERS

1. telegraphic 2. Chomsky 3. T 4. B 5. D 6. A 7. B 8. C 9. C 10. A 11. A 12. scaffolding 13. All humans need to be able to base their actions on their understanding of the intentions, desires, and beliefs of others. For example, children from Micronesia, a group of small islands in the Pacific Ocean, also develop a theory of mind at around 4 years of age (Oberle, 2009).

Human Development: Adolescence and Adulthood

Never a Grownup

One common misconception of the idea of human development is that it ends in childhood or early adolescence. At that point, you have finished growing; you are a "grownup." While our individual development might be more obvious when we are young, it is, in reality, never really over until the end of our lives. Personality theorist Erik Erikson's (1903–1994) psychosocial theory provides a good overview of the major psychological stages of development that occur during a "typical" life.

Adolescence and young adulthood is a time of exuberance and youthful searching. It also can also be a time of worry and problems. During adolescence, a person's identity and moral values come into sharper focus even as the transition to adulthood is occurring at ever-later ages. In later adulthood, we all face many additional challenges, including physical aging. Regardless, it is possible to age successfully. We also must face our own inevitable death.

arekmalang/iStockphoto.com

Let's trace Erikson's stages with a focus on adolescence and adulthood.

SURVEY QUESTIONS

15.1 What are the typical tasks and dilemmas through the lifespan?

15.2 Why is the transition from adolescence to adulthood especially challenging?

15.3 How do we develop morals and values?

15.4 What is involved in well-being during middle and later adulthood?

15.5 How do people typically react to death?

The Story of a Lifetime— Rocky Road or Garden Path?

SURVEY QUESTION 15.1: What are the typical tasks and dilemmas through the life span?

Every life is marked by a number of *developmental milestones* (Kail & Cavanaugh, 2013). These are notable events, markers, or turning points in personal development. Some examples include being born, learning to speak, going to school, graduating from school, voting for the first time, getting married, watching a child leave home (or move back!), burying a parent, becoming a grandparent, retiring, and, in the end, dying. Thus far, we have traced progress through the first few years of life. What are some of the challenges we must face during adolescence and adulthood?

Erikson's Psychosocial Theory

Perhaps the best way to get a preview of a life is to consider some of the major psychological milestones and challenges we are likely to encounter. Broad similarities between people can be found in the life stages of infancy, childhood, adolescence, young adulthood, middle adulthood, and old age.

Personality theorist Erik Erikson (1903–1994) is best known for his life-stage theory of human development.

Each developmental stage confronts a person with new **developmental tasks**, specific challenges that must be mastered for optimal development. Examples are learning to read in childhood, adjusting to sexual maturity in adolescence, and establishing a vocation as an adult.

In a highly influential book entitled *Childhood and Society*, Erik Erikson suggests that we face a specific *psychosocial dilemma*, or "crisis," at each stage of life. A **psychosocial dilemma** is a conflict between personal impulses and the social world. Resolving each dilemma creates a new balance between a person and society. A string of "successes" produces healthy development and a satisfying life. Unfavorable outcomes throw us off balance, making it harder to deal with later crises. Life becomes a "rocky road," and personal growth is stunted. ● Table 15.1 lists Erikson's (1963) dilemmas.

TABLE 15.1	Erikson's Psychosocial Dilemmas
Age	**Characteristic Dilemma**
Birth to 1 year	Trust versus mistrust
1 to 3 years	Autonomy versus shame and doubt
3 to 5 years	Initiative versus guilt
6 to 12 years	Industry versus inferiority
Adolescence	Identity versus role confusion
Young adulthood	Intimacy versus isolation
Middle adulthood	Generativity versus stagnation
Late adulthood	Integrity versus despair

© Cengage Learning

What are the major developmental tasks and life crises? A brief description of each psychosocial dilemma follows.

Stage One, First Year of Life During the first year of life, children are completely dependent on others. Erikson believes that a basic attitude of **trust or mistrust** is formed at this time. *Trust* is established when babies are given warmth, touching, love, and physical care. *Mistrust* is caused by inadequate or unpredictable care and by parents who are cold, indifferent, or rejecting. Basic mistrust may later cause insecurity, suspiciousness, or an inability to relate to others. Notice that trust comes from the same conditions that help babies become securely attached to their parents.

Stage Two, 1–3 Years In stage two, children develop **autonomy or shame and doubt**, as they express their growing self-control by climbing, touching, exploring, and trying to do things for themselves. Jay and Gloria fostered baby Joseph's *autonomy* by encouraging him to try new skills. However, his first efforts were sometimes crude, involving spilling, falling, wetting, and other "accidents." If Jay and Gloria had ridiculed or overprotected Joseph, they might have caused him to feel *shameful* about his actions and *doubt* his abilities.

Stage Three, 3–5 Years In stage three, children move beyond simple self-control to develop **initiative or guilt**. Through play, children learn to make plans and carry out tasks. Parents reinforce *initiative* by giving children freedom to play, ask questions, use imagination, and choose activities. Feelings of *guilt* about initiating activities are formed if parents criticize severely, prevent play, or discourage a child's questions.

Stage Four, 6–12 Years Many events of middle childhood are symbolized by that fateful day when you first entered school. With dizzying speed, your world expanded beyond your family, and you faced a whole series of new challenges.

The elementary school years are a child's "entrance into life." In school, children begin to learn skills valued by society, and success or failure can affect a child's feelings of **industry or inferiority**. Children learn a sense of *industry* if they win praise for productive activities, such as building, painting, cooking, reading, and studying. If a child's efforts are regarded as messy, childish, or inadequate, feelings of *inferiority* result. For the first time, teachers, classmates, and adults outside the home become as important as parents in shaping attitudes toward oneself.

Stage Five, Adolescence As we have noted, adolescence is often a turbulent time, when adolescents develop **identity or role confusion**. Erikson considers a need to answer the question "Who am I?" the primary task during this stage of life. As Joseph matures mentally and physically, he will have new feelings, a new body, and new attitudes. Like other adolescents, he will need to build a consistent *identity* out of his talents, values, life history, relationships, and the demands of his culture (Côté, 2006). His conflicting experiences as a student, friend, athlete, worker, son, lover, and so forth must be integrated into a unified sense of self. Persons who fail to develop a sense of identity suffer from *role confusion*, an uncertainty about who they are and where they are going.

Stage Six, Young Adulthood In stage six, the individual is faced with developing **intimacy or isolation** in his or her life. After establishing a stable identity, a person is prepared to share meaningful love or deep friendship with others (Beyers & Seiffge-Krenke, 2010). By *intimacy*, Erikson means an ability to care about others and to share experiences with them. And yet, marriage or sexual involvement is no guarantee of intimacy: Many adult relationships remain shallow and unfulfilling. Failure to establish intimacy with others leads to a deep sense of *isolation*—feeling alone and uncared for in life. This often sets the stage for later difficulties.

Stage Seven, Middle Adulthood According to Erikson, an interest in guiding the next generation results in **generativity or stagnation**. Erikson called this quality *generativity*. Emotional balance in middle adulthood is expressed by caring about oneself, one's children, and future generations.

Joseph may achieve generativity by guiding his own children or by helping other children, as a teacher or coach, for example (Hebblethwaite & Norris, 2011). Productive or creative work also can express generativity. In any case, a person must broaden his or his concerns and energies to include the welfare of others and society as a whole. Failure to do this is marked by a feeling of *stagnation*—concern with one's own needs and comforts. Life loses meaning, and the person feels bitter, dreary, and trapped (Friedman, 2004).

Stage Eight, Late Adulthood *What does Erikson see as the conflicts of old age?* Late adulthood is a time of reflection, leading to **integrity or despair**. According to Erikson, when Joseph grows old, it would be better if he were able to look back over his life with acceptance and satisfaction. People who have lived richly and responsibly develop a sense of *integrity*, or self-respect. This allows them to face aging and death with dignity. If previous life events are viewed with regret, the elderly person experiences *despair*, or heartache and remorse. In this case, life seems like a series of missed opportunities. The person feels like a failure, knowing it's too late to reverse what has been done. Aging and the threat of death then become sources of fear and depression.

The Whole Human To squeeze a lifetime into a few pages, we had to ignore countless details. Although much is lost, the result is a clearer picture of an entire life cycle. Is Erikson's description, then, an exact map of anyone's unique past and future?

According to Erikson, an interest in future generations characterizes optimal adult development.

Developmental tasks *Skills that must be mastered, or personal changes that must take place, for optimal development.*
Psychosocial dilemma *A conflict between personal impulses and the social world.*
Trust versus mistrust *A conflict early in life about learning to trust others and the world.*
Autonomy versus shame and doubt *A conflict created when growing self-control (autonomy) is pitted against feelings of shame or doubt.*
Initiative versus guilt *A conflict between learning to take initiative and overcoming feelings of guilt about doing so.*
Industry versus inferiority *A conflict in middle childhood centered around lack of support for industrious behavior, which can result in feelings of inferiority.*
Identity versus role confusion *A conflict of adolescence, involving the need to establish a personal identity.*
Intimacy versus isolation *The challenge of overcoming a sense of isolation by establishing intimacy with others.*
Generativity versus stagnation *A conflict of middle adulthood in which self-interest is countered by an interest in guiding the next generation.*
Integrity versus despair *A conflict in old age between feelings of integrity and the despair of viewing previous life events with regret.*

Probably not. Still, psychosocial dilemmas are major events in many lives. Knowing about them may allow you to anticipate typical trouble spots in your own life. You also may be better prepared to understand the problems and feelings of friends and relatives at various points in the life cycle.

Adolescence and Young Adulthood—The Best of Times, the Worst of Times

SURVEY QUESTION 15.2: Why is the transition from adolescence to adulthood especially challenging?

Adolescence is the culturally defined period between childhood and adulthood (Bjorklund & Hernández Blasi, 2012). Socially, the adolescent is no longer a child, yet not quite an adult. Almost all cultures recognize this transitional status. However, the length of adolescence varies greatly from culture to culture. For example, most 14-year-old girls in North America live at home and go to school. In contrast, many 14-year-old females in rural villages of many less developed countries are married and have children. In our culture, 14-year-olds are adolescents. In others, they may be adults.

Is marriage the primary criterion for adult status in North America? No, it's not even one of the top three criteria. Today, the most widely accepted standards are (1) taking responsibility for oneself, (2) making independent decisions, and (3) becoming financially independent. In practice, this typically means breaking away from parents by getting a job and setting up a separate residence (Arnett, 2010).

Puberty

Many people confuse adolescence with puberty. However, puberty is a *biological* event, not a social status. During **puberty**, hormonal changes promote rapid physical growth and sexual maturity. Biologically, most people reach reproductive maturity in the early teens. Social and intellectual maturity, however, may lie years ahead. Young adolescents often make decisions that affect their entire lives, even though they are immature mentally and socially. The tragically high rates of teenage pregnancy and drug abuse are prime examples. Despite such risks, most people manage to weather

adolescence without developing any serious psychological problems (Rathus, 2011).

How much difference does the timing of puberty make? For boys, maturing early is generally beneficial. Typically, it enhances their self-image and gives them an advantage socially and athletically. Early-maturing boys tend to be more relaxed, dominant, self-assured, and popular. However, early puberty carries some risks because early-maturing boys also are more likely to get into trouble with drugs, sex, alcohol, and antisocial behavior (Steinberg, 2001).

For girls, the advantages of early maturation are less clear-cut. In elementary school, fast-maturing girls are *less* popular and have poorer self-images, perhaps because they are larger and heavier than their classmates (Deardorff et al., 2007). This is a growing problem as more American girls are reaching puberty at earlier ages (Biro et al., 2010). By junior high, however, early development includes sexual features. This leads to a more positive body image, *greater* peer prestige, and adult approval. Early-maturing girls tend to date sooner and are more independent and more active in school. However, like their male counterparts, they also are more often in trouble at school and more likely to engage in early sex (Negriff & Trickett, 2010).

As you can see, costs and benefits are associated with early puberty. One added cost of early maturation is that it may force premature identity formation. When Joseph is a teenager and he begins to look like an adult, he may be treated like an adult. Ideally, this change can encourage greater maturity and independence. However, if the search for identity ends too soon, it may leave Joseph with a distorted, poorly formed sense of self.

The Search for Identity

Identity formation is a key challenge faced by adolescents (Schwartz, 2008). Of course, problems of identity occur at other times, too. But in a very real sense, puberty signals that it's time to begin forming a new, more mature self-image (Rathus, 2011). Many problems stem from unclear standards about the role adolescents should play within society. Are they adults or children? Should they be autonomous or dependent? Should they work or play? Such ambiguities make it difficult for young people to form clear images of themselves and how they should act.

Answering the question "Who am I?" also is spurred by cognitive development. After adolescents have attained the

Human Diversity

Ethnic Diversity and Identity

Ethnic heritage is an important aspect of personal identity (Weisskirch, 2005). For adolescents of ethnic descent, the question often is not just "Who am I?" Rather, it is "Who am I at home? Who am I at school? Who am I with friends in my neighborhood?"

As ethnic minorities in America continue to grow in status and prominence, adolescents are less and less likely to feel rejected or excluded because of their ethnic heritage as they try to find their place in society. This is fortunate because ethnic adolescents have often faced degrading stereotypes concerning their intelligence, sexuality, social status, manners, and so forth. The result can be lowered self-esteem and confusion about roles, values, and personal identity (Charmaraman & Grossman, 2010). At the same time, the increasingly multicultural nature of contemporary American society raises new questions for adolescents about what it means to be American (Schwartz, 2008).

In forming an identity, adolescents of ethnic descent face the question of how they should think of themselves. Is Lori an American or a Chinese American or both? Is Jaime a Latino, a Chicano, or a Mexican American? The answer typically depends on how strongly adolescents identify with their family and ethnic community. Teens who take pride in their ethnic heritage have higher self-esteem, a better self-image, and a stronger sense of personal identity (Galliher, Jones, & Dahl, 2011; Roberts et al., 1999). They also are less likely to engage in drug use (Marsiglia et al., 2004) or violent behavior (French, Kim, & Pillado, 2006).

Group pride, positive models, and a more tolerant society could do much to keep a broad range of options open to *all* adolescents.

stage of formal operations, they are better able to ask questions about their place in the world and about morals, values, politics, and social relationships. Then, too, being able to think about hypothetical possibilities allows the adolescent to contemplate the future and ask more realistically, "Who will I be?" (Côté, 2006; see "Ethnic Diversity and Identity").

Emerging Adulthood

Have you ever met someone who is well into his or her twenties, still living at home, not yet married, with no children, and no settled career (could we talking about you)? Today, the challenge of identity formation is further complicated by the fact that more and more young people are deferring young adulthood, preferring to prolong identity explorations into their twenties before they commit to long-term choices in love and work. Western industrialized societies, like the United States and Canada, have become increasingly tolerant of **emerging adulthood**, a socially accepted period of extended adolescence (Arnett, 2010).

Are such people still adolescents who are taking longer to find their identity? Or are they self-indulgent adults trapped in a "maturity gap" (Galambos, Barker, & Tilton-Weaver, 2003)? Either way, emerging adulthood is an unstable, in-between, self-focused period of time to explore identities and life possibilities (Arnett, 2004).

According to psychologist Jeffrey Arnett, emerging adulthood is now becoming increasingly common in affluent Westernized cultures around the world (Arnett, 2011). However, in less affluent countries, as in poorer parts of every country, including America, most adolescents continue to "become adults" at much younger ages (Arnett & Galambos, 2003). Thus, words like *adolescent* or *adulthood* cannot be defined solely in terms of physical maturation. Sociocultural factors also play a role in defining when we stop being children or become adults (Arnett, 2010).

Joseph may live with Gloria and Jay until his mid-twenties, delaying his transition to adulthood. Alternatively, he may make the transition to young adulthood during the traditional 18- to 21-year-old period. Regardless, he will eventually face the primary adult issues of marriage, children, and career. How he manages, especially in his core relationships, will determine whether he feels a sense of intimacy or feels isolated from others.

In many ways, adolescence and young adulthood are more emotionally turbulent than midlife or old age. One important aspect of this period is the struggle with right and wrong—the need to develop moral values.

Adolescence *The culturally defined period between childhood and adulthood.*
Puberty *The biologically defined period during which a person matures sexually and becomes capable of reproduction.*
Emerging adulthood *A socially accepted period of extended adolescence now quite common in Western and Westernized societies.*

Moral Development— Growing a Conscience

SURVEY QUESTION 15.3: How do we develop morals and values?

A person with a terminal illness is in great pain. She is pleading for death. Should extraordinary medical efforts be made to keep her alive? A friend of yours desperately needs to pass a test and asks you to help him cheat. Will you do it? These are *moral* questions, or questions of conscience.

Moral development starts in childhood and continues into adulthood (Nucci & Gingo, 2011). Through this process, we acquire values, beliefs, and thinking patterns that guide responsible behavior (King, 2009). Moral values are especially likely to come into sharper focus during adolescence and the transition to adulthood as capacities for self-control and abstract thinking increase (Hart & Carlo, 2005). Let's take a brief look at this intriguing aspect of personal development.

Levels of Moral Development

How are moral values acquired? In an influential account, psychologist Lawrence Kohlberg (1981) held that we learn moral values through thinking and reasoning. To study moral development, Kohlberg posed dilemmas to children of different ages. The following is one moral dilemma he used (Adapted from Kohlberg, 1969):

> A woman was near death from cancer, and there was only one drug that might save her. The druggist who discovered it was charging 10 times what it cost to make the drug. The sick woman's husband could pay only $1,000, but the druggist wanted $2,000. He asked the druggist to sell it cheaper or to let him pay later. The druggist said no. So the husband became desperate and broke into the store and stole the drug for his wife. Should he have done that? Was it wrong or right? Why?

Each child was asked what action the husband should take. Kohlberg classified the reasons given for each choice and identified three levels of moral development. Each is based not so much on the choices made, but on the reasoning used to arrive at a choice.

At the lowest, **preconventional moral reasoning** level, moral thinking is guided by the consequences of actions (punishment, reward, or an exchange of favors). For example, a person at this level might reason: "The man shouldn't steal the drug because he could get caught and sent to jail" (avoiding punishment); or "It won't do him any good to steal the drug because his wife will probably die before he gets out of jail" (self-interest).

At the second, **conventional moral reasoning**, level, thinking is based on a desire to please others or to follow accepted authority, rules, and values. For example, a person at this intermediate level might say, "He shouldn't steal the drug because others will think he is a thief. His wife would not want to be saved by thievery" (avoiding disapproval) or "Although his wife needs the drug, he should not break the law to get it. Everyone has to obey the law. His wife's condition does not justify stealing" (traditional morality of authority).

At the highest, **postconventional moral reasoning** level, moral behavior is directed by self-chosen ethical principles that tend to be general, comprehensive, or universal. People at this level place high value on justice, dignity, and equality. For example, a highly principled person might say, "He should steal the drug and then inform the authorities that he has done so. He will have to face a penalty, but he will have saved a human life" (self-chosen ethical principles).

Does everyone eventually reach the highest level? People advance at different rates, and many fail to reach the postconventional level of moral reasoning. In fact, some may not even reach the conventional level. For instance, a significant number of men in their first year of college think unwanted sexual aggression is acceptable (Tatum & Foubert, 2009).

The preconventional level is most characteristic of young children and delinquents (Forney, Forney, & Crutsinger, 2005). Conventional, group-oriented morals are typical of older children and most adults. Kohlberg estimated that only about 20 percent of the adult population achieves postconventional morality, representing self-direction and higher principles. (It would appear that few of these people enter politics!)

Developing a "moral compass" is an important part of growing up. Many of the choices we make every day involve fundamental questions of right and wrong. The ability to think clearly about such questions is essential to becoming a responsible adult.

Justice or Caring? Carol Gilligan (1982) pointed out that Kohlberg's system is concerned mainly with *justice*. Based on studies of women who faced real-life dilemmas, Gilligan argued that there also is an ethic of *caring* about others. As one illustration, Gilligan presented the following story to 11- to 15-year-old American children.

The Porcupine and the Moles

Seeking refuge from the cold, a porcupine asked to share a cave for the winter with a family of moles. The moles agreed. But because the cave was small, they soon found they were being scratched each time the porcupine moved about. Finally, they asked the porcupine to leave. But the porcupine refused, saying, "If you moles are not satisfied, I suggest that you leave."

Boys who read this story tended to opt for justice in resolving the dilemma: "It's the moles' house. It's a deal. The porcupine leaves." In contrast, girls tended to look for solutions that would keep all parties happy and comfortable, such as "Cover the porcupine with a blanket."

Gilligan's point is that male psychologists have, for the most part, defined moral maturity in terms of justice and autonomy. From this perspective, a woman's concern with relationships can look like a weakness rather than a strength. (A woman who is concerned about what pleases or helps others would be placed at the conventional level in Kohlberg's system.) But Gilligan believes that caring also is a major element of moral development, and she suggests that males may lag in achieving it (Botes, 2000; Lambert et al., 2009).

Several studies have found little or no difference in men's and women's overall moral reasoning abilities (Glover, 2001). Indeed, both men and women may use caring *and* justice to make moral decisions. The moral yardstick they use appears to depend on the situation they face (Wark & Krebs, 1996). Just the same, Gilligan deserves credit for identifying a second major way moral choices are made. It can be argued that our best moral choices combine justice and caring, reason and emotion—which may be what we mean by wisdom (Pasupathi & Staudinger, 2001).

Middle and Late Adulthood: You're an Adult Now!

SURVEY QUESTION 15.4: What is involved in well-being during middle and later adulthood?

Although Erikson's dilemmas extend into adulthood, they are not the only challenges adults face, as we discuss in this section.

Other Challenges of Adulthood

Middle-aged adults (those from about ages 35 to 64) and *later adults* (those age 65 and older) face life challenges such as financial pressures, legal conflicts, and personal tragedies, to name but a few. However, most challenges of adulthood revolve around health, careers, marriage, children, and parents (Damman, Henkens, & Kalmijn, 2011).

Health Joseph's father, Jay, just came back from his physiotherapy appointment. He put his knee out in a game of touch football (he swears the other guy did more than just "touch" him!). A high school football star, 40-year old Jay has encountered the obvious: he is getting older. Although some adults face far more serious health issues, from heart attacks to cancer, every adult faces the routine wear and tear of aging. How one deals with the inevitable slow declines during adulthood strongly influences that adult's degree of life satisfaction (Lachman, 2004). Fortunately, most of the time, declines happen slowly enough that they can be offset by increased life experience. Most adults learn to work "smarter," both physically and mentally (Santrock, 2012).

Careers The work adults do—as homemakers, volunteers, hourly workers, or in careers—also is critical to feeling successful (Sterns & Huyck, 2001). While peak earnings commonly occur during these years, growing expenses may continue to create financial pressures, from child care to tuition fees for children and from rent to mortgages. This is one reason career difficulties and unemployment can pose such serious challenges to adult well-being. Another reason, of course, is that many adults derive much of their identity from their work (Santrock, 2012).

Marriage, Children, and Parents Most adult Americans identify their social relationships—especially with children, spouses, and parents—as another important aspect of adult life (Markus et al., 2004). Creating and sustaining social

Moral development *The development of values, beliefs, and thinking abilities that act as a guide regarding what is acceptable behavior.*
Preconventional moral reasoning *Moral thinking based on the consequences of one's choices or actions (punishment, reward, or an exchange of favors).*
Conventional moral reasoning *Moral thinking based on a desire to please others or to follow accepted rules and values.*
Postconventional moral reasoning *Moral thinking based on carefully examined and self-chosen moral principles.*

relationships can involve working through the stresses of child-rearing, becoming "empty nesters" when children move away, becoming grandparents, experiencing marital strife or divorce, living as singles or in blended families, seeing parents grow old, need support, and die, to mention some of the more common social challenges faced by adults.

A Midlife Crisis? *Don't people face a "midlife crisis" at this point in their lives?* Although adulthood brings its fair share of life's challenges, only about a quarter of men and women believe they have experienced a midlife crisis (Wethington, Kessler, & Pixley, 2004). It is more common to make a "mid-course correction" at midlife than it is to survive a "crisis" (Freund & Ritter, 2009; Lachman, 2004). Ideally, the midlife transition involves reworking old identities, achieving valued goals, finding one's own truths, and preparing for old age. Taking stock may be especially valuable at midlife, but reviewing past choices to prepare for the future is helpful at any age. For some people, difficult turning points in life can serve as "wake-up calls" that create opportunities for personal growth (Weaver, 2009; Wethington, 2003).

Facing the Challenges of Adulthood

How do people maintain a state of well-being as they run the gauntlet of modern life? Psychologist Gloria Ryff believes that well-being during adulthood has six elements (Ryff & Singer, 2009; van Dierendonck et al., 2008):

1. Self-acceptance
2. Positive relations with others
3. Autonomy (personal freedom)
4. Environmental mastery
5. A purpose in life
6. Continued personal growth

Ryff found that, for many adults, age-related declines are offset by positive relationships and greater mastery of life's demands (Ryff & Singer, 2009). Thus, sharing life's joys and sorrows with others, coupled with a better understanding of how the world works, can help carry people through midlife and into their later years (Lachman et al., 2008; Ryff, Singer, & Palmersheim, 2004). It is important to note that despite the emphasis on youth in our culture, middle age and beyond can be a rich period of life in which people feel secure, happy, and self-confident (Rubenstein, 2002).

Old Age

After the late 50s, physical aging complicates personal development. However, it is wrong to believe that most elderly people are sickly, infirm, or senile. (Nowadays, 60 is the new 40, an idea with which both of your authors wholeheartedly agree!) Only about 5 percent of those older than 65 are in nursing homes. Mentally, many elderly persons are at least as capable as the average young adult. On intellectual tests, top scorers over the age of 65 match the average for men younger than 35. What sets these silver-haired stars apart? Typically, they are people who have continued to work and remain intellectually active (Hooyman & Kiyak, 2011; Salthouse, 2004). **Gerontologist**—a psychologist who studies aging and the aged—Warner Schaie (1994, 2005) found that you are most likely to stay mentally sharp in old age if:

1. You remain healthy.
2. You live in a favorable environment. (You are educated and have a stimulating occupation, an above-average income, and an intact family.)
3. You are involved in intellectually stimulating activities (reading, travel, cultural events, continuing education, clubs, and professional associations).
4. You have a flexible personality.
5. You are married to an intelligent spouse.
6. You maintain your perceptual processing speed by staying active.
7. You were satisfied with your accomplishments in midlife.

A shorter summary of this list is "Those who live by their wit die with their wits."

Successful Aging *What are the keys to successful aging?* They are not unlike the elements of well-being at midlife. The psychological characteristics shared by the healthiest, happiest older people are the following (de Leon, 2005; Vaillant, 2002):

- Optimism, hope, and an interest in the future
- Gratitude and forgiveness; an ability to focus on what is good in life
- Empathy; an ability to share the feelings of others and see the world through their eyes
- Connection with others; an ability to reach out, to give and receive social support

These are excellent guidelines for well-being at *any* stage of adulthood.

In summary, enlightened views of aging call for an end to the forced obsolescence of the elderly. As a group, older people represent a valuable source of skill, knowledge, and energy that we can't afford to cast aside. As we face the challenges of this planet's uncertain future, we need all the help we can get!

Aging and Ageism **Ageism**, which refers to discrimination or prejudice based on age, can oppress the young as well as the old (Bodner, 2009). For instance, a person applying for a job may just as well be told "You're too young" as "You're too old." In some societies, ageism is expressed as respect for the elderly. In Japan, for instance, aging is seen as positive, and greater age brings more status and respect. In most Western nations, however, ageism tends to have a negative impact on older individuals.

Ageism is often expressed through patronizing language. Older people are frequently spoken to in an overly polite, slow, loud, and simple way, implying that they are infirm, even when they are not (Nelson, 2005). Popular stereotypes of the "dirty old man," "meddling old woman," "senile old fool," and the like also help perpetuate myths about aging. But such stereotypes are clearly wrong: A tremendous diversity exists among the elderly—ranging from the infirm to aerobic-dancing grandmothers.

Shown here at her star-studded 90th birthday party in 2012, Betty White's 70+ years as a popular entertainer show that aging does not inevitably bring an end to engaging in challenging activities.

In many occupations, older workers perform well in jobs that require *both* speed and skill. Of course, people do experience a gradual loss of *fluid intelligence* (abilities requiring speed or rapid learning) as they age but, often, this can be offset by *crystallized intelligence* (abilities involving already learned knowledge and skills), such as vocabulary and stored-up facts, which may actually improve—at least into the 60s (Schaie, 2005). (Remember that infants show just the opposite pattern, being high in fluid intelligence but low in crystallized intelligence.) Overall, little loss of job performance need occur as workers grow older (Agrigoroaei & Lachman, 2011). In the professions, wisdom and expertise can usually more than compensate for any loss of mental quickness (Ericsson, 2000). Basing retirement solely on a person's age makes little sense.

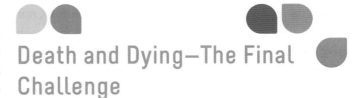

Death and Dying—The Final Challenge

SURVEY QUESTION 15.5: How do people typically react to death?

We have seen throughout this module that it is valuable to understand major trends in the course of development. With this in mind, let's explore emotional responses to death, the inevitable conclusion of every life.

Reactions to Impending Death

A highly influential account of emotional responses to death comes from the work of Elisabeth Kübler-Ross (1926–2004). Kübler-Ross was a **thanatologist** (THAN-ah-TOL-oh-jist: one who studies death). Over the years, she spent hundreds of hours at the bedsides of the terminally ill, where she observed five basic emotional reactions to impending death (Kübler-Ross, 1975):

1. **Denial and isolation.** A typical first reaction is to deny death's reality and isolate oneself from information confirming that death is really going to occur. Initially, the person may be sure that "It's all a mistake." "Surely," she or he thinks, "the doctor made an error."

Gerontologist *A psychologist who studies aging and the aged.*
Ageism *Discrimination or prejudice based on a person's age.*
Thanatologist *A specialist who studies emotional and behavioral reactions to death and dying.*

2. **Anger.** Many dying individuals feel anger and ask, "Why me?" As they face the ultimate threat of having life torn away, their anger may spill over into rage toward the living.

3. **Bargaining.** In another common reaction, the terminally ill bargain with themselves or with God. The dying person thinks, "Just let me live a little longer and I'll do anything to earn it."

4. **Depression.** As death draws near and the person begins to recognize that it cannot be prevented, feelings of futility, exhaustion, and deep depression may set in.

5. **Acceptance.** If death is not sudden, many people manage to come to terms with dying and accept it calmly. The person who accepts death is neither happy nor sad but at peace with the inevitable.

Not all terminally ill persons display all these reactions, nor do they always occur in this order. In general, one's approach to dying will mirror his or her style of living (Yedidia & MacGregor, 2001). It is a mistake to think that Kübler-Ross's list is a series of stages to go through in a particular order or that something is wrong if a person does not show all these emotions. Rather, the list describes typical reactions to impending death. Note, as well, that many of the same reactions accompany any major loss, be it divorce, loss of a home due to fire, death of a pet, or loss of a job.

Implications *How can I make use of this information?* First, it can help both the dying and survivors to recognize and cope with periods of depression, anger, denial, and bargaining. Second, it helps to realize that close friends or relatives may feel many of the same emotions before or after a person's death because they, too, are facing a loss.

Death may be inevitable, but it can be faced with dignity and sometimes even humor. Mel Blanc's famous sign-off, "That's all folks," is engraved on a marble headstone over his grave. Blanc was the voice of Bugs Bunny, Porky Pig, and many other cartoon characters.

© Michael Newman/PhotoEdit

Perhaps the most important thing to recognize is that dying persons need to share their feelings and to discuss death openly (Corr, Nabe, & Corr, 2013). Too often, dying persons feel isolated and separated from others. If someone in your life is dying, here's some advice (Dyer, 2001):

- Be yourself and relate person to person.
- Be ready to listen again and again.
- Be respectful.
- Be aware of feelings and nonverbal cues.
- Be comfortable with silence.
- Be genuine.

Most of all, be there.

Module 15: Summary

15.1 What are the typical tasks and dilemmas through the lifespan?

- **15.1.1** Erik Erikson identified a series of specific psychosocial dilemmas that occur as we age. These range from a need to gain trust in infancy to the need to live with integrity in old age.
- **15.1.2** Successful resolution of the dilemmas produces healthy development, whereas unsuccessful outcomes make it harder to deal with later crises.

15.2 Why is the transition from adolescence to adulthood especially challenging?

- **15.2.1** The timing of puberty can complicate the task of identity formation, a major task of adolescence. Identity formation is even more challenging for adolescents of ethnic descent.
- **15.2.2** In Western industrialized societies, the transition into adulthood is further complicated because it is increasingly delayed well into the 20s (emerging adulthood).

continued

Module 15: Summary, *continued*

15.3 How do we develop morals and values?

- **15.3.1** Lawrence Kohlberg identified preconventional, conventional, and postconventional levels of moral reasoning. Developing mature moral standards also is an important task of adolescence.
- **15.3.2** Most people function at the conventional level of morality, but some never get beyond the selfish, preconventional level. Only a minority of people attain the highest, or postconventional level, of moral reasoning.
- **15.3.3** Carol Gilligan distinguished between Kohlberg's justice perspective and a caring perspective. Mature adult morality likely involves both.

15.4 What is involved in well-being during middle and later adulthood?

- **15.4.1** Physical aging starts early in adulthood. Every adult must find ways to successfully cope with aging. Only a minority of people have a midlife crisis, but midlife course corrections are more common.
- **15.4.2** Well-being during adulthood consists of six elements: self-acceptance, positive relations with others, autonomy, environmental mastery, having a purpose in life, and continued personal growth.
- **15.4.3** Intellectual declines associated with aging are limited, at least through one's 70s. This is especially true of individuals who remain mentally active.
- **15.4.4** Ageism refers to prejudice, discrimination, and stereotyping on the basis of age. It affects people of all ages but is especially damaging to older people. Most ageism is based on stereotypes, myths, and misinformation.

15.5 How do people typically react to death?

- **15.5.1** Typical emotional reactions to impending death include denial, anger, bargaining, depression, and acceptance, but not necessarily in that order or in every case.
- **15.5.2** Death is a natural part of life. There is value in understanding it and accepting it.

Module 15: Knowledge Builder

Recite

1. During middle adulthood, the crisis is generativity versus

   _____ .

2. Identify formation is spurred by _____ and _____

   _____ .

3. According to Jeffrey Arnett, the trend in affluent Westernized cultures toward allowing young people to take longer to settle into their adult roles is best referred to as
   - **a.** emerging adulthood
   - **b.** hurried childhood
   - **c.** a maturity gap
   - **d.** extended adolescence

4. Gilligan regards gaining a sense of justice as the principal basis of moral development. *T or F?*

5. After age 65, a large proportion of older people show significant signs of mental disability and most require special care. *T or F?*

6. In the reaction that Kübler-Ross describes as bargaining, the dying individual asks, "Why me?" *T or F?*

Reflect

Think Critically

7. Do labels like *adolescent* or *young adult* reflect heredity or environment?

Self Reflect

See if you can think of a person you know who is facing one of Erikson's psychosocial dilemmas. Now see if you can think of specific people who seem to be coping with each of the other dilemmas.

To what extent does the concept of identity formation apply to your own experience during adolescence?

Do you think emerging adults (Are you one?) are adolescents who are taking longer to find their identity or young adults avoiding their need to establish themselves in the world of adults?

Describe three instances of ageism you have witnessed.

ANSWERS

1. Stagnation 2. puberty, cognitive development 3. a 4. F 5. F 6. F 7. Environment, rather than heredity, is the better answer. Even better, the meanings of terms like "adolescence" or "adult" vary considerably from culture to culture indicating that it is really a matter of definition (Arnett, 2011).

16 Module

Psychology in Action: Well-Being and Happiness

What Makes a Good Life?

What makes you happy? Love? Money? Music? Sports? Partying? Religion? Clearly, there is no simple, universal formula for happiness. What does it mean to have a good life? Is it a matter of health? Achievement? Friendship? Leisure? Personal growth? Again, there are no simple answers. Nevertheless, psychologists are beginning to understand some aspects of what it means to be happy and live well. Their findings provide valuable hints about how to live a successful life.

In general, both happiness and living a "good life" depend greatly on individual needs and cultural values. Most important is that your happiness and life satisfaction depend on the way you perceive, interpret, and manage events. How you frame your experiences is as important as the nature of the events. How is your sense of subjective well-being? Let's find out.

© mangostock/Shutterstock

Subjective Well-Being— Here's to a Happy Life

SURVEY QUESTION 16.1: What factors contribute most to a happy life?

To study happiness, psychologist Ed Diener and his associates have focused on what they call **subjective well-being**. According to them, feelings of well-being, or happiness, occur when people are generally satisfied with their lives, have frequent positive emotions, and have relatively few negative emotions (Diener, Scollon, & Lucas, 2009; Tay & Diener, 2011).

Life Satisfaction

What does life satisfaction mean? You are high in life satisfaction if you strongly agree with the following statements (from the "Satisfaction with Life Scale," Diener, 2009):

1. In most ways, my life is close to my ideal.
2. The conditions of my life are excellent.
3. I am satisfied with my life.
4. So far, I have gotten the important things I want in life.
5. If I could live my life over, I would change almost nothing.

These statements seem to cover much of what it means to be happy. However, Diener and his colleagues believe day-to-day emotional experiences also are important.

Emotions

Imagine that several pleasant or rewarding events have occurred today. These events caused you to experience moments of laughter, joy, delight, and satisfaction. As a result, you feel happy and life seems good. In contrast, imagine that your day was marred by a series of unpleasant or punishing events, which left you feeling sad. In reality, of course, we rarely have entirely good or entirely bad days. Life is a mixture of rewarding and punishing events, so everyone feels both positive and negative emotions. It's possible for the same person to have lots of positive feelings *and* lots of negative feelings. That's why happiness is not just a matter of having good feelings. The happiest people are those who have many positive emotional experiences and relatively few negative experiences (Diener, Scollon, & Lucas, 2009).

Life Events *Then, do good and bad events in life dictate whether a person is happy?* Happiness is related to good and bad life events, but the impact is smaller than you might imagine. This is because happiness tends to come from within a person. Subjective well-being is affected by our culture, goals, choices, emotions, values, and personality (Scollon, Koh, & Au, 2011). The way events are perceived, interpreted, and managed is as important as the nature of the events themselves. People who are good at dodging life's hard knocks tend to create their own "luck." As a result, they are happier and seem to negotiate life's demands more smoothly (Wong, 2011).

Personal Factors

What about factors such as income, age, or marital status? Are they related to happiness? Personal characteristics have only a small connection with overall happiness. Let's see why.

Wealth It is tempting to think that wealth brings happiness. Up to a certain point, it's true: More resources can bring happiness to people living in poverty (Howell & Howell, 2008). However, the overall association between money and happiness is weak. In fact, people who win lotteries often are *less* happy than they were before they won (Lutter, 2007). New stresses that instant riches usually bring into a person's life tend to cancel out any positive effects of wealth. While money may make it possible to meet your basic needs in life, it can't buy you a good life. Happiness must usually come from other sources (Diener et al., 2010; Scollon & King, 2011).

Education More-educated people tend to be a little happier than the less educated. However, this most likely is just another way of saying that there is a small connection between wealth and happiness. Higher education generally results in higher income and more social status.

Marriage Married people report greater happiness than people who are divorced, separated, or single. It could be that happier people are simply more likely to get married. But a better explanation for this association is that happy people are more likely to get married and stay married. Most people get a small boost in happiness immediately after getting married. However, most eventually return to about the same level of happiness they had before they tied the knot (Lucas et al., 2003).

Religion A small but positive association exists between happiness and holding spiritual beliefs (Diener, Tay, & Myers, 2011). Religious beliefs may add to feelings of purpose and meaning in life, resulting in greater happiness. Another possibility is that church membership may simply provide social support that softens the impact of life's negative events.

Age The stereotype of the crotchety old person who is dissatisfied with everything is inaccurate (Sorrell, 2009). Life satisfaction and happiness generally *do not* decline with age. People are living longer and staying healthier, which has greatly delayed age-related declines. When declines do occur, older people today seem better able to cope with them.

Sex Overall, men and women do not differ in happiness (Brannon, 2011). However, women do have a tendency to experience higher emotional highs and lower lows than men. Thus, more women are found among those rare individuals who are extremely happy or unhappy.

Work People who are satisfied with their jobs tend to be happier, but the association is weak. If fact, it probably just reflects the fact that people who are satisfied with their lives also tend to be satisfied with their jobs.

Personality To a degree, some people are more temperamentally disposed to be happy, regardless of life events. In general, happier people also tend to be extraverted (outgoing), optimistic, and worry-free. This combination probably influences the balance of positive and negative emotions a person feels (Lucas & Diener, 2009).

Goals and Happiness

The preceding information gives some insight into who is happy, but we can learn more by examining people's goals. To know if someone is happy, it is helpful to ask, "What is this person trying to do in life? How well is she or he succeeding at it?"

Do you want to be healthy and physically fit? To do well in school? To be liked by friends? To own a recording studio? A BMW? The goals people choose vary widely. Nevertheless, one generalization we can make is that people tend to be happy if they are meeting their personal goals. This is especially true if you feel you are making progress on a day-to-day basis on smaller goals that relate to long-term, life goals (King, Richards, & Stemmerich, 1998).

Subjective well-being *General life satisfaction combined with frequent positive emotions and relatively few negative emotions.*

The importance of personal goals helps explain why specific circumstances tell us so little about happiness. It is often difficult to know if an event is good or bad without knowing what a person is trying to achieve in life (Diener, Scollon, & Lucas, 2009).

Goals and Happiness In summary, happier persons tend to be married, comfortable with their work, extraverted, religious, optimistic, and generally satisfied with their lives. They also are making progress toward their goals. However, attaining goals that do not express our deeper interests and values may add little to happiness (Scollon & King, 2011).

What, then, makes a good life? Purpose and meaning are important sources of well-being at every point in life (Ryff & Singer, 2009). A good life is one that is happy *and* meaningful (Shrira et al., 2011).

Module 16: Summary

16.1 What factors contribute most to a happy life?

- **16.1.1** Subjective well-being (happiness) is a combination of general life satisfaction, plus more positive emotions than negative emotions.
- **16.1.2** Life events and various demographic factors have relatively little influence on happiness.
- **16.1.3** People with extraverted (outgoing), optimistic, and worry-free personalities tend to be happier.
- **16.1.4** Making progress toward one's goals is associated with happiness.
- **16.1.5** Overall well-being is a combination of happiness and meaning in life, which comes from pursuing goals that express one's deeper interests and values.

Module 16: Knowledge Builder

Recite

1. Subjective well-being consists of a mixture of _____ _____, positive emotions, and negative emotions.

2. People who experience many positive emotions are, by definition, very happy. *T or F?*

3. Happiness has only a small positive correlation with wealth. *T or F?*

4. Single persons are generally happier than those who are married. *T or F?*

5. Making progress day-by-day toward important _____, _____ is a major source of happiness.

Reflect

Think Critically

6. "To thine own self be true" may seem like a cliché, but it's not a bad place to begin a search for a happy and meaningful life. Explain what it means to be true to yourself.

Self-Reflect

How do you think you would rate on each of the three components of subjective well-being? What other factors discussed in this section are related to your own level of happiness?

It is common for students to pursue goals that are imposed on them. Which of your activities do you regard as most meaningful? How do they relate to your personal beliefs and values?

ANSWERS

1. life satisfaction 2. F 3. T 4. F 5. life goals 6. To be true to yourself is to live with *integrity*, by finding happiness through the pursuit of meaningful life goals (McGregor, McAdams, & Little, 2006).

CENGAGE brain .com

Go to **cengagebrain.com** to access **MindTap** for Coon/Mitterer *Psychology Modules for Active Learning* and other online learning tools. MindTap is a fully online learning experience that combines all the tools you need—readings, multimedia, activities, and assessments—into a singular personalized Learning Path that guides you through the course.

Sensation and Perception: Sensory Processes

The Trees Have Eyes

One of your authors was hiking in a beautiful rainforest when he had the uncanny sensation he was being watched. For several minutes, he searched fruitlessly, taking in the lush scene. There! Hanging not more than a foot from his own head was the head of a snake, staring straight at him. The snake was perfectly camouflaged, hanging motionless from an overhanging branch, looking for all the world like just another green vine (this species isn't called a green vine snake for nothing).

As this story shows, sensing the world is just a first step in perceiving the world. Even though his eyes picked up the basic visual information he needed to perceive the snake, his brain couldn't put the perceptual puzzle together. Sensory information can be interpreted (and misinterpreted) in various ways, which is step two in experiencing the world. This module addresses the first step, sensation. We explore the second step, perception, in a later module.

© Dlillc/Corbis

SURVEY QUESTIONS

17.1 In general, how do sensory systems function?

17.2 Why are we more aware of some sensations than others?

Sensory Systems—The First Step

SURVEY QUESTION 17.1: In general, how do sensory systems function?

Right now, you are bathed in a swirling kaleidoscope of electromagnetic radiation, heat, pressure, vibrations, molecules, and mechanical forces. If some of this physical energy, say in the form of light, heat, or sound, strikes your senses, an instant later, you may notice a bumblebee whiz past, the warmth of the sun on your face, or a catchy new tune on the radio. In that instant, a remarkable series of events transpires as you detect, analyze, and interpret sensory information. However, unless your senses translate these forces into a form your brain can understand, you will experience only a void of silence and darkness. Before we examine specific senses in more detail, let's explore how the senses and selective attention together reduce the amount of information the brain must process.

The primary function of the senses is to act as biological **transducers**, devices that convert one kind of energy into another (Fain, 2003; Goldstein, 2014). Each sense translates a specific type of external energy into patterns of activity (action potentials) in neurons. Information arriving from the sense organs creates **sensations**. Then the brain processes these messages. When the brain organizes sensations into meaningful patterns, we speak of **perception**. It is fascinating to realize that "seeing" and "hearing" take place in your brain, not in your eyes or ears.

Consider, for example, vision, which gives us amazingly wide access to the world. In one instant, you can view a star light years away, and in the next, you can peer into the microscopic universe of a dewdrop. Yet, vision also narrows what we can possibly observe. Like the other senses, vision acts as a *data-reduction system*. It selects and analyzes information in order to code and send to the brain only the most important data (Goldstein, 2014).

Selection

How does sensory data reduction take place? Considerable selection occurs because sensory receptors do not transduce all the energies they encounter. For example, a guitar transduces string vibrations into sound waves. Pluck a string and the guitar will produce a sound. However, stimuli that don't cause the string to move will have no effect. If you shine a light on the string, or pour cold water on it, the guitar will remain silent. (The owner of the guitar, however, might become quite loud at this point!) In a similar way, the eye transduces electromagnetic radiation, the ear transduces sound waves, and so on. Many other types of stimuli cannot be sensed directly because we lack sensory receptors to transduce their energy. For example, humans cannot sense the bioelectric fields of other living creatures, but sharks have special organs that can (Fields, 2007). (Do they *hear* the fields or *feel* them or what?)

In the field of **psychophysics**, physical energy (such as sound waves or electromagnetic radiation) is measured and related to dimensions of the resulting sensations we experience (such as loudness or brightness). Psychophysical research has shown that sense receptors transduce only part of their target energy range (Fain, 2003). For example, your eyes transduce only a tiny fraction of the entire range of electromagnetic energies—the part we call the *visible spectrum*. The eyes of honeybees can transduce, and therefore see, parts of the electromagnetic spectrum invisible to us humans. Likewise, bats *shout* at a pitch too high for humans to transduce. But they can hear their own reflected echoes. This ability, called *echolocation*, allows bats to fly in total darkness, avoid collisions, and catch insects.

Similarly, energy below a certain minimum intensity is necessary for a sensation to occur. The necessary minimum defines the **absolute threshold** for a sensory system. For example, very soft sounds (which could be heard if they were just a little louder) fall below the absolute threshold for human hearing. Of course owls, who hunt at night, have much lower absolute thresholds for hearing. As you can see, our rich sensory experiences are only a small part of what *could* be sensed and what some animals *can* sense.

Absolute thresholds define the sensory worlds of humans and animals, sometimes with serious consequences. The endangered Florida manatee (sea cow) is a peaceful, plant-eating creature that can live for more than 60 years. For the last decade, the number of manatees killed by boats has climbed alarmingly. The problem? Manatees have poor sensitivity to the low-frequency sounds made by slow-moving boats. Current laws require boats to slow down in manatee habitats, which may actually increase the risk to these gentle giants (Gerstein, 2002).

Sensory Adaptation

The flow of sensations to the brain is reduced in another way. Think about walking into a house in which fried liver, sauerkraut, and headcheese were just prepared for dinner. (Some dinner!) Although you might pass out at the door, people who had been in the house for some time wouldn't be aware of the food odors. Why? Because sensory receptors respond less to unchanging stimuli, a process called **sensory adaptation**.

Fortunately, the olfactory (smell) receptors adapt quickly. When exposed to a constant odor, they send fewer and fewer nerve impulses to the brain until the odor is no longer noticed. Adaptation to pressure from a wristwatch, waistband, ring, or glasses is based on the same principle. Because there is usually little reason to keep reminding the brain that a sensory input is unchanged, sensory receptors generally respond best to *changes* in stimulation. No one wants or needs to be reminded 16 hours a day that his or her shoes are on.

Sensory Analysis

What we experience also is influenced by **sensory analysis**. As the senses process information, they divide the world into important **perceptual features**, or basic stimulus patterns.

Figure 17.1

Visual pop-out. This pop-out is so basic that babies as young as 3 months respond to it. (Adapted from Adler & Orprecio, 2006.)

The visual system, for example, has a set of *feature detectors* that are attuned to specific stimuli, such as lines, shapes, edges, spots, colors, and other patterns (Hubel & Wiesel, 2005). Look at ● **Figure 17.1** and notice how eye-catching the single vertical line is among a group of slanted lines. This effect, which is called *visual pop-out*, occurs because your visual system is highly sensitive to these perceptual features (Hsieh, Colas, & Kanwisher, 2011).

Similarly, frog eyes are highly sensitive to small, dark, moving spots. In other words, they are "tuned" to detect bugs flying nearby (Lettvin, 1961). But the insect (spot) must be moving, or the frog's "bug detectors" won't work. A frog could starve to death surrounded by dead flies.

Although our sensitivity to perceptual features is an innate characteristic of the nervous system, it also is influenced by experiences early in life. For instance, Colin Blakemore and Graham Cooper of Cambridge University raised kittens in a room with only vertical stripes on the walls. Another set of kittens were raised seeing only horizontal stripes. When returned to normal environments, the "horizontal" cats could easily jump onto a chair, but when walking on the floor, they bumped into chair legs. "Vertical" cats, on the other hand, easily avoided chair legs, but they missed when trying to jump to horizontal surfaces. The cats raised with vertical stripes were "blind" to horizontal lines, and the "horizontal" cats acted as if vertical lines were invisible (Blakemore & Cooper, 1970). Other experiments show an actual decrease in brain cells that are tuned to the missing features (Grobstein & Chow, 1975).

Sensory Coding

As they select and analyze information, sensory systems *code* it. **Sensory coding** refers to converting important features of the world into neural messages understood by the brain (Hubel & Wiesel, 2005). For example, not every difference between two stimuli can be coded; instead, the difference must be sufficiently large. Psychophysics also involves the study of **difference thresholds**. Here, we are asking, "How different must two stimuli be before the difference becomes noticeable and, hence, codable?" For example, if you were to put one extra grain of sugar in your coffee, would you notice a difference? How much would it take? A few grains? A half spoonful? A spoonful?

To see coding at work, try closing your eyes for a moment. Then, take your fingertips and press firmly on your eyelids. Apply enough pressure to "squash" your eyes slightly. Do this for about 30 seconds and observe what happens. (Readers with eye problems or contact lenses should not try this.)

Did you "see" stars, checkerboards, and flashes of color? These are called *phosphenes* (FOSS-feens), visual sensations caused by mechanical excitation of the retina. They occur because the eye's receptor cells, which normally respond to light, also are somewhat sensitive to pressure. Notice, though, that the eye is prepared to code stimulation—including pressure—only into visual features. As a result, you experience light sensations, not pressure. Also important in producing this effect is *sensory localization* in the brain.

Transducers *Devices that convert one kind of energy into another.*
Sensation *A sensory impression; also, the process of detecting physical energies with the sensory organs.*
Perception *The mental process of organizing sensations into meaningful patterns.*
Psychophysics *Study of the relationship between physical stimuli and the sensations they evoke in a human observer.*
Absolute threshold *The minimum amount of physical energy necessary to produce a sensation.*
Sensory adaptation *A decrease in sensory response to an unchanging stimulus.*
Sensory analysis *Separation of sensory information into important elements.*
Perceptual features *Basic elements of a stimulus, such as lines, shapes, edges, or colors.*
Sensory coding *Codes the sense organs use to transmit information to the brain.*
Difference threshold *The minimum difference between two stimuli that is detectable to an observer.*

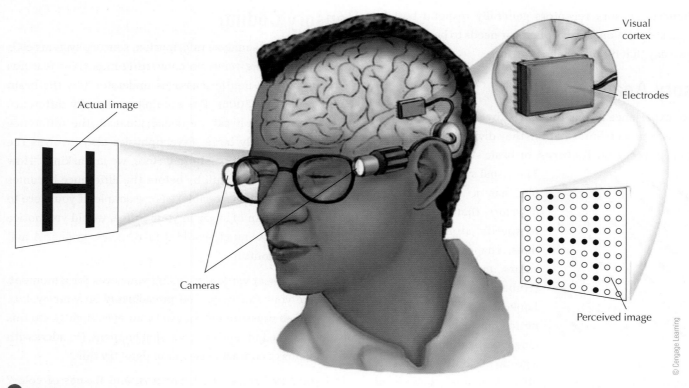

Actual image

Visual cortex

Electrodes

Cameras

Perceived image

© Cengage Learning

Figure 17.2

An artificial visual system. Video cameras translate light into electrical impulses that directly stimulate the visual cortex, resulting in rudimentary visual experiences. What do you suppose this person would experience if the electrical impulses were sent to the auditory cortex instead?

Sensory localization means that the type of sensation you experience depends on which brain area is activated. Some brain areas receive visual information; others receive auditory information, and still others receive taste or touch (see Module 9). Knowing which brain areas are active tells us, in general, what kinds of sensations you are feeling.

Sensory localization is beginning to make it possible to artificially restore sight, hearing, or other senses. In one approach, researchers used a used a miniature television camera to send electrical signals directly to the brain, bypassing damaged eyes and optic nerves (● **Figure 17.2**) (Dobelle, 2000; Warren & Normann, 2005). Using technologies like these, people who have lost their vision are now able to "see" letters, words, and some common objects like knives and forks (Nirenberg & Pandarinath, 2012).

How much control do people have over sensory data reduction? Is it anything like focusing attention on studying and deliberately ignoring other stuff going on around you? Good question. We have no real conscious control over what energy ranges our senses can transduce, analyze, or encode. Likewise, it is quite difficult to consciously control sensory adaptation. *Selective attention* is a different capability, one that you *can* control. Pay attention, now.

Selective Attention— Tuning in and Tuning Out

SURVEY QUESTION 17.2: Why are we more aware of some sensations than others?

Although the senses reduce a mixture of sights, sounds, odors, tastes, and touch sensations to more manageable amounts, they are still too much for the brain to handle. That's why the brain further filters sensory information through *selective attention*. For example, as you sit reading this page, receptors for touch and pressure in the seat of your pants are sending nerve impulses to your brain. Although these sensations have been present all along, you were probably not aware of them until just now. This "seat-of-the-pants phenomenon" is an example of **selective attention**—voluntarily focusing on a specific sensory input. Selective attention appears to be based on the ability of brain structures to select and divert incoming sensory messages (Mather, 2011). We are able to "tune in on" a single sensory message while excluding others.

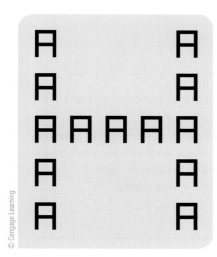

Figure 17.3

The attentional "bottleneck," or "spotlight," can be widened or narrowed. If you focus on local details in this drawing, you will see the letter *A* repeated 13 times. If you broaden your field of attention to encompass the overall pattern, you see the letter *H*.

Another familiar example of this is the cocktail party effect. When you are in a group of people, surrounded by voices, you can still select and attend to the voice of the person you are facing. Or if that person gets dull, you can eavesdrop on conversations all over the room. (Be sure to smile and nod your head occasionally!) However, no matter how interesting your companion may be, your attention will probably shift if you hear your own name spoken somewhere in the room (Koch et al., 2011). We do find what others say about us to be very interesting, don't we?

At times, we can even suffer from **inattentional blindness**, a failure to notice a stimulus because attention is focused elsewhere (Thakral, 2011). Not seeing something that is plainly before your eyes most likely occurs when your attention is narrowly focused (Bressan & Pizzighello, 2008). Inattentional blindness is vividly illustrated by a classic study in which participants were shown a film of two basketball teams, one wearing black shirts and the other wearing white. Observers were asked to watch the film closely and count how many times a basketball passed between members of one of the teams, while ignoring the other team. As observers watched and counted, a person wearing a gorilla suit walked into the middle of the basketball game, faced the camera, thumped its chest, and walked out of view. Half the observers failed to notice this rather striking event (Simons & Chabris, 1999). This effect probably explains why fans of opposing sports teams often act as if they had seen two completely different games.

In a similar way, using a cell phone while driving can cause inattentional blindness. Instead of ignoring a gorilla, you might miss seeing another car, a motorcyclist, or a pedestrian while your attention is focused on the phone. It probably goes without saying, but the more engaged you are with your cell phone while driving (like texting instead of having a conversation), the greater the problem (Fougnie & Marois, 2007).

You might find it helpful to think of selective attention as a *bottleneck*, or narrowing in the information channel linking the senses to perception. When one message enters the bottleneck, it seems to prevent others from passing through (● **Figure 17.3**). Imagine, for instance, that you are driving a car and approaching an intersection. You need to be sure the traffic light is still green. Just as you are about to check, your passenger points to a friend at the side of the road. If you then fail to notice that the light just changed to red, an accident may be seconds away.

Are some stimuli more attention getting than others? Yes. Very *intense* stimuli usually command attention. Stimuli that are brighter, louder, or larger tend to capture attention: A gunshot in a library would be hard to ignore. If a brightly colored hot-air balloon ever lands at your college campus, it almost certainly will draw a crowd.

Repetitious stimuli, repetitious stimuli, repetitious stimuli, repetitious stimuli, repetitious stimuli, repetitious stimuli also are attention getting. A dripping faucet at night makes little noise by normal standards, but because of repetition, it may become as attention getting as a single sound that is many times louder. This effect is used repeatedly, so to speak, in television and radio commercials.

ATTENTION ALSO IS **FREQUENTLY** RELATED TO contrast OR *change* IN STIMULATION. The contrasting type styles in the preceding sentence draw attention because they are *unexpected*.

Unconscious sensory data reduction, together with selective attention, reduce the flow of sensory information to the brain to a manageable level. But how do the individual senses actually function? We explore that topic in the next two modules, but first, here's a chance to pay some attention to what you've learned.

Selective attention *Giving priority to a particular incoming sensory message.*
Inattentional blindness *A failure to notice a stimulus because attention is focused elsewhere.*

PSYCHOLOGY · MODULES FOR ACTIVE LEARNING

Module 17: Summary

17.1 In general, how do sensory systems function?

- **17.1.1** The senses act as selective data-reduction systems to prevent the brain from being overwhelmed by sensory input.
- **17.1.2** Sensation begins with transduction in a receptor organ; other data-reduction processes are sensory adaptation, analysis, and coding.
- **17.1.3** Sensation can be partially understood in terms of sensory localization in the brain.

17.2 Why are we more aware of some sensations than others?

- **17.2.1** Incoming sensations are affected by selective attention, a brain-based process that allows some sensory inputs to be selected for further processing while others are ignored.
- **17.2.2** Don't use your cell phone while driving!

Module 17: Knowledge Builder

Recite

1. Sensory receptors are biological _____, or devices for converting one type of energy to another.

2. As time passes, nerve endings in the skin under your clothes send fewer signals to the brain and you become unable to feel your clothes. This process is called
   - **a.** transduction
   - **b.** difference threshold
   - **c.** reverse attention
   - **d.** sensory adaptation

3. Important features of the environment are transmitted to the brain through a process known as
   - **a.** perception
   - **b.** coding
   - **c.** detection
   - **d.** programming

4. The brain-centered ability to influence what sensations we will receive is called
   - **a.** sensory adaptation
   - **b.** psychophysics
   - **c.** selective attention
   - **d.** sensory biasing

5. Which of the following stimuli are more effective at getting attention?
   - **a.** unexpected stimuli
   - **b.** repetitious stimuli
   - **c.** intense stimuli
   - **d.** all of the above

Reflect

Think Critically

6. William James once said, "If a master surgeon were to cross the auditory and optic nerves, we would hear lightning and see thunder." Can you explain what James meant?

Self-Reflect

What if, like some other animals, you could transduce other energies? How would the sensory world in which you live change? What would it be like to be a bat? A shark?

As you sit reading this book, which sensory inputs have undergone adaptation? What new inputs can you become aware of by shifting your focus of attention?

Can you pay attention to more than one sensory input at once?

ANSWERS

1. transducers 2. d 3. b 4. c 5. d 6. The explanation is based on sensory localization. If a lightning flash caused rerouted messages from the eyes to activate auditory areas of the brain, we would experience a sound sensation. Likewise, if the ears transduced a thunderclap and sent impulses to the visual area, a sensation of light would occur. It is amazing that some people, called synesthetes, naturally experience sensory inputs in terms of other senses. For example, one synesthete experiences pain as the color orange, whereas the taste of spiced chicken is pointy (Dixon, Smilek, & Merikle, 2004).

CENGAGE**brain**.com

Go to **cengagebrain.com** to access **MindTap for Coon/Mitterer** *Psychology Modules for Active Learning* and other online learning tools. MindTap is a fully online learning experience that combines all the tools you need—readings, multimedia, activities, and assessments—into a singular personalized Learning Path that guides you through the course.

Sensation and Perception: Vision

The Most Important Sense?

Most people agree that the one sense they would least prefer to lose is their vision. And why not? In the morning, when you first open your eyes, you effortlessly become aware of the visual richness of the world around you. That visual richness obscures the fact that your eyes transduce only the tiniest fraction of the entire range of electromagnetic energies—the part we call the *visible spectrum*. You cannot "see" the vast majority of the electromagnetic spectrum, such as microwaves, cosmic rays, x-rays, or radio waves.

Similarly, the effortlessness with which normally sighted people can *see* obscures incredible complexity. How does sensory transduction actually occur in vision? What does it mean to need glasses? How can we see in the dark? How can we see in color? Many questions have been answered; yet many remain. Regardless, vision is an impressive sensory system, worthy of a detailed discussion.

Serg Zastavkin/Shutterstock.com

SURVEY QUESTION

18.1 How does the visual system function?

Vision—Catching Some Rays

SURVEY QUESTION 18.1: How does the visual system function?

What are the basic dimensions of light and vision? The *visible spectrum*—the spread of electromagnetic energies to which the eyes respond—is made up of a narrow range of wavelengths of electromagnetic radiation. Visible light starts at "short" wavelengths of 400 *nanometers* (nan-OM-et-er: one-billionth of a meter), which we sense as purple or violet. Longer light waves produce blue, green, yellow, orange, and red, which has a wavelength of 700 nanometers (● Figure 18.1).

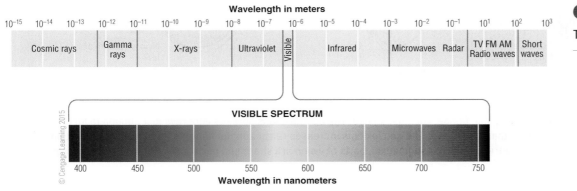

● **Figure 18.1**
The visible spectrum.

The term *hue* refers to the basic color categories of red, orange, yellow, green, blue, indigo, and violet. As just noted, various hues, or color sensations, correspond to the wavelength of the light that reaches our eyes (Mather, 2011). White light, in contrast, is a mixture of many wavelengths. Hues (colors) from a narrow band of wavelengths are very *saturated*, or pure. (An intense fire-engine red is more saturated than a muddy brick red.) A third dimension of vision, *brightness*, corresponds roughly to the amplitude, or height, of light waves. Waves of greater amplitude are taller, carry more energy, and cause the colors we see to appear brighter or more intense. For example, the same brick red would look bright under intense, high-energy illumination and drab under dim light.

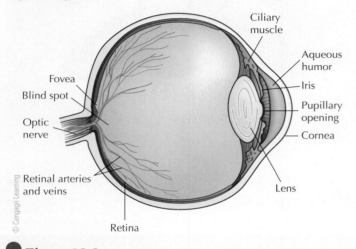

● Figure 18.2

The human eye, a simplified view.

Structure of the Eye

Although the visual system is much more complex than any digital camera, cameras and eyes have a *lens* to focus images on a light-sensitive layer at the back of an enclosed space. In a camera, it is a layer of light-sensitive pixels in the digital image sensor. In the eye, it is a layer of *photoreceptors* (light-sensitive cells) in the **retina**, which is an area about the size and thickness of a postage stamp (● Figure 18.2).

How does the eye focus? Most focusing is done at the front of the eye by the *cornea,* a clear membrane that bends light inward. The lens makes additional, smaller adjustments. Your eye's focal point changes when muscles attached to the lens alter its shape. This process is called **accommodation**. In cameras, focusing is done more simply—by changing the distance between the lens and the image sensor.

Visual Problems Focusing also is affected by the shape of the eye. If your eye is too short, nearby objects will be blurred, but distant objects will be sharp. This is called **hyperopia** (HI-per-OPE-ee-ah), or farsightedness. If your eyeball is too long, images fall short of the retina and you won't be able to focus distant objects. This results in **myopia** (my-OPE-ee-ah), or nearsightedness. When the cornea or the lens is misshapen, part of vision will be focused and part will be fuzzy. In this case, the eye has more than one focal point, a problem called **astigmatism** (ah-STIG-mah-tiz-em). All three visual defects can be corrected by placing glasses (or contact lenses) in front of the eye to change the path of light (● Figure 18.3).

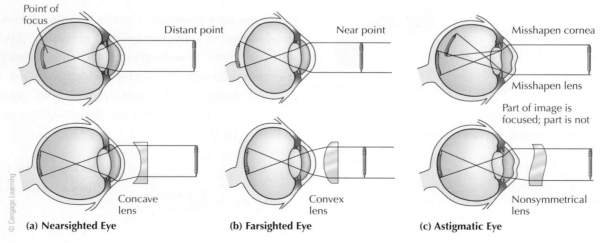

(a) Nearsighted Eye **(b) Farsighted Eye** **(c) Astigmatic Eye**

● Figure 18.3

Visual defects and corrective lenses: *(a)* A myopic (longer than usual) eye. The concave lens spreads light rays just enough to increase the eye's focal length. *(b)* A hyperopic (shorter than usual) eye. The convex lens increases refraction (bending) to focus light on the retina. *(c)* An astigmatic (lens or cornea not symmetrical) eye. In astigmatism, parts of vision are sharp and parts are unfocused. Lenses that correct astigmatism are nonsymmetrical.

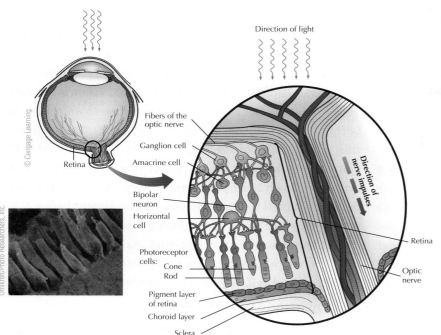

Figure 18.4

Anatomy of the retina. Note that light does not fall directly on the rods and cones. It must first pass through the cornea, the lens, the vitreous humor (a jelly-like substance that fills the eyeball), and the outer layers of the retina. Only about one-half of the light at the front of the eye reaches the rods and cones—testimony to the retina's amazing sensitivity. The lower-left photograph shows rods and cones as seen through an electron microscope. In the photograph, the cones are colored green and the rods blue.

As people age, the lens becomes less flexible and less able to accommodate. The result is **presbyopia** (prez-bee-OPE-ee-ah), from the Latin for "old vision," or farsightedness due to aging. Perhaps you have seen a grandparent or older friend reading a newspaper at arm's length because of presbyopia. If you now wear glasses for nearsightedness, you may need bifocals as you age. (Just like your authors. Sigh.) Bifocal lenses correct near vision *and* distance vision.

Rods and Cones

The eye has two types of "image sensors," consisting of receptor cells called *rods* and *cones* (Mather, 2011). The 5 million **cones** in each eye work best in bright light. They also produce color sensations and fine details. In contrast, the **rods**, numbering

about 120 million, can't detect colors (● **Figure 18.4**). Pure rod vision is black and white. However, the rods are much more sensitive to light than the cones. The rods therefore allow us to see in very dim light.

It is hard to believe, but the retina has a "hole" in it: Each eye has a *blind spot* because there are no receptors where the optic nerve passes out of the eye and blood vessels enter (Lamb, 2011; **Figure 18.5a**). The blind spot shows that vision depends greatly on the brain. If you close one eye, some of the incoming light will fall on the blind spot of your open eye. Why isn't there a gap in your vision? The answer is that the visual cortex of the brain actively fills in the gap with patterns from surrounding areas (● **Figure 18.5b**). By closing one eye, you can visually "behead" other people by placing their images on your blind spot. (Just a hint for some classroom fun.) The brain also can "erase" distracting information. Roll your eyes all the way to the right and then close your right eye. You should clearly see your nose in your left eye's field of vision. Now, open your right eye again and your nose will nearly disappear because your brain disregards its presence.

Figure 18.5

Experiencing the blind spot. *(a)* With your right eye closed, stare at the upper-right cross. Hold the book about 1 foot from your eye and slowly move it back and forth. You should be able to locate a position that causes the black spot to disappear. When it does, it has fallen on the blind spot. With a little practice, you can learn to make people or objects you dislike disappear, too! *(b)* Repeat the procedure described, but stare at the lower cross. When the white space falls on the blind spot, the black lines will appear to be continuous. This may help you understand why you do not usually experience a blind spot in your visual field.

Retina *The light-sensitive layer of cells at the back of the eye.*
Accommodation *Changes in the shape of the lens of the eye.*
Hyperopia *Difficulty focusing nearby objects (farsightedness).*
Myopia *Difficulty focusing distant objects (nearsightedness).*
Astigmatism *Defects in the cornea, lens, or eye that cause some areas of vision to be out of focus.*
Presbyopia *Farsightedness caused by aging.*
Cones *Visual receptors for colors and daylight visual acuity.*
Rods *Visual receptors for dim light that produce only black and white sensations.*

Visual Acuity The rods and cones also affect **visual acuity**, or sharpness (Foley & Matlin, 2010). The cones lie mainly at the center of the eye. In fact, the *fovea* (FOE-vee-ah), a small cup-shaped area in the middle of the retina, contains only cones—about 50,000 of them. Like high-resolution digital sensors made of many small pixels, the tightly packed cones in the fovea produce the sharpest images. Normal acuity is designated as 20/20 vision: At 20 feet in distance, you can distinguish what the average person can see at 20 feet (● **Figure 18.6**). If your vision is 20/40, you can see at 20 feet only what the average person can see at 40 feet. If your vision is 20/200, everything is a blur and you need glasses! Vision that is 20/12 means that you can see at 20 feet what the average person must be 8 feet nearer to see, indicating better than average acuity. American astronaut Gordon Cooper, who claimed to see railroad lines in northern India from 100 miles above the earth, had 20/12 vision.

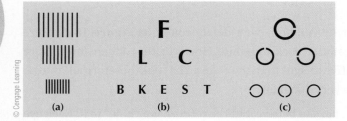

● **Figure 18.6**

Tests of visual acuity. Here are some common tests of visual acuity. In *(a)*, sharpness is indicated by the smallest grating still seen as individual lines. The Snellen chart *(b)* requires that you read rows of letters of diminishing size until you no longer can distinguish them. The Landolt rings *(c)* require no familiarity with letters. Simply note which side has a break in it.

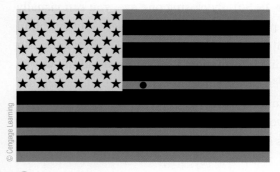

● **Figure 18.7**

Negative afterimages. Stare at the dot near the middle of the flag for at least 30 seconds. Then look immediately at a plain sheet of white paper or a white wall. You will see the American flag in its normal colors. Reduced sensitivity to yellow, green, and black in the visual system, caused by prolonged staring, results in the appearance of complementary colors. Project the afterimage of the flag on other colored surfaces to get additional effects.

Peripheral Vision *What is the purpose of the rest of the retina?* Areas outside the fovea also get light, creating a large region of **peripheral (side) vision**. The rods are most numerous about 20 degrees from the center of the retina, so much of our peripheral vision is rod vision. Although rod vision is not very high resolution, the rods are quite sensitive to *movement* in peripheral vision (Yamamoto & Philbeck, 2013). To experience this characteristic of the rods, look straight ahead and hold your hand beside your head, at about 90 degrees. Wiggle your finger and slowly move your hand forward until you can detect motion. You will become aware of the movement before you can actually "see" your finger. Seeing "out of the corner of the eye" is important for sports, driving, and walking down dark alleys. People who suffer from *tunnel vision* (a loss of peripheral vision) feel as if they are wearing blinders (Godnig, 2003).

The rods also are highly responsive to dim light. Because most rods are 20 degrees to each side of the fovea, the best night vision comes from looking *next to* an object you want to see. Test this yourself some night by looking at, and next to, a dim star.

Color Vision

How do the cones produce color sensations? The **trichromatic theory** (TRY-kro-MAT-ik) of color vision holds that there are three types of cones, each most sensitive to either red, green, or blue. Other colors result from combinations of these three.

A basic problem with the trichromatic theory is that four colors of light—red, green, blue, and yellow—seem to be primary (you can't get them by mixing other colors). Also, why is it impossible to have a reddish green or a yellowish blue? These problems led to the development of a second view, known as the **opponent-process theory**, which states that vision analyzes colors into "either-or" messages (Goldstein, 2014). That is, the visual system can produce messages for either red or green, yellow or blue, black or white. Coding one color in a pair (red, for instance) seems to block the opposite message (green) from coming through. As a result, a reddish green is impossible, but a yellowish red (orange) can occur.

According to opponent-process theory, fatigue caused by making one response produces an afterimage of the opposite color as the system recovers. *Afterimages* are visual sensations that persist after a stimulus is removed—like seeing a spot after a flashbulb goes off. To see an afterimage of the type predicted by opponent-process theory, look at ● **Figure 18.7** and follow the instructions there.

Which color theory is correct? Both! The three-color theory applies to the retina, in which three different types of cones have been found. Each contains a different type of *iodopsin* (i-oh-DOP-sin), a light-sensitive pigment that breaks down when struck by light. This triggers action potentials and sends neural messages to the brain. The three types of cones are most sensitive to red, green, or blue. Other colors result from combinations of these three. As predicted, each form of iodopsin is most sensitive to light in roughly the red, green, or blue region. Thus, the three types of cones fire nerve impulses at different rates to produce various color sensations (● **Figure 18.8**).

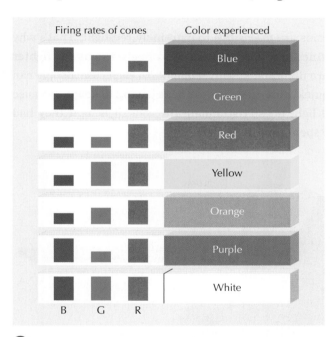

● **Figure 18.8**

Firing rates of blue, green, and red cones in response to different colors. The taller the colored bar, the higher the firing rates for that type of cone. As you can see, colors are coded by differences in the activity of all three types of cones in the normal eye. (Adapted from Goldstein, 2014.)

In contrast, the opponent-process theory better explains what happens in optic pathways and the brain *after* information leaves the eye. For example, some nerve cells in the brain are excited by the color red and inhibited by the color green. So both theories are correct. One explains what happens in the eye itself. The other explains how colors are analyzed after messages leave the eye (Gegenfurtner & Kiper, 2003).

Color Blindness and Color Weakness

Do you know anyone who regularly draws hoots of laughter by wearing clothes of wildly clashing colors? Or someone who sheepishly tries to avoid naming the color of an object? If so, you probably know someone who is color blind.

What is it like to be color blind? What causes color blindness? A person with **color blindness** cannot perceive colors. It is as if the world were a black-and-white movie. The color-blind person either lacks cones or has cones that do not function normally (Deeb, 2004; Neitz & Neitz, 2011). Such total color blindness is rare. In **color weakness**, or partial color blindness, a person can't see certain colors. Approximately 8 percent of Caucasian males (but fewer Asian, African, and Native American males and fewer than 1 percent of women) are red–green color blind. These people see reds and greens as the same color, usually a yellowish brown (● **Figure 18.9**).

(a)

(b)

(c)

● **Figure 18.9**

Color blindness and color weakness. *(a)* Photograph illustrates normal color vision. *(b)* Photograph is printed in blue and yellow and gives an impression of what a red–green color-blind person sees. *(c)* Photograph simulates total color blindness. If you are totally color blind, all three photos will look nearly identical.

Visual acuity *The sharpness of visual perception.*
Peripheral (side) vision *Vision at the edges of the visual field.*
Trichromatic theory *Theory of color vision based on three cone types: red, green, and blue.*
Opponent-process theory *Theory of color vision based on three coding systems (red or green, yellow or blue, black or white).*
Color blindness *A total inability to perceive colors.*
Color weakness *An inability to distinguish some colors.*

Another type of color weakness, involving yellow and blue, is extremely rare (National Institutes of Health, 2013).

It is surprising that some people reach adulthood without knowing that some colors are missing (Gündogan et al., 2005). If you can't see the number 5 or follow the dots from X to X in ● **Figure 18.10**, you might be red–green color blind.

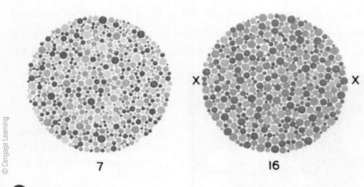

● **Figure 18.10**

A replica of two images from the widely used Ishihara test for red–green color blindness.

How can color-blind individuals drive? Don't they have trouble with traffic lights? Red–green color-blind individuals have normal vision for yellow and blue, so the main problem is telling red lights from green. In practice, that's not difficult. The red light is always on top, and the green light is brighter than the red. Also, red traffic signals have yellow light mixed in with the red and a green light is really blue-green.

Seeing in the Dark

What happens when the eyes adjust to a dark room? **Dark adaptation** is the dramatic increase in retinal sensitivity to light that occurs after a person enters the dark (Goldstein, 2014). Consider walking into a theater. If you enter from a brightly lit lobby, you practically need to be led to your seat. After a short time, however, you can see the entire room in detail (including the couple kissing over in the corner). It takes about 30 to 35 minutes of complete darkness to reach maximum visual sensitivity (● **Figure 18.11**). At that point, your eye will be 100,000 times more sensitive to light.

What causes dark adaptation? Like cones, which contain iodopsin, rods also contain a light-sensitive visual pigment, *rhodopsin* (row-DOP-sin), which allows them to see in black and white. When struck by light, visual pigments *bleach*, or break down chemically. The afterimages you have seen after looking at a flashbulb are a result of this bleaching. In fact, a few seconds of exposure to bright white light can completely wipe out dark adaptation. That's why you should avoid looking at oncoming headlights when you are driving at night—especially the new bluish-white xenon lights. To restore light sensitivity, the rhodopsin in the rods must recombine, which takes time.

The rods are *insensitive* to extremely red light. That's why submarines, airplane cockpits, and ready rooms for fighter pilots are illuminated with red light. In each case, people can move quickly into the dark without having to adapt. Because the red light doesn't stimulate the rods, it is as if they had already spent time in the dark.

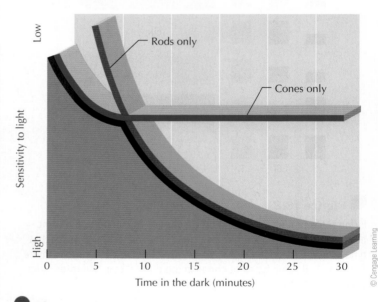

● **Figure 18.11**

Typical course of dark adaptation. The dark line shows how the threshold for vision lowers as a person spends time in the dark. (A lower threshold means that less light is needed for vision.) The blue line shows that the cones adapt first, but they soon cease adding to light sensitivity. Rods, shown by the red line, adapt more slowly. However, they continue to add to improved night vision long after the cones are fully adapted.

Dark adaptation *Increased retinal sensitivity to light.*

Module 18: Summary

18.1 How does the visual system function?

- **18.1.1** The eye is a visual system, not a photographic one. The entire visual system is structured to analyze visual information.
- **18.1.2** Four common visual defects are myopia, hyperopia, presbyopia, and astigmatism.
- **18.1.3** The rods and cones are photoreceptors in the retina of the eye.
- **18.1.4** The rods specialize in peripheral vision, night vision, seeing black and white, and detecting movement. The cones specialize in color vision, acuity, and daylight vision.

- **18.1.5** Color vision is explained by the trichromatic theory in the retina and by the opponent-process theory in the visual system beyond the eyes.
- **18.1.6** Total color blindness is rare, but 8 percent of males and 1 percent of females are red–green color blind or color weak.
- **18.1.7** Dark adaptation is caused mainly by an increase in the amount of rhodopsin in the rods.

Module 18: Knowledge Builder

Recite

1. Match:

   _____ Myopia   **A.** Farsightedness
   _____ Hyperopia   **B.** Elongated eye
   _____ Presbyopia   **C.** Misshapen cornea or lens
   _____ Astigmatism   **D.** Farsightedness due to aging

2. In dim light, vision depends mainly on the _____.
   In brighter light, color and fine detail are produced by the _____.

3. The greatest visual acuity is associated with the _____ and the _____.
   - **a.** trichromat, rods
   - **b.** vitreous humor, cones
   - **c.** fovea, cones
   - **d.** nanometer, cones

4. Colored afterimages are best explained by
   - **a.** trichromatic theory
   - **b.** the effects of astigmatism
   - **c.** sensory localization
   - **d.** opponent-process theory

5. Dark adaptation is directly related to an increase in
   - **a.** rhodopsin
   - **b.** astigmatism
   - **c.** accommodation
   - **d.** saturation

Reflect

Think Critically

6. Sensory transduction in the eye takes place first in the cornea, then in the lens, and then in the retina. True or false?

Self-Reflect

Pretend you are a beam of light. What will happen to you at each step as you pass into the eye and land on the retina? What will happen if the eye is not perfectly shaped? How will the retina know you've arrived? How will it tell what color of light you are? What will it tell the brain about you?

ANSWERS

1. B, A, D, C 2. rods, cones 3. c 4. d 5. A 6. False. Although the cornea and lens prepare incoming light rays by bending them and focusing them on the retina, they do not change light to another form of energy. No change in the *type* of energy takes place until the retina converts light to nerve impulses.

Sensation and Perception: The Other Senses

Even Pain?

We depend so much on vision that we sometimes neglect the other senses. But you need to wear earplugs for only a short time to appreciate how much we rely on hearing for communication, navigation, entertainment, and many other purposes. Similarly, skilled novelists always include descriptions of odors and tastes in their writings. Perhaps they intuitively realize that a scene is incomplete without smells and tastes. Like the other senses, the body senses also are an essential part of our sensory world. It would be very difficult to move, stay upright, or even stay alive without touch, balance, and other body senses. Even pain, which few people welcome, has its place in our lives. To appreciate pain, just imagine how much damage you might do to yourself if, for example, you could not feel any pain even though your foot was far too close to a burning campfire. Here's to the "other" senses.

stetsko/Shutterstock

SURVEY QUESTIONS

19.1 What are the mechanisms of hearing?

19.2 How do the chemical senses operate?

19.3 What are the somesthetic senses?

Hearing—Good Vibrations

SURVEY QUESTION 19.1: What are the mechanisms of hearing?

Rock, classical, jazz, blues, country, hip-hop—whatever your musical taste, you have undoubtedly been moved by the riches of sound. Hearing also collects information from all around the body, such as detecting the direction of approach of an unseen car (Johnstone, Nábělek, & Robertson, 2010). Vision, in all its glory, is limited to stimuli in front of the eyes.

What is the stimulus for hearing? If you throw a stone into a quiet pond, a circle of waves will spread in all directions. In much the same way, sound travels as a series of invisible waves of *compression* (peaks) and *rarefaction* (RARE-eh-fak-shun: valleys) in the air. Any vibrating object—a tuning fork, the string of a musical instrument, or the vocal cords—will produce sound waves (rhythmic movement of air molecules). Other materials, such as fluids or solids, also can carry sound.

The *frequency* of sound waves (the number of waves per second) corresponds to the perceived *pitch* (higher or lower tone) of a sound. The *amplitude*, or physical "height," of a sound wave tells how much energy it contains. Psychologically, amplitude corresponds to sensed *loudness* or sound intensity (● **Figure 19.1**).

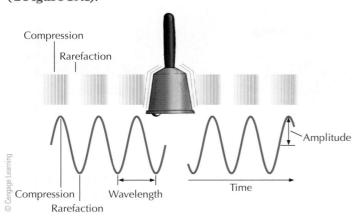

● **Figure 19.1**

Waves of compression in the air, or vibrations, are the stimulus for hearing. The frequency (or wavelength) of sound waves determines their pitch. The amplitude determines loudness.

How We Hear Sounds

How are sounds converted to nerve impulses? Hearing involves a chain of events that begins with the *pinna* (PIN-ah), the visible, external part of the ear. In addition to being a good place to hang earrings or balance pencils, the pinna acts like a funnel to concentrate sounds. After they are guided into the ear canal, sound waves collide with the *tympanic membrane* (eardrum), setting it in motion. This, in turn, causes three small bones, the *auditory ossicles* (OSS-ih-kuls), to vibrate (● **Figure 19.2**). The ossicles are the malleus (MAL-ee-us), incus, and stapes (STAY-peas). Their common names are the hammer, anvil, and stirrup. The ossicles link the eardrum with the *cochlea* (KOCK-lee-ah), a snail-shaped organ that makes up the inner ear. The stapes is attached to a membrane on the cochlea called the *oval window*. As the oval window moves back and forth, it makes waves in a fluid inside the cochlea.

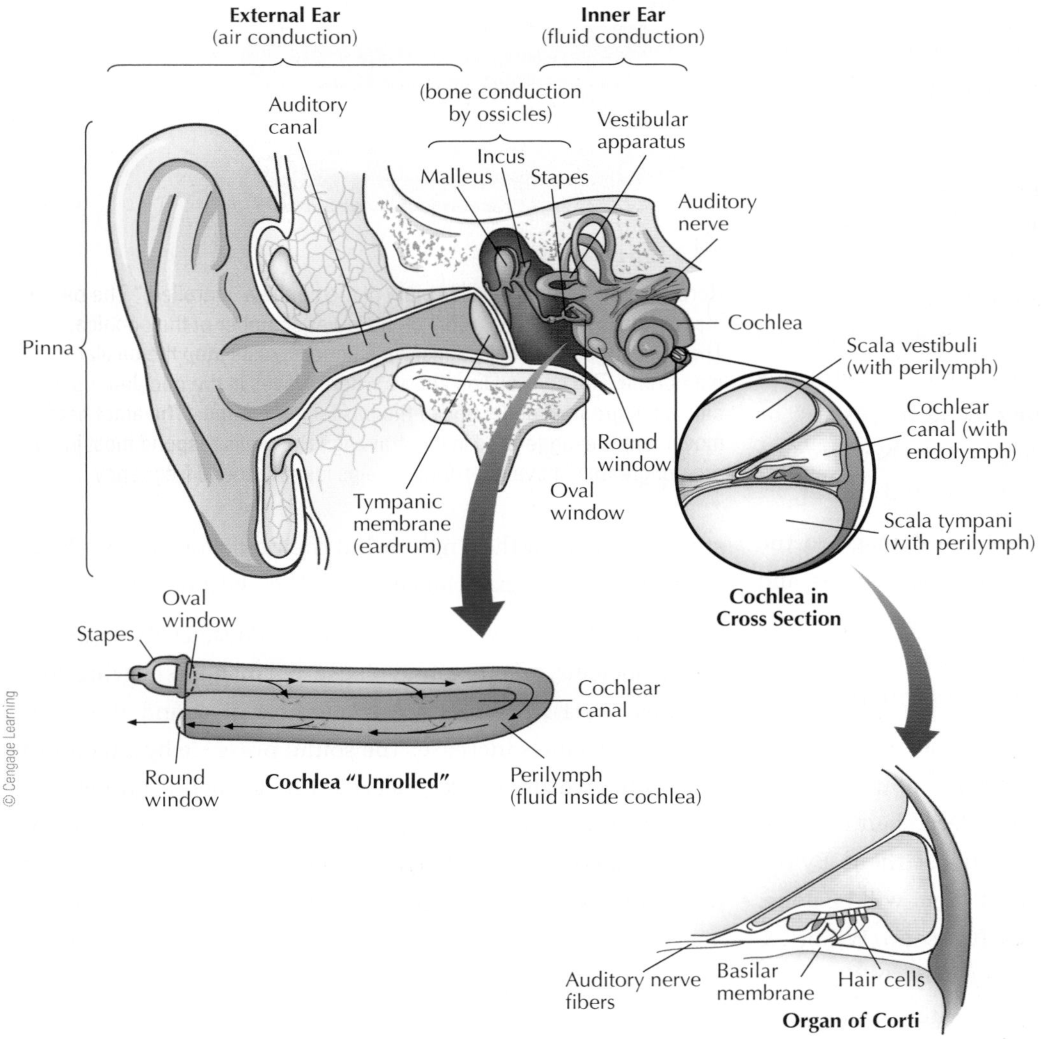

● **Figure 19.2**

Anatomy of the ear. The entire ear is a mechanism for transducing waves of air pressure into nerve impulses. The inset in the foreground ("Cochlea 'Unrolled'") shows that as the stapes moves the oval window, the round window bulges outward, allowing waves to ripple through fluid in the cochlea. The waves move membranes near the hair cells, causing cilia, or "bristles," on the tips of the cells to bend. The hair cells then generate nerve impulses carried to the brain. (See an enlarged cross section of cochlea in Figure 19.3.)

External Ear (air conduction)

Inner Ear (fluid conduction)

(bone conduction by ossicles)

Auditory canal

Incus
Malleus
Stapes

Vestibular apparatus

Auditory nerve

Cochlea

Scala vestibuli (with perilymph)

Cochlear canal (with endolymph)

Scala tympani (with perilymph)

Round window

Oval window

Pinna

Tympanic membrane (eardrum)

Cochlea in Cross Section

Oval window

Stapes

Cochlear canal

Round window

Perilymph (fluid inside cochlea)

Cochlea "Unrolled"

Auditory nerve fibers

Basilar membrane

Hair cells

Organ of Corti

Inside the cochlea, tiny **hair cells** detect waves in the fluid. The hair cells are part of the **organ of Corti** (KOR-tee), which makes up the center part of the cochlea (● **Figure 19.3**). A set of *stereocilia* (STER-ee-oh-SIL-ih-ah), or "bristles," atop each hair cell brush against the tectorial membrane when waves ripple through the fluid surrounding the organ of Corti. As the stereocilia are bent, nerve impulses are triggered, which then flow to the brain.

How are higher and lower sounds detected? The **frequency theory** of hearing states that as pitch rises, nerve impulses of a corresponding frequency are fed into the auditory nerve—that is, an 800-hertz tone produces 800 nerve impulses per second. (*Hertz* refers to the number of vibrations per second.) This explains how sounds up to about 4,000 hertz reach the brain. But what about higher tones? **Place theory** states that higher and lower tones excite specific areas of the cochlea. High tones register most strongly at the base of the cochlea (near the oval window). Lower tones, on the other hand, mostly move hair cells near the narrow outer tip of the cochlea (● **Figure 19.4**). Pitch is signaled by the area of the cochlea most strongly activated. Place theory also explains why hunters sometimes lose hearing in a narrow pitch range. "Hunter's notch," as it is called, occurs when hair cells are damaged in the area affected by the pitch of gunfire.

Hearing Loss *Are there different types of hearing loss?* The two most common types of hearing loss afflict some 36 million Americans (National Institutes of Health, 2012) and over 270 million people worldwide (Tennesen, 2007). **Conductive hearing loss** occurs when the transfer of vibrations from the outer ear to the inner ear weakens. For example, the eardrums or ossicles may be damaged or immobilized by disease or injury. In many cases, conductive hearing loss can be overcome with a hearing aid, which makes sounds louder and clearer.

Sensorineural hearing loss results from damage to the inner ear hair cells or auditory nerve. Many jobs, hobbies, and pastimes can cause **noise-induced hearing loss**, a common form of sensorineural hearing loss that occurs when very loud sounds damage fragile hair cells (as in hunter's notch).

If you work in a noisy environment or enjoy loud music, motorcycling, snowmobiling, hunting, or similar pursuits, you may be risking noise-induced hearing loss. Dead hair cells are never replaced: When you abuse them, you lose them. By the time you are 65, more than 40 percent of them will be gone, mainly those that transduce high pitches (Chisolm, Willott, & Lister, 2003; Lin et al., 2011). This explains why younger students are beginning to download very high-pitched ringtones for their cell phones: If their teacher has an aging ear, the

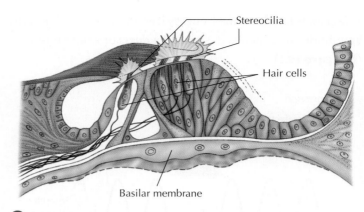

● **Figure 19.3**

A closer view of the hair cells shows how movement of fluid in the cochlea causes the bristling "hairs," or cilia, to bend, generating a nerve impulse.

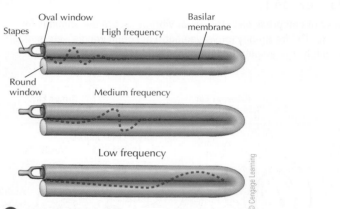

● **Figure 19.4**

Here, we see a simplified side view of the cochlea "unrolled." The basilar membrane is the elastic "roof" of the lower chamber of the cochlea. The organ of Corti, with its sensitive hair cells, rests atop the basilar membrane. The colored line shows where waves in the cochlear fluid cause the greatest deflection of the basilar membrane. (The amount of movement is exaggerated in the drawing.) Hair cells respond most in the area of greatest movement, which helps identify sound frequency.

students can hear the ringtone but their teacher cannot. (Your authors may have experienced this effect without knowing it!)

How loud must a sound be to be hazardous? Daily exposure to 85 decibels or more may cause permanent hearing loss (Mather, 2011). *Decibels* are a measure of sound intensity. Every 20 decibels increases the sound pressure by a factor of 10. In other words, a rock concert at 120 decibels is 1,000 times stronger than a voice at 60 decibels. Even short periods at 120 decibels can cause temporary hearing loss. Brief exposure to 150 decibels (a jet airplane nearby) may cause permanent hearing loss. You might find it interesting to check the decibel ratings of some of your activities in ● **Figure 19.5**. Be aware that amplified music concerts, iPod-style earbuds, and car stereos also can damage your hearing.

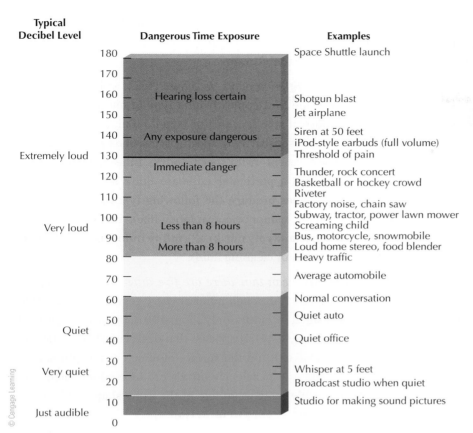

Typical Decibel Level / **Dangerous Time Exposure** / **Examples**

Typical Decibel Level	Decibel	Dangerous Time Exposure	Examples
	180		Space Shuttle launch
	170	Hearing loss certain	
	160		Shotgun blast
	150		Jet airplane
	140	Any exposure dangerous	Siren at 50 feet
Extremely loud	130		iPod-style earbuds (full volume) / Threshold of pain
	120	Immediate danger	Thunder, rock concert
	110		Basketball or hockey crowd / Riveter
	100		Factory noise, chain saw
Very loud	90	Less than 8 hours	Subway, tractor, power lawn mower / Screaming child / Bus, motorcycle, snowmobile
	80	More than 8 hours	Loud home stereo, food blender / Heavy traffic
	70		Average automobile
	60		Normal conversation
Quiet	50		Quiet auto
	40		Quiet office
	30		
Very quiet	20		Whisper at 5 feet / Broadcast studio when quiet
	10		Studio for making sound pictures
Just audible	0		

© Cengage Learning

● **Figure 19.5**

The loudness of sound is measured in decibels. Zero decibels is the faintest sound most people can hear. Sounds of 110 decibels are uncomfortably loud. Prolonged exposure to sounds above 85 decibels may damage the inner ear. Some music concerts, which can reach 120 decibels, have caused hearing loss in musicians and may affect audiences as well. Sounds of 130 decibels pose an immediate danger to hearing.

Artificial Hearing Hearing aids are no help in cases of sensorineural hearing loss because auditory messages are blocked from reaching the brain. In many cases, however, the auditory nerve is intact. This finding has spurred the development of cochlear implants that bypass hair cells and stimulate the auditory nerves directly (● **Figure 19.6**). Wires from a microphone carry electrical signals to an external coil. A matching coil under the skin picks up the signals and carries them to one or more areas of the cochlea. The latest implants use place theory to separate higher and lower tones into separate channels. This has allowed some formerly deaf persons to hear human voices, music, and other higher-frequency sounds. About 60 percent of all multichannel implant patients can understand some spoken words and appreciate music (Foley & Matlin, 2010; Leal et al., 2003). Some deaf children with implants learn to speak. Those who receive a cochlear implant before age 2 have the best chance to learn spoken language at a near normal rate (Ertmer & Jung, 2012; Gordon et al., 2011).

At present, artificial hearing remains crude. All but the most successful cochlear implant patients describe the sound as "like a radio that isn't quite tuned in." But cochlear implants are improving. And even at the current level, it is hard to argue with

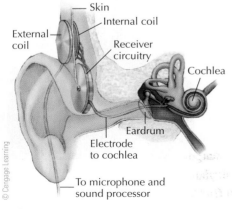

● **Figure 19.6**

A cochlear implant, or "artificial ear."

Hair cells *Receptor cells within the cochlea that transduce vibrations into nerve impulses.*
Organ of Corti *Center part of the cochlea, containing hair cells, canals, and membranes.*
Frequency theory *Holds that tones up to 4,000 hertz are converted to nerve impulses that match the frequency of each tone.*
Place theory *Theory that higher and lower tones excite specific areas of the cochlea.*
Conductive hearing loss *Poor transfer of sounds from the eardrum to the inner ear.*
Sensorineural hearing loss *Loss of hearing caused by damage to the inner ear hair cells or auditory nerve.*
Noise-induced hearing loss *Damage caused by exposing the hair cells to excessively loud sounds.*

enthusiasts like Kristen Cloud. Shortly after Kristen received an implant, she was able to hear a siren and avoid being struck by a speeding car. She says simply, "The implant saved my life."

Smell and Taste—The Nose Knows When the Tongue Can't Tell

SURVEY QUESTION 19.2: How do the chemical senses operate?

Unless you are a wine taster, a perfume blender, a chef (Ramsay?), or a gourmet, you may think of **olfaction**, or smell, and **gustation**, or taste, as minor senses. You could probably survive without these *chemical senses*—receptors that respond to chemical molecules. But don't be deceived—life without these senses can be difficult (Drummond, Douglas, & Olver, 2007). One person, for instance, almost died because he couldn't smell the smoke when his apartment building caught fire. Besides, olfaction and gustation add pleasure to our lives. Let's see how they operate.

The Sense of Smell

Smell receptors respond to airborne molecules. As air enters the nose, it flows over roughly 5 million nerve fibers embedded in the lining of the upper nasal passages (● Figure 19.7).

Receptor proteins on the surface of the fibers are sensitive to various airborne molecules. When a fiber is stimulated, it sends signals to the brain.

How are different odors detected? This is still an unfolding mystery. One hint comes from a type of *anosmia* (an-OZE-me-ah: loss of smell), a sort of "smell blindness" for a single odor. Loss of sensitivity to specific types of odors suggests the presense of receptors for specific odors. Indeed, the molecules that produce a particular odor are quite similar in shape. Specific shapes produce the following types of odors: floral (flower-like), camphoric (camphor-like), musky (have you ever smelled a sweaty musk ox?), minty (mint-like), and etherish (like ether or cleaning fluid).

Does this mean that there are five different types of olfactory receptors? Although humans carry genes for about 1,000 types of smell receptors, only about 400 of them are expressed (Sela & Sobel, 2010). It appears that different-shaped "holes," or "pockets," exist on the surface of olfactory receptors. Like a piece fits in a puzzle, chemicals produce odors when part of a molecule matches a hole of the same shape. This is the **lock-and-key theory of olfaction**.

Further, molecules trigger activity in different *combinations* of odor receptors. Thus, humans can detect at least 10,000 different odors. Just as you can make many thousands of words from the 26 letters of the alphabet, many combinations of the 400 types of receptors are possible, resulting in many different

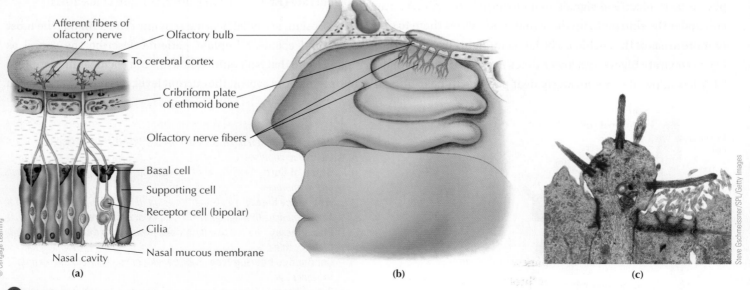

● **Figure 19.7**

Receptors for the sense of smell (olfaction). (a) Olfactory nerve fibers respond to gaseous molecules. Receptor cells are shown in cross section to the left. (b) Olfactory receptors are located in the upper nasal cavity. (c) On the right, an extreme close-up of an olfactory receptor shows fibers that sense gaseous molecules of various shapes.

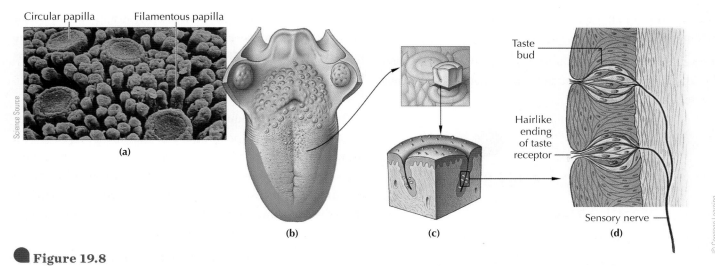

Circular papilla   Filamentous papilla

(a)   (b)   (c)   (d)

Taste bud

Hairlike ending of taste receptor

Sensory nerve

Figure 19.8

Receptors for taste: (a) The tongue is covered with small protrusions called *papillae.* (b) Most taste buds are found around the top edges of the tongue (shaded area). However, some are located elsewhere, including under the tongue. Stimulation of the central part of the tongue causes no taste sensations. All four primary taste sensations occur anywhere that taste buds exist. (c) An enlarged drawing shows that taste buds are located near the base of papillae. (d) Detail of a taste bud. These receptors also occur in other parts of the digestive system, such as the lining of the mouth.

odors. Scents also are identified, in part, by the *location* of the receptors in the nose that a particular odor activates. And finally, the *number of activated receptors* tells the brain the strength of an odor (Bensafi et al., 2004). The brain uses these distinctive patterns of messages it gets from the olfactory receptors to recognize particular scents (Sela & Sobel, 2010).

What causes anosmia? Five people out of 100 experience some degree of anosmia, including the total loss of smell (Bramerson et al., 2004). Risks include infections, allergies, and blows to the head (which may tear the olfactory nerves). Exposure to chemicals such as ammonia, paints, solvents, and hairdressing "potions" also can cause anosmia. If you value your sense of smell, be careful what you sniff (Drummond, Douglas, & Olver, 2007).

Taste and Flavors

There are at least four basic taste sensations: *sweet, salt, sour,* and *bitter.* We are most sensitive to bitter, less sensitive to sour, even less sensitive to salt, and least sensitive to sweet. This order may have helped prevent poisonings when most humans foraged for food because bitter and sour foods are more likely to be inedible.

Most experts now believe that a fifth taste quality exists (Nakamura et al., 2011). The Japanese word *umami* (oo-MAH-me) describes a pleasant savory or "brothy" taste associated with certain amino acids in chicken soup, some meat extracts, kelp, tuna, human milk, cheese, and soybeans. The receptors for *umami* are sensitive to glutamate, a substance found in mono-sodium glutamate (MSG) (Sugimoto & Ninomiya, 2005).

If there are only four or five tastes, how can there be so many different flavors? Flavors seem more varied because we include sensations of texture, temperature, smell, and even pain ("hot" chili peppers) with taste. Smell is particularly important in determining flavor (Shepherd, 2006). If you plug your nose and eat small bits of apple, potato, and onion, they will "taste" almost exactly alike. So do gourmet jelly beans! That's why food loses its "taste" when you have a cold. It is probably fair to say that subjective flavor is half smell.

MSG's reputation as a "flavor enhancer" likely arose because of the combination of savory odors of, say, chicken soup, with the taste of glutamate (which does not taste pleasant by itself) (McCabe & Rolls, 2007). At the very least, we may finally know why chicken soup is such a "comfort food." But remember to smell it first!

Taste buds, or taste-receptor cells, are located mainly on the top side of the tongue, especially around the edges. However, a few are found elsewhere inside the mouth (**Figure 19.8**). As food is chewed, it dissolves and enters the taste buds, where it sets off nerve impulses to the brain (Northcutt, 2004). Much like smell, sweet and bitter tastes appear to be based on a lock-and-key match between molecules and intricately shaped receptors. Saltiness and sourness, however, are triggered

Olfaction *The sense of smell.*
Gustation *The sense of taste.*
Lock-and-key theory of olfaction *Holds that odors are related to the shapes of chemical molecules.*
Taste buds *The receptor organs for taste.*

by a direct flow of charged atoms into the tips of taste cells (Lindemann, 2001).

If smell and taste are seen as minor senses, then the somesthetic senses are the unnoticed senses. Let's see why they merit our careful attention.

The Somesthetic Senses— Flying by the Seat of Your Pants

SURVEY QUESTION 19.3: What are the somesthetic senses?

A gymnast "flying" through a routine on the uneven bars may rely as much on the **somesthetic senses** as on vision (*soma* means "body," *esthetic* means "feel"). Even the most routine activities, such as walking, running, or passing a sobriety test, would be impossible without the **skin senses** (touch), the **kinesthetic senses** (receptors in muscles and joints that detect body position and movement), and the **vestibular senses** (receptors in the inner ear for balance, gravity, and acceleration). Because of their importance, let's begin with the skin senses.

The Skin Senses

It's difficult to imagine what life would be like without the sense of touch, but the plight of Ian Waterman gives a hint.

After an illness, Waterman permanently lost all feeling below his neck. Now, in order to know the position of his body, he must be able to see it. If he moves with his eyes closed, he has no idea where he is moving. If the lights go out in a room, he's in big trouble (Gallagher, 2004).

Skin receptors produce at least five different sensations: *light touch, pressure, pain, cold,* and *warmth.* Receptors with particular shapes appear to specialize somewhat in various sensations (**Figure 19.9**). However, free nerve endings alone can produce all five sensations (Carlson, 2013). Altogether, the skin has about 200,000 nerve endings for temperature, 500,000 for touch and pressure, and 3 million for pain.

Does the number of receptors in an area of skin relate to its sensitivity? Yes. Your skin could be "mapped" by applying heat, cold, touch, pressure, or pain to points all over your body (Hollins, 2010). Such testing would show that the number of skin receptors varies and that sensitivity generally matches the number of receptors in a given area. Broadly speaking, important areas such as the lips, tongue, face, hands, and genitals have a higher density of receptors. Of course, the sensation you ultimately feel will depend on brain activity.

Pain *Does the number of pain receptors also vary?* Yes, like the other skin senses, pain receptors vary in their distribution. About 230 pain points per square centimeter (about a half inch) are found behind the knee, 180 per centimeter on the buttocks, 60 on the pad of the thumb, and 40 on the tip of the nose. (Is it better then, to be pinched on the nose or behind the knee? It depends on what you like!)

Pain carried by *large nerve fibers* is sharp, bright, and fast and seems to come from specific body areas (McMahon & Koltzenburg, 2013). This is the body's **warning system**. Give yourself a small jab with a pin and you will feel this type of pain. As you do this, notice that warning pain quickly disappears. Much as we may dislike warning pain, it is usually a signal that the body has been, or is about to be,

Figure 19.9

The skin senses include touch, pressure, pain, cold, and warmth. This drawing shows different forms the skin receptors can take. The functions of these receptors are likely as follows: Merkel's disks sense pressure on the skin; free nerve endings sense warmth, cold, and pain; Meissner's corpuscles sense pressure; hair follicle receptors sense hair movement; Pacinian corpuscles sense pressure and vibration; and Ruffini's endings sense skin stretching (Freberg, 2010; Kalat, 2013). The feeling of being touched is likely made up of a combination of varying degrees of activity in all these receptors.

Hairy skin — Glabrous skin

Merkel's disk
Free nerve ending
Meissner's corpuscle
Hair follicle receptor
Pacinian corpuscle
Ruffini's ending

Epidermis
Dermis
Subcutaneous tissue

© Cengage Learning

damaged. Without warning pain, we would be unable to detect or prevent injury. Children who are born with a rare inherited insensitivity to pain repeatedly burn themselves, break bones, bite off parts of their tongues, and become ill without knowing it (Erez et al., 2010). As you might imagine, it's also hard for people with *congenital pain insensitivity* to have empathy for the pain of others (Danziger, Prkachin, & Willer, 2006).

A second type of somatic pain is carried by *small nerve fibers*. This type of pain is slower, nagging, aching, widespread, and very unpleasant (McMahon & Koltzenburg, 2013). It gets worse if the pain stimulus is repeated. This is the body's **reminding system**. It reminds the brain that the body has been injured. For instance, lower-back pain often has this quality. Sadly, the reminding system can cause agony long after an injury has healed, or in terminal illnesses, when the reminder is useless.

The Pain Gate You may have noticed that one type of pain will sometimes cancel another. Ronald Melzack's (1999) **gate control theory** suggests that pain messages from the different nerve fibers pass through the same neural "gate" in the spinal cord. If the gate is "closed" by one pain message, other messages may not be able to pass through (Melzack & Katz, 2006).

How is the gate closed? Messages carried by large, fast nerve fibers seem to close the spinal pain gate directly. Doing so can prevent slower, "reminding system" pain from reaching the brain. Messages from small, slow fibers seem to take a different route. After going through the pain gate, they pass on to a "central biasing system" in the brain. Under some circumstances, the brain then sends a message back down the spinal cord, closing the pain gates (● Figure 19.10). Melzack believes that gate control theory also may explain the painkilling effects of *acupuncture* (but see "The Neomatrix and Phantom Limbs").

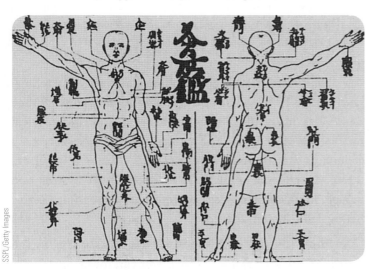

(Above) An acupuncturist's chart. (Left) Thin stainless steel needles are inserted into areas defined by the chart. Modern research has begun to explain the painkilling effects of acupuncture (see text). Acupuncture's claimed ability to cure diseases is more debatable.

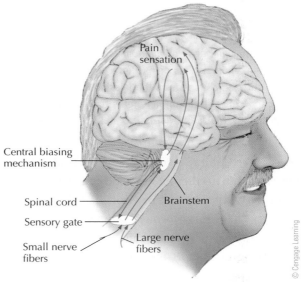

● **Figure 19.10**

Diagram of a sensory gate for pain. A series of pain impulses going through the gate may prevent other pain messages from passing through. Or pain messages may relay through a "central biasing mechanism" that exerts control over the gate, closing it to other impulses.

Somesthetic senses *Sensations produced by the skin, muscles, joints, viscera, and organs of balance.*
Skin senses *The senses of touch, pressure, pain, heat, and cold.*
Kinesthetic senses *The senses of body movement and positioning.*
Vestibular senses *The senses of balance, gravity, position in space, and acceleration.*
Warning system *Pain based on large nerve fibers; warns that bodily damage may be occurring.*
Reminding system *Pain based on small nerve fibers; reminds the brain that the body has been injured.*
Gate control theory *Proposes that pain messages pass through neural "gates" in the spinal cord.*

Brainwaves

The Neomatrix and Phantom Limbs

In the popular *Matrix* films, Neo, as played by Keanu Reeves, discovers that machines have imprisoned humans in a phantom world called the Matrix, in order to steal human energy for their own use. Actually, the idea of a "matrix" is not totally farfetched. Your own brain may create a *neuromatrix* that allows you to perceive your own body (Iannetti & Mouraux, 2010).

A person who suffers an amputation doesn't need to believe in the Matrix to encounter phantoms. Most amputees have *phantom limb* sensations, including pain, for months or years after losing a limb (Longo, Long, & Haggard, 2012; Murray et al., 2007). Because the phantom limb feels so "real," a patient with a recently amputated leg may inadvertently try to walk on it, risking further injury. Sometimes phantom limbs feel like they are stuck in awkward positions. For instance, one man can't fall asleep on his back because his missing arm feels like it is twisted behind him.

What causes the experience of phantom limbs? Gate control theory cannot explain phantom limb pain (Hunter, Katz, & Davis, 2003). Because pain can't be coming from the missing limb (after all, it's missing!), it cannot pass through pain gates to the brain. Instead, according to Ronald Melzack (Melzack & Katz, 2006), over time,

the brain creates a body image called the *neuromatrix*. This internal model of the body generates our sense of bodily self. Although amputation may remove a limb, it still exists as far as the neuromatrix is concerned.

In fact, amputees dream of intact, fully functional limbs without any phantom limb experiences. Evidently, during sleep, sensory inputs from the area of the missing limb are suppressed. In contrast, when amputees are awake, sensory inputs from the area of the missing limb conflict with the neuromatrix, which interprets the conflict as a phantom limb, complete with phantom limb pain (Alessandria et al., 2011; Giummarra et al., 2007). Functional magnetic resonance imaging (fMRI) confirms that sensory and motor areas of the brain are more active when a person feels a phantom limb (MacIver et al., 2008).

Sometimes the brain gradually reorganizes to adjust for the sensory loss (Schmalzl et al., 2011). For example, a person who loses an arm may at first have a phantom arm and hand. After many years, the phantom may shrink, until only a hand is felt at the shoulder. Perhaps more vividly than others, people with phantom limbs are reminded that the sensory world we experience is constructed, moment by moment, not by some futuristic machines but by our own brain activity.

Acupuncture is the Chinese medical art of relieving pain and illness by inserting thin needles into the body. As the acupuncturist's needles are twirled, heated, or electrified, they activate small pain fibers. These relay through the biasing system to close the gates to intense or chronic pain. Studies have shown that acupuncture produces short-term pain relief for about half of patients tested (Weidenhammer et al., 2007; Witt et al., 2011). (However, its ability to cure illness is much more debatable.)

Pain Control Gate control theory helps explain *counterirritation*, one widely used pain-control technique. Pain clinics use it by applying a mild electrical current to the skin. This causes only a mild tingling, but it can greatly reduce more agonizing pain (Köke et al., 2004). For more extreme pain, the electrical current can be applied directly to the spinal cord (Linderoth & Foreman, 2006).

You can use counterirritation to control your own pain (Schmelz, 2010). For instance, if you are having a tooth filled, try itching or pinching yourself, or digging a fingernail into a knuckle, while the dentist is working. Focus your attention on the pain you are creating, and increase it anytime the dentist's work becomes more uncomfortable or painful. This strategy may seem strange, but it works. Generations of children have used it to take the edge off a spanking.

In some cultures, people endure tattooing, stretching, cutting, and burning with little apparent pain. How do they do it? Very likely, the answer lies in relying on psychological factors that anyone can use to reduce pain, such as anxiety reduction, control, and attention (Mailis-Gagnon & Israelson, 2005). In general, unpleasant emotions such as fear and anxiety increase pain; pleasant emotions decrease it (Kerns, Sellinger, & Goodin, 2011).

Anytime you can anticipate pain (such as a trip to the doctor, dentist, or tattoo parlor), you can lower anxiety by making sure you are *fully informed*. Be sure everything that will happen is explained. In general, the more control you *feel* over a painful stimulus, the less pain is experienced (Vallerand, Saunders, & Anthony, 2007). To apply this principle, you might arrange a signal so your doctor, dentist, or body piercer will know when to start and stop a painful procedure. Finally, distraction also reduces pain. Instead of listening to the whirr of a dentist's drill, for example, you could imagine that you are lying in the sun at a beach, listening to the roar of the surf. Or take an iPod along and crank up your favorite MP3s (Bushnell, Villemure, & Duncan, 2004). At home, music also can be a good distractor from chronic pain (Mitchell et al., 2007).

The Vestibular System

Although space flight might look like fun, the likelihood of you throwing up during your first experience in orbit is about 70 percent.

Why? Weightlessness and space flight affect the vestibular system and often cause severe motion sickness. Within the vestibular system, fluid-filled sacs called *otolith* (OH-toe-lith) *organs* are sensitive to movement, acceleration, and gravity (● **Figure 19.11**). The otolith organs contain tiny crystals in a soft, gelatin-like mass. The tug of gravity or rapid head movements can cause the mass to shift. This, in turn, stimulates hair-like receptor cells, allowing us to sense gravity, acceleration, and movement through space (Lackner & DiZio, 2005).

Weightlessness presents astronauts with a real challenge in sensory adaptation. In 2007, world-famous physicist Steven Hawking, who suffers from amyotrophic lateral sclerosis (ALS, or Lou Gehrig's disease), fulfilled a lifelong dream of experiencing weightlessness. He took a flight on the "Weightless Wonder," NASA's official nickname for the high-flying airplane that provides short periods of weightlessness to train astronauts. (Unofficially, it is called the "Vomit Comet.")

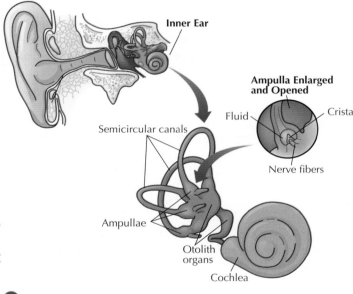

● **Figure 19.11**
The vestibular system. (See text for explanation.)

Three fluid-filled tubes—called the *semicircular canals*—are the sensory organs for balance. If you could climb inside these tubes, you would find that head movements cause the fluid to swirl about. As the fluid moves, it bends a small "flap," or "float," called the *crista*, that detects movement in the semicircular canals. The bending of each crista again stimulates hair cells and signals head rotation.

What causes motion sickness? According to **sensory conflict theory**, dizziness and nausea occur when sensations from the vestibular system don't match sensations from the eyes and body (Flanagan, May, & Dobie, 2004). On solid ground, information from the vestibular system, vision, and kinesthesis usually matches. However, in a heaving, pitching boat, car, or

airplane, or even playing a video game, a serious mismatch can occur—causing disorientation and heaving of another kind (Chang et al., 2012).

Why does sensory conflict cause nausea? You can probably blame (or thank) evolution. Many poisons disturb the vestibular system, vision, and the body. Therefore, we may have evolved so that we react to sensory conflict by vomiting to expel poison. The value of this reaction, however, may be little comfort to anyone who has ever been "green" and miserable with motion sickness. To minimize such conflicts, try to keep your head still, fix your vision on a distant immobile object, and lie down if you can (Harm, 2002).

CENGAGE brain.com

Go to **cengagebrain.com** to access **MindTap for Coon/ Mitterer *Psychology Modules for Active Learning*** and other online learning tools. MindTap is a fully online learning experience that combines all the tools you need—readings, multimedia, activities, and assessments—into a singular personalized Learning Path that guides you through the course.

Sensory conflict theory *Explains motion sickness as the result of a mismatch among information from vision, the vestibular system, and kinesthesis.*

Module 19: Summary

19.1 What are the mechanisms of hearing?

- **19.1.1** Sound waves are the stimulus for hearing. They are transduced by the eardrum, auditory ossicles, oval window, cochlea, and ultimately, the hair cells.
- **19.1.2** Frequency theory explains how we hear tones up to 4,000 hertz; place theory explains tones above 4,000 hertz.
- **19.1.3** Two basic types of hearing loss are conductive hearing loss and sensorineural hearing loss. Noise-induced hearing loss is a common form of sensorineural hearing loss caused by exposure to loud noise.

19.2 How do the chemical senses operate?

- **19.2.1** Olfaction (smell) and gustation (taste) are chemical senses that respond to airborne or liquefied molecules.
- **19.2.2** The lock-and-key theory of olfaction partially explains smell. In addition, the location of the olfactory receptors in the nose helps identify various scents.
- **19.2.3** Sweet and bitter tastes are based on a lock-and-key coding of molecule shapes. Salty and sour tastes are triggered by a direct flow of ions into taste receptors.

19.3 What are the somesthetic senses?

- **19.3.1** The somesthetic senses include the skin senses, vestibular senses, and kinesthetic senses (receptors that detect muscle and joint positioning).
- **19.3.2** The skin senses are touch, pressure, pain, cold, and warmth. Sensitivity to each is related to the number of receptors found in an area of skin.
- **19.3.3** Distinctions can be made between warning pain and reminding pain.
- **19.3.4** Selective gating of pain messages takes place in the spinal cord, as explained by gate control theory.
- **19.3.5** Pain can be reduced through counterirritation and by controlling anxiety and attention.
- **19.3.6** According to sensory conflict theory, motion sickness is caused by a mismatch of visual, kinesthetic, and vestibular sensations. Motion sickness can be avoided by minimizing sensory conflict.

Module 19: Knowledge Builder

Recite

1. The frequency of a sound wave corresponds to how loud it is. **T or F?**

2. Sensorineural hearing loss occurs when the auditory ossicles are damaged. **T or F?**

3. Daily exposure to sounds with a loudness of _____ decibels may cause permanent hearing loss.

4. Olfaction appears to be at least partially explained by the _____ _____ _____ theory of molecule shapes and receptor sites.

5. Which of the following is a somesthetic sense?
   - **a.** gustation
   - **b.** olfaction
   - **c.** rarefaction
   - **d.** kinesthesis

6. Warning pain is carried by _____ nerve fibers.

7. Head movements are detected primarily in the semicircular canals and gravity by the otolith organs. **T or F?**

Reflect

Think Critically

8. Why do you think your voice sounds so different when you hear a recording of your speech?

9. Drivers are less likely to become carsick than passengers. Why do you think drivers and passengers differ in susceptibility to motion sickness?

Self-Reflect

Close your eyes and listen to the sounds around you. As you do, try to mentally trace the events necessary to convert vibrations in the air into the sounds you hear.

What is your favorite food aroma? What is your favorite taste? Explain how you are able to sense the aroma and taste of foods.

Stand on one foot with your eyes closed. Now touch the tip of your nose with your index finger. Which of the somesthetic senses did you use to perform this feat?

Imagine you are on a boat ride with a friend who starts to feel queasy. What would you explain to your friend about the causes of motion sickness and what she or he can do to prevent it?

ANSWERS

1. F 2. F 3. 85 4. lock and key 5. d 6. large 7. T 8. The answer lies in another question: How else might vibrations from the voice reach the cochlea? Other people hear your voice only as it is carried through the air. You hear not only that sound but also vibrations conducted by the bones of your skull. 9. Drivers experience less sensory conflict because they control the car's motion. This allows them to anticipate the car's movements and to coordinate their head and eye movements with those of the car.

Sensation and Perception: Perceptual Processes

Is That a Deer?

While driving at night, a woman slams on her brakes to avoid hitting a deer. As she skids to a stop, she realizes that the "deer" is actually a bush on the roadside. Such misperceptions are common. The brain must continuously find patterns in a welter of sensations. If you look closely at this photomosaic by Robert Silver, you may see that it is made up entirely of small individual photos. An infant or newly sighted person looking closely at the same photomosaic might well see only a jumble of meaningless colors. But because the photos form a familiar pattern, you should easily see the Statue of Liberty.

How do we organize sensations into perceptions? Visual perception involves finding meaningful patterns in complex stimuli. Our brain creates our perceptions by using preexisting knowledge such as the principles of perceptual grouping and perceptual constancies to help us make sense out of sensations.

Joe Sohm/Visions of America, LLC / Alamy

SURVEY QUESTIONS

20.1 In general, how do we construct our perceptions?

20.2 How is it possible to see depth and judge distance?

Perception—The Second Step

SURVEY QUESTION 20.1: In general, how do we construct our perceptions?

Aren't you born with the ability to create perceptions out of sensations? Imagine what it would be like to have your vision restored after a lifetime of blindness. Actually, a first look at the world can be disappointing because the newfound ability to *sense* (see) the world does not guarantee that it can be *perceived.* Newly sighted persons must *learn* to identify objects, to read clocks, numbers, and letters, and to judge sizes and

distances. For instance, Mr. S. B. was a cataract patient who had been blind since birth. After an operation restored his sight at age 52, Mr. S. B. struggled to use his vision (Gregory, 2003).

Mr. S. B. soon learned to tell time from a large clock and to read block letters he had known only from touch. At a zoo, he recognized an elephant from descriptions he had heard. However, handwriting meant nothing to him for more than a year after he regained sight, and many objects were meaningless until he touched them. Thus, Mr. S. B. slowly learned to organize his *sensations* into meaningful *perceptions.* Cases like those of Mr. S. B. show that your experiences are **perceptual constructions**, or mental models of external events, that *are actively created by your brain* (Goldstein, 2014).

Of course, perceptions can be *mis*constructed as they are filtered through our needs, expectations, attitudes, values, and beliefs (● Figure 20.1). One of your authors was once approached in a supermarket by a young girl screaming, "Help! Someone is killing my father." He followed her to see two men struggling. The guy on top had his victim by the throat. Blood was everywhere. It was a murder in progress! Soon, however, it turned out that the "guy on the bottom" had passed out, hit his head, and was bleeding. The "guy on top" saw the first man fall and was loosening his collar.

● Figure 20.1

It is difficult to look at this simple drawing without perceiving depth. Yet the drawing is nothing more than a collection of flat shapes. Turn this page counterclockwise 90 degrees and you will see 3 *C*s, one within another. When the drawing is turned sideways, it seems nearly flat. However, if you turn the page upright again, a sense of depth will reappear. Clearly, you have used your knowledge and expectations to *construct* an illusion of depth. The drawing itself would be only a flat design if you didn't invest it with meaning.

Obviously, the girl misperceived what was happening to her father. Because of the dramatic influence of her words, so did your author. As this story shows, sensory information can be interpreted in various ways. The girl's description completely shaped his own initial perceptions. This perhaps is understandable. But he'll never forget the added shock he felt when he met the "murderer." The man he had seen a few moments before as vicious and horrible-looking was not even a stranger. He was a neighbor whom your author had seen dozens of times before. Clearly, we don't just believe what we see. We also see what we believe.

Illusions Perceptual *mis*construction is responsible for many illusions. In an **illusion**, length, position, motion, curvature, or direction is consistently misjudged. For example, because we have seen thousands of rooms shaped roughly like a box, we habitually construct perceptions based on this assumption. This need not be true, however. An *Ames room* (named for the man who designed it) is a lopsided space that appears square when viewed from a certain angle (● Figure 20.2). This illusion is achieved by carefully distorting the proportions of the walls, floor, ceiling, and windows. Because the left corner of the Ames room is farther from a viewer than the right, a person standing in that corner looks very small; one standing in the nearer, shorter right corner looks very large. A person who walks from the left to the right corner will seem to "magically" grow larger.

Notice that illusions are distorted perceptions of stimuli that actually exist. In a **hallucination**, people perceive objects or events that have no external reality (Boksa, 2009). For example, they hear voices that are not there (Plaze et al., 2011) (see "Staying in Touch with Reality"). If you think you

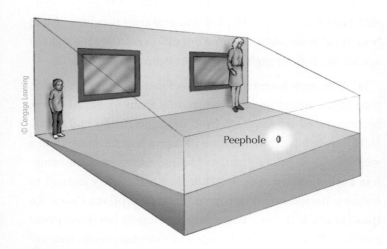

● Figure 20.2

The Ames room. From the front, the room looks normal; in reality, the right-hand corner is very short, and the left-hand corner is very tall. In addition, the left side of the room slants away from viewers. The diagram shows the shape of the room and reveals why people appear to get bigger as they cross the room toward the nearer, shorter right corner.

The Clinical File

Staying in Touch with Reality

Just imagine that often, and without warning, you hear a voice shouting, "Buckets of blood!" or see blood spattering across the walls of your bedroom. Chances are people would think you are mentally disturbed. Hallucinations are a major symptom of psychosis, dementia, epilepsy, migraine headaches, alcohol withdrawal, and drug intoxication (Plaze et al., 2011; Spence & David, 2004). They also are one of the clearest signs that a person has "lost touch with reality."

Yet consider the case of mathematician John Nash (the subject of *A Beautiful Mind,* the winner of the 2002 Oscar for best film). Even though Nash suffered from schizophrenia, he eventually learned to use his *reality testing* to sort out which of his experiences were perceptions and which were hallucinations. Unlike John Nash, however, most people who experience full-blown hallucinations have a limited ability to engage in reality testing (Hohwy & Rosenberg, 2005).

Curiously, "sane hallucinations" also occur. *Charles Bonnet syndrome* is a rare condition that afflicts mainly older people who are partially blind, but not mentally disturbed (Cammaroto et al., 2008). Animals, buildings, plants, people, and other objects may seem to appear and disappear in front of their eyes. One older man suffering from partial blindness and leukemia complained of seeing animals in his house, including cattle and bears (Jacob et al., 2004). However, people experiencing "sane hallucinations" can more easily tell that their hallucinations aren't real because their capacity for reality testing is not impaired.

Such unusual experiences show how powerfully the brain seeks meaningful patterns in sensory input and the role that reality testing plays in our normal perceptual experience.

---

are experiencing an illusion or a hallucination, try engaging in some reality testing.

Figure 20.3

The limits of pure perception. Even simple designs are easily misperceived. Fraser's spiral is actually a series of concentric circles. The illusion is so powerful that people who try to trace one of the circles sometimes follow the illusory spiral and jump from one circle to the next. (After Seckel, 2000.)

What do you mean by reality testing? In any situation having an element of doubt or uncertainty, **reality testing** involves obtaining additional information to check your perceptions (Landa et al., 2006). If you think you see a 3-foot-tall butterfly, you can confirm you are hallucinating by trying to touch its wings. To detect an illusion, you may have to measure a drawing or apply a straightedge to it. ● **Figure 20.3** shows a powerful illusion called Fraser's spiral. What appears to be a spiral is actually made of a series of closed circles. Most people cannot spontaneously see this reality. Instead, they must carefully trace one of the circles to confirm what is "real" in the design.

Let's explore the process of perceptual construction and some factors that shape or even distort it.

Bottom-Up and Top-Down Processing

Moment by moment, our perceptions are typically constructed in both *bottom-up* and *top-down* fashion. Think about the process of building a house: Raw materials, such as lumber, doors, tiles, carpets, screws, and nails, must be painstakingly fitted

Perceptual construction *A mental model of external events.*
Illusion *A misleading or misconstructed perception.*
Hallucination *An imaginary sensation—such as seeing, hearing, or smelling something that does not exist in the external world.*
Reality testing *Obtaining additional information to check on the accuracy of perceptions.*

together. At the same time, a building plan guides how the raw materials are assembled.

Our brain builds perceptions in similar ways. In **bottom-up processing**, we start constructing at the "bottom" with raw materials—that is, we begin with small sensory units (features) and build upward to a complete perception. The reverse also occurs. In **top-down processing**, preexisting knowledge is used to rapidly organize features into a meaningful whole (Goldstein, 2014). If you put together a picture puzzle you've never seen before, you are relying mainly on bottom-up processing: You must assemble small pieces until a recognizable pattern begins to emerge. Top-down processing is like putting together a puzzle you have solved many times: After only a few pieces are in place, your past experience gives you the plan to rapidly fill in the final picture.

Both types of processing are illustrated by ● **Figure 20.4**. Also, look ahead to Figure 20.7. The first time you see this photo, you will probably process it bottom-up, picking out features until it becomes recognizable. The next time you see it, because of top-down processing, you should recognize it instantly.

● **Figure 20.4**

Check out this abstract design. If you process it "bottom-up," likely all you will see are three small, dark geometric shapes near the edges. Would you like to try some top-down processing? Knowing the title of the design will help you apply your knowledge and see it in an entirely different way. The title? It's *Special K*. Can you see it now?

An excellent example of perceptual construction is found in the Gestalt organizing principles.

Gestalt Organizing Principles

How are sensations organized into perceptions? The Gestalt psychologists (see Module 3) proposed that the simplest organization involves grouping some sensations into an object, or figure, that stands out on a plainer background. **Figure-ground organization** is probably inborn because it is the first perceptual ability to appear after cataract patients like Mr. S. B. regain sight. In normal figure-ground perception, only one figure is seen. In *reversible figures,* however, figure and ground can be switched. In ● **Figure 20.5**, it is equally possible to see either a wineglass on a dark background or two facial profiles on a light background. As you shift from one pattern to the other, you should get a clear sense of what figure-ground organization means.

● **Figure 20.5**

A reversible figure-ground design. Do you see two faces in profile or a wine glass?

The Gestalt psychologists identified several other principles that bring some order to your perceptions (● **Figure 20.6**).

1. **Nearness.** All other things equal, stimuli that are near each other tend to be grouped together (Quinn, Bhatt, & Hayden, 2008). Thus, if three people stand near each other and a fourth person stands 10 feet away, the adjacent three will be seen as a group and the distant person as an outsider (see Figure 20.6*a*).

2. **Similarity.** "Birds of a feather flock together," and stimuli that are similar in size, shape, color, or form tend to be grouped together (see Figure 20.6*b*). Picture two bands marching side by side. If their uniforms are different colors, the bands will be seen as two separate groups, not as one large group.

3. **Continuation, or continuity.** Perceptions tend toward simplicity and continuity. In Figure 20.6*c*, it is easier to visualize a wavy line on a squared-off line than it is to see a complex row of shapes.

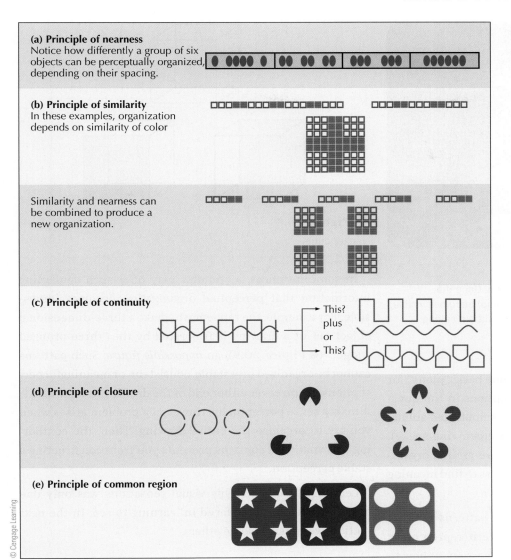

Figure 20.6
Some Gestalt organizing principles.

(a) Principle of nearness
Notice how differently a group of six objects can be perceptually organized, depending on their spacing.

(b) Principle of similarity
In these examples, organization depends on similarity of color

Similarity and nearness can be combined to produce a new organization.

(c) Principle of continuity

This? plus or This?

(d) Principle of closure

(e) Principle of common region

© Cengage Learning

4. **Closure.** Closure refers to the tendency to *complete* a figure so that it has a consistent overall form. Each of the drawings in Figure 20.6*d* has one or more gaps, yet each is perceived as a recognizable figure. The "shapes" that appear in the two drawings on the right in Figure 20.6*d* are *illusory figures* (implied shapes that are not bounded by an edge or an outline). Even young children see these shapes, despite knowing that they are "not really there." Illusory figures reveal that our tendency to form shapes—even with minimal cues—is powerful.

5. **Common region.** As you can see in Figure 20.6*e*, stimuli that are found within a common area tend to be seen as a group (Palmer & Beck, 2007). On the basis of similarity and nearness, the stars in Figure 20.6*e* should be one group and the dots another. However, the colored backgrounds define regions that create three groups of objects (four stars, two stars plus two dots, and four dots).

6. **Contiguity.** A principle that can't be shown in Figure 20.6 is contiguity, or nearness in time *and* space. Contiguity often is responsible for the perception that one thing has *caused* another (Buehner & May, 2003). A psychologist friend of ours demonstrates this principle in class by knocking on his head with one hand while knocking on a wooden table (out of sight) with the other. The knocking sound is perfectly timed with the movements of his visible hand. This leads to the irresistible perception that his head is made of wood.

Bottom-up processing *Organizing perceptions by beginning with low-level features.*
Top-down processing *Applying higher-level knowledge to rapidly organize sensory information into a meaningful perception.*
Figure-ground organization *Organizing a perception so that part of a stimulus appears to stand out as an object (figure) against a less prominent background (ground).*

Figure 20.7

A challenging example of perceptual organization. Once the camouflaged insect (known as a leaf mimic katydid) becomes visible, it is almost impossible to view the picture again without seeing the insect. Go ahead, try it!

Clearly, the Gestalt principles offer us some basic "plans" for organizing parts of our day-to-day perceptions in top-down fashion. Take a moment and look for the camouflaged animal pictured in ● **Figure 20.7** (no, it's not a green vine snake). Because camouflage patterns break up figure-ground organization, Mr. S. B. would have been at a total loss to find meaning in such a picture.

In a way, we are all detectives seeking patterns in what we see. In this sense, a meaningful pattern represents a **perceptual hypothesis**, or initial plan or guess about how to organize sensations. Have you ever seen a "friend" in the distance, only to have the person turn into a stranger as you drew closer? Preexisting ideas and expectations *actively* guide our interpretation of sensations (Most et al., 2005).

The active, constructive nature of perception is perhaps most apparent for *ambiguous stimuli* (patterns allowing more than one interpretation). If you look at a cloud, you may discover dozens of ways to organize its contours into fanciful shapes and scenes. Even clearly defined stimuli may permit more than one interpretation. Look at the Necker cube in ● **Figure 20.8** if you doubt that perception is an active process. Visualize the top cube as a wire box. If you stare at the cube, its organization will change. Sometimes it will seem to project upward, like the lower-left cube; other times it will project downward. The difference lies in how your brain interprets the same information. In short, we actively *construct* meaningful perceptions; we do not passively record the events and stimuli around us (Rolls, 2008).

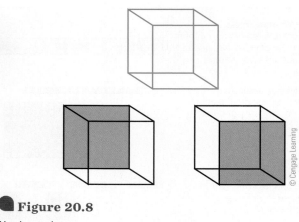

Figure 20.8
Necker cube.

In some instances, a stimulus may offer such conflicting information that perceptual organization becomes impossible. For example, the tendency to make a three-dimensional object out of a drawing is frustrated by the "three-pronged widget" (● **Figure 20.9**), an *impossible figure*. Such patterns cannot be organized into stable, consistent, or meaningful perceptions. If you cover either end of the drawing in Figure 20.9, it makes sense perceptually. However, a problem arises when you try to organize the entire drawing. Then, the conflicting information it contains prevents you from constructing a stable perception.

Learning to organize his visual sensations was only one of the hurdles Mr. S. B. faced in learning to see. In the next section, we consider some others.

Figure 20.9
An impossible figure—the "three-pronged widget."

Perceptual Constancies

When Mr. S. B. first regained his vision, he could judge distance only in familiar situations (Gregory, 1990). One day he was found crawling out of a hospital window to get a closer look at traffic on the street. It's easy to understand his curiosity, but he had to be restrained. His room was on the fourth floor!

Why would Mr. S. B. try to crawl out of a fourth-story window? Couldn't he at least tell distance from the size of the cars? No. You

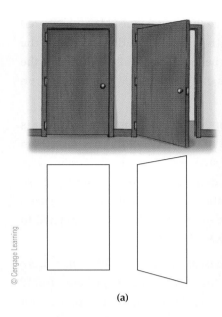

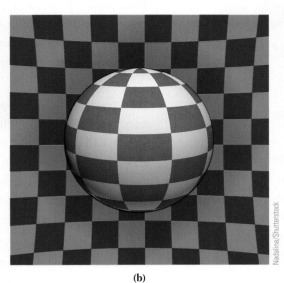

(a)   (b)

© Cengage Learning

Nadalina/Shutterstock

Figure 20.10

Shape constancy. (a) When a door is open, its image forms a trapezoid. Shape constancy is indicated because it is still perceived as a rectangle. (b) With great effort, you may be able to see this design as a collection of flat shapes. However, if you maintain shape constancy, the distorted quadrilaterals strongly suggest the surface of a sphere.

must be visually familiar with objects to use their size to judge distance. Try holding your left hand a few inches in front of your nose and your right hand at arm's length. Your right hand should appear to be about half the size of your left hand. Still, you know your right hand did not suddenly shrink, because you have seen it many times at various distances. We call this **size constancy**: The perceived size of an object remains the same, even though the size of its image on the retina changes.

To perceive your hand accurately, you had to draw on past experience to provide a top-down plan for constructing your perception. Some of these plans are so basic they seem *native*, or inborn. An example is the ability to see a line on a piece of paper. Likewise, even newborn babies show some evidence of size constancy (Granrud, 2006). However, many of our perceptions are *empirical*, or based on prior experience. For instance, cars, houses, and people look like toys when seen from a great distance or from an unfamiliar perspective, such as from the top of a skyscraper. This suggests that although some size constancy is innate, it also is affected by learning (Granrud, 2009).

In **shape constancy**, the shape of an object remains stable, even though the shape of its retinal image changes. You can demonstrate shape constancy by looking at this page from directly overhead and then from an angle. Obviously, the page is rectangular, but most of the images that reach your eyes are distorted. Yet, though the book's image changes, your perception of its shape remains constant (for additional examples, see ● **Figure 20.10**). On the highway, alcohol intoxication impairs size and shape constancy, adding to the accident rate among drunk drivers (Goldstein, 2014).

Let's say that you are outside in bright sunlight. Beside you, a friend is wearing a gray skirt and a white blouse. Suddenly a cloud shades the sun. It might seem that the blouse would grow dimmer, but it still appears to be bright white. This happens because the blouse continues to reflect a greater *proportion* of light than nearby objects. **Brightness constancy** refers to the fact that the brightness of objects appears to stay the same as lighting conditions change. However, this holds true only if the blouse and other objects are all illuminated by the same amount of light. You could make an area on your friend's gray skirt look whiter than the shaded blouse by shining a bright spotlight on the skirt.

To summarize, the energy patterns reaching our senses are constantly changing, even when they come from the same object. Size, shape, and brightness constancy rescue us from a confusing world in which objects would seem to shrink and grow, change shape as if made of rubber, and light up or fade like neon lamps.

Perceptual hypothesis *An initial guess regarding how to organize (perceive) a stimulus pattern.*
Size constancy *The perceived size of an object remains constant, despite changes in its retinal image.*
Shape constancy *The perceived shape of an object is unaffected by changes in its retinal image.*
Brightness constancy *The apparent (or relative) brightness of objects remains the same as long as they are illuminated by the same amount of light.*

Depth Perception—What If the World Were Flat?

SURVEY QUESTION 20.2: How is it possible to see depth and judge distance?

One particularly interesting example of perceptual construction is the brain's ability to construct a three-dimensional (3-D) experience of the world around us. Cross your eyes, hold your head very still, and stare at a single point across the room. Your surroundings may appear to be almost flat, like a two-dimensional (2-D) painting or photograph. This is the world that neuroscientist Susan Barry, cross-eyed from birth, lived with until, at the age of 48, she learned to see in 3-D (Barry & Sacks, 2009). Now, uncross your eyes. Suddenly, the 3-D perceptual world returns. What mechanisms underlie our ability to perceive depth and space?

Depth perception is the ability to see space and to accurately judge distances. Without 3-D depth perception, a form of perceptual construction, the world would look like a flat surface. You would have great difficulty driving a car or riding a bicycle, shooting baskets, threading a needle, or simply navigating a room (Harris & Jenkin, 2011).

Mr. S. B. had trouble with depth perception after his sight was restored. Is depth perception learned? Studies done with a visual cliff suggest that depth perception is partly learned and partly innate (Witherington et al., 2005). Basically, a visual cliff is a glass-topped table (● Figure 20.11). On one side, a checkered surface lies directly beneath the glass. On the other side, the checkered surface is 4 feet below the tabletop. This makes the glass look like a tabletop on one side and a cliff, or drop-off, on the other.

To test for depth perception, 6- to 14-month-old infants were placed in the middle of the visual cliff. This gave them a choice of crawling to the shallow side or the deep side. (The glass prevented them from doing any "skydiving" if they chose the deep side.) Most infants chose the shallow side. In fact, most refused the deep side even when their mothers tried to call them toward it (Gibson & Walk, 1960).

If the infants were at least 6 months old when they were tested, isn't it possible that they had learned to perceive depth? Yes. More recent research has shown that depth perception begins to develop as early as 2 weeks of age (Yonas, Elieff, & Arterberry, 2002). It is very likely that at least a basic level of depth perception is innate. Yet, the development of depth perception is not complete until about 6 months of age, suggesting that it depends on both brain maturation and individual experience (Nawrot, Mayo, & Nawrot, 2009).

But don't some older babies crawl off tables or beds? As soon as infants become active crawlers, they refuse to cross the deep side of the visual cliff. However, older infants who have just learned to walk must again learn to avoid the "deep" side of the visual cliff (Witherington et al., 2005). Besides, even babies who perceive depth may not be able to catch themselves if they slip. A lack of coordination—not an inability to see depth—probably explains most "crash landings" after about 4 months of age.

Mark Richards/PhotoEdit

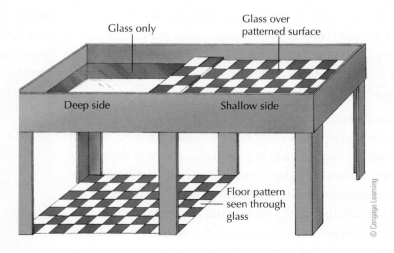

Glass only

Glass over patterned surface

Deep side

Shallow side

Floor pattern seen through glass

© Cengage Learning

● **Figure 20.11**

Human infants and newborn animals refuse to go over the edge of the visual cliff.

Stereoscopic: optic nerve transmissions from each eye are relayed to both sides of brain

Binocular: both eyes have overlapping fields of vision

Allows depth perception with accurate distance estimation

(a)

© Cengage Learning

Figure 20.12

(a) Stereoscopic vision. (b) The photographs show what the right and left eyes would see when viewing this person. Hold the page about 6 to 8 inches from your eyes. Allow your eyes to cross and focus on the overlapping image between the two photos. Then try to fuse the women into one image. If you are successful, the third dimension will appear like magic.

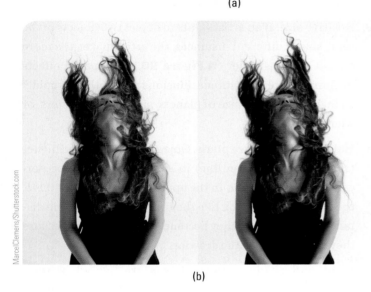

MarcelClemens/Shutterstock.com

(b)

We learn to construct our perception of 3-D space by integrating information from a variety of *depth cues* (Schiller et al., 2011). **Depth cues** are features of the environment and messages from the body that supply information about distance and space. Some cues require two eyes (**binocular depth cues**), whereas others will work with just one eye (**monocular depth cues**).

Binocular Depth Cues

The most basic source of depth perception is *retinal disparity* (a discrepancy in the images that reach the right and left eyes). Retinal disparity is based on the fact that the eyes are about 2.5 inches apart. Because of this, each eye receives a slightly different view of the world. Try this: Put a finger in front of your eyes and as close to your nose as you can. First, close one eye and then the other, over and over again. You should notice that your finger seems to jump back and forth as you view the different images reaching each eye. However, when the two different images are fused into one overall image, **stereoscopic vision** (3-D sight) occurs (Harris & Jenkin, 2011). The resulting powerful sensation of depth can be used to produce 3-D movies (● **Figure 20.12**).

Convergence is a second binocular depth cue. When you look at a distant object, the lines of vision from your eyes are parallel. You normally are not aware of it, but whenever you estimate a distance under 50 feet (as when you play catch or shoot trash can hoops with the first draft of your essay), you are using convergence. How? Muscles attached to the eyeball feed information on eye position to the brain to help it judge distance (● **Figure 20.13**).

You can feel convergence by exaggerating it: Focus on your fingertip and bring it toward your eyes until they almost cross. You can feel the muscles that control eye movement working harder and harder as your fingertip gets closer.

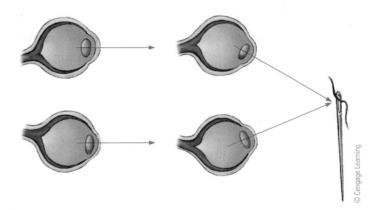

© Cengage Learning

● **Figure 20.13**

The eyes must converge, or turn in toward the nose, to focus close objects. The eyes shown are viewed from above the head.

Depth perception *The ability to see three-dimensional space and to accurately judge distances.*
Depth cues *Features of the environment and messages from the body that supply information about distance and space.*
Binocular depth cues *Perceptual features that impart information about distance and three-dimensional space which require two eyes.*
Monocular depth cues *Perceptual features that impart information about distance and three-dimensional space which require just one eye.*
Stereoscopic vision *Perception of space and depth as a result of the eyes receiving different images.*

Can a person with one eye perceive depth? Yes, but not nearly as well as a person with two eyes. Try driving a car or riding a bicycle with one eye closed. You will find yourself braking too soon or too late, and you will have difficulty estimating your speed. ("But officer, my psychology text said to....") Despite this, you will be able to drive, although it will be more difficult than usual. You can drive because your single eye can still use monocular depth cues.

Monocular Depth Cues

As their name implies, monocular depth cues can be perceived with just one eye. One such cue is *accommodation,* bending of the lens to focus on nearby objects. Sensations from muscles attached to each lens flow back to the brain. Changes in these sensations help us judge distances within about 4 feet of the eyes. This information is available even if you are using only one eye, so accommodation is a monocular cue. Beyond 4 feet, accommodation has limited value. Obviously, accommodation is more important to a watchmaker or a person trying to thread a needle than it is to a basketball player or someone driving an automobile. Other monocular depth cues are referred to as *pictorial depth cues* because a good movie, painting, or photograph can create a convincing sense of depth where none exists.

How is the illusion of depth created on a 2-D surface? **Pictorial depth cues** are features found in paintings, drawings, and photographs that impart information about space, depth, and distance. To understand how these cues work, imagine that you are looking outdoors through a window. If you trace everything you see onto the glass, you will have an excellent drawing, with convincing depth. If you then analyze what is on the glass, you will find the following features:

1. **Linear perspective.** This cue is based on the apparent convergence of parallel lines in the environment. If you stand between two railroad tracks, they appear to meet near the horizon, even though they actually remain parallel. Because you know they are parallel, their convergence implies great distance (● **Figure 20.14***a*).

2. **Relative size.** If an artist wants to depict two objects of the same size at different distances, the artist makes the more distant object smaller (● **Figure 20.14***b*). Special effects in films create sensational illusions of depth by rapidly changing the image size of planets, airplanes, monsters, or what have you.

3. **Height in the picture plane.** Objects that are placed higher (closer to the horizon line) in a drawing tend to be perceived as more distant. In the upper frame of Figure 20.14*b*, the black columns look like they are receding into the distance partly because they become smaller but also because they move higher in the drawing.

4. **Light and shadow.** Most objects are lighted in ways that create clear patterns of light and shadow. Copying such patterns of light and shadow can give a 2-D design a 3-D appearance (see ● **Figure 20.14***c*). (Also, look ahead to ● **Figure 20.15** for more information on light and shadow.)

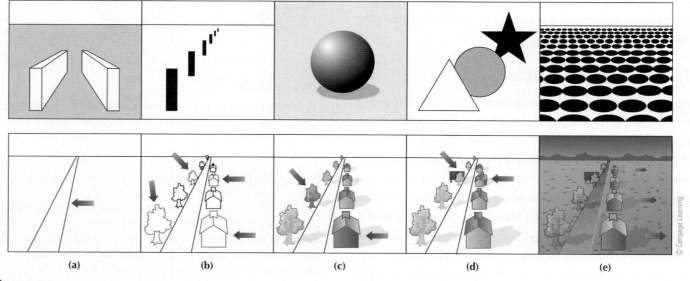

(a)   (b)   (c)   (d)   (e)

© Cengage Learning

● **Figure 20.14**

(a) Linear perspective. (b) Relative size. (c) Light and shadow. (d) Overlap. (e) Texture gradients. Drawings in the top row show fairly "pure" examples of each pictorial depth cue. In the bottom row, the pictorial depth cues are used to assemble a more realistic scene.

© Cengage Learning

Figure 20.15

(Above) When judging depth, we usually assume that light comes mainly from one direction, usually from above. Squint a little to blur the image you see here. You should perceive a collection of globes projecting outward. If you turn this page upside down, the globes should become cavities. (After Ramachandran, 1995.) *(Left)* The famed Dutch artist M. C. Escher violated our assumptions about light to create the dramatic illusions of depth found in his 1953 lithograph *Relativity*. In this print, light appears to come from all sides of the scene.

5. **Overlap.** Overlap (or *interposition*) occurs when one object partially blocks another object. Hold your hands up and ask a friend across the room which is nearer. Relative size will give the answer if one hand is much nearer to your friend than the other. But if one hand is only slightly closer than the other, your friend may not be able to tell—until you slide one hand in front of the other. Overlap then removes any doubt (see ● **Figure 20.14***d*).

6. **Texture gradients.** Changes in texture also contribute to depth perception. If you stand in the middle of a cobblestone street, the street will look coarse near your feet. However, its texture will get smaller and finer as you look into the distance (see ● **Figure 20.14***e*).

7. **Aerial perspective.** Smog, fog, dust, and haze add to the apparent distance of an object. Because of aerial perspective, distant objects tend to be hazy, washed out in color, and lacking in detail. Aerial haze often is most noticeable when it is missing. If you have ever seen a distant mountain range on a crystal-clear day, it might have looked like it was only a few miles away. In reality, you could have been viewing the mountains through 50 miles of crystal-clear air.

8. **Relative motion.** Relative motion, also known as *motion parallax* (PAIR-ah-lax), can be seen by looking out a window and moving your head from side to side. Notice that nearby objects appear to move a sizable distance as your head moves. Trees, houses, and telephone poles that are farther away appear to move slightly in relation to the

background. Distant objects like hills, mountains, or clouds don't seem to move at all.

When combined, pictorial cues can create a powerful illusion of depth. (See ● **Table 20.1** for a summary of all the depth cues we have discussed.)

TABLE 20.1	Summary of Visual Depth Cues
Binocular Depth Cues	
• Retinal disparity	
• Convergence	
Monocular Depth Cues	
• Accommodation	
• Pictorial depth cues (listed below)	
Linear perspective	
Relative size	
Height in the picture plane	
Light and shadow	
Overlap	
Texture gradients	
Aerial perspective	
Relative motion (motion parallax)	

© Cengage Learning

Pictorial depth cues *Monocular depth cues found in paintings, drawings, and photographs that impart information about space, depth, and distance.*

Is motion parallax really a pictorial cue? Strictly speaking it is not, except in the world of 2-D movies, television, or animated cartoons. However, when parallax is present, we almost always perceive depth (Yoonessi & Baker, 2011). Much of the apparent depth of a good movie comes from relative motion captured by the camera. ● **Figure 20.16** illustrates the defining feature of motion parallax. Imagine that you are in a bus

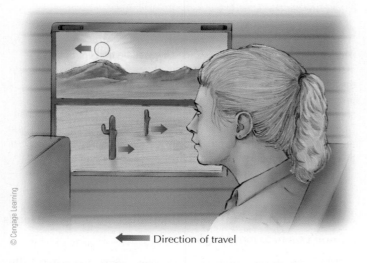

© Cengage Learning

◀── Direction of travel

and watching the passing scenery (with your gaze at a right angle to the road). Under these conditions, nearby objects will appear to rush *backward*. Those farther away, such as distant mountains, will seem to move very little or not at all. Objects that are more remote, such as the sun or moon, will appear to move in the *same* direction you are traveling. (That's why the sun appears to "follow" you when you take a stroll.)

● **Figure 20.16**

The apparent motion of objects viewed during travel depends on their distance from the observer. Apparent motion also can be influenced by an observer's point of fixation. At middle distances, objects closer than the point of fixation appear to move backward; those beyond the point of fixation appear to move forward. Objects at great distances, such as the sun or moon, always appear to move forward.

Module 20: Summary

20.1 In general, how do we construct our perceptions?

- **20.1.1** Perception is an active process of constructing sensations into a meaningful mental representation of the world.
- **20.1.2** Perceptions are based on simultaneous bottom-up and top-down processing. Complete perceptions are assembled out of small sensory features in "bottom-up" fashion, guided by preexisting knowledge applied "top-down" to help organize features into a meaningful whole.
- **20.1.3** Separating figure and ground is the most basic perceptual organization.
- **20.1.4** The following Gestalt principles also help organize sensations: nearness, similarity, continuity, closure, contiguity, and common region.
- **20.1.5** A perceptual organization may be thought of as a hypothesis held until evidence contradicts it.

- **20.1.6** In vision, the image projected on the retina is constantly changing, but the external world appears stable and undistorted because of size, shape, and brightness constancy.

20.2 How is it possible to see depth and judge distance?

- **20.2.1** A basic, innate capacity for depth perception is present soon after birth.
- **20.2.2** Depth perception depends on binocular cues of retinal disparity and convergence.
- **20.2.3** Depth perception also depends on the monocular cue of accommodation.
- **20.2.4** Monocular "pictorial" depth cues also underlie depth perception. They are linear perspective, relative size, height in the picture plane, light and shadow, overlap, texture gradients, aerial haze, and motion parallax.

Module 20: Knowledge Builder

Recite

1. In top-down processing of information, individual features are analyzed and assembled into a meaningful whole. *T or F?*

2. At times, meaningful perceptual organization represents a _____, or "guess," held until the evidence contradicts it.

3. The design known as the Necker cube is a good example of an impossible figure. *T or F?*

4. Which among the following are subject to basic perceptual constancy?

   a. figure-ground organization
   b. size
   c. ambiguity
   d. brightness
   e. continuity
   f. closure
   g. shape
   h. nearness

5. The visual cliff is used to test for infant sensitivity to linear perspective. *T or F?*

6. Write an *M* or a *B* after each of the following to indicate whether it is a monocular or binocular depth cue.

   accommodation _____
   convergence _____
   retinal disparity _____
   linear perspective _____
   motion parallax _____
   overlap _____
   relative size _____

7. Movies are especially able to create a 3-D illusion because of the _____ _____ depth cue.

Reflect

Think Critically

8. People who have taken psychedelic drugs, such as LSD or mescaline, often report that the objects and people they see appear to be changing in size, shape, and brightness. This suggests that such drugs disrupt which perceptual process?

Self-Reflect

As you look around the area where you are now, how are the Gestalt principles helping organize your perceptions? Try to find a specific example for each principle.

Why are the constancies important for maintaining a stable perceptual world?

Part of the rush of excitement produced by action movies and video games is based on the sense of depth they create. Return to the list of pictorial depth cues. What cues have you seen used to portray depth? Try to think of specific examples in a movie or game you have seen recently.

ANSWERS

8. Perceptual constancies (size, shape, and brightness). **1.** F **2.** hypothesis **3.** F **4.** b, d, g **5.** F **6.** accommodation (M), convergence (B), retinal disparity (B), linear perspective (M), motion parallax (M), overlap (M), relative size (M) **7.** motion parallax

Sensation and Perception: Perception and Objectivity

Finding Lost Balls

One of your authors (a terrible golfer) occasionally had to spend the day golfing with his father (a great golfer). Imagine watching your opponent hit the ball right down the middle of the fairway over and over while you spend much of your day looking for your lost golf ball. Now imagine that your opponent is always the one to find your lost ball. And so it was with your author. (Sigh.)

In many sports, expert players are much better than beginners at paying attention to key information. Compared with novices, experts scan actions and events more quickly and they focus on only the most meaningful information. This helps experts make decisions and react more quickly. In fact, various processes shape our perceptions, which are far from a perfect model of the world. Let's investigate some factors that affect the accuracy of our perceptual experiences.

Lars Baron/Getty Images

SURVEY QUESTIONS

21.1 How do expectations, motives, emotions, and learning alter perception?

21.2 How can I perceive events more accurately?

Perceptual Learning— Believing Is Seeing

SURVEY QUESTIONS 21.1: How do expectations, motives, emotions, and learning alter perception?

We use Gestalt organizing principles, perceptual constancies, and depth cues to construct our visual perceptions (see Module 20). All these processes and others make up the common, partly inborn, core of our perceptual abilities. In addition, we each have specific life experiences that can, in top-down fashion, affect our perceptions. For instance, what you perceive can be altered by *perceptual expectancies,* motives, emotions, and *perceptual habits.*

Perceptual Expectancies

What is a perceptual expectancy? If you are a runner in the starting blocks at a track meet, you are *set* to respond in a certain way. If a car backfires, runners at a track meet may jump the gun. Likewise, past experience, motives, context, or suggestions may create a **perceptual expectancy (set)** that prepares you to perceive in a certain way. As a matter of fact, we all frequently jump the gun when perceiving. In essence, an expectancy is a perceptual hypothesis we are *very likely* to apply to a stimulus—even if applying it is inappropriate.

Perceptual sets often lead us to see what we *expect* to see. For example, let's say while driving you just made an illegal lane change (or texted on your cell phone!?). You then see a flashing light. "Rats," you think, "busted," and wait for the police car to pull you over. But as the car draws nearer, you see it was

View I

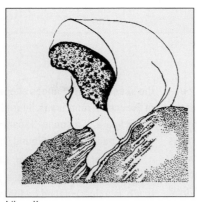
View II

View III

© Cengage Learning

Figure 21.1

"Young woman/old woman" illustrations. As an interesting demonstration of perceptual expectancy, show some of your friends view I and some view II (cover all other views). Next, show your friends view III and ask them what they see. Those who saw view I should see the old woman in view III; those who saw view II should see the young woman in view III. Can you see both? (After Leeper, 1935.)

just a car with a vivid turn signal. Most people have had similar experiences in which expectations altered their perceptions. To observe perceptual expectancies firsthand, perform the demonstration described in ● Figure 21.1.

Perceptual expectancies are frequently created by *suggestion*. In one study (wine snobs take note), participants given a taste of a $90 wine reported that it tasted better than a $10 wine. Functional MRI images confirmed that brain areas related to pleasure were indeed more active when participants tasted the more expensive wine (Plassmann et al., 2008). The twist is that the same wine was served in both cases. Suggesting that the wine was expensive created a perceptual expectancy that it would taste better. And so it did (advertisers also take note). In the same way, labeling people as "gang members," "mental patients," "queers," "illegal immigrants," "bitches," and so on is likely to distort perceptions.

Motives, Emotions, and Perception

Our motives and emotions also play a role in shaping our perceptions. For example, if you are hungry, food and even food-related words are more likely to gain your attention than non–food-related words (Mogg et al., 1998; Werthmann et al., 2011). Advertisers take advantage of two motives that are widespread in our society: *anxiety* and *sex*. Everything from automobile tires to cosmetic surgery is merchandised by using sex to gain attention (Hennink-Kaminski & Reichert, 2011). Other ads combine sex with anxiety. Deodorant, soaps, toothpaste, and countless other products are pushed in ads that play on desires to be attractive, to have "sex appeal," or to avoid embarrassment.

Our emotions also can shape our perceptions (Yiend, 2010). According to psychologist Barbara Frederickson, negative emotions generally narrow our perceptual focus, or "spotlight," increasing the likelihood of inattentional blindness. In contrast, positive emotions can broaden the scope of attention (Fredrickson & Branigan, 2005). For example, positive emotions can affect how well people recognize people from other races. In recognizing faces, a consistent *other-race effect* occurs. This is a sort of "They all look alike to me" bias in perceiving persons from other racial and ethnic groups. In tests of facial recognition, people are much better at recognizing faces of their own race than others. But when people are in positive moods, their ability to recognize people from other races improves (Johnson & Fredrickson, 2005).

The main reason for the other-race effect is that we typically have more experience with people from our own race. As a result, we become familiar with the features that help us recognize different persons. For other groups, we lack the perceptual expertise needed to accurately separate one face from another (Megreya, White, & Burton, 2011; Sporer, 2001). Such differences indicate the importance of perceptual learning, a topic we turn to next.

Okay, so maybe members of different races or ethnic groups have developed perceptual sets that lead them to see in-group faces differently, but we all see everything else the same, right? For an answer, see "Do They See What We See?"

Perceptual expectancy (set) *A readiness to perceive in a particular manner, induced by strong expectations.*

Human Diversity

Do They See What We See?

According to psychologist Richard Nisbett and his colleagues, people from different cultures do, in fact, perceive the world differently. European Americans are individualistic people who tend to focus on themselves and their sense of personal control. In contrast, East Asians are collectivist people who tend to focus on their interpersonal relationships and social responsibilities. As a consequence, European Americans tend to perceive actions in terms of internal factors ("She did it because she chose to do it"). In comparison, East Asians tend to perceive actions in terms of their social context ("He did it because it was his responsibility to his family") (Henrich, Heine, & Norenzayan, 2010; Norenzayan & Nisbett, 2000).

Do such cultural differences affect our everyday perception of objects and events? Apparently they do. In one study, American and Japanese participants were shown drawings of everyday scenes, such as a farm. Later, they saw a slightly changed version of the scene. Some of the changes were made to the focal point, or figure, of the scene. Other changes altered the surrounding context, or ground, of the scene. Americans, it turns out, were better at detecting changes in the figure of a scene. Japanese participants were better at finding alterations in the background (Nisbett & Miyamoto, 2005).

To explain this difference, Chua, Boland, and Nisbett (2005) presented American and Chinese participants with pictures of a figure (such as a tiger) placed on the ground (such as in a jungle) and monitored their eye-movement patterns. The Americans focused their eye movements on the figure; Chinese participants made more eye movements around the ground. In other words, Westerners have a relatively narrow focus of attention, whereas Easterners have a broader focus of attention (Boduroglu, Shah, & Nisbett, 2009). Apparently, the society in which we live can indeed influence even our most basic perceptual habits (Hedden et al., 2008). This difference in perceptual style even influences the artistic and aesthetic preferences expressed in Eastern and Western art (Masuda et al., 2008).

Perceptual Habits

England is one of the few countries in the world where people drive on the left side of the road. Because of this reversal, it is not unusual for visitors from other countries to step off curbs in front of cars—after carefully looking for traffic in the *wrong* direction. As this example suggests, learning has a powerful impact on top-down processing in perception.

How does learning affect perception? The term **perceptual learning** refers to changes in the brain that alter how we construct sensory information into perception (Moreno et al., 2009). For example, to use a computer, you must learn to pay attention to specific stimuli, such as icons and cursors. We also learn to tell the difference between stimuli that seemed identical at first. An example is the novice chef who discovers how to tell the difference between dried basil, oregano, and tarragon. In other situations, we learn to focus on just one part of a group of stimuli. This saves us from having to process all the stimuli in the group. For instance, a linebacker in football may be able to tell if the next play will be a run or a pass by watching one or two key players, rather than the entire opposing team (Gorman, Abernethy, & Farrow, 2011; Seitz & Watanabe, 2005).

In general, learning creates *perceptual habits*—ingrained patterns of organization and attention—that affect our daily experience. Stop for a moment and look at ● **Figure 21.2**. The face on the left looks somewhat unusual, to be sure. But the

The Gallery Collection/Corbis

● **Figure 21.2**

The effects of prior experience on perception. The doctored face looks far worse when viewed right-side up because it can be related to past experience.

distortion seems mild—until you turn the page upside down. Viewed normally, the face looks quite grotesque. Why is there a difference? Apparently, most people have little experience with upside-down faces. Perceptual learning, therefore, has less impact on our perceptions of an upside-down face. With a face in the normal position, you know what to expect and where to look. Also, you tend to see the entire face as a recognizable pattern. When a face is inverted, we are forced to perceive its individual features separately (Caharel et al., 2006).

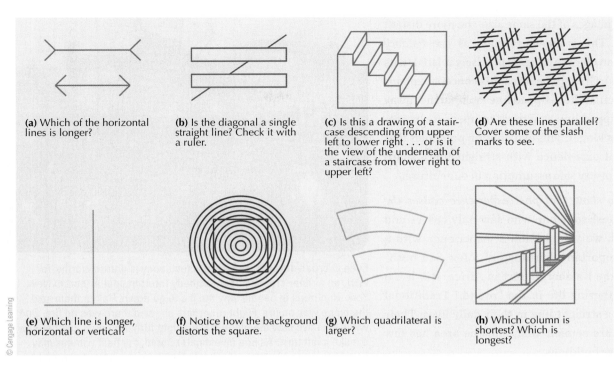

Figure 21.3
Some interesting perceptual illusions. Such illusions reveal that perceptual misconstructions are a normal part of visual perception.

(a) Which of the horizontal lines is longer?

(b) Is the diagonal a single straight line? Check it with a ruler.

(c) Is this a drawing of a staircase descending from upper left to lower right . . . or is it the view of the underneath of a staircase from lower right to upper left?

(d) Are these lines parallel? Cover some of the slash marks to see.

(e) Which line is longer, horizontal or vertical?

(f) Notice how the background distorts the square.

(g) Which quadrilateral is larger?

(h) Which column is shortest? Which is longest?

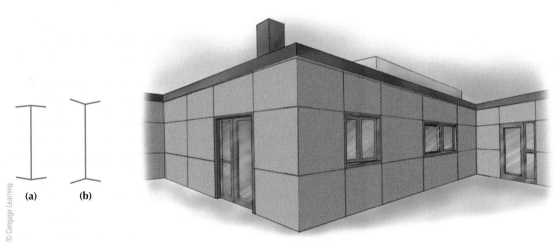

(a)   **(b)**

Figure 21.4
Why does line (b) in the Müller-Lyer illusion look longer than line (a)? Probably because it looks more like a distant corner than a nearer one. Because the vertical lines form images of the same length, the more "distant" line must be perceived as larger. As you can see in the drawing on the right, additional depth cues accentuate the Müller-Lyer illusion.

The Müller-Lyer Illusion *Can perceptual habits explain other illusions?* Perceptual habits play a role in explaining some illusions. In general, size and shape constancy, habitual eye movements, continuity, and perceptual habits combine in various ways to produce the illusions in ● **Figure 21.3**. Rather than attempt to explain all of them, let's focus on one deceptively simple example.

Consider the drawing in Figure 21.3a. This is the familiar **Müller-Lyer illusion** (MEOO-ler-LIE-er) in which the horizontal line with arrowheads appears shorter than the line with Vs. A quick measurement will show that they are the same length. How can we explain this illusion?

Evidence suggests it is based on a lifetime of experience with the edges and corners of rooms and buildings. Richard

Gregory (2000) believes you see the line with the arrowheads as if it were the nearby corner of a room joining two walls receding from it (● **Figure 21.4a**). The line with the Vs (● **Figure 21.4b**), on the other hand, suggests the farther corner of a room or building joining two walls coming closer. (If these two lines were belly buttons, (a) would be an "outie" and (b) would be an "innie.") In other words, cues that suggest a 3-D space alter our perception of a 2-D design.

Perceptual learning *Changes in perception that can be attributed to prior experience; a result of changes in how the brain processes sensory information.*
Müller-Lyer illusion *Two equal-length lines tipped with inward or outward pointing Vs appear to be of different lengths.*

© Cengage Learning

If two objects make images of the same size, the more distant object must be larger. This is known formally as *size-distance invariance* (the size of an object's image is precisely related to its distance from the eyes). Gregory believes this concept explains the Müller-Lyer illusion. If the V-tipped line looks farther away than the arrowhead-tipped line, you must compensate by seeing the V-tipped line as longer. This explanation presumes that you have had years of experience with straight lines, sharp edges, and corners—a pretty safe assumption in our culture.

Is there any way to show that past experience causes the illusion? If we could test someone who saw only curves and wavy lines as a child, we would know if experience with a "square" culture is important. Fortunately, a few San bushmen, a culture from the Kalahari desert in Africa, still live a traditional hunter-gathering life in the "round." Traditional San rarely encounter a straight line in their daily lives: Their temporary dwellings are semicircular, and the area has few straight roads or square buildings.

What happens if a San looks at the Müller-Lyer design? The typical traditional San does not experience the illusion. At most, she or he sees the V-shaped line as *slightly* longer than the other (Henrich, Heine, & Norenzayan, 2010). This seems to confirm the importance of perceptual habits in determining our view of the world.

Can perception ever be "illusion-free"? Probably not. But the next section offers some ideas on how to perceive events more accurately.

Even in broad daylight, eyewitness testimony is untrustworthy. In 2001, an airliner crashed near Kennedy International Airport in New York. Hundreds of people saw the plane go down. Half of them said the plane was on fire. Flight recorders showed there was no fire. One witness in five saw the plane make a right turn. An equal number saw it make a left turn! As one investigator noted, the best witness may be a "kid under 12 years old who doesn't have his parents around." Adults, it seems, are easily swayed by their expectations.

Becoming a Better Eyewitness to Life—Pay Attention!

SURVEY QUESTIONS 21.2: How can I perceive events more accurately?

In the courtroom, eyewitness testimony can be a key to proving guilt or innocence. The claim "I saw it with my own eyes" still carries a lot of weight with a jury. Too many jurors (unless they have taken a psychology course) tend to assume that eyewitness testimony is nearly infallible (Brewer & Wells, 2006). Even U.S. judges are vulnerable to overoptimism about eyewitness testimony (Wise et al., 2010; Wise & Safer, 2010). But, to put it bluntly, eyewitness testimony is frequently wrong (Shermer, Rose, & Hoffman, 2011). Recall, for instance, that one of your authors would have sworn in court that he had

seen a murder taking place at the supermarket—*if* he hadn't received more information to correct his misperceptions.

What about witnesses who are certain that their perceptions were accurate? Should juries believe them? Having confidence in your testimony has almost no bearing on its accuracy (Brewer & Wells, 2006)! Unfortunately, perception rarely provides an "instant replay" of events. Impressions formed when a person is surprised, threatened, or under stress are especially prone to distortion (Yuille & Daylen, 1998). One study of eyewitness cases found that the *wrong person* was chosen from police lineups 25 percent of the time (Levi, 1998). Psychologists are gradually convincing lawyers, judges, and police that eyewitness errors are common (Yarmey, 2010). Even so, thousands of people have been wrongfully convicted.

Wouldn't the victim of a crime remember more than a mere witness? Not necessarily. A classic study found that eyewitness accuracy is virtually the same for witnessing a crime (seeing a pocket calculator stolen) as it is for being a victim (seeing one's own watch stolen) (Hosch & Cooper, 1982). Placing more weight on the testimony of victims may be a serious mistake. In many crimes, victims fall prey to *weapon focus*. Understandably, they fix their entire attention on the knife, gun, or other weapon an attacker used. In doing so, they fail to notice details of appearance, dress, or other clues to identity (Pickel, French, & Betts, 2003). Additional factors that consistently lower eyewitness accuracy are summarized in ● Table 21.1.

Implications

Since DNA testing became available, over 300 people who were convicted of murder, rape, and other crimes in the United States have been exonerated. About 75 percent of these innocent people were convicted mainly on the basis of eyewitness testimony. Each also spent *years* in prison before being cleared (Innocence Project, 2012). How often are everyday perceptions as inaccurate or distorted as those of an emotional eyewitness? The answer we have been moving toward is "very frequently." Bearing this in mind may help you be more tolerant of the views of others and more cautious about your own objectivity. It also may encourage more frequent *reality testing* on your part.

If you have ever concluded that someone was angry, upset, or unfriendly without checking the accuracy of your perceptions, you have fallen into a subtle trap. Personal objectivity is an elusive quality, requiring frequent reality testing to maintain. At the very least, it pays to ask a person what she or he is feeling when you are in doubt. Clearly, most of us could learn to be better "eyewitnesses" to daily events (Siegel, 2010).

The Whole Human: Perceptual Accuracy

Do some people perceive things more accurately than others? Humanistic psychologist Abraham Maslow (1969) believed that some people perceive themselves and others with unusual accuracy. Maslow characterized these people as especially alive, open, aware, and mentally healthy. He found that their perceptual styles were marked by immersion in the present; a lack of self-consciousness; freedom from selecting, criticizing, or evaluating; and a general "surrender" to experience. The kind of perception Maslow described is like that of a mother with her newborn infant, a child at Christmas, or two people in love.

In daily life, we quickly *habituate*, or respond less, to predictable and unchanging stimuli. **Habituation** is a type of learning—basically, we learn to cease paying attention to familiar stimuli. For instance, when you download a new song from iTunes, the music initially holds your attention all the way through. But when the song becomes "old," it may play without you really attending to it. When a stimulus is repeated *without change*, our response to it habituates, or decreases.

TABLE 21.1	Factors Affecting the Accuracy of Eyewitness Perceptions
Sources of Error	**Summary of Findings**
1. Wording of questions	An eyewitness's testimony about an event can be affected by the wording of questions the witness is asked.
2. Postevent information	Eyewitness testimony about an event often reflects not only what was actually seen but also information obtained later on.
3. Attitudes, expectations	An eyewitness's perception and memory for an event may be affected by his or her attitudes and expectations.
4. Alcohol intoxication	Alcohol intoxication impairs later ability to recall events.
5. Cross-racial perceptions	Eyewitnesses are better at identifying members of their own race than they are at identifying people of other races.
6. Weapon focus	The presence of a weapon impairs an eyewitness's ability to identify the culprit's face.
7. Accuracy-confidence	An eyewitness's confidence is not a good predictor of his or her accuracy.
8. Exposure time	The less time an eyewitness has to observe an event, the less correctly she or he will perceive and remember it.
9. Unconscious transference	Eyewitnesses sometimes identify as a culprit someone they have seen in another situation or context.
10. Color perception	Judgments of color made under monochromatic light (such as an orange street light) are highly unreliable.
11. Stress	High levels of stress impair the accuracy of eyewitness perceptions.

Source: Adapted from Wells & Olson, 2003; Yarmey, 2010.

It is interesting that creative people habituate *more slowly* than average. We might expect that they would rapidly become bored with a repeated stimulus. Instead, it seems that creative people actively attend to stimuli, even those that are repeated (Colin, Moore, & West, 1996; Runco, 2012).

The Value of Paying Attention

Whereas the average person has not reached perceptual restriction of the "if you've seen one tree, you've seen them all" variety, the fact remains that most of us look at a tree and classify it in the perceptual category of "trees in general" without appreciating the miracle standing before us. How, then, can we bring about **dishabituation**—a reversal of habituation—on a day-to-day basis? Does perceptual clarity require years of effort? Fortunately, a more immediate avenue is available. The deceptively simple key to dishabituation is this: Pay attention. The following story summarizes the importance of attention:

> One day a man of the people said to Zen Master Ikkyu: "Master, will you please write for me some maxims of the highest wisdom?"
>
> Ikkyu immediately took his brush and wrote the word "Attention."
>
> "Is that all?" asked the man. "Will you not add something more?"
>
> Ikkyu then wrote twice running: "Attention. Attention."
>
> "Well," remarked the man rather irritably, "I really don't see much depth or subtlety in what you have just written."
>
> Then Ikkyu wrote the same word three times running: "Attention. Attention. Attention." Half angered, the man demanded, "What does that word 'attention' mean anyway?"
>
> And Ikkyu answered gently: "Attention means attention." (Kapleau, 1966)

To this, we can add only one thought, provided by the poet William Blake: "If the doors of perception were cleansed, man would see everything as it is, infinite."

How to Become a Better "Eyewitness" to Life

Here's an overview of some ideas from this module (and the other modules on sensation and perception) to help you maintain and enhance perceptual awareness and accuracy:

1. *Remember that perceptions are constructions of reality.* Learn to regularly question your own perceptions. Are they accurate? Could another interpretation fit the facts? What assumptions are you making? How might your assumptions be distorting your perceptions?

2. *Break perceptual habits and interrupt habituation.* Each day, try to get away from habitual, top-down processing and do some activities in new ways. For example, take different routes when you travel to work or school. Do routine activities, such as brushing your teeth or combing your hair, with your nonpreferred hand. Try to look at friends and family members as if they are persons you just met for the first time.

3. *Seek out-of-the-ordinary experiences.* The possibilities here range from trying foods you don't normally eat to reading opinions very different from your own. Experiences ranging from a quiet walk in the woods to a trip to an amusement park may be perceptually refreshing.

4. *Beware of perceptual sets.* Anytime you pigeonhole people, objects, or events, there is a danger that your perceptions will be distorted by expectations or preexisting categories. Be especially wary of labels and stereotypes. Try to see people as individuals and events as unique, one-time occurrences.

5. *Be aware of the ways motives and emotions influence perceptions.* It is difficult to avoid being swayed by your own interests, needs, desires, and emotions. But be aware of this trap and actively try to see the world through the eyes of others. Taking the other person's perspective is especially valuable in disputes or arguments. Ask yourself, "How does this look to her or him?"

6. *Make a habit of engaging in reality testing.* Actively look for additional evidence to check the accuracy of your perceptions. Ask questions, seek clarifications, and find alternate channels of information. Remember that perception is not automatically accurate. You could be wrong—we all are frequently.

7. *Pay attention.* Make a conscious effort to pay attention to other people and your surroundings. Don't drift through life in a haze. Listen to others with full concentration. Watch their facial expressions. Make eye contact. Try to get in the habit of approaching perception as if you are going to have to testify later about what you saw and heard.

Habituation *A decrease in perceptual response to a repeated stimulus.*
Dishabituation *A reversal of habituation.*

Module 21: Summary

21.1 How do expectations, motives, emotions, and learning alter preceptions?

- **21.1.1** Suggestion, motives, emotions, attention, and prior experience combine in various ways to create perceptual sets, or expectancies.
- **21.1.2** Personal motives and values often alter perceptions by changing the evaluation of what is seen or by altering attention to specific details.
- **21.1.3** Perceptual learning influences the top-down organization and interpretation of sensations.
- **21.1.4** One of the most familiar of all illusions, the Müller-Lyer illusion, seems to be related to perceptual learning, linear perspective, and size–distance invariance relationships.

21.2 How can I perceive events more accurately?

- **21.2.1** Eyewitness testimony is surprisingly unreliable. Eywitness accuracy is further damaged by weapon focus and several similar factors.
- **21.2.2** When a stimulus is repeated without change, our response to it undergoes habituation.
- **21.2.3** Perceptual accuracy is enhanced by reality testing, dishabituation, and conscious efforts to pay attention.
- **21.2.4** It also is valuable to break perceptual habits, to broaden frames of reference, to beware of perceptual sets, and to be aware of the ways motives and emotions influence perceptions.

Module 21: Knowledge Builder

Recite

1. When a person is prepared to perceive events in a particular way, it is said that a perceptual expectancy or _____ exists.

2. People around the world perceive in the same way regardless of culture. *T or F?*

3. Perceptual habits may become so ingrained that they lead us to misperceive a stimulus. *T or F?*

4. Inaccuracies in eyewitness perceptions obviously occur in "real life," but they cannot be reproduced in psychology experiments. *T or F?*

5. Victims of crimes are more accurate eyewitnesses than impartial observers. *T or F?*

6. *Reality testing* is another term for dishabituation. *T or F?*

7. A good antidote to perceptual habituation can be found in conscious efforts to
   a. reverse sensory gating
   b. pay attention
   c. achieve visual accommodation
   d. counteract shape constancy

Reflect
Think Critically

8. Cigarette advertisements in the United States are required to carry a warning label about the health risks of smoking. How have tobacco companies made these labels less visible?

Self-Reflect

You have almost certainly misperceived a situation at some time because of a perceptual expectancy or the influence of your motives and emotions. How were your perceptions influenced?

How has perceptual learning affected your ability to safely drive a car? For example, where do you habitually look as you are driving?

Because perceptions are constructions or models of external events, we should all engage in more frequent reality testing. Can you think of a recent event when a little reality testing would have saved you from misjudging a situation?

ANSWERS

1. set 2. F 3. T 4. F 5. F 6. F 7. b 8. Advertisers place health warnings in the corners of ads, where they attract the least possible attention. Also, the labels are often placed on "busy" backgrounds so they are partially camouflaged. Finally, the main images in ads are designed to strongly attract attention. This further distracts readers from seeing the warnings.

Psychology in Action: Extrasensory Perception

Are We Too Eager to Believe?

It is common sense to state that we have five basic senses that supply us with all we can possibly sense. But is this the whole story? Once, during the middle of the night, a woman away for a weekend visit suddenly had a strong impulse to return home. When she arrived, she found the house on fire with her husband asleep inside. How could she have known? Could she have used some mysterious extrasensory ability?

A surprising number of people are prepared to answer in the affirmative. About half of the general public believes in the existence of extrasensory perception. Yet few psychologists share this belief. It's surprising that even more people aren't believers. ESP and other paranormal events are treated as accepted facts in many movies and television programs. Stage

entertainers routinely "astound" their audiences. What is the evidence for and against extrasensory perception?

SURVEY QUESTION

22.1 Is extrasensory perception possible?

Extrasensory Perception— Do You Believe in Ghosts?

SURVEY QUESTION 22.1: Is extrasensory perception possible?

Extrasensory perception (ESP) is the purported ability to perceive events in ways that cannot be explained by known sensory capacities. The field of *parapsychology* studies ESP and other **psi phenomena** (events that seem to defy accepted scientific laws). (Psi is pronounced like "sigh.") Parapsychologists seek answers to the questions raised by three basic forms that ESP could take:

1. **Telepathy**. The purported ability to communicate directly with another person's mind. When the other person is dead, the communications are called *mediumship*.

2. **Clairvoyance**. The purported ability to perceive events or gain information in ways that appear unaffected by distance or normal physical barriers.

3. **Precognition**. The purported ability to perceive or accurately predict future events. Precognition may take the form of prophetic dreams that foretell the future.

While we are at it, we might as well toss in another purported psi ability:

4. **Psychokinesis**. The purported ability to exert influence over inanimate objects (such as bending spoons) by willpower ("mind over matter"). (Psychokinesis cannot be classed as a type of ESP, but parapsychologists frequently study it.)

An Appraisal of ESP

Why don't psychologists believe in ESP? Regardless of all the popular enthusiasm, psychologists as a group are highly skeptical about psi abilities (Wiseman & Watt, 2006). Let's look at the evidence for and against extrasensory perception. The formal investigation of psi events owes much to the late J. B. Rhine, who tried to study ESP objectively. Many of Rhine's experiments made use of *Zener cards* (a deck of 25 cards, each bearing one of five symbols) (● **Figure 22.1**). In a typical clairvoyance test, people try to guess the symbols on the cards as they are turned up from a shuffled deck. In a typical telepathy test, a *receiver* tries to guess the correct symbol by reading the mind of a *sender* looking at a card. Pure guessing in these tests will produce an average score of 5 "hits" out of 25 cards. Rhine and others since him have reported results much greater than might be expected by chance alone.

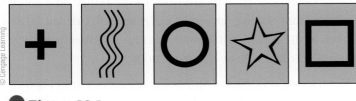

● **Figure 22.1**

ESP cards used by J. B. Rhine, an early experimenter in parapsychology.

Doesn't such evidence settle the issue? No, it doesn't, for several reasons, including fraud, poorly designed experiments, and chance.

Fraud Fraud continues to plague parapsychology. The need for skepticism is especially great any time there's money to be made from purported psychic abilities. Stage demonstrations of ESP are based on deception and tricks, as are other "for-profit" enterprises. For example, in 2002, the owners of the "Miss Cleo" television-psychic operation were convicted of felony fraud. "Miss Cleo," supposedly a Jamaican-accented psychic, was really just an actress from Los Angeles. People who paid $4.99 a minute for a "reading" from "Miss Cleo" reached one of several hundred operators. These people were hired to do "cold readings" through ads that read, "No experience necessary." Despite being entirely faked, the "Miss Cleo" scam brought in more than $1 billion before it was shut down.

Anyone can learn to do "cold readings" well enough to produce satisfied customers (Wood et al., 2003). *Cold reading* is a set of techniques that are used to lead people to believe in the truth of what a psychic or medium is saying about them. These include relying on many of the same techniques used by astrologers, such as uncritical acceptance, confirmation bias, and the Barnum effect. (Remember Module 2?)

The "psychic" begins a "reading" by making general statements about a person. The psychic then plays "hot and cold" by attending to the person's facial expressions, body language, or tone of voice. When the psychic is "hot" (on the right track), he or she continues to make similar statements about the person.

If the person's reactions signal that the psychic is "cold," the psychic drops that topic or line of thought and tries another (Hyman, 2007).

Poorly Designed Experiments Unfortunately, some of Rhine's most dramatic early experiments used badly printed Zener cards that allowed the symbols to show faintly on the back. It also is very easy to cheat by marking cards with a fingernail or by noting marks on the cards caused by normal use. There also is evidence that early experimenters sometimes unconsciously gave people cues about cards with their eyes or facial gestures. In short, none of the early studies in parapsychology were done in a way that eliminated the possibility of deliberate fraud or the accidental "leakage" of helpful information (Alcock, Burns, & Freeman, 2003).

Modern parapsychologists are now well aware of the need for double-blind experiments, security and accuracy in record keeping, meticulous control, and repeatability of experiments (Milton & Wiseman, 1997; O'Keeffe & Wiseman, 2005). In the last 10 years, hundreds of experiments have been reported in parapsychological journals. Many of them seem to support the existence of psi abilities (Aldhous, 2010).

Chance *Then why do most psychologists still remain skeptical about psi abilities?* The most important reason has to do with chance. Remember the woman who had a premonition that something bad was about to happen to her husband? She returned home early to find her house on fire with him sleeping inside (Rhine, 1953). An apparent clairvoyant or telepathic experience like this is certainly striking, but it does not confirm the existence of ESP. Such *coincidences* occur quite often. On any given night, many thousands of people around the world might act on a "premonition." If, by coincidence, one person's hunch turns out to be correct, it may be *reinterpreted* as clairvoyance (Marks, 2000; Wiseman & Watt, 2006). Then you read about it in the news the next day. No one reports the vast majority of false premonitions, which are simply forgotten.

Inconsistency in psi research is a related problem. For every published study with positive results, there are others that fail and are never published (Alcock, 2010). Even experimental "successes" are weak. Many of the most spectacular findings

Extrasensory perception (ESP) *The purported ability to perceive events in ways that cannot be explained by known capacities of the sensory organs.*

Psi phenomena *Events that seem to lie outside the realm of accepted scientific laws.*

in parapsychology simply cannot be *replicated* (reproduced or repeated) (Hyman, 1996a). Furthermore, improved research methods usually result in fewer positive results (Hyman, 1996b; O'Keeffe & Wiseman, 2005).

Even when a person seems to show evidence of psi ability, it is rare—in fact, almost unheard of—for him or her to maintain that ability over any sustained period of time (Alcock, Burns, & Freeman, 2003). This is likely because a person who only temporarily scores above chance has just received credit for a **run of luck**—a statistically unusual outcome that could occur by chance alone.

To understand the run-of-luck criticism, imagine that you flip a coin 100 times and record the results. You then flip another coin 100 times, again recording the results. The two lists are compared. For any 10 pairs of flips, we would expect heads or tails to match 5 times. Let's say you go through the list and find a set of 10 pairs in which 9 out of 10 matched. This is far above chance expectation. But does it mean that the first coin "knew" what was going to come up on the second coin? That idea is obviously silly. Now, what if a person guesses 100 times what will come up on a coin? Again, we might find a set of 10 guesses that matches the results of flipping the coin. Does this mean that the person, for a time, had precognition—then lost it?

You may be surprised to learn that some ESP researchers believe this "decline effect" shows that parapsychological skills are very fragile, like a weak cell phone connection, and fade in and out over time. If a person has a good short run of guessing, it is assumed that the person, for a time, had precognition. A subsequent run of poor guesses is interpreted to mean the person's precognition has temporarily faded.

In fact, creative interpretation is a common problem when it comes to psi. For example, former astronaut Edgar Mitchell claimed he did a successful telepathy experiment from space. Yet, news accounts never mentioned that on some trials Mitchell's "receivers" scored above chance, whereas on others they scored *below* chance. Although you might assume that below-chance trials were failures to find telepathy, Mitchell reinterpreted them as "successes," claiming that they represented intentional "psi missing." But, as skeptics have noted, if both high scores and low scores count as successes, how can you lose?

Implications After close to 130 years of investigation, it is still impossible to say conclusively whether psi events occur. As we have seen, a close look at psi experiments often reveals serious problems of evidence, procedure, and scientific rigor (Alcock, Burns, & Freeman, 2003; Hyman, 2007; Stokes, 2001). The more closely psi experiments are examined, the more likely it is that claimed successes will evaporate (Alcock, 2010; Stokes, 2001). As one critic put it, positive ESP results usually mean "Error Some Place" (Marks, 2000).

What would it take to scientifically demonstrate the existence of ESP? Quite simply, it would take a set of instructions that would allow any competent, unbiased observer to produce a psi event under standardized conditions that rule out any possibility of fraud or chance (Schick & Vaughn, 2014). In fact, professional magician and skeptic James Randi even offers a $1 million prize to anyone who can demonstrate evidence of psi events under standardized conditions. No one has yet tried for the prize. (Go ahead, claim your cool million by Googling the James Randi Educational Foundation.)

Undoubtedly, researchers will continue their attempts to supply irrefutable evidence. Others remain skeptics and consider 130 years of inconclusive efforts reason enough to abandon the concept of ESP (Marks, 2000). Yet, being a skeptic does not mean a person is against something. It means that you are unconvinced. The purpose of this discussion, then, has been to counter the *uncritical* acceptance of psi events reported in the popular press or by researchers who are uncritical "true believers." (But then, you already knew we were going to say that, didn't you?)

Of course, in many ESP tests, the outcome is beyond debate. A good example is provided by ESP experiments done through newspapers, radio, and television. The results of more than 1.5 million ESP trials done through the mass media are easy to summarize: There was no significant ESP effect (Milton & Wiseman, 1999). Clearly, lottery organizers have nothing to fear!

Run of luck *A statistically unusual outcome (as in getting five heads in a row when flipping a coin) that could still occur by chance alone.*

Module 22: Summary

22.1 Is extrasensory perception possible?

- **22.1.1** Parapsychology is the study of purported psi phenomena, including telepathy (including mediumship), clairvoyance, precognition, and psychokinesis.

- **22.1.2** Research in parapsychology remains controversial because of a variety of problems and shortcomings. The bulk of the evidence to date is against the existence of ESP.

- **22.1.3** The more carefully controlled an ESP experiment is, the less likely it is to produce evidence that ESP occurs.

Module 22: Knowledge Builder

Recite

1. Four purported psi events investigated by parapsychologists are clairvoyance, telepathy, precognition, and _____.

2. The Zener cards were used in early studies of
   - **a.** psi phenomena
   - **b.** inattentional blindness
   - **c.** the Müller-Lyer illusion
   - **d.** top-down processing

3. Natural, or "real-life," occurrences are regarded as the best evidence for the existence of ESP. *T or F?*

4. Skeptics attribute positive results in psi experiments to statistical runs of luck. *T or F?*

5. Replication rates are very high for ESP experiments. *T or F?*

Reflect

Think Critically

6. What would you estimate is the chance that two people will have the same birthday (day and month, but not year) in a group of 30 people?

7. A "psychic" on television offers to fix broken watches for viewers. Moments later, dozens of viewers call the station to say that their watches miraculously started running again. What have they overlooked?

Self-Reflect

Let's say that a friend of yours is an avid fan of television shows that feature paranormal themes. See if you can summarize for her or him what is known about ESP. Be sure to include evidence for and against the existence of ESP and some of the thinking errors associated with nonskeptical belief in the paranormal.

ANSWERS

1. psychokinesis **2.** a **3.** F **4.** T **5.** F **6.** Most people assume that this would be a relatively rare event. However, there is a 71 percent chance that two people will share a birthday in a group of thirty. Most people probably underestimate the natural rate of occurrence of many seemingly mysterious coincidences (Alcock, Burns, & Freeman, 2003). **7.** When psychologists handled watches awaiting repair at a store, 57 percent began running again, with no help from a "psychic." Believing the psychic's claim also overlooks the impact of big numbers: If the show reached a large audience, at least a few "broken" watches would start working merely by chance.

CENGAGE**brain**.com

Go to **cengagebrain.com** to access **MindTap for Coon/Mitterer** *Psychology Modules for Active Learning* and other online learning tools. MindTap is a fully online learning experience that combines all the tools you need—readings, multimedia, activities, and assessments—into a singular personalized Learning Path that guides you through the course.

Consciousness: States of Consciousness

Grand, Indeed!

- At the Grand Canyon, a hiker enters a fully conscious state of mindfulness meditation.
- In New York City, an aspiring actor is hypnotized to help reduce her stage fright.
- In a Tokyo hospital, a man lies in a deep coma after surviving a horrendous traffic accident.
- In Brisbane, a college student drifts into a pleasant daydream while sitting at the back of class.
- At a park in Amsterdam, a group of street musicians smoke a joint and sing for spare change.
- In Tucson, Arizona, one of your authors brews himself another cup of cappuccino.

Each of these people is experiencing a different state of consciousness. Some have no choice, and some are deliberately seeking to bend their minds—to alter consciousness—in different ways, to different degrees, and for different reasons. As these examples suggest, consciousness can take many forms, some grand and some not so grand. Let's explore the varieties of conscious experience.

© Galyna Andrushka/Shutterstock

SURVEY QUESTIONS

23.1 What is consciousness?

23.2 What is hypnosis?

23.3 Do meditation and mindfulness have any benefits?

States of Consciousness— the Many Faces of Awareness

SURVEY QUESTION 23.1: What is consciousness?

An unconscious person will die without constant care. Yet, as crucial as consciousness is, we can't yet really explain how it occurs (Robinson, 2008; Schwitzgebel, 2011). On the other hand, we can identify various states of consciousness and explore the role they play in our lives. To be *conscious* means to be aware. **Consciousness** consists of your sensations and perceptions of external events as well as your self-awareness of mental events, including thoughts, memories, and feelings about your experiences and yourself (Morin, 2006; Robinson, 2008). Take, for example, one hiker's profound moment at the Grand Canyon. As Eric first looked over the rim, he was "blown away" by deep feelings of insignificance and awe. In that instant, he also was fully aware that he *was* experiencing a deeply moving moment.

Although this definition of consciousness may seem obvious, it is based on your own subjective, *first-person* experience. You are the expert on what it feels like to be you. But what about other people? What does it feel like to be your mother? Or someone in a coma? What runs through a dog's mind when it sniffs other dogs? Does it feel joy?

You simply can't answer these questions about *other minds* through your own first-person perspective. The difficulty of knowing other minds is one reason the early behaviorists distrusted introspection (see Module 3). Instead, psychologists adopt an objective, *third-person* point of view. A key challenge for psychology is to use objective studies of the brain and behavior to help us understand the mind and consciousness, which are basically private phenomena (Robinson, 2008). This module, and the three that follow, summarize some of what we have learned about different states of consciousness.

Altered States of Consciousness

We spend most of our lives in **waking consciousness**, a state of clear, organized alertness. In waking consciousness, we perceive times, places, and events as real, meaningful, and familiar. But states of consciousness related to fatigue, delirium, hypnosis, drugs, and euphoria may differ markedly from normal awareness (Chalmers, 2010). Everyone experiences at least some altered states, such as sleep, dreaming, and daydreaming. Some people experience dramatically altered states, such as the lower levels of awareness associated with strokes and other forms of brain damage (Morin, 2006; Schnakers & Laureys, 2012). In everyday life, changes in consciousness may even accompany long-distance running, listening to music, making love, or other circumstances.

How are altered states distinguished from normal awareness? During an **altered state of consciousness (ASC)**, changes occur in the *quality* and *pattern* of mental activity. Typically, distinct shifts happen in our perceptions, emotions, memories, time sense, thoughts, feelings of self-control, and suggestibility (Hohwy & Fox, 2012; Siegel, 2005). Definitions aside, most people know when they have experienced an ASC. In fact, heightened self-awareness is an important feature of many ASCs (Revonsuo, Kallio, & Sikka, 2009).

Are there other causes of ASCs? In addition to the ones mentioned, we could add sensory overload (a rave, Mardi Gras crowd, or mosh pit), monotonous stimulation (such as "highway hypnotism" on long drives), unusual physical conditions (high fever, hyperventilation, dehydration, sleep loss, near-death experiences), restricted sensory input (extended periods of isolation), and many other possibilities. In some instances, altered states have important cultural meanings (see "Consciousness and Culture" for more information). Let's continue with a more detailed look at two interesting altered states, hypnosis and meditation, before turning our attention to sleep, dreams, and drug use and abuse in the modules that follow.

Human Diversity

Consciousness and Culture

Throughout history, people everywhere have found ways to alter consciousness (Siegel, 2005). A dramatic example is the sweat lodge ceremony of the Native American Sioux. During the ritual, several men sit in total darkness inside a small chamber heated by coals. Cedar smoke, bursts of steam, and sage fill the air. The men chant rhythmically. The heat builds. At last, they can stand it no more. The door is thrown open. Cooling night breezes rush in. And then? The cycle begins again—often to be repeated four or five times.

John Mitterer

In many cultures, rituals of healing, prayer, meditation, purification, or personal transformation at sites like this Buddhist temple near Hong Kong are accompanied by altered states of consciousness.

Like Buddhists engaging in meditation practices, Navaho elders drinking peyote tea, or New Zealand Maori priests performing nightlong rituals to communicate with the mythical period the Aborigines call "Dreamtime," the ritual "sweats" of the Sioux are meant to cleanse the mind and body. When they are especially intense, they bring altered awareness and personal revelation.

People seek some altered states purely for pleasure or escape, as is often true of drug intoxication. Yet as the Sioux illustrate, many cultures regard altered consciousness as a pathway to personal enlightenment. Indeed, all cultures and most religions recognize and accept some alterations of consciousness. However, the meaning given to these states varies greatly—from signs of "madness" and "possession" by spirits to life-enhancing breakthroughs. Thus, cultural conditioning greatly affects what altered states we recognize, seek, consider normal, and attain (Cardeña et al., 2011).

Consciousness *Mental awareness of sensations and perceptions of external events as well as self-awareness of internal events, including thoughts, memories, and feelings about experiences and the self.*
Waking consciousness *A state of clear, organized alertness.*
Altered state of consciousness (ASC) *A condition of awareness distinctly different in quality or pattern from waking consciousness.*

Hypnosis—Look into My Eyes

SURVEY QUESTION 23.2: What is hypnosis?

"Your body is becoming heavy. You can barely keep your eyes open. You are so tired you can't move. Relax. Let go. Relax. Close your eyes and relax." These are the last words a textbook should ever say to you, and the first a hypnotist might say. What do you know about hypnosis? Which of your beliefs are true? Which are myths? Is hypnosis real? Does it have any value?

Interest in hypnosis began in the 1700s with Austrian doctor Franz Mesmer, whose name gave us the term *mesmerize* (to hypnotize). Mesmer believed he could cure disease with magnets. Mesmer's strange "treatments" are related to hypnosis because they relied on the power of suggestion, not magnetism (Barrios, 2009; Benjafield, 2012). For a time, Mesmer enjoyed quite a following. In the end, however, his theories of "animal magnetism" were rejected and he was branded a fraud.

Ever since, stage hypnotists have entertained us with a combination of little or no hypnosis and a bit of deception. On stage, people are unusually cooperative because they don't want to "spoil the act." As a result, they readily follow almost any instruction given by the entertainer. After volunteers loosen up and respond to a few suggestions, they find that they are suddenly the stars of the show. Audience response to the antics on stage brings out the "ham" in many people. No hypnosis is required; all the "hypnotist" needs to do is direct the action.

Like stage magicians, stage hypnotists also make liberal use of deception. One of the more impressive stage tricks is to rigidly suspend a person between two chairs. This is astounding only because the audience does not question it. Anyone can do it, as is shown in the photographs and instructions in ● **Figure 23.1**. Try it!

Entertainment aside, hypnosis is a real phenomenon. The term *hypnosis* was coined by English surgeon James Braid. The Greek word *hypnos* means "sleep," and Braid used it to describe the hypnotic state. Today, we know that hypnosis is *not* sleep. Confusion about this point remains because some hypnotists give the suggestion, "Sleep, sleep." However, brain activity recorded during hypnosis is different from that observed when a person is asleep or pretending to be hypnotized (del Casale et al., 2012; Oakley & Halligan, 2010).

Theories of Hypnosis

If hypnosis isn't sleep, then what is it? That's a good question. **Hypnosis** is often defined as an altered state of consciousness, characterized by narrowed attention and an increased openness to suggestion (Kallio & Revonsuo, 2003). Notice that this definition assumes hypnosis is a distinct *state* of consciousness.

The best-known *state theory* of hypnosis was proposed by Ernest Hilgard (1904–2001), who argued that hypnosis causes a *dissociative state*, or "split" in awareness. To illustrate, he asked hypnotized participants to plunge one hand into a painful bath of ice water. Participants told to feel no pain said they felt none. The same participants were then asked if any part of their mind did feel pain. With their free hand, many wrote, "It hurts," or "Stop it, you're hurting me," while they continued to act pain free (Hilgard, 1977, 1994). Thus, one part of the hypnotized person says there is no pain and acts as if there is none. Another part, which Hilgard calls the *hidden observer*, is aware of the pain but remains in the background. The **hidden observer** is a detached part of the hypnotized person's awareness that silently observes events.

In contrast, *nonstate theorists* argue that hypnosis is not a distinct state at all. Instead, it is merely a blend of conformity,

Dennis Coon

● **Figure 23.1**

Arrange three chairs as shown. Have someone recline as shown. Ask him or her to lift slightly while you remove the middle chair. Accept the applause gracefully! (Concerning hypnosis and similar phenomena, the moral, of course, is "Suspend judgment until you have something solid to stand on.")

Discovering Psychology

Swinging Suggestions

Here's a demonstration you can use to gain insight into hypnosis. Tie a short length of string (about 6 inches) to a small, heavy object, such as a ring or a small metal nut. Hold the ring at eye level, about a foot from your face. Concentrate on the ring and notice that it will begin to move, ever so slightly. As it does, focus all your attention on the ring. Narrow your attention to a beam of energy and mentally push the ring away from you. Each time the ring swings away, push on it, using only mental force. Then release it and let it swing back toward you. Continue to mentally push and release the ring until it is swinging freely. For the best results, try this now, before reading more.

Did the ring move? If it did, you used *autosuggestion* to influence your own behavior in a subtle way. Suggestions that the ring would swing caused your hand to make tiny micromuscular movements. These, in turn, caused the ring to move—no special mental powers or supernatural forces are involved.

John Mitterer

As is true of hypnotic suggestion, the ring's movement probably seemed automatic. Obviously, you could just intentionally swing the ring. However, if you responded to suggestion, the movement seemed to happen without any effort on your part. In the same way, when people are hypnotized, their actions seem to occur without any voluntary intent. Incidentally, autosuggestion likely underlies other phenomena, such as how Ouija boards answer questions without any conscious movements by the person using the pointer. Autosuggestion also plays a role in many forms of self-therapy (Yapko, 2011).

relaxation, imagination, obedience, and role-playing (Kirsch, 2005; Lynn & O'Hagen, 2009). For example, many theorists believe that all hypnosis is really self-hypnosis *(autosuggestion)*. From this perspective, a hypnotist merely helps another person follow a series of suggestions. These suggestions, in turn, alter sensations, perceptions, thoughts, feelings, and behaviors (Lynn & Kirsch, 2006; see "Swinging Suggestions").

The Reality of Hypnosis

How is hypnosis done? Could I be hypnotized against my will? Hypnotists use many different methods. Still, all techniques encourage a person to (1) focus attention on what is being said, (2) relax and feel tired, (3) "let go" and accept suggestions easily, and (4) use vivid imagination (Barabasz & Watkins, 2005). Basically, you must cooperate to become hypnotized.

What does it feel like to be hypnotized? You might be surprised at some of your actions during hypnosis. You also might have mild feelings of floating, sinking, anesthesia, or separation from your body. Personal experiences vary widely. A key element in hypnosis is the **basic suggestion effect**—a tendency of hypnotized persons to carry out suggested actions as if they were involuntary. Hypnotized persons feel like their actions and experiences are *automatic*—they seem to happen without effort. Here is how one person described his hypnotic session:

"I felt lethargic, my eyes going out of focus and wanting to close. My hands felt real light.... I felt I was sinking deeper into the chair.... I felt like I wanted to relax more and more....

My responses were more automatic. I didn't have to *wish* to do things so much or *want* to do them.... I just did them.... I felt floating... very close to sleep" (Hilgard, 1968).

Contrary to how hypnosis is portrayed in movies, hypnotized people generally remain in control of their behavior and aware of what is going on. For instance, most people will not act out hypnotic suggestions that they consider immoral or repulsive (such as disrobing in public or harming someone) (Kirsch & Lynn, 1995).

Hypnotic Susceptibility *Can everyone be hypnotized?* About eight people out of ten can be hypnotized, but only four out of ten will be good hypnotic participants. People who are imaginative and prone to fantasy are often highly responsive to hypnosis (Kallio & Revonsuo, 2003). But people who lack these traits also may be hypnotized. If you are willing to be hypnotized, chances are good that you could be. Hypnosis depends more on the efforts and abilities of the hypnotized person than the skills of the hypnotist. But make no mistake: People who are hypnotized are not merely faking their responses.

Hypnosis *An altered state of consciousness characterized by narrowed attention and increased suggestibility.*
Hidden observer *A detached part of the hypnotized person's awareness that silently observes events.*
Basic suggestion effect *The tendency of hypnotized persons to carry out suggested actions as if they were involuntary.*

TABLE 23.1	Stanford Hypnotic Susceptibility Scale
Suggested Behavior	**Criterion of Passing**
1. Postural sway	Falls without forcing
2. Eye closure	Closes eyes without forcing
3. Hand lowering (left)	Lowers at least 6 inches by end of 10 seconds
4. Immobilization (right arm)	Arm rises less than 1 inch in 10 seconds
5. Finger lock	Incomplete separation of fingers at end of 10 seconds
6. Arm rigidity (left arm)	Less than 2 inches of arm bending in 10 seconds
7. Hands moving together	Hands at least as close as 6 inches after 10 seconds
8. Verbal inhibition (name)	Name unspoken in 10 seconds
9. Hallucination (fly)	Any movement, grimacing, acknowledgment of effect
10. Eye catalepsy	Eyes remain closed at end of 10 seconds
11. Posthypnotic (changes chairs)	Any partial movement response
12. Amnesia test	Three or fewer items recalled

Adapted from Weitzenhoffer & Hilgard, 1959.

Hypnotic susceptibility refers to how easily a person can become hypnotized. It is measured by giving a series of suggestions and counting the number of times a person responds. A typical hypnotic test is the *Stanford Hypnotic Susceptibility Scale*, shown in ● Table 23.1. In the test, various suggestions are made, and the person's response is noted. For instance, you might be told that your left arm is becoming more and more rigid and that it will not bend. If you can't bend your arm during the next 10 seconds, you have shown susceptibility to hypnotic suggestions.

Effects of Hypnosis *What can (and cannot) be achieved with hypnosis?* Many abilities have been tested during hypnosis, leading to the following conclusions:

1. **Strength.** Hypnosis has no more effect on physical strength than instructions that encourage a person to make his or her best effort (Chaves, 2000).

2. **Memory.** Some evidence shows that hypnosis can enhance memory (Wester & Hammond, 2011). However, it frequently increases the number of false memories as well (see Module 32). For this reason, many states now bar persons from testifying in court if they were hypnotized to improve their memory of a crime they witnessed.

3. **Amnesia.** A person told not to remember something heard during hypnosis may claim not to remember. In some instances, this may be nothing more than a deliberate attempt to avoid thinking about specific ideas. However,

brief memory loss of this type does seem to occur (Barnier, McConkey, & Wright, 2004).

4. **Pain relief.** Hypnosis can relieve pain (Hammond, 2008; Kohen, 2011). It can be especially useful when chemical painkillers are ineffective. For instance, hypnosis can reduce phantom limb pain (Oakley, Whitman, & Halligan, 2002). (As discussed in Module 19, amputees sometimes feel phantom pain that seems to come from a missing limb.)

5. **Age regression.** Given the proper suggestions, some hypnotized people appear to regress to childhood. However, most theorists now believe that age-regressed participants are only acting out a suggested role.

6. **Sensory changes.** Hypnotic suggestions concerning sensations are among the most effective. Given the proper instructions, a person can be made to smell a small bottle of ammonia and respond as if it were a wonderful perfume. It also is possible to alter color vision, hearing sensitivity, time sense, perception of illusions, and many other sensory responses.

Like meditation, which we explore next, hypnosis is a valuable tool in a variety of settings (Yapko, 2011). It can help people relax, feel less pain, and make better progress in therapy (Lynn, Kirsch, & Rhue, 2010). Generally, hypnosis is more successful at changing subjective experience than it is at modifying behaviors such as smoking or overeating.

Meditation and Mindfulness— Chilling, the Healthy Way

SURVEY QUESTION 23.3: Do meditation and mindfulness have any benefits?

Throughout history, meditation has been widely used as a means of altering consciousness through deep relaxation. Let's see how meditation works.

Meditation

Meditation is a mental exercise used to alter consciousness. In general, meditation focuses attention and interrupts the typical flow of thoughts, worries, and analysis. People who use meditation to reduce stress often report less daily physical tension and anxiety (Sears & Kraus, 2009; Vago & Nakamura, 2011). Brain scans (such as PET and fMRI) reveal changes during meditation in the activity of the brain, including the frontal lobes, which suggests that it may be a distinct state of consciousness (Brewer et al., 2011; Cahn & Polich, 2006).

Meditation takes two major forms. In **concentrative meditation**, you attend to a single focal point, such as an object, a thought, or your own breathing. In contrast, **mindfulness meditation** is "open," or expansive. In this case, you widen your attention to embrace a total, nonjudgmental awareness of the world (Hölzel et al., 2011). An example is losing all self-consciousness while walking in the wilderness with a quiet and receptive mind. Although it may not seem so, mindfulness meditation is more difficult to attain than concentrative meditation. For this reason, we will discuss concentrative meditation as a practical self-control method.

Performing Concentrative Meditation *How is concentrative meditation done?* The basic idea is to sit still and quietly focus on some external object or on a repetitive internal stimulus, such as your own breathing or humming. As an alternative, you can silently repeat a *mantra* (a word used as the focus of attention in concentrative meditation). Typical mantras are smooth, flowing sounds that are easily repeated. A widely used mantra is the word *om*. A mantra also could be any pleasant word or a phrase from a familiar song, poem, or prayer. If other thoughts arise as you repeat a mantra, just return attention to it as often as necessary to maintain meditation.

The Relaxation Response Medical researcher Herbert Benson believes that the core of meditation is the **relaxation response**—an innate physiological pattern that opposes your body's fight-or-flight mechanisms (Chang, Dusek, & Benson, 2011). Benson feels, quite simply, that most of us have forgotten how to relax deeply. People in his experiments learned to produce the relaxation response by following instructions like these:

Sit quietly and comfortably. Close your eyes. Relax your muscles, beginning at your feet and progressing up to your head. Relax them deeply. Become aware of breathing through your nose. As you breathe out, say a word like "peace" silently to yourself. Don't worry about how successful you are in relaxing deeply. Just let relaxation happen at its own pace. Don't be surprised by distracting thoughts. When they occur, ignore them and continue repeating "peace." (Adapted from Chang, Dusek, & Benson, 2011; Hölzel et al., 2011.)

As a stress-control technique, meditation may be a good choice for people who find it difficult to "turn off" upsetting thoughts when they need to relax. In one study, a group of college students who received just 90 minutes of training in the relaxation response experienced greatly reduced stress levels (Deckro et al., 2002). The physical benefits of meditation include lowered heart rate, blood pressure, muscle tension, and other signs of stress (Zeidan et al., 2010), as well as improved immune system activity (Davidson et al., 2003).

According to Shauna Shapiro and Roger Walsh (2006), meditation has benefits beyond relaxation. Practiced regularly, meditation may foster mental well-being and positive mental skills such as clarity, concentration, and calm. In this sense, meditation may share much in common with psychotherapy. Indeed, research has shown that mindfulness meditation relieves a variety of psychological disorders, from insomnia to excessive anxiety. It also can reduce aggression and the use of psychoactive drugs (Brewer et al., 2011; Shapiro & Walsh, 2006). Regular meditation may even help

Meditation *A mental exercise for producing relaxation or heightened awareness.*
Concentrative meditation *Mental exercise based on attending to a single object or thought.*
Mindfulness meditation *Mental exercise based on widening attention to become aware of everything experienced at any given moment.*
Relaxation response *The pattern of internal bodily changes that occurs at times of relaxation.*
Hypnotic susceptibility *One's capacity for becoming hypnotized.*

The Clinical File

Tranquility in a Tank

Imagine floating in a tank of warm water, for a short while, without the least bit of muscle tension (● **Figure 23.2**). You cannot hear anything, and it is pitch dark. You are experiencing brief *sensory deprivation*, a major reduction in the amount or variety of sensory stimulation.

● **Figure 23.2**
A sensory-deprivation chamber. Psychologists have used small flotation tanks like this one to study the effects of mild sensory deprivation. Participants float in darkness and silence. The shallow, body-temperature water contains hundreds of pounds of Epsom salts, so participants float near the surface.

What happens when stimulation is greatly reduced? A hint comes from reports by prisoners in solitary confinement, arctic explorers, high-altitude pilots, long-distance truck drivers, and radar operators. When faced with limited or monotonous stimulation, people sometimes have bizarre sensations, dangerous lapses in attention, and wildly distorted perceptions. Intense or prolonged sensory deprivation is stressful and disorienting.

Yet, oddly enough, brief periods of sensory restriction can produce a strong relaxation response (Bood et al., 2006). An hour or two spent in a flotation tank can cause a large drop in blood pressure, muscle tension, chronic pain, and other signs of stress (Bood et al., 2006; Kjellgren, Buhrkall, & Norlander, 2011).

Like other forms of meditation, mild sensory deprivation also may help with more than relaxation. Deep relaxation makes people more open to suggestion, and sensory deprivation interrupts habitual behavior patterns. This can loosen belief systems, making it easier for people to quit smoking, lose weight, and reduce their use of alcohol and drugs (Suedfeld & Borrie, 1999; van Dierendonck & Te Nijenhuis, 2005).

Mild sensory deprivation even shows promise as a way to stimulate creative thinking and enhance sports and music performance skills (Norlander, Bergman, & Archer, 1998, 1999; Vartanian & Suedfeld, 2011). Clearly, much is yet to be learned from studying "nothingness."

people develop better control over their attention, heightened self-awareness, and maturity (Hodgins & Adair, 2010; Travis, Arenander, & DuBois, 2004). For a curious way to meditate, see "Tranquility in a Tank."

Summary To summarize, research suggests that meditation, including mild sensory deprivation, is a way to elicit the relaxation response. For many people, sitting quietly and "resting" can be as effective. Similar stress reduction occurs when people set aside time daily to engage in other restful activities, such as muscle relaxation, positive daydreaming, and even leisure reading. However, if you are the type of person who finds it difficult to ignore upsetting thoughts, then concentrative meditation might be a good way to promote relaxation. Practiced regularly, meditation and mild sensory isolation may even help improve overall mental health—something almost everyone could use in our fast-paced society.

The Whole Human: Mindfulness and Well-Being

Did you "space out" anytime today? Most of us have occasional moments of reduced awareness. **Mindfulness** is the opposite of such mindless moments: It involves an open, nonjudgmental awareness of current experience. In other words, mindfulness is similar to the state that people who practice mindfulness receptive meditation are trying to achieve. A person who is mindful is fully present, moment by moment (Hölzel et al., 2011). She or he is acutely aware of every thought, emotion, or sensation, but does not judge it or react to it. The person is fully "awake" and attuned to immediate reality, just like Eric that day at the Grand Canyon.

Psychologists interested in positive mental states have begun to study the effects of mindfulness. For example, cancer patients who are taught mindfulness meditation have lower levels of distress and a greater sense of well-being. Similarly, being mindful makes it easier to quit smoking (Brewer et al., 2011). Such benefits apply to healthy people, too. In general, mindfulness is associated with self-knowledge and well-being (Friese, Messner, & Schaffner, 2012; Siegel, 2010). Anyone who has a tendency to sleepwalk through life—and that's most of us at times—would be wise to be mindful of the value of mindfulness.

Mindfulness *A state of open, nonjudgmental awareness of current experience.*

Module 23: Summary

23.1 What is consciousness?

- **23.1.1** Consciousness is a core feature of mental life consisting of sensations and perceptions of external events as well as self-awareness of mental events, including thoughts, memories, and feelings about experiences and the self.
- **23.1.2** States of awareness that differ from normal, alert, waking consciousness are called altered states of consciousness (ASCs). Altered states are especially associated with sleep and dreaming, hypnosis, meditation, and psychoactive drugs.
- **23.1.3** Cultural conditioning greatly affects what altered states a person recognizes, seeks, considers normal, and attains.

23.2 What is hypnosis?

- **23.2.1** Although not all psychologists agree, hypnosis is usually defined as an altered state characterized by narrowed attention and increased suggestibility.

- **23.2.2** Hypnosis appears capable of producing relaxation, controlling pain, and altering perceptions. It also is more capable of changing subjective experiences more than habits, such as smoking.

23.3 Do meditation and mindfulness have any benefits?

- **23.3.1** Concentrative meditation can be used to focus attention, alter consciousness, and reduce stress. Mindfulness meditation widens attention to achieve similar outcomes.
- **23.3.2** Major benefits of meditation are its ability to interrupt anxious thoughts and to elicit the relaxation response.
- **23.3.3** Mindfulness is a positive mental state that involves an open, nonjudgmental awareness of current experience.

Module 23: Knowledge Builder

Recite

1. Changes in the quality and pattern of mental activity define a(n)
   - **a.** EEG
   - **b.** REM
   - **c.** SIDS
   - **d.** ASC

2. In Ernest Hilgard's dissociative state theory of hypnosis, awareness is split between normal consciousness and
   - **a.** disinhibition
   - **b.** autosuggestion
   - **c.** memory
   - **d.** the hidden observer

3. Which of the following can most definitely be achieved with hypnosis?
   - **a.** unusual strength
   - **b.** pain relief
   - **c.** improved memory
   - **d.** sleep-like brain waves

4. The focus of attention in concentrative meditation is "open," or expansive. *T or F?*

5. Mantras are words said silently to oneself to end a session of meditation. *T or F?*

6. The most immediate benefit of meditation appears to be its capacity for producing the relaxation response. *T or F?*

Reflect

Think Critically

7. Regular meditators report lower levels of stress and a greater sense of well-being. What other explanations must we eliminate before this effect can be regarded as genuine?

Self-Reflect

Make a quick list of some altered states of consciousness you have experienced. What do they have in common? How are they different? What conditions caused them?

How have your beliefs about hypnosis changed after reading the preceding section? Can you think of specific examples in which hypnosis was misrepresented, for example, in movies, or television dramas?

Various activities can produce the relaxation response. When do you experience states of deep relaxation, coupled with a sense of serene awareness?

ANSWERS

1. d 2. d 3. b 4. F 5. F 6. T 7. Studies on the effects of meditation must control for the placebo effect and the fact that those who choose to learn meditation may not be a representative sample of the general population.

Go to **cengagebrain.com** to access **MindTap for Coon/Mitterer** *Psychology Modules for Active Learning* and other online learning tools. MindTap is a fully online learning experience that combines all the tools you need—readings, multimedia, activities, and assessments—into a singular personalized Learning Path that guides you through the course.

Consciousness: Sleep and Dreams

To Sleep, Perchance to Dream

Not all animals sleep, but like humans, those that do have powerful sleep needs. For example, dolphins must voluntarily breathe air, which means they face the choice of staying awake or drowning. A dolphin solves this problem by sleeping on just one side of its brain at a time! The other half of the brain, which remains awake, controls breathing.

Sleep is a necessity for dolphins, but how about humans? Of course, sleep will give way temporarily, especially at times of great danger. As comedian and filmmaker Woody Allen once put it, "The lion and the lamb shall lie down together, but the lamb will not be very sleepy." However, there are limits to how long we humans can go without sleep. What are they? What happens if we become sleep deprived? Why do we have to sleep, anyway? Why do some people have trouble sleeping? What are dreams? Let's find out.

Timothy Ross/The Image Works

Sleep—Catching a Few ZZZs

SURVEY QUESTIONS 24.1: What are the effects of sleep loss or changes in sleep patterns?

Each of us will spend some 25 years of life asleep. Because sleep is familiar, many people think they know all about it. But many common-sense beliefs about sleep are false. For example, you are not totally unresponsive during sleep. A sleeping mother may ignore a jet thundering overhead but wake at the slightest whimper of her child. Likewise, you are more likely to awaken if you hear your own name spoken instead of another. It's even possible to do simple tasks while asleep. In one experiment, people learned to avoid an electric shock by touching a switch each time a tone sounded. Eventually, they could do it without waking. (This is much like the basic survival skill of turning off your alarm clock without waking.) Of course, sleep does impose limitations. Don't expect to learn math, a foreign language, or other complex skills while asleep—especially if the snooze takes place in class (González-Vallejo et al., 2008). But do expect that a good sleep will help you remember what you learned the day before (Holz et al., 2012; Saxvig et al., 2008).

The Need for Sleep

How strong is the need for sleep? Sleep is an innate **biological rhythm** that never can be entirely ignored (Luyster et al., 2012). For example, a rare disease that prevents sleep always ends with stupor, coma, and death (Zhang et al., 2010).

How long could a person go without sleep? With few exceptions, four days or more without sleep becomes hell for everyone. The world record is held by Randy Gardner, who at age 17 went 264 hours (11 days) without sleep. Surprisingly, Randy needed only 14 hours of sleep to recover. As Randy found, most symptoms of **sleep deprivation**, or sleep loss, are reversed by a single night's rest (Sallinen et al., 2008).

What are the costs of sleep loss? At various times, Randy's speech was slurred, and he couldn't concentrate, remember clearly, or name common objects (Coren, 1996). Sleep loss also typically causes trembling hands, drooping eyelids, inattention, irritability, staring, increased pain sensitivity, and general discomfort (Doran, Van Dongen, & Dinges, 2001).

Most people experience *hypersomnia* (hi-per-SOM-nee-ah), or excessive daytime sleepiness, after even a few hours of sleep loss (Centers for Disease Control, 2012d). Hypersomnia is a common problem during adolescence (Carskadon, Acebo, & Jenni, 2004; Kotagal, 2012). Rapid physical changes during puberty increase the need for sleep. However, the quality and quantity of sleep time tend to decrease during the teen years.

Most people who have not slept for a day or two can still do interesting or complex mental tasks. But they have trouble paying attention, staying alert, and doing simple or boring routines (Trujillo, Kornguth, & Schnyer, 2009). They also are susceptible to **microsleeps**, which are brief shifts in brain activity to the pattern normally recorded during sleep. Imagine placing an animal on a moving treadmill, over a pool of water. Even under these conditions, animals soon drift into repeated microsleeps. For a pilot or machine operator, this can spell disaster (Hardaway & Gregory, 2005; Kaida et al., 2008). If a task is monotonous (such as factory work or air traffic control), no amount of sleep loss is safe.

When you drive, remember that microsleeps can lead to macro-accidents. Even if your eyes are open, you can fall asleep for a few seconds. More than 15 percent of fatal crashes every year are caused by sleepiness (American Academy of Sleep Medicine, 2013). Although coffee helps (Kamimori et al., 2005), if you are struggling to stay awake while driving, you should stop, quit fighting it, and take a short nap.

Severe sleep loss can even cause a temporary **sleep-deprivation psychosis**—a loss of contact with reality. Confusion, disorientation, delusions, and hallucinations are typical of this reaction. Fortunately, such "crazy" behavior is uncommon. Hallucinations and delusions rarely appear before 60 hours of wakefulness (Naitoh, Kelly, & Englund, 1989).

How can I tell how much sleep I really need? Pick a day when you feel well rested. Then sleep that night until you wake without an alarm clock. If you feel rested when you wake up, that's your natural sleep need. If you're sleeping fewer hours than you need, you're building up a sleep debt (Basner & Dinges, 2009).

Sleep Patterns

Sleep was described as an innate biological rhythm. What does that mean? Daily sleep and waking periods create a variety of sleep patterns. Rhythms of sleep and waking are so steady that they continue for many days, even when clocks and light–dark cycles are removed. However, under such conditions, humans eventually shift to sleep–waking cycles that average more than 24 hours (Czeisler et al., 1999; ● **Figure 24.1**). This suggests that external time markers, especially light and dark, help tie our sleep rhythms to days that are exactly 24 hours long. Otherwise, many of us would drift into our own unusual sleep cycles (Kovrov et al., 2012).

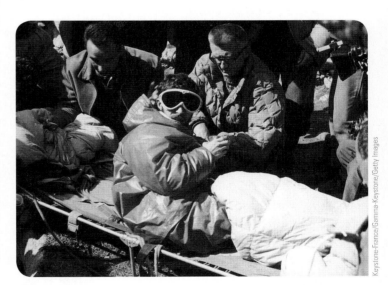

Keystone-France/Gamma-Keystone/Getty Images

● **Figure 24.1**

Frenchman Michel Siffre has spent months at a time living in caves deep underground without the usual external markers of night and day. He found that without these markers, his sleep cycles tended to get longer. During one such stay, he settled into a 48-hour sleep–waking cycle.

Biological rhythm *Any repeating cycle of biological activity, such as sleep and waking cycles or changes in body temperature.*
Sleep deprivation *Being prevented from getting desired or needed amounts of sleep.*
Microsleeps *Brief shifts in brain-wave patterns to those of sleep.*
Sleep-deprivation psychosis *A major disruption of mental and emotional functioning brought about by sleep loss.*

What is the normal range of sleep? A few rare individuals can get by on an hour or two of sleep a night—and feel perfectly fine. Only a small percentage of the population are *short sleepers*, averaging five hours of sleep or fewer per night. On the other end of the scale, we find *long sleepers*, who doze nine hours or more (Grandner & Kripke, 2004). The majority of us sleep on a familiar seven- to eight-hour-per-night schedule. Urging everyone to sleep eight hours would be like advising everyone to wear medium-size shoes.

We need less sleep as we get older, right? Yes, total sleep time declines throughout life. Those older than 50 average only six hours of sleep a night. In contrast, infants spend up to twenty hours a day sleeping, usually in two- to four-hour cycles. As they mature, most children go through a nap stage and eventually settle into a steady cycle of sleeping once a day. Perhaps we should all continue to take an afternoon siesta. Midafternoon sleepiness is a natural part of the sleep cycle. Brief, well-timed naps can help maintain alertness in people like truck drivers and hospital interns, who often must fight to stay alert (Ficca et al., 2010).

Busy people may be tempted to sleep less. However, people on *shortened* cycles—for example, three hours of sleep to six hours awake—often can't get to sleep when the cycle calls for it. That's why astronauts continue to sleep on their normal earth schedule while in space. Adapting to *longer*-than-normal days is more promising. Such days can be tailored to match natural sleep patterns, which have a ratio of two to one between time awake and time asleep (sixteen hours awake and eight hours asleep). For instance, one study showed that twenty-eight-hour "days" work for some people. Overall, sleep patterns may be bent and stretched, but they rarely yield entirely to human whims (Åkerstedt, 2007).

Stages of Sleep—The Nightly Roller Coaster

SURVEY QUESTIONS 24.2: What are some functions of sleep?

It has long been thought that sleep helps keep the body, including the brain, healthy by regulating its temperature and immune system, conserving energy, and aiding development and repair (Faraut et al., 2011; Freberg, 2010). According to **repair/restorative theories of sleep**, lowering body and brain activity and metabolism during sleep may help conserve energy and lengthen life.

According to the **dual-process hypothesis of sleep**, sleep also helps calm the brain and store important memories (Ficca & Salzarulo, 2004). The key to understanding this intriguing idea is to appreciate that whether you are awake or asleep depends on the *balance* between separate sleep and waking systems. Brain circuits and chemicals in one of the systems promote sleep (Lagos et al., 2009; Steiger, 2007). A network of brain cells in the other system responds to chemicals that inhibit sleep. The two systems seesaw back and forth, switching the brain between sleep and wakefulness. Note that the brain does not "shut down" during sleep. Rather, the *pattern* of activity changes repeatedly throughout a night's sleep.

Sleep Stages

How does brain activity change when you fall asleep? Changes in tiny electrical signals (brain waves) the brain generates can be amplified and recorded with an **electroencephalograph (EEG)** (eh-LEK-tro-en-SEF-uh-lo-graf) (Pagel, 2012). When you are awake and alert, the EEG reveals a pattern of small, fast waves called **beta waves** (● **Figure 24.2**). Immediately before sleep, the pattern shifts to larger and slower waves called **alpha waves**. (Alpha waves also occur when you are relaxed and allow your thoughts to drift.) As the eyes close, breathing becomes slow and regular, the pulse rate slows, and body temperature drops. Soon after, we descend into *slow-wave sleep* through four distinct **sleep stages**.

Stage 1 As you enter **light sleep (Stage 1 sleep)**, your heart rate slows even more. Breathing becomes more irregular. The muscles of your body relax. This may trigger a reflex muscle twitch called a *hypnic* (HIP-nik: sleep) *jerk*. (This is quite normal, so have no fear about admitting to your friends that you fell asleep with a hypnic jerk.) In Stage 1 sleep, the EEG is made up mainly of small, irregular waves, with some alpha waves. Persons awakened at this time may or may not say they were asleep.

Stage 2 As sleep deepens, body temperature drops further. Also, the EEG begins to include **sleep spindles**, which are short bursts of distinctive brain-wave activity generated by the thalamus (Caporro et al., 2012). Sleep spindles may help prevent the sleeping brain from being aroused by external stimuli, thus marking the true boundary of sleep (Dang-Vu et al., 2010). Within a few minutes after spindles appear, most people will say they were asleep.

Stage 3 In Stage 3, a new brain wave begins to appear. **Delta waves** are very large and slow. They signal a move to deeper slow-wave sleep and a further loss of consciousness.

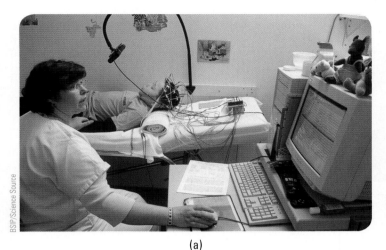

(a)

(b)

Figure 24.2

(a) Photograph of an EEG recording session. The boy in the background is asleep. (b) Changes in brain-wave patterns associated with various stages of sleep. Most wave types are present at all times, but they occur more or less frequently in various sleep stages.

Stage 4 Most people reach **deep sleep (Stage 4 sleep)**—the deepest level of normal sleep—in about an hour. Stage 4 brain waves are almost pure slow-wave delta, and the sleeper is in a state of oblivion. If a sleeper hears a loud noise during Stage 4, he or she will wake up in a state of confusion and may not remember the noise.

The Dual-Process Hypothesis of Sleep

There is much more to a night's sleep than a simple descent into Stage 4. Fluctuations in sleep hormones cause recurring cycles of deeper and lighter sleep throughout the night (Steiger, 2007). During these repeated periods of lighter sleep, a curious thing happens: The sleeper's eyes occasionally move under the eyelids. (If you ever get a chance to watch a sleeping child, roommate, or spouse, you may see these eye

movements.) **Rapid eye movements (REMs)** are associated with dreaming (● **Figure 24.3**). In addition, **REM sleep** is marked by a return of fast, irregular EEG patterns similar to Stage 1 sleep. In fact, the brain is so active during REM sleep that it looks as if the person is awake (Rock, 2004).

The two most basic states of sleep, then, are **non-REM (NREM) sleep**, which occurs during Stages 1, 2, 3, and 4, and REM sleep, with its associated dreaming (Rock, 2004). According to the *dual-process hypothesis of sleep*, NREM and REM sleep together help calm the brain and sharpen important memories.

The Function of NREM Sleep *What is the function of NREM sleep?* NREM sleep is dream free about 90 percent of the time and is deepest early in the night during the first few Stage 4 periods. Your first period of Stage 1 sleep also usually lacks REMs and dreams. Later Stage 1 periods typically include a shift into REM sleep. Dreamless, slow-wave NREM sleep increases after physical exertion and may help us recover from bodily fatigue. It also appears to calm the brain and begin memory consolidation during the earlier part of a night's sleep (Diekelmann & Born, 2010; Holz et al., 2012; Tononi & Cirelli, 2003).

Repair/restorative theories of sleep *Propose that lowering body and brain activity and metabolism during sleep may help conserve energy and lengthen life.*

Dual-process hypothesis of sleep *Proposes that NREM sleep reduces the overall level of brain activation, allowing unimportant memories to be forgotten while REM sleep sharpens memory for important events from the previous day.*

Electroencephalograph (EEG) *A device designed to detect, amplify, and record electrical activity in the brain.*

Beta waves *Small, fast brain waves associated with being awake and alert.*

Alpha waves *Large, slow brain waves associated with relaxation and falling asleep.*

Sleep stages *Levels of sleep identified by brain-wave patterns and behavioral changes.*

Light sleep (Stage 1 sleep) *Marked by small, irregular brain waves and some alpha waves.*

Sleep spindles *Distinctive bursts of brain-wave activity that indicate a person is asleep.*

Delta waves *Large, slow brain waves that occur in deeper sleep (Stages 3 and 4).*

Deep sleep (Stage 4 sleep) *The deepest form of normal sleep.*

Rapid eye movements (REMs) *Swift eye movements during sleep.*

REM sleep *Sleep marked by rapid eye movements and a return to Stage 1 EEG patterns.*

Non-REM (NREM) sleep *Non–rapid eye movement sleep characteristic of Stages 1, 2, 3, and 4.*

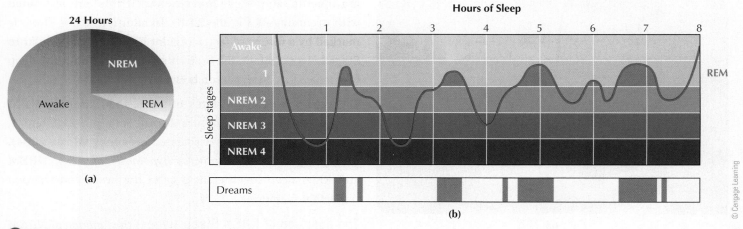

24 Hours

(a)

Hours of Sleep

(b)

Figure 24.3

(a) Average proportion of time adults spend daily in REM sleep and NREM sleep. REM periods add up to about 20 percent of total sleep time.
(b) Typical changes in stages of sleep during the night. Note that dreams mostly coincide with REM periods.

According to the dual-process hypothesis, we are bombarded by information throughout the day, which causes our neural networks to become more and more active. As a result, your brain requires more and more energy to continue functioning. Slow-wave sleep early in the night brings overall brain activation levels back down, allowing a fresh approach to the next day.

Consider for a moment the rich jumble of events that make up a day. Some experiences are worth remembering (like what you are reading right now, of course), and others are not so important (like which sock you put on first this morning). As slow-wave sleep reduces overall activation in the brain, less important experiences may fade away and be forgotten. If you wake up feeling clearer about what you studied the previous night, it might be because your brain doesn't "sweat the small stuff"!

The Function of REM Sleep *What, then, is the purpose of REM sleep?* According to the dual-process hypothesis, whereas NREM sleep calms the brain, REM sleep appears to sharpen or complete the consolidation of our memories of the previous day's more important experiences (Diekelmann & Born, 2010; Saxvig et al., 2008). Daytime stress tends to increase REM sleep, which may rise dramatically when there is a death in the family, trouble at work, a marital conflict, or other emotionally charged events. The value of more REM sleep is that it helps us sort and retain memories, especially memories about strategies for solving problems (Walker & Stickgold, 2006). This is why, after studying for a long period, you may remember more if you go to sleep rather than pulling an all-nighter. (REMember to get some REM!)

REM Sleep and Dreaming Roughly 85 percent of the time, people awakened during REMs report vivid dreams. Some eye movements correspond to dream activities. Dream that you are watching a tennis match, and you will probably move your eyes from side to side. However, people who were born blind still have REMs, so eye movements are not just a result of "watching" dream images (Shafton, 1995). REM sleep is easy to observe in pets, such as dogs and cats. Watch for eye and face movements and irregular breathing. (You can forget about your pet iguana, though. Reptiles show no signs of REM sleep.)

Brain areas associated with imagery and emotion become more active during REM sleep (Rock, 2004). This may explain why REM dreams tend to be longer, more vivid, more detailed, more bizarre, and more "dream-like" than thoughts and images that occur in NREM sleep (Hobson, Pace-Schott, & Stickgold, 2000).

Speaking very loosely, it's as if the dreaming brain were reviewing messages left on a telephone answering machine to decide which are worth keeping. During the day, when information is streaming in, the brain may be too busy to efficiently select useful memories. When the conscious brain is "off-line," we are better able to identify and solidify important new memories.

What happens to the body when a person dreams? REM sleep is a time of high emotion. The heart beats irregularly. Blood pressure and breathing waver. Both males and females appear to be sexually aroused: Men usually have an erection, and genital blood flow increases in women. This occurs for all REM sleep, so it is not strictly related to erotic dreams (Jouvet, 1999).

During REM sleep, your body becomes quite still, as if you were paralyzed. Imagine for a moment the results of acting out some of your recent dreams. Very likely, REM-sleep paralysis prevents some hilarious—and dangerous—nighttime escapades. When it fails, some people thrash violently, leap out of bed, and may attack their bed partners. A lack of muscle paralysis during REM sleep is called *REM behavior disorder* (Neikrug & Ancoli-Israel, 2012). One patient suffering from the disorder tied himself to his bed every night. That way, he couldn't jump up and crash into furniture or walls (Shafton, 1995). And yet, sometimes sleep paralysis can go a little too far. See "They Came from Outer Space?" to find out why.

We will now turn our attention to a survey of some additional sleep problems—if you are still awake.

Clinical File

They Came from Outer Space?

"Imagine opening your eyes shortly before dawn, attempting to roll over in your bed, and suddenly realizing that you are entirely paralyzed. While lying helplessly on your back and unable to cry out for help, you become aware of sinister figures lurking in your bedroom. As they move closer to your bed, your heart begins to pound violently and you feel as if you are suffocating. You hear buzzing sounds and feel electrical sensations shooting throughout your body. Within moments, the visions vanish and you can move once again. Terrified, you wonder what has just happened" (McNally & Clancy, 2005).

Sleep paralysis, which normally prevents us from moving during REM sleep, also can occur just as you begin to wake up. During such episodes, people sometimes have *hypnopompic* (hip-neh-POM-pik: "upon awakening") hallucinations, including bizarre experiences, such as sensing that an alien being is in your bedroom; feeling something pressing on your chest, suffocating you; or feeling like you are floating out of your body (Cheyne, 2005; McCarthy-Jones et al., 2011).

Although most of us shrug off these weird experiences, some people try to make sense of them. Earlier in history, people interpreted these hallucinated intruders as angels, demons, or witches and believed that their out-of-body experiences were real (Cheyne & Girard, 2009). However, as our culture changes, so do our interpretations of sleep experiences. Today, for example, some people who have sleep-related hallucinations believe they have been abducted by space aliens or sexually abused (McNally & Clancy, 2005).

Swiss artist Henry Fuseli drew on hypnopompic imagery as an inspiration for his famous painting, *The Nightmare.*

Detroit Institute of the Arts/SuperStock

Superstitions and folklore often develop as attempts to explain human experiences, including some of the stranger aspects of sleep. By studying hypnopompic hallucinations, psychologists hope to offer natural explanations for many experiences that might otherwise seem supernatural or paranormal (Cheyne & Girard, 2009).

Sleep Disorders and Disturbances— The Sleepy Time Blues

SURVEY QUESTIONS 24.3: What are some sleep disorders and unusual sleep events?

Sleep quality has taken a beating in North America. Artificial lighting, frenetic schedules, exciting pastimes, smoking, drinking, overstimulation, and many other factors have contributed to a near epidemic of sleep problems (Smith, Comella, & Högl, 2008). These disturbances range from daytime sleep attacks to sleepwalking and terrifying nightmares (● Table 24.1). Let's explore a few of the sleep problems some people face.

Insomnia Disorder

No one wants to lie awake staring at the ceiling at 2 AM. Yet, about 60 million Americans have frequent or chronic insomnia (National Institute of Neurological Disorders and Stroke, 2007). **Insomnia** includes difficulty in falling asleep, frequent nighttime awakenings, waking too early, or a combination of these problems. Insomnia can harm people's work, health, and relationships (Ebben & Spielman, 2009).

Types and Causes of Insomnia Worry, stress, and excitement can cause *temporary insomnia* and a self-defeating cycle. First, excess mental activity ("I can't stop turning things over in my mind") and heightened arousal block sleep. Then, frustration and anger over not being able to sleep cause more worry and arousal. This further delays sleep, which causes more frustration, and so on (Sateia & Nowell, 2004). A good way to beat this cycle is to avoid fighting it. Get up and do something useful or satisfying when you can't sleep. (Reading a textbook might be

Insomnia *Difficulty in getting to sleep or staying asleep.*

TABLE 24.1	Sleep Disturbances—Some of the Things That Go Wrong in the Night
Insomnia disorder	Difficulty in getting to sleep or staying asleep; also, not feeling rested after sleeping.
Hypersomnolence disorder	Excessive daytime sleepiness. This can result from depression, insomnia, narcolepsy, sleep apnea, sleep drunkenness, periodic limb movements, drug abuse, and other problems.
Narcolepsy	Sudden, irresistible, daytime sleep attacks that may last anywhere from a few minutes to a half hour. Victims may fall asleep while standing, talking, or even driving.
Sleep apneas	During sleep, breathing stops for 20 seconds or more until the person wakes a little, gulps in air, and settles back to sleep; this cycle may be repeated hundreds of times per night.
Circadian rhythm sleep–wake disorders	A mismatch between the sleep–wake schedule demanded by a person's bodily rhythm and that demanded by the environment.
Sleepwalking	During N-REM sleep, a person engages in activities that are normally engaged in while awake.
Sleep terrors	The repeated occurrence of night terrors that significantly disturb sleep.
Nightmare disorder	Vivid, recurrent nightmares that significantly disturb sleep.
REM sleep behavior disorder	A failure of normal muscle paralysis, leading to violent actions during REM sleep.
Restless legs syndrome	An irresistible urge to move the legs to relieve sensations of creeping, tingling, prickling, aching, or tension.

Source: American Psychiatric Association (2013).

© Cengage Learning

a good choice of useful activities.) Return to bed only when you begin to feel that you are struggling to stay awake. If sleeping problems last for more than three weeks, then a diagnosis of *chronic insomnia* can be made.

Drug-dependency insomnia (sleep loss caused by withdrawal from sleeping pills) also can occur. There is real irony in the billion dollars a year North Americans spend on sleeping pills.

Barbara Smaller/The New Yorker Collection/www.cartoonbank.com

"It's only insomnia if there's nothing good on."

Nonprescription sleeping pills such as Sominex, Nytol, and Sleep-Eze have little sleep-inducing effect. Barbiturates are even worse. These prescription sedatives decrease both Stage 4 sleep and REM sleep, drastically lowering sleep quality. In addition, many users become "sleeping-pill junkies" who need an ever-greater number of pills to get to sleep. Victims must be painstakingly weaned from their sleep medicines. Otherwise, terrible nightmares and "rebound insomnia" may drive them back to drug use.

It's worth remembering that although alcohol and other depressant drugs may help a person get to sleep, they greatly reduce sleep quality (Nau & Lichstein, 2005). Even newer drugs, such as Ambien and Lunesta, which induce sleep, have drawbacks. Possible side effects include amnesia, impaired judgment, increased appetite, decreased sex drive, depression, and even sleepwalking, sleep eating, and sleep driving. Rebound insomnia also is a risk, making these drugs a temporary remedy at best.

Behavioral Remedies for Insomnia *If sleeping pills are a poor way to treat insomnia, what can be done?* It is usually better to treat insomnia with lifestyle changes and behavioral techniques (McGowan & Behar, 2013; Montgomery & Dennis, 2004). Treatment for chronic insomnia usually begins with a careful analysis of a patient's sleep habits, lifestyle, stress levels, and medical problems. All the approaches discussed in the following list are helpful for treating insomnia (Ebben & Spielman, 2009; Nau & Lichstein, 2005):

1. **Stimulus control.** Insisting on a regular schedule helps establish a firm body rhythm, greatly improving sleep. This is best achieved by exercising stimulus control, which refers to linking a response with specific stimuli. It is important to get up and go to sleep at the same time each day, including weekends (Vincent, Lewycky, & Finnegan, 2008). In addition, insomniacs are told to avoid doing anything but sleeping when they are in bed. They are not to study, eat, watch television, read, pay the bills, worry, or even think in bed. (Lovemaking is okay, however.) In this way, only sleeping and relaxation become associated with going to bed at specific times.

2. **Sleep restriction.** Even if an entire night's sleep is missed, it is important not to sleep late in the morning, nap more than an hour, sleep during the evening, or go to bed early the following night. Instead, restricting sleep to normal bedtime hours avoids fragmenting sleep rhythms (Smith, Comella, & Högl, 2008; Vincent, Lewycky, & Finnegan, 2008).

3. **Paradoxical intention.** Another helpful approach is to remove the pressures of trying to go to sleep. Instead, the goal becomes trying to keep the eyes open (in the dark) and stay awake as long as possible (Nau & Lichstein, 2005). This allows sleep to come unexpectedly and lowers performance anxiety (Taylor & Roane, 2010).

4. **Relaxation.** Some insomniacs lower their arousal before sleep by using a physical or mental strategy for relaxing, such as progressive muscle relaxation (see Module 67 for more information), meditation, or blotting out worries with calming images. It also is helpful to schedule time in the early evening to write down worries or concerns and plan what to do about them the next day in order to set them aside before going to bed.

5. **Exercise.** Strenuous exercise during the day promotes sleep (Brand et al., 2010). However, exercise within three to six hours of sleep is helpful only if it is very light.

6. **Food intake.** What you eat can affect how easily you get to sleep. Eating starchy foods increases the amount of tryptophan (TRIP-tuh-fan: an amino acid) reaching the brain. More tryptophan, in turn, increases the amount of serotonin in the brain, which is associated with relaxation, a positive mood, and sleepiness (Silber & Schmitt, 2010). Thus, to promote sleep, try eating a starchy snack, such as cookies, bread, pasta, oatmeal, pretzels, or dry cereal. If you really want to drop the bomb on insomnia, try eating a baked potato (which may be the world's largest sleeping pill!).

7. **Stimulant avoidance.** Stimulants, such as coffee and cigarettes, should be avoided. It also is worth remembering that alcohol, although not a stimulant, impairs sleep quality.

Sleepwalking, Sleeptalking, and Sleepsex

Sleepsex? As strange as it may seem, many waking behaviors can be engaged in while asleep, such as driving a car, cooking, playing a musical instrument, and eating (Plazzi et al., 2005). The most famous, sleepwalking, is eerie and fascinating in its own right (Banerjee & Nisbet, 2011). Somnambulists (som-NAM-bue-lists: those who sleepwalk) avoid obstacles, descend stairways, and on rare occasions may step out of windows or in front of automobiles. Sleepwalkers have been observed jumping into lakes, urinating in garbage pails or closets (phew!), shuffling furniture around, and even brandishing weapons (Schenck & Mahowald, 2005).

The sleepwalker's eyes are usually open, but a blank face and shuffling feet reveal that the person is still asleep. If you find someone sleepwalking, you should gently guide the person back to bed. Awakening a sleepwalker does no harm, but it is not necessary.

Does sleepwalking occur during dreaming? No. Remember that people are normally immobilized during REM sleep. EEG studies have shown that somnambulism occurs during NREM Stages 3 and 4 (Kalat, 2013; Stein & Ferber, 2001). *Sleeptalking* also occurs mostly during NREM sleep. The link with deep sleep explains why sleeptalking makes little sense and why sleepwalkers are confused and remember little when awakened.

Oh, yes, you're curious about sleepsex. Of course, it has an official name: *sexsomnia* (Klein & Houlihan, 2010). Sexsomnia is not as exciting as it might sound: Just imagine being startled wide awake by your bed partner, who is asleep, attempting to have sex with you (Andersen et al., 2007).

Stimulus control *Linking a particular response with specific stimuli.*
Somnambulists *People who sleepwalk; occurs during NREM sleep.*

Nightmare Disorder and Night Terrors

Stage 4 sleep also is the realm of night terrors. These frightening episodes are quite different from ordinary nightmares. A nightmare is simply a bad dream that takes place during REM sleep. Frequently occurring nightmares (one a week or more) are associated with higher levels of psychological distress (Levin & Fireman, 2002). During a Stage 4 night terror, a person suffers total panic and may hallucinate frightening dream images into the bedroom. An attack may last 15 or 20 minutes. When it is over, the person awakens drenched in sweat but only vaguely remembers the terror. Because night terrors occur during NREM sleep (when the body is not immobilized), victims may sit up, scream, get out of bed, or run around the room. Victims remember little afterward. (Other family members, however, may have a story to tell.) Although night terrors are more common in childhood, they are not uncommon in adulthood (Belicki, Chambers, & Ogilvie, 1997; Kataria, 2004).

How to Eliminate a Nightmare

Is there any way to stop a recurring nightmare? A bad nightmare can be worse than any horror movie. It's easy to leave a theater, but we often remain trapped in terrifying dreams. Nevertheless, most nightmares can be banished by following three simple steps. First, write down your nightmare, describing it in detail. Next, change the dream any way you wish, making sure to spell out the details of the new dream. The third step is *imagery rehearsal,* in which you mentally rehearse the changed dream before you fall asleep again (Krakow & Zadra, 2006). Imagery rehearsal may work because it makes upsetting dreams familiar while a person is awake and feeling safe. Or perhaps it mentally "reprograms" future dream content. In any case, the technique has helped many people (Harb et al., 2012).

Sleep Apneas

Some sage once said, "Laugh and the whole world laughs with you; snore and you sleep alone." Nightly "wood sawing" is often harmless, but it can signal a serious problem. A person who snores loudly, with short silences and loud gasps or snorts, may suffer from *apnea* (AP-nee-ah: interrupted breathing). In sleep apnea, breathing stops for periods of twenty seconds to two minutes. As the need for oxygen becomes intense, the person wakes a little and gulps in air. She or he then settles back to sleep. But soon, breathing stops again. This cycle is repeated hundreds of times a night. Although snoring might be funny, sleep apnea is no joke. As you might guess, apnea victims are extremely sleepy during the day (Collop, 2005). They also can

have a harder time functioning during the day (Grenèche et al., 2011) and, in the long run, may suffer damage to their oxygen-hungry brains (Joo et al., 2010).

What causes sleep apnea? Central sleep apnea occurs because the brain stops sending signals to the diaphragm to maintain breathing. *Obstructive sleep apnea hypopnea syndrome* is blockage of the upper air passages. One of the most effective treatments is the use of a continuous positive airway pressure (CPAP) mask to aid breathing during sleep. The resulting improvement in sleep will often result in improved daytime function (Tregear et al., 2010). Other treatments include weight loss and surgery for breathing obstructions (Collop, 2005).

SIDS Sleep apnea is suspected as one cause of sudden infant death syndrome (SIDS), or "crib death." In the "typical" crib death, a slightly premature or small baby with some signs of a cold or cough is bundled up and put to bed. A short time later, parents find the child has died. A baby deprived of air will normally struggle to begin breathing again. However, SIDS babies seem to have a weak arousal reflex. This prevents them from changing positions and resuming breathing after an episode of apnea. SIDS is the leading cause of death in children between 1 month and 1 year of age (National Institute of Child Health and Human Development, 2012).

Babies at risk for SIDS must be carefully watched for the first 6 months of life. To aid parents in this task, a special monitor may be used that sounds an alarm when breathing or pulse becomes weak (● Figure 24.4). Babies at risk for SIDS are often premature; have a shrill, high-pitched cry; engage in "snoring," breath-holding, or frequent awakening at night; breathe mainly through an open mouth; or remain passive when their face rolls into a pillow or blanket. For these reasons, it is wise to avoid using blankets or pillows for infants.

"Back to Sleep" Sleeping position is another major risk factor for SIDS. Healthy infants are best off sleeping on their backs (sides are not as good but much better than face down) (Shapiro-Mendoza et al., 2009). (Premature babies, those with respiratory problems, and those who often vomit may need to sleep face down. Ask a pediatrician for guidance.)

Narcolepsy

Narcolepsy (NAR-koe-lep-see), or sudden, irresistible sleep attacks, is one of the most dramatic sleep problems. Victims may fall asleep anywhere for a few minutes to a half hour, while standing, talking, or even driving. Emotional excitement, especially laughter, commonly triggers narcolepsy. (Tell an

● Figure 24.4

Infants at risk for SIDS are often attached to devices that monitor breathing and heart rate during sleep. An alarm sounds to alert parents if either pulse or respiration falters. SIDS rarely occurs after an infant is 1 year old. Babies at risk for SIDS should be placed on their backs.

especially good joke and a narcoleptic may fall asleep.) Many victims also suffer from *cataplexy* (CAT-uh-plex-see), a sudden temporary paralysis of the muscles, leading to complete body collapse (Ingravallo et al., 2012). Sleep attacks and paralysis appear to occur when REM sleep intrudes into the waking state (Kalat, 2013). It's easy to understand why narcolepsy can devastate careers and relationships.

Fortunately, narcolepsy is rare. It runs in families, which suggests that it is hereditary (Chabas et al., 2003). This has been confirmed by breeding several generations of narcoleptic dogs. (These dogs, by the way, are simply outstanding at learning the trick "Roll over and play dead.") There is no known cure for narcolepsy, but a drug named sodium oxybate reduces the frequency and intensity of attacks (Lammers et al., 2010).

Dreams—A Separate Reality?

SURVEY QUESTIONS 24.4: Do dreams have meaning?

When REM sleep was discovered in 1952, it ushered in a "golden era" of dream inquiry. To conclude our discussion of sleep, let's consider some age-old questions about dreaming.

Does everyone dream? Do dreams occur in an instant? Most people dream four or five times a night, but not all people remember their dreams upon awakening in the morning.

"Nondreamers" are often surprised by their dreams when first awakened during REM sleep. Dreams are usually spaced about 90 minutes apart.

REM Rebound

How important is REM sleep for dreaming? To answer this question, sleep expert William Dement awakened volunteers each time they entered REM sleep. Soon, their need for "dream time" grew more urgent. By the fifth night, many had to be awakened 20 or 30 times to prevent REM sleep. When the volunteers were finally allowed to sleep undisturbed, they dreamed extra amounts. This effect, called a **REM rebound**, explains why alcoholics have horrible nightmares after they quit drinking. Alcohol reduces sleep quality by suppressing REM sleep, thus setting up a powerful rebound when it is withdrawn (Stein & Friedmann, 2005).

Dement's volunteers complained of memory lapses, poor concentration, and anxiety. For a while, it was thought that people deprived of REM sleep might go crazy. But later experiments showed that missing *any* sleep stage can cause a rebound for that stage. In general, daytime disturbances are related to the *total amount* of sleep lost, not to the *type* of sleep lost (Devoto et al., 1999).

Dream Theories

How meaningful are dreams? Some theorists believe that dreams have deeply hidden meanings. Others regard dreams as nearly meaningless. Yet others hold that dreams reflect our waking thoughts, fantasies, and emotions (Hartmann, 2011). Let's examine all three views.

Psychodynamic Dream Theory **Psychodynamic theories** of dreaming emphasize internal conflicts and unconscious forces (Fischer & Kächele, 2009). Sigmund Freud's (1900) landmark book, *The Interpretation of Dreams*, first advanced the idea that many dreams are based on *wish fulfillment* (an expression

Nightmare *A bad dream that occurs during REM sleep.*
Night terror *A state of panic during NREM sleep.*
Sleep apnea *Repeated interruption of breathing during sleep.*
Sudden infant death syndrome (SIDS) *The sudden, unexplained death of an apparently healthy infant.*
Narcolepsy *A sudden, irresistible sleep attack.*
REM rebound *The occurrence of extra rapid eye movement sleep following REM sleep deprivation.*
Psychodynamic theory *Any theory of behavior that emphasizes internal conflicts, motives, and unconscious forces.*

of unconscious desires). One of Freud's key proposals was that dreams express unconscious desires and conflicts as disguised **dream symbols**—images that have deeper symbolic meaning. Understanding a dream, then, requires analyzing the dream's **manifest content**, or obvious, visible meaning, to uncover its **latent content**, or hidden, symbolic meaning.

For instance, a woman who dreams of stealing her best friend's wedding ring and placing it on her own hand may be unwilling to consciously admit that she is sexually attracted to her best friend's husband. Similarly, a journey might symbolize death, and horseback riding or dancing could symbolize sexual intercourse.

Do all dreams have hidden meanings? Probably not. Freud realized that some dreams are trivial "day residues" or carryovers from ordinary waking events. On the other hand, dreams do tend to reflect a person's current concerns, so Freud wasn't entirely wrong.

The Activation-Synthesis Hypothesis

Psychiatrists Allan Hobson and Robert McCarley have a radically different view of dreaming, called the **activation-synthesis hypothesis**. They believe that during REM sleep, several lower brain centers are "turned on" *(activated)* in more or less random fashion. However, messages from those

Christie's Images/Corbis

According to psychodynamic theory, dream imagery often has symbolic meaning. How would you interpret Italian artist Mimmo Paladino's dream-like image, titled *Vespero*? The fact that dreams don't have a single unambiguous meaning is one of the shortcomings of Freudian dream theory.

cells are blocked from reaching the body, so no movement occurs. Nevertheless, the cells continue to tell higher brain areas of their activities. Struggling to interpret this random information, the brain searches through stored memories and manufactures *(synthesizes)* a dream (Hobson, 2000, 2005). Because frontal areas of the cortex, which control higher mental abilities, are mostly shut down during REM sleep, the resulting dreams are more primitive and more bizarre than daytime thoughts (Hobson, 2000).

How does that help explain dream content? According to the activation-synthesis hypothesis, dreams are usually meaningless. Let's use the classic chase dream as an example. In such dreams, we feel we are running but not going anywhere. This occurs because the brain is told the body is running, but it gets no feedback from the motionless legs. To try to make sense of this information, the brain creates a chase drama. A similar process probably explains dreams of floating or flying.

So dreams have no meaning? The activation-synthesis hypothesis rejects the idea that dreams are deliberate, meaningful messages from our unconscious. However, it does not rule out the possibility that we can find meaning in some dreams. Because dreams are created from memories and past experiences, parts of dreams can sometimes reflect each person's mental life, emotions, and concerns (Hobson, 2000).

Neurocognitive Dream Theory

Can't dreams just be about everyday stuff? Yes, they can. According to William Domhoff's **neurocognitive dream theory**, dreams have much in common with waking thoughts and emotions. Domhoff believes this is true because many brain areas that are active when we are awake remain active during dreaming (Domhoff, 2001, 2003). From this perspective, our dreams are a conscious expression of REM sleep processes that are sorting and storing daily experiences (Levin & Nielsen, 2009). Thus, we shouldn't be surprised if a student who is angry at a teacher dreams of embarrassing the teacher in class, a lonely person dreams of romance, or a hungry child dreams of food. It is not necessary to seek deeper symbolic meanings to understand these dreams.

Dream Worlds

Which dream theory is the most widely accepted? Each theory has strengths and weaknesses (Hobson & Schredl, 2011; MacDuffie & Mashour, 2010). However, studies of dream content tend to support neurocognitive theory's focus on the continuity between dreams and waking thought. Rather than seeming exotic or bizarre, most dreams reflect everyday events (Domhoff & Schneider, 2008; Pesant & Zadra, 2006).

For example, athletes tend to dream about the previous day's athletic activities (Erlacher & Schredl, 2004). In general, the favorite dream setting is a familiar room in a house. Action usually takes place between the dreamer and two or three other emotionally important people—friends, enemies, loved ones, or employers. Dream actions also are mostly familiar: running, jumping, riding, sitting, talking, and watching. About half of all dreams have sexual elements. Dreams of flying, floating, and falling occur less frequently. However, note that such dreams lend some support to the activation-synthesis hypothesis because they are not everyday events (unless you are a trapeze artist).

Even if many dreams can be viewed as just a different form of thought, many psychologists continue to believe that some dreams have deeper meaning (Halliday, 2010; Wilkinson, 2006). There seems to be little doubt that dreams can make a difference in our lives: Veteran sleep researcher William Dement once dreamed that he had lung cancer. In the dream, a doctor told Dement he would die soon. At the time, Dement was smoking two packs of cigarettes a day. He says, "I will never forget the surprise, joy, and exquisite relief of waking up. I felt reborn." Dement quit smoking the following day. (For more information about dreaming, see Module 26.)

Module 24: Summary

24.1 What are the effects of sleep loss or changes in sleep patterns?

- **24.1.1** Sleep is an innate biological rhythm essential for survival.
- **24.1.2** Moderate sleep loss affects mainly vigilance and performance on routine or boring tasks.
- **24.1.3** Higher animals and people deprived of sleep experience involuntary microsleeps.
- **24.1.4** Extended sleep loss can (somewhat rarely) produce a temporary sleep-deprivation psychosis.
- **24.1.5** Sleep patterns show some flexibility, but seven to eight hours remains average. The amount of daily sleep decreases steadily from birth to old age.

24.2 What are some functions of sleep?

- **24.2.1** Lowered body and brain activity and metabolism during sleep may help conserve energy and lengthen life.
- **24.2.2** Sleep occurs in four stages. Stage 1 is light sleep, and Stage 4 is deep sleep. The sleeper alternates between Stages 1 and 4 (passing through Stages 2 and 3) several times each night.

- **24.2.3** According to the dual-process hypothesis, non-REM (NREM) sleep "refreshes" the body and brain, and rapid eye movement (REM) sleep helps form lasting memories.
- **24.2.4** NREM sleep brings overall brain activation levels down, thus calming the brain.
- **24.2.5** REM sleep is strongly associated with dreaming. REM sleep and dreaming help us store important memories.

24.3 What are some sleep disorders and unusual sleep events?

- **24.3.1** Insomnia may be temporary or chronic. Behavioral approaches to managing insomnia, such as sleep restriction and stimulus control, are quite effective.
- **24.3.2** Sleepwalking, sleeptalking, and sleepsex occur during NREM sleep.
- **24.3.3** Night terrors occur in NREM sleep, whereas nightmares occur in REM sleep.
- **24.3.4** Sleep apnea (interrupted breathing) is one source of insomnia and daytime hypersomnia (sleepiness).

continued

Dream symbols *Images in dreams that serve as visible signs of hidden ideas, desires, impulses, emotions, relationships, and so forth.*
Manifest content (of dreams) *The surface, "visible" content of a dream; dream images as the dreamer remembers them.*
Latent content (of dreams) *The hidden or symbolic meaning of a dream, as revealed by dream interpretation and analysis.*
Activation-synthesis hypothesis *An attempt to explain how dream content is affected by motor commands in the brain that occur during sleep but are not carried out.*
Neurocognitive dream theory *Proposal that dreams reflect everyday waking thoughts and emotions.*

Module 24: Summary, *continued*

- **24.3.5** Apnea is suspected as one cause of sudden infant death syndrome (SIDS). In general, healthy infants should sleep on their backs.
- **24.3.6** Narcolepsy (sleep attacks) and cataplexy are caused by a sudden shift to Stage 1 REM patterns during normal waking hours.

24.4 Do dreams have meaning?
- **24.4.1** The Freudian, or psychodynamic, view is that dreams express unconscious wishes, frequently hidden by dream symbols.
- **24.4.2** The activation-synthesis model portrays dreaming as a physiological process.
- **24.4.3** The neurocognitive view of dreams holds that dreams are continuous with waking thoughts and emotions. Supporting the neurocognitive view, most dream content is about familiar settings, people, and actions.

Module 24: Knowledge Builder

Recite

1. Alpha waves are to presleep drowsiness as _____ are to Stage 4 sleep.

2. Rapid eye movements indicate that a person is in deep sleep. *T or F?*

3. Sharpening memories and facilitating their storage is one function of
   - **a.** activation-synthesis cycles
   - **b.** REM sleep
   - **c.** deep sleep
   - **d.** NREM sleep

4. Which of the following is *not* a behavioral remedy for insomnia?
   - **a.** daily hypersomnia
   - **b.** stimulus control
   - **c.** progressive relaxation
   - **d.** paradoxical intention

5. Night terrors, sleepwalking, and sleeptalking all occur during Stage 1, NREM sleep. *T or F?*

6. Sleep _____ is suspected as one cause of SIDS.

7. According to the activation-synthesis hypothesis of dreaming, dreams are constructed from _____ to explain messages received from nerve cells controlling eye movement, balance, and bodily activity.

Reflect

Think Critically

8. In addition to helping repair and restore the body, as well as store memories, can you think of any other biological advantages sleeping might provide?

Self-Reflect

Imagine that you are a counselor at a sleep clinic. Explain the basics of sleep and dreaming to a new client who knows little about these topics.

Almost everyone suffers from insomnia at least occasionally. Which of the techniques for combating insomnia are similar to strategies you have discovered on your own?

How many sleep disturbances can you name (including those listed in Table 24.1)? Have you experienced any of them? Which do you think would be most disruptive?

Do you think your dreams have symbolic meaning or reflect everyday concerns?

ANSWERS

1. delta waves 2. F 3. b 4. a 5. F 6. apnea 7. Memories 8. Natural selection may have favored sleep because animals that remained active at night probably had a higher chance of being killed (Freberg, 2010). (We'll bet they had more fun, though.)

Consciousness: Psychoactive Drugs

Lucy in the Sky With Diamonds

Many musicians have celebrated the use of psychoactive drugs in their music. Other artists, including writers and painters, have even attributed their creativity to drug-induced experiences. Here, the artist depicts visual experiences he had while under the influence of LSD. While positive images and songs about drug use are commonplace in today's popular culture, they tend to obscure another, darker reality.

The problem is that prescription drugs that can ease pain, induce sleep, or end depression have a high potential for abuse. So do freely available legal drugs, like nicotine and alcohol. Add to the mix the destruction wrought by illicit drugs and it's little wonder that so many lives are damaged by drug use. In fact, drug abuse may well overshadow many of the positive benefits psychoactive drugs can have when appropriately used. This module provides an overview of commonly abused substances.

Isaac Abrams/Cengage Learning

SURVEY QUESTIONS

25.1 What are the effects of the more commonly used psychoactive drugs?

25.2 What are some common stimulants?

25.3 What are some common depressants?

25.4 What is a hallucinogen?

Drug-Altered Consciousness— The High and Low of It

SURVEY QUESTIONS 25.1: What are the effects of the more commonly used psychoactive drugs?

One common way to alter human consciousness is to administer a **psychoactive drug**—a substance capable of altering attention, emotion, judgment, memory, time sense, self-control, or perception. In fact, most Americans regularly use consciousness-altering drugs (don't forget that caffeine, alcohol, and nicotine are mildly psychoactive). Psychoactive drugs alter consciousness by directly influencing brain activity (Maisto, Galizio, & Connors, 2011; see "How Psychoactive Drugs Affect the Brain"). Many psychoactive drugs can be placed on a scale ranging from stimulation to depression (● **Figure 25.1**). A **stimulant**, or *upper*, is a substance that increases activity in the body and nervous system. A **depressant**, or *downer,* does the reverse.

Most, if not all, of the drugs discussed in this module have legitimate uses (Hart, Ksir, & Ray, 2013). Some have been used for centuries in various cultures, in search of insight. Others were developed specifically to treat various mental illnesses. Still others have a variety of health benefits. The key to healthy drug use is moderation, and it is truly unfortunate that it is so very hard to keep "the monkey off your back." Because drugs like pain killers, sleep aids, and antidepressants are easy to abuse, the more powerful psychoactive drugs are controlled substances (Goldberg, 2010). Regardless, in 2011,

Drug Effects · STIMULATION · **Drug Groups**

Death

— Strychnine

Convulsions

Extreme nervousness, tremors

Anxiety, palpitations — Amphetamines — Cocaine (large dose)

Feeling of well-being, euphoria — Antidepressants — Cocaine (small dose)

Distortion of time and space — Hallucinogens (LSD, mescaline, marijuana) — Nicotine

Increased alertness — Caffeine

NEUTRAL AREA

Anxiety relief — Tranquilizers

Feeling of well-being, euphoria — Narcotics, barbiturates, alcohol (small dose)

Loss of pain — Narcotics (medium dose)

Drowsiness — Barbiturates, alcohol (medium dose)

Sleep — Hypnotics

Loss of consciousness — Narcotics, barbiturates, alcohol (large dose)

Convulsions — Anesthetics

Death

DEPRESSION

© Cengage Learning

● **Figure 25.1**

Spectrum and continuum of drug action. Many drugs can be rated on a stimulation–depression scale according to their effects on the central nervous system. Although LSD, mescaline, and marijuana are listed here, the stimulation–depression scale is less relevant to these drugs. The principal characteristic of such hallucinogens is their mind-altering quality.

almost 23 million Americans used illicit drugs, including over 3 million first-time users (Substance Abuse and Mental Health Services Administration, 2012). Drug abuse has been one of the most persistent of all social problems in Western nations.

Why is drug abuse so common? People seek drug experiences for many reasons, ranging from curiosity and a desire to belong to a group to a search for meaning or an escape from feelings of inadequacy. Many abusers turn to drugs in a self-defeating attempt to cope with life. All the frequently abused drugs produce immediate feelings of pleasure. The negative consequences follow much later. This combination of immediate pleasure and delayed punishment allows abusers to feel good on demand. In time, of course, most of the pleasure goes out of drug abuse and the abuser's problems get worse. But if an abuser merely feels better (however briefly) after taking a drug, drug taking can become compulsive (Higgins, Heil, & Lussier, 2004).

Adolescents are more likely to use and abuse drugs if they believe that the risks of drug use are low, that drugs are readily available, and that drug use by their peers is okay (Substance

Abuse and Mental Health Services Administration, 2012). Additional predictors include parental drug use, delinquency, parental maladjustment, poor self-esteem, social noncon-formity, and stressful life changes. One study found that many adolescents who abuse drugs tend to be maladjusted, alienated, impulsive, and emotionally distressed (Masse & Tremblay, 1997). Antisocial behavior, school failure, and risky sexual behavior also are commonly associated with drug abuse (Boyd, Harris, & Knight, 2012). Such patterns make it clear that taking drugs is a symptom, rather than a cause, of personal and social maladjustment (Hart, Ksir, & Ray, 2013).

Drug Dependence

Another reason drug abuse is so common is that taking most psychoactive drugs tends to create dependencies. Once you get started, it can be very hard to stop (Calabria et al., 2010). Drug dependence falls into two broad categories (Maisto, Galizio, & Connors, 2011). When a person compulsively uses a drug to main-tain bodily comfort, a **physical dependence** (addiction) exists. Addiction occurs most often with drugs that cause **withdrawal symptoms** (physical illness that follows removal of a drug). Withdrawal from drugs such as alcohol, barbiturates, and opi-ates can cause violent flu-like symptoms of nausea, vomiting, diarrhea, chills, sweating, and cramps. Addiction is often accom-panied by a **drug tolerance** (reduced response to a drug). This leads users to take larger and larger doses to get the desired effect.

Persons who develop a **psychological dependence** feel that a drug is necessary to maintain their comfort or well-being. Usually, they intensely crave the drug and its rewarding qualities. Psychological dependence can be just as powerful as physical addiction. That's why some psychologists define addiction as any compulsive habit pattern. By this definition, a person who has lost control over drug use, for whatever rea-son, is addicted. In fact, most people who answer yes to both of the following questions have an alcohol or drug problem and should seek professional help:

- In the last year, did you ever drink or use drugs more than you meant to?
- Have you felt you wanted or needed to cut down on your drinking or drug use in the last year?

Patterns of Abuse Some drugs, of course, have a higher poten-tial for abuse than others. Heroin is certainly more dangerous than caffeine. However, this is only one side of the picture. It can be as useful to classify drug-taking *behavior* as it is to rate drugs. For example, some people remain social drinkers for life, whereas others become alcoholics within weeks of taking their

Brain Waves

How Psychoactive Drugs Affect the Brain

Psychoactive drugs influence the activity of brain cells (Kalat, 2013). Typically, drugs imitate or alter the effects of neurotransmitters, the chemicals that carry messages between brain cells. Some drugs, such as Ecstasy, amphetamines, and some antidepressants, cause more neurotransmitters to be released, increasing the activity of brain cells. Other drugs, such as cocaine, slow the removal of neurotransmitters after they are released. This prolongs the action of transmitter chemicals and typically has a stimulating effect. Other drugs, such as nicotine and opiates, directly stimulate brain cells by mimicking neurotransmitters. Another possibility is illustrated by alcohol and tranquilizers. These drugs affect certain types of brain cells that cause relaxation and relieve anxiety. Some drugs fill receptor sites on brain cells and block incoming messages. Other possibilities also exist, which is why drugs can have such a wide variety of effects on the brain (Julien, 2011).

Nearly all addictive drugs stimulate the brain's reward circuitry, producing feelings of pleasure (Freberg, 2010; Kalat, 2013). In particular, addictive drugs stimulate a brain region called the *nucleus accumbens* to release the neurotransmitter dopamine, which results in intensified feelings of pleasure (● **Figure 25.2**). As one expert put it, addictive drugs fool brain–reward pathways. As a result, the reward pathway signals, "That felt good. Let's do it again. Let's remember exactly how we did it." This creates a compulsion to repeat the drug experience. It's

the hook that eventually snares the addict (National Institute on Drug Abuse, 2010). In the end, the addictive drug physically changes the brain's reward circuitry, making it even harder for the addict to overcome his or her addiction (Henry et al., 2010; Niehaus, Cruz-Bermúdez, & Kauer, 2009). Adolescents are especially susceptible to addiction because brain systems that restrain their risk-taking are not as mature as those that reward pleasure seeking (Boyd, Harris, & Knight, 2012).

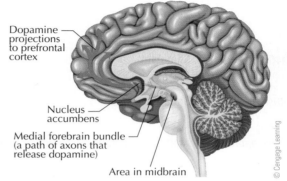

● **Figure 25.2**

Addictive drugs increase dopamine activity in the medial forebrain bundle and the nucleus accumbens, stimulating the frontal cortex and giving rise to intensified feelings of pleasure.

first drink (Robinson & Berridge, 2003). In this sense, drug use can be classified as *experimental* (short-term use based on curiosity), *social-recreational* (occasional social use for pleasure or relaxation), *situational* (use to cope with a specific problem, such as needing to stay awake), *intensive* (daily use with elements of dependence), or *compulsive* (intense use and extreme dependence). The last three categories of drug taking tend to be damaging no matter what drug is used.

Polydrug Abuse One more pattern of drug abuse bears mentioning: the abuse of more than one drug at the same time. According to the Florida Medical Examiners Commission (2012), polydrug abuse accounts for the "vast majority" of deaths due to drug overdose. When mixed, the effects of different drugs can be multiplied by a **drug interaction**—one drug enhances the effect of another—that are responsible for thousands of fatal drug overdoses every

In 2013, Cory Monteith, a star of television's *Glee*, died of an overdose of heroin combined with alcohol. Just months earlier, Chris Kelly, half of the rap duo Kriss Kross, became yet another victim of *speedballing*. Involving the injection of a combination of heroin and cocaine, this form of polydrug abuse has already claimed the lives of many entertainers, including John Belushi, River Phoenix, Chris Farley, Layne Staley, and Hillel Slovak.

Psychoactive drug *A substance capable of altering attention, memory, judgment, time sense, self-control, mood, or perception.*
Stimulant *A substance that increases activity in the body and nervous system.*
Depressant *A substance that decreases activity in the body and nervous system.*
Physical dependence *Physical addiction, as indicated by the presence of drug tolerance and withdrawal symptoms.*
Withdrawal symptoms *Physical illness and discomfort following the withdrawal of a drug.*
Drug tolerance *A reduction in the body's response to a drug.*
Psychological dependence *Drug dependence that is based primarily on emotional or psychological needs.*
Drug interaction *A combined effect of two drugs that exceeds the addition of one drug's effects to the other.*

year (Goldberg, 2010). This is true whether the mixed drugs were legally or illegally obtained. Combining barbiturates or tranquilizers with alcohol is especially risky. All too often, depressants are gulped down with alcohol or added to a spiked punch bowl.

Drugs of Abuse Table 25.1 reveals that the drugs most likely to lead to physical dependence are alcohol, amphetamines, barbiturates, cocaine, codeine, heroin, methadone, morphine, and nicotine (tobacco). Using *most* of the drugs listed in Table 25.1 also can result in psychological dependence.

TABLE 25.1	**Comparison of Psychoactive Drugs**		
Name	**Classification**	**Medical Use**	**Duration of Effect**
Alcohol	Sedative-hypnotic	Solvent, antiseptic, sedative	1–4 hours
Amphetamines	Stimulant	Relief of mild depression, control of narcolepsy and hyperactivity	4 hours
Barbiturates	Sedative-hypnotic	Sedation, relief of high blood pressure, anticonvulsant, antianxiety	1–16 hours
Benzodiazepines	Anxiolytic (antianxiety drug)	Tranquilizer	10 minutes–8 hours
Caffeine	Stimulant	Counteract depressant drugs, treatment of migraine headaches	Varies
Cocaine	Stimulant, local anesthetic	Local anesthesia	Varied, 1–4 hours
Codeine	Narcotic	Ease pain and coughing	3–6 hours
GHB	Sedative-hypnotic	Experimental treatment of narcolepsy, alcoholism	1–3 hours
Heroin	Narcotic	Pain relief	3–6 hours
LSD	Hallucinogen	Experimental study of mental function, alcoholism	8–12 hours
Marijuana (THC)	Relaxant, euphoriant; in high doses, hallucinogen	Treatment of glaucoma and side effects of chemotherapy	2–4 hours
MDMA	Stimulant/hallucinogen	None	4–6 hours
Mescaline	Hallucinogen	None	8–12 hours
Methadone	Narcotic	Pain relief	12–24 hours
Morphine	Narcotic	Pain relief	3–6 hours
PCP	Anesthetic	None	4–6 hours, plus 12-hour recovery
Psilocybin	Hallucinogen	None	Varies
Tobacco (nicotine)	Stimulant	Emetic (nicotine)	Varies

Question marks indicate conflict of opinion. It should be noted that illicit drugs are frequently mixed with unknown and possibly dangerous substances and thus pose possible hazards to the user.

Note also that people who take drugs intravenously are at high risk for developing hepatitis and AIDS (see Module 48). The discussion that follows focuses on the drugs most often abused by students.

Effects Sought	Long-Term Symptoms	Physical Dependence Potential	Psychological Dependence Potential	Organic Damage Potential
Sense alteration, anxiety reduction, sociability	Cirrhosis, toxic psychosis, neurologic damage, addiction	Yes	Yes	Yes
Alertness, activeness, relieve fatigue	Loss of appetite, delusions, hallucinations, toxic psychosis	Yes	Yes	Yes
Anxiety reduction, euphoria	Addiction with severe withdrawal symptoms, possible convulsions, toxic psychosis	Yes	Yes	Yes
Anxiety relief	Irritability, confusion, depression, sleep disorders	Yes	Yes	No, but can affect fetus
Wakefulness, alertness	Insomnia, heart arrhythmias, high blood pressure	No?	Yes	Yes
Excitation, talkativeness	Depression, convulsions	Yes	Yes	Yes
Euphoria, prevent withdrawal discomfort	Addiction, constipation, loss of appetite	Yes	Yes	No
Intoxication, euphoria, relaxation	Anxiety, confusion, insomnia, hallucinations, seizures	Yes	Yes	No?
Euphoria, prevent withdrawal discomfort	Addiction, constipation, loss of appetite	Yes	Yes	No*
Insightful experiences, exhilaration, distortion of senses	May intensify existing psychosis, panic reactions	No	No?	No?
Relaxation; increased euphoria, perceptions, sociability	Possible lung cancer, other health risks	Yes	Yes	Yes?
Excitation, euphoria	Personality change, hyperthermia, liver damage	No	Yes	Yes
Insightful experiences, exhilaration, distortion of senses	May intensify existing psychosis, panic reactions	No	No?	No?
Prevent withdrawal discomfort	Addiction, constipation, loss of appetite	Yes	Yes	No
Euphoria, prevent withdrawal discomfort	Addiction, constipation, loss of appetite	Yes	Yes	No*
Euphoria	Unpredictable behavior, suspicion, hostility, psychosis	Debated	Yes	Yes
Insightful experiences, exhilaration, distortion of senses	May intensify existing psychosis, panic reactions	No	No?	No?
Alertness, calmness, sociability	Emphysema, lung cancer, mouth and throat cancer, cardiovascular damage, loss of appetite	Yes	Yes	Yes

*Persons who inject drugs under nonsterile conditions run a high risk of contracting AIDS, hepatitis, abscesses, or circulatory disorders.
© Cengage Learning

Uppers—Amphetamines, Cocaine, MDMA, Caffeine, Nicotine

SURVEY QUESTION 25.2: What are some common stimulants?

Some of the most common *uppers* are amphetamines, cocaine, MDMA, caffeine, and nicotine.

Amphetamines

Amphetamines are synthetic stimulants. Some common street names for amphetamine are *speed, bennies, dexies, amp*, and *uppers*. These drugs were once widely prescribed for weight loss or depression. Today, the main legitimate medical use of amphetamines is to treat childhood hyperactivity and overdoses of depressant drugs. Illicit use of amphetamines is widespread, however, especially by people seeking to stay awake and by those who rationalize that such drugs can improve mental or physical performance (DeSantis & Hane, 2010).

Adderall and Ritalin, two popular "study drugs," are both mixes of amphetamines used to treat **attention deficit/hyperactivity disorder (ADHD)**. People with ADHD have difficulty controlling their attention and are prone to displaying hyperactive and impulsive behavior (American Psychiatric Association, 2013). Increasing numbers of normal college students are illegally taking these drugs in the hopes they also will be able to focus better while doing schoolwork (Dodge et al., 2012).

Is it true that those drugs actually can help students study? Taking "study drugs" may produce slight improvements in problem-solving performance; however, this may be offset by a slight loss of creativity (Farah et al., 2009). Most important, all amphetamines have side effects that are worrisome, as we will see shortly.

Methamphetamine is a more potent variation of amphetamine. It can be snorted, injected, or eaten. Of the various types of amphetamine, methamphetamine has created the largest drug problem. *Bergs, glass, meth, crank*, or *crystal*, as it is known on the street, can be made cheaply in backyard labs and sold for massive profits. In addition to ruining lives through addiction, it has fueled a violent criminal subculture.

Amphetamines rapidly produce a drug tolerance. Most abusers end up taking ever-larger doses to get the desired effect. Eventually, some users switch to injecting methamphetamine directly into the bloodstream. True "speed freaks" typically go on binges lasting several days, after which they "crash" from lack of sleep and food.

Abuse *How dangerous are amphetamines?* Large doses can cause nausea, vomiting, extremely high blood pressure, fatal heart attacks, and disabling strokes. It is important to realize that amphetamines speed up the use of the body's resources; they do not magically supply energy. After an amphetamine binge, people suffer from crippling fatigue, depression, confusion, uncontrolled irritability, and aggression. Repeated amphetamine use damages the brain. Amphetamines also can cause *amphetamine psychosis*, a loss of contact with reality. Affected users have paranoid delusions that someone is out to get them. Acting on these delusions, they may become violent, resulting in suicide, self-injury, or injury to others (Scott, 2012).

A potent smokable form of crystal methamphetamine has added to the risks of stimulant abuse. This drug, known as *ice* on the street, is highly addictive. Like *crack*, the smokable form of cocaine, it produces an intense high. But also like crack (discussed in a moment), crystal methamphetamine very rapidly leads to compulsive abuse and severe drug dependence.

Cocaine

Cocaine (coke, snow, blow, snuff, flake) is a powerful central nervous system stimulant extracted from the leaves of the coca plant. Cocaine produces feelings of alertness, euphoria, well-being, power, boundless energy, and pleasure (Julien, 2011). At the turn of the twentieth century, dozens of nonprescription potions and cure-alls contained cocaine. It was during this time that Coca-Cola was indeed the "real thing." From 1886

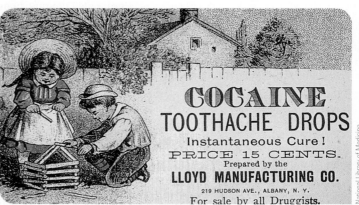

Cocaine was the main ingredient in many nonprescription elixirs before the turn of the twentieth century. Today, cocaine is recognized as a powerful and dangerous drug. Its high potential for abuse has damaged the lives of countless users.

until 1906, when the U.S. Pure Food and Drug Act was passed, Coca-Cola contained cocaine (which has since been replaced with caffeine).

How does cocaine differ from amphetamines? The two are very much alike in their effects on the central nervous system. The main difference is that amphetamine effects typically lasts longer than those of cocaine, which is more quickly metabolized.

Abuse *How dangerous is cocaine?* Cocaine's capacity for abuse and social damage rivals that of heroin. Rats and monkeys given free access to cocaine find it irresistible. Many, in fact, end up dying of convulsions from self-administered overdoses of the drug. Even casual or first-time users risk having convulsions, a heart attack, or a stroke. Cocaine increases the chemical messengers *dopamine* (DOPE-ah-meen) and *noradrenaline* (nor-ah-DREN-ah-lin). Noradrenaline arouses the brain, and dopamine produces a "rush" of pleasure. This combination is so powerfully rewarding that cocaine users run a high risk of becoming compulsive abusers (Ridenour et al., 2005).

A person who stops using cocaine does not experience heroin-like withdrawal symptoms. Instead, the brain adapts to cocaine abuse in ways that upset its chemical balance, causing depression when cocaine is withdrawn. First, there is a jarring "crash" of mood and energy. Within a few days, the person enters a long period of fatigue, anxiety, paranoia, boredom, and **anhedonia** (an-he-DAWN-ee-ah), an inability to feel pleasure. Before long, the urge to use cocaine becomes intense. So, although cocaine does not fit the classic pattern of addiction, it is ripe for compulsive abuse. Even a person who gets through withdrawal may crave cocaine months or years later (Washton & Zweben, 2009). If cocaine were cheaper, nine out of ten users would progress to compulsive abuse. In fact, rock cocaine (*crack, rock,* or *roca*), which is cheaper, produces very high abuse rates.

Anyone who thinks she or he has a cocaine problem should seek advice at a drug clinic or a Cocaine Anonymous meeting. Although quitting cocaine is extremely difficult, three out of four abusers who remain in treatment succeed in breaking their coke dependence (Sinha et al., 2006). Hope also is on the horizon in the form of a vaccine currently undergoing clinical trials that prevents cocaine from stimulating the nervous system (Kosten et al., 2012).

MDMA (Ecstasy)

The drug *MDMA* (methylenedioxymethamphetamine, or *Ecstasy*) also is chemically similar to amphetamine. In addition to producing a rush of energy, users say it makes them feel closer to others and heightens sensory experiences. Ecstasy causes brain cells to release extra amounts of serotonin as well as prolonging its effects. The physical effects of MDMA include dilated pupils, elevated blood pressure, jaw clenching, loss of appetite, and elevated body temperature (National Institute on Drug Abuse, 2012a). Although some users believe that Ecstasy increases sexual pleasure, it *diminishes* sexual performance, impairing erection in 40 percent of men and delaying orgasm in both men and women (Zemishlany, Aizenberg, & Weizman, 2001).

Abuse Ecstasy use in North America has declined slightly from a peak around 2002, perhaps because of widespread negative publicity. Regardless, in 2011, over 900,000 Americans tried Ecstasy for the first time (Substance Abuse and Mental Health Services Administration, 2012). Every year, emergency room doctors see many MDMA cases, including MDMA-related deaths. Some of these incidents are caused by elevated body temperature (hyperthermia) or heart arrhythmias, which can lead to collapse. Ecstasy users at "rave" parties try to prevent overheating by drinking water to cool themselves. This may help to a small degree, but the risk of fatal heat exhaustion is real.

MDMA also can cause severe liver damage, which can be fatal (National Institute on Drug Abuse, 2012a). In addition, Ecstasy users are more likely to abuse alcohol and other drugs, to neglect studying, to party excessively, and to engage in risky sex (Strote, Lee, & Wechsler, 2002). Ironically, Ecstasy use at "rave" parties does intensify the impact of the music. We say ironically because the end result is often overstimulation of the brain, which can result in a rebound depression (Iannone et al., 2006).

Ecstasy use also has long-term effects. Feelings of anxiety or depression can persist for months after a person stops taking Ecstasy. In addition, heavy users typically do not perform well in tests of learning and memory and show some signs of underlying brain damage (National Institute on Drug Abuse, 2012a; Quednow et al., 2006). Fortunately, however, the long-term consequences are not as severe as once feared (Advisory Council on the Misuse of Drugs, 2009).

Attention deficit/hyperactivity disorder (ADHD) *A behavioral problem characterized by short attention span, restless movement, and impaired learning capacity.*
Anhedonia *An inability to feel pleasure.*

Caffeine

Caffeine is the most frequently used psychoactive drug in North America. (And that's not counting Seattle!) Many people have a hard time starting a day (or writing another paragraph) without a cup because caffeine suppresses drowsiness and increases alertness, especially when combined with sugar (Adan & Serra-Grabulosa, 2010; Smith, Christopher, & Sutherland, 2013). Physically, caffeine can cause sweating, talkativeness, tinnitus (ringing in the ears), and hand tremors (Nehlig, 2004). Caffeine stimulates the brain by blocking chemicals that normally inhibit or slow nerve activity (Maisto, Galizio, & Connors, 2011). Its effects become apparent with doses as small as 50 milligrams, the amount found in about one-half cup of brewed coffee.

How much caffeine did you consume today? It is common to think of coffee as the major source of caffeine, but there are many others. Caffeine is found in tea, many soft drinks (especially colas), chocolate, and cocoa. Thousands of nonprescription drugs also contain caffeine, including stay-awake pills, cold remedies, and many name-brand aspirin products.

Abuse *Are there any serious drawbacks to using caffeine?* Overuse of caffeine may result in an unhealthy dependence known as *caffeinism.* Insomnia, irritability, loss of appetite, chills, racing heart, and elevated body temperature are all signs of caffeinism. Many people with these symptoms drink 15 or 20 cups of coffee a day. However, even as few as 2.5 cups of coffee a day (or the equivalent) can intensify anxiety and other psychological problems (Hogan, Hornick, & Bouchoux, 2002). People who consume even such modest amounts may experience anxiety, depression, fatigue, headaches, and flu-like symptoms during withdrawal (Juliano & Griffiths, 2004).

Caffeine poses a variety of other health risks. Caffeine encourages the growth of breast cysts in women, and it may contribute to bladder cancer, heart problems, and high blood pressure. Pregnant women who consume as little as two cups of coffee a day increase the risk of having a miscarriage (Cnattingius et al., 2000). It is wise to remember that caffeine *is* a drug and to use it in moderation.

Nicotine

Next to caffeine and alcohol, *nicotine* is the most widely used psychoactive drug (Julien, 2011). A natural stimulant found mainly in tobacco, nicotine is so toxic that it is sometimes used to kill insects! In large doses, it causes stomach pain, vomiting and diarrhea, cold sweats, dizziness, confusion, and muscle tremors. In very large doses, nicotine may cause convulsions, respiratory failure, and death. For a nonsmoker, 50 to 75 milligrams of nicotine taken in a single dose could be lethal. (Chain-smoking a pack of cigarettes can produce this dosage.) Most first-time smokers get sick on one or two cigarettes. In contrast, regular smokers build a tolerance for nicotine. A heavy smoker may inhale several packs a day without feeling ill.

Abuse *How addictive is nicotine?* A vast array of evidence confirms that nicotine is very addictive (Dani & Balfour, 2011). Most smokers begin when they are teenagers, which is unfortunate because young people are even more vulnerable to addiction than are adults (Counotte et al., 2011). Although 35 million Americans each year want to quit smoking, more than 85 percent of them relapse, many within a week (National Institute on Drug Abuse, 2012b). As humorist Mark Twain once whimsically lamented, "Giving up smoking is the easiest thing in the world. I know because I've done it thousands of times."

This should come as no surprise because withdrawal from nicotine causes headaches, sweating, cramps, insomnia, digestive upset, irritability, and a sharp craving for cigarettes. These symptoms may last from two to six weeks and may even be worse than heroin withdrawal. Just a few puffs will make that all go away until the next time the smoker works up the courage to quit.

Impact on Health *How serious are the health risks of smoking?* Smoking is the leading cause of preventable deaths worldwide. Every year, 6 million people around the globe, including almost 450,000 Americans, die from tobacco use (National Institute on Drug Abuse, 2012b; World Health Organization, 2011). Tens of millions more live diminished lives because they smoke.

A burning cigarette releases a large variety of potent *carcinogens* (car-SIN-oh-jins: cancer-causing substances). Smoking causes widespread damage to the body, leading to an increased risk of many cancers (such as lung cancer), cardiovascular diseases (such as stroke), respiratory diseases (such as chronic bronchitis), and reproductive disorders (such as decreased fertility). Together, these health risks combine to reduce the life expectancy of the average smoker by 10 to 15 years.

By the way, urban cowboys and Skoal bandits, the same applies to chewing tobacco and snuff. A 30-minute exposure to one pinch of smokeless tobacco is equivalent to smoking three or four cigarettes. Along with all the health risks of smoking, users of smokeless tobacco also run a higher risk of developing oral cancer (Oral Cancer Foundation, 2013).

E-cigarettes are electrical devices that look and feel like cigarettes because they vaporize a smokeless mist that can mimic tobacco smoke. When they deliver no nicotine, or a reduced dose, they may help people quitting smoking by allowing the smoker to enjoy the ritual of smoking while withdrawing from nicotine. However, when they are used as a smokeless way to deliver the usual dose, they become just another delivery device that must be medically regulated (Cobb & Abrams, 2011).

Smokers don't just risk their own health; they also endanger those who live and work nearby. Secondary smoke causes about 3,500 lung cancer deaths and as many as 70,000 heart disease deaths each year in the United States alone. It is particularly irresponsible of smokers to expose young children, who are especially vulnerable, to secondhand smoke (American Lung Association, 2013).

Quitting Smoking *If it is so hard to quit, how do some people manage to succeed?* Whatever approach is taken, quitting smoking is not easy. It is especially difficult to try quitting alone, without any support. Many people find that using nicotine patches or gum and/or other medications, such as *bupropion*, helps them suppress their cravings during the withdrawal period (Bolt et al., 2012). The best chance of success comes when the smoker combines the desire to quit with both medication and some sort of counseling (Centers for Disease Control, 2013).

Some smokers try to quit cold turkey, whereas others try to taper down gradually. Although going cold turkey has its advocates, gradually quitting works better for more people. Going cold turkey makes quitting an all-or-nothing proposition. Smokers who smoke even one cigarette after "quitting forever" tend to feel they've failed. Many figure they might just as well resume smoking. Those who quit gradually accept that success may take many attempts, spread over several months. Either way, you will have a better chance of success if you decide to quit *now* rather than at some time in the future and don't delay your quit date too often (Hughes & Callas, 2011).

The best way to taper off is *scheduled gradual reduction* (Riley et al., 2002). Smoking can be gradually reduced in many ways. For example, the smoker can (1) delay having a first cigarette in the morning and then try to delay a little longer each day, (2) gradually reduce the total number of cigarettes smoked each day, or (3) quit completely, but for just 1 week, and then quit again, a week at a time, for as many times as necessary to make it stick. Deliberately scheduling and then gradually stretching the length of time between cigarettes is a key part of this program. Scheduled smoking apparently helps people learn to cope with the urge to smoke.

It is also worth noting that smoking is more than a nicotine delivery system for most smokers. The entire ritual of smoking is itself a positive experience. Just holding a cigarette, dangling it between the lips, or even seeing a favorite smoking chair can give a smoker pleasure. For this reason, behavioral self-management techniques can be very useful for breaking habits such as smoking (see Module 31 and Module 69). In recent years, *e-cigarettes* have become popular as a way to simulate smoking either with or without delivering any nicotine. Anyone trying to quit should be prepared to make several attempts before succeeding. But the good news is that tens of millions of people have quit.

Downers—Narcotics, Sedatives, Tranquilizers, and Alcohol

SURVEY QUESTIONS 25.3: What are some common depressants?

While narcotics, like *heroin* and *morphine*, may be more powerful, both as drugs of abuse and as painkillers, the most widely used downers, or depressant drugs, are alcohol, barbiturates, GHB, and benzodiazepine (ben-zoe-die-AZ-eh-peen) tranquilizers. These drugs are much alike in their effects. In fact, barbiturates and tranquilizers are sometimes referred to as "solid alcohol." Let's examine the properties of each.

Narcotics

Opium poppies have been cultivated throughout recorded history (Dikotter, Laamann, & Xun, 2008). Raw opium, secreted by poppy seedpods, has been used for centuries to produce pain relief. Two narcotics refined from opium, morphine and codeine, are still widely used for that purpose. That narcotics are highly addictive also has long been recognized; *heroin (big H, dope, horse)*, derived by further refining morphine, is widely thought to be the most addictive drug of all.

Narcotics can produce a powerful feeling of euphoria ("rush") accompanied by a reduction of anxiety, relaxation, and, of course, pain relief. At higher doses, breathing can be impaired, leading to death. A new wave of narcotics addiction, notable for the number of younger abusers involved, has followed the more recent introduction of oxycodone (Oxycontin), another opium derivative (Substance Abuse and Mental Health Services Administration, 2012).

Another narcotic, *methadone,* also bears mentioning. Narcotics addicts are often treated with methadone, which reduces a narcotic's "rush," making it much easier to go through withdrawal. Methadone is often freely given to addicts as part of a *harm-reduction strategy* meant to reduce the negative consequences of addiction without requiring drug abstinence (McKeganey, 2012). Harm-reduction programs are controversial because it can seem as if they merely support substance abusers in their addiction (supplying clean needles for drug injections is another example); in reality, they are often the only hope for addicts who would otherwise cause more harm to themselves and to others (Centre for Addiction and Mental Health, 2012).

Barbiturates

Barbiturates are sedative drugs that depress brain activity. Common barbiturates include amobarbital, pentobarbital, secobarbital, and tuinal. On the street, they are known as *downers, blue devils, yellow jackets, lows, goof balls, reds, pink ladies, rainbows,* or *tooies.* Medically, barbiturates are used to calm patients or to induce sleep. At mild dosages, barbiturates have an effect similar to alcohol intoxication. Higher dosages can cause severe mental confusion or even hallucinations. Barbiturates are often taken in excess amounts because a first dose may be followed by others, as the user becomes uninhibited or forgetful. Overdoses first cause a loss of consciousness. Then they severely depress brain centers that control heartbeat and breathing. The result is often death (Grilly & Salamone, 2012).

GHB

Would you swallow a mixture of degreasing solvent and drain cleaner to get high? Apparently, a lot of people would.

A mini-epidemic of GHB (gamma-hydroxybutyrate) use has taken place in recent years, especially at nightclubs and raves. GHB *(goop, scoop, max, Georgia Home Boy)* is a central nervous system depressant that relaxes and sedates the body. Users describe its effects as similar to those of alcohol (Johnson & Griffiths, 2013). Mild GHB intoxication tends to produce euphoria, a desire to socialize, and a mild loss of inhibitions. GHB's intoxicating effects typically last a few hours, depending on the dosage.

Abuse At lower dosages, GHB can relieve anxiety and produce relaxation. However, as the dose increases, its sedative effects may result in nausea, a loss of muscle control, and either sleep or a loss of consciousness. Potentially fatal doses of GHB are only three times the amount typically taken by users. This narrow margin of safety has led to numerous overdoses, especially when GHB was combined with alcohol. An overdose causes coma, breathing failure, and death. GHB also inhibits the gag reflex, so some users choke to death on their own vomit.

In 2000, the U.S. government classified GHB as a controlled substance, making possession a felony. Evidence increasingly suggests that GHB is addictive and a serious danger to users. Two out of three frequent users have lost consciousness after taking GHB. Chronic use leads to brain damage (Pedraza, García, & Navarro, 2009). Heavy users who stop taking GHB have withdrawal symptoms that include anxiety, agitation, tremor, delirium, and hallucinations (Miotto et al., 2001).

As if the preceding weren't reason enough to be leery of GHB, here's one more to consider: GHB is often manufactured in homes with recipes and ingredients purchased on the Internet. As mentioned earlier, it can be produced by combining degreasing solvent with drain cleaner. If you want to degrease your brain, GHB will do the trick.

Tranquilizers

Tranquilizers lower anxiety and reduce tension. Doctors prescribe benzodiazepine tranquilizers to alleviate nervousness and stress. Valium is the best-known drug in this family; others are Xanax, Halcion, and Librium. Even at normal dosages, these drugs can cause drowsiness, shakiness, and confusion. When used at too high a dosage or for too long, benzodiazepines are addictive (McKim, 2013).

A drug sold under the trade name Rohypnol (ro-HIP-nol) has added to the problem of tranquilizer abuse. This drug, which is related to Valium, is cheap and 10 times more potent. It lowers inhibitions and produces relaxation or intoxication.

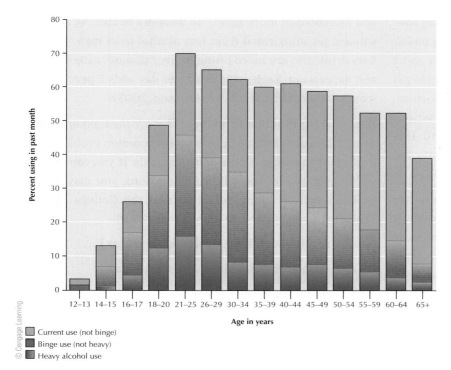

© Cengage Learning

Current use (not binge)
Binge use (not heavy)
Heavy alcohol use

Figure 25.3

Many Americans of all ages abuse alcohol. According to this 2010 survey, about 40 percent of young adults aged 18–29 admitted to heavy alcohol use or binge drinking in the month before the survey was administered (Substance Abuse and Mental Health Services Administration, 2012).

Large doses induce short-term amnesia and sleep. *Roofies,* as they are known on the street, are odorless and tasteless. They have occasionally been used to spike drinks, which are given to the unwary. Victims of this "date rape" drug are then sexually assaulted or raped while they are unconscious (Nicoletti, 2009). (Be aware, however, that drinking too much alcohol is by far the most common prelude to date rape.)

Abuse Repeated use of barbiturates can cause physical dependence. Some abusers suffer severe emotional depression that may end in suicide. Similarly, when tranquilizers are used at too high a dosage or for too long, addiction can occur. Many people have learned the hard way that their legally prescribed tranquilizers are as dangerous as many illicit drugs (Goldberg, 2010).

Alcohol

Alcohol is the common name for ethyl alcohol, the intoxicating element in fermented and distilled liquors. Contrary to popular belief, alcohol is not a stimulant. The noisy animation at drinking parties is due to alcohol's effect as a *depressant.* Small amounts of alcohol reduce inhibitions and produce feelings of relaxation and euphoria. Larger amounts cause greater impairment of the brain until the drinker loses consciousness. Alcohol also is not an aphrodisiac. Rather than enhancing sexual arousal, it usually impairs performance, especially in males. As William Shakespeare observed long ago, drink "provokes the desire, but it takes away the performance."

Some people become relaxed and friendly when they are drunk. Others become aggressive and want to argue or fight. How can the same drug have such different effects? Some people drink for pleasure while others drink to cope with negative emotions, such as anxiety and depression. That's why alcohol abuse increases with the level of stress in people's lives. People who drink to relieve bad feelings are at great risk of becoming alcoholics (Roberto & Koob, 2009).

Also, when a person is drunk, thinking and perception become dulled or shortsighted, a condition that has been called *alcohol myopia* (my-OH-pea-ah) (Giancola et al., 2010). Only the most obvious and immediate stimuli catch a drinker's attention. Worries and "second thoughts" that would normally restrain behavior are banished from the drinker's mind. That's why many behaviors become more extreme when a person is drunk. On college campuses, drunken students tend to have accidents, get into fights, sexually assault others, or engage in risky sex. They also destroy property and disrupt the lives of students who are trying to sleep or study (Brower, 2002).

Abuse Alcohol, the world's favorite depressant, breeds our biggest drug problem. More than 20 million people in the United States and Canada have serious drinking problems. One American dies every 20 minutes in an alcohol-related car crash. Significant percentages of Americans of all ages abuse alcohol (●**Figure 25.3**).

Tranquilizer *A drug that lowers anxiety and reduces tension.*

It is especially worrisome to see binge drinking among adolescents and young adults. **Binge drinking** is defined as downing five or more drinks (four drinks for women) in a short time. Apparently, many students think it's entertaining to get completely wasted and throw up on their friends (Norman, Conner, & Stride, 2012). However, binge drinking is a serious sign of alcohol abuse (Beseler, Taylor, & Leeman, 2010). It is responsible for 1,800 U.S. college student deaths each year and thousands of trips to the emergency room (Mitka, 2009).

Binge drinking is of special concern because the brain continues to develop into the early twenties. Research has shown that teenagers and young adults who drink too much may lose as much as 10 percent of their brain power—especially their memory capacity (Brown et al., 2000). Such losses can have a long-term impact on a person's chances for success in life. In short, getting drunk is a slow but sure way to get stupid (Le Berre et al., 2012).

Binge drinking and alcohol abuse have become serious problems among college students (Tewksbury, Higgins, & Mustaine, 2008).

Edward Frazer/Corbis

At Risk Children of alcoholics and those who have other relatives who abuse alcohol are at greater risk for becoming alcohol abusers themselves. The increased risk appears to be partly genetic (Starkman, Sakharkar, & Pandey, 2012). It is based on the fact that some people have stronger cravings for alcohol after they drink (Hutchison et al., 2002). Women also face some special risks. For one thing, alcohol is absorbed faster and metabolized more slowly by women's bodies. As a result, women get intoxicated from less alcohol than men. Women who drink also are more prone to liver disease, osteoporosis, and depression. Each extra drink per day adds 7 percent to a woman's risk of breast cancer (Aronson, 2003).

Recognizing Problem Drinking *What are the signs of alcohol abuse?* Because alcohol abuse is such a common problem, it is important to recognize the danger signals. If you can answer yes to even one of the following questions, you may have a problem with drinking (adapted from the College Alcohol Problems Scale, revised; Maddock et al., 2001):

As a result of drinking alcoholic beverages I . . .

1. engaged in unplanned sexual activity.
2. drove under the influence.
3. did not use protection when engaging in sex.
4. engaged in illegal activities associated with drug use.
5. felt sad, blue, or depressed.
6. was nervous or irritable.
7. felt bad about myself.
8. had problems with appetite or sleeping.

Moderated Drinking Almost everyone has been to a party spoiled by someone who drank too much too fast. Those who avoid overdrinking have a better time, and so do their friends. But how do you avoid drinking too much? After all, as one wit once observed, "The conscience dissolves in alcohol." It takes skill to regulate drinking in social situations, where the temptation to drink can be strong. If you choose to drink, here are some guidelines that may be helpful (adapted from Miller & Munoz, 2005; National Institute on Alcohol Abuse and Alcoholism, 2008):

Moderated Drinking

1. Think about your drinking beforehand, plan how you will manage it, and keep track of how much you drink.
2. Drink slowly (no more than one drink an hour), eat while drinking or drink on a full stomach, and make every other drink (or more) a nonalcoholic beverage.
3. Limit drinking primarily to the first hour of a social event or party.
4. Practice how you will politely but firmly refuse drinks.
5. Learn how to relax, meet people, and socialize without relying on alcohol.

And remember, research has shown that you are likely to overestimate how much your fellow students are drinking (Maddock & Glanz, 2005). So don't let yourself be lured into overdrinking just because you have the (probably false) impression that other students are drinking more than you. Limiting your own drinking may help others as well. When people are tempted to drink too much, their main reason for stopping is that "other people were quitting and deciding they'd had enough" (Johnson, 2002).

Treatment Treatment for alcohol dependence begins with sobering up the person and cutting off the supply. This phase is referred to as **detoxification** (literally, "to remove poison"). It frequently produces all the symptoms of drug withdrawal and can be extremely unpleasant. The next step is to try to restore the person's health. Heavy abuse of alcohol usually causes severe damage to body organs and the nervous system. After alcoholics have "dried out" and some degree of health has been restored, they may be treated with tranquilizers, antidepressants, or psychotherapy. Unfortunately, the success of these procedures has been limited.

One mutual-help approach that has been fairly successful is Alcoholics Anonymous (AA). AA takes a spiritual approach while acting on the premise that it takes a former alcoholic to understand and help a current alcoholic. Participants at AA meetings admit that they have a problem, share feelings, and resolve to stay "dry" one day at a time. Other group members provide support for those struggling to end dependency (Teresi & Haroutunian, 2011). (Other "12-step" programs, such as Cocaine Anonymous and Narcotics Anonymous, use the same approach.)

Other groups offer a rational, nonspiritual approach to alcohol abuse that better fits the needs of some people. Examples include Rational Recovery and Secular Organizations for Sobriety (SOS). Other alternatives to AA include medical treatment, group therapy, mindfulness meditation, and individual psychotherapy (Huebner & Kantor, 2011; Jacobs-Stewart, 2010). There is a strong tendency for abusive drinkers to deny they have a problem. The sooner they seek help, the better.

Hallucinogens—Tripping the Light Fantastic

SURVEY QUESTIONS 25.4: What is a hallucinogen?

Although a **hallucinogen** (hal-LU-sin-oh-jen) is generally a mild stimulant, its main effect is to alter sensory impressions. The most common hallucinogens include LSD, PCP,

mescaline, psilocybin, and marijuana. In fact, *marijuana* is the most popular illicit drug in America (Substance Abuse and Mental Health Services Administration, 2012).

LSD, PCP, Mescaline, and Psilocybin

The drug LSD (lysergic acid diethylamide, or *acid*) is perhaps the best-known hallucinogen. Even when taken in tiny amounts, LSD can produce hallucinations and psychotic-like disturbances in thinking and perception. Two other common hallucinogens are mescaline (peyote) and psilocybin (*magic mushrooms*, or *shrooms*). Incidentally, the drug PCP (phencyclidine, or *angel dust*) can have hallucinogenic effects. However, PCP, which is an anesthetic, also has stimulant and depressant effects. This potent combination can cause extreme agitation, disorientation, violence, and—too often—tragedy. Like other psychoactive drugs, all of the hallucinogens, including marijuana, typically affect neurotransmitter systems that carry messages between brain cells (Maisto, Galizio, & Connors, 2011).

Marijuana

Marijuana and hashish are derived from the hemp plant *Cannabis sativa*. Marijuana (*pot, grass, reefer, MJ*) consists of the dried leaves and flowers of the hemp plant. Hashish is a resinous material scraped from cannabis buds. The main active chemical in marijuana is *tetrahydrocannabinol* (tet-rah-hydro-cah-NAB-ih-nol), or THC for short.

Marijuana's psychological effects include a sense of euphoria or well-being, relaxation, altered time sense, and perceptual distortions. At high dosages, however, paranoia, hallucinations, and delusions can occur (Hart, Ksir, & Ray, 2013). All considered, marijuana intoxication is relatively subtle by comparison to drugs such as LSD or alcohol. Despite this, driving a car while high on marijuana can be extremely hazardous (National Institute on Drug Abuse, 2012c). As a matter of fact, driving under the influence of any intoxicating drug is dangerous.

No overdose deaths from marijuana have been reported. However, marijuana cannot be considered harmless. Particularly worrisome is the fact that THC accumulates in the body's fatty tissues, especially in the brain and reproductive organs.

Binge drinking *Consuming five or more drinks in a short time (four for women).*
Detoxification *In the treatment of alcoholism, the withdrawal of the patient from alcohol.*
Hallucinogen *A substance that alters or distorts sensory impressions.*

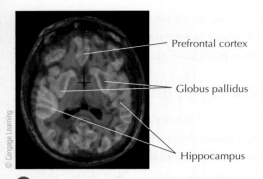

Prefrontal cortex

Globus pallidus

Hippocampus

Figure 25.4

The red and yellow areas in this PET scan show where the brain is rich in THC receptors. The prefrontal cortex plays a role in human consciousness, the globus pallidus is involved in the control of coordinated movement, and the hippocampus plays a role in memory (Freberg, 2010). This may explain why marijuana use negatively affects memory and coordination (but what about the munchies?).

Even if a person smokes marijuana just once a week, the body is never entirely free of THC. Scientists have located a specific receptor site on the surface of brain cells where THC binds to produce its effects (● **Figure 25.4**). These receptor sites are found in several parts of the brain, including the prefrontal cortex, which is the seat of human consciousness (Julien, 2011). In addition, THC receptors are found in areas involved in the control of skilled movement. Naturally occurring chemicals similar to THC may help the brain cope with pain and stress. However, when THC is used as a drug, high doses can cause paranoia, hallucinations, and dizziness (Maisto, Galizio, & Connors, 2011).

Abuse *Does marijuana produce physical dependence?* Yes, according to recent studies (Filbey et al., 2009; Lichtman & Martin, 2006). Frequent users of marijuana find it very difficult to quit, so dependence is a risk (Budney & Hughes, 2006). But marijuana's potential for abuse lies primarily in the realm of psychological dependence, not physical addiction.

For about a day after a person smokes marijuana, his or her attention, coordination, and short-term memory are impaired. Frequent marijuana users show small declines in learning, memory, attention, and thinking abilities (Solowij et al., 2002). When surveyed, nonusers are healthier, earn more, and are more satisfied with their lives than people who smoke marijuana regularly (Allen & Holder, 2013; Ellickson, Martino, & Collins, 2004). In fact, marijuana use is associated with a variety of mental health problems (Buckner, Ecker, & Cohen, 2010; National Institute on Drug Abuse, 2012c).

People who smoke regularly score lower on IQ tests (Kuehn, 2012). This is enough to dull their learning capacity. In fact,

many people who have stopped using marijuana say they quit because they were bothered by short-term memory loss and concentration problems. Fortunately, IQ scores and other cognitive measures rebound about a month after a person quits using marijuana (Grant et al., 2001). In other words, people who smoke dope may act like dopes, but if they quit, there's a good chance they will regain their mental abilities.

Long-Term Health Risks Marijuana's long-term effects include the following health risks:

1. Marijuana smoke contains more cancer-causing hydrocarbons and tar than does tobacco smoke. In regular users, marijuana increases the risk of a variety of cancers, including prostate and cervical cancer (Hashibe et al., 2005).

2. THC may interfere with menstrual cycles and ovulation as well as cause a higher rate of miscarriages. It also can reach the developing fetus: Children whose mothers smoked marijuana during pregnancy show lowered ability to succeed in challenging, goal-oriented activities (National Institute on Drug Abuse, 2012c; Noland et al., 2005). As is true for so many other drugs, marijuana should be avoided during pregnancy.

3. THC can suppress the body's immune system, increasing the risk of disease.

4. Chronic marijuana users are more prone to develop psychosis (Castle et al., 2012).

5. THC impairs memory functions (Patel & Khazeni, 2012).

6. Activity levels in the cerebellum are lower than normal in marijuana abusers. This may explain why chronic marijuana users tend to show some loss of coordination (Volkow et al., 1996).

7. Some evidence shows that THC impairs memory functions (Patel & Khazeni, 2012).

Although much is still unknown, marijuana appears to pose a wide range of health risks. Only future research will tell for sure "what's in the pot."

CENGAGEbrain.com

Module 25: Summary

25.1 What are the effects of the more commonly used psychoactive drugs?

- **25.1.1** Psychoactive drugs affect the brain in ways that alter consciousness. Most psychoactive drugs can be placed on a scale ranging from stimulation to depression.
- **25.1.2** Psychoactive drugs are highly prone to abuse. Drug abuse is related to personal maladjustment, the reinforcing qualities of drugs, peer group influences, and expectations about drug effects.
- **25.1.3** Drugs may cause a physical dependence (addiction), a psychological dependence, or both. Physically addicting drugs are alcohol, amphetamines, barbiturates, cocaine, codeine, GHB, heroin, marijuana, methadone, morphine, nicotine, and tranquilizers. All psychoactive drugs can lead to psychological dependence.
- **25.1.4** Drug use can be classified as experimental, recreational, situational, intensive, and compulsive. Drug abuse is most often associated with the last three.

25.2 What are some common stimulants?

- **25.2.1** Stimulant drugs are readily abused because of the period of depression that often follows stimulation. The greatest risks are associated with amphetamines (especially methamphetamine), cocaine, MDMA, and nicotine, but even caffeine can be a problem.
- **25.2.2** Nicotine includes the added risk of lung cancer, heart disease, and other health problems.

25.3 What are some common depressants?

- **25.3.1** Narcotics are highly addictive because they produce intense feelings of euphoria. Narcotics addiction is often treated with a harm reduction strategy.
- **25.3.2** Barbiturates and tranquilizers are depressant drugs whose action is similar to that of alcohol. The overdose level for barbiturates and GHB is close to the intoxication dosage, making them dangerous drugs. Mixing barbiturates, tranquilizers, or GHB and alcohol may result in a fatal drug interaction.
- **25.3.3** Alcohol is the most heavily abused drug in common use today. Binge drinking is a problem among college students. It is possible to pace the consumption of alcohol.

25.4 What is a hallucinogen?

- **25.4.1** Hallucinogens such as PSD, PCP, and marijuana alter sensory impressions.
- **25.4.2** Studies have linked chronic marijuana use with cancer, various mental impairments, and other health problems.

Module 25: Knowledge Builder

Recite

1. Addictive drugs stimulate the brain's reward circuitry by affecting
   - **a.** neurotransmitters
   - **b.** alpha waves
   - **c.** tryptophan levels
   - **d.** delta spindles

2. Which of the following drugs are known to cause physical dependence?
   - **a.** heroin
   - **b.** morphine
   - **c.** codeine
   - **d.** methadone
   - **e.** barbiturates
   - **f.** alcohol
   - **g.** marijuana
   - **h.** amphetamines
   - **i.** nicotine
   - **j.** cocaine
   - **k.** GHB

3. Amphetamine psychosis is similar to extreme _____, in which the individual feels threatened and suffers from delusions.

4. Cocaine is very similar to which of the following in its effects on the central nervous system?
   - **a.** Seconal
   - **b.** codeine
   - **c.** cannabis
   - **d.** amphetamine

5. MDMA and GHB are classified as depressants. *T or F?*

6. College students may overdrink as they try to keep up with how much they falsely imagine that their peers drink. *T or F?*

Reflect

Think Critically

7. Why do you think there is such a contrast between the laws regulating marijuana and those regulating alcohol and tobacco?

Self-Reflect

What legal drugs did you use in the last year? Did any have psychoactive properties? How do psychoactive drugs differ from other substances in their potential for abuse?

ANSWERS

Psychology in Action:
Exploring and Using Dreams

Dream a Little Dream for Me

Insight can come to us in a surprising variety of ways. Even our dreams can be avenues for growth. One possibility is that our dreams are trying to tell us something important about ourselves. How would you try to find the meaning of a dream? A traditional approach is to look for symbolic messages as well as literal meanings. If you find yourself wearing a mask in a dream, for instance, it could relate to important roles that you play at school, work, or home. It also could mean that you want to hide or that you are looking forward to a costume party. However, to accurately interpret a dream, it is important to learn your own "vocabulary" of dream images and meanings.

It may even be possible to turn dreams into tools to deliberately foster creativity and deeper understanding. Lucid dreaming is a dramatic example of what is possible if you take your dream life seriously. Let's check it out.

Elisa Lazo de Valdez/Corbis

SURVEY QUESTION

26.1 How can dreams be used to promote personal understanding?

Exploring Your "Dreamworks"

SURVEY QUESTION 26.1: **How can dreams be used to promote personal understanding?**

No matter what theory of dreaming we favor, dreams can be thought of as a message *from* yourself *to* yourself. Thus, the way to understand dreams is to remember them, write them down, look for the messages they contain, and become deeply acquainted with *your own* symbol system. Here's how:

How to Catch a Dream

1. Before going to sleep, plan to remember your dreams. Keep a pen and paper or a digital recorder beside your bed.

2. If possible, arrange to awaken gradually without an alarm. Natural awakening almost always follows soon after a REM period.

3. If you rarely remember your dreams, you may want to set an alarm clock to go off an hour before you usually awaken. Although less desirable than awakening naturally, this may let you catch a dream.

4. Upon awakening, lie still and review the dream images with your eyes closed. Try to recall as many details as possible.

5. If you can, make your first dream record (whether by writing or by recording) with your eyes closed. Opening your eyes will disrupt dream recall.

6. Review the dream again and record as many additional details as you can remember. Dream memories disappear

quickly. Be sure to describe feelings as well as the plot, characters, and actions of the dream.

7. Put your dreams into a permanent dream diary. Keep dreams in chronological order and review them periodically. This procedure will reveal recurrent themes, conflicts, and emotions. It almost always produces valuable insights.

8. Remember, several drugs, including alcohol, amphetamines, barbiturates, cocaine, opiates, and valium, suppress dreaming by interfering with REM sleep.

Dream Work

At one time or another, almost everyone has had a dream that seemed to have deep meaning (Rock, 2004). Exploring everyday dream life can be a source of personal enrichment and personal growth (Halliday, 2010). What strategies do psychologists use to interpret dreams? Let's start with Sigmund Freud's pioneering approach.

To unlock dreams, Freud identified four **dream processes**, or mental filters, that disguise the meanings of dreams. The first is **condensation**, in which several people, objects, or events are combined into a single dream image. A dream character who looks like a teacher, acts like your father, talks like your mother, and is dressed like your employer might be a condensation of authority figures in your life.

Displacement is a second way of disguising dream content. Displacement may cause important emotions or actions of a dream to be redirected toward safe or seemingly unimportant images. Thus, a student angry with his parents might dream of accidentally wrecking their car instead of directly attacking them.

A third dream process is **symbolization**. Freud believed that dreams are often expressed in images that are symbolic rather than literal. That's why it helps to ask what feelings or ideas a dream image might symbolize. Let's say, for example, that a student dreams of coming to class naked. A literal interpretation would be that the student is an exhibitionist! A more likely symbolic meaning is that the student feels vulnerable or unprepared in the class.

Secondary elaboration is the fourth method by which dream meanings are disguised. **Secondary elaboration** is the tendency to make a dream more logical and to add details when remembering it. The fresher a dream memory, the more useful it is likely to be.

Looking for condensation, displacement, symbolization, and secondary elaboration may help you unlock your dreams. But other techniques also may be effective. Fritz Perls, the originator of Gestalt therapy, considered most dreams a special message about what's missing in our lives, what we avoid doing, or feelings that need to be "re-owned." Perls believed that dreams are a way of filling in gaps in personal experience (Perls, 1969).

An approach that Perls found helpful is to "take the part of" or "speak for" each of the characters and objects in the dream. In other words, if you dream about a strange man standing behind a doorway, you would speak aloud to the man, and then answer for him. To use Perls's method, you would even speak for the door, perhaps saying something like, "I am a barrier. I keep you safe, but I also keep you locked inside. The stranger has something to tell you. You must risk opening me to learn it."

Another theorist, Ernest Hartmann, suggests that dreams arise as our brains seek to make creative connections. Ignoring the elements of a dream that merely replay a day's events and focusing instead on unusual dream elements is central to unlocking the dream's meaning (Hartmann, 2010, 2011). Hartmann adds that the overall *emotional tone* (underlying mood) of a dream is another major clue to its meaning (Hartmann, 2008). Is the dream comical, threatening, joyous, or depressing? Were you lonely, jealous, frightened, in love, or angry?

Because each dream has several possible meanings or levels of meaning, there is no fixed way to work with it (Halliday, 2010). Telling the dream to others and discussing its meaning can be a good start. Describing it may help you relive some of the feelings in the dream. Also, family members or friends may be able to offer interpretations to which you might be blind. Watch for verbal or visual puns and other playful elements in dreams. For example, if you dream that you are in a wrestling match and your arm is pinned behind your back, it may mean that you feel someone is "twisting your arm" in real life.

The meaning of most dreams will yield to a little detective work. Try asking a series of questions about dreams you would like to understand:

Probing Dreams

1. Who was in the dream? Were there humans, animals, or mythical characters? Do you recognize any of the characters?

Dream processes *Mental filters that hide the true meanings of dreams.*
Condensation *Combining several people, objects, or events into a single dream image.*
Displacement *Directing emotions or actions toward safe or unimportant dream images.*
Symbolization *The nonliteral expression of dream content.*
Secondary elaboration *Making a dream more logical and complete while remembering it.*

2. What social interactions were taking place? Were those interactions friendly? Aggressive? Sexual?

3. What activities were taking place? Were they physical activities?

4. Was there striving? Was the striving successful or not?

5. Was the dream about good fortune or misfortune?

6. What emotions were present in the dream? Was there anger, apprehension, confusion, happiness, or sadness?

7. What were the physical surroundings? What was the setting? Were any physical objects present? (Adapted from the Hall-Van de Castle system of dream content analysis; Domhoff, 2003.)

A particularly interesting dream exercise is to continue a dream as waking fantasy so that it may be concluded or carried on to a more meaningful ending. As the world of dreams and your personal dream language become more familiar, you will doubtless find many answers, paradoxes, intuitions, and insights into your own behavior.

Using Your Dreams

It is possible to learn to use dreams for our own purposes. For example, as mentioned previously (see Module 24), nightmare sufferers can use imagery rehearsal to modify their own nightmares (Germain et al., 2004; Harb et al., 2012; Krakow & Zadra, 2006). Similarly, it is possible to use your dreams to enhance creativity (Stickgold & Walker, 2004).

Dreams and Creativity

History is full of cases in which dreams have been a pathway to creativity and discovery. A striking example is provided by Dr. Otto Loewi, a pharmacologist and winner of a Nobel Prize. Loewi had spent years studying the chemical transmission of nerve impulses. A tremendous breakthrough in his research came when he dreamed of an experiment three nights in a row. On the third night, he got up after having the dream, went straight to his laboratory, and performed the crucial experiment. Loewi later said that if the experiment had occurred to him while awake, he would have rejected it.

Loewi's experience gives some insight into using dreams to produce creative solutions. Inhibitions are reduced during dreaming, which may be especially useful in solving problems that require a fresh point of view. Even unimaginative people may create amazing worlds each night in their dreams. For many of us, this rich ability to create is lost in the daily rush of sensory input.

The ability to take advantage of dreams for problem solving is improved if you "set" yourself before retiring for the night. Before you go to bed, try to visualize or think intently about a problem you want to solve. Steep yourself in the problem by stating it clearly and reviewing all relevant information. Then use the suggestions listed previously to catch your dreams. Although this method is not guaranteed to produce a novel solution or a new insight, it is certain to be an adventure.

Lucid Dreaming If you would like to press further into the territory of dreams, you may want to learn lucid dreaming, a relatively rare but fascinating experience. During a **lucid dream**, a person feels as if she or he is fully awake within the dream world and capable of normal thought and action. If you ask yourself, "Could this be a dream?" and answer "Yes," you are having a lucid dream (Dresler et al., 2012).

Stephen LaBerge and his colleagues at the Stanford University Sleep Research Center have used a unique approach to show that lucid dreams are real and that they occur during REM sleep. In the sleep lab, lucid dreamers agree to make prearranged signals when they become aware they are dreaming. One such signal is to look up abruptly in a dream, causing a distinct upward eye movement. Another signal is to clench the right and left fists (in the dream) in a prearranged pattern. In other words, lucid dreamers can partially overcome REM sleep paralysis. Such signals show very clearly that lucid dreaming and voluntary action in dreams are possible (LaBerge, 2000).

Can a person learn to have lucid dreams? In short, yes (Stumbrys et al., 2012). Try following this simple routine: When you awake spontaneously from a dream, take a few minutes to try to memorize it. Next, engage in 10 to 15 minutes of reading or any other activity requiring full wakefulness. Then, while lying in bed and returning to sleep, say to yourself, "Next time I'm dreaming, I want to remember I'm dreaming." Finally, visualize yourself lying in bed asleep while in the dream you just rehearsed. At the same time, picture yourself realizing that you are dreaming. Follow this routine each time you awake (substitute a dream memory from another occasion if you don't awaken from a dream).

Why would anyone want to have more lucid dreams? Researchers are interested in lucid dreams because they provide a tool for understanding dreaming (Paulsson & Parker, 2006). Using participants who can signal when they are dreaming makes it possible to explore dreams with firsthand data from the dreamer's world.

On a more personal level, lucid dreaming can convert dreams into a nightly "workshop" for emotional growth. Consider, for example, a recently divorced woman who kept dreaming that she was being swallowed by a giant wave. The woman was asked to try swimming the next time the wave engulfed her. She did, with great determination, and the nightmare lost its terror. More important, her revised dream made her feel that she could cope with life again.

For reasons such as this, people who have lucid dreams tend to feel a sense of emotional well-being (Taitz, 2011). Dream expert Allan Hobson believes that learning to voluntarily enter altered states of consciousness (through lucid dreaming or self-hypnosis, for example) has allowed him to have enlightening experiences without the risks of taking mind-altering drugs (Hobson, 2001, 2009). So, day or night, don't be afraid to dream a little.

Module 26: Summary

26.1 How can dreams be used to promote personal understanding?

- **26.1.1** Collecting and interpreting your dreams can promote self-awareness.
- **26.1.2** Freud held that the meaning of dreams is hidden by condensation, displacement, symbolization, and secondary elaboration. Perls emphasized the technique of speaking for dream elements, and Hartmann's view of dreams as creative connections guided by emotions suggests focusing on unusual dream elements and emotions.
- **26.1.3** Dreams may be used for creative problem solving, especially when dream awareness is achieved through lucid dreaming.

Module 26: Knowledge Builder

Recite

1. Which is *not* one of the four dream processes Freud identified?
   - *a.* condensation
   - *b.* lucidity
   - *c.* displacement
   - *d.* symbolization

2. In secondary elaboration, one dream character stands for several others. *T or F?*

3. Fritz Perls's approach to dream interpretation emphasizes taking the part of characters and even objects portrayed in a dream. *T or F?*

4. Ernest Hartmann stresses that dreaming is a relatively mechanical process having little personal meaning. *T or F?*

5. Recent research shows that lucid dreaming occurs primarily during NREM sleep or micro-awakenings. *T or F?*

Reflect

Think Critically

6. The possibility of having a lucid dream raises an interesting question: If you were dreaming right now, how could you prove it?

Self-Reflect

Some people are very interested in remembering and interpreting their dreams. Others pay little attention to dreaming. What importance do you place on dreams? Do you think dreams and dream interpretation can increase self-awareness?

ANSWERS

1. b 2. F 3. T 4. F 5. F 6. In waking consciousness, our actions have consequences that produce immediate sensory feedback. Dreams lack such external feedback. Thus, trying to walk through a wall or doing similar tests would reveal if you were dreaming.

Lucid dream *A dream in which the dreamer feels awake and capable of normal thought and action.*

Conditioning and Learning:
Associative and Cognitive Learning

Rats!

Larry still vividly remembers the day he learned to fear rats. At the age of six, he overheard his mother tearfully describe how, as a little girl, she was terrified by a rat scampering out of a woodpile.

As an adult, Larry read about irrational fears and realized that a form of *associative learning* called *vicarious classical conditioning* explained his dread of rats. Armed with this knowledge, he tried to hold a rat in a local pet store and was shocked to discover that his newfound knowledge was no help at all. All his abstract "book learning," a form of *cognitive learning,* was powerless to protect him in the presence of a rat. Larry eventually went to a therapist who used classical conditioning to help him overcome his fear. He now has a pet rat named Einstein.

Oleg Kozlov/Shutterstock

Different forms of learning reach into every corner of our lives. Are you ready to learn more?

SURVEY QUESTIONS

27.1 What is learning?

27.2 What are some types of associative learning?

27.3 What are some types of cognitive learning?

27.4 Does learning occur by imitation?

Learning—One Way or Another

SURVEY QUESTION 27.1: What is learning?

Most behavior is learned. Imagine if you suddenly lost all you had ever learned. What could you do? You would be unable to read, write, or speak. You couldn't feed yourself, find your way home, drive a car, play the clarinet, or "party." Needless to say, you would be totally incapacitated. (Dull, too!)

Learning is a relatively permanent change in behavior due to experience (Chance, 2014). Notice that this definition excludes both temporary changes and more permanent changes caused by motivation, fatigue, maturation, disease,

injury, or drugs. Each of these can alter behavior, but none qualifies as learning.

As Larry's rat experience illustrates, there are different types of learning (Lefrançois, 2012; Shanks, 2010). **Associative learning** occurs whenever a person or an animal forms a simple association among various stimuli and/or behaviors. Associative learning requires relatively little awareness or thought. Regardless, we humans share the important capacity for associative learning with many other species. In this and the next few modules, we explore associative learning in depth.

Is all learning just an association between stimuli and responses? Much learning can be explained by associative learning. But humans also engage in **cognitive learning**, which refers to understanding, knowing, anticipating, or otherwise making use of information-rich higher mental processes. In contrast with associative learning, more complex forms of cognitive learning, such as learning from written language, are unique to humans. However, some animals do engage in simpler forms of cognitive learning, as we will see later on in this module.

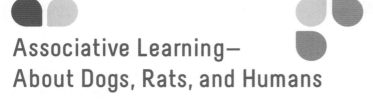

Associative Learning— About Dogs, Rats, and Humans

SURVEY QUESTION 27.2: What are some types of associative learning?

For early psychologists, such as Ivan Pavlov, John Watson, and Edward Thorndike (see Module 3), associative learning was a fairly mechanical process of "stamping in" associations between objective stimuli and objective responses, or behaviors (Hergenhahn & Henry, 2014). No subjective "thinking" was thought to be required.

Types of Associative Learning

There are two main types of associative learning: In Russia, Ivan Pavlov discovered *classical conditioning* and, in North America, Edward Thorndike discovered what is today called *operant conditioning*. It is well worth understanding both forms of associative learning because they help us make sense of much animal and human behavior.

Unlocking the secrets of associative learning begins with noting what happens before and after a particular behavior. Events that precede a behavior are **antecedents**. For example, Ashleigh, who is three, runs to the front door whenever Daddy gets home. She has recently begun running as soon as she hears his truck pull into the driveway. She has associated running to the door with the antecedent sound of the truck. Effects that follow a behavior are **consequences**. The hug she gets from her father strengthens Ashleigh's tendency to run to the door. As this suggests, paying careful attention to the "before and after" of associative learning is a key to understanding it.

Classical conditioning is a type of associative learning based on what happens *before* we respond. It begins with a stimulus that reliably triggers a behavior as a response. Imagine, for example, that a puff of air (the stimulus) is aimed at your eye. The air puff will make you blink (a response) every time. The eyeblink is a **reflex** (automatic, nonlearned response). Now,

assume that we sound a horn (another stimulus) just before each puff of air hits your eye. If the horn and the air puff occur together many times, what happens? Soon, the horn alone will make you blink. Clearly, you've learned something. Before, the horn didn't make you blink. Now it does.

In **classical conditioning**, an antecedent stimulus that doesn't produce a response is linked with one that does (a horn is associated with a puff of air to the eye, for example). We can say that learning has occurred when the new stimulus also will elicit (bring forth) responses (● **Figure 27.1**).

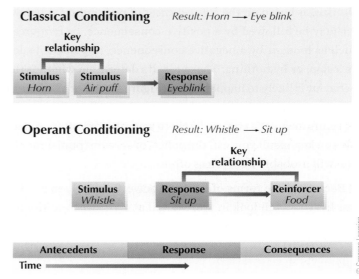

● Figure 27.1

In classical conditioning, a stimulus that does not produce a response is paired with a stimulus that does elicit a response. After many such pairings, the stimulus that previously had no effect begins to produce a response. In the example shown, a horn precedes a puff of air to the eye. Eventually, the horn alone will produce an eyeblink. In operant conditioning, a response that is followed by a reinforcing consequence becomes more likely to occur on future occasions. In the example shown, a dog learns to sit up when it hears a whistle.

Learning *Any relatively permanent change in behavior that can be attributed to experience.*

Associative learning *The formation of simple associations between various stimuli and responses.*

Cognitive learning *Higher-level learning involving thinking, knowing, understanding, and anticipation.*

Antecedents *Events that precede a response.*

Consequences *Effects that follow a response.*

Reflex *An innate, automatic response to a stimulus, for example, an eyeblink.*

Classical conditioning *A form of learning in which reflex responses are associated with new stimuli.*

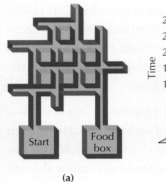

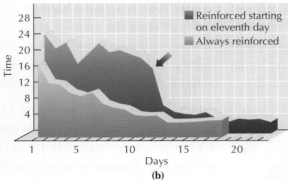

(a)   (b)

Figure 27.2

Latent learning. (*a*) The maze used by Tolman and Honzik to demonstrate latent learning by rats. (*b*) Results of the experiment. Notice the rapid improvement in performance that occurred when food was made available to the previously unreinforced animals. This indicates that learning had occurred but that it remained hidden or unexpressed. (Adapted from Tolman & Honzik, 1930.)

The other form of associative learning, **operant conditioning**, is based on the *consequences* of responding. A behavior may be followed by a positive consequence, or *reinforcer,* such as food; or by a negative consequence, or *punisher,* such as a slap; or by nothing. These results determine whether the behavior is likely to happen again (Figure 27.1). For example, if you wear a particular hat and get lots of compliments (reward or reinforcement), you are likely to wear it more often. If people snicker, insult you, call the police, or scream (punishment), you will probably wear it less often.

Because these forms of learning powerfully influence all of our lives, we will look in more detail at classical conditioning in Module 28 and operant conditioning in Modules 29 and 30.

Latent Learning

As stated previously, a core assumption of early theories of associative learning was that learning did not require any thinking, or cognition. Animals, it was widely assumed, did not have "minds" and certainly could not "think" in any way that resembles how we humans think. A classic series of studies conducted in the 1930s by University of California, Berkeley, psychologist Edward Tolman began to challenge this assumption (Olson & Hergenhahn, 2013).

In one of Tolman's experiments, two groups of rats were allowed to explore a maze. The animals in one group found food at the far end of the maze. Soon, they learned to rapidly make their way through the maze when released. Rats in the second group were unrewarded and showed no signs of learning. But later, when the "uneducated" rats were given food, they ran the maze as quickly as the rewarded group (Tolman & Honzik, 1930). Although there was no outward sign of it, the unrewarded animals had nevertheless learned their way around the maze (● **Figure 27.2**). Their learning was **latent learning**, occurring without obvious reinforcement and remaining hidden until reinforcement was provided (Davidson, 2000; Gershman & Niv, 2010).

How did the rats learn without any reinforcement? We now know that many animals (and, of course, humans) learn just to satisfy their curiosity (Harlow & Harlow, 1962). In humans, latent learning also is related to cognitive abilities, such as anticipating future reward. For example, even if you are not being reinforced for it, if you give an attractive classmate a ride home, you may make mental notes about how to get to his or her house, even if a date is only a remote future possibility.

Cognitive Maps Tolman's research made it hard to disagree that even the lowly rat—not exactly a mental giant (well, except for our Einstein)—can form *cognitive maps* to remember *where* food is found in a maze, not just which turns to make to reach the food (Tolman, Ritchie, & Kalish, 1946). A **cognitive map** is an internal representation of an area, such as a maze, city, or campus.

How do you navigate the town in which you live? Have you simply learned to make a series of right and left turns to get from one point to another? More likely, you have an overall mental picture of how the town is laid out. This cognitive map acts as a guide even when you must detour or take a new route (Foo et al., 2005; Lew, 2011).

If you have ever learned your way through some of the levels found in many video games, you will have a good idea of what constitutes a cognitive map. In a sense, cognitive maps also apply to other types of knowledge. For instance, it could be said that you have been developing a "map" of psychology while reading this book. That's why students sometimes find it helpful to draw pictures or diagrams of how they envision concepts fitting together.

Cognitive Learning— Beyond Conditioning

SURVEY QUESTION 27.3: What are some types of cognitive learning?

After Edward Tolman's trailblazing maze studies, the focus of psychology began to shift from mechanical, associative theories to theories which accepted that not all learning requires external reinforcement or punishment. As humans, we are greatly affected by information, expectations, perceptions, mental images, and the like. Today, there is no doubt that human learning includes a large *cognitive,* or mental, dimension (Goldstein, 2011; Lefrançois, 2012).

As noted earlier, cognitive learning extends beyond basic conditioning into the realms of memory, thinking, problem solving, and language. Because these topics are covered in later modules, our discussion here is limited to a first look at learning beyond conditioning. Consider, for example, the cognitive concept of *feedback.*

Feedback

Her eyes are driven and blazing and her body contorts. One hand jerks up and down while the other one furiously spins in circular motions. Does this describe some strange neurological disorder? Actually, it depicts little Nikki as she plays a Wii animated fishing adventure.

How did Nikki learn the complex movements needed to excel at virtual fishing? After all, she was not rewarded with food or money. The answer lies in the fact that Nikki's video game provides **feedback**, a key element that underlies cognitive learning. Feedback—information about the effect a response had—is particularly important in human cognitive learning (Lefrançois, 2012).

Every time a player does something, a video game responds instantly with sounds, animated actions, and a higher or lower score. The machine's responsiveness and the information flow it provides can be very motivating if you want to win. The same principle applies to many other learning situations: If you are trying to learn to use a computer, to play a musical instrument, to cook, to play a sport, or to solve math problems, receiving feedback that you achieved a desired result can be reinforcing in its own right.

The adaptive value of feedback helps explain why much human learning occurs in the absence of obvious reinforcers, such as food or water. Humans readily learn responses that merely have a desired effect or that bring a goal closer. Let's explore this idea further.

Knowledge of Results Imagine that you are asked to throw darts at a target. Each dart must pass over a screen that prevents you from telling if you hit the target. If you threw 1,000 darts, we would expect little improvement in your performance because no feedback is provided. Nikki's video game did not explicitly reward her for correct responses. Yet, because it provided feedback, rapid learning took place.

How can feedback be applied? Increased feedback—also called **knowledge of results**—almost always improves learning and performance (Snowman & McCown, 2012; Vojdanoska, Cranney, & Newell, 2010). If you want to learn to play a musical instrument, to sing, to speak a second language, or to deliver a speech, recorded feedback can be very helpful. In sports, video replays are used to provide feedback on everything from tennis serves to pick-off moves in baseball. Whenever you are trying to learn a complex skill, it pays to get more feedback (Eldridge, Saltzman, & Lahav, 2010; Jaehnig & Miller, 2007). (Also see "Learning and Conservation.")

Learning Aids *How can feedback be applied?* Because increased feedback almost always improves learning and performance, it makes sense to design learning aids to supply effective feedback (Snowman & McCown, 2012). Feedback is most effective when it is *frequent, immediate,* and *detailed.* **Programmed instruction** teaches students in a format that presents information in small amounts, gives immediate practice, and provides continuous feedback to learners. Frequent feedback keeps learners from practicing errors. It also lets students work at their own pace.

Operant conditioning *Learning based on the consequences of responding.*

Latent learning *Learning that occurs without obvious reinforcement and that remains unexpressed until reinforcement is provided.*

Cognitive map *Internal images or other mental representations of an area (maze, city, campus, and so forth) that underlie an ability to choose alternative paths to the same goal.*

Feedback *Information returned to a person about the effects a response has had; also known as knowledge of results.*

Knowledge of results (KR) *Informational feedback.*

Programmed instruction *Any learning format that presents information in small amounts, gives immediate practice, and provides continuous feedback to learners.*

Discovering Psychology

Learning and Conservation

Psychologists enjoy helping people solve practical problems. One area of behavior much in need of attention is our "throw-away" society. We burn fossil fuels; destroy forests; use chemical products; and strip, clear, and farm the land. In doing so, we alter the very face of the Earth. What can be done?

One approach involves changing the *consequences* of wasteful energy use, polluting, and the like. For example, energy taxes can be used to increase the cost of using fossil fuels. On the reinforcement side of the equation, rebates can be offered for installing insulation or buying energy-efficient appliances or cars, and tax breaks can be given to companies that take steps to preserve the environment. Recycling also is more effective when entire families participate, with some family members (usually Mom, of course) reinforcing the recycling behavior of other family members (Meneses & Beerlipalacio, 2005).

Feedback also is important. Environmental psychologists have long known that a lack of prompt feedback is a major barrier to conservation (Carrico & Riemer, 2010; McCalley, de Vries, & Midden, 2011). When families, work groups, factories, and dorms receive feedback on a weekly basis about how much they recycled, they typically recycle more. New tools, such as *ecological footprint calculators,* make it much easier for individuals to get feedback about their individual resource consumption (Global Footprint Network, 2012b). With growing public concern over global warming, many people are now calculating their individual *carbon footprint,* the volume of greenhouse gases their individual consumption adds to the atmosphere (The Nature Conservancy, 2013).

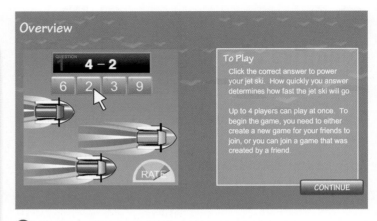

Figure 27.3

Computer-assisted instruction. To increase interest and motivation, this math game allows students to compete in a speedboat race rather than just complete a series of subtraction problems. The more quickly correct answers are selected, the faster the student's boat speeds toward the finish line. (Screenshot from "Island Chase Subtraction." http://www.arcademicskillbuilders.com/games/island_chase/island_chase.html. Copyright © 2012, Arcademics. Reprinted by permission.)

partner, sound effects, and rich computer graphics to increase interest and motivation (Charsky, 2010; Connolly et al., 2012; see ● **Figure 27.3**).

Educational *simulations,* the most complex serious games, allow students to explore an imaginary situation or "microworld" to learn to solve real-world problems (● **Figure 27.4**). By seeing the effects of their choices, students discover basic principles in a variety of subjects (Helle & Säljö, 2012; Herold, 2010).

To get a sense of the programmed instruction format, finish reading this module and complete the *Knowledge Builder* when you encounter it (just like you do with *all* of the Knowledge Builders you come across, right?). Work through the *Recite* questions one at a time, checking your answer before moving on. In this way, your correct (or incorrect) responses will be followed by immediate feedback.

Today, programmed instruction is often presented via computer (Davis, 2011; Mayer, 2011). You may know it as CAI *(computer-assisted instruction)* or drill-and-practice (or, affectionately, drill-and-kill). In addition to giving learners immediate feedback, the computer can give hints about why an answer was wrong and what is needed to correct it (Jaehnig & Miller, 2007). Increasingly, CAI programs called *serious games* are using game formats such as stories, competition with a

Figure 27.4

Boeing 747 Airline Training Simulator. Student pilots can learn all the ins and outs of flying a jumbo jet in this flight simulator. Aren't you glad they don't have to do that with real planes (and passengers)? Your authors sure are!

CAI software can save teachers and learners much time and effort, although the final level of skill or knowledge gained is not necessarily higher. In addition, people often do better with feedback from a computer because they can freely make mistakes and learn from them (Mayer, 2011; Ward & Parr, 2010).

Discovery Learning

Much of what is meant by cognitive learning is summarized by the word *understanding*. Each of us has, at times, learned ideas by **rote learning**—mechanical repetition and memorization. Although rote learning can be efficient, many psychologists believe that learning is more lasting and flexible when people *discover* facts and principles on their own. In **discovery learning**, skills are gained by insight and understanding instead of by rote (Snowman & McCown, 2012).

As long as learning occurs, what difference does it make if it is by discovery or by rote? ● **Figure 27.5** illustrates the difference. Two groups of students were taught to calculate the area of a parallelogram by multiplying the height by the length of the base. Some were encouraged to see that a "piece" of a parallelogram could be "moved" to create a rectangle. Later, they were better able to solve unusual problems in which the height times base formula didn't seem to work. Students who simply memorized a rule were confused by similar problems (Wertheimer, 1959). As this implies, discovery can lead to a better understanding of new or unusual problems.

When possible, people should try new strategies and discover new solutions during learning. However, this doesn't mean that students are supposed to stumble around and rediscover the principles of math, physics, or chemistry. The best teaching strategies are based on *guided discovery*, in which students are given enough freedom to actively think about problems and enough guidance so that they gain useful knowledge (Mayer, 2004, 2011).

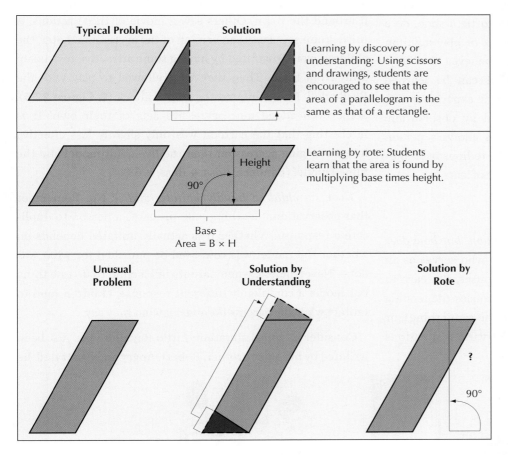

Typical Problem **Solution**

Learning by discovery or understanding: Using scissors and drawings, students are encouraged to see that the area of a parallelogram is the same as that of a rectangle.

Height
90°
Base
Area = B × H

Learning by rote: Students learn that the area is found by multiplying base times height.

Unusual Problem **Solution by Understanding** **Solution by Rote**

?
90°

● **Figure 27.5**

Learning by understanding and by rote. For some types of learning, understanding may be superior, although both types of learning are useful. (Adapted from Wertheimer, 1959.)

Rote learning *Learning that takes place mechanically, through repetition and memorization, or by learning rules.*
Discovery learning *Learning based on insight and understanding.*

Observational Learning— Do as I Do, Not as I Say

SURVEY QUESTION 27.4: Does learning occur by imitation?

Many skills are learned by what Albert Bandura (1971) calls **observational learning (modeling)**—watching and imitating the actions of another person or noting the consequences of those actions. We humans share the capacity for observational learning with many mammals (Tennie et al., 2010; Zentall, 2011).

Observational learning often imparts large amounts of information that would be difficult to obtain by reading instructions or memorizing rules.

The value of learning by observation is obvious: Imagine trying to *tell* someone how to tie a shoe, do a dance step, or play a guitar. Bandura believes that anything that can be learned from direct experience can be learned by observation. Often, this allows a person to skip the tedious trial-and-error stage of learning.

Observational Learning

It seems obvious that we learn by observation, but how does it occur? By observing a model—someone who serves as an example, a person may (1) learn new responses, (2) learn to carry out or avoid previously learned responses (depending on what happens to the model for doing the same thing), or (3) learn a general rule that can be applied to various situations (Lefrançois, 2012).

For observational learning to occur, several things must take place. First, the learner must pay *attention* to the model and *remember* what was done. (A beginning surgeon might be interested enough to watch an operation but unable to remember all the steps.) Next, the learner must be able to *reproduce* the modeled behavior. (Sometimes this is a matter of practice, but it may be that the learner will never be able to perform the behavior. We may admire the feats of world-class musicians, but most of us could never reproduce them, no matter how much we practiced.) If a model is *successful* at a task or *rewarded* for a response, the learner is more likely to imitate the behavior. Finally, once a new response is tried, *normal reinforcement or feedback determines whether it will be repeated thereafter.* (Notice the similarity to latent learning, described earlier.)

Imitating Models Modeling has a powerful effect on behavior. In a classic experiment, children watched an adult attack a large blow-up "Bo-Bo the Clown" doll. Some children saw an adult sit on the doll, punch it, hit it with a hammer, and kick it around the room. Others saw a movie of these actions. A third group saw a cartoon version of the aggression. Later, the children were frustrated by having some attractive toys taken away from them. Then they were allowed to play with the Bo-Bo doll. Most imitated the adult's attack (● **Figure 27.6**). Some even added new aggressive acts of their own! It is interesting that the cartoon was only slightly less effective in encouraging aggression than the live adult model and the filmed model (Bandura, Ross, & Ross, 1963).

Then, do children blindly imitate adults? No. Remember that observational learning only prepares a person to duplicate a response. Whether it is actually imitated depends on whether the model was rewarded or punished for what was done. Nevertheless, when parents tell a child to do one thing but model a completely different response, children tend to imitate what the parents *do,* and *not* what they *say.*

Consider a typical situation: Little Raymond has just been irritated by his older brother, Robert. Angry and frustrated, he

● **Figure 27.6**

A nursery school child imitates the aggressive behavior of an adult model he has just seen in a movie.

Critical Thinking

You Mean Video Games Might Be Bad for Me?

Today's kids can experience more gore in a day than most people used to experience in a lifetime, even during military combat. For example, one video game begins as zombies graphically attack a little girl, turning her into one of them. She viciously attacks her father, only to be flung several stories to her death.

What effects do such experiences have on people who play violent video games? Many reviews have concluded that violent video games increase aggressive behavior in children and young adults (Anderson, 2004; Krahé & Möller, 2010). As with television, younger children appear to be especially susceptible to fantasy violence in video games (Anderson et al., 2003; Bensley & Van Eenwyk, 2001). In fact, the more personalized, intimate experience of video games may heighten their impact (Fischer, Kastenmüller, & Greitemeyer, 2010).

Unfortunately, much of the early research may have led to overly strong conclusions (Adachi & Willoughby, 2011a; Valadez & Ferguson, 2012). For example, in one earlier study, college students played a violent *(Mortal Kombat)* or nonviolent *(PGA Tournament Golf)* video game. Next, they competed with another student (actually an actor) in a task that allowed aggression and retaliation to take place. Students who played the violent game were much more likely to aggress by punishing their competitor (Bartholow & Anderson, 2002). However, these two games differed not only in their degree of violence; they also differed in degree of competitiveness, difficulty, and pace of action.

A more recent study compared a violent action game *(Conan)* and a nonviolent racing game *(Fuel)* that were equally competitive, difficult, and fast-paced. In a subsequent task, college students who played the violent game were no more likely to be aggressive than those who played the nonviolent game (Adachi & Willoughby, 2011b). In other words, it is entirely possible that the competitiveness, difficulty, or pacing of a game influences aggression levels just as much, if not more, than the violent content of the game.

Until further research can more definitively disentangle these issues, the question of whether playing violent video games triggers aggression toward others remains unresolved. Regardless, before you write off video games altogether, read "You Mean Video Games Might Be Good for Me?" in Module 40.

swats Robert. This behavior interrupts his father Frank, who is watching television. Father promptly spanks little Raymond, saying, "This will teach you to hit your big brother." And it will. The message Frank has given the child is clear: "You have frustrated me; therefore, I will hit you." The next time little Raymond is frustrated, it won't be surprising if he imitates his father and hits his brother. (So why does everybody love Raymond, anyway?)

Thus, through modeling, children learn not only attitudes, gestures, emotions, and personality traits but fears, anxieties, and bad habits as well. For example, adolescents are much more likely to begin smoking if their parents, siblings, and friends smoke (Wilkinson & Abraham, 2004). More tragically, children who witness domestic violence are more likely to commit it themselves (Murrell, Christoff, & Henning, 2007).

Modeling and the Media

Much of what we learn, good and bad, comes from media. Today's children and young adults spend less time in the classroom than they do engaged with various media, including television, video games, movies, the Internet, music, and print (Rideout, Foehr, & Roberts, 2010). It should come as no surprise, then, that many parents and educators have worried about the effects of experiencing high levels of media violence.

Media Violence By the time the average American has graduated from high school, she or he will have "witnessed" thousands of murders and countless acts of robbery, arson, bombing, torture, and beatings. Even G-rated cartoons average 10 minutes of violence per hour (Yokota & Thompson, 2000). But does all of this media mayhem promote the observational learning of aggression? Early studies appeared to confirm that children who watch a great deal of televised violence are more prone to behave aggressively (Anderson, Gentile, & Buckley, 2007; Miller et al., 2012).

Does the same conclusion apply to video games? Children tend to imitate what they observe in all media (Kirsh, 2010). From professional wrestling (Bernthal, 2003) to rap music (Wingood et al., 2003) to video games (Carnagey & Anderson, 2004), children have plenty of opportunities to observe and imitate both the good and the bad (and the ugly?). (See "You Mean Video Games Might Be Bad for Me?")

Observational learning (modeling) *Learning achieved by watching and imitating the actions of another or noting the consequences of those actions.*
Model (in learning) *A person who serves as an example in observational learning.*

How might media violence increase aggressive behavior? We have already suggested that experiencing media violence may teach people how to be more aggressive in real life (Kirsh, 2010; Unsworth & Ward, 2001). Another possibility is that repeated exposure to media violence may desensitize people, making them less likely to react negatively to violence and hence more prone to engage in it (Funk, 2005; Krahé et al., 2011).

Either way, according to clinical psychologist Christopher Ferguson, experiencing media violence does not invariably "cause" any given person to become more aggressive. At best, it can make aggression more *likely* (Ferguson & Dyck, 2012). Many other factors, such as personality characteristics, family conflict, depression, and negative peer influences, also affect the chances that hostile thoughts will be turned into actions (Ferguson, Miguel, & Hartley, 2009).

Parents and educators who worry that violent media are turning young people into a generation of sadistic criminals can take heart from the data shown in ● **Figure 27.7**. In recent years, the violent crime rate among youth has declined, even as sales of violent video games have risen. However, none of this is to say that we should be unconcerned about the long-term

Media regularly portray violent and often incredible feats. Fortunately, only a few "jackasses" actually try to imitate them despite the usual warning: "Do not try this at home."

effects of experiencing violent media, including imitation, desensitization, and vicarious traumatization. This is especially true for younger children, who are more likely to be influenced because they don't always fully recognize that media characters and stories are fantasies (McKenna & Ossoff, 1998).

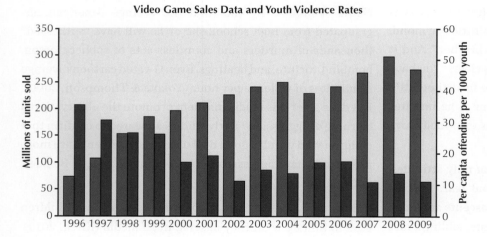

Video Game Sales Data and Youth Violence Rates

● **Figure 27.7**

This graph shows that the rate of violent crimes among youth declined between the years 1996 to 2007. Yet, during the same period, sales of violent video games increased. While correlational data such as these are not by themselves conclusive, they do help us put the issue of violence in video games into perspective. (Ferguson, C. J., & Garza, A. (2011). Call of (civic) Duty: Action games and civic behavior in a large sample of youth. Computers in Human Behavior, 27, 770–775. doi:10.1016/j.chb.2010.10.026.)

■ Video Games Units Sold
■ Youth Violence (Serious Violent Crimes)

Module 27: Summary

27.1 What is learning?

- **27.1.1** Learning is a relatively permanent change in behavior due to experience.
- **27.1.2** Associative learning is a simple type of learning that affects many aspects of daily life.
- **27.1.3** Cognitive learning involves higher mental processes, such as understanding, knowing, or anticipating.

27.2 What are some types of associative learning?

- **27.2.1** Classical conditioning and operant conditioning are two basic types of associative learning.
- **27.2.2** In classical conditioning, a neutral stimulus is followed by an unconditioned stimulus. With repeated pairings, the neutral stimulus begins to elicit a response.
- **27.2.3** In operant conditioning, responses that are followed by reinforcement occur more frequently.
- **27.2.4** In latent learning, learning remains hidden or unseen until a reward or incentive for performance is offered.
- **27.2.5** Even in relatively simple learning situations, animals and people seem to form cognitive maps (internal representations of relationships).

27.3 What are some types of cognitive learning?

- **27.3.1** Feedback, or knowledge of results, also aids learning and improves performance. It is most effective when it is immediate, detailed, and frequent.
- **27.3.2** Programmed instruction breaks learning into a series of small steps and provides immediate feedback. Computer-assisted instruction (CAI) has the added advantage of providing alternative exercises and information when needed.
- **27.3.3** Discovery learning emphasizes insight and understanding, in contrast to rote learning.

27.4 Does learning occur by imitation?

- **27.4.1** Learning can occur by merely observing and imitating the actions of another person or by noting the consequences of the person's actions.
- **27.4.2** Observational learning is influenced by the personal characteristics of the model and the success or failure of the model's behavior. Aggression can be learned and released by modeling.
- **27.4.3** Media characters can act as powerful models for observational learning. Media violence can increase the likelihood of aggression by viewers.

Module 27: Knowledge Builder

Recite

1. The concept of forming an association applies to both
   - **a.** associative and cognitive learning
   - **b.** latent and discovery learning
   - **c.** classical and operant conditioning
   - **d.** imitation and modeling

2. Learning that suddenly appears when a reward or incentive for performance is given is called
   - **a.** discovery learning
   - **c.** rote learning
   - **b.** latent learning
   - **d.** reminiscence

3. Knowledge of results also is known as _____.

4. Psychologists use the term _____ to describe observational learning.

5. If a model is successful, or rewarded, the model's behavior is
   - **a.** less difficult to reproduce
   - **b.** less likely to be attended to
   - **c.** more likely to be imitated
   - **d.** more subject to positive transfer

6. Children who observed a live adult behave aggressively became more aggressive; those who observed movie and cartoon aggression did not. **_T or F?_**

Reflect

Think Critically

7. Can you imagine different forms of feedback?

Self-Reflect

Try to think of at least one personal example of each of these concepts: cognitive map, latent learning, discovery learning, modeling.

What entertainment or sports personalities did you identify with when you were a child? How did it affect your behavior?

ANSWERS

1. c 2. b 3. feedback 4. modeling 5. c 6. F 7. Knowledge of results means you find out if your response was right or wrong. Knowledge of correct response also tells you what the correct response should have been. Elaboration feedback adds additional information, such as an explanation of the correct answer. Adding knowledge of correct response and/or some elaboration is more effective than knowledge of results alone (Jaehnig & Miller, 2007).

Learning: Classical Conditioning

The Nobel Drool

At the beginning of the twentieth century, something happened in the lab of Russian physiologist Ivan Pavlov that gained him the Nobel Prize: His subjects drooled at him. Actually, Pavlov was studying digestion by putting dogs in harnesses and placing some food tidbit on their tongues. By arranging for a tube to carry saliva from the dogs' mouths to a lever that activated a recording device, he was able to measure the resulting flow of saliva.

However, after repeating his procedure many times, Pavlov noticed that his dogs began salivating *before* the food reached their mouths. Later, the dogs even began to salivate when they saw Pavlov enter the room. Pavlov realized that some type of learning had occurred and soon began investigating "conditioning." He did this by presenting various stimuli along with a

dish of food placed next to the dog while measuring how much the dog salivated. Let's explore what he found.

SURVEY QUESTIONS

28.1 How does classical conditioning occur?

28.2 Does conditioning affect emotions?

Classical Conditioning— Does the Name Pavlov Ring a Bell?

SURVEY QUESTION 28.1: How does classical conditioning occur?

Pavlov initially believed that salivation is an automatic, inherited reflex. It really shouldn't change from one day to the next. His dogs were *supposed* to salivate when he put food in their mouths, but they were *not supposed* to salivate when they merely saw him. This change in behavior was due to experience. Because of its place in history, this form of learning is now called **classical conditioning** (also known as *Pavlovian conditioning* or *respondent conditioning*) (Schultz & Schultz, 2012).

Pavlov's Experiment

How did Pavlov study conditioning? To begin, he rang a bell. At first, the bell was a neutral stimulus (the dogs did not respond to it by salivating). Immediately after, he placed meat powder on the dogs' tongues, which caused reflex salivation. This sequence was repeated a number of times: bell, meat powder, salivation; bell, meat powder, salivation. Eventually (as conditioning took place), the dogs began to salivate when they heard the bell (● **Figure 28.1**). By association, the bell, which before had no effect, began to evoke the same response as food. This was shown by sometimes ringing the bell alone. The dogs still salivated, even though no food had been placed in their mouths.

Psychologists use several terms to describe these events. The meat powder is an **unconditioned stimulus (US)**—a stimulus innately capable of producing a response (salivation in this case). Notice that the dog did not have to learn to respond to the US. Such stimuli naturally trigger reflexes or emotional

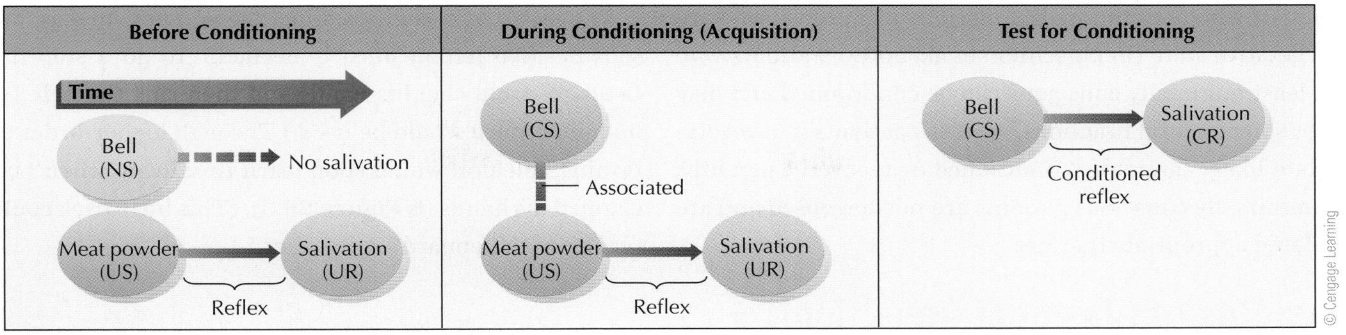

Figure 28.1
The classical conditioning procedure.

TABLE 28.1	Elements of Classical Conditioning			
Element	**Symbol**	**Description**		**Example**
Unconditioned stimulus	US	A stimulus innately capable of eliciting a response		Meat powder
Unconditioned response	UR	An innate reflex response elicited by an unconditioned stimulus		Reflex salivation *to the US*
Neutral stimulus	NS	A stimulus that does not evoke the unconditioned response		Bell *before conditioning*
Conditioned stimulus	CS	A stimulus that evokes a response because it has been repeatedly paired with an unconditioned stimulus		Bell *after conditioning*
Conditioned response	CR	A learned response elicited by a conditioned stimulus		Salivation *to the CS*

reactions. Because a reflex is innate, or "built in," it is called an **unconditioned response (UR)**, or nonlearned response. Reflex salivation was the UR in Pavlov's experiment.

The bell starts out as a **neutral stimulus (NS)**. In time, the bell becomes a **conditioned stimulus (CS)**—a stimulus that, because of learning, elicits a response. When Pavlov's bell also produced salivation, the dog was making a new response. Thus, salivation also had become a **conditioned response (CR)**, or learned response (see Figure 28.1). Table 28.1 summarizes the important elements of classical conditioning.

Are all these terms really necessary? Yes, because they help us recognize similarities in various instances of learning. Let's summarize the terms using an earlier example:

Before Conditioning	Example
US → UR	Puff of air → eye blink
NS → no effect	Horn → no effect

After Conditioning	Example
CS → CR	Horn → eye blink

As trivial as it might seem to use classical conditioning to condition blinking, it has great clinical potential (Laasonen et al.,

2012). For example, remember Kate Adamson, the courageous woman with locked-in syndrome, who we met in Module 10? Because she was totally paralyzed, doctors assumed she was brain dead. Fortunately, Kate discovered she could communicate by deliberately blinking her eyes. But what if she couldn't do even that? Worse still, what if she were only *minimally conscious* instead of brain dead (in a *vegetative state*)?

One exciting possibility is that eyeblink conditioning may be useful for distinguishing locked-in individuals from those with more severe brain damage and even severely brain-damaged

Classical conditioning *A form of learning in which reflex responses are associated with new stimuli.*
Unconditioned stimulus (US) *A stimulus innately capable of eliciting a response.*
Unconditioned response (UR) *An innate reflex response elicited by an unconditioned stimulus.*
Neutral stimulus (NS) *A stimulus that does not evoke a response.*
Conditioned stimulus (CS) *A stimulus that evokes a response because it has been repeatedly paired with an unconditioned stimulus.*
Conditioned response (CR) *A learned response elicited by a conditioned stimulus.*

individuals who are minimally conscious from those who are in a vegetative state (Bekinschtein et al., 2009). Patients who are at least minimally conscious can be conditioned and may recover some mental functions, whereas patients in a vegetative state likely cannot be conditioned or recover. Currently, some minimally conscious patients are misdiagnosed and are not offered appropriate therapy.

Principles of Classical Conditioning

Suppose a scientist named Leonard wants to study conditioning by conditioning his friend Sheldon. To observe conditioning, he could ring a bell and squirt lemon juice into Sheldon's mouth. By repeating this procedure several times, he could condition Sheldon to salivate to the bell. Sheldon might then be used to explore other aspects of classical conditioning.

Acquisition During **acquisition**, or training, a conditioned response must be established and strengthened (● **Figure 28.2**). Classical conditioning occurs when the NS is followed by, or associated with, a US. As this association is strengthened, the NS increasingly elicits the UR; it is becoming a CS capable of eliciting a CR. For Sheldon, the bell is an NS on the way to becoming a CS, the sour lemon juice is a US, and salivating is a UR on the way to becoming a CR. For the bell to elicit salivation, we must link the bell with the lemon juice. Conditioning will be most rapid if the US (lemon juice) follows *immediately* after the CS (the bell). With most classical conditioning, the optimal delay between CS and US is from ½ second to about 5 seconds (Olson & Hergenhahn, 2013).

Higher-Order Conditioning Once a response is learned, it can bring about **higher-order conditioning**. In this case, a well-learned CS is used to condition further learning (Lefrançois, 2012)—that is, the CS has become strong enough to be used like an unconditioned stimulus. Let's illustrate again with Sheldon.

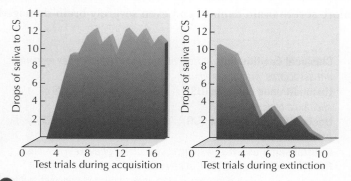

● **Figure 28.2**

Acquisition and extinction of a conditioned response. (After Pavlov, 1927.)

As a result of earlier learning, the bell now makes Sheldon salivate. (No lemon juice is needed.) To go a step further, Leonard could clap his hands and then ring the bell. (Again, no lemon juice would be used.) Through higher-order conditioning, Sheldon would soon learn to salivate when Leonard clapped his hands (● **Figure 28.3**). (This little trick could be a real hit with Leonard's colleagues.)

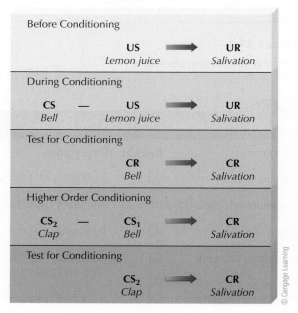

● **Figure 28.3**

Higher-order conditioning takes place when a well-learned conditioned stimulus is used as if it were an unconditioned stimulus. In this example, Sheldon is first conditioned to salivate to the sound of a bell. In time, the bell will elicit salivation. At that point, Leonard could clap his hands and then ring the bell. Soon, after repeating the procedure, Sheldon would learn to salivate when Leonard clapped his hands.

Higher-order conditioning extends learning one or more steps beyond the original conditioned stimulus. Many advertisers use this effect by pairing images that evoke good feelings (such as people, including celebrities, smiling and having fun) with pictures of their products. They hope that you will learn, by association, to feel good when you see their products (Chen, Lin, & Hsiao, 2012; Till, Stanley, & Priluck, 2008).

Expectancies Pavlov believed that classical conditioning does not involve any cognitive processes. Today, many psychologists think that classical conditioning does have cognitive origins because it is related to information that might aid survival. According to this **informational view**, we look for associations among events (Schultz & Helmstetter, 2010). Doing so creates new mental **expectancies**, or thoughts about how events are interconnected.

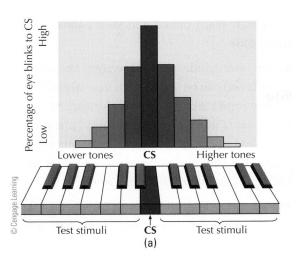

Figure 28.4

(*a*) Stimulus generalization. Stimuli similar to the CS also elicit a response. (*b*) This cat has learned to salivate when it sees a cat food box. Because of stimulus generalization, it also salivates when shown a similar-looking detergent box.

How does classical conditioning alter expectancies? Notice that the conditioned stimulus reliably precedes the unconditioned stimulus. Because it does, the CS *predicts* the US (Rescorla, 1987). During conditioning, the brain learns to *expect* that the US will follow the CS. As a result, the brain prepares the body to respond to the US. Here's an example: When you are about to get a shot with a hypodermic needle, your muscles tighten and there is a catch in your breathing. Why? Because your body is preparing for pain. You have learned to expect that getting poked with a needle will hurt. This expectancy, which was acquired during classical conditioning, changes your behavior.

Extinction and Spontaneous Recovery *Once an association has been classically conditioned, will it ever go away?* If the US stops following the CS, conditioning will fade away, or extinguish. Let's return to Sheldon. If Leonard rings the bell many times and does not follow it with lemon juice, Sheldon's expectancy that "bell precedes lemon juice" will weaken. As it does, he will lose his tendency to salivate when he hears the bell. Thus, we see that classical conditioning can be weakened by removing the connection between the conditioned and the unconditioned stimulus (see Figure 28.2). This process is called **extinction**.

If conditioning takes a while to build up, shouldn't it take time to reverse? Yes. In fact, it may take several extinction sessions to completely reverse conditioning. Let's say that Leonard rings the bell until Sheldon quits responding. It might seem that extinction is complete. However, Sheldon will probably respond to the bell again on the following day, at least at first (Rescorla, 2004). The return of a learned response after apparent extinction is called **spontaneous recovery**. It explains why people who have had a car accident may need many slow, calm rides before their fear of driving completely extinguishes.

Generalization After conditioning, other stimuli similar to the CS also may trigger a response. This is called **stimulus**

generalization. For example, Leonard might find that Sheldon salivates to the sound of a ringing telephone or doorbell, even though they were never used as conditioning stimuli.

It is easy to see the value of stimulus generalization. Consider the child who burns her finger while playing with matches. Most likely, lighted matches will become conditioned fear stimuli for her. Because of stimulus generalization, she also may have a healthy fear of flames from lighters, fireplaces, stoves, and so forth. It's fortunate that generalization extends learning to related situations. Otherwise, we would all be far less adaptable.

As you may have guessed, stimulus generalization has limits. As stimuli become less like the original CS, responding decreases. If you condition a person to blink each time you play a particular note on a piano, blinking will decline as you play higher or lower notes. If the notes are *much* higher or lower, the person will not respond at all (● **Figure 28.4**). Stimulus generalization partly explains why many stores carry imitations of nationally known products. For many customers, positive attitudes conditioned to the original products tend to generalize to the cheaper knockoffs (Till & Priluck, 2000).

Acquisition *The period in conditioning during which a response is reinforced.*

Higher-order conditioning *Classical conditioning in which a conditioned stimulus is used to reinforce further learning—that is, a CS is used as if it were a US.*

Informational view *Perspective that explains learning in terms of information imparted by events in the environment.*

Expectancy *An anticipation concerning future events or relationships.*

Extinction *The weakening of a conditioned response through removal of reinforcement.*

Spontaneous recovery *The reappearance of a learned response after its apparent extinction.*

Stimulus generalization *The tendency to respond to stimuli similar to, but not identical to, a conditioned stimulus.*

Discrimination Let's consider one more idea with Sheldon (who by now must be ready to explode in a big bang). Suppose Leonard again conditions Sheldon with a bell as the CS. As an experiment, he also occasionally sounds a buzzer instead of ringing the bell. However, the buzzer is never followed by the US (lemon juice). At first, Sheldon salivates when he hears the buzzer (because of generalization). But after Leonard sounds the buzzer several times more, Sheldon will stop responding to it. Why? In essence, Sheldon's generalized response to the buzzer has extinguished. As a result, he has learned to *discriminate,* or respond differently, to the bell and the buzzer.

Stimulus discrimination is the ability to respond differently to various stimuli. As an example, you might remember the feelings of anxiety or fear you had as a child when your mother's or father's voice changed to the dreaded put-away-that-PlayStation-controller tone. Most children quickly learn to discriminate voice tones associated with punishment from those associated with praise or affection.

Classical Conditioning in Humans—An Emotional Topic

SURVEY QUESTION 28.2: Does conditioning affect emotions?

Is much human learning actually based on classical conditioning? At its simplest, classical conditioning depends on unconditioned reflex responses. As mentioned earlier, a reflex is a dependable, inborn stimulus-and-response connection. For example, your hand reflexively draws back from pain. Bright light causes the pupils of your eyes to narrow. A puff of air directed at your eye will make you blink. Various foods elicit salivation. Any of these reflexes, and others as well, can be associated with a new stimulus. At the very least, you have probably noticed how your mouth waters when you see or smell a bakery. Even pictures of food may make you salivate (a photo of a sliced lemon is great for this).

Conditioned Emotional Responses

More complex *emotional,* or "gut," responses also may be associated with new stimuli. For instance, if your face reddened when you were punished as a child, you may blush now when you are embarrassed or ashamed. Or, think about the effects of associating pain with a dentist's office during your first visit.

On later visits, did your heart pound and your palms sweat *before* the dentist began?

Many *involuntary,* autonomic nervous system responses ("fight-or-flight" reflexes) can be linked with new stimuli and situations by classical conditioning. For example, learned reactions worsen many cases of hypertension (high blood pressure). Traffic jams, arguments with a spouse, and similar situations can become conditioned stimuli that trigger a dangerous rise in blood pressure (Reiff, Katkin, & Friedman, 1999).

Of course, emotional conditioning also applies to animals. One of the most common mistakes people make with pets (especially dogs) is hitting them if they do not come when called. Calling the animal then becomes a conditioned stimulus for fear and withdrawal. No wonder the pet disobeys when called on future occasions. Parents who belittle, scream at, or physically abuse their children make the same mistake.

Learned Fears In 1920, pioneering psychologist John Watson reported classically conditioning a young child named Little Albert to fear rats (Beck, Levinson, & Irons, 2009). Since then, it has been widely accepted that many phobias (FOE-bee-ahs) begin as a **conditioned emotional response (CER)**, or learned emotional reaction to a previously neutral stimulus (Laborda & Miller, 2011). A *phobia* is a fear that persists even when no realistic danger exists. Fears of animals, water, heights, thunder, fire, bugs, elevators, and the like are common.

People who have phobias can often trace their fears to a time when they were frightened, injured, or upset by a particular stimulus, especially in childhood (King, Muris, & Ollendick, 2005). One bad experience in which you were frightened or disgusted by a spider may condition fears that last for years (de Jong & Muris, 2002). Stimulus generalization and higher-order conditioning can spread CERs to other stimuli. As a result, what began as a limited fear may become a disabling phobia (● **Figure 28.5**).

Systematic Desensitization During a CER, an area of the brain called the amygdala becomes more active, producing feelings of fear (Schweckendiek et al., 2011). The amygdala is part of the limbic system, which is responsible for other emotions as well (see Module 10). Cognitive learning has little effect on these lower brain areas (Olsson, Nearing, & Phelps, 2007). Perhaps that's why fears and phobias cannot be readily eased by merely reading about how to control fears—as our friend Larry discovered with his rat phobia. However, conditioned fears

(a)   (b)

(c)   (d)

© Cengage Learning

🔵 **Figure 28.5**

Hypothetical example of a CER becoming a phobia. A child approaches dog (*a*) and is frightened by it (*b*). This fear generalizes to other household pets (*c*) and later to virtually all furry animals (*d*).

do respond to a therapy called **systematic desensitization**. This is done by gradually exposing the phobic person to feared stimuli while she or he remains calm and relaxed. For example, people who fear heights can be slowly taken to ever-higher elevations until their fears extinguish. Similarly, people can overcome their fear of spiders by slowly getting closer and closer to actual spiders. Systematic desensitization even works when computer graphics are used to simulate the experience of the phobic object or event (Michaliszyn et al., 2010; Price et al., 2011). (See Module 67 for more information about therapies based on learning principles.)

Undoubtedly, we acquire many of our likes, dislikes, and fears as conditioned emotional responses. As noted before, advertisers try to achieve the same effect by pairing products with pleasant images and music. So do many students on a first date.

Vicarious, or Secondhand, Conditioning

Conditioning also can occur indirectly. Let's say, for example, that you watch another person get an electric shock. Each time, a signal light comes on before the shock is delivered. Even if you don't receive a shock yourself, you will soon develop a CER to the light. Children who learn to fear thunder by watching their parents react to it have undergone similar conditioning. Many Americans were traumatized as a consequence of watching media coverage of the September 11, 2001, terrorist attacks in

New York and Washington (Blanchard et al., 2004). Similarly, people who counsel traumatized victims of sexual abuse can themselves develop vicarious trauma (Jordan, 2010).

Vicarious classical conditioning occurs when we learn to respond emotionally to a stimulus by observing another person's emotional reactions (Cohen & Collens, 2012). Such "secondhand" learning affects feelings in many situations. Being told that "snakes are dangerous" may not explain the child's *emotional* response. More likely, the child has observed others reacting fearfully to the word *snake* or to snake images on television (King, Muris, & Ollendick, 2005). That is exactly how Larry, who we met previously, developed his fear of rats. As children grow up, the emotions of parents, friends, and relatives undoubtedly add to fears of snakes, caves, spiders, heights, and other terrors. Even "horror" movies filled with screaming actors can have a similar effect.

The emotional attitudes we develop toward foods, political parties, ethnic groups, escalators—whatever—are probably conditioned not only by direct experiences but vicariously as well. No one is born prejudiced—all attitudes are learned. Parents may do well to look in a mirror if they wonder how or where a child "picked up" a particular fear or emotional attitude.

CENGAGE**brain**.com

Go to **cengagebrain.com** to access **MindTap for Coon/ Mitterer** *Psychology Modules for Active Learning* and other online learning tools. MindTap is a fully online learning experience that combines all the tools you need—readings, multimedia, activities, and assessments—into a singular personalized Learning Path that guides you through the course.

Stimulus discrimination *The learned ability to respond differently to similar stimuli.*
Conditioned emotional response (CER) *An emotional response that has been linked to a previously nonemotional stimulus by classical conditioning.*
Systematic desensitization *Reducing fear or anxiety by repeatedly exposing a person to emotional stimuli while the person is deeply relaxed.*
Vicarious classical conditioning *Classical conditioning brought about by observing another person react to a particular stimulus.*

Module 28: Summary

28.1 How does classical conditioning occur?

- **28.1.1** Classical conditioning, studied by Pavlov, occurs when a neutral stimulus (NS) is associated with an unconditioned stimulus (US).
- **28.1.2** The US causes a reflex called the unconditioned response (UR). If the NS is consistently paired with the US, it becomes a conditioned stimulus (CS) capable of producing a conditioned (learned) response (CR).
- **28.1.3** When the conditioned stimulus is repeatedly followed by the unconditioned stimulus, an association between the two is established and strengthened.
- **28.1.4** Higher-order conditioning occurs when a well-learned conditioned stimulus is used as if it were an unconditioned stimulus, bringing about further learning.
- **28.1.5** From an informational view, conditioning creates expectancies, which alter response patterns. In classical conditioning, the CS creates an expectancy that the US will follow.

- **28.1.6** When the CS is repeatedly presented alone, conditioning is extinguished (weakened or inhibited). After extinction seems to be complete, a rest period may lead to the temporary reappearance of a conditioned response. This is called spontaneous recovery.
- **28.1.7** Through stimulus generalization, stimuli similar to the conditioned stimulus also will produce a response. Generalization gives way to stimulus discrimination when an organism learns to respond to one stimulus but not to similar stimuli.

28.2 Does conditioning affect emotions?

- **28.2.1** Conditioning applies to visceral or emotional responses as well as simple reflexes. As a result, conditioned emotional responses (CERs) also occur.
- **28.2.2** Irrational fears called *phobias* may be CERs. Conditioning of emotional responses can occur vicariously (secondhand) as well as directly.

Module 28: Knowledge Builder

Recite

1. You smell the odor of cookies being baked and your mouth waters. Apparently, the odor of cookies is a _____ and your salivation is a _____.
   - **a.** CR, CS
   - **b.** CS, CR
   - **c.** consequence, neutral stimulus
   - **d.** reflex, CS

2. The informational view says that classical conditioning is based on changes in mental _____ about the CS and US.

3. After you have acquired a conditioned response, it may be weakened by repeated
   - **a.** spontaneous recovery
   - **b.** stimulus generalization
   - **c.** presentation of the CS alone
   - **d.** presentation of the CS followed by the US

4. When a conditioned stimulus is used to reinforce the learning of a second conditioned stimulus, higher-order conditioning has occurred. *T or F?*

5. Psychologists theorize that many phobias begin when a CER generalizes to other, similar situations. *T or F?*

6. Three-year-old Josh sees a neighbor's dog chase his five-year-old sister. Now Josh is as afraid of the dog as his sister is. Josh's fear is a result of
   - **a.** stimulus discrimination
   - **b.** vicarious conditioning
   - **c.** spontaneous recovery
   - **d.** higher-order conditioning

Reflect

Think Critically

7. Lately, you have been getting a shock of static electricity every time you touch a door handle. Now, you hesitate before you approach a door handle. Can you analyze this situation in terms of classical conditioning?

Self-Reflect

US, CS, UR, CR—How will you remember these terms? First, note that we are interested in either a stimulus (S) or a response (R). Each S or R can be either conditioned (C) or unconditioned (U). If a stimulus provokes a response before any learning, then it's a US. If you have to learn to respond, then it's a CS. Does a response occur without being learned? Then it's a UR. If it has to be learned, then it's a CR.

ANSWERS

Conditioning and Learning: Operant Conditioning

Shape Up!

The principles of *operant conditioning,* another form of associative learning, are among the most powerful tools in psychology. You won't regret learning how to use them. Almost all living creatures learn through operant conditioning. In fact, a few simple operant concepts explain much day-to-day behavior.

For example, operant learning is strengthened each time a response is followed by a satisfying state of affairs. Similarly, it is weakened if it is followed by an unsatisfying state of affairs. You are much more likely to keep telling a joke if people laugh at it. If the first three people frown when they hear the joke, you may not tell it again.

Operant conditioning can be used to deliberately alter the behavior of pets, children, other adults, and your own behavior.

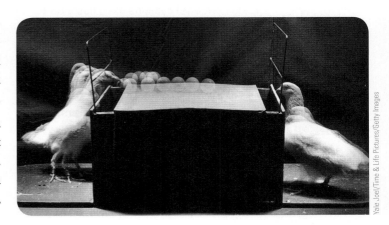

Operant principles were even used to train these pigeons to play Ping-Pong. Let's find out how.

SURVEY QUESTIONS

29.1 How does operant conditioning occur?

29.2 What is stimulus control?

Operant Conditioning— Ping-Pong Playing Pigeons?

SURVEY QUESTION 29.1: How does operant conditioning occur?

As stated previously (see Module 27), in **operant conditioning** (also known as *instrumental learning*), we associate responses with their consequences. The basic principle is simple: Acts that are followed by a positive consequence tend to be repeated (Lefrançois, 2012). A dog is much more likely to keep searching for food under a pillow if it finds food there. The dog will likely stop looking there if it fails to find food or finds something frightening. Pioneer learning theorist Edward L. Thorndike called this the **law of effect**: The probability of a response is altered by the effect it has had (Benjafield, 2012).

In operant conditioning, the learner actively "operates on" the environment. Thus, operant conditioning refers mainly to learning *voluntary* responses. For example, pushing buttons on a television remote control is a learned operant response. Pushing a particular button is reinforced by gaining the consequence you desire, such as changing channels or muting an obnoxious commercial. In contrast, classical conditioning is passive. It simply "happens to" the learner when a US follows a CS. (See ● Table 29.1 for a further comparison of classical and operant conditioning.)

Positive Reinforcement

Isn't reinforcement *another term for* reward? Not exactly. To be correct, it is better to say *reinforcer.* Why? Because rewards do not always increase responding. If you give chocolate to a child as a "reward" for good behavior, it will work only if the child likes chocolate. What is reinforcing for one person may not be for another. As a practical rule of thumb, psychologists

TABLE 29.1	Comparison of Classical and Operant Conditioning	
	Classical Conditioning	**Operant Conditioning**
Nature of response	Involuntary, reflex	Spontaneous, voluntary
Timing of learning	Occurs *before* response (CS paired with US)	Occurs *after* response (Response is followed by reinforcing stimulus or event.)
Role of learner	Passive (Response is *elicited* by US.)	Active (Response is emitted.)
Nature of learning	Neutral stimulus becomes a CS through association with a US	Probability of making a response is altered by consequences that follow it.
Learned expectancy	US will follow CS.	Response will have a specific effect.

© Cengage Learning

define an **operant reinforcer** as any event that follows a response and increases its probability of occurring again (● **Figure 29.1**).

Acquiring an Operant Response

Many studies of operant conditioning in animals use an **operant conditioning chamber (Skinner box)**, which was invented by B. F. Skinner (Skinner, 1938; ● **Figure 29.2**). The walls are bare except for a metal lever and a tray into which food pellets can be dispensed. The fact that there's not much to do in a Skinner box increases the chances that a subject will make

the desired response, which is pressing the bar. Also, hunger keeps the animal motivated to seek food and actively *emit*, or freely give off, a variety of responses. A look into a typical Skinner box will clarify the process of operant conditioning.

Einstein Snags a Snack

A smart and hungry rat (yes, it's Larry's rat Einstein) is placed in an operant conditioning chamber. For a while, Einstein walks around, grooms, sniffs at the corners, or stands on his hind legs—all typical rat behaviors. Then it happens. He places his paw on the lever to get a better view of the top of the cage. *Click!* The lever depresses, and a food pellet drops into the tray. The rat scurries to the tray, eats the pellet, and then grooms himself. Up and exploring the cage again, he leans on the lever. *Click!* After a trip to the food tray, he returns to the bar and sniffs it, and then puts his foot on it. *Click!* Soon Einstein settles into a smooth pattern of frequent bar pressing.

Day 1
doll
duh
dat

Day 5
doll
duh
dat

Day 10
doll
duh
dat

Day 20
doll
duh
dat

© Cengage Learning

● **Figure 29.1**

Assume that a child who is learning to talk points to her favorite doll and says either "doll," "duh," or "dat" when she wants it. Day 1 shows the number of times the child uses each word to ask for the doll (each block represents one request). At first, she uses all three words interchangeably. To hasten learning, her parents decide to give her the doll only when she names it correctly. Notice how the child's behavior shifts as operant reinforcement is applied. By day 20, saying "doll" has become the most probable response.

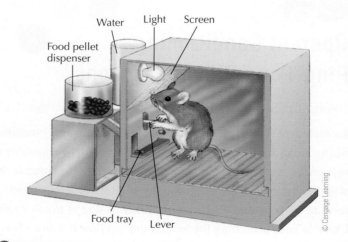

© Cengage Learning

● **Figure 29.2**

The Skinner box. This simple device, invented by B. F. Skinner, allows careful study of operant conditioning. When the rat presses the bar, a pellet of food or a drop of water is automatically released. (A photograph of a Skinner box appears in Module 3.)

Notice that the rat did not acquire a new skill in this situation. He already was able to press the bar. Reinforcement only alters how *frequently* he presses the bar. In operant conditioning, new behavior patterns are molded by changing the probability that various responses will be made.

Information and Contingency Like classical conditioning, we can think of operant learning as based on information and expectancies (Lefrançois, 2012). In operant conditioning, *we learn to expect that a certain response will have a certain effect at certain times*—that is, we learn that a particular response is associated with reinforcement. Further, operant reinforcement works best when it is *response contingent* (kon-TIN-jent)—that is, it must be given only after a desired response has occurred. From this point of view, a reinforcer tells a person or an animal that a response was "right" and worth repeating.

For example, reinforcement was used to teach, Jay, a 3-year-old autistic child, to answer questions with a "Yes" or a "No" (Shillingsburg et al., 2009). (Recall from Module 9 that autistic children have an impaired ability to communicate with other people.) If he answered "Yes" to questions like "Do you want a cookie?" (a preferred food), he was reinforced with a cookie and verbal praise. Similarly, if he answered "No" to questions like "Do you want corn?" (a nonpreferred food), he was reinforced with verbal praise. In addition, he was praised if he answered "Yes" to questions like "Does a cow say 'moo'?" or "No" to a question like (upon seeing a photo of a boat) "Is this a shoe?"

In similar ways, operant principles greatly affect behavior in homes, schools, and businesses. It is always worthwhile to arrange reinforcers so that they encourage productive and responsible behavior.

The Timing of Reinforcement

Operant reinforcement is most effective when it rapidly follows a correct response (Powell & Honey, 2013). For rats in a Skinner box, little or no learning occurs if the delay between bar pressing and receiving food exceeds 50 seconds (● **Figure 29.3**). In general, you will be most successful if you present a reinforcer *immediately* after a response you want to change. Thus, a child who is helpful or courteous should be immediately praised for her good behavior. In fact, tight timing is all that is required for learning to occur. (See "Are We Less Superstitious Than Pigeons?")

Let's say I work hard all semester in a class to get an A. Wouldn't the delay in reinforcement keep me from learning anything? No, for several reasons. First, as a mature human, you

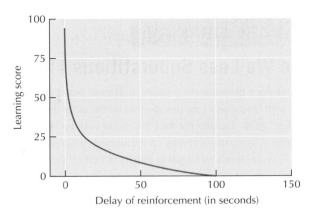

Figure 29.3

The effect of delay of reinforcement. Notice how rapidly the learning score drops when reward is delayed. Animals learning to press a bar in a Skinner box showed no signs of learning if food reward following a bar press took more than 100 seconds.

can anticipate future reward. Second, you get reinforced by quiz and test grades all through the semester. Third, a single reinforcer can often maintain a long **response chain**—a linked series of actions that lead to reinforcement.

An example of response chaining is provided by the sport of dog agility training. Dogs are taught to navigate a variety of obstacles. These include jumping over hurdles, walking over seesaws, climbing up and jumping off inclined walls, and running through tunnels made of cloth (Helton, 2007, 2009). During competitions, a trainer can reinforce a dog with a snack or a hug only after the dog completes the entire response chain. The winning dog is the one who finishes the course with the fewest mistakes and the fastest time. (Good dog!)

Many of the things we do every day involve similar response chains. The long series of events necessary to prepare a meal is rewarded by the final eating. A violinmaker may carry out thousands of steps for the final reward of hearing a first musical note. And as a student, you have built up long response chains for the final reward of getting good grades (right?).

Operant conditioning (Instrumental Learning) *Learning based on the consequences of responding.*
Law of effect *Responses that lead to desirable effects are repeated; those that produce undesirable results are not.*
Operant reinforcer *Any event that reliably increases the probability or frequency of responses it follows.*
Operant conditioning chamber (Skinner box) *An apparatus designed to study operant conditioning in animals.*
Superstitious behavior *A behavior repeated because it seems to produce reinforcement, even though it is actually unnecessary.*
Response chain *A series of actions that eventually lead to reinforcement.*

Critical Thinking

Are We Less Superstitious Than Pigeons?

Skinner once placed some pigeons in Skinner boxes and reinforced them with food every now and then no matter what they were doing (Domjan, 2010). Despite the fact that there was no real connection between their behavior and its consequences, each pigeon acted as if there were. One bird began to flap its left wing, another to hop on one leg, a third to turn around in complete circles, and so on, despite these behaviors being quite unnecessary to receive reinforcement. (Silly birds!)

But humans wouldn't behave that way, right? Don't bet on it. When Skinner did this research, he had in mind human behavior like that of a golfer who always taps her club on the ground three times before hitting a shot. This probably started because once, by chance, the golfer tapped her club three times immediately before hitting a great shot. The tapping behavior was followed by success, and was hence reinforced, even though it had nothing to do with the great shot (which was due to her correct swing). Reinforcers affect not only the specific response they follow but also other responses that occur shortly before. After happening a few more times, this golfer ended up tapping her club three times before every shot. (Silly human!)

Skinner even used the term **superstitious behavior** to describe a behavior that is repeated because it appears to produce reinforcement, even though it is unnecessary. Some examples of actual superstitious behaviors of athletes include drawing four lines in the dirt before getting in the batter's box, eating chicken before each game, and always playing in the same athletic supporter—for four years (phew!) (Brevers et al., 2011; Wright & Erdal, 2008).

Skinner's idea helps explain many human superstitions. If you walk under a ladder and then hurt yourself, you may avoid ladders in the future. Each time you avoid a ladder and nothing bad happens, your superstitious action is reinforced. Belief in magic also can be explained along such lines. Rituals to bring rain, ward off illness, or produce abundant crops likely earn the faith of participants because they occasionally appear to succeed (Abbott & Sherratt, 2011; Jahoda, 2007). So keep your fingers crossed!

Dogs must build up long response chains to compete in agility training competitions or serve as police dogs or guide dogs.

Shaping

How is it possible to reinforce responses that rarely occur? Even in a barren Skinner box, it could take a long time for a rat (even one as smart as Einstein) to accidentally press the bar and get a food pellet. We might wait forever for more complicated chains of responses to occur. For example, you would have to wait a long time for a duck to accidentally walk out of its cage, turn on a light, play a toy piano, turn off the light, and walk back to its cage. If this is what you wanted to reward, you would never get the chance.

Then, how are the animals on television and at amusement parks taught to perform complicated tricks? The answer lies in **shaping**, which is the gradual molding of responses to a desired pattern. Let's look again at our favorite rat, Einstein.

Shape Up, Einstein

Instead of waiting for Einstein's first accidental bar press, which might have taken a long time, we could have shaped his behavior. Assume that Einstein has not yet learned to press the bar. At first, we settle for just getting him to face the bar. Any time he turns toward the bar, he is reinforced with a bit of food. Soon Einstein spends much of his time facing the bar. Next, we reinforce him every time he takes a step toward the bar. If he turns toward the bar and walks away, nothing happens. But when he faces the bar and takes a step forward, *click!* His responses are being shaped.

By changing the rules about what makes a successful response, we can gradually train the rat to approach the bar and press it. In other words, *successive approximations* (ever-closer matches) to a desired response are reinforced during shaping. B. F. Skinner once taught two pigeons to play Ping-Pong in this way. Humans also can be shaped (Lamb et al., 2010). Let's say you want to study more, clean the house more often, or exercise more. In each case, it would be best to set a series of gradual, daily goals. Then you can reward yourself for small steps in the right direction (Watson & Tharp, 2014).

Operant Extinction

Would a rat stop bar pressing if no more food arrived? Yes, but not immediately. Through **operant extinction**, learned responses that are not reinforced fade away gradually. Just as acquiring an operant response takes time, so does extinction. For example, if a television program repeatedly bores you, watching the program will likely extinguish over time.

Even after extinction seems complete, the previously reinforced response may return. If a rat is removed from a Skinner box after extinction and given a short rest, the rat will press the bar again when returned to the box. Similarly, a few weeks after they give up on buying lottery tickets, many people are tempted to try again.

Does extinction take as long the second time? If reinforcement is still withheld, a rat's bar pressing will extinguish again, usually more quickly. The brief return of an operant response after extinction is another example of *spontaneous recovery* (mentioned earlier regarding classical conditioning). Spontaneous recovery is very adaptive. After a rest period, the rat responds again in a situation that produced food in the past: "Just checking to see if the rules have changed!"

Marked changes in behavior occur when reinforcement and extinction are combined. For example, parents often unknowingly reinforce children for *negative attention seeking* (using misbehavior to gain attention). Children are generally ignored when they are playing quietly. They get attention when they become louder and louder, yell "Hey, Mom!" at the top of their lungs, throw tantrums, show off, or break something. Granted, the attention they get is often a scolding, but attention is a powerful reinforcer, nevertheless. Parents report dramatic improvements when they praise or attend to a child who is quiet or playing constructively and *ignore* their children's disruptive behavior.

Negative Reinforcement

Until now, we have stressed **positive reinforcement**, which occurs when a pleasant or desirable event follows a response. How else could operant learning be reinforced? The time has come to consider **negative reinforcement**, which occurs when making a response removes an unpleasant event. Don't be fooled by the word *negative*. Negative reinforcement also increases responding. However, it does so by ending (*negating*, or taking away) discomfort.

Let's say that you have a headache and take a painkiller. Your painkiller-taking will be negatively reinforced if the headache stops. Likewise, a rat could be taught to press a bar to get food (positive reinforcement), or the rat could be given a continuous mild shock (through the floor of its cage) that is turned off by a bar press (negative reinforcement). Either way, the rat will learn to press the bar more often. Why? Because it leads to a desired state of affairs (food or an end to pain). Here are two additional examples of negative reinforcement:

- While walking outside, your hands get so cold they hurt. You take a pair of gloves out of your backpack and put them on, ending the pain. (Putting on gloves is negatively reinforced.)
- A politician who irritates you is being interviewed on the evening news. You change channels so you won't have to listen to him. (Channel changing is negatively reinforced.)

Punishment

Many people mistake negative reinforcement for punishment. However, *punishment* usually refers to following a response with an *aversive* (unpleasant) consequence. This form of punishment also is known as **positive punishment (punishment)**. Again, don't be fooled by the word *positive*. Positive punishment *decreases* the likelihood that the response will occur again. However, it does so by initiating (*adding*) discomfort. As noted, negative reinforcement *increases* responding.

The difference can be seen in a hypothetical example. Let's say you live in an apartment and your neighbor's stereo is blasting so loudly that you can't concentrate on reading this book. If you pound on the wall and the volume suddenly drops (you have been negatively reinforced), you will be more likely to pound on the wall in the future. But if you pound on the wall and the volume increases (you have been positively punished) or if the neighbor comes over and pounds on you (more positive punishment), your wall pounding becomes less likely.

Shaping *Gradually molding responses to a final desired pattern.*
Operant extinction *The weakening or disappearance of a nonreinforced operant response.*
Positive reinforcement *Occurs when a response is followed by a reward or other positive event.*
Negative reinforcement *Occurs when a response is followed by an end to discomfort or by the removal of an unpleasant event.*
Positive punishment (punishment) *Any event that follows a response and decreases its likelihood of occurring again; the process of suppressing a response.*

TABLE 29.2   **Behavioral Effects of Various Consequences**

	Consequence of Making a Response	Example	Effect on Response Probability
Positive reinforcement	Good event begins	Food given	Increase
Negative reinforcement	Bad event ends	Pain stops	Increase
Positive punishment	Bad event begins	Pain begins	Decrease
Negative punishment (response cost)	Good event ends	Food removed	Decrease
Nonreinforcement	Nothing	—	Decrease

© Cengage Learning

Here are two more examples of positive punishment, in which an unpleasant result follows a response:

- You are driving your car too fast. You are caught in a radar trap and given a speeding ticket. Henceforth, you will be less likely to speed. (Speeding was positively punished by a fine.)
- Every time you give advice to a friend, she suddenly turns cold and distant. Lately, you've stopped offering her advice. (Giving advice was positively punished by rejection.)

Isn't it also punishing to have privileges, money, or other positive things taken away for making a particular response? Yes. Punishment also occurs when a reinforcer or positive state of affairs is removed, such as losing privileges. This second type of punishment is called **negative punishment (response cost)**. One more time, don't be fooled by the word *negative*. Negative punishment also decreases responding. However, it does so by ending (*negating*, or taking away) something pleasant.

The best-known form of response cost is *time-out*, in which children are removed from situations that normally allow them to gain reinforcement. When your parents put you in time-out by sending you to your room, they denied you the reinforcement of being with the rest of your family or hanging out with your friends. For your convenience, ● Table 29.2 summarizes five basic consequences of making a response.

Stimulus Control—Red Light, Green Light

SURVEY QUESTION 29.2: What is stimulus control?

When you are driving, your behavior at intersections is controlled by the red or green light. In similar fashion, many of the stimuli we encounter each day act like stop or go signals that guide our behavior. To state the idea more formally, stimuli that consistently precede a rewarded response tend to influence when and where the response will occur. This effect is called **stimulus control**. Notice how it works with our friend Einstein.

Lights Out for Einstein

While learning the bar-pressing response, Einstein has been in a Skinner box illuminated by a bright light. During several training sessions, the light is alternately turned on and off. When the light is on, a bar press will produce food. When the light is off, bar pressing goes unrewarded. We soon observe that the rat presses vigorously when the light is on and ignores the bar when the light is off.

In this example, the light signals what consequences will follow if a response is made. A similar example of stimulus control would be a child learning to ask for candy when her mother is in a good mood but not asking at other times. Evidence for stimulus control could be shown by turning the food delivery *on* when the light is *off*. A well-trained animal might never discover that the rules had changed (Powell & Honey, 2013). Likewise, we pick up phones that are ringing but rarely answer phones that are silent.

Generalization

Two important aspects of stimulus control are generalization and discrimination. Let's return to dogs to illustrate these concepts. First, generalization.

Is generalization the same in operant conditioning as it is in classical conditioning? Basically, yes. **Operant stimulus generalization** is the tendency to respond in the presence of stimuli similar to those that preceded operant reinforcement—that is, a reinforced response tends to be made again when similar antecedents are present.

Assume, for instance, that your dog has begun to jump up at you whenever you are eating dinner at the kitchen table. (Bad dog!) Mind you, that's because you have been rewarding its behavior with table scraps. (Bad master!) Then, your dog begins to jump up any time you sit at the kitchen table. The dog has learned that reinforcement tends to occur when you are at the kitchen table. The dog's behavior has come under stimulus control. Now, let's say that you have some other tables in your house. Because they are similar, your dog will likely jump up if you sit at any of them because the jumping response *generalized* to other tables. Similar generalization explains why children may temporarily call all men *Daddy*—much to the embarrassment of their parents.

Discrimination

Meanwhile, back at the table. . . . As stated earlier, to discriminate means to respond differently to varied stimuli. Because one table signaled the availability of reinforcement to your dog, it also began jumping up while you sat at other tables (generalization). If you do not feed your dog while sitting at any other table, the jumping response that originally generalized to them will extinguish because of *nonreinforcement*.

Carleton Ray/Photo Researchers, Inc.

Stimulus control. Operant shaping was used to teach this whale to "bow" to an audience. Fish were used as reinforcers. Notice the trainer's hand signal, which serves as a discriminative stimulus to control the performance.

Thus, your dog's jumping response is consistently rewarded in the presence of a specific table. The same response to different tables is extinguished. Through **operant stimulus discrimination**, your dog has learned to differentiate between antecedent stimuli that signal reward and nonreward. As a result, the dog's response pattern will shift to match these **discriminative stimuli**—stimuli that precede reinforced and nonreinforced responses.

Stimulus discrimination is aptly illustrated by the "sniffer" dogs that locate drugs and explosives at airports and border crossings. Operant discrimination is used to teach these dogs to recognize contraband. During training, they are reinforced only for approaching containers baited with drugs or explosives.

Stimulus discrimination also has a tremendous impact on human behavior. Learning to recognize different automobile brands, birds, animals, wines, types of music, and even the answers on psychology tests all depends, in part, on operant discrimination learning.

A discriminative stimulus with which most drivers are familiar is a police car on the freeway. This stimulus is a clear signal that a specific set of reinforcement contingencies applies. As you have probably observed, the presence of a police car brings about rapid reductions in driving speed, lane changes, and tailgating.

Would using different ringtones on my cellphone be an example of using discriminative stimuli? Excellent! Suppose you use one ringtone for people you want to speak to, one for people you don't, and yet another for calls from strangers. In no time at all, you will show different telephone-answering behavior in response to different ringtones.

Negative punishment (response cost) *Removal of a positive reinforcer after a response is made.*

Stimulus control *Stimuli present when an operant response is acquired tend to control when and where the response is made.*

Operant stimulus generalization *The tendency to respond to stimuli similar to those that preceded operant reinforcement.*

Operant stimulus discrimination *The tendency to make an operant response when stimuli previously associated with reward are present and to withhold the response when stimuli associated with nonreward are present.*

Discriminative stimuli *Stimuli that precede rewarded and nonrewarded responses in operant conditioning.*

Module 29: Summary

29.1 How does operant conditioning occur?

- **29.1.1** Operant conditioning occurs when a voluntary action is followed by a reinforcer (which increases the frequency of the response) or a punisher (which decreases the frequency of the response).

- **29.1.2** Delaying reinforcement greatly reduces its effectiveness, but a single reinforcer may maintain long chains of responses.

- **29.1.3** Superstitious behaviors often become part of response chains because they appear to be associated with reinforcement.

- **29.1.4** By rewarding successive approximations to a particular response, behavior can be shaped into desired patterns.

- **29.1.5** If an operant response is not reinforced, it may extinguish (disappear). However, after extinction seems complete, it may temporarily reappear (spontaneous recovery).

- **29.1.6** Both positive reinforcement and negative reinforcement increase the likelihood that a response will be repeated. Positive and negative punishment decreases the likelihood that the response will occur again.

29.2 What is stimulus control?

- **29.2.1** Stimuli that precede a reinforced response tend to control the response on future occasions (stimulus control). Two aspects of stimulus control are generalization and discrimination.

- **29.2.2** In generalization, an operant response tends to occur when stimuli similar to those preceding reinforcement are present.

- **29.2.3** In discrimination, responses are given in the presence of discriminative stimuli associated with reinforcement and withheld in the presence of stimuli associated with nonreinforcement.

Module 29: Knowledge Builder

Recite

1. Responses in operant conditioning are _____ or _____, whereas those in classical conditioning are passive, _____, or _____ responses.

2. Changing the rules in small steps so that an animal (or person) is gradually trained to respond as desired is called _____.

3. Extinction in operant conditioning also is subject to _____ of a response.
   - **a.** successive approximations
   - **b.** shaping
   - **c.** automation
   - **d.** spontaneous recovery

4. Positive reinforcers increase the rate of responding, and negative reinforcers decrease it. *T or F?*

5. Responding tends to occur in the presence of discriminative stimuli associated with reinforcement and tends not to occur in the presence of discriminative stimuli associated with nonreinforcement. *T or F?*

Reflect

Think Critically

6. Can you think of any reasons that engaging in superstitious behaviors might actually improve performance?

Self-Reflect

A friend of yours punishes his dog all the time. What advice would you give him about how to use reinforcement, extinction, and shaping instead of punishment?

Doors that are meant to be pushed outward have metal plates on them. Those that are meant to be pulled inward have handles. Do these discriminative stimuli affect your behavior?

ANSWERS

1. voluntary or emitted, involuntary or elicited 2. shaping 3. d 4. F 5. T 6. Even though you know tapping your club on the ground three times is not causing a better golf shot, it might nevertheless help settle you down or help you focus your attention on your swing (Damisch, Stoberock, & Mussweiler, 2010).

Conditioning and Learning:
Reinforcement and Punishment in Detail

One-Armed Bandits

Earlier, we examined reinforcement and punishment. However, if you want to influence operant learning, you need to know more about these two concepts. For example, how do different types and patterns of reinforcement affect behavior? Imagine that a mother wants to reward her child for turning off the lights when he leaves a room. Contrary to what you might think, it is better to reinforce only some of her son's correct responses. Why should this be so? You'll find the answer in this module, along with the secret of slot machines.

Spankings, reprimands, fines, jail sentences, firings, failing grades, and the like also are commonly used to control behavior. Unfortunately, too many people tend to rely exclusively on punishment to shape operant behavior. Yet, punishment, especially severe punishment, is worth avoiding, if

Eric Raptosh Photography/Blend Images/Getty Images

at all possible. Why? Clearly, the story of operant learning is unfinished without a return to the topic of punishment.

SURVEY QUESTIONS

30.1 Are there different types of operant reinforcement?

30.2 How are we influenced by patterns of reward?

30.3 What does punishment do to behavior?

Types of Operant Reinforcement—What's Your Pleasure?

SURVEY QUESTION 30.1: Are there different types of operant reinforcement?

For humans, learning may be reinforced by anything from a candy bar to a word of praise. In categorizing reinforcers, a useful distinction can be made between *primary reinforcers* and *secondary reinforcers*.

Primary Reinforcers

Primary reinforcers produce comfort, end discomfort, or fill an immediate physical need: They are natural, nonlearned, and rooted in biology. Food, water, and sex are obvious examples. Every time you open the refrigerator, walk to a drinking fountain, turn up the heat, or order a double latte, your actions reflect primary reinforcement.

In addition to obvious examples, there are other, less obvious, primary reinforcers, such as psychoactive drugs. One of the most powerful reinforcers is *intracranial self-stimulation,* which involves the direct activation of "pleasure centers" in the brain. (See "Tickling Your Own Fancy.")

Brainwaves

Tickling Your Own Fancy

Suppose you could have an electrode implanted in your brain and connected to a remote control. Slide the controller upward and electrical impulses stimulate one of your brain's "pleasure centers." The few humans who have had a chance to try direct brain stimulation report feeling intense pleasure that is better than food, water, sex, drugs, or any other primary reinforcer (Heath, 1963; ● **Figure 30.1**).

Most of what we know about such intracranial self-stimulation comes from studying rats with similar implants (Vlachou & Markou, 2011). A rat "wired for pleasure" can be trained to press the bar in a Skinner box to deliver electrical stimulation to its own limbic system (refer to Figure 30.1). Some rats will press the bar thousands of times per hour to obtain brain stimulation. After 15 or 20 hours of constant pressing, animals sometimes collapse from exhaustion. When they revive, they begin pressing again. If the reward circuit is not turned off, an animal will ignore food, water, and sex in favor of bar pressing.

Many natural primary reinforcers activate the same pleasure pathways in the brain that make intracranial self-stimulation so powerful (Powell & Honey, 2013). So do psychoactive drugs, such as alcohol and cocaine (Galankin, Shekunova, & Zvartau, 2010; Rodd et al., 2005). In fact, rats also will self-administer nicotine. When they do, they are even more likely to engage in intracranial self-stimulation (Kenny & Markou, 2006). Apparently, nicotine further increases the sensitivity of pleasure pathways in the brain.

© Cengage Learning

● **Figure 30.1**

Humans have been "wired" for brain stimulation, as shown in (*a*). However, in humans, this has been done only as an experimental way to restrain uncontrollable outbursts of violence. Implants have not been done merely to produce pleasure. Most research has been carried out with rats. Using the apparatus shown in (*b*), the rat can press a bar to deliver mild electric stimulation to a "pleasure center" in the brain.

One shudders to think what might happen if brain implants were easy and practical to do. (They are not.) Every company from Playboy to Microsoft would have a device on the market, and we would have to keep a closer watch on politicians than usual!

Secondary Reinforcers

Although human learning is still strongly tied to food, water, and other primary reinforcers, humans also respond to a much broader range of rewards and reinforcers. Money, praise, attention, approval, success, affection, grades, and the like, all serve as learned or **secondary reinforcers**.

How does a secondary reinforcer gain its ability to promote learning? Some secondary reinforcers are simply associated with a primary reinforcer. For example, if you want to train a dog to follow you ("heel") when you take a walk, you could reward the dog with small food treats for staying near you. If you praise the dog each time you give it a treat, praise will become a secondary reinforcer. In time, you will be able to skip giving treats and simply praise your pup for doing the right thing. The same principle applies to children. One reason that parents' praise becomes a secondary reinforcer is because it is frequently associated with food, candy, hugs, and other primary reinforcers.

Tokens and Token Economies Secondary reinforcers that can be *exchanged* for primary reinforcers gain their value more directly (Powell & Honey, 2013). Printed money obviously has little or no value of its own. You can't eat it, drink it, or sleep with it. However, it can be exchanged for food, water, lodging, and other necessities.

A **token reinforcer** is a tangible secondary reinforcer, such as money, gold stars, poker chips, and the like. In a series of classic experiments, chimpanzees were taught to work for tokens. The chimps were first trained to put poker chips into a vending machine (● **Figure 30.2**). Each chip dispensed a few grapes or raisins. Once the animals had learned to exchange tokens for food, they would learn new tasks to earn the chips. To maintain the value of the tokens, the chimps were occasionally allowed to use the "Chimp-O-Mat" (Cowles, 1937).

A major advantage of tokens is that they don't lose reinforcing value as quickly as primary reinforcers. For instance, if you use candy to reinforce a developmentally disabled child

Figure 30.2

Poker chips normally have little or no value for chimpanzees, but this chimp will work hard to earn them once he learns that the "Chimp-O-Mat" will dispense food in exchange for them.

for correctly naming things, the child might lose interest when he or she is no longer hungry. It would be better to use tokens as immediate rewards for learning. Later, the child can exchange tokens for candy, toys, or other treats.

Token economies, systems for managing and altering behavior through reinforcement of selected responses, have been used with troubled children and adults in special programs and even in ordinary school classrooms (Alberto & Troutman, 2013; Maggin et al., 2011; ● Figure 30.3). In each case, the goal is to provide an immediate reward for learning. Typically, tokens may be exchanged for food, special privileges, or trips to movies, amusement parks, and so forth. Many parents find that tokens greatly reduce discipline problems with younger children. For example, children can earn points or gold stars during the week for good behavior. If they earn enough tokens, they are allowed on the weekend to choose one item out of a grab bag of small prizes.

Social Reinforcers

As we have noted, learned desires for attention and approval, which are called **social reinforcers**, often influence human behavior. This fact can be used in a classic, if somewhat mischievous, demonstration.

Shaping a Teacher

For this activity, about one-half (or more) of the students in a classroom must participate. First, select a target behavior. This should be something like "lecturing from the right side of the room." (Keep it simple, in case your teacher is a slow learner.) Begin training in this way: Each time the instructor turns toward the right or takes a step in that direction, participating students should look *really* interested. Also, smile, ask questions, lean forward, and make eye contact. If the teacher turns to the left or takes a step in that direction, participating students should lean back, yawn, check out their split ends, close their eyes, or generally look bored. Soon, without being aware of why, the instructor should be spending most of his or her time each class period lecturing from the right side of the classroom.

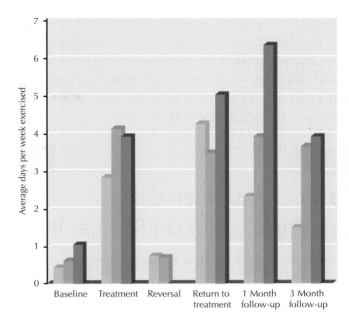

Figure 30.3

Reinforcement in a token economy. Children with cystic fibrosis (a hereditary lung disease) benefit from exercise that clears blocked airways. This graph shows the effects of using tokens to reward aerobic exercise in three children with cystic fibrosis. The number of minutes of aerobic exercise each day was measured. Tokens earned could be exchanged for rewards such as going to see a movie or staying up past bedtime. The graph shows that all three children exercised relatively infrequently without the reinforcement (*baseline* and *reversal* phases) and relatively more when the reinforcement was in place (*training* and return to *treatment* phases). It is encouraging to note that exercise rates remained heightened for months after the token economy was first implemented. (Adapted from Bernard, Cohen, & Moffett, 2009.)

This trick has been a favorite of psychology graduate students for decades. For a time, one of your author's professors delivered all her lectures from the right side of the room while toying with the cords on the window shades. (The students added the cords the second week!) The point to remember from this example is that attention and approval can change

Primary reinforcers *Nonlearned reinforcers; usually those that satisfy physiological needs.*
Secondary reinforcer *A learned reinforcer; often one that gains reinforcing properties by association with a primary reinforcer.*
Token reinforcer *A tangible secondary reinforcer such as money, gold stars, poker chips, and the like.*
Social reinforcer *Reinforcement based on receiving attention, approval, or affection from another person.*

the behavior of children, family members, friends, roommates, and coworkers. Be aware of what you are reinforcing. Also be aware that you may be *unaware* of some of the reinforcers that are changing your own behavior! (In fact, such automatic associative learning is a hallmark of experiential processing, but more about that is included in Module 37.)

Partial Reinforcement— Las Vegas, a Human Skinner Box?

SURVEY QUESTION 30.2: How are we influenced by patterns of reward?

Until now, we have treated operant reinforcement as if it were continuous. **Continuous reinforcement** means that a reinforcer follows every correct response. At the start, continuous reinforcement is useful for learning new responses (Chance, 2014). To teach your dog to come to you, it is best to reinforce your dog every time it comes when called. Curiously, once your dog has learned to come when called, it is best to shift to **partial reinforcement**, in which reinforcers do not follow every response. Responses acquired by partial reinforcement are highly resistant to extinction, a phenomenon known as the **partial reinforcement effect** (Chance, 2014; Horsley et al., 2012).

How does getting reinforced part of the time make a habit stronger? If you have ever visited a casino, you have probably seen row after row of people playing slot machines. To gain insight into the distinction between continuous and partial reinforcement, imagine that you put a dollar in a slot machine and pull the handle. Ten dollars spills into the tray. Let's say this continues for several minutes. Every pull is followed by a payoff. Because you are being reinforced on a continuous schedule, you quickly "get hooked" (and begin to plan your retirement). But, alas, suddenly each pull is followed by nothing. Obviously, you would respond several times more before giving up. However, when continuous reinforcement is followed by extinction, the message quickly becomes clear: No more payoffs (or early retirement).

Contrast this with partial reinforcement. This time, imagine that you put a dollar in a slot machine five times without a payoff. You are just about to quit, but decide to play once more. Bingo! The machine returns $20. After this, payoffs continue on a partial schedule; some are large, and some are

small. All are unpredictable. Sometimes you hit two in a row, and sometimes 20 or 30 pulls go unrewarded. Now let's say the payoff mechanism is turned off again. How many times do you think you would respond this time before your handle-pulling behavior is extinguished? Because you have developed the expectation that any play may be "the one," it will be hard to resist just one more play . . . and one more . . . and one more. Also, because partial reinforcement might include long periods of nonreward, it will be harder to distinguish between periods of reinforcement and extinction. It is no exaggeration to say that the partial reinforcement effect has left many people penniless. Even psychologists visiting a casino may get "cleaned out." (Not your authors, of course!)

To return to our examples, after using continuous reinforcement to teach a child to turn off the lights or a dog to come when called, it is best to shift to partial reinforcement. That way, the new behavior will become more *resistant to extinction* (Horsley et al., 2012).

Schedules of Partial Reinforcement

Partial reinforcement can be given in several patterns, or partial **schedules of reinforcement**—plans for determining which responses will be reinforced (Chance, 2014). Let's consider the four most basic, which have some interesting effects on us. Typical responses to each pattern are shown in ⬤ **Figure 30.4**. Results such as these are obtained when a recorder is connected to a Skinner box. Rapid responding results in a steep line; a horizontal line indicates no response. Small tick marks on the lines show when a reinforcer was given.

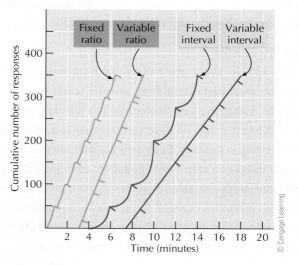

⬤ **Figure 30.4**

Typical response patterns for partial reinforcement schedules.

Fixed Ratio What would happen if a reinforcer followed only every other response? What if we followed every third, fourth, fifth, or other number of responses with reinforcement? Each of these patterns is a **fixed ratio (FR) schedule**—a set number of correct responses must be made to obtain a reinforcer. Notice that in an FR schedule, the ratio of reinforcers to responses is fixed: FR-3 means that every third response is reinforced; FR-10 means that 10 responses must be made to obtain a reinforcer.

Fixed ratio schedules produce *very high response rates* (see Figure 30.4). A hungry rat on an FR-10 schedule will quickly run off 10 responses, pause to eat, and then run off 10 more. A similar situation occurs when factory employees or farmworkers are paid on a piecework basis. When a fixed number of items must be produced for a set amount of pay, work output is high.

Variable Ratio In a **variable ratio (VR) schedule**, a varied number of correct responses must be made to get a reinforcer. Instead of reinforcing every fourth response (FR-4), for example, a person or animal on a VR-4 schedule gets rewarded *on average* every fourth response. Sometimes two responses must be made to obtain a reinforcer; sometimes it's five; sometimes four; and so on. The actual number varies, but it averages out to four (in this example). Variable ratio schedules also produce high response rates.

VR schedules seem less predictable than FR. Does that have any effect on extinction? Yes. Because reinforcement is less predictable, VR schedules tend to produce greater resistance to extinction than fixed ratio schedules. Playing a slot machine is an example of behavior maintained by a variable ratio schedule. Another would be a plan to sporadically reward a child for turning off the lights, once he or she has learned to do so. Golf, tennis, baseball, and many other sports also are reinforced on a variable ratio basis: Even the best batters in baseball rarely get a hit more than an average of three out of every ten times they are at bat.

Fixed Interval In another pattern, reinforcement is given only when a correct response is made after a fixed amount of time has passed. This time interval is measured from the last reinforced response. Responses made during the time interval are not reinforced. In a **fixed interval (FI) schedule**, the first correct response made after the time period has passed is reinforced. Thus, a rat on an FI-30-second schedule has to wait 30 seconds after the last reinforced response before a bar press will pay off again. The rat can press the bar as often as it wants during the interval, but it will not be rewarded.

Fixed interval schedules produce *moderate response rates*. Animals working on an FI schedule seem to display a keen sense of the passage of time (Zentall, 2010). Few responses occur just after a reinforcement is delivered and a spurt of activity occurs just before the next reinforcement is due. (See "Are Animals Stuck in Time?")

Is getting paid weekly an FI schedule? Pure examples of fixed interval schedules are rare, but getting paid each week at work does come close. Notice, however, that most people do not work faster just before payday, as an FI schedule predicts. A closer parallel would be having a report due every two weeks for a class. Right after turning in a paper, your work would probably drop to zero for a week or more (Chance, 2014).

Variable Interval A **variable interval (VI) schedule** is a variation on a fixed interval schedule. Here, reinforcement is given for the first correct response made after a varied amount of time. On a VI-30-second schedule, reinforcement is available after an interval that *averages* 30 seconds.

VI schedules produce *slow, steady response rates* and tremendous resistance to extinction (Lattal, Reilly, & Kohn, 1998). If you check your email every now and then while awaiting an important message, your reward (getting the message) is on a VI schedule. You may have to wait a few minutes or hours. If you are like most people, you will doggedly check over and over until you get your message. Success in fishing also is on a VI schedule—which may explain the bulldog tenacity of many anglers (Domjan, 2010).

Continuous reinforcement *A pattern in which a reinforcer follows every correct response.*
Partial reinforcement *A pattern in which only a portion of all responses are reinforced.*
Partial reinforcement effect *Responses acquired with partial reinforcement are more resistant to extinction.*
Schedules of reinforcement *Rules or plans for determining which responses will be reinforced.*
Fixed ratio (FR) schedule *A set number of correct responses must be made to get a reinforcer. For example, a reinforcer is given for every four correct responses.*
Variable ratio (VR) schedule *A varied number of correct responses must be made to get a reinforcer. For example, a reinforcer is given after three to seven correct responses; the actual number changes randomly.*
Fixed interval (FI) schedule *A reinforcer is given only when a correct response is made after a set amount of time has passed since the last reinforced response. Responses made during the time interval are not reinforced.*
Variable interval (VI) schedule *A reinforcer is given for the first correct response made after a varied amount of time has passed since the last reinforced response. Responses made during the time interval are not reinforced.*

Critical Thinking

Are Animals Stuck in Time?

We humans are *cognitive time travelers,* regularly zooming back and forth through time in our minds. You can, for example, think about past events, such as what you had for breakfast this morning. We also can imagine events in the future. But what about animals? Are they less cognitive and hence "stuck in time" (Clayton, Russell, & Dickinson, 2009)? Do dogs ever think about how hot it was yesterday or what they plan to do tomorrow? To answer such questions, psychologists have used operant conditioning as a research tool.

Conditioning studies have repeatedly shown that animals are sensitive to the passage of time (Zentall, 2010). For example, pigeons and rats reinforced on fixed interval schedules stop responding immediately after they receive a reinforcer and do not start again until just before the next scheduled reinforcement (Roberts, 2002). In one study, pigeons were put in a Skinner box with a pecking key on each wall. They quickly learned to peck only at Key 1 if it was 9:30 in the morning and at Key 3 if it was 4:00 in the afternoon (Saksida & Wilkie, 1994).

Another study focused on scrub jays. These birds are hoarders; they store excess food at different locations and then go back later to eat it. Scrub jays were allowed to hoard some nuts in one location and some worms in another. If they were released four hours later, they went directly to the worms. However, if they were released five days later, they went straight for the nuts. Worms are a scrub jay's favorite food, which explains their choice after four hours. But worms decay after a day or so, whereas nuts stay edible. It seems that the jays knew exactly where they stored each type of food and how much time had passed (Clayton, Yu, & Dickinson, 2001).

Although these studies are suggestive, they are part of an ongoing debate about animal cognition, including whether animals are stuck in time (Roberts & Roberts, 2002; Zentall, 2010). Nevertheless, be careful if you forget to feed your beloved dog, Rover, at his usual mealtime. If he has been conditioned to think it's time to eat, he may settle for your favorite flip-flops instead of dog food!

Consequences of Punishment—Putting the Brakes on Behavior

SURVEY QUESTION 30.3: What does punishment do to behavior?

Recall that **punishment** lowers the probability that a response will occur again. To be most effective, punishment must be given contingently (only after an undesired response occurs). Punishers, like reinforcers, are defined by observing

Punishers are consequences that lower the probability that a response will be made again. Receiving a traffic citation is directly punishing because the driver is delayed and reprimanded. Paying a fine and higher insurance rates add to the punishment in the form of response cost.

their effects on behavior. A **punisher** is any consequence that reduces the frequency of a target behavior.

It is not always possible to know ahead of time what will act as a punisher for a particular person. For example, when Jason's mother reprimanded him for throwing toys, he stopped doing it. In this instance, the reprimand was a punisher. However, Chris is starved for attention of any kind from his parents, who both work full-time. For Chris, a reprimand, or even a spanking, might actually reinforce toy throwing. Remember, too, that a punisher can be either the onset of an unpleasant event (*positive punishment*) or the removal of a pleasant state of affairs (*negative punishment or response cost*).

Variables Affecting Punishment

How effective is punishment? The effectiveness of punishers depends greatly on their *timing, consistency,* and *intensity.* Punishment works best when it occurs as the response is being made, or *immediately* afterward (timing), and when it is given *each time* a response occurs (consistency). Thus, if simply refusing to feed your dog table scraps is not enough to stop it from jumping at you when you sit at a table, you could effectively (and humanely) punish it by spraying water on its nose each time it jumps up. About 10 to 15 such treatments are usually enough. This would not be the case if you applied punishment haphazardly or long after the jumping stopped. If you discover that your dog dug up a tree and ate it while you were gone, punishing the dog hours later will do little good. Likewise, the commonly heard childhood threat,

"Wait 'til your father comes home, then you'll be sorry," just makes the father a feared brute; it doesn't effectively punish an undesirable response.

Severe punishment (following a response with an intensely aversive or unpleasant stimulus) can be extremely effective in stopping behavior. If 10-year-old Beavis sticks his finger in a light socket and gets a shock, that may be the last time he *ever* tries it (the little butthead!). Intense punishment may permanently suppress responding, even for actions as basic as eating.

However, mild punishment only temporarily *suppresses* a response. If the response is still reinforced, punishment may be particularly ineffective. This fact was demonstrated by slapping rats on the paw as they were bar pressing in a Skinner box. Two groups of well-trained rats were placed on extinction. One group was punished with a slap for each bar press, and the other group was not. It might seem that the slap would cause bar pressing to extinguish more quickly. Yet, this was not the case, as you can see in ● Figure 30.5. Punishment temporarily slowed responding, but it did not cause more rapid extinction. Slapping the paws of rats or children has little permanent effect on a reinforced response.

The Downside of Punishment

Are there drawbacks to using punishment? Using punishment has several drawbacks, all of which become more of a problem as punishment increases in severity. Basically, punishment is *aversive* (painful or uncomfortable). As a result, people and situations associated with punishment tend, through classical conditioning, to become feared, resented, or disliked. The aversive nature of punishment makes it an especially poor

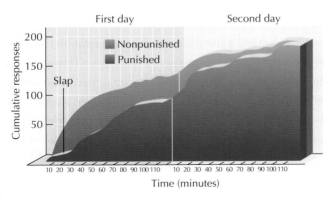

● **Figure 30.5**

The effect of punishment on extinction. Immediately after punishment, the rate of bar pressing is suppressed, but by the end of the second day, the effects of punishment have disappeared. (After B. F. Skinner, 1938.)

method to use when teaching children to eat politely or in toilet training (Miltenberger, 2012).

Escape and Avoidance A second major problem is that aversive stimuli encourage escape and avoidance learning, a regular part of daily experience (Schlund & Cataldo, 2010). In **escape learning**, we learn to make a response in order to end an aversive stimulus. For example, if you work with a loud and obnoxious person, you may at first escape from conversations with him to obtain relief. (Notice that escape learning is based on negative reinforcement.) Later, you may dodge him altogether. This is an example of **avoidance learning**)—making a response in order to postpone or prevent discomfort. Each time you sidestep him, your avoidance is again reinforced by a sense of relief. In many situations involving frequent punishment, similar desires to escape and avoid are activated. For example, children who run away from punishing parents (escape) may soon learn to lie about their behavior (avoidance) or to spend as much time away from home as possible (also an avoidance response).

Aggression A third problem with punishment is that it can greatly increase *aggression*. Animals react to pain by attacking whomever or whatever else is around. A common example is the faithful dog that nips its owner during a painful procedure at the veterinarian's office. Likewise, humans who are in pain have a tendency to lash out at others. When spanked, a child may feel angry, frustrated, and hostile. What if that child then goes outside and hits a brother, a sister, or a neighbor? The danger is that aggressive acts may feel good because they release anger and frustration. If so, aggression has been rewarded and will tend to occur again in other frustrating situations.

Studies have found that children who are physically punished are more likely to engage in aggressive, impulsive, antisocial behavior (Taylor et al., 2010). Similarly, a classic study of angry adolescent boys found that they were severely punished at home. This suppressed their misbehavior at home but made them more aggressive elsewhere. Parents were often surprised to learn that their "good boys" were in trouble for

Punishment *Any event that follows a response and decreases its likelihood of occurring again; the process of suppressing a response.*
Punisher *Any event that decreases the probability or frequency of responses it follows.*
Escape learning *Learning to make a response in order to end an aversive stimulus.*
Avoidance learning *Learning to make a response in order to postpone or prevent discomfort.*

fighting at school (Simons & Wurtele, 2010). Fortunately, at least for younger children, if parents change to less punitive parenting, their children's levels of aggression will decline (Thomas, 2004).

In the classroom, physical punishment, yelling, and humiliation also are generally ineffective. Positive reinforcement, in the form of praise, approval, and reward, is much more likely to quell classroom disruptions, defiance, and inattention (Alberto & Troutman, 2013).

Using Punishment Wisely

In light of its limitations and drawbacks, should punishment be used to control behavior? Parents, teachers, animal trainers, and the like have three basic tools to control simple learning: (1) Reinforcement strengthens responses. (2) Nonreinforcement causes responses to extinguish. (3) Punishment suppresses responses. (Consult ● **Figure 30.6** to refresh your memory about the different types of reinforcement and punishment.) These tools work best in combination. It is usually best to begin by making liberal use of positive reinforcement, especially praise, to encourage good behavior (Martin & Pear, 2011). Also, try extinction first: See what happens if you ignore a problem behavior, or shift attention to a desirable activity and then reinforce it with praise. Remember, it is much more

effective to strengthen and encourage desirable behaviors than it is to punish unwanted behaviors (Olson & Hergenhahn, 2013). When all else fails, it may be necessary to use punishment to help manage the behavior of an animal, child, or even another adult. For those times, here are some tips to keep in mind:

1. *Avoid harsh punishment.* Harsh or excessive punishment has serious negative drawbacks (never slap a child's face, for instance). "Sparing the rod" will not spoil a child. In fact, the reverse is true. As we just discussed, harsh punishment can lead to negative emotional reactions, avoidance and escape behaviors, and increased aggression (Aucoin, Frick, & Bodin, 2006; Simons & Wurtele, 2010). It can even lead to long-term mental health problems (Afifi et al., 2006).

   What about spanking? Parents should minimize spanking or avoid it entirely (Gershoff & Bitensky, 2007). Although most children show no signs of long-term damage from spanking if it is backed up by supportive parenting, emotional damage does occur if spankings are severe, frequent, or coupled with harsh parenting (Maguire-Jack, Gromoske, & Berger, 2012; Stacks et al., 2009). Like all harsh punishment, frequent spanking tends to increase aggression and leads to more problem behaviors, not fewer (Simons & Wurtele, 2010). In fact, antispanking laws have been passed in a number of countries around the world (Isaacs, 2011).

2. *Use the minimum punishment necessary to suppress misbehavior.* If punishment is used at all, it should be mild. In a situation that poses immediate danger, such as when a child reaches for something hot or a dog runs into the street, mild punishment may prevent disaster. Punishment in such cases works best when it produces actions *incompatible* with the response you want to suppress. Let's say a child reaches toward a stove burner. Would a swat on the bottom serve as an effective punisher? Probably so. It would be better, however, to slap the child's outstretched hand so that it will be *withdrawn* from the source of danger. Negative punishment (response cost) such as taking away privileges or other positive reinforcers is usually best for older children and adults. A verbal rebuke or a scolding is often enough.

3. *Apply punishment during, or immediately after, misbehavior.* Of course, immediate punishment is not always possible. With older children and adults, you can bridge the delay by clearly stating what act you are punishing. If you cannot punish an animal or young child immediately, wait for the next instance of misbehavior.

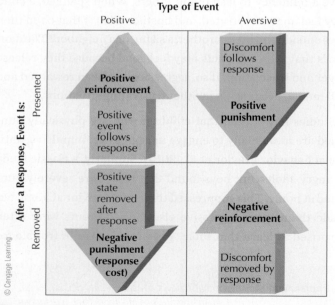

● **Figure 30.6**

Types of reinforcement and punishment. The impact of an event depends on whether it is presented or removed after a response is made. Each square defines one possibility: Arrows pointing upward indicate that responding is increased; downward-pointing arrows indicate that responding is decreased.

4. *Be consistent.* Be very clear about what you regard as misbehavior. Punish every time the misbehavior occurs. Don't punish for something one time and ignore it the next. If you are usually willing to give a child three chances, don't change the rule and explode without warning after a first offense. Both parents should try to punish their children for the same things and in the same way.

5. *Use counterconditioning.* Mild punishment tends to be ineffective if reinforcers are still available in the situation. That's why it is best to also reward an alternate, desired response. For example, Sally, who has a habit of taking toys from her sister, should not just be reprimanded for it. She should be *counterconditioned,* or rewarded, for displaying any behavior that is *counter* to the unacceptable behavior, such as cooperative play or sharing her toys. As desired behaviors become more frequent, undesired behaviors become less frequent. Sally can't very well share her toys *and* take them from her sister at the same time.

   Remember, punishment tells a person or an animal only that a response was "wrong." Punishment does not say what the "right" response is, so it *does not teach new behaviors.* If reinforcement is missing, punishment becomes less effective (Gershoff & Bitensky, 2007).

6. *Expect anger from a punished person.* Briefly acknowledge this anger, but be careful not to reinforce it. Be willing to admit your mistake if you wrongfully punish someone or if you punished too severely.

7. *Punish with kindness and respect.* Avoid punishing when you are angry. It is easy to get carried away and become abusive (Gershoff & Bitensky, 2007; Gonzalez et al., 2008). Two-thirds of child abuse cases start out as attempts at physical punishment (Trocmé et al., 2001). One way to guard against doing harm is to punish with kindness and respect. Doing so also allows the punished person to retain self-respect. For instance, do not punish a person in front of others, if possible. A strong, trusting relationship tends to minimize behavior problems. Ideally, others should want to behave well to get your praise, not because they fear punishment.

To summarize, an unfortunately common error is to rely too much on punishment for training or discipline. The overall emotional adjustment of a child or pet disciplined mainly by reward is usually superior to one disciplined mainly by punishment. Frequent punishment makes a person or an animal unhappy, confused, anxious, aggressive, and fearful (Gershoff & Bitensky, 2007; Olson & Hergenhahn, 2013).

Parents and teachers also should be aware that using punishment can be "habit forming." When children are noisy, messy, disrespectful, or otherwise misbehave, the temptation to punish them can be strong. The danger is that punishment often works. When it does, a sudden end to the adult's irritation acts as a negative reinforcer. This encourages the adult to use punishment more often in the future (Alberto & Troutman, 2013). Immediate silence may be "golden," but its cost can be very high in terms of a child's emotional health.

Module 30: Summary

30.1 Are there different types of operant reinforcement?

- **30.1.1** Operant learning may be based on primary reinforcers (which are rooted in biology) and secondary reinforcers (such as tokens and social reinforcers).
- **30.1.2** Primary reinforcers are "natural," physiologically based rewards. Intracranial stimulation of "pleasure centers" in the brain also can serve as a primary reinforcer.

- **30.1.3** Secondary reinforcers are learned. They typically gain their reinforcing value by direct association with primary reinforcers or because they can be exchanged for primary reinforcers. Tokens and money gain their reinforcing value in this way.

30.2 How are we influenced by patterns of reward?

- **30.2.1** Reward or reinforcement may be given continuously (after every response) or on a schedule of partial reinforcement. Partial reinforcement produces greater resistance to extinction.

continued

Module 30: Summary, *continued*

- **30.2.2** The four most basic partial schedules of reinforcement are fixed ratio, variable ratio, fixed interval, and variable interval. Each produces a distinct pattern of responding.

30.3 What does punishment do to behavior?

- **30.3.1** Punishment decreases response frequency.
- **30.3.2** Punishment occurs when a response is followed by the onset of an aversive event (positive punishment) or by the removal of a positive event (negative punishment or response cost).
- **30.3.3** Punishment is most effective when it is immediate, consistent, and intense.

- **30.3.4** Although severe punishment can virtually eliminate a particular behavior, mild punishment usually only temporarily suppresses responding. Reinforcement must be used to make lasting changes in the behavior of a person or an animal.
- **30.3.5** The undesirable side effects of punishment include the conditioning of fear to punishing agents and situations associated with punishment, the learning of escape and avoidance responses, and the encouragement of aggression.

Module 30: Knowledge Builder

Recite

1. Primary reinforcers are those learned through classical conditioning. ***T or F?***

2. Which is a correct match?
   - ***a.*** social reinforcer–primary reinforcement
   - ***b.*** token reinforcer–secondary reinforcement
   - ***c.*** intracranial stimulation–secondary reinforcement
   - ***d.*** negative reinforcer–punishment

3. Partial reinforcement tends to produce slower responding and reduced resistance to extinction. ***T or F?***

4. The schedule of reinforcement associated with playing slot machines and other types of gambling is
   - ***a.*** fixed ratio
   - ***b.*** variable ratio
   - ***c.*** fixed interval
   - ***d.*** variable interval

5. Negative reinforcement increases responding; punishment suppresses responding. ***T or F?***

6. Mild punishment tends to only temporarily _____ a response that also is reinforced.
   - ***a.*** enhance
   - ***b.*** aggravate
   - ***c.*** replace
   - ***d.*** suppress

7. Three undesired side effects of punishment are (1) conditioning of fear and resentment, (2) encouragement of aggression, and (3) the learning of escape or _____ responses.

Reflect

Think Critically

8. Using the concept of partial reinforcement, can you explain why inconsistent punishment is especially ineffective?

9. Escape and avoidance learning have been applied to encourage automobile seat belt use. Can you explain how?

Self-Reflect

See if you can think of at least one everyday example of the five basic schedules of reinforcement (continuous reinforcement and the four types of partial reinforcement).

Think of how you were punished as a child. Was the punishment immediate? Was it consistent? What effect did these factors have on your behavior? Was the punishment effective? Which of the side effects of punishment have you witnessed or experienced?

ANSWERS

1. F 2. B 3. F 4. B 5. T 6. d 7. avoidance **8.** An inconsistently punished response will continue to be reinforced on a partial schedule, which can make it even more resistant to extinction. **9.** Many automobiles have an unpleasant buzzer that sounds if the ignition key is turned before the driver's seat belt is fastened. Most drivers quickly learn to fasten the belt to stop the annoying sound. This is an example of escape conditioning. Avoidance conditioning is evident when a driver learns to buckle up before the buzzer sounds.

Psychology in Action: Behavioral Self-Management

Control Yourself

Marta wants to stop telling jokes that hurt others. Fatima is interested in cutting down on watching so much television. Ignacio is tired of snacking so much that he doesn't feel hungry at dinnertime. Brent is worried he is smoking too much. Jackie needs to spend more time studying. Like Marta, Fatima, Ignacio, Brent, and Jackie, do you have behaviors you would like to change? Would you like to get more exercise, attend more of those early morning classes, cut down on smoking, study longer, or read more books?

This is an invitation to use the principles of operant conditioning to carry out a self-management project of your own. Let's explore how to identify, track, and modify the behaviors you want to reduce or increase in frequency. As such, this

Lucky Business/Shutterstock.com

could be the start of one of the most personal applications of psychology in this book.

SURVEY QUESTION

31.1 How does conditioning apply to everyday problems?

Self-Management— A Rewarding Project

SURVEY QUESTION 31.1: How does conditioning apply to everyday problems?

The principles of operant conditioning can be adapted to manage your own behavior (Miltenberger, 2012; Watson & Tharp, 2014). Here's how:

1. **Choose a target behavior.** Identify the activity you want to change.

2. **Record a baseline.** Record how much time you currently spend performing the target activity, or count the number of desired or undesired responses you make each day.

3. **Establish goals.** Remember the principle of shaping, and set realistic goals for gradual improvement on each successive week. Also, set daily goals that add up to the weekly goal.

4. **Choose reinforcers.** If you meet your daily goal, what reward will you allow yourself? Daily rewards might be watching television, eating a candy bar, socializing with friends, listening to your iPod, or whatever you enjoy. Also establish a weekly reward. If you reach your weekly goal, what reward will you allow yourself? A movie? A dinner out? Some time playing a game like Guitar Hero? A weekend hike?

5. **Record your progress.** Keep accurate records of the amount of time spent each day on the desired activity or the number of times you make the desired response.

6. **Reward successes.** If you meet your daily goal, collect your reward. If you fall short, be honest with yourself and skip the reward. Do the same for your weekly goal.

7. **Adjust your plan as you learn more about your behavior.** Overall progress will reinforce your attempts at self-management.

If you have trouble thinking of rewards, remember that anything done often can serve as reinforcement. This is known as the **Premack principle**, named after David Premack, the psychologist who popularized its use. For example, if you like to watch television every night and want to study more, make it a rule not to turn on the set until you have studied for an hour (or whatever length of time you choose). Then lengthen the requirement each week. Here is a sample of Jackie's plan:

1. *Target behavior:* number of hours spent studying.
2. *Recorded baseline:* an average of 25 minutes per day for a weekly total of 3 hours.
3. *Goal for the first week:* an increase in study time to 40 minutes per day; weekly goal of 5 hours total study time. *Goal for second week:* 50 minutes per day and 6 hours per week. *Goal for third week:* 1 hour per day and 7 hours per week. *Ultimate goal:* to reach and maintain 14 hours per week study time.
4. *Daily reward for reaching goal:* 1 hour of guitar playing in the evening; no playing if the goal is not met. *Weekly reward for reaching goal:* going to a movie or buying a DVD.

Self-Recording

Even if you find it difficult to give and withhold rewards, **self-recording**—keeping records of response frequencies, a form of feedback—can make a difference all by itself. This is because we tend to react to being observed, even when we are the ones watching our own behavior. In general, when you systematically (and honestly) observe yourself, you are more likely to engage in desired behaviors and less likely to perform undesired behaviors (Fireman, Kose, & Solomon, 2003; Watson & Tharp, 2014).

Keep track of the number of times that you exercise, arrive late to class, eat vegetables, smoke a cigarette, study, watch television, drink a cappuccino, swear, or whatever you are interested in changing. A simple tally on a piece of paper will do, or you can get a small mechanical counter like those used to keep golf scores or count calories. Record keeping helps break patterns, and the feedback can be motivating as you begin to make progress.

Good Ways to Break Bad Habits

Are there any extra tips for breaking bad habits? By using the methods we have discussed, you can *decrease* unwanted behaviors, such as swearing, biting your nails, criticizing others, smoking, drinking coffee, watching too much television, or engaging in any other behavior you choose to target. However, breaking bad habits may require some additional techniques. Here are four strategies to help you change bad habits.

Alternate Responses A good strategy for change is to try to get the same reinforcement with a new response.

Example: Marta often tells jokes at the expense of others. Her friends sometimes feel hurt by her sharp-edged humor. Marta senses this and wants to change. What can she do? Usually, Marta's joke telling is reinforced by attention and approval. She could just as easily get the same reinforcement by giving other people praise or compliments. Making a change in her behavior should be easy because she will continue to receive the reinforcement she seeks.

Extinction Try to discover what is reinforcing an unwanted response and remove, avoid, or delay the reinforcement.

Example: Fatima has developed a habit of taking longer and longer "breaks" to watch television when she should be studying. Obviously, television watching is reinforcing her break taking. To improve her study habits, Fatima could delay reinforcement by studying at the library or some other location a good distance from her television.

Response Chains Break up response chains that precede an undesired behavior; this will help break the bad habit. The key idea is to scramble the chain of events that leads to an undesired response (Watson & Tharp, 2014).

Example: Most nights Ignacio comes home from work, logs in to his favorite role-playing game, and eats a whole bag of cookies or chips. He then takes a shower and changes clothes. By dinnertime, he has lost his appetite. Ignacio realizes he is substituting junk food for dinner. Ignacio could solve the problem by breaking the response chain that precedes dinner. For instance, he could shower immediately when he gets home or delay logging in until after dinner.

Cues and Antecedents Try to avoid, narrow down, or remove stimuli that elicit the bad habit.

Example: Brent wants to cut down on smoking. He can take many smoking cues out of his surroundings by removing ashtrays, matches, and extra cigarettes from his house, car, and office. Drug cravings are strongly related to cues conditioned to the drug, such as the odor of cigarettes. Brent can narrow antecedent stimuli even more. He could begin by smoking only in the lounge at work, never in his office or in his car. He could then limit his smoking to home. Then to only one room at home. Then to one chair at home. If he succeeds in getting this far, he may want to limit his smoking to only one unpleasant place, such as a bathroom, basement, or garage (Riley et al., 2002).

Contracting If you try the techniques described here and have difficulty sticking with them, you may want to try behavioral contracting. In a **behavioral contract**, you state a specific problem behavior you want to control or a goal you want to achieve. Also state the rewards you will receive, privileges you will forfeit, or punishments you must accept. The contract should be signed by you and a person you trust.

A behavioral contract can be quite motivating, especially when mild punishment is part of the agreement. Here's a classic example, reported by Nurnberger and Zimmerman (1970): A student working on his PhD had completed all requirements but his dissertation, yet for two years he had not written a single page. A contract was drawn up for him in which he agreed to meet weekly deadlines on the number of pages he would complete. To make sure he would meet the deadlines, he wrote postdated checks. These were to be forfeited if he failed to reach his goal for the week. The checks were made out to organizations he despised (the Ku Klux Klan and American Nazi Party). From the time he signed the contract until he finished his degree, the student's work output was greatly improved.

Getting Help

Attempting to manage or alter your own behavior may be more difficult than it sounds. If you feel you need more information, consult the books listed. You also will find helpful advice in Module 69. If you do try a self-modification project but find it impossible to reach your goals, be aware that professional advice is available.

Miltenberger, R. G. (2012). *Behavior modification: Principles and procedures* (5th ed.). Belmont, CA: Cengage Learning/Wadsworth.

Watson, D. L., & Tharp, R. G. (2014). *Self-directed behavior: Self-modification for personal adjustment* (10th ed.). Belmont, CA: Wadsworth.

Module 31: Summary

31.1 How does conditioning apply to everyday problems?

- **31.1.1** By applying operant conditioning principles, it is possible to change or manage your own behavior.

- **31.1.2** Four strategies that can help change bad habits are reinforcing alternative responses, promoting extinction, breaking response chains, and avoiding antecedent cues.
- **31.1.3** When managing behavior, self-reinforcement, self-recording, feedback, and behavioral contracting are all helpful.

Premack principle *Any high-frequency response can be used to reinforce a low-frequency response.*
Self-recording *Self-management based on keeping records of response frequencies.*
Behavioral contract *A formal agreement stating behaviors to be changed and consequences that apply.*

Module 31: Knowledge Builder

Recite

1. After a target behavior has been selected for reinforcement, it's a good idea to record a baseline so that you can set realistic goals for change. *T or F?*

2. Self-recording, even without the use of extra rewards, can bring about desired changes in target behaviors. *T or F?*

3. The Premack principle states that behavioral contracting can be used to reinforce changes in behavior. *T or F?*

4. A self-management plan should use the principle of shaping by setting a graduated series of goals. *T or F?*

Reflect

Think Critically

5. How does setting daily goals in a behavioral self-management program help maximize the effects of reinforcement?

Self-Reflect

Even if you don't expect to carry out a self-management project right now, outline a plan for changing your own behavior. Be sure to describe the behavior you want to change, set goals, and identify reinforcers.

ANSWERS

1. T 2. T 3. F 4. T 5. Daily performance goals and rewards reduce the delay of reinforcement, which maximizes its impact.

Memory: Memory Systems

Fuhgeddaboudit

That advice, offered New York City style, may not seem helpful at exam time. After all, the less you forget, the better, right? On the one hand, most people would be upset if they found they couldn't, for example, remember their mother. On the other hand, consider the woman pictured here. Although her mother died five years ago, she still can't "let go" and move on with her life. In a very real sense, who we are is determined by what we remember *and* what we forget.

Do you remember what you had for breakfast this morning? Or any of what happened last month? Of course you do. But how is it possible to so easily "travel back in time"? An interesting series of events must occur before we can say, "I remember." As you read this module—and others on memory and forgetting—you'll almost certainly discover ways to improve your memory.

Ansgar Photography/Corbis

SURVEY QUESTIONS

32.1 How does memory work?

32.2 What are the features of short-term memory?

32.3 What are the features of long-term memory?

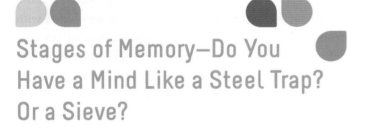

Stages of Memory—Do You Have a Mind Like a Steel Trap? Or a Sieve?

SURVEY QUESTION 32.1: How does memory work?

Many people think of memory as a passive "library of facts." In reality, human **memory** is a series of active systems that receive, store, organize, alter, and recover information (Baddeley, Eysenck, & Anderson, 2009). For information to be stored for a long time—like, say, between when you study and when you need to remember it for an exam—it must pass through three successive memories: sensory memory, short-term memory, and long-term memory.

To be remembered, information also must be encoded, stored, and retrieved in each of the three memories. Incoming information is first **encoded**, or changed into a usable form. Next, information is **stored**, or held, in the memory system. Finally, to be useful, information must be **retrieved**, or located and taken out of storage.

If you're going to remember all of the 9,856 new terms on your next psychology exam, you must successfully encode them in sensory memory, move them through short-term

Memory *The active mental system for receiving, encoding, storing, organizing, altering, and retrieving information.*
Encoding *Converting information into a form in which it will be retained in memory.*
Storage *Holding information in memory for later use.*
Retrieval *Recovering information from storage in memory.*

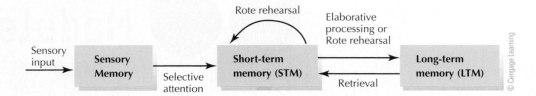

Figure 32.1

The Atkinson-Shiffrin model. Successful long-term remembering involves three stages of memory. Sensory memory encodes and stores sensory information for a second or two. Selectively attending to that information encodes small amounts in short-term memory, where it may be processed. Any resulting meaningful information may be encoded in long-term memory, where it may be stored until it is needed, at which time it may be retrieved as needed. The preceding is a useful, but highly simplified, *model* of memory; it may not be literally true regarding what happens in the brain.

memory, and eventually successfully retrieve them from long-term memory. These stages are summarized by the *Atkinson-Shiffrin model of memory*, shown in ● **Figure 32.1** (Atkinson & Shiffrin, 1968; Reed, 2013). It is well worth tracing the series of memory events that must occur before you can pass that exam. Let's start with a quick overview.

Sensory Memory

Let's say you sit down to memorize a few terms from this textbook for your exam next month. As you read, information is first automatically encoded in sensory memory, which can hold an exact copy of what you are seeing for a few seconds or less. We are normally unaware of the functioning of our sensory memories, which hold information just long enough for it to be retrieved and encoded into short-term memory (Radvansky, 2011).

For instance, look at a definition in this book and then quickly close your eyes. If you are lucky, a fleeting "photocopy" of the letters will persist. Iconic (eye-KON-ick) memories—visual sensory images—are typically stored for about a half second (Keysers et al., 2005). Similarly, when you hear information, sensory memory stores it for up to 2 seconds as an echoic memory, a brief flurry of activity in the auditory system (Cheng & Lin, 2012).

If you are *selectively attending* (focusing on a selected portion of sensory input) to the terms you are studying, they most likely will be automatically retrieved from sensory memory and encoded in short-term memory. Background events, such as a voice on the television announcing a new episode of *Honey Boo Boo*, will not. However, if you are just looking at the words on the page but not paying attention (maybe you are too busy sneaking peeks at the television), that does not bode well for your exam. As your elementary teacher might have commented, reading is more than just passing your eyes over the page.

Short-Term Memory

Even though you might normally be unaware of your sensory memory, you cannot fail to be aware of your short-term memory. Carefully read the definition contained in the next two sentences. Short-term memory (STM) stores small amounts of information. We are consciously aware of short-term memories for a dozen seconds or so (Jonides et al., 2008). That's right, what you're aware of right now *is* in your short-term memory. So, as you encode information in short-term memory, you become consciously aware of it. Back to those definitions you are studying. You pay attention to what you are reading and so become aware of the definitions when they are encoded in STM.

Working Memory Short-term memory is often used for more than just storing information. When STM is combined with other mental processes, it acts more like a sort of "mental scratchpad," or working memory, in which we do much of our thinking (Nevo & Breznitz, 2013). That is, working memory briefly holds the information we need when we are thinking and solving problems (Chein & Fiez, 2010). Whenever you read a book, do mental arithmetic, put together a puzzle, plan a meal, or follow directions, you are using working memory (Baddeley, 2012; Prime & Jolicoeur, 2010).

Long-Term Memory

If STM is so limited, how do we remember for longer periods? Information that is important or meaningful is retrieved from STM and encoded in long-term memory (LTM), which acts as a lasting storehouse for knowledge. LTM contains everything you know about the world—from aardvark to zebra, math to *The Walking Dead*, facts to fantasy. Yet, there appears to be no danger of running out of room. LTM can store nearly limitless amounts of information. In fact, the more you know, the easier it becomes to add new information to memory. This is the reverse of what we would expect if LTM could be "filled up" (Goldstein, 2011). It also is one of many reasons for getting an education.

The Relationship Between STM and LTM

Although sensory memory is involved every time we store information, we are most likely to notice STM and LTM. To summarize their connection, picture a small desk (STM) at the front of a huge warehouse full of filing cabinets (LTM). As information enters the warehouse, it is first placed on the desk. Because the desk is small, it must be quickly cleared off to make room for new information. While unimportant items are simply tossed away, personally or culturally meaningful information is placed in the files (Wang & Conway, 2004).

When we want to use knowledge from LTM to answer a question, the information is returned to STM. Or, in our analogy, a folder is retrieved from the files (LTM) and moved to the desk (STM), where it can be used. Now that you have a general picture of memory, it is time to explore STM and LTM in more detail.

Short-Term Memory—Do You Know the Magic Number?

SURVEY QUESTION 32.2: What are the features of short-term memory?

How are short-term memories encoded? Short-term memories can be encoded as images. But most often they are encoded *phonetically* (by sound), especially when it comes to words and letters (Barry et al., 2011). If you are introduced to Tim at a party and you forget his name, you are more likely to call him by a name that sounds like Tim (Jim, Kim, or Slim, for instance), rather than a name that sounds different, such as Bob or Mike. If a friend interrupts to ask what you are studying, you may be lucky if you don't say "axon potential" instead of "action potential," or "depression" instead of "repression"!

Rehearsing Information in STM

How long is a short-term memory stored? It depends, because you can prolong it by silently repeating it, a process called **maintenance rehearsal** (see Figure 32.1). In a sense, rehearsing information allows you to "hear" it many times, not just once (Tam et al., 2010). You have probably used maintenance rehearsal to keep a phone number active in your mind while looking at your cell phone and dialing it.

What if rehearsal is prevented so a memory cannot be recycled or moved to LTM? Without maintenance rehearsal, STM storage disappears rapidly. In one experiment, participants heard meaningless syllables like "xar," followed by a number like 67. As soon as participants heard the number, they began counting backward by threes (to prevent them from repeating the syllable). After a delay of between 12 and 18 seconds, their memory for the syllables fell to zero (Peterson & Peterson, 1959). That's why, when you are introduced to someone, that person's name can easily slip out of STM. To avoid embarrassment, pay careful attention to the name, rehearse it several times, and try to use it in the next sentence or two—before you lose it (Radvansky, 2011).

You also have likely noticed that STM is very sensitive to *interruption*, or *displacement*. You've probably had something like this happen: Someone gives you a phone number to call. You rehearse the number as you start to dial. He or she then asks you a question. You answer and return to dialing only to find that your memory of the number was displaced by processing the question. Because STM can handle only small amounts of information, it can be difficult to do more than one task at a time (Mercer & McKeown, 2010; Oberauer & Göthe, 2006). At the same time, this feature of short-term memory prevents our minds from more permanently storing useless names, dates, telephone numbers, and other trivia.

Sensory memory *The first, normally unconscious, stage of memory, which holds an exact record of incoming information for a few seconds or less.*

Iconic memory *A mental image or visual representation.*

Echoic memory *A brief continuation of sensory activity in the auditory system after a sound is heard.*

Short-term memory (STM) *The memory system used to hold small amounts of information in our conscious awareness for about a dozen seconds.*

Working memory *Another name for short-term memory, especially as it is used for thinking and problem solving.*

Long-term memory (LTM) *The memory system used for relatively permanent storage of meaningful information.*

Maintenance rehearsal *Silently repeating or mentally reviewing information to hold it in short-term memory.*

Isn't saying stuff to yourself over and over also a way of studying? It *is* true that the more times a short-term memory is rehearsed, the greater are its chances of being stored in LTM (Goldstein, 2011; refer to Figure 32.1). This is **rote rehearsal (rote learning)**—learning by simple repetition. But rote learning is not a very effective way to study.

Elaborative processing, which makes information more meaningful, is a far better way to form lasting memories. When encoding information for the first time, it is best to elaborate on links between that information and memories that are already in LTM. When you are studying, you will remember more if you elaborate on the meaning of the information (Raposo, Han, & Dobbins, 2009). As you read, try to reflect frequently. Ask yourself "why" questions, such as, "Why would that be true?" (Toyota & Kikuchi, 2005). Also, try to relate new ideas to your own experiences and knowledge (Karpicke & Smith, 2012). If you do not already recognize this advice, consider (re?)reading Module 1, if only to elaborate on your processing of the idea of elaborative processing.

The Capacity of Short-Term Memory

How much information can be held in short-term memory? For an answer, read the following numbers once, and then close the book and write as many as you can in the correct order.

8	5	1	7	4	9	3

This is called a *digit-span* test—a measure of attention and short-term memory. Most adults can correctly repeat about seven digits. Now try to memorize the following list, again reading it only once.

7	1	8	3	5	4	2	9	1	6	3	4

This series was likely beyond your short-term memory capacity. Psychologist George Miller found that short-term memory is limited to the "magic number" of seven (plus or minus two) **information bits** (Miller, 1956). A bit is a single meaningful "piece" of information, such as a digit. It is as if short-term memory has seven "slots" or "bins" into which separate items can be placed. A few people can remember up to nine bits, and for some types of information, five bits is the limit. Thus, an *average* of seven information bits can be stored in short-term memory (Radvansky, 2011).

When all of the "slots" in STM are filled, there is no room for new information. Picture how this works at a party: Let's say your hostess begins introducing everyone who is there, "Chun, Dasia, Sandra, Roseanna, Cholik, Shawn, Kyrene . . . ." *Stop*, you think to yourself. But she continues, "Nelia, Jay, Frank, Patty,

Amit, Ricky." The hostess leaves, satisfied that you have met everyone. You spend the evening talking with Chun, Dasia, and Ricky, the only people whose names you remember!

Chunking

Before we continue, try your short-term memory again, this time on letters. Read the following letters once, and then look away and try to write them in the proper order.

T	V	I	B	M	U	S	N	Y	M	C	A

Notice that there are twelve letters, or "bits" of information. If you studied the letters one at a time, this should be beyond the seven-item limit of STM. However, you may have noticed that some of the letters can be grouped, or *chunked*, together. For example, you may have noticed that NY is the abbreviation for New York. If so, the two bits N and Y became one chunk. **Information chunks** are made up of bits of information grouped into larger units.

Does chunking make a difference? Chunking *recodes* (reorganizes) information into units that are already in LTM. In a classic experiment that used lists like this one, people remembered best when the letters were read as familiar meaningful chunks: TV, IBM, USN, YMCA (Bower & Springston, 1970). If you recoded the letters this way, you organized them into four *chunks* of information and probably remembered the entire list. If you didn't, go back and try it again; you'll notice a big difference.

Chunking suggests that STM holds about five to seven of whatever units we are using. A single chunk could be made up of numbers, letters, words, phrases, or familiar sentences. Picture STM as a small desk again. Through chunking, we combine several items into one "stack" of information. This allows us to place seven stacks on the desk, whereas before there was room for only seven separate items. While you are studying, try to find ways to link two, three, or more separate facts or ideas into larger chunks, and your short-term memory will improve. In fact, some psychologists believe that STM may actually hold only four items, unless some chunking has occurred (Jonides et al., 2008; Mathy & Feldman, 2012).

The clear message is that creating information chunks is the key to making good use of your short-term memory (Gilchrist, Cowan, & Naveh-Benjamin, 2009; Jones, 2012). This means, for example, that it is well worthwhile to find or create meaningful chunks when you study. When meaningful organizations are elusive, even artificial ones (mnemonics; see Module 36) are better than none at all.

Speaking of meaning, let's move on to explore long-term memory.

Long-Term Memory—A Blast from the Past

SURVEY QUESTION 32.3: What are the features of long-term memory?

Are long-term memories also encoded as images or sounds? They can be. But typically, long-term memories are encoded on the basis of *meaning*. For example, try to memorize this story:

> With hocked gems financing him, our hero bravely defied all scornful laughter. "Your eyes deceive," he had said. "An egg, not a table, correctly typifies this unexplored planet." Now three sturdy sisters sought proof. Forging along, days became weeks as many doubters spread fearful rumors about the edge. At last from nowhere welcome winged creatures appeared, signifying momentous success. (Adapted from Dooling & Lachman, 1971.)

This odd story emphasizes the impact that meaning has on memory. You can, of course, memorize the words without understanding their meaning. But people given the title of the story find it much more meaningful, and memorable, than those not given a title. See if the title helps you as much as it did them: "Columbus Discovers America."

Back to your psychology exam: If you make an error in LTM, it probably will be related to meaning. For example, if you are trying to recall the phrase *test anxiety*, you are more likely to mistakenly write down *test nervousness* or *test worry* than *text anxiety* or *tent anxiety*.

One important way to gain meaning is to link information currently in STM to knowledge already stored in LTM. This makes it easier to encode in LTM and, hence, remember. For example, if you can relate the definition of *test anxiety* to a memory of a time when you or a friend were nervous about taking a test, you are more likely to remember the definition.

Now that my understanding of the definitions has been encoded in LTM, all I have to do is store them until the exam, right? While you do have to retain your understanding in LTM, don't forget that you must be able to retrieve those definitions if necessary. Tune in to Modules 34 and 35 for more on retrieval from LTM.

Storage in LTM

An electrode touched the patient's brain. Immediately, she said, "Yes, sir, I think I heard a mother calling her little boy somewhere. It seemed to be something happening years ago. It was somebody in the neighborhood in which I live." A short time later, the electrode was applied to the same spot. Again the patient said, "Yes, I hear the same familiar sounds. It seems to be a woman calling, the same lady" (Penfield, 1958). A woman made these statements while she was undergoing brain surgery. The brain has no pain receptors, so the patient was awake while her brain was electrically stimulated (● Figure 32.2). When activated, some brain areas seemed to produce vivid memories of long-forgotten events (Jacobs, Lega, & Anderson, 2012).

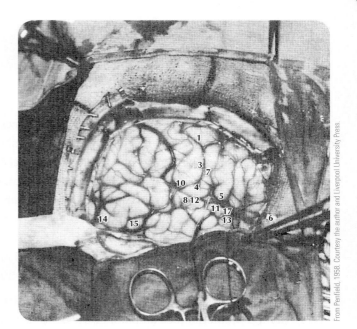

● **Figure 32.2**
Exposed cerebral cortex of a patient undergoing brain surgery. Numbers represent points that reportedly produced "memories" when electrically stimulated. A critical evaluation of such reports suggests that they are more like dreams than memories. This fact raises questions about claims that long-term memories are permanently accurate.

Rote rehearsal (rote learning) *Learning by simple repetition.*
Elaborative processing *Making memories more meaningful through processing that encodes links between new information and existing memories and knowledge, either at the time of the original encoding or on subsequent retrievals.*
Information bits *Meaningful units of information, such as numbers, letters, words, or phrases.*
Information chunks *Information bits grouped into larger units.*

Are all our experiences permanently recorded in memory? Results like those described led neurosurgeon Wilder Penfield to propose that the brain records the past like a "strip of movie film, complete with sound track" (Penfield, 1957). However, as you already know, this is an exaggeration because many events never get past sensory or short-term memory. Also, most reports of memory-like experiences resemble dreams more than memories, and many are clearly imaginary. Memory experts now believe that, except for a few rare individuals, long-term memories are only relatively permanent (Goldstein, 2011).

Try It Yourself: How's Your Memory?

To better appreciate the next topic, pause for a moment and read the words you see here. Read through the list once, and then continue reading the next section of this module.

> bed dream blanket doze pillow nap
> snore mattress alarm clock rest slumber
> nod sheet bunk cot cradle groggy

Elaborating False Memories

There's another reason to doubt that all our experiences are permanently recorded. Although elaborative processing is helpful when you're making meaningful connections between new information and what you already know, it also can lead to *memories* of things that never happened. Gaps in memory, which are common, may be filled in by logic, guessing, or new information (Schacter & Addis, 2008). The result is often the storage of new long-term memories as older memories might be revised or even lost (Baddeley, Eysenck, & Anderson, 2009).

To illustrate this point, Elizabeth Loftus and John Palmer (1974) showed people a filmed automobile accident. Afterward, some participants were asked to estimate how fast the cars were going when they "smashed" into one another. For others, the words "bumped," "contacted," or "hit" replaced "smashed." One week later, each person was asked, "Did you see any broken glass?" Those asked earlier about the cars that "smashed" into one another were more likely to say yes, even though no broken glass was shown in the film. The new information ("smashed") was incorporated into the original memories, elaborating them and producing a **false memory**. Such "memories" can seem accurate, but they never happened (such as remembering broken glass at an accident when there was none) (Loftus, 2003; Weinstein & Shanks, 2010).

Try It Yourself: Old or New?

Now, without looking back to the list of words you read a few minutes ago, see if you can tell which of the following are "old"

words (items from the list you read) and which are "new" words (items that weren't on the list). Mark each of the following words as old or new:

> sofa sleep lamp kitchen

In another study, people who had visited a Disney resort were shown several fake ads for Disney that featured Bugs Bunny. Later, about 16 percent of the people who saw these fake ads claimed that they had met Bugs at Disneyland. This is impossible, of course, because Bugs Bunny is a Warner Brothers character who would never show his face at Disneyland (Braun, Ellis, & Loftus, 2002).

Could elaborative processing be used to deliberately manipulate memory? Yup. According to one theory, advertisers do it all the time. (See "Do You Like Jam with Your Memory?")

Try It Yourself: And Now, the Results

Return now and look at the labels you wrote on the "old or new" word list. Contrary to what you may think you "remembered," all of the listed words are "new." None was on the original list!

Critical Thinking

Do You Like Jam with Your Memory?

Why do companies that sell huge quantities of extremely familiar products (such as soft drinks or beer) continue to advertise heavily? If you believe that the point of the advertising is to familiarize people with a product, it *is* a mystery. But if you think about the elaborative nature of memory, the mystery is solved. According to economist Jesse Shapiro (2006), the intent of much advertising is to "jam" your memory with positive impressions of a product.

How does "memory jamming" work? How many times have you had a bottle or can of your favorite beer or soft drink? And how many commercials for those beverages have you watched? Every commercial potentially adds one more positive memory of the beverage to your long-term memory. Here's a typical commercial: Boy goes to cool party, sees a hot girl, flashes favorite beer, gets the girl. (Yes, beer commercials mainly target young men.)

According to Shapiro (2006), the more positive fictional commercials we see, the less likely we are to remember a negative experience with a product. The end result is that you might remember that you enjoy drinking a particular beverage more than you do in reality. In effect, the positive, fictional memories "jam," or block, our ability to remember actual negative memories when deciding whether to buy a product. Jam. Yum!

If you thought you "remembered" that "sleep" was on the original list, you elaborated a false memory. The word *sleep* is associated with most of the words on the original list, which creates a strong impression that you saw it before (Roediger & McDermott, 1995).

As the preceding examples show, thoughts, inferences, and mental associations may be mistaken for true memories (Scoboria et al., 2012). False memories are a common problem in police work. For example, a witness may select a photo of a suspect from police files or see a photo in the news. Later, the witness identifies the suspect in a lineup or in court. Did the witness really remember the suspect from the scene of the crime? Or was it from the more recently seen photograph?

Eyewitness memories are notoriously inaccurate. By the time witnesses are asked to testify in court, information they learned after an incident may blend into their original memories.

Does new information always "overwrite" existing memories? No. Sometimes elaborative processing makes us vulnerable to **source confusion**, which occurs when the origins of a memory are misremembered (Fandakova, Shing, & Lindenberger, 2012; Rosa & Gutchess, 2011). This can, for example, lead witnesses to "remember" a face that they actually saw somewhere other than the crime scene (Ruva, McEvoy, & Bryant, 2007). Many tragic cases of mistaken identity occur this way. One famous example involved memory expert Donald Thomson. After appearing live on Australian television, he was accused of rape. It turns out that the victim was watching him on television when the actual rapist broke into her apartment (Schacter, 1996). She correctly remembered her attacker's face but attributed it to the wrong *source*.

To summarize, forming and using long-term memories is an active, creative, highly personal process. Our memories are colored by emotions, judgments, and quirks of personality. If you and a friend were joined at the hip and you went through life side by side, you would still have different memories. What we remember depends on what we pay attention to, what we regard as meaningful or important, how we elaborate our memory, and what we feel strongly about.

Organizing Memories

Long-term memory stores huge amounts of information during a lifetime. How are we able to quickly find specific memories? The answer is that each person's "memory index" is highly organized.

Does that mean that information is arranged alphabetically, as in a dictionary? Not usually. Information in LTM may be arranged according to rules, images, categories, symbols, similarity, formal meaning, or personal meaning (Baddeley, Eysenck, & Anderson, 2009). Psychologists believe that a **network model** best explains the *structure*, or organization, of memories. *Memory structure* refers to the pattern of associations among items of information. According to this view, LTM is organized as a network of linked ideas.

With ● **Figure 32.3** in mind, assume that Erica was given two statements to which she must quickly answer yes or no: (1) *Classical conditioning forms simple associations.* (2) *Classical conditioning is due to experience.* Which will she answer more quickly? Erica most likely will say yes that *Classical conditioning forms simple associations* faster than she can say yes that *Classical conditioning is due to experience* (Collins & Quillian, 1969).

Why should this be so? When ideas are "farther" apart, it takes a longer chain of associations to connect them. The more two items are separated, the longer it takes to answer. In terms of information links, *classical conditioning* is probably "closer" to *forms simple associations* in Erica's "memory file." *Is due to experience* and *classical conditioning* are farther apart. Remember that this has nothing to do with alphabetical order. We are talking about a system of linked meanings.

False memory *A memory that can seem accurate but is not.*
Source confusion (in memory) *Occurs when the origins of a memory are misremembered.*
Network model *A model of memory that views it as an organized system of linked information.*

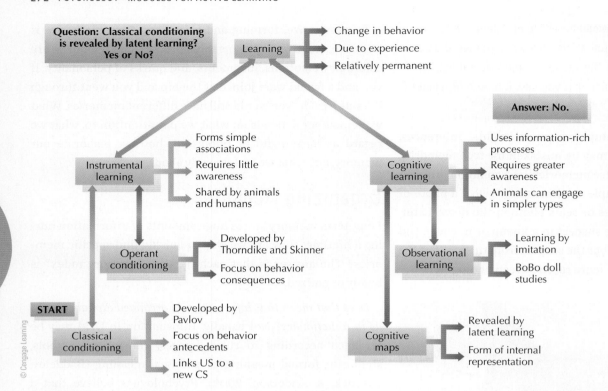

Figure 32.3

Erica, a first-year psychology major, has just completed studying for an exam on conditioning and learning. This figure presents a network model of a part of what she just learned. Small networks of ideas such as this are probably organized into larger and larger units and higher levels of meaning.

Redintegration Memory networks also may help explain a common experience: Imagine finding a picture taken on your sixth birthday or at your high school graduation. As you look at the photo, one memory leads to another, which leads to another, and another. Soon you have unleashed a flood of seemingly forgotten details. This process is called **redintegration** (reh-DIN-tuh-GRAY-shun).

The key idea in redintegration is that one memory serves as a cue to trigger another. As a result, an entire past experience may be reconstructed from one small recollection. Many people find that redintegration can be touched off by distinctive odors from the past—from a farm visited in childhood, Grandma's kitchen, the seashore, the perfume or aftershave of a former lover, and so on (Willander & Larsson,

Figure 32.4

Hypothetical networks of two students' encoding of the concept of reinforcement. Only part of Erica's more elaborated network is shown here. (See text for explanation.)

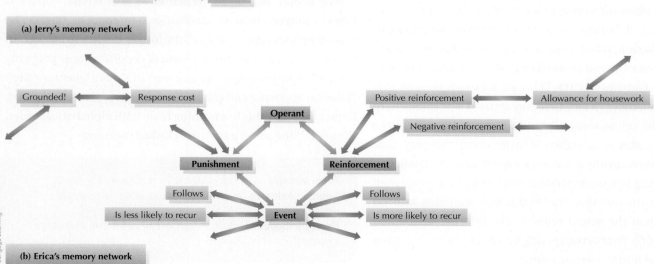

Critical Thinking

Telling Wrong from Right in Forensic Memory

Imagine you are a forensic psychologist investigating a crime. Unfortunately, your witness can't remember much of what happened. As a "memory detective," what can you do to help?

Could hypnosis improve the witness's memory? It might seem so. In one case in California, 26 children were abducted from a school bus and held captive for ransom. Under hypnosis, the bus driver recalled the license plate number of the kidnappers' van. This memory helped break the case. Such successes seem to imply that hypnosis can improve memory. But does it?

Research has shown that hypnosis increases false memories more than it reveals true ones. Eighty percent of the new memories produced by hypnotized subjects in one classic experiment were *incorrect* (Dywan & Bowers, 1983). This is in part because a hypnotized person is more likely than normal to use imagination to fill in gaps in memory. Also, if a questioner asks misleading or suggestive questions, hypnotized persons tend to elaborate the questioner's information into their memories (Scoboria et al., 2002). To make matters worse, even when a memory is completely false, the hypnotized person's confidence in it can be unshakable (Burgess & Kirsch, 1999).

Thus, hypnosis sometimes uncovers more information, as it did with the bus driver (Schreiber & Schreiber, 1999). However, in the absence of corroborating evidence, there is no sure way to tell which memories are false and which are true (Mazzoni, Heap, & Scoboria, 2010).

Is there a better way to improve eyewitness memory? To help police detectives, R. Edward Geiselman and Ron Fisher created the **cognitive interview**, a technique which uses *redintegration* to improve the memory of eyewitnesses (Fisher & Geiselman, 1987). The key to this approach is re-creating the crime scene. Witnesses revisit the scene in their imaginations or in person. That way, aspects of the crime scene, such as sounds, smells, and objects, provide helpful retrieval cues (stimuli associated with a memory). Back in the context of the crime, the witness is encouraged to recall events in different orders and from different viewpoints. Every new memory, no matter how trivial it may seem, can serve as a cue to trigger the retrieval of yet more memories.

When used properly, the cognitive interview produces 35 percent more correct information than standard questioning (Centofanti & Reece, 2006; Geiselman et al., 1986). This improvement comes without adding to the number of false memories elicited, as occurs with hypnosis (Holliday et al., 2012). The result is a procedure that is more effective in actual police work, even across cultures (Memon, Meissner, & Fraser, 2010; Stein & Memon, 2006).

2006). Redintegration has even been used to help improve the memory of witnesses. (See "Telling Wrong from Right in Forensic Memory.")

From Encoding to Retrieval in Long-Term Memory Let's get back to passing that psychology exam. On one recent exam, Jerry, another introductory psychology student, studied using rote learning, whereas Erica made extensive use of elaborative processing. ● **Figure 32.4** shows what their memory networks might look like for the concept of reinforcement (Module 29).

Because Jerry spent most of his time in rote rehearsal, his memory network for the concept of reinforcement is quite sparse. He managed to get the definition right. Also, during rote learning, it occurred to him that extra soldiers joining a battle also were reinforcements. In contrast, while studying, Erica asked herself how reinforcement and punishment differ and what were the kinds of reinforcement (and punishment); she also tried to think of personal examples. In addition, she checked out the difference between operant and respondent learning.

That means Erica has a better chance of doing well on the psychology exam, right? Much better. To begin, Jerry used rote learning, so his memories will be weaker because he cannot be as sure as Erica that he understood the concept of reinforcement. Also, suppose Jerry cannot directly retrieve the definition of reinforcement during his exam. His only other hope is to remember soldiers so that redintegration might pop up the needed definition.

In sharp contrast, for Erica to successfully encode her more elaborated network, she *had* to understand the concept of reinforcement. Hence, she is more likely than Jerry to directly retrieve that information if she needs it. On the off-chance Erica does not immediately remember the needed definition,

Redintegration *Process by which memories are reconstructed or expanded by starting with one memory and then following chains of association to other, related memories.*
Cognitive interview *Use of various cues and strategies to improve the memory of eyewitnesses.*

she has many retrieval cues to help her. Remembering punishment, or an example of reinforcement, or even the time she got grounded, could well trigger redintegration of "reinforcement."

In summary, more elaborative processing results in more elaborate memory networks and, hence, more retrieval cues to help with redintegration. Time spent in elaborative processing is time well spent, at least if you want to do well on exams.

Types of Long-Term Memory

How many types of long-term memory are there? It is becoming clear that more than one type of long-term memory exists. For example, a curious thing happens to many people who develop amnesia. Amnesic patients may be unable to learn a telephone number, an address, or a person's name. Yet, the same patients can learn to solve complex puzzles in a normal amount of time (Cavaco et al., 2004; ● **Figure 32.5**). These and other observations have led many psychologists to conclude that long-term memories fall into at least two categories (Lum & Bleses, 2012). One is called *procedural memory* (or skill memory). The other is *declarative memory* (sometimes called fact memory).

Procedural Memory
Procedural memory includes basic conditioned responses and learned actions, such as those involved in typing, driving, or swinging a golf club. Memories such as these can be fully expressed only as actions (or know-how). It is likely that skill memories register in "lower" brain areas, especially the basal ganglia and the cerebellum. They represent the more basic "automatic" elements of conditioning, learning, and memory (Freberg, 2010; Lum & Bleses, 2012).

Declarative Memory
Declarative memory stores specific factual information, such as names, faces, words, dates, and ideas. Declarative memories are expressed as words or symbols. For example, knowing that *Apple* is both a fruit and a computer company is a declarative memory. This is the type of memory that a person with amnesia lacks and that most of us take for granted. Declarative memory can be further divided into *semantic memory* and *episodic memory* (Tulving, 2002).

Semantic Memory
Much of our basic factual knowledge about the world is almost totally immune to forgetting. The names of objects, the days of the week or months of the year, simple

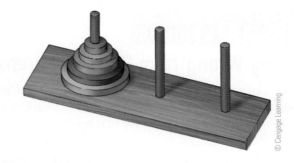

● **Figure 32.5**

The tower puzzle. In this puzzle, all the colored disks must be moved to another post without ever placing a larger disk on a smaller one. Only one disk may be moved at a time, and a disk must always be moved from one post to another (it cannot be held aside). An amnesic patient learned to solve the puzzle in 31 moves, the minimum possible. Even so, each time he began, he protested that he did not remember ever solving the puzzle before and that he did not know how to begin. Evidence like this suggests that memories for skills are distinct from memories for facts.

math skills, the seasons, words and language, and other general facts are all quite lasting. Such impersonal facts make up a part of LTM called **semantic memory**, which serves as a mental dictionary or encyclopedia of basic knowledge.

Episodic Memory
Semantic memory has no connection to times or places. It would be rare, for instance, to remember when and where you first learned the names of the seasons. In contrast, **episodic memory** (ep-ih-SOD-ik) is an "autobiographical" record of personal experiences. It stores life events (or episodes) day after day, year after year. Can you remember your seventh birthday? Your first date? What you did yesterday? All are episodic memories. Note that episodic memories are about the "what," "where," and "when" of our lives. More than simply storing information, they allow us to mentally travel back in time and *re-experience* events (Kirchhoff, 2009; Philippe, Koestner, & Lekes, 2013).

Are episodic memories as lasting as semantic memories? Either type of memory can last indefinitely. However, unless episodic memories are important, they are easily forgotten. In fact, it is the forgetting of episodic information that results in the formation of semantic memories. At first, you remembered when and where you were when you learned the names of the seasons. ("Mommy, Mommy, guess what I learned in preschool today!") Over time, you forgot the episodic details but will likely remember the names for the rest of your life.

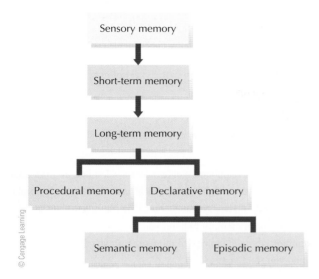

© Cengage Learning

Figure 32.6

In the model shown, long-term memory is divided into procedural memory (learned actions and skills) and declarative memory (stored facts). Declarative memories can be either semantic (impersonal knowledge) or episodic (personal experiences associated with specific times and places).

How Many Types of Long-Term Memory Exist? In answer to the question posed at the beginning of this section, it is likely that three kinds of long-term memories exist: procedural memory and two types of declarative memory, semantic and episodic (● **Figure 32.6**).

Module 32: Summary

32.1 How does memory work?

- **32.1.1** Memory is an active system that encodes, stores, and retrieves information.
- **32.1.2** The Atkinson-Shiffrin model of memory includes three stages of memory (sensory memory, short-term or working memory, and long-term memory) that hold information for increasingly longer periods.
- **32.1.3** Sensory memories are encoded as iconic memories or echoic memories.
- **32.1.4** Selective attention determines what information moves from sensory memory, which is exact but very brief, on to STM.
- **32.1.5** Short-term memories tend to be encoded by sound and are sensitive to interruption, or displacement.
- **32.1.6** Long-term memories are encoded by meaning.

32.2 What are the features of short-term memory?

- **32.2.1** Short-term memories are brief; however, they can be prolonged by maintenance rehearsal.
- **32.2.2** For transferring information to LTM, rote rehearsal is less effective than elaborative processing.
- **32.2.3** STM has a capacity of about five to seven bits of information, but this limit can be extended by chunking.

32.3 What are the features of long-term memory?

- **32.3.1** Long-term memories are relatively permanent. LTM seems to have an almost unlimited storage capacity.
- **32.3.2** Elaborative processing can have the effect of altering memories. Remembering is an active process. Our memories are frequently lost, altered, revised, or distorted.
- **32.3.3** LTM is highly organized. The structure of memory networks is the subject of current research.
- **32.3.4** In redintegration, memories are reconstructed as one bit of information leads to others, which then serve as cues for further recall.
- **32.3.5** LTM contains procedural (skill) and declarative (fact) memories. Declarative memories can be semantic or episodic.

Procedural memory *Long-term memories of conditioned responses and learned skills.*
Declarative memory *That part of long-term memory containing specific factual information.*
Semantic memory *A subpart of declarative memory that records impersonal knowledge about the world.*
Episodic memory *A subpart of declarative memory that records personal experiences that are linked with specific times and places.*

Module 32: Knowledge Builder

Recite

Match: **A.** Sensory memory **B.** STM **C.** LTM

1. _____ Information tends to be stored phonetically
2. _____ Holds information for a few seconds or less
3. _____ Stores an iconic memory or echoic memory
4. _____ Relatively permanent, unlimited capacity
5. _____ Temporarily holds small amounts of information
6. _____ Selective attention determines its contents
7. Elaborative processing is often responsible for creating false memories. *T or F?*
8. Which of the following is a synonym for skill memory?
   a. semantic memory
   b. declarative memory
   c. episodic memory
   d. procedural memory

Reflect

Think Critically

9. Why is sensory memory important to filmmakers?

Self-Reflect

In the United States, telephone numbers are divided into an area code (three digits) and a seven-digit number that is divided into three digits plus four more. Can you relate this practice to STM chunking and recoding?

How is long-term memory helping you read this sentence? If your understanding of the meanings of the words wasn't already stored in LTM, could you read at all?

Think about how you've used your memory in the last hour. Can you identify an example of each of the following: a procedural memory, a declarative memory, a semantic memory, and an episodic memory?

ANSWERS

1. B 2. A 3. A 4. C 5. B 6. B 7. T 8. D 9. Without sensory memory, a movie would look like a series of still pictures. The split-second persistence of visual images helps blend one motion-picture frame into the next.

CENGAGE brain.com

Go to **cengagebrain.com** to access **MindTap for Coon/Mitterer** *Psychology Modules for Active Learning* and other online learning tools. MindTap is a fully online learning experience that combines all the tools you need—readings, multimedia, activities, and assessments—into a singular personalized Learning Path that guides you through the course.

Memory: Measuring Memory

On the Tip of Your Tongue?

Janelle fumed as she handed in her written answers at the end of the examination. She studied hard and expected to do well. However, she was frustrated when she got to a question worth a lot of marks. She *knew* she knew the answer. It tortured her . . . for the remainder of the exam.

Perhaps you, too, have experienced this. You read an exam question and immediately the answer is on the tip of your tongue. Yet, it doesn't come to mind. You know what often happens next, right? As soon as you leave the exam, the answer "pops" into your head. (Professor, I *knew* my stuff!)

Whether you "remember" depends on how you are tested. For example, police lineups use *recognition* memory. However, unless great care is taken, false identifications are still possible.

Is the lineup pictured here fair? Let's find out more about the ins and outs of measuring memory.

SURVEY QUESTION

33.1 How is memory measured?

Measuring Memory—The Answer Is on the Tip of My Tongue

SURVEY QUESTION 33.1: How is memory measured?

You either remember something or you don't, right? Wrong. Partial memories are common. For instance, have you, like Janelle, ever tried to remember something only to find yourself stuck in a **tip-of-the-tongue (TOT) state**? This is the feeling that a memory is **available**—stored in your memory—and yet you cannot **access**—locate or retrieve—the complete memory (Brown, 2012).

In a classic TOT study, university students read the definitions of words such as *sextant, sampan,* and *ambergris.* Students who "drew a blank" and couldn't name a defined word were asked to give any other information they could. Often, they could guess the first and last letter and the number of syllables of the word they were seeking. They also gave words that sounded like or meant the same thing as the defined word (Brown & McNeill, 1966).

Closely related to the TOT state is the fact that people can often tell beforehand if they are likely to remember something. This is called the *feeling of knowing* (Thomas, Bulevich, & Dubois, 2011; Widner, Otani, & Winkelman, 2005). Feeling-of-knowing reactions are easy to observe on television game shows, where they occur just before contestants are allowed to answer.

Déjà vu, the feeling that you have already experienced a situation that you are experiencing for the first time, may be another example of partial memory (Brown & Marsh, 2010). If a new experience triggers vague memories of a past experience, without yielding *any* details at all, you might be left saying to yourself, "I feel like I've seen it before." The new experience seems familiar even though the older memory is too weak to rise to the level of awareness.

Because memory is not an all-or-nothing event, it can be measured in several ways. Three commonly used methods of measuring memory are *recall*, *recognition*, and *relearning*. Let's see how they differ.

Recalling Information

What is the name of the first song on your favorite playlist? Who won the World Series last year? Who wrote *Hamlet?* If you can answer these questions, you are using **recall**, a direct retrieval of facts or information. Tests of recall often require *verbatim* (word-for-word) memory. If you study a poem until you can recite it without looking at it, you are recalling it. If you complete a fill-in-the-blank question, you are using recall. When you answer an essay question by providing facts and ideas, you also are using recall, even though you didn't learn your essay verbatim.

The order in which information is memorized has an interesting effect on recall. To experience it, try to memorize the following list, reading it only once:

> bread, apples, soda, ham, cookies, rice, lettuce, beets, mustard, cheese, oranges, ice cream, crackers, flour, eggs

If you are like most people, it will be hardest for you to recall items from the middle of the list. ● **Figure 33.1** shows the results of a similar test. Notice that most errors occur with middle items of an ordered list. This is the **serial position** **effect** (Bonk & Healy, 2010). You can remember the last items on a list because they are still in STM. The first items also are remembered well because they entered an "empty" short-term memory. This allows you to rehearse the items so they move into long-term memory (Addis & Kahana, 2004). The middle items are neither held in short-term memory nor moved to long-term memory, so they are often lost.

Recognizing Information

Try to write down everything you can remember learning from a class you took last year. If you actually did this, you might conclude that you had learned very little. However, a more sensitive test based on recognition could be used. In **recognition**, previously learned material is correctly identified. For instance, you could take a multiple-choice test on facts and ideas from the course. Because you would have to recognize only correct answers, you probably would find that you had learned a lot.

Recognition can be amazingly accurate for pictures and photographs (Oates & Reder, 2011). In one classic study, people viewed 2,560 photographs at a rate of one every 10 seconds. Each person was then shown 280 pairs of photographs. Each pair included an "old" picture (from the first set of photos) and a similar "new" image. Participants could tell 85 to 95 percent of the time which photograph they had seen before (Haber, 1970). This finding may explain why we rarely need to see our friends' vacation photos more than once.

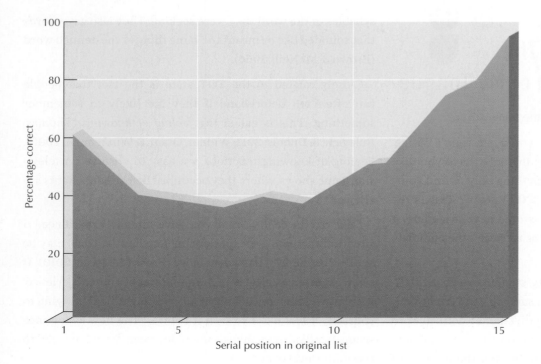

● **Figure 33.1**

The serial position effect. The graph shows the percentage of participants correctly recalling each item in a 15-item list. Recall is best for the first and last items. (Data from Craik, 1970.)

Recognition is usually superior to recall. That's why people so often say, "I may forget a name, but I never forget a face." (You can't recall the name but can recognize the face.) That's also why police departments use photographs or a lineup to identify criminal suspects. Witnesses who disagree when they try to recall a suspect's height, weight, age, or eye color often agree completely when they merely need to recognize the person.

Is recognition always superior? It depends greatly on the kind of *distractors* used (Flowe & Ebbese, 2007). Distractors are false items included with an item to be recognized. If distractors are similar to the correct item, memory may be poor. A reverse problem occurs when only one choice looks like it could be correct. This can produce a *false positive*, or false sense of recognition.

Many hundreds of people have been put in jail on the basis of mistaken eyewitness memories (Lampinen, Neuschatz, & Cling, 2012; Wade, Green, & Nash, 2010). In some instances, witnesses have described a criminal as black, tall, or young. Then a lineup was held in which a suspect was the only African American among whites, the only tall suspect, or the only young person. In such cases, a false identification is very likely. To avoid tragic mistakes, it's better to have *all* the distractors look like the person witnesses described. Also, to reduce false positives, witnesses should be warned that the culprit *may not be present*. It also may better to show witnesses one photo at a time (a sequential lineup). For each photo, the witness must decide whether the person is the culprit before another photo is shown (Mickes, Flowe, & Wixted, 2012; Wells & Olsen, 2003).

Relearning Information

In another classic experiment, a psychologist read a short passage in Greek to his son every day when the boy was between 15 months and 3 years of age. At age 8, the boy was asked if he remembered the Greek passage. He showed no evidence of recall. He was then shown selections from the passage he heard and selections from other Greek passages. Could he recognize the one he heard as an infant? "It's all Greek to me!" he said, indicating a lack of recognition (and drawing a frown from everyone in the room).

Had the psychologist stopped, he might have concluded that no memory of the Greek remained. However, the child was then asked to memorize the original quotation and others of equal difficulty. This time, his earlier learning became evident. The boy memorized the passage he had heard in childhood

25 percent faster than the others (Burtt, 1941). As this experiment suggests, **relearning** is typically the most sensitive measure of memory.

When a person is tested by relearning, how do we know a memory still exists? As with the boy described, relearning is measured by a *savings score* (the amount of time saved when relearning information). Let's say it takes you 1 hour to memorize all the names in a telephone book. (It's a small town.) Two years later, you relearn them in 45 minutes. Because you "saved" 15 minutes, your savings score would be 25 percent (15 divided by 60 times 100). Savings of this type are a good reason for studying a wide range of subjects. It may seem that learning algebra, history, or a foreign language is wasted if you don't use the knowledge immediately. But when you do need such information, you will be able to relearn it quickly.

Explicit and Implicit Memories

Who were the last three presidents of the United States? What did you have for breakfast today? What is the title of Taylor Swift's latest album? Explicit memory is used in answering each of these questions. An **explicit memory** is a past experience that is consciously brought to mind. Recall, recognition, and the tests you take in school rely on explicit memories.

In contrast, an **implicit memory** lies outside awareness (Gopie, Craik, & Hasher, 2011). That is, we are not aware that a memory exists. For example, if you know how to type, it is apparent that you know where the letters are on

---

Tip-of-the-tongue (TOT) state *The feeling that a memory is available but not quite retrievable.*

Availability (in memory) *Memories currently stored in memory are available.*

Accessibility (in memory) *Memories currently stored in memory that can be retrieved when necessary are both available and accessible.*

Recall *To supply or reproduce memorized information with a minimum of external cues.*

Serial position effect *The tendency to make the most errors in remembering the middle items of an ordered list.*

Recognition *An ability to correctly identify previously learned information.*

Relearning *Learning again something that was previously learned. Used to measure memory of prior learning.*

Explicit memory *A memory that a person is aware of having; a memory that is consciously retrieved.*

Implicit memory *A memory that a person does not know exists; a memory that is retrieved unconsciously.*

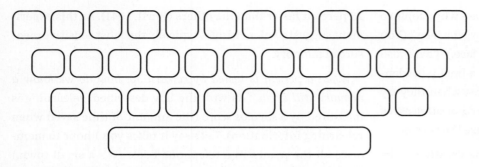

Can you label the letter keys on this blank keyboard? If you can, you probably used implicit memory to do it.

the keyboard. But how many typists could correctly label blank keys in a drawing of a keyboard? Many people find that they cannot directly remember such information, even though they "know" it. Nevertheless, implicit memories—such as unconsciously knowing where the letters are on a keyboard—greatly influence our behavior (Voss, Lucas, & Paller, 2012).

Priming *How is it possible to show that a memory exists if it lies outside awareness?* Psychologists first noticed implicit memory while studying memory loss caused by brain injuries. Let's say, for example, that a patient is shown a list of common words, such as *chair, tree, lamp, table,* and so on. Later, the patient fails to recall any words from the list.

Now, instead of asking the patient to explicitly recall the list, we could "prime" his memory by giving him the first two letters of each word. "Just say whatever word comes to mind that begins with these letters," we tell him. Of course, many words could be made from each pair of letters. For example, the first item (from "chair") would be the letters CH. The patient could say "child," "chalk," "chain," "check," or many other words. Instead, he says "chair," a word from the original list. The patient is not aware that he is remembering the list, but as he gives a word for each letter pair, almost all are from the list. Apparently, the letters **primed** (activated) hidden memories, which then influenced his answers.

Similar effects have been found for people with normal memories. As the preceding example implies, implicit memories are often revealed by giving a person limited cues, such as the first letter of words or partial drawings of objects. Typically, the person believes that he or she is just saying whatever comes to mind. Nevertheless, information previously seen or heard affects his or her answers (Lavigne et al., 2012).

Module 33: Summary

33.1 How is memory measured?

- **33.1.1** The tip-of-the-tongue state shows that memory is not an all-or-nothing event. Memories may be revealed by recall, recognition, relearning, or priming.
- **33.1.2** In recall, memories are retrieved without explicit cues, as in an essay exam. Recall of listed information often reveals a serial position effect.

- **33.1.3** A common test of recognition is the multiple-choice question.
- **33.1.4** In relearning, material that seems to be forgotten is learned again, and memory is revealed by a savings score.
- **33.1.5** Recall, recognition, and relearning mainly measure explicit memories. Other techniques, such as priming, are necessary to reveal implicit memories.

Priming *Facilitating the retrieval of an implicit memory by using cues to activate hidden memories.*

Module 33: Knowledge Builder

Recite

1. Four techniques for measuring or demonstrating memory are the following:

   _____ _____

   _____ _____

2. Essay tests require _____ of facts or ideas.

3. As a measure of memory, a savings score is associated with
   - **a.** recognition
   - **b.** priming
   - **c.** relearning
   - **d.** reconstruction

4. The two most sensitive tests of memory are
   - **a.** recall and redintegration
   - **b.** recall and relearning
   - **c.** recognition and relearning
   - **d.** recognition and digit-span

5. Priming is used to reveal which type of memories?
   - **a.** explicit
   - **b.** sensory
   - **c.** skill
   - **d.** implicit

Reflect

Think Critically

6. When asked to explain why they may have failed to recall some information, people often claim it must be because the information is no longer in their memory. Why does the existence of implicit memories challenge this explanation?

Self-Reflect

Do you prefer tests based primarily on recall or recognition? Have you observed a savings effect while relearning information you studied in the past (such as in high school)?

What things do you do that are based on implicit memories? For instance, how do you know which way to turn various handles in your house, apartment, or dorm? Do you have to explicitly think, "Turn it to the right," before you act?

ANSWERS

1. recall, recognition, relearning, priming 2. recall 3. c 4. c 5. d 6. It is possible to have an implicit memory that cannot be consciously recalled. Memories like these (*available* in memory even though they are not consciously *accessible*) show that failing to recall something does not guarantee it is no longer in memory (Voss, Lucas, & Paller, 2012).

CENGAGE**brain**.com

Go to **cengagebrain.com** to access **MindTap for Coon/Mitterer** *Psychology Modules for Active Learning* and other online learning tools. MindTap is a fully online learning experience that combines all the tools you need—readings, multimedia, activities, and assessments—into a singular personalized Learning Path that guides you through the course.

Memory: Forgetting

Where's My Car?

Forgetting is not always a bad thing. Consider Mr. S., who made a living as a professional memorizer, or *mnemonist*. He regularly wowed audiences with his ability to memorize, with equal ease, long strings of digits, meaningless consonants, mathematical formulas, and poems in foreign languages. Don't be too quick to envy Mr. S.'s abilities. He had to devise ways to *forget* unimportant information—such as writing it on a piece of paper and then burning it.

Lucky Mr. S aside, why do most of us lose some memories so quickly? It turns out that we forget for a variety of reasons. For example, if you park your car in a different place every day, you may have experienced forgetting caused by *interference*. Today's memory about your car's location is easily confused with memories from yesterday, and the day before, and the day before that. Let's read more about some explanations for forgetting.

Duncan McKenzie/Photographer's Choice/Getty Images

SURVEY QUESTIONS

34.1 Why do we forget?

34.2 How does the brain form and store memories?

Forgetting—Why We, Uh, Let's See . . . . Why We, Uh . . . Forget!

SURVEY QUESTION 34.1: Why do we forget?

We don't expect sensory memories and short-term memories to remain with us for long. But when you deliberately encode and store information in long-term memory, you want it to stay there (after all, it's supposed to be *long*-term). For example, when you study for an exam, you count on your long-term memory to retain the information at least until you take your exam.

Why do we forget long-term memories? The more you know about how we "lose" memories, the better you will be able to hang on to them. Most forgetting tends to occur immediately

The New Yorker Collection. Mick Stevens/Cartoonbank.com

after memorization. Herman Ebbinghaus (1885) famously tested his own memory at various intervals after learning. To be sure he would not be swayed by prior learning, he memorized *nonsense syllables*. These are meaningless three-letter words such as *cef, wol,* and *gex*. The importance of using meaningless words is shown by the fact that *Vel, Fab,* and *Duz* are no longer used on memory tests. People who recognize these words as detergent names find them easy to remember. This is another reminder that relating new information to what you already know can improve memory.

By waiting various lengths of time before testing himself, Ebbinghaus plotted a *curve of forgetting*. This graph shows the amount of information remembered after varying lengths of time (● **Figure 34.1**). Notice that forgetting is rapid at first and is then followed by a slow decline (Hintzman, 2005; Sternberg, 2012). The same applies to meaningful information, but the forgetting curve is stretched over a longer time. As you might expect, recent events are recalled more accurately than those from the remote past. Thus, you are more likely to remember that *Argo* won the Best Picture Academy Award for 2013 than you are to remember that *No Country for Old Men* won it for 2008.

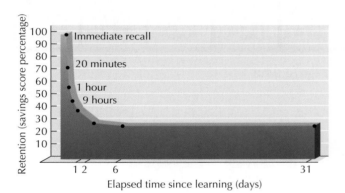

● **Figure 34.1**

The curve of forgetting. This graph shows the amount remembered (measured by relearning) after varying lengths of time. Notice how rapidly forgetting occurs. The material learned was nonsense syllables. Forgetting curves for meaningful information also show early losses followed by a long gradual decline, but overall, forgetting occurs much more slowly. (After Ebbinghaus, 1885.)

As a student, you should note that a short delay between studying and taking a test minimizes forgetting. However, this is no reason for cramming. Most students make the error of only cramming. If you cram, you don't have to remember for very long, but you may not learn enough in the first place. If you use short, daily study sessions and review intensely before a test, you will get the benefit of good preparation and a minimum time lapse.

The Ebbinghaus curve shows less than 30 percent remembered after only two days have passed. Is forgetting really that rapid?

No, not always. Meaningful information is not lost nearly as quickly as nonsense syllables. After three years, students who took a university psychology course had forgotten about 30 percent of the facts they learned. After that, little more forgetting occurred (Conway, Cohen, & Stanhope, 1992).

Although the Ebbinghaus curve gives a general picture of forgetting from long-term memory, it doesn't explain it. For explanations, we must search further. (Before we do, look at "Card Magic!" and you will find an interesting demonstration.) In Module 32, we pointed out that three processes are involved in successfully remembering: encoding, storage, and retrieval. Conversely, forgetting can be due to the failure of any one of these three processes.

When Memory Encoding Fails

Whose head is on a U.S. penny? Which way is it facing? What is written at the top of a penny? Can you accurately draw and label a penny? In an interesting experiment, Ray Nickerson and Marilyn Adams (1979) asked a large group of students to draw a penny. Few could. In fact, few could even recognize a drawing of a real penny among fakes (● **Figure 34.4**). Can you?

The most obvious reason for forgetting is also the most commonly overlooked. Obviously, few of us ever encode the details of a penny. Similarly, we may not encode the details of what we are reading in a book or studying for an exam. In such cases, we "forget" because of **encoding failure** (Johnson, Nessler, & Friedman, 2012). That is, a memory was never formed in the first place (the card trick you just saw is another example). If you are bothered by frequent forgetting or absentmindedness, it is wise to ask yourself, "Have I been encoding the information in the first place?" (Kirchhoff, 2009). By the way, if you like to study while watching television or instant messaging, beware. Dividing your attention between studying and other activities increases the likelihood of encoding failure (Johnson, Nessler, & Friedman, 2012; Naveh-Benjamin, Guez, & Sorek, 2007).

Actively focusing on the information you are learning (elaborative processing) is a good way to prevent encoding failure (Hall et al., 2007; Wong, 2012). You'll find more memory strategies in Module 1, "How to Study Psychology." Check it out, if you haven't already.

Encoding failure *Failure to store sufficient information to form a useful memory.*

Discovering Psychology

Card Magic!

● Figure 34.2

Pick a card from the six shown in ● **Figure 34.2** above. Look at it closely and be sure you can remember which card is yours. Now, snap your fingers and look at the cards in ● **Figure 34.3**, below. Poof! Only five cards remain, and the card you chose has disappeared. Obviously, you could have selected any one of the six cards in Figure 34.2. How did we know which one to remove?

This trick is based entirely on an illusion of memory. Recall that you were asked to concentrate on one card among the six cards in Figure 34.2. That prevented you from paying attention to the other cards, so they weren't stored in your memory (Naveh-Benjamin, Guez, & Sorek, 2007). The five cards you see below are all new (none is shown in Figure 34.3). Because you couldn't find it in the "remaining five," your card seemed to disappear. What looked like "card magic" is memory magic. Now, return to "When Memory Encoding Fails" and continue reading to learn more about forgetting.

● Figure 34.3

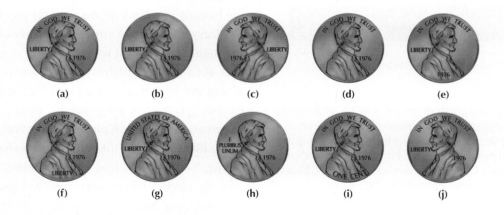

● Figure 34.4

Some of the distractor items used in a study of recognition memory and encoding failure. Penny A is correct but was seldom recognized. Pennies G and J were popular wrong answers. (Adapted from Nickerson & Adams, 1979.)

College Students: They're All Alike! Encoding failures can even affect our memories of people. Imagine yourself in this situation: As you are walking on campus, a young man, who looks like a college student, approaches you and asks for directions. While you are talking, two workers carrying a door pass between you and the young man. While your view is blocked by the door, another man takes the place of the first. Now you are facing a different person than the one who was there just seconds earlier. If this happened to you, do you think you would notice the change? Remarkably, only half the people tested in this way noticed the switch (Simons & Levin, 1998)!

How could anyone fail to notice that one stranger was replaced by another? The people who didn't remember the first man were all older adults. College students weren't fooled by the switch. Apparently, older adults encoded the first man in very general terms as a "college student." As a result, that's all they remembered. Because his replacement also looked like a college student, they thought he was the same person.

We all tend to categorize strangers in general terms: Is the person young or old, male or female, a member of my ethnic group or another one? This tendency is one reason eyewitnesses are better at identifying members of their own ethnic group than persons from other groups (Wallis, Lipp, & Vanman, 2012). It may seem harsh to say so, but during brief social contacts, people really do act as if members of other ethnic groups "all look alike." Of course, this bias disappears when people get acquainted and learn more about one another as individuals (Bukach et al., 2012).

When Memory Storage Fails

One view of forgetting holds that **memory traces**—changes in nerve cells or brain activity—decay (fade or weaken) over time. **Memory decay** is a factor in the loss of sensory memories and short-term memory. Information stored in these memories seems to initiate a brief flurry of activity in the brain that quickly dies out. Sensory memory and short-term memory, therefore, operate like "leaky buckets": New information constantly pours in, but it rapidly fades away and is replaced by still-newer information.

Disuse *Does decay also occur in long-term memory?* Evidence exists that memories not retrieved and "used" or rehearsed become weaker over time—that is, some long-term memory traces may fade from **disuse** (infrequent retrieval) and eventually become too weak to retrieve. However, disuse alone cannot fully explain forgetting (Della Sala, 2010). Disuse doesn't seem to account for our ability to recover seemingly forgotten memories through redintegration, relearning, and priming. It also fails to explain why some unused memories fade, whereas others are carried for life.

A third contradiction will be recognized by anyone who has spent time with the elderly. People growing senile may become so forgetful that they can't remember what happened a week ago. Unfortunately, this is often due to conditions like *Alzheimer's disease* and other *dementias*, which slowly strangle the brain's ability to process and store information (Hanyu et al., 2010; Verma & Howard, 2012). Yet, at the same time that your Uncle Oscar's recent memories are fading, he may have vivid memories of trivial and long-forgotten events from the past. "Why, I remember it as clearly as if it were yesterday," he will say, forgetting that the story he is about to tell is one he told earlier the same day (twice). In short, disuse offers no more than a partial explanation of long-term forgetting.

When Memory Retrieval Fails

If encoding failure and storage failure don't fully explain forgetting from long-term memory, what does? If you have encoded and stored information, that leaves retrieval failure as a likely cause of forgetting (Della Sala, 2010; Guerin et al., 2012). Even if memories are *available* (stored in your memory), you still have to be able to *access* them (locate or retrieve them) in order to remember. For example, as we mentioned earlier, you might have had the experience of knowing you know the answer to an exam question (you knew it was available) but being unable to retrieve it during the exam (it was inaccessible).

Cue-Dependent Forgetting One reason retrieval may fail is **retrieval cues**—stimuli associated with a memory—are missing when the time comes to retrieve information. For instance, if you were asked, "What were you doing on Monday afternoon of the third week in May, two years ago?" your reply might be, "Come on, how should I know?" However, if you were reminded, "That was the day the courthouse burned," or "That was the day Stacy had her automobile accident," you might remember immediately.

The presence of appropriate cues almost always enhances memory. As we saw previously, more elaborately encoded memories are more likely to be remembered because more retrieval cues are associated with any particular piece of information. Memory will even tend to be better if you study in the same room where you will be tested. Because this is often impossible, when you study, try to visualize the room where you will be tested. Doing so can enhance memory later (Jerabek & Standing, 1992).

Memory traces *Physical changes in nerve cells or brain activity that take place when memories are stored.*
Memory decay *The fading or weakening of memories assumed to occur when memory traces become weaker.*
Disuse *Theory that memory traces weaken when memories are not periodically used or retrieved.*
Retrieval cues *Stimuli associated with a memory. Retrieval cues usually enhance memory.*

External cues like those found in a photograph, in a scrapbook, or during a walk through an old neighborhood often aid recall of seemingly lost memories. For many veterans, finding a familiar name engraved in the Vietnam Veterans Memorial unleashes a flood of memories.

State-Dependent Learning Have you heard the one about the drunk who misplaced his wallet and had to get drunk again to find it? This is not too farfetched. The bodily state that exists during learning also can be a strong retrieval cue for later memory, an effect known as **state-dependent learning** (Radvansky, 2011). Being very thirsty, for instance, might prompt you to remember events that took place on another occasion when you were thirsty. Because of such effects, information learned under the influence of a drug is best remembered when the drugged state occurs again (Koek, 2011; Mariani et al., 2011). However, this is a laboratory finding. In school, it's far better to study with a clear mind in the first place.

A similar effect applies to emotional states (Wessel & Wright, 2004). For instance, Gordon Bower (1981) found that people who learned a list of words while in a happy mood recalled them better when they were again happy. People who learned while they felt sad remembered best when they were sad (**Figure 34.5**). Similarly, if you are in a happy mood, you are more likely to remember recent happy events. If you are in a bad mood, you will tend to have unpleasant memories. Such links between emotional cues and memory could explain why couples who quarrel often end up remembering—and rehashing—old arguments.

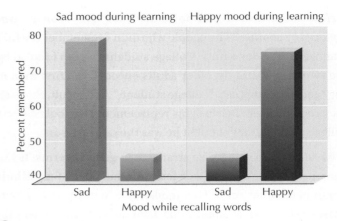

Figure 34.5

The effect of mood on memory. Participants best remembered a list of words when their mood during testing was the same as their mood when they learned the list. (Adapted from Bower, 1981.)

Interference

Further insight into forgetting comes from a classic experiment in which college students learned lists of nonsense syllables. After studying, students in one group slept for eight hours and were then tested for memory of the lists. A second group stayed awake for eight hours and went about business as usual. When members of the second group were tested, they remembered *less* than the group that slept (**Figure 34.6**). This difference is based on the fact that new learning can interfere with the ability to retrieve previous learning. (Sleep can improve

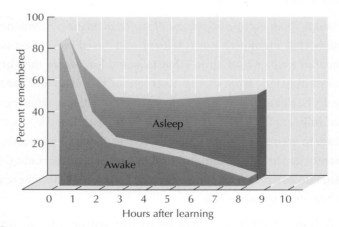

Figure 34.6

The amount of forgetting after a period of sleep or of being awake. Notice that sleep causes less memory loss than activity while one is awake. (After Jenkins & Dallenbach, 1924.)

memory in another way: REM sleep and dreaming appear to also help us form memories. See Module 24.) **Interference** refers to the tendency for new memories to impair retrieval of older memories (and the reverse). It seems to apply to both short-term and long-term memory (Radvansky, 2011; Rodríguez-Villagra et al., 2012).

It is not completely clear whether new memories alter existing memory traces or whether they make it harder to retrieve earlier memories. In any case, there is no doubt that interference is a major cause of forgetting (Radvansky, 2011). In one classic study, college students who memorized 20 lists of words (one list each day) were able to recall only 15 percent of the last list. Students who learned

only one list remembered 80 percent (Underwood, 1957) (● Figure 34.7).

The sleeping college students who studied nonsense syllables remembered more because the type of interference called retroactive (RET-ro-AK-tiv) interference was held to a minimum. **Retroactive interference** refers to the tendency for new learning to inhibit retrieval of old learning. Avoiding new learning prevents retroactive interference. This doesn't exactly mean you should hide in a closet after you study for an exam. However, you should, if possible, avoid studying other subjects until the exam. Sleeping after study can help you retain memories, and reading, writing, or even watching television may cause interference.

Retroactive interference is easily demonstrated in the laboratory by this arrangement:

Experimental group:	**Learn A**	**Learn B**	**Test A**
Control group:	**Learn A**	**Rest**	**Test A**

Imagine yourself as a member of the experimental group. In task A, you learn a list of telephone numbers. In task B, you learn a list of Social Security numbers. How do you score on a test of task A (the telephone numbers)? If you do not remember as much as the control group that learns *only* task A, then retroactive interference has occurred. The second thing learned interfered with memory of the first thing learned; the interference went "backward," or was "retroactive" (● Figure 34.8).

Proactive (pro-AK-tiv) interference is the second type of interference. **Proactive interference** occurs when prior learning inhibits recall of later learning. A test for proactive interference would take this form:

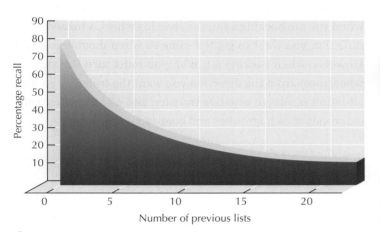

● **Figure 34.7**

Effects of interference on memory. The graph shows the approximate relationship between percentage recalled and number of different word lists memorized. (Adapted from Underwood, 1957.)

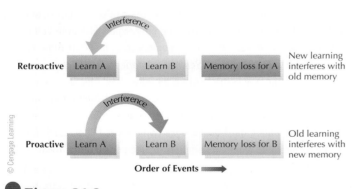

● **Figure 34.8**

Retroactive and proactive interference. The order of learning and testing shows whether interference is retroactive (backward) or proactive (forward).

Experimental group:	**Learn A**	**Learn B**	**Test B**
Control group:	**Rest**	**Learn B**	**Test B**

State-dependent learning *Memory influenced by one's physical state at the time of learning and at the time of retrieval. Improved memory occurs when the physical states match.*
Interference *The tendency for new memories to impair retrieval of older memories, and the reverse.*
Retroactive interference *The tendency for new memories to interfere with the retrieval of old memories.*
Proactive interference *The tendency for old memories to interfere with the retrieval of newer memories.*

Let's assume that the experimental group remembers less than the control group on a test of task B. In that case, learning task A interfered with memory for task B.

Then, proactive interference goes "forward"? Yes. For instance, if you cram for a psychology exam and then later the same night cram for a history exam, your memory for the second subject studied (history) will be less accurate than if you had studied only history. (Because of retroactive interference, your memory for psychology also would probably suffer.) The greater the similarity in the two subjects studied, the more interference takes place. The moral, of course, is don't procrastinate in preparing for exams. The more you can avoid competing information, the more likely you are to recall what you want to remember (Wixted, 2004).

The interference effects we have described apply primarily to memories of verbal information, such as the contents of this module. When you are learning a skill, similarity can sometimes be beneficial, rather than disruptive. The next section explains how this occurs.

Transfer of Training Two people begin mandolin lessons. One already plays the violin. The other is a trumpet player. All other things being equal, which person will initially do better in learning the mandolin? If you chose the violin player, you have an intuitive grasp of the meaning of positive transfer. (The strings on a mandolin are tuned the same as a violin.) **Positive transfer** takes place when mastery of one task aids mastery of a second task. Another example would be learning to balance and turn on a bicycle before learning to ride a motorcycle or motor scooter. Likewise, surfing and skateboarding skills transfer to snowboarding.

In **negative transfer**, skills developed in one situation conflict with those required to master a new task. Learning to back a car with a trailer attached to it is a good example. Normally, when you are backing a car, the steering wheel is turned in the direction you want to go, the same as when moving forward. However, when backing a trailer, you must turn the steering wheel *away* from the direction you want the trailer to go. This situation results in negative transfer, and often creates comical scenes at campgrounds and boat-launching ramps.

Clinical File

The Recovered Memory/False Memory Debate

Many sexually abused children develop problems that persist into adulthood. In some instances, they repress all memory of the abuse. According to some psychologists, uncovering these hidden memories can be an important step toward regaining emotional health (Colangelo, 2007; Haaken & Reavey, 2010).

Although the preceding may be true, the search for repressed memories of sexual abuse has itself been a problem. Families have been torn apart by accusations of sexual abuse that later turned out to be completely false. For example, when Meridith Maran thought she had recovered vivid memories of being molested by her father, she withdrew herself and her children from any further contact with him. It was not until nine years later that she realized that her "memories" were not true and finally apologized to her father (Maran, 2010). Things have gotten much worse for other people as some cases have gone to court, some innocent people have gone to jail, and some actual sexual abuse victims have been accused of making false claims about their very real memories.

Why would anyone have false memories about such disturbing events? Several popular books and a few misguided therapists have actively encouraged people to find repressed memories of abuse. Hypnosis, guided visualization, suggestion, age regression,

administering the so-called truth drug Amytal, and similar techniques can elicit fantasies that are mistaken for real memories. As we saw earlier, it is easy to create false memories, especially by using hypnosis (Weinstein & Shanks, 2010).

In an effort to illustrate how easy it is to create false memories, and to publicize *false memory syndrome,* memory expert Elizabeth Loftus once deliberately implanted a false memory in actor Alan Alda. As the host of the television series *Scientific American Frontiers*, he was scheduled to interview Loftus. Before the interview, Alda was asked to fill out a questionnaire about his tastes in food. When he arrived, Loftus told Alda that his answers revealed that he must have gotten sick once after eating hard-boiled eggs (which was false). Later that day, at a picnic, Alda would not eat hard-boiled eggs (Loftus, 2003).

Certainly, some memories of abuse that return to awareness are genuine and must be dealt with. However, there is little doubt that some "recovered" memories are pure fantasy. No matter how real a recovered memory may seem, it could be false, unless it can be verified by others or by court or medical records (Bernstein & Loftus, 2009; Otgaar & Smeets, 2010). The saddest thing about such claims is that they deaden public sensitivity to actual abuse. Childhood sexual abuse is widespread. Awareness of its existence must not be repressed.

On a more serious note, many tragic crashes caused by negative transfer finally led to greater standardization of airplane cockpits. Fortunately, negative transfer is usually brief, and it occurs less often than positive transfer. Negative transfer is most likely to occur when a new response must be made to an old stimulus (Besnard & Cacitti, 2005). If you have ever encountered a pull-type handle on a door that must be pushed open, you will appreciate this point.

Repression and Suppression of Memories

Take a moment and scan the events of the last few years of your life. What kinds of things most easily come to mind? Many people remember happy, positive events better than disappointments and irritations (Moore & Zoellner, 2007). This tendency is called **repression**, or motivated forgetting. Through repression, painful, threatening, or embarrassing memories are held out of consciousness. An example is provided by soldiers who have repressed some of the horrors they saw during combat (Anderson & Huddleston, 2012).

Forgetting past failures, upsetting childhood events, the names of people you dislike, or appointments you don't want to keep may reveal repression (Goodman, Quas, & Ogle, 2010). People who are extremely sensitive to emotional events tend to use repression to protect themselves from threatening thoughts. See "The Recovered Memory/False Memory Debate" for further cautions.

If I try to forget a test I failed, am I repressing it? Probably not. Repression can be distinguished from **suppression**, an active, conscious attempt to put something out of mind (Anderson et al., 2011). By not thinking about the test, you have merely suppressed a memory. If you choose, you can remember the test. Clinicians consider true repression an *unconscious* event and one of the major psychological defenses we use against emotional threats. (See Module 57 for details.) When a memory is repressed, we may be unaware that forgetting has even occurred.

Although some psychologists have questioned whether repression exists, evidence suggests that we can choose to actively suppress upsetting memories (Ceylan & Sayin, 2012; Neufeind et al., 2009). If you have experienced a painful emotional event, you will probably avoid all thoughts associated with it. This tends to keep cues out of mind that could trigger a painful memory. In time, your active suppression of the memory may become true repression.

Memory and the Brain— Some "Shocking" Findings

SURVEY QUESTION 34.2: How does the brain form and store memories?

One possibility overlooked in our discussion of forgetting is that memories may be lost as they are being formed (Papanicolaou, 2006). For example, a head injury may cause a "gap" in memories preceding the accident. **Retrograde amnesia**, as this is called, involves forgetting events that occurred before an injury or trauma (MacKay & Hadley, 2009). In contrast, **anterograde amnesia** involves forgetting events that follow an injury or trauma (Dewar et al., 2010). (We discuss an example of this type of amnesia in a moment.)

Consolidation

We can explain retrograde amnesia by assuming that it takes time to form a lasting memory, a process called **consolidation** (Nadel et al., 2012). You can think of consolidation as being somewhat like writing your name in wet concrete. Once the concrete is set, the information (your name) is fairly lasting. But while the concrete is setting, the information can be wiped out (amnesia) or scribbled over (interference).

Consider a classic experiment on consolidation, in which a rat is placed on a small platform. The rat steps down to the floor and receives a painful electric shock. After one shock, the rat can be returned to the platform repeatedly, but it will not step down. Obviously, the rat remembers the shock. Would it remember if consolidation were disturbed?

Positive transfer *Mastery of one task aids learning or performing another.*
Negative transfer *Mastery of one task conflicts with learning or performing another.*
Repression *Unconsciously pushing unwanted memories out of awareness.*
Suppression *A conscious effort to put something out of mind or to keep it from awareness.*
Retrograde amnesia *Loss of memory for events that preceded a head injury or other amnesia-causing event.*
Anterograde amnesia *Loss of the ability to form or retrieve memories for events that occur after an injury or trauma.*
Consolidation *Process by which relatively permanent memories are formed in the brain.*

Curiously, one way to prevent consolidation is to give a different kind of shock called *electroconvulsive shock (ECS)*. ECS is a mild electric shock to the brain. It does not harm the animal, but it does destroy any memory that is being formed. If each painful shock (the one the animal remembers) is followed by ECS (which wipes out memories during consolidation), the rat will step down over and over. Each time, ECS erases the memory of the painful shock. (ECS is employed as a psychiatric treatment for severe depression in humans; see Module 68.)

What would happen if ECS were given several hours after the learning? Recent memories are more easily disrupted than older memories. If enough time is allowed to pass between learning and ECS, the memory will be unaffected because consolidation is already complete. That's why people with mild head injuries lose only memories from just before the accident, whereas older memories remain intact (Baddeley, Eysenck, & Anderson, 2009). Likewise, you would forget more if you studied, stayed awake eight hours, and then slept eight hours than you would if you studied, slept eight hours, and were awake for eight hours. Either way, sixteen hours would pass. However, less forgetting would occur in the second instance because more consolidation would occur before interference begins.

Where does consolidation take place in the brain? Many parts of the brain are responsible for memory, but the **hippocampus** is particularly important (Squire & Wixted, 2011). The hippocampus acts as a sort of "switching station" between short-term and long-term memory (Hardt, Einarsson, & Nader, 2010). The hippocampus does this, in part, by growing new neurons (nerve cells) and by making new connections within the brain (Leuner & Gould, 2010).

If the hippocampus is damaged, patients usually develop anterograde amnesia and show a striking inability to consolidate new memories. A man described by Brenda Milner (1965) provides a dramatic example. Two years after an operation damaged his hippocampus, the 29-year-old H. M. continued to give his age as 27 and reported that the operation had just taken place. His memory of events before the operation remained clear, but he found forming new long-term memories almost impossible. When his parents moved to a new house a few blocks away on the same street, he could not remember the new address. Month after month, he read the same magazines over and over without finding them familiar. If you were to meet this man, he would seem fairly normal because he still has short-term memory. But if you were to leave the room and return 15 minutes later, he would act as if he had never seen you before. Lacking the ability to form new lasting memories, he lived eternally in the present until his death in 2008 at the age of 82 (Bohbot & Corkin, 2007).

Memory, Stress, and Emotion Many older people can still remember when they first learned about the terrorist attacks on New York City's World Trade Center in 2001. They can even recall lots of detail, including how they reacted. They have **flashbulb memories** for 9/11 (Paradis et al., 2004). A flashbulb memory is an especially vivid image that seems to be frozen in memory at times of emotionally significant personal or public events (Lanciano, Curci, & Semin, 2010). Depending on your age, you also may have a flashbulb memory for the assassinations of John F. Kennedy or Martin Luther King, Jr., the death of Princess Diana, or the massive tsunami and earthquake that struck Japan in 2011 (Curci & Luminet, 2006).

Does the brain handle flashbulb memories differently? Powerfully exciting or stressful experiences activate the limbic system, a part of the brain that processes emotions. Heightened activity in the limbic system, in turn, appears to intensify memory consolidation (LaBar, 2007). As a result, flashbulb memories tend to form at times of intense emotion.

Although flashbulb memories are often related to public tragedies, memories of both positive and negative events can have "flashbulb" clarity. Would you consider any of the following to be a flashbulb memory: Your first kiss or your prom night? How about a time you had to speak in front of a large audience? A car accident you were in or witnessed?

Mark Wilson/Getty Images

Do you have a flashbulb memory for Super Storm Sandy, which struck the United States in 2012? You do if you were caught in the storm and can still remember it like it happened yesterday. You even do if you saw the news on TV and you have clear memories of how you reacted.

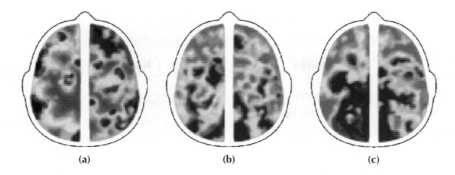

(a)   (b)   (c)

Figure 34.9

Patterns of blood flow in the cerebral cortex (wrinkled outer layer of the brain) change as areas become more or less active. Thus, blood flow can be used to draw "maps" of brain activity. This drawing, which views the brain from the top, shows the results of measuring cerebral blood flow while people were thinking about a semantic memory (*a*) or an episodic memory (*b*). In the map, green indicates areas that are more active during semantic thinking. Red shows areas of greater activity during episodic thinking. The brain in view *c* shows the difference in activity between views *a* and *b*. The resulting pattern suggests that the front of the cortex is related to episodic memory. Areas toward the back and sides of the brain, especially the temporal lobes, are more associated with semantic memory (Tulving, 1989, 2002). Copyright © Tulving, E. (1989). "Remembering and knowing the past." *American Scientist*, 77(4), 361–367. Reprinted by permission.

The term *flashbulb memories* was first used to describe recollections that seemed to be unusually vivid and permanent (Brown & Kulik, 1977). It has become clear, however, that flashbulb memories are not particularly accurate (Talarico & Rubin, 2007). More than anything else, what sets flashbulb memories apart is that we tend to place great *confidence* in them—even when they are wrong (Niedzwienska, 2004). Perhaps that's because we review emotionally charged events over and over and tell others about them. Also, public events such as wars, earthquakes, and elections reappear many times in the news, which highlights them in memory. Over time, flashbulb memories tend to crystallize into consistent, if not entirely accurate, landmarks in our lives (Lanciano, Curci, & Semin, 2010).

Some memories go beyond flashbulb clarity and become so intense that they may haunt a person for years. Extremely traumatic experiences, such as military combat or maltreatment as a child, can produce so much limbic system activation that the resulting memories and "flashbacks" leave a person emotionally handicapped (Goodman, Quas, & Ogle, 2010).

Long-Term Memory and the Brain

Somewhere within the 3-pound mass of the human brain lies all we know: ZIP codes, faces of loved ones, history, favorite melodies, the taste of an apple, and much, much more. Where is this information? According to neuroscientists, many parts of the brain become active when we form and retrieve long-term memories, but some areas are more important for different types of memory and memory processes (Squire & Wixted, 2011).

For example, patterns of blood flow in the cerebral cortex (the wrinkled outer layer of the brain) can be used to map brain activity. ● **Figure 34.9** shows the results of measuring blood flow while people were thinking about a semantic memory or an episodic memory. The resulting pattern indicates that we use the front of the cortex for episodic memory. Back areas are more associated with semantic memory (Tulving, 1989, 2002). As another example, different parts of the cortex are activated when we are engaging in memory retrieval and suppression (Mecklinger, 2010).

Let's summarize (and simplify greatly). Earlier, we noted that the hippocampus handles memory consolidation (Wang & Morris, 2010). Once declarative long-term memories are formed, they appear to be stored and retrieved in the cortex of the brain (episodic in the front, semantic in the back) (Mecklinger, 2010; Squire, 2004). Long-term procedural (skill) memories are stored in the basal ganglia and cerebellum, parts of the brain that also are responsible for muscular coordination (Freberg, 2010; Lum & Bleses, 2012).

Hippocampus *A brain structure associated with emotion and the transfer of information from short-term memory to long-term memory.*
Flashbulb memory *Especially vivid memory created at a time of high emotion.*

How are memories recorded in the brain? Scientists are beginning to identify the exact ways nerve cells record information. For example, Eric Kandel and his colleagues have studied learning in the marine snail *aplysia* (ah-PLEEZ-yah). Learning in the *aplysia* occurs when certain nerve cells in a circuit alter the amount of transmitter chemicals it releases (Bailey & Kandel, 2004). Learning also alters the activity, structure, and chemistry of brain cells. Such changes determine which connections get stronger and which become weaker.

Scientists continue to study various chemicals, especially neurotransmitters, that affect memory (Xu & Yao, 2010). Their research may eventually help the millions of persons who suffer from memory impairment (Elli & Nathan, 2001; see "The Long-Term Potential of a Memory Pill").

© Daniel Gotshall/Visuals Unlimited/Corbis

An *aplysia.* The relatively simple nervous system of this sea animal allows scientists to study memory as it occurs in single nerve cells.

Brainwaves

The Long-Term Potential of a Memory Pill

At long last, scientists may have found the chemical "signature" that records memories in everything from snails to rats to humans. If two or more interconnected brain cells become more active at the same time, the connections between them grow stronger (Kalat, 2013). This process is called *long-term potentiation.* After it occurs, an affected brain cell will respond more strongly to messages from the other cells. The brain appears to use this mechanism to form lasting memories (Blundon & Zakharenko, 2008; Kimura et al., 2012).

How has that been demonstrated? Electrically stimulating parts of the brain involved in memory, such as the hippocampus, can decrease long-term potentiation (Eckert & Racine, 2006; Ivanco & Racine, 2000). As we saw earlier, using electroconvulsive shock to overstimulate memory areas in the brains of rats interferes with long-term potentiation. It also causes memory loss—just as it does when humans are given ECS for depression.

Will researchers ever produce a "memory pill" for people with normal memory? It's a growing possibility, although one early candidate, *ginkgo biloba*, has yielded disappointing results in research trials (Snitz et al., 2009). Yet, drugs that increase long-term potentiation also tend to improve memory (Farah et al., 2004). For example, rats administered such drugs could remember the correct path through a maze better than rats not given the drug (Service, 1994). Such findings suggest that memory can be and will be artificially enhanced. However, the possibility of something like a "physics pill" or a "math pill" still seems remote.

Module 34: Summary

34.1 Why do we forget?

- **34.1.1** Forgetting is most rapid immediately after learning.
- **34.1.2** Failure to encode information is a common cause of "forgetting."
- **34.1.3** Forgetting in sensory memory and STM is due to a failure of storage through a weakening (decay) of memory traces. STM forgetting also occurs through displacement. Decay of memory traces due to disuse also may explain some LTM losses.
- **34.1.4** Failures of retrieval occur when information that resides in memory is nevertheless not retrieved. A lack of retrieval cues can produce retrieval failure. State-dependent learning is related to the effects of retrieval cues.
- **34.1.5** Much forgetting in LTM is caused by interference. In retroactive interference, new learning interferes with the ability to retrieve earlier learning. Proactive interference occurs when old learning interferes with the retrieval of new learning.

- **34.1.6** Memories can be consciously suppressed and they may be unconsciously repressed.

34.2 How does the brain form and store memories?

- **34.2.1** It takes time to consolidate memories. In the brain, memory consolidation takes place in the hippocampus. Until they are consolidated, long-term memories are easily destroyed, resulting in retrograde amnesia.
- **34.2.2** Intensely emotional experiences can result in flashbulb memories.
- **34.2.3** After memories have been consolidated, they appear to be stored in the cortex of the brain.
- **34.2.4** Lasting memories are recorded by changes in the activity, structure, and chemistry of nerve cells as well as how they interconnect.

Module 34: Knowledge Builder

Recite

1. Which explanation(s) seem(s) to account for the loss of short-term memories?
   - **a.** decay
   - **b.** disuse
   - **c.** repression
   - **d.** displacement

2. When memories are available but not accessible, forgetting may be cue dependent. **T or F?**

3. When learning one thing makes it more difficult to recall another, forgetting may be caused by _____.

4. You are asked to memorize long lists of telephone numbers. You learn a new list each day for ten days. When tested on list three, you remember less than a person who learned only the first three lists. Your larger memory loss is probably caused by
   - **a.** disuse
   - **b.** retroactive interference
   - **c.** regression
   - **d.** proactive interference

5. If you consciously succeed at putting a painful memory out of mind, you have used
   - **a.** redintegration
   - **b.** suppression
   - **c.** negative rehearsal
   - **d.** repression

6. Retrograde amnesia results when consolidation is speeded up. **T or F?**

Reflect

Think Critically

7. Based on state-dependent learning, why do you think music often strongly evokes memories?

Self-Reflect

Which of the following concepts best explains why you have missed some answers on psychology tests: encoding failure, disuse, memory cues, interference?

Do you know someone whose name you have a hard time remembering? Do you like or dislike that person? Do you think your difficulty is an instance of repression? Suppression? Interference? Retrieval failure?

ANSWERS

CENGAGE **brain**.com

Go to **cengagebrain.com** to access **MindTap for Coon/Mitterer** *Psychology Modules for Active Learning* and other online learning tools. MindTap is a fully online learning experience that combines all the tools you need—readings, multimedia, activities, and assessments—into a singular personalized Learning Path that guides you through the course.

Memory: Superior Memory

Lights, Camera, Action!

Regardless of how good your memory may be, at times you probably wish it were better. In this module, we explore exceptional memories. Is superior memory, such as having a "photographic" memory, a biological gift? Or do excellent memorizers merely make better-than-average use of normal memory capacities?

For example, actors can remember large amounts of complex information for many months, even when learning new roles between existing roles. During testing, they remember their lines best when they are allowed to move and gesture as they would when performing. Apparently, their movements supply cues that aid recall. Similarly, by practicing chunking, a long-distance runner named Steve learned to memorize lists of up to 80 digits at a time.

While we're waiting around for the arrival of a memory pill, this module also describes some ways to immediately improve your memory skills.

SURVEY QUESTIONS

35.1 What are photographic memories?

35.2 How can I improve my memory?

Exceptional Memory— Wizards of Recall

SURVEY QUESTION 35.1: What are photographic memories?

The occasional rare individual has a truly exceptional memory, like Mr. S., the professional memorizer we met in the previous module (Luria, 1968). But, as we noted, this is not necessarily a good thing. Consider what Jill Price thinks about her "perfect" memory: "My memory has ruled my life. . . . Whenever I see a date flash on the television (or anywhere else for that matter), I automatically go back to that day and remember where I was, what I was doing, what day it fell on, and on and on and on and on. It is nonstop, uncontrollable, and totally exhausting. . . . Most have called it a gift, but I call it a burden. I run my entire life through my head every day and it drives me crazy!!!" (Parker, Cahill, & McGaugh, 2006; Price & Davis, 2009).

Mental Imagery

Is it necessary to have a photographic memory, like Jill Price, to have a superior memory? In rare instances, mental images may be so vivid and persistent that it is reasonable to say that a person has "photographic memory." However, the term *photographic memory* is more often used to describe an uncommon memory ability called eidetic imagery.

Eidetic imagery (eye-DET-ik) occurs when a person has visual images clear enough to be "scanned" or retained for at least 30 seconds. Internal mental images can be "viewed" mentally with the eyes closed. In contrast, eidetic images are "projected" in front of a person—that is, they are best "seen" on a plain surface, such as a blank piece of paper. In this respect, eidetic images are somewhat like the afterimages you might have after looking at a flashbulb or a brightly lit neon sign (Brang & Ramachandran, 2010). Eidetic memory is more common in childhood and becomes rare by adulthood (Haber & Haber, 2000).

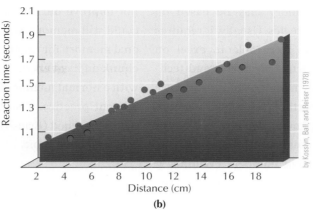

🔵 Figure 35.1

(*a*) "Treasure map" similar to the one used by Kosslyn, Ball, and Reiser (1978) to study images in memory. (*b*) This graph shows how long it took participants to move a visualized spot various distances on their mental images of the map. (See text for explanation.)

Whether or not you have an exceptional memory, however, the odds are you use mental imagery. Can you remember how many doors are in your house or apartment? To answer a question like this, many people form **mental images**—mental pictures—of each room and count the doorways they visualize. As this example implies, many memories are processed and stored as mental images (Ganis, 2013; Shorrock & Isaac, 2010).

Stephen Kosslyn, Thomas Ball, and Brian Reiser (1978) found an interesting way to show that memories do exist as images. Participants first memorized a sort of treasure map similar to the one shown in 🔵 **Figure 35.1a**. They were then asked to picture a black dot moving from one object, such as one of the trees, to another, such as the hut at the top of the island. Did people really form an image to do this task? It seems they did. As shown in 🔵 **Figure 35.1b**, the time it took to "move" the dot was directly related to actual distances on the map.

Memory Champions

Few adults possess naturally amazing memory abilities, such as photographic memory, eidetic imagery, or the near-perfect recall of Jill Price and Mr. S., who we met in Module 34. Most superior memorizers must work hard to develop their memory skills.

Each year, the World Memory Championship is held in England. Contestants must rapidly memorize daunting amounts of information, such as long lists of unrelated words and numbers. Psychologists John Wilding and Elizabeth Valentine saw this event as an opportunity to study exceptional memory and persuaded the contestants to take some additional memory tests. These ranged from ordinary (recall a story), to challenging (recall the telephone numbers of six different people), to diabolical (recall 48 numerals arranged in rows and columns) (Maguire et al., 2003; Wilding & Valentine, 1994).

Exceptional memorizers are identified by the following traits:

This number matrix is similar to the ones contestants in the World Memory Championship had to memorize. To be scored as correct, digits had to be recalled in their proper positions (Wilding & Valentine, 1994).

- They have naturally superior memory abilities, often including vivid mental images.
- They don't have superior intellectual abilities or different brains.
- They have specialized interests and knowledge that make certain types of information easier to encode and recall.
- They use memory strategies and techniques.

Eidetic imagery *The ability to retain a "projected" mental image long enough to use it as a source of information.*
Mental images *Mental pictures or visual depictions used in memory and thinking.*

In other words, exceptional memory may be based on either natural ability or learned strategies. Usually, it requires both. Several memory contestants were able to excel on tasks that prevented the use of learned strategies and techniques, implying that exceptional memory ability can be a "gift" (Yi & Qian, 2009). More important for us mere memory mortals, specialized interests and knowledge also helped for some tasks. For example, one contestant, a mathematician, was exceedingly good at memorizing numbers (Wilding & Valentine, 1994). Many of the contestants also actively used memory strategies, including special memory "tricks" called *mnemonics* (nee-MON-iks).

Most good memorizers are selective in what and how they choose to remember (unlike, say, Mr. S., who had to develop strategies to *forget*). If you didn't have selective memory, you would recall all the ingredients on your cereal box, every street number you've seen, and countless other scraps of information. In other words, most good memorizers have learned effective strategies for remembering.

Learning to Chunk

As an example of an effective strategy for remembering, consider Steve. At first, this intrepid student volunteer could remember seven digits. Could he improve with practice? For twenty months (!), Steve practiced memorizing ever-longer lists of digits. Ultimately, he was able to memorize approximately eighty digits, like this sample:

```
9284204805084226895399019025291280799970660657417173106010
805852697260263573323135
```

How did Steve do it? Basically, he worked by chunking digits into meaningful groups containing three or four digits each. Steve's avid interest in long-distance running helped greatly. For instance, to him the first three digits in the preceding group represented 9 minutes and 28 seconds, a good time for a 2-mile run. When running times wouldn't work, Steve used other associations, such as ages or dates, to chunk digits (Ericsson & Chase, 1982). It is apparent that Steve's success was based on learned strategies. By using similar memory systems, other people have trained themselves to equal Steve's feat (Bellezza, Six, & Phillips, 1992). In fact, the ability to organize information into chunks underlies expertise in many fields (Gilchrist, Cowan, & Naveh-Benjamin, 2009; Gobet, 2005).

Psychologist Anders Ericsson believes that exceptional memory is often a learned extension of normal memory. As evidence, he notes that Steve's short-term memory did not improve during months of practice. For example, Steve could still memorize only seven consonants. Steve's phenomenal memory for numbers grew as he figured out new ways to chunk digits at encoding and store them in LTM. Steve began with a normal memory for digits. He extended his memory by diligent practice. Clearly, superior memory can be, to some degree, learned (Ericsson et al., 2004). Let's delve further into this important topic.

Improving Memory—Keys to the Memory Bank

SURVEY QUESTION 35.2: How can I improve my memory?

Let's see how you can improve your memory. To begin, you can do very little to improve your brain's ability to store long-term memories. The jury is still out on the use of drugs, herbs (such as *ginkgo biloba*), and vitamins (such as vitamin E) to improve human memory (McDaniel, Maier, & Einstein, 2002; McGaugh & Roozendaal, 2009). However, until there's a memory pill, you can immediately use meaning-based strategies to improve memory encoding and memory retrieval (Fry, 2012; Hancock, 2011). Most superior memorizers use these strategies to augment whatever natural talents they have. Some of their strategies are described in the remainder of this section. Later, mnemonics are explored in Module 36. Please do remember to read it.

Encoding Strategies

One way to improve your memory is to be sure to fully encode information. That way, you can avoid forgetting due to encoding failure. Following are some steps you can take to become a better encoder:

Use Elaborative Processing Let us reiterate: The more you *rehearse* (mentally review) information as you read, the better you will remember it. Even repeatedly thinking about facts helps link them together in memory. But remember that maintenance rehearsal alone is not very effective. Elaborative processing, in which you rehearse by looking for connections to existing knowledge, is far better. To learn college-level information, you must make active use of more reflective study strategies (Halonen & Santrock, 2013).

Be Selective The Dutch scholar Erasmus said that a good memory should be like a fishnet: It should keep all the big fish and let the little ones escape. If you boil down the paragraphs in most textbooks to one or two important terms or ideas, your memory chores will be more manageable. Practice selective marking in your texts and use marginal notes to further summarize ideas. Most students mark their texts too much instead of too little. If everything is underlined, you haven't been selective. And, very likely, you didn't pay much attention in the first place.

Organize Assume that you must memorize the following list of words: north, man, red, spring, woman, east, autumn, yellow, summer, boy, blue, west, winter, girl, green, south. This rather difficult list could be reorganized into *chunks* as follows: north-east-south-west, spring-summer-autumn-winter, red-yellow-green-blue, man-woman-boy-girl. Organizing class notes and summarizing modules or chapters can be quite helpful (Ellis, 2013). You may even want to summarize your summaries so that the overall network of ideas becomes clearer and simpler. Summaries improve memory by encouraging better encoding of information (Anderson, 2010a).

Consider Whole Versus Part Learning If you have to memorize a speech, is it better to try to learn it from beginning to end or in smaller parts like paragraphs? It depends. For fairly short, organized information, it is usually better to practice whole packages of information rather than smaller parts *(whole learning)*. Learning parts is usually better for extremely long, complicated information. In *part learning*, subparts of a larger body of information are studied (such as sections of a textbook module or chapter). To decide which approach to use, remember to study the *largest meaningful amount of information* you can at one time.

For very long or complex material, try the *progressive-part method*, by breaking a learning task into a series of short sections. At first, you study part A until it is mastered. Next, you study parts A and B; then A, B, and C; and so forth. This is a good way to learn the lines of a play, a long piece of music, or a poem (Ash & Holding, 1990). After the material is learned, you also should practice by starting at points other than A (at C, D, or B, for example). This helps prevent getting "lost" or going blank in the middle of a performance.

Beware Serial Position Whenever you must learn something in *order*, be aware of the serial position effect. As you will recall, this is the tendency to make the most errors in remembering the middle of a list. If you are introduced to a long line of people, the names you are likely to forget will be those in the middle, so you should make an extra effort to attend to them.

You also should give extra practice to the middle of a list, poem, or speech. Try to break long lists of information into short sublists, and make the middle sublists the shortest of all.

Encode Retrieval Cues The best *retrieval cues* (stimuli that aid retrieval) are those that were present during encoding (Anderson, 2010a). For example, students in one classic study had the daunting task of trying to recall a list of 600 words. As they read the list (which they did not know they would be tested on), the students gave three other words closely related in meaning to each listed word. In a test given later, the words each student supplied were used as cues to jog memory. The students recalled an astounding 90 percent of the original word list (Mantyla, 1986).

Now, read the following sentence:

The fish bit the swimmer.

If you were tested a week from now, you would be more likely to recall the sentence if you were given a retrieval cue. And, surprisingly, the word *shark* would work better as a reminder than *fish* because most people think of a shark when they read the sentence. As a result, *shark* becomes a potent retrieval cue.

The preceding example shows, once again, that it often helps to *elaborate* information as you learn. When you study, try to use new names, ideas, or terms in several sentences. Also, form images that include the new information and relate it to knowledge you already have. Your goal should be to knit meaningful cues into your memory code to help you retrieve information when you need it.

Overlearn Numerous studies have shown that memory is greatly improved when you *overlearn* or continue to study beyond bare mastery. After you have learned material well enough to remember it once without error, you should continue studying. Overlearning is your best insurance against going blank on a test because of nervousness.

Use Spaced Practice To keep boredom and fatigue to a minimum, try alternating short study sessions with brief rest periods. This pattern, called **spaced practice**, is generally superior to **massed practice**, in which little or no rest is given between learning sessions (Radvansky, 2011). By improving attention

Spaced practice *A practice schedule that alternates study periods with brief rests.*
Massed practice *A practice schedule in which studying continues for long periods, without interruption.*

and consolidation, three 20-minute study sessions can produce more learning than 1 hour of continuous study.

Perhaps the best way to use spaced practice is to *schedule* your time. To make an effective schedule, designate times during the week before, after, and between classes when you will study particular subjects. Then treat these times just as if they are classes you have to attend.

Retrieval Strategies

Once you have successfully encoded information, you still have to retrieve it. Following are some strategies to help you avoid retrieval failure:

Rely on Retrieval Practice Learning proceeds best when feedback allows you to check your progress. Feedback can help you identify ideas that need extra practice. In addition, it is rewarding to know that you have remembered or answered correctly. A prime way to provide feedback for yourself while studying is *recitation*. If you are going to remember something, eventually you have to retrieve it. *Recitation* refers to summarizing aloud while you are learning. Recitation forces you to practice retrieving information. When you are reading a textbook, you should stop frequently and try to remember what you have just read by restating it in your own words. In one classic experiment, the best memory score was earned by a group of students who spent 80 percent of their time reciting and only 20 percent reading (Gates, 1917). Maybe students who talk to themselves aren't crazy after all.

If you have spaced your practice and overlearned, retrieval practice in the form of review will be like icing on your study cake (Karpicke & Blunt, 2011). Reviewing shortly before an exam cuts down the time during which you must remember details that may be important for the test. When reviewing, hold the amount of new information you try to memorize to a minimum. It may be realistic to take what you have learned and add a little more to it at the last minute by cramming. But remember that more than a little new learning may interfere with what you already know.

Use a Strategy to Aid Recall Successful retrieval is usually the result of a planned *search* of memory (Reed, 2013). For example, one study found that students were most likely to recall names that eluded them if they made use of partial information (Reed & Bruce, 1982). The students were trying to answer questions such as, "He is best remembered as the scarecrow in the Judy Garland movie *The Wizard of Oz*." (The answer is Ray Bolger.) Partial information that helped

students remember included impressions about the length of the name, letter sounds within the name, similar names, and related information (such as the names of other characters in the movie). A similar helpful strategy is to go through the alphabet, trying each letter as the first sound of a name or word you are seeking.

The *cognitive interview* described in Module 32 (see "Telling Wrong from Right in Forensic Memory") offers some further hints for recapturing context and jogging memories:

1. Say or write down *everything* you can remember that relates to the information you are seeking. Don't worry about how trivial any of it seems; each bit of information you remember can serve as a cue to bring back other information.

2. Try to recall events or information in different orders. Let your memories flow backward or out of order, or start with whatever impressed you the most.

3. Recall from different viewpoints. Review events by mentally standing in a different place. Or try to view information as another person would remember it. When taking a test, for instance, ask yourself what other students or your professor would remember about the topic.

4. Mentally put yourself back in the situation where you learned the information. Try to mentally re-create the learning environment or relive the event. As you do, include sounds, smells, details of weather, nearby objects, other people present, what you said or thought, and how you felt as you learned the information (Milne & Bull, 2002).

Extend How Long You Remember When you are learning new information, practice retrieval repeatedly. As you do, gradually lengthen the amount of time that passes before you test yourself again. For example, if you are studying German words on flash cards, look at the first card and then move it a few cards back in the stack. Do the same with the next few cards. When you get to the first "old" card, test yourself on it and check the answer. Then, move it farther back in the stack. Do the same with other "old" cards as they come up. When "old" cards come up for the third time, put them clear to the back of the stack.

Mind Your Sleep Remember that sleeping after study reduces interference. However, unless you are a night person, late evening may not be a very efficient time for you to study. Also, you obviously can't sleep after every study session or study everything just before you sleep. That's why your study schedule should include ample breaks between subjects as described earlier (see "Use Spaced Practice"). The breaks and free time in your schedule are as important as your study periods.

Mind Your Hunger On the one hand, it is better to study before eating rather than after (Diano et al., 2006). On the other hand, people who are hungry almost always score lower on memory tests. So Mother was right, it's a good idea to make sure you've had a good breakfast or lunch before you take tests at school (Smith, Clark, & Gallagher, 1999). A cup of coffee won't hurt your test performance, either (Smith, Christopher, & Sutherland, 2013).

A Look Ahead Psychologists still have much to learn about the nature of memory and how to improve it. For now, one thing stands out clearly: People who have good memories excel at organizing meaningful information. Sometimes, however, you are faced with the need to memorize information without much inherent meaning. For example, a shopping list is just a list of more or less unrelated items. Not much of a meaningful relationship is present among carrots, rolls of toilet paper, TV dinners, and Twinkies except that you need more of them. With this in mind, in Module 36, you learn how to use mnemonics to better memorize when meaning-based strategies, like those described in this module, are not helpful.

Module 35: Summary

35.1 What are "photographic" memories?

- **35.1.1** Eidetic imagery (photographic memory) occurs when a person is able to project an image onto a blank surface. Eidetic imagery is rarely found in adults. However, many adults have internal mental images, which can be very vivid.
- **35.1.2** Exceptional memory may be based on natural ability or learned strategies. Usually, it involves both.

35.2 How can I improve my memory?

- **35.2.1** Superior memory abilities are based on using strategies and techniques that make learning efficient and that compensate for natural weaknesses in human memory.

- **35.2.2** Memory can be improved through better encoding strategies, such as elaborating, selecting, and organizing information as well as whole learning, the progressive part method, encoding retrieval cues, overlearning, and spaced practice.
- **35.2.3** Memory also can be improved through better retrieval strategies, such as retrieval practice, which involves feedback, recitation, and review and active search strategies.
- **35.2.4** When you are studying or memorizing, you also should keep in mind the effects of serial position, sleep, and hunger.

Module 35: Knowledge Builder

Recite

1. For most people, having an especially good memory is based on
   - **a.** maintenance rehearsal
   - **b.** elaborative processing
   - **c.** phonetic imagery
   - **d.** learned strategies

2. As new information is encoded, it is helpful to elaborate on its meaning and connect it to other information. *T or F?*

3. Organizing information while studying has little effect on memory because long-term memory is already highly organized. *T or F?*

4. To improve memory, it is reasonable to spend as much or more time reciting as reading. *T or F?*

5. The cognitive interview helps people remember more by providing
   - **a.** retrieval cues
   - **b.** a serial position effect
   - **c.** phonetic priming
   - **d.** massed practice

Reflect

Think Critically

6. What are the advantages of taking notes as you read a textbook, as opposed to underlining words in the text?

Self-Reflect

What kinds of information are you good at remembering? Why do you think your memory is better for those topics?

Return to the topic headings in the preceding pages that list techniques for improving memory. Review any you didn't mark and think of a specific example of how you could use each technique at school, at home, or at work.

ANSWERS

1. d 2. T 3. F 4. T 5. a 6. Properly done, note-taking is a form of elaborative processing; it encourages active reflection and facilitates the organization and selection of important ideas, and your notes can be used for review.

CENGAGE**brain**.com

Psychology in Action: Mnemonics

On Old Olympus' Towering Top

Imagine the poor biology or psychology student who is required to learn the names of the 12 cranial nerves (in order, of course). Although the spinal nerves connect the brain to the body through the spinal cord, the cranial nerves do so directly. Just in case you want to know, the names are olfactory, optic, oculomotor, trochlear, trigeminal, abducens, facial, vestibulocochlear, glossopharyngeal, vagus, spinal accessory, and hypoglossal.

As you might imagine, most of us find it difficult to successfully encode this list. In the absence of any obvious meaningful relationship among these terms, it is difficult to apply the memory strategies we discussed in Module 35. Instead, we are tempted to resort to *rote* learning (learning by simple repetition). Fortunately, there *is* an alternative: mnemonics. The basic idea is to impose an artificial organization on material if none is naturally present. By practicing mnemonics,

Mnemonics can be an aid in preparing for tests. However, because mnemonics help most in the initial stages of storing information, it is important to follow through with other elaborative learning strategies.

you should be able to greatly improve your memory with little effort.

SURVEY QUESTION

36.1 What are mnemonics?

Mnemonics—Tricks of the (Memory) Trade

SURVEY QUESTION 36.1: What are mnemonics?

A **mnemonic** (nee-MON-ik) is any kind of memory system or aid. The superiority of mnemonic learning as opposed to rote learning has been demonstrated many times (Saber & Johnson, 2008; Worthen & Hunt, 2010).

Some mnemonic systems are so common that almost everyone knows them. If you are trying to remember how many days there are in a month, you may find the answer by reciting, "Thirty days hath September. . . ." Physics teachers often help students remember the colors of the spectrum by giving them the mnemonic "Roy G. Biv": **R**ed, **O**range, **Y**ellow, **G**reen, **B**lue, **I**ndigo, **V**iolet. The budding sailor who has trouble telling port from starboard may remember that "port" and "left" both have four letters or may remind herself, "I *left* port." And what beginning musician hasn't remembered the notes represented by the lines and spaces of the musical staff by learning "F-A-C-E" and "**E**very **G**ood **B**oy **D**oes **F**ine."

Generations of students have learned the names of the spinal nerves by memorizing the sentence "**O**n **O**ld **O**lympus' **T**owering **T**op **A** **F**amous **V**ocal **G**erman **V**iewed **S**ome **H**ops." This mnemonic, which uses the first letter of each of the cranial nerves to generate a nonsense sentence, indeed produces better recall of the cranial nerves. Such *acrostics* are even more effective if you make up your own (Fry, 2012).

Here, then, are some basic principles of mnemonics:

1. **Make things meaningful.** In general, transferring information from short-term memory to long-term memory is aided by making it meaningful. If you encounter technical terms that have little or no immediate meaning for you, *give* them meaning, even if you have to stretch the term to do so. (This point is clarified by the examples following this list.)

2. **Make information familiar.** Another way to get information into long-term memory is to connect it to information already stored there. If some facts or ideas in a module or chapter seem to stay in your memory easily, associate other more difficult facts with them.

3. **Use mental pictures.** Visual pictures, or images, are generally easier to remember than words. Turning information into mental pictures is therefore very helpful. Make these images as vivid as possible (Soemer & Schwan, 2012).

4. **Form bizarre, unusual, or exaggerated mental associations.** Forming images that make sense is better in most situations. However, when associating two ideas, terms, or especially mental images, you may find that the more outrageous and exaggerated the association, the more likely you are to remember. Bizarre images make stored information more *distinctive* and therefore easier to retrieve (Worthen & Hunt, 2010). Imagine, for example, that you have just been introduced to Mr. Rehkop. To remember his name, you could picture him wearing a police uniform. Then replace his nose with a ray gun. This bizarre image will provide two hints when you want to remember Mr. Rehkop's name: *ray* and *cop.*

This technique works for other kinds of information, too. College students who used exaggerated mental associations to remember the names of unfamiliar animals outperformed students who just used rote memory (Carney & Levin, 2001). Bizarre images help improve mainly immediate memory, and they work best for fairly simple information (Fritz et al., 2007). Nevertheless, they can be a first step toward learning.

A sampling of typical applications of mnemonics should make these four points clearer to you.

Example 1 Let's say you have some new vocabulary words to memorize in Spanish. You can proceed by rote memorization (repeat them over and over until you begin to get them), or you can learn them with little effort by using the **keyword method,** in

Exaggerated mental images can link two words or ideas in ways that aid memory. Here, the keyword method is used to link the English word *letter* with the Spanish word *carta.*

which a familiar word or image is used to link two other words or items (Campos, Camino, & Pérez-Fabello, 2011; Fritz et al., 2007). To remember that the word *pajaro* (pronounced PAH-hah-ro) means bird, you can link it to a "key" word in English: *Pajaro* sounds a bit like "parked car-o." Therefore, to remember that *pajaro* means bird, you might visualize a parked car jam-packed with birds. You should try to make this image as vivid and exaggerated as possible, with birds flapping and chirping and feathers flying everywhere. Similarly, for the word *carta* (which means letter), you might imagine a shopping *cart* filled with postal letters.

If you link similar keywords and images for the rest of the list, you may not remember them all, but you will get most without much more practice. As a matter of fact, if you have formed the *pajaro* and *carta* images, it will be almost impossible for you to see these words again without remembering what they mean.

What about a year from now? How long do keyword memories last? Mnemonic memories work best in the short run. Later, they may be more fragile than conventional memories. That's why it's usually best to use mnemonics during the initial stages of learning (Carney & Levin, 2003; Fry, 2012). To create more lasting memories, you need to use the techniques discussed in Module 35.

Example 2 Suppose you have to learn the names of all the bones and muscles in the human body. To remember that the jawbone is the *mandible,* you can associate it to a *man nibbling,* or maybe you can picture a *man dribbling* a basketball with his jaw (make this image as ridiculous as possible). If the muscle name *latissimus dorsi* gives you trouble, familiarize it by turning it into *"the ladder misses the door, sigh."* Then picture a ladder glued to your back where the muscle is found. Picture the ladder leading up to a small door at your shoulder. Picture the ladder missing the door. Picture the ladder sighing like an animated character in a cartoon.

This seems like more to remember, not less; and it seems like it might lead to misspelling things. Mnemonics are an aid, not a complete substitute for normal memory. Mnemonics are not likely to be helpful unless you make extensive use of *images* (Worthen & Hunt, 2010). Your mental pictures will come back to you easily. As for misspellings, mnemonics can be thought of as a built-in hint in your memory. Often, when taking a test, you will find that the slightest hint is all you need to remember correctly. A mnemonic image is like having someone leaning over your shoulder who says, "Psst, the name of that muscle sounds like 'ladder misses the door, sigh.'" If misspelling continues to be a problem, try to create memory aids for spelling, too.

Two more examples will help you appreciate the flexibility of a mnemonic approach to studying.

Example 3 Your art history teacher expects you to be able to name the artist when you are shown slides as part of exams. You have seen many of the slides only once before in class. How will you remember them? As the slides are shown in class, make each artist's name into an object or image. Then, picture the object *in* the paintings done by the artist. For example, you can picture Van Gogh as a *van* (automobile) *going* through the middle of each Van Gogh painting. Picture the van running over things and knocking things over. Or, if you remember that Van Gogh cut off his ear, picture a giant bloody ear in each of his paintings.

Example 4 If you have trouble remembering history, try to avoid thinking of it as something from the dim past. Picture each historical personality as a person you know right now (a friend, teacher, parent, and so on). Then picture these people doing whatever the historical figures did. Also, try visualizing battles or other events as if they were happening in your town, or you could make parks and schools into countries. Use your imagination.

How can mnemonics be used to remember things in order? Here are three helpful techniques:

1. **Form a story or a chain.** To remember lists of ideas, objects, or words in order, try forming an exaggerated association (mental image) connecting the first item to the second and then the second to the third, and so on. To remember the following short list in order—elephant, doorknob, string, watch, rifle, oranges—picture a full-size *elephant* balanced on a *doorknob* playing with a *string* tied to him. Picture a *watch* tied to the string, and a *rifle* shooting *oranges* at the watch. This technique can be used quite successfully for lists of 20 or more items. In one test, people who used a linking mnemonic did much better at remembering lists of 15 and 22 errands (Higbee et al., 1990). Try it next time you go shopping and leave your list at home. Another helpful strategy is to make up a short story that links all the items on a list you want to remember (McNamara & Scott, 2001; Worthen & Hunt, 2010).

2. **Take a mental walk.** Ancient Greek orators had an interesting way to remember ideas in order when giving a speech. Their method was to take a mental walk along a familiar path. As they did, they associated topics with the images of statues found along the walk. You can do the same thing by "placing" objects or ideas along the way as you mentally take a familiar walk (Radvansky, 2011).

3. **Use a system.** As we have already seen, many times the first letters or syllables of words or ideas can be formed into another word that serves as a reminder of order. "Roy G. Biv" is an example. As an alternative, learn the following: 1 is a bun, 2 is a shoe, 3 is a tree, 4 is a door, 5 is a hive, 6 is sticks, 7 is heaven, 8 is a gate, 9 is a line, 10 is a hen. To remember a list in order, form an image associating bun with the first item on your list. For example, if the first item is *frog,* picture a "frog-burger" on a bun to remember it. Then, associate shoe with the second item, and so on.

If you have never used mnemonics, you may still be skeptical, but give this approach a fair trial. Most people find they can greatly extend their memory using mnemonics. But remember, like most things worthwhile, remembering takes effort (Hancock, 2011).

Mnemonic *Any kind of memory system or aid.*
Keyword method *As an aid to memory, using a familiar word or image to link two items.*

Module 36: Summary

36.1 What are mnemonics?

- **36.1.1** Memory systems (mnemonics) greatly improve immediate memory. However, conventional learning tends to create the most lasting memories.

- **36.1.2** Mnemonic systems use mental images and unusual associations to link new information with familiar memories already stored in LTM.

- **36.1.3** Effective mnemonics tend to rely on mental images and bizarre or exaggerated mental associations.

Module 36: Knowledge Builder

Recite

1. Memory systems and aids are referred to as _____.

2. Which of the following is least likely to improve memory?
   - *a.* using exaggerated mental images
   - *b.* forming a chain of associations
   - *c.* turning visual information into verbal information
   - *d.* associating new information to information that is already known or familiar

3. Bizarre images make stored information more distinctive and therefore easier to retrieve. **T or F?**

4. In general, mnemonics improve only memory for related words or ideas. **T or F?**

Reflect

Think Critically

5. How are elaborative processing and mnemonics alike?

Self-Reflect

The best mnemonics are your own. As an exercise, see if you can create a better acrostic for the 12 cranial nerves. One student generated **O**ld **O**tto **O**ctavius **T**ried **T**rigonometry **A**fter **F**acing **V**ery **G**rim **V**irgin's **S**ad **H**usbands (Bloom & Lamkin, 2006).

ANSWERS

CENGAGE**brain**.com

Go to **cengagebrain.com** to access **MindTap for Coon/Mitterer** *Psychology Modules for Active Learning* and other online learning tools. MindTap is a fully online learning experience that combines all the tools you need—readings, multimedia, activities, and assessments—into a singular personalized Learning Path that guides you through the course.

Cognition and Intelligence: Modes of Thought

Homo Sapiens

Unlike other species, humans owe their success more to thinking abilities than to physical strength or speed. That's why we are called *Homo sapiens* (from the Latin for *man* and *wise*). Our mental abilities make us highly adaptable. We live in deserts, jungles, mountains, frenzied cities, placid retreats, and even space stations.

Consider Steven Hawking. Lou Gehrig's disease has ravaged his spinal cord, short-circuiting messages between his brain and muscles. Today, confined to a wheelchair, he "speaks" by controlling a speech synthesizer through cheek movements. Yet despite his severe disabilities, his brain is unaffected by the disease and remains fiercely active. He can still *think*. Steven is a theoretical physicist and one of the best-known scientific minds of modern times.

But *how* do we think? What does language have to do with thought? How are we able to solve problems? What is intelligence? What is wisdom? Let's think this through.

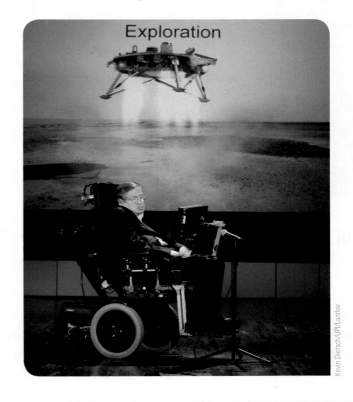

Exploration

Kevin Dietsch/UPI/Landov

SURVEY QUESTIONS

37.1 What is the nature of thought?

37.2 In what ways are images related to thinking?

37.3 What are concepts and how are they learned?

37.4 What is language and what role does it play in thinking?

What Is Thinking?— Brains over Brawn

SURVEY QUESTION 37.1: What is the nature of thought?

At its most basic, **cognition (thinking)** refers to processing a *mental representation* (mental expression) of a problem or situation (Sternberg, 2012). Let's do some thinking while looking at ● **Figure 37.1**. On the left *(a)*, is this face happy or sad? Chances are you *knew* the answer just by looking at the photo. You were engaging in more or less passive, effortless, and automatic **experiential processing**. Now, looking at *(b)*,

what is the sum of these numbers? Chances are, experiential processing was not enough in this case; you likely had to deliberately concentrate as you engaged in **reflective processing** (Kahneman, 2011; Norman, 1994). (The difference between these two types of cognition is relevant to how well you understand and remember what you are learning; see Module 1, How to Study Psychology.)

In Module 27, we saw that animals can engage in simple forms of cognitive learning. In contrast, human cognition can take many forms, from experiential daydreaming to more reflective problem solving and reasoning. Consider, for example, the relatively reflective process of planning. Picture a television interviewer who mentally tries out several lines of questioning before beginning a live interview. By *planning* her

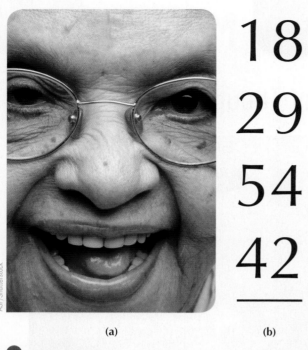

18

29

54

42

(a)   (b)

● **Figure 37.1**

An experiential processing task (*a*) versus a reflective processing task (*b*). See the text for an explanation. (After Kahneman, 2011.)

moves, she can avoid many mistakes. Imagine planning what to study for an exam, what to say at a job interview, or how to get to your spring break hotel. Better yet, in each of these cases, imagine what might happen if you didn't, or couldn't, plan at all.

Some Basic Units of Thought

The power of being able to mentally represent problems is dramatically illustrated by chess grand master Miguel Najdorf, who once simultaneously played 45 chess games while blindfolded. How did Najdorf do it? Like most people, he used the basic units of thought: images, concepts, and language (or symbols). **Images** are picture-like mental representations. **Concepts** are ideas that represent categories of objects or events. **Language** consists of words or symbols and rules for combining them. Thinking often involves all three units. For example, blindfolded chess players rely on visual images, concepts ("Game 2 begins with a strategy called an English opening"), and the notational system, or "language," of chess.

In a moment, we delve further into imagery, concepts, and language. Be aware, however, that thinking involves attention,

pattern recognition, memory, decision making, intuition, knowledge, and more (Reed, 2013). This module is only a sample of what cognitive psychology is about.

Mental Imagery—Does a Frog Have Lips?

SURVEY QUESTION 37.2: In what ways are images related to thinking?

Almost everyone has visual and auditory images. More than half of us also experience imagery for movement, touch, taste, smell, and pain. Thus, mental images are often more than just "pictures." For example, your image of a bakery also may include its delicious aroma. Some people even have a rare form of imagery called *synesthesia* (sin-es-THEE-zyah). For these individuals, images cross normal sensory barriers (Craver-Lemley & Reeves, 2013). For one such person, spiced chicken tastes "pointy"; for another, pain is the color orange; and for a third, human voices unleash a flood of colors and tastes (Dixon, Smilek, & Merikle, 2004; Robertson & Sagiv, 2005). Despite such variations, most of us use images to think, remember, and solve problems. For instance, we may use mental images to do the following:

- Make a decision or solve a problem (choose what clothes to wear; figure out how to arrange furniture in a room)

- Change feelings (think of pleasant images to get out of a bad mood; imagine yourself as thin to stay on a diet)

- Improve a skill or prepare for some action (use images to improve a tennis stroke; mentally rehearse how you will ask for a raise)

- Aid memory (picture Mr. Cook wearing a chef's hat, so you can remember his name)

The Nature of Mental Images

Mental images are not flat, like photographs. Researcher Stephen Kosslyn showed this by asking people, "Does a frog have lips and a stubby tail?" Unless you often kiss frogs, you probably will tackle this question by using mental images. Most people picture a frog, "look" at its mouth, and then

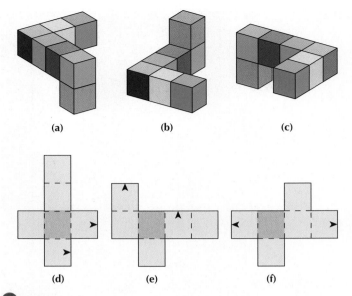

Figure 37.2

Imagery in thinking. (*Top*) Participants were shown a drawing similar to (*a*) and drawings of how (*a*) would look in other positions, such as (*b*) and (*c*). Participants could recognize (*a*) after it had been "rotated" from its original position. However, the more (*a*) was rotated in space, the longer it took to recognize it. This result suggests that people formed a three-dimensional image of (*a*) and rotated the image to see if it matched (Shepard, 1975). (*Bottom*) Try your ability to manipulate mental images: Picture each of these shapes as a piece of paper that can be folded to make a cube. After they have been folded, on which cubes do the arrow tips meet (Kosslyn, 1985)?

mentally "rotate" the frog in mental space to check its tail (Kosslyn, 1983). Mental rotation is partly based on imagined movements (● **Figure 37.2**). That is, we can mentally "pick up" an object and turn it around or even fold it (Harris, Hirsh-Pasek, & Newcombe, 2013; Wraga, 2010).

"Reverse Vision" *What happens in the brain when a person has visual images?* Seeing something in your "mind's eye" is similar to seeing real objects. Information from the eyes normally activates the brain's primary visual area, creating an image (● **Figure 37.3**). Other brain areas then help us recognize the image by relating it to stored knowledge. When you form a mental image, the system works in reverse. Brain areas in which memories are stored send signals back to the visual cortex, where once again an image is created (Borst & Kosslyn, 2010; Ganis, Thompson, & Kosslyn, 2004). For example, if you visualize a friend's face right now, the area of your brain that specializes in perceiving faces will become more active (Prochnow et al., 2013).

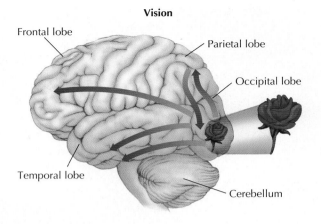

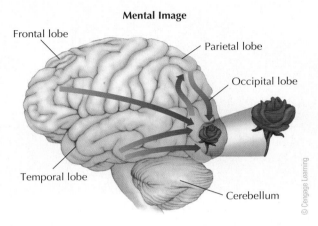

Figure 37.3

(*Top*) When you see a flower, its image is represented by activity in the primary visual area of the cortex at the back of the brain. Information about the flower also is relayed to other brain areas. (*Bottom*) If you form a mental image of a flower, information follows a reverse path. The result, once again, is activation of the primary visual area.

Using Mental Images *How are images used to solve problems?* Let's say you are asked, "How many ways can you use an empty egg carton?" You might begin by picturing uses

Cognition (thinking) *The process of mentally processing information (images, concepts, words, rules, and symbols).*
Experiential processing *Thought that is passive, effortless, and automatic.*
Reflective processing *Thought that is active, effortful, and controlled.*
Image *Most often, a mental representation that has picture-like qualities; an icon.*
Concept *A generalized idea representing a category of related objects or events.*
Language *Words or symbols, and rules for combining them, that are used for thinking and communication.*

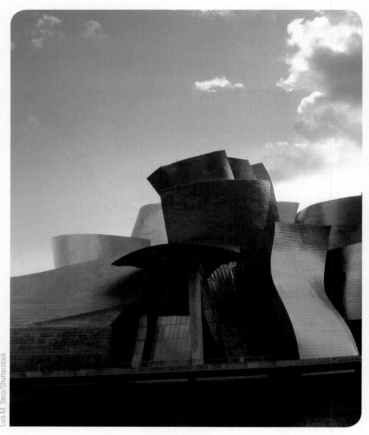

The Guggenheim Museum in Bilbao, Spain, was designed by architect Frank Gehry. Could a person lacking mental imagery design such a masterpiece? Most artists, architects, designers, sculptors, and filmmakers have excellent visual imagery.

Rock climbers use kinesthetic imagery to learn climbing routes and to plan their next few moves (Smyth & Waller, 1998).

you have already seen, such as sorting buttons. To give more original answers, you might assemble or invent new images. Thus, an artist may completely picture a proposed sculpture before beginning work. People with good imaging abilities tend to score higher on tests of creativity, even if they are blind (Eardley & Pring, 2007; Morrison & Wallace, 2001).

Kinesthetic Imagery In a sense, we think with our bodies as well as our heads. *Kinesthetic (motor) images* are created from muscular sensations (Grangeon, Guillot, & Collet, 2011; Guillot et al., 2009). Such images help us think about movements and actions.

As you think and talk, kinesthetic sensations can guide the flow of ideas. For example, if a friend calls and asks you the combination of a lock you loaned her, you may move your hands as if twirling the dial on the lock. Or, try answering this question: Which direction do you turn the hot-water handle in your kitchen to shut off the water? If you haven't memorized the words "leftie loosie" and "rightie tightie," you may "turn" the faucet in your imagination before answering. You may even make a turning motion with your hand before answering.

Kinesthetic images are especially important in movement-oriented skills such as music, sports, dance, skateboarding, and martial arts. An effective way to improve such skills is to practice by rehearsing kinesthetic images of yourself performing flawlessly (Anema & Dijkerman, 2013).

Concepts—I'm Positive, It's a Whatchamacallit

SURVEY QUESTION 37.3: What are concepts and how are they learned?

As noted earlier, a *concept* is an idea that represents a category of objects or events. Concepts help us identify important features of the world. That's why experts in various areas of knowledge are good at classifying objects. Bird-watchers, tropical fish fanciers, 5-year-old dinosaur enthusiasts, and other experts all learn to look for identifying details that beginners tend to miss. If you are knowledgeable about a topic, such as horses, flowers, or football, you literally see things differently than less well-informed people (Harel et al., 2010; Ross, 2006).

Forming Concepts

How are concepts learned? **Concept formation** is the process of classifying information into meaningful categories (Ashby & Maddox, 2005; Newell, 2012). At its most basic, concept formation is based on experience with *positive* and *negative instances* (examples that belong, or do not belong, to the concept class). Concept formation is not as simple as it might seem. Imagine a child learning the concept of *dog*:

Dog Daze

A child and her father go for a walk. At a neighbor's house, they see a medium-sized dog. The father says, "See the dog." As they pass the next yard, the child sees a cat and says, "Dog!" Her father corrects her, "No, that's a *cat*." The child now thinks, "Aha, dogs are large and cats are small." In the next yard, she sees a Pekingese and says, "Cat!" "No, that's a dog," replies her father.

The child's confusion is understandable. At first, she might even mistake a Pekingese for a dust mop. However, with more positive and negative instances, the child will eventually recognize everything from Great Danes to Chihuahuas as members of the same category—dogs.

As adults, we often acquire concepts by learning or forming *conceptual rules*, guidelines for deciding whether objects or events belong to a concept class. For example, a triangle must be a closed shape with three sides made of straight lines. Rules are an efficient way to learn concepts, but examples remain important. It's unlikely that memorizing rules would allow a new listener to accurately categorize *rhythm and blues, hip-hop, fusion, salsa, rock, country,* and *rap* music.

Types of Concepts

Are there different kinds of concepts? Yes, **conjunctive concepts**, or "and concepts," are defined by the presence of two or more features (Reed, 2013). In other words, an item must have "this feature *and* this feature *and* this feature." For example, a *motorcycle* must have two wheels *and* an engine *and* handlebars.

Relational concepts are based on how an object relates to something else, or how its features relate to one another. All of the following are relational concepts: *larger, above, left, north,* and *upside down.* Another example is *brother,* which is defined as "a male considered in his relation to another person having the same parents."

Disjunctive concepts have *at least one* of several possible features. These are "either/or" concepts. To belong to the category,

an item must have "this feature *or* that feature *or* another feature." For example, in baseball, a *strike* is *either* a swing and a miss *or* a pitch over the plate *or* a foul ball. The either/or quality of disjunctive concepts makes them harder to learn.

Prototypes When you think of the concept *bird,* do you mentally list the features of birds? Probably not. In addition to rules and features, we use **prototypes,** or ideal models, to identify concepts (Rosch, 1977; Tunney & Fernie, 2012). A robin, for example, is a prototypical bird; an ostrich is not. In other words, some items are better examples of a concept than others are (Smith, Redford, & Haas, 2008). Which of the drawings in ● **Figure 37.4** best represents a cup? At some point, as a cup grows taller or wider, it becomes a vase or a bowl. How do we know when the line is crossed? Probably, we mentally compare objects to an "ideal" cup, like number 5. That's why it's hard to identify concepts when we can't come up with relevant prototypes (Minda & Smith, 2011).

Faulty Concepts Using inaccurate concepts often leads to thinking errors. For example, *social stereotypes* are oversimplified concepts of groups of people (Le Pelley, et al., 2010). Stereotypes about men, African Americans, women,

● **Figure 37.4**

When does a cup become a bowl or a vase? Deciding if an object belongs to a conceptual class is aided by relating it to a prototype, or ideal example. Participants in one experiment chose Number 5 as the "best" cup. (After Labov, 1973.)

Concept formation *The process of classifying information into meaningful categories.*
Conjunctive concept *A class of objects that have two or more features in common. (For example, to qualify as an example of the concept, an object must be both red and triangular.)*
Relational concept *A concept defined by the relationship between features of an object or between an object and its surroundings (for example, "greater than," "lopsided").*
Disjunctive concept *A concept defined by the presence of at least one of several possible features. (For example, to qualify, an object must be either blue or circular.)*
Prototype *An ideal model used as a prime example of a particular concept.*

conservatives, liberals, police officers, or other groups often muddle thinking about members of the group. (See Module 73 for more information about stereotypes, prejudice, and discrimination.) A related problem is *all-or-nothing thinking* (one-dimensional thought). In this case, we classify things as absolutely right or wrong, good or bad, fair or unfair, black or white, honest or dishonest. Thinking this way prevents us from appreciating the subtleties of most life problems (Alberts, Thewissen, & Raes, 2012).

Connotative Meaning Generally speaking, concepts have two types of meaning. The **denotative meaning** of words or concepts is their exact definition. The **connotative meaning** is the emotional or personal meaning of words. The denotative meaning of the word *naked* (having no clothes) is the same for a nudist as it is for a movie censor, but we could expect their connotations to differ.

Can you clarify what a connotative meaning is? Yes, connotative meaning can be measured with a technique called the *semantic differential*, as shown in ●**Figure 37.5**. When we rate words or concepts, most of their connotative meaning boils down to the dimensions *good/bad, strong/weak,* and *active/passive*. These dimensions give words very different connotations, even when their denotative meanings are similar. For example, I am *conscientious*; you are *careful*; he is *nitpicky*! Because we are conscientious. (Not nitpicky, right?)

Connotative differences can influence how we think about issues. Would you rather eat *rare prime beef* or *bloody slab of dead cow*? The arts of *political spin* and *propaganda* often amount to manipulating connotations. For example, facing a terminal illness, would you rather engage in *end-of-life counseling* or attend a *death panel* (Payne, 2009)? Let's further explore language.

Language—Don't Leave Home Without It

SURVEY QUESTION 37.4: What is language and what role does it play in thinking?

As we have seen, thinking may occur without language. Everyone has searched for a word to express an idea that exists as a vague image or feeling. Nevertheless, most thinking relies heavily on language, because words *encode* (translate) the world into symbols that are easy to manipulate (●**Figure 37.6**). And, as we saw earlier, the words we choose to use can greatly affect our thinking. (See "What's North of My Fork?")

The study of meaning in words and language is known as **semantics** (Traxler, 2011). It is here that the link between language and thought becomes most evident. Suppose, on an

Rate this word: **JAZZ**

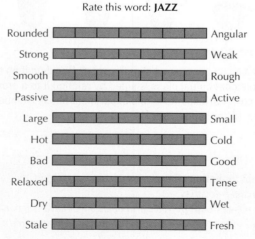

●**Figure 37.5**

This is an example of Osgood's semantic differential. The connotative meaning of the word *jazz* can be established by rating it on the scales. Mark your own rating by placing dots or Xs in the spaces. Connect the marks with a line; then, have a friend rate the word and compare your responses. It might be interesting to do the same for *rock and roll, classical,* and *hip-hop.* You also might want to try the word *psychology.* (Adapted from Osgood, 1952.)

●**Figure 37.6**

Wine tasting illustrates the encoding function of language. To communicate their experiences to others, wine connoisseurs must put taste sensations into words. The wine you see here is "Marked by deeply concentrated nuances of plum, blackberry, and currant, with a nice balance of tannins and acid, building to a spicy oak finish." (Don't try this with a Pop-Tart!)

Critical Thinking

What's North of My Fork?

It is clear that our thoughts influence the words we use. But might the reverse be true? Do the words we use affect our thoughts and actions? The answer may lie in a remote part of northeastern Australia. Cognitive psychologist Lera Boroditsky has reported that aboriginal children from Cape York can accurately point to any compass direction as early as age 5. In contrast, most Americans cannot do this even as adults (Boroditsky, 2011).

But why? According to Boroditsky, unlike English, Kuuk Thaayorre, the language of the Cape York Australian aboriginals, relies exclusively on *absolute* directional references. Like English, Kuuk Thaayorre has words for "north," "south," and so on. Unlike English, Kuuk Thaayorre lacks words for *relative* directional references, such as "left" and "right."

For long distances, an English speaker might say, "Chicago is north of here." But for short distances, the same speaker will shift to a relative reference and might say, "My brother is sitting to my right." In contrast, a speaker of Kuuk Thaayorre always uses absolute directional references, saying things like "My friend is sitting southeast of me" and "The dessert spoon is west of the coffee cup." If you are a young aboriginal child, you had best master your absolute directions, or most conversations will be impossible to follow.

Another interesting consequence for speakers of Kuuk Thaayorre is how they arrange time. In one study, English speakers given a set of cards depicting a series of events (for example, a person getting older or a meal being cooked and eaten) and asked to put them in order usually arranged them from left to right. Hebrew speakers usually arranged the cards from right to left, presumably because this is the direction in which Hebrew is written. In contrast, speakers of Kuuk Thaayorre arrange temporal sequences from east to west. If the sorter is facing north, the cards are arranged from right to left, but if the sorter is facing south, the cards are arranged from left to right, and so on (Boroditsky & Gaby, 2010).

Findings like these lend support to the **linguistic relativity hypothesis**, the idea that the words we use not only reflect our thoughts but can shape them as well. So the next time you think your future is "ahead" of you and your past is "behind," think again. For speakers of Aymara, a South American language, it is the past that is "ahead" (Miles et al., 2010). So watch your back.

---

intelligence test, you were asked to circle the word that does not belong in this series:

| SKYSCRAPER | CATHEDRAL | TEMPLE | PRAYER |

If you circled *prayer,* you answered as most people do. Now try another problem, again circling the odd item:

| CATHEDRAL | PRAYER | TEMPLE | SKYSCRAPER |

Did you circle *skyscraper* this time? The new order subtly alters the meaning of the last word (Mayer, 1995). This occurs because words get much of their meaning from *context.* For example, the word *shot* means different things when we are thinking of marksmanship, bartending, medicine, photography, or golf (Carroll, 2008).

More subtle effects also occur. For example, most people have difficulty quickly naming the color of the ink used to print the words in the bottom two rows of ● **Figure 37.7.** The automatic processing of word meanings is just too strong to ignore.

Language also plays a major role in defining ethnic communities and other social groups. Thus, language can be a bridge or a barrier between cultures. Translating languages can cause a rash of semantic problems. Perhaps the San Jose, California, public library can be excused for once displaying a large banner that was supposed to say "You are welcome" in a

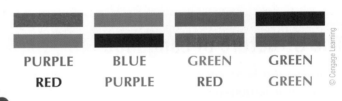

| PURPLE | BLUE | GREEN | GREEN |
| **RED** | PURPLE | RED | GREEN |

● **Figure 37.7**

The Stroop interference task. Test yourself by naming the colors in the top two rows as quickly as you can. Then name the colors of the ink used to print the words in the bottom two rows. (Do not read the words themselves.) Was it harder to name the ink colors in the bottom rows?

---

native Philippine language. The banner actually said "You are circumcised." However, in more important situations, such as in international business and diplomacy, avoiding semantic confusion may be vital. (See "Bilingualism—*Si o No, Oui ou Non,* Yes or No?")

Denotative meaning *The exact, dictionary definition of a word or concept; its objective meaning.*
Connotative meaning *The subjective, personal, or emotional meaning of a word or concept.*
Semantics *The study of meanings in words and language.*
Linguistic relativity hypothesis *The idea that the words we use not only reflect our thoughts but can shape them as well.*

Human Diversity

Bilingualism—*Si o No, Oui ou Non,* Yes or No?

Are there advantages to being able to speak more than one language? Definitely. **Bilingualism** is the ability to speak two languages. Studies have found that students who learn to speak two languages well have better mental flexibility, general language skills, control of attention, and problem-solving abilities (Bialystok & Barac, 2012; Bialystok & DePape, 2009).

Unfortunately, millions of minority American children who do not speak English at home experience *subtractive bilingualism.* Immersed in English-only classrooms, in which they are expected to "sink or swim," they usually end up losing some of their native language skills. Such children risk becoming less than fully competent in *both* their first and second languages. In addition, they tend to fall behind educationally. As they struggle with English, their grasp of arithmetic, social studies, science, and other subjects also may suffer. In short, English-only instruction can leave them poorly prepared to succeed in the majority culture (Durán, Roseth, & Hoffman, 2010; Matthews & Matthews, 2004).

For the majority of children who speak English at home, the picture can be quite different because learning a second language is almost always beneficial. It poses no threat to the child's home language and improves a variety of cognitive skills. This has been called *additive*

bilingualism because learning a second language adds to a child's overall competence (Hermanto, Moreno, & Bialystok, 2012).

An approach called **two-way bilingual education** can help children benefit from bilingualism and avoid its drawbacks (Benitz, 2009; Lessow-Hurley, 2013). In such programs, majority group children and children with limited English skills are taught part of the day in English and part in a second language. Both majority and minority language speakers become fluent in two languages, and they perform as well as or better than single-language students in English and general academic abilities.

Then, why isn't two-way bilingual education more widely used? Bilingual education tends to be politically unpopular among majority language speakers (Garcia, 2008). Language is an important sign of group membership. Even where the majority culture is highly dominant, some of its members may feel that recent immigrants and "foreign languages" are eroding their culture. Regardless, an ability to think and communicate in a second language is a wonderful gift. Given the cognitive benefits, fostering bilingualism also may turn out to be one of the best ways to improve competitiveness in our rapidly globalizing information economy.

The Structure of Language

What does it take to make a language? First, a language must provide *symbols* that stand for objects and ideas (Harley, 2008). The symbols we call words are built out of **phonemes** (FOE-neems: basic speech sounds) and **morphemes** (MOR-feems: speech sounds collected into meaningful units, such as syllables or words). For instance, in English the sounds *m, b, w,*

Albanian	mak, mak
Chinese	gua, gua
Dutch	rap, rap
English	quack, quack
French	coin, coin
Italian	qua, qua
Spanish	cuá, cuá
Swedish	kvack, kvack
Turkish	vak, vak

John Mitterer

● **Figure 37.8**

Animals around the world make pretty much the same sounds. Notice, however, how various languages use slightly different phonemes to express the sound a duck makes.

and *a* cannot form a syllable *mbwa.* In Swahili, they can. (Also see ● **Figure 37.8.**)

Next, a language must have a **grammar**, or set of rules for making sounds into words and words into sentences (Reed, 2013). One part of grammar, known as **syntax**, concerns rules for word order. Syntax is important because rearranging words almost always changes the meaning of a sentence: "Dog bites man" versus "Man bites dog."

Traditional grammar is concerned with "surface" language—the sentences we actually speak. Linguist Noam Chomsky has focused instead on the unspoken rules we use to change core ideas into various sentences. Chomsky (1986) believes that we do not learn all the sentences we might ever say. Rather, we actively *produce* them by applying **transformation rules** to universal, core patterns. We use these rules to change a simple declarative sentence to other voices or forms (past tense, passive voice, and so forth). For example, the core sentence "Dog bites man" can be transformed to these patterns (and others):

Past: The dog bit the man.

Passive: The man was bitten by the dog.

Negative: The dog did not bite the man.

Question: Did the dog bite the man?

Children seem to be using transformation rules when they say things such as "I runned home"—that is, the child applied the normal past tense rule to the irregular verb *to run*.

A true language is, therefore, *productive*—it can generate new thoughts or ideas. In fact, words can be rearranged to produce a nearly infinite number of sentences. Some are silly: "Please don't feed me to the goldfish." Some are profound: "We hold these truths to be self-evident, that all men are created equal." In either case, the productive quality of language makes it a powerful tool for thinking.

Gestural Languages

Contrary to common belief, language is not limited to speech. Consider the case of Ildefonso, a young man who was born deaf. At age 24, Ildefonso had never communicated with another human, except by mime. Then, at last, Ildefonso had a breakthrough: After much hard work with a sign language teacher, he understood the link between a cat and the gesture for it. At that magic moment, he grasped the idea that "cat" could be communicated to another person, just by signing the word.

American Sign Language (ASL), a gestural language, made Ildefonso's long-awaited breakthrough possible. ASL is a true language, like German, Spanish, or Japanese (Liddell, 2003). In fact, people who use other gestural languages, such as French Sign, Mexican Sign, or Old Kentish Sign, may not easily understand ASL (Lucas & Bayley, 2011; Shaw & Delaporte, 2011).

Although ASL has a *spatial* grammar, syntax, and semantics all its own (● **Figure 37.9**), both speech and signing follow

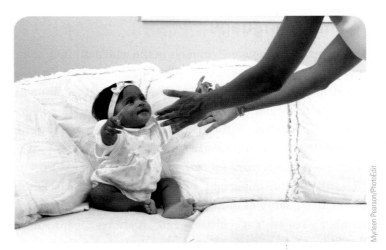

Infants can express the idea "pick me up" in gestures before they can make the same request in words. Their progression from gestures to speech may mirror the evolution of human language abilities (Genty et al., 2009).

similar universal language patterns. Signing children pass through the stages of language development at about the same age as speaking children. Some psychologists now believe that speech evolved from gestures, far back in human and primate history (Slocombe, Waller, & Liebal, 2011). Gestures help us string words together as we speak (Moreno-Cabrera, 2011). Some people would have difficulty speaking with their hands tied to their sides. Do you ever make hand gestures when you are speaking on the phone? If so, you may be displaying a remnant of the gestural origins of language. Perhaps that's also why the same brain areas become more active when a person speaks or signs (Enrici et al., 2011).

Sign languages naturally arise out of a need to communicate visually. But they also embody a personal identity and define a distinct community. Those who "speak" sign share not just a language but a rich culture as well (West & Sutton-Spence, 2012).

Look at

Stare

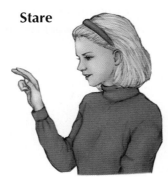

● **Figure 37.9**

ASL has only 3,000 root signs, compared with roughly 600,000 words in English. However, variations in signs make ASL a highly expressive language. For example, the sign LOOK-AT can be varied in ways to make it mean look at me, look at her, look at each, stare at, gaze, watch, look for a long time, look at again and again, reminisce, sightsee, look forward to, predict, anticipate, browse, and many more variations.

Bilingualism   *The ability to speak two languages.*
Two-way bilingual education   *A program in which English-speaking children and children with limited English proficiency are taught half the day in English and half in a second language.*
Phonemes   *The basic speech sounds of a language.*
Morphemes   *The smallest meaningful units in a language, such as syllables or words.*
Grammar   *A set of rules for combining language units into meaningful speech or writing.*
Syntax   *Rules for ordering words when forming sentences.*
Transformation rules   *Rules by which a simple declarative sentence may be changed to other voices or forms (past tense, passive voice, and so forth).*

Animal Language

Do animals use language? Animals in the wild definitely communicate. The cries, gestures, and mating calls of animals have broad meanings immediately understood by other animals of the same species (Bradbury & Vehrencamp, 2011). For the most part, however, natural animal communication is quite limited. Even apes and monkeys make only a few dozen distinct cries, which carry messages such as "attack," "flee," or "food here." More important, animal communication lacks the productive quality of human language. For example, when a monkey gives an "eagle distress call," it always means something like, "I see an eagle." The monkey has no way of saying, "I don't see an eagle," or "Thank heavens that wasn't an eagle," or "That sucker I saw yesterday was some huge eagle" (Pinker & Jackendoff, 2005).

What about trying to teach language to animals? To this point, numerous chimps and gorillas, as well as an assortment of dolphins, sea lions, and parrots, have been taught to communicate with word symbols of various kinds. The "champion" is probably a pygmy chimpanzee named Kanzi.

Kanzi's Lexigrams

Since the 1980s, Duane Rumbaugh and Sue Savage-Rumbaugh have been teaching Kanzi to communicate by pushing buttons on a computer keyboard. Each of the 250 buttons is marked with a *lexigram*, or geometric word-symbol (● **Figure 37.10**). Some of the lexigrams Kanzi knows are quite abstract, like symbols for "bad" and "good" (Lyn, Franks, & Savage-Rumbaugh, 2008). Using the lexigrams, Kanzi can create primitive sentences several words long. He also can understand about 650 spoken sentences.

Kanzi's sentences consistently follow correct word order. Like a child learning language, Kanzi picked up some rules

● **Figure 37.10**

Kanzi's language learning has been impressive. He can comprehend spoken English words. He can identify lexigram symbols when he hears corresponding words. He can use lexigrams when the objects to which they refer are absent, and he can, if asked, lead someone to the object. All these skills were acquired through observation, not conditioning (Segerdahl, Fields, & Savage-Rumbaugh, 2005).

from his caregivers (Segerdahl, Fields, & Savage-Rumbaugh, 2005). However, he has developed other patterns on his own (Gillespie-Lynch et al., 2011). For example, Kanzi usually places action symbols in the order he wants to carry them out, such as "chase tickle" or "chase hide."

In these respects, Kanzi's vocabulary and ability to invent a simple grammar are on a par with 2-year-olds. After about 30 years of training, Kanzi's language use is certainly noteworthy and may yet help us better understand the roots of human language (Slocombe, Waller, & Liebal, 2011). On the other hand, as Chomsky insists, if chimps were biologically capable of language, they would use it on their own.

Module 37: Summary

37.1 What is the nature of thought?

- **37.1.1** Thinking is the manipulation of internal representations of external stimuli or situations.
- **37.1.2** Thinking can be either automatic experiential processing or more effortful reflective processing.
- **37.1.3** Three basic units of thought are images, concepts, and language (or symbols).

37.2 In what ways are images related to thinking?

- **37.2.1** Most people have internal images of one kind or another. Sometimes they cross normal sense boundaries in a type of imagery called synesthesia.
- **37.2.2** Images may be three-dimensional and they may be rotated in space.
- **37.2.3** The same brain areas are involved in both vision and visual imagery.
- **37.2.4** Kinesthetic images are used to represent movements and actions.

37.3 What are concepts and how are they learned?

- **37.3.1** A concept is a generalized idea of a class of objects or events.
- **37.3.2** Concept formation may be based on positive and negative instances or rule learning.
- **37.3.3** Concepts may be conjunctive ("and" concepts), disjunctive ("either/or" concepts), or relational.
- **37.3.4** In practice, concept identification frequently makes use of prototypes, or ideal models.
- **37.3.5** The denotative meaning of a word or concept is its dictionary definition. Connotative meaning is personal or emotional.

37.4 What is language and what role does it play in thinking?

- **37.4.1** Language encodes events into symbols for easy mental manipulation. The study of meaning in language is called semantics.
- **37.4.2** Bilingualism is a valuable ability. Two-way bilingual education allows children to develop additive bilingualism while in school.
- **37.4.3** Language carries meaning by combining a set of symbols according to a set of rules (grammar), which includes rules about word order (syntax).
- **37.4.4** True languages are productive and can be used to generate new ideas or possibilities.
- **37.4.5** Complex gestural systems, such as American Sign Language, are true languages.
- **37.4.6** Chimpanzees and other primates have learned to use word symbol systems about as well as 2-year-old humans.

Module 37: Knowledge Builder

Recite

1. Reflective processing is automatic and effortless. *T or F?*
2. Our reliance on imagery in thinking means that problem solving is impaired by the use of language or symbols. *T or F?*
3. Humans can form three-dimensional images that can be moved or rotated in mental space. *T or F?*
4. A *mup* is defined as anything that is small, blue, and hairy. *Mup* is a _____ concept.
5. Stereotyping is an example of oversimplification in thinking. *T or F?*
6. True languages are _____ because they can be used to generate new possibilities.
7. The basic speech sounds are called _____; the smallest meaningful units of speech are called _____.
8. Noam Chomsky believes that we can create an infinite variety of sentences by applying _____ _____ to universal language patterns.

Reflect

Think Critically

9. A Democrat and a Republican are asked to rate the word *democratic* on the semantic differential. Under what conditions would their ratings be most alike?

Self-Reflect

Name some ways you have used imagery in the thinking you have done today.

Write a conceptual rule for the following idea: *unicycle*. Were you able to define the concept with a rule? Would positive and negative instances help make the concept clearer for others?

Just for fun, see if you can illustrate the productive quality of language by creating a sentence that no one has ever before spoken.

ANSWERS

Cognition and Intelligence: Problem Solving

At Least They Weren't Tigers

You can imagine Pie's surprise. He had anchored his little motorboat 10 miles from an island and gone snorkelling. He returned to the boat only to discover that two seals had settled in for a quick nap. He climbed into his boat and immediately began to cruise toward the island at 7 miles per hour. Just then the two seals woke up, indignantly jumped into the water, and also swam toward the island. At the same instant, Pie's friend left the island in a sailboat at 3 miles per hour, coming out to rendezvous with the motorboat. The seals swam back and forth between the motorboat and sailboat at a speed of 8 miles per hour.

John Mitterer

A good way to start a discussion of problem solving is to solve a problem, so, how far will the seals have swum when the two boats meet?

SURVEY QUESTION

38.1 What do we know about problem solving?

Problem Solving—Go Figure

SURVEY QUESTION 38.1: What do we know about problem solving?

Problem solving can be as commonplace as figuring out how to make a nonpoisonous meal out of leftovers or as significant as developing a cure for cancer. No matter what form a problem takes, it is usually best faced *mindfully* (Hayes, Strosahl, & Wilson, 2012). Did you enter reflective processing mode and tackle the seals and boats problem? If you didn't immediately see the answer to this problem, try it again. (The answer is revealed in the "Insightful Solutions" section.)

Mechanical Solutions

For routine problems, a **mechanical solution** may be adequate. Mechanical solutions are achieved by trial and error or by rote (Goldstein, 2011). If you forget the combination to your bike lock, you may be able to discover it by trial and error. When a problem is solved by *rote*, thinking is guided by an **algorithm**,

or learned set of rules that always leads to an answer. A simple example of an algorithm is the steps you used to add up the numbers in Figure 37.1 (whether you did it in your head or by using a calculator). Becoming a problem-solving expert in any particular field involves, at a minimum, becoming familiar with the algorithms available in that field. Imagine wanting to be a mathematician and yet being unwilling to learn any algorithms.

If you have a good background in math, you may have solved the problem of the seals and the boats by rote. (Your authors hope you didn't. There is an easier solution.)

Solutions by Understanding

Many problems cannot be solved mechanically. In that case, **understanding** (deeper comprehension of a problem) is necessary. Try this problem:

> A person has an inoperable stomach tumor. A device is available that produces rays that at high intensity will destroy tissue (both healthy and diseased). How can the tumor be destroyed without damaging surrounding tissue? (Also see the sketch in
> ● Figure 38.1.)

Figure 38.1

A schematic representation of Duncker's tumor problem. The dark spot represents a tumor surrounded by healthy tissue. How can the tumor be destroyed without injuring surrounding tissue? (Adapted from Duncker, 1945.)

What does this problem show about problem solving? German psychologist Karl Duncker gave college students this problem in a classic series of studies. Duncker asked them to think aloud as they worked. He found that successful students first had to discover the *general properties* of a correct solution. A **general solution** defines the requirements for success but not in enough detail to guide further action. This phase was complete when students realized that the intensity of the rays had to be lowered on their way to the tumor. Then, in the second phase, they proposed a number of **functional solutions**, or workable solutions, and selected the best one (Duncker, 1945). (One solution is to focus weak rays on the tumor from several angles. Another is to rotate the person's body to minimize exposure of healthy tissue.)

Here's another example. Amateur naturalists usually begin painfully identifying the birds, butterflies, mammals, or plants they find by mechanically (i.e., rote) searching through published field guides until they find the correct species name and description. In time, those who persist begin to identify more and more species from memory and others based on the general properties they have learned through experience. With enough practice, this is exactly how novices become experts in a wide variety of fields.

Heuristics

"You can't get there from here," or so it often seems when facing a problem. Solving problems often requires a strategy. If the number of alternatives is small, a *random search strategy* may work. This is another example of trial-and-error thinking in which all possibilities are tried, more or less randomly. Imagine that you are traveling and you decide to look up an old FBI friend, Olivia Dunham, in a big city you are visiting. You search an online directory and find a dozen O. Dunhams listed. Of course, you could dial each number until you find the right one. "Forget it," you say to yourself. "Is there any way I can narrow the search?" "Oh, yeah! I remember hearing that Olivia lives by the beach." Then you use a map and call only the numbers with addresses near the waterfront.

The approach used in this example is a **heuristic** (hew-RIS-tik)—a strategy for identifying and evaluating problem solutions. Typically, a heuristic is a "rule of thumb" that *reduces the number of alternatives* thinkers must consider (Benjafield, Smilek, & Kingstone, 2010). Expert problems solvers are good at using heuristic strategies like these:

- Try to identify how the current state of affairs differs from the desired goal. Then find steps that will reduce the difference.
- Try working backward from the desired goal to the starting point or current state.
- If you can't reach the goal directly, try to identify an intermediate goal or subproblem that at least gets you closer.
- Represent the problem in other ways—with graphs, diagrams, or analogies, for instance.
- Generate a possible solution and test it. Doing so may eliminate many alternatives, or it may clarify what is needed for a solution.

In closing, notice that although heuristics like these raise the odds of success, they do not guarantee a solution.

Insightful Solutions

A thinker who suddenly solves a problem has experienced **insight** (Cushen & Wiley, 2012). Insights are usually based on reorganizing a problem. This allows us to see problems in new ways and makes their solutions seem obvious (Hélie & Sun, 2010).

Let's return now to the problem of the boats and the seals. The best way to solve it is by insight. Because the boats will cover the 10-mile distance in exactly 1 hour, and the seals swim 8 miles per hour, the seals will have swum 8 miles when the boats meet. Very little math is necessary if you have insight

---

Mechanical solution *A problem solution achieved by trial and error or by a fixed procedure based on learned rules.*
Algorithm *A learned set of rules that always leads to the correct solution of a problem.*
Understanding *In problem solving, a deeper comprehension of the nature of the problem.*
General solution *A solution that correctly states the requirements for success but not in enough detail for further action.*
Functional solution *A detailed, practical, and workable solution.*
Heuristic *Any strategy or technique that aids problem solving, especially by limiting the number of possible solutions to be tried.*
Insight *A sudden mental reorganization of a problem that makes the solution obvious.*

Water lilies

Problem: Water lilies growing in a pond double in area every 24 hours. On the first day of spring, only one lily pad is on the surface of the pond. Sixty days later, the pond is entirely covered. On what day is the pond half-covered?

Twenty dollars

Problem: Jessica and Blair both have the same amount of money. How much must Jessica give Blair so that Blair has $20 more than Jessica?

How many pets?

Problem: How many pets do you have if all of them are birds except two, all of them are cats except two, and all of them are dogs except two?

Between 2 and 3

Problem: What one mathematical symbol can you place between 2 and 3 that results in a number greater than 2 and less than 3?

One word

Problem: Rearrange the letters NEWDOOR to make one word.

● Figure 38.2

Some insight problems.

---

into this problem. **● Figure 38.2** lists some additional insight problems you may want to try (the answers can be found in **● Table 38.1**).

The Nature of Insight Psychologist Janet Davidson (2003) believes that insight involves three abilities. The first is *selective encoding,* which refers to selecting information that is relevant to a problem while ignoring distractions. For example, consider the following problem:

> If you have white socks and black socks in your drawer, mixed in the ratio of 4 to 5, how many socks will you have to take out to ensure you have a pair of the same color?

A person who recognizes that "mixed in a ratio of 4 to 5" is irrelevant will be more likely to come up with the correct answer of 3 socks.

Insight also relies on *selective combination,* or bringing together seemingly unrelated bits of useful information. Try this sample problem:

> With a 7-minute hourglass and an 11-minute hourglass, what is the simplest way to time boiling an egg for 15 minutes?

The answer requires using both hourglasses in combination. First, the 7-minute and the 11-minute hourglasses are started.

When the 7-minute hourglass runs out, it's time to begin boiling the egg. At this point, 4 minutes remain on the 11-minute hourglass. Thus, when it runs out, it is simply turned over. When it runs out again, 15 minutes will have passed.

A third source of insights is *selective comparison.* This is the ability to compare new problems with old information or with problems already solved. A good example is the hat rack problem, in which participants must build a structure that can support an overcoat in the middle of a room. Each person is given only two long sticks and a C-clamp to work with. The solution, shown in **● Figure 38.3**, is to clamp the two sticks together so that they are wedged between the floor and ceiling. If you were given this problem, you would be more likely to solve it if you first thought of how pole lamps are wedged between the floor and ceiling.

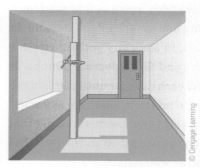

● Figure 38.3

A solution to the hat rack problem.

Fixations One of the most important barriers to problem solving is **fixation**, the tendency to get "hung up" on wrong solutions or to become blind to alternatives (Sternberg, 2012). This usually occurs when we, without giving it any thought, place unnecessary restrictions on our thinking (McCaffrey, 2012). How, for example, could you plant four small trees so that each is an equal distance from all the others? (The answer is shown in ● Figure 38.4.)

● Figure 38.4

Four trees can be placed equidistant from one another by piling dirt into a mound. Three of the trees are planted equal distances apart around the base of the mound. The fourth tree is planted on the top of the mound. If you were fixated on arrangements that involve level ground, you may have been blind to this three-dimensional solution.

A prime example of restricted thinking is **functional fixedness**. This is an inability to see new uses (functions) for familiar objects or for things that were used in a particular way (Bernstein & Lucas, 2008). If you have ever used a dime as a screwdriver, you've overcome functional fixedness.

How does functional fixedness affect problem solving? Karl Duncker once asked students to mount a candle on a vertical board so the candle could burn normally. He gave each student three candles, some matches, some cardboard boxes, some thumbtacks, and other items. Half of Duncker's participants received these items *inside* the cardboard boxes. The others were given all the items, including the boxes, spread out on a tabletop.

Duncker found that when the items were in the boxes, solving the problem was very difficult. Why? If students saw the boxes as *containers*, they didn't realize the boxes might be part of the solution (if you haven't guessed the solution, check ● **Figure 38.5**). Undoubtedly, we could avoid many fixations by being more flexible in categorizing the world (Kalyuga & Hanham, 2011; Langer, 2000). For instance, creative thinking could be facilitated in the container problem by saying "This *could be* a box," instead of "This *is* a box."

When tested with the candle problem, 5-year-old children show no signs of functional fixedness. Apparently, this is because they have had less experience with the use of various objects. It is sometimes said that to be more creative, you should try to see the world without preconceptions, as if

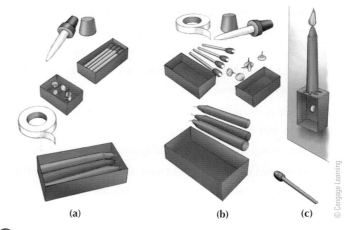

(a)   (b)   (c)

● Figure 38.5

Materials for solving the candle problem were given to participants in boxes (*a*) or separately (*b*). Functional fixedness caused by condition (*a*) interfered with solving the problem. The solution to the problem is shown in (*c*).

through the eyes of a child. In the case of functional fixedness, that may be true (German & Defeyter, 2000).

Common Barriers to Problem Solving

Functional fixedness is just one of the mental blocks that prevent insight (Reed, 2013). Here's an example of another: A $5 bill is placed on a table and a stack of objects is balanced precariously on top of the bill. How can the bill be removed without touching, moving, or toppling the objects? A good answer is to split the bill on one of its edges. Gently pulling from opposite ends will tear the bill in half and remove it without toppling the objects. Many people fail to see this solution because they have learned not to destroy money (Adams, 2001). Notice again the impact of placing something in a category—in this case, "things of value" (which should not be destroyed). Other common mental blocks can hinder problem solving:

1. **Emotional barriers:** Inhibition and fear of making a fool of oneself, fear of making a mistake, inability to tolerate ambiguity, excessive self-criticism

   Example: An architect is afraid to try an unconventional design because she fears that other architects will think it is frivolous.

Fixation (in problem solving) *The tendency to repeat wrong solutions or faulty responses, especially as a result of becoming blind to alternatives.*

Functional fixedness *A rigidity in problem solving caused by an inability to see new uses for familiar objects.*

2. **Cultural barriers:** Values that hold that fantasy is a waste of time; that playfulness is for children only; that reason, logic, and numbers are good; that feelings, intuitions, pleasure, and humor are bad or have no value in the serious business of problem solving

    Example: A corporate manager wants to solve a business problem but becomes stern and angry when members of his marketing team joke playfully about possible solutions.

3. **Learned barriers:** Conventions about uses (functional fixedness), meanings, possibilities, taboos

    Example: A cook doesn't have any clean mixing bowls and fails to see that he could use a pot as a bowl.

4. **Perceptual barriers:** Habits leading to a failure to identify important elements of a problem

    Example: A beginning artist concentrates on drawing a vase of flowers without seeing that the "empty" spaces around the vase are part of the composition, too.

TABLE 38.1	Solutions to Insight Problems

Water lilies: Day 59

Twenty dollars: $10

How many pets?: Three (one bird, one cat, and one dog)

Between 2 and 3: A decimal point

One word: ONE WORD (You may object that the answer is two words, but the problem called for the answer to be "one word," and it is.)

© Cengage Learning

Experts and Novices

So far, we have seen that problem-solving expertise is based on *acquired strategies* (learned heuristics) and specific *organized knowledge* (systematic information). Experts are better able to see the true nature of problems and to define them more flexibly in terms of general principles (Anderson, 2010a; Kalyuga & Hanham, 2011). For example, chess experts are much more likely than novices to have heuristics available for solving problems. However, what really sets master players apart is their ability to intuitively recognize *patterns* that suggest what lines of play should be explored next. This helps eliminate a large number of possible moves. The chess master, therefore, does not waste time exploring unproductive pathways (Ross, 2006).

In other words, becoming a star performer does not come from some general strengthening of the mind. Master chess players don't necessarily have better memories than

beginners (except for realistic chess positions) (Gobet & Simon, 1996; Goldstein, 2011; see ● **Figure 38.6**). And, typically, they don't explore more moves ahead than do lesser players.

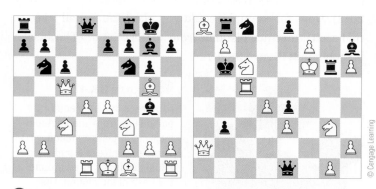

© Cengage Learning

● **Figure 38.6**

The left chessboard shows a realistic game. The right chessboard is a random arrangement of pieces. Expert chess players can memorize the left board at a glance, yet they are no better than beginners at memorizing the random board (Ross, 2006). Expert performance at most thinking tasks is based on acquired strategies and knowledge. If you want to excel at a profession or a mental skill, plan on adding to your knowledge every day (Reed, 2013).

You might think experts are always in reflective processing mode. Oddly enough, just the opposite is true. Expertise involves more experiential, *automatic* processing, or fast, fairly effortless thinking based on experience with similar problems. Automatic processing frees "space" in short-term memory, making it easier to work on the problem (Kalyuga, Renkl, & Paas, 2010). At the highest skill levels, expert performers tend to rise above rules and plans. Their decisions, thinking, and actions become rapid, fluid, and insightful (Hélie & Sun, 2010). Thus, when a chess master recognizes a pattern on the chessboard, the most desirable tactic comes to mind almost immediately. Mind you, this capacity comes at a price of time and effort. Expert chess players can automatically recognize 50,000 to 100,000 patterns, a level of skill that takes about 10 years of mindful, reflective processing to build up (Ross, 2006).

To develop expertise in a field, then, requires us to learn available heuristic solution strategies as well as to develop a deeper general understanding of the field. Throw into the mix that expertise also involves learning thousands of patterns and practicing solving many problems and you can see that developing expertise involves years of hard work. Think about that the next time someone says of an expert, "She makes it look easy."

Module 38: Summary

38.1 What do we know about problem solving?

- **38.1.1** The solution to a problem may be arrived at mechanically (by trial and error or by rote application of rules), but mechanical solutions are often inefficient.
- **38.1.2** Solutions by understanding usually begin with discovery of the general properties of an answer, followed by a functional solution.
- **38.1.3** Problem solving is aided by heuristics, which narrow the search for solutions.

- **38.1.4** When understanding leads to a rapid solution, insight has occurred. Three elements of insight are selective encoding, selective combination, and selective comparison.
- **38.1.5** Insight can be blocked by fixations. Functional fixedness is a common fixation, but emotional blocks, cultural values, learned conventions, and perceptual habits also are problems.
- **38.1.6** Problem-solving experts also engage in automatic processing and pattern recognition.

Module 38: Knowledge Builder

Recite

1. Insight refers to rote, or trial-and-error, problem solving. **T or F?**
2. The first phase in problem solving by understanding is to discover the general properties of a correct solution. **T or F?**
3. Problem-solving strategies that guide the search for solutions are called _____.
4. A common element underlying insight is that information is encoded, combined, and compared
   - **a.** mechanically
   - **b.** by rote
   - **c.** functionally
   - **d.** selectively
5. Functional fixedness is a major barrier to
   - **a.** insightful problem solving
   - **b.** using random search strategies
   - **c.** mechanical problem solving
   - **d.** achieving fixations through problem solving
6. Organized knowledge, acquired heuristics, and the ability to recognize patterns are all characteristics of human expertise. **T or F?**

Reflect

Think Critically

7. Do you think that it is true that "a problem clearly defined is a problem half solved"?
8. In captivity, white-handed gibbons (a type of ape), have been observed building swings to swing on. Does this qualify as thinking?

Self-Reflect

Identify at least one problem you have solved mechanically. Now identify a problem you solved by understanding. Did the second problem involve finding a general solution, a functional solution, or both? What heuristics did you use to solve the problem?

What is the most insightful solution you've ever come up with? Did it involve selective encoding, combination, or comparison?

Can you think of a time when you overcame functional fixedness to solve a problem?

ANSWERS

1. F 2. T 3. heuristics 4. d 5. a 6. T 7. Although this might be an overstatement, it is true that clearly defining a starting point and the desired goal can serve as a heuristic in problem solving. 8. It certainly involves tool use. Thinking also may be implicated because the actions appear to be planned with an awareness of likely results (Bentley-Condit & Smith, 2010).

Go to **cengagebrain.com** to access **MindTap for Coon/Mitterer** *Psychology Modules for Active Learning* and other online learning tools. MindTap is a fully online learning experience that combines all the tools you need—readings, multimedia, activities, and assessments—into a singular personalized Learning Path that guides you through the course.

Cognition and Intelligence: Creative Thinking and Intuition

No One-Hit Wonders

Original ideas have changed the course of human history. Much of what we now take for granted in art, medicine, music, technology, and science were once regarded as radical or impossible. How do creative thinkers like Steven Hawking achieve the breakthroughs that advance us into new realms?

For a start, creative thinkers are usually continuously creative. Mozart produced more than 600 pieces of music. Inventor Thomas Edison held over 1,000 U.S. patents for his inventions. Emily Dickinson wrote 597 poems. Salvador Dali (shown here) created more than 1,500 paintings as well as sculptures, drawings, illustrations, books, and even an animated cartoon. Not all of these works were masterpieces. However, a fluent outpouring of ideas fed the creative efforts of each of these geniuses.

Psychologists have learned a great deal about how creativity occurs and how to promote it. Besides noting the fluency of creative thinkers, what else have they found?

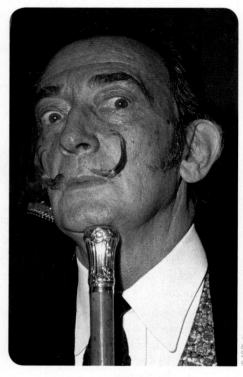

© AP Photo

SURVEY QUESTIONS

39.1 What is the nature of creative thinking?

39.2 How accurate is intuition?

Creative Thinking— Down Roads Less Traveled

SURVEY QUESTION 39.1: What is the nature of creative thinking?

We have seen that problem solving may be mechanical, insightful, or based on understanding. To this, we can add that thinking may be **inductive**—going from specific facts or observations to general principles—or **deductive**—going from general principles to specific situations. Thinking also may be **logical**—proceeding from given information to new conclusions on the basis of explicit rules—or **illogical**—intuitive, associative, or personal.

What distinguishes creative thinking from more routine problem solving? Whereas problem solving is usually a consciously reflective processing activity, creativity more likely involves apparently unconscious experiential processing (Ritter, van Baaren, & Dijksterhuis, 2012). Creative thinking also involves *fluency, flexibility,* and *originality*.

Let's say that you would like to find creative uses for the billions of plastic containers discarded each year. The creativity of your suggestions could be rated in this way: **Fluency** is defined as the total number of suggestions you are able to make. **Flexibility** is the number of times you shift from one class of possible uses to another. **Originality** refers to how novel or unusual your ideas are. By counting the number of times you showed fluency, flexibility, and originality, we could rate your creativity, or capacity for *divergent thinking* (Runco, 2012; Runco & Acar, 2012).

In routine problem solving or thinking, there is one correct answer, and the problem is to find it. This leads to **convergent thinking** (lines of thought converge on the answer). **Divergent thinking** is the reverse, in which many possibilities are developed from one starting point. (See ● Table 39.1 for some examples.) Rather than repeating learned solutions, creative thinking produces new answers, ideas, or patterns (Davidovitch & Milgram, 2006).

Tests of Creativity

Divergent thinking can be measured in several ways (Kaufman, 2009; Runco & Acar, 2012). In the *Unusual Uses test*, you would be asked to think of as many uses as possible for some object, such as the plastic containers mentioned earlier. In the *Consequences test*, you would list the consequences that would follow a basic change in the world. For example, you might be

TABLE 39.1	Convergent and Divergent Problems

Convergent Problems
- What is the area of a triangle that is 3 feet wide at the base and 2 feet tall?
- Erica is shorter than Zoey but taller than Carlo, and Carlo is taller than Jared. Who is the second tallest?
- If you simultaneously drop a baseball and a bowling ball from a tall building, which will hit the ground first?

Divergent Problems
- What objects can you think of that begin with the letters BR?
- How could discarded aluminum cans be put to use?
- Write a poem about fire and ice.

© Cengage Learning

asked, "What would happen if everyone suddenly lost their sense of balance and could no longer stay upright?" People try to list as many reactions as possible. If you were to take the *Anagrams test*, you would be given a word such as *creativity* and asked to make as many new words as possible by rearranging the letters. Each of these tests can be scored for fluency, flexibility, and originality. (For an example of other tests of divergent thinking, see ● Figure 39.1.)

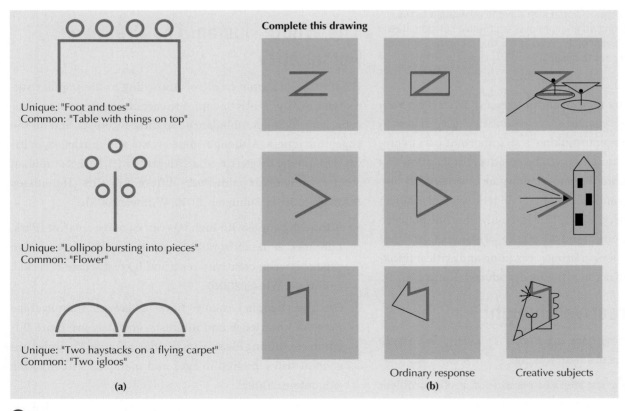

 Figure 39.1

Some tests of divergent thinking. Creative responses are more original and more complex. [(*a*) Adapted from Wallach & Kogan, 1965; (*b*) adapted from Barron, 1958.]

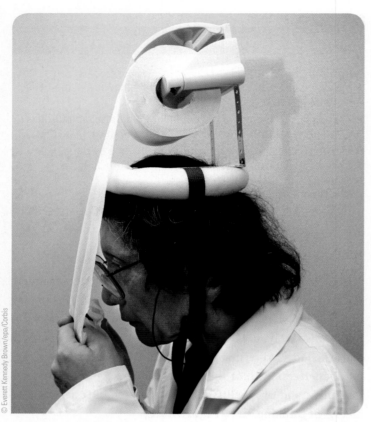

Whimsical Japanese inventor Kenji Kawakami created the "hay fever hat" so no one with allergies would ever have to go without tissue paper. In addition to being original or novel, a creative solution must be high quality and relevant of the problem. Is this a creative solution to the "problem" of access to tissues?

Isn't creativity more than divergent thought? What if a person comes up with a large number of useless answers to a problem? A good question. Divergent thinking is an important part of creativity, but there is more to it. To be creative, the solution to a problem must be more than novel, unusual, or original. It also must be *high quality* and *relevant* to solving the original problem (Kaufman & Sternberg, 2010). This is the dividing line between a "harebrained scheme" and a "stroke of genius." In other words, the creative person brings reasoning and critical thinking to bear on new ideas once they are produced (Runco, 2012).

Stages of Creative Thought

Does creative thinking have a pattern? Typically, five stages occur during creative problem solving:

1. **Orientation.** As a first step, the person defines the problem and identifies its most important dimensions.

2. **Preparation.** In the second stage, creative thinkers saturate themselves with as much information about the problem as possible.

3. **Incubation.** Most major problems will have a period during which all attempted solutions are futile. At this point, problem solving may proceed on a subconscious level: Although the problem seems to have been set aside, it is still "cooking" in the background.

4. **Illumination.** The incubation stage is often ended by a rapid insight or series of insights. These produce the "Aha!" experience, often depicted in cartoons as a light bulb appearing over the thinker's head.

5. **Verification.** The final step is to test and critically evaluate the solution obtained during the illumination stage. If the solution proves faulty, the thinker reverts to the stage of incubation.

Of course, creative thought is not always so neat. Nevertheless, the stages listed are a good summary of the most typical sequence of events.

Some psychologists believe that truly exceptional creativity requires a rare combination of thinking skills, personality, and a supportive social environment. This mix, they believe, accounts for creative giants such as Edison, Freud, Mozart, Picasso, and others (Robinson, 2010; Simonton, 2009).

The Whole Human: The Creative Personality

What makes a person creative? According to the popular stereotype, highly creative people are eccentric, introverted, neurotic, socially inept, unbalanced in their interests, and on the edge of madness. Although some artists and musicians cultivate this public image, there is little truth in it. Direct studies of creative individuals paint a very different picture (Hennessey & Amabile, 2010; Robinson, 2010; Winner, 2003):

1. Although people with high IQs can be quite creative (Park, Lubinski, & Benbow, 2008), generally, little correlation exists between creativity tests and IQ test scores (Preckel, Holling, & Wiese, 2006).

2. Creative people usually have a greater-than-average range of knowledge and interests, and they are more fluent in combining ideas from various sources. They also are good at using mental images and metaphors in thinking (Riquelme, 2002).

3. Creative people are open to a wide variety of experiences. They accept irrational thoughts and are uninhibited about their feelings and fantasies. They tend to use broad categories, question assumptions, and break mental sets, and they

find order in chaos. They also experience more unusual states of consciousness, such as vivid dreams and mystical experiences (Ayers, Beaton, & Hunt, 1999).

4. Creative people enjoy symbolic thought, ideas, concepts, and possibilities. They tend to be interested in truth, form, and beauty, rather than in fame or success. Their creative work is an end in itself (Robinson, 2010; Sternberg & Lubart, 1995).

5. Creative people value their independence and prefer complexity. However, they are unconventional and nonconforming primarily in their work; otherwise, they do not have unusual, outlandish, or bizarre personalities. Don't forget to read Module 41 for more on creativity.

Can creativity be learned? It is beginning to look as if some creative thinking skills can be learned. In particular, you can become more creative by practicing divergent thinking and by taking risks, asking unusual questions, analyzing ideas, and seeking odd connections between ideas (Bucher, 2011; Sternberg, 2012).

Intuitive Thought—Mental Shortcut? Or Dangerous Detour?

SURVEY QUESTION 39.2: How accurate is intuition?

At the same time that experiential, intuitive thought may contribute to creative problem solving, it also can lead to thinking errors (Kahneman, 2011). To see how this can happen, try the following problems:

Problem 1 An epidemic breaks out, and 600 people are about to die. Doctors have two choices. If they give drug A, 200 lives will be saved. If they give drug B, there is a one-third chance that 600 people will be saved and a two-thirds chance that none will be saved. Which drug should they choose?

Problem 2 Again, 600 people are about to die, and doctors must make a choice. If they give drug A, 400 people will die. If they give drug B, there is a one-third chance that no one will die and a two-thirds chance that 600 will die. Which drug should they choose?

Most people choose drug A for the first problem and drug B for the second. This is fascinating because the two problems are identical. The only difference is that the first is stated in terms of lives saved, the second in terms of lives lost. Yet, even people who realize that their answers are contradictory find it difficult to change them (Kahneman, 2011; Kahneman & Tversky, 1972).

Intuition

As the example of the two problems shows, we often make decisions intuitively, rather than logically or rationally. **Intuition** is quick, impulsive thought. It may provide fast answers, but it also can be misleading and sometimes disastrous. (See "Have You Ever Thin-Sliced Your Teacher?")

Two noted psychologists, Daniel Kahneman (KON-eh-man) and Amos Tversky (tuh-VER-ski) (1937–1996), studied how we make decisions in the face of uncertainty. They found that human judgment is often seriously flawed (Kahneman, 2011; Kahneman, Slovic, & Tversky, 1982). Let's explore some common intuitive thinking errors, so you will be better prepared to avoid them.

Representativeness One very common pitfall in judgment is illustrated by the following question: Which is more probable?

A. The New York Yankees will not be in the lead after the first half of the baseball season but will win their division.

B. The New York Yankees will not be in the lead after the first half of the baseball season.

According to Tversky and Kahneman (1982), people who follow baseball are likely to regard a statement like A as more probable than B (For those of you not in the know, the Yankees are often competitive in post-season play). However, this intuitive answer overlooks an important fact: The likelihood of two events occurring together is lower than the probability

---

Inductive thought *Thinking in which a general rule or principle is gathered from a series of specific examples; for instance, inferring the laws of gravity by observing many falling objects.*

Deductive thought *Thought that applies a general set of rules to specific situations; for example, using the laws of gravity to predict the behavior of a single falling object.*

Logical thought *Drawing conclusions on the basis of formal principles of reasoning.*

Illogical thought *Thought that is intuitive, haphazard, or irrational.*

Fluency *In tests of creativity, refers to the total number of solutions produced.*

Flexibility *In tests of creativity, flexibility is indicated by how many different types of solutions are produced.*

Originality *In tests of creativity, originality refers to how novel or unusual solutions are.*

Convergent thinking *Thinking directed toward discovery of a single established correct answer; conventional thinking.*

Divergent thinking *Thinking that produces many ideas or alternatives; a major element in original or creative thought.*

Intuition *Quick, impulsive thought that does not use formal logic or clear reasoning.*

Critical Thinking

Have You Ever Thin-Sliced Your Teacher?

Think back to your least favorite teacher. (Not your current one, of course!) How long did it take you to figure out that he or she wasn't going to make your list of star teachers?

In an intriguing study, psychologist Nalini Ambady asked people to watch video clips of teachers they did not know. After watching three 10-second segments, participants were asked to rate the teachers. Amazingly, their ratings correlated highly with year-end course evaluations made by actual students (Ambady & Rosenthal, 1993). Ambady obtained the same result when she presented an even thinner "slice" of teaching behavior, just three 2-second clips. A mere 6 seconds is all that participants needed to form intuitive judgments of the instructors' teaching!

In his book *Blink*, Malcolm Gladwell (2005) argues that this was not a case of hurried irrationality. Instead, it was "thin-slicing," or quickly making sense of thin slivers of experience. According to Gladwell, these immediate, intuitive, experiential reactions can sometimes form the basis of more carefully reasoned, reflective judgments. They are a testament to the power of the cognitive unconscious, which is a part of the brain that does automatic, unconscious processing (Wilson, 2002). Far from being irrational, intuition may be an important part of how we think (Ritter, van Baaren, & Dijksterhuis, 2012).

The trick, of course, is figuring out when thin-slicing can be trusted and when it can't. After all, first impressions aren't always right. For example, have you ever had a teacher you came to appreciate only after classes were well under way or only after the course was over? In many circumstances, quick impressions are most valuable when you take the time to verify them through more reflective observation (Tom, Tong, & Hesse, 2010).

of either one alone. (For example, the probability of getting one head when flipping a coin is one-half, or .5. The probability of getting two heads when flipping two coins is one-fourth, or .25.) Therefore, A is less likely to be true than B.

According to Tversky and Kahneman, such faulty conclusions are based on the **representativeness heuristic**—that is, we tend to give a choice greater weight if it seems to be representative of what we already know. Thus, you probably compared the information about the Yankees with your mental model of what a successful professional baseball team's behavior should be like. Therefore, A seems more likely than answer B, even though it isn't. In courtrooms, jurors are more likely to think a defendant is guilty if the person appears to fit the profile of a person likely to commit

a crime (Davis & Follette, 2002). For example, a young single male from a poor neighborhood would be more likely to be judged guilty of theft than a middle-aged married father from an affluent suburb.

Underlying Odds A second common error in judgment involves ignoring the **base rate**, or underlying probability of an event. People in one experiment were told that they would be given descriptions of 100 people—70 lawyers and 30 engineers. Participants were then asked to guess, without knowing anything about a person, whether she or he was an engineer or a lawyer. All correctly stated the probabilities as 70 percent for lawyer and 30 percent for engineer. Participants were then given this description:

> Eric is a 30-year-old man. He is married with no children. A man of high ability and high motivation, he promises to be quite successful in his field. He is well liked by his colleagues.

Notice that the description gives no new information about Eric's occupation. He could still be either an engineer or a lawyer. Therefore, the odds should again be estimated as 70–30. However, most people changed the odds to 50–50. Intuitively, it seems that Eric has an equal chance of being either an engineer or a lawyer. But this guess completely ignores the underlying odds.

Perhaps it is fortunate that at times we do ignore underlying odds. Were this not the case, how many people would get married in the face of a 50 percent divorce rate? Or how many would start high-risk businesses? On the other hand, people who smoke, drink and then drive, or skip wearing auto seatbelts ignore rather high odds of injury or illness. In many high-risk situations, ignoring base rates is the same as thinking you are an exception to the rule.

Framing The most general conclusion about intuition is that the way a problem is stated, or **framed**, affects decisions (Kahneman, 2011; Tversky & Kahneman, 1981). As the first example in this discussion revealed, people often give different answers to the same problem if it is stated in slightly different ways. To gain some added insight into framing, try another thinking problem:

> A couple is divorcing. Both parents seek custody of their only child, but custody can be granted to just one parent. If you had to make a decision based on the following information, to which parent would you award custody of the child?

> **Parent A:** Average income, average health, average working hours, reasonable rapport with the child, relatively stable social life

Parent B: Above-average income, minor health problems, lots of work-related travel, very close relationship with the child, extremely active social life

Most people choose to award custody to Parent B, the parent who has some drawbacks but also several advantages (such as above-average income). That's because people tend to look for *positive qualities* that can be *awarded* to the child. However, how would you choose if you were asked this question: Which

Critical Thinking

"Extra Hot, Decaf, Double-Shot . . .

… sugar-free, venti with vanilla soy, light whip, peppermint white chocolate mocha, nonfat, no foam with extra syrup, double-cupped, please." Overhearing the order while standing in line at their favorite coffee shop, the older woman remarked to her husband, "Don't you miss the days when all you could order was a coffee with cream and sugar?" Behind them, a young man whispered in his friend's ear, "Poor old people!" One stereotype of elderly people is that they have trouble coping with modern life. But are the elderly the only ones sometimes bewildered by tasks as "simple" as ordering a cup of coffee?

Isn't the freedom of having a wide variety of choices a good thing (Leotti, Iyengar, & Ochsner, 2010)? Maybe not. According to behavioral economist Dilip Soman (2010), we are all struggling to make choices in an ever more complex world.

In one study, consumers were given an option to purchase jam. Half of them could choose from six different flavors, the other half had twenty-four flavors from which to choose. Although consumers with more choice expressed more interest, they were ten times *less* likely to purchase *any* jam (Iyengar & Lepper, 2000). Similarly, restaurants with menus that feature a broader variety of choices often find that patrons are more likely to order from a smaller number of familiar choices (Soman, 2010). Apparently, businesses that increase the variety of their product offerings are not guaranteed increased sales (Gourville & Soman, 2005).

It may be faintly amusing that people have trouble exercising choice in a coffee shop, grocery store, or restaurant. It's not that funny when more important issues are involved, such as choosing the best medicine or medical procedure. Imagine, for example, facing too many options when deciding whether to remove a seriously ill infant from life support (Botti, Orfali, & Iyengar, 2009).

Why are more complex choices so tough to make? Researchers like Soman have identified a number of factors, such as increased stress, cognitive overload, difficulty remembering all the choices, and confusion about the possibilities (Soman, 2010). Although the growing complexity of modern life may increase our freedom, our choices may be expanding beyond our capacity to cope. So try ordering a coffee with cream and sugar sometime.

parent should be denied custody? In this case, most people choose to deny custody to Parent B. Why is Parent B a good choice one moment and a poor choice the next? It's because the second question asked who should be *denied* custody. To answer this question, people tend to look for *negative qualities* that would *disqualify* a parent. As you can see, the way a question is framed can channel us down a narrow path so we attend to only part of the information provided, rather than weighing all the pros and cons.

Usually, the *broadest* way of framing or stating a problem produces the best decisions. However, people often state problems in increasingly narrow terms until a single, seemingly "obvious" answer emerges. For example, to select a career, it would be wise to consider pay, working conditions, job satisfaction, needed skills, future employment outlook, and many other factors. Instead, such decisions are often narrowed to thoughts such as, "I like to write, so I'll be a journalist," "I want to make good money and law pays well," or "I can be creative in photography." Framing decisions so narrowly greatly increases the risk of making a poor choice. If you would like to think more critically and analytically, it is important to pay attention to how you are defining problems before you try to solve them. Remember, shortcuts to answers often short-circuit clear thinking.

"Hot" Cognition   One final factor bears mentioning: Emotions also tend to affect good judgment. When we must make a choice, our emotional reactions to various alternatives can determine what intuitively seems to be the right answer. Of course, taking action in the heat of anger, passion, or stress may not be the wisest move. It may be better to cool down a bit before picking that bar fight, running off and eloping, or immediately declining that daunting job offer (Johnson, Batey, & Holdsworth, 2009). Personal rituals, such as counting to ten, meditating for a moment, and even engaging in superstitious behaviors like crossing your fingers before moving ahead, can be calming (Damisch, Stoberock, & Mussweiler, 2010).

Even mild emotions, such as low-level stress, can subtly influence how we think and act. (For an example, see "Extra Hot, Decaf, Double-Shot….") Emotions such as fear, hope, anxiety, liking, or disgust can eliminate possibilities

Representativeness heuristic   *A tendency to select wrong answers because they seem to match pre-existing mental categories.*
Base rate   *The basic rate at which an event occurs over time; the basic probability of an event.*
Framing   *In thought, the terms in which a problem is stated or the way that it is structured.*

from consideration or promote them to the top of the list (Kahneman, 2011). For many people, choosing which political candidate to vote for is a good example of how emotions can cloud clear thinking. Rather than comparing candidates' records and policies, it is tempting to vote for the person we like rather than the person who is most qualified for the job.

Module 39: Summary

39.1 What is the nature of creative thinking?

- **39.1.1** To be creative, a solution must be practical and sensible as well as original. Creative thinking requires divergent thought, characterized by fluency, flexibility, and originality. Tests of creativity measure these qualities.
- **39.1.2** Five stages often seen in creative problem solving are orientation, preparation, incubation, illumination, and verification.
- **39.1.3** Studies suggest that the creative personality has a number of characteristics, most of which contradict popular stereotypes. Only a very small correlation exists between IQ and creativity.
- **39.1.4** Some creative thinking skills can be learned.

39.2 How accurate is intuition?

- **39.2.1** Intuitive thinking can be fast and accurate but also often leads to errors. Wrong conclusions may be drawn when an answer seems highly representative of what we already believe is true.
- **39.2.2** A second problem is ignoring the base rate (or underlying probability) of an event.
- **39.2.3** Clear thinking is usually aided by stating or framing a problem in broad terms.
- **39.2.4** Emotions also lead to intuitive thinking and poor choices.

Module 39: Knowledge Builder

Recite

1. Fluency, flexibility, and originality are characteristics of
   - **a.** convergent thought
   - **b.** deductive thinking
   - **c.** creative thought
   - **d.** trial-and-error solutions

2. Reasoning and critical thinking tend to block creativity; these are noncreative qualities. *T or F?*

3. To be creative, an original idea also must be high quality and relevant. *T or F?*

4. Intelligence and creativity are highly correlated; the higher a person's IQ, the more likely he or she is to be creative. *T or F?*

5. Our decisions are greatly affected by the way a problem is stated, a process called
   - **a.** framing
   - **b.** base rating
   - **c.** induction
   - **d.** selective encoding

Reflect
Think Critically

6. A coin is flipped four times with one of the following results: (a) H T T H, (b) T T T T, (c) H H H H, (d) H H T H. Which sequence would most likely precede getting a head on the fifth coin flip?

Self-Reflect

Make up a question that would require convergent thinking to answer. Now, do the same for divergent thinking.

On which of the tests of creativity described in the text do you think you would do best? (Look back if you can't remember them all.)

Explain in your own words how representativeness and base rates contribute to thinking errors.

ANSWERS

1. c 2. F 3. T 4. F 5. a 6. The chance of getting heads on the fifth flip is the same in each case. Each time you flip a coin, the chance of getting a head is 50 percent, no matter what happened before. However, many people intuitively think that b is the answer because a head is "overdue" or that c is correct because the coin is "on a roll" for heads.

Cognition and Intelligence: Intelligence

How Intelligent Is the Idea of Intelligence?

What does it mean to say that a person like the brilliant physicist Steven Hawking is "intelligent"? You might assume that most psychologists agree on the meaning of this everyday word. After all, Hawking *is* a genius, right? IQ tests measure intelligence, and Hawking would score high, wouldn't he? (When Hawking was once asked about his IQ, he claimed he didn't know and joked, "People who boast about their IQ are losers.")

You might be surprised to learn that many questions about "intelligence" remain unanswered. Can intelligence be accurately measured? What does it mean to have extremely high or low intelligence? Is intelligence all about "book learning"? What about "street smarts"? Is athletic brilliance another form of "intelligence" or something else altogether?

These questions and others concerning intelligence have fascinated psychologists for more than 100 years. Let's see what has been learned and what issues are still debated.

Noah Graham/Contributor/National Basketball Association/Getty Images

SURVEY QUESTIONS

40.1 How is human intelligence defined and measured?

40.2 How much does intelligence vary from person to person?

40.3 What are some issues in the study of intelligence?

Human Intelligence—The IQ and You

SURVEY QUESTION 40.1: How is human intelligence defined and measured?

Like many important concepts in psychology, intelligence cannot be observed directly. Nevertheless, we feel certain it exists. Let's compare two children:

> When she was 14 months old, Anne wrote her own name. She taught herself to read at age 2. At age 5, she astounded her kindergarten teacher by bringing an iPad to class—on which she was reading an encyclopedia. At 10, she breezed through an entire high school algebra course in 12 hours.

> Billy, who is 10 years old, can write his name and can count, but he has trouble with simple addition and subtraction problems and finds multiplication impossible. He has been held back in school twice and is still incapable of doing the work his 8-year-old classmates find easy.

Anne is considered a genius; Billy, a slow learner. There seems little doubt that they differ in intelligence.

Wait! Anne's ability is obvious, but how do we know that Billy isn't just lazy? That's the same question that Alfred Binet faced in 1904 (Benjafield, 2012; Jarvin & Sternberg, 2003). The French minister of education wanted to find a way to distinguish slower students from the more capable (or the capable but lazy). In a flash of brilliance, Binet and an associate created a test made up of "intellectual" questions and problems. Next, they learned which questions an average child could answer at each age. By giving children the test, they could tell whether a child was performing up to his or her potential (Kaplan & Saccuzzo, 2013; Kaufman, 2000).

Binet's approach gave rise to modern intelligence tests. At the same time, it launched an ongoing debate. Part of the debate is related to the basic difficulty of defining intelligence (Sternberg et al., 2011).

Defining Intelligence

Isn't there an accepted definition of intelligence? Broadly speaking, yes. **Intelligence** is the overall capacity to act purposefully, to think rationally, and to adapt to one's surroundings (Barber, 2010; Flynn, 2012). Beyond this, however, there is much disagreement. Some theorists propose that the core of intelligence is a small set of general mental abilities (called the **g-factor**) like those we explored earlier in this module, such as reasoning, problem solving, knowledge, and memory (Sternberg, 2004; Ziegler et al., 2011). Some theorists question just which general mental abilities together constitute intelligence. Others question the idea of the *g-factor* itself, proposing instead that there are different "intelligences."

In fact, many psychologists simply accept an operational definition of intelligence by spelling out the procedures they use to measure it (Neukrug & Fawcett, 2010). Thus, by selecting items for an intelligence test, a psychologist is saying in a direct way, "This is what *I* mean by intelligence." A test that measures memory, reasoning, and verbal fluency offers a very different

Modern intelligence tests are widely used to measure intellectual abilities. When properly administered, such tests provide an operational definition of intelligence.

definition of intelligence than one that measures strength of grip, shoe size, hunting skills, or the person's best *Guitar Hero* score (Goldstein, 2011).

Measuring Intelligence

American psychologists quickly saw the value of Alfred Binet's test. In 1916, Lewis Terman and others at Stanford University revised it for use in North America. After more revisions, the *Stanford-Binet Intelligence Scales, Fifth Edition* (SB5), continue to be widely used. The SB5 primarily is made up of age-ranked questions that get a little harder at each age level. The SB5 is appropriate for people from age 2 to 85+ years, and scores on the test are very reliable (Decker, Brooks, & Allen, 2011; Raid & Tippin, 2009).

The SB5 measures five cognitive factors (types of mental abilities) that make up general intelligence: fluid reasoning, knowledge, quantitative reasoning, visual-spatial processing, and working memory. Each factor is measured with verbal questions (those involving words and numbers), and nonverbal questions (items that use pictures and objects). If you were to take the SB5, it would yield a score for your general intelligence, verbal intelligence, nonverbal intelligence, and each of the five cognitive factors (Decker, Brooks, & Allen, 2011). Let's see what each factor looks like.

Fluid Reasoning Questions like the following are used to test fluid reasoning:

How are an apple, a plum, and a banana different from a beet?

An apprentice is to a master as a novice is to an _____.

"I knew my bag was going to be in the last place I looked, so I looked there first." What is silly or impossible about that?

Other items ask people to fill in the missing shape in a group of shapes and to tell a story that explains what's going on in a series of pictures.

Knowledge The knowledge factor assesses the person's knowledge about a wide range of topics:

Why is yeast added to bread dough?

What does "cryptic" mean?

What is silly or impossible about this picture? (For example, a bicycle has square wheels.)

Quantitative Reasoning Test items for quantitative reasoning measure a person's ability to solve problems involving numbers. Here are some samples:

TABLE 40.1	Sample Items Similar to Those Used on the WAIS-IV
Verbal Comprehension	**Sample Items or Descriptions**
Similarities	In what way are a wolf and a coyote alike? In what way are a screwdriver and a chisel alike?
Vocabulary	The test consists of asking, "What is a _____?" or "What does _____ mean?" The words range from more to less familiar and difficult.
Information	How many wings does a butterfly have? Who wrote *Romeo and Juliet?*
Perceptual Reasoning	
Block Design	Copy designs with blocks (as shown at right).
Matrix Reasoning	Select the item that completes the matrix.
Visual Puzzles	Choose the pieces that go together to form a figure.
Working Memory	
Digit Span	Repeat from memory a series of digits, such as 8 5 7 0 1 3 6 2, after hearing it once.
Arithmetic	Four girls divided 28 jellybeans equally among themselves. How many jellybeans did each girl receive? If 3 peaches take 2 minutes to find and pick, how long will it take to find and pick a dozen peaches?

(*continued*)

If I have six marbles and you give me another one, how many marbles will I have?

Given the numbers 3, 6, 9, 12, what number would come next?

If a shirt is being sold for 50 percent of the normal price, and the price tag is $60, what is the cost of the shirt?

Visual-Spatial Processing People who have visual-spatial skills are good at putting picture puzzles together and copying geometric shapes (such as triangles, rectangles, and circles). Visual-spatial processing questions ask test takers to reproduce patterns of blocks and choose pictures that show how a piece of paper would look if it were folded or cut. Verbal questions also can require visual-spatial abilities:

Suppose that you are going east, then turn right, then turn right again, then turn left. In what direction are you facing now?

Working Memory The working memory part of the SB5 measures the ability to use short-term memory. Some typical memory tasks include the following:

Correctly remember the order of colored beads on a stick.

After hearing several sentences, name the last word from each sentence.

Repeat a series of digits (forward or backward) after hearing them once.

The Wechsler Tests

Is the Stanford-Binet the only intelligence test? A widely used alternative is the *Wechsler Adult Intelligence Scale—Fourth Edition* (WAIS-IV). A version for children is called the *Wechsler Intelligence Scale for Children—Fourth Edition* (WISC-IV) (Kaplan & Saccuzzo, 2013). Like the Stanford-Binet, the Wechsler tests yield a single overall intelligence score. In addition, these tests also separate scores for **performance (nonverbal) intelligence** and **verbal intelligence**—language- or symbol-oriented intelligence. The abilities measured by the Wechsler tests and some sample test items are listed in ● Table 40.1.

Intelligence *An overall capacity to think rationally, act purposefully, and adapt to one's surroundings.*
***g*-factor** *A general ability factor proposed to underlie intelligence; the core of general intellectual ability that involves reasoning, problem-solving ability, knowledge, and memory.*
Performance (nonverbal) intelligence *Intelligence measured by solving puzzles, assembling objects, completing pictures, and other nonverbal tasks.*
Verbal intelligence *Intelligence measured by answering questions involving vocabulary, general information, arithmetic, and other language- or symbol-oriented tasks.*

TABLE 40.1	Sample Items Similar to Those Used on the WAIS-If *(continued)*

Processing Speed

Symbol Search	Match symbols appearing in separate groups.	

Symbol Search

Coding	Fill in the symbols:

1	2	3	4
X	III	I	0

3	4	1	3	4	2	1	2

Items like those on the Wechsler Adult Intelligence Scale, Fourth Edition *(Wechsler, 2008).*

Group Tests

The SB5 and the Wechsler tests are *individual* intelligence tests, which are given to a single person by a trained specialist. In contrast, *group* intelligence tests can be given to large groups of individuals with minimal supervision. Group tests usually require people to read, to follow instructions, and to solve problems of logic, reasoning, mathematics, or spatial skills. If you're wondering if you have ever taken an intelligence test, the answer is probably yes. The well-known SAT Reasoning Test (SAT) measures aptitudes for language, math, and reasoning. The SAT is designed to predict your chances for success in college. Because it measures a number of different mental aptitudes, it also can be used to estimate general intelligence.

Intelligence Quotients

What is an IQ? Imagine that a child named Yuan can answer intelligence test questions that an average 7-year-old can answer. We could say that 7 is her **mental age** (average intellectual performance). How smart is Yuan? We can't say yet, because we don't know how old she is. If she is 10, she's not very smart. If she's 5, she is very bright. To estimate a child's intelligence, then, we need to compare her mental age and her *chronological age* (age in years). When the Stanford-Binet was first used, mental age (MA) was divided by chronological age (CA). The resulting *quotient* was then multiplied by 100 to give a whole number, rather than a decimal, yielding an **intelligence quotient (IQ)**:

$$\frac{MA}{CA} \times 100 = IQ$$

In this way, children with different chronological and mental ages could be compared. For instance, 10-year-old Justin has a mental age of 12. Thus, his IQ is 120. Justin's friend Suke also has a mental age of 12. However, Suke's chronological age is 12, so his IQ is 100. The IQ shows that 10-year-old Justin is brighter than his 12-year-old friend Suke, even though their intellectual skills are about the same. Notice that a person's IQ will be 100 whenever mental age equals chronological age. This is why an IQ score of 100 is defined as average intelligence.

"The five candles represent his mental age."

Kes/CartoonStock.Ltd

Then, does a person with an IQ score below 100 have below average intelligence? Not unless the IQ is well below 100. Average intelligence is usually defined as any score from 90 to 109. The important point is that IQ scores will be over 100 when mental age is higher than age in years. IQ scores below 100 occur when a person's age in years exceeds his or her mental age.

Deviation IQs Although the preceding examples may give you insight into IQ scores, it's no longer necessary to directly calculate IQs. Instead, modern tests use **deviation IQs**. Tables supplied with the test are used to convert a person's relative standing in the group to an IQ score—that is, they tell how far above or below average the person's score falls. For example, if you score at the 50th percentile, half the people your age who take the test score higher than you and half score lower. In this case, your IQ score is 100. If you score at the 84th percentile, your IQ score is 115. If you score at the 97th percentile, your IQ score is 130. (For more information, see Module 79.)

Variations in Intelligence— Curved Like a Bell

SURVEY QUESTION 40.2: How much does intelligence vary from person to person?

IQ scores are classified as shown in ● **Figure 40.1**. The distribution (or scattering) of IQ scores approximates a bell-shaped or **normal curve**—that is, most scores fall close to the average and few are found at the extremes.

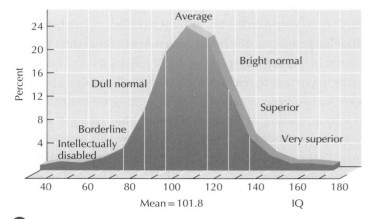

● **Figure 40.1**

Distribution of Stanford-Binet Intelligence Test scores for 3,184 children. (After Terman & Merrill, 1937/1960.)

The Mentally Gifted

How high is the IQ of a genius? Only 2 people out of 100 score above 130 on IQ tests. These bright individuals are usually described as "gifted." Less than one-half of one percent of the population scores above 140. These people are certainly gifted or perhaps even "geniuses." However, some psychologists reserve the term *genius* for people with even higher IQs or those who are exceptionally creative (Hallahan, Kauffman, & Pullen, 2011).

Gifted Children *Do high IQ scores in childhood predict later ability?* To directly answer this question, Lewis Terman selected 1,500 children with IQs of 140 or more. Terman followed this gifted group (the "Termites" as he called them) into adulthood and found that most were quite successful. A majority finished college, earned advanced degrees, or held professional positions, and many had written books or scientific articles (Terman & Oden, 1959).

In general, the correlation between IQ scores and school grades is .50, a sizable association. The link would be even stronger, but motivation, special talents, off-campus learning, and many other factors also affect grades. The same is true of real-world success beyond school. IQ is not at all good at predicting success in art, music, writing, dramatics, science, and leadership. Creativity is much more strongly related to doing well in these areas (Preckel, Holling, & Wiese, 2006; Runco, 2012).

Were all the Termites superior as adults? No. Although the gifted tend to be well adjusted psychologically (Dai, 2010; Garland & Zigler, 1999), some had committed crimes, were unemployable, or were unhappy misfits. Remember that a high IQ reveals *potential*. It does not guarantee success. Nor does a lower IQ guarantee failure. Nobel Prize–winning physicist Richard Feynman, whom many regard as a genius, had an IQ of 122 (Michalko, 2001; 2006).

Mental age *The average mental ability displayed by people of a given age.*
Intelligence quotient (IQ) *An index of intelligence defined as a person's mental age divided by his or her chronological age and multiplied by 100.*
Deviation IQ *An IQ obtained statistically from a person's relative standing in his or her age group—that is, how far above or below average the person's score is relative to other scores.*
Normal curve *A bell-shaped curve characterized by a large number of scores in a middle area, tapering to very few extremely high and low scores.*

It is wise to remember that a child may be gifted in many ways. Many schools now offer Gifted and Talented Education programs for students who have a variety of special abilities—not just for those who score well on IQ tests.

How did Terman's more successful Termites differ from the less successful? Most of them had educated parents who valued learning and encouraged them to do the same. In general, successful gifted persons tend to have strong *intellectual determination*—a desire to know, to excel, and to persevere (Winner, 2003). Gifted or not, most successful persons tend to be *persistent* and *motivated* to learn (Reis & Renzulli, 2010). No one is paid to sit around being *capable* of achievement. What you do is always more important than what you should be able to do. That's why a child's talents are most likely to blossom when she or he is nurtured with support, encouragement, education, and effort (Callahan, 2006).

Identifying Gifted Children *How might a parent spot an unusually bright child?* Early signs of giftedness are not always purely "intellectual." **Giftedness** can be either the possession of a high IQ or of special talents or aptitudes (Kreger Silverman, 2013). The following signs may reveal that a child is gifted: a tendency to seek out older children and adults; an early fascination with explanations and problem solving; talking in complete sentences as early as 2 or 3 years of age; an unusually good memory; precocious talent in art, music, or number skills; an early interest in books, along with early reading (often by age 3); showing kindness, understanding, and cooperation toward others (Dai, 2010; Distin, 2006).

Notice that this list goes beyond straight g-factor, or general "academic" intelligence. In fact, if artistic talent, mechanical aptitude, musical aptitude, athletic potential, and so on are considered, many children have a special "gift" of one kind or another. Limiting giftedness to a high IQ can shortchange children with special talents or potentials. This is especially true of ethnic minority children, who may be the victims of subtle biases in standardized intelligence tests. These children, as well as children with physical disabilities, are less likely to be recognized as gifted (Castellano & Frazier, 2011; Kornilov et al., 2012).

In the next section, we discuss intellectual disability.

Intellectual Disability

Before you begin this section, take a few moments to read "Meet the Rain Man," in which you will find information about a remarkable mixture of brilliance and intellectual disability. And please keep Kim Peek in mind as you read on. Intellectually disabled people usually have much more to them than what is shown by the results of IQ testing (Treffert, 2010). It is especially important to realize that intellectually disabled persons have no handicap concerning feelings. They are easily hurt by rejection, teasing, or ridicule. Likewise, they respond warmly to love and acceptance. They have a right to self-respect and a place in the community (Montreal Declaration on Intellectual Disabilities, 2004). This is especially important during childhood, when support from others adds greatly to each person's chances of becoming a well-adjusted member of society.

A person with mental abilities far below average is termed *intellectually disabled* (the former term, *mentally retarded,* is

The Clinical File

The Rain Man

Meet Kim Peek, the model for Dustin Hoffman's character in the Academy Award–winning movie *Rain Man* (Peek & Hanson, 2007). By the time of Kim's death in 2009, he could recite from memory more than 9,000 books. He knew all the ZIP codes and area codes in the United States and could give accurate travel directions between any two major U.S. cities. He also could discuss hundreds of pieces of classical music in detail and could play most of it quite well. Amazingly, though, for someone with such skills, Kim had difficulty with abstract thinking and tests of general intelligence. He was poorly coordinated and couldn't button his own clothes (Treffert, 2010; Treffert & Christensen, 2005).

Kim Peek had *savant syndrome*, in which a person of limited general intelligence nevertheless shows exceptional mental ability in one or more narrow areas, such as mental arithmetic, calendar calculations, art, or music (Crane et al., 2010; Young, 2005).

Do savants have special mental powers not shared by most people? According to one theory, many savants have suffered some form of damage to their left hemispheres, freeing them from the "distractions" of language, concepts, and higher-level thought. This allows them to

Once, four months after reading a novel, Kim was asked about a character. He immediately named the character, gave the page number on which a description appeared, and accurately recited several paragraphs about the character (Treffert & Christensen, 2005).

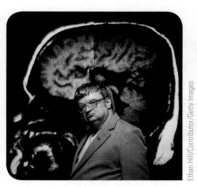

focus with crystal clarity on music, drawing, prime numbers, license plates, television commercials, and other specific information (Young, 2005). Another theory holds that the performances of many savants result from intense practice. Perhaps each of us harbors embers of mental brilliance that intense practice could fan into full flame (Snyder et al., 2006; Treffert, 2010).

Although savant syndrome hasn't been fully explained, it does show that extraordinary abilities can exist apart from general intelligence.

---

now regarded as offensive). According to the definition listed in the American Psychiatric Association's *Diagnostic and Statistical Manual of Mental Disorders (DSM-5)*, **intellectual disability (intellectual developmental disorder)** begins at an IQ of approximately 70 or below. However, a person's ability to perform *adaptive behaviors* (basic skills such as dressing, eating, communicating, shopping, and working) is more important in evaluating this disability (American Psychiatric Association, 2013; Kirk et al., 2011).

Causes of Intellectual Disability *What causes intellectual disability?* Intellectual disability can be caused by a wide range of factors. Some of the most common are the following:

- **Genetic abnormalities.** A variety of genetic abnormalities, such as missing genes, extra genes, or defective genes, can result in an intellectual disability. For example, *Down syndrome* children have an extra 21st chromosome. This condition, also called trisomy 21, results from flaws in the parents' egg or sperm cells. Although Down syndrome is *genetic*, it is not usually *hereditary* (it doesn't "run in the family"). In contrast, children with *PKU (phenylketonuria)* have an inherited inability to control a destructive chemical that builds up in their bodies.

- **Fetal damage.** As we saw in Module 12, the developing fetus can be damaged by a variety of teratogens such as disease, infection, or drugs. *Fetal alcohol syndrome (FAS)*, caused by heavy drinking during pregnancy, is, unfortunately, one of the most common causes of intellectual disability (Jones & Streissguth, 2010).

- **Birth injuries.** Birth injuries such as a lack of oxygen during delivery or an overly premature delivery also can result in intellectual disability.

- **Postnatal problems.** Malnutrition and exposure to lead, PCBs, and other toxins early in childhood also can cause organic intellectual disability (Beirne-Smith, Patton, & Shannon, 2006). In many cases, no known biological problem can be identified. Often, other family members also are mildly intellectually disabled. *Familial intellectual disability*, as this is called, occurs mostly in very poor households where nutrition, intellectual stimulation, medical care, and emotional support may be inadequate (Harris, 2010).

Giftedness *The possession of either a high IQ or special talents or aptitudes.*
Intellectual disability (intellectual developmental disorder) *The presence of a developmental disability, a formal IQ score below 70, and a significant impairment of adaptive behavior.*

This young woman exhibits the classical features of Down syndrome, including almond-shaped eyes, a slightly protruding tongue, a stocky build, and stubby hands with deeply creased palms. Although she is mildly intellectually disabled, she is very loving and has a right to self-respect and a place in the community.

Questioning Intelligence— More Questions Than Answers?

SURVEY QUESTION 40.3: What are some issues in the study of intelligence?

In this section, we consider a sampling of the issues that have arisen in the study of intelligence. Most stem from questions about the traditional assumptions that intelligence can be defined in terms of a small set of general mental abilities and measured with IQ tests like the SB5 or the Wechsler scales. One criticism has been that this approach is too vague; according to researchers in the field of artificial intelligence, a better approach is to specify what we mean by intelligent behavior in enough detail that we can program computers to act intelligently. Others have wondered if maybe the traditional approach is too narrow and doesn't apply across cultures. Still others have questioned the value of defining intelligence in terms of any general intelligence factor at all. Finally, many have challenged the often implicit assumption that intelligence is mainly inherited from our parents.

Artificial Intelligence

While most efforts have focused on measuring intelligence in humans, a small group of psychologists and computer scientists have taken an entirely different approach. Their basic idea is to build machines that display **artificial intelligence (AI)**. This usually refers to creating computer programs capable of doing things that require intelligence when done by people (Müller, 2012; Russell & Norvig, 2010).

As computer scientist Aaron Sloman explains it, "Human brains don't work by magic, so whatever it is they do should be doable by machine" (Brooks, 2009; Sloman, 2008). The resulting programs can then help us understand how people do those same things. While a robot like RuBot II might do a spiffy job of solving Rubik's Cube puzzles, it also can be thought of as a *computer simulation*, a program that attempts to duplicate specific human behaviors, especially thinking, decision making, and problem solving. Here, the computer acts as a "laboratory" for testing models of cognition. If a computer program behaves as humans do (including making the same errors), then the program may be a good model of how we think.

So, how intelligent are computers? You may be surprised to learn that the answer, to date, is "not very." Computers have been most successful in specific situations where complex skills can be converted into clearly stated rules a computer can follow. The resulting *expert systems* can already predict the weather, analyze geological formations, diagnose disease, play chess, read, tell when to buy or sell stocks, harmonize music, and perform many other tasks better than humans (Giarratano & Riley, 2004). Consider, for example, IBM's "Watson" supercomputer, which outperforms even expert humans at playing the television game *Jeopardy* (Markoff, 2011).

RuBot II, the *Cubinator*, recently held the computer world record for solving the Rubik's Cube, taking just 20 seconds. The fastest human, you ask? Six seconds! To what extent is the way the Cubinator comes up with solutions helpful for understanding how humans do it?

Another example is world chess champion Garry Kasparov's loss, in 1997, to a computer called Deep Blue. However, before you get too impressed, don't forget that outside their little corners of expertise, these "expert systems" are as dumb as a bag of nails. Deep Blue plays chess. Period.

To see why expert systems are not the whole story, it helps to get Siri-ous. As you likely already know, *Siri* is an "intelligent personal assistant" on Apple's iPhone. You can talk to Siri and "she" talks back. Although there is no limit to what you can ask, Siri operates in a simple question-and-answer mode and cannot engage in a believable free-flowing conversation. In contrast, we humans can mentally "shift gears" from one topic to another with incredible flexibility that is not easily described by expert system rules. You may be surprised to learn that, to date, no machine has proven able to keep up an open-ended conversation (Floridi, Taddeo, & Turilli, 2009).

Regardless, intelligent personal assistants like Siri can already be very helpful. If you say, "Siri, remind me to call home," she might reply "When should I remind you?" Once you tell her "noon," she sets an alarm to go off at noon. However, Siri often misunderstands questions and can offer famously oddball responses. One that went viral was her answer to the question "Where can I hide a body?" She would respond with something like "What kind of place are you looking for? Mines, reservoirs, metal foundries, dumps, or swamps?" At least she has a sense of humor!

Make no mistake, however. Intelligent personal assistants and other computers and robots will continue to improve over time as they help psychologists and computer scientists better understand human intelligence (Cassimatis, 2012).

Culture and Intelligence

Imagine giving the Stanford-Binet 5 to a young Bushman hunter. If he values and is good at tracking prey, then what would it mean if (when?) he got a low IQ score? In other words, not every culture values the same set of metal abilities as those assessed by current IQ tests. (For a glimpse at how some other cultures define "intelligence," see "Intelligence—How Would a Fool Do It?")

Cultural values, knowledge, language patterns, and traditions can greatly affect performance on tests designed for Western cultures (Nisbett et al., 2012; Sternberg & Grigorenko, 2005). Psychologist Jerome Kagan once remarked, "If the Wechsler and Binet scales were translated into Spanish, Swahili, and Chinese and given to every 10-year-old in Latin America, East Africa, and China, the majority would obtain IQ scores in the mentally retarded range." Certainly, we cannot believe that children of other cultures are all intellectually disabled. The fault must lie with the test (Castles, 2012).

Human Diversity

Intelligence—How Would a Fool Do It?

You have been asked to sort some objects into categories. Wouldn't it be smart to put the clothes, containers, implements, and foods in separate piles? Not necessarily. When members of the Kpelle culture in Liberia were asked to sort objects, they grouped them together by function. For example, a potato (food) would be placed together with a knife (implement). When the Kpelle were asked why they grouped the objects this way, they often said that was how a wise man would do it. The researchers finally asked the Kpelle, "How would a fool do it?" Only then did the Kpelle sort the objects into the nice, neat categories that we Westerners prefer.

This anecdote, related by cultural psychologist Patricia Greenfield (1997), illustrates serious questions about general definitions of intelligence. For example, among the Cree of Northern Canada, "smart" people are those who have the skills needed to find food on the frozen tundra (Darou, 1992). For the Puluwat people in the South

How important do you think the mental abilities assessed in modern intelligence tests are to this Bushman hunter in Africa's Kalahari Desert?

Pacific, smart means having the ocean-going navigation skills necessary to get from island to island (Sternberg, 2004). And so it goes, as each culture teaches its children how the wise man would do it, not the fool (Barber, 2010; Correa-Chávez, Rogoff, & Arauz, 2005).

Artificial intelligence (AI) *Any artificial system (often a computer program) that is capable of human-like problem solving or intelligent responding.*

In view of such problems, psychologists have tried to create "culture-fair" intelligence tests that do not disadvantage certain groups. A **culture-fair test** is designed to minimize the importance of skills and knowledge that may be more common in some cultures than in others. (For a sample of culture-fair test items, see ● Figure 40.2.)

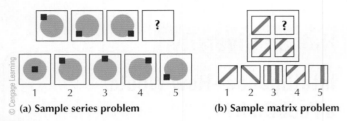

(a) Sample series problem   (b) Sample matrix problem

© Cengage Learning

● **Figure 40.2**

Sample items like those often found on culture-fair intelligence tests. (*a*) Sample series problem. Which pattern correctly continues the series of patterns shown at the top left? (Number 4.) (*b*) Sample matrix problem. Which pattern fits best completes the matrix of patterns shown at the top right? (Number 1.) The idea is that the ability to read and the mastery of culturally relevant knowledge should not be necessary to do well. Nevertheless, do you think illiterate street orphans from Sao Paulo, Brazil or Aboriginals living in the desert of the Australian outback would find these items as easy to complete as you did? If not, can you think of any alternative truly culture-fair ways to test intelligence across different cultures?

Culture-fair tests attempt to measure intelligence without, as much as possible, being influenced by a person's verbal skills, cultural background, and educational level. Their value lies not just in testing people from other cultures. They also are useful for testing children in the United States who come from poor communities, rural areas, or ethnic minority families (Stephens et al., 1999). However, no intelligence test can be entirely free of cultural influences. For instance, our culture is very "visual" because children are constantly exposed to television, movies, video games, and the like. Thus, compared with children in developing countries, a child who grows up in the United States may be better prepared to take both nonverbal tests and traditional IQ tests.

Because the concept of intelligence exhibits diversity across cultures, many psychologists have begun to stress the need to rethink the concept of intelligence itself (Greenfield, 1997; Sternberg & Grigorenko, 2005). If we are to find a truly culture-fair way to measure intelligence, we first need to identify the core cognitive skills that lie at the heart of human intelligence the world around (Gardner, 2008; Henrich, Heine, & Norenzayan, 2010).

Multiple Intelligences

Defining intelligence as a g-factor (general ability) also has been questioned. As we just noted, there may be many ways to be smart. For example, consider William, a grade-school student two years behind in reading, who shows his teacher how to solve a difficult computer-programming problem. What about his classmate, Malika, who is poor in math but plays intricate pieces of piano music? Both these children show clear signs of intelligence. Yet, each might score below average on a traditional IQ test. And, as we have seen, autistic savants like Kim Peek have even more extreme intellectual strengths and weaknesses. Such observations have convinced many psychologists that it is time to forge new, broader definitions of intelligence. Their basic goal is to better predict real-world success—not just the likelihood of success in school (Richardson, 2013; Sternberg & Grigorenko, 2006).

One such psychologist is Howard Gardner of Harvard University. Gardner (2008, 2011) theorizes that there are eight distinctly different kinds of intelligence. These are different mental "languages" that people use for thinking. Each is listed below, with examples of pursuits that use them:

1. *Language* (linguistic abilities)—writer, lawyer, comedian
2. *Logic and math* (numeric abilities)—scientist, accountant, programmer
3. *Visual and spatial* (pictorial abilities)—engineer, inventor, artist
4. *Music* (musical abilities)—composer, musician, music critic
5. *Bodily-kinesthetic* (physical abilities)—dancer, athlete, surgeon
6. *Intrapersonal* (self-knowledge)—poet, actor, minister
7. *Interpersonal* (social abilities)—psychologist, teacher, politician
8. *Naturalist* (ability to understand the natural environment)—biologist, medicine man, organic farmer

To simplify a great deal, people can be *word smart, number smart, picture smart, music smart, body smart, self smart, people smart,* and/or *nature smart*. It could be argued that to be *self smart* and *other smart*, one must take emotions into account. For an interesting take on defining intelligence, see Module 45 on emotional intelligence. Most of us are probably strong in only a few types of intelligence. In contrast, geniuses like Albert Einstein seem to be able to use nearly all of the intelligences, as needed, to solve problems.

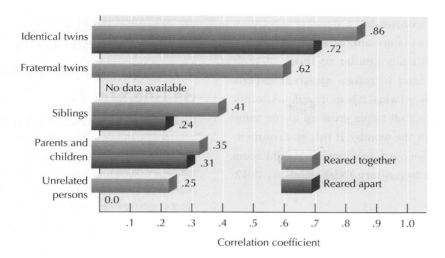

● Figure 40.3

Approximate correlations between IQ scores for persons with varying degrees of genetic and environmental similarity. Notice that the correlations grow smaller as the degree of genetic similarity declines. Also note that a shared environment increases the correlation in all cases. (Estimates from Bouchard, 1983; Henderson, 1982.)

If Gardner's theory of **multiple intelligences** is correct, traditional IQ tests measure only a part of real-world intelligence—namely, linguistic, logical-mathematical, and spatial abilities (Roberts & Lipnevich, 2012). A further implication is that our schools may be wasting a lot of human potential. For example, some children might find it easier to learn math or reading if these topics were tied into art, music, dance, drama, and so on. Many schools are now using Gardner's theory to cultivate a wider range of skills and talents (Campbell, 2008).

Let's end this module with a look at the controversial question of how much intelligence is inherited from our parents.

IQ and Heredity

Most people are aware of a moderate similarity in the intelligence of parents and their children or between brothers and sisters. As ● **Figure 40.3** shows, the closer two people are on a family tree, the more alike their IQs are likely to be.

Does this indicate that intelligence is hereditary? Not necessarily. Brothers, sisters, and parents share similar environments as well as similar genes (Grigorenko, 2005). To separate nature and nurture, **twin studies** may be done. Such studies compare the IQs of twins who were raised together or separated at birth. This allows us to estimate how much heredity and environment affect intelligence.

Twin Studies Notice in Figure 40.3 that the IQ scores of fraternal twins are more alike than the IQs of ordinary brothers and sisters. *Fraternal twins* come from two separate eggs that

are fertilized at the same time. They are no more genetically alike than ordinary siblings. Why, then, should the twins' IQ scores be more similar? The reason is environmental: Parents treat twins more alike than ordinary siblings, resulting in a closer match in IQs.

More striking similarities are observed with *identical twins,* who develop from a single egg and have identical genes. At the top of Figure 40.3, you can see that identical twins who grow up in the same family have highly correlated IQs. This is what we would expect with identical heredity and very similar environments. Now, let's consider what happens when identical twins are reared apart. As you can see, the correlation drops, but only from .86 to .72. Psychologists who emphasize genetics believe figures like these show that differences in adult intelligence are roughly 50 percent hereditary (Jacobs et al., 2008; Nisbett et al., 2012).

How do environmentalists interpret the figures? They point out that some separated identical twins differ by as much as 20 IQ points. In every case in which this occurs, there are

Culture-fair test *A test (such as an intelligence test) designed to minimize the importance of skills and knowledge that may be more common in some cultures than in others.*

Multiple intelligences *Howard Gardner's theory that there are several specialized types of intellectual ability.*

Twin study *A comparison of the characteristics of twins who were raised together or separated at birth; used to identify the relative impact of heredity and environment.*

large educational and environmental differences between the twins. Also, separated twins are almost always placed in homes socially and educationally similar to those of their birth parents. This would tend to inflate apparent genetic effects by making the separated twins' IQs more alike. Another frequently overlooked fact is that twins grow up in the same environment before birth (in the womb). If this environmental similarity is taken into account, intelligence would seem to be less than 50 percent hereditary (Nisbett et al., 2012; Turkheimer et al., 2003).

IQ and Environment Some evidence for an environmental view of intelligence comes from families having one adopted child and one biological child. As ● **Figure 40.4** shows, parents contribute genes and environment to their biological child. With an adopted child, they contribute only environment. If intelligence is highly genetic, the IQs of biological children should be more like their parents' IQs than the IQs of adopted children. However, studies show that children reared by the same mother resemble her in IQ to the same degree. It doesn't matter whether they share her genes (Kamin, 1981; Weinberg, 1989).

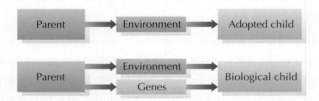

● **Figure 40.4**

Comparison of an adopted child and a biological child reared in the same family. (After Kamin, 1981.)

How much can environment alter intelligence? It depends on the quality of the environment (Nisbett et al., 2012). One way to look at environmental effects is to compare children adopted by parents of high or low *socioeconomic status (SES)*. As you might predict, children who grow up in high SES homes develop higher IQs than those reared by lower SES parents. Presumably, the higher SES homes provide an enriched environment, with better nutrition, greater educational opportunities, and other advantages (Nisbett et al., 2012).

More important, children adopted *out of* low SES environments can experience great relative gains in intelligence. That is, the IQs of low SES children may be more dramatically

Critical Thinking

You Mean Video Games Might Be Good for Me?

Even though the Flynn effect suggests that environmental factors influence intelligence (Flynn, 2012), we are left with the question: "Which factors?" Writer Steven Johnson (2005) believes that contemporary culture is responsible. Although he agrees that much popular media content is too violent or sexual in nature, he points out that video games, the Internet, and even television are becoming more complex. As a result, they demand ever greater cognitive effort from us. In other words, it is as important to understand *how* we experience the environment as it is to understand *what* we experience.

For example, most early video games, such as *Pong* or *Pac Man*, offered simple, repetitive visual experiences. In contrast, many of today's best-selling games, such as *Call of Duty* or *Mass Effect*, offer rich, complicated experiences that can take many hours of intense game play and problem solving to complete. Furthermore, players must usually figure out the rules by themselves. Instructions for completing popular games, which have been created by fans, can be much longer than the longest modules in this textbook. Only a complex and engaging game would prompt players to use such instructions, much less write them for others to use (Johnson, 2005).

According to Johnson, other forms of popular culture also have become more complex, including the Internet and computer software. Even popular television has become more cognitively demanding. For example, compared with television dramas of the past, modern dramas weave plot lines and characters through an entire season of programs. In the end, popular culture may well be inviting us to read, reflect, and problem solve more than ever before (Jaeggi et al., 2008). (Before you uncritically embrace video games, read "You Mean Video Games Might Be Bad for Me?" in Module 27.)

influenced by environmental factors than the IQs of high SES children (Henrich, Heine, & Norenzayan, 2010). In one study, striking increases in IQ occurred in 25 children who were moved from an orphanage and were eventually adopted by parents who gave them love, a family, and a stimulating home environment. Once considered intellectually disabled and unadoptable, the children gained an average of 29 IQ points. A second group of initially less intellectually disabled children who stayed in the orphanage lost an average of 26 IQ points (Skeels, 1966).

A particularly dramatic environmental effect is the fact that 14 nations have shown average IQ gains of from 5 to 25 points during the last 30 years (Dickens & Flynn, 2001; Flynn, 2012). Referred to as the *Flynn effect*, after New Zealand psychologist James Flynn, these IQ boosts occurred in far too short a time to be explained by genetics. It is more likely that the gains reflect environmental forces, such as improved education and nutrition and living in a technologically complex society (Barber, 2010; Johnson, 2005). If you've ever tried to play a computer game or set up a wireless network in your home, you'll understand why people may be getting better at answering IQ test questions. (See "You Mean Video Games Might Be Good for Me?")

IQ and Race Historically, African-American children in the United States scored an average of about 15 points lower on standardized IQ tests than European-American children (although this gap has been reduced by one-third since 1972; Nisbett et al., 2012). As a group, Japanese-American children scored above average in IQ. Could such differences be genetic? One persistent, but disputed, claim is that African Americans score below average in IQ because they are genetically incapable of climbing out of poverty (Hernstein & Murray, 1994; Rushton & Jensen, 2005). Psychologists have responded to such claims with several counterarguments.

To begin, it is no secret that as a group African Americans are more likely than European Americans to live in environments that are physically, educationally, and intellectually impoverished. When unequal education is part of the equation, IQs may tell us little about how heredity affects intelligence (Sternberg et al., 2011; Suzuki & Aronson, 2005). Indeed, one study found that placing poor African-American children into European-American adoptive families increased the children's IQs by an average of 13 points, bringing them into line with those of European-American children (Nisbett, 2005, 2009). That is, providing African-American children with the same environmental experiences available to European-American children erased IQ differences.

Furthermore, although IQ predicts school performance, it does not predict later career success (McClelland, 1994). In this regard, "street smarts," or what psychologist Robert Sternberg calls *practical intelligence*, may be seen by minority cultures as more important than "book learning," or what Sternberg calls *analytic intelligence* (Stemler & Sternberg, 2006; Wagner, 2011).

Most psychologists have concluded that there is no scientific evidence that group differences in average IQ are based on genetics. In fact, studies that used actual blood group testing found no significant correlations between ethnic ancestry and IQ scores. This is because it does not even make sense to talk about "races" at all—obvious external markers, like skin color, have little to do with underlying genetic differences (Bonham, Warshauer-Baker, & Collins, 2005; Sternberg, 2007). Group differences in IQ scores are based on cultural and environmental diversity as much as on heredity (Nisbett, 2009; Nisbett et al., 2012). To conclude otherwise reflects political beliefs and biases, not scientific facts.

The Whole Human: Wisdom

In the final analysis, intelligence reflects development as well as potential, nurture as well as nature (Richardson, 2013). Moreover, the fact that intelligence is partly determined by heredity tells us little of any real value. Genes are fixed at birth. Improving the environments in which children learn and grow is the main way we can ensure that they reach their full potential (Grigorenko & Sternberg, 2003; Roberts & Lipnevich, 2012).

Perhaps most important, people can be intelligent without being wise. For example, a person who does well in school and on IQ tests may make a total mess of his or her life. Likewise, people can be intelligent without being creative; and clear, rational thinking can lead to correct, but uninspired, answers (Solomon, Marshall, & Gardner, 2005). In many areas of human life, wisdom represents a mixture of convergent thinking, intelligence, and reason, spiced with creativity and originality (Meeks & Jeste, 2009). People who are wise approach life with openness and tolerance (Le, 2011).

Module 40: Summary

40.1 How is human intelligence defined and measured?

- **40.1.1** Intelligence refers to the general capacity (or g-factor) to act purposefully, think rationally, and adapt to the environment.

- **40.1.2** In practice, intelligence is operationally defined by intelligence tests, which provide a useful but narrow estimate of real-world intelligence.

- **40.1.3** The first practical intelligence test was assembled by Alfred Binet. A modern version of Binet's test is the Stanford-Binet Intelligence Scales—Fifth Edition (SB5).

- **40.1.4** A second major intelligence test is the Wechsler Adult Intelligence Scale—Fourth Edition (WAIS-IV). Wechsler's children's version is the Wechsler Intelligence Scale for Children—Fourth Edition (WISC-IV).

- **40.1.5** Intelligence is expressed as an intelligence quotient (IQ), defined as mental age divided by chronological age and then multiplied by 100.

40.2 How much does intelligence vary from person to person?

- **40.2.1** The distribution of IQ scores approximates a normal curve. Most people score in the middle range on intelligence tests. Only a small percentage of people have exceptionally high or low IQ scores.

- **40.2.2** People with IQs in the gifted or "genius" range of above 140 tend to be superior in many respects. However, by criteria other than IQ, many children can be considered gifted or talented in one way or another.

- **40.2.3** The term *intellectually disabled* is applied to those whose IQ falls below 70 and who lack various adaptive behaviors. Causes include genetic abnormalities, fetal damage, birth injures, and postnatal problems.

40.3 What are some issues in the study of intelligence?

- **40.3.1** *Artificial intelligence* refers to any artificial system that can perform tasks that require intelligence when done by people. Two principal areas of artificial intelligence research on particular human skills are computer simulations and expert systems.

- **40.3.2** Traditional IQ tests often suffer from a degree of cultural and racial bias. For this and other reasons, it is wise to remember that IQ is merely an index of intelligence and that intelligence is narrowly defined by most tests.

- **40.3.3** Many psychologists have begun to forge new, broader definitions of intelligence. Howard Gardner's theory of multiple intelligences is a good example.

- **40.3.4** Intelligence is partially determined by heredity. However, environment also is important, as revealed by IQ increases as a result of education and stimulating environments.

Module 40: Knowledge Builder

Recite

1. If we define intelligence by writing a test, we are using a(n) _____ definition.

2. By definition, a person has average intelligence when
   a. MA = CA
   b. CA = 100
   c. MA = 100
   d. MA × CA = 100

3. The distribution of IQs approximates a _____ (bell-shaped) curve.

4. Many cases of intellectual disability without known organic causes appear to be _____.

5. The claim that heredity accounts for racial differences in average IQ scores ignores environmental differences and the cultural bias inherent in standard IQ tests. *T or F?*

6. From a practical point of view, intelligence can most readily be increased by
   a. genetics
   b. teaching adaptive behaviors
   c. stimulating environments
   d. applying deviation IQs

Reflect

Think Critically

7. Is it ever accurate to describe a machine as "intelligent"?

8. Some people treat IQ as if it were a fixed number, permanently stamped on the forehead of each child. Why is this view in error?

Self-Reflect

If you were going to write an intelligence test, what kinds of questions would you include? How much would they resemble the questions found on the SB5, the WAIS-III, or culture-fair tests? Can you think of any type of question that wouldn't favor the mental skills emphasized by some culture, somewhere in the world?

How has your understanding of the following concepts changed: IQ, giftedness, intellectual disability?

A friend says to you, "I think intelligence is entirely inherited from parents." What could you tell your friend to make sure she or he is better informed?

ANSWERS

1. operational 2. a 3. normal 4. familial 5. T 6. c 7. Rule-driven expert systems may appear "intelligent" within a narrow range of problem solving. However, they are "stone stupid" at everything else. This is usually not what we have in mind when discussing human intelligence. 8. Because one's IQ depends on the intelligence test used to measure it: Change the test and you will, to some extent, change the score. Also, heredity establishes a range of possibilities; it does not automatically preordain a person's intellectual capacities.

CENGAGE brain.com

Go to **cengagebrain.com** to access **MindTap for Coon/Mitterer** *Psychology Modules for Active Learning* and other online learning tools. MindTap is a fully online learning experience that combines all the tools you need—readings, multimedia, activities, and assessments—into a singular personalized Learning Path that guides you through the course.

Psychology in Action: Enhancing Creativity

Brainstorms

Life is not a standardized test with a single set of correct answers. It is much more like a blank canvas on which you can create designs that uniquely express your talents and interests. In other words, feel free to be creative and "think outside the box."

Whether you *brainstorm* by yourself or in a group, the key is to keep the production of ideas separate from their evaluation. In other words, don't "pooh-pooh" ideas right away just because they seem odd. Instead, try to produce as many ideas as possible without fear of criticism. Feel free to modify or combine ideas freely. Try to generate lots of ideas. Let your imagination run amok! Seek unusual, remote, or wild ideas. Absolutely do not criticize ideas until you have elaborated or improved on the most promising ideas.

Let's continue with a look at some more creative ideas about how to get more creative ideas.

SURVEY QUESTION

41.1 What can be done to improve thinking and promote creativity?

Enhancing Creativity— Get Out of the Box

SURVEY QUESTION 41.1: What can be done to improve thinking and promote creativity?

Thomas Edison explained his creativity by saying, "Genius is 1 percent inspiration and 99 percent perspiration." Many studies of creativity show that "genius" and "eminence" owe as much to persistence and dedication as they do to inspiration (Robinson, 2010; Winner, 2003). Once it is recognized that creativity can be worked at, then something can be done to enhance it. Here are some suggestions:

Break Mental Sets and Challenge Assumptions

A **mental set** is the tendency to perceive a problem in a way that blinds us to possible solutions. Mental sets are a major barrier to creative thinking. They usually trap us "in a box," leading us to see a problem in preconceived terms that impede our problem-solving attempts (Hurson, 2008). (Fixations and functional fixedness, which were described in Module 39, are specific types of mental sets.)

Try the problems pictured in ● **Figure 41.1**. If you have difficulty, try asking yourself what assumptions you are making. The problems are designed to demonstrate the limiting effects of a mental set. (The answers to these problems,

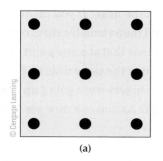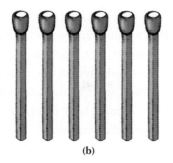

(a)   (b)

Figure 41.1

(*a*) Nine dots are arranged in a square. Can you connect them by drawing four continuous straight lines without lifting your pencil from the paper? (*b*) Six matches must be arranged to make four triangles. The triangles must be the same size, with each side equal to the length of one match. (The solutions to these problems appear in Figure 41.2.)

along with an explanation of the sets that prevent their solution, are found in ● **Figure 41.2**.)

Now that you have been forewarned about the danger of faulty assumptions, see if you can correctly answer the following questions. If you get caught on any of them, consider it an additional reminder of the value of actively challenging the assumptions you are making in any instance of problem solving.

1. Some months have 30 days, some have 31. How many months have 28 days?

2. It is not unlawful for a man living in Winston-Salem, North Carolina, to be buried west of the Mississippi River. T or F?

3. I have two coins that together total 30 cents. One of the coins is not a nickel. What are the two coins?

These questions are designed to cause thinking errors. Here are the answers: 1. All of them. 2. It is against the law to bury a living person anywhere. 3. A quarter and a nickel. One of the coins is not a nickel, but the other one is!

Frame Problems Broadly

An effective way to break mental sets is to frame the problem broadly (Thurson, 2008; Reed, 2013). For instance, assume that your problem is to design a better doorway. This is likely to lead to ordinary solutions. Why not change the problem to design a better way to get through a wall? Now your solutions will be more original. Best of all might be to state the problem as follows: Find a better way to define separate areas for living and working. This could lead to truly creative solutions.

Let's say you are leading a group that's designing a new can opener. Wisely, you ask the group to think broadly about opening in general, rather than about can openers. This was just the approach that led to the pop-

top can. As the design group discussed the concept of opening, one member suggested that nature has its own openers, like the soft seam on a pea pod. Instead of a new can-opening tool, the group invented the self-opening can (Stein, 1974).

Restate the Problem in Different Ways

Stating problems in novel ways also tends to produce more creative solutions. See if you can cross out six letters to make a single word out of the following:

C S R I E X L E A T T T E R E S

If you're having difficulty, it may be that you need to restate the problem. Were you trying to cross out six letters? The real solution is to cross out the letters in the words "six letters," which yields the word CREATE.

One way to restate a problem is to imagine how another person would view it. What would a child, engineer, professor, mechanic, artist, psychologist, judge, or minister ask about the problem? Also, don't be afraid to ask "silly" or playful questions such as: If the problem were alive, what would it look like? If the problem were edible, how would it taste? Is any part of the problem pretty? Ugly? Stupid? Friendly?

At the very least, you should almost always ask the following questions: What information do I have? What don't I know? Have I used all of the information? What additional information do I need? What are the parts of the problem? How are the parts related? How could the parts be related? Remember, to think more creatively, you must find ways to jog yourself out of mental sets and habitual modes of thought (Michalko, 1998; Simonton, 2009).

Mental set *A predisposition to perceive or respond in a particular way.*

Seek Varied Input

Remember, creativity requires divergent thinking. Rather than dig deeper with logic, you attempt to shift your mental "prospecting" to new areas. As an example of this strategy, Edward de Bono (1992) recommends that you randomly look up words in the dictionary and relate them to the problem. Often the words will trigger a fresh perspective or open a new avenue. For instance, let's say you are asked to come up with new ways to clean oil off a beach. Following de Bono's suggestion, you could read the following randomly selected words, relate each to the problem, and see what thoughts are triggered: *weed, rust, poor, magnify, foam, gold, frame, hole, diagonal, vacuum, tribe, puppet, nose, link, drift, portrait, cheese, coal.* You may get similar benefits from relating various objects to a problem. Or, take a walk, skim through a newspaper, or look through a stack of photographs to see what thoughts they trigger (Michalko, 2001; 2006). Exposing yourself to a wide variety of information is a good way to encourage divergent thinking (Gilhooly et al., 2007).

Look for Analogies

Many "new" problems are really old problems in new clothing (Siegler, 1989). Representing a problem in a variety of ways is often the key to a solution. Most problems become easier to solve when they are effectively represented. For example, consider this problem:

> Two backpackers start up a steep trail at 6 AM. They hike all day, resting occasionally, and arrive at the top at 6 PM. The next day, they start back down the trail at 6 AM. On the way down, they stop several times and vary their pace. They arrive back at 6 PM. On the way down, one of the hikers, who is a mathematician, tells the other that she has realized that they will pass a point on the trail at exactly the same time as they did the day before. Her non-mathematical friend finds this hard to believe because on both days they have stopped and started many times and changed their pace. The problem: Is the mathematician right?

Perhaps you will see the answer to this problem immediately. If not, think of it this way: What if there were two pairs of backpackers, one going up the trail, the second coming down, and both hiking *on the same day?* As one pair of hikers goes up the trail and the other goes down, they *must* pass one other at some point on the trail, right? Therefore, at that point, they will be at the same place at the same time. Now, would your conclusion change if one of the pairs was going up the trail one day and

the other was coming down the trail the next? If you mentally draw their path up the mountain and then visualize them coming back down it the next day, do you see that at some point, the two paths will meet at the same point at the same time on both days? Well, what if the same pair of hikers were going up one day and coming back down the next? As you can now see, the mathematician was right.

Allow Time for Incubation

If you are feeling hurried by a sense of time pressure, you are almost always less likely to think creatively (Amabile, Hadley, & Kramer, 2002). You need to be able to revise or embellish initial solutions, even those based on rapid insight. Incubation is especially fruitful when you are exposed to external cues that relate to the problem. For example, Johannes Gutenberg, creator of the printing press, realized while at a wine harvest that the mechanical pressure used to crush grapes could also be used to imprint letters on paper (Dorfman, Shames, & Kihlstrom, 1996).

Delay Evaluation

Various studies suggest that people are most likely to be creative when they are given the freedom to play with ideas and solutions without having to worry about whether they will be evaluated. In the first stages of creative thinking, it is important to avoid criticizing your efforts. Worrying about the correctness of solutions tends to inhibit creativity (Basadur, Runco, & Vega, 2000).

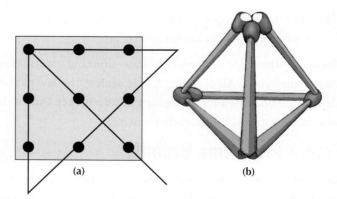

Figure 41.2

Problem solutions. (*a*) The dot problem can be solved by extending the lines beyond the square formed by the dots. Most people assume incorrectly that they may not do this. (*b*) The match problem can be solved by building a three-dimensional pyramid. Most people assume that the matches must be arranged on a flat surface. If you remembered the four-tree problem from an earlier module, the match problem may have been easy to solve.

Live More Creatively

Many people who think in conventional ways live intelligent, successful, and fulfilling lives. Just the same, creative thinking can add spice to life and lead to exciting personal insights (Kaufman, 2009). Psychologist Mihalyi Csikszentmihalyi (sik-sent-me-HALE-yee) (1997) makes these recommendations about how to become more creative:

- Find something that surprises you every day.
- Try to surprise at least one person every day.
- If something sparks your interest, follow it.

- Make a commitment to doing things well.
- Seek challenges.
- Take time for thinking and relaxing.
- Start doing more of what you really enjoy and less of what you dislike.
- Try to look at problems from as many viewpoints as you can.

Even if you don't become more creative by following these suggestions, they are still good advice. To live more creatively, you must be ready to seek new ways of doing things. Try to surprise at least one person today—yourself, if no one else.

Module 41: Summary

41.1 What can be done to improve thinking and promote creativity?

- **41.1.1** Various strategies that promote divergent thinking tend to enhance creative problem solving.

Module 41: Knowledge Builder

Recite

1. Fixations and functional fixedness are specific types of mental sets. *T or F?*
2. The incubation period in creative problem solving usually lasts just a matter of minutes. *T or F?*
3. Exposure to creative models has been shown to enhance creativity. *T or F?*
4. One way to live more creatively is to surprise yourself every day. *T or F?*

Reflect

Think Critically

5. Do you think there is any connection between your mood and your creativity?

Self-Reflect

Review the preceding pages and note which methods you could use more often to improve the quality of your thinking. Now, mentally summarize the points you especially want to remember.

ANSWERS

1. T 2. F 3. T 4. T 5. In general, more intense moods are associated with higher creativity (Davis, 2009).

Personality: Overview of Personality

Even Cowgirls Get the Blues

Sissy waved from her porch, obviously happy to see long-lost friends arrive. If anyone was suited for a move to the "wilds" of Wyoming, it was Sissy, a strong and resourceful woman. Still, it was hard to imagine a more radical change. After going through the "blues" when she separated from her husband, she traded a comfortable life in Manhattan for rougher times on a ranch. Although her friends worried that she might be changed, she was, on the contrary, more her "old self" than ever.

Have you had a similar experience? After years of separation, it is always intriguing to see an old friend. You probably will be delighted to discover that the semi-stranger before you is still the person you once knew. It is exactly this core of consistency that psychologists have in mind when they use the term *personality*. But how is *personality* defined and measured? Read on to find out.

Hans Marie Frei/DigA-Pals/Glow Images

SURVEY QUESTIONS

50.1 How do psychologists use the term *personality*?

50.2 Can personality be measured?

The Psychology of Personality— Do You Have Personality?

SURVEY QUESTION 50.1: How do psychologists use the term *personality*?

"Sissy has a very optimistic personality." "Ramiro's not handsome, but he has a great personality." "My father's business friends think he's a nice guy. They should see him at home where his real personality comes out." "It's hard to believe Tanya and Nikki are sisters. They have such opposite personalities."

It's obvious that we all frequently use the term *personality*. But if you think that personality means "charm," "charisma," or "style," you have misused the term. Many people also confuse personality with the term **character**, which implies that a person has been evaluated as possessing positive qualities, not just described as having them (Bryan & Babelay, 2009). If, by saying someone has "personality," you mean the person is friendly, outgoing, and upstanding, you might be describing what we regard as good character in our culture. But in some cultures, it is deemed good for people to be fierce, warlike, and cruel.

Does this man have personality? Do you?

CBS/Courtesy Everett Collection

Psychologists regard **personality** as a person's unique long-term pattern of thinking, emotions, and behavior (Engler, 2014; Ewen, 2009). In other words, personality refers to the consistency in who you are, have been, and will become. It also refers to the special blend of talents, values, hopes, loves, hates, and habits that makes each of us a unique person. So, everyone in a particular culture has personality, whereas not everyone has character—or at least not good character. (Do you know any good characters?)

Psychologists use a large number of concepts and theories to explain personality. It might be wise, therefore, to start with a few key ideas to help you keep your bearings as you read more about personality.

Traits

We use the idea of traits every day to talk about personality. For instance, Daryl is *sociable*, *orderly*, and *intelligent*. His sister Hollie is *shy*, *sensitive*, and *creative*. Personality traits like these can be quite stable (Allemand, Steiger, & Hill, 2013; Rantanen et al., 2007). Think about how little your best friends have changed in the last five years. It would be strange indeed to feel like you were talking with a different person every time you met a friend or an acquaintance. In general, then, **personality traits** like these are stable qualities that a person shows in most situations (Mõttus, Johnson, & Deary, 2012).

Typically, traits are inferred from behavior. If you see Daryl talking to strangers—first at a supermarket and later at a party—you might deduce that he is "sociable." Once personality traits are identified, they can be used to predict future behavior. For example, noting that Daryl is outgoing might lead you to predict that he will be sociable at school or at work. In fact, such consistencies can span many years (Mõttus, Johnson, & Deary, 2012).

Traits even influence our health as well as our marital and occupational success (Donnellan et al., 2012; Roberts et al., 2007). For example, who do you think will be more successful in her chosen career: Jane, who is conscientious, or Sally, who is not (Brown et al., 2011; Ng & Feldman, 2010)?

Types

Have you ever asked the question, "What type of person is she (or he)?" A **personality type** refers to people who have *several traits in common* (Larsen & Buss, 2010). Informally, your own thinking might include categories such as the executive type, the athletic type, the motherly type, the hip-hop type, the

Tyler Stableford/Getty Images

Psychologists and employers are especially interested in the personality traits of individuals who hold high-risk, high-stress positions involving public safety, such as police, firefighters, air-traffic controllers, and nuclear power plant employees.

techno geek, and so forth. If you tried to define these informal types, you would probably list a different collection of traits for each one.

How valid is it to speak of personality "types"? Over the years, psychologists have proposed many ways to categorize personalities into types. For example, Swiss psychiatrist Carl Jung (pronounced *yoong*) proposed that people are either *introverts* or *extroverts*. An **introvert** is a shy, reserved person whose attention is usually focused inward. An **extrovert** is a bold, outgoing person whose attention is usually directed outward. These terms are so widely used that you may think of yourself and your friends as being one type or the other. However, knowing if someone is extroverted or introverted tells you

Character *Personal characteristics that have been judged or evaluated; a person's desirable or undesirable qualities.*
Personality *A person's unique and relatively stable patterns of thinking, emotions, and behavior.*
Personality trait *A stable, enduring quality that a person shows in most situations.*
Personality type *A style of personality defined by a group of related traits.*
Introvert *A person whose attention is focused inward; a shy, reserved, self-focused person.*
Extrovert *A person whose attention is directed outward; a bold, outgoing person.*

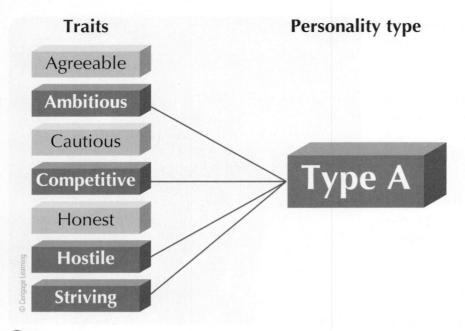

Traits   **Personality type**

Agreeable

Ambitious

Cautious

Competitive

Honest

Hostile

Striving

Type A

© Cengage Learning

Figure 50.1

Personality types are defined by the presence of several specific traits. For example, several possible personality traits are shown in the left column. A person who has a Type A personality typically possesses all or most of the highlighted traits. Type A persons are especially prone to heart disease (see Module 58).

little about how conscientious she is, or how kind or open to new ideas he is. In short, two categories (or even several) are often inadequate to fully capture differences in personality. That's why rating people on a list of traits tends to be more informative than classifying them into two or three types (Engler, 2014).

Even though types tend to oversimplify personality, they do have value. Most often, types are a shorthand way to label people who have several key traits in common. For example, in Module 58, we discuss Type A and Type B personalities. Type A people have personality traits that increase their chance of suffering a heart attack; Type B people take a more laid-back approach to life (see ● **Figure 50.1**). Similarly, in Module 63, you read about unhealthy personality types such as the paranoid personality, the dependent personality, and the antisocial personality. Each problem type is defined by a specific collection of traits that are not adaptive.

Self-Concept

Self-concepts provide another way of understanding personality. Your **self-concept** consists of all your ideas, perceptions, stories, and feelings about who you are. It is the mental

"picture" you have of your own personality (Jonkmann et al., 2012; Ritchie et al., 2011).

We creatively build our self-concepts out of daily experiences. Then we slowly revise them as we have new experiences. Once a stable self-concept exists, it tends to guide what we pay attention to, remember, and think about. Because of this, self-concepts can greatly affect our behavior and personal adjustment—especially when they are inaccurate (Wouters, et al., 2011). For instance, Alesha is a student who thinks she is stupid, worthless, and a failure, despite getting good grades. With such an inaccurate self-concept, she tends to be depressed regardless of how well she does.

Self-Esteem Note that in addition to having a faulty self-concept, Alesha has low self-esteem (a negative self-evaluation). A person with high **self-esteem** is confident, proud, and self-respecting. One who has low self-esteem is insecure, lacking in confidence, and self-critical. Like Alesha, people with low self-esteem are usually anxious and unhappy. People who have low self-esteem typically also suffer from poor self-knowledge. Their self-concepts are inconsistent, inaccurate, and confused (see Module 54).

Self-esteem tends to rise when we experience success or praise. It also buffers us against negative experiences (Brown, 2010). A person who is competent and effective and who is loved, admired, and respected by others will almost always have high self-esteem (Baumeister et al., 2003; Buss, 2012). The reasons for having high self-esteem, however, can vary

Self-concepts can be remarkably consistent. In an interesting study, old people were asked how they had changed over the years. Almost all thought they were essentially the same person they were when they were young (Troll & Skaff, 1997). Well over 90 years old, Nelson Mandela, has thought of himself as a highly committed human rights activist for his entire adult life.

Tom Stoddart Archive/Getty Images

Human Diversity

Self-Esteem and Culture—Hotshot or Team Player?

You and some friends are playing soccer. Your team wins, in part because you make some good plays. After the game, you bask in the glow of having performed well. You don't want to brag about being a hotshot, but your self-esteem gets a boost from your personal success.

In Japan, Shinobu and some of his friends are playing soccer. His team wins, in part because he makes some good plays. After the game, Shinobu is happy because his team did well. However, Shinobu also dwells on the ways in which he let his team down. He thinks about how he could improve, and he resolves to be a better team player.

These sketches illustrate a basic difference in Eastern and Western psychology. In individualistic cultures such as the United States, self-esteem is based on personal success and outstanding performance (Buss, 2012; Ross et al., 2005). For us, the path to higher self-esteem

lies in self-enhancement. We are pumped up by our successes and tend to downplay our faults and failures.

Japanese and other Asian cultures place a greater emphasis on collectivism or interdependence among people. For them, self-esteem is based on a secure sense of belonging to social groups. As a result, people in Asian cultures are more apt to engage in self-criticism (Kitayama, Markus, & Kurokawa, 2000; Tafarodi et al., 2011). By correcting personal faults, they add to the well-being of the group. And, when the *group* succeeds, individual members feel better about themselves, which raises their self-esteem.

Perhaps self-esteem is still based on success in both Eastern and Western cultures (Brown et al., 2009). However, it is fascinating that cultures define success in such different ways (Buss, 2012; Schmitt & Allik, 2005).

---

in different cultures. See "Self-Esteem and Culture" for more information.

What if you "think you're hot," but you're not? Genuine self-esteem is based on an accurate appraisal of your strengths and weaknesses. A positive self-evaluation that is bestowed too easily may not be healthy (Kernis & Lakey, 2010; Twenge & Campbell, 2001). People who think very highly of themselves (and let others know it) may at first seem confident, but their arrogance quickly turns off other people.

The Whole Human: Personality Theories

As you can already see, it would be easy to get lost without a framework for understanding the richness of human personality. How do our thoughts, actions, and feelings relate to one another? How does personality develop? Why do some people suffer from psychological problems? How can they be helped? To answer such questions, psychologists have created a dazzling array of theories. A **personality theory** is a system of concepts, assumptions, ideas, and principles proposed to explain personality. Although many detailed personality theories have been put forward, they can be categorized into four major perspectives:

1. **Trait theories** attempt to learn what traits make up personality and how they relate to actual behavior.

2. **Psychodynamic theories** focus on the inner workings of personality, especially internal conflicts and struggles.

3. **Humanistic theories** stress private, subjective experience, and personal growth.

4. **Behaviorist and social learning theories** place importance on the external environment and on the effects of conditioning and learning. Social learning theories attribute differences in personality to socialization, expectations, and mental processes.

Which of the personality theories is right? To date, each major personality theory has added to our understanding by providing a sort of lens through which human behavior can be viewed. Nevertheless, theories can't be fully proved or disproved. We can only ask, "Does the evidence tend to support this theory or disconfirm it?" Yet, although theories are neither true nor false, their implications or predictions may be. The best way to judge a theory, then, is in terms of its *usefulness*. Does the theory adequately explain behavior? Does it stimulate new

Self-concept *A person's perception of his or her own personality traits.*
Self-esteem *Regarding oneself as a worthwhile person; a positive evaluation of oneself.*
Personality theory *A system of concepts, assumptions, ideas, and principles used to understand and explain personality.*

TABLE 50.1   Comparison of Personality Theories

	Trait Theories	Psychoanalytic Theory	Humanistic Theories	Behaviorist and Social Learning Theories
Role of inheritance (genetics)	Maximized	Stressed	Minimized	Minimized
Role of environment	Recognized	Recognized	Maximized	Maximized
View of human nature	Neutral	Negative	Positive	Neutral
Is behavior free or determined?	Determined	Determined	Free will	Determined
Principal motives	Depends on one's traits	Sex and aggression	Self-actualization	Drives of all kinds
Personality structure	Traits	Id, ego, superego	Self	Habits, expectancies
Role of unconscious	Minimized	Maximized	Minimized	Practically nonexistent
Conception of conscience	Traits of honesty, etc.	Superego	Ideal self, valuing process	Self-reinforcement, punishment history
Developmental emphasis	Combined effects of heredity and environment	Psychosexual stages	Development of self-image	Critical learning situations, identification, and imitation
Barriers to personal growth	Unhealthy traits	Unconscious conflicts, fixations	Conditions of worth, incongruence	Maladaptive habits, unhealthy environment

© Cengage Learning

research? Does it suggest how to treat psychological disorders? Each theory has fared differently in these areas (Cervone & Pervin, 2013). ● Table 50.1 provides an overview of the four principal approaches to personality. In the final analysis, the challenge now facing personality theorists is how to integrate the four major perspectives into a unified, systematic explanation of personality (Mayer, 2005; McAdams & Pals, 2006). With these broad perspectives in mind, let's explore some of the ways psychologists have attempted to assess personality.

Personality Assessment— Psychological Yardsticks

SURVEY QUESTION 50.2: Can personality be measured?

Because the concept of personality is so broad, psychologists use interviews, observation, questionnaires, and projective tests to assess personality (Engler, 2014). Each method has strengths and limitations. For this reason, they are often used in combination.

Formal personality measures are refinements of more casual ways of judging a person. At one time or another, you have probably "sized up" a potential date, friend, or roommate by engaging in conversation (interview). Perhaps you have had the following conversation with a friend: "When I'm delayed, I get mad. Do you?" (questionnaire). Maybe you watch your professors when they are angry or embarrassed to learn what they are "really" like when they're caught off-guard (observation). Or possibly you have noticed that when you say, "I think people feel . . .," you may be expressing your own feelings (projection). Let's see how psychologists apply each of these methods to probe personality.

Interviews

In an **interview**, direct questioning is used to learn about a person's life history, personality traits, or current mental state (Craig, 2013; Murphy & Dillon, 2011). In an **unstructured interview**, conversation is informal and topics are taken up freely as they arise. In a **structured interview**, information is gathered by asking a planned series of questions.

How are interviews used? Interviews are used to identify personality disturbances; to select people for jobs, college, or special programs; and to study the dynamics of personality. Interviews also provide information for counseling or therapy. For instance, a counselor might ask a depressed person, "Have you ever contemplated suicide? What were the circumstances?" The counselor might then follow by asking,

"How did you feel about it?" or, "How is what you are now feeling different from what you felt then?"

In addition to providing information, interviews make it possible to observe a person's tone of voice, hand gestures, posture, and facial expressions. Such "body language" cues are important because they may radically alter the message sent, such as when a person claims to be "completely calm" but trembles uncontrollably.

Limitations Interviews give rapid insight into personality, but they have limitations. For one thing, interviewers can be swayed by preconceptions. A person identified as a "housewife," "college student," "high school athlete," "punk," "geek," or "ski bum" may be misjudged because of an interviewer's personal biases. Second, an interviewer's own personality, gender, or ethnicity may influence a client's behavior. When this occurs, it can accentuate or distort the person's apparent traits (Perry, Fowler, & Howe, 2008; Pollner, 1998). A third problem is that people sometimes try to deceive interviewers. For example, a person accused of a crime might try to avoid punishment by pretending to be mentally disabled.

A fourth problem is the **halo effect**, which is the tendency to generalize a favorable (or unfavorable) impression to an entire personality (Hartung et al., 2010). Because of the halo effect, a person who is likable or physically attractive may be rated more mature, intelligent, or mentally healthy than she or he actually is. The halo effect is something to keep in mind at job interviews.

Even with their limitations, interviews are a respected method of assessment. In many cases, interviews are the first step in evaluating personality and an essential prelude to therapy. Nevertheless, interviews usually are not revealing enough and must be supplemented by other measures and tests (Meyer et al., 2001; Murphy & Dillon, 2011).

Direct Observation and Rating Scales

Are you fascinated by airports, bus depots, parks, taverns, subway stations, or other public places? Many people relish a chance to observe the actions of others. When used for assessment, looking at behavior by **direct observation** is a simple extension of this natural interest in "people watching." For instance, a psychologist might arrange to observe a disturbed child as she plays with other children. Is the child withdrawn? Does she become hostile or aggressive without warning? By careful observation, the psychologist can identify the girl's personality traits and clarify the nature of her problems.

Wouldn't observation be subject to the same problems of misperception as an interview? Yes. Misperceptions can be a difficulty, which is why rating scales are sometimes used (● **Figure 50.2**). A **rating scale** is a list of personality traits or aspects of behavior that can be used to evaluate a person (Siefert, 2010). Rating scales limit the chance that some traits will be overlooked while others are exaggerated (Synhorst et al., 2005). Perhaps they should be a standard procedure for choosing a roommate, spouse, or lover!

An alternative approach is to do a **behavioral assessment** by counting the frequency of specific behaviors (Cipani & Schock, 2010). In this case, observers record *actions,* not what traits they think a person has. For example, a psychologist working with hospitalized mental patients might note the frequency of a patient's aggression, self-care, speech, and unusual behaviors. Behavioral assessments also can be used to probe thought processes. In one study, for example, couples were

What is your impression of the person wearing the beige suit? If you think that she looks friendly, attractive, or neat, your other perceptions of her might be altered by that impression. Interviewers are often influenced by the halo effect (see text).

Interview (personality) *A face-to-face meeting held for the purpose of gaining information about an individual's personal history, personality traits, current psychological state, and so forth.*
Unstructured interview *An interview in which conversation is informal and topics are taken up freely as they arise.*
Structured interview *An interview that follows a prearranged plan, usually a series of planned questions.*
Halo effect *The tendency to generalize a favorable or unfavorable particular impression to unrelated details of personality.*
Direct observation *Assessing behavior through direct surveillance.*
Rating scale *A list of personality traits or aspects of behavior on which a person is rated.*
Behavioral assessment *Recording the frequency of various behaviors.*

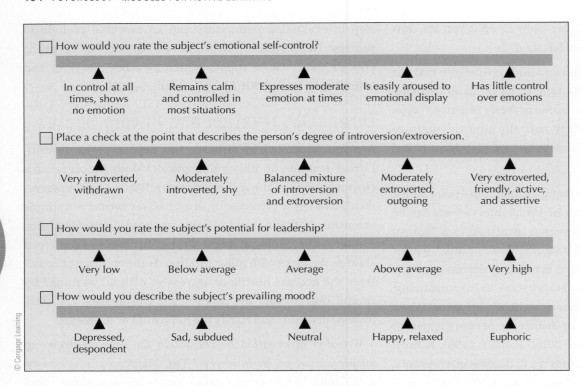

Figure 50.2

Sample rating scale items. To understand how the scale works, imagine someone you know well. Where would you place check marks on each of the scales to rate that person's characteristics?

assessed while talking with each other about their sexuality. Couples with sexual difficulties were less likely to be receptive to discussing their sexuality and more likely to blame each other than were couples with no sexual difficulties (Kelly, Strassberg, & Turner, 2006).

Situational Testing In **situational testing**, a type of direct observation, real-life conditions are simulated so that a person's spontaneous reactions can be observed. Such tests assume that the best way to learn how people react is to put them in realistic situations and watch what happens. Situational tests expose people to frustration, temptation, pressure, boredom, or other conditions capable of revealing personality characteristics (Weekley & Polyhart, 2006). Some popular reality TV programs, such as *American Idol, Survivor,* and *The Amazing Race* bear some similarity to situational tests—which may account for their ability to attract millions of viewers.

How are situational tests done? An interesting example of situational testing is the judgmental firearms training provided by many police departments. At times, police officers must make split-second decisions about using their weapons. A mistake could be fatal. In a typical shoot–don't-shoot test, actors play the part of armed criminals. As various high-risk scenes are acted out live, on DVD, or by computer, officers must decide to shoot or hold fire.

A police special tactics team undergoes judgmental firearms training. Variations on this situational test are used by many police departments. All officers must score a passing grade.

Personality Questionnaires

Personality questionnaires are paper-and-pencil tests that reveal personality characteristics. Questionnaires are more objective than interviews or observation. (An **objective test** gives the same score when different people correct it.) Questions, administration, and scoring are all standardized so that scores are unaffected by any biases an examiner may have. A good test also must be reliable and valid (Kaplan & Saccuzzo, 2013). A test is **reliable** if it yields close to the same score each time it is given to the same person. A test has **validity** if it measures what it claims to measure. Unfortunately, many personality tests you will encounter, such as those in magazines or on the Internet, have little or no validity.

Dozens of personality tests are available, including the *Guilford-Zimmerman Temperament Survey*, the *California Psychological Inventory*, the *Allport-Vernon Study of Values*, the 16 PF, and many more. One of the best-known and most widely used objective tests is the **Minnesota Multiphasic Personality Inventory-2 (MMPI-2)** (Butcher, 2011). The MMPI-2 is composed of 567 items to which a test taker must respond "true" or "false." Items include statements such as the following.

Everything tastes the same.

I am very normal, sexually.

I like birds.

I usually daydream in the afternoon.

Mostly, I stay away from other people.

Someone has been trying to hurt me.

Sometimes I think strange thoughts.*

How can these items show anything about personality? For instance, what if a person has a cold so that "everything tastes the same"? For an answer (and a little bit of fun), read the following items. Answer "Yes," "No," or "Don't bother me, I can't cope!"

I have a collection of 1,243 old pizza cartons.

I enjoy the thought of eating liver-flavored ice cream.

I love the smell of napalm in the morning.

I hate the movie *Apocalypse Now*.

I can't add numbers correctly.

Bathing sucks.

I like rats and dry hand towels.

I absolutely adore this textbook.

These items were written by your authors to satirize personality questionnaires. (Why not try writing some of your own?) Such questions may seem ridiculous, but they are not very different from the real thing. How, then, do the items on tests such as the MMPI-2 reveal anything about personality? The answer is that a single item tells little about personality. For example, a person who agrees that "Everything tastes the same" might simply have a cold. It is only through *patterns* of response that personality dimensions are revealed.

Items on the MMPI-2 were selected for their ability to correctly identify persons with particular psychological problems

---

*MMPI-2 statements themselves cannot be reproduced, to protect the validity of the test.

(Butcher, 2011). For instance, if depressed persons consistently answer a series of items in a particular way, it is assumed that others who answer the same way also are prone to depression. As silly as the gag items in the preceding list may seem, it is possible that some could work in a legitimate test. But before an item could be part of a test, it would have to be shown to correlate highly with some trait or dimension of personality.

The MMPI-2 measures 10 major aspects of personality (listed in ● Table 50.2). After the MMPI-2 is scored, results

TABLE 50.2	MMPI-2 Basic Clinical Subscales

1. **Hypochondriasis** (HI-po-kon-DRY-uh-sis). Exaggerated concern about one's physical health

2. **Depression.** Feelings of worthlessness, hopelessness, and pessimism

3. **Hysteria.** The presence of physical complaints for which no physical basis can be established

4. **Psychopathic deviate.** Emotional shallowness in relationships and a disregard for social and moral standards

5. **Masculinity/femininity.** One's degree of traditional "masculine" aggressiveness or "feminine" sensitivity

6. **Paranoia.** Extreme suspiciousness and feelings of persecution

7. **Psychasthenia** (sike-as-THEE-nee-ah). The presence of obsessive worries, irrational fears (phobias), and compulsive (ritualistic) actions

8. **Schizophrenia.** Emotional withdrawal and unusual or bizarre thinking and actions

9. **Mania.** Emotional excitability, manic moods or behavior, and excessive activity

10. **Social introversion.** One's tendency to be socially withdrawn

(Reproduced by permission. © 1943, renewed 1970 by the University of Minnesota. Published by the Psychological Corporation, New York. All rights reserved.)

Situational test *Simulating real-life conditions so that a person's reactions may be directly observed.*

Personality questionnaire *A paper-and-pencil test consisting of questions that reveal aspects of personality.*

Objective test *A test that gives the same score when different people correct it.*

Reliability *The ability of a test to yield nearly the same score each time it is given to the same person.*

Validity *The ability of a test to measure what it purports to measure.*

Minnesota Multiphasic Personality Inventory-2 (MMPI-2) *One of the best-known and most widely used objective personality questionnaires.*

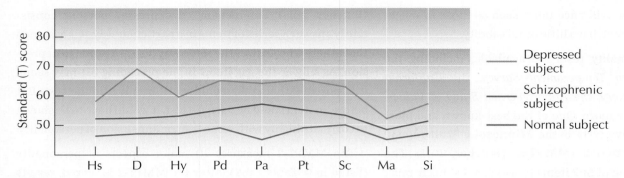

● Figure 50.3

MMPI-2 Profiles. The MMPI-2 can even track progress in therapy. At the start of treatment, the scores of a group of severely troubled individuals were elevated on most of the individual scales. (Note that the masculinity/femininity scores are not included.) After three years of therapy, their scores have declined significantly and are much more similar to normal scores, which usually fall in the 45–50 range. An unusually low score (40 and below) also may reveal personality characteristics or problems. (Adapted from Gordon, 2001.)

are charted graphically as an *MMPI-2 profile* (● **Figure 50.3**). By comparing a person's profile with scores produced by typical, normal adults, a psychologist can identify various personality disorders. Additional scales can identify substance abuse, eating disorders, Type A (heart-attack prone) behavior, repression, anger, cynicism, low self-esteem, family problems, inability to function in a job, and other problems (Butcher, 2011).

How accurate is the MMPI-2? Personality questionnaires are accurate only if people tell the truth about themselves. Because of this, the MMPI-2 has additional *validity scales* that reveal whether a person's scores should be discarded. The validity scales detect attempts by test takers to "fake good" (make themselves look good) or "fake bad" (make it look like they have problems) (Scherbaum et al., 2013). Other scales uncover defensiveness or tendencies to exaggerate shortcomings and troubles. When taking the MMPI-2, it is best to answer honestly and not try to second-guess the test.

A clinical psychologist trying to decide whether a person has emotional problems would be wise to take more than the MMPI-2 into account. Test scores are informative, but they can incorrectly label some people (Kaplan & Saccuzzo, 2013). Fortunately, clinical judgments usually rely on information from interviews, tests, and other sources. Also, despite their limitations, it is reassuring to note that psychological assessments are at least as accurate as commonly used medical tests (Neukrug & Fawcett, 2010).

Projective Tests of Personality

Projective tests take a different approach to personality. Interviews, observation, rating scales, and inventories try to directly identify overt, observable traits. By contrast, projective tests seek to uncover deeply hidden or *unconscious* wishes, thoughts, and needs (Burger, 2011; McGrath & Carroll, 2012).

As a child, you may have delighted in finding faces and objects in cloud formations. Or perhaps you have learned something about your friends' personalities from their reactions to movies or paintings. If so, you have some insight into the rationale for projective tests. In a **projective test**, a person is asked to describe ambiguous stimuli or make up stories about them. Describing an unambiguous stimulus (a picture of an automobile, for example) tells little about your personality. But when you are faced with an unstructured stimulus, you must organize what you see in terms of your own life experiences. Everyone sees something different in a projective test, and what is perceived can reveal the inner workings of personality.

Projective tests have no right or wrong answers, which makes them difficult to fake. Moreover, projective tests can be a rich source of information because responses are not restricted to simple true/false or yes/no answers.

The Rorschach Inkblot Test *Is the inkblot test a projective technique?* The **Rorschach Inkblot Test** (ROAR-shock) is one of the oldest and most widely used projective tests. Developed by Swiss psychologist Hermann Rorschach in the 1920s, it consists of 10 standardized inkblots. These vary in color, shading, form, and complexity.

How does the test work? First, a person is shown each blot and asked to describe what she or he sees in it (● **Figure 50.4**). Later, the psychologist may return to a blot, asking the person to identify specific sections of it, to expand previous descriptions, or to give new impressions about what it contains. Obvious differences in content—such as "blood dripping from

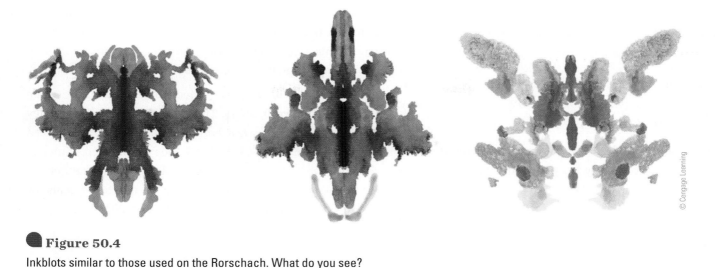

Figure 50.4

Inkblots similar to those used on the Rorschach. What do you see?

a dagger" versus "flowers blooming in a basket"—are important for identifying personal conflicts and fantasies. But surprisingly, content is less important than what parts of the inkblot are used to organize images. These factors allow psychologists to detect emotional disturbances by observing how a person perceives the world (Bornstein, 2012). Schizophrenia and other psychotic disorders are associated with severe disturbances in thinking and perception. Such disturbances are usually readily apparent during projective testing (Moore et al., 2013). (See Module 61.)

Figure 50.5

This is a picture like those used for the Thematic Apperception Test. If you want to simulate the test, tell a story that explains what led up to the pictured situation, what is happening now, and how the action will end.

The Thematic Apperception Test Another popular projective test is the **Thematic Apperception Test (TAT)**, developed by personality theorist Henry Murray (1893–1988).

How does the TAT differ from the Rorschach? The TAT consists of 20 sketches depicting various scenes and life situations (● **Figure 50.5**). During testing, a person is shown each sketch and asked to make up a story about the people in it. Later, the person looks at each sketch a second or a third time and elaborates on previous stories or creates new stories.

To score the TAT, a psychologist analyzes the content of the stories. Interpretations focus on how people feel, how they interact, what events led up to the incidents depicted in the sketch, and how the story will end. For example, TAT stories told by bereaved college students typically include themes of death, grief, and coping with loss (Balk et al., 1998).

A psychologist might also count how many times the central figure in a TAT story is angry, overlooked, apathetic, jealous, or threatened. A student wrote the following story to describe Figure 50.5:

> The girl has been seeing this guy her mother doesn't like. The mother is telling her that she better not see him again. The mother says, "He's just like your father." The mother and father

Projective tests *Psychological tests that use ambiguous or unstructured stimuli.*
Rorschach Inkblot Test *A projective test that consists of 10 standardized inkblots.*
Thematic Apperception Test (TAT) *A projective test consisting of 20 different scenes and life situations about which respondents make up stories.*

are divorced. The mother is smiling because she thinks she is right. But she doesn't really know what the girl wants. The girl is going to see the guy again, anyway.

As this example implies, the TAT is especially good at revealing feelings about a person's social relationships (Aronow et al., 2001; Teglasi, 2010).

Limitations of Projective Testing Although projective tests have been popular, their validity is open to question (Bornstein, 2012; Wood et al., 2003). Objectivity and reliability (consistency) also are low for different users of the TAT and Rorschach. Note that after a person interprets an ambiguous stimulus, the scorer must interpret the person's (sometimes) ambiguous responses. In a sense, the interpretation of a projective test may be a projective test for the scorer!

Despite their drawbacks, projective tests still have value (McGrath & Carroll, 2012). This is especially true when they are used as part of a *test battery* (collection of assessment devices and interviews). In the hands of a skilled clinician, projective tests can be a good way to detect major conflicts, to get clients to talk about upsetting topics, and to set goals for therapy (Garcia-Barrera et al., 2013; Teglasi, 2010).

Module 50: Summary

50.1 How do psychologists use the term personality?

- **50.1.1** *Personality* refers to a person's consistent and unique patterns of thinking, emotion, and behavior.
- **50.1.2** Personality traits are lasting personal qualities that are inferred from behavior.
- **50.1.3** Personality types group people into categories on the basis of shared traits.
- **50.1.4** Behavior is influenced by self-concept, which is a perception of one's own personality traits. A positive self-evaluation leads to high self-esteem. Low self-esteem is associated with stress, unhappiness, and depression.
- **50.1.5** Each of the four major theories of personality—trait, psychodynamic, humanistic, and behaviorist and social learning—combines interrelated assumptions, ideas, and principles and is useful for understanding some aspects of personality.

50.2 Can personality be measured?

- **50.2.1** Techniques typically used for personality assessment are interviews, observation, questionnaires, and projective tests.

- **50.2.2** Structured and unstructured interviews provide much information, but they are subject to interviewer bias and misperceptions. The halo effect also may lower the accuracy of an interview.
- **50.2.3** Direct observation, sometimes involving situational tests, behavioral assessment, or the use of rating scales, allows evaluation of a person's actual behavior.
- • **50.2.4** Personality questionnaires, such as the *Minnesota Multiphasic Personality Inventory-2 (MMPI-2)*, are objective and reliable, but their validity is open to question.
- **50.2.5** Projective tests ask a person to project thoughts or feelings to an ambiguous stimulus or unstructured situation. Two well-known examples are the *Rorschach Inkblot Test* and the *Thematic Apperception Test (TAT)*.
- **50.2.6** Projective tests are low in validity and objectivity. Nevertheless, they are considered useful by many clinicians, particularly as part of a test battery.

Module 50: Knowledge Builder

Recite

1. An individual's perception of his or her own personality constitutes that person's _____.

2. The halo effect can be a serious problem in accurate personality assessment that is based on
   - **a.** projective testing
   - **b.** behavioral recording
   - **c.** interviewing
   - **d.** the TAT

3. Doing a behavioral assessment requires direct observation of the person's actions or a direct report of the person's thoughts. **T or F**?

4. A test is considered valid if it consistently yields the same score when the same person takes it on different occasions. **T or F**?

5. Which of the following is considered the most objective measure of personality?
   - **a.** rating scales
   - **b.** personality questionnaires
   - **c.** projective tests
   - **d.** TAT

6. The use of ambiguous stimuli is most characteristic of
   - **a.** interviews
   - **b.** projective tests
   - **c.** personality inventories
   - **d.** direct observation

Reflect

Think Critically

7. In what way would memory contribute to the formation of an accurate or inaccurate self-image?

8. Projective testing would be of greatest interest to which type of personality theorist?

Self-Reflect

See if you can define or describe the following terms in your own words: *personality, character, trait, type, self-concept, self-esteem.*

How do *you* assess personality? Do you informally use any of the methods described in this module?

ANSWERS

1. self-concept 2. c 3. T 4. F 5. b 6. b 7. As discussed in Module 32, memory is highly selective, and long-term memories are often distorted by recent information. Such properties add to the moldability of self-concept. 8. Psychodynamic; projective testing is designed to uncover unconscious thoughts, feelings, and conflicts.

CENGAGE brain.com

Go to **cengagebrain.com** to access **MindTap for Coon/Mitterer** *Psychology Modules for Active Learning* and other online learning tools. MindTap is a fully online learning experience that combines all the tools you need—readings, multimedia, activities, and assessments—into a singular personalized Learning Path that guides you through the course.

Personality: Trait Theories

Conscientious Drivers Always Check Their Rear-Views

Sam's a good guy and a great friend. He's talkative, curious, and good-natured. Conscientious? Not so much. Sam's more likely to be found socializing at the local students' pub than studying at the library.

Trait theories seek to describe personality in terms of a small number of underlying personality traits or factors, like the adjectives we used to describe Sam. The trait approach is currently the dominant method for studying personality. Of the various trait theories, The *Five Factor Personality Model (Big Five)* is currently the most influential. According to this theory, all personalities can be described as varying along five key factors: *extroversion, agreeableness, conscientiousness, neuroticism,* and *openness to experience.*

Knowing where a person stands on the "Big Five" personality factors helps predict his or her behavior. For example, people who score high on conscientiousness tend to be safe

Eleanor Bentall/Corbis

drivers who are less likely to have automobile accidents (Sam, Sam, what have you done! lol).

SURVEY QUESTION

51.1 Are some personality traits more basic or important than others?

The Trait Approach— Describe Yourself in 18,000 Words or Less

SURVEY QUESTION 51.1: Are some personality traits more basic or important than others?

Take a moment to read through ● **Table 51.1** and check the traits that describe your personality. Don't worry if some of your key traits aren't in the table. More than 18,000 English words refer to personal characteristics. Are the traits you checked of equal importance? Are some stronger or more

basic than others? Do any overlap? For example, if you checked "dominant," did you also check "confident" and "bold"? Answers to these questions would interest a trait theorist.

To better understand personality, **trait theorists** attempt to analyze, classify, and interrelate traits. In addition, trait theorists often think of traits as *biological predispositions,* a hereditary readiness of humans to behave in particular ways. (We encountered this idea before, in Module 14, in which we humans were described as having a biological predisposition to learn language.)

As we have noted, traits are stable dispositions that a person shows in most situations (Mõttus, Johnson, & Deary, 2012). For example, if you are usually friendly, optimistic, and cautious, these qualities are traits of your personality.

TABLE 51.1	Adjective Checklist		
Check the traits you feel are characteristic of your personality. Are some more basic than others?			
Aggressive	Organized	Ambitious	Clever
Confident	Loyal	Generous	Calm
Warm	Bold	Cautious	Reliable
Sensitive	Mature	Talented	Jealous
Sociable	Honest	Funny	Religious
Dominant	Dull	Accurate	Nervous
Humble	Uninhibited	Visionary	Cheerful
Thoughtful	Serious	Helpful	Emotional
Orderly	Anxious	Conforming	Good-natured
Liberal	Curious	Optimistic	Kind
Meek	Neighborly	Passionate	Compulsive

© Cengage Learning

What if I also am sometimes shy, pessimistic, or uninhibited? The original three qualities are still traits as long as they are most *typical* of your behavior. Let's say our friend Sissy approaches most situations with optimism but tends to expect the worst each time she applies for a job and worries that she won't get it. If her pessimism is limited to this situation or just a few others, it is still accurate and useful to describe her as an optimistic person.

Predicting Behavior

As we have noted, separating people into broad types, such as "introvert" or "extrovert," may oversimplify personality. However, introversion/extroversion also can be thought of as a trait. Knowing how you rate on this single dimension allows us to predict how you will behave in a variety of settings. How, for example, do you prefer to meet people—face-to-face or through the Internet? Researchers have found that students high in the trait of introversion are more likely to prefer the Internet because they find it easier to talk with people online (Mitchell et al., 2011; Rice & Markey, 2009). Other interesting links exist between traits and behavior. See "What's Your MUSIC Personality?"

Classifying Traits

Are there different types of traits? Yes. Psychologist Gordon Allport (1961) identified several kinds. **Common traits** are characteristics shared by most members of a culture. Common

traits tell us how people from a particular nation or culture are similar or which traits a culture emphasizes. In America, for example, competitiveness is a fairly common trait. Among the Hopi of northern Arizona, however, it is relatively rare.

Of course, common traits don't tell us much about individuals. Although many people are competitive in American culture, various people you know may rate high, medium, or low in this trait. Usually, we also are interested in **individual traits**, which describe a person's unique qualities.

Here's an analogy to help you separate common traits from individual traits: If you decide to buy a pet dog, you will want to know the general characteristics of the dog's breed (its common traits). In addition, you will want to know about the "personality" of a specific dog (its individual traits) before you decide to take it home.

Allport also made distinctions among *cardinal traits, central traits*, and *secondary traits*. **Cardinal traits** are so basic that all of a person's activities can be traced to the trait. For instance,

Trait theorist *A psychologist interested in classifying, analyzing, and interrelating traits to understand personality.*
Common traits *Personality traits that are shared by most members of a particular culture.*
Individual traits *Personality traits that define a person's unique individual qualities.*
Cardinal trait *A personality trait so basic that all of a person's activities relate to it.*

Discovering Psychology

What's Your MUSIC Personality?

Even if you like all kinds of music, you probably prefer some styles to others. Of the styles listed here, which three do you enjoy the most? (Circle your choices.)

alternative blues classical contemporary adult country dance electronic folk funk hard rock heavy metal hip-hop jazz opera pop punk r&b rap religious rock-n-roll soft rock soul world

In a series of studies, Peter Rentfrow found that the types of music people prefer tend to be associated with their personality characteristics (Rentfrow & Gosling, 2003). See if your musical tastes match one of their *MUSIC* (*M*ellow, *U*npretentious, *S*ophisticated, *I*ntense, *C*ontemporary) categories (Rentfrow et al., 2012; Rentfrow, Goldberg, & Levitin, 2011):

- **Mellow:** People who are relaxed, thoughtful, unaggressive, and quiet tend to appreciate smooth and relaxing music (contemporary adult, r&b, soft rock, soul).

- **Unpretentious:** People who are cheerful, conventional, extroverted, reliable, helpful, and conservative tend to

enjoy upbeat conventional music (country, pop, religious, rock-n-roll).

- **Sophisticated:** People who value aesthetic experiences, have good verbal abilities, and are liberal and tolerant of others tend to like music that is reflective and complex (blues, classical, folk, jazz, opera, world).

- **Intense:** People who are curious about new experiences, enjoy taking risks, and are physically active prefer intense, rebellious music (alternative, hard rock, heavy metal, punk).

- **Contemporary:** People who are talkative, full of energy, forgiving, and physically attractive and who reject conservative ideals tend to prefer energetic, rhythmic music (dance, electronic, funk, hip-hop, rap).

Unmistakably, personality traits are related to our everyday behavior (Rentfrow, 2012).

---

compassion was an overriding trait of Mother Teresa's personality. Likewise, Abraham Lincoln's personality was dominated by the cardinal trait of honesty. According to Allport, few people have cardinal traits.

Central Traits *How do central and secondary traits differ from cardinal traits?* **Central traits** are the basic building blocks of personality. A surprisingly small number of central traits can capture the essence of a person. For instance, just six traits would provide a good description of Jacintha's personality: dominant, sociable, honest, cheerful, intelligent, and optimistic. When college students were asked to describe someone they knew well, they mentioned an average of seven central traits (Allport, 1961).

Secondary traits are more superficial personal qualities, such as food preferences, attitudes, political opinions, musical tastes, and so forth. In Allport's terms, a personality description might therefore include the following items:

Name: Jane Doe

Age: 22

Cardinal traits: None

Central traits: Possessive, autonomous, artistic, dramatic, self-centered, trusting

Secondary traits: Prefers colorful clothes, likes to work alone, politically liberal, always late

Source Traits *How can you tell whether a personality trait is central or secondary?* Raymond B. Cattell (1906–1998) tried to answer this question by directly studying the traits of a large number of people. Cattell began by measuring visible features of personality, which he called **surface traits**. Soon, Cattell noticed that these surface traits often appeared together in groups. In fact, some traits clustered together so often that they seemed to represent a single, more basic trait. Cattell called these deeper characteristics, or dimensions, **source traits (factors)** (Cattell, 1965). They are the core of an individual's personality.

How do source traits differ from Allport's central traits? Allport classified traits subjectively, and it's possible that he was wrong at times. To look for connections among traits, Cattell used **factor analysis**, a statistical technique used to correlate multiple measurements and identify general underlying factors. For example, he found that imaginative people are almost always inventive, original, curious, creative, innovative, and ingenious. If you are an imaginative person, we automatically know that you have several other traits. Thus, *imaginative* is a source trait, or factor. For example, ● **Figure 51.1** shows one of the first trait theories, composed of two factors, introversion–extroverison and emotionally stable–unstable.

Cattell (1973) identified 16 source traits. According to him, all 16 are needed to fully describe a personality. Source traits

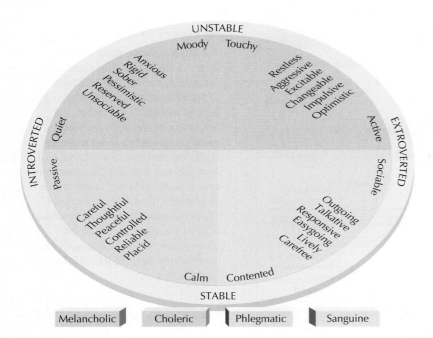

Figure 51.1

English psychologist Hans Eysenck (1916–1997) proposed the personality theory that many personality traits are related to whether you are mainly introverted or extroverted and whether you tend to be emotionally stable or unstable (highly emotional). These characteristics, in turn, are related to four basic types of temperament first recognized by the early Greeks. The types are: *melancholic* (sad, gloomy), *choleric* (hot-tempered, irritable), *phlegmatic* (sluggish, calm), and *sanguine* (cheerful, hopeful). (Adapted from Eysenck, 1981.)

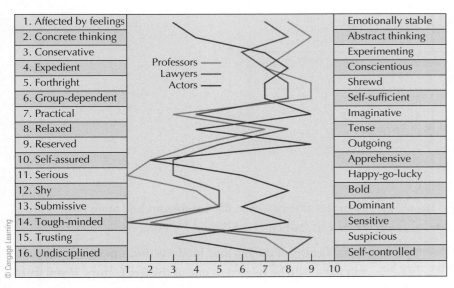

Figure 51.2

The 16 source traits measured by Cattell's (1973) 16 PF are listed beside the graph. Scores can be plotted as a profile for an individual or a group. The hypothetical profiles shown here are group averages for college professors, lawyers, and professional actors. Notice the similarities between professors and lawyers and the differences between these two groups and professional actors. (Of course, your authors may only be expressing the common stereotype that professors and lawyers are more reserved abstract thinkers than actors or that actors are less emotionally stable and more happy-go-lucky than professors and lawyers. What do you think?)

are measured by a test called the *Sixteen Personality Factor Questionnaire* (often referred to as the *16 PF*). Like many personality tests, the 16 PF can be used to produce a **trait profile**, or graph of a person's score on each trait. Trait profiles draw a "picture" of individual personalities, which makes it easier to compare them (**Figure 51.2**).

The Big Five

Noel is outgoing and friendly, conscientious, even-tempered, and curious. His brother Joel is reserved, hostile, irresponsible, temperamental, and disinterested in ideas. You will be spending a week in a space capsule with either Noel or Joel. Who would you choose? If the answer seems obvious, it's because Noel and Joel were described with the **five-factor**

model, a system that identifies the five most basic dimensions of personality.

Central traits *The core traits that characterize an individual personality.*
Secondary traits *Traits that are inconsistent or relatively superficial.*
Surface traits *The visible or observable traits of one's personality.*
Source traits (factors) *Basic underlying traits, or dimensions, of personality; each source trait is reflected in a number of surface traits.*
Factor analysis *A statistical technique used to correlate multiple measurements and identify general underlying factors.*
Trait profile *A graph of the scores obtained on several personality traits.*
Five-factor model *Proposes that personality has five universal dimensions.*

Figure 51.3

The Big Five. According to the five-factor model, basic differences in personality can be "boiled down" to the dimensions shown here. Rate yourself on each factor. The five-factor model answers these essential questions about a person: Is she/he extroverted or introverted? Agreeable or difficult? Conscientious or irresponsible? Emotionally stable or unstable? Smart or unintelligent? These questions cover a large measure of what we might want to know about someone's personality. (Trait descriptions adapted from McCrae & Costa, 2001.)

Five Key Dimensions The "Big Five" factors listed in ● **Figure 51.3** attempt to further reduce Cattell's 16 factors to just five universal dimensions, or source traits (Costa & McCrae, 2006; Noftle & Fleeson, 2010). The Big Five may be the best answer of all to the question, What is the essence of human personality?

If you would like to compare the personalities of two people, try rating them informally on the five dimensions shown in Figure 51.3. For Factor 1, *extroversion*, rate how introverted or extroverted each person is. Factor 2, *agreeableness*, refers to how friendly, nurturant, and caring a person is, as opposed to cold, indifferent, self-centered, or spiteful. A person who is *conscientious* (Factor 3) is self-disciplined, responsible, and achieving. People low on this factor are irresponsible, careless, and undependable. Factor 4, *neuroticism*, refers to negative, upsetting emotions. People who are high in neuroticism tend to be anxious, emotionally "sour," irritable, and unhappy. Finally, people who rate high on Factor 5,

openness to experience, are intelligent and open to new ideas (Ashcraft, 2012).

The beauty of the Big Five model is that almost any trait you can name will be related to one of the five factors. If you were selecting a college roommate, hiring an employee, or answering a post at a singles site, you would probably want to know all the personal dimensions covered by the Big Five. Now, try rating yourself as you read "Which Personality Are You (and Which Is Best)?"

The Big Five traits have been related to different brain systems and chemicals (DeYoung et al., 2010; Nettle, 2008). They also predict how people will act in various circumstances (Sutin & Costa, 2010). For example, people who score high in conscientiousness tend to perform well at work, do well in school, and rarely have automobile accidents (Brown et al., 2011; Chamorro-Premuzic & Furnham, 2003). They are healthier and even live longer (Hampson et al., 2013; Martin, Friedman, & Schwartz, 2007).

Discovering Psychology

Which Personality Are You (and Which Is Best)?

According to the *five-factor model*, your rating on each of five basic personality dimensions, or factors, gives a good overall description of your personality. Try rating yourself (see Figure 51.3). How well do you think your ratings describe you? When you were rating yourself, did you notice that some of the traits don't seem very attractive? After all, who would want to score low in *extroversion?* What could be good about being a quiet, passive, and reserved loner? In other words, aren't some personality patterns better than others?

OK, so what is the best personality pattern? You might be surprised to learn that there is no one "best" personality pattern. For example, extroverts tend to earn more during their careers than introverts and they have more sexual partners. But they also are more likely to take risks than introverts (and to land in the hospital with an injury). Extroverts also are more likely to divorce. Because of this, extroverted men are less likely to live with their children. In other words, extroversion tends to open the doors to some life experiences and close doors to others (Cain, 2012; Nettle, 2005).

The same is true for *agreeableness.* Agreeable people attract more friends and enjoy strong social support from others. But agreeable people often put the interests of friends and family ahead of their own.

This leaves agreeable people at a disadvantage. To do creative, artistic work or to succeed in the business world often involves putting your own interests first (Nettle, 2008).

How about conscientiousness? Up to a point, conscientiousness is associated with high achievement. However, having impossibly high standards, a trait called *perfectionism*, can be a problem. As you might expect, college students who are perfectionists tend to get good grades. Yet, some students cross the line into maladaptive perfectionism, which typically *lowers* performance at school and elsewhere (Weiner & Carton, 2012). Authentic Navajo rugs always have a flaw in their intricate designs. Navajo weavers intentionally make a "mistake" in each rug as a reminder that humans are not perfect. There is a lesson in this: It is not always necessary, or even desirable, to be "perfect." To learn from your experiences, you must feel free to make mistakes. Success, in the long run, is more often based on seeking "excellence" rather than "perfection" (Enns, Cox, & Clara, 2005).

Except for very extreme personality patterns, which are often maladaptive, most "personalities" involve a mix of costs and benefits (Turiano et al., 2013). We all face the task of pursuing life experiences that best suit our own unique personality patterns (Nettle, 2008).

Module 51: Summary

51.1 Are some personality traits more basic or important than others?

- **51.1.1** Trait theories identify qualities that are most lasting or characteristic of a person.
- **51.1.2** Allport made useful distinctions between common traits and individual traits and among cardinal, central, and secondary traits.

- **51.1.3** Cattell's theory attributes visible surface traits to the existence of 16 underlying source traits.
- **51.1.4** Source traits are measured by the *Sixteen Personality Factor Questionnaire* (16 PF).
- **51.1.5** The five-factor model identifies five universal dimensions of personality: extroversion, agreeableness, conscientiousness, neuroticism, and openness to experience.

Module 51: Knowledge Builder

Recite

1. Eysenck's early trait theory was composed of two factors, emotional stability–instability and _____.

2. Traits are stable dispositions that a person shows in most _____.

3. Central traits are those shared by most members of a culture. **T or F?**

4. Cattell believes that clusters of _____ traits reveal the presence of underlying _____ traits.

5. Which of the following is *not* one of the Big Five personality factors?
   - *a.* submissiveness
   - *b.* agreeableness
   - *c.* extroversion
   - *d.* neuroticism

Reflect

Think Critically

6. Can you think of a Big Five trait besides conscientiousness that might be related to academic achievement?

Self-Reflect

List six or seven traits that best describe your personality. Which system of traits seems to best match your list, Allport's, Cattell's, or the Big Five?

Choose a prominent trait from your list. Does its expression seem to be influenced by specific situations? Do you think that heredity contributed to the trait?

ANSWERS

1. introversion-extraversion 2. situations 3. F 4. surface, source 5. a 6. In one study, conscientiousness was positively related to academic performance, as you might expect. Students high in neuroticism also were better academic performers, but only if they were not too stressed (Kappe & van der Flier, 2010).

CENGAGEbrain.com

Go to **cengagebrain.com** to access **MindTap for Coon/Mitterer** *Psychology Modules for Active Learning* and other online learning tools. MindTap is a fully online learning experience that combines all the tools you need—readings, multimedia, activities, and assessments—into a singular personalized Learning Path that guides you through the course.

Personality: Psychodynamic and Humanistic Theories

The Why of Personality

Meghan is self-conscious around strangers. You could almost say she is shy. This has been a life-long personality trait. But *why*, she often wonders. So, too, do psychodynamic theorists, who are not content with studying traits. Instead, they try to probe under the surface of personality—to learn what drives, conflicts, and energies animate us. A psychodynamic theorist would explain Meghan's shyness in terms of hidden, or *unconscious*, thoughts, needs, and emotions.

While humanistic theorists also seek to explain personality, they tend to focus on *conscious* thoughts, needs, and emotions. For example, humanists consider self-image a central determinant of behavior and personal adjustment. Humanistic theories also pay special attention to the fuller use of human potentials, and they help bring balance to our overall views of personality. A humanist might ask what it is about the attitudes Meghan holds regarding herself that makes her feel self-conscious.

So, which is it, Meghan? Let's look into it.

Shai_Halud/Shutterstock

SURVEY QUESTIONS

52.1 How do psychodynamic theories explain personality?

52.2 What are humanistic theories of personality?

Psychoanalytic Theory— Id Came to Me in a Dream

SURVEY QUESTION 52.1: How do psychodynamic theories explain personality?

Psychoanalytic theory, the first, and best-known, psychodynamic approach, grew out of the work of Sigmund Freud, a Viennese physician. As a doctor, Freud was fascinated by patients whose problems seemed to be more emotional than physical. From about 1890 until his death in 1939, Freud evolved a theory of personality that deeply influenced modern thought (Schultz & Schultz, 2013; Tauber, 2010). Let's consider some of its main features.

The Structure of Personality

How did Freud view personality? Freud's model portrays personality as a dynamic system directed by three mental structures: the *id*, the *ego*, and the *superego*. According to Freud, most behavior involves activity of all three systems. (Freud's theory includes a large number of concepts. For your convenience, they are defined in ● Table 52.1 rather than in glossary boxes.)

The Id The **id** is made up of innate biological instincts and urges. The id operates on the **pleasure principle**. It is self-serving, irrational, impulsive, and totally unconscious—that is,

TABLE 52.1	Key Freudian Concepts

Anal stage The psychosexual stage corresponding roughly to the period of toilet training (ages 1 to 3).

Anal-expulsive personality A disorderly, destructive, cruel, or messy person.

Anal-retentive personality A person who is obstinate, stingy, or compulsive and who generally has difficulty "letting go."

Conscience The part of the superego that causes guilt when its standards are not met.

Conscious The region of the mind that includes all mental contents a person is aware of at any given moment.

Ego The executive part of personality that directs rational behavior.

Ego ideal The part of the superego representing ideal behavior; a source of pride when its standards are met.

Electra conflict A girl's sexual attraction to her father and feelings of rivalry with her mother.

Erogenous zone Any body area that produces pleasurable sensations.

Eros Freud's name for the "life instincts."

Fixation A lasting conflict developed as a result of frustration or overindulgence.

Genital stage Period of full psychosexual development, marked by the attainment of mature adult sexuality.

Id The primitive part of personality that remains unconscious, supplies energy, and demands pleasure.

Latency According to Freud, a period in childhood when psychosexual development is more or less interrupted.

Libido In Freudian theory, the force, primarily pleasure oriented, that energizes the personality.

Moral anxiety Apprehension felt when thoughts, impulses, or actions conflict with the superego's standards.

Neurotic anxiety Apprehension felt when the ego struggles to control id impulses.

Oedipus conflict A boy's sexual attraction to his mother and feelings of rivalry with his father.

Oral stage The period when infants are preoccupied with the mouth as a source of pleasure and means of expression.

Oral-aggressive personality A person who uses the mouth to express hostility by shouting, cursing, biting, and so forth. Also, one who actively exploits others.

Oral-dependent personality A person who wants to passively receive attention, gifts, love, and so forth.

Phallic personality A person who is vain, exhibitionistic, sensitive, and narcissistic.

Phallic stage The psychosexual stage (roughly ages 3 to 6) when a child is preoccupied with the genitals.

Pleasure principle A desire for immediate satisfaction of wishes, desires, or needs.

Preconscious An area of the mind containing information that can be voluntarily brought to awareness.

Psyche The mind, mental life, and personality as a whole.

Psychosexual stages The oral, anal, phallic, and genital stages, during which various personality traits are formed.

Reality principle Delaying action (or pleasure) until it is appropriate.

Superego A judge or censor for thoughts and actions.

Thanatos The **death instinct** postulated by Freud.

Unconscious The region of the mind that is beyond awareness, especially impulses and desires not directly known to a person.

it seeks to freely express pleasure-seeking urges of all kinds. If we were solely under control of the id, the world would be chaotic beyond belief.

The id acts as a power source for the entire **psyche** (sigh-KEY), or personality. This energy, called **libido** (lih-BEE-doe), flows from the **life instincts (Eros)**. According to Freud, libido underlies our efforts to survive, as well as our sexual desires and pleasure seeking. Freud also described a **death instinct** (Thanatos)—although today it is more often thought of as an impulse toward aggression and destructive urges. Freud offered humanity's long history of wars and violence as evidence of such urges. Most id energies, then, are aimed at discharging tensions related to sex and aggression.

The Ego The **ego** is sometimes described as the "executive" because it directs energies supplied by the id. The id is like a blind warrior whose power is awesome but who must rely on

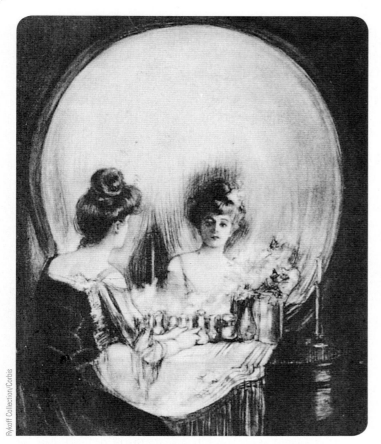

Freud considered personality an expression of two conflicting forces: life instincts and the death instinct. Both are symbolized in this drawing by Allan Gilbert. (If you don't immediately see the death symbolism, stand farther from the drawing.)

others to carry out orders. The id can only form mental images of things it desires. The ego wins power to direct behavior by relating the desires of the id to external reality.

Are there other differences between the ego and the id? Yes. Recall that the id operates on the pleasure principle. The ego, in contrast, is guided by the **reality principle**. The ego is the system of thinking, planning, problem solving, and deciding. It is in conscious control of the personality and often delays action until it is practical or appropriate.

The Superego *What is the role of the superego?* The **superego** acts as a judge or censor for the thoughts and actions of the ego. One part of the superego, called the **conscience**, reflects actions for which a person has been punished. When standards of the conscience are not met, you are punished internally by *guilt* feelings.

A second part of the superego is the **ego ideal**. The ego ideal reflects all behavior one's parents approved or rewarded. The ego ideal is a source of goals and aspirations. When its standards are met, we feel *pride*.

The superego acts as an "internalized parent" to bring behavior under control. In Freudian terms, a person with a weak superego will be a delinquent, criminal, or antisocial personality. In contrast, an overly strict or harsh superego may cause inhibition, rigidity, or unbearable guilt.

The Dynamics of Personality

How do the id, ego, and superego interact? Freud didn't picture the id, ego, and superego as parts of the brain or as "little people" running the human psyche. Instead, they are conflicting mental processes. Freud theorized a delicate balance of power among the three. For example, the id's demands for immediate pleasure often clash with the superego's moral restrictions. Perhaps an example will help clarify the role of each part of the personality.

Freud in a Nutshell

Let's say you are sexually attracted to an acquaintance. The id clamors for immediate satisfaction of its sexual desires but is opposed by the superego (which finds the very thought of sex shocking). The id says, "Go for it!" The superego icily replies, "Never even think that again!" And what does the ego say? The ego says, "I have a plan!"

This example is, of course, a drastic simplification, but it does capture the core of Freudian thinking. To reduce tension, the ego could begin actions leading to friendship, romance, courtship, and marriage. If the id is unusually powerful, the ego may give in and attempt a seduction. If the superego prevails, the ego may be forced to *displace* or *sublimate* sexual energies to other activities (sports, music, dancing, push-ups, cold showers). According to Freud, internal struggles and rechanneled energies typify most personality functioning.

Is the ego always caught in the middle? Basically, yes, and the pressures on it can be intense. In addition to meeting the conflicting demands of the id and superego, the overworked ego must deal with external reality.

According to Freud, you feel anxiety when your ego is threatened or overwhelmed. Impulses from the id cause **neurotic anxiety** when the ego can barely keep them under control. Threats of punishment from the superego cause **moral anxiety**. Each person develops habitual ways of calming these anxieties, and many resort to using *ego-defense mechanisms*

Psychoanalytic theory *Freudian theory of personality that emphasizes unconscious forces and conflicts.*

to lessen internal conflicts. Defense mechanisms are mental processes that deny, distort, or otherwise block out sources of threat and anxiety. (The ego defense mechanisms that Freud identified are used as a form of protection against stress, anxiety, and threatening events. See Module 57.)

Levels of Awareness Like other psychodynamic theorists, Freud believed that our behavior often expresses unconscious (or hidden) forces. The **unconscious** holds repressed memories and emotions, plus the instinctual drives of the id. It is interesting that modern scientists have found brain circuits that do, in fact, seem to underlie repression and the triggering of unconscious emotions and memories (Berlin, 2011; Ceylan & Sayın, 2012).

Even though they are beyond awareness, unconscious thoughts, feelings, or urges may slip into behavior in disguised or symbolic form (Reason, 2000; yes, these are *Freudian slips*). For example, if you meet someone you would like to know better, you may unconsciously leave a book or a jacket at that person's house to ensure another meeting.

Are the actions of the ego and superego also unconscious, like the id? At times, yes, but they also operate on two other levels of awareness (● Figure 52.1). The **conscious** level includes everything you are aware of at a given moment, including thoughts, perceptions, feelings, and memories. The **preconscious** contains material that can be easily brought to awareness. If you stop to think about a time when you felt angry or rejected, you are moving this memory from the preconscious to the conscious level of awareness.

The superego's activities also reveal differing levels of awareness. At times, we consciously try to live up to moral codes or standards. Yet, at other times, a person may feel guilty without knowing why. Psychoanalytic theory credits such guilt to unconscious workings of the superego. Indeed, Freud believed that the unconscious origins of many feelings cannot be easily brought to awareness.

Personality Development

How does psychoanalytic theory explain personality development? Freud theorized that the core of personality is formed before age 6 in a series of **psychosexual stages**. Freud believed that erotic urges in childhood have lasting effects on development (Ashcraft, 2012). As you might expect, this is a controversial idea. However, Freud used the terms *sex* and *erotic* very broadly to refer to many physical sources of pleasure.

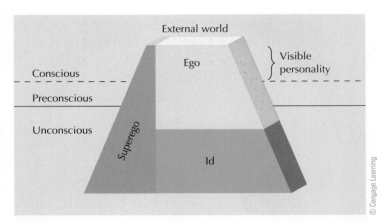

● Figure 52.1

The approximate relationship between the id, ego, and superego, and the levels of awareness.

A Freudian Fable? Freud identified four psychosexual stages, **oral**, **anal**, **phallic**, and **genital**. (He also described a period of "latency" between the phallic and genital stages. Latency is explained in a moment.) At each stage, a different part of the body becomes a child's primary **erogenous zone**—an area capable of producing pleasure. Each area then serves as the main source of pleasure, frustration, and self-expression. Freud believed that many adult personality traits can be traced to fixations in one or more of the stages.

What is a fixation? A **fixation** is an unresolved conflict or emotional hang-up caused by overindulgence or by frustration. As we describe the psychosexual stages, you'll see why Freud considered fixations important.

The Oral Stage During the first year of life, most of an infant's pleasure comes from stimulation of the mouth. If a child is overfed or frustrated, oral traits may be created. Adult expressions of oral needs include gum chewing, nail biting, smoking, kissing, overeating, and alcoholism.

What if there is an oral fixation? Fixation early in the oral stage produces an **oral-dependent personality**. Oral-dependent persons are gullible (they swallow things easily!) and

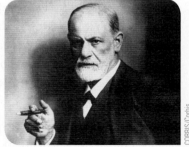

Was Freud's ever-present cigar a sign of an oral fixation? Was it a phallic symbol? Was it both? Or was it neither? Once, when he was asked, Freud himself apparently replied, "Sometimes a cigar is just a cigar." An inability to say for sure is one of the shortcomings of psychoanalytic theory.

passive and need lots of attention (they want to be mothered and showered with gifts). Frustrations later in the oral stage may cause aggression, often in the form of biting. Fixations here create cynical, **oral-aggressive** adults who exploit others. They also like to argue. ("Biting sarcasm" is their forte!)

The Anal Stage

Between the ages of 1 and 3, the child's attention shifts to the process of elimination. When parents attempt toilet training, the child can gain approval or express rebellion or aggression by "holding on" or by "letting go." Therefore, harsh or lenient toilet training can cause an anal fixation that may lock such responses into personality. Freud described a "holding-on," or **anal-retentive personality**, as obstinate, stingy, orderly, and compulsively clean. (If someone accuses you of being "anal," blame Freud.) The "letting-go," or **anal-expulsive personality**, is disorderly, destructive, cruel, or messy.

The Phallic Stage

Adult traits of the **phallic personality** are vanity, exhibitionism, sensitive pride, and narcissism (self-love). Freud theorized that phallic fixations develop between the ages of 3 and 6. At this time, increased sexual interest causes the child to be physically attracted to the parent of the opposite sex. In males, this attraction leads to an **Oedipal conflict**. In it, the boy feels a rivalry with his father for the affection of his mother. Freud believed that the male child feels threatened by the father (specifically, the boy fears castration). To ease his anxieties, the boy must *identify* with the father. Their rivalry ends when the boy seeks to become more like his father. As he does, he begins to accept the father's values and forms a conscience (Kupfersmid, 2012).

What about the female child? Girls experience an **Electra conflict**. In this case, the girl loves her father and competes with her mother. However, according to Freud, the girl identifies with the mother more gradually.

Freud believed that females already feel castrated. Because of this, they are less driven to identify with their mothers than boys are with their fathers. This, he said, is less effective in creating a conscience. This particular part of Freudian thought has been thoroughly—and rightfully—rejected by modern experts in the psychology of women. It is better understood as a reflection of the male-dominated times in which Freud lived.

Latency

According to Freud, there is a period of latency from age 6 to puberty. **Latency** is not so much a stage as it is a quiet time during which psychosexual development is dormant. Freud's belief that psychosexual development is "on hold" at this time is hard to accept. Nevertheless, Freud saw latency as a relatively quiet time compared with the stormy first six years of life.

The Genital Stage

At puberty, an upswing in sexual energies activates all the unresolved conflicts of earlier years. This upsurge, according to Freud, is the reason adolescence can be filled with emotion and turmoil. The genital stage begins at puberty. It is marked, during adolescence, by a growing capacity for responsible social–sexual relationships. The genital stage ends with a mature capacity for love and the realization of full adult sexuality.

Critical Comments

Is Freudian theory still widely accepted? Although few psychologists wholeheartedly embrace Freud's theory today, it remains influential for several reasons. First, it pioneered the general idea of unconscious processes. Contemporary psychodynamic theorists generally agree that some part of the human mind is unconscious and yet plays an important role in shaping human behavior, even if they do not share Freud's (over?)focus on the motivating power of sex and death (Epstein, 2003). Other motives and cognitive factors are today seen as having equal importance.

Second, the general idea that critical events during the first years of life help shape adult personality remains widely accepted. For example, Freud was among the first to propose that development proceeds through a series of stages (Shaffer, 2009). (Erik Erikson's psycho*social* stages, which cover development from birth to old age, are a modern offshoot of Freudian thinking. See Module 15.)

However, when it comes to the details, Freud clearly was often wrong. His portrayal of the elementary school years (latency) as free from sexuality and unimportant for personality development is hard to believe. His idea of the role of a stern or threatening father in the development of a strong conscience in males also has been challenged. Studies show that a son is more likely to develop a strong conscience if his father is affectionate and accepting rather than stern and punishing.

In addition, Freud's ideas on the development of women have been thoroughly discredited (Hyde & Else-Quest, 2013). For example, Freud has been heavily criticized for his views of patients who believed they were sexually molested as children (Marcel, 2005). Freud assumed that such events were merely childhood fantasies. This view led to a long-standing tendency to disbelieve children who have been molested and women who have been raped (Brannon, 2011).

Another important criticism is that Freud's concepts are almost impossible to verify scientifically. His theories provide numerous ways to explain almost any thought, action, or feeling *after* it has occurred. However, they lead to few predictions, which makes their claims difficult to test. Although more criticisms of Freud could be listed, the fact remains that much of what he said has an element of truth (Moran, 2010; Tauber, 2010).

Humanistic Theory—Peak Experiences and Personal Growth

SURVEY QUESTION 52.2: What are humanistic theories of personality?

Humanism focuses on human experience, problems, potentials, and ideals. As we saw in Module 3, the core of humanism is a positive image of humans as creative beings capable of **free will**—an ability to choose that is not determined by genetics, learning, or unconscious forces. In short, humanists seek ways to encourage our potentials to blossom.

Humanism is sometimes called a "third force" in that it is opposed to both psychodynamic and behaviorist theories of personality. Humanism is a reaction to the pessimism of psychoanalytic theory. It rejects the Freudian view of personality as a battleground for instincts and unconscious forces. Instead, humanists view **human nature**—the traits, qualities, potentials, and behavior patterns most characteristic of the human species—as inherently good. Humanists also oppose the machine-like overtones of the behaviorist view of human nature (which we discuss in Module 53). We are not, humanists say, merely a bundle of moldable responses.

To a humanist, the person you are today is largely the product of all the choices you have made. Humanists also emphasize immediate **subjective experience**—private perceptions of reality—rather than prior learning. They believe that there are as many "real worlds" as there are people. To understand behavior, we must learn how a person subjectively views the world—what is "real" for her or him.

Who are the major humanistic theorists? Many psychologists have added to the humanistic tradition. Of these, the best known are Abraham Maslow (1908–1970) and Carl Rogers (1902–1987). Because Maslow's idea of self-actualization was introduced in Module 3, let's begin with a more detailed look at this facet of his thinking.

Maslow and Self-Actualization

Abraham Maslow became interested in people who were living unusually effective lives (Hoffman, 2008). How were they different? To find an answer, Maslow began by studying the lives of great men and women from history, such as Albert Einstein, William James, Jane Addams, Eleanor Roosevelt, Abraham Lincoln, John Muir, and Walt Whitman. From there, he moved on to directly study living artists, writers, poets, and other creative individuals.

Along the way, Maslow's thinking changed radically. At first, he studied only people of obvious creativity or high achievement. However, it eventually became clear that anyone could live a rich, creative, and satisfying life (Davidson, Bromfield, & Beck, 2007). Maslow referred to the process of fully developing personal potentials as **self-actualization** (Maslow, 1954). The heart of self-actualization is a continuous search for personal fulfillment (Peterson & Park, 2010; Reiss & Havercamp, 2005).

Characteristics of Self-Actualizers A *self-actualizer* is a person who is living creatively and fully using his or her potentials. In his studies, Maslow found that self-actualizers share many similarities. Whether famous or unknown, well-schooled or uneducated, rich or poor, self-actualizers tend to fit the following profile:

1. **Efficient perceptions of reality.** Self-actualizers are able to judge situations correctly and honestly. They are very sensitive to the fake and dishonest.

2. **Comfortable acceptance of self, others, and nature.** Self-actualizers accept their own human nature with all its flaws. The shortcomings of others and the contradictions of the human condition are accepted with humor and tolerance.

3. **Spontaneity.** Maslow's subjects extended their creativity into everyday activities. Actualizers tend to be unusually alive, engaged, and spontaneous.

4. **Task centering.** Most of Maslow's subjects had a mission to fulfill in life or some task or problem outside themselves to pursue. Humanitarians such as Albert Schweitzer and Mother Teresa represent this quality.

5. **Autonomy.** Self-actualizers are free from reliance on external authorities or other people. They tend to be resourceful and independent.

6. **Continued freshness of appreciation.** The self-actualizer seems to constantly renew appreciation of life's basic goodness. A sunset or a flower is experienced as intensely

time after time as it was first experienced. Self-actualizers have an "innocence of vision" like that of an artist or child.

7. **Fellowship with humanity.** Maslow's subjects felt a deep identification with others and the human situation in general.

8. **Profound interpersonal relationships.** The interpersonal relationships of self-actualizers are marked by deep, loving bonds.

9. **Comfort with solitude.** Despite their satisfying relationships with others, self-actualizing persons value solitude and are comfortable being alone.

10. **Nonhostile sense of humor.** This refers to the wonderful capacity to laugh at oneself. It also describes the kind of humor possessed by a man like Abraham Lincoln. Lincoln probably never made a joke that hurt anybody. His wry comments were a gentle prodding of human shortcomings.

11. **Peak experiences.** All of Maslow's subjects reported the frequent occurrence of **peak experiences**, or temporary moments of self-actualization. These occasions were marked by feelings of ecstasy, harmony, and deep meaning. Self-actualizers reported feeling at one with the universe, stronger and calmer than ever before, filled with light, beautiful and good, and so forth.

In summary, self-actualizers feel safe, nonanxious, accepted, loved, loving, and alive.

Although Maslow tried to investigate self-actualization empirically, his choice of people for study was subjective. Undoubtedly, one can make full use of personal potential in many ways. Maslow's primary contribution was to draw our attention to the possibility of lifelong personal growth (Peterson & Park, 2010).

What steps can be taken to promote self-actualization? Maslow found no magic formula for leading a more creative life. Self-actualization is primarily a *process,* not a goal or an end point. As such, it requires hard work, patience, and commitment. Nevertheless, some helpful suggestions can be gleaned from his writings (Maslow, 1954, 1967, 1971). Here are some ways to begin:

1. **Be willing to change.** Continually ask yourself, "Am I living in a way that is deeply satisfying to me and that truly expresses me?" If not, be prepared to make changes in your life.

2. **Take responsibility.** You can become an architect of self by acting as if you are personally responsible for every aspect of your life. Avoid the habit of blaming others for your own shortcomings.

3. **Examine your motives.** Self-discovery involves an element of risk. If your behavior is restricted by a desire for safety or security, it may be time to test some limits.

4. **Experience honestly and directly.** Wishful thinking is another barrier to personal growth. Self-actualizers trust themselves enough to accept all kinds of information without distorting it to fit their fears and desires. Try to see yourself as others do.

5. **Make use of positive experiences.** Maslow considered peak experiences temporary moments of self-actualization. Therefore, you might actively repeat activities that have caused feelings of awe, amazement, exaltation, renewal, reverence, humility, fulfillment, or joy.

6. **Be prepared to be different.** Maslow felt that everyone has a potential for "greatness," but most fear becoming what they might. As part of personal growth, be prepared to trust your own impulses and feelings; don't automatically judge yourself by the standards of others.

7. **Get involved.** With few exceptions, self-actualizers tend to have a mission or "calling" in life. For these people, "work" is not done just to fill deficiency needs, but to satisfy higher yearnings for truth, beauty, community, and meaning. Turn your attention to problems outside yourself.

8. **Assess your progress.** There is no final point at which one becomes self-actualized. It's important to gauge your progress frequently and to renew your efforts. If you feel bored at school, at a job, or in a relationship, consider it a challenge. Have you been taking responsibility for your own personal growth?

Humanism *An approach that focuses on human experience, problems, potentials, and ideals.*
Free will *The ability to freely make choices that are not controlled by genetics, learning, or unconscious forces.*
Human nature *Those traits, qualities, potentials, and behavior patterns most characteristic of the human species.*
Subjective experience *Reality as it is perceived and interpreted, not as it exists objectively.*
Self-actualization *The process of fully developing personal potentials.*
Peak experiences *Temporary moments of self-actualization.*

The Whole Person: Thriving

It could be said that self-actualizing people are thriving, not just surviving. Like Maslow, proponents of positive psychology have tried to scientifically study positive personality traits that contribute to happiness and well-being (Ryan, Curren, & Deci, 2013; Seligman, 2003). Although their work does not always fall within the humanistic tradition, their findings are relevant here.

Martin Seligman, Christopher Peterson, and others have identified six human strengths that contribute to well-being and life satisfaction. Each strength is expressed by the positive personality traits listed here (Peterson & Seligman, 2004):

- **Wisdom and knowledge:** Creativity, curiosity, open-mindedness, love of learning, perspective
- **Courage:** Bravery, persistence, integrity, vitality
- **Humanity:** Love, kindness, social intelligence
- **Justice:** Citizenship, fairness, leadership
- **Temperance:** Forgiveness, humility, prudence, self-control
- **Transcendence:** Appreciation of beauty and excellence, gratitude, hope, humor, spirituality

Which of the positive personality traits are most closely related to happiness? One study found that traits of hope, vitality, gratitude, love, and curiosity are strongly associated with life satisfaction (Park, Peterson, & Seligman, 2004). These characteristics, in combination with Maslow's descriptions of self-actualizers, provide a good guide to the characteristics that help people live happy, meaningful lives.

Carl Rogers's Self Theory

Carl Rogers, another well-known humanist, also emphasized the human capacity for inner peace and happiness (Elliott & Farber, 2010). The **fully functioning person**, he said, lives in harmony with his or her deepest feelings and impulses. Such people are open to their experiences, and they trust their inner urges and intuitions (Rogers, 1961). Rogers believed that this attitude is most likely to occur when a person receives ample amounts of love and acceptance from others.

Personality Structure and Dynamics Rogers's theory emphasizes the **self**, a flexible and changing perception of personal identity. Much behavior can be understood as an attempt to maintain consistency between our *self-image* and our actions. (Your **self-image** is a total subjective perception of your body and personality.) For example, people who think of themselves as kind tend to be considerate in most situations.

Let's say I know a person who thinks she is kind, but she really isn't. How does that fit Rogers's theory? According to Rogers, we allow experiences that match our self-image into awareness, where they gradually change the self. Information or feelings inconsistent with the self-image are said to be incongruent. Thus, a person who thinks she is kind but really isn't is in a state of **incongruence**. In other words, there is a discrepancy between her experiences and her self-image. As another example, it would be incongruent to believe that you are a person who "never gets angry" if you spend much of each day seething inside.

Experiences seriously incongruent with the self-image can be threatening and are often distorted or denied conscious recognition. Blocking, denying, or distorting experiences prevents the self from changing. This creates a gap between the self-image and reality (Ryckman, 2013). As the self-image grows more unrealistic, the *incongruent person* becomes confused, vulnerable, dissatisfied, or seriously maladjusted (● **Figure 52.2**). In line with Rogers's observations, a study of college students confirmed that being *authentic* is vital for healthy functioning—that is, we need to feel that our behavior accurately expresses who we are (Wenzel & Lucas-Thompson, 2012). Please note, however, that being authentic doesn't mean you can do whatever you want. Being true to yourself is no excuse for acting irresponsibly or ignoring the feelings of others (Kernis & Goldman, 2005).

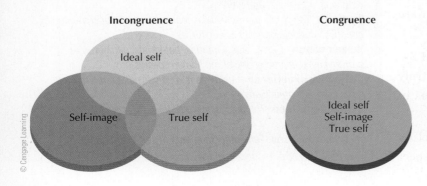

● **Figure 52.2**

Incongruence occurs when there is a mismatch between any of these three entities: the ideal self (the person you would like to be); your self-image (the person you think you are); and the true self (the person you actually are). Self-esteem suffers when there is a large difference between one's ideal self and self-image. Anxiety and defensiveness are common when the self-image does not match the true self.

The Clinical File

Telling Stories About Ourselves

You know these two student stereotypes: the carefree party animal and the conscientious bookworm. Perhaps you even think of yourself as one or the other. Is there any truth to these (stereo)types? Can you change your type?

In general, our personality traits are relatively stable characteristics (McAdams & Pals, 2006). As a result, a person high in the Big Five traits of extroversion and agreeableness tends to embrace a carefree college lifestyle. In comparison, someone high in conscientiousness will find it easier to hit the books (McGregor, McAdams, & Little, 2006).

Does that mean a partier can't become a bookworm (or vice versa)? It depends: Do you mean over a week? Or a lifetime? Personality traits do slowly change as we age (Mõttus, Johnson, & Deary, 2012). In particular, we tend to become more agreeable, conscientious, and emotionally stable as we grow older (Roberts & Mroczek, 2008).

Oh, you need to change by the end of the semester? That's a taller order. In that case, you might want to try telling yourself stories about possible selves you could become. The *narrative approach* to personality asserts that our personalities are shaped by the stories we tell about ourselves (Frazier, 2012; Lodi-Smith et al., 2009). In other words,

alternate life stories are not just fantasies or daydreams. They actually influence who we are and who we become.

So, if you feel that you are being too careless and carefree at school, start imagining yourself studying more, getting to classes on time, and getting good grades. Listen to the stories of successful students and use them to revise your own story. Visit your campus counseling center to learn more about how to succeed at school. In other words, imagine yourself as a bit more of a bookworm. (Don't worry, your carefree nature won't desert you!)

If you feel you are too conscientious and working too hard, imagine yourself going out with friends more often. Listen to the stories of your extroverted classmates. Imagine the benefits of balancing work and play in your life. If you are shy or perfectionistic, visit your campus counseling center to learn how to become more sociable or relaxed. And, again, don't worry: Having more fun won't make you irresponsible.

Whatever possible self you choose to pursue, you are more likely to become what you imagine if you elaborate your story, making it more detailed and "real" as you gradually adopt new patterns. You *can* create a new narrative identity for yourself (Bauer, McAdams, & Pals, 2008; Nelson et al., 2012).

When your self-image is consistent with what you really think, feel, do, and experience, you are best able to actualize your potentials. Rogers also considered it essential to have congruence between the self-image and the **ideal self**. The ideal self is similar to Freud's ego ideal. It is an image of the person you would most like to be (Przybylski et al., 2012).

Is it really incongruent not to live up to your ideal self? Rogers was aware that we never fully attain our ideals. Nevertheless, the greater the gap between the way you see yourself and the way you would like to be, the more tension and anxiety you will experience.

Rogers emphasized that to maximize our potentials, we must accept information about ourselves as honestly as possible. In accord with his thinking, researchers have found that people with a close match between their self-image and ideal self tend to be socially poised, confident, and resourceful. Those with a poor match tend to be depressed, anxious, and insecure (Boldero et al., 2005).

According to psychologists Hazel Markus and Paula Nurius (1986), our ideal self is only one of a number of **possible selves**—persons we could become or are afraid of becoming.

Consider William, an intellectually gifted African-American student. He simultaneously welcomes the possible self who continues to broaden his intellectual horizons and fears the possible self of the stereotyped gangsta wearing baggy pants (Frazier, 2012). Like William, you may have pondered many possible personal identities. (See "Telling Stories About Ourselves.")

Possible selves translate our hopes, fears, fantasies, and goals into specific images of who we *could* be. Thus, a beginning law student might picture herself as a successful attorney,

Fully functioning person *A person living in harmony with her or his deepest feelings, impulses, and intuitions.*

Self *A continuously evolving conception of one's personal identity.*

Self-image *Total subjective perception of one's body and personality (another term for self-concept).*

Incongruence *A state that exists when there is a discrepancy between one's experiences and self-image or between one's self-image and ideal self.*

Ideal self *An idealized image of oneself (the person one would like to be).*

Possible selves *A collection of thoughts, beliefs, feelings, and images concerning the person one could become.*

an enterprising college student might imagine himself as an Internet entrepreneur, and a person on a diet might imagine both slim and morbidly obese possible selves. Such images tend to direct our future behavior (Barreto & Frazier, 2012; Oyserman et al., 2004).

Of course, almost everyone over age 30 has probably felt the anguish of realizing that some cherished possible selves will never be realized. Nevertheless, there is value in asking yourself not just "Who am I?" but also "Who would I like to become?" As you do, remember Maslow's advice that everyone has a potential for "greatness," but most fear becoming what they might.

Humanistic View of Development

Why do mirrors, photographs, video cameras, and the reactions of others hold such fascination and threat for many people? Carl Rogers's theory suggests it is because they provide information about one's self. The development of a self-image depends greatly on information from the environment. It begins with a sorting of perceptions and feelings: my body, my toes, my nose, I want, I like, I am, and so on. Soon, it expands to include self-evaluation: I am a good person, I did something bad just now, and so forth.

How does development of the self contribute to later personality functioning? Rogers believed that positive and negative evaluations by others cause children to develop internal standards of evaluation called **conditions of worth**. In other words, we learn that some actions win our parents' love and approval, whereas others are rejected. More important,

parents may label some *feelings* as bad or wrong. For example, a child might be told that it is wrong to feel angry toward a brother or sister—even when anger is justified. Likewise, a little boy might be told that he must not cry or show fear, two very normal emotions.

Learning to evaluate some experiences or feelings as "good" and others as "bad" is directly related to a later capacity for self-esteem, positive self-evaluation, or **positive self-regard**, to use Rogers's term. To think of yourself as a good, lovable, worthwhile person, your behavior and experiences must match your internal conditions of worth. The problem is that this can cause incongruence by leading to the denial of many true feelings and experiences.

To put it simply, Rogers blamed many adult emotional problems on attempts to live by the standards of others (Ashcraft, 2012). He believed that congruence and self-actualization are encouraged by replacing conditions of worth with **organismic valuing**, a natural, undistorted, full-body reaction to an experience. Organismic valuing is a direct, gut-level response to life that avoids the filtering and distortion of incongruence. It involves trusting one's own feelings and perceptions. Rogers felt that organismic valuing most likely develops when children (or adults) receive **unconditional positive regard**, unshakable love and approval, from others—when they are "prized" as worthwhile human beings, just for being themselves, without any conditions or strings attached. Although this may be a luxury few people enjoy, we are more likely to move toward our ideal selves if we receive affirmation and support from a close partner (Drigotas et al., 1999).

Conditions of worth *Internal standards used to judge the value of one's thoughts, actions, feelings, or experiences.*
Positive self-regard *Thinking of oneself as a good, lovable, worthwhile person.*
Organismic valuing *A natural, undistorted, full-body reaction to an experience.*
Unconditional positive regard *Unshakable love and approval given without qualification.*

Module 52: Summary

52.1 How do psychodynamic theories explain personality?

- **52.1.1** Like other psychodynamic approaches, Sigmund Freud's psychoanalytic theory emphasizes unconscious forces and conflicts within the personality.

- **52.1.2** In Freud's theory, personality is made up of the id, ego, and superego.

- **52.1.3** Libido, derived from the life instincts, is the primary energy running the personality. Conflicts within the personality may cause neurotic anxiety or moral anxiety and motivate us to use ego-defense mechanisms.

- **52.1.4** The personality operates on three levels: the conscious, preconscious, and unconscious.

- **52.1.5** The Freudian view of personality development is based on a series of psychosexual stages: the oral, anal, phallic, and genital stages. According to Freud, fixation at any stage can leave a lasting imprint on personality.

52.2 What are humanistic theories of personality?

- **52.2.1** Humanistic theories stress subjective experience, free will, self-actualization, and positive models of human nature.

- **52.2.2** Abraham Maslow found that self-actualizers share characteristics that range from efficient perceptions of reality to frequent peak experiences.

- **52.2.3** Positive psychologists have identified six human strengths that contribute to well-being and life satisfaction: wisdom and knowledge, courage, humanity, justice, temperance, and transcendence.

- **52.2.4** Carl Rogers viewed the self as an entity that emerges from personal experience. We tend to become aware of experiences that match our self-image and exclude those that are incongruent with it.

- **52.2.5** The incongruent person has a highly unrealistic self-image and/or a mismatch between the self-image and the ideal self. The congruent or fully functioning person is flexible and open to experiences and feelings.

- **52.2.6** As parents apply conditions of worth to children's behavior, thoughts, and feelings, children begin to do the same. Internalized conditions of worth then contribute to incongruence that disrupts the organismic valuing process.

Module 52: Knowledge Builder

Recite

1. Freud stated that the mind functions on three levels: the conscious, the unconscious, and the
   - a. psyche
   - b. preconscious
   - c. superego
   - d. subconscious

2. List the three divisions of personality postulated by Freud: _____ _____ _____

3. Freud proposed the existence of a life instinct known as Thanatos. *T or F?*

4. Freud's view of personality development is based on the concept of _____ stages.

5. Humanists view human nature as basically good and they emphasize the effects of subjective learning and unconscious choice. *T or F?*

6. Maslow thought of peak experiences as temporary moments of
   - a. congruence
   - b. positive self-regard
   - c. self-actualization
   - d. self-reinforcement

7. According to Rogers, a close match between the self-image and the ideal self creates a condition called incongruence. *T or F?*

8. Carl Rogers believed that personal growth is encouraged when conditions of worth are replaced by
   - a. self-efficacy
   - b. instrumental worth
   - c. latency
   - d. organismic valuing

Reflect

Think Critically

9. What role would your self-image and "possible selves" have in the choice of a college major?

Self-Reflect

Try to think of at least one time when your thoughts, feelings, or actions seemed to reflect the workings of each of the following: the id, the ego, and the superego.

Do you know anyone who seems to have oral, anal, or phallic personality traits? Do you think Freud's concept of fixation explains their characteristics?

Do you know anyone who seems to be making especially good use of his or her personal potential? Does that person fit Maslow's profile of a self-actualizer?

How much difference do you think there is among your self-image, your ideal self, and your true self?

ANSWERS

1. b 2. id, ego, superego 3. F 4. psychosexual 5. F 6. c 7. F 8. d 9. Career decisions almost always involve, in part, picturing oneself occupying various occupational roles. Such possible "future selves" play a role in many of the major decisions we make (Masters & Holley, 2006).

Personality: Behavioral and Social Learning Theories

A Boy Named Sue

Why is little Sue so aggressive? No, we're not kidding. His daddy named him Sue after an old country song. Freud believed that aggressive urges are "instinctual." Unlike psychodynamic and humanistic theorists, behavioral theories assume that personal characteristics such as aggressiveness are learned. Might Sue's aggression be the result of observational learning, harsh punishment, or prior reinforcement?

Sue will tell you himself that his name always triggers giggles from girls. Boys always laugh at and taunt him. The resulting fights are, to Sue, an inevitable part of his life. So why did his father name him Sue, you ask? To toughen him up, the dirty, mangy dog said, before he abandoned his family when Sue turned three.

All kidding aside, behavioral and social learning theories are based on scientific research, which makes them especially

Phanie/RGB Ventures LLC dba SuperStock/Alamy

powerful ways of looking at personality and developing therapies to help people change, if they should so desire.

SURVEY QUESTIONS

53.1 What do behaviorists and social learning theorists emphasize in their approach to personality?

53.2 How do heredity and environment affect personality?

Learning Theories of Personality—Habit I Seen You Before?

SURVEY QUESTION 53.1 What do behaviorists and social learning theorists emphasize in their approach to personality?

How do behaviorists approach personality? According to some critics, as if people are robots. Actually, the behaviorist position is not nearly that mechanistic, and its value is well established. Behaviorists have shown repeatedly that children can *learn* things like kindness, hostility, generosity, or destructiveness. What does this have to do with personality? Everything, according to the behavioral viewpoint.

Behavioral personality theories emphasize that personality is no more (or less) than a collection of relatively stable learned behavior patterns. Personality, like other learned behavior, is acquired through classical and operant conditioning, observational learning, reinforcement, extinction, generalization, and discrimination. When Mother says, "It's not nice to make mud pies with Mommy's blender. If we want to grow up to be a big girl, we won't do it again, will we?" she serves as a model and in other ways shapes her daughter's personality.

Strict **learning theorists** reject the idea that personality is made up of traits. They would assert, for instance, that there is no such thing as a *trait* of "honesty" (Mischel, 2004).

Certainly some people are honest and others are not. How can honesty not be a trait? Remember, for many trait theorists, traits are biological dispositions. According to learning theorists, they are, instead, stable learned responses. If his parents consistently reward little Alexander for honesty, he is more likely to become an honest adult. If his parents are less scrupulous, Alexander might well grow up differently (Schultz & Schultz, 2013).

Learning theorists also stress the external causes, or **situational determinants**, of actions. Knowing that someone is honest does not automatically allow us to predict whether that person will be honest in a specific situation. It would not be unusual, for example, to find that a person honored for returning a lost wallet had cheated on a test, bought a term paper, or broken the speed limit. If you were to ask a learning theorist, "Are you an honest person?" the reply might be, "In what situation?"

A good example of how situations can influence behavior is a study in which people were intentionally overpaid for doing an assigned task. Under normal circumstances, 80 percent kept the extra money without mentioning it. But as few as 17 percent were dishonest if the situation were altered. For instance, if people thought the money was coming out of the pocket of the person doing the study, far fewer were dishonest (Bersoff, 1999). Thus, situations always interact with our prior learning to activate behavior.

Seventy-five percent of American college students admit that they have been academically dishonest in one way or another. What can be done about these high rates of dishonesty? The behavioral perspective holds that honesty is determined as much by circumstances as it is by personality. In line with this, simple measures like announcing in classes that integrity codes will be enforced can significantly reduce cheating. Using multiple forms of exams and web-based plagiarism software and educating students about plagiarism also tend to deter dishonesty (Altschuler, 2001; McKeever, 2006).

How Situations Affect Behavior

Situations vary greatly in their impact. Some are powerful. Others are trivial and have little effect on behavior. The more powerful the situation, the easier it is to see what is meant by *situational determinants*. For example, each of the following situations would undoubtedly have a strong influence on your behavior: An armed person walks into your classroom; you accidentally sit on a lighted cigarette; you find your lover in bed with your best friend. Yet, even these situations could provoke very different reactions from different personalities. That's why behavior is always a product of both prior learning and the situations in which we find ourselves (Mischel & Shoda, 2010; Mischel, Shoda, & Smith, 2008).

Ultimately, what is predictable about personality is that we respond in fairly consistent ways to certain situations. Consider, for example, two people who are easily angered: One person might get angry when she is delayed (for example, in traffic or a checkout line) but not when she misplaces something at home; the other person might get angry whenever she misplaces things but not when she is delayed. Overall, the two women are equally prone to anger, but their anger tends to occur in different patterns and different situations (Mischel, 2004).

Personality = Behavior

How do learning theorists view the structure of personality? The behavioral view of personality can be illustrated with an early theory proposed by John Dollard and Neal Miller (1950). In their view, learned behavior patterns, or **habits**, make up the structure of personality. As for the dynamics of personality, habits are governed by four elements of learning: *drive, cue, response*, and *reward*. A *drive* is any stimulus strong enough to goad a person to action (such as hunger, pain, lust, frustration, or fear). *Cues* are signals from the environment. These signals guide *responses* (actions) so that they are most likely to bring about *reward* (positive reinforcement).

How does that relate to personality? Let's say a child named Amina is frustrated by her older brother Kelvin, who takes a toy from her. Amina could respond in several ways: She could throw a temper tantrum, hit Kelvin, tell her mother, and so forth. The response she chooses is guided by available cues and the previous effects of each response. If telling her mother has paid off in the past, and her mother is present, telling may be Amina's immediate response. If a different set of cues exists (if her mother is absent or if Kelvin looks particularly menacing), Amina may select some other response. To an outside observer, Amina's actions seem to reflect her personality. To a learning theorist, they simply express the combined effects of drive, cue, response, and reward. Behavioral theories have contributed greatly to the creation of therapies for various psychological problems and disorders. See the discussion of behavior therapy in Module 67.

Doesn't this analysis leave out a lot? Yes. Learning theorists originally set out to provide a simple, clear model of personality. But they eventually had to face a fact that they previously tended to set aside: People think. Contemporary behavioral psychologists—whose views include perception, thinking, expectations, and other mental events—are called *social learning theorists*. Learning principles, modeling, thought patterns, perceptions, expectations, beliefs, goals, emotions, and social relationships are combined in **social learning theory** to explain personality (Mischel, Shoda, & Smith, 2008; Santrock, 2012).

Social Learning Theory

The "cognitive behaviorism" of social learning theory can be illustrated by three classic concepts proposed by Julian Rotter: the psychological situation, expectancy, and reinforcement value (Rotter & Hochreich, 1975). Let's examine each.

Someone trips you. How do you respond? Your reaction probably depends on whether you think it was planned or an accident. It is not enough to know the setting in which a person responds. We also need to know the person's **psychological situation** (how the person interprets or defines the situation). As another example, let's say you score low on an exam. Do you consider it a challenge to work harder, a sign that you should drop the class, or an excuse to get drunk? Again, your interpretation is important.

Our actions are affected by an **expectancy**, or anticipation, that making a response will lead to reinforcement. To continue the example, if working harder has paid off in the past, it is a likely reaction to a low test score. But to predict your response, we also would have to know if you *expect* your efforts to pay off in the present situation. In fact, expected reinforcement may be more important than actual past reinforcement. And what about the *value* you attach to grades, school success, or personal ability? The third concept, **reinforcement value**, states that we attach different subjective values to various activities or rewards. You will likely choose to study harder if passing your courses and obtaining a degree is highly valued. This, too, must be taken into account to understand personality.

Self-Efficacy An ability to control your own life is the essence of what it means to be human (Corey & Corey, 2014). Because of this, Albert Bandura believes that one of the most important expectancies we develop concerns **self-efficacy** (EF-uh-keh-see)—a capacity for producing a desired result. Believing that our actions will produce desired results influences the activities and environments we choose (Bandura, 2001; Schultz & Schultz, 2013). You're attracted to someone in your anthropology class. Will you ask him or her out? You're beginning to consider a career in psychology. Will you take the courses you need to get into graduate school? You'd like to exercise more on the weekends. Will you join a hiking club? In these and countless other situations, efficacy beliefs play a key role in shaping our lives (Byrne, Barry, & Petry, 2012; Prat-Sala & Redford, 2012).

Self-Reinforcement One more idea deserves mention. At times, we all evaluate our actions and may reward ourselves with

Spring break in Key West. We can reward ourselves through self-reinforcement for personal achievements and other "good" behavior. (At least that's the theory, right?)

Behavioral personality theory *Any model of personality that emphasizes learning and observable behavior.*
Learning theorist *A psychologist interested in the ways that learning shapes behavior and explains personality.*
Situational determinants *External conditions that strongly influence behavior.*
Habit *A deeply ingrained, learned pattern of behavior.*
Social learning theory *An explanation of personality that combines learning principles, cognition, and the effects of social relationships.*
Psychological situation *A situation as it is perceived and interpreted by an individual, not as it exists objectively.*
Expectancy *Anticipation about the effect a response will have, especially regarding reinforcement.*
Reinforcement value *The subjective value a person attaches to a particular activity or reinforcer.*
Self-efficacy *Belief in your capacity to produce a desired result.*

special privileges or treats for "good behavior." With this in mind, social learning theory adds the concept of self-reinforcement to the behaviorist view. **Self-reinforcement** refers to praising or rewarding yourself for having made a particular response (such as completing a school assignment). Thus, habits of self-praise and self-blame become an important part of personality (Schultz & Schultz, 2013). In fact, self-reinforcement can be thought of as the social learning theorist's counterpart to the superego.

Self-reinforcement is closely related to high self-esteem. The reverse also is true: Mildly depressed college students tend to have low rates of self-reinforcement. It is not known if low self-reinforcement leads to depression, or the reverse. In either case, higher rates of self-reinforcement are associated with less depression and greater life satisfaction (Seybolt & Wagner, 1997). From a behavioral viewpoint, there is value in learning to be "good to yourself."

Behaviorist View of Development

How do learning theorists account for personality development? Many of Freud's ideas can be restated in terms of learning theory. John Dollard and Neal Miller (1950) agree with Freud that the first six years are crucial for personality development, but for different reasons. Rather than thinking in terms of psychosexual urges and fixations, they ask, "What makes early learning experiences so lasting in their effects?" Their answer is that childhood is a time of urgent drives, powerful rewards and punishments, and crushing frustrations. Also important is **social reinforcement**, which is based on praise, attention, or approval from others. These forces combine to shape the core of personality (Shaffer, 2009).

Critical Situations Dollard and Miller believe that during childhood, four **critical situations** are capable of leaving a lasting imprint on personality. These are (1) feeding, (2) toilet or cleanliness training, (3) sex training, and (4) learning to express anger or aggression. (Does this remind you of Freud?)

Why are these of special importance? Feeding serves as an illustration. If children are fed when they cry, it encourages them to actively manipulate their parents. The child allowed to cry without being fed learns to be passive. Thus, a basic active or passive orientation toward the world may be created by early feeding experiences. Feeding also can affect later social relationships because the child learns to associate people with pleasure or with frustration and discomfort.

Toilet and cleanliness training can be a particularly strong source of emotion for both parents and children. Rashad's parents were aghast the day they found him smearing feces about with joyful abandon. They reacted with sharp punishment, which frustrated and confused Rashad. Many attitudes toward cleanliness, conformity, and bodily functions are formed at such times. Studies also have long shown that severe, punishing, or frustrating toilet training can have undesirable effects on personality development (Christophersen & Mortweet, 2003). Because of this, toilet and cleanliness training demand patience and a sense of humor.

What about sex and anger? When, where, and how a child learns to express anger and sexual feelings can leave an imprint on personality. Specifically, permissiveness for sexual and aggressive behavior in childhood is linked to adult needs for power (McClelland & Pilon, 1983). This link probably occurs because permitting such behaviors allows children to get pleasure from asserting themselves. Sex training also involves learning socially defined "male" and "female" gender roles—which, in turn, affects personality (Cervone & Pervin, 2013).

Personality and Gender *What does it mean to have a "masculine" or "feminine" personality?* From birth onward, children are labeled as boys or girls and encouraged to learn appropriate **gender roles**—the favored pattern of behavior expected of each sex (Fine, 2010; Orenstein, 2011). According to social learning theory, identification and imitation contribute greatly to personality development and to sex training. **Identification** refers to the child's emotional attachment to admired adults, especially those who provide love and care. Identification typically encourages **imitation**, a desire to act like the admired person. Many "male" or "female" traits come from children's attempts to imitate a same-sex parent with whom they identify (Helgeson, 2012).

Adult personality is influenced by identification with parents and imitation of their behavior.

If children are around parents of both sexes, why don't they imitate behavior typical of the opposite sex as well as of the same sex? You may recall from Module 28 that learning takes place vicariously as well as directly. This means that we can learn without direct reward by observing and remembering the actions of others. But the actions we choose to imitate depend on their outcomes. For example, boys and girls have equal chances to observe adults and other children acting aggressively. However, girls are less likely than boys to imitate directly aggressive behavior (shouting at or hitting another person). Instead, girls are more likely to rely on indirectly aggressive behavior (excluding others from friendship, spreading rumors). This could be because expressing direct aggression is considered inappropriate for girls.

As a consequence, girls do not as often see direct female aggression rewarded or approved (Field et al., 2009). In others words, "girlfighting" is likely a culturally reinforced pattern (Brown, 2005). It is intriguing that over the last few years, girls have become more willing to engage in direct aggression as popular culture presents more and more images of directly aggressive women (Artz, 2005).

We have considered only a few examples of the links between social learning and personality. Nevertheless, the connection is unmistakable. When parents accept their children and give them affection, the children become sociable, positive, and emotionally stable and they have high self-esteem. When parents are rejecting, punishing, sarcastic, humiliating, or neglectful, their children become hostile, unresponsive, unstable, and dependent and have impaired self-esteem (Cervone & Pervin, 2013; Triandis & Suh, 2002).

Traits and Situations—The Great Debate

SURVEY QUESTION 53.2: How do heredity and environment affect personality?

Personality theorists have long grappled with the relative roles of nature and nurture in shaping personalities. Some theories, such as trait theory and psychoanalytic theory, stress the role of inherited biological predispositions, whereas others, including humanist and behavioral theories, stress the role of learning and life experiences. Let's look at the roles that heredity and biological predispositions (nature) and environmental situations (nurture) play in forming personality.

Do We Inherit Personality?

Even newborn babies differ in temperament, which implies that it is hereditary. **Temperament**, the "raw material" from which personalities are formed, refers to the hereditary aspects of your personality, such as biological predispositions to be sensitive, irritable, and distractible and to display a typical mood (Shiner et al., 2012). Temperament has a large impact on how infants interact with their parents.

At what age are personality traits firmly established? Personality starts to stabilize at around age 3 and continues to "harden" well past age 50 (Caspi, Roberts, & Shiner, 2005; Hopwood et al., 2011). However, as mentioned earlier, personality slowly matures during old age as most people continue to become more conscientious, agreeable, and emotionally stable (Roberts & Mroczek, 2008). It appears that stereotypes of the "grumpy old man" and "cranky old woman" are largely unfounded.

Does the stability of personality traits mean that they are affected by heredity? Some breeds of dogs have reputations for being friendly, aggressive, intelligent, calm, or emotional. Such differences fall in the realm of **behavioral genetics**, the study of inherited behavioral traits. We know that facial features, eye color, body type, and many other physical characteristics are inherited. So are many of our behavioral dispositions (Bouchard, 2004; Kalat, 2013). Genetic studies have shown that intelligence, language, some mental disorders, temperament, and other complex qualities are influenced by heredity. In view of such findings, it wouldn't be a surprise to find that genes affect personality as well (Nettle, 2006).

Self-reinforcement *Praising or rewarding oneself for having made a particular response (such as completing a school assignment).*
Social reinforcement *Praise, attention, approval, and/or affection from others.*
Critical situations *Situations during childhood that are capable of leaving a lasting imprint on personality.*
Gender roles *The pattern of behaviors that are regarded as "male" or "female" by one's culture; sometimes also referred to as a sex role.*
Identification *Feeling emotionally connected to a person and seeing oneself as like him or her.*
Imitation *An attempt to match one's own behavior to another person's behavior.*
Temperament *The hereditary aspects of personality, including sensitivity, activity levels, prevailing mood, irritability, and adaptability.*
Behavioral genetics *The study of inherited behavioral traits and tendencies.*

Wouldn't comparing the personalities of identical twins help answer the question? It would indeed—especially if the twins were separated at birth or soon after.

Twins and Traits For several decades, psychologists at the University of Minnesota have been studying identical twins who grew up in different homes. Medical and psychological tests reveal that reunited twins are very much alike, even when they are reared apart (Bouchard, 2004; Johnson et al., 2009). If one twin excels at art, music, dance, drama, or athletics, the other is likely to as well—despite wide differences in childhood environment. They may even be similar in voice quality, facial gestures, hand movements, and nervous tics, such as nail biting. However, as "The Amazing Twins" explains, it's wise to be cautious about some reports of extraordinary similarities in reunited twins.

Summary Studies of twins make it clear that heredity has a sizable effect on each of us. All told, it seems reasonable to conclude that heredity is responsible for about 25 to 55 percent of the variation in many personality traits (Caspi, Roberts, & Shiner, 2005; Kandler, 2012). Notice, however, that the same figures imply that personality is shaped as much, or more, by environment as it is by biological predispositions (Johnson et al., 2009).

Each personality, then, is a unique blend of heredity and environment, nature and nurture, biology and culture. We are not—thank goodness—genetically programmed robots whose behavior and personality traits are "wired in" for life. Where you go in life is the result of the choices you make. Although these choices are influenced by inherited tendencies, they are not merely a product of your genes (Funder, 2010).

Critical Thinking

The Amazing Twins

Many reunited twins in the Minnesota study (the Minnesota Twins?) have displayed similarities far beyond what would be expected on the basis of heredity. The "Jim twins," James Lewis and James Springer, are one famous example. Both Jims had married and divorced women named Linda. Both had undergone police training. One named his firstborn son James Allan, the other named *his* firstborn son James Alan. Both drove Chevrolets and vacationed at the same beach each summer. Both listed carpentry and mechanical drawing among their hobbies. Both had built benches around trees in their yards, and so forth (Holden, 1980).

Are all identical twins so, well, identical? No, they aren't. Consider identical twins Carolyn Spiro and Pamela Spiro Wagner who, unlike the "Jim twins," lived together throughout their childhood. While in sixth grade, they found out that President Kennedy had been assassinated. Carolyn wasn't sure why everyone was so upset. Pamela heard voices announcing that she was responsible for his death. After years of hiding her voices from everyone, Pamela tried to commit suicide while the twins were attending Brown University. She was diagnosed with schizophrenia. Never to be cured, she has gone on to write award-winning poetry. Carolyn eventually became a Harvard psychiatrist (Spiro Wagner & Spiro, 2005). Some twins reared apart appear very similar; some reared together appear rather different.

So why are some identical twins, like the Jim twins, so much alike even if they were reared apart? Although genetics is important, it is preposterous to suggest that there are child-naming genes and bench-building genes. How, then, do we explain the eerie similarities in some separated twins' lives? Imagine that you were separated at birth from a twin brother or sister. If you were reunited with your twin today, what would you do? Quite likely, you would spend the next several days comparing every imaginable detail of your lives. Under such circumstances,

it is virtually certain that you and your twin would notice and compile a long list of similarities. ("Wow! I use the same brand of toothpaste you do!") Yet, two unrelated persons of the same age, sex, and race could probably rival your list—*if* they were as motivated to find similarities.

In fact, one study compared twins with unrelated pairs of students. The unrelated pairs, who were the same age and sex, were almost as alike as the twins. They had highly similar political beliefs, musical interests, religious preferences, job histories, hobbies, favorite foods, and so on (Wyatt

Courtesy of Pam Wagner

Identical twins Pam (left) and Carolyn (right) were raised together. Regardless, Carolyn became a psychiatrist while Pamela developed schizophrenia and went on to become an award-winning poet (Spiro Wagner & Spiro, 2005). Their story illustrates the complex interplay of forces that shape our adult personalities.

et al., 1984). Why were the unrelated students so similar? Basically, it's because people of the same age and sex live in the same historical times and select from similar societal options. As just one example, in nearly every elementary school classroom, you will find several children with the same first name.

It appears then that many of the seemingly "astounding" coincidences shared by reunited twins may be yet another example of confirmation bias, described in Module 2. Reunited twins tend to notice the similarities and ignore the differences.

Personality and Environment

Sally was always quite calm and peaceful. Then one day in a bar, she decked a man who was harassing her. How could that happen? Before we try to provide an answer, take a moment to answer the questions that follow. Doing so will add to your understanding of a long-running controversy in the psychology of personality.

Rate Yourself: How Do You View Personality?

1. My friends' actions are fairly consistent from day to day and in different situations. T or F?

2. Whether a person is honest or dishonest, kind or cruel, a hero or a coward depends mainly on circumstances. T or F?

3. Most people I have known for several years have pretty much the same personalities now as they did when I first met them. T or F?

4. People in some professions (such as teachers, lawyers, or doctors) seem so much alike because their work requires that they act in particular ways. T or F?

5. One of the first things I would want to know about a potential roommate is what the person's personality is like. T or F?

6. I believe that immediate circumstances usually determine how people act at any given time. T or F?

7. To be comfortable in a particular job, a person's personality must match the nature of the work. T or F?

8. Almost anyone would be polite at a wedding reception; it doesn't matter what kind of personality the person has. T or F?

Now count the number of times you marked true for the odd-numbered items. Do the same for the even-numbered items. If you agreed with most of the odd-numbered items, you tend to view behavior as strongly influenced by personality traits or lasting personal dispositions, whether biological or learned. If you agreed with most of the even-numbered items, you view behavior as strongly influenced by external situations and circumstances.

What if I answered true about equally for odd and even items? Then you place equal weight on traits and situations as ways to explain behavior. This is the view now held by many personality psychologists (Funder, 2010; Mischel, Shoda, & Smith, 2008).

Does that mean that to predict how a person will act, it is better to focus both on personality traits and external circumstances? Yes, it's best to take both into account. Because personality *traits* are consistent, they can predict such things as job performance, dangerous driving, or a successful marriage (Burger, 2011). Yet, as we mentioned earlier in the module, *situations* also greatly influence our behavior. A person's normally calm demeanor, for example, might become aggressive only because of an unusual and extreme situation.

Can all unusual behaviors be "blamed" on unusual situations? Great question. Consider Fred Cowan, a model student in school and described by those who knew him as quiet, gentle, and a man who loved children. Despite his size (6 feet tall, 250 pounds), Fred was described by a coworker as "someone you could easily push around." Two weeks after he was suspended from his job, Fred returned to work determined to get even with his supervisor. Unable to find the man, he killed four coworkers and a policeman before taking his own life (Lee, Zimbardo, & Bertholf, 1977).

Sudden murderers like Fred Cowan tend to be quiet, overcontrolled individuals. They are likely to be especially violent if they ever lose control. Although their attacks may be triggered by a minor irritation or frustration, the attack reflects years of unexpressed feelings of anger and belittlement. When sudden murderers finally release the strict controls they have maintained on their overcontrolled behavior, a furious and frenzied attack ensues (Cartwright, 2002). Usually, it is totally out of proportion to the offense against them, and many have amnesia for their violent actions. So, unlike Sally, who reacted in an unexpected way to an unusual situation, Fred Cowan's overreaction was typical of people who share his personality pattern.

Trait–Situation Interactions It would be unusual for you to dance at a movie or read a book at a football game. Likewise, few people sleep in roller coasters or tell off-color jokes at funerals. However, your personality traits may predict whether you choose to read a book, go to a movie, or attend a football game in the first place. Typically, traits *interact* with situations to determine how we will act (Mischel, 2004).

In a **trait–situation interaction**, external circumstances influence the expression of a personality trait. For instance, imagine what would happen if you moved from a church to a classroom to a party to a football game. As the setting changed, you would probably become louder and more boisterous. This change would show situational effects on behavior. At the same time, your personality traits also would be apparent: If you were quieter than average in church and class, you would probably be quieter than average in the other settings, too.

Trait–situation interaction *The influence that external settings or circumstances have on the expression of personality traits.*

Module 53: Summary

53.1 What do behaviorists and social learning theorists emphasize in their approach to personality?

- **53.1.1** Behavioral theories of personality emphasize learning, conditioning, and immediate effects of the environment (situational determinants).
- **53.1.2** Learning theorists Dollard and Miller consider habits the basic core of personality. Habits express the combined effects of drive, cue, response, and reward.
- **53.1.3** Social learning theory adds cognitive elements, such as perception, thinking, and understanding to the behavioral view of personality.
- **53.1.4** Social learning theory is exemplified by Julian Rotter's concepts of the psychological situation, expectancies, and reinforcement value.

- **53.1.5** The behaviorist view of personality development holds that social reinforcement in four situations is critical. The situations are feeding, toilet or cleanliness training, sex training, and anger or aggression training.
- **53.1.6** Identification and imitation are of particular importance in learning to be "male" or "female."

53.2 How do heredity and environment affect personality?

- **53.2.1** Temperament refers to the hereditary and physiological aspects of one's emotional nature.
- **53.2.2** Behavioral genetics and studies of identical twins suggest that heredity contributes significantly to adult personality traits.
- **53.2.3** Biological predispositions (traits) interact with environment (situations) to explain our behavior.

Module 53: Knowledge Builder

Recite

1. Learning theorists believe that personality "traits" really are _____ acquired through prior learning. They also emphasize _____ determinants of behavior.
2. Dollard and Miller consider cues the basic structure of personality. ***T or F?***
3. To explain behavior, social learning theorists include mental elements, such as _____ (the anticipation that a response will lead to reinforcement).
4. Self-reinforcement is to behavioristic theory as superego is to psychoanalytic theory. ***T or F?***
5. Which of the following is *not* a "critical situation" in the behaviorist theory of personality development?
   - **a.** feeding
   - **b.** sex training
   - **c.** language training
   - **d.** anger training
6. In addition to basic rewards and punishments, a child's personality also is shaped by _____ reinforcement.
7. Social learning theories of development emphasize the impact of identification and _____.

Reflect
Think Critically

8. Rotter's concept of *reinforcement value* is closely related to a motivational principle discussed in Module 42. Can you name it?

Self-Reflect

Some people love to shop; others hate it. How have the psychological situation, expectancy, and reinforcement value affected your willingness to "shop til you drop"?

One way to describe personality is in terms of a set of "If–Then" rules that relate situations to traits (Kammrath, Mendoza-Denton, & Mischel, 2005). For example, Sally has a trait of independence. But she is not independent in every situation. Here are some If–Then rules for Sally: *If* Sally is working at home, *Then* she is independent. *If* Sally is in a bar being hassled by a man, *Then* she is very independent. *If* Sally has to go for a medical checkup, *Then* she is not very independent. Can you write some If–Then rules that describe your personality?

ANSWERS

1. habits, situational **2.** F **3.** expectancies **4.** T **5.** c **6.** social **7.** imitation **8.** Incentive value

Psychology in Action: Understanding Shyness

Why Shy?

Do you find it hard to talk to strangers? Lack confidence around people? Feel uncomfortable in social situations? Feel nervous with people who are not close friends? You might be shy. But why? And, more important, can you do anything about it?

Almost everyone feels anxious in at least some social situations. But there is a key difference in how shy and not-shy persons *label* this anxiety. Shy persons tend to consider their social anxiety a *lasting personality trait*. Shyness, in other words, becomes part of their self-concept. In contrast, not-shy persons believe that *external situations* cause their occasional feelings of shyness. When not-shy persons feel anxiety or "stage fright," they assume that almost anyone would feel as they do under the same circumstances.

Joshua Rainey Photography/Shutterstock

To read more about the role of *self-defeating bias* in perpetuating shyness, and for some advice on how to overcome it, don't be shy. Read on.

SURVEY QUESTION

54.1 What causes shyness, and what can be done about it?

Understanding Shyness— Barriers and Bridges

SURVEY QUESTION 54.1: What causes shyness, and what can be done about it?

As a personality trait, **shyness** refers to a tendency to avoid others, accompanied by feelings of anxiety, preoccupation, and social inhibition (uneasiness and strain when socializing) (Flowers, 2011). Shy persons fail to make eye contact, retreat when spoken to, speak too quietly, and display little interest or animation in conversations (Brunet, Mondloch, & Schmidt, 2010).

Almost half of all American adolescents report being shy to some extent, while about 8 percent report that they are extremely shy. While mild shyness may be no more than a nuisance, extreme shyness may be diagnosed as *social anxiety disorder* or *social phobia* and is often associated with depression, loneliness, fearfulness, social anxiety, inhibition, and low self-esteem (Baker & McNulty, 2010; Burstein, Ameli-Grillon, & Merikangas, 2011).

Elements of Shyness

What causes shyness? To begin, shyness is often rooted in **social anxiety**—a feeling of apprehension in the presence of others. Almost everyone feels nervous in some social situations (such as meeting an attractive stranger). Typically, this is a reaction to **evaluation fears**—fears of being inadequate, embarrassed, ridiculed, or rejected. Although fears of rejection are common, they are much more frequent or intense for shy persons (Bradshaw, 2006).

Also, shy people can, over time, develop a distortion in their thinking called **self-defeating bias**. Specifically, shy persons almost always blame themselves when a social encounter doesn't go well. To compound matters further, because shy people tend to avoid social situations, they fail to develop *social skills*—proficiency at interacting with others. Many simply have not learned how to meet people or how to start a conversation and keep it going.

Dynamics of Shyness Shyness is most often triggered by *novel* or *unfamiliar* social situations. A person who does fine with family or close friends may become socially anxious and awkward when meeting a stranger. Shyness also is magnified by formality, meeting someone of higher status, being noticeably different from others, or being the focus of attention (as in giving a speech) (Larsen & Buss, 2010).

Don't most people become cautious and inhibited in such circumstances? Yes. That's why we need to discuss how the personalities of shy and not-shy persons differ. There is a tendency to think that shy persons are wrapped up in their own feelings and thoughts. But surprisingly, researchers Jonathan Cheek and Arnold Buss (1979) found no connection between shyness and **private self-consciousness**—attention to inner feelings, thoughts, and fantasies. Instead, they discovered that shyness is linked to **public self-consciousness**, or acute awareness of oneself as a social object.

Persons who rate high in public self-consciousness are intensely concerned about what others think of them (Cowden, 2005; Fenigstein, 2009). They are unnecessarily self-critical in social situations. They worry about saying the wrong thing or appearing foolish. In public, they may feel "naked" or as if others can "see through them." Such feelings trigger anxiety or outright fear during social encounters, leading to awkwardness and inhibition (Cowden, 2005). The shy person's anxiety, in turn, often causes her or him to misperceive others in social situations.

Self-Defeating Bias and Shyness Shyness affects *self-esteem*. In general, not-shy persons tend to have higher self-esteem than shy persons. This is because not-shy persons give themselves credit for their social successes and recognize that failures are often due to circumstances (Burgess et al., 2006). In contrast, shy people blame themselves for social failures, never give themselves credit for successes, and expect to be rejected (Jackson et al., 2002).

What can be done to reduce shyness? Shyness is often maintained by several unrealistic or self-defeating beliefs (Antony & Swinson, 2008; Butler, 2008). Becoming mindful of these beliefs is an important first step in reducing their impact (Flowers, 2011). Here's a sample of such beliefs:

1. *If you wait around long enough at a social gathering, something will happen.*

   Comment: This is a cover-up for fear of starting a conversation. For two people to meet, at least one has to make an effort, and it might as well be you.

2. *Other people who are popular are just lucky when it comes to being invited to social events or asked out.*

   Comment: Except for times when a person is formally introduced to someone new, this is false. People who are more active socially typically make an effort to meet and spend time with others. They join clubs, invite others to do things, strike up conversations, and generally leave little to luck.

3. *The odds of meeting someone interested in socializing are always the same, no matter where I am.*

   Comment: This is another excuse for inaction. It pays to seek out situations that have a higher probability of leading to social contact, such as clubs, teams, and school events.

4. *If someone doesn't seem to like you right away, they really don't like you and never will.*

   Comment: This belief leads to much needless shyness. Even when a person doesn't show immediate interest, it doesn't mean the person dislikes you. Liking takes time and opportunity to develop.

Unproductive beliefs like the preceding can be replaced with statements such as the following (adapted from Antony & Swinson, 2008; Butler, 2008):

1. I've got to be active in social situations.

2. I can't wait until I'm completely relaxed or comfortable before taking a social risk.

3. I don't need to pretend to be someone I'm not; it just makes me more anxious.

4. I may think other people are harshly evaluating me, but actually I'm being too hard on myself.

5. I can set reasonable goals for expanding my social experience and skills.

6. Even people who are very socially skillful are unlikely to be successful anyway near 100 percent of the time. I shouldn't get so upset when an encounter goes badly.

Social Skills and Shyness

Because shy people avoid social encounters, they have fewer opportunities to learn and practice social skills (Carducci & Fields, 2007; Miller, 2012). There is nothing "innate" about knowing how to meet people or start a conversation. Social skills can be directly practiced in a variety of ways. It can be helpful, for instance, to record yourself and listen to several of your conversations. You may be surprised by the way you pause, interrupt, miss cues, or seem disinterested. Similarly, it can be useful to look at yourself in a mirror and exaggerate facial expressions of surprise, interest, dislike, pleasure, and so forth. By such methods, most people can learn to put more animation and skill into their self-presentation. (For a discussion of related skills, see the section on self-assertion in Module 71.)

One of the easiest social skills to develop is how to ask questions during conversation. A good series of questions shifts attention to the other person and shows you are interested. Nothing fancy is needed. You can do fine with questions such as, "Where do you (work, study, live)? Do you like (dancing, travel, music)? How long have you (been at this school, worked here, lived here)?" After you've broken the ice, the best questions are often those that are *open ended* (they can't be answered yes or no):

"What parts of the country have you seen?" (as opposed to: "Have you ever been to Florida?")

"What's it like living on the West Side?" (as opposed to: "Do you like living on the West Side?")

"What kinds of food do you like?" (as opposed to: "Do you like Chinese cooking?")

It's easy to see why open-ended questions are helpful. In replying to open-ended questions, people often give "free information" about themselves. This extra information can be used to ask other questions or to lead into other topics of conversation.

This brief sampling of ideas is no substitute for actual practice. Overcoming shyness requires a real effort to test old beliefs and attitudes and learn new skills. It may even require the help of a counselor or therapist. At the very least, a shy person must be willing to take social risks. Breaking down the barriers of shyness will always include some awkward or unsuccessful encounters. Nevertheless, the rewards are powerful: human companionship and personal freedom.

Shyness *A tendency to avoid others, plus uneasiness and strain when socializing.*
Social anxiety *A feeling of apprehension in the presence of others.*
Evaluation fears *Fears of being inadequate, embarrassed, ridiculed, or rejected.*
Self-defeating bias *A distortion of thinking that impairs behavior.*
Private self-consciousness *Preoccupation with inner feelings, thoughts, and fantasies.*
Public self-consciousness *Intense awareness of oneself as a social object.*

Module 54: Summary

54.1 What causes shyness, and what can be done about it?

- **54.1.1** Shyness typically involves social anxiety, evaluation fears, heightened public self-consciousness, self-defeating bias,

a tendency to regard one's shyness as a lasting trait, and a lack of social skills.
- **54.1.2** Shyness can be reduced by replacing self-defeating beliefs with more supportive thoughts and by learning social skills.

Module 54: Knowledge Builder

Recite

1. Social anxiety and evaluation fears are seen almost exclusively in shy individuals; the not-shy rarely have such experiences. **T or F?**

2. Unfamiliar people and situations most often trigger shyness. **T or F?**

3. Contrary to what many people think, shyness is *not* related to
   a. private self-consciousness
   b. social anxiety
   c. self-esteem
   d. blaming oneself for social failures

4. Shy persons tend to consider their social anxiety to be a
   a. situational reaction
   b. personality trait
   c. public efficacy
   d. habit

5. Changing personal beliefs and practicing social skills can be helpful in overcoming shyness. **T or F?**

Reflect
Think Critically

6. Shyness is a trait of Vonda's personality. Like most shy people, Vonda is most likely to feel shy in unfamiliar social settings. Vonda's shy behavior demonstrates that the expression of traits is governed by what concept?

Self-Reflect

If you are shy, see if you can summarize how social skills, social anxiety, evaluation fears, self-defeating thoughts, and public self-consciousness contribute to your social inhibition. If you're not shy, imagine how you would explain these concepts to a shy friend.

ANSWERS

1. F 2. T 3. a 4. b 5. T 6. trait–situation interactions (again)

CENGAGE**brain**.com

Go to **cengagebrain.com** to access **MindTap for Coon/Mitterer** *Psychology Modules for Active Learning* and other online learning tools. MindTap is a fully online learning experience that combines all the tools you need—readings, multimedia, activities, and assessments—into a singular personalized Learning Path that guides you through the course.

Health Psychology: Overview of Health Psychology

Mee Jung's Term from Heck

What a year! Mee Jung barely managed to survive the rush of make-or-break term papers, projects, and classroom presentations. Sleep deprivation, gallons of coffee, junk food, and equal portions of cramming and complaining had carried her through finals. She was off for a summer of karate. At last, she could kick back, relax, and have some fun. Or could she? Just four days after school ended, Mee Jung got a bad cold, followed by bronchitis that lasted for nearly a month.

Mee Jung's term from heck (well, that's not exactly what *she* called it) illustrates what happens when personal habits, stress, and health collide. Though the timing of her cold might have been a coincidence, odds are it wasn't. Periods of stress are frequently followed by illness. In this module, we explore how our health is affected by a variety of behavioral health risks, including stress.

SURVEY QUESTION

55.1 What is health psychology, and how do cognition and behavior affect health?

Health Psychology— Here's to Your Good Health

SURVEY QUESTION 55.1: What is health psychology, and how do cognition and behavior affect health?

For centuries, the *medical model* has dominated Western thinking (Ghaemi, 2010). From this perspective, health is an absence of illness and your body is a complex biological machine that can break down and become ill. Sometimes an external cause, such as a virus, is the culprit. Sometimes you inflict the damage yourself through poor lifestyle choices, such as smoking or overeating. In either event, the problem is physical or biological, and your "mind" has little to do with it. Moreover, physical problems call for physical treatments ("Take your medicine."), so your mind also has little to do with your recovery. In the medical model, *any* impact of the mind on health is dismissed as a mere placebo effect. (To remind yourself about placebo effects, see Module 4.)

Over the last 50 years, the medical model has slowly begun to give way to the **biopsychosocial model**, which states that diseases are caused by a combination of biological, psychological, and social factors (Suls, Luger, & Martin, 2010). More often than you might think, psychological and social processes play a role in influencing the progress and outcome of "biological" diseases. It is becoming clear that medicine works best when doctors help people *make sense* of their medical condition to maximize healing (Benedetti, 2009; Moerman, 2002). Further, the biopsychosocial model defines health as a state of well-being that we can *actively* attain and maintain (Oakley, 2004). As you take responsibility for your own well-being, remember that in some ways health *is* all in your mind.

Most of us agree that our health is priceless. Yet, many diseases and well over half of all deaths each year in North America can be traced to our unhealthy behaviors (Danaei et al., 2009). **Health psychology**, then, aims to use cognitive and behavioral principles to prevent illness and death and to promote health (Harrington, 2013). Psychologists working in the allied field of **behavioral medicine** apply psychology to manage medical problems, such as diabetes or asthma. Their interests include pain control, helping people cope with chronic illness, stress-related diseases, self-screening for diseases (such as breast cancer), and similar topics (Brannon, Feist, & Updegraff, 2014).

Behavioral Risk Factors

A century ago, people died primarily from infectious diseases and accidents. Today, people generally die from **lifestyle diseases**, which are related to health-damaging personal habits (Kozica et al., 2012). Examples include heart disease, stroke, HIV/AIDS, and lung cancer (● **Figure 55.1**). Clearly, some lifestyles promote health, whereas others lead to illness and death (Hales, 2013). As one observer put it, "If you don't take care of yourself, the undertaker will overtake that responsibility for you."

What are some unhealthy behaviors? Some causes of illness are beyond our control, but many behavioral risks can be

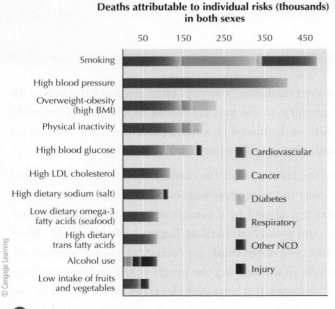

Deaths attributable to individual risks (thousands) in both sexes

● Figure 55.1

The leading causes of preventable deaths in the United States are tobacco and alcohol consumption, along with poor diet and exercise habits. Together they account for over half of all premature deaths and cause no end of day-to-day health problems. (Data adapted from Danaei et al., 2009. NCD = noncommunicable diseases.)

reduced. **Behavioral risk factors** are actions that increase the chances of disease, injury, or early death. For example, about 450,000 Americans die every year from smoking-related diseases—about 20 percent of all deaths, regardless of the cause (National Institute on Drug Abuse, 2012b). Similarly, roughly two-thirds of all American adults are overweight. Of those, half are extremely overweight, or *obese* (Flegal et al., 2010). In fact, being overweight may soon overtake smoking as the main cause of preventable death (Danaei et al., 2009). A person who is overweight at age 20 can expect to lose 5 to 20 years of life expectancy (Fontaine et al., 2003).

Each of the following factors is a major behavioral risk (Brannon, Feist, & Updegraff, 2014): high levels of stress, untreated high blood pressure, cigarette smoking, abuse of alcohol or other drugs, overeating, inadequate exercise, unsafe sexual behavior, exposure to toxic substances, violence, excess sun exposure, reckless driving, and disregarding personal safety (avoidable accidents). Seventy percent of all medical costs are related to just six of the listed factors—smoking, alcohol abuse, drug abuse, poor diet, insufficient exercise, and risky sexual practices (Brannon, Feist, & Updegraff, 2014; Orleans, Gruman, & Hollendonner, 1999). (Unsafe sex is discussed in Module 48.)

The personal habits you have by the time you are 18 or 19 greatly affect your health, happiness, and life expectancy years later (Gurung, 2014; Hales, 2013). ● Table 55.1 shows how many American high school students engage in various kinds of risky behaviors.

Specific risk factors are not the only concern. Some people have a general **disease-prone personality** that leaves them depressed, anxious, hostile, and frequently ill. In contrast, people who are intellectually resourceful, compassionate, optimistic, and nonhostile tend to enjoy good health (Li et al., 2009; Taylor, 2012). Depression, in particular, is likely to damage health (Luppa et al., 2007). People who are depressed eat poorly, sleep poorly, rarely exercise, fail to use seat belts in cars, smoke more, and so on.

Lifestyle In your mind's eye, fast-forward an imaginary film of your life all the way to old age. Do it twice—once with a lifestyle including a large number of behavioral risk factors and again without them. It should be obvious that many small risks can add up, dramatically raising the chance of illness. If stress is a frequent part of your life, visualize your body seething with emotion, day after day. If you smoke, picture a lifetime's worth of cigarette smoke blown through your lungs in a week. If you drink, take a lifetime of alcohol's assaults on the brain, stomach, and liver and squeeze them into a month:

Your body would be poisoned, ravaged, and soon dead. If you eat a high-fat, high-cholesterol diet, fast-forward a lifetime of heart-killing plaque clogging your arteries.

TABLE 55.1	Percentage of U.S. High School Students Who Engaged in Health-Endangering Behaviors
Risky Behavior	**Percentage**
Rode with drinking driver (previous 30 days)	24
Were in a physical fight (previous 12 months)	33
Carried a weapon (previous 30 days)	17
Drank alcohol (previous 30 days)	38
Used marijuana (previous 30 days)	23
Engaged in sexual intercourse (previous 90 days)	34
Did not use condom (during last sexual intercourse)	40
Smoked cigarettes (previous 30 days)	18
Did not have any fruit (previous 7 days)	5
Did not have any vegetables (previous 7 days)	6
Played 3 or more hours of video games (average school day)	31

Source: Eaton et al., 2012.

In the long run, behavioral risk factors and lifestyles do make a difference in health and life expectancy.

We don't mean to sermonize. We just want to remind you that risk factors make a big difference. To make matters worse, unhealthy lifestyles almost always create multiple risks—that is, people who smoke also are likely to drink excessively. Those who overeat usually do not get enough exercise, and so on (Lippke, Nigg, & Maddock, 2012). Even infectious diseases are often linked to behavioral risks. For example, pneumonia and other infections occur at higher rates in people who have cancer, heart disease, lung disease, or liver disease. Thus, many deaths attributed to infections can be traced back to smoking, poor diet, or alcohol abuse (Mokdad et al., 2004).

Health-Promoting Behaviors

To prevent disease, health psychologists first try to reduce behavioral risk factors. All the medicine in the world might not be enough to restore health without changes in behavior. We all know someone who has had a heart attack or lung disease who couldn't change the habits that led to his or her illness.

In some cases, lifestyle diseases can be treated or prevented by making specific, minor changes in behavior. For example, hypertension (high blood pressure) can be deadly. Yet, consuming less sodium (salt) can help fend off this "silent killer." Losing weight, using alcohol sparingly, and getting more exercise also will help (Edenfield & Blumenthal, 2011; Hales, 2013).

In addition to removing specific risk factors, psychologists are interested in getting people to increase behaviors that promote health. Health-promoting behaviors include obvious practices such as getting regular exercise, controlling smoking and alcohol use, maintaining a balanced diet, getting good medical care, and managing stress (Zarcadoolas, Pleasant, & Greer, 2006). In one study, the risk of dying during

Biopsychosocial model *Approach which acknowledges that biological, psychological, and social factors interact to influence illness and health.*
Health psychology *Study of the ways cognitive and behavioral principles can be used to prevent illness and promote health.*
Behavioral medicine *The study of behavioral factors in medicine, physical illness, and medical treatment.*
Lifestyle disease *A disease related to health-damaging personal habits.*
Behavioral risk factors *Behaviors that increase the chances of disease, injury, or premature death.*
Disease-prone personality *A personality type associated with poor health; marked by persistent negative emotions, including anxiety, depression, and hostility.*

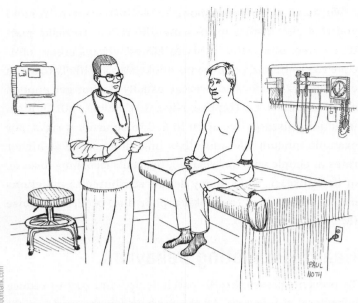

"Will I still be able to not exercise?"

a 10-year period was cut by 65 percent for adults who were careful about diet, alcohol, exercise, and smoking (Knoops et al., 2004).

Health-promoting behaviors don't have to be restrictive or burdensome. For instance, maintaining a healthy diet doesn't mean surviving on tofu and wheatgrass. The healthiest people in the study just described ate a tasty "Mediterranean diet" higher in fruit, vegetables, and fish and lower in red meat and dairy products. Likewise, you don't need to exercise like an Olympic athlete to benefit from physical activity. All you need is 30 minutes of exercise (the equivalent of a brisk walk) three or four times a week. Almost everyone can fit such "lifestyle physical activity" into his or her schedule (Pescatello, 2001).

What about alcohol? Moderation in drinking doesn't mean that you must be a teetotaler. Consuming one or two alcoholic drinks per day is generally safe for most people, especially if you remain alcohol-free two or three days a week. A glass of red wine daily may even be healthy (Anekonda, 2006). However, having three or more drinks a day greatly increases the risk for stroke, cirrhosis of the liver, cancer, high blood pressure, heart disorders, and other diseases (Knoops et al., 2004; Lamont et al., 2011).

To summarize, a small number of behavioral patterns accounts for many common health problems (Eaton et al., 2012; Straub, 2012). ● Table 55.2 lists several major ways to promote good health. (To explore an interesting social factor that may underlie common health problems, see "Unhealthy Birds of a Feather.")

Early Prevention

Of the behavioral risks we have discussed, smoking is the largest preventable cause of death and the single most lethal factor (National Center for Chronic Disease Prevention and Health Promotion, 2011). As such, it illustrates the prospect for preventing illness.

What have health psychologists done to lessen the risks of smoking? Attempts to "immunize" youths against pressures to start smoking are a good example. When humorist Mark

TABLE 55.2	Major Health-Promoting Behaviors
Source	**Desirable Behaviors**
Tobacco	Do not smoke; do not use smokeless tobacco.
Nutrition	Eat a balanced, low-fat diet; have appropriate caloric intake; maintain a healthy body weight.
Exercise	Engage in at least 30 minutes of aerobic exercise 5 days per week.
Blood pressure	Lower blood pressure with diet and exercise or medicine if necessary.
Alcohol and drugs	Drink no more than 2 drinks per day; abstain from using drugs.
Sleep and relaxation	Avoid sleep deprivation; provide for periods of relaxation every day.
Sex	Practice safer sex; avoid unplanned pregnancy.
Injury	Curb dangerous driving habits; use seat belts; minimize sun exposure; forgo dangerous activities.
Stress	Learn stress management; lower hostility.

Discovering Psychology

Unhealthy Birds of a Feather

Would you like to eat better, exercise more, or quit smoking? Researchers Nicholas Christakis and James Fowler believe they know why it can be difficult to alter unhealthy behaviors. Often, social factors are a barrier to change. If you are a smoker, do your friends also smoke? Are your family members fast-food junkies just like you? Are your friends all drinkers? Unhealthy behaviors such as overeating or smoking seem to spread almost like a "mental virus" (Christakis & Fowler, 2009; Lyons, 2011).

One study of social contagion found that people were 57 percent more likely to become obese if they had a friend who became fat first (Christakis & Fowler, 2007). Similarly, smokers tend to "hang out" with other smokers (Christakis & Fowler, 2008). Another study found that spending time with drinkers increases alcohol consumption (Ali & Dwyer, 2010). Apparently, we tend to flock together with like-minded people and adopt many of their habits.

Does that mean I am doomed to be unhealthy if my family and friends have unhealthy habits? Not necessarily. Social networks also can spread healthy behaviors (Fowler & Christakis, 2010). If one smoker in a group of smokers quits, others are more likely to follow suit. If your spouse quits smoking, you are 67 percent more likely to quit. If a good friend quits smoking, your chances of abandoning tobacco go up by 36 percent (Christakis & Fowler, 2008). The growing social unpopularity of smoking may be the best explanation of why fewer and fewer American adults (now only 19 percent) still smoke (Centers for Disease Control, 2012c).

The implication? Don't wait for your friends or family to adopt healthier habits. Take the lead and get them to join you. Failing that, start hanging out with a healthier crowd. You might catch something healthy.

Twain said, "Giving up smoking is the easiest thing in the world. I know because I've done it thousands of times," he stated a basic truth—only one smoker in ten has long-term success at quitting (Krall, Garvey, & Garcia, 2002). Thus, the best way to deal with smoking is to prevent it before it becomes a lifelong habit. For example, prevention programs in schools discourage smoking with quizzes about smoking, multimedia presentations, antismoking art contests, poster and T-shirt giveaways, antismoking pamphlets for parents, and questions for students to ask their parents (Flynn et al., 2011; Prokhorov et al., 2010). Such efforts are designed to persuade kids that smoking is dangerous and "uncool."

Some antismoking programs include **refusal skills training**. In such training, youths learn to resist pressures to begin smoking (or using other drugs). For example, junior high students can role-play ways to resist smoking pressures from peers, adults, and cigarette ads. Similar methods can be applied to other health risks, such as sexually transmitted diseases and teen pregnancy (Wandersman & Florin, 2003; Witkiewitz et al., 2011).

Many health programs also teach students general life skills. The idea is to give kids skills that will help them cope with day-to-day stresses. That way, they will be less tempted to escape problems through drug use or other destructive behaviors. **Life skills training** includes practice in stress reduction, self-protection, decision making, goal setting, self-control, and social skills (Allen & Williams, 2012; Corey & Corey, 2014).

Centers for Disease Control and Prevention

Celebrities also can help persuade young people to not start smoking in the first place.

Refusal skills training *Program that teaches youths how to resist pressures to begin smoking (also can be applied to other drugs and health risks).*

Life skills training *A program that teaches stress reduction, self-protection, decision making, self-control, and social skills.*

Community Health

In addition to early prevention, health psychologists have had some success with **community health campaigns**. These are community-wide education projects designed to lessen major risk factors (Lounsbury & Mitchell, 2009). Health campaigns inform people of risks such as stress, alcohol abuse, high blood pressure, high cholesterol, smoking, sexually transmitted diseases, or excessive sun exposure. This is followed by efforts to motivate people to change their behavior. Campaigns sometimes provide *role models* (positive examples) who show people how to improve their own health. They also direct people to services for health screening, advice, and treatment. Health campaigns may reach people through the mass media, public schools, health fairs, workplaces, or self-help programs.

Stress

Stress can be a major behavioral risk factor if it is prolonged or severe, but it isn't always bad. As Canadian stress research pioneer Hans Selye (SEL-yay) (1978) observed, "To be totally without stress is to be dead." That's because **stress** is the mental and physical condition that occurs when we adjust or adapt to the environment. Unpleasant events such as work pressures, marital problems, or financial woes naturally produce stress. But so do travel, sports, a new job, rock climbing, dating, and other positive activities. Even if you aren't a thrill seeker, a healthy lifestyle may include a fair amount of *eustress* (good stress). Activities that provoke "good stress" are usually challenging, rewarding, and energizing.

Regardless of whether it is triggered by a pleasant or an unpleasant event, **stress reaction** begins with the same autonomic nervous system (ANS) arousal that occurs during emotion. Imagine you are standing at the top of a wind-whipped ski jump for the first time. Internally, you experience a rapid surge in your heart rate, blood pressure, respiration, muscle tension, and other ANS responses. *Short-term* stresses of this kind can be uncomfortable, but they rarely do any damage. (Your landing might, however.) *Long-term* stresses are another matter entirely.

General Adaptation Syndrome

The impact of long-term stresses can be understood by examining the body's defenses against stress, a pattern known as the **general adaptation syndrome (GAS)**. The GAS is a series of bodily reactions to prolonged stress. Selye (1978) noticed that the first symptoms of almost any disease or trauma

(poisoning, infection, injury, or stress) are almost identical. The body responds in the same way to any stress, be it infection, failure, embarrassment, a new job, trouble at school, or a stormy romance.

How does the body respond to stress? The GAS consists of three stages: an alarm reaction, a stage of resistance, and a stage of exhaustion (● **Figure 55.2**; Selye, 1978).

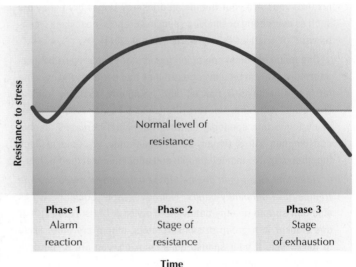

● **Figure 55.2**

The General Adaptation Syndrome. During the initial alarm reaction to stress, resistance falls below normal. It rises again as body resources are mobilized, and it remains high during the stage of resistance. Eventually, resistance falls again as the stage of exhaustion is reached. (Based on Selye, 1978.)

In the **alarm reaction**, your body mobilizes its resources to cope with added stress. The pituitary gland signals the adrenal glands to produce more adrenaline, noradrenaline, and cortisol. As these stress hormones are dumped into the bloodstream, some bodily processes are speeded up and others are slowed. This allows bodily resources to be applied where they are needed.

We should all be thankful that our bodies automatically respond to emergencies. But brilliant as this emergency system is, it also can cause problems. In the first phase of the alarm reaction, people have symptoms such as headache, fever, fatigue, sore muscles, shortness of breath, diarrhea, upset stomach, loss of appetite, and a lack of energy. Notice that these also are the symptoms of being sick, of stressful travel, of high-altitude sickness, of final exams week, and (possibly) of falling in love!

During the **stage of resistance**, bodily adjustments to stress stabilize. As the body's defenses come into balance, symptoms of the alarm reaction disappear. Outwardly, everything seems normal. However, this appearance of normality comes at a high cost. The body is better able to cope with the original stressor, but its resistance to other stresses is lowered. For example, animals placed in extreme cold become more resistant to the cold but more susceptible to infection. It is during the stage of resistance that the first signs of psychosomatic disorders (physical disorders triggered by psychological factors) begin to appear.

Continued stress leads to the **stage of exhaustion**, in which the body's resources are drained and stress hormones are depleted. Some of the typical signs or symptoms of impending exhaustion include the following (Friedman, 2002; Gurung, 2014):

Emotional signs: Anxiety, apathy, irritability, mental fatigue

Behavioral signs: Avoidance of responsibilities and relationships, extreme or self-destructive behavior, self-neglect, poor judgment

Physical signs: Excessive worry about illness, frequent illness, exhaustion, overuse of medicines, physical ailments and complaints

The GAS may sound melodramatic if you are young and healthy or if you've never endured prolonged stress. However, do not take stress lightly. Unless a way of relieving stress is found, the result will be a psychosomatic disease, a serious loss of health, or complete collapse. When Selye examined animals in the later stages of the GAS, he found that their adrenal glands were enlarged and discolored. Intense shrinkage of internal organs, such as the thymus, spleen, and lymph nodes, was evident, and many animals had stomach ulcers. In addition to such direct effects, stress can disrupt the body's immune system.

Health psychology pays special attention to the effect that stress has on health and sickness. Understanding stress and learning to control it can improve not only your health but the quality of your life as well (Allen, Carlson, & Ham, 2007). (For these reasons, a discussion of stress and stress management follows in Modules 56, 57, 58, and 59.)

The Whole Human: Subjective Well-Being

Health is not just an absence of disease (Diener & Chan, 2011; Tay & Diener, 2011). People who are truly healthy enjoy a positive state of **subjective well-being**. Maintaining subjective well-being is a lifelong pursuit and, hopefully, a labor of love. People who attain optimal subjective well-being are both physically and psychologically healthy. They are happy, optimistic, self-confident individuals who can bounce back emotionally from adversity. People who enjoy a sense of well-being also have supportive relationships with others, do meaningful work, and live in a clean environment. Many of these aspects of subjective well-being are addressed elsewhere in this book.

Tubol Evgeniya/Shutterstock

Stress and negative emotions lower immune system activity and increase inflammation. This, in turn, raises our vulnerability to infection, worsens illness, and delays recovery.

Community health campaign *A community-wide education program that provides information about how to lessen risk factors and promote health.*

Stress *The mental and physical condition that occurs when a person must adjust or adapt to the environment.*

Stress reaction *The physical response to stress, consisting mainly of bodily changes related to autonomic nervous system arousal.*

General adaptation syndrome (GAS) *A series of bodily reactions to prolonged stress; occurs in three stages: alarm, resistance, and exhaustion.*

Alarm reaction *First stage of the GAS, during which bodily resources are mobilized to cope with a stressor.*

Stage of resistance *Second stage of the GAS, during which the bodily adjustments to stress stabilize, but at a high physical cost.*

Stage of exhaustion *Third stage of the GAS, at which time the body's resources are exhausted and serious health consequences occur.*

Subjective well-being *A positive state of good health; more than the absence of disease.*

Module 55: Summary

55.1 What is health psychology, and how do cognition and behavior affect health?

- **55.1.1** Health psychologists are interested in how cognition and behavior help maintain and promote health.
- **55.1.2** Studies of health and illness have identified several behavioral risk factors that have a major effect on general health and life expectancy.
- **55.1.3** At the minimum, it is important to maintain health-promoting cognitions and behaviors with respect to diet, alcohol, exercise, and smoking.
- **55.1.4** Health psychologists have pioneered efforts to prevent the development of unhealthy habits and to improve well-being through community health campaigns.

- **55.1.5** Stress is a normal part of life that occurs when demands are placed on an organism to adjust or adapt. However, it also is a major risk factor for illness and disease.
- **55.1.6** The body reacts to stress in a series of stages called the general adaptation syndrome (GAS). The stages of the GAS are alarm, resistance, and exhaustion. Bodily reactions in the GAS follow the pattern observed in the development of psychosomatic disorders.
- **55.1.7** Maintaining good health is a personal responsibility, not a matter of luck. Wellness is based on minimizing risk factors and engaging in health-promoting behaviors.

Module 55: Knowledge Builder

Recite

1. Adjustment to chronic illness and the control of pain are topics that would more likely be of interest to a specialist in _____ rather than a health psychologist.

2. With respect to health, which of the following is *not* a major behavioral risk factor?
   - **a.** overexercise
   - **b.** cigarette smoking
   - **c.** stress
   - **d.** high blood pressure

3. Lifestyle diseases related to just six behaviors account for 70 percent of all medical costs. The behaviors are smoking, alcohol abuse, drug abuse, poor diet, insufficient exercise, and
   - **a.** driving too fast
   - **b.** excessive sun exposure
   - **c.** unsafe sex
   - **d.** exposure to toxins

4. Health psychologists tend to prefer _____ rather than modifying habits (like smoking) that become difficult to break once they are established.

5. The disease-prone personality is marked by _____, anxiety, and hostility.

6. The first signs of psychosomatic disorders begin to appear during the stage of
   - **a.** alarm
   - **b.** exhaustion
   - **c.** resistance
   - **d.** appraisal

Reflect

Think Critically

7. The general public is increasingly well informed about health risks and healthful behavior. Can you apply the concept of reinforcement to explain why so many people fail to act on this information?

Self-Reflect

Make a list of the major behavioral risk factors that apply to you. Are you laying the foundation for a lifestyle disease?

Which of the health-promoting behaviors listed in Table 55.1 would you like to increase?

If you were designing a community health campaign, who would you use as role models of healthful behavior?

Are you experiencing any signs of GAS? (Not a joke, guys ☺.) What are they?

ANSWERS

1. behavioral medicine 2. a 3. c 4. prevention 5. depression 6. c 7. Many of the health payoffs are delayed by months or years, greatly lessening the immediate rewards for healthful behavior (Watson & Tharp, 2014).

Health Psychology: Stressors

The Luckiest Girl in the World

Darya was the luckiest girl in the world. After marrying her sweetheart, they enjoyed a spectacular honeymoon in Jamaica. Now they were moving to new apartment to begin their lives together. So why was she feeling run over by a truck?

What Darya was learning firsthand is that prolonged or severe stress can lead to health problems, even if it is triggered by positive events. Over the last few months, she had experienced quite a few major life changes. It had all added up and now she had a bad cough and a fever.

We begin this module with the commonsense idea that stressful events "happen to" people. Although this is sometimes the case, more often stress is a matter of how we perceive events and react to them. We also explore some of the factors that determine the intensity of a stressor and close with a look at some different types of stressors, including frustration and conflict.

Cardinal/Creative/Corbis

SURVEY QUESTIONS

56.1 What is a stressor and what factors determine its severity?

56.2 What are some types of stressors?

Stress—Threat or Thrill?

SURVEY QUESTION 56.1: What is a stressor and what factors determine its severity?

It goes almost without saying that some events are more likely to cause stress than others. A **stressor** is a condition or event that challenges or threatens a person. But what makes an event a stressor?

Appraising Stressors

Sometimes stressful events do "just happen," but as noted in Module 44, our emotions are greatly affected by how we appraise situations. That's why some people are distressed by events that others view as a thrill or a challenge (*eustress*). Ultimately, stress depends on how you perceive a situation. Our friend Akihito would find it stressful to listen to five of his son's hip-hop CDs in a row. His son Takashi would find it stressful to listen to *one* of his father's opera CDs. To know if you are stressed, we must know what meaning you place on events. Whenever a stressor is appraised as a *threat* (potentially harmful), a powerful stress reaction follows (Lazarus, 1991a; Smith & Kirby, 2011).

"Am I Okay or in Trouble?" You have been selected to give a speech to 300 people. Or a doctor tells you that you must undergo a dangerous and painful operation. Or the one true love of your life walks out the door. What would be your emotional response to these events?

According to Richard Lazarus (1991a), there are two important steps in managing a threat. The first is a **primary appraisal**, in which you decide whether a situation is relevant or irrelevant, positive or threatening. In essence, this step answers the question, "Am I okay or in trouble?" Then, you make a **secondary appraisal**, in which you assess your resources and choose a way to meet the threat or challenge. ("What can I do about this situation?") Thus, the way a situation is "sized up" greatly affects our ability to cope with it (● **Figure 56.1**). Public speaking, for instance, can be appraised as an intense threat or as a chance to perform. Emphasizing the threat—by imagining failure, rejection, or embarrassment—obviously invites disaster (Tripp et al., 2011). (For an example of how changing your appraisal may make a big difference in your life, see "So You Think You're Poor.")

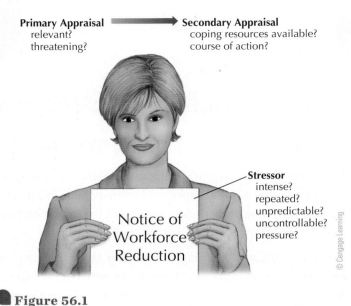

Primary Appraisal
relevant?
threatening?

Secondary Appraisal
coping resources available?
course of action?

Stressor
intense?
repeated?
unpredictable?
uncontrollable?
pressure?

© Cengage Learning

● **Figure 56.1**

Stress is the product of an interchange between a person and the environment.

Human Diversity

So You Think You're Poor

Being poor is no fun. It probably will not surprise you to learn it's no good for your health, either (Fuller-Rowell, Evans, & Ong, 2012). In general, the poorer people are, the more their health suffers and the lower is their life expectancy. According to the World Health Organization, 1.2 *billion* people around the world live in *absolute poverty*, surviving on less than a dollar a day. Tragically, absolute poverty wreaks havoc on people's health (World Health Organization, 2013). But that's not the whole story. For example, physician Stephen Bezruchka has shown that Greeks earn, on average, less than half of what Americans earn and yet have a longer life expectancy (Bezruchka as cited in Sapolsky, 2005).

How could this be? A hint to one possible answer is revealed in a study that found poorer women in California are *more* likely to die if they live in better-off neighborhoods than if they live in poorer neighborhoods (Winkleby, Ahn, & Cubbin, 2006). Apparently, being constantly reminded that you are *relatively poor* piles on an extra measure of stress (Bjornstrom, 2011; Wilkinson & Pickett, 2006, 2007). Add to that the fact that the United States currently has the largest income inequalities in the developed world. Constantly living with an awareness of their relative poverty, then, may help explain why Americans have shorter life expectancies than Greeks.

No one should pretend that relative poverty in the United States is anywhere near as big a problem as absolute poverty around the world. Nevertheless, it is a growing problem in the United States as the gap between the rich and poor continues to widen (Emerson, 2009; Oishi, Kesebir, & Diener, 2011).

janine wiedel/Alamy

Although being poor in the United States may mean living above an absolute poverty level, it also means constantly living with the stress of dramatic income inequality (Wilkinson & Pickett, 2009).

What should I do if I always feel poor? That may be part of the reason you are reading this book. First, commit to changing your circumstances through education and hard work. That's called *problem-focused coping* (you'll read about it in Module 57). In the meantime, remember Lazarus's (1991a) point about appraisal: It's only a stressor if you appraise it as one. A realistic appraisal of your situation may reveal that you are "richer" than you think. Maybe the best things in life are not all free, but why make yourself sick comparing yourself to people much better off than you (Wilkinson & Pickett, 2009)?

The Nature of Threat

Once an event has been appraised as a threat, several factors contribute to the intensity of that threat. Certainly, in most day-to-day situations, it doesn't mean you think your life is in danger. (Unless, of course, you owe money to Tony Soprano.) Threat has more to do with the idea of *control*. We are particularly prone to feel stressed when we can't—or think we can't—control our immediate environment. In short, a *perceived* lack of control is just as threatening as a real lack of control. For example, college students who feel overloaded experience stress even though their workload may not be any heavier than that of their classmates (Jacobs & Dodd, 2003).

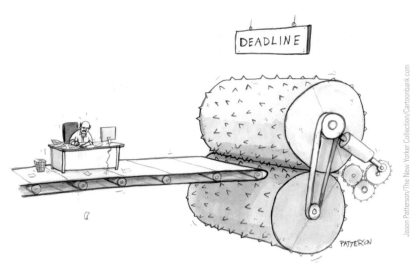

A sense of control also comes from believing you can reach desired goals. It is threatening to feel that we lack *competence* to cope with life's demands (Bandura, 2001; Leiter, Gascón, & Martínez-Jarreta, 2010). Because of this, the intensity of your body's stress reaction often depends on what you think and tell yourself about a stressor. That's why it's valuable to learn to think in ways that ward off the body's stress response. (Some strategies for controlling upsetting thoughts are described in Module 59.)

Unpredictability is another important factor. Police officers, for instance, suffer from a high rate of stress-related diseases. The threat of injury or death—plus occasional confrontations with angry, drunk, or hostile citizens—takes a toll. A major factor is the *unpredictable* nature of police work. An officer who stops a car to issue a traffic ticket never knows if a cooperative citizen or an armed gang member is waiting inside.

A revealing study shows how unpredictability adds to stress. In a series of 1-minute trials, college students breathed air through a mask. In some trials, the air contained 20 percent more carbon dioxide (CO_2) than normal. If you were to inhale this air, you would feel anxious, stressed, and a little like you were suffocating. Students tested this way hated the "surprise" doses of CO_2. They found it much less stressful to be told in advance which trials would include a choking whiff of CO_2 (Lejuez et al., 2000).

Pressure is another element of stress, especially job stress. **Pressure** occurs when a person must meet *urgent* external demands or expectations (Szollos, 2009). For example, we feel pressured when activities must be speeded up, when deadlines must be met, when extra work is added, or when we must work near maximum capacity for long periods. Most students who have survived final exams are familiar with the effects of pressure.

What if I set deadlines for myself? Does the source of the pressure make a difference? Yes. People generally feel more stress in situations over which they have little or no control (Leiter,

Air traffic control is stressful work. Employees must pay intense attention for long periods of time and have little control over the pace of work, and the consequences of making a mistake can be dire.

Stressor *A specific condition or event in the environment that challenges or threatens a person.*
Primary appraisal *Deciding if a situation is relevant to oneself and if it is a threat.*
Secondary appraisal *Deciding how to cope with a threat or challenge.*
Pressure *A stressful condition that occurs when a person must meet urgent external demands or expectations.*

TABLE 56.1	The Top 10 Work Stresses	
Work Stress		**Rank**
Low salary		1
Lack of opportunity for growth		2
Workload too heavy		3
Hours too long		4
Job expectations uncertain		5
Job expectations unrealistic		6
Work interferes with personal time		7
Job insecurity		8
Lack of participation in decision making		9
Inflexible hours		10

Source: Data from American Psychological Association (2012).

Gascón, & Martínez-Jarreta, 2010; Taris et al., 2005). In one study, nurses with a high sense of control (e.g., over the pacing of work and the physical arrangement of the working environment) were less likely to get sick, either physically or mentally, than nurses with a low sense of control (Ganster, Fox, & Dwyer, 2001).

To summarize, when emotional "shocks" are *uncontrollable, unpredictable,* and linked to *pressure,* stress is magnified and damage is likely to result. At work, people face many of these sources of stress every day. (See ● Table 56.1 for a list of the most common sources of stress at work.) In fact, chronic job stress sometimes results in *burnout.*

Burnout

Burnout occurs when workers are physically, mentally, and emotionally drained (Leiter, Gascón, & Martínez-Jarreta, 2010). When people become burned out, they experience emotional exhaustion, cynicism or detachment, and feelings of reduced personal accomplishment (Gallavan & Newman, 2013).

Burnout may occur in any job, but it is a special problem in emotionally demanding helping professions, such as nursing, teaching, social work, child care, counseling, or police work. Also, people who are more passionate about their work are more vulnerable to burnout (Saban et al., 2013; Vallerand et al., 2010). If we want to keep caring people in the helping professions, it may be necessary to adjust workloads, rewards,

and the amount of control people have in their jobs (Leiter & Maslach, 2005).

Can college students experience burnout? Yes, they can (Parker & Salmela-Aro, 2011). If you have a negative attitude toward your studies and feel that your college workload is too heavy, you may be vulnerable to burnout (Jacobs & Dodd, 2003). On the other hand, if you have a positive attitude toward your studies, participate in extracurricular activities, and enjoy good social support from your friends, rock on!

Types of Stressors

SURVEY QUESTION 56.2: What are some types of stressors?

From major life events, like getting married or moving to another country, to minor hassles, like getting cut off by the car in front of you or having too many things to do, and from frustrations to conflicts, almost anything can become a stressor under the right circumstances. Let's look at stressors in more detail.

Life Events and Stress

Disaster, depression, and sorrow often precede illness (Harrington, 2013). More surprising is the finding that *life changes*—both good *and* bad—can increase susceptibility to accidents or illness. Major changes in our surroundings or routines require us to be on guard and ready to react. Over long periods, this can be quite stressful (Sternberg, 2009).

How can I tell if I am subjecting myself to too much stress? Psychiatrist Thomas Holmes and graduate student Richard Rahe developed the first rating scale to estimate the health hazards we face when stresses add up (Holmes & Rahe, 1967). Still widely used today, a version of the **Social Readjustment Rating Scale (SRRS)** is reprinted in ● Table 56.2 (Miller & Rahe, 1997; Woods, Racine, & Klump, 2010). Notice that the impact of life events is expressed in *life change units (LCUs)* (numerical values assigned to each life event).

Why is going on vacation on the list? Positive life events can be stressful as well. (For example, marriage rates a 50 and Christmas a 30, even though they usually are happy events.) Even a change in social activities rates 27 LCUs, whether the change is due to an improvement or a decline. A stressful adjustment may be required in either case. To use the scale

TABLE 56.2 Social Readjustment Rating Scale

Rank	Life Event	Life Change Units	Rank	Life Event	Life Change Units
1	Death of spouse or child	119	23	Mortgage or loan greater than $10,000	44
2	Divorce	98	24	Change in responsibilities at work	43
3	Death of close family member	92	25	Change in living conditions	42
4	Marital separation	79	26	Change in residence	41
5	Fired from work	79	27	Begin or end school	38
6	Major personal injury or illness	77	28	Trouble with in-laws	38
7	Jail term	75	29	Outstanding personal achievement	37
8	Death of close friend	70	30	Change in work hours or conditions	36
9	Pregnancy	66	31	Change in schools	35
10	Major business readjustment	62	32	Christmas	30
11	Foreclosure on a mortgage or loan	61	33	Trouble with boss	29
12	Gain of new family member	57	34	Change in recreation	29
13	Marital reconciliation	57	35	Mortgage or loan less than $10,000	28
14	Change in health or behavior of family member	56	36	Change in personal habits	27
15	Change in financial state	56	37	Change in eating habits	27
16	Retirement	54	38	Change in social activities	27
17	Change to different line of work	51	39	Change in number of family get-togethers	26
18	Change in number of arguments with spouse	51	40	Change in sleeping habits	26
19	Marriage	50	41	Vacation	25
20	Spouse begins or ends work	46	42	Change in church activities	22
21	Sexual difficulties	45	43	Minor violations of the law	22
22	Child leaving home	44			

Source: Reprinted from Miller & Rahe (1997). Journal of Psychosomatic Research, *Vol. 43, No. 3.*

shown in Table 56.2, add up the LCUs for all life events you have experienced during the last year and compare the total to the following standards:

0–150: No significant problems
150–199: Mild life crisis (33 percent chance of illness)
200–299: Moderate life crisis (50 percent chance of illness)
300 or more: Major life crisis (80 percent chance of illness)

You have a higher chance of illness or accident when your LCU total exceeds 300 points. A more conservative rating of stress can be obtained by totaling LCU points for only the

Burnout *A work-related condition of mental, physical, and emotional exhaustion.*
Social Readjustment Rating Scale (SRRS) *A scale that rates the impact of various life events on the likelihood of illness.*

previous six months. The health of college students also is affected by stressful events, such as entering college, changing majors, or experiencing a breakup in a steady relationship.

Evaluation People differ greatly in their reactions to the same event. For this reason, stress scales like the SRRS at best provide a rough index of stress. Nevertheless, research has shown that if your stress level is too high, an adjustment in your activities or lifestyle may be needed. In one classic study, people were deliberately exposed to the virus that causes common colds. The results were nothing to sneeze at: If a person had a high stress score, she or he was much more likely to actually get a cold (Cohen, Tyrrell, & Smith, 1993). In view of such findings, higher levels of stress should be taken seriously (Hales, 2013). Remember, "To be forewarned is to be forearmed."

The Hazards of Hassles

There must be more to stress than major life changes. Isn't there a link between ongoing stresses and health? In addition to having a direct impact, major life events spawn countless daily frustrations and irritations (Henderson, Roberto, & Kamo, 2010). Also, many of us face ongoing stresses at work or at home that do not involve major life changes (Pett & Johnson, 2005). Such minor but frequent stresses are called **hassles (microstressors)**. (See ● Table 56.3 for some examples of hassles faced by college students.)

Table 56.3	Examples of Common Hassles Faced by College Students
Too many things to do
Not enough money for housing
Feeling discriminated against
People making gender jokes
Communication problems with friends
Driving to school
People making fun of my religion
Fear of losing valuables
Work schedule
Getting into shape
Parents' expectations

Source: Pett & Johnson, 2005.

In a yearlong study, 100 men and women recorded the hassles they endured. Participants also reported on their physical and mental health. Frequent and severe hassles turned out to be better predictors of day-to-day health than major life events. However, major life events did predict changes in health one or two years after the events took place. It appears that daily hassles are closely linked to immediate health and psychological well-being (Crowther et al., 2001). Major life changes have more of a long-term impact and exacerbate the effects of daily hassles (Woods, Racine, & Klump, 2010).

One way to guarantee that you will experience a large number of life changes and hassles is to live in a foreign culture. "Acculturative Stress—Stranger in a Strange Land" offers a brief glimpse into some of the consequences of culture shock.

Frustration

Frustration is a negative emotional state that occurs when people are prevented from reaching desired goals. If your goal of finding a parking space is blocked by another car, you may be frustrated and experience stress.

Obstacles of many kinds cause frustration. A useful distinction can be made between external and personal sources of frustration. *External frustration* is based on conditions outside a person that impede progress toward a goal. The following are external frustrations: getting stuck with a flat tire; having a marriage proposal rejected; finding the cupboard bare when you go to get your poor dog a bone; and being chased out of the house by your starving dog. In other words, external frustrations are based on *delays, failure, rejection, loss,* and other direct blocking of motivated behavior.

Notice that external obstacles can be either *social* (slow drivers, tall people in theaters, people who cut in lines) or *nonsocial* (stuck doors, a dead battery, rain on the day of the game). If you ask your friends what has frustrated them recently, most will probably mention someone's behavior ("My sister wore one of my dresses when I wanted to wear it," "My supervisor is unfair," or "My history teacher grades too hard"). As social animals, we humans are highly sensitive to social sources of frustration (Taylor, 2012). That's probably why unfair treatment associated with racial or ethnic prejudice is a major source of frustration and stress in the lives of many African Americans and other minority group members (Brondolo et al., 2011; Gurung, 2014).

Frustration usually increases as the *strength, urgency,* or *importance* of a blocked motive increases. An escape artist submerged in a tank of water and bound with 200 pounds of

Human Diversity

Acculturative Stress—Stranger in a Strange Land

Around the world, an increasing number of emigrants and refugees must adapt to dramatic changes in language, dress, values, and social customs. For many, the result is a period of culture shock or acculturative stress—stress caused by adapting to a foreign culture. Typical reactions to acculturative stress are anxiety, hostility, depression, alienation, physical illness, or identity confusion. For many young immigrants, acculturative stress is a major source of mental health problems (Choi & Dancy, 2009; Mejía & McCarthy, 2010; Yeh, 2003).

The severity of acculturative stress is related, in part, to how a person adapts to a new culture. Here are four main patterns (Berry et al., 2005; Sam & Berry, 2010):

- **Integration:** Maintain your old cultural identity but participate in the new culture.
- **Separation:** Maintain your old cultural identity and avoid contact with the new culture.

One of the best antidotes for acculturative stress is a society that tolerates or even celebrates ethnic diversity. Although some people find it hard to accept new immigrants, the fact is, nearly everyone's family tree includes people who were once strangers in a strange land.

- **Assimilation:** Adopt the new culture as your own and have contact with its members.
- **Marginalization:** Reject your old culture but suffer rejection by members of the new culture.

To illustrate each pattern, let's consider a family that has immigrated to the United States from the imaginary country of Heinleinia:

The father favors integration. He is learning English and wants to get involved in American life. At the same time, he is a leader in the Heinleinian-American community and spends much of his leisure time with other Heinleinian Americans. His level of acculturative stress is low.

The mother speaks only the Heinleinian language and interacts only with other Heinleinian Americans. She remains almost completely separate from American society. Her stress level is high.

The teenage daughter is annoyed by hearing Heinleinian spoken at home, by her mother's serving only Heinleinian food, and by having to spend her leisure time with her extended Heinleinian family. She would prefer to speak English and to be with her American friends. Her desire to assimilate creates moderate stress.

The son doesn't particularly value his Heinleinian heritage, yet his schoolmates reject him because he speaks with a Heinleinian accent. He feels trapped between two cultures. His position is marginal, and his stress level is high.

To summarize, those who feel marginalized tend to be highly stressed; those who seek to remain separate also are highly stressed; those who pursue integration into their new culture are minimally stressed; and those who assimilate are moderately stressed.

As you can see, integration and assimilation are the best options. However, a big benefit of assimilating is that people who embrace their new culture experience fewer social difficulties. For many, this justifies the stress of adopting new customs and cultural values (Gurung, 2014; Sam & Berry, 2010).

---

chain would become *quite* frustrated if a trick lock jammed. Remember, too, that motivation becomes stronger as we near a goal. As a result, frustration is more intense when a person runs into an obstacle when very close to a goal. If you've ever missed an A grade by five points, you were probably very frustrated. If you've missed an A by one point—well, frustration builds character, right?

A final factor affecting frustration is summarized by the old phrase "the straw that broke the camel's back." The effects of *repeated* frustrations can accumulate until a small irritation

sets off an unexpectedly violent response. A case in point is the fact that people with long daily commutes are more likely to display "road rage" (angry, aggressive driving) (Sansone & Sansone, 2010).

Hassle (microstressor) *Any distressing, day-to-day annoyance.*
Frustration *A negative emotional state that occurs when one is prevented from reaching a goal.*
Acculturative stress *Stress caused by the many changes and adaptations required when a person moves to a foreign culture.*

Personal frustrations are based on personal characteristics. If you are 4 feet tall and aspire to be a professional basketball player, you very likely will be frustrated. If you want to go to medical school but can earn only D grades, you likewise will be frustrated. In both examples, frustration is based on personal limitations, yet failure may be *perceived* as externally caused. We return to this point in a discussion of stress management. In the meantime, let's look at some typical reactions to frustration.

Reactions to Frustration
Aggression is any response made with the intent of harming a person or an object. It is one of the most persistent and frequent responses to frustration (Shaver & Mikulincer, 2011).

Does frustration always cause aggression? Aren't there other reactions? Although the connection is strong, frustration does not always incite aggression. More often, frustration is met first with *persistence,* often in the form of more vigorous efforts and varied responses (● **Figure 56.2**). For example, if you put your last dollar in a vending machine and pressing the button has no effect, you probably will press harder and faster (vigorous effort). Then, you will press all the other buttons (varied response). Persistence may help you reach your goal by getting *around* a barrier. However, if the machine *still* refuses to

Paintball seems to bring out aggressive impulses in many players. Wild shoot-outs are part of the fun, but are some players displacing aggressive urges related to frustration in other areas of their lives?

deliver or return your dollar, you may become aggressive and kick the machine (or at least tell it what you think of it).

Persistence can be very adaptive. Overcoming a barrier ends the frustration and allows the need or motive to be satisfied. The same is true of aggression that removes or destroys a barrier. Picture a small band of nomadic humans, parched by thirst but separated from a water hole by a menacing animal. It is easy to see that attacking the animal may ensure their survival. In modern society, such direct aggression is seldom acceptable. If you find a long line at the drinking fountain, aggression is hardly appropriate. Because direct aggression is discouraged, it is frequently *displaced* (Reijntjes et al., 2013).

How is aggression displaced? Directing aggression toward a source of frustration may be impossible, or it may be too dangerous. If you are frustrated by your boss at work or by a teacher at school, the cost of direct aggression may be too high (losing your job or failing a class). Instead, the aggression may be displaced, or redirected, toward whomever or whatever is available. Targets of **displaced aggression** tend to be safer, or less likely to retaliate, than the original source of frustration. At one time or another, you have probably lashed out at a friend or relative who was not the real cause of your annoyance. As this suggests, excessive anger over a minor irritation is a common form of displaced aggression (Miller et al., 2003).

Psychologists attribute much hostility to displaced aggression. A disturbing example is the finding that unemployment and divorce are associated with increased child abuse (Weissman, Jogerst, & Dawson, 2003). In a pattern known as

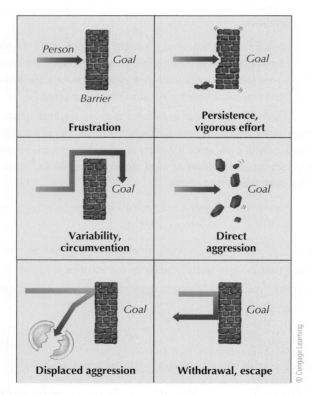

● **Figure 56.2**

Frustration and common reactions to it.

scapegoating, a person or a group is blamed for conditions not of their making. A *scapegoat* is a person who has become a habitual target of displaced aggression. Despite recent progress, many minority groups continue to face hostility based on scapegoating (Vasquez, Lickel, & Hennigan, 2010). Think, for example, about the hostility expressed toward illegal immigrants during times of economic hardship. In many communities, layoffs and job losses are closely linked to increased violence (Glick, 2008). Or, think about the hostility expressed toward anyone in the United States who looks even vaguely "foreign" right after a terrorist attack.

I have a friend who dropped out of school to hitchhike around the country. He seemed very frustrated before he quit. What type of response to frustration is that? Another major reaction to frustration is escape, or withdrawal. It is stressful and unpleasant to be frustrated. If other reactions do not reduce frustration, a person may try to escape. Escape may mean actually leaving a source of frustration (dropping out of school, quitting a job, leaving an unhappy marriage), or it may mean psychologically escaping. Two common forms of psychological escape are feigned apathy (pretending not to care) and the use of drugs such as cocaine, alcohol, marijuana, or narcotics. Notice that these are examples of ineffective *emotion-focused coping* (see Module 57).

Coping with Frustration

In a classic experiment, a psychologist studying frustration placed rats on a small platform at the top of a tall pole. Then, he forced them to jump off the platform toward two elevated doors, one locked and the other unlocked. If the rat chose the correct door, it swung open and the rat landed safely on another platform. Rats that chose the locked door bounced off it and fell into a net far below them.

The problem of choosing the open door was made unsolvable and very frustrating by randomly alternating which door was locked. After a time, most rats adopted a stereotyped response—that is, they chose the same door every time. This door was then permanently locked. All the rat had to do was jump to the other door to avoid a fall, but time after time, the rat bounced off the locked door (Maier, 1949).

Isn't that an example of persistence? No. Persistence that is *inflexible* can turn into "stupid," stereotyped behavior like that of a rat on a jumping platform. When dealing with frustration, you must know when to quit and establish a new direction. Here are some suggestions to help you avoid needless frustration:

1. Try to identify the source of your frustration. Is it external or personal?

2. Is the source of frustration something that can be changed? How hard would you have to work to change it? Is it under your control at all?

3. If the source of your frustration can be changed or removed, are the necessary efforts worth it?

The answers to these questions help determine whether persistence will be futile. There is value in learning to accept gracefully those things that cannot be changed.

Conflict

Conflict occurs whenever a person must choose between contradictory needs, desires, motives, or demands. Choosing between college and work, marriage and single life, or study and failure are common conflicts. There are three basic forms of conflict. As we will see, each has its own properties (● Figure 56.3 and ● Figure 56.4).

● Figure 56.3

Three basic forms of conflict. For this woman, choosing between pie and ice cream is a minor approach–approach conflict; deciding whether to take a job that will require weekend work is an approach–avoidance conflict; and choosing between paying higher rent and moving is an avoidance–avoidance conflict.

Aggression *Any response made with the intent of causing harm.*
Displaced aggression *Redirecting aggression to a target other than the actual source of one's frustration.*
Scapegoating *Blaming a person or a group of people for conditions not of their making.*
Escape *Reducing discomfort by leaving frustrating situations or by psychologically withdrawing from them.*
Conflict *A stressful condition that occurs when a person must choose between incompatible or contradictory alternatives.*

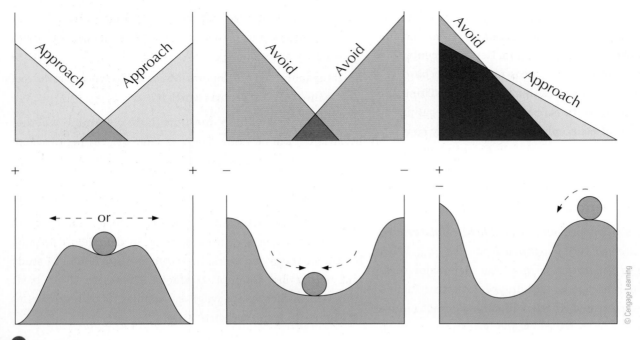

Figure 56.4

Conflict diagrams. As shown by the colored areas in the graphs, desires to approach and to avoid increase near a goal. The effects of these tendencies are depicted below each graph. The "behavior" of the ball in each example illustrates the nature of the conflict above it. An approach–approach conflict *(left)* is easily decided. Moving toward one goal increases its attraction *(graph)* and leads to a rapid resolution. (If the ball moves in either direction, it will go all the way to one of the goals.) In an avoidance–avoidance conflict *(center)*, tendencies to avoid are deadlocked, resulting in inaction. In an approach–avoidance conflict *(right)*, approach proceeds to the point where desires to approach and avoid cancel each other. Again, these tendencies are depicted *(below)* by the action of the ball. (Graphs after Miller, 1944.)

Approach–Approach Conflicts An **approach–approach conflict** comes from having to choose between two positive, or desirable, alternatives. Choosing between tutti-frutti-coconut-mocha-champagne ice and orange-marmalade-peanut-butter-coffee swirl at the ice cream parlor may throw you into a temporary conflict. However, if you really like both choices, your decision will be quickly made. Even when more important decisions are at stake, approach–approach conflicts tend to be the easiest to resolve. The old fable about the mule that died of thirst and starvation while standing between a bucket of water and a bucket of oats is obviously unrealistic. When both options are positive, the scales of decision are easily tipped one direction or the other.

Avoidance–Avoidance Conflicts Being forced to choose between two negative, or undesirable, alternatives creates an **avoidance–avoidance conflict**. A person in an avoidance conflict is caught between "the devil and the deep blue sea," "the frying pan and the fire," or "a rock and a hard place." In real life, double-avoidance conflicts involve dilemmas such as choosing between unwanted pregnancy and abortion, the

dentist and tooth decay, a monotonous job and poverty, or dorm food and starvation.

Suppose that I consider any pregnancy sacred and not to be tampered with. Or, suppose I don't object to abortion. Like many other stressful situations, these examples can be defined as conflicts only on the basis of personal needs and values. If a woman would not consider abortion under any circumstances, she experiences no conflict. If she wants to end a pregnancy and does not object to abortion, she also experiences no conflict.

Avoidance conflicts often have a "damned if you do, damned if you don't" quality. In other words, both choices are negative, but *not choosing* may be impossible or equally undesirable. To illustrate, imagine the plight of a person trapped in a hotel fire 20 stories from the ground. Should she jump from the window and almost surely die on the pavement? Or, should she try to dash through the flames and almost surely die of smoke inhalation and burns? When faced with a choice such as this, it is easy to see why people often *freeze,* finding it impossible to decide or take action. In actual disasters of this sort, people are often found dead in their rooms, victims of an inability to take action.

Indecision, inaction, and freezing are not the only reactions to double-avoidance conflicts. Because avoidance conflicts are stressful and difficult to solve, people sometimes pull out of them entirely. This reaction, called *leaving the field,* is another form of escape. It may explain the behavior of a student who could not attend school unless he worked. However, if he worked, he could not earn passing grades. His solution after much conflict and indecision? He joined the navy.

Approach-Avoidance Conflicts

Approach–avoidance conflicts also are difficult to resolve. In some ways, they are more troublesome than avoidance conflicts because people seldom escape them. A person in an approach–avoidance conflict is "caught" by being attracted to, and repelled by, the same goal or activity. Attraction keeps the person in the situation, but its negative aspects cause turmoil and distress. For example, a high school student arrives to pick up his date for the first time. He is met at the door by her father, who is a professional wrestler—7 feet tall, 300 pounds, and entirely covered with hair. The father gives the boy a crushing handshake and growls that he will break him in half if the girl is not home on time. The student considers the girl attractive and has a good time. But does he ask her out again? It depends on the relative strength of his attraction and his fear. Almost certainly he will feel *ambivalent* about asking her out again, knowing that another encounter with her father awaits him.

Ambivalence (mixed positive and negative feelings) is a central characteristic of approach–avoidance conflicts. Ambivalence is usually translated into *partial approach* (Miller, 1944). Because our student is still attracted to the girl, he may spend time with her at school and elsewhere. But he may not actually date her again. Some more realistic examples of approach–avoidance conflicts are planning to marry someone your parents strongly disapprove of, wanting to be in a play but suffering stage fright, wanting to buy a car but not wanting to make monthly payments, and wanting to eat when you're already overweight. Many of life's important decisions have approach–avoidance dimensions.

Multiple Conflicts

Aren't real-life conflicts more complex than the ones described here? Yes. Conflicts are rarely as clear-cut as those described. People in conflict are usually faced with several dilemmas at once, so several types of conflict may be intermingled. In real life, it is common to face multiple approach–avoidance conflicts, in which you are simultaneously attracted to and repelled by each of several alternatives. For example, you are offered two jobs: One is in a good city and pays well but offers poor hours and dull work; the other is in a city you don't like so much and pays poorly but offers interesting work and excellent hours. Which do you select? These situations are more typical of the choices we must usually make. The options are neither completely positive nor completely negative.

As with single approach–avoidance conflicts, people faced with multiple approach–avoidance conflicts tend to feel ambivalent about each choice. This causes them to vacillate, or waver, between the alternatives. Just as you are about to choose one such alternative, its undesirable aspects tend to loom large. What do you do? You swing back toward the other choice. If you have ever been romantically attracted to two people at once—each having qualities you like and dislike—then you have probably experienced vacillation. Another example that may be familiar is trying to decide between two college majors, each with advantages and disadvantages.

When multiple approach–avoidance conflicts involve major life decisions, such as choosing a career, a school, a mate, or a job, they can add greatly to the amount of stress we experience.

Managing Conflicts

How can I handle conflicts more effectively? Most of the suggestions made earlier concerning frustration also apply to conflicts. However, here are some additional things to remember when you are in conflict or must make a difficult decision:

1. Don't be hasty when making important decisions. Hasty decisions are often regretted. Even if you do make a faulty decision, it will trouble you less if you know that you did everything possible to avoid a mistake.

2. Try out important decisions *partially* when possible. If you are thinking about moving to a new town, try to spend a few days there first. If you are choosing between colleges, do the same. If classes are in progress, sit in on some. If you want to learn to scuba dive, rent equipment for a reasonable length of time before buying.

Approach–approach conflict *Choosing between two positive, or desirable, alternatives.*

Avoidance–avoidance conflict *Choosing between two negative, undesirable alternatives.*

Approach–avoidance conflict *Being attracted to and repelled by the same goal or activity.*

Multiple approach–avoidance conflict *Being simultaneously attracted to and repelled by each of several alternatives.*

3. Look for workable compromises. Again, it is important to get all available information. If you think that you have only one or two alternatives and they are undesirable or unbearable, seek the aid of a teacher, counselor, minister, or social service agency. You may be overlooking possible alternatives these people will know about.

4. When all else fails, make a decision and live with it. Indecision and conflict exact a high cost. Sometimes it is best to select a course of action and stick with it unless it is obviously wrong after you have taken it.

Conflicts are a normal part of life. With practice, you can learn to manage many of the conflicts you will face.

Module 56: Summary

56.1 What is a stressor and what factors determine its severity?

- **56.1.1** Any condition or event that challenges or threatens a person is a stressor.
- **56.1.2** Making a primary appraisal greatly affects our emotional responses to a situation. Stress is intensified when a situation is appraised as a threat.
- **56.1.3** During a secondary appraisal, we select a way to manage stress. Stress also is intensified when a person does not feel competent to cope with it.
- **56.1.4** Stress is more damaging in situations involving a lack of control, unpredictability of the stressor, and pressure.
- **56.1.5** In work settings, prolonged stress can lead to burnout.

56.2 What are some types of stressors?

- **56.2.1** Work with stress scales like the *Social Readjustment Rating Scale* indicates that multiple life changes tend to increase long-range susceptibility to accident or illness.
- **56.2.2** Immediate physical and psychological health is more closely related to the intensity and severity of daily hassles (microstressors).

- **56.2.3** Frustration is the negative emotional state that occurs when progress toward a goal is blocked. External frustrations are based on delay, failure, rejection, loss, and other direct blocking of motives. Personal frustration is related to personal characteristics over which one has little control.
- **56.2.4** Major behavioral reactions to frustration include persistence, more vigorous responding, circumvention, direct aggression, displaced aggression (including scapegoating), and escape or withdrawal.
- **56.2.5** Four major types of conflict are approach–approach, avoidance–avoidance, approach–avoidance, and multiple approach–avoidance.
- **56.2.6** Approach–approach conflicts are usually the easiest to resolve.
- **56.2.7** Avoidance–avoidance conflicts are difficult to resolve and are characterized by inaction, indecision, freezing, and a desire to escape (called leaving the field).
- **56.2.8** People usually remain in approach–avoidance conflicts but fail to fully resolve them. Approach–avoidance conflicts are associated with ambivalence and partial approach.
- **56.2.9** Vacillation is a common reaction to multiple approach–avoidance conflicts.

Module 56: Knowledge Builder

Recite

Stressors

1. The SRRS appears to predict long-range changes in health, whereas the frequency and severity of daily microstressors is closely related to immediate ratings of health. *T or F?*

2. According to Richard Lazarus, choosing a way to meet a threat or challenge takes place during the
   - *a.* primary stress reaction
   - *b.* secondary stress reaction
   - *c.* primary appraisal
   - *d.* secondary appraisal

3. Stress tends to be greatest when a situation is appraised as a _____ and a person does not feel _____ to cope with the situation.

4. Emotional exhaustion, cynicism, and reduced accomplishment are characteristics of job _____.

5. Which of the following is *not* a common reaction to frustration?
   - *a.* ambivalence
   - *b.* aggression
   - *c.* displaced aggression
   - *d.* persistence

6. Displaced aggression is closely related to the pattern of behavior known as
   - *a.* scapegoating
   - *b.* leaving the field
   - *c.* stereotyped responding
   - *d.* burnout

7. You would be most likely to experience vacillation if you found yourself in
   - *a.* an approach–approach conflict
   - *b.* an avoidance–avoidance conflict
   - *c.* a multiple approach–avoidance conflict
   - *d.* the condition called emotion-focused coping

Reflect

Think Critically

8. Being frustrated is unpleasant. If some action, including aggression, ends frustration, why might we expect the action to be repeated on other occasions?

Self-Reflect

Do you think there is more of a connection between major life events and your health? Or, have you observed more of a connection between microstressors and your health?

Suppose you moved to a foreign country. How much acculturative stress do you think you would face? Which pattern of adaptation do you think you would adopt?

Think of a time when you were frustrated. What was your goal? What prevented you from reaching it? Was your frustration external or personal?

Have you ever displaced aggression? Why did you choose another target for your hostility?

Review the major types of conflict and think of a conflict you have faced that illustrates each type.

ANSWERS

1. T 2. d 3. threat, competent 4. burnout 5. a 6. a 7. c 8. If a response ends discomfort, the response has been negatively reinforced. This makes it more likely to occur in the future (see Module 29).

CENGAGE brain.com

Go to **cengagebrain.com** to access **MindTap for Coon/Mitterer** *Psychology Modules for Active Learning* and other online learning tools. MindTap is a fully online learning experience that combines all the tools you need—readings, multimedia, activities, and assessments—into a singular personalized Learning Path that guides you through the course.

Module

Health Psychology: Coping with Stress

Between a Rock and a Hard Place

There is no doubt that mountain climber Aron Ralston experienced a trauma. After suffering a fall, his arm became impossibly wedged between two boulders. Remarkably, he overcame his trauma through a combination of problem-focused and emotion-focused coping. Left with no choice, he amputated his own arm with a dull knife and survived to climb again. Ralston told his story in his 2004 book, *Between a Rock and a Hard Place*, which inspired the 2010 film *127 Hours*.

Stressful and threatening experiences often produce anxiety. (You can be sure Ralston experienced plenty of that!) How do we handle this unpleasant state? Psychodynamic psychologists have identified various defense mechanisms that shield us from anxiety. You might not always be aware of it, but you have probably used several of the defenses described here. You'll also find an interesting perspective on helplessness and depression in this module, with a special section on the "college blues."

AP Photo/E. Pablo Kosmicki

SURVEY QUESTIONS

57.1 What are problem-focused and emotion-focused coping?

57.2 What are defense mechanisms?

57.3 What do we know about coping with feelings of helplessness and depression?

Coping Styles—Making the Best of It

SURVEY QUESTION 57.1: What are problem-focused and emotion-focused coping?

You have appraised a situation as stressful. What will you do next? You have two major choices. Both involve thinking and acting in ways that help us handle stressors. **Problem-focused coping** is aimed at managing or correcting the distressing situation. Some examples are making a plan of action or concentrating on your next step. In contrast, in **emotion-focused coping**, we try to control our emotional reactions to the situation. For example, a distressed person may distract herself by listening to music, taking a walk to relax, or seeking emotional support from others (Herman & Tetrick, 2009; Smith & Kirby, 2011).

Couldn't both types of coping occur together? Yes. Sometimes the two types of coping aid one another. For instance, quieting your emotions may make it easier for you to find a way to solve a problem. Say, for example, that you feel anxious as you step in front of your class to give a presentation. If you take a few deep breaths to reduce your anxiety (emotion-focused coping), you will be better able to glance over your notes to improve your delivery (problem-focused coping).

The Clinical File

Coping with Traumatic Stress

Traumatic experiences produce psychological injury or intense emotional pain. Victims of **traumatic stresses**, such as war, torture, rape, assassination, plane crashes, natural disasters, and street violence, may suffer from nightmares, flashbacks, insomnia, irritability, nervousness, grief, emotional numbing, and depression (Durand & Barlow, 2013). For example, the 2012 Superstorm Sandy, along with the resulting chaos, was undoubtedly a traumatically stressful event.

People who personally witness or survive a disaster are most affected by traumatic stress. Twenty percent of the people who lived close to the World Trade Center in New York City suffered serious stress disorders after the 9/11 terrorist attack (Galea et al., 2002). Yet, even those who experience horror at a distance may be traumatized (Galea & Resnick, 2005). Forty-four percent of U.S. adults who only saw the 9/11 attacks on television had at least some stress symptoms (Schuster et al., 2001). For example, Americans faced elevated risks of hypertension and heart problems for three years after 9/11 (Holman et al., 2008). Indirect exposure to such terrorist attacks, coupled with the ongoing risk of more attacks, has ensured that many people will suffer ongoing stress into the foreseeable future (Marshall et al., 2007).

Traumatic stress produces feelings of helplessness and vulnerability. Victims realize that disaster could strike again without warning. In addition to feeling threatened, many victims sense that they are losing control of their lives (Fields & Margolin, 2001; Ford, 2012).

What can people do about such reactions? Psychologists recommend the following:

- Identify what you are feeling and talk to others about your fears and concerns.
- Think about the skills that have helped you overcome adversity in the past and apply them to the present situation.
- Continue to do the things that you enjoy and that make life meaningful.
- Get support from others. This is a major element in recovery from all traumatic events.
- Give yourself time to heal. Fortunately, most people are more resilient than they think.

When traumatic stresses are severe or repeated, some people have even more serious symptoms (Durand & Barlow, 2013). They suffer from crippling anxiety or become emotionally numb. Typically, they can't stop thinking about the disturbing event, they anxiously avoid anything associated with the event, and they are constantly fearful or nervous. (These are the symptoms of *stress disorders,* which are discussed in Module 63.) Such reactions can leave victims emotionally handicapped for months or years after a disaster. The consequences can last a lifetime for children who are the victims of trauma (Gillespie & Nemeroff, 2007; Salloum & Overstreet, 2012). If you feel that you are having trouble coping with a severe emotional shock, consider seeking help from a psychologist or other professional (Bisson et al., 2007).

It also is possible for coping efforts to clash. For instance, if you have to make a difficult decision, you may suffer intense emotional distress. In such circumstances, it is tempting to make a quick, unreflective choice, just to end the suffering (Arnsten, Mazure, & Sinha, 2012). Doing so may allow you to cope with your emotions, but it shortchanges problem-focused coping.

In general, problem-focused coping tends to be especially useful when you are facing a controllable stressor—that is, a situation you can actually do something about. Emotion-focused efforts are best suited to managing your reaction to stressors you cannot control (Folkman & Moskowitz, 2004; Smith & Kirby, 2011).

So far, our discussion has focused on everyday stresses. How do people react to the extreme stresses imposed by war, violence, or disaster? "Coping with Traumatic Stress" discusses this important topic.

Psychological Defense— Mental Karate?

SURVEY QUESTION 57.2: What are defense mechanisms?

Threatening situations tend to produce **anxiety**. When you are anxious, you feel tense, uneasy, apprehensive, worried,

Problem-focused coping *Directly managing or remedying a stressful or threatening situation.*
Emotion-focused coping *Managing or controlling one's emotional reaction to a stressful or threatening situation.*
Traumatic stresses *Extreme events that cause psychological injury or intense emotional pain.*
Anxiety *Apprehension, dread, or uneasiness similar to fear but based on an unclear threat.*

and vulnerable. This unpleasant state can lead to emotion-focused coping that is defensive in nature (Kramer et al., 2010). Psychodynamic psychologists have identified various defense mechanisms that allow us to reduce anxiety caused by stressful situations or our own shortcomings. You might not always be aware of it, but you have probably used several of the defenses described here.

What are psychological defense mechanisms, and how do they reduce anxiety? A **defense mechanism** is any mental process used to avoid, deny, or distort sources of threat or anxiety, especially threats to one's self-image. Many of the defenses were first identified by Sigmund Freud, who assumed they operate *unconsciously*. Often, defense mechanisms create large blind spots in awareness. For instance, you might know an extremely stingy person who is completely unaware that he is a tightwad.

Everyone has at one time or another used defense mechanisms. Let's consider some of the most common; a more complete listing is given in ● Table 57.1.

Denial One of the most basic defenses is **denial**—protecting oneself from an unpleasant reality by refusing to accept it or believe it. We are prone to deny death, illness, and similar painful and threatening events. For instance, if you were told

that you had only three months to live, how would you react? Your first thoughts might be, "Aw, come on, someone must have mixed up the X-rays," or, "The doctor must be mistaken," or simply, "It can't be true!" Similar denial and disbelief are common reactions to the unexpected death of a friend or relative: "It's just not real. I don't believe it!"

Repression Freud noticed that his patients had tremendous difficulty recalling shocking or traumatic events from childhood. It seemed that powerful forces were holding these painful memories from awareness. Freud called this **repression** and said we use it to protect ourselves by blocking out threatening thoughts and impulses. Feelings of hostility toward a family member, the names of people we dislike, and past failures are common targets of repression. Research suggests that you are most likely to repress information that threatens your self-image (Axmacher et al., 2010; Mendolia, 2002).

Reaction Formation In a **reaction formation**, impulses are not just repressed; they also are held in check by exaggerating opposite behavior. For example, a mother who unconsciously resents her children may, through reaction formation, become absurdly overprotective and overindulgent. Her real thoughts of "I hate them" and "I wish they were gone" are replaced by "I love them" and "I don't know what I would do without

TABLE 57.1	Psychological Defense Mechanisms
Compensation	Counteracting a real or imagined weakness by emphasizing desirable traits or seeking to excel in the area of weakness or in other areas
Denial	Protecting oneself from an unpleasant reality by refusing to perceive it
Fantasy	Fulfilling unmet desires in imagined achievements or activities
Identification	Taking on some of the characteristics of an admired person, usually as a way to compensate for perceived personal weaknesses or faults
Intellectualization	Separating emotion from a threatening or anxiety-provoking situation by talking or thinking about it in impersonal "intellectual" terms
Isolation	Separating contradictory thoughts or feelings into "logic-tight" mental compartments so that they do not come into conflict
Projection	Attributing one's own feelings, shortcomings, or unacceptable impulses to others
Rationalization	Justifying your behavior by giving reasonable and "rational," but false, reasons for it
Reaction formation	Preventing dangerous impulses from being expressed in behavior by exaggerating opposite behavior
Regression	Retreating to an earlier level of development or to earlier, less demanding habits or situations
Repression	Unconsciously preventing painful or dangerous thoughts from entering awareness
Sublimation	Working off unmet desires, or unacceptable impulses, in activities that are constructive

them." The mother's hostile impulses are traded for "smother" love so that she won't have to admit she hates her children. Thus, the basic idea in a reaction formation is that the individual acts out an opposite behavior to block threatening impulses or feelings.

Regression In its broadest meaning, regression refers to any return to earlier, less demanding situations or habits. Most parents who have a second child have to put up with at least some regression by the older child. Threatened by a new rival for affection, an older child may regress to childish speech, bed-wetting, or infantile play after the new baby arrives. If you've ever seen a child get homesick at summer camp or on a vacation, you've observed regression. The child wants to go home, where it's "safe." An adult who throws a temper tantrum or a married adult who "goes home to mother" also is regressing.

Projection Projection is an unconscious process that protects us from the anxiety we would feel if we were to discern our faults. A person who is projecting tends to see his or her own feelings, shortcomings, or unacceptable impulses in others. Projection lowers anxiety by exaggerating negative traits in others. This justifies one's own actions and directs attention away from personal failings.

One of your authors once worked for a greedy shop owner who cheated many of his customers. This same man considered himself a pillar of the community and very moral and religious. How did he justify to himself his greed and dishonesty? He believed that everyone who entered his store was bent on cheating *him* any way they could. In reality, few, if any, of his customers shared his motives, but he projected his own greed and dishonesty onto them.

Rationalization Every teacher is familiar with this strange phenomenon: On the day of an exam, an incredible wave of disasters sweeps through the city. Mothers, fathers, sisters, brothers, aunts, uncles, grandparents, friends, relatives, and pets of students become ill or die. Motors suddenly fall out of cars. Books are lost or stolen. Alarm clocks go belly-up and ring no more. All manner of computer equipment malfunctions.

The making of excuses comes from a natural tendency to explain our behavior. Rationalization refers to justifying personal actions by giving "rational" but false reasons for them. When the explanation you give for your behavior is reasonable and convincing—but not the real reason—you are *rationalizing*. For example, Mee Jung failed to turn in an assignment given at the beginning of the semester in one of her classes. Here's the explanation she gave her professor:

My car broke down two days ago, and I couldn't get to the library until yesterday. Then I couldn't get all the books I needed because some were checked out, but I wrote what I could. Then last night, as the last straw, the ink cartridge in my printer ran out, and because all the stores were closed, I couldn't finish the paper on time.

When asked why she left the assignment until the last minute (the real reason it was late), Mee Jung offered another set of rationalizations. Like many people, Mee Jung had difficulty seeing herself without the protection of her rationalizations.

All the defense mechanisms described seem pretty undesirable. Do they have a positive side? People who overuse defense mechanisms become less adaptable because they consume great amounts of emotional energy to control anxiety and maintain an unrealistic self-image. Defense mechanisms do have value, though. Often, they help keep us from being overwhelmed by immediate threats. This can provide time for a person to learn to cope in a more effective, problem-focused manner. If you recognize some of your own behavior in the descriptions here, it is hardly a sign that you are hopelessly defensive. As noted earlier, most people occasionally use defense mechanisms.

Two defense mechanisms that have a decidedly more positive quality are compensation and sublimation.

Compensation Compensatory reactions are defenses against feelings of inferiority. A person who has a defect or weakness (real or imagined) may go to unusual lengths to overcome the weakness or to compensate for it by excelling in other areas. One of the pioneers of "pumping iron" was Jack LaLanne, who opened the first modern health club in America. LaLanne made a successful career out of bodybuilding in spite of the

---

Defense mechanism *A habitual and often unconscious psychological process used to reduce anxiety.*

Denial *Protecting oneself from an unpleasant reality by refusing to perceive it.*

Repression *Unconsciously preventing painful or dangerous thoughts from entering awareness.*

Reaction formation *Preventing dangerous impulses from being expressed in behavior by exaggerating opposite behavior.*

Regression *Retreating to an earlier level of development or to earlier, less demanding habits or situations.*

Projection *Attributing one's own feelings, shortcomings, or unacceptable impulses to others.*

Rationalization *Justifying your behavior by giving reasonable and "rational," but false, reasons for it.*

Compensation *Counteracting a real or imagined weakness by emphasizing desirable traits or seeking to excel in the area of weakness or in other areas.*

fact that he was thin and sickly as a young man. Perhaps it would be more accurate to say *because* he was thin and sickly. You can find dozens of examples of compensation at work. A childhood stutterer may excel in debate at college. As a child, Helen Keller was unable to see or hear, but she became an outstanding thinker and writer. Perhaps Ray Charles, Stevie Wonder, Andrea Bocelli, and other blind entertainers were drawn to music because of their disability.

Sublimation The defense called **sublimation** (sub-lih-MAY-shun) is defined as working off frustrated desires (especially sexual desires) through socially acceptable activities. Freud believed that art, music, dance, poetry, scientific investigation, and other creative activities could serve to rechannel sexual energies into productive behavior. Freud also felt that almost any strong desire could be sublimated. For example, a very aggressive person may find social acceptance as a professional soldier, boxer, or football player. Greed may be refined into a successful business career. Lying may be sublimated into storytelling, creative writing, or politics.

For some players—and fans—football probably allows sublimation of aggressive urges. *Call of Duty, Mass Effect,* and similar computer games may serve the same purpose.

Sexual motives appear to be the most easily and widely sublimated (Moran, 2010). Freud would have had a field day with such modern pastimes as surfing, motorcycle riding, drag racing, and dancing to or playing rock music, to name but a few. People enjoy each of these activities for a multitude of reasons, but it is hard to overlook the rich sexual symbolism apparent in each.

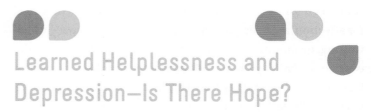

Learned Helplessness and Depression—Is There Hope?

SURVEY QUESTION 57.3: What do we know about coping with feelings of helplessness and depression?

What would happen if a person's defenses failed or if the person appraised a threatening situation as hopeless? Martin Seligman studied the case of a young Marine who seemed to have adapted to the stresses of being held prisoner during the Vietnam War. The Marine's health was related to a promise made by his captors: If he cooperated, they said, he would be released on a certain date. As the date approached, his spirits soared. Then came a devastating blow. He had been deceived. His captors had no intention of ever releasing him. He immediately lapsed into a deep depression, refused to eat or drink, and died shortly thereafter.

That seems like an extreme example. Does anything similar occur outside concentration camps? Apparently so. For example, researchers in San Antonio, Texas, asked older people if they were hopeful about the future. Those who answered "No" died at elevated rates (Stern, Dhanda, & Hazuda, 2001).

Learned Helplessness

To explain such patterns, psychologists have focused on the concept of **learned helplessness**, an acquired inability to overcome obstacles and avoid aversive stimuli (Seligman, 1989). To observe learned helplessness, let's see what happens when animals are tested in a shuttle box (● **Figure 57.1**). If placed in one side of a divided box, dogs quickly learn to leap to the other side to escape an electric shock. If they are given a warning before the shock occurs (for example, a light that dims), most dogs learn to avoid the shock by leaping the barrier before the shock arrives. This is true of most dogs, but not those who have learned to feel helpless (Overmier & LoLordo, 1998).

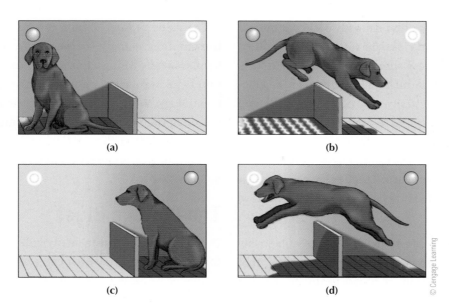

Figure 57.1

In the normal course of escape and avoidance learning, a light dims shortly before the floor is electrified (*a*). Because the light does not yet have meaning for the dog, the dog receives a shock (noninjurious, by the way) and leaps the barrier (*b*). Dogs soon learn to watch for the dimming of the light (*c*) and to jump before receiving a shock (*d*). Dogs made to feel "helpless" rarely even learn to escape shock, much less to avoid it.

How is a dog made to feel helpless? Before being tested in the shuttle box, a dog can be placed in a harness (from which the dog cannot escape) and then given several painful shocks. The animal is helpless to prevent these shocks. When placed in the shuttle box, dogs prepared this way react to the first shock by crouching, howling, and whining. None of them try to escape. They helplessly resign themselves to their fate. After all, they have already learned that there is nothing they can do about getting shocked.

As the shuttle box experiments suggest, helplessness is a psychological state that occurs when events *appear to be uncontrollable* (Seligman, 1989). Helplessness also afflicts humans (Domjan, 2010; Reivich et al., 2013). It is a common reaction to repeated failure and to unpredictable or unavoidable punishment. A prime example is college students who feel helpless about their schoolwork. Such students tend to procrastinate, give up easily, and drop out of school (Perry, 2003).

Where humans are concerned, attributions (discussed in Module 44) have a large effect on helplessness. Persons who are made to feel helpless in one situation are more likely to act helpless in other situations if they attribute their failure to *lasting, general* factors. An example would be concluding "I must be stupid" after doing poorly on a test in a biology class. In contrast, attributing a low score to specific factors in the situation ("I'm not too good at the type of test my biology

professor uses" or "I'm not very interested in biology") tends to prevent learned helplessness from spreading (Peterson & Vaidya, 2001; Prochaska & Norcross, 2010).

Depression

Seligman and others have pointed out the similarities between learned helplessness and **depression**. Both are marked by feelings of despondency, powerlessness, and hopelessness. "Helpless" animals display decreased activity, lowered aggression, blunted appetite, and a loss of sex drive. Humans suffer from similar effects and also tend to see themselves as failing, even when they're not (Brown & Barlow, 2011; LoLordo, 2001).

Depression is one of the most widespread emotional problems, and it undoubtedly has many causes. However, learned helplessness seems to explain many cases of depression and hopelessness. For example, Seligman (1972) describes the fate of Archie, a 15-year-old boy. For Archie, school is

Sublimation *Working off unmet desires, or unacceptable impulses, in activities that are constructive.*
Learned helplessness *A learned inability to overcome obstacles or to avoid punishment; learned passivity and inaction to aversive stimuli.*
Depression *A state of despondency marked by feelings of powerlessness and hopelessness.*

an unending series of shocks and failures. Other students treat him as if he's stupid; in class, he rarely answers questions because he doesn't know some of the words. He feels knocked down everywhere he turns. These may not be electric shocks, but they are certainly emotional "shocks," and Archie has learned to feel helpless to prevent them. When he leaves school, his chances of success are poor. He has learned to passively endure whatever shocks life has in store for him. Archie is not alone in this regard. Hopelessness is almost always a major element of depression (Durand & Barlow, 2013; Reivich et al., 2013).

Recognizing Depression Most people know, obviously enough, when they are "down." You should assume that more than a minor fluctuation in mood is involved when the following conditions exist (National Institute of Mental Health, 2012a):

1. Persistent sad, anxious, or "empty" feelings
2. Feelings of guilt, worthlessness, and/or helplessness
3. Difficulty concentrating, remembering details, and making decisions
4. Feelings of hopelessness and/or pessimism
5. Loss of interest in activities or hobbies once pleasurable, including sex

Hope *Does Seligman's research give any clues about how to "unlearn" helplessness?* With dogs, an effective technique is to forcibly drag them away from shock into the "safe" compartment. After this is done several times, the animals regain "hope" and feelings of control over the environment. Just how this can be done with humans is a question psychologists are exploring. It seems obvious, for instance, that someone like Archie would benefit from an educational program that would allow him to "succeed" repeatedly.

In **mastery training**, responses that lead to mastery of a threat or control over one's environment are reinforced. Animals that undergo such training become more resistant to learned helplessness (Volpicelli et al., 1983). For example, animals that first learn to escape shock become more persistent in trying to flee inescapable shock. In effect, they don't give up, even when the situation really is "hopeless."

Such findings suggest that we might be able to "immunize" people against helplessness and depression by allowing them to master difficult challenges (Miltenberger, 2012). The Outward Bound schools, in which people pit themselves against the rigors of mountaineering, white-water canoeing, and wilderness survival, might serve as a model for such a program.

The value of hope should not be overlooked. As fragile as this emotion seems, it is a powerful antidote to depression and helplessness (Weingarten, 2010). As an individual, you may find hope in religion, nature, human companionship, or even technology. Wherever you find it, remember its value: Hope is among the most important of all human emotions. Having positive beliefs, such as optimism, hope, and a sense of meaning and control, is closely related to overall well-being (Diener & Chan, 2011).

The College Blues

During the school year, many college students suffer symptoms of depression, which can exert a toll on academic performance (Lindsey, Fabiano, & Stark, 2009). In one study, students diagnosed with depression scored half a grade point below nondepressed students (Hysenbegasi, Hass, & Rowland, 2005). Why do students get "blue"? Various problems contribute to depressive feelings. Here are some of the most common (Aselton, 2012; Enns, Cox, & Clara, 2005; Gonzalez, Reynolds, & Skewes, 2011):

1. Stresses from college work and pressures to choose a career can leave students feeling that they are missing out on fun or that all their hard work is meaningless.
2. Isolation and loneliness are common when students leave their support groups behind. In the past, family, a circle of high school friends, and often a boyfriend or girlfriend could be counted on for support and encouragement.
3. Problems with studying and grades frequently trigger depression. Many students start college with high aspirations and little prior experience with failure. At the same time, many lack basic skills necessary for academic success and are afraid of failure.
4. Depression can be triggered by the breakup of an intimate relationship, either with a former boyfriend or girlfriend or with a newly formed college romance.
5. Students who find it difficult to live up to their idealized images of themselves are especially prone to depression.
6. An added danger is that depressed students are more likely to abuse alcohol, which is a depressant.

Coping with the College Blues Bouts of the college blues are closely related to stressful events. Learning to manage college work and to challenge self-critical thinking can help alleviate mild school-related depression (Halonen & Santrock, 2013). For example, if you don't do well on a test or a class assignment, how do you react? If you see it as a small, isolated setback, you probably won't feel too bad. However, if you feel like you have "blown it" in a big way, depression may follow. Students who strongly link everyday events to long-term goals (such as a successful career or high income) tend to overreact to day-to-day disappointments (McIntosh, Harlow, & Martin, 1995; Halonen & Santrock, 2013).

What does the preceding tell us about the college blues? The implication is that it's important to take daily tasks one step at a time and chip away at them (Watson & Tharp, 2014). That way, you are less likely to feel overwhelmed, helpless, or hopeless. When you feel "blue," you should make a daily schedule for yourself (Burka & Yuen, 2008). Try to schedule activities to fill up every hour during the day. It is best to start with easy activities and progress to more difficult tasks. Check off each item as it is completed. That way, you will begin to break the self-defeating cycle of feeling helpless and falling further behind. (Depressed students spend much of their time sleeping.) A series of small accomplishments, successes, or pleasures may be all that you need to get going again. However, if you are lacking skills needed for success in college, ask for help in getting them. Don't remain "helpless."

Feelings of worthlessness and hopelessness are usually supported by self-critical or negative thoughts. Consider writing down such thoughts as they occur, especially those that immediately precede feelings of sadness (Pennebaker & Chung, 2007). After you have collected these thoughts, write a rational answer to each. For example, the thought "No one loves me" should be answered with a list of those who do care. One more point to keep in mind is this: When events begin to improve, try to accept it as a sign that better times lie ahead. Positive events are most likely to end depression if you view them as stable and continuing rather than temporary and fragile.

Attacks of the college blues are common and should be distinguished from more serious cases of depression. Severe depression is a serious problem that can lead to suicide or a major impairment of emotional functioning. In such cases, it would be wise to seek professional help (Corsini & Wedding, 2011).

Module 57: Summary

57.1 What are problem-focused and emotion-focused coping?

- **57.1.1** Problem-focused coping involves directly managing or remedying a stressful or threatening situation. Emotion-focused coping relies on managing or controlling one's emotional reaction to a stressful or threatening situation.

57.2 What are defense mechanisms?

- **57.2.1** Defense mechanisms are mental processes used to avoid, deny, or distort sources of threat or anxiety, including threats to one's self-image. Overuse of defense mechanisms makes people less adaptable.
- **57.2.2** Several defense mechanisms have been identified, including compensation, denial, fantasy, intellectualization, isolation, projection, rationalization, reaction formation, regression, repression, and sublimation.

57.3 What do we know about coping with feelings of helplessness and depression?

- **57.3.1** Learned helplessness can be used as a model for understanding depression. Depression is a major, and surprisingly common, emotional problem.
- **57.3.2** Actions and thoughts that counter feelings of helplessness tend to reduce depression. Mastery training, optimism, and hope all act as antidotes for learned helplessness or depression.
- **57.3.3** The college blues are a relatively mild form of depression. Learning to manage college work and to challenge self-critical thinking can help alleviate the college blues.

Mastery training *Reinforcement of responses that lead to mastery of a threat or control over one's environment.*

Module 57: Knowledge Builder

Recite

1. Stress is always better dealt with through problem-focused coping? **T or F?**

2. Fulfilling frustrated desires in imaginary achievements or activities defines the defense mechanism of
   - **a.** compensation
   - **b.** isolation
   - **c.** fantasy
   - **d.** sublimation

3. In compensation, one's own undesirable characteristics or motives are attributed to others. **T or F?**

4. Of the defense mechanisms, two that are considered relatively constructive are
   - **a.** compensation
   - **b.** denial
   - **c.** isolation
   - **d.** projection
   - **e.** regression
   - **f.** rationalization
   - **g.** sublimation

5. Depression in humans is similar to _____ observed in animal experiments.

6. Learned helplessness tends to occur when events appear to be
   - **a.** frustrating
   - **b.** in conflict
   - **c.** uncontrollable
   - **d.** problem focused

7. Frequent self-criticism and self-blame are a natural consequence of doing college work. **T or F?**

Reflect

Think Critically

8. Learned helplessness is closely related to which of the factors that determine the severity of stress?

Self-Reflect

What type of coping do you tend to use when you face a stressor such as public speaking or taking an important exam?

We tend to be blind to our own reliance on defense mechanisms. See if you can think of one example of each defense that you have observed yourself or someone else using.

Have you ever felt helpless in a particular situation? What caused you to feel that way?

Imagine that a friend of yours is suffering from the college blues. What advice would you give your friend?

ANSWERS

1. F 2. c 3. F 4. a, g 5. learned helplessness 6. c 7. F 8. Feelings of incompetence and lack of control

CENGAGE**brain**.com

Health Psychology: Stress and Health

Type A

Have you ever become ill after facing a stressful final exam period? Or gotten sick after experiencing one or more positive life events, like getting married? Was it a coincidence? Maybe you even got accused of faking it, of being a *hypochondriac*, or of having a *psychosomatic* problem and needing a psychiatrist. Antoine, a college wide receiver, got teased when his teammates found out he had chronic high blood pressure. They even nicknamed him "Type A."

What do all of these terms mean? Psychologists have now firmly established that stress affects our bodily health. Let's begin to see how this powerful mind–body connection is explained by the field of *psychoneuroimmunology*. (Try dropping that word into a conversation sometime if you want to see a stress reaction!).

We also explore some factors that limit the health risks we face. Because we live in a fast-paced and often stressful society, these are topics worth stressing.

Ariel Skelley/Blend Images/SuperStock

SURVEY QUESTION

58.1 How is stress related to health and disease?

Stress and Health— Unmasking a Hidden Killer

SURVEY QUESTION 58.1: How is stress related to health and disease?

How can stress result in a physical illness? An answer can be found in your body's immune system, which mobilizes defenses (such as white blood cells) against invading microbes and other disease agents. The immune system is regulated, in part, by the brain. Because of this link, stress and upsetting emotions can affect the immune system in ways that increase susceptibility to disease (Janusek, Cooper, & Mathews, 2012; Zachariae, 2009).

By the way, the study of links among behavior, stress, disease, and the immune system is called **psychoneuroimmunology** (Daruna, 2012; Kendall-Tackett, 2010).

Studies show that the immune system is weakened in students during major exam times, as you may already have unfortunately discovered. Immunity also is lowered by divorce, bereavement, a troubled marriage, job loss, poor sleep, depression, and similar stresses (Motivala & Irwin, 2007; Segerstrom & Miller, 2004). Lowered immunity explains why the "double whammy" of getting sick when you are trying to cope with prolonged or severe stress is so common (Pedersen, Bovbjerg, & Zachariae, 2011). Stress causes the body to release substances that increase inflammation. This is part of the body's self-protective response to threats, but it can prolong infections and delay healing (Kiecolt-Glaser, 2010).

It's also worth noting again the value of positive emotions. Happiness, laughter, and delight tend to strengthen immune system response. Doing things that make you happy also can protect your health (Diener & Chan, 2011; Rosenkranz et al., 2003).

Could reducing stress help prevent illness? Yes. Various psychological approaches, such as support groups, relaxation exercises, guided imagery, and stress-management training, can actually boost immune system functioning (Kottler & Chen, 2011). By doing so, they help promote and restore health. For example, stress management reduced the severity of cold and flu symptoms in a group of university students (Reid, Mackinnon, & Drummond, 2001).

There is even evidence that stress management can improve the chances of survival in people with life-threatening diseases, such as cancer, heart disease, and HIV/AIDS. With some successes to encourage them, psychologists are now searching for the best combination of treatments to help people resist disease (Phillips et al., 2012; Schneiderman et al., 2001).

Psychosomatic Disorders

As we have seen, chronic or repeated stress can damage physical health as well as upset emotional well-being. Prolonged stress reactions are closely related to a large number of psychosomatic (SIKE-oh-so-MAT-ik) illnesses. In **psychosomatic disorders** (*psyche:* mind; *soma:* body), psychological factors contribute to actual bodily damage or to damaging changes in bodily functioning (Asmundson & Taylor, 2005; Bourgeois et al., 2009). Psychosomatic problems, therefore, are *not* the same as hypochondria. **Hypochondriacs** (HI-po-KON-dree-aks) imagine that they have diseases. There is nothing imaginary about asthma, a migraine headache, or high blood pressure.

The most common psychosomatic problems are gastrointestinal and respiratory (stomach pain and asthma, for example), but many others exist. Typical problems include eczema (skin rash), hives, migraine headaches, rheumatoid arthritis, hypertension (high blood pressure), colitis (ulceration of the colon), and heart disease. And these are only the major problems. Many lesser health complaints also are stress related. Typical examples include sore muscles, headaches, neckaches, backaches, indigestion, constipation, chronic diarrhea, fatigue, insomnia, premenstrual problems, and sexual dysfunctions (Taylor, 2012). Severe psychosomatic disorders can even be fatal. Thus, the person who says, "Oh, it's *just* psychosomatic" doesn't understand how serious stress-related diseases really are. For some of these problems, biofeedback may be helpful. The next section explains how.

Biofeedback

Psychologists have discovered that people can learn to control bodily activities once thought to be involuntary. This is done by applying informational feedback to bodily control, a process called **biofeedback**. If you were asked to raise the temperature of your right hand, you probably couldn't because you wouldn't know if you were succeeding. To make your task easier, a sensitive thermometer could be attached to your hand. The thermometer could be wired so that an increase in temperature would activate a signal light. Then, all you would have to do is try to keep the light on as much as possible. With practice and the help of biofeedback, you could learn to raise your hand temperature at will.

Biofeedback holds promise as a way to treat some psychosomatic problems (● **Figure 58.1**). For instance, people have been trained to prevent migraine headaches with biofeedback.

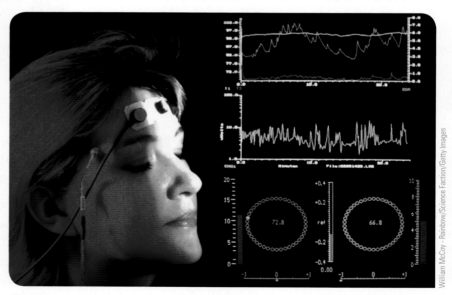

● **Figure 58.1**

In biofeedback training, bodily processes are monitored and processed electronically. A signal is then routed back to the patient through headphones, signal lights, or other means. This information helps the patient alter bodily activities not normally under voluntary control. This woman is learning to control her brain waves in order to relax.

Sensors are taped to patients' hands and foreheads. Patients then learn to redirect blood flow away from the head to their extremities. Because migraine headaches involve excessive blood flow to the head, biofeedback helps patients reduce the frequency of their headaches (Larsson et al., 2005; Stokes & Lappin, 2010).

Biofeedback also can help relieve muscle-tension headaches and chronic pain (Middaugh & Pawlick, 2002; Sousa et al., 2009). It shows promise for lowering blood pressure and controlling heart rhythms (Olsson et al., 2010; Wheat & Larkin, 2010). The technique has been used with some success to control epileptic seizures and hyperactivity in children (Demos, 2005). Insomnia also responds to biofeedback therapy (Gathchel & Oordt, 2003; McLay & Spira, 2009).

How does biofeedback work? Some researchers believe that many of its benefits arise from *general relaxation*. Others stress that the method simply acts as a "mirror" to help a person perform tasks involving *self-regulation*. Just as a mirror does not comb your hair, biofeedback does not do anything by itself. It can, however, help people make desired changes in their behavior.

The Cardiac Personality

It would be a mistake to assume that stress is the sole cause of psychosomatic diseases. Genetic differences, organ weaknesses, and learned reactions to stress combine to do damage. Personality also enters the picture. As mentioned earlier, a general disease-prone personality type exists. To a degree, there also are "headache personalities," "asthma personalities," and so on. The best documented of such patterns is the "cardiac personality"—a person at high risk for heart disease.

In a landmark study of heart problems, two cardiologists, Meyer Friedman and Ray Rosenman, classified people as either **Type A personalities**, those who run a high risk for heart attack, or **Type B personalities**, those who are unlikely to have a heart attack. In an eight-year follow-up, they found more than twice the rate of heart disease in Type A's than in Type B's (Friedman & Rosenman, 1983).

Type A *What is the Type A personality like?* Type A people are hard driving, ambitious, highly competitive, achievement oriented, and striving. Type A people believe that with enough effort they can overcome any obstacle, and they "push" themselves

accordingly. Perhaps the most telltale signs of a Type A personality are *time urgency* and chronic *anger* or *hostility* (Allan, 2011).

Type A's hurry from one activity to another, racing the clock in self-imposed urgency. As they do, they feel a constant sense of frustration and anger. Feelings of anger and hostility, in particular, are strongly related to increased risk for heart attack (Boyle et al., 2004; Bunde & Suls, 2006). One study found that 15 percent of a group of 25-year-old doctors and lawyers who scored high on a hostility test were dead by age 50. The most damaging pattern may occur in hostile persons who keep their anger "bottled up." Such people seethe with anger but don't express it outwardly. This increases their pulse rate and blood pressure and puts a tremendous strain on the heart (Bongard, al'Absi, & Lovallo, 1998).

TYPE Z BEHAVIOR

Psychoneuroimmunology *Study of the links among behavior, stress, disease, and the immune system.*

Psychosomatic disorders *Illnesses in which psychological factors contribute to bodily damage or to damaging changes in bodily functioning.*

Hypochondriac *(HI-po-KON-dree-ak) A person who complains about illnesses that appear to be imaginary.*

Biofeedback *Information given to a person about his or her ongoing bodily activities; aids voluntary regulation of bodily states.*

Type A personality *A personality type with an elevated risk of heart disease; characterized by time urgency, anger, and hostility.*

Type B personality *All personality types other than Type A; a low-cardiac-risk personality.*

TABLE 58.1	Characteristics of the Type A Person

Check the items that apply to you. Do you:

_____ Find yourself constantly creating overly tight schedules?

_____ Impatiently interrupt other people to finish their sentences yourself?

_____ Read only the headlines and summaries in newspapers rather than the entire articles?

_____ Feel road rage and "line rage" when traffic or lineups move slowly?

_____ Usually feel events are unfolding too slowly?

_____ Never stop to "smell the roses" or enjoy a beautiful sunset?

_____ Frequently try to be more efficient by doing several things at the same time?

_____ Tend to overstress key words in your speech even when you don't need to? (You are really BUGGING me. GO AWAY.)

_____ Usually feel a bit guilty if you do try to relax, go on vacation, or have nothing in particular that you need to get done?

_____ Focus on achievement (your income, how much you win at sports, your academic average at school) rather than enjoyment?

_____ Always fidget (repetitively bounce your leg, twirl a ring or a lock of hair, tap your fingers)?

_____ Have difficulty *listening* to other people talk to you instead of thinking about other things?

_____ Always end up overloading yourself by taking on too much?

_____ Never take time for a casual meal or a calm stroll?

Source: Created by your authors to illustrate characteristics of the Type A person.

To summarize, there is growing evidence that anger or hostility may be the core lethal factor of Type A behavior (Lemogne et al., 2010; Smith & Traupman, 2011). In view of this, Type A's would be wise to take their increased health risks seriously.

How are Type A people identified? Characteristics of Type A people are summarized in the short self-identification test presented in ● Table 58.1. If most of the list applies to you, you might be a Type A. However, confirmation of your type requires more powerful testing methods. Also, remember that the original definition of Type A behavior was probably too broad. The key psychological factors that increase heart disease risk appear to be anger, hostility, and mistrust (Myrtek, 2007; Smith et al., 2004). Also, although Type A behavior appears to promote heart disease, depression or distress may be what finally triggers a heart attack (Denollet & Van Heck, 2001; Dinan, 2001).

Because our society places a premium on achievement, competition, and mastery, it is not surprising that many people develop Type A personalities. The best way to avoid the self-made stress this causes is to adopt behavior that is the opposite of that listed in Table 58.1 (Williams, Barefoot, & Schneiderman, 2003). It is entirely possible to succeed in life without sacrificing your health or happiness in the process.

People who frequently feel angry and hostile toward others may benefit from the advice of Redford Williams (1989). According to Williams, reducing hostility involves three goals. First, you must stop mistrusting the motives of others. Second, you must find ways to reduce how often you feel anger, indignation, irritation, and rage. Third, you must learn to be kinder and more considerate. It is entirely possible to succeed in life without sacrificing your health or happiness in the process.

The Hardy Personality

How do Type A people who do not develop heart disease differ from those who do? Psychologist Salvatore Maddi has studied people who have a **hardy personality**. Such people seem to be unusually resistant to stress (Maddi et al., 2009; Stix, 2011). The first study of hardiness began with two groups of managers at a large utility company. All the managers held high-stress positions. Yet, some tended to get sick after stressful events, whereas others were rarely ill. How did the people who were thriving differ from their "stressed-out" colleagues? Both groups seemed to have traits typical of the Type A personality, so that wasn't the explanation. They also were quite similar in most other respects. The main difference was that the hardy group seemed to hold a worldview that consisted of three traits (Maddi, 2006; Maddi et al., 2009):

1. They had a sense of personal *commitment* to self, work, family, and other stabilizing values.
2. They felt that they had *control* over their lives and their work.
3. They had a tendency to see life as a series of *challenges,* rather than as a series of threats or problems.

How do such traits protect people from the effects of stress? Persons strong in *commitment* find ways of turning whatever they are doing into something that seems interesting and important. They tend to get involved rather than feel alienated.

Persons strong in *control* believe that more often than not they can influence the course of events around them. This prevents them from passively seeing themselves as victims of circumstance.

Finally, people strong in *challenge* find fulfillment in continual growth. They seek to learn from their experiences rather than accept easy comfort, security, and routine. Indeed, many "negative" experiences can enhance personal growth—if you have support from others and the skills needed to cope with challenge (Garrosa et al., 2008; Stix, 2011).

The Whole Human: Hardiness, Optimism, and Happiness

Good and bad events occur in all lives. What separates happy people from those who are unhappy is largely a matter of attitude. Happy people tend to see their lives in more positive terms, even when trouble comes their way. For example, happier people tend to find humor in disappointments. They look at setbacks as challenges. They are strengthened by losses (Lyubomirsky & Tucker, 1998). In short, happiness tends to be related to hardiness (Cohn et al., 2009; Maddi et al., 2009).

Why is there a connection? As psychologist Barbara Fredrickson has pointed out, positive emotions tend to broaden our mental focus. Emotions such as joy, interest, and contentment create an urge to play, to be creative, to explore, to savor life, to seek new experiences, to integrate, and to grow. When you are stressed, experiencing positive emotions can make it more likely that you will find creative solutions to your problems. Positive emotions also tend to reduce the bodily arousal that occurs when we are stressed, possibly limiting stress-related damage (Diener & Chan, 2011; Fredrickson, 2003).

We should again note the value of optimism, which goes hand in hand with hardiness and happiness. Optimists tend to expect that things will turn out well. This motivates them to actively cope with adversity. They are less likely to be stopped by temporary setbacks and more likely to deal with problems head-on. Pessimists are more likely to ignore or deny problems. The result of such differences is that optimists are less stressed and anxious than pessimists. They also are in better health than pessimists. In general, optimists tend to take better care of themselves because they believe that their efforts to stay healthy will succeed (Peterson & Chang, 2003; Taylor, 2011).

A Look Ahead The work we reviewed here has drawn new attention to the fact that each of us has a personal responsibility for maintaining and promoting health. In Module 59, we look at what you can do to better cope with stress and the health risks that it entails. But first, the following questions may help you maintain a healthy grade on your next psychology test.

Hardy personality *A personality style associated with superior stress resistance.*

Module 58: Summary

58.1 How is stress related to health and disease?

- **58.1.1** Studies of psychoneuroimmunology show that stress lowers the body's resistance to disease by weakening the immune system.
- **58.1.2** Intense or prolonged stress may cause damage in the form of psychosomatic problems.
- **58.1.3** During biofeedback training, bodily processes are monitored and converted to a signal that tells what the body is doing.

Biofeedback allows people to alleviate some psychosomatic illnesses by altering bodily activities.

- **58.1.4** People with Type A personalities are competitive, striving, hostile, impatient, and prone to having heart attacks.
- **58.1.5** People who have the traits of a hardy personality seem to be unusually resistant to stress.
- **58.1.6** Optimism and positive emotions tend to buffer stress.

Module 58: Knowledge Builder

Recite

1. Students taking stressful final exams are more susceptible to the cold virus, a pattern best explained by the concept of
   a. the disease-prone personality
   b. psychoneuroimmunology
   c. emotion-focused coping
   d. reaction formation

2. Ulcers, migraine headaches, and hypochondria frequently are psychosomatic disorders. *T or F?*

3. Two major elements of biofeedback training appear to be relaxation and self-regulation. *T or F?*

4. Evidence suggests that the most important feature of the Type A personality is a sense of time urgency rather than feelings of anger and hostility. *T or F?*

5. A sense of commitment, challenge, and control characterizes the hardy personality. *T or F?*

6. In many ways, a person who has a hardy personality is the opposite of a person who has
   a. a high STD score   c. Type A traits
   b. a low LCU score   d. Type B traits

Reflect

Think Critically

7. People with a hardy personality type appear to be especially resistant to which of the problems discussed in Module 57?

Self-Reflect

Mindy complains about her health all the time, but she seems to be just fine. An acquaintance of Mindy's dismisses her problems by saying, "Oh, she's not really sick. It's just psychosomatic." What's wrong with this use of the term *psychosomatic*?

Do you think you are basically a Type A or a Type B personality? To what extent do you possess traits of the hardy personality?

ANSWERS

1. B 2. F 3. T 4. F 5. T 6. C 7. Learned helplessness

CENGAGE**brain**.com

Go to **cengagebrain.com** to access **MindTap for Coon/Mitterer** *Psychology Modules for Active Learning* and other online learning tools. MindTap is a fully online learning experience that combines all the tools you need—readings, multimedia, activities, and assessments—into a singular personalized Learning Path that guides you through the course.

Psychology in Action: Stress Management

Blog On!

They were tough times for Freddy. "I was facing a cancer scare, my girlfriend and I broke up, my student loan money ran out, and final exams were just around the corner. Stressed out for months, I didn't know what to do next."

Freddy decided to visit the student counseling center where a counselor suggested he write about his troubles. Never one to share his feelings, he had to overcome some serious misgivings. But he did start blogging to his family and a few close friends. Freddy was surprised to find that expressing his emotions was very helpful. After he received some emotional support and constructive feedback from his family and friends, he realized that they could act as a buffer against stress. Oh, yes, and spending time with his dog, Boo, helped as well. What else can someone like Freddy do to help with life's stresses and strains?

william casey/Shutterstock

SURVEY QUESTION

59.1 What are the best strategies for managing stress?

Health Psychology— Here's to Your Good Health

SURVEY QUESTION 59.1: What are the best strategies for managing stress?

Stress management is the use of cognitive and behavioral strategies to reduce stress and improve coping skills. As promised, this section describes strategies for managing stress. Before you continue reading, if you haven't yet had the chance, you may want to make sure you go back and assess your level of stress using the *Social Readjustment Rating Scale* (Table 56.2). High scores on the *SRRS* suggest that you have been exposed to health-threatening levels of stress. But remember, stress is an internal state. If you are good at coping with stressors, a high score may not be a problem for you.

Now that you have a picture of your current level of stress, what can you do about it? The simplest way of coping with stress is to modify or remove its source—by leaving a stressful job, for example. Obviously, this is often impossible, which is why learning to manage stress is so important.

As shown in ● **Figure 59.1**, stress triggers *bodily effects, upsetting thoughts,* and *ineffective behavior.* Not shown is the fact that each element worsens the others in a vicious cycle. Indeed, once this cycle begins, you can find yourself spiraling out of control—unless you take action to break the cycle. The information that follows tells how.

Managing Bodily Reactions

Much of the immediate discomfort of stress is caused by fight-or-flight emotional responses. The body is ready to act, with tight muscles and a pounding heart. If action is prevented, we merely remain "uptight." A sensible remedy is to learn a reliable, drug-free way to relax.

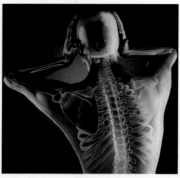

Bodily Reactions	Ineffective Behavior	Upsetting Thoughts
• Fight-or-flight response	• Too fast-paced	• Negative self-statements
• Tight muscles	• Too disorganized	• Fearful
• Pounding heart	• Too unbalanced	• Worried
• Shallow breathing	• Unrealistic	• Distracted
• Poor sleep	• Indecisive	• Obsessive
• Tiredness	• Avoidant	• Excessively body aware
• Stress-based illness	• Inefficient	• Health fears
• Poor digestion	• Aggressive	• Self-doubt

Figure 59.1

The effects of stress on body, behavior, and thought.

Exercise Stress-based arousal can be dissipated by using the body. Any full-body exercise can be effective. Our intrepid student, Mee Jung, enjoys karate. Swimming, dancing, jumping rope, yoga, most sports, and especially walking are valuable outlets. Regular exercise alters hormones, circulation, muscle tone, and several other aspects of physical functioning. Together, such changes can reduce anxiety and lower the risks for disease (Brannon, Feist, & Updegraff, 2014; Edenfield & Blumenthal, 2011).

Be sure to choose activities that are vigorous enough to relieve tension, yet enjoyable enough to be done repeatedly. Exercising for stress management is most effective when it is done daily. As little as 30 minutes of total exercise per day, even if it occurs in short 10- to 20-minute sessions, can improve mood and energy (Hansen, Stevens, & Coast, 2001).

Meditation Many stress counselors recommend meditation for quieting the body and promoting relaxation. Meditation is one of the most effective ways to relax (Sears & Kraus, 2009; Zeidan et al., 2010). Be aware that listening to or playing music, taking nature walks, enjoying hobbies, and the like can be meditative. Anything that reliably interrupts upsetting thoughts and promotes relaxation can be helpful. For now, it is enough to state that meditation is easy to learn—taking an expensive commercial course is unnecessary. To learn more about meditation and its effects, read Module 23.

Progressive Relaxation It is possible to relax systematically, completely, and by choice. The basic idea of **progressive relaxation** is to tighten all the muscles in a given area of your body (the arms, for instance) and then voluntarily relax them. By first tensing and relaxing each area of the body (also called the *tension-release method*), you can learn what muscle tension feels like. Then, when each area is relaxed, the change is more noticeable and more controllable. In this way, it is possible, with practice, to greatly reduce tension. To learn the details of how this is done, consult Module 67.

Guided Imagery In a technique called **guided imagery**, people visualize images that are calming, relaxing, or beneficial in other ways. Relaxation, for instance, can be promoted by visualizing peaceful scenes. Pick several places where you feel safe, calm, and at ease. Typical locations might be a beach or lake, the woods, floating on an air mattress in a warm pool, or lying in the sun at a quiet park. To relax, vividly imagine yourself in one of these locations. In the visualized scene, you should be alone and in a comfortable position. It is important to visualize the scene as realistically as possible. Try to feel, taste, smell, hear, and see what you would experience in the calming scene. Practice forming such images several times a day for about five minutes each time. When your scenes become familiar and detailed, they can be used to reduce anxiety and encourage relaxation. Remember, too, imagining that a supportive friend or a loving pet is nearby also can reduce tension and anxiety (Allen, Blascovich, & Mendes, 2002; Smith, Ruiz, & Uchino, 2004).

Modifying Ineffective Behavior

Stress is often made worse by our misguided responses to it. The following suggestions may help you deal with stress more effectively.

Slow Down Remember that stress can be self-generated. Try to deliberately do things at a slower pace—especially if your pace has speeded up over the years. Tell yourself, "What counts most is not if I get there first, but if I get there at all," or "My goal is distance, not speed."

Organize Disorganization creates stress. Try to take a fresh look at your situation and get organized. Setting priorities can be a real stress fighter. Ask yourself what's really important, and concentrate on the things that count. Learn to let go of trivial but upsetting irritations. And above all, when you are feeling stressed, remember to K.I.S.: **K**eep **I**t **S**imple. (Some people prefer K.I.S.S: Keep It Simple, Stupid.)

Strike a Balance Work, school, family, friends, interests, hobbies, recreation, community, church—a satisfying life has many important elements. Damaging stress often comes from letting one element—especially work or school—get blown out of proportion. Your goal should be quality in life, not quantity. Try to strike a balance between challenging "good stress" and relaxation. Remember, when you are "doing nothing," you are doing something very important: Set aside time for "me acts" such as loafing, browsing, puttering, playing, and napping.

Recognize and Accept Your Limits Many of us set unrealistic and perfectionist goals. Given that no one can ever be perfect, this attitude leaves many people feeling inadequate, no matter how well they have performed. Set gradual, achievable goals for yourself. Also, set realistic limits on what you try to do on any given day. Learn to say no to added demands or responsibilities.

Seek Social Support Social support—close, positive relationships with others—facilitates good health and morale (Ai et al., 2013; Winfree & Jiang, 2010). People with close, supportive relationships have better immune responses and better health (Smith, Ruiz, & Uchino, 2004; Taylor & Master, 2011). Apparently, support from family, friends, and even pets serves as a buffer to cushion the impact of stressful events (Allen, Blascovich, & Mendes, 2002).

Women tend to make better use of social support than men. Women who are stressed seek support and they nurture others. Men are more likely to become aggressive or to withdraw emotionally (Taylor, 2012). This may be why "manly men" won't ask for help, whereas women in trouble call their friends! Where stress is concerned, many men could benefit from adopting women's tendency to nurture and befriend others.

How else might social support help? Most people share positive events, such as marriages, births, graduations, and birthdays, with others. When things go well, we like to tell others. Sharing such events tends to amplify positive emotions and to further increase social support. In many ways, sharing good news is an important means by which positive events contribute to individual well-being (Gable et al., 2004).

Write about Your Feelings If you don't have someone you can talk to about stressful events, you might try expressing your thoughts and feelings in writing. Several studies have found that students who write about their upsetting experiences, thoughts, and feelings are better able to cope with stress. They also experience fewer illnesses, and they get better grades (Smyth & Pennebaker, 2008). Writing about your feelings tends to leave your mind clearer. This makes it easier to pay attention to life's challenges and come up with effective coping strategies. Thus, after you write about your feelings, it helps to make specific plans for coping with upsetting experiences (Klein & Boals, 2001; Smyth, Pennebaker, & Arigo, 2012).

As an alternative, you might want to try writing about positive experiences. In one study, college students who wrote about intensely positive experiences had fewer illnesses over the next three months. Writing just twenty minutes a day for three days improved the students' moods and had a surprisingly long-lasting effect on their health (Burton & King, 2004).

Counteract Upsetting Thoughts

Assume you are taking a test. Suddenly you realize that you are running short of time. If you say to yourself, "Oh no, this is terrible, I've blown it now," your body's response will probably be sweating, tenseness, and a knot in your stomach. On the other hand, if you say, "I should have watched the time, but getting upset won't help; I'll just take one question at a time," your stress level will be much lower.

As stated earlier, stress is greatly affected by the views we take of events. Physical symptoms and a tendency to make poor decisions are increased by negative thoughts or "self-talk." In many cases, what you say to yourself can mean the difference between coping and collapsing (Smith & Kirby, 2011).

Coping Statements Psychologist Donald Meichenbaum has popularized a technique called **stress inoculation**. In it, clients learn to fight fear and anxiety with an internal monologue

Stress management *The application of cognitive and behavioral strategies to reduce stress and improve coping skills.*
Progressive relaxation *A method for producing deep relaxation of all parts of the body.*
Guided imagery *Intentional visualization of images that are calming, relaxing, or beneficial in other ways.*
Social support *Close, positive relationships with other people.*
Stress inoculation *Use of positive coping statements to control fear and anxiety.*

of positive coping statements. First, clients learn to identify and monitor **negative self-statements**—self-critical thoughts that increase anxiety. Negative thoughts are a problem because they tend to directly elevate physical arousal. To counter this effect, clients learn to replace negative statements with coping statements from a supplied list. Eventually, they are encouraged to make their own lists (Meichenbaum, 2009).

How are coping statements applied? **Coping statements** are reassuring and self-enhancing. They are used to block out, or counteract, negative self-talk in stressful situations. Before giving a short speech, for instance, you would replace "I'm scared," "I can't do this," "My mind will go blank and I'll panic," or "I'll sound stupid and boring" with "I'll give my speech on something I like," or "I'll breathe deeply before I start my speech," or "My pounding heart just means I'm psyched up to do my best." Additional examples of coping statements follow.

Preparing for Stressful Situation

- I'll just take things one step at a time.
- If I get nervous, I'll just pause a moment.
- Tomorrow, I'll be through it.
- I've managed to do this before.
- What exactly do I have to do?

Confronting the Stressful Situation

- Relax now, this can't really hurt me.
- Stay organized, focus on the task.

- There's no hurry, take it step by step.
- Nobody's perfect, I'll just do my best.
- It will be over soon, just be calm.

Meichenbaum cautions that saying the "right" things to yourself may not be enough to improve stress tolerance. You must practice this approach in actual stress situations. Also, it is important to develop your own personal list of coping statements by finding what works for you. Ultimately, the value of learning this, and other stress-management skills, ties back into the idea that much stress is self-generated. Knowing that you can manage a demanding situation is in itself a major antidote for stress. In one study, college students who learned stress inoculation not only had less anxiety and depression but better self-esteem as well (Schiraldi & Brown, 2001).

Lighten Up Humor is worth cultivating as a way to reduce stress. A good sense of humor can lower your distress/stress reaction to difficult events (Morrison, 2012). In addition, an ability to laugh at life's ups and downs is associated with better immunity to disease (Earleywine, 2011). Don't be afraid to laugh at yourself and at the many ways we humans make things difficult for ourselves. You've probably heard the following advice about everyday stresses: "Don't sweat the small stuff" and "It's all small stuff." Humor is one of the best antidotes for anxiety and emotional distress because it helps put things into perspective (Crawford & Caltabiano, 2011; Kuiper & McHale, 2009). The vast majority of events are only as stressful as you allow them to be. Have some fun. It's perfectly healthy.

Negative self-statements *Self-critical thoughts that increase anxiety and lower performance.*
Coping statements *Reassuring, self-enhancing statements that are used to stop self-critical thinking.*

Module 59: Summary

59.1 What are the best strategies for managing stress?

- **59.1.1** Stress-management techniques focus on one of three areas: bodily effects, ineffective behavior, and upsetting thoughts.
- **59.1.2** All of the following are good ways to manage bodily reactions to stress: exercise, meditation, progressive relaxation, and guided imagery.

- **59.1.3** To minimize ineffective behavior when you are stressed, you can slow down, get organized, balance work and relaxation, accept your limits, seek social support, and write about your feelings.
- **59.1.4** Learning to use coping statements is a good way to combat upsetting thoughts.

Module 59: Knowledge Builder

Recite

1. Exercise, meditation, and progressive relaxation are considered effective ways to counter negative self-statements. ***T or F?***

2. A person using progressive relaxation for stress management is most likely trying to control which component of stress?
   - **a.** bodily reactions
   - **b.** upsetting thoughts
   - **c.** ineffective behavior
   - **d.** the primary appraisal

3. Research shows that social support from family and friends has little effect on the health consequences of stress. ***T or F?***

4. While taking a stressful classroom test, you say to yourself, "Stay organized, focus on the task." It's obvious that you are using
   - **a.** guided imagery
   - **b.** coping statements
   - **c.** LCUs
   - **d.** guided relaxation

Reflect

Think Critically

5. Steve always feels extremely pressured when the due date arrives for his major term papers. How could he reduce stress in such instances?

Self-Reflect

If you were going to put together a "tool kit" for stress management, what items would you include?

_____

ANSWERS

1. F 2. a 3. F 4. b 5. The stress associated with doing term papers can be almost completely eliminated by breaking up a long-term assignment into many small daily or weekly assignments (Anderson, 2010a; Ariely & Wertenbroch, 2002). Students who habitually procrastinate are often amazed at how pleasant college work can be once they renounce "brinkmanship" (pushing things off to the limits of tolerance).

Psychological Disorders: Normality and Psychopathology

One Can Short of a Six Pack

It can be amusing to hear or use phrases like "That guy is really wacko. His porch lights are dimming" or "The butter's sliding off his waffle. He's ready to go postal." Amusing or not, phrases like these offer little insight into what it means to be "crazy." To even draw the line between normal and psychopathological, we must weigh some complex issues.

Consider Ella. Her friends are worried. Two years ago, her husband of twenty-five years unexpectedly died of a heart attack right in front of her. She still dresses in black and spends much of her time missing him. She sits alone at home feeling profoundly depressed. Is she experiencing normal grief, or is a depression this long and deep a sign of mental illness?

Let's begin with some factors that affect judgments of normality before surveying some of the major disorders that psychologists and psychiatrists diagnose and treat.

Fotoduki/Shutterstock

Normality—What's Normal?

SURVEY QUESTION 60.1: How is abnormality defined?

The statistics are grim. The direct cost of treating people who seek help for mental illness is almost $60 billion a year. Add the indirect costs, such as lost earnings, and the total exceeds $315 billion a year. Hidden by the dollar signs is the immense human cost. More than a quarter of American adults suffer from a diagnosable mental disorder in any given year (Kessler, 2010; National Institute of Mental Health, 2013). In 2011, more than 38,000 Americans committed suicide (Hoyert & Xu, 2012). About 90 percent of them had a diagnosable mental disorder (National Institute of Mental Health, 2010a).

The scientific study of mental, emotional, and behavioral disorders is known as **psychopathology**. The term also refers to mental disorders themselves, such as schizophrenia or depression, and to behavior patterns that make people unhappy and impair their personal growth (Sue et al., 2013). Even though this definition may seem obvious, to seriously classify people as psychologically unhealthy raises complex and age-old issues (Luyten & Blatt, 2011). The conservative, churchgoing housewife down the street might be flagrantly psychotic and a lethal danger to her children. The reclusive eccentric who hangs out at the park could be the sanest person in town.

Let's begin with the idea of statistical abnormality, which some psychologists use to define normality more objectively. **Statistical abnormality** refers to scoring very high or low on some dimension, such as intelligence, anxiety, or depression. Anxiety, for example, is a feature of several psychological disorders. To measure it, we could create a test to learn how many people show low, medium, or high levels of anxiety. Usually, the results of such tests will form a *normal* (bell-shaped) *curve*. (*Normal* in this case refers only to the *shape* of the curve.) Notice that most people score near the middle of a normal curve; very few have extremely high or low scores (● **Figure 60.1**). A person who deviates from the average by being anxious all the time (high anxiety) might be abnormal. So, too, might a person who never feels anxiety.

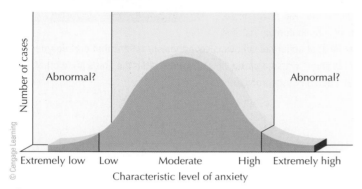

● **Figure 60.1**

The number of people displaying a personal characteristic may help define what is statistically abnormal.

Then, statistical abnormality tells us nothing about the meaning of deviations from the norm? Right. It is as statistically "abnormal" (unusual) for a person to score above 145 on an IQ test as it is to score below 55. However, only the lower score is regarded as "abnormal" or undesirable. In the same sense, it is unusual for a person to speak four languages or to win an event at the Olympics, but these are desirable, if rare, accomplishments.

Statistical definitions also can't tell us *where to draw the line* between normality and abnormality. For example, we could obtain the average frequency of sexual intercourse for persons of a particular age, sex, sexual orientation, and marital status. Clearly, a person who feels driven to have sex dozens of times a day has a problem. But as we move back toward the norm, we face the problem of drawing lines. How often does a normal behavior have to occur before it becomes abnormal? As you can see, statistical boundary lines tend to be somewhat arbitrary (Comer, 2013).

Another approach is to focus on the nonconformity that may be associated with some disorders. **Social nonconformity** refers to disobeying public standards for acceptable conduct.

Extreme nonconformity can lead to destructive, self-destructive, or illegal behavior. (Think, for instance, of a drug abuser or a prostitute.)

However, we must be careful to separate unhealthy nonconformity from creative lifestyles. Many eccentric "characters" are charming and emotionally stable. Note, too, that strictly following social norms is no guarantee of mental health. In some cases, psychopathology involves rigid conformity (see "Crazy for a Day").

Social nonconformity does not automatically indicate psychopathology.

Further, before we can even begin to judge a behavior as abnormal or nonconforming, we also must consider the *situational context* (social situation, behavioral setting, or general circumstances) in which it occurs. A young woman ties a thick rubber cord around her ankles, screams hysterically, and jumps headfirst off a bridge. Forty years ago, the woman's behavior might have seemed completely crazy. Today, it is a routine form of entertainment—bungee jumping. Is it abnormal to stand outside and water a lawn with a hose? It depends on whether it is raining. Is it nonconforming for a grown man to remove his pants and expose himself to another man or woman in a place of business? It depends on whether the other person is a bank clerk or a doctor.

Almost any imaginable behavior can be considered normal in some contexts. For example, in 2003, a man sawed off his own arm. Mind you, he was a mountain climber who had fallen into a crevasse, trapping his arm between two boulders. After five days of trying to free his arm, and nearing unconsciousness, he did what he needed to do to survive (Ralston, 2004).

As implied by our earlier discussion of social norms, culture is one of the most influential contexts in which any behavior

Psychopathology *The scientific study of mental, emotional, and behavioral disorders; also maladaptive behavior.*
Statistical abnormality *Abnormality defined on the basis of an extreme score on some dimension, such as IQ or anxiety.*
Social nonconformity *Failure to conform to societal norms or the usual minimum standards for social conduct.*

Discovering Psychology

Crazy for a Day

Performing a mildly abnormal behavior is a good way to get a sense of how social norms define "normality" in daily life. Here's your assignment: Do something strange in public and observe how people react to you. (Please don't do anything dangerous, harmful, or offensive—and don't get arrested!) Here are some deviant behaviors that other students have staged:

- Sit in the dining area of a fast-food restaurant and loudly carry on a conversation with an imaginary companion.
- Stand in a busy hallway on campus and adopt a kung fu stance. Remain in that position for 10 minutes.
- Walk around campus on a sunny day wearing a raincoat and carrying an open umbrella. Keep the umbrella over your head when you are inside buildings.
- Stick one finger in your nose and another in your ear. Walk through a busy shopping mall.

- Wear a *Planet of the Apes* mask for a day.

Mikeledray/Shutterstock

Does the idea of performing any of these actions make you uncomfortable? If so, you may not need to do anything more to appreciate how powerfully social norms constrain our actions. As we have noted, social nonconformity is just one facet of abnormal behavior. Nevertheless, actions that are regarded as "strange" within a particular culture are often the first sign to others that a person has a problem.

---

is judged (Fabrega, 2004; Whitbourne & Halgin, 2013). In some cultures, it is considered normal to defecate or urinate in public or to appear naked in public. In our culture, such behaviors would be considered unusual or abnormal. In some Muslim cultures, women who remain completely housebound are considered normal or even virtuous. In some Western cultures, they might be diagnosed as suffering from a disorder called agoraphobia. (Agoraphobia is described in Module 63.)

Thus, *cultural relativity* (the idea that judgments are made relative to the values of one's culture) can affect the diagnosis of psychological disorders. Still, *all* cultures classify people as abnormal if they fail to communicate with others or are consistently unpredictable in their actions.

Yet another approach is to characterize psychopathology by *subjective discomfort* (private feelings of pain, unhappiness, or emotional distress).

But couldn't a person experience serious distress without psychopathology, and couldn't someone be seriously disturbed without feeling discomfort? Yes on both counts. People who have, for example, lost a loved one, like Ella, or lived through a natural disaster like a hurricane normally take some time to overcome their distress. Also, psychopathology doesn't always cause personal anguish. A person suffering from mania might feel elated and "on top of the world." A *lack* of discomfort may actually reveal a problem.

For example, if you showed no signs of grief or distress after the violent death of a close friend, we might suspect psychopathology. In practice, though, subjective discomfort explains most instances in which people voluntarily seek professional help.

Core Feature of Disordered Behavior

If abnormality is so hard to define, how are judgments of psychopathology made? Although the standards we have discussed thus far are *relative,* psychopathological behavior does have a core feature: It is maladaptive. Rather than helping people cope successfully, maladaptive behavior arises from an underlying psychological or biological dysfunction that makes it more difficult for them to meet the demands of day-to-day life (American Psychiatric Association, 2013). Maladaptive behavior most often results in serious psychological discomfort, disability, and/or *loss of control* of thoughts, behaviors, or feelings.

For example, gambling is not a problem if people bet for entertainment and can maintain self-control. However, compulsive gambling is a sign of psychopathology. Hearing uncontrollable voices is a prime example of what it means to lose control of one's thoughts. In the most extreme cases, people become a danger to themselves or others, which is clearly maladaptive (Bennett, 2011).

In practice, deciding that a person needs help usually occurs when the person *does something* (assaults a person, hallucinates, stares into space, collects too many old pizza cartons, and so forth) that *annoys* or *gains the attention* of a person in a *position of power* in the person's life (an employer, teacher, parent, spouse, or the person himself or herself). That person then does something about it. The person may voluntarily seek help, the person may be urged to see a psychologist, a police officer may be called, or a relative may start commitment proceedings.

Legal Insanity and the Insanity Defense

What are commitment proceedings? Commitment proceedings are legal proceedings that may result in the finding of **insanity**, which is a legal, not a psychological, term (Fuller, 2012). It refers to an inability to manage one's affairs or foresee the consequences of one's actions. People who are declared insane are not legally responsible for their actions. If necessary, they can be involuntarily committed to a mental hospital.

Legally, insanity is established by testimony from *expert witnesses* (psychologists and psychiatrists) recognized by a court of law as qualified to give opinions on a specific topic. Involuntary commitments happen most often when people are brought to emergency rooms or are arrested for committing a crime. People who are involuntarily committed are usually judged to be a danger to themselves or to others, or they are severely intellectually disabled.

What is the insanity defense? Someone accused of a crime may argue that he or she is *not guilty by reason of insanity*. In practice, this means that the accused, due to a diagnosable psychological disorder, was unable to realize that what he or she did was wrong (Gowensmith, Murrie, & Boccaccini, 2013). This may be distinguished from *not guilty by reason of diminished responsibility*, which is more likely to apply in other situations, such as cases of intellectual disability, like autism or brain damage.

You may be surprised to learn that being diagnosed with a psychological disorder does not automatically imply a successful insanity defense. For example, someone diagnosed with, say, an anxiety disorder who commits murder might nevertheless be well aware that murder is against the law. In fact, very few criminal trials end with this verdict (Fuller, 2012; Martin & Weiss, 2010).

Classifying Mental Disorders—Problems by the Book

SURVEY QUESTION 60.2: What are the major psychological disorders?

Psychological problems are classified by using the most recent version of the *DSM*, the *Diagnostic and Statistical Manual of Mental Disorders (5th Edition)* (American Psychiatric Association, 2013). The *DSM-5* influences most activities in mental health settings—from diagnosis to therapy to insurance company billing (American Psychiatric Association, 2013).

A **mental disorder** is a significant impairment in psychological functioning. If you were to glance through the *DSM-5*, you would see many disorders described. It's impossible here to discuss all these problems; however, a simplified list of the major types of *DSM-5* disorders can be found in ● **Table 60.1**. Those disorders are described in the next section.

An Overview of Psychological Disorders

As even a quick scan of the *DSM-5* makes clear, a wide variety of psychological disorders are currently diagnosed and treated. Various forms of damage to the nervous system can result in various forms of psychopathology. Problems arising before adulthood, such as *autism*, are termed **neurodevelopmental disorders**, whereas problems not arising until adulthood, such as *Alzheimer's disease*, are termed **neurocognitive disorders**.

Maladaptive behavior *Behavior arising from an underlying psychological or biological dysfunction that makes it difficult to adapt to the environment and meet the demands of day-to-day life.*
Insanity *A legal term that refers to a mental inability to manage one's affairs or to be aware of the consequences of one's actions.*
Mental disorder *A significant impairment in psychological functioning.*
Neurodevelopmental disorders *Psychopathologies due to various forms of damage to the nervous system arising before adulthood.*
Neurocognitive disorders *Psychopathologies due to various forms of damage to the nervous system not arising until adulthood.*

TABLE 60.1   Major *DSM-5* Categories of Psychopathology

Problem	Primary Symptom	Typical Signs of Trouble	Examples
Neurodevelopmental Disorders	Impairment of nervous system development before adulthood	You have intellectual, communication, attentional, or motor problems that emerge early in your life.	Intellectual developmental disorder, Autism spectrum disorder, Attention deficit/hyperactivity disorder, Tourette's disorder
Schizophrenia spectrum and other psychotic disorders	Loss of contact with reality	You hear or see things that others don't; your mind has been playing tricks on you.	Delusional disorder, Brief psychotic disorder, Schizophrenia
Bipolar and related disorders	Alternating mania and depression	You feel depressed; or you talk too loud and too fast and have a rush of ideas and feelings that others think are unreasonable.	Bipolar I disorder, Bipolar II disorder, Cyclothymic disorder
Depressive disorders	Depression	You feel sad and hopeless.	Major depressive disorder, Persistent depressive disorder (dysthymia)
Anxiety disorders	High anxiety or anxiety-related distortions of behavior	You have anxiety attacks and feel like you are going to die; or you are afraid to do things that most people can do.	Specific phobia, Social phobia, Panic disorder, Agoraphobia, Generalized anxiety disorder
Obsessive-compulsive and related disorders	Unnecessarily repetitious behavior	You spend unusual amounts of time doing things like washing your hands or counting your heartbeats.	Obsessive compulsive disorder, Hoarding disorder, Trichotillomania (hair-pulling disorder)
Trauma- and stressor-related disorders	Difficulty dealing with a traumatic or stressful event	You persistently reexperience a traumatic event; you have an exceptionally strong negative reaction to a traumatic event such as becoming highly anxious, depressed, or being unable to sleep.	Posttraumatic stress disorder, Acute stress disorder, Adjustment disorder
Dissociative disorders	Amnesia, feelings of unreality, multiple identities	There are major gaps in your memory of events; you feel like you are a robot or a stranger to yourself; others tell you that you have done things that you don't remember doing.	Dissociative identity disorder, Dissociative amnesia, Depersonalization/derealization disorder
Somatic symptom disorders	Body complaints without an organic (physical) basis	You feel physically sick, but your doctor says nothing is wrong with you; you suffer from pain that has no physical basis; or you are preoccupied with thoughts about being sick.	Somatic symptom disorder, Conversion disorder, Factitious disorder

TABLE 60.1   Major *DSM-5* Categories of Psychopathology (*Continued*)

Problem	Primary Symptom	Typical Signs of Trouble	Examples
Feeding and eating disorders	Disturbance of food intake into the body	You eat nonfood items (pica) or have difficulty eating enough food to remain healthy.	Pica, Anorexia nervosa, Bulimia nervosa
Elimination disorders	Disturbance of waste elimination from the body	You have trouble controlling the elimination of urine (enuresis) or feces (encopresis).	Enuresis, Encopresis
Sleep–wake disorders	Troubles falling asleep, staying asleep, or waking up.	You have difficulty getting a healthy night's sleep; you snore, have nightmares, or fall asleep inappropriately (narcolepsy).	Insomnia disorder, Hypersomnolence disorder, Narcolepsy, Nightmare disorder
Sexual dysfunctions	Problems in sexual adjustment	You have problems with sexual desire, arousal, or performance.	Erectile disorder, Female sexual interest/arousal disorder, Genito-pelvic pain/penetration disorder, Male hypoactive sexual desire disorder
Gender dysphoria	Disturbed gender identity	You feel that you are a man trapped in a woman's body (or the reverse).	Gender dysphoria
Disruptive, impulse control and conduct disorders	Difficulties of self-control	You are defiant and aggressive; you set fires (pyromania) or are a chronic thief (kleptomania).	Oppositional defiant disorder, Conduct disorder, Pyromania, Kleptomania,
Substance use and addictive disorders	Disturbances related to drug abuse or dependence as well as other addictive behaviors	You have been drinking too much, using illegal drugs, taking prescription drugs more often than you should, or gambling too much.	Opioid-related disorders, Stimulant-related disorders, Gambling disorder
Neurocognitive disorders	Impairment of nervous system development while in adulthood	Your ability to think and remember has suffered a dramatic decline in adulthood.	Delirium, Neurocognitive disorder due to Alzheimer's disease, Neurocognitive disorder due to Parkinson's disease, Neurocognitive disorder due to HIV Infection
Personality disorders	Unhealthy personality patterns	Your behavior patterns repeatedly cause problems at work, at school, and in your relationships with others.	Antisocial personality disorder, Borderline personality disorder
Paraphilic disorders	Deviant sexual behavior	You can gain sexual satisfaction only by engaging in highly atypical sexual behavior.	Voyeuristic disorder, Exhibitionistic disorder, Pedophilic disorder, Fetishistic disorder

Source: American Psychiatric Association (2013).

People suffering from **schizophrenia spectrum and other psychotic disorders** have "retreated from reality"—that is, they suffer from hallucinations and delusions and are socially withdrawn. Psychotic disorders are severely disabling and often lead to hospitalization. Typically, psychotic patients cannot control their thoughts and actions. Psychotic symptoms occur in *schizophrenia, delusional disorders,* and even in some *mood disorders.*

Mood disorders are defined primarily by the presence of extreme, intense, and long-lasting emotions. When the mood is one of deep *depression,* one of the **depressive disorders** is involved. When depression alternates with periods of *mania,* meaning the person is agitated, elated, and hyperactive, one of the **bipolar and related disorders** is involved (Ellison-Wright & Bullmore, 2010).

Anxiety-related disorders are marked by fear or anxiety and by distorted behavior. Particular **anxiety disorders** involve feelings of *panic.* Others take the form of *phobias* (irrational fears) or just overwhelming anxiety and nervousness. The **obsessive-compulsive and related disorders** involve extreme preoccupations with certain thoughts and compulsive performance of certain behaviors. **Trauma- and stressor-related disorders** are behavior patterns also associated with high anxiety brought on by experiencing traumatic stresses. A person with one of the **dissociative disorders** may have temporary amnesia or multiple personalities. Also included in this category are frightening episodes of depersonalization, in which people feel like they are outside their bodies, are behaving like robots, or are lost in a dream world. **Somatic symptom and related disorders** occur when a person has physical symptoms that mimic disease or injury (e.g., paralysis, blindness, illness, chronic pain) for which there is no identifiable physical cause. In such cases, psychological factors appear to explain the symptoms.

Personality disorders are deeply ingrained, unhealthy personality patterns. Such patterns usually appear in adolescence and continue through much of adult life. They include paranoid (overly suspicious), narcissistic (overly self-loving), dependent, borderline, and antisocial personality types as well as others.

Disorders of the digestive system include **feeding and eating disorders** like *anorexia nervosa,* a life-threatening failure to maintain sufficient body weight (see Module 43), and **elimination disorders** like *enuresis,* which is difficulty controlling urination.

Sleep–wake disorders include difficulties falling asleep, staying asleep, and/or waking up (see Module 24).

Disorders of human sexuality include any of a wide range of difficulties with sexual adjustment, gender identity, or deviant sexual behavior. **Sexual dysfunctions** include problems in sexual desire, arousal, or response (see Module 49). **Gender dysphoria** is said to occur when gender identity does not match a person's physical sex, and the person may seek a sex-change operation (see Module 47). Deviations in sexual behavior known as **paraphilic disorders** include pedophilia, exhibitionism, fetishism, voyeurism, and so on (see Module 48).

Disruptive, impulse control, and conduct disorders usually involve difficulties of self-control, such as *oppositional-defiant disorder* or *pyromania* (setting of fires).

Substance-related disorders involve abuse of, or dependence on, psychoactive drugs. Typical culprits include alcohol, barbiturates, opiates, cocaine, amphetamines, hallucinogens, marijuana, and nicotine. A person with a substance-related disorder cannot stop using the drug and also may suffer from withdrawal symptoms, delirium, amnesia, psychosis, emotional outbursts, sexual problems, and sleep disturbances. (Problems with drug abuse and dependence are discussed in Module 25.)

In addition to the formal mental disorders we have reviewed, many cultures have names for "unofficial" psychological "disorders." See "Running Amok with Cultural Maladies" for some examples.

Comorbidity

Many disturbed people are **comorbid**—that is, they suffer from more than one mental disorder at the same time. One way comorbidity develops is when a *primary* problem causes *secondary* problems. For example, someone like Ella, experiencing a prolonged and deep depression, might turn to drugs, legal or otherwise, for treatment and become addicted, complicating the primary disorder with a secondary, substance-related disorder (Fenton et al., 2012).

According to sociologist Ronald Kessler, comorbidity is quite common; more than 40 percent of all people with mental disorders are comorbid (Kessler, 2010). Not only does comorbidity increase these people's misery it also makes it much more difficult for health care providers to diagnose and treat them.

Human Diversity

Running Amok with Cultural Maladies

Every culture recognizes the existence of psychopathology, and most have at least a few folk names for afflictions you won't find in the *DSM-5*. Here are some examples of *culture-bound syndromes* from around the world (Durand & Barlow, 2013; López & Guarnaccia, 2000; Teo & Gaw, 2010):

- **Amok:** Men in Malaysia, Laos, the Philippines, and Polynesia who believe they have been insulted are sometimes known to go *amok*. After a period of brooding, they erupt into an outburst of violent, aggressive, or homicidal behavior randomly directed at people and objects.

- **Susto:** Among Latin Americans, the symptoms of *susto* include insomnia, irritability, phobias, and an increase in sweating and heart rate. Susto can result if someone is badly frightened by a black magic curse. In extreme cases, *voodoo death* can result because the person is literally scared to death.

- **Ghost sickness:** Among many Native American tribes, people who become preoccupied with death and the deceased are said to suffer from *ghost sickness*. The symptoms of ghost sickness include bad dreams, weakness, loss of appetite, fainting, dizziness, fear, anxiety, hallucinations, loss of consciousness, confusion, feelings of futility, and a sense of suffocation.

- **Koro:** In South Asia and East Asia, a man may experience sudden and intense anxiety that his penis (or, in females, the vulva and nipples) will recede into the body. In addition to the terror this incites, victims also believe that advanced cases of *koro* can cause death. A similar fear of shrinking genitals has also been reported from West Africa (Dzokoto & Adams, 2005).

- **Hikikomori:** In Japanese society, adolescents or young adults who refuse to leave their parents' homes for months at a time are experiencing an extreme form of social withdrawal called *hikikomori*.

It is clear that people everywhere have a need to label and categorize troubled behavior. With some cultural sensitivity, it is often possible to understand these unusual experiences (Flaskerud, 2009). Regardless, the terms listed here provide little guidance about the true nature of a person's problems or the best ways to treat them. That's why the *DSM-5* is based on empirical data and clinical observations. Otherwise, psychologists and psychiatrists would be no better than folk healers when making diagnoses (Ancis, Chen, & Schultz, 2004).

By the way, culture-bound syndromes occur in all societies. For example, American psychologists Pamela Keel and Kelly Klump believe that the eating disorder bulimia is primarily a syndrome of Western cultures like the United States (Keel & Klump, 2003).

The Fluidity of Psychiatric Diagnosis

You might be surprised to learn that definitions of mental disorders change over time. For example, when the *DSM-I* was first published in 1952, *neurosis* was included. The term was dropped in later editions because it is too imprecise. Even though *neurosis* is an outdated term, you may still hear it used to loosely refer to problems involving excessive anxiety. Similarly, *homosexuality* was omitted as a diagnosis in 1974.

Published in 2013, the *DSM-5* reflects updated research (American Psychiatric Association, 2013; Birgegård, Norring, & Clinton, 2012). Regardless, the process leading up to publication of the *DSM-5* was controversial and full of disagreement (Frances, 2012; Marecek & Gavey, 2013). Perhaps the most important and certainly the most contentious change has been the proliferation of diagnoses. The original *DSM* contained about 100 diagnoses; today, it contains over 350. Critics charge that more and more "normal" people are being diagnosed as "mentally ill" (Frances, 2012; Lane, 2009). For example,

Schizophrenia spectrum and other psychotic disorders *Severe mental disorders characterized by a retreat from reality, by hallucinations and delusions, and by social withdrawal.*

Depressive disorders *Major mood disturbances involving deep depression.*

Bipolar and related disorders *Major mood disturbances in which depression alternates with periods of mania, meaning the person is agitated, elated, and hyperactive.*

Anxiety disorders *Disruptive feelings of fear, apprehension, or anxiety, or distortions in behavior that are directly anxiety related.*

Obsessive-compulsive and related disorders *Extreme preoccupations with certain thoughts and compulsive performance of certain behaviors.*

Trauma- and stressor-related disorders *Behavior patterns brought on by traumatic stresses.*

Dissociative disorders *Temporary amnesia, multiple personality, or depersonalization.*

Somatic symptom and related disorders *Physical symptoms that mimic disease or injury (e.g., paralysis, blindness, illness, chronic pain) for which there is no identifiable physical cause.*

Personality disorders *Maladaptive personality patterns.*

Feeding and eating disorders *Difficulty managing food intake such as a life-threatening failure to maintain sufficient body weight.*

attention deficit hyperactivity disorder was not a diagnosis in the original *DSM*. Since its inclusion, it has become one of the most widely diagnosed disorders among young boys, prompting critics to decry the diagnosis as "pathologizing boyhood" (Bruchmüller, Margraf, & Schneider, 2012).

A related concern is that diagnoses are getting easier and easier to apply. For example, changes to the *DSM-5* make it easier to diagnose someone like Ella, who lost her husband, as suffering from *major depressive disorder* rather than grief (Frances, 2012).

At the same time, some changes are more widely accepted. For example, after considerable debate, the now-outdated term *gender identity disorder* appears in the *DSM-5* as *gender dysphoria* (American Psychiatric Association, 2012; De Cuypere, Knudson, & Bockting, 2011). Opponents of the old terminology argued that many people whose physical sex does not match their gender identity are well adjusted and should not be labeled as "disordered" (Hein & Berger, 2012). The new diagnosis reflects this because it applies only to individuals who are deeply troubled by their gender variance.

Each of the problems listed in the *DSM* can seriously disrupt a person's life, so perhaps they *should* be part of the *DSM*. It is hoped that the changes in the *DSM-5* will lead to better diagnosis and treatment for those of us who need help.

General Risk Factors

What causes psychological disorders like those listed in Table 60.1? Here are some general risk factors that contribute to psychopathology:

- **Biological/organic factors:** Genetic defects or inherited vulnerabilities, poor prenatal care, very low birth weight, chronic physical illness or disability, exposure to toxic chemicals or drugs, head injuries (● **Figure 60.2**)
- **Psychological factors:** Stress, low intelligence, learning disorders, lack of control or mastery
- **Family factors:** Parents who are immature, mentally disturbed, criminal, or abusive; severe marital strife; extremely poor child discipline; disordered family communication patterns
- **Social conditions:** Poverty, stressful living conditions, homelessness, social disorganization, overcrowding

Before we explore some specific disorders and their causes, let's take a detour into the issues involved in psychiatric labeling.

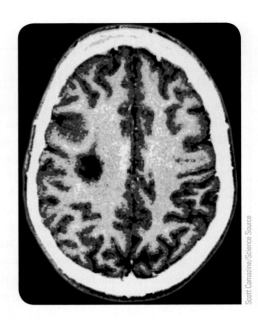

Scott Camazine/Science Source

● **Figure 60.2**

This MRI scan of a human brain (viewed from the top) reveals a tumor (dark spot). Mental disorders sometimes have organic causes of this sort. However, in many instances, no obvious organic damage can be found.

Disorders in Perspective—Psychiatric Labeling

SURVEY QUESTION 60.3: How can psychiatric labeling be misused?

The terms we encounter in this module are meant to aid communication about human problems. But if used maliciously or carelessly, they can hurt people. (See "A Disease Called Freedom.") Everyone has felt or acted "crazy" during brief periods of stress or high emotion. People with psychological disorders have problems that are more severe or long lasting than most of us experience. Otherwise, they may not be that different from the rest of us.

A fascinating classic study carried out by psychologist David Rosenhan illustrates the impact of psychiatric labeling. Rosenhan and several colleagues had themselves committed to mental hospitals with a diagnosis of "schizophrenia" (Rosenhan, 1973). After being admitted, each of these "pseudopatients" dropped all pretense of mental illness. Yet, even though they acted completely normal, none of the researchers was ever recognized by hospital *staff* as a phony patient.

Human Diversity

A Disease Called Freedom

The year is 1840. You are a slave who has tried repeatedly to escape from a cruel and abusive master. You want to be free. An expert is consulted about your "abnormal" behavior. His conclusion? You are suffering from "drapetomania," a mental "disorder" that causes slaves to run away (Wakefield, 1992). Your "cure"? The expert cuts off your toes.

As this example suggests, psychiatric terms are easily abused. Historically, some have been applied to culturally disapproved behaviors that are not disorders. Another of our personal favorites is the long-outdated diagnosis of "anarchia," a form of insanity that leads one to seek a more democratic society (Brown, 1990).

All of the following were once considered disorders: childhood masturbation, lack of vaginal orgasm, self-defeating personality (applied mainly to women), homosexuality, and nymphomania (a woman with a healthy sexual appetite) (Wakefield, 1992). Even today, race, gender, and social class continue to affect the diagnosis of various disorders (Mizock & Harkins, 2011; Poland & Caplan, 2004).

Gender is probably the most common source of bias in judging normality because standards tend to be based on males (Fine, 2010; Nolen-Hoeksema, 2011). According to psychologist Paula Caplan, women are penalized both for conforming to female stereotypes and for ignoring them. If a woman is independent, aggressive, and unemotional, she may be considered "unhealthy." Yet at the same time, a woman who is vain, emotional, irrational, and dependent on others (all "feminine" traits in our culture) may be classified as having a personality disorder. Indeed, a majority of persons classified as having dependent personality disorder are women. In view of this, Paula Caplan asks, why isn't there a category called "delusional dominating personality disorder" for obnoxious men (Caplan, 1995)?

Because biases can influence perceptions of disorder and normality, it is worth being cautious before you leap to conclusions about or label the mental health of others (American Psychiatric Association, 2013). (*Ape-mask-wearing disorder*? They might be doing an assignment for their psychology class!)

Real patients were not so easily fooled: It was not unusual for a patient to say to one of the researchers, "You're not crazy, you're checking up on the hospital!" or "You're a journalist."

To record his observations, Rosenhan took notes by carefully jotting things on a small piece of paper hidden in his hand. However, he soon learned that stealth was totally unnecessary. Rosenhan simply walked around with a clipboard, recording observations. No one questioned this behavior. Rosenhan's note-taking was just regarded as another symptom of his "illness." This observation clarifies why staff members failed to detect the fake patients. Because they were in a mental ward and because they had been *labeled* schizophrenic, anything the pseudopatients did was seen as a symptom of psychopathology.

As Rosenhan's study implies, it is better to label *problems* than to label people. Think of the difference in impact between saying, "You are experiencing a serious psychological disorder" and "You're a schizophrenic." Which statement would you prefer to have said about yourself?

Social Stigma

An added problem with psychiatric labeling is that it frequently leads to prejudice and discrimination—that is, the mentally ill in our culture are often *stigmatized* (rejected and disgraced). People who have been labeled mentally ill (at any time in their lives) are less likely to be hired. They also tend to be denied housing and are more likely to be falsely accused of crimes. Sadly, the fear of stigmatization, including self-stigmatization, is one major reason many people do not seek help for their mental illness (Mojtabai et al., 2011). Thus, people who are grappling with mental illness may be harmed by social stigma as well as by their immediate psychological problems (Elkington et al., 2012).

Elimination disorders *Difficulty managing the elimination of bodily wastes, for example, difficulty controlling urination.*
Sleep–wake disorders *Difficulties falling asleep, staying asleep, and/or waking up, such as insomnia disorder.*
Sexual dysfunctions *Problems with sexual desire, arousal, or response.*
Gender dysphoria *Distress that may occur when gender identity does not match a person's physical sex.*
Paraphilic disorders *Deviations in sexual behavior such as pedophilia, exhibitionism, fetishism, voyeurism, and so on.*
Disruptive, impulse control, and conduct disorders *Difficulties of self-control, such as oppositional-defiant disorder or pyromania (setting of fires).*
Substance-related disorders *Abuse of or dependence on a mood- or behavior-altering drug.*
Comorbidity (in mental disorders) *The simultaneous presence in a person of two or more mental disorders.*

An Important Note—You're Okay, Really! We hope that you have not already fallen prey to "medical student's disease." Medical students, it seems, have a predictable tendency to notice in themselves the symptoms of each dreaded disease they study. As a psychology student, you may notice what seem to be abnormal tendencies in your own behavior. If so, don't panic. In most instances, this only shows that pathological behavior is an *exaggeration* of normal defenses and reactions, not that your behavior is abnormal. Keep this in mind as you read the next four modules, where we explore some disorders in more detail, beginning with psychotic disorders. Regardless, before we go on, here's a study break to help you diagnose your grasp of psychopathology.

Module 60: Summary

60.1 How is abnormality defined?

- **60.1.1** *Psychopathology* refers to the scientific study of mental disorders and to maladaptive behavior.
- **60.1.2** Factors that typically affect judgments of abnormality include statistical abnormality, nonconformity, context, culture, and subjective discomfort.
- **60.1.3** The key element in judgments of disorder is that a person's behavior is maladaptive. The result is usually serious psychological discomfort or disability and loss of control.
- **60.1.4** *Insanity* is a legal term defining whether a person may be held responsible for his or her actions. Insanity is determined in court on the basis of testimony by expert witnesses.

60.2 What are the major psychological disorders?

- **60.2.1** Psychological problems are classified by using the *Diagnostic and Statistical Manual of Mental Disorders (5th Edition)* (*DSM-5*).
- **60.2.2** Culture-bound syndromes are not found in the *DSM-5* and are unique to every culture.
- **60.2.3** General risk factors that contribute to psychopathology include biological/organic factors, psychological factors, family factors, and social conditions.

60.3 How can psychiatric labeling be misused?

- **60.3.1** Psychiatric labels can be misused to harm and stigmatize people.

Module 60: Knowledge Builder

Recite

1. The core feature of abnormal behavior is that it is
   - **a.** statistically unusual
   - **b.** maladaptive
   - **c.** socially nonconforming
   - **d.** a source of subjective discomfort

2. One of the most powerful contexts in which judgments of normality and abnormality are made is
   - **a.** the family
   - **b.** occupational settings
   - **c.** religious systems
   - **d.** culture

3. Which of the following is a *legal* concept?
   - **a.** neurosis
   - **b.** psychosis
   - **c.** drapetomania
   - **d.** insanity

4. People are said to have "retreated from reality" when they suffer from
   - **a.** psychotic disorders
   - **b.** mood disorders
   - **c.** somatic symptom disorders
   - **d.** personality disorders

5. Amnesia, multiple identities, and depersonalization are possible problems in
   - **a.** mood disorders
   - **b.** somatic symptom disorders
   - **c.** psychosis
   - **d.** dissociative disorders

6. Someone who engages in one of the paraphilias has what type of disorder?
   - **a.** dissociative
   - **b.** somatic symptom
   - **c.** substance
   - **d.** sexual

7. *Comorbidity* is said to occur when a person suffers from

   _____.

Reflect

Think Critically

8. Many states began to restrict use of the insanity defense after John Hinkley, Jr., who tried to murder former President Ronald Reagan, was acquitted by reason of insanity. What does this trend reveal about insanity?

Self-Reflect

Think of an instance of abnormal behavior you have witnessed. By what formal standards would the behavior be regarded as abnormal? In every society? Was the behavior maladaptive in any way?

How are the mentally ill stigmatized in movies and television dramas? Can you think of any positive portrayals (such as the film *A Beautiful Mind*)? How do you think such portrayals affect attitudes about mental disorders?

ANSWERS

1. b 2. d 3. d 4. a 5. d 6. d 7. more than one disorder 8. It emphasizes that insanity is a legal concept, not a psychiatric diagnosis. Laws reflect community standards. When those standards change, lawmakers may seek to alter definitions of legal responsibility.

CENGAGE brain.com

Go to **cengagebrain.com** to access **MindTap for Coon/Mitterer** *Psychology Modules for Active Learning* and other online learning tools. MindTap is a fully online learning experience that combines all the tools you need—readings, multimedia, activities, and assessments—into a singular personalized Learning Path that guides you through the course.

Psychological Disorders: Psychosis, Delusional Disorders, and Schizophrenia

Dark Side of the Moon

Imagine that someone you know (Floyd?) has been hearing voices, has covered his head with aluminum foil, and believes that houseflies are speaking to him in code. He talks very strangely; recently he commented "When you do the 25 of time, it means that you leave the house 25 before Syd comes to mail a package so they can wish you quiet desperation . . . and they know where you're going. They are animals. Wish you were here."

If you observed such symptoms, would you be concerned? Of course you would, and rightly so. Psychotic disorders, which usually involve a break with reality, are among the most serious of all mental problems. They also are among the most difficult to treat. Drug therapies offer some hope; however, many psychotic individuals end up in prison or committed to a mental hospital.

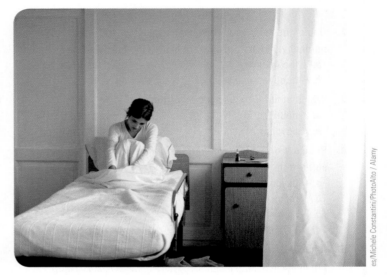

es/Michele Constantini/PhotoAlto / Alamy

Let's take a look at the general characteristics and major types of the psychotic disorders.

SURVEY QUESTIONS

61.1 What are the general characteristics of psychotic disorders?

61.2 What is the nature of a delusional disorder?

61.3 What is schizophrenia and what causes it?

Psychotic Disorders— Loss of Contact

SURVEY QUESTION 61.1: What are the general characteristics of psychotic disorders?

A person who is psychotic undergoes striking changes in thinking, behavior, and emotion. Basic to all these changes is the fact that **psychosis** (psychosis, singular; psychoses, plural) reflects a loss of contact with shared views of reality (Durand & Barlow, 2013.)

What are the major symptoms of psychotic disorders? You might find it helpful to distinguish between *positive* and *negative symptoms* (Rollins et al., 2010).

Positive symptoms, such as delusions and hallucinations, are excesses or exaggerations compared to normal behavior. People who suffer from **delusions** hold exaggerated false beliefs that they insist are true, regardless of how much the facts contradict them. An example is a 34-year-old woman who was convinced she would become "President of the United States of the World" (Mendelson & Goes, 2011). Some common types of delusions are: (1) *depressive* delusions, in which people feel that they have committed horrible crimes or sinful deeds, (2) *somatic* delusions, in which people believe their

TABLE 61.1	*DSM-5* Classification of Psychotic Disorders
Problem	**Typical Signs of Trouble**
Neurocognitive Disorders	
Alzheimer's Disease	You slowly lose the ability to think clearly and remember.
Schizophrenia Spectrum and Other Psychotic Disorders	
Delusional Disorder	You have some deeply held and bizarre but false beliefs.
Schizophrenia	Your personality has disintegrated; you have hallucinations and/or delusions.
Catatonia	You remain mute while holding odd postures for hours or even days at a time.

Sources: American Psychiatric Association (2013); Durand & Barlow (2013).

bodies are "rotting away" or emitting foul odors, (3) delusions of *grandeur*, in which people think they are extremely important, (4) delusions of *influence*, in which people feel they are being controlled or influenced by others or by unseen forces, (5) delusions of *persecution*, in which people believe that others are "out to get them," and (6) delusions of *reference*, in which people give great personal meaning to unrelated events (Kearney & Trull, 2012).

Hallucinations are imaginary sensations, such as seeing, hearing, or smelling things that don't exist in the real world. The most common psychotic hallucination is hearing voices. Sometimes these voices command patients to hurt themselves. Unfortunately, sometimes people obey (Barrowcliff & Haddock, 2006). More rarely, psychotic people may feel "insects crawling under their skin," taste "poisons" in their food, or smell "gas" their "enemies" are using to "get" them. Sensory changes, such as anesthesia (numbness, or a loss of sensation) or extreme sensitivity to heat, cold, pain, or touch also can occur.

In contrast, *negative symptoms* are absences or deficiencies compared to normal behavior. During a psychotic episode, emotions are often severely disturbed. For instance, the psychotic person may be wildly elated or hyperemotional. But sometimes, psychotic patients may be depressed or apathetic and display a lack of emotion, or *flat affect*, a condition in which the face is frozen in a blank expression. Brain images from psychotic patients with "frozen faces" reveal that their brains process emotions abnormally (Lepage et al., 2011).

Similarly, a reduced capacity to communicate verbally is a nearly universal symptom of psychosis. In fact, psychotic speech can be so garbled and chaotic that it sometimes sounds like a "word salad." For this reason, psychotic symptoms are sometimes thought of as a primitive type of communication— that is, many patients may be using their actions to say "I need help" or "I can't handle it anymore."

Major disturbances such as those just described—as well as added problems with thinking, memory, and attention—bring about personality disintegration and a break with reality. *Personality disintegration* occurs when a person's thoughts, actions, and emotions are no longer coordinated. When psychotic disturbances and a fragmented personality are evident for weeks or months, the person has suffered a psychosis (American Psychiatric Association, 2013; Sue et al., 2013) (● Table 61.1).

Neurocognitive Disorders

In a sense, all psychoses (and most, if not all, other mental illnesses) are partly organic—that is, they involve physical changes in the brain. But some psychoses are directly caused

Psychosis *A withdrawal from reality marked by hallucinations and delusions, disturbed thoughts and emotions, and personality disorganization.*
Delusion *A false belief held against all contrary evidence.*
Hallucination *An imaginary sensation, such as seeing, hearing, or smelling things that don't exist in the real world.*

by physical damage to the brain. For example, poisoning by lead or mercury can damage the brain, causing intellectual disability, hallucinations, delusions, and a loss of emotional control (Kern et al., 2012) (● **Figure 61.1**). Children with higher levels of lead in their blood are more likely to be arrested as adults for criminal offenses (Wright et al., 2008). On a much larger scale, "poisoning" of another type, in the form of drug abuse, also can produce deviant behavior and psychotic symptoms (American Psychiatric Association, 2013).

The *neurocognitive disorders* are serious mental impairments in old age caused by deterioration of the brain (Treves & Korczyn, 2012). In these disorders, we see major disturbances in memory, reasoning, judgment, impulse control, and personality. This combination usually leaves people confused, suspicious, apathetic, or withdrawn. Some common causes of neurocognitive disorders are circulatory problems, repeated strokes, or general shrinkage and atrophy of the brain.

Alzheimer's disease (ALLS-hi-merz) is the most common neurocognitive disorder. Alzheimer's victims slowly lose the ability to work, cook, drive, read, write, or do arithmetic. Eventually, they are mute and bedridden. Alzheimer's disease appears to be caused by unusual webs and tangles in the brain that damage areas important for memory and learning (Hanyu et al., 2010; Stix, 2010). Genetic factors can increase the risk of developing this devastating disease (Treves & Korczyn, 2012).

Courtesy of Galerie Beckel-Odille-Boïcos, Paris

Artist William Utermohlen painted haunting images portraying his decline into the grasp of Alzheimer's disease.

Besides neurocognitive disorders, psychotic disorders are mainly characterized by psychosis. Two major types of schizophrenia spectrum and other psychotic disorders are *delusional disorders* and *schizophrenia*.

Bettmann/Corbis

● **Figure 61.1**

The Mad Hatter, from Lewis Carroll's *Alice's Adventures in Wonderland.* History provides numerous examples of psychosis caused by toxic chemicals. Carroll's Mad Hatter character is modeled after an occupational disease of the eighteenth and nineteenth centuries. In that era, hatmakers were heavily exposed to mercury used in the preparation of felt. Consequently, many suffered brain damage and became psychotic, or "mad" (Kety, 1979).

Delusional Disorders—An Enemy Behind Every Tree

SURVEY QUESTION 61.2: What is the nature of a delusional disorder?

People with delusional disorders usually do *not* suffer from hallucinations, emotional excesses, or personality disintegration. Even so, their break with reality is unmistakable. The main feature of a **delusional disorder** is the presence of deeply held false beliefs, which may take the following forms (American Psychiatric Association, 2013; Sue et al., 2013):

- **Erotomanic type:** In this disorder, people have erotic delusions that they are loved by another person, especially by someone famous or of higher status. As you might imagine, some celebrity stalkers suffer from erotomania.

- **Grandiose type:** In this case, people suffer from the delusion that they have some great, unrecognized talent, knowledge, or insight. They also may believe that they have a special relationship with an important person or with God or that they are a famous person. (If the famous person is alive, the deluded person regards her or him as an imposter.)

- **Jealous type:** An example of this type of delusion would be having an all-consuming, but unfounded, belief that your spouse or lover is unfaithful.

- **Persecutory type:** Delusions of persecution involve belief that you are being conspired against, cheated, spied on, followed, poisoned, maligned, or harassed.

- **Somatic type:** People suffering from somatic delusions typically believe that their bodies are diseased or rotting, infested with insects or parasites, or that parts of their bodies are defective.

Although false and sometimes far-fetched, all these delusions are about experiences that could conceivably occur in real life. In other types of psychosis, delusions tend to be more bizarre (Brown & Barlow, 2011). For example, a person with schizophrenia might believe that space aliens have replaced all his internal organs with electronic monitoring devices. In contrast, people with ordinary delusions merely believe that someone is trying to steal their money, that they are being deceived by a lover, that the FBI is watching them, and the like.

Paranoid Psychosis

The most common delusional disorder, **paranoid psychosis**, centers on delusions of persecution. Many self-styled reformers, crank letter writers, conspiracy theorists, and the like suffer paranoid delusions. Paranoid individuals often believe that they are being cheated, spied on, followed, poisoned, harassed, or plotted against. Usually, they are intensely suspicious, believing they must be on guard at all times.

The evidence such people find to support their beliefs usually fails to persuade others. Every detail of the paranoid person's existence is woven into a private version of "what's really going on." For instance, buzzing during a telephone conversation may be interpreted as "someone listening," or a stranger who comes to the door asking for directions may be seen as "really trying to get information."

It is difficult to treat people suffering from paranoid delusions because it is almost impossible for them to accept that they need help. Anyone who suggests that they have a problem simply becomes part of the "conspiracy" to "persecute" them. Consequently, paranoid people frequently lead lonely, isolated, and humorless lives dominated by constant suspicion and hostility.

Although paranoid people are not necessarily dangerous to others, they can be. People who believe that the Mafia, "government agents," terrorists, or a street gang is slowly closing in on them may be moved to violence by their irrational fears. Imagine that a stranger comes to the door to ask a paranoid person for directions. If the stranger has his hand in his coat pocket, he could become the target of a paranoid attempt at "self-defense."

Delusional disorders are rare. By far, the most common form of psychosis is schizophrenia. Let's explore schizophrenia in more detail and see how it differs from a delusional disorder.

Schizophrenia—Shattered Reality

SURVEY QUESTION 61.3: What is schizophrenia and what causes it?

Do people with schizophrenia have two personalities? No. How many times have you heard people say something like, "Laurence was so warm and friendly yesterday, but today he's as cold as ice. He's so schizophrenic that I don't know how to react." Such statements show how often the term *schizophrenic* is misused. As we will see in Module 63, a person who displays two or more *integrated* personalities has a dissociative disorder and is *not* schizophrenic. Neither, of course, is a person like Laurence, whose behavior is merely inconsistent.

Symptoms of Schizophrenia

Like the other psychotic disorders, **schizophrenia** (SKIT-soh-FREN-ee-uh) is characterized by a disintegration or

---

Alzheimer's disease *(ALLS-hi-merz) An age-related disease characterized by memory loss, mental confusion, and, in its later stages, a nearly total loss of mental abilities.*

Delusional disorder *A psychosis marked by severe delusions of grandeur, jealousy, persecution, or similar preoccupations.*

Paranoid psychosis *A delusional disorder centered especially on delusions of persecution.*

Schizophrenia *(SKIT-soh-FREN-ee-uh) A psychosis characterized by delusions, hallucinations, apathy, and a "split" between thought and emotion.*

"splitting" apart of the normally integrated personality with a consequent loss of contact with reality. One person in 100 has schizophrenia in any given year (National Institute of Mental Health, 2013). Schizophrenia is often marked by thinking abnormalities, such as delusions and hallucinations, mood abnormalities, such as apathy, and behavioral abnormalities, such as *catatonia*.

Abnormal Cognition Many schizophrenic symptoms appear to be related to problems with *selective attention*. In other words, it is hard for people with schizophrenia to focus on one item of information at a time. Having an impaired "sensory filter" in their brains may be why they are overwhelmed by a jumble of thoughts, sensations, images, and feelings (Cellard et al., 2010; Heinrichs, 2001).

Paranoia is a common symptom in schizophrenia. As in paranoid delusional disorders, **paranoia** in schizophrenia centers on delusions of grandeur and persecution. However, schizophrenics with paranoia also hallucinate, and their delusions are more bizarre and unconvincing than those in a delusional disorder (Corcoran, 2010; Freeman & Garety, 2004). Schizophrenic delusions may include the idea that the person's thoughts and actions are being controlled, that thoughts are being broadcast (so others can hear them), that thoughts have been "inserted" into the person's mind, or that thoughts have been removed. Schizophrenics whose predominant symptom is paranoia are sometimes referred to as *paranoid schizophrenics* (● **Figure 61.2**).

Thinking that God, the government, or "cosmic rays from space" are controlling their minds or that someone is trying to poison them, people suffering from paranoid schizophrenia may feel forced into violence to "protect" themselves. An example is James Huberty, who brutally murdered 21 people at a McDonald's restaurant in San Ysidro, California. Huberty, who had paranoid schizophrenia, felt persecuted and cheated by life. Shortly before he announced to his wife that he was "going hunting humans," Huberty had been hearing hallucinated voices.

How dangerous are the mentally ill? Horrific crimes, like the San Ysidro murders, lead many people to believe that the mentally ill are dangerous. Although sensationalized media reports tend to exaggerate the connection between mental illness and violence, the reality is just the opposite (Markowitz, 2011). According to the largest study ever conducted on this question, mentally ill individuals who are not also substance abusers are no more prone to violence than normal individuals (Monahan et al., 2001). In general, only persons who are *actively psychotic* and *currently* experiencing psychotic symptoms are at increased risk for violence. In fact, the risk of violence from mental patients is many times lower than that from persons who have the following attributes: young, male, poor, and intoxicated (Corrigan & Watson, 2005).

Abnormal Affect In schizophrenia, emotions may become blunted or very inappropriate. For example, if a person with schizophrenia is told his mother just died, he might smile, giggle, or show no emotion at all (*flat affect*).

Abnormal Behavior Schizophrenia often involves withdrawal from contact with others, a loss of interest in external activities, a breakdown of personal habits, and an inability to deal with daily events (Neufeld et al., 2003; Ziv, Leiser, & Levine, 2011).

Schizophrenics sometimes display **catatonia**, remaining *mute* (not speaking) while holding odd postures for hours or even days at a time. These periods of stupor may be similar to the tendency to "freeze" at times of great emergency or panic. Catatonic individuals appear to be struggling desperately to control their inner turmoil (Fink, Shorter, & Taylor, 2010; Fink, 2013). One sign of this is the fact that stupor may occasionally give way to agitated outbursts or violent behavior. As you might imagine, catatonic patients are difficult to "reach."

HO/U.S. Marshals Service/Reuters/Landov

● **Figure 61.2**

In 2011, Jared Lee Loughner went on a shooting rampage in Tucson, Arizona, severely injuring his intended target, U. S. Representative Gabrielle Giffords. Of the other 18 people he shot, 12 died of their wounds. Diagnosed with paranoid schizophrenia, he was nevertheless found competent to stand trial. He was convicted and sentenced to life in prison.

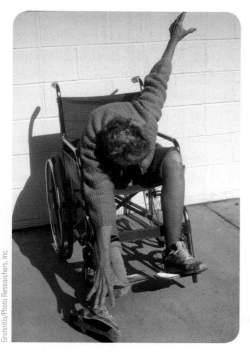

Catatonia, with its rigid postures and stupor, is recognized by the *DSM-5* as a disorder of its own. It also can co-occur with schizophrenia, bipolar disorder, depression, and several other conditions, including drug abuse (Fink, 2013).

Schizophrenics whose predominant symptom is catatonia are sometimes referred to as *catatonic schizophrenics*.

Disorganized Schizophrenia Not all symptoms are equally prominent in every schizophrenic. Similarly, the different symptoms in any individual can become more or less prominent over time. For these reasons, the various manifestations of schizophrenia are referred to as *schizophrenia spectrum disorders* (American Psychiatric Association, 2013). However, when a person's personality disintegration is almost complete and thinking, feeling, and behavior are *all* highly disorganized, the result comes close to matching the stereotyped images of "madness" seen in movies. Such schizophrenics, sometimes referred to as *disorganized* or *hebephrenic*, can display silliness, laughter, and bizarre or obscene behavior, as shown by this intake interview of a patient named Edna:

Dr.: Tell me, how do you feel?

Patient: London's bell is a long, long dock. Hee! Hee! (Giggles uncontrollably.)

Dr.: Do you know where you are now?

Patient: D_____n! S_____t on you all who rip into my internals! The grudgerometer will take care of you all! (Shouting) I am the Queen, see my magic, I shall turn you all into smidgelings forever!

Dr.: Your husband is concerned about you. Do you know his name?

Patient: (Stands, walks to and faces the wall) Who am I, who are we, who are you, who are they, (turns)

I … I … I … I! (Makes grotesque faces.)

Edna was placed in the women's ward where she proceeded to masturbate. Occasionally, she would scream or shout obscenities. At other times, she giggled to herself. She was known to attack other patients. She began to complain that her uterus was attached to a "pipeline to the Kremlin" and that she was being "infernally invaded" by Communism (Suinn, 1975[1]).

_____

[1] From Fundamentals of Behavior Pathology by R. M. Suinn. Copyright © 1975. Reprinted by permission of John Wiley & Sons, Inc.

In disorganized schizophrenia, behavior is marked by silliness, laughter, and bizarre or obscene behavior.

Paranoia *Symptom marked by a preoccupation with delusions related to a single theme, especially grandeur or persecution.*
Catatonia *Considered a disorder in its own right, marked by stupor; rigidity; unresponsiveness; posturing; mutism; and, sometimes, agitated, purposeless behavior.*

Such extreme schizophrenia typically develops in adolescence or young adulthood. Chances of improvement are limited, and social impairment is usually extreme (American Psychiatric Association, 2013).

Causes of Schizophrenia

What causes schizophrenia? Former British Prime Minister Winston Churchill once described a question that perplexed him as "a riddle wrapped in a mystery inside an enigma." The same words might describe the causes of schizophrenia.

Environment An increased risk of developing schizophrenia may begin at birth or even before. Women who are exposed to the influenza (flu) virus or to rubella (German measles) during the middle of pregnancy have children who are more likely to become schizophrenic (Durand & Barlow, 2013; Vuillermot et al., 2010). Malnutrition during pregnancy and complications at the time of birth can have a similar impact. Possibly, such events disturb brain development, leaving people more vulnerable to a psychotic break with reality (Walker et al., 2004).

Early **psychological trauma**—a psychological injury or shock—also may add to the risk. Often, the victims of schizophrenia were exposed to violence, sexual abuse, death, divorce, separation, or other stresses in childhood (Walker et al., 2004). Living in a troubled family is a related risk factor. In a disturbed family environment, stressful relationships, communication patterns, and negative emotions prevail. Deviant communication patterns cause anxiety, confusion, anger, conflict, and turmoil. Typically, disturbed families interact in ways that are laden with guilt, prying, criticism, negativity, and emotional attacks (Bressi, Albonetti, & Razzoli, 1998; Davison & Neale, 2006).

Although they are attractive, environmental explanations alone are not enough to account for schizophrenia. For example, when the children of schizophrenic parents are raised away from their chaotic home environment, they still are more likely to become psychotic (Walker et al., 2004).

Heredity *Does that mean that heredity affects the risk of developing schizophrenia?* There is now little doubt that heredity is a factor in schizophrenia (Gejman, Sanders, & Duan, 2010). It appears that some individuals inherit a *potential* for developing schizophrenia. They are, in other words, more *vulnerable* to the disorder (Levy et al., 2010; Walker et al., 2004).

How has that been shown? If one identical twin becomes schizophrenic (remember, identical twins have identical genes), then the other twin has a 48 *percent* chance of also becoming schizophrenic (Insel, 2010a; Lenzenweger & Gottesman, 1994). The figure for twins can be compared with the risk of schizophrenia for the population in general, which is 1 percent. (See ● **Figure 61.3** for other relationships.) In general, schizophrenia is clearly more common among close relatives and tends to

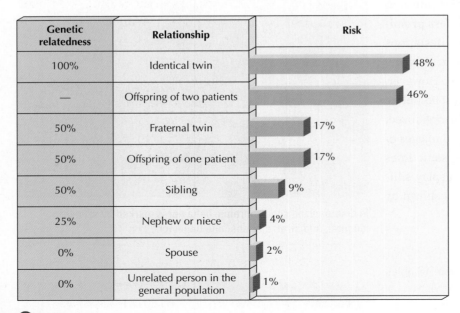

Genetic relatedness	Relationship	Risk
100%	Identical twin	48%
—	Offspring of two patients	46%
50%	Fraternal twin	17%
50%	Offspring of one patient	17%
50%	Sibling	9%
25%	Nephew or niece	4%
0%	Spouse	2%
0%	Unrelated person in the general population	1%

● **Figure 61.3**

Lifetime risk of developing schizophrenia is associated with how closely a person is genetically related to a schizophrenic person. A shared environment also increases the risk. [Lenzenweger, M. F., & Gottesman, I. I. (1994). Schizophrenia. In V. S. Ramachandran (Ed.), Encyclopedia of human behavior (Vol 4, pp. 41–59). San Diego, CA: Academic.]

run in families. There's even a case on record of *four* identical quadruplets *all* developing schizophrenia (Mirsky et al., 2000). In light of such evidence, researchers are beginning to search for specific genes related to schizophrenia (Curtis et al., 2011; Hyman, 2011; Roffman et al., 2011).

A problem exists with current genetic explanations of schizophrenia: Very few people with schizophrenia have children (Bundy, Stahl, & MacCabe, 2011). How could a genetic defect be passed from one generation to the next if afflicted people don't reproduce? One possibility is suggested by the fact that the older a man is (even if he doesn't suffer from schizophrenia) when he fathers a child, the more likely it is that the child will develop schizophrenia (Helenius, Munk-Jørgensen, & Steinhausen, 2012). Apparently, genetic mutations occur in aging male reproductive cells and increase the risk of schizophrenia (as well as other medical problems) (Sipos et al., 2004).

Brain Chemistry Amphetamine, LSD, PCP (angel dust), and similar drugs produce effects that partially mimic the symptoms of schizophrenia. Also, the same drugs (phenothiazines) used to treat LSD overdoses tend to alleviate psychotic symptoms. Facts such as these suggest that biochemical abnormalities (disturbances in brain chemicals or neurotransmitters) may occur in schizophrenic people. It is possible that the schizophrenic brain produces some substance similar to a *psychedelic* (mind-altering) drug. At present, one likely candidate is *dopamine* (DOPE-ah-meen), an important chemical messenger found in the brain.

Many researchers believe that schizophrenia is related to disturbances in brain dopamine systems (Citrome, 2011). Dopamine receptors in one part of the brain appear to become super-responsive to normal amounts of dopamine, triggering a flood of unrelated thoughts, feelings, and perceptions, which may account for the positive symptoms (voices, hallucinations, and delusions) of schizophrenia (Madras, 2013). The implication is that schizophrenic people may be on a sort of drug trip caused by their own bodies (● **Figure 61.4**).

Dopamine is not the only brain chemical that has caught scientists' attention. The neurotransmitter glutamate also appears to be related to schizophrenia. People who take the hallucinogenic drug PCP, which affects glutamate, have symptoms that closely mimic schizophrenia (Javitt et al., 2012). This occurs because glutamate influences brain activity in areas that control emotions and sensory information (Citrome, 2011). Another tantalizing connection is the fact

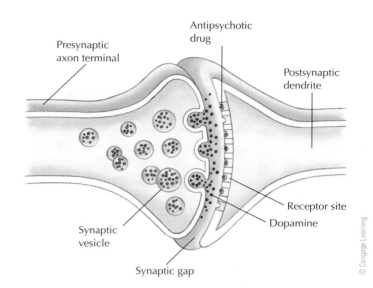

● Figure 61.4

Dopamine normally crosses the synapse between two neurons, activating the second cell. Antipsychotic drugs bind to the same receptor sites as does dopamine, blocking its action. In people suffering from schizophrenia, a reduction in dopamine activity can quiet a person's agitation and psychotic symptoms.

that stress alters glutamate levels, which in turn alters dopamine systems (Holloway et al., 2013; Moghaddam, 2002). The story is far from complete, but it appears that dopamine, glutamate, and other brain chemicals partly explain the devastating symptoms of schizophrenia (Walker et al., 2004). See "The Schizophrenic Brain" to learn how brain imaging techniques are improving our understanding of this condition.

Implications

In summary, the emerging picture of psychotic disorders such as schizophrenia takes this form: Anyone subjected to enough stress may be pushed to a psychotic break. (Battlefield psychosis is an example.) However, some people inherit a difference in brain chemistry or brain structure that makes them more susceptible to developing psychotic disorders—even when experiencing normal life stresses.

Thus, the right mix of inherited potential and environmental stress brings about mind-altering changes in brain chemicals and brain structure. This explanation is called a **stress-vulnerability model**. It attributes psychotic disorders

Psychological trauma *A psychological injury or shock, such as that caused by violence, abuse, neglect, separation, and so forth.*

Stress-vulnerability model *Attributes mental illness to a combination of environmental stress and inherited susceptibility.*

Brainwaves

The Schizophrenic Brain

Several brain imaging methods (see Module 8) have made it possible to directly observe the living schizophrenic brain. Computed tomography (CT) scans and magnetic resonance imaging (MRI) scans, which can reveal brain structure, suggest that the brains of schizophrenics have shrunk, or atrophied (Bora et al., 2011). For example, ● Figure 61.5 shows a CT scan (a computer-enhanced X-ray image) of the brain of John Hinkley, Jr., who shot former President Ronald Reagan and three other men in 1981. In the ensuing trial, Hinkley was declared insane. As you can see, his brain had wider than normal surface fissuring.

Similarly, MRI scans indicate that schizophrenic people tend to have enlarged ventricles (fluid-filled spaces within the brain), again suggesting that surrounding brain tissue has withered (Andreasen et al., 2011; Barkataki et al., 2006). One possible explanation is that the schizophrenic brain may be unable to continually create new neurons to replace old ones that have died. In contrast, normal brains continue to produce new neurons (a process referred to as neurogenesis) throughout life. It is telling that the affected areas are crucial for regulating motivation, emotion, perception, actions, and attention (DeCarolis & Eisch, 2010; Inta, Meyer-Lindenberg, & Gass, 2011; Kawada et al., 2009).

Other methods provide images of brain activity, including positron emission tomography (PET) scans. To make a PET scan, a radioactive sugar solution is injected into a vein. When the sugar reaches the brain, an electronic device measures how much is used in each area. These data are then translated into a color map, or scan, of brain activity (● Figure 61.6). Researchers are finding patterns in such

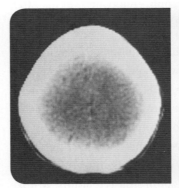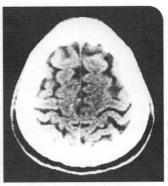

Dennis Brack/Black Star

● Figure 61.5

(*left*) CT scan of would-be presidential assassin John Hinkley, Jr., taken when he was 25. The X-ray image shows widened fissures in the wrinkled surface of Hinkley's brain. (*right*) CT scan of a normal 25-year-old's brain. In most young adults, the surface folds of the brain are pressed together too tightly to be seen. As a person ages, surface folds of the brain normally become more visible. Pronounced brain fissuring in young adults may be a sign of schizophrenia, chronic alcoholism, or other problems.

scans that are consistently linked with schizophrenia, affective disorders, and other problems. For instance, activity tends to be abnormally low in the frontal lobes of the schizophrenic brain (Durand & Barlow, 2013; Roffman et al., 2011). In the future, PET scans may be used to accurately diagnose schizophrenia. For now, such scans show that there is a clear abnormality in schizophrenic brain activity.

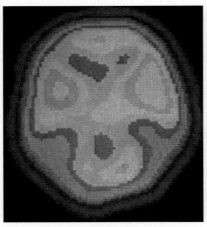 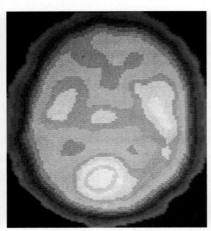 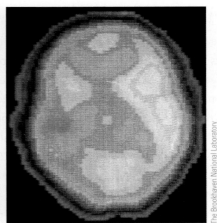

| Normal | Schizophrenic | Manic Depressive |

The Brookhaven National Laboratory

● Figure 61.6

Positron emission tomography produces PET scans of the human brain. In the scans shown here, red, pink, and orange indicate lower levels of brain activity; white and blue indicate higher activity levels. Notice that activity in the schizophrenic brain is quite low in the frontal lobes (top area of each scan) (Velakoulis & Pantelis, 1996). Activity in the manic-depressive brain is low in the left-brain hemisphere and high in the right-brain hemisphere. The reverse is more often true of the schizophrenic brain. Researchers are trying to identify consistent patterns like these to aid diagnosis of mental disorders.

to a blend of environmental stress and inherited susceptibility (Jones & Fernyhough, 2007; Walker et al., 2004). This idea has been applied to other forms of psychopathology as well, such as depression (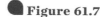 **Figure 61.7**).

Despite advances in our understanding, psychosis remains "a riddle wrapped in a mystery inside an enigma." Let's hope that recent progress toward a cure for schizophrenia will continue.

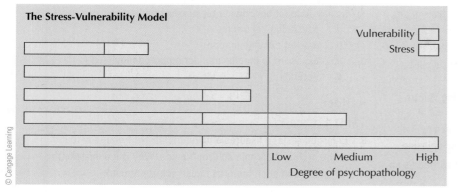

Figure 61.7

Various combinations of vulnerability and stress may produce psychological problems. The top bar shows low vulnerability and low stress. The result? No problem. The same is true of the next bar down, in which low vulnerability is combined with moderate stress. Even high vulnerability (third bar) may not lead to problems if stress levels remain low. However, when high vulnerability combines with moderate or high stress (bottom two bars) the person "crosses the line" and suffers from psychopathology.

Module 61: Summary

61.1 What are the general characteristics of psychotic disorders?

- **61.1.1** Psychosis is a break in contact with reality that is marked by delusions, hallucinations, sensory changes, disturbed emotions, disturbed communication, and personality disintegration.
- **61.1.2** Some psychoses are due to known injuries or diseases of the brain, such as poisoning and drug abuse. Neurocognitive disorders, such as Alzheimer's disease, strike in old age.

61.2 What is the nature of a delusional disorder?

- **61.2.1** Delusional disorders are almost totally based on the presence of deeply held false beliefs of grandeur, persecution, infidelity, romantic attraction, or physical disease.
- **61.2.2** Paranoid psychosis is the most common delusional disorder. Paranoid persons may be violent if they believe they are threatened.

61.3 What is schizophrenia and what causes it?

- **61.3.1** Schizophrenia spectrum disorder involves varying degrees of abnormal cognition (delusions, hallucinations), abnormal mood (flat or inappropriate affect), abnormal behavior (inability to cope, catatonia), and a disintegrated personality.
- **61.3.2** Paranoia involves delusions of grandeur and persecution.
- **61.3.3** Catatonia is associated with stupor, mutism, and odd postures. Sometimes, violent and agitated behavior also occurs.
- **61.3.4** Environmental factors that increase the risk for schizophrenia include viral infection or malnutrition during the mother's pregnancy, birth complications, early psychological trauma, and a disturbed family environment.
- **61.3.5** Heredity is a major factor in schizophrenia. Recent biochemical studies have focused on the neurotransmitters glutamate and dopamine and their receptor sites.
- **61.3.6** The dominant explanation of schizophrenia, and other problems as well, is the stress-vulnerability model, which emphasizes a combination of inherited susceptibility and environmental stress.

Module 61: Knowledge Builder

Recite

1. Angela wrongly believes that her body is "rotting away." She is suffering from
   - a. depressive hallucinations
   - b. a delusion
   - c. flat affect
   - d. Alzheimer's disease

2. Colin, who has suffered a psychotic break, is hearing voices. This symptom is referred to as
   - a. flat affect
   - b. a hallucination
   - c. a word salad
   - d. an organic delusion

3. A psychosis caused by lead poisoning would be regarded as an organic disorder. *T or F?*

4. Hallucinations and personality disintegration are the principal features of paranoid psychosis. *T or F?*

5. Environmental explanations of schizophrenia emphasize emotional trauma and
   - a. manic parents
   - b. schizoaffective interactions
   - c. psychedelic interactions
   - d. disturbed family relationships

6. Biochemical explanations of schizophrenia have focused on excessive amounts of _____ in the brain.
   - a. radioactive sugar
   - b. webs and tangles
   - c. PCP
   - d. dopamine and glutamate

7. The stress-vulnerability model of mental disorders explains them as a product of environmental stresses and
   - a. psychological trauma
   - b. deviant communication
   - c. exposure to the flu virus during pregnancy
   - d. heredity

Reflect

Think Critically

8. Enlarged surface fissures and ventricles are frequently found in the brains of chronic schizophrenics. Why is it a mistake to conclude that such features cause schizophrenia?

Self-Reflect

If you were writing a "recipe" for psychosis, what would be the main "ingredients"?

If you were asked to play the role of a paranoid person for a theater production, what symptoms would you emphasize?

You have been asked to explain the causes of schizophrenia to the parents of a schizophrenic teenager. What would you tell them?

ANSWERS

1. b 2. b 3. T 4. F 5. d 6. d 7. d 8. Because correlation does not confirm causation. Structural brain abnormalities are merely *correlated* with schizophrenia. They could be additional symptoms, rather than causes, of the disorder.

CENGAGE brain .com

Go to **cengagebrain.com** to access **MindTap for Coon/Mitterer** *Psychology Modules for Active Learning* and other online learning tools. MindTap is a fully online learning experience that combines all the tools you need—readings, multimedia, activities, and assessments—into a singular personalized Learning Path that guides you through the course.

Psychological Disorders: Mood Disorders

Mood Swings

For some people, minor bouts of depression are as common as colds. But extreme swings of mood can be as disabling as a serious physical illness. In fact, depression can be deadly because depressed persons may be suicidal. It is difficult to imagine how bleak and hopeless the world looks to a person who is deeply depressed.

By the same token, it can be "crazy" to ride a wave of true mania. Manic patients may go bankrupt in a matter of days, get arrested, or go on a binge of promiscuous sex and then have to deal with the consequences of their actions. In the most severe cases of depression and/or mania, the person may even lose touch with reality and display psychotic symptoms.

Unfortunately, mood disorders have resisted adequate explanation and treatment. Nevertheless, scientific progress continues to be made, so let's explore mood disorders and their causes.

Erica Shires/Corbis

SURVEY QUESTION

62.1 What are mood disorders and what causes them?

Mood Disorders— Peaks and Valleys

SURVEY QUESTIONS 62.1: What are mood disorders and what causes them?

Nobody loves you when you're down and out—or so it seems. Psychologists have come to realize that *mood disorders*—major disturbances in emotion—are among the most serious of all psychological conditions. In any given year, roughly 9.5 percent of the U.S. population suffers from a mood disorder (National Institute of Mental Health, 2013). Two general types of mood disorders are depressive disorders and bipolar disorders (see ● Table 62.1.)

Depressive Disorders

In *depressive disorders*, sadness and despondency are exaggerated, prolonged, or unreasonable. Signs of a depressive disorder are dejection, hopelessness, and an inability to feel pleasure or to take interest in anything. Other common symptoms are fatigue, disturbed sleep and eating patterns, feelings of worthlessness, a very negative self-image, and thoughts of suicide.

Some mood disorders are long-lasting but relatively moderate. If a person is mildly depressed for at least two years, the problem is called a **persistent depressive disorder (dysthymia)** (dis-THY-mee-ah). Even at this level, depressive disorders can be debilitating. However, major depressions are much more damaging.

TABLE 62.1	*DSM-5* Classification of Mood Disorders
Problem	**Typical Signs of Trouble**
Depressive Disorders	
Persistent depressive disorder (dysthymia)	You feel down and depressed more days than not; your self-esteem and energy levels have been low for many months.
Major depressive disorder	You feel extremely sad, worthless, fatigued, and empty; you are unable to feel pleasure; you are having thoughts of suicide.
Bipolar and Related Disorders	
Cyclothymic disorder	You have been experiencing upsetting emotional ups and downs for many months.
Bipolar I disorder	At times, you have little need for sleep, you can't stop talking, your mind races, and everything you do is of immense importance; at other times, you feel extremely sad, worthless, and empty.
Bipolar II disorder	Most of the time, you feel extremely sad, worthless, fatigued, and empty; however, at times, you feel unusually good, cheerful, energetic, or "high."

Sources: American Psychiatric Association (2013); Durand & Barlow (2013).

In a **major depressive disorder**, the depression is much deeper. Everything looks bleak and hopeless. The person has feelings of failure, worthlessness, and total despair. In serious cases of depression, it is impossible for a person to function at work or at school. Sometimes, depressed individuals cannot even feed or dress themselves. Suffering is intense, and the person may become extremely subdued, withdrawn, or intensely suicidal. Suicide attempted during a major depression is rarely a "plea for help." Usually, the person intends to succeed and may give no prior warning.

Bipolar and Related Disorders

Unlike depressive disorders, in *bipolar disorder and related disorders*, people go both "up" and "down" emotionally (American Psychiatric Association, 2013). A long-lasting but relatively moderate alternation between depression and periods when the person's mood is cheerful, expansive, or irritable is a **cyclothymic disorder** (SIKE-lo-THY-mik). Like depressive disorders, however, major bipolar disorders are much more severe.

In a **bipolar I disorder**, people experience both extreme mania and deep depression. During manic episodes, the person is loud, elated, hyperactive, grandiose, and energetic. During periods of depression, the person is deeply despondent and possibly suicidal.

In a **bipolar II disorder**, the person is mostly sad and guilt ridden but has had one or more mildly manic episodes (called

hypomania). That is, in a bipolar II disorder, both elation and depression occur, but the person's mania is not as extreme as in a bipolar I disorder. Bipolar II patients who are hypomanic usually just manage to irritate everyone around them. They are excessively cheerful, aggressive, or irritable, and they may brag, talk too fast, interrupt conversations, or spend too much money (Nolen-Hoeksema, 2011).

Causes of Mood Disorders

Because the mood disorders often appear to be **endogenous** (en-DODGE-eh-nus: produced from within), some scientists are focusing on the biology of mood changes. They are interested in brain chemicals and transmitter substances, especially serotonin, noradrenaline, and dopamine levels. The findings are incomplete, but progress has been made. For example, the chemical lithium carbonate can be effective for treating some cases of bipolar depression (Malhi et al., 2012).

Other researchers seek psychological explanations. Psychoanalytic theory, for instance, holds that depression is caused by repressed anger. This rage is displaced and turned inward as self-blame and self-hate. As discussed in Module 57, behavioral theories of depression emphasize learned helplessness (Durand & Barlow, 2013; Reivich et al., 2013). Cognitive psychologists believe that self-criticism and negative, distorted, or self-defeating thoughts underlie many cases of depression. (This view is discussed in Module 66.) Clearly, life stresses trigger many mood disorders (Calabrese et al., 2009).

This is especially true for people who have personality traits and thinking patterns that make them vulnerable to depression (Dozois & Dobson, 2002).

Gender and Depression

Overall, women are 50 percent more likely than men to experience depression (National Institute of Mental Health, 2013). Hormonal fluctuations likely play a role in cases of depression involving pregnancy, menstruation, and menopause (Lokuge et al., 2011). Nevertheless, researchers believe that social and environmental conditions are the main reason for this difference (Jack & Ali, 2010; McGuinness, Dyer, & Wade, 2012). Psychosocial factors that contribute to women's greater risk for depression include conflicts about birth control and pregnancy, work and parenting, and the strain of providing emotional support for others. Marital strife, sexual and physical abuse, and poverty also are factors. Nationwide, women and children are most likely to live in poverty. As a result, poor women frequently suffer the stresses associated with single parenthood, loss of control over their lives, poor housing, and dangerous neighborhoods (Grant et al., 2011; Stoppard & McMullen, 2003).

Postpartum Depression

One source of women's depression is fairly easy to identify. After pregnancy and childbirth, many women face a high risk of becoming depressed (Phillips et al., 2010). An estimated 25 to 50 percent of women experience *maternity blues*, a mild depression that usually lasts from one to two days after childbirth. These "third-day blues" are marked by crying, fitful sleep, tension, anger, and irritability. For most women, such reactions are a normal part of adjusting to childbirth. The depression is usually brief and not too severe.

For some women, maternity blues can be the beginning of a serious depression. Roughly 13 percent of all women who give birth develop **postpartum depression**, a moderately severe depression that begins within three months following childbirth. Typical signs of postpartum depression are mood swings, despondency, feelings of inadequacy, an inability to cope with the new baby, and an increased risk of self-harm (Healey et al., 2013; Insel, 2010b). Unlike other types of depression, postpartum depression also features unusually high levels of restlessness and difficulty concentrating (Bernstein et al., 2008). Depression of this kind may last anywhere from two months to about a year. Women are not the only ones to suffer when postpartum depression strikes. A depressed mother can seriously affect her child's development (Cooper & Murray, 2001; Tikotzky et al., 2012).

Stress and anxiety before birth and negative attitudes toward child rearing increase the risk of postpartum depression (Phillips et al., 2010). A troubled marriage and lack of support from the father also are danger signs. Part of the problem may be hormonal: After a woman gives birth, her estrogen levels can drop, altering her mood (Fernandez, Grizzell, & Wecker, 2013). Educating new parents about the importance of supporting one another may reduce the risk of depression. Groups where new mothers can discuss their feelings also are helpful. If depression is severe or long-lasting, new mothers should seek professional help.

Biology and Depression

Is heredity involved in the major mood disorders? Yes, especially in bipolar disorders (Curtis et al., 2011; Scharinger et al., 2010). As a case in point, if one identical twin is depressed, the other has a 67 percent chance of suffering depression, too. For fraternal twins, the probability is 19 percent. This difference may be related to the finding that people who have a particular version of a gene are more likely to become depressed when they are stressed (Halmai et al., 2013). As we have noted, psychological causes are important in many cases of depression. But for major mood disorders, biological factors seem to play a larger role. Surprisingly, one additional source of depression is related to the seasons.

Seasonal Affective Disorder

Unless you have experienced a winter of "cabin fever" in the far north, you may be surprised to learn that the rhythms of the seasons underlie **seasonal affective disorder (SAD)**, or depression that occurs only during the fall and winter months. Almost anyone can get a

Persistent depressive disorder (dysthymia) *(dis-THY-mee-ah) Moderate depression that persists for two years or more.*
Major depressive disorder *A mood disorder in which the person has suffered one or more intense episodes of depression.*
Cyclothymic disorder *(SIKE-lo-THY-mik) Moderate manic and depressive behavior that persists for two years or more.*
Bipolar I disorder *A mood disorder in which a person has episodes of mania (excited, hyperactive, energetic, grandiose behavior) and also periods of deep depression.*
Bipolar II disorder *A mood disorder in which a person is mostly depressed (sad, despondent, guilt ridden) but also has had one or more episodes of mild mania (hypomania).*
Endogenous (en-DODGE-eh-nus) (in depression) *Depression that appears to be produced from within (perhaps by chemical imbalances in the brain), rather than as a reaction to life events.*
Postpartum depression *A mild to moderately severe depression that begins within three months following childbirth.*
Seasonal affective disorder (SAD) *Depression that occurs only during fall and winter; presumably related to decreased exposure to sunlight.*

little depressed when days are short, dark, and cold. But when a person's symptoms are lasting and disabling, the problem may be SAD.

Starting in the fall, people with SAD sleep longer but more poorly. During the day they feel tired and drowsy, and they tend to overeat. With each passing day, they become sadder, anxious, irritable, and socially withdrawn (Rosenthal, 2013). Although their depressions are usually not severe, many victims of SAD face each winter with a sense of foreboding. SAD is especially prevalent in northern latitudes (think of countries like Sweden and Canada), where days are very short during the winter (Kegel et al., 2009; ● Figure 62.1). For instance, one study found that 13 percent of college students living in northern New England showed signs of suffering from SAD (Low &

Feissner, 1998). The students most likely to be affected were those who had moved from the south to attend college!

Seasonal depressions are related to the release of more melatonin during the winter. This hormone, which is secreted by the pineal gland in the brain, regulates the body's response to changing light conditions (Delavest et al., 2012). That's why 80 percent of SAD patients can be helped by a remedy called phototherapy (● Figure 62.2). **Phototherapy** involves exposing SAD patients to one or more hours of very bright fluorescent light each day. This is best done early in the morning, where it simulates dawn in the summer (Rosenthal, 2013; Vandewalle et al., 2011). For many SAD sufferers, a hearty dose of morning "sunshine" appears to be the next best thing to vacationing in the tropics.

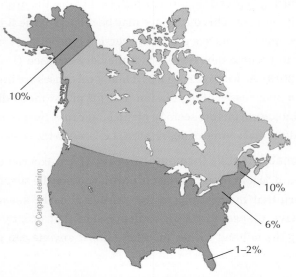

Rates of seasonal affective disorder, by latitude

● Figure 62.1

Seasonal affective disorder (SAD) appears to be related to reduced exposure to daylight during the winter. SAD affects 1 to 2 percent of Florida's population, about 6 percent of the people living in Maryland and New York City, and nearly 10 percent of the residents of New Hampshire and Alaska (Booker & Hellekson, 1992).

● Figure 62.2

An hour or more of bright white or blue light a day can dramatically reduce the symptoms of seasonal affective disorder. Treatment is usually necessary from fall through spring. Light therapy is best done early in the morning, when it simulates dawn in the summer (Avery et al., 2001). An hour or more of bright light a day can dramatically reduce the symptoms of seasonal affective disorder. Treatment is usually necessary from fall through spring. Light therapy typically works best when a bright white or blue light is used early in the morning.

Phototherapy *A treatment for seasonal affective disorder that involves exposure to bright, full-spectrum light.*

Module 62: Summary

62.1 What are mood disorders and what causes them?

- **62.1.1** Mood disorders primarily involve disturbances of mood or emotion, producing manic or depressive states. Severe mood disorders may include psychotic features.
- **62.1.2** In a persistent depressive disorder (dysthymia), depression is long-lasting, though moderate. In contrast, major depressive disorder involves extreme sadness and despondency.
- **62.1.3** Bipolar disorders combine mania and depression. In a cyclothymic disorder, people suffer from long-lasting, though moderate, swings between depression and elation. In a bipolar I disorder, the person swings between severe mania and severe depression. In a bipolar II disorder, the person is mostly depressed but has had periods of mild mania.

- **62.1.4** Mood disorders are partially explained by genetic vulnerability and changes in brain chemistry. Mood disorders also are partially explained by psychological factors such as loss, anger, learned helplessness, stress, and self-defeating thinking patterns.
- **62.1.5** Women are more likely than men to become depressed. Risk factors include hormonal fluctuations and stressful social and environmental conditions.
- **62.1.6** After birth, many women experience a short bout of the maternity blues. Some women suffer from a more serious and lasting condition called postpartum depression.
- **62.1.7** Seasonal affective disorder (SAD), which occurs during the winter months, is another common form of depression. SAD is typically treated with phototherapy.

Module 62: Knowledge Builder

Recite

1. Dysthymic disorder is to depression as cyclothymic disorder is to manic depression. *T or F?*
2. Mood disorders often appear to be endogenous. *T or F?*
3. Learned helplessness is emphasized by _____ theories of depression.
   - *a.* humanistic
   - *b.* biological
   - *c.* behaviorist
   - *d.* psychoanalytic
4. The drug lithium carbonate has been shown to be an effective treatment for anxiety disorders. *T or F?*
5. Roughly 13 percent of all new mothers experience the maternity blues, which are the first stage of postpartum depression. *T or F?*
6. Depression that occurs only in the winter is likely to be classified as
   - *a.* SAD
   - *b.* PTSD
   - *c.* bipolar
   - *d.* endogenous

Reflect

Think Critically

7. How might relationships contribute to the higher rates of depression experienced by women?

Self-Reflect

Have you ever suffered a bout of the "blues" or got "on a roll"? What is the difference between normal mood swings and a mood disorder?

ANSWERS

CENGAGE brain.com

Go to **cengagebrain.com** to access **MindTap** for Coon/Mitterer *Psychology Modules for Active Learning* and other online learning tools. MindTap is a fully online learning experience that combines all the tools you need—readings, multimedia, activities, and assessments—into a singular personalized Learning Path that guides you through the course.

Psychological Disorders: Anxiety-Related Disorders and Personality Disorders

High Anxiety

Imagine that you are waiting to find out whether you have a serious illness. It would be quite normal for you to experience some *anxiety*—feelings of apprehension, dread, or uneasiness. However, people who suffer from extreme anxiety are miserable most of the time, and their behavior can become distorted and self-defeating.

Anxiety can arise in many ways. It can be generalized and unrelated to any particular life stressor or it may be triggered by specific life events. The annual U.S. tornado season upsets many lives. In the aftermath of such disasters, many survivors suffer from stress reactions that can affect them for years. In this module, we begin by discussing anxiety-related disorders and why they occur.

You probably know someone whose personality characteristics make life difficult for her or him. Imagine that person's

FEMA/Alamy

traits becoming more extreme. If they did, the person would have a personality disorder, our second topic in this module.

SURVEY QUESTIONS

63.1 What problems result when a person suffers high levels of anxiety?

63.2 How do psychologists explain anxiety-related disorders?

63.3 What is a personality disorder?

Anxiety-Related Disorders— When Anxiety Rules

SURVEY QUESTION 63.1: What problems result when a person suffers high levels of anxiety?

If anxiety is a normal emotion, when does it signify a problem? Anxiety only becomes a problem when it becomes so intense that it prevents people from doing what they want or need to do. Also, their anxieties are out of control—they simply cannot stop worrying. People with anxiety-related problems feel threatened and often can't do anything constructive about it.

They struggle to control themselves but remain ineffective and unhappy (Cisler et al., 2010; Rachman, 2013).

An example is a college student named Jian, who became unbearably anxious when he took exams. By the time Jian went to see a counselor, he had skipped several tests and was in danger of flunking out of school. In general, people with anxiety-related problems like Jian's display the following characteristics:

- High levels of anxiety and/or restrictive, self-defeating behavior patterns

- A tendency to use elaborate defense mechanisms or avoidance responses to get through the day

- Pervasive feelings of stress, insecurity, inferiority, and dissatisfaction with life

We begin this module by examining the *anxiety disorders*. Then, we look at several types of disorders that are in some way related to anxiety: *obsessive-compulsive and related disorders, trauma- and stressor-related disorders, dissociative disorders*, and *somatic symptom and related disorders*

Anxiety Disorders

In most *anxiety disorders*, distress seems greatly out of proportion to a person's circumstances. For example, consider the following description of Adrian H:

> She becomes very anxious that her children "might have been hurt or killed if they were out of the neighborhood playing and she hadn't heard from them in a couple of hours." She also worries all the time about her job performance and her relationships with men. Adrian believes that men rarely call back after a date or two because "they can sense I'm not a fun person." She never really relaxes, has difficulty focusing at work, has frequent headaches, and suffers from insomnia. (Adapted from Brown & Barlow, 2011.)

Distress like Adrian H's is a key ingredient in anxiety disorders. In any given year, roughly 18 percent of the adult population suffers from an anxiety disorder (National Institute of Mental Health, 2013). Anxiety also may underlie obsessive-compulsive, trauma- and stressor-related, dissociative, and somatic symptom disorders, where maladaptive behavior serves to reduce anxiety and discomfort (● Table 63.1). To deepen your understanding, let's directly examine the anxiety disorders. Then, we'll see how anxiety contributes to the other stress-related problems.

Generalized Anxiety Disorder
A person with a **generalized anxiety disorder** has been extremely anxious and worried for at least six months. Sufferers typically complain of sweating, a racing heart, clammy hands, dizziness, upset stomach, rapid breathing, irritability, and poor concentration. Overall, more women than men have these symptoms (Brown & Barlow, 2011).

Was Adrian H's problem a generalized anxiety disorder? Yes. However, if she also experienced *anxiety attacks*, then she would likely be diagnosed with panic disorder (Batelaan et al., 2010).

Panic Disorder
In a **panic disorder**, people are highly anxious and also feel sudden, intense, unexpected panic. During a *panic attack*, victims experience chest pain, a racing heart, dizziness, choking, feelings of unreality, trembling, or fears of losing control. Many believe that they are having a heart attack, are going insane, or are about to die. Needless to say, this pattern leaves victims unhappy and uncomfortable much of the time. Again, the majority of people who suffer from panic disorder are women (Foot & Koszycki, 2004).

To get an idea of how a panic attack feels, imagine that you are trapped in your stateroom on a sinking ocean liner (the Titanic?). The room fills with water. When only a small air space remains near the ceiling and you are gasping for air, you'll know what a panic attack feels like.

Agoraphobia
Agoraphobia (ah-go-rah-FOBE-ee-ah) involves the *fear that something extremely embarrassing will happen* if the person leaves home or enters an unfamiliar situation. Often, an agoraphobic person may refuse to go outside because he or she fears having a sudden attack of dizziness, diarrhea, shortness of breath, or a panic attack. Going outside the home alone, being in a crowd, standing in line, crossing a bridge, or riding in a car can be impossible for an agoraphobic person. As a result, some agoraphobics are prisoners in their own homes (American Psychiatric Association, 2013).

Although they are considered to be separate disorders, agoraphobia and panic attacks can occur together in the same individual. About 4.2 percent of all adults suffer from agoraphobia (with or without panic) during their lifetime (Grant et al., 2006).

Specific Phobia
Phobias are intense, irrational fears that a person cannot shake off, even when there is no real danger. In a **specific phobia**, the person's fear, anxiety, and avoidance are focused on particular objects, activities, or situations. People affected by phobias recognize that their fears are unreasonable, but they cannot control them. For example, a person with a spider phobia would find it impossible to ignore a picture of a spider, even though a photograph can't bite anyone (Lipka, Miltner, & Straube, 2011). Specific phobias can be linked to nearly any object or situation (Stinson et al., 2007).

Generalized anxiety disorder *A chronic state of tension and worry about work, relationships, ability, or impending disaster.*
Panic disorder *A chronic state of anxiety and also brief moments of sudden, intense, unexpected panic.*
Agoraphobia *(ah-go-rah-FOBE-ee-ah) The fear that something extremely embarrassing will happen if one leaves the house or enters an unfamiliar situation.*
Specific phobia *An intense, irrational fear of specific objects, activities, or situations.*

TABLE 63.1 — *DSM-5* Classification of Anxiety-Related Disorders

Type of Disorder	Typical Signs of Trouble
Anxiety Disorders	
Generalized anxiety disorder	You have been extremely anxious or worried for six months.
Panic disorder	You are anxious much of the time and have sudden panic attacks. You have panic attacks and are afraid that they might occur in public places, so you rarely leave home.
Agoraphobia	You fear that something extremely embarrassing will happen if you leave home (but you don't have panic attacks).
Specific phobia	You have an intense fear of specific objects, activities, or locations.
Social phobia	You fear social situations in which people can watch, criticize, embarrass, or humiliate you.
Obsessive-Compulsive Disorders	
Obsessive-compulsive disorder	Your thoughts make you extremely nervous and compel you to rigidly repeat certain actions or routines.
Hoarding disorder	You collect things and have difficulty throwing or giving them away.
Trauma- and Stressor-Related Disorders	
Adjustment disorder	A normal life event has triggered troublesome anxiety, apathy, or depression.
Acute stress disorder	You are tormented for less than a month by the emotional aftereffects of horrible events you have experienced.
Post-traumatic stress disorder	You are tormented for more than a month by the emotional aftereffects of horrible events you have experienced.
Dissociative Disorders	
Dissociative amnesia	You can't remember your name, address, or past.
Dissociative fugue	You took a sudden, unplanned trip and are confused about who you are.
Dissociative identity disorder	You have two or more separate identities or personality states.
Somatic Symptom and Related Disorders	
Somatic symptom disorder	You are preoccupied with bodily functions and disease.
Factitious disorder (Munchausen syndrome)	You are deliberately faking medical problems to gain attention.
Conversion disorder	You are "converting" severe emotional conflicts into symptoms that closely resemble a physical disability.

Sources: American Psychiatric Association (2013); Durand & Barlow (2013).

In descending order of prevalence, the most common specific phobias among Americans are the following:

Phobia of insects, birds, snakes, or other animals (including, of course, arachnophobia, the fear of spiders, and zoophobia, fear of animals)

Acrophobia—fear of heights

Astraphobia—fear of storms, thunder, lightning

Aquaphobia—fear of being on or in water

Aviophobia—fear of airplanes

Claustrophobia—fear of closed spaces

Agoraphobia—fear of crowds

Shown here watching a basketball game, war hero Senator John McCain is no fan of the number 13. Apparently he always carries 31 cents with him (the opposite of 13). Once, when a campaign office was located on the 13th floor of a building, the floor was quickly renamed the "Mth floor" (Wargo, 2008).

By combining the appropriate root word with the word "phobia," any number of fears can be named. Some are: triskaidekaphobia, fear of the number 13; xenophobia, fear of strangers; and hematophobia, fear of blood. One of your authors' favorites is coulrophobia, fear of clowns. Another is arachibutyrophobia, fear of peanut butter sticking to the roof of the mouth.

Almost everyone has a few mild phobias, such as fear of heights, closed spaces, or bugs and crawly things. True phobias may lead to overwhelming fear, vomiting, wild climbing and running, or fainting. For a phobic disorder to exist, the person's fear must disrupt his or her daily life. Phobic persons are so threatened that they will go to almost any length to avoid the feared object or situation, such as driving 50 miles out of the way to avoid crossing a bridge. About 8.7 percent of all adults have a specific phobic disorder in any given year (National Institute of Mental Health, 2013).

Social Phobia In social phobia, people fear situations in which they can be observed, evaluated, embarrassed, or humiliated by others. This leads them to avoid certain social situations, such as eating, writing, using the restroom, or speaking in public. When such situations cannot be avoided, people endure them with intense anxiety or distress. It is common for them to have uncomfortable physical symptoms, such as a pounding heart, shaking hands, sweating, diarrhea, mental confusion, and blushing. Social phobias greatly impair a person's ability to work, attend school, and form personal relationships (American Psychiatric Association, 2013). About 6.8 percent of all adults are affected by social phobias in a given year (National Institute of Mental Health, 2013).

Obsessive-Compulsive and Related Disorders

While the *DSM-5* categorizes the obsessive-compulsive and related disorders separately from the anxiety disorders, they are nevertheless clear examples of coping with anxiety.

People who suffer from obsessive-compulsive disorder are preoccupied with certain distressing thoughts and feel compelled to perform certain behaviors. You have probably experienced a mild obsessional thought, such as a song or stupid commercial jingle that repeats over and over in your mind. This may be irritating, but it's usually not terribly disturbing. True obsessions are images or thoughts that force their way into awareness against a person's will. They are so disturbing that they cause intense anxiety. The main types of obsessions are (1) about being "dirty" or "unclean," (2) about whether one has performed some action (such as locking the door), (3) about putting things "in order," and (4) about taboo thoughts or actions (such as one's spouse being poisoned or committing immoral acts). A related disorder, hoarding disorder, is about excessively collecting various things (Rasmussen, Eisen, & Greenberg, 2013).

Obsessions usually give rise to compulsions. These are irrational acts that a person feels driven to repeat. Often, compulsive acts help control or block out anxiety caused by an obsession. For example, a minister who finds profanities popping into her mind might start compulsively counting her heartbeat. Doing this would prevent her from thinking "dirty" words. Some compulsive people are *checkers* or *cleaners*. For instance, a young mother who repeatedly pictures a knife plunging into her baby might check once an hour to make sure all the knives in her house are locked away. Doing so may reduce her anxieties, but it also will probably take over her life. Likewise, a person who feels "contaminated" from touching ordinary objects because "germs are everywhere" may be driven to wash his hands hundreds of times a day.

Social phobia *An intense, irrational fear of being observed, evaluated, embarrassed, or humiliated by others in social situations.*
Obsessive-compulsive disorder *An extreme preoccupation with certain thoughts and compulsive performance of certain behaviors.*
Hoarding disorder *Excessively collecting various things.*

Hoarders are obsessive about collecting things, which they also have great difficulty discarding (Hayward & Coles, 2009).

Of course, not all obsessive-compulsive disorders are so dramatic. Many simply involve extreme orderliness and rigid routine. Compulsive attention to detail and rigid following of rules help keep activities totally under control and make the highly anxious person feel more secure (Challacombe, Oldfield, & Salkovskis, 2011). (If such patterns are long-standing but less intense, they are classified as personality disorders, which we discuss later in more detail.)

Trauma- and Stressor-Related Disorders

If a situation causes distress, anxiety, or fear, we tend to "put it behind us" and avoid it in the future. This is a normal survival instinct. *Trauma- and stressor-related disorders* occur when people experience traumas or stresses outside their ability to cope.

How is this different from an anxiety disorder? The outward symptoms are similar. However, people suffering from anxiety disorders seem to generate their own misery, regardless of what's happening around them. They feel that they must be on guard against *future* threats that *could happen* at any time (Butcher, Mineka, & Hooley, 2010). In contrast, trauma- and stressor-related disorders are rooted in a person's specific life circumstances and may improve as life circumstances improve (Kramer et al., 2010).

Do stress and trauma problems cause a "nervous breakdown"? People suffering from *trauma- and stressor-related disorders* may be miserable, but they rarely experience a "breakdown." Actually, the term *nervous breakdown* has no formal meaning.

Nevertheless, a problem known as an *adjustment disorder* does come close to being something of a "breakdown."

An **adjustment disorder** occurs when ordinary stresses push people beyond their ability to cope with life. Examples of such stresses are a job loss, intense marital strife, and chronic physical illness. People suffering from an adjustment disorder may be extremely irritable, anxious, apathetic, or depressed. They also have trouble sleeping, lose their appetite, and suffer from various physical complaints. Often, their problems can be relieved by rest, sedation, supportive counseling, and a chance to "talk through" their fears and anxieties (Ben-Itzhak et al., 2012).

More extreme reactions can occur when traumas or stresses fall outside the range of normal human experience, such as floods, tornadoes, earthquakes, or horrible accidents. They affect many political hostages; combat veterans; prisoners of war; victims of terrorism, torture, violent crime, child molestation, rape, or domestic violence; and people who have witnessed a death or serious injury (Hughes et al., 2011; Polusny et al., 2011).

Symptoms of more extreme stress disorders include repeated reliving of the traumatic event, avoidance of reminders of the event, and blunted emotions. Also common are insomnia, nightmares, wariness, poor concentration, irritability, and explosive anger or aggression. If such reactions last *less* than a month after a traumatic event, the problem is called an **acute stress disorder**. If they last *more* than a month, the person is suffering from **post-traumatic stress disorder (PTSD)** (Gupta, 2013; Sue et al., 2013).

About 3.5 percent of American adults suffer from post-traumatic stress in any given year (National Institute of Mental Health, 2013). And yet up to 20 percent of military veterans returning from combat develop PTSD, including soldiers involved in combat in Iraq and Afghanistan (Rosen et al., 2012; Salisbury & Burker, 2011). The constant threat of death and the gruesome sights and sounds of war take a terrible toll.

Dissociative Disorders

In the *dissociative disorders*, we see striking episodes of *amnesia, fugue,* or *multiple identity*. **Dissociative amnesia** is an inability to recall one's name, address, or past. **Dissociative fugue** (fewg) involves sudden, unplanned travel away from home and confusion about personal identity. In such cases, forgetting personal identity and fleeing unpleasant situations appear to be defenses against intolerable anxiety. A person suffering from a **dissociative identity disorder** has two or more separate identities or personality states. (Don't forget that identity disorders are not the same as schizophrenia. Schizophrenia, which is a psychotic disorder, was discussed in Module 62.)

One famous and dramatic example of multiple identities is described in the book *Sybil* (Schreiber, 1973). Sybil reportedly had 16 different personality states. Each identity had a distinct voice, vocabulary, and posture. One personality could play the piano (not Sybil), but the others could not.

When an identity other than Sybil was in control, Sybil experienced a "time lapse," or memory blackout. Sybil's amnesia and alternate identities first appeared during childhood. As a girl she was beaten, locked in closets, perversely tortured, sexually abused, and almost killed. Sybil's first dissociations allowed her to escape by creating another person who would suffer torture in her place. Identity disorders often begin with unbearable childhood experiences, like those that Sybil endured. A history of childhood trauma, especially sexual abuse, is found in a high percentage of persons whose personalities split into multiple identities (McLewin & Muller, 2006).

Flamboyant cases like Sybil's have led some experts to question the existence of multiple personalities (Boysen & VanBergen, 2013; Piper, 2008). However, a majority of psychologists continue to believe that multiple identity is a real, if rare, problem (Boysen, 2011; Dell, 2009). Therapy for dissociative identity disorders may make use of hypnosis, which allows contact with the various personality states. The goal of therapy is *integration* and *fusion* of the identities into a single, balanced personality.

Somatic Symptom and Related Disorders

Have you ever known someone who appeared to be healthy but seemed to constantly worry about disease? These people are preoccupied with bodily functions, such as their heartbeat or breathing or digestion. Minor physical problems—even a small sore or an occasional cough—may convince them that they have cancer or some other dreaded disease. Typically, they can't give up their fears of illness, even if doctors find no medical basis for their complaints (Dimsdale, 2011).

Are you describing hypochondria? Partly. **Somatic symptom disorder** ("body-form" disorder) is a new *DSM-5* disorder combining the features of three older disorders, *hypochondriasis* (HI-po-kon-DRY-uh-sis), *somatization disorder*, and

The Clinical File

Sick of Being Sick

At 14, Ben was in the hospital again for his sinus problem. He had already undergone 40 surgeries since the age of 8. In addition, he had been diagnosed at various times with bipolar disorder, oppositional defiant disorder, and attention deficit disorder. Ben was taking 19 different medications, and his mother said she desperately wanted him to be "healed." She sought numerous tests and never missed an appointment. But at long last, it became clear that there was nothing wrong with Ben. Left alone with doctors, Ben revealed that he was "sick of being sick."

In reality, it was Ben's mother who was sick. She was eventually diagnosed as suffering from **factitious disorder** (Awadallah et al., 2005). A factitious disorder is called *Munchausen syndrome* if the person fakes his or her own medical problems, and, as in the case with Ben, *Munchausen by proxy syndrome* if the person fakes the medical problems of someone in his or her care. As in Ben's case, most people with the syndrome are mothers who fabricate their children's illnesses (Day & Moseley, 2010). Sometimes they even deliberately harm their children. For example, one mother injected her son with 7-Up (Reisner, 2006).

But why? People who suffer from factitious disorder appear to have a pathological need to seek attention and sympathy from medical professionals. They also may win praise for being health conscious or a good parent (Day & Moseley, 2010).

Adjustment disorder *Emotional disturbance caused by ongoing stressors within the range of common experience.*

Acute stress disorder *A psychological disturbance lasting up to one month following stresses that would produce anxiety in anyone who experienced them.*

Post-traumatic stress disorder (PTSD) *A psychological disturbance lasting more than one month following stresses that would produce anxiety in anyone who experienced them.*

Dissociative amnesia *Loss of memory (partial or complete) for important information related to personal identity.*

Dissociative fugue *(fewg) Sudden travel away from home, plus confusion about one's personal identity.*

Dissociative identity disorder *The presence of two or more distinct personalities (multiple personality).*

Factitious disorder (Munchausen syndrome) *To gain attention, an affected person fakes his or her medical problems or those of someone in his or her care.*

Somatic symptom disorder *Includes one or more of the following: interpreting normal bodily sensations as proof of disease (hypochondria); expressing anxieties through bodily complaints; and/or disabling pain with no identifiable physical basis.*

pain disorder (American Psychiatric Association, 2013). People with this disorder typically display some combination of the following: (1) interpreting normal bodily sensations as proof that they have a terrible disease (hypochondria), (2) expressing *their* anxieties through various bodily complaints, and (3) disabling pain that has no identifiable physical basis. Such individuals may suffer from problems such as vomiting or nausea, shortness of breath, difficulty swallowing, or painful menstrual periods. Typically, the person feels ill much of the time and visits doctors repeatedly. Most sufferers take medicines or other treatments, but no physical cause can be found for their distress. (See "Sick of Being Sick" for a related disorder with a curious twist).

In **conversion disorder**, another rare disorder, severe emotional conflicts are "converted" into symptoms that actually disturb physical functioning or closely resemble a physical disability. For instance, a soldier might become deaf or lame or develop "glove anesthesia" just before a battle.

Glove anesthesia? Glove anesthesia is a loss of sensitivity in the areas of the skin that would normally be covered by a glove. Glove anesthesia shows that conversion symptoms often contradict known medical facts. The system of nerves in the hands does not form a glove-like pattern and could not cause such symptoms (● **Figure 63.1**).

Age fotostock/SuperStock

Uncontrollable sneezing, which may continue for days or weeks, is often a conversion disorder. In such cases, sneezing is atypical in rate and rhythm. In addition, the person's eyes do not close during a sneeze and sneezing does not occur during sleep. (A normal sneeze is shown here.) All these signs suggest that the cause of the sneezing is psychological, not physical (Fochtmann, 1995).

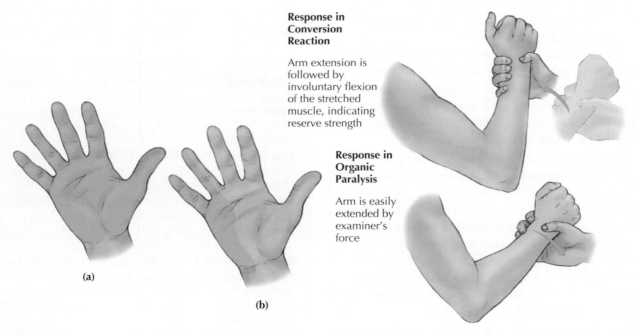

Response in Conversion Reaction

Arm extension is followed by involuntary flexion of the stretched muscle, indicating reserve strength

Response in Organic Paralysis

Arm is easily extended by examiner's force

(a)

(b)

● **Figure 63.1**

(*left*) "Glove anesthesia" is a conversion reaction involving loss of feeling in areas of the hand that would be covered by a glove (*a*). If the "anesthesia" were physically caused, it would follow the pattern shown in (*b*). (*right*) To test for organic paralysis of the arm, an examiner can suddenly extend the arm, stretching the muscles. A conversion reaction is indicated if the arm pulls back involuntarily. (Adapted from Weintraub, 1983.)

If symptoms disappear when a victim is asleep, hypnotized, or anesthetized, a conversion reaction must be suspected (Russo et al., 1998). Another sign to note is that victims of conversion reactions are strangely unconcerned about suddenly being disabled.

Anxiety and Disorder—Four Pathways to Trouble

SURVEY QUESTION 63.2: How do psychologists explain anxiety-related disorders?

Anxiety-related disorders also may be best explained by the stress-vulnerability model. Susceptibility to anxiety-related disorders appears to be partly inherited (Rachman, 2013). Studies show that being high-strung, nervous, or emotional runs in families. For example, 60 percent of children born to parents suffering from panic disorder have a fearful, inhibited temperament. Such children are irritable and wary as infants, shy and fearful as toddlers, and quiet and cautious introverts in elementary school. By the time they reach adulthood, they are at high risk for anxiety problems, such as panic attacks (Barlow, 2000; Durand & Barlow, 2013).

There are at least four major psychological perspectives on the causes of the anxiety-related disorders: (1) the *psychodynamic* approach, (2) the *humanistic-existential* approach, (3) the *behavioral* approach, and (4) the *cognitive* approach.

Psychodynamic Approach

The term *psychodynamic* refers to internal motives, conflicts, unconscious forces, and other dynamics of mental life. Freud was the first to propose a psychodynamic explanation for what he called "neurosis." According to Freud, disturbances like those we have described represent a raging conflict among subparts of the personality—the id, ego, and superego.

Freud emphasized that intense anxiety can be caused by forbidden id impulses for sex or aggression that threaten to break through into behavior. The person constantly fears doing something "crazy" or forbidden. She or he also may be tortured by guilt, which the superego uses to suppress forbidden impulses. Caught in the middle, the ego is eventually overwhelmed. This forces the person to use rigid defense mechanisms and misguided, inflexible behavior to prevent a disastrous loss of control (see Module 57).

Humanistic-Existential Approaches

Humanistic theories emphasize subjective experience, human problems, and personal potentials. Humanistic psychologist Carl Rogers regarded disorders of emotion, including the anxiety-related disorders, as the end product of a faulty self-image or self-concept (Rogers, 1959). Rogers believed that anxious individuals have built up unrealistic mental images of themselves. This leaves them vulnerable to contradictory information. Let's say, for example, that an essential part of Cheyenne's self-image is the idea that she is highly intelligent. If Cheyenne does poorly in school, she may begin to deny or distort her perceptions of herself and the situation. Should Cheyenne's anxiety become severe, she may resort to using defense mechanisms. A conversion reaction, anxiety attacks, or similar symptoms also may result from threats to her self-image. These symptoms, in turn, might become new threats that provoke further distortions. Soon, she could fall into a vicious cycle of maladjustment and anxiety that feeds on itself once started.

Existentialism focuses on the elemental problems of existence, such as death, meaning, choice, and responsibility. Psychologists who take a more existential view stress that unhealthy anxiety reflects a loss of *meaning* in one's life. According to them, we must show *courage* and *responsibility* in our choices if life is to have meaning. Too often, they say, we give in to "existential anxiety" and back away from life-enhancing choices. Existential anxiety is the unavoidable anguish that comes from knowing we are personally responsible for our lives. Hence, we have a crushing need to choose wisely and courageously as we face life's empty and impersonal void. Adolescents may experience considerable existential anxiety as they develop their identity (Berman, Weems, & Stickle, 2006).

From the existential view, people who are anxious are living in "bad faith"; that is, they have collapsed in the face of the awesome responsibility to choose a meaningful existence. In short, they have lost their way in life. From this point of view, making choices that don't truly reflect what you value, feel, and believe can make you sick.

Conversion disorder *A bodily symptom that mimics a physical disability but is actually caused by anxiety or emotional distress.*

Behavioral Approach

Behaviorist approaches emphasize overt, observable behavior and the effects of learning and conditioning. Behaviorists assume that the "symptoms" we have discussed are learned, just as other behaviors are learned. You might recall from Module 28, for instance, that phobias can be acquired through classical conditioning. Similarly, anxiety attacks may reflect conditioned emotional responses that generalize to new situations, and the hypochondriac's "sickness behavior" may be reinforced by the sympathy and attention he or she gets. One point on which all theorists agree is that disordered behavior is ultimately self-defeating because it makes the person more miserable in the long run, even though it temporarily lowers anxiety.

But if the person becomes more miserable in the long run, how does the pattern get started? The behavioral explanation is that self-defeating behavior begins with avoidance learning (described in Module 30). Avoidance learning occurs when making a response delays or prevents the onset of a painful or unpleasant stimulus. Here's a quick review to refresh your memory:

> An animal is placed in a special cage. After a few minutes a light comes on, followed a moment later by a painful shock. Quickly, the animal escapes into a second chamber. After a few minutes, a light comes on in this chamber, and the shock is repeated. Soon the animal learns to avoid pain by moving before the shock occurs. Once an animal learns to avoid the shock, it can be turned off altogether. A well-trained animal may avoid the non-existent shock indefinitely.

The same analysis can be applied to human behavior. A behaviorist would say that the powerful reward of immediate relief from anxiety keeps self-defeating avoidance behaviors alive. This view, known as the **anxiety reduction hypothesis**, seems to explain why the behavior patterns we have discussed often look very "stupid" to outside observers.

Cognitive Approach

The cognitive view is that distorted thinking causes people to magnify ordinary threats and failures, which leads to distress (Steinman et al., 2013). For example, Bonnie, who is socially phobic, constantly has upsetting thoughts about being evaluated at school. One reason for such thoughts is that people with social phobias tend to be perfectionists. Like other social phobics, Bonnie is excessively concerned about making mistakes.

She also perceives criticism when none exists. If Bonnie expects that a social situation will focus too much attention on her, she avoids it (Brown & Barlow, 2011). Even when socially phobic persons are successful, distorted thoughts lead them to believe they have failed. In short, changing the thinking patterns of anxious individuals like Bonnie can greatly lessen their fears (Arch et al., 2013).

Implications All four psychological explanations probably contain a core of truth. For this reason, understanding anxiety-related disorders may be aided by combining parts of each perspective. Each viewpoint also suggests a different approach to treatment. Because many possibilities exist, therapy is discussed in later modules.

Personality Disorders— Blueprints for Maladjustment

SURVEY QUESTION 63.3: What is a personality disorder?

"Get out of here and leave me alone so I can die in peace," Judy screamed at her nurses in the seclusion room of the psychiatric hospital. Long, dark-red marks on one of her arms mingled with the scars of previous suicide attempts. Judy once bragged that her record was 67 stitches. Today, the nurses had to strap her into restraints to keep her from gouging her own eyes. She was given a sedative and slept for 12 hours. She woke calmly and asked for her therapist—even though her latest outburst began when he canceled a morning appointment and changed it to afternoon.

Judy has a condition called *borderline personality disorder*. Although she is capable of working, Judy has repeatedly lost jobs because of her turbulent relationships with other people. At times, she can be friendly and a real charmer. At other times, she is extremely unpredictable, moody, and even suicidal. Being a friend to Judy can be a fearsome challenge. Canceling an appointment, forgetting a special date, uttering a wrong turn of phrase—these and similar small incidents may trigger Judy's rage or a suicide attempt. Like other people with borderline personality disorder, Judy is extremely sensitive to ordinary criticism, which leaves her feeling rejected and abandoned. Typically, she reacts with anger, self-hatred, and impulsive behavior. These "emotional storms" damage her personal relationships and leave her confused about who she is (Siever & Koenigsberg, 2000).

TABLE 63.2	*DSM-5* Classification of Personality Disorders
Type of Personality Disorder	**Typical Signs of Trouble**
Paranoid	You deeply distrust others and are suspiciousness of their motives, which you perceive as insulting or threatening.
Schizoid	You feel very little emotion and can't form close personal relationships with others.
Schizotypal	You are a loner, you engage in extremely odd behavior, and your thought patterns are bizarre, but you are not actively psychotic.
Antisocial	You are irresponsible, lack guilt or remorse, and engage in antisocial behavior, such as aggression, deceit, or recklessness.
Borderline	Your self-image, moods, and impulses are erratic, and you are extremely sensitive to any hint of criticism, rejection, or abandonment by others.
Histrionic	You are dramatic and flamboyant; you exaggerate your emotions to get attention from others.
Narcissistic	You think you are wonderful, brilliant, important, and worthy of constant admiration.
Avoidant	You are timid, uncomfortable in social situations, and fear evaluation.
Dependent	You lack confidence, and you are extremely submissive and dependent on others (clinging).
Obsessive-compulsive	You demand order, perfection, control, and rigid routine at all times.

Sources: American Psychiatric Association (2013); Durand & Barlow (2013).

Maladaptive Personality Patterns

As stated earlier, a person with a personality disorder has maladaptive personality traits. For example, people with a *paranoid personality disorder* are suspicious, hypersensitive, and wary of others. *Narcissistic persons* need constant admiration and they are lost in fantasies of power, wealth, brilliance, beauty, or love. Celebrities appear more likely to be narcissistic than noncelebrities, perhaps because they receive so much attention (Young & Pinsky, 2006). The *dependent personality* suffers from extremely low self-confidence. Dependent persons allow others to run their lives, and they place everyone else's needs ahead of their own. People with a *histrionic personality disorder* constantly seek attention by dramatizing their emotions and actions.

Typically, patterns such as the ones just described begin during adolescence or even childhood. Thus, *personality disorders* are deeply rooted and usually span many years. The list of personality disorders is long (● Table 63.2), so let's focus on the antisocial personality.

Antisocial Personality

What are the characteristics of an antisocial personality? A person with an **antisocial personality** lacks a conscience. Such people are impulsive, selfish, dishonest, emotionally shallow,

and manipulative (Visser et al., 2010). Antisocial persons, who are sometimes called *sociopaths* or *psychopaths*, are poorly socialized and seem to be incapable of feeling guilt, shame, fear, loyalty, or love (American Psychiatric Association, 2013).

Are sociopaths dangerous? Sociopaths tend to have a long history of conflict with society. Many are delinquents or criminals who may be a threat to the general public (Bateman & Fonagy, 2012; Lobbestael, Cima, & Arntz, 2013). However, sociopaths are rarely the crazed murderers you may have seen portrayed in the media. In fact, many sociopaths are "charming" at first. Their "friends" only gradually become aware of the sociopath's lying and self-serving manipulation. One study found that psychopaths are "blind" to signs of disgust in others. This may add to their capacity for cruelty and their ability to use others (Kosson et al., 2002). Many successful businesspersons, entertainers, politicians, and other seemingly normal people have sociopathic leanings. Basically, antisocial persons coldly use others and cheat their way through life (Ogloff, 2006).

Anxiety reduction hypothesis *Explains the self-defeating nature of avoidance responses as a result of the reinforcing effects of relief from anxiety.*
Antisocial personality (antisocial/psychopathic personality) *A person who lacks a conscience; is emotionally shallow, impulsive, selfish; and tends to manipulate others.*

Causes *What causes sociopathy?* Typically, people with antisocial personalities showed similar problems in childhood (Burt et al., 2007). Adult sociopaths also display subtle neurological problems (● Figure 63.2). For example, they have unusual brain-wave patterns that suggest underarousal of the brain. This may explain why sociopaths tend to be thrill seekers. Quite likely, they are searching for stimulation strong enough to overcome their chronic underarousal and feelings of "boredom" (Hare, 2006; Pemment, 2013).

In a revealing study, sociopaths were shown extremely grisly and unpleasant photographs of mutilations. The photos were so upsetting that they visibly startled normal people. The sociopaths, however, showed no startle response to the photos (Levenston et al., 2000). (They didn't "bat an eyelash.") Those with antisocial personalities might therefore be described as *emotionally cold.* They simply do not feel normal pangs of conscience, guilt, or anxiety (Blair et al., 2006). Again, this coldness seems to account for an unusual ability to calmly lie, cheat, steal, or take advantage of others.

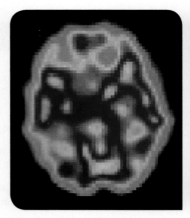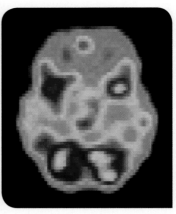

Courtesy of Robert Hare

● **Figure 63.2**

Using PET scans, Canadian psychologist Robert Hare found that the normally functioning brain (*left*) lights up with activity when a person sees emotion-laden words such as "maggot" or "cancer." But the brain of a psychopath (*right*) remains inactive, especially in areas associated with feelings and self-control. When Dr. Hare showed the right image to several neurologists, one asked, "Is this person from Mars?"

Can sociopathy be treated? Antisocial personality disorders are rarely treated with success (Bateman & Fonagy, 2012). All too often, sociopaths manipulate therapy, just like any other situation. If it is to their advantage to act "cured," they will do so. However, they return to their former behavior patterns as soon as possible. On a more positive note, antisocial behavior does tend to decline somewhat after age 40, even without treatment, because people tend to become more "mellow" as they age (Laub & Sampson, 2003).

A Look Ahead Treatments for psychological problems range from counseling and psychotherapy to mental hospitalization and drug therapy. Because they vary greatly, a complete discussion of therapies is found in Modules 65–68. For now, it's worth noting that many milder mental disorders can be treated successfully. Even major disorders may respond well to drugs and other techniques. It is wrong to fear "former mental patients" or to exclude them from work, friendships, and other social situations. A struggle with major depression or a psychotic episode does not inevitably lead to lifelong dysfunction. Too often, however, it does lead to unnecessary rejection based on groundless fears (Elkington et al., 2012; Sarason & Sarason, 2005).

Let's conclude by noting a widely misunderstood mental health problem: By the time you finish reading this page, someone in the United States will have attempted suicide. What can be done about suicide? Consider reading Module 64 for some answers.

Halfdark/fStop/Alamy

Many prison inmates have been diagnosed with antisocial personality disorder (Bateman & Fonagy, 2012).

Module 63: Summary

63.1 What problems result when a person suffers high levels of anxiety?

- **63.1.1** Anxiety disorders and anxiety-related disorders (obsessive-compulsive and related disorders, trauma- and stressor-related disorders, dissociative disorders, and somatic symptom and related disorders) are characterized by high levels of anxiety, rigid defense mechanisms, and self-defeating behavior patterns.

- **63.1.2** Anxiety disorders include generalized anxiety disorder, panic disorder, agoraphobia, specific phobias, and social phobia.

- **63.1.3** The obsessive-compulsive and related disorders include obsessive-compulsive disorder and hoarding disorder.

- **63.1.4** Trauma- and stressor-related disorders include adjustment disorder, acute stress disorder and post-traumatic stress disorder. In an adjustment disorder, ordinary stresses push people beyond their ability to cope with life.

- **63.1.5** Dissociative disorders may take the form of amnesia, fugue, or multiple identities.

- **63.1.6** Somatic symptom and related disorders center on physical complaints that mimic disease or disability. Three examples are somatic symptom disorder, factitious disorder (Munchausen syndrome), and conversion disorder.

63.2 How do psychologists explain anxiety-related disorders?

- **63.2.1** Susceptibility to anxiety-related disorders appears to be partly inherited.

- **63.2.2** The psychodynamic approach emphasizes unconscious conflicts as the cause of disabling anxiety.

- **63.2.3** The humanistic approach emphasizes the effects of a faulty self-image.

- **63.2.4** The behaviorists emphasize the effects of previous learning, particularly avoidance learning.

- **63.2.5** Cognitive theories of anxiety focus on distorted thinking and being fearful of others' attention and judgments.

63.3 What is a personality disorder?

- **63.3.1** Personality disorders are persistent, maladaptive personality patterns.

- **63.3.2** Sociopathy is a common personality disorder. Antisocial persons seem to lack a conscience. They are emotionally unresponsive, manipulative, shallow, and dishonest.

Module 63: Knowledge Builder

Recite

1. Excessive anxiety over ordinary life stresses is characteristic of which of the following disorders?
   - *a.* PTSD
   - *b.* agoraphobia
   - *c.* hypochondriasis
   - *d.* adjustment disorder

2. Panic disorder can occur with or without agoraphobia, but agoraphobia cannot occur alone, without the presence of a panic disorder. *T or F?*

3. Alice has a phobic fear of closed spaces. What is the formal term for her fear?
   - *a.* nyctophobia
   - *b.* claustrophobia
   - *c.* pathophobia
   - *d.* pyrophobia

4. The symptoms of acute stress disorders last less than one month; post-traumatic stress disorders last more than one month. *T or F?*

5. Which of the following is *not* a dissociative disorder?
   - *a.* fugue
   - *b.* amnesia
   - *c.* conversion reaction
   - *d.* multiple identity

6. According to the _____ view, anxiety disorders are the end result of a loss of meaning.
   - *a.* psychodynamic
   - *b.* humanistic
   - *c.* behaviorist
   - *d.* cognitive

7. Antisocial personality disorders are difficult to treat, but typically, antisocial behavior declines a year or two after adolescence. *T or F?*

Reflect

Think Critically

8. In this module, we met Ben's mother, who was deliberately faking her son's "illnesses." How could someone get away with Munchausen by proxy syndrome? Wouldn't doctors figure out that something was fishy with Ben long before he had 40 surgeries for a faked sinus disorder?

Self-Reflect

Which of the anxiety disorders would you *least* want to suffer from? Why?

What minor obsessions or compulsions have you experienced?

Which of the four psychological explanations of anxiety-related disorders do you find most convincing?

Many of the qualities that define personality disorders exist to a minor degree in normal personalities. Try to think of a person you know who has some of the characteristics described for each type of personality disorder.

ANSWERS

1. d. 2. F. 3. b. 4. T. 5. c. 6. b. 7. F. 8. No one doctor tolerates false symptoms for long. Once a doctor refuses further treatment, the Munchausen sufferer moves on to another. Also, more than one doctor is often being seen.

Psychology in Action: Suicide

Too Permanent a Solution?

Talk show host Phil Donahue once commented that "suicide is a permanent solution to a temporary problem." If this is so obvious, then why is suicide so distressingly common? In North America, for every three people who die by homicide, five kill themselves. And, there may be ten times as many suicide attempts for every "successful" suicide. Sooner or later, you are likely to be affected by the suicide attempt of someone you know.

It is estimated that about two-thirds of all suicide attempts are made by people who do not really want to die. Almost a third more are *ambivalent* or undecided about dying. Very few suicide cases involve people who really want to die. Most people, therefore, are relieved when someone comes to their aid. Remember that suicide is almost always a cry for help and that you *can* help. Let's find out how.

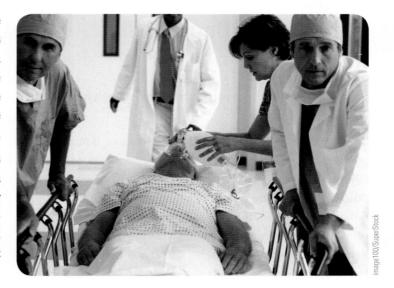
image100/SuperStock

SURVEY QUESTION

64.1 Why do people commit suicide, and can they be stopped?

Suicide—A Permanent Solution?

SURVEY QUESTION 64.1: Why do people commit suicide, and can they be stopped?

Why do people try to kill themselves? The best explanation for suicide may simply come from a look at the conditions that precede it. A diagnosable mental disorder (usually depression or substance abuse disorder) is a factor in 90 percent of all suicides (National Institute of Mental Health, 2011). Suicidal people usually have a history of trouble with family, a lover, or a spouse. Often they have drinking or drug abuse problems, sexual adjustment problems, or job difficulties.

The following are all major risk factors for suicide (National Institute of Mental Health, 2010a, 2011; Joiner, 2010): drug or alcohol abuse; a prior suicide attempt; depression or other mood disorder; feelings of hopelessness or worthlessness; antisocial, impulsive, or aggressive behavior; severe anxiety; panic attacks; a family history of suicidal behavior; shame, humiliation, failure, or rejection; and the availability of a firearm. Among ethnic adolescents, loss of face, acculturative stress, racism, and discrimination have been identified as additional risk factors (Goldston et al., 2008).

Typically, suicidal people isolate themselves from others; feel worthless, helpless, and misunderstood; and want to die. An extremely negative self-image and severe feelings of hopelessness are warnings that the risk for suicide is very high (Britton et al., 2008; Heisel, Flett, & Hewitt, 2003). However, a long history of such conditions is not always necessary to produce a desire for suicide. Anyone may temporarily reach a state of depression severe enough to impulsively attempt suicide. Most dangerous for the average person are times of divorce, separation, rejection, failure, and bereavement.

Such situations can seem intolerable and motivate an intense desire to escape, to obtain relief, or to die (Boergers, Spirito, & Donaldson, 1998). For young people, feelings of anger and hostility add to the danger. When the impulse to harm others is turned inward, the risk for suicide increases dramatically.

Factors Affecting Suicide Rates

Suicide rates vary greatly, but some general patterns do emerge.

Sex Men are "better" at suicide than women. Four times as many men *complete* suicide, but women make more attempts (Denney et al., 2009; National Institute of Mental Health, 2010). Male suicide attempts are more lethal because men typically use a gun or an equally fatal method. Women most often attempt a drug overdose, so there's a better chance of help arriving before death occurs. Sadly, women are beginning to use more deadly methods and may soon equal men in their likelihood of death by suicide.

Ethnicity Suicide rates vary dramatically from country to country (Colucci, 2013). The rate in the United States is almost ten times higher than the rate in Azerbaijan, and, in turn, the rate in Hungary is more than three times the U.S. rate (Lester & Yang, 2005). Within the United States, Caucasians generally have higher suicide rates than non-Caucasians (● **Figure 64.1**), although rates have increased among African-Americans in recent years (National Institute of Mental Health, 2010a). Sadly, the suicide rate among Native Americans is by far the highest in the country (suicide rates also are elevated among the aboriginal peoples of other countries) (Goldston et al., 2008; Sveticic, Milner, & De Leo, 2012).

Age Suicide rates increase with advancing age. More than half of all suicide victims are over 45 years old (see Figure 64.1). White males 65 years and older are particularly at risk. Of special concern is the rate of suicide among younger people. Between 1950 and 1990, suicide rates for adolescents and young adults doubled (Durand & Barlow, 2013). In fact, suicide is the third leading cause of death among 15- to 24-year-olds (National Institute of Mental Health, 2010a). School is a factor in some suicides, but only in the sense that suicidal students were not living up to their own extremely high standards. Many were good students. Other important factors in student suicide are cocaine or alcohol use (Garlow, Purselle, & Heninger, 2007), chronic health problems (real or imagined), and interpersonal difficulties. (Some who commit suicide are rejected lovers, but others are simply withdrawn and friendless people.)

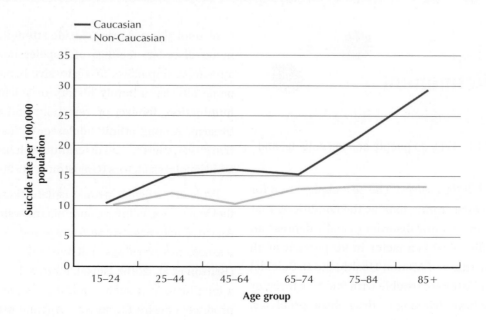

● **Figure 64.1**

In the United States, in general, suicide rates for Caucasians are higher than those for non-Caucasians. Also, older people have higher suicide rates than younger people (Centers for Disease Control, 2003; National Institute of Mental Health, 2008).

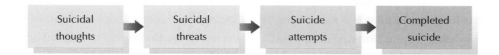

● Figure 64.2

Suicidal behavior usually progresses from suicidal thoughts, to threats, to attempts. A person is unlikely to make an attempt without first making threats. Thus, suicide threats should be taken seriously (Leenaars, A. A., Lester, D., & Wenckstern, S. (2005). Coping with suicide: The art and the research. In R. I. Yufit & D. Lester (Eds.), Assessment, treatment, and prevention of suicidal behavior (pp. 347–377). New York: Wiley).

Marital Status Marital status also is related to suicide rates. Married individuals have lower suicide rates than divorced, widowed, or single persons (Yip & Thorburn, 2004), at least among men (Denney et al., 2009).

Preventing Suicide

Is it true that people who talk about or threaten suicide are rarely the ones who try it? No, this is a major fallacy. Of every ten potential suicides, eight give warning beforehand. A person who threatens suicide should be taken seriously (see ● **Figure 64.2**). A suicidal person may say nothing more than "I feel sometimes like I'd be better off dead." Warnings also may come indirectly. If a friend gives you a favorite ring and says, "Here, I won't be needing this anymore" or comments, "I guess I won't get my watch fixed—it doesn't matter anyway," it may be a plea for help.

The warning signs in the list that follows, especially if they are observed in combination, can signal an impending suicide attempt (Leenaars, Lester, & Wenckstern, 2005; National Institute of Mental Health, 2011):

- Direct threats to commit suicide
- Preoccupation with death
- Depression/hopelessness
- Rage/anger or seeking revenge
- Aggression and/or risk taking
- Alcohol/drug use
- Withdrawal from contact with others
- No sense of purpose in life
- Sudden swings in mood
- Personality change
- Gift giving of prized possessions
- Recent occurrence of life crisis or emotional shock

Is it true that suicide can't be prevented, that the person will find a way to do it anyway? No. Suicide attempts usually come when a person is alone, depressed, and unable to view matters objectively. You *should* intervene if someone seems to be threatening suicide.

How to Help

What is the best thing to do if someone hints they are thinking about suicide? It helps to know some of the common characteristics of suicidal thoughts and feelings (Leenaars, Lester, & Wenckstern, 2005):

1. **Escape.** At times, everyone feels like running away from an upsetting situation. Running away from home, quitting school, abandoning a marriage—these are all departures. Suicide, of course, is the ultimate escape. It helps when suicidal persons see that the natural wish for escape doesn't have to be expressed by ending it all.

2. **Unbearable psychological pain.** Emotional pain is what the suicidal person is seeking to escape. A goal of anyone hoping to prevent suicide should be to reduce the pain in any way possible. Ask the person, "Where does it hurt?" Suicide occurs when pain exceeds a person's resources for coping with pain.

3. **Frustrated psychological needs.** Often, suicide can be prevented if a distressed person's frustrated needs can be identified and eased. Is the person deeply frustrated in his or her search for love, achievement, trust, security, or friendship?

4. **Constriction of options.** The suicidal person feels helpless and decides that death is the *only* solution. The person has narrowed all his or her options solely to death. The rescuer's goal, then, is to help broaden the person's perspective. Even when all the choices are unpleasant, suicidal persons can usually be made to see that their *least unpleasant option* is better than death.

Knowing these patterns will give some guidance in talking to a suicidal person. In addition, your most important task may be to establish *rapport* (a harmonious connection) with the person. You should offer support, acceptance, and legitimate caring.

Remember that a suicidal person feels misunderstood. Try to accept and understand the feelings the person is expressing. It is completely acceptable to ask, "Are you thinking of suicide?"

Establishing communication with suicidal persons may be enough to carry them through a difficult time. You also may find it helpful to get day-by-day commitments from them to meet for lunch, share a ride, and the like. Let the person know you *expect* her or him to be there. Such commitments, even though small, can be enough to tip the scales when a person is alone and thinking about suicide.

Don't end your efforts too soon. A dangerous time for suicide is when a person suddenly seems to get better after a severe depression. This often means the person has finally decided to end it all. The improvement in mood is deceptive because it comes from an anticipation that suffering is about to end.

Crisis Intervention

Most cities have mental health crisis intervention teams or centers for suicide prevention trained to talk with suicidal persons over the phone (Spencer-Thomas & Jahn, 2012). Give a person who seems to be suicidal the number of one of these services. Urge the person to call you or the other number if she or he becomes frightened or impulsive. Or better yet, help the person make an appointment to get psychological treatment (Kleiman, Miller, & Riskind, 2012; Weishaar, 2006).

The preceding applies mainly to persons who are having mild suicidal thoughts. If a person actually threatens suicide, or if a suicide attempt seems to be imminent, don't worry about overreacting. Immediately seek professional assistance by calling the police, crisis intervention, or a rescue unit. If that is not feasible, ask how the person plans to carry out the suicide. A person who has a *specific*, *workable plan*, and the means to carry it out should be asked to accompany you to the emergency ward of a hospital.

Needless to say, you should call for help immediately if a person is in the act of attempting suicide or if a drug has already been taken. The majority of suicide attempts come at temporary low points in a person's life and may never be repeated. Get involved—you may save a life!

Module 64: Summary

64.1 Why do people commit suicide, and can they be stopped?
- **64.1.1** Suicide is a relatively frequent cause of death that can, in many cases, be prevented.
- **64.1.2** Suicide is statistically related to such factors as sex, ethnicity, age, and marital status.

- **64.1.3** In individual cases, the potential for suicide is best identified by a desire to escape, unbearable psychological pain, and frustrated psychological needs.
- **64.1.4** People contemplating suicide narrow their options until death seems like the only way out.
- **64.1.5** The impulse to attempt suicide is usually temporary. Efforts to prevent suicide are worthwhile.

Module 64: Knowledge Builder

Recite

1. More women than men use guns in their suicide attempts. *T or F?*
2. While the overall suicide rate has remained about the same, adolescent suicides have decreased. *T or F?*
3. Suicide is equally a problem in all countries. *T or F?*
4. The highest suicide rates are found among the divorced. *T or F?*
5. The majority (two-thirds) of suicide attempts are made by people who do not really want to die. *T or F?*
6. The risk that a person may attempt suicide is greatest if the person has
    a. a concrete, workable plan
    b. had a recent life crisis
    c. withdrawn from contact with others
    d. frustrated psychological needs

Reflect

Think Critically

7. If you follow the history of popular music, see if you can answer this question: What two major risk factors contributed to the 1994 suicide of Kurt Cobain, lead singer for the rock group Nirvana?

Self-Reflect

You're working a suicide hotline and you take a call from a very distressed young man. What risk factors will you look for as he tells you about his anguish?

What are the common characteristics of suicidal thoughts and feelings? If a friend of yours were to express any of these thoughts or feelings, how would you respond?

ANSWERS

1. F 2. F 3. F 4. T 5. T 6. a 7. Drug or alcohol abuse and availability of a firearm

CENGAGE brain.com

Go to **cengagebrain.com** to access **MindTap for Coon/Mitterer** *Psychology Modules for Active Learning* and other online learning tools. MindTap is a fully online learning experience that combines all the tools you need—readings, multimedia, activities, and assessments—into a singular personalized Learning Path that guides you through the course.

Therapies: Treating Psychological Distress

Like a Duck

Joe stared through the window in his professor's office at the ducks, quacking away on the campus pond. His teacher was surprised. Joe's excellent work in class and his healthy, casual appearance left her unprepared when he murmured, "I feel like I'm losing my mind." He told her about working hard to hide a world of crippling fear, anxiety, and depression. At work, he was deathly afraid to talk to coworkers and customers. Several disastrous romances had left him terrified of women. As Joe described his own personal hell, it became clear he felt like the ducks outside, appearing peaceful on the surface, but madly paddling underneath.

This module offers an overview of methods used to alleviate problems like Joe's. We begin with a look at the origins of modern therapy and identify both the ways contemporary psychotherapies differ and the core features all successful therapies share.

Warren Goldswain/Shutterstock

SURVEY QUESTIONS

65.1 How did psychotherapy originate?

65.2 How do contemporary psychotherapies differ?

65.3 What do various psychotherapies have in common and are they effective?

Origins of Therapy— Bored Out of Your Skull

SURVEY QUESTION 65.1: How did psychotherapy originate?

Early treatments for mental problems give good reasons to appreciate modern therapies (Sharf, 2012). Archaeological findings dating to the Stone Age suggest that most premodern approaches were marked by fear and superstitious belief in spirits, demons, witchcraft, and magic (McNamara, 2011). If Joe had been unlucky enough to be born several thousand years ago, his "treatment" might have left him feeling "bored." One of the more dramatic "cures" practiced by primitive "therapists" was a process called *trepanning* (treh-PAN-ing), also

sometimes spelled *trephining* (Terry, 2006). In modern usage, trepanning is any surgical procedure in which a hole is bored in the skull. In the hands of primitive therapists, it meant boring, chipping, or bashing holes in a patient's head. Presumably, this was done to relieve pressure or release the spirits "possessing" him or her (● Figure 65.1).

Joe would not have been much better off during the Middle Ages. Then, treatments for mental illness in Europe focused on demonology, the study of demons and persons plagued by them. Medieval "therapists" commonly blamed abnormal behavior on supernatural forces, such as possession by the devil, or on curses from witches and wizards. As a cure, they used exorcism to "cast out evil spirits." For the fortunate, exorcism was a religious ritual. More often, physical torture was used to make the body an inhospitable place for the devil to reside.

Figure 65.1

Primitive "treatment" for mental disorders sometimes took the form of boring a hole in the skull. This example shows signs of healing, which means the patient survived the treatment. Many didn't.

Modern analyses of "demonic possession" suggest that many victims may have been suffering from epilepsy, schizophrenia, dissociative disorders, Tourette's syndrome, and depression (McNamara, 2011; Mirsky & Duncan, 2005; Thase, 2006; van der Hart, Lierens, & Goodwin, 1996). Thus, many people "treated" by demonologists may have been doubly victimized.

Then, in 1793, a French doctor named Philippe Pinel changed the Bicêtre Asylum in Paris from a squalid "madhouse" into a mental hospital by unchaining the inmates (Schuster, Hoertel, & Limosin, 2011). Finally, the emotionally disturbed were regarded as "mentally ill" and given compassionate treatment. Although it has been more than 200 years since Pinel began more humane treatment, the process of improving care continues today.

When was psychotherapy developed? In contrast to medical therapies, which are physical in nature, the first true **psychotherapy**—a psychological technique that can bring about positive changes in personality, behavior, or personal adjustment—was created by Sigmund Freud little more than

100 years ago (Borch-Jacobsen & Shamdasani, 2011). As a physician in Vienna, Freud was intrigued by cases of *hysteria*. People suffering from hysteria have physical symptoms (such as paralysis or numbness) for which no physical causes can be found. (Such problems are now called *somatic symptom disorders*, as discussed in Module 63.) Slowly, Freud became convinced that hysteria was related to deeply hidden unconscious conflicts and developed *psychoanalysis*, his "talking cure," to help patients gain insight into those conflicts (Knafo, 2009).

Psychotherapy Since Freud

Since the development of psychoanalysis, psychotherapy has undergone dramatic change, beginning with Freud's own followers, the neo-Freudians (see Module 3). Today, a wide variety of psychotherapeutic options are available.

Further, therapy has often been depicted as a complete personal transformation—a sort of "major overhaul" of the psyche. But years of research and clinical experience have made it clear that psychotherapy is *not* equally effective

(*left*) Many early asylums were no more than prisons with inmates held in chains. (*right*) One late-nineteenth-century "treatment" was based on swinging the patient in a harness—presumably to calm the patient's nerves.

Demonology *In medieval Europe, the study of demons and the treatment of persons "possessed" by demons.*

Psychotherapy *Any psychological technique used to facilitate positive changes in a person's personality, behavior, or adjustment.*

for all problems. Chances of improvement are fairly good for phobias, low self-esteem, some sexual problems, and marital conflicts. More complex problems can be difficult to solve and may, as in Joe's case, require medical treatment. The most extreme cases may not respond to psychotherapy at all, leaving a medical therapy as the only viable treatment option.

In short, it is often unrealistic to expect psychotherapy to undo a person's entire past. For many people, the major benefit of psychotherapy is that it provides comfort, support, and a way to make constructive changes. Yet even when problems are severe, therapy may help a person gain a new perspective or learn behaviors to better cope with life. Psychotherapy can be hard work for both clients and therapists, but when it succeeds, few activities are more worthwhile.

It also is a mistake to think that psychotherapy is used only to solve problems or end a crisis. Even if a person is already doing well, therapy can be a way to promote personal growth (Burns, 2010). Therapists in the positive psychology movement are developing ways to help people use their personal strengths. Rather than trying to fix what is "wrong" with a person, they seek to nurture positive traits such as self-awareness and

motivation for personal growth (Compton & Hoffman, 2013). ● Table 65.1 lists some of the elements of positive mental health that therapists seek to restore or promote.

In Modules 66, 67, and 68, we look in depth at five main types of modern therapy: psychodynamic, humanistic, cognitive, behavior, and medical therapies. Before then, let's get an overview of the various forms that contemporary psychotherapies can take.

Dimensions of Therapy— The Many Paths to Health

SURVEY QUESTION 65.2: How do contemporary psychotherapies differ?

Psychotherapy is usually based on a dialogue between therapists and their clients, although some therapists also use learning principles to directly alter troublesome behaviors. Therapists have many approaches from which to choose and, as we will see, each therapy emphasizes different concepts and methods. For this reason, the best approach for a particular person or problem may vary. The terms in the list that follows describe some basic aspects of various psychotherapies (Corsini & Wedding, 2011; Prochaska & Norcross, 2010; Sharf, 2012):

- **Insight versus action therapy:** Does the therapy aim to bring clients to a deeper understanding of their thoughts, emotions, and behavior? Or is it designed to bring about direct changes in troublesome thoughts, habits, feelings, or behavior without seeking insight into their origins or meanings?

- **Nondirective versus directive therapy:** Does the therapist provide strong guidance and advice? Or does the therapist assist clients, who are responsible for solving their own problems?

- **Open-ended versus time-limited therapy:** Is the time allotted for therapy open-ended or time-limited?

- **Individual versus group therapy:** Does the therapy involve one therapist with one client? Or can several clients participate at the same time?

- **Face-to-face versus distance therapy:** Must the therapist and client meet face-to-face, or can they successfully communicate over the telephone or the Internet?

Notice that more than one term may apply to a particular therapy. For example, it is possible to have an action-oriented,

TABLE 65.1	Elements of Positive Mental Health

- Personal autonomy and independence
- A sense of identity
- Feelings of personal worth
- Skilled interpersonal communication
- Sensitivity, nurturance, and trust
- Genuineness and honesty with self and other
- Self-control and personal responsibility
- Committed and loving personal relationships
- Capacity to forgive others and oneself
- Personal values and a purpose in life
- Self-awareness and motivation for personal growth
- Adaptive coping strategies for managing stresses and crises
- Fulfillment and satisfaction in work
- Good habits of physical health

Sources: Adapted from Burns (2010); Compton & Hoffman (2013).

directive, open-ended group therapy meeting via the Internet or an insight-oriented, nondirective, individual, time-limited therapy meeting face-to-face. In what follows, we explore these dimensions of therapies in a bit more detail.

Insight Versus Action Therapy

Freud's initial intent in developing psychoanalysis was to help patients gain insight into previously unconscious psychodynamic conflicts. A psychoanalyst might use free association and dream analysis to enable Joe to realize that his anxieties originate, say, in an unconscious fear of dying. Joe was approaching the age at which his namesake uncle Joe died prematurely of a heart attack 22 years ago. Psychoanalysts expect this insight will "discharge" Joe's unconscious pressures and alleviate his general sense of anxiety. In contrast, a more action-oriented therapist might be less concerned with *why* Joe felt anxious; she might help Joe learn some relaxation techniques and new ways of thinking about his feelings to directly relieve his anxieties whenever they get too strong. In Modules 66 and 67, we encounter psychoanalysis and the humanistic insight therapies as well as the cognitive and behavioral action therapies.

Nondirective Versus Directive Therapy

Psychoanalysis is a relatively directive therapy. Based on his analysis of Joe's free associations and dreams, his psychoanalyst might direct Joe's awareness toward his unconscious fear of dying. Without this direction, Joe might *resist* gaining the insight needed to overcome his anxiety. In a less directive therapy like *client-centered therapy*, it would be assumed that Joe must articulate his own problems and actively seek to resolve them himself. His nondirective therapist's role is to support him in his growing understanding, not to tell Joe what is "wrong" with him or how to "fix it." We further explore nondirective and directive therapies in Modules 66 and 67.

Open-Ended Versus Time-Limited Therapy

Traditional psychoanalysis was open-ended, calling for three to five therapy sessions a week, often for many years. Today, most patients are seen only once or twice per week, but treatment may still go on for years.

Most psychodynamic therapists have switched to doing time-limited, **brief psychodynamic therapy**, which uses direct questioning to reveal unconscious conflicts (Binder,

2004). Modern therapists also actively provoke emotional reactions that will lower defenses and provide insights. It is interesting that brief therapy appears to accelerate recovery. Patients seem to realize that they need to get to the heart of their problems quickly (Lemma, Target, & Fonagy, 2011).

Interpersonal Psychotherapy One example of a brief dynamic therapy is **interpersonal psychotherapy (IPT)**, which was first developed to help depressed people improve their relationships with others (Teyber & McClure, 2011). Research has confirmed that IPT is effective for depressive disorders, as well as eating disorders, substance abuse, social phobias, and personality disorders (Cuijpers et al., 2011; Fiore et al., 2008; Hoffart, 2005; Talbot & Gamble, 2008).

Liona's therapy is a good example of IPT (Brown & Barlow, 2011). Liona was suffering from depression that a therapist helped her trace to a conflict with her parents. When her father was absent, Liona adopted the role of her mother's protector and friend. However, when her father was home, she was expected to resume her role as a daughter. She was angry with her father for frequently abandoning her mother and upset about having to switch roles so often. Liona's IPT sessions (which sometimes included her mother) focused on clarifying Liona's family roles. Her mood improved a lot after her mother urged her to "stick to being herself."

Individual Versus Group Therapy

Many psychotherapies can be adapted for use in groups (Corey, 2012). Surprisingly, **group therapy**—psychotherapy done with more than one person—has turned out to be just as effective as individual therapy, and even has some special advantages (Burlingame, Fuhriman, & Mosier, 2003).

What are the advantages? In group therapy, a person can *act out* or directly experience problems. Doing so often produces insights that might not occur from merely talking about an issue. In addition, other group members with similar problems can offer support and useful input. Group therapy is especially good for helping people understand their personal relationships (Corey, 2012; McCluskey, 2002). For reasons such as

---

Brief psychodynamic therapy *A modern therapy based on psychoanalytic theory but designed to produce insights more quickly.*
Interpersonal psychotherapy (IPT) *A brief dynamic psychotherapy designed to help people by improving their relationships with other people.*
Group therapy *Psychotherapy conducted in a group setting to make therapeutic use of group dynamics.*

A group therapy session. Group members offer mutual support while sharing problems and insights.

Ghislain & Marie David de Lossy/Cultura Creative/Alamy

these, several specialized groups have emerged. Because they range from Alcoholics Anonymous to Marriage Encounter, we share only a few examples.

Psychodrama One of the first group therapies was developed by Jacob Moreno (1953), who called his technique *psychodrama*. In **psychodrama**, clients act out personal conflicts with others who play supporting roles (Blatner, 2006; McVea, Gow, & Lowe, 2011). Through role-playing, the client reenacts incidents that cause problems in real life. For example, Don, a disturbed teenager, might act out a typical family fight, with the therapist playing his father and with other clients playing his mother, brothers, and sisters. Moreno believed that insights gained in this way transfer to real-life situations.

Therapists using psychodrama often find that role reversals are helpful. A **role reversal** involves taking the part of another person to learn how he or she feels. For instance, Don might role-play his father or mother to better understand their feelings. A related method is the **mirror technique**, in which clients observe another person reenact their behavior. Thus, Don might briefly join the audience and watch as another group member plays his role. This would allow him to see himself as others see him. Later, the group may summarize what happened and reflect on its meaning.

Family and Couples Therapy Family relationships are the source of great pleasure and, all too often, great pain. In **family therapy**, parents and children work as a group to resolve the problems of each family member. This is called *couples therapy* when children are not involved (Scheinkman, 2008). Family and couples therapy tends to be time-limited and focused

on specific problems, such as frequent fights or a depressed teenager. For some types of problems, family therapy may be superior to other approaches (Eisler et al., 2007; Trull & Prinstein, 2013).

Family therapists believe that a problem experienced by one family member is the whole family's problem (Teyber & McClure, 2011). If the entire pattern of behavior in a family doesn't change, improvements in any single family member may not last. Family members, therefore, work together to improve communication, change destructive patterns, and see themselves and each other in new ways (Goldenberg & Goldenberg, 2013; Griffin, 2002).

Does the therapist work with the whole family at once? Family therapists treat the family as a unit, but they may not meet with the entire family at each session (Eisler et al., 2007). If a family crisis is at hand, the therapist may first try to identify the most resourceful family members who can help solve the immediate problem.

Face-to-Face Versus Distance Therapy

While it is generally preferable to meet with a therapist face-to-face, it is not always possible. Today, psychological services are available in the home through radio, television, telephone, and the Internet (Goss & Anthony, 2009). Not only is this generally less expensive, it also makes therapy available to people who, for a variety of reasons, cannot easily attend a traditional face-to-face session.

Mass Media Therapists By now, you have probably heard a phone-in radio psychologist or watched one on television.

Popular TV psychologist Phillip McGraw was awarded a President's Citation from the American Psychological Association for his work in publicizing mental health issues (Meyers, 2006). Media psychologists have been urged to educate without actually doing therapy on the air. Some overstep this boundary, however. Do you think Dr. Phil ever goes too far?

Participants typically describe problems ranging from child abuse to phobias and sexual adjustment to depression. The media psychologist then offers reassurance, advice, or suggestions for getting help. Such programs may seem harmless, but they raise some important questions. For instance, is it reasonable to give advice without knowing anything about a person's background? Could the advice do harm? What good can a psychologist do in three minutes or even an hour?

In their own defense, mass media psychologists point out that listeners and viewers may learn solutions to their problems by hearing others talk. Many also stress that their work is educational, not therapeutic. Nevertheless, the question arises: When does advice become therapy? The American Psychological Association urges media psychologists to discuss problems only of a general nature and not to actually counsel anyone.

Telephone and Internet Therapists Of course, mass media psychologists must entertain as well as educate. Most distance therapy is conducted one-on-one via telephone or the Internet. Regardless of how a therapist and client communicate, perhaps the *key* feature of successful therapy is the establishment of an effective relationship between therapist and client. This could be a problem if, for example, only texting is used. Smiley faces and text message shorthand are poor substitutes for real human interaction, which includes interpersonal cues such as facial expressions and body language. ☺ lol. Similarly, brief e-mail messages are no way to make a diagnosis. However, the Internet also makes it possible to create two-way audio–video links. Conducting therapy this way lacks the close personal contact of face-to-face interaction, but it also removes many of the objections to doing therapy at a distance.

It is worth noting that distance therapy does have some distinct advantages and disadvantages. For one thing, clients can more easily remain anonymous. (But beware that e-mail counseling may not be completely confidential and could be intercepted and misused.) Thus, a person who might hesitate to see a psychologist can seek help privately, on the phone or online. Of special concern is the fact that distance therapists may or may not be trained professionals (Bloom, 1998). Even if they are, questions exist about whether a psychologist licensed in one state can legally do therapy in another state via the telephone or the Internet.

In closing, under the right circumstances, distance therapies can be successful (Bauer et al., 2011; Brenes, Ingram, & Danhauer, 2011). For example, telephone counseling helps people quit smoking (Rabius, Wiatrek, & McAlister, 2012). Other studies have shown that depressed people as well as people with social phobia and panic disorder benefit from

Psychodrama *A therapy in which clients act out personal conflicts and feelings in the presence of others who play supporting roles.*
Role reversal *Taking the role of another person to learn how one's own behavior appears from the other person's perspective.*
Mirror technique *Observing another person reenact one's own behavior, like a character in a play; designed to help persons see themselves more clearly.*
Family therapy *Technique in which all family members participate, both individually and as a group, to change destructive relationships and communication patterns.*

TABLE 65.2	Comparison of Psychotherapies			
	Insight or Action?	**Nondirective or Directive?**	**Individual or Group?**	**Therapy's Strength**
Psychoanalysis	Insight	Directive	Individual	Searching honesty
Brief psychodynamic therapy	Insight	Directive	Individual	Productive use of conflict
Client-centered therapy	Insight	Nondirective	Both	Acceptance, empathy
Existential therapy	Insight	Both	Individual	Personal empowerment
Gestalt therapy	Insight	Directive	Both	Focus on immediate awareness
Behavior therapy	Action	Directive	Both	Observable changes in behavior
Cognitive therapy	Action	Directive	Individual	Constructive guidance
Rational-emotive behavior therapy	Action	Directive	Individual	Clarity of thinking and goals
Psychodrama	Insight	Directive	Group	Constructive reenactments
Family therapy	Both	Directive	Group	Shared responsibility for problems

Sources: Adapted from Corsini & Wedding (2011); Prochaska & Norcross (2010).

Internet therapy (Carlbring et al., 2007; Klein, Richards, & Austin, 2006; Titov, 2011).

Summary For a summary of major differences among the psychotherapies discussed in this module, as well as in Modules 66 and 67, see ● Table 65.2. To add to your understanding, let's briefly summarize what all successful psychotherapies have in common.

Therapies—An Overview

SURVEY QUESTION 65.3: What do various psychotherapies have in common and are they effective?

In this section, let's ask whether the psychotherapies, regardless of what form they take, work and what, if anything, they have in common.

Core Features of Psychotherapy

What do psychotherapies have in common? Psychotherapies of various types share all or most of the following goals: understanding a client's perspective to help the client restore hope, courage, and optimism; gain insight; resolve conflicts; improve one's sense of self; change unacceptable patterns of behavior; find purpose; mend interpersonal relations; and learn to approach problems rationally (Frank & Frank, 2004; Trull & Prinstein, 2013).

Understanding another person's perspective is especially important when cultural differences may create a barrier between a client and therapist (Jun, 2010). (See "Therapy and Culture—A Bad Case of 'Ifufunyane.'"). Regardless, to accomplish these goals, psychotherapies offer the following:

1. Perhaps more than any other single factor, effective therapy provides a **therapeutic alliance**, a *caring relationship* that unites the client and therapist as they work together to solve the client's problems. The strength of this alliance

Human Diversity

Therapy and Culture—A Bad Case of "Ifufunyane"

At the age of 23, the patient was clearly suffering from "ifufunyane," a form of bewitchment common in the Xhosa culture of South Africa. However, he was treated at a local hospital by psychiatrists, who said he had schizophrenia and gave him antipsychotic drugs. The drugs helped, but his family shunned his fancy medical treatment and took him to a traditional healer who gave him herbs for his ifufunyane. Unfortunately, he got worse and was readmitted to the hospital. This time, the psychiatrists included the patient's family in his treatment. Together, they agreed to treat him with a combination of antipsychotic drugs *and* traditional herbs. This time, the patient got much better and his ifufunyane was alleviated, too (Niehaus et al., 2005).

As this example illustrates, **culturally skilled therapists** are trained to work with clients from various cultural backgrounds. To be culturally skilled, a counselor must be able to do all of the following (American Psychological Association, 2003b, 2008a; Brammer, 2012):

- Adapt traditional theories and techniques to meet the needs of clients from non-European ethnic or racial groups.

- Be aware of his or her own cultural values and biases.
- Establish rapport with a person from a different cultural background.
- Be open to cultural differences without resorting to stereotypes.
- Treat members of racial or ethnic communities as individuals.
- Be aware of a client's ethnic identity and degree of acculturation to the majority society.
- Use existing helping resources within a cultural group to support efforts to resolve problems.

Cultural awareness has helped broaden our ideas about mental health and optimal development (Brammer, 2012). It also is worth remembering that cultural barriers apply to communication in all areas of life, not just therapy. Although such differences can be challenging, they also are frequently enriching (Fowers & Davidov, 2006).

---

has a major impact on whether therapy succeeds (Meier et al., 2006; Muran & Barber, 2010). The basis for this relationship is emotional rapport, warmth, friendship, understanding, acceptance, and empathy.

2. Therapy offers a *protected setting* in which emotional *catharsis* (release) can take place. Therapy is a sanctuary in which the client is free to express fears, anxieties, and personal secrets without fearing rejection or loss of confidentiality.

3. All therapies to some extent offer an *explanation* or *rationale* for the client's suffering. In addition, they propose a line of action that will end this suffering.

4. Therapy provides clients with a *new perspective* about themselves and their situations and a chance to practice *new behaviors* (Prochaska & Norcross, 2010). Insights gained during therapy can bring about lasting changes in clients' lives (Grande et al., 2003).

Effectiveness of Psychotherapy

OK. So how effective is psychotherapy? Judging the outcome of therapy is tricky. In a national survey, nine out of ten people who have sought mental health care say their lives improved as a result of the treatment (Kotkin, Daviet, & Gurin, 1996). Unfortunately, you can't just take people's word for it. An old

joke among doctors is that a cold lasts a week without treatment and seven days with it. Perhaps the same is true of therapy. Someone who feels better after six months of therapy may have experienced a *spontaneous remission*—they just feel better because so much time has passed. Or perhaps the crisis that triggered the therapy is now nearly forgotten. Or maybe some sort of therapy placebo effect has occurred. Also, it's possible that the person has received help from other people, such as family, friends, or clergy.

To find out if therapy works, we could randomly place clients in an experimental group that receives therapy and a control group that does not. When this is done, the control group may show some improvement, even without receiving therapy (Lambert & Ogles, 2002; Schuck, Keijsers, & Rinck, 2011). Thus, we can conclude that the therapy is effective only if people in the experimental group improve more than those in the control group.

Therapeutic alliance *A caring relationship that unites a therapist and a client in working to solve the client's problems.*
Culturally skilled therapist *A therapist who has the awareness, knowledge, and skills necessary to treat clients from diverse cultural backgrounds.*

But isn't it unethical to withhold treatment from someone who really needs therapy? That's right. One way to deal with this is to use a *waiting-list control group*. In this case, people who are waiting to see a therapist are compared with those who receive therapy. Later, those on the waiting list also eventually receive therapy.

Empirically Supported Therapies Using appropriately designed studies, psychologists are making steady progress in identifying "empirically supported" (or "evidence-based") therapies (Duncan & Reese, 2013; Westen & Bradley, 2005). Hundreds of studies show a strong pattern of positive effects for psychotherapy, counseling, and other psychological treatments (Barlow, Boswell, & Thompson-Hollands, 2013; Shedler, 2010). In addition, studies have revealed that some therapies work best for specific problems (Bradley et al., 2005; Eddy et al., 2004). For example, behavioral, cognitive, and drug therapies are most helpful in treating obsessive-compulsive disorder.

As well as relying on guidelines developed through clinical practice, clinicians are seeking guidance from research experiments (David & Montgomery, 2011; Elkins, 2012). The end result is a better understanding of which therapies "work" best for specific types of problems. This trend also is helping weed out fringe "therapies" that have little or no value.

Of course, results vary in individual cases. For some people, therapy is immensely helpful; for others, it is unsuccessful. Overall, it is effective for more people than not. Speaking more subjectively, a real success, in which a person's life is changed for the better, can be worth the frustration of several cases in which little progress is made.

Although it is common to think of therapy as a long, slow process, this is not normally the case (Shapiro et al., 2003). Research shows that most clients feel better after between eight and twenty-one weekly therapy sessions (Harnett, O'Donovan, & Lambert, 2010). This means that the majority of clients improve after six months of therapy. Such rapid improvement is impressive in view of the fact that people often suffer for several years before seeking help. Unfortunately, because of high costs and limited insurance coverage, the average client receives only five therapy sessions, after which only 20 percent of all patients feel better (Hansen, Lambert, & Forman, 2002).

Module 65: Summary

65.1 How did psychotherapy originate?

- **65.1.1** Early approaches to mental illness were dominated by superstition and moral condemnation.
- **65.1.2** Demonology attributed mental disturbance to demonic possession and prescribed exorcism as the cure.
- **65.1.3** More humane treatment began in 1793 with the work of Philippe Pinel in Paris.
- **65.1.4** Sigmund Freud developed psychoanalysis, the first psychotherapy, little more than a hundred years ago.

65.2 How do contemporary psychotherapies differ?

- **65.2.1** All psychotherapy aims to facilitate positive changes in personality, behavior, or adjustment.
- **65.2.2** Psychotherapies may be classified as insight, action, nondirective, directive, and combinations of these.
- **65.2.3** Therapies may be open-ended or time-limited, conducted either individually or in groups, and either face-to-face or at a distance.

- **65.2.4** In psychodrama, individuals enact roles and incidents resembling their real-life problems. In family therapy, the family group is treated as a unit.
- **65.2.5** Telephone counselors and Internet therapists can provide some effective mental health services at a distance.

65.3 What do various psychotherapies have in common and are they effective?

- **65.3.1** Most psychotherapies are based on the therapeutic alliance, a protected setting, catharsis, insights, new perspectives, and a chance to practice new behaviors.
- **65.3.2** The culturally skilled counselor must be able to establish rapport with a person from a different cultural background and adapt traditional theories and techniques to meet the needs of clients from non-European ethnic groups.
- **65.3.3** Psychotherapy is generally effective, although no single form of therapy is superior to others.

Module 65: Knowledge Builder

Recite

Match: **A.** Change behavior **B.** Place responsibility on the client

C. The client is guided strongly **D.** Seek understanding

_____1.   Directive therapies

_____2.   Action therapies

_____3.   Insight therapies

_____4.   Nondirective therapies

5. In psychodrama, people attempt to form meaningful wholes out of disjointed thoughts, feelings, and actions. *T or F?*

6. The mirror technique is frequently used in
   - *a.* exposure therapy
   - *b.* psychodrama
   - *c.* family therapy
   - *d.* ECT

7. To date, the most acceptable type of "distance therapy" is
   - *a.* media psychology
   - *b.* commercial telephone counseling
   - *c.* emoticon-based therapy
   - *d.* based on two-way audio and video links

8. Emotional rapport, warmth, understanding, acceptance, and empathy are the core of
   - *a.* the therapeutic alliance
   - *b.* large-group awareness training
   - *c.* role reversals
   - *d.* action therapy

9. Culturally skilled therapists do all but one of the following. Which one does *not* apply?
   - *a.* Are aware of the client's degree of acculturation
   - *b.* Use helping resources within the client's cultural group
   - *c.* Adapt standard techniques to match cultural stereotypes
   - *d.* Are aware of their own cultural values

Reflect

Think Critically

10. In your opinion, do psychologists have a duty to protect others who may be harmed by their clients? For example, if a patient has homicidal fantasies about his ex-wife, should she be informed?

Self-Reflect

The use of trepanning, demonology, and exorcism all implied that the mentally ill were "cursed." To what extent are the mentally ill rejected and stigmatized today?

Can you think of any personal experiences of spontaneous remission (times when a psychological issue resolved itself without any intervention on your part)?

Make a list describing what you think it means to be mentally healthy. How well does your list match the items in Table 65.1?

What lies at the "heart" of psychotherapy? How would you describe it to a friend?

ANSWERS

1. C 2. A 3. D 4. B 5. F 6. F 7. d 8. a 9. c 10. According to the law, there is a duty to protect others when a therapist could, with little effort, prevent serious harm. However, this duty can conflict with a client's rights to confidentiality and with client–therapist trust. Therapists often must make difficult choices in such situations.

CENGAGE brain.com

Go to **cengagebrain.com** to access **MindTap for Coon/Mitterer** *Psychology Modules for Active Learning* and other online learning tools. MindTap is a fully online learning experience that combines all the tools you need—readings, multimedia, activities, and assessments—into a singular personalized Learning Path that guides you through the course.

Therapies: Psychodynamic, Humanistic, and Cognitive Therapies

The Talking Cures

Imagine lying back on a couch, talking about whatever comes to mind. That's just how psychotherapy got started, on this famous couch with Sigmund Freud sitting out of sight, taking notes, and offering interpretations. This procedure was supposed to encourage a free flow of thoughts and images from the unconscious.

When most people picture psychotherapists at work, they imagine them talking with their clients. Let's sample a variety of talk-oriented approaches. Psychodynamic therapies, of which Freudian psychoanalysis was the first, tend to stress the need to gain insight into the *unconscious* forces assumed to control us all. While humanistic therapies also are insight therapies, they focus on helping clients gain deeper insight into their *conscious* thoughts, emotions, and behavior. In contrast to both psychodynamic and humanistic therapies, cognitive therapies tend to be less concerned with insight than with

Peter Aprahamian/Encyclopedia/Corbis

helping people change harmful thinking patterns. Let's start with some insight.

SURVEY QUESTIONS

66.1 Is Freudian psychoanalysis still used?

66.2 What are the major humanistic therapies?

66.3 How does cognitive therapy change thoughts and emotions?

Psychodynamic Therapies— The Talking Cure

SURVEY QUESTION 66.1: Is Freudian psychoanalysis still used?

How did Freud treat psychological problems? Freud's theory stressed that "neurosis" and "hysteria" are caused by repressed memories, motives, and conflicts—particularly those stemming from instinctual drives for sex and aggression. Although they are hidden, these forces remain active in the personality and cause some people to develop rigid ego defenses and compulsive, self-defeating behavior. Thus, the main goal of **psychoanalysis** is to reduce internal conflicts that lead to emotional suffering (Fayek, 2010).

Psychoanalysis

Freud developed four basic techniques to uncover the unconscious roots of neurosis (Freud, 1949): *free association, dream analysis, analysis of resistance,* and *analysis of transference.*

Free Association The basis for **free association** is saying whatever comes to mind without worrying whether ideas are painful, embarrassing, or illogical. Thoughts are simply allowed to move freely from one idea to the next, without self-censorship. The purpose of free association is to lower defenses so that unconscious thoughts and feelings can emerge (Lavin, 2012; Spence et al., 2009).

Dream Analysis

Freud believed that dreams disguise consciously unacceptable feelings and forbidden desires in dream form (Fischer & Kächele, 2009; Rock, 2004). The psychoanalyst can use this "royal road to the unconscious" to help the patient work past the obvious, visible meaning of the dream (its *manifest content*) to uncover the hidden, symbolic meaning (its *latent content*). This is achieved by analyzing *dream symbols* (images that have personal or emotional meanings; see Module 26).

Suppose that a young man dreams of pulling a pistol from his waistband and aiming at a target as his wife watches. The pistol repeatedly fails to discharge, and the man's wife laughs at him. Freud might have seen this as an indication of repressed feelings of sexual impotence, with the gun serving as a disguised image of the penis.

Analysis of Resistance

A central concern of psychoanalysis is the fact that patients who come to analysis for help nevertheless often *resist* changing when it is necessary to become healthier (Levenson, 2012). For example, when free associating or describing dreams, patients may resist talking about or thinking about certain topics. Such resistances—blockages in the flow of insights and ideas—reveal particularly important unconscious conflicts. As analysts become aware of resistances, they bring them to the patient's awareness so the patient can deal with them realistically. Rather than being roadblocks in therapy, resistances can be clues and challenges (Engle & Arkowitz, 2006).

Analysis of Transference

Transference is the tendency to "transfer" feelings to a therapist similar to those the patient had for important persons in his or her past. At times, the patient may act as if the analyst is a rejecting father, an unloving or overprotective mother, or a former lover, for example. As the patient reexperiences repressed emotions, the therapist can help the patient recognize and understand them. Troubled persons often provoke anger, rejection, boredom, criticism, and other negative reactions from others. Effective therapists learn to avoid reacting like others and playing the patient's habitual resistance and transference games. This, too, contributes to therapeutic change (Fayek, 2010).

Psychoanalysis Today

What is the status of psychoanalysis today? Psychoanalysis made a major contribution to modern therapies by highlighting the importance of unconscious conflicts (Borch-Jacobsen & Shamdasani, 2011; Friedman, 2006). However, traditional psychoanalysis took a long time and considerable effort. This resulted in the development of newer, more streamlined dynamic therapies, in part due to questions about whether traditional psychoanalysis "works." In a classic criticism, Hans Eysenck (1994) suggested that psychoanalysis simply takes so long that patients experience a spontaneous remission of symptoms—improvement due to the mere passage of time.

How seriously should the possibility of spontaneous remission be taken? It's true that problems ranging from hyperactivity to anxiety do improve with the passage of time. Regardless, researchers have confirmed that psychoanalysis and related psychotherapies do, in fact, produce improvement in a majority of patients (Doidge, 1997; Shedler, 2010).

The real value of Eysenck's critique is that it encouraged psychologists to try new ideas and techniques. Researchers began to ask, "When psychoanalysis works, why does it work? Which parts of it are essential and which are unnecessary?" Modern therapists have given surprisingly varied answers to these questions.

Humanistic Therapies— Liberating Human Potential

SURVEY QUESTION 66.2: What are the major humanistic therapies?

Better self-knowledge was the goal of traditional psychoanalysis. However, Freud claimed that his patients could expect only to change their "hysterical misery into common

Psychoanalysis *A Freudian therapy that emphasizes the use of free association, dream interpretation, resistances, and transference to uncover unconscious conflicts.*

Free association *In psychoanalysis, the technique of having a client say anything that comes to mind, regardless of how embarrassing or unimportant it may seem.*

Resistance *A blockage in the flow of insight and ideas during analysis; topics the client resists thinking or talking about.*

Transference *The tendency of patients to transfer feelings to a therapist that correspond to those the patient had for important persons in his or her past.*

Spontaneous remission *Improvement of symptoms due to the mere passage of time.*

unhappiness"! Humanistic therapists are more optimistic and believe that humans have a natural urge to seek health and self-growth. Most assume that it is possible for people to use their potentials fully and live rich, rewarding lives. Here, we discuss three of the most popular humanistic therapies: client-centered therapy, existential therapy, and Gestalt therapy.

Client-Centered Therapy

What is client-centered therapy? How is it different from psychoanalysis? Whereas psychoanalysis is directive and based on insights from the *un*conscious, **client-centered therapy (person-centered therapy)** is *non*directive and based on insights from *conscious* thoughts and feelings (Brodley, 2006; Rogers, 1959). The psychoanalyst tends to take a position of authority, stating what dreams, thoughts, or memories "mean." In contrast, Carl Rogers (1902–1987), who originated client-centered therapy, believed that what is right or valuable for the therapist may be wrong for the client. (Rogers preferred the term *client* to *patient* because *patient* implies that a person is sick and needs to be cured.)

Consequently, in client-centered therapy, therapists do not try to "fix" clients. Instead, clients must actively seek to solve their problems because they determine what will be discussed during each session (Cooper & McLeod, 2011). The therapist's job is to create a safe "atmosphere of growth" by providing opportunities for change.

How do therapists create such an atmosphere? Rogers believed that effective therapists maintain four basic conditions. First, the therapist offers the client **unconditional**

Psychotherapist Carl Rogers, who originated client-centered therapy.

positive regard, or unshakable personal acceptance. The therapist refuses to react with shock, dismay, or disapproval to anything the client says or feels. Total acceptance by the therapist is the first step to self-acceptance by the client.

Second, the therapist attempts to achieve genuine **empathy** by trying to see the world through the client's eyes and feeling some part of what the client is feeling (Grant, 2010).

As a third essential condition, the therapist strives to be **authentic** (genuine and honest). The therapist must not hide behind a professional role. Rogers believed that phony fronts destroy the growth atmosphere sought in client-centered therapy.

Fourth, the therapist does not make interpretations, propose solutions, or offer advice. Instead, the therapist **reflects**—rephrases, summarizes, or repeats—the client's thoughts and feelings. This enables the therapist to act as a psychological "mirror" so clients can see themselves more clearly. Rogers theorized that a person armed with a realistic self-image and greater self-acceptance will gradually discover solutions to life's problems.

Existential Therapy

According to the existentialists, "being in the world" (existence) creates deep anxiety. Each of us must deal with the realities of death. We must face the fact that we create our private worlds by making choices. We must overcome isolation on a vast and indifferent planet. Most of all, we must confront feelings of meaninglessness (Craig, 2012; Schneider, Galvin, & Serlin, 2009).

What do these concerns have to do with psychotherapy? **Existential therapy** focuses on the problems of existence, such as meaning, choice, and responsibility. Like client-centered therapy, it promotes self-knowledge. However, there are important differences. Client-centered therapy seeks to uncover a "true self" hidden behind a screen of defenses. In contrast, existential therapy emphasizes free will, the human ability to make choices. Accordingly, existential therapists believe you can *choose to become* the person you want to be.

Existential therapists try to give clients the *courage* to make rewarding and socially constructive choices. Typically, therapy focuses on *death, freedom, isolation*, and *meaninglessness*, the "ultimate concerns" of existence (Vontress, 2013). These universal human challenges include an awareness of one's mortality, the responsibility that comes with freedom to choose, being alone in your own private world, and the need to create meaning in your life.

One example of existential therapy is Victor Frankl's *logotherapy*, which emphasizes the need to find and maintain meaning in life. Frankl (1904–1997) based his approach on experiences he had as a prisoner in a Nazi concentration camp. In the camp, Frankl saw countless prisoners break down as they were stripped of all hope and human dignity (Frankl, 1955). Those who survived with their sanity did so because they managed to hang on to a sense of meaning *(logos)*. Even in less dire circumstances, a sense of purpose in life adds greatly to psychological well-being (Prochaska & Norcross, 2010).

What does the existential therapist do? The therapist helps clients discover self-imposed limitations in personal identity. To be successful, the client must fully accept the challenge of changing his or her life (Bretherton & Orner, 2004). It is interesting that Buddhists seek a similar state that they call "radical acceptance" (Brach, 2003). A key aspect of existential therapy is *confrontation,* in which clients are challenged to be mindful of their values and choices and to take responsibility for the quality of their existence (Claessens, 2009).

An important part of confrontation is the unique, intense, here-and-now *encounter* between two human beings. When existential therapy is successful, it brings about a renewed sense of purpose and a reappraisal of what's important in life. Some clients even experience an emotional rebirth, as if they had survived a close brush with death. As Marcel Proust wrote, "The real voyage of discovery consists not in seeing new landscapes but in having new eyes."

Gestalt Therapy

Gestalt therapy is based on the idea that perception, or *awareness,* is disjointed and incomplete in maladjusted persons. The German word *Gestalt* means "whole" or "complete." **Gestalt therapy** helps people rebuild thinking, feeling, and acting into connected wholes. This is achieved by expanding personal awareness; by accepting responsibility for one's thoughts, feelings, and actions; and by filling in gaps in experience (Frew, 2013).

What are "gaps in experience"? Gestalt therapists believe that we often shy away from expressing or "owning" upsetting feelings. This creates a gap in self-awareness that may become

a barrier to personal growth. For example, a person who feels anger after the death of a parent might go for years without fully expressing it. This and similar threatening gaps may impair emotional health.

The Gestalt approach is more directive than client-centered or existential therapy, and it is less insight-oriented, instead emphasizing immediate experience. Working either one-to-one or in a group setting, the Gestalt therapist encourages clients to become more aware of their moment-to-moment thoughts, perceptions, and emotions (Levin, 2010). Rather than discussing *why* clients feel guilt, anger, fear, or boredom, the therapist encourages them to have these feelings in the "here and now" and become fully aware of them. The therapist promotes awareness by drawing attention to a client's posture, voice, eye movements, and hand gestures. Clients also may be asked to exaggerate vague feelings until they become clear. Gestalt therapists believe that expressing such feelings allows people to "take care of unfinished business" and break through emotional impasses (Masquelier, 2006).

Gestalt therapy is often associated with the work of Fritz Perls (1969). According to Perls, emotional health comes from knowing what you *want* to do, not dwelling on what you *should* do, *ought* to do, or *should want* to do (Brownell, 2010). In other words, emotional health comes from taking full responsibility for one's feelings and actions. For example, it means changing "I can't" to "I won't," or "I must" to "I choose to."

Client-centered (or person-centered) therapy *A nondirective therapy based on insights gained from conscious thoughts and feelings; emphasizes accepting one's true self.*

Unconditional positive regard *An unqualified, unshakable acceptance of another person.*

Empathy *A capacity for taking another's point of view; the ability to feel what another is feeling.*

Authenticity *In Carl Rogers's terms, the ability of a therapist to be genuine and honest about his or her own feelings.*

Reflection *In client-centered therapy, the process of rephrasing or repeating thoughts and feelings expressed by clients so they can become aware of what they are saying.*

Existential therapy *An insight therapy that focuses on the elemental problems of existence, such as death, meaning, choice, and responsibility; emphasizes making courageous life choices.*

Gestalt therapy *An approach that focuses on immediate experience and awareness to help clients rebuild thinking, feeling, and acting into connected wholes; emphasizes the integration of fragmented experiences.*

How does Gestalt therapy help people discover their real wants? Above all else, Gestalt therapy emphasizes *present* experience (Levin, 2010; Yontef, 2007). Clients are urged to stop intellectualizing and talking *about* feelings. Instead, they learn to live now; live here; stop imagining; experience the real; stop unnecessary thinking; taste and see; express rather than explain, justify, or judge; give in to unpleasantness and pain just as to pleasure; and surrender to being as you are. Gestalt therapists believe that, paradoxically, the best way to change is to become who you really are (Brownell, 2010).

Cognitive Therapy—Think Positive!

SURVEY QUESTION 66.3: How does cognitive therapy change thoughts and emotions?

Whereas psychodynamic and humanistic therapies usually seek to foster insight, cognitive therapies usually try to directly change what people think, believe, and feel, and, as a consequence, how they act (Rosner, 2012). In general, cognitive therapy helps clients change thinking patterns that lead to troublesome emotions or behaviors (Davey, 2008; Power, 2010).

For example, Janice is a hoarder whose home is crammed full with things she has acquired over two decades. If she seeks help from a therapist concerned with insight, she will try to better understand why she began collecting stuff. In contrast, if she seeks help from a cognitive therapist, she may spend little time examining her past. Instead, she will work to actively change her thoughts and beliefs about hoarding. With either approach, the goal is to give up hoarding. Further, in practice, humanistic therapies often also result in active change, and cognitive therapies often also yield deeper insight.

Cognitive therapy has been successfully used as a remedy for many problems, ranging from generalized anxiety disorder and post-traumatic stress disorder to marital distress and anger (Butler et al., 2006). For example, compulsive hand washing can be greatly reduced by changing a client's thoughts and beliefs about dirt and contamination (Jones & Menzies, 1998). Cognitive therapy has been especially successful in treating depression (Hollon, Stewart, & Strunk, 2006).

Cognitive Therapy for Depression

As you may recall from Module 62, cognitive psychologists believe that negative, self-defeating thoughts underlie depression. According to Aaron Beck (1991), depressed persons see themselves, the world, and the future in negative terms because of major distortions in thinking. The first is selective perception, which refers to perceiving only certain stimuli in a larger array. If five good things and three bad things happen during the day, depressed people focus only on the bad. A second thinking error in depression is overgeneralization, the tendency to think that an upsetting event applies to other, unrelated situations. An example would be Billy's considering himself a total failure or completely worthless if he were to lose a part-time job or fail a test. To complete the picture, depressed persons tend to magnify the importance of undesirable events by engaging in all-or-nothing thinking. They see events as completely good or bad, right or wrong, and themselves as either successful or failing miserably (Lam & Mok, 2008).

How do cognitive therapists alter such patterns? Cognitive therapists make a step-by-step effort to correct negative thoughts that lead to depression or similar problems. At first, clients are taught to recognize and keep track of their own thoughts. The client and therapist then look for ideas and beliefs that cause depression, anger, and avoidance (Segal, Williams, & Teasdale, 2013).

Next, clients are asked to gather information to test their beliefs. For instance, a depressed person might list his or her activities for a week. The list is then used to challenge all-or-nothing thoughts, such as "I had a terrible week" or "I'm a complete failure." With more coaching, clients learn to alter their thoughts in ways that improve their moods, actions, and relationships.

Cognitive therapy is at least as effective as drugs for treating many cases of depression. More important, people who have adopted new thinking patterns are less likely to become depressed again—a benefit that drugs can't impart (Eisendrath, Chartier, & McLane, 2011; Hollon, Stewart, & Strunk, 2006).

In an alternate approach, cognitive therapists look for an *absence* of effective coping skills and thinking patterns, not for the *presence* of self-defeating thoughts (Dobson, Backs-Dermott, & Dozois, 2000). The aim is to teach clients how to cope with anger, depression, shyness, stress, and similar problems. Stress inoculation, which was described in Module 59, is a good example of this approach.

Discovering Psychology

Ten Irrational Beliefs—Which Do You Hold?

Rational-emotive behavior therapists have identified numerous beliefs that commonly lead to emotional upsets and conflicts. See if you recognize any of the following irrational beliefs:

1. I must be loved and approved by almost every significant person in my life or it's awful and I'm worthless.

   Example: "One of my classmates doesn't seem to like me. I must be a big loser."

2. I should be completely competent and achieving in all ways to be a worthwhile person.

   Example: "I don't understand my physics class. I guess I really am just stupid."

3. It's terribly upsetting when things don't go my way.

   Example: "I should have gotten a B in that class. The teacher is a total creep."

4. It's not my fault I'm unhappy; I can't control my emotional reactions.

   Example: "You make me feel awful. I would be happy if it weren't for you."

5. I should never forget it if something unpleasant happens.

   Example: "I'll never forget the time my boss insulted me. I think about it every day at work."

6. It is easier to avoid difficulties and responsibilities than to face them.

   Example: "I don't know why my girlfriend is angry. Maybe it will just pass if I ignore it."

7. A lot of people I have to deal with are bad. I should severely punish them for it.

   Example: "The students renting next door are such a pain. I'm going to play my stereo even louder the next time they complain."

8. I should depend on others who are stronger than me.

   Example: "I couldn't survive if she left me."

9. Because something once strongly affected me, it will do so forever.

   Example: "My girlfriend dumped me during my junior year in college. I can never trust a woman again."

10. There is always a perfectly obvious solution to human problems, and it is immoral if this solution is not put into practice.

    Example: "I'm so depressed about politics in this country. It all seems hopeless."*

If any of the listed beliefs sound familiar, you may be creating unnecessary emotional distress for yourself by holding on to unrealistic expectations.

Adapted from Dryden 2011; Ellis & Ellis 2011; Teyber & McClure 2011.

Cognitive therapy is a rapidly expanding specialty. Before we leave the topic, let's explore another widely used cognitive therapy.

Rational-Emotive Behavior Therapy

Rational-emotive behavior therapy (REBT) attempts to change irrational beliefs that cause emotional problems. According to Albert Ellis (1913–2007), the basic idea of REBT is as easy as A-B-C (Ellis, 1995, Ellis & Ellis, 2011). Ellis assumed that people become unhappy and develop self-defeating habits because they have unrealistic or faulty *beliefs*.

How are beliefs important? Ellis analyzed problems in this way: The letter A stands for an *activating experience*, which the person assumes to be the cause of C, an *emotional consequence*. For instance, a person who is rejected (the activating experience) feels depressed, threatened, or hurt (the consequence). Rational-emotive behavior therapy shows the client that the real problem is what comes between A and C: B, which is the client's irrational and unrealistic *beliefs*. In this example, an unrealistic belief leading to unnecessary suffering is: "I must be loved and approved by everyone at all times." REBT holds that events do not *cause* us to have feelings. We feel as we do because of our beliefs (Dryden, 2011; Kottler & Shepard, 2011).

Cognitive therapy *A therapy directed at changing the maladaptive thoughts, beliefs, and feelings that underlie emotional and behavioral problems.*

Selective perception *Perceiving only certain stimuli among a larger array of possibilities.*

Overgeneralization *Blowing a single event out of proportion by extending it to a large number of unrelated situations.*

All-or-nothing thinking *Classifying objects or events as absolutely right or wrong, good or bad, acceptable or unacceptable, and so forth.*

Rational-emotive behavior therapy (REBT) *An approach that states that irrational beliefs cause many emotional problems and that such beliefs must be changed or abandoned.*

The Clinical File

You've Got to Know When to Fold 'Em

Seventeen-year-old Jonathan just lost his shirt again. This time, he did it playing online blackjack. Jonathan started out making $5 bets and then doubled his bet over and over. Surely, he thought, his luck would eventually change. However, he ran out of money after just eight straight hands, having lost more than $1,000. Last week, he lost a lot of money playing Texas Hold 'Em. Now Jonathan is in tears—he has lost most of his summer earnings, and he is worried about having to drop out of school and tell his parents about his losses. Jonathan has had to admit that he is part of the growing ranks of underage gambling addicts (Blinn-Pike, Worthy, & Jonkman, 2010; Volberg, 2012).

Like many problem gamblers, Jonathan suffers from several cognitive distortions related to gambling. Here are some mistaken beliefs about gambling (adapted from Toneatto, 2002; Wickwire, Whelan, & Meyers, 2010):

Magnified gambling skill: Your self-confidence is exaggerated, despite the fact that you lose persistently.

Attribution errors: You ascribe your wins to skill but blame losses on bad luck.

Gambler's fallacy: You believe that a string of losses soon must be followed by wins.

Selective memory: You remember your wins but forget your losses.

Overinterpretation of cues: You put too much faith in irrelevant cues such as bodily sensations or a feeling that your next bet will be a winner.

Luck as a trait: You believe that you are a lucky person in general.

Probability biases: You have incorrect beliefs about randomness and chance events.

Do you have any of these mistaken beliefs? Taken together, Jonathan's cognitive distortions created an illusion of control—that is, he believed that if he worked hard enough, he could figure out how to win. Fortunately, a cognitive therapist helped Jonathan *cognitively restructure* his beliefs. He now no longer believes he can control chance events. Jonathan still gambles a bit, but he does so only recreationally, keeping his losses within his budget and enjoying himself in the process.

Ocean/Corbis

Gambling addiction is a growing problem among young people (LaBrie & Shaffer, 2007).

(For some examples, see "Ten Irrational Beliefs—Which Do You Hold?")

Ellis (1979; Ellis & Ellis, 2011) says that most irrational beliefs come from three core ideas, each of which is unrealistic:

1. I *must* perform well and be approved of by significant others. If I don't, then it is awful, I cannot stand it, and I am a rotten person.

2. You *must* treat me fairly. When you don't, it is horrible, and I cannot bear it.

3. Conditions *must* be the way I want them to be. It is terrible when they are not, and I cannot stand living in such an awful world.

It's easy to see that such beliefs can lead to much grief and needless suffering in a less-than-perfect world. Rational-emotive behavior therapists are very directive in their attempts to change a client's irrational beliefs and "self-talk." The therapist may directly attack clients' logic, challenge their thinking, confront them with evidence contrary to their beliefs, and even assign "homework." Here, for instance, are some examples of statements that dispute irrational beliefs (adapted from Dryden, 2011; Ellis & Ellis, 2011; Kottler & Shepard, 2011):

- "Where is the evidence that you are a loser just because you didn't do well this one time?"
- "Who said the world should be fair? That's your rule."
- "What are you telling yourself to make yourself feel so upset?"
- "Is it really terrible that things aren't working out as you would like? Or is it just inconvenient?"

Many of us would probably do well to give up our irrational beliefs. Improved self-acceptance and a better tolerance of daily annoyances are the benefits of doing so (see "You've Got to Know When to Fold 'Em").

Cognitive Behavior Therapy

One last point, before we go on to explore behavior therapies in Module 67: Did you notice that the B in REBT stands for "behavior"? Today, most therapists realize that changing maladaptive thoughts and doing the same for maladaptive behaviors can be done simultaneously. **Cognitive behavior therapy (CBT)** combines cognitive and behavioral therapies to optimize treatment outcomes (Mahoney & McEvoy, 2012). For example, compulsive hoarders respond well to therapy when it *both* corrects distorted thinking about hoarding *and* actively modifies hoarding behavior (Steketee et al., 2010). In fact, CBT is currently the most popular approach to nonmedical therapy (Pilgrim, 2011). Anyway, onward to the behavior therapies.

Module 66: Summary

66.1 Is Freudian psychoanalysis still used?

- **66.1.1** As the first true psychotherapy, Freud's psychoanalysis gave rise to modern psychodynamic therapies.

- **66.1.2** The psychoanalyst uses free association, dream analysis, and analysis of resistance and transference to reveal health-producing insights.

- **66.1.3** Psychoanalysts have become relatively rare because psychoanalysis is expensive and time intensive.

- **66.1.4** Some critics argue that traditional psychoanalysis receives credit for spontaneous remissions of symptoms. However, psychoanalysis is successful for many patients.

66.2 What are the major humanistic therapies?

- **66.2.1** Client-centered (or person-centered) therapy is nondirective, based on insights gained from conscious thoughts and feelings, and dedicated to creating an atmosphere of growth.

- **66.2.2** Unconditional positive regard, empathy, authenticity, and reflection are combined to give the client a chance to solve his or her own problems.

- **66.2.3** Existential therapies focus on the end result of the choices one makes in life. Clients are encouraged through confrontation and encounter to exercise free will and to take responsibility for their choices.

- **66.2.4** Gestalt therapy emphasizes immediate awareness of thoughts and feelings. Its goal is to rebuild thinking, feeling, and acting into connected wholes and to help clients break through emotional blockages.

66.3 How does cognitive therapy change thoughts and emotions?

- **66.3.1** Cognitive therapy emphasizes changing thought patterns that underlie emotional or behavioral problems. Its goals are to correct distorted thinking and/or teach improved coping skills.

- **66.3.2** Aaron Beck's cognitive therapy focuses on changing several major distortions in thinking: selective perception, overgeneralization, and all-or-nothing thinking.

- **66.3.3** In Albert Ellis's variation of cognitive therapy, called rational-emotive behavior therapy (REBT), clients learn to recognize and challenge the irrational beliefs that are at the core of their maladaptive thinking patterns.

Cognitive behavior therapy (CBT) *An approach combining cognitive and behavioral therapies to optimize treatment outcomes.*

Module 66: Knowledge Builder

Recite

1. In psychoanalysis, what is an emotional attachment to the therapist by the patient?
   - **a.** free association
   - **b.** manifest association
   - **c.** resistance
   - **d.** transference

Match:

_____ 2. Client-centered therapy   **A.** Changing thought patterns

_____ 3. Gestalt therapy   **B.** Unconditional positive regard

_____ 4. Existential therapy   **C.** Gaps in awareness

_____ 5. REBT   **D.** Choice and becoming

6. The Gestalt therapist tries to *reflect* a client's thoughts and feelings. *T or F?*

7. Confrontation and encounter are concepts of existential therapy. *T or F?*

8. The B in the A-B-C of REBT stands for
   - **a.** behavior
   - **b.** belief
   - **c.** being
   - **d.** Beck

Reflect

Think Critically

9. According to Freud's concept of *transference*, patients "transfer" their feelings onto the psychoanalyst. In light of this idea, to what might the term *countertransference* refer?

10. How might using the term *patient* affect the relationship between an individual and a therapist?

Self-Reflect

Try to free associate (aloud) for 10 minutes. Did anything interesting surface?

You are going to play the role of a therapist for a classroom demonstration. How would you act if you were a psychoanalyst? A client-centered therapist? A Gestalt therapist? A rational-emotive behavior therapist? A cognitive behavior therapist?

We all occasionally engage in negative thinking. Can you remember a time recently when you engaged in selective perception? Overgeneralization? All-or-nothing thinking?

ANSWERS

1. d 2. B 3. C 4. D 5. A 6. F 7. T 8. a 9. Psychoanalysts (and therapists in general) also are human. They may transfer their own unresolved, unconscious feelings onto their patients. This sometimes complicates the therapeutic process (Kim & Gray, 2009). 10. The terms *doctor* and *patient* imply a large gap in status and authority between the individual and his or her therapist. Client-centered or person-centered therapy attempts to narrow this gap by making the person the final authority concerning solutions to his or her problems. Also, the word *patient* implies that a person is "sick" and needs to be "cured." Many regard this as an inappropriate way to think about human problems.

CENGAGE**brain**.com

Go to **cengagebrain.com** to access **MindTap for Coon/Mitterer** *Psychology Modules for Active Learning* and other online learning tools. MindTap is a fully online learning experience that combines all the tools you need—readings, multimedia, activities, and assessments—into a singular personalized Learning Path that guides you through the course.

Therapies: Behavior Therapies

Testing Her Wings

Shanika had a big problem. It wasn't the free Caribbean vacation she unexpectedly won in a contest so much as her fear of flying there in the first place. Realizing that she should have done it years ago, she enrolled in a program designed to help her overcome her fear. Little did she know that phobias like hers responded well to a behavior therapy called systematic desensitization.

In just a few weeks, her program treated her fear of flying by combining systematic desensitization, relaxation, group support, and lots of direct exposure to airliners. She was amazed at how calm she was when her program concluded with an actual brief flight so that participants could "test their wings."

Behavior therapists seek to directly change behavior patterns so that people can function more comfortably and effectively.

John Lund/Marc Romanelli/Blend Images/Corbis

This module describes some innovative, and very successful, behavioral therapies, including systematic desensitization.

SURVEY QUESTIONS

67.1 What is behavior therapy?

67.2 What role do operant principles play in behavior therapy?

Therapies Based on Classical Conditioning—Healing by Learning

SURVEY QUESTION 67.1: What is behavior therapy?

In general, how does behavior therapy work? A breakthrough occurred when psychologists realized they could use learning principles to solve human problems. **Behavior therapy** is an action therapy that uses learning principles to make constructive changes in behavior. Behavior therapists believe that deep insight into one's problems is often unnecessary for improvement. Instead, they try to directly alter troublesome actions and thoughts. Shanika didn't need to probe into her past or her emotions and conflicts; she simply wanted to overcome her fear of flying.

Behavior therapists assume that people have *learned* to be the way they are. If they have learned responses that cause problems, then they can change them by *relearning* more appropriate behaviors. Broadly speaking, **behavior modification** refers to any use of classical or operant conditioning to directly alter human behavior (Miltenberger, 2012; Spiegler & Guevremont, 2010). (Some therapists prefer to call this approach *applied behavior analysis*.) Behavioral approaches include aversion therapy, systematic desensitization, token economies, and other techniques (Spiegler, 2013a,b).

How does classical conditioning work? Perhaps a brief review would be helpful. Classical conditioning is a form of learning in which simple responses (especially reflexes) are associated with new stimuli. In classical conditioning, a neutral stimulus is followed by an *unconditioned stimulus (US)* that consistently produces an unlearned reaction, called the *unconditioned response (UR)*. Eventually, the previously neutral stimulus

Harris, S/CSL, CartoonStock Ltd.

begins to produce this response directly. The response is then called a *conditioned response (CR)*, and the stimulus becomes a *conditioned stimulus (CS)*. Thus, for a child, the sight of a hypodermic needle (CS) is followed by an injection (US), which causes anxiety or fear (UR). Eventually, the sight of a hypodermic (the conditioned stimulus) may produce anxiety or fear (a conditioned response) *before* the child gets an injection. (For a more thorough review of classical conditioning, return to Module 28.)

What does classical conditioning have to do with behavior modification? Classical conditioning can be used, for example, to associate discomfort with a bad habit. More powerful versions of this approach are called aversion therapy.

Aversion Therapy

Imagine that you are eating an apple. Suddenly, you discover that you just bit a large green worm in half. You vomit. Months later, you cannot eat an apple without feeling ill. It's apparent that you have developed a conditioned aversion to apples. (A *conditioned aversion* is a learned dislike or negative emotional response to some stimulus.)

In **aversion therapy**, an individual learns to associate a strong aversion to an undesirable habit such as smoking, drinking, or gambling. Aversion therapy has been used to treat hiccups, sneezing, stuttering, vomiting, nail-biting, bed-wetting, compulsive hair-pulling, alcoholism, and the smoking of tobacco, marijuana, or crack cocaine. Actually, aversive conditioning happens every day. For example, not many physicians who treat lung cancer patients are smokers, nor do many emergency room doctors drive without using their seat belts (Eifert & Lejuez, 2000).

Puffing Up an Aversion The fact that nicotine is toxic makes it easy to create an aversion that helps people give up smoking. Behavior therapists have found that electric shock, nauseating drugs, and similar aversive stimuli are not required to make smokers uncomfortable. All that is needed is for the smoker to smoke—rapidly, for a long time, at a forced pace. During *rapid smoking,* clients are told to smoke continuously, taking a puff every 6 to 8 seconds. Rapid smoking continues until the smoker is miserable and can stand it no more. By then, most people are thinking, "I never want to see another cigarette for the rest of my life."

Rapid smoking has long been known as an effective behavior therapy for smoking (McRobbie & Hajek, 2007). Nevertheless, anyone tempted to try rapid smoking should realize that it is very unpleasant. Without the help of a therapist, most people quit too soon for the procedure to succeed. In addition, rapid smoking can be dangerous. It should be done only with professional supervision. (An alternative method that is more practical is described in Module 69.)

Aversive Therapy for Drinking Another excellent example of aversion therapy was pioneered by Roger Vogler and his associates (1977). Vogler worked with alcoholics who were unable to stop drinking and for whom aversion therapy was a last chance. While drinking an alcoholic beverage, clients receive a painful (although not injurious) electric shock to the hand. Most of the time, these shocks occur as the client is beginning to take a drink of alcohol.

These *response-contingent shocks* (shocks that are linked to a response) obviously take the pleasure out of drinking. Shocks also cause the alcohol abuser to develop a conditioned aversion to drinking. Normally, the misery caused by alcohol abuse comes long after the act of drinking—too late to have much effect. But if alcohol can be linked with *immediate* discomfort, then drinking will begin to make the individual very uncomfortable.

Is it really acceptable to treat clients this way? People are often disturbed (shocked?) by such methods. However, clients usually *volunteer* for aversion therapy because it helps them overcome a destructive habit. Indeed, commercial aversion programs for overeating, smoking, and alcohol abuse have attracted many willing customers. More important, aversion therapy can be justified by its benefits. Many people prefer the short-term discomfort of aversion therapy to the long-term pain caused by a lifetime of struggling with a maladaptive habit.

Discovering Psychology

Feeling a Little Tense? Relax!

The key to desensitization is relaxation. To inhibit fear, you must *learn* to relax. One way to voluntarily relax is by using the **tension-release method**. To achieve deep-muscle relaxation, try the following exercise:

> Tense the muscles in your right arm until they tremble. Hold them tight as you slowly count to ten and then let go. Allow your hand and arm to go limp and to relax completely. Repeat the procedure. Releasing tension two or three times will allow you to feel whether your arm muscles have relaxed. Repeat the tension-release procedure with your left arm. Compare it with your right arm. Repeat until the left arm is equally relaxed. Apply the tension-release technique to your right leg; to your left leg; to your abdomen; to your chest and shoulders. Clench and release your chin, neck, and throat. Wrinkle and release your forehead and scalp. Tighten and release your mouth and face muscles. As a last step, curl your toes and tense your feet and then release.

If you carried out these instructions, you should be noticeably more relaxed than you were before you began. Practice the tension-release method until you can achieve complete relaxation quickly (5 to 10 minutes). After you have practiced relaxation once a day for a week or two, you will begin to be able to tell when your body (or a group of muscles) is tense. Also, you will begin to be able to relax on command. This is a valuable skill that you can apply in any situation that makes you feel tense or anxious.

Systematic Desensitization

Can behavior therapy be used to treat phobias, fears, and anxieties? Another behavioral technique, *systematic desensitization*, is used primarily to help people unlearn phobias (intense, unrealistic fears) or strong anxieties. For example, each of these people might be a candidate: a teacher with stage fright; a student with test anxiety; a salesperson who fears people; a newlywed with an aversion to sexual intimacy; or a person like Shanika, who is afraid of flying.

Suppose a behavior therapist wanted to help Curtis overcome his fear of heights (acrophobia). How might she proceed? Simply forcing Curtis to go out onto a balcony on the top (35th) floor of his apartment building could be a psychological disaster (after all, Curtis is a ground floor kinda guy). The behavior therapist (and Curtis) would be better off using **systematic desensitization**—a guided reduction in fear, anxiety, or aversion attained by gradually approaching a feared stimulus while maintaining relaxation (Head & Gross, 2009).

Performing Systematic Desensitization *How is systematic desensitization done?* Curtis and the therapist begin by constructing his **fear hierarchy**—a list of fear-provoking situations, arranged from least disturbing to most frightening. In addition, Curtis is taught exercises that produce deep relaxation. (See "Feeling a Little Tense? Relax!") Then, once Curtis is relaxed, he tries to perform the least disturbing item on his fear of heights hierarchy, which might be (1) Stand on a chair. The first item is repeated until Curtis feels no anxiety. Any change from complete relaxation is a signal that Curtis must relax again before continuing. Slowly, Curtis moves up the hierarchy: (2) Climb to the top of a small stepladder, (3) Look down one flight of stairs, and so on, until the last item is performed without fear. (20) Stand on the balcony on the top floor.

How does systematic desensitization work? Working through his fear hierarchy allows Curtis to gradually undergo *adaptation*. Systematic desensitization also is based on **reciprocal inhibition**—using one emotional state to block another (Heriot & Pritchard, 2004). For instance, it is impossible to be anxious and relaxed at the same time. If we can get Curtis onto the building staircase in a relaxed state, his anxiety and fear will be inhibited. Repeated visits to the staircase should cause fear to disappear in this situation. When Curtis has conquered his fear, we can say that *desensitization* has occurred (Spiegler & Guevremont, 2010).

For many phobias, desensitization works best when people are directly exposed to the stimuli and situations they fear (Bourne, 2010; Miltenberger, 2012). For something like a

Behavior therapy *Any therapy designed to actively change behavior.*
Behavior modification *The application of learning principles to change human behavior, especially maladaptive behavior.*
Aversion therapy *Suppressing an undesirable response by associating it with aversive (painful or uncomfortable) stimuli.*
Tension-release method *A procedure for systematically achieving deep relaxation of the body.*
Systematic desensitization *A reduction in fear, anxiety, or aversion brought about by planned exposure to aversive stimuli.*
Fear hierarchy *A list of fears, arranged from least fearful to most fearful, for use in systematic desensitization.*
Reciprocal inhibition *The presence of one emotional state can inhibit the occurrence of another, such as joy preventing fear or anxiety inhibiting pleasure.*

simple spider phobia, this exposure can even be done in groups and may be completed in a single session (Müller et al., 2011).

Vicarious Desensitization

What if it's not practical to directly act out the steps of a fear hierarchy? For a fear of heights, the steps of the fear hierarchy might be acted out, just as Curtis did. However, if this is impractical, as it might be in the case of a fear of flying, the problem can be handled by having clients observe *models* who are performing the feared behavior (Eifert & Lejuez, 2000; Bourne, 2010; ● Figure 67.1). A model is a person (either live or filmed) who serves as an example for observational learning. If such vicarious desensitization—secondhand learning—can't be used, there is yet another option. Fortunately, desensitization works almost as well when a person *vividly imagines* each step in the hierarchy (Yahnke, Sheikh, & Beckman, 2003). If the steps can be visualized without anxiety, fear in the actual situation is reduced. Because imagining feared stimuli can be done at a therapist's office, it is the most common way of doing desensitization.

Virtual Reality Exposure

Desensitization is an *exposure therapy*. Similar to other such therapies, it involves exposing people to feared stimuli until their fears extinguish. In an important recent development, psychologists are now using virtual reality to treat phobias. Virtual reality is a computer-generated, three-dimensional "world" that viewers enter by wearing a head-mounted video display. **Virtual reality exposure**

● Figure 67.1

Treatment of a snake phobia by vicarious desensitization. These classic photographs show models interacting with snakes. To overcome their own fears, phobic subjects observed the models (Bandura, Blanchard, & Ritter, 1969).

presents computerized fear stimuli to clients in a realistic yet carefully controlled fashion (Wiederhold & Wiederhold, 2005; Riva, 2009). It has already been used to treat fears of flying, driving, and public speaking as well as acrophobia (fear of heights), claustrophobia, and spider phobias (Meyerbröker & Emmelkamp, 2010; Müller et al., 2011; ● Figure 67.2). Virtual

● Figure 67.2

(*left*) A person in the head-mounted display explores a virtual reality system used to expose people to feared stimuli. (*right*) A computer image from a virtual Iraq or Afghanistan. Veterans suffering from post-traumatic stress disorder (PTSD) can reexperience their traumas. For example, someone whose checkpoint was suddenly attacked by a carload of terrorists can relive that moment, complete with sights, sounds, vibrations, and even smells. Successive exposures result in a reduction of PTSD symptoms (Gerardi et al., 2008; McLay, 2012).

reality exposure also has been used to create immersive distracting environments for helping patients reduce the experience of pain (Keefe et al., 2012).

Desensitization has been one of the most successful behavior therapies. A relatively new technique may provide yet another way to lower fears, anxieties, and psychological pain.

Eye Movement Desensitization Traumatic events produce painful memories. Disturbing flashbacks often haunt victims of accidents, disasters, molestations, muggings, rapes, or emotional abuse. To help ease traumatic memories and post-traumatic stress, Dr. Francine Shapiro developed **eye movement desensitization and reprocessing (EMDR)**.

In a typical EMDR session, the client is asked to visualize the images that most upset her or him. At the same time, a pencil (or other object) is moved rapidly from side to side in front of the person's eyes. Watching the moving object causes the person's eyes to dart swiftly back and forth. After about 30 seconds, clients describe any memories, feelings, and thoughts that emerged and discuss them with the therapist. These steps are repeated until troubling thoughts and emotions no longer surface (Shapiro, 2012; Shapiro & Forrest, 2004).

Several studies suggest that EMDR lowers anxieties and takes the pain out of traumatic memories (Fleming, 2012; Oren & Solomon, 2012). However, EMDR is controversial. Some studies, for example, have found that eye movements add nothing to the treatment. The apparent success of EMDR may simply be based on gradual exposure to upsetting stimuli, as in other forms of desensitization (Albright & Thyer, 2010). On the other hand, some researchers continue to find that EMDR is superior to traditional therapies (Greenwald, 2006; Solomon, Solomon, & Heide, 2009; Tarquinio et al., 2012).

Is EMDR a breakthrough? Given the frequency of traumas in modern society, it shouldn't be long before we find out.

Operant Therapies—All the World Is a Skinner Box?

SURVEY QUESTION 67.2: What role do operant principles play in behavior therapy?

Aversion therapy and desensitization are based on classical conditioning. Where does operant conditioning fit in? As you may recall, *operant conditioning* refers to learning based on

the consequences of making a response. Behavior therapists most often use the following operant principles to deal with human behavior:

1. **Positive reinforcement.** Responses that are followed by reinforcement tend to occur more frequently. If children whine and get attention, they will whine more frequently. If you get straight *A*s in your psychology class, you may become a psychology major.

2. **Nonreinforcement and extinction.** A response that is not followed by reinforcement will occur less frequently. If a response is not followed by reward after it has been repeated many times, it will extinguish entirely. After winning three times, you pull the handle on a slot machine 30 times more without a payoff. What do you do? You go away. So does the response of handle pulling (for that particular machine, at any rate).

3. **Punishment.** If a response is followed by discomfort or an undesirable effect, the response will be suppressed (but not necessarily extinguished).

4. **Shaping.** Shaping means reinforcing actions that are closer and closer approximations to a desired response. For example, to reward an intellectually challenged child for saying "ball," you might begin by reinforcing the child for saying anything that starts with a *b* sound.

5. **Stimulus control.** Responses tend to come under the control of the situation in which they occur. If you set your clock 10 minutes fast, it may be easier to leave the house on time in the morning. Your departure is under the stimulus control of the clock, even though you know it is fast.

6. **Time-out.** A time-out procedure usually involves removing the individual from a situation in which reinforcement occurs. Time-out is a variation of response cost: It prevents reward from following an undesirable response. For example, children who fight with each other can be sent to separate rooms and allowed out only when they are able to

Vicarious desensitization *A reduction in fear or anxiety that takes place vicariously (secondhand) when a client watches models perform the feared behavior.*
Virtual reality exposure *Use of computer-generated images to present fear stimuli. The virtual environment responds to a viewer's head movements and other inputs.*
Eye movement desensitization and reprocessing (EMDR) *A technique for reducing fear or anxiety; based on holding upsetting thoughts in mind while rapidly moving the eyes from side to side.*

behave more calmly. (For a more thorough review of operant learning, return to Modules 29 and 30.)

As simple as these principles may seem, they have been used very effectively to overcome difficulties in work, home, school, and industrial settings. Let's see how.

Nonreinforcement and Extinction

An extremely overweight mental patient had a persistent and disturbing habit: She stole food from other patients. No one could persuade her to stop stealing or to diet. For the sake of her health, a behavior therapist assigned her a special table in the ward dining room. If she approached any other table, she was immediately removed from the dining room. Any attempt to steal from others caused the patient to miss her own meal (Ayllon, 1963). Because her attempts to steal food went unrewarded, they rapidly disappeared.

What operant principles did the therapist in this example use? The therapist used *nonreinforcement* to produce *extinction*. The most frequently occurring human behaviors lead to some form of reward. An undesirable response can be eliminated by *identifying* and *removing* the rewards that maintain it. But people don't always do things for food, money, or other obvious rewards. Most of the rewards maintaining human behavior are subtler. *Attention, approval,* and *concern* are common yet powerful reinforcers for humans (● **Figure 67.3**).

Nonreward and extinction can eliminate many problem behaviors, especially in schools, hospitals, and institutions. Often, difficulties center on a limited number of particularly disturbing responses. *Time-out* is a good way to remove such responses, usually by refusing to pay attention to a person who is misbehaving. For example, 14-year-old Terrel periodically appeared in the nude in the activity room of a training center for disturbed adolescents. This behavior always generated a great deal of attention from staff and other patients. As an experiment, the next time he appeared nude, counselors and other staff members greeted him normally and then ignored him. Attention from other patients rapidly subsided. Sheepishly, he returned to his room and dressed.

Reinforcement and Token Economies

Institutional settings, such as mental hospitals, halfway houses, schools for the intellectually challenged, programs for delinquents, and ordinary classrooms, also use reinforcement, in the form of *tokens* (symbolic rewards that can be exchanged for real rewards). Tokens may be printed slips of paper, check marks, points, or gold stars. Whatever form they take, tokens serve as rewards because they may be exchanged for candy, food, cigarettes, recreation, or privileges, such as private time with a therapist, outings, or watching television. They usually produce improvements in behavior (Maggin et al., 2011; Matson & Boisjoli, 2009).

By using tokens, positive responses can be *immediately rewarded.* For maximum impact, therapists select specific *target behaviors* (actions or other behaviors the therapist seeks to modify). Target behaviors are then reinforced with tokens. For example, a mute mental patient might first be given a token each time he or she says a word. Next, tokens may be given for

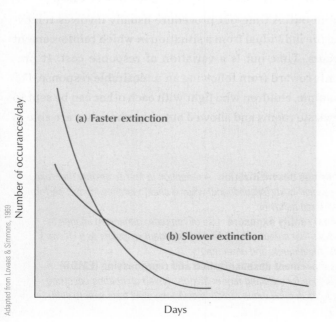

● **Figure 67.3**

Children with developmental difficulties sometimes engage in self-harm, like head banging. Since such behavior can be maintained by parental attention, it can be worth trying to extinguish such behavior by ignoring it (and instead paying attention when the child is **not** engaged in self-harm). The graph gives two hypothetical but realistic examples showing that such behaviors can sometimes be extinguished in this way.

Credit Card

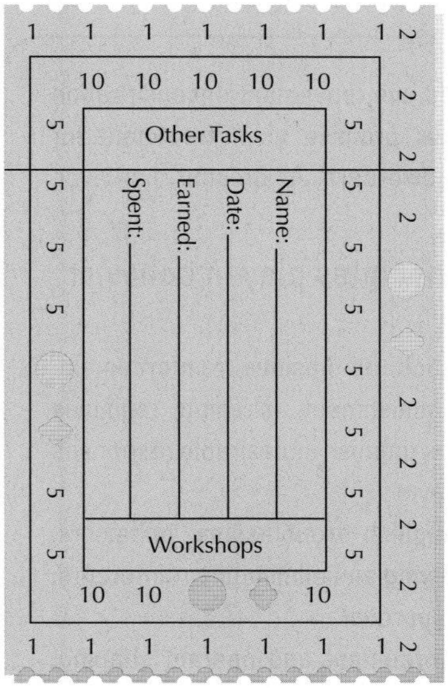

OXNARD DAY TREATMENT CENTER CREDIT INCENTIVE SYSTEM			
EARN CREDITS BY		**SPEND CREDITS FOR**	
MONITOR DAILY	15	COFFEE	5
MENU PLANNING CHAIRMAN	50	LUNCH	10
PARTICIPATE	5	EXCEPT THURSDAY	15
BUY FOOD AT STORE	10	BUS TRIP	5
COOK FOR/PREPARE LUNCH	5	BOWLING	8
WIPE OFF KITCHEN TABLE	3	GROUP THERAPY	5
WASH DISHES	5–10	PRIVATE STAFF TIME	5
DRY AND PUT AWAY DISHES	5	DAY OFF	5–20
MAKE COFFEE AND CLEAN URN	15	WINDOW SHOPPING	5
CLEAN REFRIGERATOR	20	REVIEW WITH DR.	10
ATTEND PLANNING CONFERENCE	1	DOING OWN THING	1
OT PREPARATION	1–5	LATE 1 PER EVERY 10 MIN	
COMPLETE OT PROJECT	5	PRESCRIPTION FROM DR.	10
RETURN OT PROJECT	2		
DUST AND POLISH TABLES	5		
PUT AWAY GROCERIES	3		
CLEAN TABLE	5		
CLEAN 6 ASH TRAYS	2		
CLEAN SINK	5		
CARRY OUT CUPS & BOTTLES	5		
CLEAN CHAIRS	5		
CLEAN KITCHEN CUPBOARDS	5		
ASSIST STAFF	5		
ARRANGE MAGAZINES NEATLY	3		
BEING ON TIME	5		
MONITOR-ANN			

● **Figure 67.4**
Shown here is a token used in one token economy system. In this instance, the token is a card that records the number of credits earned by a patient. Also pictured is a list of credit values for various activities. Tokens may be exchanged for items or for privileges listed on the board. (After photographs by Robert P. Liberman.)

speaking a complete sentence. Later, the patient could gradually be required to speak more often, then to answer questions, and eventually to carry on a short conversation in order to receive tokens. In this way, deeply withdrawn patients have been returned to the world of normal communication.

The full-scale use of tokens in an institutional setting produces a *token economy*. In a **token economy**, patients are rewarded with tokens for a wide range of socially desirable or productive activities (Spiegler & Guevremont, 2010). They must *pay* tokens for privileges and when they engage in problem behaviors (● **Figure 67.4**). For example, tokens are given to patients who dress themselves, take required medication, arrive for meals on time, and so on. Constructive activities, such as gardening, cooking, or cleaning, also may earn tokens. Patients must *exchange* tokens for meals and private rooms, movies, passes, off-ward activities, and other privileges. They are *charged* tokens for disrobing in public, talking to themselves, fighting, crying, and similar target behaviors (Morisse et al., 1996; Spiegler & Guevremont, 2010).

Token economies can radically change a patient's overall adjustment and morale. Patients are given an incentive to change, and they are held responsible for their actions. The use of tokens may seem manipulative, but it empowers patients. Many "hopelessly" intellectually challenged, mentally ill, and delinquent people have been returned to productive lives by means of token economies (Boerke & Reitman, 2011).

By the time they are ready to leave, patients may be earning tokens on a weekly basis for maintaining sane, responsible, and productive behavior (Miltenberger, 2012). Typically, the most effective token economies are those that gradually switch from tokens to *social rewards* such as praise, recognition, and approval. Such rewards are what patients will receive when they return to their family, friends, and community.

CENGAGE brain.com

Go to **cengagebrain.com** to access **MindTap for Coon/ Mitterer *Psychology Modules for Active Learning*** and other online learning tools. MindTap is a fully online learning experience that combines all the tools you need—readings, multimedia, activities, and assessments—into a singular personalized Learning Path that guides you through the course.

Token economy *A therapeutic program in which desirable behaviors are reinforced with tokens that can be exchanged for goods, services, activities, and privileges.*

Module 67: Summary

67.1 What is behavior therapy?

- **67.1.1** Behavior therapists use the learning principles of classical or operant conditioning to directly change human behavior.
- **67.1.2** In aversion therapy, classical conditioning is used to associate maladaptive behavior (such as smoking or drinking) with pain or other aversive events to inhibit undesirable responses.
- **67.1.3** In desensitization, gradual adaptation and reciprocal inhibition break the link between fear and particular situations. Typical steps in desensitization are the following: construct a fear hierarchy; learn to produce total relaxation; and perform items on the hierarchy (from least to most disturbing).
- **67.1.4** Desensitization may be carried out with real settings or it may be done by vividly imagining the fear hierarchy or by watching models perform the feared responses.
- **67.1.5** In some cases, virtual reality exposure can be used to present fear stimuli in a controlled manner.

- **67.1.6** A new technique called eye movement desensitization and reprocessing (EMDR) shows promise as a treatment for traumatic memories and stress disorders. At present, however, EMDR is controversial.

67.2 What role do operant principles play in behavior therapy?

- **67.2.1** Operant principles, such as positive reinforcement, nonreinforcement, extinction, punishment, shaping, stimulus control, and time-out, are used to extinguish undesirable responses and to promote constructive behavior.
- **67.2.2** Nonreward can extinguish troublesome behaviors. Often this is done by simply identifying and eliminating reinforcers, particularly attention and social approval.
- **67.2.3** To apply positive reinforcement and operant shaping, tokens are often used to reinforce selected target behaviors.
- **67.2.4** Full-scale use of tokens in an institutional setting produces a token economy. Toward the end of a token economy program, patients are shifted to social rewards such as recognition and approval.

Module 67: Knowledge Builder

Recite

1. Shock, pain, and discomfort play what role in conditioning an aversion?
   - **a.** conditioned stimulus
   - **b.** unconditioned response
   - **c.** unconditioned stimulus
   - **d.** conditioned response

2. When desensitization is carried out through the use of live or filmed models, it is called
   - **a.** cognitive therapy
   - **b.** flooding
   - **c.** covert desensitization
   - **d.** vicarious desensitization

3. Systematic desensitization has three basic steps: constructing a hierarchy, flooding the person with anxiety, and imagining relaxation. *T or F?*

4. In EMDR therapy, computer-generated virtual reality images are used to expose clients to fear-provoking stimuli. *T or F?*

5. Behavior modification programs aimed at extinction of an undesirable behavior typically use what operant principles?
   - **a.** punishment and stimulus control
   - **b.** punishment and shaping
   - **c.** nonreinforcement and time-out
   - **d.** stimulus control and time-out

6. Attention can be a powerful _____ for humans.

Reflect

Think Critically

7. A natural form of desensitization often takes place in hospitals. Can you guess what it is?

Self-Reflect

Can you describe three problems for which you think behavior therapy would be an appropriate treatment?

Have you ever become naturally desensitized to a stimulus or situation that at first made you anxious (for instance, heights, public speaking, or driving on freeways)? How would you explain your reduced fear?

See if you can give a personal example of how the following principles have affected your behavior: positive reinforcement, extinction, punishment, shaping, stimulus control, and time-out.

ANSWERS

1. c 2. d 3. F 4. F 5. c 6. reinforcer 7. Doctors and nurses learn to relax and remain calm at the sight of blood and other bodily fluids because of their frequent exposure to them.

Therapies: Medical Therapies

When Talk Won't Do

Psychotherapy can be used to treat many mental disorders, but it may not always be successful. How can you talk someone through their illness if they are suffering a complete psychotic break from reality? Besides, if the primary problem is due to, say, a biochemical imbalance in the brain, wouldn't it be better to treat the imbalance itself, perhaps with medication? For reasons like these, severe mental disorders, such as schizophrenia or major depressive disorders, are more often treated medically—although combinations of medication and psychotherapy also are often helpful. With appropriate treatment, many seriously mentally ill individuals have gone on to lead happy and productive lives.

The work of artist Rodger Casier illustrates the value of psychiatric care. Despite having a form of schizophrenia, Casier produces artwork, like his *Self-Portrait* shown here, that has received public acclaim and has been featured in professional journals.

Rodger Casier

SURVEY QUESTION

68.1 How do psychiatrists treat psychological disorders?

Medical Therapies—Psychiatric Care

SURVEY QUESTION 68.1: How do psychiatrists treat psychological disorders?

Three main types of **somatic therapy,** or physical body therapy, are *pharmacotherapy (drug therapies), brain stimulation therapy,* and *psychosurgery.* Somatic therapy is often done in the context of psychiatric hospitalization. All somatic approaches have a strong medical slant and are typically administered by psychiatrists, who are trained as medical doctors.

Drug Therapies

The atmosphere in psychiatric wards and mental hospitals changed radically in the mid-1950s with the widespread adoption of **pharmacotherapy** (FAR-meh-koe-THER-eh-pea), the use of drugs to treat psychopathology. Drugs may relieve the anxiety attacks and other discomforts of milder psychological disorders. More often, however, they are used to combat schizophrenia and major mood disorders (Julien, 2011).

What sort of drugs are used in pharmacotherapy? Three major types of drugs are used. All achieve their effects by influencing the activity of different brain neurotransmitters (Kalat, 2013). **Anxiolytics** (ANG-zee-eh LIT-iks), such as Valium, produce relaxation or reduce anxiety. **Antidepressants,** such as Prozac, are mood-elevating drugs that combat depression.

Antipsychotics (major tranquilizers), such as Risperdal, have tranquilizing effects and reduce hallucinations and delusions. (See ● Table 68.1 for examples of each class of drugs.)

Are drugs a valid approach to treatment? Definitely. Drugs have shortened hospital stays, and they have greatly improved the chances that people will recover from major psychological disorders. Drug therapy also has made it possible for many people to return to the community, where they can be treated on an outpatient basis.

Limitations of Drug Therapy

Regardless of their benefits, all drugs involve risks. For example, 15 percent of patients taking major tranquilizers for long periods develop a neurological disorder that causes rhythmic facial and mouth movements (Chakos et al., 1996). Similarly, although the drug *clozapine* (Clozaril) can relieve the symptoms of schizophrenia, 2 out of 100 patients taking the drug suffer from a potentially fatal blood disease (Mustafa, 2013).

Is the risk worth it? Many experts think it is because chronic schizophrenia robs people of almost everything that makes life worth living. It's possible, of course, that newer drugs will improve the risk/benefit ratio in the treatment of severe problems like schizophrenia. For example, the drugs risperidone (Risperdal) and olanzapine (Zyprexa) appear to be as effective as clozapine, without the same degree of lethal risk.

But even the best new drugs are not cure-alls. They help some people and relieve some problems, but not all. As noted earlier, for serious mental disorders, a combination of medication and psychotherapy almost always works better than drugs alone (Manber et al., 2008; Oestergaard & Møldrup, 2011). Nevertheless, where schizophrenia and major mood disorders are concerned, drugs will undoubtedly remain the primary mode of treatment (Leucht et al., 2011; Vasa, Carlino, & Pine, 2006).

Brain Stimulation Therapy

In contrast to drug therapies, brain stimulation therapies achieve their effects by altering the electrical activity of the brain.

Electroconvulsive Therapy (ECT)

Electroconvulsive therapy (ECT) is the first, and most dramatic, of the brain stimulation therapies. Widely used since the 1940s, it remains controversial to this day (Case et al., 2013; Hirshbein & Sarvananda, 2008). Although ECT is mainly used to treat depression, it is still used to treat other disorders (Cusin et al., 2013; Weiss, Allan, & Greenaway, 2012). In ECT, a 150-volt electrical current is passed through the brain for slightly less than a second.

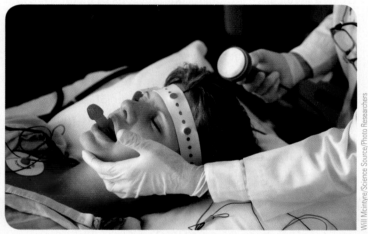

In electroconvulsive therapy (ECT), electrodes are attached to the head and a brief electrical current is passed through the brain. ECT is used in the treatment of severe depression.

TABLE 68.1	Commonly Prescribed Psychiatric Drugs		
Class	**Examples (Trade Names)**	**Effects**	**Main Mode of Action**
Anxiolytics (minor tranquilizers)	Ativan, Halcion, Librium, Restoril, Valium, Xanax	Reduce anxiety, tension, fear	Enhance effects of GABA
Antidepressants	Anafranil, Elavil, Nardil, Norpramin, Parnate, Paxil, Prozac, Tofranil, Zoloft	Counteract depression	Enhance effects of serotonin or dopamine
Antipsychotics (major tranquilizers)	Clozaril, Haldol, Mellaril, Navane, Risperdal, Thorazine	Reduce agitation, delusions, hallucinations, thought disorders	Reduce effects of dopamine

Source: Adapted from Julien, 2011; Kalat, 2013.

This rather drastic medical treatment for depression triggers a convulsion and causes the patient to lose consciousness for a short time. Muscle relaxants and sedative drugs are given before ECT to soften its impact. Treatments are given in a series of sessions spread over several weeks or months.

How does shock help? It is the seizure activity—not the shock—that is believed to be helpful. Proponents of ECT claim that shock-induced seizures alter or "reset" the biochemical and hormonal balance in the brain and body, bringing an end to severe depression and suicidal behavior as well as improving long-term quality of life (McCall et al., 2006; Medda et al., 2009). Others have charged that ECT works only by confusing patients so they can't remember why they were depressed.

Not all professionals support the use of ECT. However, most experts seem to agree on the following: (1) At best, ECT produces only temporary improvement—it gets the patient out of a bad spot, but it must be combined with other treatments, (2) ECT can cause memory loss in some patients (Sienaert et al., 2010), (3) ECT should be used only after other treatments have failed, and (4) to lower the chance of a relapse, ECT should be followed by antidepressant drugs (McCall et al., 2011). All told, ECT is considered by many to be a valid treatment for selected cases of depression—especially when it rapidly ends wildly self-destructive or suicidal behavior (Medda et al., 2009). It's interesting to note that most ECT patients feel that the treatment helped them. Most, in fact, would have it done again (Bernstein et al., 1998; Smith et al., 2009).

Deep Brain Stimulation Unlike ECT, **deep brain stimulation (DBS)** requires surgery to implant electrodes but allows for electrical stimulation of precisely targeted brain regions. (See Module 8 for more information about electrical stimulation of the brain.) In some studies, depressed patients who hadn't benefited from drug therapy and ECT improved when a specific brain region was stimulated (Kennedy et al., 2011; Sartorius et al., 2010). Stimulating pleasure centers in the brains of another group of patients also relieved depression (Schlaepfer et al., 2008). Also, unlike ECT, DBS can be used to treat disorders other than depression, such as obsessive-compulsive disorder (Haq et al., 2010).

Transcranial Magnetic Stimulation Neuroscience research continues to probe the functioning of the brain and its various parts in ever-greater detail. As a result, more precisely targeted medical therapies with fewer side effects continue to be discovered (Barr et al., 2013; Kalat, 2013). For example, a new technique called **transcranial magnetic stimulation (TMS)** uses magnetic pulses to temporarily block activity in specific parts of the brain (● Figure 68.1).

By applying TMS to parts of the frontal lobe, Paulo Boggio and his colleagues (2010) were able to change the way people made decisions while gambling. It is not a long stretch to imagine that this technique might become a powerful adjunct

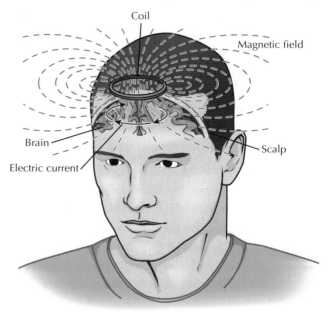

● Figure 68.1

Transcranial magnetic stimulation (TMS) uses a small coil held near the surface of the scalp to create magnetic pulses that induce electrical activity in the underlying brain tissue. The result is a temporary blockage of normal brain activity. TMS can be used to study brain function and has already been applied as a medical therapy (Mantovani et al., 2010).

Somatic therapy *Any bodily therapy, such as drug therapy, electroconvulsive therapy, or psychosurgery.*

Pharmacotherapy *(FAR-meh-koe-THER-eh-pea) The use of drugs to treat psychopathology.*

Anxiolytics *(ANG-zee-eh LIT-iks) Drugs (such as Valium) that produce relaxation or reduce anxiety.*

Antidepressants *Mood-elevating drugs.*

Antipsychotics (major tranquilizers) *Drugs that, in addition to having tranquilizing effects, also tend to reduce hallucinations and delusional thinking.*

Electroconvulsive therapy (ECT) *A treatment for severe depression, consisting of an electric shock passed directly through the brain, which induces a convulsion.*

Deep brain stimulation (DBS) *Electrical stimulation of precisely targeted brain regions; a surgical procedure is necessary to implant electrodes in the brain that allow for the stimulation.*

Transcranial magnetic stimulation (TMS) *Device that uses magnetic pulses to temporarily block activity in specific parts of the brain.*

therapy to cognitive therapy to treat compulsive gambling (Ladouceur, Lachance, & Fournier, 2009). Similarly, patients with obsessive-compulsive disorder have shown marked improvement when TMS disrupted brain areas involved in compulsive behavior (Mantovani et al., 2010).

Psychosurgery

Psychosurgery—any surgical alteration of the brain intended to treat a psychological disorder—is the most extreme medical treatment. The oldest and most radical psychosurgery is the lobotomy. In *prefrontal lobotomy*, the frontal lobes are surgically disconnected from other brain areas. This procedure was supposed to calm persons who didn't respond to any other type of treatment.

When the lobotomy was first introduced in the 1940s, there were enthusiastic claims for its success. But later studies suggested that some patients were calmed, some showed no change, and some became mental "vegetables." Lobotomies also produced a high rate of undesirable side effects, such as seizures, blunted emotions, major personality changes, and stupor. About the same time that such problems became apparent, the first antipsychotic drugs became available. Soon after, the lobotomy was abandoned (Mashour, Walker, & Martuza, 2005).

To what extent is psychosurgery used now? Psychosurgery is still considered valid by many neurosurgeons. However, most now use *deep lesioning*, in which small target areas are destroyed in the brain's interior. The appeal of deep lesioning is that it can have value as a remedy for some very specific disorders. For instance, patients suffering from a severe type of obsessive-compulsive disorder may be helped by psychosurgery (Anderson & Booker, 2006; Greenspan & Coghill et al., 2008).

It is worth remembering that psychosurgery cannot be reversed. Whereas a drug can be given or taken away and electrical stimulation can be turned off, you can't take back psychosurgery. Critics argue that psychosurgery should be banned altogether; others continue to report success with brain surgery. Nevertheless, it may have value as a remedy for some very specific disorders (Sachdev & Chen, 2009).

Hospitalization

In 2008, about 7.5 percent of all Americans received inpatient treatment for a mental health problem (National Institute of Mental Health, 2013). **Mental hospitalization** involves placing a person in a protected setting where medical therapy is provided. Hospitalization by itself can be a form of treatment. Staying in a hospital takes patients out of situations that may be sustaining their problems. For example, people with drug addictions may find it nearly impossible to resist the temptations for drug abuse in their daily lives. Hospitalization can help them make a clean break from their self-destructive behavior patterns (André et al., 2003).

At their best, hospitals are sanctuaries that provide diagnosis, support, refuge, and therapy. This is frequently true of psychiatric units in general hospitals and private psychiatric hospitals. At its worst, confinement to an institution can be a brutal experience that leaves people less prepared to face the world than when they arrived. This is more often the case in large state mental hospitals. In most instances, hospitals are best used as a last resort, after other forms of treatment within the community have been exhausted.

Peter Turnley/Turnley/Corbis

Depending on the quality of the institution, hospitalization may be a refuge or a brutalizing experience. Many state "asylums" or mental hospitals are antiquated and in need of drastic improvement.

Another trend in treatment is **partial hospitalization** (Bales & Bateman, 2012). In this approach, some patients spend their days in the hospital but go home at night. Others attend therapy sessions during the evening. A major advantage of partial hospitalization is that patients can go home and practice what they've been learning. Overall, partial hospitalization can be just as effective as full hospitalization (Drymalski & Washburn, 2011; Kiser, Heston, & Paavola, 2006).

Deinstitutionalization In the last 60 years, the population in large mental hospitals has dropped by two-thirds. This is largely a result of **deinstitutionalization**, or reduced use of full-time commitment to mental institutions. Long-term "institutionalization" can lead to dependency, isolation, and continued emotional disturbance (Novella, 2010). Deinstitutionalization was meant to remedy this problem.

How successful has deinstitutionalization been? In truth, its success has been limited (Paulson, 2012). Many states reduced mental hospital populations primarily to save money. The upsetting result is that many chronic patients have been discharged to hostile communities without adequate care. Many former patients have joined the ranks of the homeless. Others are repeatedly jailed for minor crimes. Sadly, patients who trade hospitalization for unemployment, homelessness, and social isolation all too often end up rehospitalized, in jail, or even as suicides (Markowitz, 2011; Yoon & Bruckner, 2009).

Large mental hospitals may no longer be warehouses for society's unwanted, but many former patients are no better off in bleak nursing homes, single-room hotels, board-and-care homes, shelters, or jails. For every mentally ill American in a hospital, three are trapped in the criminal justice system (National Institute of Mental Health, 2010b). These figures suggest that jails are replacing mental hospitals as our society's "solution" for mental illness (Markowitz, 2011). Yet, ironically, high-quality care is available in almost every community. As much as anything, a simple lack of money prevents large numbers of people from getting the help they need.

Halfway houses may be a better way to ease a patient's return to the community (Soyez & Broekaert, 2003). **Halfway houses** are short-term group living facilities for people making the transition from an institution (mental hospital, prison, and so forth) to independent living. Typically, they offer supervision and support, without being as restricted and medically oriented as hospitals. They also keep people near their families. Most important, halfway houses can ease a person's return to "normal" life and reduce chances of being readmitted to a hospital (Davidson et al., 2010).

Community Mental Health Programs

Community mental health centers, which offer a wide range of mental health services and psychiatric care, are a bright spot in the area of mental health care. Such centers try to help people avoid hospitalization, find answers to mental health problems, and improve mental health literacy (Jorm, 2012; Mark et al., 2013). Typically, they do this by providing short-term treatment, counseling, outpatient care, emergency services, and suicide prevention.

A well-run halfway house can be a humane and cost-effective way to ease former mental patients back into the community.

Mental health centers also are concerned with *prevention*. Consultation, education, and **crisis intervention** (skilled management of a psychological emergency) are used to prevent problems before they become serious. Also, some centers attempt to raise the general level of mental health in a community by combating unemployment, delinquency, and drug abuse (Mancini & Wyrick-Waugh, 2013).

Have community mental health centers succeeded in meeting their goals? In practice, they have concentrated much more on providing clinical services than they have on preventing problems. This appears to be primarily the result of wavering government support (translation: money). Overall, community mental health centers have succeeded in making psychological services more accessible than ever. Many of their programs rely on **paraprofessionals**,

Psychosurgery *Any surgical alteration of the brain designed to bring about desirable behavioral or emotional changes.*

Mental hospitalization *Placing a person in a protected, therapeutic environment staffed by mental health professionals.*

Partial hospitalization *An approach in which patients receive treatment at a hospital during the day but return home at night.*

Deinstitutionalization *Reduced use of full-time commitment to mental institutions to treat mental disorders.*

Halfway house *A community-based facility for individuals making the transition from an institution (mental hospital, prison, and so forth) to independent living.*

Community mental health center *A facility offering a wide range of mental health services, such as prevention, counseling, consultation, and crisis intervention.*

Crisis intervention *Skilled management of a psychological emergency.*

Paraprofessional *An individual who works in a near-professional capacity under the supervision of a more highly trained person.*

individuals who work in a near-professional capacity under the supervision of more highly trained staff. Some paraprofessionals are ex-addicts, ex-alcoholics, or ex-patients who have "been there." Many more are persons (paid or volunteer) who have skills in tutoring, crafts, or counseling or who are simply warm, understanding, and skilled at communication. Often, paraprofessionals are more approachable than doctors. This encourages people to seek mental health services that they might otherwise be reluctant to use (Farrand et al., 2009).

Module 68: Summary

68.1 How do psychiatrists treat psychological disorders?

- **68.1.1** Three medical, or somatic, approaches to treatment are pharmacotherapy, brain stimulation therapy (including electroconvulsive therapy [ECT]), and psychosurgery.

- **68.1.2** Hospitalization, including partial hospitalization, involves placing a person in a protected setting where medical therapy is provided.
- **68.1.3** Community mental health centers seek to avoid or minimize mental hospitalization. They also seek to prevent mental health problems through education, consultation, and crisis intervention.

Module 68: Knowledge Builder

Recite

1. Major tranquilizers also are known as
   - **a.** anxiolytics
   - **b.** antipsychotics
   - **c.** antidepressants
   - **d.** prefrontal sedatives
2. ECT is a modern form of pharmacotherapy. *T or F?*
3. Currently, the frontal lobotomy is the most widely used form of psychosurgery. *T or F?*
4. Deinstitutionalization is an advanced form of partial hospitalization. *T or F?*

Reflect

Think Critically

5. Residents of Berkeley, California, once voted on a referendum to ban the use of ECT within city limits. Do you think that the use of certain psychiatric treatments should be controlled by law?

Self-Reflect

Keeping in mind that all therapies, and especially medical therapies, have side effects (see, e.g., Casselle, 2009), when is it appropriate to use a medical therapy to treat someone with a mental illness? Why not use psychotherapy instead?

Why might you choose to combine a medical therapy and a psychotherapy? Can you frame your reasons in terms of the stress–vulnerability model introduced in Module 61?

ANSWERS

1. b **2.** F **3.** F **4.** F **5.** The question of who can prescribe drugs, perform surgery, and administer ECT is controlled by law. However, psychiatrists strongly object to residents, city councils, or government agencies making *medical* decisions.

CENGAGE**brain**.com

Psychology in Action: Facing Mental Health Issues

I Really Wanna Quit

Trouble quitting smoking? Try vividly imagining one of the following scenes every time you crave a smoke:

"I am in a doctor's office. The doctor looks at some reports and tells me I have lung cancer. She says a lung will have to be removed and sets a date for the operation."

"I am in bed under an oxygen tent. My chest feels caved in. There is a tube in my throat. I can barely breathe."

"I wake up in the morning and smoke a cigarette. I begin coughing up blood."

"My lover won't even kiss me because my breath smells bad."

This technique, known as *covert sensitization*, is one of the self-control techniques we explore in this module. Because not every mental health issue can be overcome this way, we also explore how to find help if you need it.

Lawrence Manning/Corbis

SURVEY QUESTIONS

69.1 How are behavioral principles applied to everyday problems?

69.2 What are some basic counseling skills?

69.3 How could a person find professional help?

Self-Management— Boosting Your "Willpower"

SURVEY QUESTION 69.1: How are behavioral principles applied to everyday problems?

You should definitely seek professional help when a significant problem exists. For lesser difficulties, you may want to try applying behavioral principles yourself (Martin & Pear, 2011; Watson & Tharp, 2014). (See also Modules 31 and 67.)

Covert Sensitization and Reward

Although the behavior therapies are no cure-all, they do offer some simple tools that can help you modify your own behavior by making your less desirable behaviors less frequent while increasing the frequency of your more desired behaviors. Let's explore some of them.

Covert Sensitization In **covert sensitization**, aversive imagery is used to reduce the occurrence of an undesired response, such as smoking, overeating, and other habits (Kearney, 2006; Watson & Tharp, 2014). For example, Jay repeatedly and vividly imagined himself going into a store to steal something. He then pictured himself being caught and turned over to the police, who handcuffed him and hauled him off to jail. Once there, he imagined calling his wife to tell her he had been arrested for shoplifting. He became very distressed as he faced her anger and his son's disappointment (Kohn & Antonuccio, 2002).

Why would anyone imagine such a thing? Jay's behavior is not as strange as it may seem. His goal was self-control: Jay is a *kleptomaniac* (a compulsive thief). The method he chose (called *covert sensitization*) is a form of behavior therapy (Prochaska & Norcross, 2010).

Covert sensitization can be used in any situation that tests your self-control. Here's how it's done: Obtain six cards and on each write a brief description of a scene related to the habit you want to control. The scene should be so *disturbing* or *disgusting* that thinking about it would temporarily make you very uncomfortable about indulging in the habit. For overeating, the cards might read:

- "I reach for a spoonful of my favorite dessert but it is crawling with maggots."

- "Someone just vomited something green all over my pizza."

- "As I bring a French fry to my mouth, I notice that it smells like ripe manure."

Other cards would continue along the same line. The trick is to get yourself to imagine or picture vividly each of these disturbing scenes *several times* a day. Imagining the scenes can be accomplished by placing them under *stimulus control*. Simply choose something you do *frequently* each day (such as getting a snack). Next, make a rule: Before you can get a cup of coffee or get up from your chair, or whatever you have selected as a cue, you must take out your cards and *vividly picture* yourself engaging in the action you wish to curb (eating or smoking, for example). Then *vividly picture* the scene described on the top card. Imagine the scene for 30 seconds.

After visualizing the top card, move it to the bottom, so the cards are rotated. Make up new cards each week. The scenes can be made much more upsetting than the samples given here, which are toned down to keep you from being "grossed out." Covert sensitization may sound as if you are "playing games with yourself," but it can be a great help if you want to cut down on a bad habit (Kearney, 2006). Try it!

Thought Stopping

As discussed in Module 67, behavior therapists accept that thoughts, like visible responses, also can cause trouble. Think of times when you have repeatedly "put yourself down" mentally or when you have been preoccupied by needless worries, fears, or other negative and upsetting thoughts. If you want to gain control over such thoughts, thought stopping may help you do it.

In **thought stopping**, aversive stimuli are used to interrupt or prevent upsetting thoughts (Bakker, 2009). The simplest thought-stopping technique uses mild punishment to suppress upsetting mental images and internal "talk." Simply place a large, flat rubber band around your wrist. As you go through the day, apply this rule: Each time you catch yourself thinking the upsetting image or thought, pull the rubber band away from your wrist and snap it. You need not make this terribly painful. Its value lies in drawing your attention to how often you form negative thoughts and in interrupting the flow of thoughts.

A second thought-stopping procedure requires only that you interrupt upsetting thoughts each time they occur. Begin by setting aside time each day during which you will deliberately think the unwanted thought. As you begin to form the thought, shout "Stop!" aloud, with conviction. (Obviously, you should choose a private spot for this part of the procedure!)

Repeat the thought-stopping procedure ten to twenty times for the first two or three days. Then switch to shouting "Stop!" covertly (to yourself) rather than aloud. Thereafter, thought stopping can be carried out throughout the day, whenever upsetting thoughts occur. After several days of practice, you should be able to stop unwanted thoughts whenever they occur.

Covert Reinforcement

Earlier, we discussed how punishing images can be used to decrease undesirable responses, such as smoking or overeating. Many people also find it helpful to covertly *reinforce* desired actions. **Covert reinforcement** is the use of positive imagery to reinforce desired behavior. For example, suppose your target behavior is, once again, not eating dessert. If this were the case, you could do the following (Kearney, 2006; Watson & Tharp, 2014):

> Imagine that you are standing at the dessert table with your friends. As dessert is passed, you politely refuse and feel good about staying on your diet.

These images would then be followed by imagining a pleasant, reinforcing scene:

> Imagine that you are your ideal weight. Someone you really like says to you, "Gee, you've lost weight. I've never seen you look so good."

For many people, of course, actual direct self-reinforcement (as described in Module 31) is the best way to alter behavior. Nevertheless, covert or "visualized" reinforcement can have similar effects. To make use of covert reinforcement, choose one or more target behaviors and rehearse them mentally. Then follow each rehearsal with a vivid, rewarding image.

Self-Directed Desensitization

You have prepared for two weeks to give a speech in a large class. As your turn approaches, your hands begin to tremble. Your heart pounds, and you find it difficult to breathe. You say to your body, "Relax!" What happens? Nothing! That's why the first step in desensitization is learning to relax voluntarily by using the tension-release method described in Module 67. As an alternative, you might want to try imagining a very safe, pleasant, and relaxing scene. Some people find such images as relaxing as the tension-release method (Rosenthal, 1993). Another helpful technique is to do some deep breathing. Typically, a person who is breathing deeply is relaxed. Shallow breathing involves little movement of the diaphragm. If you place your hand on your abdomen, it will move up and down if you are breathing deeply.

Once you have learned to relax, the next step is to identify the fear you want to control and construct a *fear hierarchy*.

Procedure for Constructing a Fear Hierarchy Make a list of situations (related to the fear) that make you anxious. Try to list at least 10 situations. Some should be very frightening and others only mildly frightening. Write a short description of each situation on a separate card. Place the cards in order from the least disturbing situation to the most disturbing. Here is a sample hierarchy for a student afraid of public speaking:

1. Being given an assignment to speak in class
2. Thinking about the topic and the date the speech must be given
3. Writing the speech; thinking about delivering the speech
4. Watching other students speak in class the week before the speech date
5. Rehearsing the speech alone; pretending to give it to the class
6. Delivering the speech to my roommate; pretending my roommate is the teacher
7. Reviewing the speech on the day it is to be presented
8. Entering the classroom; waiting and thinking about the speech
9. Being called; standing up; facing the audience
10. Delivering the speech

Using the Hierarchy When you have mastered the relaxation exercises and have the hierarchy constructed, set aside time each day to work on reducing your fear. Begin by performing the relaxation exercises. When you are completely relaxed, visualize the scene on the first card (the least frightening scene). If you can *vividly* picture and imagine yourself in the

first situation twice *without a noticeable increase in muscle tension,* proceed to the next card. Also, as you progress, relax yourself between cards.

Each day, stop when you reach a card that you cannot visualize without becoming tense in three attempts. Each day, begin one or two cards before the one on which you stopped the previous day. Continue to work with the cards until you can visualize the last situation without experiencing tension (techniques are based on Wolpe, 1974).

By using this approach, you should be able to reduce the fear or anxiety associated with things such as public speaking, entering darkened rooms, asking questions in large classes, heights, talking to members of the opposite sex, and taking tests (Watson & Tharp, 2014). Even if you are not always able to reduce a fear, you will have learned to place relaxation under voluntary control. This alone is valuable because controlling unnecessary tension can increase energy and efficiency.

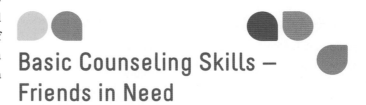

Basic Counseling Skills — Friends in Need

SURVEY QUESTION 69.2: What are some basic counseling skills?

While you may not currently be experiencing any mental health problems, perhaps you have a friend who is. If someone close to you asks to talk about his or her troubles, it helps to be prepared.

Before we review some general counseling skills, it is important to remember that only a licensed professional possesses the full set of skills necessary to counsel more serious mental health problems. The *instant* you realize that your friend's problem is beyond your own ability to properly address, help your friend find a more qualified counselor (see the next section of this module). Referring your friends for more professional counseling is not a sign of failure on

---

Covert sensitization *Use of aversive imagery to reduce the occurrence of an undesired response.*

Thought stopping *Use of aversive stimuli to interrupt or prevent upsetting thoughts.*

Covert reinforcement *Using positive imagery to reinforce desired behavior.*

your part; it is a testimony to your own wisdom. Although your textbook authors are psychologists, we are not licensed counselors and quite frequently refer students to our college counseling centers.

Basic Counseling Skills

Several general helping skills can be distilled from the various approaches to therapy. Keep these points in mind if you are ever called on to comfort a person in distress, such as a troubled friend or relative (Kottler & Shepard, 2011; Sharf, 2012) (● Table 69.1).

TABLE 69.1	Helping Behaviors

To help another person gain insight into a personal problem, it is valuable to keep the following comparisons in mind:

Behaviors That Help	Behaviors That Hinder
Active listening	Probing painful topics
Acceptance	Judging/moralizing
Reflecting feelings	Criticism
Open-ended questioning	Threats
Supportive statements	Rejection
Respect	Ridicule/sarcasm
Patience	Impatience
Genuineness	Placing blame
Paraphrasing	Opinionated statements

Source: Adapted from Kottler & Shepard (2011).

Be an Active Listener People frequently talk "at" each other without really listening. A person with problems needs to be heard. Make a sincere effort to listen to and understand the person. Try to accept the person's message without judging it or leaping to conclusions. Let the person know you are listening, through eye contact, posture, your tone of voice, and your replies (Kottler & Shepard, 2011).

Reflect Thoughts and Feelings One of the best things you can do when offering support to another person is to give feedback by simply restating what is said. This also is a good way to encourage a person to talk. If your friend seems to be at a loss for words, *restate* or *paraphrase* his or her last sentence. Here's an example:

Friend: I'm really down about school. I can't get interested in any of my classes. I flunked my Spanish test, and somebody stole my notebook for psychology.

You: So you're really upset about school?

Friend: Yeah, and my parents are hassling me about my grades again.

You: You're feeling pressured by your parents?

Friend: Yeah.

You: It must make you angry to be pressured by them.

As simple as this sounds, it is very helpful to someone trying to sort out feelings. Try it. If nothing else, you'll develop a reputation as a fantastic conversationalist!

Don't Be Afraid of Silence Counselors tend to wait longer before responding than do people in everyday conversations. Pauses of 5 seconds or more are not unusual, and interrupting is rare. Listening patiently lets the person feel unhurried and encourages her or him to speak freely.

Ask Open-Ended Questions Because your goal is to encourage free expression, *open-ended questions* tend to be the most helpful. A *closed question* is one that can be answered yes or no. Open-ended questions call for an open-ended reply. Say, for example, that a friend tells you, "I feel like my boss has it in for me at work." A closed question would be, "Oh, yeah? So, are you going to quit?" Open-ended questions such as, "Do you want to talk about it?" or "How do you feel about it?" are more likely to be helpful.

Clarify Problems People who have a clear idea of what is wrong in their lives are more likely to discover solutions. Try to understand the problem from the person's point of view. As you do, check your understanding often. For example, you might ask, "Are you saying that you feel depressed just at school? Or in general?" Remember, a problem well defined is often half solved.

Focus on Feelings Feelings are neither right nor wrong. By focusing on feelings, you can encourage the outpouring of emotion that is the basis for catharsis. Passing judgment on what is said just makes people defensive. For example, a friend confides that he has failed a test. Perhaps you know that he studies very little. If you say, "Just study more and you will do better," he will probably become defensive or hostile. Much more can be accomplished by saying, "You must feel very frustrated" or simply, "How do you feel about it?"

Avoid Giving Advice Many people mistakenly think that they must solve problems for others. Remember that your goal is to provide understanding and support, not solutions. Of course, it is reasonable to give advice when you are asked for it, but beware of the trap of the "Why don't you . . . ? Yes, but . . ." game. According to psychotherapist Eric Berne (1964), this "game" follows a pattern: Someone says, "I have this problem." You say, "Why don't you do this?" The person replies, "Yes, but . . ." and then tells you why your suggestion won't work. If you make a new suggestion, the reply once again will be, "Yes, but. . . ." Obviously, the person either knows more about his or her personal situation than you do, or he or she has reasons for avoiding your advice. The student described earlier knows he needs to study. His problem is to understand why he doesn't *want* to study.

Accept the Person's Frame of Reference Because we all live in different psychological worlds, there is no "correct" view of a life situation. Try to resist imposing your views on the problems of others. A person who feels that his or her viewpoint has been understood feels freer to examine it objectively and to question it.

Maintain Confidentiality Your efforts to help will be wasted if you fail to respect the privacy of someone who has confided in you. Put yourself in the person's place. Don't gossip.

Remember, these guidelines are not an invitation to play "junior therapist." Professional therapists are trained to approach serious problems with skills far exceeding those described here. However, the points made help define the qualities of a therapeutic relationship. They also emphasize that each of us can supply two of the greatest mental health resources available at any cost: friendship and honest communication.

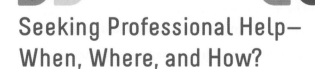

Seeking Professional Help— When, Where, and How?

SURVEY QUESTION 69.3: How could a person find professional help?

Chances are good that at some point you, a friend, or a family member will benefit from mental health services of one kind or another. In 2008, 13.4 percent of all Americans received treatment for a mental health problem (National Institute of Mental Health, 2013).

How would I know if I should seek professional help at some point in my life? Although this question has no simple answer, the following guidelines may be helpful:

1. If your level of psychological discomfort (unhappiness, anxiety, or depression, for example) is comparable to a level of physical discomfort that would cause you to see a doctor or dentist, you should consider seeing a psychologist or a psychiatrist.

2. Another signal to watch for is significant changes in behavior, such as the quality of your work (or schoolwork), your rate of absenteeism, your use of drugs (including alcohol), or your relationships with others.

3. Perhaps you have urged a friend or relative to seek professional help and were dismayed because he or she refused to do so. If *you* find friends or relatives making a similar suggestion, recognize that they may be seeing things more clearly than you are.

4. If you have persistent or disturbing suicidal thoughts or impulses, seek help immediately.

Locating a Therapist

If I wanted to talk to a therapist, how would I find one? Here are some suggestions that can help you get started:

1. **Your family physician.** Your family physician, if you have one, often will be able to help you find the help you are seeking.

2. **Colleges and universities.** If you are a student, don't overlook counseling services offered by a student health center or special student counseling facilities.

3. **Workplaces.** If you have a job, check with your employer. Some employers have employee assistance programs that offer confidential free or low-cost therapy for employees.

4. **Community or county mental health centers.** Most counties and many cities offer public mental health services. (These are listed in the phone book or can be found by searching the Internet.) Public mental health centers usually provide counseling and therapy services directly, and they can refer you to private therapists.

5. **Mental health associations.** Many cities have mental health associations organized by concerned citizens. Groups such as these usually keep listings of qualified therapists and other services and programs in the community.

6. **The Yellow Pages.** Psychologists are listed in the telephone book or on the Internet under "Psychologists," or in some

cases under "Counseling Services." Psychiatrists are generally listed as a subheading under "Physicians." Counselors are usually found under the heading "Marriage and Family Counselors." These listings will usually put you in touch with individuals in private practice.

7. **Crisis hotlines.** A typical crisis hotline is a phone service staffed by volunteers. These people are trained to provide information concerning a wide range of mental health problems. They also have lists of organizations, services, and other resources in the community where you can go for help.

Table 69.2 summarizes the sources for psychotherapy, counseling, and referrals we have discussed as well as some additional possibilities.

TABLE 69.2	Mental Health Resources

- Family doctors (for referrals to mental health professionals)
- Mental health specialists, such as psychiatrists, psychologists, social workers, and mental health counselors
- Religious leaders/counselors
- Health maintenance organizations (HMOs)
- Community mental health centers
- Hospital psychiatry departments and outpatient clinics
- University- or medical school-affiliated programs
- State hospital outpatient clinics
- Family service/social agencies
- Private clinics and facilities
- Employee assistance programs
- Local medical, psychiatric, or psychological societies

Source: National Institute of Mental Health (2012b).

Options *How would I know what kind of a therapist to see? How would I pick one?* The choice between a psychiatrist and a psychologist is somewhat arbitrary. Both are trained to do psychotherapy and can be equally effective as therapists. Although a psychiatrist can administer somatic therapy and prescribe drugs, so can psychologists in New Mexico and Louisiana (Munsey, 2006). A psychologist also can work in conjunction with a physician if such services are needed.

Fees for psychiatrists are usually higher, averaging about $160 to $200 an hour. Psychologists average about $100 an hour. Counselors and social workers typically charge about $80 per hour. Group therapy averages only about $40 an hour because the therapist's fee is divided among several people.

Be aware that most health insurance plans will pay for psychological services. If fees are a problem, keep in mind that many therapists charge on a sliding scale, or ability-to-pay basis, and that community mental health centers almost always charge on a sliding scale. In one way or another, help is almost always available for anyone who needs it.

Some communities and college campuses have counseling services staffed by sympathetic paraprofessionals or peer counselors. These services are free or very low cost. As mentioned earlier, paraprofessionals are people who work in a near-professional capacity under professional supervision. **Peer counselors** are nonprofessional persons who have learned basic counseling skills. There is a natural tendency, perhaps, to doubt the abilities of paraprofessionals. However, paraprofessional counselors are often as effective as professionals (Farrand et al., 2009).

Also, don't overlook **self-help groups**, which can add valuable support to professional treatment. Members of a self-help group typically share a particular type of problem, such as eating disorders or coping with an alcoholic parent. Self-help groups offer members mutual support and a chance to discuss problems. In many instances, helping others also serves as therapy for those who give help. For some problems, self-help groups may be the best choice of all (Dadich, 2010; Galanter et al., 2005).

Qualifications You can usually find out about a therapist's qualifications simply by asking. A reputable therapist will be glad to reveal his or her background. If you have any doubts, credentials may be checked and other helpful information can be obtained from local branches of any of the following organizations. You also can browse the websites listed here:

American Association for Marriage and Family Therapy (www.aamft.org)

American Family Therapy Academy (www.afta.org)

American Psychiatric Association (www.psych.org)

American Psychological Association (www.apa.org)

Association of Humanistic Psychology (www.ahpweb.org)

Canadian Psychiatric Association (www.cpa-apc.org)

Canadian Psychological Association (www.cpa.ca)

National Mental Health Association (www.nmha.org)

The question of how to pick a particular therapist remains. The best way is to start with a short consultation with a respected psychiatrist, psychologist, or counselor. This allows the person you consult to evaluate your difficulty and recommend a type of therapy or a therapist who is likely to be helpful. As an alternative, you might ask the person teaching this course for a referral.

Evaluating a Therapist *How would I know a therapist is being effective?* A balanced look at psychotherapies suggests that all techniques can be equally successful. However, all *therapists* are not equally successful (Elliott & Williams, 2003). Former clients consistently rate the person doing the therapy as more important than the type of therapy used (Elliott & Williams, 2003).

Ask yourself if you feel you are establishing a *therapeutic alliance* with your therapist. A therapist who is working *with* you is usually willing to use whatever method seems most helpful for a client. He or she also can be evaluated on personal characteristics of warmth, integrity, sincerity, and empathy (Okiishi et al., 2003; Prochaska & Norcross, 2010). The *relationship* between a client and therapist is the therapist's most basic tool (Hubble, Duncan, & Miller, 1999; Prochaska & Norcross, 2010). This is why you must trust and easily relate to a therapist for therapy to be effective. Here are some danger signals to watch for in psychotherapy:

- Sexual advances by a therapist
- A therapist who makes repeated verbal threats or is physically aggressive
- A therapist who is excessively blaming, belittling, hostile, or controlling
- A therapist who makes excessive small talk; talks repeatedly about his or her own problems
- A therapist who encourages prolonged dependence on him or her
- A therapist who demands absolute trust or tells client not to discuss therapy with anyone else

An especially important part of the therapeutic alliance is agreement about the goals of therapy (Meier et al., 2006). It is therefore a good idea to think about what you want to accomplish by entering therapy. Write down your goals and discuss them with your therapist during the first session. Your first meeting with a therapist should also answer all of the following questions:

- Will the information I reveal in therapy remain completely confidential?
- What risks do I face if I begin therapy?
- How long do you expect treatment to last?
- What form of treatment do you expect to use?
- Are there alternatives to therapy that might help me as much or more?

It's always tempting to avoid facing up to personal problems. With this in mind, you should give a therapist a fair chance and not give up too easily. But don't hesitate to change therapists or to terminate therapy if you lose confidence in the therapist or if you don't relate well to the therapist as a person.

Peer counselor *A nonprofessional person who has learned basic counseling skills.*
Self-help group *A group of people who share a particular type of problem and provide mutual support to one another.*

Module 69: Summary

69.1 How are behavioral principles applied to everyday problems?

- **69.1.1** Some personal problems can be successfully treated using self-management techniques, such as covert sensitization, thought stopping, covert reinforcement, and self-directed desensitization.
- **69.1.2** In covert sensitization, aversive images are used to discourage unwanted behavior.
- **69.1.3** Thought stopping uses mild punishment to prevent upsetting thoughts.
- **69.1.4** Covert reinforcement is a way to encourage desired responses by mental rehearsal.
- **69.1.5** Desensitization pairs relaxation with a hierarchy of upsetting images in order to lessen fears.

69.2 What are some basic counseling skills?

- **69.2.1** All of the following are helping skills that can be learned: active listening, acceptance, reflection, open-ended questioning, support, respect, patience, genuineness, and paraphrasing.

69.3 How could a person find professional help?

- **69.3.1** Various psychotherapies are generally equally successful, but some therapists are more effective than others. If you need help, it is worth the effort required to find a well-qualified, highly recommended therapist.
- **69.3.2** In most communities, a competent and reputable therapist can be located with public sources of information or through a referral.
- **69.3.3** Practical considerations such as cost and qualifications enter into choosing a therapist. However, the therapist's personal characteristics are of equal importance.

Module 69: Knowledge Builder

Recite

1. Covert sensitization and thought stopping combine aversion therapy and cognitive therapy. *T or F?*

2. Like covert aversion conditioning, covert reinforcement of desired responses also is possible. *T or F?*

3. Exercises that bring about deep-muscle relaxation are an essential element in covert sensitization. *T or F?*

4. Items in a desensitization hierarchy should be placed in order from the least disturbing to the most disturbing. *T or F?*

5. The first step in desensitization is to place the visualization of disturbing images under stimulus control. *T or F?*

6. Persistent emotional discomfort is a clear sign that professional psychological counseling should be sought. *T or F?*

7. Community mental health centers rarely offer counseling or therapy themselves; they only do referrals. *T or F?*

8. In many instances, a therapist's personal qualities have more of an effect on the outcome of therapy than the type of therapy used. *T or F?*

Reflect

Think Critically

9. Would it be acceptable for a therapist to urge a client to break all ties with a troublesome family member?

Self-Reflect

How could you use covert sensitization, thought stopping, and covert reinforcement to change your behavior?

Just for practice, make a fear hierarchy for a situation you find frightening. Does vividly picturing items in the hierarchy make you tense or anxious? If so, can you intentionally relax using the tension-release method?

Which of the basic counseling skills would improve your ability to help a person in distress (or even just have an engaging conversation)?

Take some time to find out what mental health services are available to you.

ANSWERS

1. T 2. T 3. F 4. T 5. F 6. T 7. F 8. T 9. Such decisions must be made by clients themselves. Therapists can help clients evaluate important decisions and feelings about significant persons in their lives. However, actively urging a client to sever a relationship borders on unethical behavior.

Social Psychology: Social Behavior and Cognition

No One Is an Island

On April 15, 2013, two bombs exploded at the finish line of the Boston Marathon, killing three people and injuring hundreds more. Why did two young men decide to carry out such a despicably antisocial act? Why did so many strangers rush to help the wounded and dying, despite the risk of being exposed to another explosion? Questions like these about human behavior can almost always be better answered by taking the perspective of social psychology.

Families, teams, crowds, tribes, companies, parties, troops, bands, sects, gangs, crews, clans, communities, and nations: We are all entwined in many, many social networks. As the poet John Donne wrote nearly 400 years ago, "No man is an island, entire of itself." We are all strongly influenced by our social networks. In the next few modules, we begin to look at some ways social situations affect all of us. We hope you will find the topics interesting and thought provoking.

David L. Ryan/The Boston Globe/Getty Images

SURVEY QUESTIONS

70.1 How do social situations affect our behavior?

70.2 How do social situations affect how we think about ourselves and others?

70.3 How are attitudes acquired and changed?

70.4 Under what conditions is persuasion most effective?

Humans in a Social Context— Mind Your Manners

SURVEY QUESTION 70.1: How do social situations affect our behavior?

Social psychology is the scientific study of how individuals behave, think, and feel in social situations—that is, in the presence, actual or implied, of others. Every day, there is a fascinating interplay between our own behavior and that of the people around us. We are born into organized societies. Established values, expectations, and behavior patterns are present when we arrive. So, too, is *culture*, an ongoing pattern of life that is passed from one generation to the next. To appreciate the impact of society and culture, think about how you have been affected by language, marriage customs, concepts of ownership, and sex roles (Matsumoto & Juang, 2013).

Social Roles

We all belong to many overlapping social groups, and in each, we occupy a *position* in the *structure* of the group. **Social roles** are patterns of behavior expected of persons in various social positions (Baumeister & Bushman, 2014). For instance, playing the role of mother, boss, or student involves different sets of behaviors and expectations. Some roles are *ascribed* (they are assigned to a person or are not under personal control): male or female, son, adolescent, inmate. *Achieved roles* are voluntarily attained by special effort: spouse, teacher, scientist, bandleader, criminal.

Sven Hagolani/Corbis

Ascribed roles have a powerful impact on social behavior. What kinds of behavior do you expect from your teachers or your coaches? What behaviors do they expect from you? What happens if either of you fails to match the other's expectations?

What effect does role-playing have on behavior? Roles streamline daily interactions by allowing us to anticipate what others will do. When a person is acting as a doctor, mother, clerk, or police officer, we expect certain behaviors. However, roles have a negative side, too.

In an infamous experiment, Phil Zimbardo at Stanford University paid normal healthy male college students to play the role of either "prisoners" or "guards" in a simulated prison (Drury et al., 2012; Zimbardo, Haney, & Banks, 1973). Within a few days, the "guards" clamped down with increasing brutality. In a surprisingly short time, the fake convicts looked like real prisoners: They were dejected, traumatized, passive, and dehumanized. After six days, the experiment had to be halted.

What had happened? Apparently, the ascribed social roles—prisoner and guard—were so powerful that in just a few days, the experiment became "reality" for those involved. We tend to think of people as inherently good or bad. But students in the Stanford prison study were randomly assigned to be prisoners or guards. Clearly, the origins of many destructive human relationships can be found in destructive roles.

Many people also experience **role conflicts**, in which two or more roles make conflicting demands on them (Gordon et al.,

2012; Valentine, Godkin, & Varca, 2010). Consider, for example, a teacher who must flunk a close friend's son, a mother who has a demanding full-time job, or a soccer coach whose daughter is on the team but isn't a very good athlete. Likewise, the clashing demands of work, family, and school create role conflicts for many students (Senécal, Julien, & Guay, 2003). Role conflicts at work (such as being a good team player versus being a strong manager) can lead to job burnout and negative health outcomes (Jawahar, Stone, & Kisamore, 2007; Pomaki, Supeli, & Verhoeven, 2007).

Group Structure, Cohesion, and Norms

Are there other dimensions of group membership? Two important dimensions of any group are its structure and its cohesiveness (Forsyth, 2014). **Group structure** consists of the network of roles, communication pathways, and power in a group. Organized groups such as an army or an athletic team have a high degree of structure. Informal friendship groups may or may not be very structured.

Group cohesiveness refers to the degree of attraction among group members or the strength of their desire to remain in the group. Members of cohesive groups literally stick together: They tend to stand or sit close together, they pay more attention to one another, and they show more signs of mutual affection. Also, their behavior tends to be closely coordinated (Chansler, Swamidass, & Cammann, 2003; Lin & Peng, 2010). Cohesiveness is the basis for much of the power that groups exert over us. Therapy groups, businesses, sports teams, and the like seek to increase cohesion because it helps people work together better (Burlingame, McClendon, & Alonso, 2011; Casey-Campbell & Martens, 2009).

In-Groups Cohesiveness is particularly strong for **in-groups**—groups with which a person mainly identifies. Very likely, your own in-groups are defined by a combination of prominent social dimensions, such as nationality, ethnicity, age, education, religion, income, political values, gender, sexual orientation, and so forth. In-group membership helps define who we are socially. Predictably, we tend to attribute positive characteristics to our in-group and negative qualities to **out-groups**—groups with which we do not identify. We also tend to exaggerate differences between members of out-groups and our own groups. This sort of "us-and-them" thinking seems to be a basic fact of social life. It also sets the stage for conflict between groups and for racial and ethnic prejudice, which can find expression in violence such as the Boston Marathon bombings—topics we explore in Module 73.

Social Status In addition to defining roles, a person's social position within groups determines his or her **social status**, or level of social power and importance. Higher social status bestows special privileges and respect (Albrecht & Albrecht, 2011). For example, in one experiment, a man walked into several bakeries and asked for a pastry while claiming he did not have enough money to pay for it. Half the time he was well dressed and half the time he was poorly dressed. If the man was polite when he asked, he was equally likely to be given a free pastry no matter how he was dressed (95 versus 90 percent). However, if he was impolite when he asked, he was much less likely to get a pastry if he was poorly dressed than if he was well dressed (75 versus 20 percent) (Guéguen & Pascual, 2003).

You don't have to be in a bakery for this to work. In most situations, we are more likely to comply with a request made by a high-status (well-dressed) person (Guéguen & Lamy, 2012). Perhaps the better treatment given "higher status" persons, even when they are impolite, explains some of our society's preoccupation with expensive clothes, cars, and other status symbols.

Norms We also are greatly affected by group norms (Matsumoto & Juang, 2013). A **norm** is a widely accepted (but often unspoken) standard for appropriate behavior. If you have the slightest doubt about the power of norms, try this test: Walk into a crowded supermarket, get in a checkout line, and begin singing loudly in your fullest voice. Are you the 1 person in 100 who could actually carry out these instructions?

The impact of norms is shown by a classic study of littering. The question was, "Does the amount of trash in an area affect littering?" To find out, people were given flyers as they walked into a public parking garage. As you can see in ● **Figure 70.1**, the more litter there was on the floor, the more likely people were to add to it by dropping their flyer. Apparently, seeing that others had already littered implied a lax norm about whether littering is acceptable. The moral? The cleaner a public area is kept, the less likely people are to "trash" it (Cialdini, Reno, & Kallgren, 1990; Göckeritz et al., 2010).

In the next section, we see that the people around us affect not only how we behave, they also influence how we think about ourselves and others. For example, one common way that we understand ourselves is by comparing ourselves to others, a process called . . . wait for it . . . *social comparison* (Brakel et al., 2011).

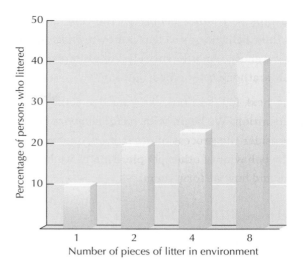

● **Figure 70.1**

Results of an experiment on norms concerning littering. The prior existence of litter in a public setting implies that littering is acceptable. This encourages others to "trash" the area. (From Cialdini, Reno, & Kallgren, 1990.)

Social Comparisons and Attributions—Behind Our Masks

SURVEY QUESTION 70.2: How do social situations affect how we think about ourselves and others?

Social cognition is the process of thinking about ourselves and others in a social context (Shook, 2013; Strack & Förster, 2009). Despite the fact that we are immersed in social

Social psychology *The scientific study of how individuals behave, think, and feel in social situations.*
Social role *Expected behavior patterns associated with particular social positions (such as daughter, worker, student).*
Role conflict *Trying to occupy two or more roles that make conflicting demands on behavior.*
Group structure *The network of roles, communication pathways, and power in a group.*
Group cohesiveness *The degree of attraction among group members or their commitment to remaining in the group.*
In-group *A group with which a person identifies.*
Out-group *A group with which a person does not identify.*
Social status *An individual's position in a social structure, especially with respect to power, privilege, or importance.*
Norm *A widely accepted (but often unspoken) standard of conduct for appropriate behavior.*
Social cognition *The process of thinking about ourselves and others in a social context.*

relationships with other people all the time and can freely *observe* their behavior, as well as our own, *understanding* that behavior is another matter entirely. For example, we know the Boston Marathon was bombed, but *why*?

In the next few sections, we consider some examples of social cognition. We begin with *social comparison*. We move on to consider the process of *attribution*, one way we understand the behavior of other people. Finally, we have a look at *attitudes* and how we form them.

Social Comparison

If you want to know how heavy you are, you simply get on a scale. But how do you know if you are a good athlete, worker, parent, or friend? How do you know if your views on politics, religion, or music are unusual or widely shared? When there are no objective standards, the only available yardstick is provided by comparing yourself with others (Baumeister & Bushman, 2014; Dvash et al., 2010).

Social psychologist Leon Festinger (1919–1989) theorized that group membership fills needs for **social comparison**—comparing your own actions, feelings, opinions, or abilities to those of others. Have you ever "compared notes" with other students after taking an exam? ("How did you do?" "Wasn't that last question hard?") If you have, you were satisfying needs for social comparison (Festinger, 1957; Johnson & Lammers, 2012).

High school class reunions are notorious for the rampant social comparisons they often encourage. Apparently, it's hard to resist comparing yourself with former classmates to see how you are doing in life.

Typically, we don't make social comparisons randomly or on some absolute scale. Meaningful evaluations are based on comparing yourself with people of similar backgrounds, abilities, and circumstances (Stapel & Marx, 2007). To illustrate, let's ask a student named Wendy if she is a good tennis player. If Wendy compares herself with a professional, the answer will be no. But this tells us little about her *relative* ability. Within her tennis group, Wendy is regarded as an excellent player. On a fair scale of comparison, Wendy knows she is good and she takes pride in her tennis skills. In the same way, thinking of yourself as successful, talented, responsible, or fairly paid depends entirely on whom you choose for comparison. Thus, a desire for social comparison provides a motive for associating with others and influences which groups we join (Franzoi & Klaiber, 2007; Johnson & Stapel, 2010).

Let's shift gears now to examine another form of social cognition. Vonda just insulted Sutchai. But why? Why did Nick change his college major? Why does Kirti talk so fast when she's around men? In answering such questions, we *attribute* people's behavior to various causes. Whether we are right or wrong about the causes of their behavior, our conclusions affect how *we* act. To learn how we fill in the "person behind the mask," let's explore the making of attributions.

Making Attributions

Every day, we must guess how people will act, often from small shreds of evidence. We do this through a form of social cognition called **attribution**. As we observe others, we make inferences about them. For example, two people enter a restaurant and order different meals. Nell tastes her food and then salts it. Bert salts his food before he tastes it. How would you explain their behavior? In Nell's case, you might assume that the *food* needed salt. If so, you have attributed her actions to an *external cause* (one that lies outside a person). With Bert, you might be more inclined to conclude that he must really *like* salt. If so, the cause of his behavior is internal. *Internal causes*, such as needs, personality traits, and Bert's taste for salt, lie within the person.

What are the effects of such interpretations? It is difficult to fully understand social behavior without considering the attributions that we make. For instance, let's say that at the last five parties you've attended, you've seen a woman named Macy. Based on this, you assume that Macy likes to socialize. You see Macy at yet another gathering and mention that she seems to like parties. She says, "Actually, I hate these parties, but I get invited to play my tuba at them. My music teacher says I need to practice in front of an audience, so I keep attending these dumb events. Want to hear a Sousa march?"

We seldom know the real reasons for others' actions. That's why we tend to infer causes from *circumstances*. However, in doing so, we often make mistakes like the one with Macy. The most common error is to attribute the actions of others to internal causes (Riggio & Garcia, 2009; Watson, 2008). This mistake is called the **fundamental attribution error**. We tend to think the actions of others have internal causes even if in reality they are caused by external forces or circumstances. One amusing example of this error is the tendency of people to attribute the actions of actors playing a role to their personalities rather than the obvious external cause (that they are playing a character) (Tal-Or & Papirman, 2007).

In 2013, Tom Hanks was the most trusted person in America, according to a *Reader's Digest* poll, ranking above many politicians, judges, religious leaders, and sports figures. Is Tom Hanks actually *that* trustworthy? Or is it that he has played many trustworthy characters in popular films? We are more prone than you might think to attribute to actors the personality traits of the characters they play (Tal-Or & Papirman, 2007).

Where our own behavior is concerned, we are more likely to think that external causes explain our actions. In other words, an **actor–observer bias** is present in how we explain behavior. As *observers,* we attribute the behavior of others to their wants, motives, and personality traits (this is the fundamental attribution error). As *actors,* however, we tend to find external explanations for our own behavior (Aronson, Wilson, & Akert, 2013; Gordon & Kaplar, 2002). No doubt you chose your major in school because of what it has to offer. Other students choose *their* majors because of the kind of people they are. Other people who don't leave tips in restaurants are cheapskates. If you don't leave a tip, it's because the service was bad. And, of course, other people are always late because they are irresponsible. You are late because you were held up by events beyond your control.

As you can see, attribution theory summarizes how we think about ourselves and others, including the errors we tend to make.

Attitudes—Got Attitude?

SURVEY QUESTION 70.3: How are attitudes acquired and changed?

Our tastes, friendships, votes, preferences, goals, and behavior in many other situations are all touched by attitudes (Baumeister & Bushman, 2014).

What, specifically, is an attitude? An **attitude** is a mixture of belief and emotion that predisposes a person to respond to other people, objects, or groups in a positive or negative way. Attitudes summarize your *evaluation* of objects (Bohner & Dickel, 2010). As a result, they predict or direct future actions.

"Your attitude is showing," is sometimes said. Actually, attitudes are expressed through beliefs, emotions, and actions. The *belief component* of an attitude is what you believe about a particular object or issue. The *emotional component* consists of your feelings toward the attitudinal object. The *action component* refers to your actions toward various people, objects, or institutions. Consider, for example, your attitude toward gun control. You will have beliefs about whether gun control would affect rates of crime or violence. You will respond emotionally to guns, finding them either attractive and desirable or threatening and destructive. And you will have a tendency to seek out or avoid gun ownership. The action component of your attitude may well include support of organizations that urge or oppose gun control. As you can see, attitudes orient us to the social world. In doing so, they prepare us to act in certain ways (Forgas, Cooper, & Crano, 2010). (For another example, see ● **Figure 70.2**.)

Social comparison *Making judgments about ourselves through comparison with others.*
Attribution *The process of making inferences about the causes of one's own behavior and that of others.*
Fundamental attribution error *The tendency to attribute the behavior of others to internal causes (personality, likes, and so forth).*
Actor–observer bias *The tendency to attribute the behavior of others to internal causes while attributing one's own behavior to external causes (situations and circumstances).*
Attitude *A learned tendency to respond to people, objects, or institutions in a positive or negative way.*

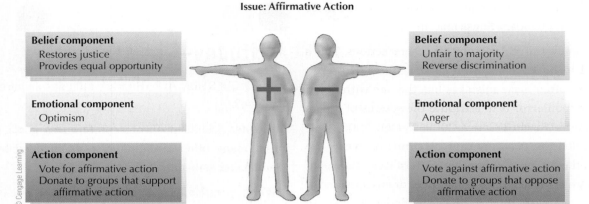

Issue: Affirmative Action

Belief component
Restores justice
Provides equal opportunity

Emotional component
Optimism

Action component
Vote for affirmative action
Donate to groups that support
affirmative action

Belief component
Unfair to majority
Reverse discrimination

Emotional component
Anger

Action component
Vote against affirmative action
Donate to groups that oppose
affirmative action

© Cengage Learning

Figure 70.2

Elements of positive and negative attitudes toward affirmative action.

Forming Attitudes

How do people acquire attitudes? Attitudes are acquired in several basic ways. Sometimes attitudes come from *direct contact* (personal experience) with the object of the attitude—such as opposing pollution when a nearby factory ruins your favorite river (Ajzen, 2005). Some attitudes are simply formed through *chance conditioning* (learning that takes place by chance or coincidence) (Albarracín, Johnson, & Zanna, 2005). Let's say, for instance, that you have had three encounters in your lifetime with psychologists. If all three were negative, you might take an unduly dim view of psychology. In the same way, people often develop strong attitudes toward cities, foods, or parts of the country on the basis of one or two unusually good or bad experiences (Ledgerwood & Trope, 2010).

Attitudes also are learned through *interaction with others*—that is, through discussion with people holding a particular attitude. For instance, if three of your good friends are volunteers at a local recycling center and you talk with them about their beliefs, you may well come to favor recycling, too. More generally, there is little doubt that many of our attitudes are influenced by *group membership*. In most groups, pressures to conform shape our attitudes, just as they do our behavior. *Child rearing* (the effects of parental values, beliefs, and practices) also affects attitudes (Bartram, 2006; Guidetti et al., 2012). For example, if both parents belong to the same political party, chances are that their children will belong to that party as adults.

Finally, there is no doubt that attitudes are influenced by the media, such as newspapers, television, and the Internet (Mahler, Beckerley, & Vogel, 2010). Every day we are coaxed, persuaded,

Monika Graff/UPI/Landov

Attitudes are an important dimension of social behavior. They are often greatly influenced by the attitudes of parents and the groups to which they belong.

and skillfully manipulated by messages in mass media. Young people today spend at least 50 hours a week immersed in media, such as television, video games, movies, the Internet, music, and print (Rideout, Foehr, & Roberts, 2010). The information thus channeled into homes has a powerful impact. For instance, frequent television viewers mistrust others and overestimate their own chances of being harmed. This suggests that a steady diet of television violence leads some people to develop a *mean worldview*, in which they regard the world as a dangerous and threatening place (Nellis & Savage, 2012).

Attitudes and Behavior

Why are some attitudes acted on, whereas others are not? To answer this question, let's consider an example. Assume that a woman named Lorraine knows that automobiles are expensive to operate and add to air pollution. Besides, she hates smog. Why would Lorraine continue to drive to work every day? Probably, it is because the *immediate consequences* of our actions weigh heavily on the choices we make. No matter what Lorraine's attitude may be, it is difficult for her to resist the immediate convenience of driving.

Our expectations of how *others will evaluate* our actions also are important. Lorraine may resist taking public transit to work for fear that her coworkers will be critical of her environmental stand. By taking this factor into account, researchers have been able to predict family planning choices, alcohol use by teenagers, reenlistment in the National Guard, voting on a nuclear power plant initiative, and so forth (Cialdini, 2009). Finally, we must not overlook the effects of long-standing *habits* (Oskamp & Schultz, 2005). Let's say that after years of driving to work, Lorraine finally vows to shift to public transit. Two months later, it would not be unusual if she found herself driving again because of habit, despite her good intentions.

In short, there are often large differences between attitudes and behavior—particularly between privately held attitudes and public behavior (Johnson & Boynton, 2010). However, barriers to action typically fall when a person holds an attitude with *conviction*. If you have *conviction* about an issue, it evokes strong feelings, you think about it and discuss it often, and you are knowledgeable about it. Attitudes held with passionate conviction often lead to major changes in personal behavior (Oskamp & Schultz, 2005).

Attitude Change— Meet the "Seekers"

SURVEY QUESTION 70.4: Under what conditions is persuasion most effective?

Although attitudes are fairly stable, they do change (Forgas, Cooper, & Crano, 2010; Izuma, 2013). Some attitude change can be understood in terms of a **reference group**—any group an individual uses as a standard for social comparison. It is not necessary to have face-to-face contact with other people for them to be a reference group. It depends instead on with whom you identify or whose attitudes and values you care about (Ajzen, 2005; Larimer et al., 2011).

In the 1930s, Theodore Newcomb studied real-life attitude change among students at Bennington College (Alwin, Cohen, & Newcomb, 1991). Most students came from conservative homes, but Bennington was a very liberal school. Newcomb found that most students shifted significantly toward more liberal attitudes during their four years at Bennington. Those who didn't change kept their parents and hometown friends as primary reference groups. Those who did change identified primarily with the campus community. Notice that all students could count the college and their families as *membership* groups. However, one group or the other tended to become their point of reference.

Do you exercise regularly? Like students in the Bennington study, your intentions to exercise are probably influenced by the exercise habits of your reference groups (Ajzen, 2005; Terry & Hogg, 1996).

Persuasion

What about advertising and other direct attempts to change attitudes? Are they effective? **Persuasion** is any deliberate attempt to change attitudes or beliefs through information and arguments (Gass & Seiter, 2014; Perloff, 2010). Businesses, politicians, and others who seek to persuade us obviously believe that attitudes can be changed. Billions of dollars are spent yearly on advertising in the United States and Canada alone. Persuasion can range from the daily blitz of media commercials to personal discussions among friends. In most cases, the success or failure of persuasion can be understood if we consider the *communicator,* the *message,* and the *audience.*

Reference group *Any group that an individual uses as a standard for social comparison.*
Persuasion *A deliberate attempt to change attitudes or beliefs with information and arguments.*

Persuasion. Are you likely to be swayed by this group's message? Successful persuasion is related to characteristics of the communicator, the message, and the audience.

At a community meeting, let's say you have a chance to promote an issue important to you (for or against building a new mall nearby, for instance). Whom should you choose to make the presentation, and how should that person present it? Research suggests that attitude change is encouraged when certain conditions are met. You should have little trouble seeing how the following principles are applied to sell everything from underarm deodorants to presidents (Aronson, 2012; Oskamp & Schultz, 2005; Perloff, 2010):

1. The communicator is likable, expressive, trustworthy, an expert on the topic, and similar to the audience in some respect.

2. The communicator appears to have nothing to gain if the audience accepts the message.

3. The message appeals to emotions, particularly to fear or anxiety.

4. The message also provides a clear course of action that will, if followed, reduce fear or produce personally desirable results.

5. The message states clear-cut conclusions.

6. The message is backed up by facts and statistics.

7. The message is repeated as frequently as possible.

8. Both sides of the argument are presented in the case of a well-informed audience.

9. Only one side of the argument is presented in the case of a poorly informed audience.

As we have just seen, we sometimes change our attitudes in response to external persuasion (Gass & Seiter, 2014). Sometimes, however, the internal process of *cognitive dissonance* also can lead to attitude change.

Cognitive Dissonance Theory

What happens if people act in ways that are inconsistent with their attitudes or self-images? Cognitions are thoughts. *Dissonance* means clashing. The influential theory of **cognitive dissonance** states that contradicting or clashing thoughts cause discomfort—that is, we have a need for *consistency* in our thoughts, perceptions, and images of ourselves (Cooper, 2007; Festinger, 1957). Inconsistency, then, can motivate people to make their thoughts or attitudes agree with their actions (Gawronski, 2012).

For example, smokers are told on every pack that cigarettes endanger their lives. They light up and smoke anyway. How do they resolve the tension between this information and their actions? They could quit smoking, but it may be easier to convince themselves that smoking is not really so dangerous. To do this, a smoker might seek examples of heavy smokers who have lived long lives, spend time with other smokers, and avoid information about the link between smoking and cancer. Or he or she might just suppress thinking of the health consequences altogether (Kneer, Glock & Rieger, 2012). According to cognitive dissonance theory, we also tend to reject new information that contradicts ideas we already hold. We're all guilty of this "don't bother me with the facts, my mind is made up" strategy at times.

A famous example of cognitive dissonance in action involves a woman named Mrs. Keech, who claimed she was in communication with beings on a planet called Clarion (Festinger, 1957). The messages foretold the destruction of North America. Mrs. Keech and her followers, the Seekers, were to be rescued by a flying saucer. The news media became involved and reported on the proceedings. When nothing happened, the Seekers suffered a bitter and embarrassing disappointment.

Did the group break up then? Amazingly, instead of breaking up, the Seekers became *more* convinced than ever before that they were right. Mrs. Keech announced that she had received a new message explaining that the Seekers had saved the world. Before, the Seekers were uninterested in persuading other people that the world was coming to an end. Now they called newspapers and radio stations to convince others of their accomplishment.

TABLE 70.1	Strategies for Reducing Cognitive Dissonance

LeShawn, who is a college student, has always thought of himself as an environmental activist. Recently, LeShawn "inherited" a car from his parents, who were replacing the family "barge." In the past, LeShawn biked or used public transportation to get around. His parents' old car is an antiquated gas-guzzler, but he has begun to drive it every day. How might LeShawn reduce the cognitive dissonance created by the clash between his environmentalism and his use of an inefficient automobile?

Strategy	Example
Change your attitude.	"Cars are not really a major environmental problem."
Add consonant thoughts.	"This is an old car, so keeping it on the road makes good use of the resources consumed when it was manufactured."
Change the importance of the dissonant thoughts.	"It's more important for me to support the environmental movement politically than it is to worry about how I get to school and work."
Reduce the amount of perceived choice.	"My schedule has become too hectic. I really can't afford to bike or take the bus anymore."
Change your behavior.	"I'm only going to use the car when it's impossible to bike or take the bus."

Source: Franzoi, 2002.

Why did their belief in Mrs. Keech's messages increase after the world failed to end? Why did the group suddenly become interested in convincing others that they were right? Cognitive dissonance theory explains that after publicly committing themselves to their beliefs, they had a strong need to maintain consistency (Tavris & Aronson, 2007). In effect, convincing others was a way of adding proof that they were correct (● Table 70.1).

Acting contrary to one's attitudes doesn't always bring about change. How does cognitive dissonance explain that? The amount of justification for acting contrary to your attitudes and beliefs affects how much dissonance you feel. (*Justification* is the degree to which a person's actions are explained by rewards or other circumstances.) In a classic study, college students did an extremely boring task (turning wooden pegs on a board) for a *long* time. Afterward, they were asked to help lure others into the experiment by pretending that the task was interesting and enjoyable. Students paid $20 for lying to others did not change their own negative opinion of the task: "That was *really* boring!" Those who were paid only $1 later rated the task as "pleasant" and "interesting." How can we explain these results? Apparently, students paid $20 experienced no dissonance. These students could reassure themselves that anybody would tell a little white lie for $20. Those paid $1 were faced with the conflicting thoughts: "I lied" and "I had no good reason to do it." Rather than admit to themselves that they had lied, these students changed their attitude toward what they had done (Festinger & Carlsmith, 1959; see ● Figure 70.3).

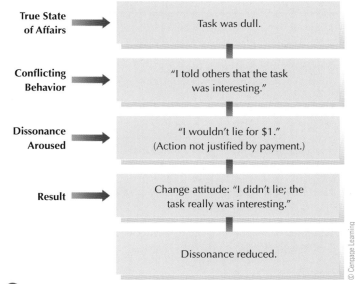

True State of Affairs → Task was dull.

Conflicting Behavior → "I told others that the task was interesting."

Dissonance Aroused → "I wouldn't lie for $1." (Action not justified by payment.)

Result → Change attitude: "I didn't lie; the task really was interesting."

Dissonance reduced.

© Cengage Learning

● **Figure 70.3**

Summary of the Festinger and Carlsmith (1959) study from the viewpoint of a person experiencing cognitive dissonance.

Cognitive dissonance *An uncomfortable clash between self-image, thoughts, beliefs, attitudes, or perceptions and one's behavior.*

Module 70: Summary

70.1 How do social situations affect our behavior?

- **70.1.1** Social psychology studies humans as social animals enmeshed in complex networks of social and cultural contexts.
- **70.1.2** Social roles, which may be achieved or ascribed, define one's position in groups and particular behavior patterns associated with those social roles. When two or more contradictory roles are held, role conflict may occur.
- **70.1.3** *Group structure* refers to the organization of roles, communication pathways, and power within a group. *Group cohesiveness* is basically the degree of attraction among group members.
- **70.1.4** Positions within groups typically carry higher or lower levels of social status. High social status is associated with special privileges and respect.
- **70.1.5** Norms are standards of conduct enforced (formally or informally) by groups.

70.2 How do social situations affect how we think about ourselves and others?

- **70.2.1** Social comparison theory holds that we affiliate to evaluate our actions, feelings, and abilities.
- **70.2.2** Attribution theory is concerned with how we make inferences about behavior.

- **70.2.3** The fundamental attribution error is to ascribe the actions of others to internal causes. Because of actor–observer differences, we tend to attribute our own behavior to external causes.

70.3 How are attitudes acquired and changed?

- **70.3.1** Attitudes are learned dispositions made up of a belief component, an emotional component, and an action component.
- **70.3.2** Attitudes may be formed by direct contact, interaction with others, child-rearing practices, and group pressures. Peer group influences, reference group membership, the media, and chance conditioning also appear to be important in attitude formation.

70.4 Under what conditions is persuasion most effective?

- **70.4.1** Effective persuasion occurs when characteristics of the communicator, the message, and the audience are well matched. In general, a likable and believable communicator who repeats a credible message that arouses emotion in the audience and states clear-cut conclusions will be persuasive.
- **70.4.2** Maintaining and changing attitudes is closely related to cognitive dissonance and our need to be consistent in our thoughts and actions.

Module 70: Knowledge Builder

Recite

1. Social psychology is the study of how people behave in _____.

2. *Social status* refers to a set of expected behaviors associated with a social position. ***T or F?***

3. Social comparisons are made pretty much at random. ***T or F?***

4. The fundamental attribution error is to attribute the actions of others to internal causes. ***T or F?***

5. Which of the following is associated with attitude formation?
   - *a.* group membership
   - *b.* mass media
   - *c.* chance conditioning
   - *d.* childrearing
   - *e.* all of the preceding
   - *f.* a and d only

6. In presenting a persuasive message, it is best to give both sides of the argument if the audience is already well informed on the topic. ***T or F?***

7. The amount of cognitive dissonance a person feels is related to how much _____ exists for his or her actions.
   - *a.* reciprocity
   - *b.* justification
   - *c.* chance conditioning
   - *d.* reference

Reflect

Think Critically

8. The Stanford prison experiment also illustrates a major concept of personality theory (see Module 53), especially social learning theory. Can you name it?

9. Cognitive dissonance theory predicts that false confessions obtained during brainwashing are not likely to bring about lasting changes in attitudes. Why?

Self-Reflect

What are the most prominent roles you play? What conflicts do they create?

How has social comparison affected your behavior?

How often do you commit the fundamental attribution error? Try to think of a specific personal example that illustrates the concept.

Which of the various sources of attitudes best explain your own attitudes?

How would you explain cognitive dissonance theory to a person who knows nothing about it?

ANSWERS

1. social situations or the presence of others **2.** F **3.** F **4.** T **5.** e **6.** T **7.** b **8.** It is the idea that behavior is often strongly influenced by situations rather than by personal traits. **9.** There is strong justification for such actions. As a result, little cognitive dissonance is created when a prisoner makes statements that contradict his or her beliefs.

Social Psychology: Social Influence

Question Authority?

Explaining people's behavior often comes down to understanding various forms of social influence. It is one thing to notice, for example, the similarities in the clothes worn by this group of men. It is another thing entirely to understand why they are all dressed the same way. Is this an example of conformity; did these friends spontaneously and freely change their behavior to bring it into agreement with each other? Or is it an example of obedience to the commands of some authority?

What are the limits of your willingness to comply with the requests of strangers or with the commands of authorities? How much should you resist attempts at coercion? You've probably seen a bumper sticker that says "Question Authority." Actually, that's not bad advice if it means "Think Critically." When, though, is it appropriate to comply with or to resist authority? These are essential questions about how we are affected by social influence.

Hill Street Studios/Blend/Glow Images

SURVEY QUESTIONS

71.1 What have social psychologists learned about the various forms of social influence?

71.2 How does self-assertion differ from aggression?

Social Influence— Follow the Leader

SURVEY QUESTION 71.1: What have social psychologists learned about the various forms of social influence?

No topic lies nearer the heart of social psychology than **social influence**—changes in behavior induced by the actions of others. When people interact, they almost always affect one another's behavior (Baer, Cialdini, & Lueth, 2012; Kassin, Fein, & Markus, 2014). For example, in a classic sidewalk experiment, various numbers of people stood on a busy New York City street. On cue, they all looked at a sixth-floor window across the street. A camera recorded how many passersby also stopped to stare. The larger the influencing group, the more people were swayed to join in staring at the window (Milgram, Bickman, & Berkowitz, 1969).

Are there different kinds of social influence? Social influence ranges from milder to stronger. The gentlest form of social influence is *mere presence* (changing behavior just because other people are nearby). We *conform* when we spontaneously change our behavior to bring it into agreement with others. Compliance is a more directed form of social influence. We *comply* when we change our behavior in response to another person who has little or no social power or authority. Obedience is an even stronger form of social influence. We *obey* when we change our behavior in direct response to the demands of an authority. The strongest form of social influence is *coercion*, or changing behavior because you are forced to.

Mere Presence

Suppose you just happened to be alone in a room, picking your nose. (We know, none of us would do that, right?) Would you continue if a stranger entered the room? **Mere presence** refers to the tendency for people to change their behavior just because of the presence of other people. (You *would* quit picking your nose, wouldn't you?) Let's explore some of the ways mere presence can induce us to modify our behavior.

Imagine you are riding your mountain bike when another rider pulls up beside you. Will you pick up your pace? Slow down? Completely ignore the other rider? In 1898, psychologist Norman Triplett's investigation of just such a social situation was the first published social psychology experiment (Strubbe, 2005). According to Triplett, you are more likely to speed up. This is **social facilitation**, the tendency to perform better when in the presence of others (Cole, Barrett, & Griffiths, 2011).

Does mere presence always improve performance? No. If you are confident in your abilities, your behavior will most likely be facilitated in the presence of others. If you are not, your performance is more likely to be impaired (Uziel, 2007). Another classic study focused on college students shooting pool at a student union. Good players who were confident (sharks?) normally made 71 percent of their shots. Their accuracy improved to 80 percent when others were watching them. Less confident, average players (marks?) who normally made 36 percent of their shots dropped to 25 percent accuracy when someone was watching them (Michaels et al., 1982).

Social loafing is another consequence of having other people nearby. People tend to work less hard (loaf) when they are part of a group than they do when they are solely responsible for their work (Ferrari & Pychyl, 2012; Najdowski, 2010). In one study, people playing tug-of-war while blindfolded pulled harder if they thought they were competing alone. When they thought others were on their team, they made less of an effort (Ingham et al., 1974).

Conformity

We show **conformity** when we bring our behavior into agreement with the actions, norms, or values of others in the absence of any direct pressure. When Harry met Sally, they fell in love and were not shy about expressing themselves around campus. Increasingly, Sally noticed other students staring at her and Harry when they were, well, expressing their love. Although they never made a conscious decision to conform, in another week their publicly intimate moments were a thing of the past. Perhaps the most basic of all group norms is, as Harry and Sally discovered, "Thou shalt conform." Like it or not, life is filled with instances of conformity (Baron, Byrne, & Branscombe, 2012).

As mentioned earlier, all groups have unspoken norms. The broadest norms, defined by society as a whole, establish "normal" or acceptable behavior in most situations. Comparing hairstyles, habits of speech, dress, eating habits, and social customs in two or more cultures makes it clear that we all conform to social norms. In fact, a degree of uniformity is necessary if we are to interact comfortably. Imagine being totally unable to anticipate the actions of others. In stores, schools, and homes, this would be frustrating and disturbing. On the highways, it would be lethal.

The Asch Experiment *How strong are group pressures for conformity?* One of the first experiments on conformity was staged by Solomon Asch (1907–1996). To fully appreciate it, imagine yourself as a participant. Assume that you are seated at a table with six other students. Your task is actually quite simple: You are shown three lines on a card and you must select the line that matches a "standard" line (● **Figure 71.1**).

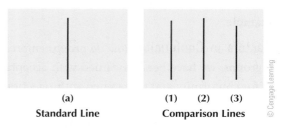

(a)
Standard Line

(1) (2) (3)
Comparison Lines

© Cengage Learning

● **Figure 71.1**

Stimuli used in Solomon Asch's conformity experiments.

As the testing begins, each person announces an answer for the first card. When your turn comes, you agree with the others. "This isn't hard at all," you say to yourself. For several more trials, your answers agree with those of the group. Then comes a shock. All six people announce that line 1 matches the standard, and you were about to say line 2 matches. Suddenly you feel alone and upset. You nervously look at the lines again. The room falls silent. Everyone seems to be staring at you. The experimenter awaits your answer. Do you yield to the group?

In this study, the other "students" were all actors who gave the wrong answer on about a third of the trials to create

Social influence *Changes in a person's behavior induced by the presence or actions of others.*
Mere presence *The tendency for people to change their behavior just because of the presence of other people.*
Social facilitation *The tendency to perform better when in the presence of others.*
Social loafing *The tendency of people to work less hard when part of a group than when they are solely responsible for their work.*
Conformity *Bringing one's behavior into agreement or harmony with norms or with the behavior of others in a group in the absence of any direct pressure.*

group pressure (Asch, 1956). Real students conformed to the group on about one-third of the critical trials. Of those tested, 75 percent yielded at least once. People who were tested alone erred in less than 1 percent of their judgments. Clearly, those who yielded to group pressures were denying what their eyes told them.

Are some people more susceptible to group pressures than others? People with high needs for structure or certainty are more likely to conform. So are people who are anxious, low in self-confidence, or concerned with the approval of others. People who live in cultures that emphasize group cooperation (such as many Asian cultures) also are more likely to conform (Bond & Smith, 1996; Fu et al., 2007).

In addition to personal characteristics, certain situations tend to encourage conformity—sometimes with disastrous results. "Groupthink—Agreement at Any Cost" offers a prime example.

Group Factors in Conformity

How do groups enforce norms? In most groups, we have been rewarded with acceptance and approval for conformity and threatened with rejection or ridicule for nonconformity. These reactions are called *group sanctions*. Negative sanctions range from laughter, staring, or social disapproval to complete rejection or formal exclusion. If you've ever felt the sudden chill of disapproval by others, you understand the power of group sanctions—just as Harry and Sally did.

The more important group membership is to a person, the more he or she will be influenced by other group members. The risk of being rejected can be a threat to our sense of personal identity (Baer, Cialdini, & Lueth, 2012). That's why the Asch experiments are impressive. Because these were only temporary groups, sanctions were informal and rejection had no lasting importance. Just the same, the power of the group was evident. In Asch's face-to-face groups, the size of the majority also made a difference, but a surprisingly small one. Even more important than the size of the majority is its *unanimity* (total agreement). Having at least one person in your corner can greatly reduce pressures to conform.

Compliance

Pressures to "fit in" and conform are usually indirect. In contrast, the term **compliance** refers to situations in which one person bends to the requests of another person who has little or no authority (Cialdini, 2009). These more direct pressures to comply are quite common. You *passively comply* when, for example, you suffer, without protest, someone smoking near you in a nonsmoking zone or talking loudly while you are

Critical Thinking

Groupthink—Agreement at Any Cost

Yale psychologist Irving Janis (1918–1990) first proposed the concept of groupthink in an attempt to understand a series of disastrous decisions made by government officials (Janis, 1989, 2007). The core of **groupthink** is misguided loyalty—an urge by decision makers to maintain each other's approval, even at the cost of critical thinking (Singer, 2005). Group members are hesitant to "rock the boat," question sloppy thinking, or tolerate alternative views. This self-censorship leads people to believe they agree more than they actually do (Henningsen et al., 2006; Mintz et al., 2010).

Groupthink has been blamed for contributing to many crises, such as the invasion and occupation of Iraq (Houghton, 2008; Post, 2011), the *Columbia* space shuttle disaster in 2003, and the loss of the $165 million *Mars Climate Orbiter* in 1999. Analyses of many international crises have found that groupthink contributed to most of them (Schafer & Crichlow, 1996; 2010).

To prevent groupthink, group leaders should take the following steps:

- Define each group member's role as a "critical evaluator."
- Avoid revealing any personal preferences in the beginning. State the problem factually, without bias.
- Invite a group member or outside person to play devil's advocate. Make it clear that group members will be held accountable for decisions.
- Encourage open inquiry and a search for alternate solutions (Baron, 2005; Janis, 2007).

In addition, Janis suggested that a "second-chance" meeting should be held to reevaluate important decisions—that is, each decision should be reached twice.

In fairness to our decision makers, it is worth noting that the presence of too many alternatives can lead to *deadlock,* which can delay taking necessary action (Kowert, 2002). Regardless, in an age clouded by the threat of war, global warming, and terrorism, even stronger solutions to the problem of groupthink would be welcome. Perhaps we should form a group to think about it!

trying to study in the library. You *actively comply* when, for example, you hand over your cell phone to a stranger who asks to borrow it to make a call or loan money to a coworker who requests it to buy a cappuccino.

What determines whether a person will comply with a request? Many factors could be listed, but three stand out as especially interesting (Cialdini & Griskevicius, 2010). We are more likely to comply with a request if it does three things:

1. Comes from someone we know rather than a stranger
2. Is consistent with our previous actions
3. Allows us to reciprocate a prior gift, favor, or service

These factors allow us to better understand several strategies that can be used to gain compliance. Because strangers must work harder to gain compliance, salespeople depend heavily on appealing to your tendency to be *consistent* and to *reciprocate*.

The Foot-in-the-Door Effect

People who sell door-to-door have long recognized that once they get a foot in the door, a sale is almost a sure thing. To state the foot-in-the-door effect more formally, a person who first agrees to a small request is later more likely, to be *consistent*, to comply with a larger demand (Pascual et al., 2013). For instance,

Would you be willing to help this young woman retrieve an item off a high shelf? What if she subsequently asked you to carry her purchases out to her car? If you did, you might have fallen victim to the foot-in-the-door effect. (That is, unless you were attracted to her and were trying to get your own foot in the door!)

if someone asked you to put a large, ugly sign in your front yard to promote safe driving, you would probably refuse. If, however, you had first agreed to put a small sign in your window, you would later be much more likely to allow the big sign in your yard.

The Door-in-the-Face Effect

Let's say that a neighbor comes to your door and asks you to feed his dogs, water his plants, and mow his yard while he is out of town for a month. This is quite a major request—one that most people would probably turn down. Feeling only slightly guilty, you tell your neighbor that you're sorry but you can't help him. Now, what if the same neighbor returns the next day and asks if you would at least pick up his mail while he is gone. Chances are very good that you would honor this request, even if you might have originally turned it down, too.

Psychologist Robert Cialdini coined the term door-in-the-face effect to describe the tendency for a person who has refused a major request to agree to a smaller request. In other words, after a person has turned down a major request ("slammed the door in your face"), he or she may be more willing to comply with a lesser demand. This strategy works because a person who abandons a large request appears to have given up something. In response, many people feel that they must *reciprocate* by giving in to the smaller request (Cialdini, 2009; Guéguen, Jacob, & Meineri, 2011). In fact, a good way to get another person to comply with a request is to first do a small favor for the person.

The Lowball Technique

Anyone who has purchased an automobile will recognize a third way of inducing compliance. Automobile dealers are notorious for convincing customers to buy cars by offering "lowball" prices that undercut the competition. The dealer first gets the customer to agree to buy at an attractively low price. Then, once the customer is committed, various techniques are used to bump the price up before the sale is concluded.

Compliance *Bending to the requests of a person who has little or no authority or other form of social power.*
Groupthink *A compulsion by members of decision-making groups to maintain agreement, even at the cost of critical thinking.*
Foot-in-the-door effect *The tendency for a person who has first complied with a small request to be more likely later to fulfill a larger request.*
Door-in-the-face effect *The tendency for a person who has refused a major request to subsequently be more likely to comply with a minor request.*

The **lowball technique** consists of getting a person committed to act and then making the terms of acting less desirable (Guéguen, Pascual, & Dagot, 2002). In this case, because you have already complied with a large request, it would be *inconsistent* to deny the follow-on smaller additional request. Here's another example: A fellow student asks to borrow $25 for a day. This seems reasonable and you agree. However, once you have given your classmate the money, he explains that it would be easier to repay you after payday, in two weeks. If you agree, you've succumbed to the lowball technique. Here's another example: Let's say you ask someone to give you a ride to school in the morning. Only after the person has agreed do you tell her that you have to be there at 6 a.m.

Obedience

If ordered to do so, would you shock a man with a heart condition who is screaming and asking to be released? Certainly, few people would obey. Or would they? In Nazi Germany, obedient soldiers (who were once average citizens) helped slaughter more than 6 million people in concentration camps. Do such inhumane acts reflect deep character flaws? Are they the acts of heartless psychopaths or crazed killers? Or are they simply the result of obedience to authority? These are questions that puzzled social psychologist Stanley Milgram (1965) when he began a provocative series of studies on **obedience**, a special type of conformity to the demands of an *authority*.

How did Milgram study obedience? As was true of the Asch experiments, Milgram's research is best appreciated by imagining yourself as a participant. Place yourself in the following situation.

Milgram's Obedience Studies Imagine answering a newspaper ad to take part in a "learning" experiment at Yale University. When you arrive, a coin is flipped and a second participant, a pleasant-looking man in his fifties, is designated the "learner." By chance, you have become the "teacher."

Your task is to read a list of word pairs. The learner's task is to memorize them. You are to punish him with an electric shock each time he makes a mistake. The learner is taken to an adjacent room, and you watch as he is seated in an "electric chair" apparatus. Electrodes are attached to his wrists. You are then escorted to your position in front of a "shock generator." On this device is a row of 30 switches marked from 15 to 450 volts. Corresponding labels range from "Slight Shock" to "Extreme Intensity Shock" and, finally, "Danger Severe Shock." Your instructions are to shock the learner each time he makes a mistake. You must begin with 15 volts and then move one switch (15 volts) higher for each additional mistake (● **Figure 71.2**).

The experiment begins, and the learner soon makes his first error. You flip a switch. More mistakes. Rapidly you reach the 75-volt level. The learner moans after each shock. At 100 volts, he complains that he has a heart condition. At 150 volts, he says he no longer wants to continue and demands to be released. At 300 volts, he screams and says he no longer can give answers.

At some point, you begin to protest to the experimenter. "That man has a heart condition," you say. "I'm not going to kill that man." The experimenter says, "Please continue." Another shock and another scream from the learner and you say, "You mean I've got to keep going up the scale? No, sir. I'm not going to give him 450 volts!" The experimenter says,

● **Figure 71.2**

Scenes from Stanley Milgram's study of obedience: the "shock generator," strapping a "learner" into his chair, and a "teacher" being told to administer a severe shock to the learner.

"The experiment requires that you continue." For a time, the learner refuses to answer any more questions and screams with each shock (Milgram, 1965). Then he falls chillingly silent for the rest of the experiment.

It's hard to believe many people would do this. What happened? Milgram also doubted that many people would obey his orders. When he polled a group of psychiatrists before the experiment, they predicted that less than 1 percent of those tested would obey. The astounding fact is that 65 percent obeyed completely by going all the way to the 450-volt level. Virtually no one stopped short of 300 volts ("Severe Shock") (● **Figure 71.3**).

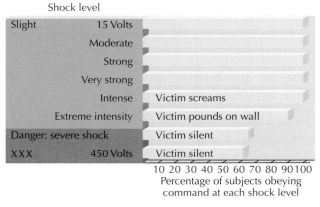

Shock level

● **Figure 71.3**

Results of Milgram's obedience experiment. Only a minority of participants refused to provide shocks, even at the most extreme intensities. The first substantial drop in obedience occurred at the 300-volt level [Milgram, S. (1963). Behavioral study of obedience. Journal of Abnormal & Social Psychology, 67, 371–378.doi:10.1037/h0040525].

Was the learner injured? The "learner" was actually an actor who turned a tape recorder on and off in the shock room. No shocks were ever administered, but the dilemma for the "teacher" was quite real. Participants protested, sweated, trembled, stuttered, bit their lips, and laughed nervously. Clearly, they were disturbed by what they were doing. Nevertheless, most obeyed the experimenter's orders.

Milgram's Follow-Up *Why did so many people obey?* Some have suggested that the prestige of Yale University added to participants' willingness to obey. Could it be that they assumed the professor running the experiment would not really allow anyone to be hurt? To test this possibility, the study was rerun in a shabby office building in nearby Bridgeport, Connecticut. Under these conditions, fewer people obeyed (48 percent), but the reduction was minor.

Milgram was disturbed by the willingness of people to knuckle under to authority and senselessly shock someone. In later experiments, he tried to reduce obedience. He found that the distance between the teacher and the learner was important. When participants were in the *same room* as the learner, only 40 percent obeyed fully. When they were *face-to-face* with the learner and were required to force his hand down on a simulated "shock plate," only 30 percent obeyed (● **Figure 71.4**). Distance from the authority also had an effect. When the experimenter gave his orders over the phone, only 22 percent obeyed. You may doubt that Milgram's study of obedience applies to you. If so, take a moment to read "Moo Like a Cow."

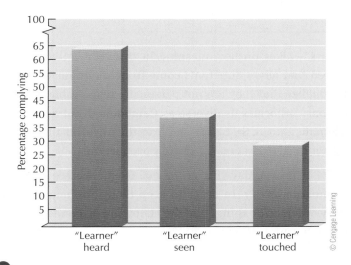

● **Figure 71.4**

Physical distance from the "learner" had a significant effect on the percentage of participants obeying orders.

Implications *Surely people wouldn't act the same way if Milgram conducted his research today, right?* Don't be so sure. Psychologist Jerry Burger of Santa Clara University recently partially replicated Milgram's study and obtained very similar results (Burger, 2009). Milgram's research raises nagging questions about our willingness to commit antisocial or inhumane acts commanded by a "legitimate authority." The excuse so often given by war criminals—"I was only following

Lowball technique *A strategy in which commitment is gained first to reasonable or desirable terms, which are then made less reasonable or desirable.*
Obedience *Conformity to the demands of an authority.*

Discovering Psychology

Moo Like a Cow

Imagine your response to the following events. On the first day of class, your psychology professor begins to establish the basic rules of behavior for the course. Draw a line under the first instruction you think you would refuse to carry out.

1. Seats are assigned and you are told to move to a new location.
2. You are told not to talk during class.
3. Your professor tells you that you must have permission to leave early.
4. You are told to bring your textbook to class at all times.
5. Your professor tells you to use only a pencil for taking notes.
6. You are directed to take off your watch.
7. The professor tells you to keep both hands on your desktop at all times.
8. You are instructed to keep both of your feet flat on the floor.
9. You are told to stand up and clap your hands three times.
10. Your professor says, "Stick two fingers up your nose and moo like a cow."

At what point would you stop obeying such orders? In reality, you might find yourself obeying a legitimate authority long after that person's demands had become unreasonable (Aronson, Wilson, & Akert, 2013). What would happen, though, if a few students resisted orders early in the sequence? Would that help free others to disobey? For an answer, return to the discussion of Milgram's experiment for some final remarks.

---

orders"—takes on new meaning in this light. Milgram suggested that when directions come from an authority, people rationalize that they are not personally responsible for their actions. In locales as diverse as Cambodia, Rwanda, Bosnia, Vietnam, Darfur, Sri Lanka, and Iraq, the tragic result has been "sanctioned massacres" of chilling proportions.

Even in everyday life, crimes of obedience are common (Zimbardo, 2007). In order to keep their jobs, many people obey orders to do things that they know are dishonest, unethical, or harmful (Hinrichs, 2007).

Isn't that an overly negative view of obedience? Obedience to authority is obviously necessary and desirable in many circumstances. Just the same, it is probably true, as C. P. Snow (1961) observed, "When you think of the long and gloomy history of man, you will find more hideous crimes have been committed in the name of obedience than in the name of rebellion." With this in mind, let's end on a more positive note. In one of his experiments, Milgram found that group support can greatly reduce destructive obedience. When real participants saw two other "teachers" (both actors) resist orders and walk out of the experiment, only 10 percent continued to obey. Thus, a personal act of courage or moral fortitude by one or two members of a group may free others to disobey misguided or unjust authority.

Coercion

We close this section on social influence by examining some forms of *coercion,* the most extreme type of social influence. You are being subjected to **coercion** if you are forced to change your beliefs or your behavior against your will (Baumeister & Bushman, 2014; Moghaddam, 2013).

If you're a history enthusiast, you may associate *brainwashing* with techniques used by the Communist Chinese on prisoners during the Korean War (Jowett, 2006). Through various types of "thought reform," the Chinese were able to coerce some prisoners to sign false confessions.

Brainwashing *How does brainwashing differ from other persuasive techniques?* As we have noted, advertisers, politicians, educators, religious organizations, and others actively seek to alter attitudes and opinions. To an extent, their persuasive efforts resemble brainwashing, but there is an important difference: *Brainwashing,* or forced attitude change, requires a captive audience. If you are offended by a television commercial, you can tune it out. Prisoners are completely at the mercy of their captors. Complete control over the environment allows a degree of psychological manipulation that would be impossible in a normal setting.

How does captivity facilitate coercion? Brainwashing typically begins by making the target person feel completely helpless. Physical and psychological abuse, lack of sleep, humiliation, and isolation serve to *unfreeze,* or loosen, former values and beliefs. When exhaustion, pressure, and fear become unbearable, *change* occurs as the person begins to abandon former beliefs. Prisoners who reach the breaking point may sign a false confession or cooperate to gain relief. When they do, they are suddenly rewarded with praise, privileges, food, or rest. From that point on, a mixture of hope and fear plus pressures to conform serve to *refreeze* (solidify) new attitudes (Taylor, 2004).

How permanent are changes coerced by brainwashing? In most cases, the dramatic shift in attitudes brought about by brainwashing is temporary. Most "converted" prisoners who returned to the United States after the Korean War eventually reverted to their original beliefs. Nevertheless, brainwashing can be powerful, as shown by the success of cults in recruiting new members.

Cults Exhorted by their leader, some 900 members of the Reverend Jim Jones's People's Temple drank Kool-Aid laced with the deadly poison cyanide. Some even forced their own children to join in. The People's Temple is a classic example of a **cult**, an authoritarian group in which the leader's personality is more important than the beliefs he or she preaches. Cult members give their allegiance to this person, who is regarded as infallible, and they follow his or her dictates without question. Almost always, cult members are victimized by their leaders in one way or another.

Aftermath of the mass suicide at Jonestown. How do cult-like groups recruit new devotees?

Psychologically, the mass suicide at Jonestown in 1978 is not so incredible as it might seem (Dein & Littlewood, 2005). The inhabitants of Jonestown were isolated in the jungles of Guyana, intimidated by guards, and lulled with sedatives. They also were cut off from friends and relatives and totally accustomed to obeying rigid rules of conduct, which primed them for Jones's final "loyalty test." Of greater psychological interest is the question of how people reach such a state of commitment and dependency (Galanter, 2013).

How are people recruited into groups such as the People's Temple? People are often initially attracted to cults when they are undergoing distress, such as depression, indecision, or alienation from family and friends. At such times, people are more easily persuaded that joining the group is all they need to do to be happy again (Hunter, 1998; Richmond, 2004). Cults exploit this vulnerability through a powerful blend of guilt, manipulation, isolation, deception, fear, and escalating commitment. In this respect, cults employ high-pressure indoctrination techniques not unlike those used in brainwashing (Singer, 2003; Singer & Addis, 1992).

Potential recruits are initially "love bombed" with intense displays of affection and understanding. Next comes isolation from noncult members and drills, discipline, and rituals (all-night meditation or continuous chanting, for instance). These rituals wear down physical and emotional resistance, discourage critical thinking, and generate feelings of commitment (Langone, 2002). Recruits are asked to make an escalating series of commitments ending in signing over a bank account or property to the group, moving in with the group, and so forth. Making such major public commitments creates a powerful cognitive dissonance effect. Before long, it becomes virtually impossible for converts to admit they have made a mistake. Conversion is complete when recruits are cut off from family and friends and come to think of themselves more as group members than as individuals. At this point, obedience is nearly total (Coates, 2012; Wexler, 1995).

If a lesson is to be learned from such destructive cults, it is this: All true spiritual leaders have taught love and compassion. They also encourage followers to question their beliefs

Coercion *Being forced to change your beliefs or your behavior against your will.*
Cult *A group that professes great devotion to some person and follows that person almost without question; cult members are typically victimized by their leaders in various ways.*

and to reach their own conclusions about how to live. In contrast, destructive cults show how dangerous it is to trade personal independence and critical thinking for security (Cowan & Bromley, 2008; Goldberg, 2001).

Assertiveness—Stand Up for Your Rights

SURVEY QUESTION 71.2: How does self-assertion differ from aggression?

Most of us have been rewarded, first as children and later as adults, for compliant, obedient, or "good" behavior. Perhaps this is why so many people find it difficult to assert themselves. Or perhaps not asserting yourself is related to anxiety about "making a scene" or feeling disliked by others. Whatever the causes, some people suffer tremendous anguish in any situation requiring poise, self-confidence, or self-assertion. Have you ever done any of the following?

- Hesitated to question an error on a restaurant bill because you were afraid of making a scene
- Backed out of asking for a raise or a change in working conditions
- Said yes when you wanted to say no
- Been afraid to question a grade that seemed unfair

If you have ever had difficulty asserting yourself in similar situations, it might be worth practicing how to be self-assertive (Tavakoli et al., 2009; Wolpe, 1974). The first step is to convince yourself of three basic rights: You have the right to refuse, to request, and to right a wrong. **Self-assertion**

Associated Press photographer Jeff Widener snapped this timeless photo of a lone protester literally standing up on his own behalf while he halted a column of tanks during the 1989 pro-democracy rallies in Tiananmen Square in Beijing, China. How many of us would find the courage to assert ourselves against such direct expressions of authority?

involves standing up for these rights by speaking out in your own behalf.

Is self-assertion just getting things your own way? Not at all. A basic distinction can be made between *self-assertion* and *aggressive* behavior. Self-assertion is a direct, honest expression of feelings and desires. It is not exclusively self-serving. People who are nonassertive are usually patient to a fault. Sometimes their pent-up anger explodes with unexpected fury, which can damage relationships. In contrast to assertive behavior, **aggression** involves hurting another person or achieving one's goals at the expense of another. Aggression does not take into account the feelings or rights of others. It is an attempt to get one's own way no matter what. Assertion techniques emphasize firmness, not attack (● Table 71.1).

TABLE 71.1	Comparison of Assertive, Aggressive, and Nonassertive Behavior	
	Actor	**Receiver of Behavior**
Nonassertive behavior	Self-denying, inhibited, hurt, and anxious; lets others make choices; goals not achieved	Feels sympathy, guilt, or contempt for actor; achieves goals at actor's expense
Aggressive behavior	Achieves goals at others' expense; expresses feelings, but hurts others; chooses for others or puts them down	Feels hurt, defensive, humiliated, or taken advantage of; does not meet own needs
Assertive behavior	Self-enhancing; acts in own best interests; expresses feelings; respects rights of others; goals usually achieved; self-respect maintained	Needs respected and feelings expressed; may achieve goal; self-worth maintained

The basic idea is that each assertive action is practiced until it can be repeated even under stress. For example, let's say it really angers you when a store clerk waits on several people who arrived after you did. To improve your assertiveness in this situation, you would begin by *rehearsing* the dialogue, posture, and gestures you would use to confront the clerk or the other customer. Working in front of a mirror can be very helpful. If possible, you should *role-play* the scene with a friend. Be sure to have your friend take the part of a really aggressive or irresponsible clerk as well as a cooperative one.

Rehearsal and role-playing also should be used when you expect a possible confrontation with someone—for example, if you are going to ask for a raise, challenge a grade, or confront a landlord.

To summarize, self-assertion does not supply instant poise, confidence, or self-assurance. However, it is a way of combating anxieties associated with life in an impersonal and sometimes intimidating society (Sarkova et al., 2013). If you are interested in more information, you can consult a book titled *Your Perfect Right* by Alberti and Emmons (2008).

Module 71: Summary

71.1 What have social psychologists learned about the various forms of social influence?

- **71.1.1** Social influence refers to alterations in behavior brought about by the behavior of others. Social influence ranges from milder (mere influence, conformity, and compliance) to stronger (obedience and coercion).

- **71.1.2** The mere presence of others may facilitate (or inhibit) performance. People may also engage in social loafing, working less hard when they are part of a group.

- **71.1.3** The famous Asch experiments demonstrated that group sanctions encourage conformity.

- **71.1.4** *Groupthink* refers to compulsive conformity in group decision making. Group members who succumb to groupthink seek to maintain each other's approval, even at the cost of critical thinking.

- **71.1.5** Three strategies for gaining compliance are the foot-in-the-door technique, the door-in-the-face approach, and the low-ball technique.

- **71.1.6** Most people have a strong tendency to obey legitimate authority. Usually, this is desirable, but it can be damaging when social power is used in misguided or unscrupulous ways.

- **71.1.7** Obedience in Milgram's studies decreased when the victim was in the same room, when the victim and participant were face to face, when the authority figure was absent, and when others refused to obey.

- **71.1.8** Coercion involves forcing people to change their beliefs or behavior against their will. Cults are groups that rely on coercion.

- **71.1.9** Three steps in brainwashing (forced attitude change) are unfreezing, changing, and refreezing attitudes and beliefs.

71.2 How does self-assertion differ from aggression?

- **71.2.1** Self-assertion involves standing up for yourself; aggression involves achieving your goals at the expense of another.

Self-assertion *A direct, honest expression of feelings and desires.*
Aggression *Hurting another person or achieving one's goals at the expense of another person.*

Module 71: Knowledge Builder

Recite

1. The mere presence of others always improves performance. *T or F?*

2. In Solomon Asch's conformity experiment, participants yielded to group pressure on about _____ of the critical trials.
   a. 1 percent
   b. 10 percent
   c. one-third
   d. two-thirds

3. Nonconformity is punished by negative group _____.

4. The term *compliance* refers to situations in which a person complies with commands made by a person who has authority. *T or F?*

5. Obedience in Milgram's experiments was related to
   a. distance between learner and teacher
   b. distance between experimenter and teacher
   c. obedience of other teachers
   d. all of these

6. Brainwashing differs from other persuasive attempts in that brainwashing requires a _____ _____.

7. Cult members are almost always victimized by their leaders in one way or another. *T or F?*

8. In assertiveness training, people learn techniques for getting their way in social situations and angry interchanges. *T or F?*

Reflect

Think Critically

9. Is it possible to be completely nonconforming—that is, to not conform to some group norm?

10. Modern warfare allows killing to take place impersonally and at a distance. How does this relate to Milgram's experiments?

Self-Reflect

Have you ever encountered a social loafer? (*You* were never one, right?) How did you react?

Identify a recent time when you conformed in some way. How did norms, group pressure, sanctions, and unanimity contribute to your tendency to conform?

You would like to persuade people to donate to a deserving charity. How, specifically, could you use compliance techniques to get people to donate?

Are you surprised that so many people obeyed orders in Milgram's experiments? Do you think you would have obeyed? How actively do you question authority?

To what extent are governments entitled to use coercion to modify the attitudes or behavior of their citizens?

Pick a specific instance when you could have been more assertive. How would you handle the situation if it occurs again?

ANSWERS

1. F 2. c 3. sanctions 4. F 5. d 6. captive audience 7. T 8. F 9. A person who did not follow at least some norms concerning normal social behavior very likely would be perceived as extremely bizarre, disturbed, or psychotic. 10. There is a big difference between someone killing someone in hand-to-hand combat and killing someone by lining up images on a video screen. Milgram's research suggests that it is easier for a person to follow orders to kill another human when the victim is at a distance and removed from personal contact.

CENGAGE**brain**.com

Go to **cengagebrain.com** to access **MindTap for Coon/Mitterer** *Psychology Modules for Active Learning* and other online learning tools. MindTap is a fully online learning experience that combines all the tools you need—readings, multimedia, activities, and assessments—into a singular personalized Learning Path that guides you through the course.

Social Psychology: Prosocial Behavior

The "Snuggle" for Survival

One common misunderstanding of human nature is that we are engaged in a perennial struggle for survival against one another. In fact, we cooperate with the people around us at least as much as we are in conflict with them. Although at times you want to be left alone, the fact is that we humans are social animals. Imagine if you were deprived of all contact with your family and friends. You would probably find it painfully lonely and disorienting. If deprived of all human contact, you might have difficulty even surviving.

The various forms of *prosocial behavior* all involve having a positive effect on people around us. From the desire for intimacy with family to the impulse to help strangers, we are drawn to other people. What brings people together to help

Blend Images/Shutterstock

each other, to seek friendship, and to find love? Let's further explore the "snuggle" for survival.

SURVEY QUESTIONS

72.1 Why do we affiliate and what factors influence interpersonal attraction?

72.2 How are liking and loving different?

72.3 What factors influence our willingness to help other people?

Affiliation and Attraction— Come Together

SURVEY QUESTIONS 72.1: Why do we affiliate and what factors influence interpersonal attraction?

Prosocial behavior is any behavior that has a positive impact on other people. (In contrast, *antisocial behavior* is any behavior that has a negative impact on other people.) We are social beings with a **need to affiliate**—a need to associate with other people—rooted in basic human desires to get and to give approval, support, friendship, and love (Baumeister & Bushman, 2014). We also affiliate to help us think about ourselves by comparing ourselves with others (see Module 70). We even seek the company of others to alleviate fear or anxiety.

Don't people also affiliate out of attraction for one another? Of course they do. Let's see why.

Interpersonal Attraction

Interpersonal attraction—affinity to another person—is the basis for most voluntary social relationships (Berscheid, 2010; Berscheid & Regan, 2005). To form friendships, we must first identify potential friends and then get to know them. Deciding whether you would like to get to know another person can happen very quickly, sometimes within just minutes of meeting (Sunnafrank, Ramirez, & Metts, 2004). That may be because you usually don't randomly choose people to encounter.

What initially attracts people to each other? "Birds of a feather flock together." "Familiarity breeds contempt." "Opposites attract." Are these statements true? At best, the folklore is a mixture of fact and fiction. As you might expect, we look for friends and lovers who will be kind and understanding and who appear to have attractive personalities (Bradbury & Karney, 2010; Park & Lennon, 2008). Let's explore some other factors that influence our initial attraction to people.

Familiarity In general, we are attracted to people with whom we are familiar (Reis et al., 2011). (That's one reason actors costarring in movies often become romantically involved.) In fact, our choice of friends (and even lovers) is based more on *physical proximity* (nearness) than we might care to believe. Proximity promotes attraction by increasing the *frequency of contact* between people.

The closer people live to each other, the more likely they are to become friends. Likewise, lovers like to think they have found the "one and only" person in the universe for them. In reality, they have probably found the best match in a 5-mile radius (Reis et al., 2011). Marriages are not made in heaven—they are made in local schools, businesses, churches, bars, clubs, and neighborhoods.

In short, there does seem to be a "boy-next-door" or "girl-next-door" effect in romantic attraction, and a "folks-next-door" effect in friendship. Notice, however, that the Internet is making it increasingly easier to stay in constant "virtual contact," which is leading to more and more long-distance friendships and romances (Aron, 2012; Sautter, Tippett, & Morgan, 2010).

Similarity Take a moment to make a list of your closest friends. What do they have in common (other than the joy of knowing you)? It is likely that their ages are similar to yours and you are of the same sex and ethnicity. There will be exceptions, of course. But similarity on these three dimensions is the general rule for friendships.

Similarity refers to how alike you are to another person in background, age, interests, attitudes, beliefs, and so forth. In everything from casual acquaintance to marriage, similar people are attracted to each other (Miller, 2012; Montoya & Horton, 2013). And why not? It's reinforcing to see our beliefs and attitudes shared by others. It shows we are "right" and reveals that they are clever people as well!

So similarity also influences mate selection? Yes, in choosing a mate, we tend to marry someone who is like us in almost every way, a pattern called *homogamy* (huh-MOG-ah-me) (Kalmijn, 2010; Schramm et al., 2012). Studies show that married couples are highly similar in age, education, ethnicity, and religion. To a lesser degree, they also are similar in attitudes and opinions, mental abilities, status, height, weight, and eye color. In case you're wondering, homogamy also applies to unmarried couples who are living together (Blackwell & Lichter, 2004).

Physical Attractiveness People who are *physically attractive* are regarded as good-looking by others. Beautiful people are generally rated as more appealing than average. This is due, in part, to the *halo effect*, a tendency to generalize a favorable impression to unrelated personal characteristics. Because of it, we assume that attractive people also are likable, intelligent, warm, witty, mentally healthy, and socially skilled. Basically, we act as if "what is beautiful is good" (Lorenzo, Biesanz, & Human, 2010).

In reality, physical attractiveness has almost *no* connection to intelligence, talents, or abilities. Perhaps that's why beauty affects mainly our initial interest in getting to know others (Keller & Young, 1996; Reis et al., 2011). Later, more meaningful qualities gain in importance. As you discover that someone has a good personality, he or she will start looking even more attractive to you. It takes more than appearance to make a lasting relationship (Berscheid, 2010; Lewandowski, Aron, & Gee, 2007; Miller, 2012).

Reciprocity Okay, so he or she is someone with whom you are familiar, appears to share a lot in common with you, and is even hot. What else do you need to know before taking it to the next level? Well, it would be nice to know if he or she also is the least bit interested in you (Greitemeyer, 2010). In fact, *reciprocity*, which occurs when people respond to each other in similar ways, may be the most important factor influencing the development of relationships. Most people find it easier to reciprocate someone else's overtures than to be the initiator (Montoya & Insko, 2008). That way, at least the embarrassment of an outright rejection can be avoided.

Self-Disclosure

Once initial contact has been made, it's time to get to know each other. This is done mainly through the process of **self-disclosure** as you begin to share private thoughts and feelings and reveal yourself to others. To get acquainted, you must be willing to talk about more than just the weather, sports, or nuclear physics. In general, as friends talk, they gradually deepen the level of liking, trust, and self-disclosure (Levesque, Steciuk, & Ledley, 2002). We more often reveal ourselves to persons we like than to those we find unattractive. Disclosure also requires a degree of trust. Many people play it safe, or "close to the vest," with people they do not know well. Indeed, self-disclosure is governed by unspoken rules about what's acceptable (Phillips, Rothbard, & Dumas, 2009).

Moderate self-disclosure leads to increased reciprocity. In contrast, *overdisclosure* exceeds what is appropriate for a relationship or social situation, giving rise to suspicion and reducing attraction. For example, imagine standing in line at a store and having the stranger in front of you say, "Lately I've been thinking about how I really feel about myself. I think I'm pretty well adjusted, but I occasionally have some questions about my sexual adequacy."

Excessive self-disclosure is a staple of many television talk shows. Guests frequently reveal intimate details about their personal lives, including private family matters, sex and dating, physical or sexual abuse, major embarrassments, and criminal activities. Viewers probably find such intimate disclosures entertaining, rather than threatening, because they don't have to reciprocate.

When self-disclosure proceeds at a moderate pace, it builds trust, intimacy, reciprocity, and positive feelings. When it is too rapid or inappropriate, we are likely to "back off" and wonder about the person's motives. It's interesting to note that on the Internet (and especially on social networking sites like Facebook), people often feel freer to express their true feelings, which can lead to personal growth and genuine, face-to-face friendships. However, it also can lead to some very dramatic overdisclosure (Jiang, Bazarova, & Hancock, 2013; Special & Li-Barber, 2012; Valkenburg, Sumter, & Peter, 2011).

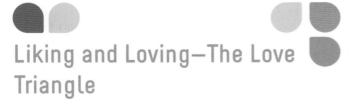

Liking and Loving—The Love Triangle

SURVEY QUESTION 72.2: How are liking and loving different?

How does love differ from interpersonal attraction? It depends on what you mean by the word *love*. **Romantic love**, for example, is based on interpersonal attraction, but it also involves high levels of passion: emotional arousal and/or sexual desire (Berscheid & Regan, 2005; Marazziti & Baroni, 2012). You are experiencing romantic love as you are "falling in love" (Aron et al., 2008).

To get another (tri?)angle on love, psychologist Robert Sternberg (1988) created his influential *triangular theory of love*. According to Sternberg, different forms of love arise from different combinations of three basic components (● Figure 72.1):

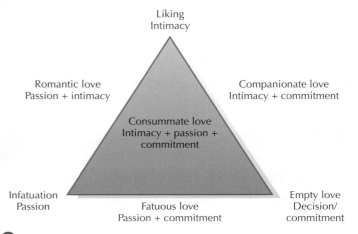

● **Figure 72.1**

The Triangle of Love. Each of the three basic components of love (intimacy, passion, and commitment) appears at one corner of the triangle and is associated with a form of love. Pairs of components and their associated form of love appear on lines of the triangle. Consummate love, which involves all three components, is pictured at the center of the triangle. [Sternberg, R. J. (1988). The triangle of love. New York: Basic.]

Intimacy refers to feelings of connectedness and affection.

Passion refers to deep emotional and/or sexual feelings.

Commitment involves the determination to stay in a long-term relationship with another person.

Prosocial behavior *Behavior toward others that is helpful, constructive, or altruistic.*
Need to affiliate *The desire to associate with other people.*
Interpersonal attraction *Social attraction to another person.*
Self-disclosure *The process of revealing private thoughts, feelings, and one's personal history to others.*
Romantic love *Love that is associated with high levels of interpersonal attraction, heightened arousal, mutual absorption, and sexual desire.*
Intimacy *Feelings of connectedness and affection for another person.*
Passion *Deep emotional and/or sexual feelings for another person.*
Commitment *The determination to stay in a long-term relationship with another person.*

How does this triangle work? Try it for yourself. Think of a person you love. Now read ● Table 72.1 as you ask yourself three yes/no questions: Do I feel intimate with this person? Do I feel passion for this person? Am I committed to this person? Find the kind of love that fits your answers. For example, if you answered *yes* to intimacy but *no* to passion and commitment, you like that person; you are friends. Alternately, if you answered *yes* to intimacy and commitment but *no* to passion, then you are feeling companionate love. This form of love is more common among couples who have been together for a long time. Such couples often describe themselves as "being in love" rather than "falling in love" (Riela et al., 2010).

Does that mean that the most complete form of love is consummate love? You've got it! We experience consummate love when we feel intimacy and passion for another person, *and* we are strongly committed to him or her.

TABLE 72.1	Sternberg's Triangular Theory of Love		
Combinations of intimacy, passion, and commitment			
Type of love	**Intimacy**	**Passion**	**Commitment**
Nonlove			
Liking	Yes		
Infatuated love		Yes	
Empty love			Yes
Romantic love	Yes	Yes	
Companionate love	Yes		Yes
Fatuous love		Yes	Yes
Consummate love	Yes	Yes	Yes

Source: Sternberg (1988).

Romantic love differs from friendship in another interesting way. In contrast to simple liking, romantic love usually involves deep *mutual absorption.* In other words, lovers (unlike friends) attend almost exclusively to one another (Riela et al., 2010).

What do lovers see when they gaze into each other's eyes? A final interesting characteristic of romantic love is lovers' ability to see their partners in idealized ways (Barelds & Dijkstra, 2009). Nobody's perfect, of course. That's why it's no surprise that relationships are most likely to persist when lovers idealize one another. Doing so doesn't just blind them to their partner's faults; it actually helps them create the relationship they want (Murray, Holmes, & Griffin, 2003).

Evolution and Mate Selection

Evolutionary psychology is the study of the evolutionary origins of human behavior patterns (Confer et al., 2010). Many psychologists believe that evolution left an imprint on men and women that influences everything from sexual attraction and infidelity to jealousy and divorce. According to David Buss, the key to understanding human mating patterns is to understand how evolved behavior patterns guide our choices (Buss, 2007, 2012).

In a study of 37 cultures on six continents, Buss found the following patterns: Compared with women, men are more interested in casual sex; they prefer younger, more physically attractive partners; and they get more jealous over real or imagined sexual infidelities than they do over a loss of emotional commitment. Compared with men, women prefer slightly older partners who appear to be industrious, higher in status, or economically successful; women are more upset by a partner who becomes emotionally involved with someone else, rather than one who is sexually unfaithful (Buss, 2012; Regan et al., 2000; ● Figure 72.2).

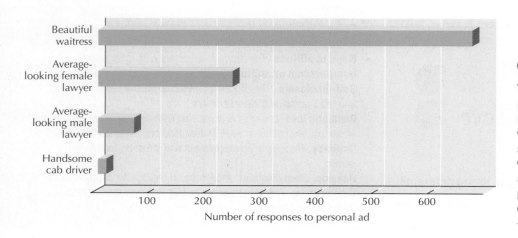

● **Figure 72.2**

What do people look for when considering potential dating partners? Here are the results of a study in which personal ads were placed in newspapers. As you can see, men were more influenced by looks and women by success [Goode, E. (1996). Gender and courtshipentitlement: Responses to personalads. Sex Roles, 34(3-4), 141–1F9. doi:10.1007/BF01544293].

Why do such differences exist? Buss and others believe that mating preferences evolved in response to the differing reproductive challenges faced by men and women (Buss, 2007, 2012; Confer et al., 2010). As a rule, women must invest more time and energy in reproduction and nurturing their young than men. Consequently, women evolved an interest in whether their partners will stay with them and whether their mates have the resources to provide for their children.

According to evolutionary psychologists, women tend to be concerned with whether mates will devote time and resources to a relationship. Men place more emphasis on physical attractiveness and sexual fidelity.

In contrast, the reproductive success of men depends on their mates' fertility. Men, therefore, tend to look for health, youth, and beauty in a prospective mate as signs of suitability for reproduction. Evolutionary theory further proposes that the male emphasis on mates' sexual fidelity is based on concerns about the paternity of offspring. From a biological perspective, men do not benefit from investing resources in children they did not sire (Buller, 2005).

Although some evidence supports the evolutionary view of mating, it is important to remember that evolved mating tendencies are subtle at best and easily overruled by other factors. Some mating patterns may simply reflect the fact that men still tend to control the power and resources in most societies (Feingold, 1992; Fine, 2010). Also, early research may be misleading because women tend to give "polite" answers to questions about jealousy. Privately, they may be just as furious about a mate's sexual infidelity as would any man (Harris, 2004).

Whatever the outcome of the debate about evolution and mate selection, it is important to remember this: Potential mates are rated as most attractive if they are kind, secure, intelligent, and supportive (Klohnen & Luo, 2003; Regan et al., 2000). These qualities are love's greatest allies.

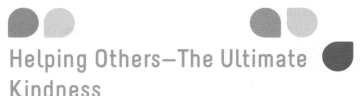

Helping Others—The Ultimate Kindness

SURVEY QUESTION 72.3: What factors influence our willingness to help other people?

It is entirely understandable to act kindly toward people to whom you're attracted or with whom you are friends or lovers. But what about total strangers? There is no doubt that showing kindness to strangers, especially when they are in need, is perhaps the most tender of prosocial acts (Mikulincer & Shaver, 2010).

Every year, awards are given to people who risk their lives while saving the lives of others. These heroes are typically honored for saving people from fires, drowning, animal attacks, electrocution, and suffocation. In the aftermath of the 2013 Boston Marathon bombings, many heroic first responders, including private citizens, rushed to help the victims, demonstrating once again the prosocial side of human nature.

The majority of people who perform such heroic acts are men, perhaps because of the physical dangers involved. However, other heroic, prosocial acts also save lives and involve personal risk. Examples are kidney donors, Peace Corps volunteers, and Doctors of the World volunteers. In such endeavors, we find as many women as men, and often more. It is important to remember, perhaps, that sensational and highly visible acts of heroism are only one of many ways in which people engage in selfless, altruistic behavior (Becker & Eagly, 2004). People who serve as community volunteers, tutors, coaches, blood donors, and the like don't just help others. Often, their efforts contribute to personal growth and make themselves healthier and happier. Thus, it can be said that "We do well by doing good" (Piliavin, 2003).

Liking *A relationship based on intimacy but lacking passion and commitment.*
Companionate love *Form of love characterized by intimacy and commitment but not passion.*
Consummate love *Form of love characterized by intimacy, passion, and commitment.*
Evolutionary psychology *Study of the evolutionary origins of human behavior patterns.*

But do we always help? In April 2010, a homeless man helped a young woman fend off an attacker in Queens, New York. For his trouble, he was stabbed and fell to the sidewalk where he laid in a pool of his own blood. When emergency aid arrived over an hour later, Hugo Tale-Yax was already dead. Compounding the horror, surveillance video revealed that 25 people walked past him as he lay dying on the street (Livingston, Doyle, & Mangan, 2010).

This recent case, and others like it, dating back to the 1964 murder of a young woman named Kitty Genovese, which was witnessed by 38 bystanders (Manning, Levine, & Collins, 2007), make us wonder why no one helped. Perhaps it is understandable that no one wanted to get involved. After all, it might have meant risking personal injury. But what prevented these people from at least calling the police?

Isn't this an example of the alienation of city life? News reports often treat such incidents as evidence of a breakdown in social ties caused by the impersonality of the city. Although it is true that urban living can be dehumanizing, this does not fully explain such *bystander apathy* (the unwillingness of bystanders to offer help during emergencies; this also is referred to as the **bystander effect**). According to landmark work by psychologists John Darley and Bibb Latané (1968), failure to help is related to the number of people present. Over the years, many studies have shown that when *more* potential helpers are present, the *less* likely are people to help (Fischer et al., 2011; Zoccola et al., 2011).

Why would people be less willing to help when others are present? Basically, we are likely to assume *someone else* will help.

Does the person lying on the ground need help? What factors determine whether a person in trouble will receive help in an emergency? Surprisingly, the presence of more potential helpers tends to lower the chances that help will be given.

The dynamics of this effect are easily illustrated: Suppose that two motorists have stalled at the roadside, one on a sparsely traveled country road and the other on a busy freeway. Who gets help first?

On the freeway, where hundreds of cars pass every minute, each driver can assume that someone else will help. Personal responsibility for helping is spread so thin that no one takes action. On the country road, one of the first few people to drive by will probably stop because the responsibility is clearly theirs. In general, Darley and Latané assume that bystanders are not apathetic or uncaring: They are inhibited by the presence of others.

Bystander Intervention

People must pass through four decision points before giving help. First, they must notice that something is happening. Next, they must define the event as an emergency. Then they must take responsibility. Finally, they must select a course of action (● **Figure 72.3**). Laboratory experiments have shown that each step can be influenced by the presence of other people.

Noticing What would happen if you fainted and collapsed on the sidewalk? Would someone stop to help? Would people think you were drunk? Would they even notice you? Darley and Latané suggest that if the sidewalk is crowded, few people will even see you. This has nothing to do with people blocking each other's vision. Instead, it is related to widely accepted norms against staring at others in public. People in crowds typically "keep their eyes to themselves."

To test this idea, students were asked to fill out a questionnaire either alone or in a room full of people. As the students worked, a thick cloud of smoke was blown into the room through a vent.

Most students left alone in the room noticed the smoke immediately. Few of the people in groups noticed the smoke until it became difficult to see through it. Participants working in groups politely kept their eyes on their papers and avoided looking at others (or the smoke). In contrast, those who were alone scanned the room from time to time.

Defining an Emergency The smoke-filled room also shows the influence others have on defining a situation as an emergency. When participants in groups finally noticed the smoke, they cast sidelong glances at others in the room. (Remember *social comparison*?) Apparently, they were searching for clues to help interpret what was happening. No one wanted to

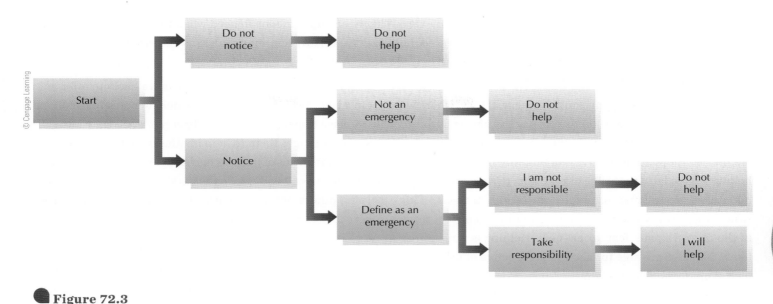

© Cengage Learning

● **Figure 72.3**

This decision tree summarizes the steps a person must take before making a commitment to offer help, according to Latané and Darley's model.

overreact or act like a fool if there was no emergency. However, as participants coolly surveyed the reactions of others, they were themselves being watched. In real emergencies, people sometimes "fake each other out" and underestimate the need for action because each person attempts to appear calm. In short, until someone acts, no one acts.

Taking Responsibility Perhaps the most crucial step in helping is assuming responsibility. In this case, groups limit helping by causing a *diffusion of responsibility* (spreading responsibility among several people).

Is that like the unwillingness of drivers to offer help on a crowded freeway? Exactly. It is the feeling that no one is personally responsible for helping. This problem was demonstrated in an experiment in which students participated in a group discussion over an intercom system. However, each group had only one real participant; the others were tape-recorded actors. Each participant was placed in a separate room (supposedly to maintain confidentiality), and discussions of college life were begun. During the discussion, one of the "students" simulated an epileptic-like seizure and called out for help. In some cases, participants thought they were alone with the seizure victim. Others believed they were members of three- or six-person groups.

People who thought they were alone with the "victim" of this staged emergency reported it immediately or tried to help. Some participants in the three-person groups failed to

respond, and those who did were slower. In the six-person groups, over a third of the participants took no action at all. People in this experiment were obviously faced with a conflict like that in many real emergencies: Should they be helpful and responsible, or should they mind their own business? Many were influenced toward inaction by the presence of others.

People do help in some emergencies. How are these different? Helping behavior is complex and influenced by many variables (Baumeister & Bushman, 2014). One naturalistic experiment staged in a New York City subway gives a hint of the kinds of things that may be important. When a "victim" (actor) "passed out" in a subway car, he received more help when carrying a cane than when carrying a liquor bottle (Piliavin, Rodin, & Piliavin, 1969). To better answer the question, we need to consider some factors not included in Latané and Darley's account of helping.

Who Will Help Whom?

Higher costs (such as possible embarrassment, great effort, and especially personal risk) almost always decrease helping

Bystander effect (bystander apathy) *Unwillingness of bystanders to offer help during emergencies or to become involved in others' problems.*

(Zoccola et al., 2011). In one study, the presence of an extra, passive bystander doing nothing to help actually *increased* the likelihood of people stopping to help in a potentially dangerous situation (Fischer & Greitemeyer, 2013).

Regardless of risk, many studies suggest that when we see a person in trouble, it tends to cause *heightened arousal* (Batson, 2010; Dovidio et al., 2006). This aroused, keyed-up feeling can motivate us to give aid, but only if the rewards of helping outweigh the costs. In addition to general arousal, potential helpers may also feel **empathic arousal**. This means they empathize with the person in need or feel some of the person's pain, fear, or anguish. Helping is much more likely when we are able to take the perspective of others and feel sympathy for their plight (Batson & Powell, 2003; Myers & Hodges, 2013).

Empathic arousal is especially likely to motivate helping when the person in need seems to be similar to ourselves (Guéguen, Martin, & Meineri, 2011; Batson, 2010). In fact, a feeling of connection to the victim may be one of the most important factors in helping. Tragically, Hugo Tale-Yax's disheveled homelessness was undoubtedly one reason no one stopped to help him.

This, perhaps, is why being in a good mood also increases helping. When we are feeling successful, happy, or fortunate, we also may feel more connected to others (Dovidio & Penner, 2001; Lamy, Fischer-Lokou, & Guéguen, 2012). In summary, there is a strong **empathy-helping relationship**: We are most likely to help someone in need when we "feel for" that person and experience emotions such as empathy, sympathy, and compassion (Batson, 2006, 2010).

People who see others helping are more likely to offer help themselves. Also, persons who give help in one situation tend to perceive themselves as helpful people. This change in self-image encourages them to help in other situations. One more point is that norms of fairness encourage us to help others who have helped us (Dovidio & Penner, 2001). For all these reasons, helping others not only assists them directly, it encourages others to help, too.

"De-victimize" Yourself If you should find yourself in need of help during an emergency, what can you do to avoid being a victim of bystander apathy? The work we have reviewed here suggests that you should make sure that you are noticed, that people realize there's an emergency, and that they need to take action. Being noticed can be promoted in some situations by shouting "Fire!" Bystanders who might run away from a robbery or an assault may rush to see where the fire is. At the very least, remember to not just scream. Instead, you should call out "Help" or "I need help right now." Whenever possible, define your situation for bystanders. Say, for instance, "I'm being attacked, call the police." Or, "Stop that man, he has my purse." You also can directly assign responsibility to a bystander by pointing to someone and saying, "You, call the police" or "I'm injured, I need you to call an ambulance."

Empathic arousal *Emotional arousal that occurs when you feel some of another person's pain, fear, or anguish.*
Empathy-helping relationship *Observation that we are most likely to help someone else when we feel emotions such as empathy and compassion.*

Module 72: Summary

72.1 Why do we affiliate and what factors influence interpersonal attraction?

- **72.1.1** Affiliation is tied to needs for approval, support, friendship, and information. Also, affiliation can reduce anxiety.
- **72.1.2** Interpersonal attraction is increased by proximity, frequent contact, beauty, competence, and similarity.
- **72.1.3** Mate selection is characterized by a large degree of similarity on many dimensions.
- **72.1.4** Self-disclosure follows a reciprocity norm: Low levels of self-disclosure are met with low levels in return; moderate self-disclosure elicits more personal replies. However, overdisclosure tends to inhibit self-disclosure by others.

72.2 How are liking and loving different?

- **72.2.1** In comparison with liking, romantic love involves higher levels of emotional arousal and is accompanied by mutual absorption between lovers. Consummate love, involving intimacy, passion, *and* commitment, is the most complete form of love.

- **72.2.2** Evolutionary psychology attributes human mating patterns to the differing reproductive challenges faced by men and women during the course of evolution.

72.3 What factors influence our willingness to help other people?

- **72.3.1** Four decision points must be passed before a person gives help: noticing, defining an emergency, taking responsibility, and selecting a course of action. Helping is less likely at each point when other potential helpers are present.
- **72.3.2** Helping is encouraged by general arousal, empathic arousal, being in a good mood, low effort or risk, and perceived similarity between the victim and the helper.
- **72.3.3** For several reasons, giving help tends to encourage others to help, too.

Module 72: Knowledge Builder

Recite

1. Interpersonal attraction is increased by all but one of the following. (Which does not fit?)
   - **a.** physical proximity
   - **b.** physical attractiveness
   - **c.** similarity
   - **d.** overdisclosure
2. High levels of self-disclosure are reciprocated in most social encounters. *T or F?*
3. In Sternberg's triangular theory, infatuated love involves passion but not commitment or intimacy. *T or F?*
4. The most striking finding about marriage patterns is that most people choose mates whose personalities are quite unlike their own. *T or F?*
5. Compared with men, women tend to be more upset by sexual infidelity than by a loss of emotional commitment on the part of their mates. *T or F?*
6. _____ behavior refers to actions that are constructive, altruistic, or helpful to others.
7. People are more likely to help another who is in trouble if
   - **a.** many other helpers are present
   - **b.** a diffusion of responsibility occurs
   - **c.** they experience empathic arousal
   - **d.** desensitization takes place

Reflect

Think Critically

8. How has the Internet altered the effects of proximity on interpersonal attraction?

Self-Reflect

How has social comparison affected your behavior? Has it influenced with whom you associate?

Think of three close friends. Which of the attraction factors described earlier apply to your friendships?

To what extent does Sternberg's triangular theory of love apply to your own relationships?

An elderly woman is at the side of the road, trying to change a flat tire. She obviously needs help. You are approaching her in your car. What must happen before you are likely to stop and help her?

ANSWERS

1. d 2. F 3. T 4. F 5. F 6. prosocial 7. c 8. As mentioned earlier, the Internet makes actual physical proximity less crucial in interpersonal attraction because frequent contact is possible even at great distances. Internet romances are a good example of this possibility.

Social Psychology: Antisocial Behavior

The Struggle for Survival

It might seem that the horrors of war and the ravages of terrorism would lead to a worldwide revulsion for killing. Yet, violent and aggressive behavior remains so commonplace it is often viewed as entertainment. Aggression is only one form of *antisocial behavior*, all of which involve having a negative effect on people around us. For example, while love and friendship bring people together, prejudice and discrimination, which are marked by suspicion, fear, or hatred, have the opposite effect.

How "natural" is aggressive behavior? What causes aggression? Can violence be reduced? What are the origins of prejudice and discrimination? How can such hurtful attitudes be reduced? Around the world, we are becoming ever more interdependent. At the same time, it is becoming easier for even a "lone wolf" to cause widespread damage. Finding answers to questions like those posed here becomes even more important. If nothing else, we owe it to the victims, past and future.

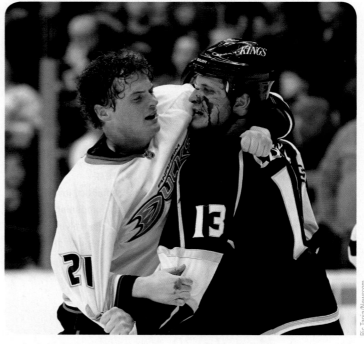

Ric Tapia/Newscom

SURVEY QUESTIONS

73.1 How do psychologists explain human aggression?

73.2 What causes prejudice and intergroup conflict?

Aggression—The World's Most Dangerous Animal

SURVEY QUESTION 73.1: How do psychologists explain human aggression?

Bluntly put, we humans are capable of hatred and cruelty as well as love. In this module, we turn our attention to the dark side of social behavior. **Antisocial behavior** is any behavior that has a negative impact on other people. Let's begin with *aggression*, which refers to any action carried out with the intention of harming another person. The human capacity for aggression is staggering. More than 180 million humans were killed by other humans (an average of nearly one person every 18 seconds) during the twentieth century (Pinker, 2011). War,

homicide, riots, family violence, assassination, rape, assault, forcible robbery, and other violent acts offer sad testimony to the realities of human aggression (Shaver & Mikulincer, 2011).

It is worth noting that aggression can be expressed in many ways, from the truly horrific, such as ethnic cleansing and gangland executions, to the more mundane, such as harassment and the one-finger salute. As an example, one pervasive form is **bullying**, any behavior that deliberately and repeatedly exposes a person to negative experiences (Powell & Ladd, 2010). Bullies tend to deal with everyday situations by resorting to aggression. Bullying can be *verbal* (name-calling, insults, teasing) or *physical* (hitting, pushing, confining), and it also can be *direct* ("in your face") or *indirect* (intentional exclusion, spreading rumors). Whereas male bullies are more likely than females to engage in direct physical aggression, female bullies tend to specialize in indirect verbal aggression (Field et al., 2009).

Bullying is a worldwide phenomenon. It occurs among all age groups and in all settings. It can even be found online, in the form of *cyberbullying* (Bonanno & Hymel, 2013). Childhood bullying can have long-term consequences for the mental health of both bullies and their victims (Sansone, Leung, & Wiederman, 2013; Twemlow & Sacco, 2012). Adolescent and adult bullying can lead to serious violence, including murder and suicide.

What causes aggression such as bullying? Aggression has many potential causes (DeWall & Anderson, 2011). Let's look at some of the major possibilities.

Instincts

Some theorists argue we are naturally aggressive, having inherited a "killer instinct" from our animal ancestors (Buss, 2012). While this idea has an intuitive appeal, many psychologists question it (Rhee & Waldman, 2011). Just labeling a behavior as *instinctive* does little to explain it. More important, we are left with the question of why some individuals or human groups (the Arapesh, the Senoi, the Navajo, the Eskimo, and others) show little hostility or aggression. And, thankfully, the vast majority of humans *do not* kill or harm others.

Biology

Despite problems with the instinctive view, aggression does have biological roots (Rhee & Waldman, 2011). Physiological studies have shown that some brain areas are capable of triggering or ending aggressive behavior. Also, researchers have found a relationship between aggression and such physical factors as hypoglycemia (low blood sugar), allergy, alcohol and drug use, and specific brain injuries and diseases. For both men and women, higher levels of the hormone testosterone may be associated with more aggressive behavior (McDermott et al., 2007; Montoya et al., 2012). Perhaps because of their higher testosterone levels, men are more likely to engage in physical aggression than women (Anderson & Bushman, 2002).

Regardless, none of these biological factors can be considered a direct *cause* of aggression (Moore, 2001; Popma et al., 2007). Instead, they probably lower the threshold for aggression, making hostile behavior more likely to occur (Tackett & Krueger, 2011). The fact that we are biologically *capable* of aggression does not mean that aggression is inevitable or "part of human nature." Humans are fully capable of learning to inhibit aggression. For example, American Quakers and Amish, who live in this increasingly violent country, adopt nonviolence as a way of life.

Frustration

Step on a dog's tail and you may get nipped. Frustrate a human and you may get insulted. As we also discuss in Module 56, frustration tends to lead to aggression, a relationship known as the **frustration-aggression hypothesis**.

Jose Luis Pelaez, Inc./Corbis

Road rage and some freeway shootings may be a reaction to the stress and frustration of traffic congestion. The fact that automobiles provide anonymity, or a loss of personal identity, also may encourage aggressive actions that would not otherwise occur.

Does frustration always produce aggression? Although the connection is strong, a moment's thought will show that frustration does not *always* lead to aggression. Frustration, for instance, may lead to stereotyped responding or perhaps to a state of "learned helplessness" (see Module 57). Also, aggression can occur in the absence of frustration. This possibility is illustrated by sports spectators who start fights, throw bottles, tear down goalposts, and so forth—after their team has *won*.

Aversive Stimuli Frustration probably encourages aggression because it is uncomfortable. Various *aversive stimuli*, which produce discomfort or displeasure, can heighten hostility and aggression (Anderson, Anderson, & Deuser, 1996; Morgan, 2005; ● **Figure 73.1**). Examples include insults, high air temperatures, pain, and even disgusting scenes or odors. Such stimuli probably raise overall arousal levels so that we

Antisocial behavior *Any behavior that has a negative impact on other people.*
Bullying *The deliberate and repeated use of verbal or physical, direct or indirect, aggression as a tactic for dealing with everyday situations.*
Frustration-aggression hypothesis *States that frustration tends to lead to aggression.*

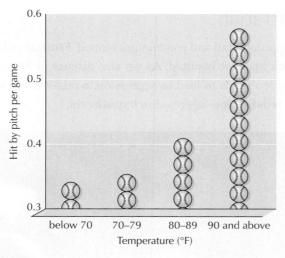

Figure 73.1

Personal discomfort caused by aversive (unpleasant) stimuli can make aggressive behavior more likely. For example, studies of crime rates show that the incidence of highly aggressive behavior, such as murder, rape, and assault, rises as the air temperature goes from warm to hot to sweltering (Anderson, 1989). The results you see here further confirm the heat-aggression link. The graph shows that there is a strong association between the temperatures at major league baseball games and the number of batters hit by a pitch during those games. When the temperature goes over 90°, watch out for that fastball [Reifman, A. S., Larrick, R. P., & Fein, S.(1991). Temper and temperature on the diamond: The heat-aggressionrelationship in major league baseball. Personality & Social PsychologyBulletin, 17(5), 580–585.doi:10.1177/0146167291175013].

become more sensitive to *aggression cues* (signals that are associated with aggression) (Schwenzer, 2008). Aversive stimuli also tend to activate ideas, memories, and expressions associated with anger and aggression (Morgan, 2005).

Some cues for aggression are internal (angry thoughts, for instance). Many are external: Certain words, actions, and gestures made by others are strongly associated with aggressive responses. A raised middle finger, for instance, is an almost universal invitation to aggression in North America. Weapons serve as particularly strong cues for aggressive behavior (Morgan, 2005). The implication of this *weapons effect* seems to be that the symbols and trappings of aggression encourage aggression. A prime example is the fact that murders are more likely to occur in homes in which guns are kept (Miller, Hemenway, & Azraela, 2007).

Social Learning

One of the most widely accepted explanations of aggression is also the simplest. **Social learning theory** holds that we learn to be aggressive by observing aggression in others (Bandura, 2001; Lefrançois, 2012). Social learning theory combines learning principles with cognitive processes, socialization,

and modeling to explain behavior. According to this view, there is no instinctive human programming for fistfighting, pipe bombing, knife wielding, gun loading, 95-mile-an-hour "bean balls," or other violent or aggressive behaviors. Hence, aggression must be learned (● **Figure 73.2**). Is it any wonder that people who were victims of violence during childhood are more likely to become violent themselves (Murrell, Christoff, & Henning, 2007)?

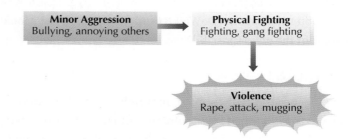

Figure 73.2

Violent behavior among delinquent boys doesn't appear overnight. Usually, their capacity for violence develops slowly as they move from minor aggr n early adolescence as boys gain physical strength and more access to weapons [Loeber, R., & Hay, D. (1997). Key issues in the development of aggression and violence from childhood to early adulthood. Annual Review of Psychology, 48, 371–410. doi:10.1146/annurev.psych.48.1.371].

Social learning theorists predict that people growing up in nonaggressive cultures will themselves be nonaggressive. Those raised in a culture with aggressive models and heroes will learn aggressive responses. Considered in such terms, it is no wonder that America has become one of the more violent countries. A violent crime occurred every 26 seconds in the United States during 2011 (Federal Bureau of Investigation, 2012). (On the bright side, the violent crime rate has declined by over 15 percent in the last decade.) Over 40 percent of U.S. households own at least one firearm (Agresti & Smith, 2012). Children and adults are treated to an almost nonstop parade of aggressive models, in the media as well as in actual behavior. We are, without a doubt, an aggressive culture.

Media Violence In Module 27, we reviewed evidence that media exposure to violence may play a role in the social learning of aggressive behavior. Today's children and adolescents spend an average of 50 hours a week exploring various media, witnessing a strong dose of violence along the way (Rideout, Foehr, & Roberts, 2010). The Internet is of special concern because it not only allows children to vicariously experience violence, it also allows them to directly engage in *electronic aggression* through bullying or harassment of others (David-Ferdon & Hertz, 2009).

As Albert Bandura showed in his studies of imitation, children may learn new aggressive actions by watching violent or aggressive behavior, or they may learn that violence is "okay." In addition to teaching new antisocial actions, media such as television and video games may disinhibit dangerous impulses that viewers already have. *Disinhibition* (the removal of inhibition) results in acting out behavior that normally would be restrained. Another worry about media violence is that it may cause a *desensitization* (reduced emotional sensitivity) to violent acts (Carnagey, Anderson, & Bushman, 2007; Krahé et al., 2011).

How much does media violence actually affect children and adolescents? While some evidence suggests that widespread exposure to media violence contributes to aggression (Anderson, Gentile, & Buckley, 2007; Miller et al., 2012), there is disagreement as to the power or pervasiveness of the impact (Adachi & Willoughby, 2011a, b; Valadez & Ferguson, 2012).

Preventing Aggression

What can be done about aggression? Social learning theory implies that "aggression begets aggression." For example, children who are physically abused at home, those who suffer severe physical punishment, and those who merely witness violence in the community are more likely to be involved in fighting, aggressive play, and antisocial behavior at school (Bartholow, Sestir, & Davis, 2005; Margolin & Gordis, 2000).

Accordingly, one way to lower aggression may to reduce exposure to violent media. Parents can make a big difference if they do the following (Frydman, 1999; McKenna & Ossoff, 1998; Thoman, 2011):

1. Start by creating a safe, warm environment at home and school and by modeling positive ways of getting along in the world.

2. Limit total media time so that television and computer games do not dominate your child's view of the world. Don't use media as a babysitter.

3. Closely monitor what your child does experience. Change channels or turn off the television if you object to a program. Be prepared to offer games and activities that stimulate your child's imagination and creativity as well as model positive behavior and social attitudes.

4. Explore media with your child so that you can counter what is shown. Help your young child distinguish between reality and fantasy in media.

Let's close with some possible good news. Harvard University psychologist Steven Pinker has suggested that if you compare the amount of violence in the modern world with the more distant past, it appears we humans are losing our taste for aggression (Pinker, 2011). Improving human rights around the globe, along with reductions in slavery, executions, and torture are all signs that "the better angels of our nature" are in ascendancy.

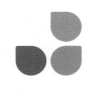

Prejudice—Attitudes That Injure

SURVEY QUESTION 73.2: What causes prejudice and intergroup conflict?

Love and friendship bring people together. Prejudice, which is marked by suspicion, fear, or hatred, has the opposite effect. **Prejudice**, an all too common part of daily life, is a negative emotional attitude held toward members of a specific social group (Biernat & Danaher, 2013). What are the origins of prejudice? How can prejudice and hurtful attitudes be reduced? Psychologists have provided valuable insights into these questions.

Prejudices may be reflected in the policies of police departments, schools, or government institutions (Harrell & Medford, 2012). In such cases, prejudice is referred to as *racism, sexism, ageism,* or *heterosexism,* depending on the group affected (Payne et al., 2010). Because it is so prevalent and damaging, let's focus on racism (Miller & Garran, 2008).

Both racial prejudice and racism lead to **discrimination**, or unequal treatment of people who should have the same rights as others. Discrimination prevents people from doing things they should be able to do, such as buying a house, getting a job, or attending a high-quality school (Whitley & Kite, 2010). For example, in many cities, African Americans have been the targets of "racial profiling," in which police stop them without reason. Sometimes, they are merely questioned, but many are cited for minor infractions, such as a cracked taillight or an illegal lane change. For many law-abiding citizens, being detained in this manner is a rude awakening (Plous, 2003). It's also one reason many African Americans and other minority persons in America distrust police and the legal system

Social learning theory *Combines learning principles with cognitive processes, socialization, and modeling to explain behavior.*
Prejudice *A negative emotional attitude held against members of a particular group of people.*
Discrimination *Treating members of various social groups differently in circumstances where their rights or treatment should be identical.*

(Dovidio et al., 2002). As distinguished African-American psychologist Kenneth Clark said, "Racial prejudice...debases all human beings—those who are its victims, those who victimize, and in quite subtle ways, those who are merely accessories."

Becoming Prejudiced

How do prejudices develop? One major theory suggests that prejudice is a form of *scapegoating* (blaming a person or a group for the actions of others or for conditions not of their making). Scapegoating is a type of *displaced aggression* in which hostilities triggered by frustration are redirected at "safer" targets (Glick, 2008; Nelson, 2006). One interesting classic test of this hypothesis was conducted at a summer camp for young men. The men were given a difficult test they were sure to fail. In addition, completing the test caused them to miss a trip to the movies, which was normally the high point of their weekly entertainment. Attitudes toward Mexicans and Japanese were measured before the test and after the men had failed the test and missed the movie. Participants in this study, all European Americans, consistently rated members of the two ethnic groups lower after being frustrated (Miller & Bugelski, 1948). This effect has been easy to observe since the September 11, 2001, terrorist attacks in the United States, as people who look "foreign" have become targets for displaced anger and hostility (Ahluwalia & Pellettiere, 2010).

At times, the development of prejudice (like other attitudes) can be traced to direct experiences with members of the rejected group. A child who is repeatedly bullied by members of a particular ethnic group might develop a lifelong dislike for all members of the group. Yet even subtle influences, such as parents' attitudes, the depiction of people in books and on television, and exposure to children of other races can have an impact. By the time they are three years old, many children show signs of race bias (Katz, 2003). Sadly, once prejudices are established, they prevent us from accepting more positive experiences that could reverse the damage (Wilder, Simon, & Faith, 1996).

Distinguished psychologist Gordon Allport (1958) concluded that there are two important sources of prejudice. *Personal prejudice* occurs when members of another ethnic group are perceived as a threat to one's own interests. For example, members of another group may be viewed as competitors for jobs. *Group prejudice* occurs when a person conforms to group norms. Let's say, for instance, that you have no personal reason for disliking out-group members. Nevertheless, your friends, acquaintances, or coworkers expect it of you.

The Prejudiced Personality

Other research suggests that prejudice can be a general personality characteristic. Theodore Adorno and his associates (1950) described what they called the *authoritarian personality*. These researchers started out by studying anti-Semitism. In the process, they found that people who are prejudiced against one group tend to be prejudiced against *all* out-groups (Kteily, Sidanius, & Levin, 2011; McAvoy, 2012).

What are the characteristics of the prejudice-prone personality? The **authoritarian personality** is marked by rigidity, inhibition, prejudice, and oversimplification (black-and-white thinking). In addition, authoritarians exhibit *right wing authoritarianism*, placing a highly value on social conformity (Duckitt & Sibley, 2010; Feldman, 2003). Authoritarians also tend to be very *ethnocentric*. **Ethnocentrism** refers to placing one's own group "at the center," usually by rejecting all other groups. In fact, authoritarians have a general *social dominance orientation* and think they are superior to everyone who is different, not just other ethnic groups (Altemeyer, 2004; Duckitt & Sibley, 2010).

To measure these qualities, the *F scale* was created (the *F* stands for *fascism*). This scale is made up of statements such as the ones that follow—to which authoritarians readily agree (Adorno et al., 1950):

Authoritarian Beliefs

- Obedience and respect for authority are the most important virtues children should learn.

- People can be divided into two distinct classes: the weak and the strong.

- If people would talk less and work more, everybody would be better off.

- What this country needs most, more than laws and political programs, is a few courageous, tireless, devoted leaders, in whom the people can put their faith.

- Nobody ever learns anything really important except through suffering.

- Every person should have complete faith in some supernatural power whose decisions are obeyed without question.

- Certain religious sects that refuse to salute the flag should be forced to conform to such patriotic action or else be abolished.

As you can see, authoritarians are rather close-minded (Butler, 2000; Roets & Van Hiel, 2011). As children, most were severely punished. As a result, they learned to fear authority (and to covet it) at an early age. In general, people are more likely to express authoritarian beliefs when they feel threatened. An example would be calling for more severe punishment in schools when the economy is bad and job insecurities are high.

It should be readily apparent from the list of authoritarian beliefs that the F scale is slanted toward politically conservative authoritarians. To be fair, rigid and authoritarian personalities can be found at both ends of the political scale (Ray, 1983). It may be better, therefore, preferred to describe rigid and intolerant thinking as dogmatism, an unwarranted certainty in matters of belief or opinion. Dogmatic persons find it difficult to change their beliefs, even when the evidence contradicts them (Butler, 2000; White-Ajmani & Bursik, 2011).

Even if we discount the obvious bigotry of the authoritarian personality, racial prejudice runs deep in many nations. Let's probe deeper into the roots of such prejudiced behavior.

Intergroup Conflict—The Roots of Prejudice

An unfortunate by-product of group membership is that it often limits contact with people in other groups. In addition, groups themselves may come into conflict. Both events tend to foster hatred and prejudice toward the out-group. The bloody clashes of opposing forces in the Middle East, Africa, Ireland, and Hometown, U.S.A. are reminders that intergroup conflict is widespread. Daily, we read of jarring strife between political, religious, or ethnic groups. How much of a role, we wonder, did factors such as these influence the 2013 Boston Marathon bombings?

Shared beliefs concerning *superiority, injustice, vulnerability,* and *distrust* are common triggers for hostility between groups. Pick almost any group in conflict with others and you will find people thinking along these lines: "We are special people who are superior to other groups, but we have been unjustly exploited, wronged, or humiliated [superiority and injustice]. Other groups are a threat to us [vulnerability]. They are dishonest and have repeatedly betrayed us [distrust]. Naturally, we are hostile toward them. They don't deserve our respect or cooperation" (Eidelson & Eidelson, 2003; Whitley & Kite, 2010).

In addition to hostile beliefs about other groups, conflicts are almost always amplified and even justified by stereotyped images of out-group members (Crandall et al., 2011; Pereira, Estramiana, & Gallo, 2010).

What exactly is a stereotype? Social stereotypes are oversimplified images of people in various groups. There is a good chance that you have stereotyped images of some of the following: African Americans, European Americans, Hispanics, Jews, women, Christians, old people, men, Asian Americans, blue-collar workers, rednecks, politicians, business executives, teenagers, or billionaires (● Figure 73.3). In general, the top three categories on which most stereotypes are based are sex, age, and race (Fiske et al., 2002).

Sam Forencich/National Basketball Association/Getty Images

● **Figure 73.3**

Racial stereotypes are common in sports. For example, a study confirmed that many people actually believe that "white men can't jump." This stereotype implies that black basketball players are naturally superior in athletic ability. White players, in contrast, are falsely perceived as smarter and harder working than black players. Such stereotypes set up expectations that distort the perceptions of fans, coaches, and sportswriters. The resulting misperceptions, in turn, help perpetuate the stereotypes (Stone, Perry, & Darley, 1997).

Authoritarian personality *A personality pattern characterized by rigidity, inhibition, prejudice, and an excessive concern with power, authority, and obedience.*
Ethnocentrism *Placing one's own group or race at the center—that is, tending to reject all other groups but one's own.*
Dogmatism *An unwarranted positiveness or certainty in matters of belief or opinion.*
Social stereotypes *Oversimplified images of the traits of individuals who belong to a particular social group.*

Human Diversity

Choking on Stereotypes

Bill, a retired aircraft mechanic, has agreed to talk to a group of high school students about the early days of commercial aviation. During his talk, Bill is concerned that any slip in his memory will confirm stereotypes about older people being forgetful. Because he is anxious and preoccupied about possible memory lapses, Bill actually "chokes" as he suffers problems with his memory (Mazerolle et al., 2012).

As Bill's example suggests, negative stereotypes can have a self-fulfilling quality. This is especially true in situations in which a person's abilities are evaluated. For example, African American and other minority group students must often cope with negative stereotypes about their academic abilities (Steele & Aronson, 1995; Owens & Massey, 2011). Could such stereotypes actually impair school performance?

Psychologist Claude Steele has amassed evidence that victims of stereotyping tend to feel **stereotype threat**. They can feel threatened when they think they are being judged in terms of a stereotype.

The anxiety that this causes can then lower performance, seemingly confirming the stereotype (Inzlicht & Schmader, 2012). An experiment Steele did demonstrates this effect. In the study, African-American and European-American college students took a very difficult verbal test. Some students were told the test measured *academic ability*. Others were told that the test was a laboratory *problem-solving task* unrelated to ability. In the ability condition, African-American students performed worse than European Americans. In the problem-solving condition, they performed the same as European Americans (Steele, 1997; Steele & Aronson, 1995). A similar effect occurs with women, who score lower on math and finance tests after being reminded of the stereotype that "women aren't good at math" (Cadinu et al., 2005; Carr & Steele, 2010).

In light of such findings, Steele and others are currently working on ways to combat stereotype threat, so that all students can use their potentials more fully (Bowen, Wegmann, & Webber, 2013; Alter et al., 2010; Cohen et al., 2009).

Stereotypes tend to simplify people into "us" and "them" categories. However, aside from the fact that they always oversimplify, stereotypes often include a mixture of *positive* or *negative* qualities. Even though stereotypes sometimes include positive traits, they are mainly used to control people. When a person is stereotyped, the easiest thing to do is to abide by others' expectations—even if they are demeaning. That's why no one likes to be stereotyped. Being forced into a small, distorted social "box" is limiting and insulting. Stereotypes rob people of their individuality (Maddox, 2004).

It is especially damaging when people begin to *self-stereotype*, halfway believing the stereotypes applied to them or at least worrying about how they appear in the presence of stereotypers (Latrofa et al., 2010; Tine & Gotlieb, 2013); see "Choking on Stereotypes." Without stereotypes, there would be far less hate, prejudice, exclusion, and conflict.

Today's racism is often disguised by **symbolic prejudice**—that is, many people realize that crude and obvious racism is socially unacceptable. However, this may not stop them from expressing prejudice in subtly veiled forms when they state their opinions about affirmative action, busing, immigration, crime, and so on (Anderson, 2010b). In effect, modern racists find ways to rationalize their prejudice so that it seems to be based on issues other than raw racism.

Michel Friang/Alamy

Ethnic pride is slowly replacing stereotypes and discrimination. For example, different Native American groups publicly celebrate their own festivals with pride. However, despite affirmations of ethnic heritage, the problem of prejudice is far from solved.

For instance, an African American candidate and a European American candidate apply for a job. Both are only moderately qualified for the position. If the person making the hiring decision is European American, who gets the job? As you might guess, the European American candidate is much more likely to be hired. In other words, the European American candidate will be given "the benefit of the doubt" about his or her abilities, whereas the African American candidate won't. People making such decisions often believe that they aren't being prejudiced, but they unconsciously discriminate against minorities (Berg, 2013; Dovidio et al., 2002).

Note, too, that when a prejudiced person meets a pleasant or likable member of a rejected group, the out-group member tends to be perceived as "an exception to the rule," not as evidence against the stereotype. This prevents prejudiced persons from changing their stereotyped beliefs (Asgari, Dasgupta, & Stout, 2012). In addition, some elements of prejudice are unconscious, which makes them difficult to change (Dovidio et al., 2002).

How do stereotypes and intergroup tensions develop? Two experiments, both in unlikely settings and both using children as participants, offer some insight into these problems.

Experiments in Prejudice

What is it like to be discriminated against? In a unique experiment, elementary school teacher Jane Elliott sought to give her pupils direct experience with prejudice. On the first day of the experiment, Elliott announced that brown-eyed children were to sit in the back of the room and that they could not use the drinking fountain. Blue-eyed children were given extra recess time and got to leave first for lunch. At lunch, brown-eyed children were prevented from taking second helpings because they would "just waste it." Brown-eyed and blue-eyed children were kept from mingling, and the blue-eyed children were told they were "cleaner" and "smarter" (Peters, 1971).

Eye color might seem like a trivial basis for creating prejudices. However, people use primarily skin color to make decisions about the race of another person (Glenn, 2009). Surely this is just as superficial a way of judging people as using eye color, especially given recent biological evidence that it does not even make genetic sense to talk about "races" (Bonham, Warshauer-Baker, & Collins, 2005; see "Understand That Race Is a Social Construction" in Module 74).

At first, Elliott made an effort to constantly criticize and belittle the brown-eyed children. To her surprise, the blue-eyed children rapidly joined in and were soon outdoing her in the viciousness of their attacks. The blue-eyed children began to feel superior, and the brown-eyed children felt just plain awful. Fights broke out. Test scores of the brown-eyed children fell.

Are these children of different "races"? Yes, this *is* a trick question. Only skin color differentiates these nonidentical twins. The odds, by the way, of mixed race parents having a pair of twins like these two are one in a million. How fair will it be when these two children experience differential treatment based solely on their skin color?

How lasting were the effects of this experiment? The effects were short lived, because two days later the children's roles were reversed. Before long, the same destructive effects occurred again, but this time in reverse. The implications of this experiment are unmistakable. In less than one day it was possible to get children to hate each other because of eye color and *status inequalities*—differences in power, prestige, or privileges. Certainly the effects of a lifetime of real-life racial or ethnic prejudice are infinitely more powerful and destructive. (See "Is America Purple?") Racism is a major source of stress in the lives of many people of color. Over time, prejudice can have a negative impact on a person's physical and emotional health (Brondolo et al., 2011).

Combatting Prejudice

What can be done to combat prejudice? Several lines of thought (including cognitive dissonance theory) suggest that more frequent *equal-status contact* between groups in conflict should reduce prejudice and stereotyping (Koschate & van Dick, 2011; Wernet et al., 2003). Equal-status contact refers to interacting on an equal footing, without obvious differences in power or status. In various studies, mixed-race

Stereotype threat *The anxiety caused by the fear of being judged in terms of a stereotype.*
Symbolic prejudice *Prejudice that is expressed in disguised fashion.*

Critical Thinking

Is America Purple?

As research shows, it is easy to create prejudice. Pick any simplistic way to divide a group of people into "us" and "them" and popularize it. That's what teacher Jane Elliott did when she divided her class into the brown-eyed kids and the blue-eyed kids. In no time at all, the groups were prejudiced against each other.

But that was just an experiment. It couldn't happen in the real world, right? According to psychologists Conor Seyle and Matthew Newman (2006), we are witnessing just such a real-world example in America today. In order to graphically convey the outcome of the presidential vote in the 2000 election, *USA Today* created a state-by-state map, color-coded red and blue to denote states that had voted for the Republican candidate or the Democratic candidate.

Just a few years later, "red" and "blue" have become a national shorthand for dividing Americans into opposing camps. The "reds" are supposed to be Republican, conservative, middle-class, rural, religious, and live in the American heartland. The "blues" are supposed to be Democrat, liberal, upper class, urban, nonreligious, and live on the coasts. The end result is that the complex American social world is reduced to two oversimplified stereotypes, leading to an increase in between-group prejudice (Binning et al., 2010; Mundy, 2004).

This oversimplification ignores the fact that, in many states, the presidential votes are very close. Thus, a state that is "red" by 51 percent is nevertheless 49 percent "blue." Besides, many different combinations exist. Former President Bill Clinton is originally from Arkansas (a "red" state), identifies himself as a Southern Baptist, and worships in a Methodist church. Is he "blue"? How do you categorize someone from California (a "blue" state) who is an economic conservative, attends church occasionally, lives in San Francisco, supports gay marriage, and yet votes Republican?

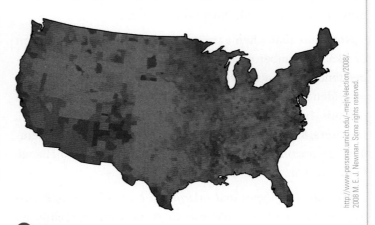

● **Figure 73.4**

Purple America map. Counties within states voting more than 70 percent Republican appear in red; areas voting more than 70 percent Democratic appear in blue. Shades of purple represent intermediate percentages of voters. (Reprinted by permission of the authors, Michael Gastner, Cosma Shalizi, and Mark Newman, University of Michigan.)

According to Seyle & Newman (2006), a better approach is to recognize that America is made of a full spectrum of political, social, religious, and economic views and that most Americans are "purple." Thinking this way also highlights the fact that Americans of all political persuasions share more similarities than they do differences when compared with the citizens of other countries. This more tolerant, less polarizing view of America is reflected in the "purple America" map (Gastner, Shalizi, & Newman, 2005; ● **Figure 73.4**). Thinking purple just might result in a more productive national discussion about the important issues facing America today. ·

groups have been formed at work, in the laboratory, and at schools. The conclusion from such research is that personal contact with a disliked group tends to induce friendly behavior, respect, and liking. However, these benefits occur only when personal contact is cooperative and on an equal footing (Grack & Richman, 1996).

Superordinate Goals Let's now consider a revealing study done with 11-year-old boys. When the boys arrived at a summer camp, they were split into two groups and housed in separate cabins. At first, the groups were kept apart to build up separate identities and friendships. Soon each group had a flag and a name (the "Rattlers" and the "Eagles") and each had staked out its territory. At this point, the two groups were placed in competition with each other. After several clashes, dislike between the groups bordered on hatred: The boys baited each other, started fights, and raided each other's cabins (Sherif et al., 1961).

Were they allowed to go home hating each other? As an experiment in reducing intergroup conflict, and to prevent the boys from remaining enemies, various strategies to reduce tensions were tried. Holding meetings between group leaders did nothing. When the groups were invited to eat together, the event turned into a free-for-all. Finally, emergencies that required *cooperation* among members of both groups were staged at the camp. For example, the water supply was damaged so that all the boys had to work together to repair it. These emergencies created **superordinate goals** that exceeded or overrode the lesser competitive goals. Creating this and other superordinate goals helped restore peace between the two groups.

Many school districts in the United States require students to wear uniforms. Appearance (including gang colors) is one of the major reasons kids treat each other differently. Uniforms help minimize status inequalities and in-group/out-group distinctions. In Long Beach, California, a switch to uniforms was followed by a 91 percent drop in student assaults, thefts, vandalism, and weapons and drug violations (Ritter, 1998).

Cooperation and shared goals seem to help reduce conflict by encouraging people in opposing groups to see themselves as members of a single, larger group (Gaertner et al., 2000). Superordinate goals, in other words, have a "we're all in the same boat" effect on perceptions of group membership. The power of superordinate goals can be seen in the unity that prevailed in the United States (and throughout much of the rest of the world) for months after the September 11 terrorist attacks. Superordinate goals also are an important factor in helping peacekeepers constructively engage with people from other nationalities (Boniecki & Britt, 2003; Whitley & Kite, 2010).

Can such goals exist on a global scale? One example might be a desire to deal with the current global energy crisis. Another is the need to preserve the natural environment on a global scale. Still another is the continuing threat posed by terrorism and religious extremism. Politically, such goals may be far from universal. But their superordinate quality is clearly evident.

"Jigsaw" Classrooms Contrary to the hopes of many, integrating public schools often has little positive effect on racial prejudice. In fact, prejudice may be made worse, and the self-esteem of minority students frequently decreases (Aronson, 2012; Binder et al., 2009).

If integrated schools provide equal-status contact, shouldn't prejudice be reduced? Theoretically, yes. But in practice, minority group children often enter schools unprepared to compete on an equal footing. The competitive nature of schools almost guarantees that children will *not* learn to like and understand each other.

With the preceding in mind, social psychologist Elliot Aronson pioneered a way to apply superordinate goals to ordinary classrooms. According to Aronson, such goals are effective because they create **mutual interdependence**—that is, people must depend on one another to meet each person's goals. When individual needs are linked, cooperation is encouraged (Deutsch, 1993; Güth, Levati, & von Wangenheim, 2010).

How has that idea been applied? Aronson has created "jigsaw" classrooms that emphasize cooperation rather than competition. The term *jigsaw* refers to the pieces of a jigsaw puzzle. In a **jigsaw classroom**, each child is given a "piece" of the information needed to complete a project or prepare for a test.

In a typical session, children are divided into groups of five or six and given a topic to study for a later exam. Each child is given his or her "piece" of information and asked to learn it. For example, one child might have information on Thomas Edison's invention of the light bulb; another, facts about his invention of the long-playing phonograph record; and a third, information about Edison's childhood. After the children have learned their parts, they teach them to others in the group. Even the most competitive children quickly realize that they cannot do well without the aid of everyone in the group. Each child makes a unique and essential contribution, so the children learn to listen to and respect each other.

Does the jigsaw method work? Compared with children in traditional classrooms, children in jigsaw groups are less prejudiced, they like their classmates more, they have more positive attitudes toward school, their grades improve, and their self-esteem increases (Aronson, 2012; Walker & Crogan, 1998). Such results are quite encouraging.

To summarize, prejudice will be reduced when the following happens:

- Members of different groups have equal status *within the situation* that brings them together.
- Members of all groups seek a common goal.
- Group members must cooperate to reach the goal.
- Group members spend enough time together for cross-group friendships to develop.

Superordinate goal *A goal that exceeds or overrides all others; a goal that renders other goals relatively less important.*
Mutual interdependence *A condition in which two or more persons must depend on one another to meet each person's needs or goals.*
Jigsaw classroom *A method of reducing prejudice; each student receives only part of the information needed to complete a project or prepare for a test.*

Module 73: Summary

73.1 How do psychologists explain human aggression?

- **73.1.1** Aggression is a fact of life, but humans are not inevitably aggressive. The same factors that help explain aggression can form the basis for preventing it.
- **73.1.2** Instinctual explanations of aggression attribute it to inherited instincts. Biological explanations of aggression emphasize brain mechanisms and physical factors that lower the threshold for aggression.
- **73.1.3** According to the frustration-aggression hypothesis, frustration and aggression are closely linked.
- **73.1.4** Frustration is only one of many aversive stimuli that can arouse a person and make aggression more likely. Aggression is especially likely to occur when aggression cues are present.
- **73.1.5** Social learning theory has focused attention on the role of aggressive models in the development of aggressive behavior.

73.2 What causes prejudice and intergroup conflict?

- **73.2.1** Prejudice is a negative attitude held toward members of various out-groups.
- **73.2.2** One theory attributes prejudice to scapegoating. A second account says that prejudices may be held for personal reasons (personal prejudice) or simply through adherence to group norms (group prejudice).
- **73.2.3** Prejudiced individuals tend to have an authoritarian or dogmatic personality, characterized by rigidity, inhibition, intolerance, oversimplification, and ethnocentrism.
- **73.2.4** Intergroup conflict gives rise to hostility and the formation of social stereotypes. Status inequalities tend to build prejudice. Equal-status contact tends to reduce it.
- **73.2.5** Superordinate goals are a key to reducing intergroup conflict.
- **73.2.6** On a smaller scale, jigsaw classrooms (which encourage cooperation through mutual interdependence) have been shown to be an effective way of combating prejudice.

Module 73: Knowledge Builder

Recite

1. The *weapons effect* refers to the impact that _____ have on behavior.
   a. just-world beliefs
   b. aggression cues
   c. self-fulfilling prophecies
   d. televised models

2. The point of view most at odds with the idea that humans are instinctively aggressive is
   a. social learning theory
   b. the frustration-aggression hypothesis
   c. ethology
   d. the aversive stimuli effect

3. Heavy exposure to media results in lowered emotional sensitivity to violence. *T or F?*

4. Some expressions of prejudice can be thought of as scapegoating or
   a. displaced aggression
   b. empathic arousal
   c. reference group reversal
   d. external attribution

5. The authoritarian personality tends to be prejudiced against all out-groups, a quality referred to as _____.

6. The term *symbolic prejudice* refers to racism or prejudice that is expressed in disguised or hidden form. *T or F?*

7. Jigsaw classrooms use _____ to create mutual interdependence.
   a. social competition
   b. just-world beliefs
   c. self-fulfilling prophecies
   d. superordinate goals

Reflect

Think Critically

8. In court trials, defense lawyers sometimes try to identify and eliminate prospective jurors who have authoritarian personality traits. Can you guess why?

Self-Reflect

Which concepts or theories do you think best explain your own aggressive actions? Does the most rigid person you know match the profile of the authoritarian personality? Stereotypes exist for many social categories, even ordinary ones such as "college student" or "unmarried young adult." What stereotypes do you think you face in daily life? Do they generate stereotype threat in you?

The director of a youth recreation center is concerned about the amount of conflict she is seeing between boys and girls from different racial and ethnic groups. What advice can you give the director?

ANSWERS

1. b 2. a 3. T 4. a 5. ethnocentrism 6. T 7. d 8. Authoritarians tend to believe that punishment is effective so they are more likely to vote for conviction.

CENGAGE brain.com

Psychology in Action: Multiculturalism

Tolerance and Acceptance

Most people publicly support policies of equality and fairness. Yet, many still have lingering biases and negative images of African Americans, Latinos, Muslim Americans, and other ethnic minorities. How can we make sense of such conflicting attitudes? While it is an admirable step, making a conscious decision to forsake prejudice does not immediately eliminate *implicit prejudice*, unconscious prejudiced thoughts and feelings about members of other ethnic groups. Quite likely, this reflects lingering stereotypes and prejudices learned in childhood.

For many people, becoming less prejudiced begins by accepting the value of *openness to the other*, the ability to genuinely appreciate those who differ from us culturally. It is important to remember that being open to someone else does not mean that you have to agree with that person or turn

John Wilkes/Bridge/Corbis

your back on your own culture. Openness, in turn, leads to the acceptance of the values of tolerance and equality. Are you open to openness? If so, read on.

SURVEY QUESTION

74.1 How can we promote multiculturalism and social harmony?

Multiculturalism—Living with Diversity

SURVEY QUESTION 74.1: How can we promote multiculturalism and social harmony?

Today's society is more like a "tossed salad" than a cultural "melting pot." Rather than expecting everyone to be alike, psychologists believe that we must learn to respect and appreciate our differences. **Multiculturalism**, as this is called, gives equal status to different ethnic, racial, and cultural groups. It is a recognition and acceptance of human diversity (Alleyne, 2011; Moghaddam, 2007).

Breaking the Prejudice Habit

People who value tolerance resist intolerant thoughts or feelings, which motivates them to try to alter their own biased reactions

(Binning et al., 2010; Dovidio & Gaertner, 1999). But doing so is not easy. Typically, to overcome unconscious **implicit prejudice** requires repeated efforts to learn to think, feel, and act differently (Anderson, 2010b; Nosek, Greenwald, & Banaji, 2005). Nevertheless, many people have succeeded in overcoming the "prejudice habit" and have become more open to life experiences in general (Fowers & Davidov, 2006). If you would like to be more open and tolerant, the following points may be helpful.

Beware of Stereotyping Stereotypes make the social world more manageable. But placing people in categories almost always causes them to appear more similar than they really are. As a result, we tend to see out-group members as very much alike, even when they are as varied as our friends and family. People who are not prejudiced work hard to actively inhibit stereotyped thoughts and to emphasize fairness and equality.

Seek Individuating Information A good way to tear down stereotypes is to get to know individuals from various ethnic and cultural groups (Inzlicht, Gutsell, & Legault, 2012; Roets & Van Hiel, 2011). Typically, we are most tempted to apply stereotypes when we have only minimal information about a person. Stereotypes help us guess what a person is like and how he or she will act. Unfortunately, these inferences are usually wrong.

One of the best antidotes for stereotypes is **individuating information**—information that helps us see a person as an individual rather than as a member of a group (Cameron & Trope, 2004; Lan Yeung & Kashima, 2010). Anything that keeps us from placing a person in a particular social category tends to negate stereotyped thinking. When you meet individuals from various backgrounds, focus on the *person*, not the *label* attached to him or her.

A good example of the effects of individuating information comes from a Canadian study of English-speaking students in a French language program. Students who were "immersed" (spent most of their waking hours with French Canadians) became more positive toward them. Immersed students were more likely to say they had come to appreciate and like French Canadians; they were more willing to meet and interact with them; and they saw themselves as less different from French Canadians (Lambert, 1987). In fact, with more subtle kinds of symbolic prejudice, such contact may be the best way to reduce intergroup conflict (Dovidio & Gaertner, 1999).

Don't Fall Prey to Just-World Beliefs
Do you believe that the world is basically fair? Even if you don't, you may believe that the world is sufficiently just so that people generally get what they deserve. It may not be obvious, but such beliefs can directly increase prejudiced thinking (Bizer, Hart, & Jekogian, 2012; Hafer & Bègue, 2005).

As a result of discrimination, social conditions, and circumstances (such as recent immigration), minorities may occupy lower socioeconomic positions (Whitley & Kite, 2010). **Just-world beliefs**—beliefs that people generally get what they deserve—can lead us to assume that minority group members wouldn't be in such positions if they weren't inferior in some way. This bit of faulty thinking amounts to blaming people who are *victims* of prejudice and discrimination for their plight. For example, assuming that a poor person is lazy may overlook the fact that discrimination in hiring has made it very difficult for him or her to find a job.

Be Aware of Self-Fulfilling Prophecies
As noted elsewhere (see, for example, Module 71), people tend to act in accordance with the behavior expected by others. If you hold strong stereotypes about members of various groups, a vicious cycle can occur. When you meet someone who is different from yourself, you may treat him or her in a way that is consistent with your stereotypes. If the other person is influenced by your behavior, he or she may act in ways that seem to match your stereotype. For example, a person who believes that members of another ethnic group are hostile and unfriendly will probably treat people in that group in ways that provoke hostile and unfriendly response. This creates a **self-fulfilling prophecy**—an expectation that prompts people to act in ways that make the expectation come true—in turn reinforcing belief in the stereotype.

Remember, Different Does Not Mean Inferior
Some conflicts between groups cannot be avoided. What *can* be avoided is unnecessary **social competition**—rivalry among groups, each of which regards itself as superior to others. The concept of social competition refers to the fact that some individuals seek to enhance their self-esteem by identifying with a group. However, this works only if the group can be seen as superior to others. Because of social competition, groups tend to view themselves as better than their rivals (Baron, Byrne, & Branscombe, 2012). In one survey, every major ethnic group in the United States rated itself as better than any other group (Njeri, 1991).

A person who has high self-esteem does not need to treat others as inferior in order to feel good about himself or herself. Similarly, it is not necessary to degrade other groups in order to feel positive about one's own group identity (Fowers & Davidov, 2006). In fact, each ethnic group has strengths that members of other groups could benefit from emulating. For instance, African Americans, Asian Americans, and Latinos emphasize family networks that help buffer them from some of the stresses of daily life (Suinn, 1999).

Understand That Race Is a Social Construction
From the viewpoint of modern genetics, the concept of race has absolutely no meaning (Bonham, Warshauer-Baker, & Collins,

---

Multiculturalism *Giving equal status, recognition, and acceptance to different ethnic and cultural groups.*

Implicit prejudice *Unconscious prejudiced thoughts and feelings about members of other ethnic groups.*

Individuating information *Information that helps define a person as an individual, rather than as a member of a group or social category.*

Just-world beliefs *Beliefs that people generally get what they deserve.*

Self-fulfilling prophecy *An expectation that prompts people to act in ways that make the expectation come true.*

Social competition *Rivalry among groups, each of which regards itself as superior to others.*

2005; Sternberg, Grigorenko, & Kidd, 2005). Members of various groups are so varied genetically and human groups have intermixed for so many centuries that it is impossible to tell, biologically, to what "race" any given individual belongs. Thus, race is an illusion based on superficial physical differences and learned ethnic identities. Certainly people *act as if* different races exist (Glenn, 2009). But this is a matter of social labeling, not biological reality. To assume that any human group is biologically superior or inferior is simply wrong. In fact, the best available evidence suggests that all people are descended from the same ancient ancestors. The origins of our species lie in Africa, about 100,000 years ago. Among early human populations, darker skin was a protective adaptation to sun exposure near the equator (Jablonski & Chaplin, 2000). Biologically, we are all brothers and sisters under the skin (Graves, 2001; Smedley & Smedley, 2005).

Look for Commonalities We live in a society that puts a premium on competition and individual effort. One problem with this is that competing with others fosters desires to demean, defeat, and vanquish them. When we cooperate with others, we tend to share their joys and suffer when they are in distress (Aronson, 2012). If we don't find ways to cooperate and live in greater harmony, everyone will suffer. That, if nothing else, is one thing we all have in common. Everyone knows what it feels like to be different. Greater tolerance comes from remembering those times.

Tolerance and Cultural Awareness

Living comfortably in a multicultural society means being open to other groups. Getting acquainted with a person whose cultural background is different from your own can be a wonderful learning experience (Matsumoto & Juang, 2008). No one culture has all the answers or the best ways of doing things. Multicultural populations enrich a community's food, music, arts, and philosophy. Likewise, openness toward different racial, cultural, and ethnic groups can be personally rewarding (Fowers & Davidov, 2006).

The importance of cultural awareness often lies in subtleties and details. For example, in large American cities, many small stores are owned by Korean immigrants. Some of these Korean-American merchants have been criticized for being cold and hostile to their customers. Refusing to place change directly in customers' hands, for instance, helped trigger an African-American boycott of Korean grocers in New York City. The core of the problem was a lack of cultural awareness on both sides.

In America, if you walk into a store, you expect the clerk to be courteous to you. One way of showing politeness is by smiling. But in the Confucian-steeped Korean culture, a smile is reserved for family members and close friends. If a Korean or Korean American has no reason to smile, he or she just doesn't smile. There's a Korean saying: "If you smile a lot, you're silly." Expressions such as "thank you" and "excuse me" also are used sparingly, and strangers rarely touch each other—not even to return change.

Here's another example of how ignorance of cultural practices can lead to needless friction and misunderstanding: An African-American woman who wanted to ease racial tensions took a freshly baked pie to her neighbors across the way, who were Orthodox Jews. At the front door the woman extended her hand, not knowing that Orthodox Jews don't shake women's hands unless the woman is a close family member. Once she was inside, she picked up a kitchen knife to cut the pie, not knowing the couple kept a kosher household and used different knives for different foods. The woman's well-intentioned attempt at neighborliness ended in an argument! Knowing a little more about each other's cultures could have prevented both the conflicts just described.

Module 74: Summary

74.1 How can we promote multiculturalism and social harmony?

- **74.1.1** Multiculturalism is a recognition and acceptance of human diversity.
- **74.1.2** Multicultural harmony can be attained through conscious efforts to be more tolerant of others.

- **74.1.3** Greater tolerance can be encouraged by neutralizing stereotypes with individuating information; by looking for commonalities with others; and by avoiding the effects of just-world beliefs, self-fulfilling prophecies, and social competition.
- **74.1.4** Cultural awareness is a key element in promoting greater social harmony.

Module 74: Knowledge Builder

Recite

1. *Multiculturalism* refers to the belief that various subcultures and ethnic groups should be blended into a single emergent culture. **T or F?**

2. Many people who don't have prejudiced beliefs still have prejudiced thoughts and feelings in the presence of minority group individuals. **T or F?**

3. One of the best antidotes for stereotypes is
   a. accepting just-world beliefs
   b. individuating information
   c. accepting self-fulfilling prophecies
   d. honest social competition

4. Just-world beliefs are the primary cause of social competition. **T or F?**

Reflect

Think Critically

5. Why is it valuable to learn the terms by which members of various groups prefer to be addressed (for example, Mexican-American, Latino [or Latina], Hispanic, or Chicano [Chicana])?

Self-Reflect

Which strategies for breaking the prejudice habit do you already use? How could you apply the remaining strategies to become more tolerant?

_____

ANSWERS

1. F 2. T 3. b 4. F 5. Labels might have negative meanings that are not apparent to persons outside the group. People who are culturally aware allow others to define their own identities, rather than imposing labels on them.

CENGAGE brain.com

Go to **cengagebrain.com** to access **MindTap for Coon/Mitterer** *Psychology Modules for Active Learning* and other online learning tools. MindTap is a fully online learning experience that combines all the tools you need—readings, multimedia, activities, and assessments—into a singular personalized Learning Path that guides you through the course.

Applied Psychology: Industrial/Organizational Psychology

Punching the Clock

Have you ever had a job that made you feel like a cog in a machine? Charlie Chaplin captured this feeling in his 1936 film *Modern Times*. Fortunately, the world of work has changed since Chaplin's day. Consider Armando, a software engineer working long hours developing a novel way to predict hurricanes for a satellite weather system. His work efficiency cannot easily be measured or improved. Instead, Armando's success depends on his own initiative, creativity, and commitment to his work. Armando quit his last job because it made him feel like he was "punching the clock," which is something he does not want to do.

Do you believe you should live to work or work to live? Whatever your attitude, the simple fact is that most adults work for a living. Whether you are already employed or plan to

CHAPLIN/UNITED ARTISTS/THE KOBAL COLLECTION

begin a career after college, it helps to know something about the psychology of work and organizations.

SURVEY QUESTION

75.1 How is psychology applied in business and industry?

Industrial/Organizational Psychology—Psychology at Work

SURVEY QUESTION 75.1: How is psychology applied in business and industry?

Applied psychology refers to the use of psychological principles and research methods to solve practical problems. The largest applied areas are clinical and counseling psychology, but there are many others, such as community psychology, educational psychology, military psychology, consumer psychology, sports psychology, health psychology, and space psychology.

Industrial/organizational (I/O) psychology, the study of people at work and in organizations, is one of the most important applied areas (Aamodt, 2013; Bryan & Vinchur,

2013). The efforts of I/O psychologists likely will affect how you are selected for a job and tested, trained, or evaluated for promotion. Most I/O psychologists are employed by the government, industry, and businesses. Typically, they work in two major areas: (1) studying jobs to identify underlying skills, which can then guide efforts to select people and train them for those jobs (the *industrial* part), and (2) studying organizations to understand how to create structures and company cultures that will improve worker performance (the *organizational* part). To get a better idea of what I/O psychologists do, look at ● Table 75.1. As you can see, their interests are quite varied.

A key person in any organization is its leader (Hodson & Sullivan, 2012). Family therapist and rabbi Edwin Friedman once remarked, "Leadership can be thought of as a capacity to define oneself to others in a way that clarifies and expands a vision of the future." How do great business leaders inspire their followers?

TABLE 75.1	Topics of Special Interest to Industrial/ Organizational Psychologists
Absenteeism	Minority workers
Decision making	Pay schedules
Design of organizations	Personnel selection
Employee stress	Personnel training
Employee turnover	Productivity
Interviewing	Promotion
Job enrichment	Task analysis
Job satisfaction	Task design
Labor relations	Work behavior
Leadership	Work environment
Machine design	Work motivation
Management styles	Worker evaluations

© Cengage Learning

Theory X Leadership

During many lunch hours at a major computer game developer, most of the employees, including the top executives, eat together while playing computer games (and no, the "bosses" don't always win), talking, and joking. To say the least, these are unusual working conditions. To understand the rationale behind them, let's consider two basic theories of leadership.

One of the earliest attempts to improve worker efficiency was made in 1923 by Frederick Taylor, an engineer. To speed up production, Taylor standardized work routines and stressed careful planning, control, and orderliness. Today, versions of Taylor's approach are called **scientific management**, or **theory X leadership** for reasons explained shortly. Scientific management uses time-and-motion studies, task analysis, job specialization, assembly lines, pay schedules, and the like to increase productivity (Crowley et al., 2010; Paton, 2013).

It sounds like scientific management treats people as if they were machines. Is that true? To some extent it is. In Taylor's day, many large companies were manufacturers with giant assembly lines. People had to be efficient cogs in the manufacturing machinery. Leaders who follow Theory X have a task orientation, focusing on the work to be done, rather than a person orientation, focusing on the people doing the work. As such, they tend to assume that workers must be goaded or

guided into being productive. Many psychologists working in business, of course, are concerned with improving **work efficiency**, defined as maximum output at lowest cost. As a result, they alter conditions they believe will affect workers (such as time schedules, work quotas, bonuses, and so on). Some might even occasionally wish that people would act like well-oiled machines.

However, most recognize that psychological efficiency is just as important as work efficiency. **Psychological efficiency** refers to maintaining good morale, labor relations, employee satisfaction, and similar aspects of work behavior. Leadership styles that ignore or mishandle the human element can be devastatingly costly. Studies have consistently found that happy workers are productive workers (Dik, Byrne, & Steger, 2013; Lerner & Henke, 2008).

Theory Y Leadership

The term *Theory X* was coined by psychologist Douglas McGregor (1960) as a way to distinguish the leadership style associated with scientific management from *Theory Y*, a newer approach, which emphasizes human relations at work.

How is this approach different? **Theory Y leaders** have a person orientation rather than a task orientation and tend to assume that workers enjoy autonomy and are willing to accept responsibility. They also assume that a worker's needs and goals can be meshed with the company's goals and that people are not naturally passive or lazy.

Aren't women more person-oriented than men? And doesn't that imply that women would make better Theory Y leaders? Good thinking. As person-oriented Theory Y leadership styles have become more popular, women have been slowly gaining acceptance as leaders (Ayman & Korabik, 2010; Eagly, 2013). (See "From Glass Ceiling to Labyrinth.")

Applied psychology *The use of psychological principles and research methods to solve practical problems.*
Industrial/organizational (I/O) psychology *A field that focuses on the psychology of work and on behavior within organizations.*
Theory X leadership (scientific management) *An approach to leadership that emphasizes work efficiency.*
Work efficiency *Maximum output (productivity) at lowest cost.*
Psychological efficiency *Maintenance of good morale, labor relations, employee satisfaction, and similar aspects of work behavior.*
Theory Y leadership *A leadership style that emphasizes human relations at work and that views people as industrious, responsible, and interested in challenging work.*

Critical Thinking

From Glass Ceiling to Labyrinth

Nearly a quarter of all American organizations have female CEOs (Martin, 2007). Studies have even shown that companies with more women in leadership roles perform better financially (Carter, Simkins, & Simpson, 2003; Krishnan & Park, 2005).

And yet, according to psychologist Alice Eagly, women continue to face unique challenges. Increasingly, cracks are appearing in the *glass ceiling,* the invisible barrier that has prevented women from moving into leadership positions. But the glass ceiling is being replaced by a labyrinth created by a clash between leadership stereotypes and stereotypes of women (Brescoll, Dawson, & Uhlmann, 2010; Eagly & Carli, 2007). On the one hand, most people expect good leaders to be *agentic:* independent, confident, ambitious, objective, dominant, and forceful. On the other hand, they expect women to be more *communal:* dependent, caring, nurturing, tender, sensitive, and sympathetic. According to traditional gender role stereotypes (see Module 47), it is men who are agentic and, therefore, better leaders, despite evidence to the contrary (Eagly, 2013).

What does this mean for a woman who moves into a leadership role? If she practices communal, Theory Y leadership, she is seen as weak. She is "not tough enough" or does not "have the right stuff" to be a leader. Yet, if she acts more assertively and

confidently, she is scorned for "trying to be a man" (Kark & Eagly, 2010). This conflict has been perfectly expressed by Carly Fiorina, former CEO of Hewlett-Packard, who wrote, "In the chat rooms around Silicon Valley ... I was routinely referred to as either a 'bimbo' or a 'bitch'— too soft or too hard, and presumptuous, besides" (Fiorina, 2006, p. 173).

As traditional gender stereotypes fade, and as Theory Y styles gain wider acceptance, perhaps women will add escaping the leadership labyrinth to their many other successes.

As the CEO of Hewlett-Packard, Carley Fiorina constantly faced the incongruity between leadership stereotypes and stereotypes of women (Fiorina, 2006).

In short, Theory Y assumes that people are industrious, creative, and rewarded by challenging work. It appears that given the proper conditions of freedom and responsibility, many people *will* work hard to gain competence and use their talents. This is especially true for **knowledge workers** (Marks & Baldry, 2009; Maruta, 2012), people who add value to a company by creating and manipulating information and who usually think of their work as a career rather than as a job. Some examples are bankers, teachers, lawyers, computer engineers, writers, and scientists. Over the last 60 years, manufacturing has declined in North America, whereas *knowledge companies* have become much more common. Today in North America, four of every five persons in the workforce are knowledge workers (Drucker, 1993).

Transformational Leadership Today's harsh economic realities often require more of leaders than a person-oriented Theory Y style. **Transformational leadership** seeks to transform employees to exceed expectations and look beyond self-interest to help the organization better compete (Avolio, Walumbwa, & Weber, 2009; Guay, 2013). The transformational leader achieves these goals in four ways:

1. Idealized influence: Employees are encouraged to work ethically, emphasizing values such as trust.

2. Inspirational motivation: Employees are inspired to see their work as meaningful and challenging.

3. Intellectual stimulation: Employees are empowered to "think outside the box" to find new solutions to problems.

4. Individualized consideration: Employees' individual needs, goals, and abilities are valued; appropriate professional development is available as required.

Leadership Strategies

Two techniques that make Theory Y and transformational leadership methods effective are *shared leadership* and *management by objectives.* In **shared leadership (participative management)**, employees at all levels are directly involved in decision making (Pearce, Manz, & Sims, 2009). By taking part in decisions that affect them, employees come to see work as a cooperative effort—not as something imposed on them by an egotistical leader. The benefits include greater

Shared leadership techniques encourage employees at all levels to become involved in decision making. Quite often, this arrangement leads to greater job satisfaction.

productivity, more involvement in work, greater job satisfaction, and less job-related stress (Pearce, Conger, & Locke, 2007; Raes et al., 2013).

What is management by objectives? In **management by objectives**, workers are given specific goals to meet so they can tell whether they are doing a good job (Antoni, 2005). Typical objectives include reaching a certain sales total, making a certain number of items, or reducing waste by a specific percentage. In any case, workers are free to choose (within limits) how they will achieve their goals. As a result, they feel more independent and take personal responsibility for their work. Workers are especially productive when they receive feedback about their progress toward goals. Clearly, people like to know what the target is and whether they are succeeding (Horn et al., 2005; Lefrançois, 2012).

Many companies also give *groups* of workers even greater freedom and responsibility. This is typically done by creating self-managed teams. A **self-managed team** is a group of employees who work together toward shared goals. Self-managed teams can typically choose their own methods of achieving results, as long as they are effective. Self-managed teams tend to make good use of the strengths and talents of individual employees. They also promote new ideas and improve motivation. Most of all, they encourage cooperation and teamwork within organizations (Woods & West, 2010). Workers in self-managed teams are much more likely to feel that they are being treated fairly at work and to

develop a positive team atmosphere (Chansler, Swamidass, & Cammann, 2003; Gilboa & Tal-Shmotkin, 2012).

How can workers below the management level be involved more in their work? One answer is the use of **quality circles**. These are voluntary discussion groups that seek ways to solve business problems and improve efficiency (Aamodt, 2013). In contrast to self-managed teams, quality circles usually do not have the power to put their suggestions into practice directly. But good ideas speak for themselves and many are adopted by company leaders. Quality circles do have many limitations, but nevertheless, studies verify that greater personal involvement can lead to better performance and job satisfaction (Beyer et al., 2003).

Job Satisfaction

It often makes perfect sense to apply Theory X methods to work. However, doing so without taking worker needs into account can be a case of winning the battle while losing the war—that is, immediate productivity may be enhanced while job satisfaction is lowered. And when job satisfaction is low, absenteeism skyrockets, morale falls, and there is a high rate of employee turnover, leading to higher training costs and inefficiency (Wright & Bonett, 2007).

Understandably, many of the methods used by enlightened Theory Y leaders ultimately improve **job satisfaction**, or the degree to which a person is pleased with his or her work. Job satisfaction is well worth cultivating because positive moods are associated with more cooperation, better performance, a greater willingness to help others, more creative problem solving, and less absenteeism (Bowling, 2010; Brief & Weiss, 2002).

Knowledge workers *Workers who add value to their company by creating and manipulating information.*

Transformational leadership *Leadership aimed at transforming employees to exceed expectations and look beyond self-interest to help the organization better compete.*

Shared leadership (participative management) *A leadership approach that allows employees at all levels to participate in decision making.*

Management by objectives *A management technique in which employees are given specific goals to meet in their work.*

Self-managed team *A work group that has a high degree of freedom with respect to how it achieves its goals.*

Quality circle *An employee discussion group that makes suggestions for improving quality and solving business problems.*

Job satisfaction *The degree to which a person is comfortable with or satisfied with his or her work.*

Under what conditions is job satisfaction highest? Basically, job satisfaction comes from a good fit between work and a person's interests, abilities, needs, and expectations. The major factors determining job satisfaction are noted in the following list. Think of a job you have held. It's likely that the more these factors were present, the higher was your job satisfaction (Aamodt, 2013; Landy & Conte, 2009):

1. My job meets my expectations.   Y or N?
2. My needs, values, and wants are met by my job.   Y or N?
3. The tasks I have to do are enjoyable.   Y or N?
4. I enjoy my supervisors and coworkers.   Y or N?
5. My coworkers are outwardly happy.   Y or N?
6. I am rewarded fairly for doing a good job.   Y or N?
7. I have a chance to grow and be challenged.   Y or N?

We should note that job satisfaction is not entirely a matter of work conditions. Anyone who has ever been employed has probably encountered at least one perpetually grumpy coworker. In other words, workers don't leave their personalities at home. Happy people are more often happy at work, and they are more likely to focus on what's good about their job rather than what's bad. Understandably, the most productive employees are those who are happy at work (Aamodt, 2013; Brown, Charlwood, & Spencer, 2012). This connection can be seen clearly when employees are allowed to participate in various forms of *flexible work*.

Flexible Work If you've ever worked "9 to 5" in an office, you know that traditional time schedules can be confining. They also doom many workers to a daily battle with rush-hour traffic. To improve worker morale, I/O psychologists recommend the use of a variety of flexible work arrangements, of which the best known is **flextime**, or flexible working hours (Kossek & Michel, 2011). The basic idea of flextime is that starting and quitting times are flexible as long as employees are present during a core work period. For example, employees might be allowed to arrive between 7:30 AM and 10:30 AM and depart between 3:30 PM and 6:30 PM. In a variation called a *compressed workweek*, employees might work fewer days but put in more hours per day.

With **flexplace** (also called *telework* or *telecommuting*), work is done outside the workplace, usually at home (Lautsch, Kossek, & Eaton, 2009; Nätti & Häikiö, 2012).

Is flexible work really an improvement? Generally speaking, yes (Yang & Zheng, 2011). For example, flextime typically has a positive effect on workers' productivity, job satisfaction, absenteeism, and comfort with their work schedules (Baltes

Connecting with work through the Internet makes it possible to telecommute, or work from home (Golden, Veiga, & Simsek, 2006).

et al., 1999). Similarly, flexplace is especially effective when it allows valued employees to maintain their homes in other cities (Atkin & Lau, 2007). Psychologists theorize that flexible work lowers stress and increases feelings of independence, both of which increase productivity and job satisfaction.

Of course, not everyone wants a compressed workweek or to work from home. Ideally, flexible working arrangements should fit the needs of employees (Troup & Rose, 2012). Regardless, most large organizations now use flexible work arrangements. Perhaps we can conclude that it is better, when possible, to bend working arrangements instead of people.

Job Enrichment For years, the trend in business and industry was to make work more streamlined and efficient and to tie better pay to better work. Ample evidence now shows that incentives such as bonuses, earned time off, and profit sharing can increase productivity. However, far too many jobs are routine, repetitive, boring, and unfulfilling. To combat the discontent this can breed, many psychologists recommend a strategy called *job enrichment*.

Job enrichment involves making a job more personally rewarding, interesting, or intrinsically motivating. Large corporations such as IBM, Maytag, Western Electric, Chrysler, and Polaroid have used job enrichment with great success. It usually leads to lower production costs, increased job satisfaction, reduced boredom, and less absenteeism (Gregory, Albritton, & Osmonbekov, 2010; Niehoff et al., 2001).

How is job enrichment done? Merely assigning a person more tasks is usually not enriching. Overloaded workers just

The Clinical File

Desk Rage and Healthy Organizations

Like road rage on the highways, "desk rage," or workplace anger, is a frequent occurrence and, at times, erupts into workplace violence (Niven, Sprigg, & Armitage, 2013). It's not difficult to understand the common triggers for workplace anger: intense anger triggered by job-related stresses (such as feeling that one has been treated unfairly), perceived threats to one's self-esteem, and work-related conflicts with others (Einarsen & Hoel, 2008; Spector, 2012).

What can be done about anger and aggression at work? Most larger companies now offer mental health services to troubled employees and trauma counseling if violence erupts in the workplace. More important, healthy organizations actively promote the well-being of people. They do this by openly confronting problems, empowering employees, and encouraging participation, cooperation, and full use of human potential. Healthy organizations also support well-being in the following ways (Hodson & Sullivan, 2012; Martinko, Douglas, & Harvey, 2006):

- Rather than always complaining and blaming, group members express sincere gratitude for the efforts of others.
- Everyone makes mistakes. The culture in caring organizations includes a capacity to forgive.

- Everyone needs encouragement at times. Encouragement can inspire workers and give them hope, confidence, and courage.
- Showing sensitivity to others can dramatically change the work environment. Sensitivity can take the form of expressing interest in others and in how they are doing. It also includes respecting the privacy of others.
- Compassion for others is a good antidote for destructive competitiveness and petty game playing.
- People have very different needs, values, and experiences. Tolerance and respect for the dignity of others goes a long way toward maintaining individual well-being.

The economic pressures that organizations face can lead to hostile and competitive work environments. However, even in economically difficult times, productivity and quality of life at work are closely intertwined. Effective organizations seek to optimize both (Fuqua & Newman, 2002). For example, companies who pay more attention to the quality of life at work generally suffer fewer productivity losses if they are forced to downsize (reduce the size of their workforce; Iverson & Zatzick, 2011).

feel stressed, and they tend to make more errors. Instead, job enrichment applies many of the principles we have discussed. Usually, it involves removing some of the controls and restrictions on employees, thus giving them greater freedom, choice, and authority. In some cases, employees also switch to doing a complete cycle of work—that is, they complete an entire item or project instead of doing an isolated part of a larger process. Whenever possible, workers are given direct feedback about their work or progress.

True job enrichment increases workers' feeling of *empowerment* and *knowledge*—that is, workers are encouraged to continuously learn and exercise a broad range of options, skills, and information related to their occupations (Gregory, Albritton, & Osmonbekov, 2010; Sessa & London, 2006). In short, most people enjoy being good at what they do.

Organizational Culture

Businesses and other organizations, whether they are large or small, develop distinct cultures. **Organizational culture** refers to a blend of customs, beliefs, values, attitudes, and rituals. These characteristics give each organization its

unique "flavor" (Chamorro-Premuzic & Furnham, 2010). Organizational culture includes such things as how people are hired and trained, disciplined, and dismissed. It encompasses how employees dress, communicate, resolve conflicts, share power, identify with organizational goals and values, negotiate contracts, and celebrate special occasions.

People who fit well into a particular organization tend to contribute to its success in ways that are not specifically part of their job description. For example, they are helpful, conscientious, and courteous. They also display good sportsmanship by avoiding pettiness, gossiping, complaining, and making

Flextime *A work schedule that allows flexible starting and quitting times.*
Flexplace *An approach to flexible work that involves working from away from the office but using a computer to stay connected throughout the workday.*
Job enrichment *Making a job more personally rewarding, interesting, or intrinsically motivating; typically involves increasing worker knowledge.*
Organizational culture *The blend of customs, beliefs, values, attitudes, and rituals within an organization.*

small problems into big ones (see "Desk Rage and Healthy Organizations"). Like good citizens, the best workers keep themselves informed about organizational issues by attending meetings and taking part in discussions. Workers with these characteristics display what could be called **organizational citizenship**. Understandably, managers and employers highly value workers who are good organizational citizens (Woods & West, 2010).

Personnel Psychology

Companies also can enhance their chances of success by hiring the right employees in the first place. **Personnel psychology** is concerned with testing, selection, placement, and promotion of employees (Campbell, 2013; Woods & West, 2010). At present, nine out of ten people are or will be employed in business or industry. Thus, nearly everyone who holds a job is sooner or later placed under the "psychological microscope" of personnel selection. Clearly, it is valuable to know how selection for hiring and promotion is done.

How do personnel psychologists select employees? Personnel selection begins with **job analysis**, a detailed description of the skills, knowledge, and activities required by a particular job (Sackett, Walmsley, & Laczo, 2013; Stetz, Button, & Porr, 2009). A job analysis may be done by interviewing expert workers or supervisors, giving them questionnaires, directly observing work, or identifying *critical incidents*. **Critical incidents** are situations with which competent employees must be able to cope. The ability to deal calmly with a mechanical emergency, for example, is a critical incident for airline pilots. Once job requirements are known, psychologists can state what skills, aptitudes, and interests are needed (●**Figure 75.1**). In addition, some psychologists are now doing a broader "work analysis." In this case, they try to identify general characteristics that a person must have to succeed in a variety of work roles, rather than in just a specific job (Sackett & Lievens, 2008).

After desirable skills and traits are identified, the next step is to learn who has them. Today, the methods most often used for evaluating job candidates include collecting *biodata,* conducting *interviews,* giving *standardized psychological tests,* and employing the *assessment center* approach. Let's see what each entails.

Biodata As simple as it may seem, one good way to predict job success is to collect detailed biographical information (**biodata**) from applicants (Schultz & Schultz, 2010). The idea behind biodata is that looking at past behavior is a good way to

Tom Sheppard/Stone/Getty Images

●**Figure 75.1**

Analyzing complex skills also has been valuable to the U.S. Air Force. When million-dollar aircraft and the lives of pilots are at stake, it makes good sense to do as much training and research as possible on the ground. Air Force psychologists use flight simulators like the one pictured here to analyze the complex skills needed to fly jet fighters. Skills can then be taught without risk on the ground. The General Electric simulator shown here uses a computer to generate full-color images that respond realistically to a pilot's use of the controls.

predict future behavior. By learning in detail about a person's life, it is often possible to say whether the person is suited for a particular type of work (Schmitt & Golubovich, 2013).

Some of the most useful items of biodata include past athletic interests, academic achievements, scientific interests, extracurricular activities, religious activities, social popularity, conflict with brothers and sisters, attitudes toward school, and parents' socioeconomic status (Woods & West, 2010). (It is worth pointing out that there are civil liberty and privacy concerns relating to the collection of sensitive biodata.) Such facts tell quite a lot about personality, interests, and abilities. In addition to past experiences, a person's recent life activities also help predict job success. For instance, you might think that college grades are unimportant, but college grade point average (GPA) predicts success in many types of work (Sackett & Lievens, 2008).

Interviews The traditional personal interview is still one of the most popular ways to select people for jobs or promotions. In a **personal interview**, job applicants are questioned about their qualifications. At the same time, interviewers gain an impression of the applicant's personality (Chamorro-Premuzic & Furnham, 2010). (Or personalities—but that's another story!)

As discussed in Module 72, interviews are subject to the halo effect and similar problems. (Recall that the *halo effect* is the tendency of interviewers to extend favorable or unfavorable

Discovering Psychology

Some Job Interview Tips

Applying for a job? Here are a few time-tested tips. In general, indirect efforts to make a good impression, like dressing well, wearing cologne, and flattering the interviewer, are less effective in interviews than direct efforts such as emphasizing your positive traits and past successes (Kleinmann & Klehe, 2011; Kristof-Brown, Barrick, & Franke, 2002). However, beware of blatant self-promotion. Excessively "blowing your own horn" tends to lower interviewers' perceptions of competence and suitability for a job.

Make sure you are prepared for your interview. Know about the company and job for which you are interviewing. Review your job qualifications and your résumé. Think about the kinds of questions you may be asked at the interview and outline broad answers in advance. Consider practicing the interview with a family member or friend.

Be on time for your interview and bring your Social Security card, résumé, and references. Also, make sure you are well groomed, dressed appropriately, and well mannered. Don't smoke or chew gum. Don't bring your pet or your mother or father. (We're not kidding.) For sure, *do not* telephone or text message others during an interview. (Once again, we're not kidding.)

Learn your interviewer's name and shake his or her hand firmly. Relax and answer all questions politely, promptly, and concisely. Cooperate enthusiastically, use positive body language, and avoid slang. Don't be afraid to ask questions about the potential job and the company interviewing you. Just be sure the answers aren't already easily available on the company website. Avoid questions about salary and benefits unless a job offer is coming. (Adapted from Doyle, 2013; Workopolis, 2013.)

---

impressions to unrelated aspects of an individual's personality, such as his or her appearance.) In addition, interviewees actively engage in *impression management,* seeking to portray a positive image to interviewers (Kleinmann & Klehe, 2011; see "Some Job Interview Tips").

It is for reasons like these that psychologists continue to look for ways to improve the accuracy of interviews. For instance, recent studies suggest that interviews can be improved by giving them more structure (Sackett & Lievens, 2008; Tsai, Chen, & Chiu, 2005). For example, each job candidate should be asked the same questions. However, even with their limitations, interviews can be a valid and effective way of predicting how people will perform on the job (Hodson & Sullivan, 2012; Landy, Shankster, & Kohler, 1994).

Psychological Testing *What kinds of tests do personnel psychologists use?* General mental ability tests (intelligence tests) tell a great deal about a person's chances of succeeding in various jobs (Aamodt, 2013; Schmidt & Hunter, 1998). So do general personality tests (described in Module 50; Hough & Connelly, 2013). In addition, personnel psychologists often use **vocational interest tests.** These tests assess people's interests and match them to interests found among successful workers in various occupations (Van Iddekinge, Putka, & Campbell, 2011). Tests such as the *Kuder Occupational Interest Survey* and the *Strong-Campbell Interest Inventory* probe interests with items like the following:

I would prefer to **a.** visit a museum **b.** read a good book **c.** take a walk outdoors

Interest inventories typically measure six major themes identified by John Holland (● Table 75.2). If you take an interest test and your choices match those of people in a given occupation, it is assumed that you, too, would be comfortable doing the work they do (Holland, 1997).

Aptitude tests are another mainstay of personnel psychology. Such tests rate a person's potential to learn tasks or skills used in various occupations. Tests exist for clerical, verbal, mechanical, artistic, legal, and medical aptitudes, plus many others (● Figure 75.2). For example, tests of clerical aptitude emphasize the capacity to do rapid, precise, and accurate

---

Organizational citizenship *Making positive contributions to the success of an organization in ways that go beyond one's job description.*

Personnel psychology *Branch of industrial/organizational psychology concerned with testing, selection, placement, and promotion of employees.*

Job analysis *A detailed description of the skills, knowledge, and activities required by a particular job.*

Critical incidents *Situations that arise in a job with which a competent worker must be able to cope.*

Biodata *Detailed biographical information about a job applicant.*

Personal interview *Formal or informal questioning of job applicants to learn their qualifications and to gain an impression of their personalities.*

Vocational interest test *A paper-and-pencil test that assesses a person's interests and matches them to interests found among successful workers in various occupations.*

Aptitude test *A test that rates a person's potential to learn skills required by various occupations.*

TABLE 75.2 **Vocational Interest Themes**

Themes	Sample College Majors	Sample Occupations
Realistic	Agriculture	Mechanic
Investigative	Physics	Chemist
Artistic	Music	Writer
Social	Education	Counselor
Enterprising	Business	Sales
Conventional	Economics	Clerk

Source: Holland, 1997.

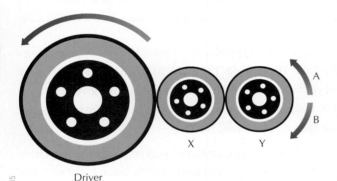

Driver

1. If the driver turns in the direction shown, which direction will wheel Y turn?   A   B

2. Which wheel will turn the slowest?   Driver   X   Y

● **Figure 75.2**

Sample questions like those found on tests of mechanical aptitude. (The answers are A and the Driver.)

office work. One section of a clerical aptitude test might therefore ask a person to mark all identical numbers and names in a long list of pairs like those shown here:

49837266	49832766
Global Widgets, Inc.	Global Wigets, Inc.
874583725	874583725
Sevanden Corp.	Sevanden Corp.
Cengage Publishing	Cengage Puhlishing

After college, chances are good that you will encounter an *assessment center*. Many large organizations use **assessment**

centers to do in-depth evaluations of job candidates. This approach has become so popular that the list of businesses using it—Ford, IBM, Kodak, Exxon, Sears, and thousands of others—reads like a corporate *Who's Who*.

How do assessment centers differ from the selection methods already described? Assessment centers are primarily used to fill management and executive positions. First, applicants are tested and interviewed. Then, they are observed and evaluated in simulated work situations. Specifically, **situational judgment tests** are used to present difficult but realistic work situations to applicants (Christian, Edwards, & Bradley, 2010; Lievens & Sackett, 2006). For example, in one exercise, applicants are given an **in-basket test** that simulates the decision-making challenges executives face. The test consists of a basket full of memos, requests, and typical business problems. Each applicant is asked to quickly read all the materials and to take appropriate action. In another, more stressful test, applicants take part in a **leaderless group discussion**. This is a test of leadership that simulates group decision making and problem solving. While the group grapples with a realistic business problem, "clerks" bring in price changes, notices about delayed supplies, and so forth. By observing applicants, it is possible to evaluate leadership skills and to see how job candidates cope with stress (Chamorro-Premuzic & Furnham, 2010).

How well does this approach work? Assessment centers have had considerable success in predicting performance in a variety of jobs, careers, and advanced positions (Chamorro-Premuzic & Furnham, 2010; Landy, Shankster, & Kohler, 1994).

Although we have only scratched the surface of industrial/organizational psychology, it is time to move on for a look at another applied area of great personal relevance. Before we begin, here's a chance to enhance your learning.

Assessment center *A program set up within an organization to conduct in-depth evaluations of job candidates.*
Situational judgment test *Presenting realistic work situations to applicants in order to observe their skills and reactions.*
In-basket test *A testing procedure that simulates the individual decision-making challenges that executives face.*
Leaderless group discussion *A test of leadership that simulates group decision making and problem solving*

© Cengage Learning 2015

Module 75: Summary

75.1 How is psychology applied in business and industry?

- **75.1.1** Applied psychology refers to the use of psychological principles and research to solve practical problems.
- **75.1.2** Industrial/organizational psychologists enhance the quality of work by studying jobs to better match people to them and by studying organizational structures and culture to improve worker performance.
- **75.1.3** Three basic leadership styles are Theory X (scientific management), Theory Y (human relations approaches), and transformational leadership (inspiring employees to exceed expectations and look beyond self-interest). Theory X is mostly concerned with work efficiency, whereas Theory Y emphasizes psychological efficiency.

- **75.1.4** Theory Y and transformational methods include shared leadership (participative management), management by objectives, self-managed teams, and quality circles.
- **75.1.5** Job satisfaction influences productivity, absenteeism, morale, employee turnover, and other factors that affect business efficiency. Job satisfaction comes from a good fit between work and a person's interests, abilities, needs, and expectations. Job enrichment tends to increase job satisfaction.
- **75.1.6** To match people with jobs, personnel psychologists combine job analysis with selection procedures, such as gathering biodata, interviewing, giving standardized psychological tests, and using assessment centers.

Module 75: Knowledge Builder

Recite

1. Theory X leadership, or scientific management, is concerned primarily with improving _____ _____.
2. Shared leadership management is often a feature of businesses with leaders who adhere to Theory Y. *T or F?*
3. For the majority of workers, job satisfaction is almost exclusively related to the amount of pay received. *T or F?*
4. Job enrichment is a direct expression of scientific management principles. *T or F?*
5. Identifying critical work incidents is sometimes included in a thorough _____ _____.
6. Detailed biographical information about a job applicant is referred to as _____.
7. A leaderless group discussion is most closely associated with which approach to employee selection?
   - *a.* aptitude testing
   - *b.* personal interviews
   - *c.* job analysis
   - *d.* assessment center

Reflect

Think Critically

8. In what area of human behavior other than work would a careful task analysis be helpful?

Self-Reflect

If you were leading people in a business setting, which of the leadership concepts do you think you would be most likely to use?

Do you think women can make effective leaders? In business? In politics?

Think of a job you know well. Could job enrichment be applied to the work? What would you do to increase job satisfaction for people doing similar work?

Which of the various ways of evaluating job applicants do you regard as most valid? Which would you prefer to have applied to yourself?

ANSWERS

1. work (or task) efficiency 2. T 3. F 4. F 5. job analysis 6. biodata 7. d 8. One such area is sports psychology. As described later in Module 77, sports skills can be broken into subparts so key elements can be identified and taught. Such methods are an extension of techniques first used for job analyses. To a large extent, attempts to identify the characteristics of effective teaching also rely on task analysis.

Applied Psychology: Environmental Psychology

Boots Too Big?

The environment has a significant impact on people. The reverse also is now known to be true: People have a significant impact on the environment. Each of us generates an *ecological footprint* as we consume the resources it takes to sustain life. Every time we eat a meal, or discard some junk, or travel somewhere, or even just sit and breathe, we enlarge our footprints.

Multiply the average ecological footprint by a bit over 7 billion, the current global population, and you get a giant *world footprint*, covering our entire planet, and another half to boot. For every year of human resource consumption, it will take Earth 1.5 years to recover. By 2030, we will be using two Earth's worth of resources every year. How is our one Earth to cope? Because of this, environmental psychologists are

Franck Fotos/Alamy

concerned with some of the most serious problems facing humanity. Let's look into environmental psychology.

SURVEY QUESTIONS

76.1 What have psychologists learned about the effects of our physical and social environments?

76.2 What effect are humans having on the natural environment?

Environmental Influences—People, People Everywhere

SURVEY QUESTION 76.1: What have psychologists learned about the effects of our physical and social environments?

Environmental psychology is the specialty concerned with the relationship between environments and human behavior (Winter & Koger, 2010). Environmental psychologists are interested in both **social environments**, defined by groups of people, such as a dance, business meeting, or party, and **physical environments**, constructed or natural. They also give special attention to **behavioral settings**, smaller areas within an environment whose use is well defined, such as an office, locker room, church, casino, or classroom. As you have no doubt noticed, various environments and behavioral settings tend to "demand" certain actions. Consider, for example,

the difference between a library and a campus center lounge. In which would a conversation be more likely to occur?

Other major interests of environmental psychologists are crowding, stressful environments, architectural design, environmental protection, and many related topics (● Table 76.1). One of the more "personal" topics in environmental psychology concerns the efforts we make to regulate the space around our bodies. Let's begin with a look at how personal space norms and territoriality affect our behavior.

Personal Space

The next time you are talking with an acquaintance, move in closer and watch the reaction. Most people show signs of discomfort and step back to reestablish their original distance. Those who hold their ground may turn to the side, look away, or position an arm in front of themselves as a barrier. If you persistently edge toward your subjects, it should be easy to move them back several feet.

Peter M. Fisher/Corbis

Various behavioral settings place strong demands on people to act in expected ways. Consider, for example, the difference between a library and a campus center lounge. In which would a conversation be more likely to occur?

TABLE 76.1	Topics of Special Interest to Environmental Psychologists
Architectural design	Noise
Behavioral settings	Personal space
Cognitive maps	Personality and environment
Constructed environments	Pollution
Crowding	Privacy
Energy conservation	Proxemics
Environmental stressors	Resource management
Heat	Territoriality
Human ecology	Urban planning
Littering	Vandalism
Natural environment	

© Cengage Learning 2015

In this case, your mere (and close) presence amounted to an invasion of that person's **personal space**, an area surrounding the body that is regarded as private and subject to personal control (Novelli, Drury, & Reicher, 2010). Basically, personal space extends "I" or "me" boundaries past the skin to the immediate environment. Personal space also is illustrated by the fact that many train commuters prefer to stand up if it means they can avoid sitting too close to strangers (Evans & Wener, 2007). The systematic study of norms concerning the use of personal space is called **proxemics** (prok-SEE-miks) (Harrigan, 2005). Such norms may explain why people who feel offended by another person sometimes say, "Get out of my face."

Would approaching "too close" work with a good friend? Possibly not. Norms governing comfortable or acceptable distances vary according to relationships as well as activities. Hall (1966) identified four basic zones: *intimate, personal, social,* and *public* distance (● Figure 76.1).

Spatial Norms

Cultural differences also affect spatial norms (Beaulieu, 2004). In many Middle Eastern countries, people hold their faces only inches apart while talking. In Western Europe, the English sit closer together when conversing than do the French. The Dutch, on the other hand, sit farther apart than the French (Remland, Jones, & Brinkman, 1991). The following distances apply to face-to-face interactions in North America:

1. **Intimate distance.** For the majority of people, the most private and exclusive space extends about 18 inches out from the skin. Entry within this space (face to face) is reserved for special people or special circumstances. Lovemaking, comforting others, and cuddling children all take place within this space.

2. **Personal distance.** This is the distance maintained in comfortable interaction with friends. It extends from about 18 inches to 4 feet from the body. Personal distance basically keeps people within "arm's reach" of each other.

Environmental psychology *The formal study of how environments affect behavior.*

Social environment *An environment defined by a group of people and their activities or interrelationships (such as a parade, revival meeting, or sports event).*

Physical environments *Natural settings, such as forests and beaches, as well as environments built by humans, such as buildings, ships, and cities.*

Behavioral setting *A smaller area within an environment whose use is well defined, such as a bus depot, waiting room, or lounge.*

Personal space *An area surrounding the body that is regarded as private and subject to personal control.*

Proxemics *Systematic study of the human use of space, particularly in social settings.*

Intimate distance *The most private space immediately surrounding the body (up to about 18 inches from the skin).*

Personal distance *The distance maintained when interacting with close friends (about 18 inches to 4 feet from the body).*

© Cengage Learning 2015

Intimate (0–1.5) Personal (1.5–4) Social (4–12) Public (12+)

Figure 76.1

Typical spatial zones (in feet) for face-to-face interactions in North America. Often, we must stand within intimate distance of others in crowds, buses, subways, elevators, and other public places. At such times, privacy is maintained by avoiding eye contact, by standing shoulder to shoulder or back to back, and by positioning a purse, bag, package, or coat as a barrier to spatial intrusions.

3. **Social distance.** Impersonal business and casual social gatherings take place in a range of about 4 to 12 feet. This distance eliminates most touching, and it formalizes conversation by requiring greater voice projection. "Important people" in many business offices use the imposing width of their desks to maintain social distance. A big smelly cigar helps, too.

4. **Public distance.** This is the distance at which formal interactions occur (about 12 feet or more from the body). When people are separated by more than 12 feet, they look "flat" and they must raise their voices to speak to one another. Formal speeches, lectures, business meetings, and the like are conducted at public distance.

Because spatial behavior is very consistent, you can learn about your relationship to others by observing the distance you comfortably hold between yourselves. But remember to be aware of cultural differences. When two people of different nationalities have different norms for personal space, an amusing "dance" may occur. Both are likely to be uncomfortable when talking. One tries to move closer and the other keeps moving back. This can lead to misunderstandings in which one person feels that the other is being too familiar, yet at the same time, the person moving closer feels rejected (Beaulieu, 2004).

Territoriality As we move farther from the body, it becomes apparent that personal space also extends to adjacent areas that we claim as our "territory." **Territorial behavior** refers to actions that define a space as one's own or that protect it from intruders (Costa, 2012). For example, in the library, you might protect your space with a coat, handbag, book, or other personal belonging. "Saving a place" at a theater or a beach also demonstrates the tendency to identify a space as "ours." Even sports teams are territorial, usually showing a home team advantage by playing better on their own home territory than while playing in another team's territory (Jamieson, 2010; Sánchez et al., 2009).

Respect for the temporary ownership of space also is widespread. It is not unusual for a person to "take over" an entire table or study room by looking annoyed when others intrude. Your own personal territory may include your room, specific seats in many of your classes, or a particular table in the campus center or library that "belongs" to you and your friends.

Researchers have found that the more attached you are to an area, the more likely you are to adorn it with obvious **territorial markers** that signal your "ownership." Typical markers include decorations, plants, photographs, or posters. College dorms and business offices are prime places to observe this type of territorial marking. It is interesting to note that obvious territorial markers, such as fences (even if small), parked cars, lawn furniture, exterior lights, and security signs can help create a more *defensible space* by deterring crime (Reynald & Elffers, 2009). (A highly territorial bulldog may help, too.) The "gated communities" that have sprung up in many cities are a good example.

John Mitterer

Graffiti, one of the blights of urban life, is an obvious form of territorial marking.

Environmental Influences on Behavior

Much of our behavior is influenced, in part, by specific types of environments. For example, a variety of environmental factors influence the amount of vandalism that occurs in public places (Brown & Devlin, 2003). On the basis of psychological research, many architects now "harden" and "de-opportunize" public settings to discourage vandalism and graffiti. Some such efforts limit opportunities for vandalism (doorless toilet stalls, tiled walls). Others weaken the lure of likely targets. (Oddly enough, raised flowerbeds around signs help protect them because people resist trampling the flowers to get to the sign.)

Similarly, many shopping malls and department stores are designed like mazes. Their twisting pathways encourage shoppers to linger and wander while looking at merchandise. Likewise, in every city, more assaults and burglaries take place near the few restaurants or bars where likely offenders tend to hang out (Buchanan, 2008). Even public bathrooms influence behavior. Because the seating is limited, few people hold meetings there!

Given the personal impact of environments, it is important to know how we are affected by stressful or unhealthy environments—a topic we consider next.

Stressful Environments

Large cities are usually thought of as stressful places to live. Traffic congestion, pollution, crime, and impersonality are urban problems that immediately come to mind. To this list, psychologists have added crowding, noise, and overstimulation as major sources of urban stress. Psychological research has begun to clarify the impact of each of these conditions on human functioning (Malan et al., 2008; Marsella, 1998).

Crowding Nowhere are the effects of urbanization more evident than in the teeming cities of many underdeveloped nations (Malan et al., 2012). Closer to home, the jammed buses, subways, and living quarters of our own large cities are ample testimony to the stresses of crowding.

Is there any way to assess the effect crowding has on people? One approach is to study the effects of overcrowding among animals. Although the results of animal experiments cannot be considered conclusive for humans, they point to some disturbing effects.

For example? In an influential classic experiment, John Calhoun (1962) let a group of laboratory rats breed without limit in a confined space. Calhoun provided plenty of food, water, and nesting material for the rats. All that the rats lacked

was space. At its peak, the colony numbered 80 rats. Yet, it was housed in a cage designed to comfortably hold about 50. Overcrowding in the cage was heightened by the actions of the two most dominant males. These rascals staked out private territory at opposite ends of the cage, gathered harems of eight to ten females, and prospered. Their actions forced the remaining rats into a small, severely crowded middle area.

What effect did crowding have on the animals? A high rate of pathological behavior developed in both males and females. Females gave up nest building and caring for their young. Pregnancies decreased, and infant mortality ran extremely high. Many of the animals became indiscriminately aggressive and went on rampaging attacks against others. Abnormal sexual behavior was rampant, with some animals displaying hypersexuality and others total sexual passivity. Many of the animals died, apparently from stress-caused diseases. The link between these problems and overcrowding is unmistakable.

But does that apply to humans? Many of the same pathological behaviors can be observed in crowded inner-city ghettos. It is therefore tempting to assume that violence, social disorganization, and declining birthrates as seen in these areas are directly related to crowding. However, the connection has not been so clearly demonstrated with humans (Evans et al., 2010). People living in the inner city suffer disadvantages in nutrition, education, income, and health care. These conditions, more than crowding, may deserve the blame for pathological behaviors. In fact, most laboratory studies using human subjects have failed to produce any serious ill effects by crowding people into small places. Most likely, this is because *crowding* is a psychological condition that is separate from **density** (the number of people in a given space).

How does crowding differ from density? **Crowding** refers to subjective feelings of being overstimulated by social inputs or a loss of privacy. Whether high density is experienced as

Social distance *The distance at which impersonal interaction takes place (about 4 to 12 feet from the body).*

Public distance *The distance at which formal interactions, such as giving a speech, occur (about 12 feet or more from the body).*

Territorial behavior *Any behavior that tends to define a space as one's own or that protects it from intruders.*

Territorial markers *Objects and other signals whose placement indicates to others the "ownership" or control of a particular area.*

Density *The number of people in a given space or, inversely, the amount of space available to each person.*

Crowding *A subjective feeling of being overstimulated by a loss of privacy or by the nearness of others (especially when social contact with them is unavoidable).*

Kevin Downs/Corbis

Times Square in New York, New Year's Eve, 2013. High densities do not automatically produce feelings of crowding. The nature of the situation and the relationships among crowd members also are important.

crowding may depend on relationships among those involved. In an elevator, subway, or prison, high densities may be uncomfortable. In contrast, a musical concert, party, or reunion may be most pleasant at higher densities. Thus, physical crowding may interact with situations to intensify existing stresses or pleasures (Evans, Lercher, & Kofler, 2002). However, when crowding causes a *loss of control* over one's immediate social environment, stress and health problems are likely to result (Solari & Mare, 2012; Steiner & Wooldredge, 2009).

Stress probably explains why death rates increase among prison inmates and mental hospital patients who live in crowded conditions. Even milder instances of crowding can have a negative impact. People who live in crowded conditions often become more aggressive or guarded and withdrawn from others (Regoeczi, 2008).

Attentional Overload One unmistakable result of high densities and crowding is a state that psychologist Stanley Milgram called **attentional overload**. This is a stressful condition that occurs when sensory stimulation, information, and social contacts make excessive demands on attention. Large cities, in particular, tend to bombard residents with continuous input. The resulting sensory and cognitive overload can be quite stressful.

Milgram (1970) believed that city dwellers learn to prevent attentional overload by engaging only in brief, superficial social contacts, by ignoring nonessential events, and by fending off others with cold and unfriendly expressions. In short, many city dwellers find that a degree of callousness is essential for survival (Wilson & Kennedy, 2006). Thus, a blunting of sensitivity to the needs of others may be one of the more serious costs of urban stresses and crowding. As described next,

noise also contributes to the sensory assault many people endure in urban environments.

The High Cost of Noise *How serious are the effects of daily exposure to noise?* A classic study of children attending schools near Los Angeles International Airport suggests that constant noise can be quite damaging. Children from the noisy schools were compared with similar students attending schools farther from the airport (Cohen et al., 1981). The comparison students were from families of similar social and economic makeup. Testing showed that children attending the noisy schools had higher blood pressure than those from the quieter schools. They were more likely to give up attempts to solve a difficult puzzle. And they were poorer at proofreading a printed paragraph—a task that requires close attention and concentration. Other studies of children living near other airports or in noisy neighborhoods have found similar signs of stress, poor reading skills, and other damaging effects (Evans, 2006; Linting et al., 2013; Sörqvist, 2010).

The tendency of the noise-battered children to give up or become distracted is a serious handicap. It may even reveal a state of "learned helplessness" (described in Module 57) caused by daily, uncontrollable blasts of sound. Even if such damage proves to be temporary, it is clear that **noise pollution**—annoying and intrusive noise—is a major source of environmental stress.

Human Influences on the Natural Environment—Sustaining Spaceship Earth

SURVEY QUESTION 76.2: What effect are humans having on the natural environment?

Overpopulation and its environmental impact rank as the most serious problems facing the world today. World population has exploded in the last 150 years (● **Figure 76.2**). The world's population is now more than 7 billion people and may exceed 10 billion by 2080 (United Nations, 2011).

All that human activity drastically changes the natural environment (Miller & Spoolman, 2013). We burn fossil fuels, destroy forests, use chemical products, and strip, clear, and farm the land. In doing so, we alter natural cycles, animal populations, and the very face of the Earth. The long-range impact of such activities is already becoming evident through

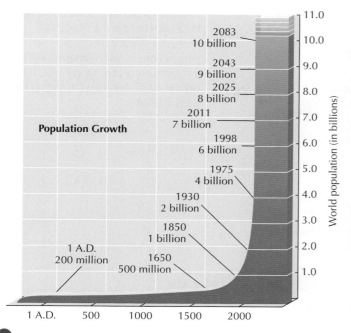

Figure 76.2

Population growth has exploded since 1850 and already exceeds 7 billion. Overpopulation and rapid population growth are closely connected with environmental damage, international tensions, and rapid depletion of nonrenewable resources. Some demographers predict that if population growth is not limited voluntarily before it reaches 10 billion, it will be limited by widespread food shortages, disease, infant mortality, and early death (Global Footprint Network, 2012a; United Nations, 2011).

In April 2010, an oil rig in the Gulf of Mexico exploded and burned, unleashing a major environmental catastrophe. In March 2011, a Japanese nuclear reactor suffered a catastrophic failure in reaction to a giant earthquake and tsunami. As the late Carl Sagan once said, "When you look closely, you find so many things going wrong with the environment, you are forced to reassess the hypothesis of intelligent life on Earth."

global warming, the extinction of plants and animals, a hole in the ozone layer, and polluted land, air, water, and oceans (Winter & Koger, 2010).

On a smaller scale, there is plenty of evidence that unchecked environmental damage will be costly to our children and descendants. For example, exposure to toxic hazards, such as radiation, pesticides, and industrial chemicals, leads to an elevated risk of physical and mental disease (Evans, 2006).

How many more people can the forests, oceans, croplands, and atmosphere support? Experts estimate that the maximum sustainable population of the Earth is between 5 billion and 20 billion persons. This means the Earth has already entered the lower range of its carrying capacity. The most pessimistic experts believe we have *already* exceeded the number of people the Earth can sustain indefinitely (Global Footprint Network, 2012a). Further population increases at the present rate could be disastrous.

Sustainable Lifestyles

A worldwide ecological crisis is brewing, and humans must change course to avoid vast human misery and permanent

damage (Moran, 2010). Of course, corporations and governments do much environmental damage. Thus, many of the solutions require changes in politics and policies. Ultimately, the solutions also require changes in individual behavior. Most of the environmental problems we face can be traced back to the human tendency to overuse natural resources (Global Footprint Network, 2012b; Huang & Rust, 2011).

Attentional overload *A stressful condition caused when sensory stimulation, information, and social contacts make excessive demands on attention.*

Noise pollution *Stressful and intrusive noise; usually artificially generated by machinery, but also includes noises made by animals and humans.*

Beef: 4,905 lbs.

Fish: 1,123 lbs.

Eggs: 18,046

Wood: 5,777 cubic feet

Vegetables: 13,653 lbs.

Coal: 290 tons

Coffee: 688 lbs.

Pesticides: 280 lbs.

Potatoes: 3,728 lbs.

Water: 41,289,000 gallons

Petroleum: 80,598 gallons

What will it cost the world to provide for a baby born in the year 2000? Without a major conservation effort, a person born in North America will over a lifetime consume, on average, the resources shown here ("Bringing Up Baby," 1999).

Monkey Business Images/Shutterstock

Wasted Resources The rapid worldwide consumption of natural resources is a devastating social problem. Resource consumption can be measured as an **ecological footprint**, the amount of land and water area required to replenish the resources that a human population consumes. According to the Global Footprint Network (2012a), humans are already consuming more than the Earth can regenerate. Industrialized nations, in particular, are consuming world resources at an alarming rate. North America, for instance, has an ecological footprint about 10 times higher than that of Asia or Africa. In the face of projected shortages and squandered resources, what can be done to encourage conservation on a personal level?

Conservation Try as you might to reduce your use of resources (electricity, for instance), you may find it difficult (Stall-Meadows & Hebert, 2011). Environmental psychologists have long known that a lack of *control* and *feedback* is a major barrier (Abrahamse et al., 2005). (See Module 27.)

For example, programmable home thermostats and energy-saving settings on appliances and electronics make it possible for conservation-conscious consumers to more precisely control their energy consumption. However, feedback about electricity use usually arrives long after the temptation to turn up the heat or to leave lights on (the monthly electricity bill). Psychologists aware of this problem have shown that lower energy bills result from simply giving families and work groups daily feedback about their use of gas or electricity (Carrico & Riemer, 2011).

Savings are magnified further with the addition of programs that give monetary rewards for energy conservation. *Smart meters*, one recent example, can provide continuous feedback about energy usage to both consumers and their energy suppliers (U.S. Department of Energy, 2010). With this information, electricity utilities can, for example, offer electricity at lower prices during periods of low demand. Savvy consumers not only can more easily conserve electricity, but they also can save even more money by, say, running their dishwasher in the evening rather than during the day.

Effective feedback about overall resource use also is finally becoming widely available as several organizations provide *ecological footprint calculators*, websites that allow individuals to calculate, and therefore track their individual resource consumption (Global Footprint Network, 2011). With growing public concern over global warming, many people are now calculating their individual **carbon footprint**, the volume of greenhouse gases individual consumption adds to the atmosphere (The Nature Conservancy, 2013).

It is now easier than ever to conserve energy (by installing energy-efficient lights, for example) and see an immediate reduction in your carbon footprint. It also is becoming

Discovering Psychology

Reuse and Recycle

While reducing consumption can lighten the environmental impact of our "throw-away" society, personally reusing products and materials that would normally be thrown away also is important. In addition, we can recycle materials such as paper, steel, glass, aluminum, and plastic that can be used to make new products.

What can be done to encourage people to recycle? Psychological research has shown that all of the following strategies promote recycling (Duffy & Verges, 2009; Winter & Koger, 2010):

- **Educate.** Learning about environmental problems and pro-environment values at home, school, and work has been one of the most effective ways to encourage pro-environmental behavior, including recycling (Carrico & Riemer, 2011; Matthies, Selge, & Klöckner, 2012).

- **Provide monetary rewards.** As mentioned before, monetary rewards encourage conservation. Requiring refundable deposits on glass bottles is a good example of using incentives to increase recycling.

- **Remove barriers.** Anything that makes recycling more convenient helps. A good example is cities that offer curbside pickup of household recyclables. Another is businesses that help customers recycle old computers, printers, and the like. On campus, simply putting marked containers in classrooms is a good way to encourage recycling.

- **Use persuasion.** Many recycling programs benefit from media campaigns to persuade people to participate.

- **Obtain public commitment.** People who feel they have committed themselves to recycling are more likely to follow through and actually recycle. Sometimes, people are asked to sign "pledge cards" on which they promise to recycle. Another technique involves having people sign a list committing themselves to recycling. Such lists may or may not be published in a local newspaper. They are just as effective either way.

People are much more likely to recycle if proper attention is given to psychological factors that promote recycling behavior. For example, this Washington State recycling bin is designed to be visually appealing.

- **Encourage goal setting.** People who set their own goals for recycling tend to meet them. Goal setting has been used successfully with families, dorms, neighborhoods, offices, factories, and so forth.

- **Give feedback.** To reiterate, feedback proves to be very valuable. Recycling typically increases when families, work groups, dorms, and the like are simply told, on a periodic basis, how much they recycled (Kim, Oah, & Dickinson, 2005). In one study, signs were placed on recycling containers on a college campus. The signs showed how many aluminum cans had been deposited in the previous week. This simple procedure increased recycling by 65 percent (Larson, Houlihan, & Goernert, 1995).

- **Revise attitudes.** Even people who believe that recycling is worthwhile are likely to regard it as a boring task. Thus, people are most likely to continue recycling if they emphasize the sense of satisfaction they get from contributing to the environment (Nigbur, Lyons, & Uzzell, 2010).

---

more popular to offset some *carbon debt*—by planting trees, for example. Prompt and accurate information and feedback about energy use are making it possible to aspire to a *carbon-neutral lifestyle,* in which your energy consumption is reduced and the remainder offset so that your overall impact on global warming is zero. Similar factors can greatly increase recycling, as described in "Reuse and Recycle."

Social Dilemmas

Why is it so difficult to get people to take better care of the environment? A pattern of behavior called a *social dilemma*

contributes to many environmental problems. A **social dilemma** is any social situation that rewards actions that have undesired effects in the long run (Van Lange et al., 2013; Van Vugt, 2009). In a typical social dilemma, no one individual

Ecological footprint *The amount of land and water area required to replenish the resources that a human population consumes.*
Carbon footprint *The volume of greenhouse gases individual consumption adds to the atmosphere.*
Social dilemma *A social situation that tends to provide immediate rewards for actions that will have undesired effects in the long run.*

intentionally acts against the group interest, but if many people act alike, collective harm is done. For example, the rapid transit systems in many large cities are underused. At the same time, the roads are jammed. Why? Too many individuals decide that it is convenient to own and drive a separate car (to run errands and so on). However, each person's behavior affects the welfare of others. Because everyone wants to drive for "convenience," driving becomes inconvenient: The mass of cars in most cities causes irritating traffic snarls and a lack of parking spaces. It also contributes to pollution and global warming. Each car owner has been drawn into a dilemma.

The Tragedy of the Commons Social dilemmas are especially damaging when we are enticed into overuse of scarce resources that must be shared by many people. Again, each person acts in his or her self-interest, but collectively, everyone ends up suffering. Ecologist Garrett Hardin (1968) calls such situations the **tragedy of the commons**. An example we have already discussed is the lack of individual incentives to conserve gasoline, water, or electricity. Whenever personal comfort or convenience is involved, it is highly tempting to "let others worry about it." Yet in the long run everyone stands to lose (Van Vugt, 2009).

Why does such misguided behavior so often prevail? Again, we see a social dilemma at work: If one person pollutes a river or trashes the roadside, it has little noticeable effect. But as many people do the same, problems that affect everyone quickly mount. Throwing away one plastic bag may seem inconsequential, but across the world hundreds of billions of plastic bags are used every year and it takes hundreds of years for the environment to recycle them. Plastic bags are major polluters of the world's oceans.

As another example, consider the farmer who applies pesticides to a crop to save it from insect damage. The farmer benefits immediately. However, if other farmers follow suit, the local water system may be permanently damaged. In most cases of environmental pollution, immediate benefits are gained for polluting, but the major, long-term costs are delayed. What can we do to avoid such dilemmas?

Escaping Dilemmas Persuasion and education have been used with some success to get individuals and businesses to voluntarily reduce destructive activities. Effective appeals may be based on self-interest (cost savings), the collective good (protecting one's own children and future generations), or simply a personal desire to take better care of the planet (Pelletier,

Baxter, & Huta, 2011; Winter & Koger, 2010). It really helps if conservation is seen as a group effort. There is evidence that in most social dilemmas, people are more likely to restrain themselves when they believe others will, too (Kugler & Bornstein, 2013; Nigbur, Lyons, & Uzzell, 2010). Otherwise, they are likely to think, "Why should I be a sucker? I don't think anyone else is going to conserve" (fuel, electricity, water, paper, or whatever).

In some cases, it is possible to dismantle social dilemmas by rearranging rewards and costs. For example, many companies are tempted to pollute because it saves them money and increases profits. To reverse the situation, a pollution tax could be levied so that it would cost more, not less, for a business to pollute. Likewise, incentives could be offered for responsible behavior. An example is the rebates offered for installing insulation or buying energy-efficient appliances (Schmuck & Vlek, 2003). Another is offering lower electricity rates for shifting use to off-peak times (U.S. Department of Energy, 2010).

Some problems may be harder to solve: What, for instance, can be done about truck drivers who cause dangerous traffic jams because they will not pull over on narrow roads? How can littering be discouraged or prevented? How would you make carpooling or using public transportation the first choice for most people? How could people simply be encouraged to stagger their departure times to and from work? All these and more are social dilemmas that need solving. It is important that we not fall into the trap of ignoring them (van Dijk, Parks, & van Lange, 2013).

Environmental Problem Solving

How do psychologists find solutions to problems like overcrowding, pollution, and overuse of resources? Solutions can more easily be found by doing **environmental assessments** to see how environments influence the behavior and perceptions of the people using them.

For example, anyone who has ever lived in a college dorm knows that at times a dorm hall can be quite a "crazy house." In one well-known environmental assessment, Baum and Valins (1977) found that students housed in long, narrow, corridor-design dormitories often feel crowded and stressed. The crowded students tended to withdraw from others and even made more trips to the campus health center than students living in less-crowded buildings.

Through **architectural psychology**, the study of the effects buildings have on behavior, psychologists are often able to suggest design changes that solve or avoid problems

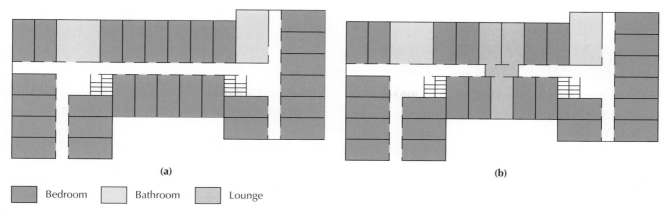

(a)   (b)

◾ Bedroom   ◾ Bathroom   ◾ Lounge

● **Figure 76.3**

An architectural solution for crowding. Psychologists divided a dorm hall like that shown in the left diagram (*a*) into two shorter halls separated by unlocked doors and a lounge area (*b*). This simple change minimized unwanted social contacts and greatly reduced feelings of crowding among dorm residents. [Baum, A., & Davis, G. E. (1980). Reducing the stress of high-density living: An architectural intervention. *Journal of Personality & Social Psychology, 38*, 471–481].

(Zeisel, 2006). For example, Baum and Valins (1979) studied two basic dorm arrangements. One dorm had a long corridor with one central bathroom. As a result, residents were constantly forced into contact with one another. The other dorm had rooms clustered in threes. Each of these suites shared a small bathroom. Even though the amount of space available to each student was the same in both dorms, students in the long-corridor dorm reported feeling more crowded. They also made fewer friends in their dorm and showed greater signs of withdrawing from social contact.

What sort of solution does this suggest? A later study showed that small architectural changes can greatly reduce stress in high-density living conditions. Baum and Davis (1980) compared students living in a long-corridor dorm housing 40 students with those living in an altered long-corridor dorm. In the altered dorm, Baum and Davis divided the hallway in half with unlocked doors and made three center bedrooms into a lounge area (● **Figure 76.3**). At the end of the term, students living in the divided dorm reported less stress from crowding. They also formed more friendships and were more open to social contacts. In comparison, students in the long-corridor dorm felt more crowded, stressed, and unfriendly, and they kept their doors shut much more frequently—presumably because they "wanted to be alone."

Similar improvements have been made by altering the interior design of businesses, schools, apartment buildings, mental hospitals, and prisons. In general, the more spaces one must pass through to get from one part of a building to another,

the less stressed and crowded people feel (Evans, Lepore, & Schroeder, 1996; Zeisel, 2006).

Conclusion

We have had room here only to hint at the creative and highly useful work being done in environmental psychology. Although many environmental problems remain, it is encouraging to see that behavioral solutions exist for at least some of them. Surely, creating and maintaining healthy environments is one of the major challenges facing coming generations (Des Jardins, 2013; Winter & Koger, 2010).

We have discussed work and the environment at some length because both have major effects on our lives. To provide a fuller account of the diversity of applied psychology, let's conclude by briefly sampling four additional topics of interest: educational psychology, legal psychology, sports psychology, and human factors psychology.

Tragedy of the commons *A social dilemma in which individuals, each acting in his or her immediate self-interest, overuse a scarce group resource.*
Environmental assessment *Measurement and analysis of the effects an environment has on the behavior and perceptions of people within that environment.*
Architectural psychology *Study of the effects buildings have on behavior and the design of buildings using behavioral principles.*

Module 76: Summary

76.1 What have psychologists learned about the effects of our physical and social environments?

- **76.1.1** Environmental psychologists are interested in behavioral settings, physical and social environments, sustainability, and human territoriality, among other topics.
- **76.1.2** The study of personal space is called proxemics. The nature of many relationships is revealed by the distance you are comfortable maintaining between yourself and another person.
- **76.1.3** Territorial behaviors, including territorial markers, are used to define a space as one's own or that protect it from intruders.
- **76.1.4** Environmental problems such as crowding, pollution, and wasted resources are based on human behavior; they can be solved only by changing behavior patterns.
- **76.1.5** Animal experiments indicate that excessive crowding can be unhealthy. However, human research shows that psychological

feelings of crowding do not always correspond to density. One major consequence of crowding is attentional overload.

76.2 What effect are humans having on the natural environment?

- **76.2.1** The origins of many environmental disasters lie in overpopulation and overconsumption.
- **76.2.2** Providing feedback about resource use is an effective way to promote conservation. Research indicates that various psychological strategies can promote recycling.
- **76.2.3** Social dilemmas, such as the tragedy of the commons, arise when people are enticed into overuse of scarce, shared resources.
- **76.2.4** Environmental psychologists offer solutions to many practical problems—from noise pollution to architectural design. Their work often begins with a careful environmental assessment.

Module 76: Knowledge Builder

Recite

1. If two people position themselves 5 feet apart while conversing, they are separated by a gap referred to as _____ distance.

2. Although male rats in Calhoun's crowded animal colony became quite pathological, female rats continued to behave in a relatively normal fashion. *T or F?*

3. Milgram believed that many city dwellers prevent attentional overload by limiting themselves to superficial social contacts. *T or F?*

4. Using tools like smart meters and ecological footprint calculators to provide feedback is one effective approach for bringing about energy conservation. *T or F?*

5. So far, the most successful approach for bringing about energy conservation is to add monetary penalties to monthly bills for excessive consumption. *T or F?*

6. Performing an environmental _____ might be a good prelude to redesigning college classrooms to make them more comfortable and conducive to learning.

Reflect

Think Critically

7. Many of the most damaging changes to the environment being caused by humans will not be felt until sometime in the future. How does this complicate the problem of preserving environmental quality?

Self-Reflect

What is the nature of your current natural environment, constructed environment, social environment, and behavioral setting?

What forms of territorial behavior are you aware of in your own actions?

Have you ever experienced a stressful level of crowding? Was density or control the key factor?

Have you ever calculated your carbon footprint? Why not try it? You might be surprised by what you find.

ANSWERS

1. social 2. F 3. T 4. T 5. F 6. assessment 7. A delay of consequences (rewards, benefits, costs, and punishments) tends to reduce their impact on immediate behavior.

Applied Psychology: The Psychology of Law, Education, and Sports

Enough for the Death Penalty?

In May 2013, a jury of her peers convicted Jodi Arias of brutally murdering her former boyfriend while in a fit of jealous rage. The jury reached their verdict after more than four months of often lurid testimony. And then it got even more traumatic because the original jury could not decide whether or not to sentence Arias to death for her crime. When most people think about psychology and the law, they think about *Criminal Minds*. Yet, understanding the minds of jurors is at least as important to the legal process.

Three of the best places to see psychology in action are in a courthouse, in a classroom, and at sporting events. These settings are all capable of bringing out some of the best and worst of human behavior. It is worth applying psychology to foster

AP Photo/The Arizona Republic, Rob Schumacher, Pool

the best rather than the worst. Let's begin with a look at the psychology of juries.

SURVEY QUESTIONS

77.1 What does psychology reveal about juries and court verdicts?

77.2 How has psychology improved education?

77.3 Can psychology enhance athletic performance?

Psychology and Law—Judging Juries

SURVEY QUESTION 77.1: What does psychology reveal about juries and court verdicts?

One of the best places to see psychology in action is the local courthouse. Jury trials are often fascinating studies in human behavior. Does the defendant's appearance affect the jury's decision? Do the personality characteristics or attitudes of jurors influence how they vote? These and many more questions have been investigated by psychologists interested in law. Specifically, the **psychology of law** is the study of the

behavioral dimensions of the legal system (Greene & Heilbrun, 2014; see ● Table 77.1).

Jury Behavior

When a case goes to trial, jurors must listen to days or weeks of testimony and then decide guilt or innocence. How do they reach their decision? Psychologists use **mock juries**, or simulated juries, to probe such questions. In some mock juries, volunteers are simply given written evidence and arguments to read before making a decision. Others watch videotaped trials staged by actors. Either way, studying the behavior of mock juries helps us understand what determines how real jurors vote (Pezdek, Avila-Mora, & Sperry, 2010).

Some of the findings of jury research are unsettling (Peoples et al., 2012). Studies show that jurors are rarely able to put

TABLE 77.1	Topics of Special Interest in the Psychology of Law	
Arbitration	Juror attitudes
Attitudes toward law	Jury decisions
Bail setting	Jury selection
Capital punishment	Mediation
Conflict resolution	Memory
Criminal personality	Parole board decisions
Diversion programs	Police selection
Effects of parole	Police stress
Expert testimony	Police training
Eyewitness testimony	Polygraph accuracy
Forensic hypnosis	Sentencing decisions
Insanity plea	White-collar crime

© Cengage Learning

aside their biases, attitudes, and values while making a decision (Buck & Warren, 2010; Stawiski, Dykema-Engblade, & Tindale, 2012). For example, appearance can be unduly influential (see Module 72). Jurors are less likely to find attractive defendants guilty (on the basis of the same evidence) than unattractive defendants. In one mock jury study, defendants were less likely to be convicted if they were wearing eyeglasses than if they were not. Presumably, eyeglasses imply intelligence and, hence, that the defendant wouldn't do anything as foolish as what he or she was accused of (Brown, Henriquez, & Groscup, 2008; Perlman & Cozby, 1983).

Another major problem is that jurors are not very good at separating evidence from other information, such as their perceptions of the defendant, attorneys, witnesses, and what they think the judge wants. For example, if complex scientific evidence is presented, jurors tend to be swayed more by the expertise of the witness than by the evidence itself (Cooper, Bennett, & Sukel, 1996; Hans et al., 2011). Similarly, today's jurors place too much confidence in DNA evidence because crime-solving programs like *CSI* and *Forensic Files* make it seem simple (Myers, 2007). Further, jurors who have been exposed to pretrial publicity tend to inappropriately incorporate that information into their jury deliberations, often without being aware it has happened (Ruva, McEvoy, & Bryant, 2007).

Often the jurors' final verdict is influenced by inadmissible evidence, such as mention of a defendant's prior conviction. When jurors are told to ignore information that slips out in court, they find it very hard to do so. A related problem occurs when jurors take into account the severity of the punishment a defendant faces (Sales & Hafemeister, 1985). Jurors are not supposed to let this affect their verdict, but many do.

Yet another area of difficulty arises because jurors usually cannot suspend judgment until all the evidence is presented. Typically, they form an opinion early in the trial. It then becomes hard for them to fairly judge evidence that contradicts their opinion.

Problems like these are troubling in a legal system that prides itself on fairness. However, all is not lost. The more severe the crime and the more clear-cut the evidence, the less a jury's quirks affect the verdict. Although it is far from perfect, the jury system works reasonably well in most cases (Greene & Heilbrun, 2014).

Jury Selection

In many cases, the composition of a jury has a major effect on the verdict of a trial (Kovera & Cutler, 2013). Before a trial begins, opposing attorneys are allowed to disqualify potential jurors who may be biased. For example, a person who knows anyone connected with the trial can be excluded. Beyond this, attorneys try to use jury selection to remove people who may cause trouble for them. For instance, juries composed of women are more likely to vote for conviction in child sexual assault trials (Eigenberg et al., 2012; Golding et al., 2007).

Only a limited number of potential jurors can be excused. As a result, many attorneys ask psychologists for help in identifying people who will favor or harm their efforts. In **scientific jury selection**, social science principles are applied to the process of choosing a jury (Lieberman, 2011; Lieberman & Sales, 2007). Several techniques are typically used. As a first step, *demographic information* may be collected for each juror. Much can be guessed by knowing a juror's age, sex, race, occupation, education, political affiliation, religion, and socioeconomic status. Most of this information is available from public records.

To supplement demographic information, a *community survey* may be done to find out how local citizens feel about the case. The assumption is that jurors probably have attitudes similar to people with backgrounds like their own. Although

Critical Thinking

Death-Qualified Juries

People in a **death-qualified jury** must favor the death penalty or at least be indifferent to it. That way, jurors are capable of voting for the death penalty if they think it is justified.

Death-qualified juries may be a necessity for the death penalty to have meaning. However, psychologists have discovered that the makeup of such juries tends to be biased. Specifically, death-qualified juries are likely to contain a disproportionate number of people who are male, white, high income, conservative, and authoritarian. Given the same facts, jurors who favor the death penalty are more likely to read criminal intent into a defendant's actions (Goodman-Delahunty, Greene, & Hsiao, 1998; Summers, Hayward, & Miller, 2010) and are much more likely than average to convict a defendant (Allen, Mabry, & McKelton, 1998; Butler, 2007).

Could death-qualified juries be too willing to convict? It is nearly impossible to say how often the bias inherent in death-qualified juries results in bad verdicts. However, the possibility that some innocent persons have been executed may be one of the inevitable costs of using death as the ultimate punishment.

Tim Wright/CORBIS

talking with potential jurors outside the courtroom is not permitted, other information networks are available. For instance, a psychologist may interview relatives, acquaintances, neighbors, and coworkers of potential jurors.

Back in court, psychologists also often watch for *authoritarian personality* traits in potential jurors. Authoritarians tend to believe that punishment is effective, and they are more likely to vote for conviction (Devine et al., 2001; see Module 73). At the same time, the psychologist typically observes potential jurors' *nonverbal behavior*. The idea is to try to learn from body language which side the person favors.

In the United States, murder trials require a special jury—one made up of people who are not opposed to the death penalty. "Death-Qualified Juries" examines the implications of this practice.

In the well-publicized case of O. J. Simpson, who was accused of brutally killing his wife and her friend, a majority of African Americans thought Simpson was innocent during the early stages of the trial. In contrast, the majority of European Americans thought he was guilty. The opinions of both groups changed little over the course of the yearlong trial. (Simpson was eventually acquitted, but he later lost a civil lawsuit brought by the victims' families.) The fact that

emerging evidence and arguments had little effect on what people believed shows why jury makeup can sometimes decide the outcome of a trial (Cohn et al., 2009).

Cases like Simpson's raise troubling ethical questions. Wealthy clients have the advantage of scientific jury selection—something most people cannot afford. Attorneys, of course, can't be blamed for trying to improve their odds of winning a case. And because both sides help select jurors, the net effect in most instances is probably a more balanced jury. At its worst, jury analysis leads to unjust verdicts. At its best, it helps to identify and remove only people who would be highly biased (Kovera & Cutler, 2013).

Jury research is perhaps the most direct link between psychology and law, but there are others. Psychologists evaluate people for sanity hearings, do counseling in prisons, profile criminals,

Psychology of law Study of the psychological and behavioral dimensions of the legal system.
Mock jury A group that realistically simulates a courtroom jury.
Scientific jury selection Using social science principles to choose members of a jury.
Death-qualified jury A jury composed of people who favor the death penalty or at least are indifferent to it.

advise lawmakers on public policy, help select and train police cadets, and more (Greene & Heilbrun, 2014; Wrightsman & Fulero, 2009). In the future, it is quite likely that psychology will have a growing impact on law and the courts.

Educational Psychology—An Instructive Topic

SURVEY QUESTION 77.2: How has psychology improved education?

You have just been asked to teach a class of fourth graders for a day. What will you do? (Assume that bribery, showing them movies, and a field trip to an amusement park are out.) If you ever do try teaching, you might be surprised at how challenging it is. Effective teachers must understand learning, instruction, classroom dynamics, and testing.

What are the best ways to teach? Is there an optimal teaching style for different age groups, topics, or individuals? These and related questions lie at the heart of educational psychology (● Table 77.2). Specifically, **educational psychology** seeks to understand how people learn and how teachers instruct (Snowman & McCown, 2013).

TABLE 77.2	Topics of Special Interest to Educational Psychologists	
Aptitude testing	Language learning
Classroom management	Learning theory
Classroom motivation	Moral development
Classroom organization	Student adjustment
Concept learning	Student attitudes
Curriculum development	Student needs
Disabled students	Teacher attitudes
Exceptional students	Teaching strategies
Gifted students	Teaching styles
Individualized instruction	Test writing
Intellectual development	Transfer of learning
Intelligence testing	

Educational psychologists are interested in enhancing learning and improving teaching.

Elements of a Teaching Strategy

Whether it's "breaking in" a new coworker, instructing a friend in a hobby, or helping a child learn to read, the fact is, we all teach at times. The next time you are asked to share your knowledge, how will you do it? One good way to become more effective is to use a specific **teaching strategy**, or planned method of instruction. The example that follows was designed for classroom use, but it applies to many other situations as well (Ormrod, 2014):

Step 1: Learner preparation. Begin by gaining the learner's attention and focus interest on the topic at hand.

Step 2: Stimulus presentation. Present instructional stimuli (information, examples, and illustrations) deliberately and clearly.

Step 3: Learner response. Allow time for the learner to respond to the information presented (by repeating correct responses or asking questions, for example).

Step 4: Reinforcement. Give positive reinforcement (praise, encouragement) and feedback ("Yes, that's right," "No, this way," and so on) to strengthen correct responses.

Step 5: Evaluation. Test or assess the learner's progress so that both you and the learner can make adjustments when needed.

Step 6: Spaced review. Periodic review is an important step in teaching because it helps strengthen responses to key stimuli.

Effects of Learning and Teaching Styles *Isn't there more to teaching than following a particular teaching strategy?* Effective teachers don't just use a teaching strategy to present material to their students. They also recognize that different students may have different *learning styles* and that it is possible to use different *teaching styles*.

There are many different approaches to the topic of learning styles. One stems from Howard Gardner's theory of multiple intelligences (see Module 40). Someone high in language ability may learn best by hearing or reading, someone high in visual intelligence may learn best through pictures, someone high in interpersonal intelligence may learn best working in groups, and so on (Gardner, 2008; Kornhaber & Gardner, 2006).

There also is little doubt that teachers can greatly affect student interest, motivation, and creativity. But what styles have what effects? To answer this question, psychologists have compared several teaching styles. Two of the most basic are *direct instruction* and *discovery learning*.

In **direct instruction**, factual information is presented by lecture, demonstration, and rote practice. In **discovery learning**, teachers create conditions that encourage students to discover or construct knowledge for themselves (Dean & Kuhn, 2007). As it turns out, both approaches have certain advantages. Students of direct instruction do slightly better on achievement tests than students in discovery classrooms (Klahr & Nigam, 2004). However, students of discovery learning do somewhat better on tests of abstract thinking, creativity, and problem solving. They also tend to be more independent, curious, and positive in their attitudes toward school (Scruggs & Mastropieri, 2007). At present, it looks as if a balance of teaching styles goes hand in hand with a balanced education.

Although we have viewed only a small sample of educational theory and research, its value for improving teaching and learning should be apparent (Snowman & McCown, 2012). Before we leave the topic of education, "Peanut Butter for the Mind: Designing Education for Everyone" offers a peek at where education is going in the future.

Sports Psychology—Psyched!

SURVEY QUESTION 77.3: Can psychology enhance athletic performance?

What does psychology have to do with sports? **Sports psychology** is the study of the behavioral dimensions of sports performance (Cox, 2011). As almost all serious athletes soon learn, peak performance requires more than physical training.

Mental and emotional "conditioning" also are important. Recognizing this fact, many teams, both professional and amateur, now include psychologists on their staffs. On any given day, a sports psychologist might teach an athlete how to relax, how to ignore distractions, or how to cope with emotions. The sports psychologist also might provide personal counseling for performance-lowering stresses and conflicts (LeUnes, 2008). Other psychologists are interested in studying factors that affect athletic achievement, such as skill learning, the personality profiles of champion athletes, the effects of spectators, and related topics (● Table 77.3). In short, sports psychologists seek to understand and improve sports performance and to enhance the benefits of participating in sports (Cox, 2011).

Sports often provide valuable information on human behavior in general. For example, one study of adolescents found a link between sports participation and physical self-esteem

TABLE 77.3	Topics of Special Interest to Sports Psychologists	
Achievement motivation	Hypnosis
Athletic personality	Mental practice
Athletic task analysis	Motor learning
Coaching styles	Peak performance
Competition	Positive visualization
Control of attention	Self-regulation
Coping strategies	Skill acquisition
Emotions and performance	Social facilitation
Exercise and mental health	Stress reduction
Goal setting	Team cooperation
Group (team) dynamics	Training procedures

© Cengage Learning

Educational psychology *The field that seeks to understand how people learn and how teachers instruct.*
Teaching strategy *A plan for effective teaching.*
Direct instruction *Presentation of factual information by lecture, demonstration, and rote practice.*
Discovery learning *Instruction based on encouraging students to discover or construct knowledge for themselves.*
Sports psychology *Study of the psychological and behavioral dimensions of sports performance.*

Human Diversity

Peanut Butter for the Mind: Designing Education for Everyone

"Education is the key to unlock the golden door of freedom," said George Washington Carver. Born in 1860, a son of slaves, he invented that universally popular food, peanut butter. In today's ever-more-complicated world, Carver's words ring truer than ever. Yet educators face an increasingly diverse mix of students: "regular" students, adult learners, students who have disabilities, students who speak English as a second language, and students at risk for dropping out (Bowe, 2000). In response, educators have begun to apply an approach called *Universal Design for Instruction* (Holbrook, Moore, & Zoss, 2010). The basic idea is to design lessons so richly that they will benefit most, if not all, students and their diverse needs and learning styles.

One principle of Universal Design for Instruction is to use a variety of instructional methods, such as a lecture, a podcast of the lecture, a group activity, an Internet discussion list, and perhaps student blogs. That way, for example, students with hearing or visual impairments can find at least one learning approach they can use.

Likewise, adult learners who can't always get to class because of work or family responsibilities can get course information in other ways. Ultimately, everyone benefits because we all learn better if we can choose among different ways of gaining knowledge. Besides, it's not a bad idea to work through learning materials more than once in different ways.

Another principle is to make learning materials simple and intuitive by removing unnecessary complexity. For instance, students can be given clear grading standards, accurate and complete course outlines, and handbooks to guide them through difficult topics. Again, such materials are not just better for special groups of students. They make learning easier for all of us.

Are these principles being applied to learning in colleges and universities? In short, yes they are (McGuire & Scott, 2002; Orr & Hammig, 2009; Thoma, Bartholomew, & Scott, 2009). Universal instruction has broad appeal—like peanut butter—but fortunately it won't stick to the roof of your mind!

---

that was, in turn, linked with overall self-esteem (Bowker, 2006). In other work, psychologists have learned that such benefits are most likely to occur when competition, rejection, criticism, and the "one-winner mentality" are minimized. When working with children in sports, it also is important to emphasize fair play, intrinsic rewards, self-control of emotions, independence, and self-reliance.

Adults, of course, also may benefit from sports through reduced stress, better self-image, and improved general health (Khan et al., 2012; Williams, 2010). Running, for instance, is associated with lower levels of tension, anxiety, fatigue, and depression than are found in the nonrunning population.

Before the advent of sports psychology, it was debatable whether athletes improved because of "homespun" coaching methods or in spite of them. For example, in early studies of volleyball and gymnastics, it became clear that people teaching these sports had very little knowledge of crucial, underlying skills (Salmela, 1974, 1975).

How has psychology helped? An ability to do detailed studies of complex skills has been one of the major contributions. In a **task analysis**, sports skills are broken into subparts so that key elements can be identified and taught (Hewit, Cronin, & Hume, 2012). Such methods are an extension of techniques first used for job analyses, as described earlier. For example, it doesn't take much to be off target in the Olympic sport of

Baltimore Sun/McClatchy-Tribune/Getty Images

Testing by psychologists has shown that umpires can call balls and strikes more accurately if they stand behind the outside corner of home plate. This position supplies better height and distance information because umpires are able to see pitches pass in front of the batter (Ford et al., 1999).

---

marksmanship. The object is to hit a bull's-eye the size of a dime at the end of a 165-foot-long shooting range. Nevertheless, an average of 50 bull's-eyes out of 60 shots is not unusual in international competition (prone position).

What does it take—beyond keen eyes and steady hands—to achieve such accuracy? The answer is surprising. Sports psychologists have found that top marksmen consistently squeeze the trigger *between* heartbeats (● **Figure 77.1**).

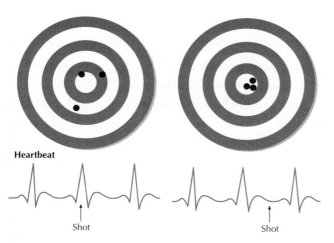

Heartbeat

Shot   Shot

● **Figure 77.1**

The target on the left shows what happens when a marksman fires during the heart's contraction. Higher scores, as shown by the three shots on the right, are more likely when shots are made between heartbeats. (Adapted from Pelton, 1983.)

Apparently, the tiny tremor induced by a heartbeat is enough to send the shot astray (Pelton, 1983). Without careful psychological study, it is doubtful that this element of marksmanship would have been identified. Now that its importance is known, competitors have begun to use various techniques—from relaxation training to biofeedback—to steady and control their heartbeat. In the future, the best marksmen may be those who set their sights on mastering their hearts.

Motor Skills Sports psychologists are very interested in how we learn motor skills (Hodges & Williams, 2012). A **motor skill** is a series of actions molded into a smooth and efficient performance. Typing, walking, pole-vaulting, shooting baskets, playing golf, driving a car, writing, and skiing are all motor skills.

A basketball player may never make exactly the same shot twice in a game. This makes it almost impossible to practice every shot that might occur. How, then, do athletes become skillful? Typically, athletic performances involve learning *motor programs*. A **motor program** is a mental plan or model of what a skilled movement should be like. Motor programs allow an athlete—or a person simply walking across a room—to perform complex movements that fit changing conditions. If, for example, you have learned a "bike-riding" motor program, you can easily ride bicycles of different sizes and types on a large variety of surfaces.

Throughout life, you will face the challenge of learning new motor skills. How can psychology make your learning more effective? Studies of sports skills suggest that you should keep the following points in mind for optimal skill learning (Karagheorgis & Terry, 2011; Williams, 2010):

1. Begin by observing and imitating a *skilled model*. Modeling provides a good mental picture of the skill. At this point, try simply to grasp a visual image of the skilled movement.

2. Learn *verbal rules* to back up motor learning. Such rules are usually most helpful in the early phases of skill learning. When first learning cross-country skiing, for example, it is helpful to say, "left arm, right foot, right arm, left foot." Later, as a skill becomes more automated, internal speech may actually get in the way.

3. Practice should be as *lifelike* as possible so that artificial cues and responses do not become a part of the skill. A competitive diver should practice on the board, not on a trampoline. If you want to learn to ski, try to practice on snow, not straw.

4. Get *feedback* from a mirror, videotape, coach, or observer. Whenever possible, get someone experienced in the skill to direct attention to *correct responses* when they occur.

5. When possible, it is better to practice *natural units* rather than break the task into artificial parts. When learning to type, it is better to start with real words rather than nonsense syllables.

6. Learn to *evaluate* and *analyze* your own performance. Remember, you are trying to learn a motor program, not just train your muscles. In reality, motor skills are quite mental.

The last point leads to one more suggestion. Research has shown that **mental practice**, or merely imagining a skilled performance, can aid learning (Blumenstein & Orbach, 2012). This technique seems to help by refining motor programs. Of course, mental practice is not superior to actual practice. Mental practice tends to be most valuable after you have mastered a task at a basic level. When you begin to get really good at a skill, give mental practice a try. You may be surprised at how effective it can be (Caliari, 2008; Short, Ross-Stewart, & Monsma, 2006).

Task analysis *Breaking complex skills into their subparts.*
Motor skill *A series of actions molded into a smooth and efficient performance.*
Motor program *A mental plan or model that guides skilled movement.*
Mental practice *Imagining a skilled performance to aid learning.*

The Whole Human: Peak Performance

One of the most interesting topics in sports psychology is the phenomenon of *peak performance*. During **peak performance**, physical, mental, and emotional states are harmonious and optimal. Many athletes report episodes during which they felt almost as if they were in a trance. The experience also has been called *flow* because the athlete becomes one with his or her performance and flows with it. At such times, athletes experience intense concentration, detachment, a lack of fatigue and pain, a subjective slowing of time, and feelings of unusual power and control (Dietrich & Stoll, 2010; Hartley, 2012). It is at just such times that "personal bests" tend to occur.

A curious aspect of flow is that it cannot be forced to happen. In fact, if a person stops to think about it, the flow state goes away. Psychologists are now seeking to identify conditions that facilitate peak performance and the unusual mental state that usually accompanies it (Harmison, 2011).

Even though flow may be an elusive state, there is much that athletes can do mentally to improve performance (Williams, 2010). A starting point is to make sure that their *arousal level is appropriate for the task* at hand. For a sprinter at a track meet, that may mean elevating arousal to a very high level. The sprinter could, for example, try to become angry by picturing a rival cheating. For a golfer or a gymnast, lowering arousal may be crucial, in order to avoid "choking" during a big event. One way of controlling arousal is to go through a *fixed routine* before each game or event. Athletes also learn to use *imagery and relaxation techniques* to adjust their degree of arousal (LeUnes, 2008).

Imaging techniques can be used to *focus attention* on the athlete's task and to *mentally rehearse* it beforehand. For example, golf great Jack Nicklaus "watches a movie" in his head before each shot. During events, athletes learn to *use cognitive-behavioral strategies to guide their efforts* in a supportive, positive way (Johnson et al., 2004). For instance, instead of berating herself for being behind in a match, a soccer player could use the time between points to savor a good shot or put an error out of mind. In general, athletes benefit from avoiding negative, self-critical thoughts that distract them and undermine their confidence (Cox, 2011). Finally, top athletes tend to use more *self-regulation strategies*, in which they evaluate their performance and make adjustments to keep it at optimum levels (Anshel, 1995; Puente & Anshel, 2010).

At present, sports psychology is a young field and still much more an art than a science. Nevertheless, interest in the field is rapidly expanding (Gallucci, 2008).

A Look Ahead Although we have sampled several major areas of applied psychology, by no means are they the only applied specialties. Others that immediately come to mind are community psychology, military psychology, and health psychology. The upcoming "Psychology in Action" module explores one of the most important applied fields: human factors psychology.

Peak performance *A performance during which physical, mental, and emotional states are harmonious and optimal.*

Module 77: Summary

77.1 What does psychology reveal about juries and court verdicts?

- **77.1.1** The psychology of law includes studies of courtroom behavior and other topics that pertain to the legal system. Psychologists also serve various consulting and counseling roles in legal, law enforcement, and criminal justice settings.
- **77.1.2** Studies of mock juries show that jury decisions are often far from objective.
- **77.1.3** Scientific jury selection is used in attempts to choose jurors who have particular characteristics. In some instances, this may result in juries that have a particular bias or that do not represent the community as a whole.
- **77.1.4** A bias toward convicting defendants is characteristic of many death-qualified juries.

77.2 How has psychology improved education?

- **77.2.1** Educational psychologists improve the quality of learning and teaching.
- **77.2.2** Educational psychologists seek to understand how people learn and teachers instruct. They are particularly interested

in teaching strategies, learning styles, and teaching styles, such as direct instruction and discovery learning.

77.3 Can psychology enhance athletic performance?

- **77.3.1** Sports psychologists seek to enhance sports performance and the benefits of sports participation. A task analysis of sports skills is a major tool for improving coaching and performance.
- **77.3.2** A motor skill is a nonverbal response chain assembled into a smooth performance. Motor skills are guided by internal mental models called motor programs.
- **77.3.3** Motor skills are refined through direct practice, but mental practice also can contribute to improvement.
- **77.3.4** During moments of peak performance, physical, mental, and emotional states are optimal.
- **77.3.5** Top performers in sports often use a variety of self-regulation strategies to focus their attention and maintain optimal levels of arousal.

Module 77: Knowledge Builder

Recite

1. Despite their many limitations, one thing that jurors are good at is setting aside inadmissible evidence. **T or F?**

2. Which of the following is *not* commonly used by psychologists to aid jury selection?
   - **a.** mock testimony
   - **b.** information networks
   - **c.** community surveys
   - **d.** demographic data

3. Evaluation of learning is typically the first step in a systematic teaching strategy. **T or F?**

4. Compared to direct instruction, discovery learning produces better scores on achievement tests. **T or F?**

5. Universal Design for Instruction aims to create educational materials that are useful to _____ students.

6. Learning verbal rules to back up motor learning is usually most helpful in the early stages of acquiring a skill. **T or F?**

7. The flow experience is closely linked with instances of _____ performance.

Reflect

Think Critically

8. When an athlete follows a set routine before an event, what source of stress has she or he eliminated?

Self-Reflect

What advice would you give a person who is about to serve on a jury if she or he wants to make an impartial judgment?

You are going to tutor a young child in arithmetic. How could you use a teaching strategy to improve your effectiveness? Would you use direct instruction or discovery learning?

How could you apply the concepts of task analysis, mental practice, and peak performance to a sport in which you are interested?

ANSWERS

1. F **2.** b **3.** F **4.** F **5.** all **6.** T **7.** peak **8.** As discussed in Module 55, stress is reduced when a person feels in control of a situation. Following a routine helps athletes maintain a sense of order and control so that they are not overaroused when the time comes to perform.

Psychology in Action: Human Factors Psychology

At the Tip of Your Finger

Smartphones, MP3 players, gaming consoles, notebook computers. By now, we're all used to the seemingly endless explosion of digital technologies. But it's not so easy to ignore their impact. Consumers have bought hundreds of millions of these devices. Digital gaming, social networking, the music business, the movie industry, and even book publishing will never be the same.

The success of these technologies almost always depends on engineers and psychologists coming up with ever-more-usable technical designs. Touch-based devices use a *multi-touch interface* to allow easy access to the full range of available digital materials. Voice recognition allows hands-free control, while gaming systems can be controlled through gesture alone.

Whether it is the computer mouse, multi-touch sensing, gestural sensing, voice-activation, or computerized systems that users with disabilities can control with brain power alone, human factors psychologists depend on understanding human behavior to help design better computer tools. Check it out.

Gregor Schuster/Corbis

SURVEY QUESTION

78.1 How are tools designed to better serve human needs?

Human Factors Psychology— Who's the Boss Here?

SURVEY QUESTION 78.1: How are tools designed to better serve human needs?

Should we serve machines or should they serve us? The demands that machines can make are all too familiar if you have ever struggled with a new cell phone or failed to put together that "easy-to-assemble" home gym. Despite all they do for us, machines are of little value unless we humans can operate them effectively. An awkward digital camera might just as well be a paperweight. An automobile design that creates large blind spots in the driver's vision could be deadly.

Designing for Human Use

The goal of **human factors psychology (ergonomics)** is to design machines and work environments so they are *compatible* with our sensory and motor capacities (Buckle, 2011; Gamache, 2004). Some areas in which human factors psychologists seek better designs can be found in ● Table 78.1.

For example, displays must be easy to perceive, controls must be easy to use, and the tendency to make errors must be minimized ● Figure 78.1. (A *display* is any dial, screen, light, or other device used to provide information about a machine's activity to a human user. A *control* is any knob, handle, button, lever, or other device used to alter the activity of a machine.)

Psychologist Donald Norman (1994) refers to successful human factors engineering as **natural design** because it is based on perceptual signals that people understand naturally,

TABLE 78.1	Topics of Special Interest to Human Factors Psychologists	
Analysis of cognitive work		Human performance in space
Augmented cognition		Human performance modeling
Aviation automation		Intercepting moving objects
Cardiovascular workload		Slips and falls
Computer-based training procedures		Navigation system design
Creativity support tools		Neuroimaging
Crew resource management training		Performance in nursing
Design of effective warnings		Physical workload
Driving safety		Primary health care efficiency
Electromyography		Product safety and effectiveness
Furniture design		Railroad human factors
Guidelines for multimedia instruction		Situation awareness
Handheld digital devices		Surgical visualization
Haptic (touch) interaction		Task interruption
Hearing in noise		Technology and aging
Human error in medicine		Transportation accident investigation
Human factors evaluation methods		Usability assessment methods
Human factors in offices		User-centered design
Human factors of homeland security		Visual display design
Human factors of information visualization		Workflow efficiency

Gahan Wilson/The New Yorker Collection/www.cartoonbank.com

"The machine's done something really weird to Mr. Hendrickson."

without needing to learn them. An example is the row of vertical buttons in elevators that mimic the layout of the floors. This is simple, natural, and clear. One way to create more natural designs is to use *metaphors* (one thing used to describe another) to create resemblances between different subjects. One famous example is the *desktop metaphor* (Terkourafi & Petrakis, 2010). The design of all current personal computers presents a visual "desktop" with images of "files," "folders," and even a "trashcan." That way, you can use your knowledge

Human factors psychology (ergonomics) *A specialty concerned with making machines and work environments compatible with human perceptual and physical capacities.*
Natural design *Human factors engineering that uses naturally understood perceptual signals.*

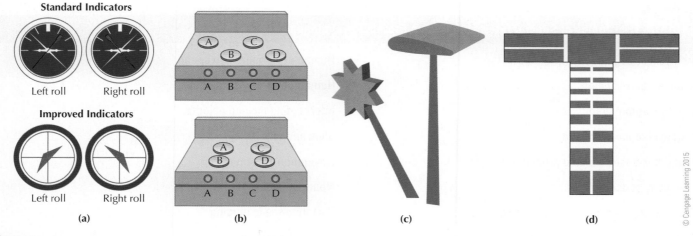

● **Figure 78.1**

Human factors engineering. (*a*) Early roll indicators in airplanes were perceptually confusing and difficult to read (top). Improved displays are clear even to nonpilots. Which would you prefer if you were flying an airplane in heavy fog? (*b*) Even on a stove, the placement of controls is important. During simulated emergencies, people made no errors in reaching for the controls on the top stove. In contrast, they erred 38 percent of the time with the bottom arrangement (Chapanis & Lindenbaum, 1959). (*c*) Sometimes the shape of a control is used to indicate its function, to discourage errors. For example, the left control might be used to engage and disengage the gears of an industrial machine, whereas the right control might operate the landing flaps on an airplane. (*d*) This design depicts a street intersection viewed from above. Psychologists have found that painting white lines across the road makes drivers feel like they are traveling faster. This effect is even stronger if the lines get progressively closer together. Placing lines near dangerous intersections or sections of highway has dramatically lowered accident rates.

of real desktops to immediately begin to use the virtual "desktop" on your computer. Earlier personal computer interfaces, which required you to type coded instructions, were much harder to use. Similarly, digital cameras are designed to look a lot like film cameras. That way, people who are familiar with film cameras can use their knowledge of how such cameras work to start using a digital camera.

Effective design also provides *feedback* (information about the effect of making a response). The artificial sounds engineered into many otherwise quiet electric cars make it easier for pedestrians to detect their presence. As Norman points out, the cause of many accidents is not just "human error." The real culprit is poor design. Human factors psychologists helped design many of the tools we rely on each day, such as "user-friendly" computers, home appliances, cameras, personal digital assistants (PDAs), airplane controls, and traffic signals.

Usability Testing To design useful tools, human factors psychologists do **usability testing**—that is, they directly measure the ease with which people can learn to use a machine (Bruno & Muzzupappa, 2010; Hamel, 2012). Health and safety also are important targets of usability testing. For example, construction workers who install steel rods in the floors of large buildings spend most of their workdays awkwardly bent over. To avoid injuries and to minimize fatigue, machines have been designed that allow workers to do the job while standing

upright. People using these machines are faster, and they spend less time in backbreaking positions (Vi, 2006).

One interesting form of usability testing is the *thinking aloud protocol*. In this case, people are asked to say everything they are thinking as they use a machine. By comparing their actual performance with what they were thinking, it is often possible to fine-tune the details of a design (Gerjets, Kammerer, & Werner, 2011; McDonald, Edwards, & Zhao, 2012).

Human–Computer Interaction

Using human factors methods to design computers and software is referred to as **human–computer interaction (HCI)** (Fuchs & Obrist, 2010; Hickling & Bowie, 2013). Traditionally, machines were designed to make us stronger (such as the automobile, which moves us faster and farther than we could go on our own). In contrast, computers are meant to make us smarter (such as software that can balance a checkbook more quickly and accurately than you could on your own). In the world of HCI, controls are called input devices and displays are called output devices. Humans communicate with computers through the *interface,* or set of input and output devices a computer provides.

The typical laptop computer today relies on a keyboard, touch pad, and perhaps voice recognition for input. Output is handled by a display screen and audio speakers. Many experts believe that current computer interfaces are too unnatural and limited when compared with the richness of human communication (Terkourafi & Petrakis, 2010).

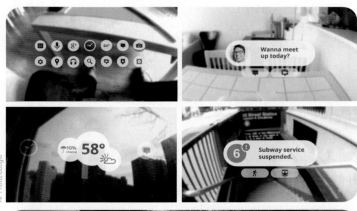

Human–computer interaction designers are actively seeking new ways to interface people with computers. Here, a Google Glass wearer gazes at various scenes. Because this wearable computer can tell where she is and in what direction she is looking, Glass can retrieve and display information about what she is looking at as she is looking.

Accordingly, the search is on for ways to open up new channels of communication between humans and computers. The Wii wand allows players using the Nintendo Wii game console to interface with games through more natural hand and body movements. Microsoft's Kinect offers an even more natural interface by eliminating the handheld controller, allowing players to play just by moving and speaking to the computer (Barras, 2010). More recently, Google's "Glass" wearable computer has broken new ground by combining a "heads-up" display with voice-controlled hands-free input.

In addition to projecting a person's actions into a virtual world, computer interfaces can create a sense of being present in a remote location (Andersson et al., 2013). *Telepresence,* as this is called, was illustrated in 2001 when a surgeon in New York first used *telesurgery* to remove the diseased gallbladder of a patient an ocean away in France. In this instance, the surgeon controlled robotic hands to perform the surgery. Because a good surgeon relies on the sense of touch, it will be important to improve telepresence systems so they provide touch feedback to users (Jin, 2010; Kitada et al., 2010).

Using Tools Effectively

Even the best-designed tools, whether for the body or the mind, can be misused or underused. Do you feel like you are in control of the tools in your life, or do you sometimes worry that they control you? The following tips will help make sure you get the most out of the tools you use.

Understand Your Task Using a tool like a digital camera, a cell phone, or social networking software can be challenging, especially if you are not sure what it can do. Begin by finding out more about what specific tasks your new tool is designed to help you accomplish. For example, if you are buying photo-editing software for your digital camera, find out what tools it offers to adjust, improve, and transform photographs.

In our hectic modern world, **satisficing**, or just getting by rather than doing things really well, is often tempting (Güth, Levati, & Ploner, 2009). Satisficing is not just a matter of being lazy. Getting by can be a survival skill, but it does not always take full advantage of the tools available to us. For example, if you know a little about photography and jump into using your new digital camera, you may be satisfied with just being able to take a basic photo. However, if you stop there, you will have used about 10 percent of what your camera is capable of doing.

Understand Your Tools As tempting as it may be to just dive in and use your new tool, do take a peek at the instruction manual. Many modern tools, especially electronic devices, have valuable capacities hidden several layers down in menus. Without reading a manual, you might never find some of them, no matter how user-friendly the device's interface may be.

Usability testing *The empirical investigation of the ease with which users can learn to use a machine.*
Human–computer interaction (HCI) *The application of human factors to the design of computers and computer software.*
Satisficing *Engaging in behavior that achieves an acceptable result, rather than an optimal result.*

Space Habitats

Let's conclude on a high note: Nowhere are the demands on human factors psychology greater than in space flight. Every machine, tool, and environment in a spacecraft must be carefully adapted for human use (Mulavara et al., 2010). Already, we have discovered that life on the International Space Station isn't easy, physically or mentally. For months at a time, residents are restricted to tiny living quarters with little privacy. These conditions, and other sources of stress, make it clear that the design of space habitats must take many human needs into account. For instance, researchers have learned that astronauts prefer rooms that clearly define "up" and "down"—even in the weightlessness of space. This can be done by color-coding walls, floors, and ceilings and by orienting furniture and controls so they all face the "ceiling" (Suedfeld & Steel, 2000).

Ideally, there should be some flexibility in the use of living and work areas inside a space station. Behavior patterns change over time, and being able to control one's environment helps lower stress. At the same time, people need stability. Psychologists have found, for instance, that eating becomes an important high point in monotonous environments. Eating at least one meal together each day can help keep crew members working as a social unit.

Sleep cycles must be carefully controlled in space to avoid disrupting body rhythms (Kanas & Manzey, 2008; Suedfeld & Steel, 2000). In past space missions, some astronauts found they couldn't sleep while other crew members continued to work and talk. Problems with sleep can be worsened by the constant noise on a space station. At first, such noise is annoying. After weeks or months, it can become a serious stressor. Researchers are experimenting with various earmuffs, eyeshades, and sleeping arrangements to alleviate such difficulties.

Sensory Restriction
Sensory monotony can be a problem in space—even the magnificent vistas of Earth become repetitive (Kanas & Manzey, 2008). (How many times would you have to see the North American continent before you lost interest?)

Researchers are developing stimulus environments that use music, movies, and other diversions to combat monotony and boredom. Again, they are trying to provide choice and

The International Space Station provides a habitat in which men and women can live and work in space for extended periods. Solving the behavioral problems of living in space will be an important step toward human exploration of the solar system.

control for space crews. Studies of confined living in the Arctic and elsewhere make it clear that one person's symphony is another's grating noise. Where music is concerned, individual earphones may be all that is required to avoid problems.

Most people in restricted environments find that they prefer solitary pastimes such as reading, listening to music, looking out windows, writing, and watching films or television. As much as anything, this preference may again show the need for privacy. Reading or listening to music is a good way to psychologically withdraw from the group. Experiences with confining environments on Earth (such as Biosphere 2) suggest that including live animals and plants in space habitats could reduce stress and boredom (Suedfeld & Steel, 2000).

Life on Spaceship Earth It is curiously fitting that the dazzling technology of space travel has highlighted the inevitable importance of human behavior. Here on Earth, as in space, we cannot count on cleverly designed machines or technology alone to solve problems. The threat of nuclear war, social conflict, crime, prejudice, infectious disease, overpopulation, environmental damage, famine, homicide, economic disaster, and most other major problems facing us are behavioral.

Will spaceship Earth endure? It's a psychological question.

Module 78: Summary

78.1 How are tools designed to better serve human needs?

- **78.1.1** Human factors psychologists (also known as ergonomists) design tools to be compatible with our sensory and motor capacities.
- **78.1.2** Successful human factors engineering uses natural design, which uses perceptual signals that people understand naturally.
- **78.1.3** Human factors psychologists rely on usability testing to empirically confirm that machines are easy to learn and use.

- **78.1.4** Human–computer interaction (HCI) is the application of human factors to the design of computers and computer software.
- **78.1.5** To use tools effectively, it is useful to know something about the tool and the task you are using it to complete. Be aware of satisficing.
- **78.1.6** Space habitats must be designed with special attention to the numerous human factors issues raised by space flight.

Module 78: Knowledge Builder

Recite

1. Human factors psychologists are interested in finding ways to help people adapt to working with machines. *T or F?*

2. According to Donald Norman, successful human factors engineering makes use of perceptual signals that people understand naturally. *T or F?*

3. Usability testing is used to empirically investigate machine designs. *T or F?*

4. To use tools effectively, it is worth
   - *a.* understanding your tool
   - *b.* satisficing
   - *c.* understanding your task
   - *d.* overcoming writer's block

5. Researchers have learned that astronauts don't really care if living quarters have clearly defined "up" and "down" orientations. *T or F?*

Reflect
Think Critically

6. Check out this photo of a men's urinal in Amsterdam's Schiphol Airport. Is that fly real? If not, why is it there?

Self-Reflect

Is there a machine whose design you admire? Can you express why the design works for you?

Have you thought about how you write? Are you using your word processor to your best advantage? What could you be improving?

John Mitterer

This fly is not real; it is painted onto this urinal from Amsterdam's Schiphol Airport. Why?

ANSWERS

1. F 2. T 3. T 4. a and c 5. F 6. Men tend to aim at the "fly" and hence are more accurate when they urinate. The result is much cleaner men's washrooms.

Appendix: Behavioral Statistics

Why Numbers?

Jackson decided to major in psychology after he began to seriously study martial arts. He was quite surprised by how much his martial arts workouts improved his ability to concentrate on everything, including his schoolwork. But his psychology studies almost came to a premature end when he found out he needed to take a statistics course to graduate. "Numbers," he muttered. "Why numbers? Doesn't psychology study people?"

Thankfully, Jackson's curiosity about martial arts and concentration in particular, and human behavior in general, was stronger than his apprehension about statistics. By the time Jackson got to his third year and began to design research projects and collect data, he understood that the results of psychological studies are often expressed as numbers, which psychologists must summarize and interpret before they have any meaning. What follows is an overview of how statistics are used in psychology.

Lucy Baldwin/Shutterstock

SURVEY QUESTIONS

79.1 What are descriptive statistics?

79.2 How are statistics used to identify an average score?

79.3 What statistics do psychologists use to measure how much scores differ from one another?

79.4 How are correlations used in psychology?

79.5 What are inferential statistics?

Descriptive Statistics— Psychology by the Numbers

SURVEY QUESTION 79.1: What are descriptive statistics?

Statistics bring greater clarity and precision to psychological thought and research (Gravetter & Wallnau, 2013). In fact, it is difficult to make scientific arguments about human behavior without depending on statistics. Psychologists depend on two major types of statistics. **Descriptive statistics** describe and summarize, or "boil down," data collected from research participants so the results become more meaningful and easier to communicate to others. In comparison, **inferential statistics** are used for decision making, for generalizing from small samples, and for drawing conclusions. Psychologists must often base decisions on limited data. Such decisions are much easier to make with the help of inferential statistics.

Let's begin by considering three basic types of descriptive statistics: *graphical statistics,* measures of *central tendency,* and measures of *variability*.

Graphical Statistics

Graphical statistics present numbers pictorially, so they are easier to visualize. At one point, Jackson got a chance to study differences in concentration. ● Table 79.1 shows the scores he obtained when he gave a test of concentration to 100 college students. With such disorganized data, it is hard to form an overall picture of the differences in concentration. But by using a *frequency distribution*, large amounts of information can be neatly organized and summarized. A **frequency distribution** is made by breaking down the entire range of possible scores into classes of equal size. Next, the number of scores falling into each class is recorded. In ● Table 79.2, Jackson's raw data from Table 79.1 have been condensed into a frequency distribution. Notice how much clearer the pattern of scores for the entire group becomes.

Frequency distributions are often shown *graphically* to make them more "visual." A **histogram**, or graph of a frequency distribution, is made by labeling class intervals on the *abscissa* (X axis or horizontal line) and frequencies (the number of scores in each class) on the *ordinate* (Y axis or vertical line). Next, bars are drawn for each class interval; the height of each bar is determined by the number of scores in each class (● **Figure 79.1**). An alternate way of graphing scores is the more familiar **frequency polygon** (● **Figure 79.2**). Here, points are placed at the center of each class interval to indicate the number of scores. Then the dots are connected by straight lines.

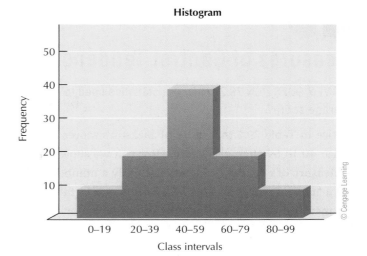

Figure 79.1

Frequency histogram of concentration scores contained in Table 79.2.

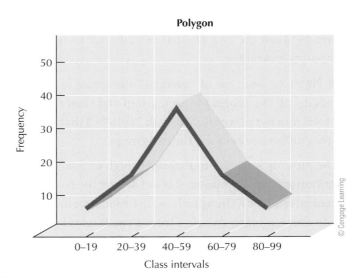

Figure 79.2

Frequency polygon of concentration scores contained in Table 79.2.

TABLE 79.1	Raw Scores of Concentration								
55	86	52	17	61	57	84	51	16	64
22	56	25	38	35	24	54	26	37	38
52	42	59	26	21	55	40	59	25	57
91	27	38	53	19	93	25	39	52	56
66	14	18	63	59	68	12	19	62	45
47	98	88	72	50	49	96	89	71	66
50	44	71	57	90	53	41	72	56	93
57	38	55	49	87	59	36	56	48	70
33	69	50	50	60	35	67	51	50	52
11	73	46	16	67	13	71	47	25	77

TABLE 79.2	Frequency Distribution of Scores
Class Interval	**Number of Persons in Class**
0–19	10
20–39	20
40–59	40
60–79	20
80–99	10

Descriptive statistics *Mathematical tools used to describe and summarize numeric data.*
Inferential statistics *Mathematical tools used for decision making, for generalizing from small samples, and for drawing conclusions.*
Graphical statistics *Techniques for presenting numbers pictorially, often by plotting them on a graph.*
Frequency distribution *A table that divides an entire range of scores into a series of classes and then records the number of scores that fall into each class.*
Histogram *A graph of a frequency distribution in which the number of scores falling in each class is represented by vertical bars.*
Frequency polygon *A graph of a frequency distribution in which the number of scores falling in each class is represented by points on a line.*

Measures of Central Tendency

SURVEY QUESTION 79.2: How are statistics used to identify an average score?

Notice in Table 79.2 that more of Jackson's scores fall in the range 40 to 59 than elsewhere. How can we show this fact? A measure of **central tendency** is simply a number describing a "typical score" around which other scores fall. A familiar measure of central tendency is the *mean,* or "average." But as we shall see in a moment, other types of averages can be used. To illustrate each, we need an example: ● Table 79.3 shows the raw data for one of Jackson's experiments, in which two groups of participants were given a test of concentration. Assume that one group was given a drug that might improve concentration (let's call the drug Focusil). The second group received a placebo. Is there a difference in concentration scores between the two groups? It's difficult to tell without computing an average.

The Mean As one type of "average," the **mean** is calculated by adding all the scores for each group and then dividing by the total number of scores. Notice in Table 79.3 that the means reveal a difference between the two groups.

The mean is sensitive to extremely high or low scores in a distribution. For this reason, it is not always the best measure of central tendency. (Imagine how distorted it would be to calculate average yearly incomes from a small sample of people that happened to include a billionaire, such as Oprah Winfrey.) In such cases, the middle score in a group of scores—called the *median*—is used instead.

The Median The **median** is found by arranging scores from the highest to the lowest and selecting the score that falls in the middle. In other words, half the values in a group of scores fall below the median and half fall above it. Consider, for example, the following weights obtained from a small class of college students: 105, 111, 123, 126, 148, 151, 154, 162, 182. The median for the group is 148, the middle score. Of course, if there is an even number of scores, there will be no middle score. This problem is handled by averaging the two scores that "share" the middle spot. This procedure yields a single number to serve as the median. (See the bottom panel of Table 79.3.)

The Mode A final measure of central tendency is the *mode.* The **mode** is simply the most frequently occurring score in a group of scores. If you were to take the time to count the

scores in Table 79.3, you would find that the mode of Group 1 is 65 and the mode of Group 2 is 60. Although the mode is usually easy to obtain, it can be an unreliable measure, especially in a small group of scores. The mode's advantage is that it gives the score actually obtained by the greatest number of people.

TABLE 79.3	Raw Scores on a Concentration Test for Subjects Taking Focusil or Placebo	
Subject	**Group 1 Focusil**	**Group 2 Placebo**
1	65	54
2	67	60
3	73	63
4	65	33
5	58	56
6	55	60
7	70	60
8	69	31
9	60	62
10	68	61
Sum	650	540
Mean	65	54
Median	66	60

$$\text{Mean} = \frac{\Sigma X}{N} \text{ or } \frac{\text{Sum of all scores, X}}{\text{number of scores}}$$

$$\text{Mean Group 1} = \frac{65 + 67 + 73 + 65 + 58 + 55 + 70 + 69 + 60 + 68}{10}$$

$$= \frac{650}{10} = 65$$

$$\text{Mean Group 2} = \frac{54 + 60 + 63 + 33 + 56 + 60 + 60 + 31 + 62 + 61}{10}$$

$$= \frac{540}{10} = 54$$

Median = the middle score or the mean of the two middle scores*

Median Group 1 = 55 58 60 65 $\boxed{65 \ 67}$ 68 69 70 73

$$= \frac{65 + 67}{2} = 66$$

Median Group 2 = 31 33 54 56 60 $\boxed{60 \ 60}$ 61 62 63

$$= \frac{60 + 60}{2} = 60$$

* $\boxed{}$ Indicates middle score(s).

Measures of Variability

SURVEY QUESTION 79.3: What statistics do psychologists use to measure how much scores differ from one another?

Let's say a researcher discovers two drugs that lower anxiety in agitated patients. However, let's also assume that one drug consistently lowers anxiety by moderate amounts, whereas the second sometimes lowers it by large amounts, sometimes has no effect, or may even increase anxiety in some patients. Overall, there is no difference in the *average* (mean) amount of anxiety reduction. Even so, an important difference exists between the two drugs. As this example shows, it is not enough to simply know the average score in a distribution. Usually, we would also want to know if scores are grouped closely together or scattered widely.

Measures of **variability** provide a single number that tells how "spread out" scores are. When the scores are widely spread, this number gets larger. When they are close together, it gets smaller. If you look again at the example in Table 79.3, you will notice that the scores within each group vary widely. How can we show this fact?

The Range The simplest way would be to use the **range**, which is the difference between the highest and the lowest scores. In Group 1 of our experiment, the highest score is 73, and the lowest is 55; thus, the range is 18 ($73 - 55 = 18$). In Group 2, the highest score is 63, and the lowest is 31; this makes the range 32. Scores in Group 2 are more spread out (are more variable) than those in Group 1.

The Standard Deviation A better measure of variability is the **standard deviation (SD)**—an index of how much a typical score differs from the mean of a group of scores. To obtain the SD, we find the deviation (or difference) of each score from the mean and then square it (multiply it by itself). These squared deviations are then added and averaged (the total is divided by the number of deviations). Taking the square root of this average yields the standard deviation (● Table 79.4). Notice again that the variability for Group 1 (5.4) is smaller than that for Group 2 (where the SD is 11.3).

TABLE 79.4	Computation of the Standard Deviation	
Group 1 Mean = 65		
Score Mean	Deviation (d)	Deviation Squared (d^2)
65 − 65 =	0	0
67 − 65 =	2	4
73 − 65 =	8	64
65 − 65 =	0	0
58 − 65 =	−7	49
55 − 65 =	−10	100
70 − 65 =	5	25
69 − 65 =	4	16
60 − 65 =	−5	25
68 − 65 =	3	9
		292

$$SD = \sqrt{\frac{\text{sum of } d^2}{n}} = \sqrt{\frac{292}{10}} = \sqrt{29.2} = 5.4$$

Group 2 Mean = 54		
Score Mean	Deviation (d)	Deviation Squared (d^2)
54 − 54 =	0	0
60 − 54 =	6	36
63 − 54 =	9	81
33 − 54 =	−21	441
56 − 54 =	2	4
60 − 54 =	6	36
60 − 54 =	6	36
31 − 54 =	−23	529
62 − 54 =	8	64
61 − 54 =	7	49
		1276

$$SD = \sqrt{\frac{\text{sum of } d^2}{n}} = \sqrt{\frac{1276}{10}} = \sqrt{127.6} = 11.3$$

Central tendency *The tendency for a majority of scores to fall in the midrange of possible values.*

Mean *A measure of central tendency calculated by adding a group of scores and then dividing by the total number of scores.*

Median *A measure of central tendency found by arranging scores from the highest to the lowest and selecting the score that falls in the middle—that is, half the values in a group of scores fall above the median and half fall below it.*

Mode *A measure of central tendency found by identifying the most frequently occurring score in a group of scores.*

Variability *The tendency for a group of scores to differ in value. Measures of variability indicate the degree to which a group of scores differs from one another.*

Range *The difference between the highest and lowest scores in a group of scores.*

Standard deviation *An index of how much a typical score differs from the mean of a group of scores.*

Standard Scores

A particular advantage of the standard deviation is that it can be used to "standardize" scores in a way that gives them greater meaning. For example, Jackson and his twin sister Jackie both took psychology midterms, but in different classes. Jackson earned a score of 118, and Jackie scored 110. Who did better? It is impossible to tell without knowing what the average score was on each test, and whether Jackson and Jackie scored at the top, middle, or bottom of their classes. We would like to have one number that gives all this information. A number that does this is the z-score.

To convert an original score to a **z-score**, we subtract the mean from the score. The resulting number is then divided by the standard deviation for that group of scores. To illustrate, Jackie had a score of 110 in a class with a mean of 100 and a standard deviation of 10. Therefore, her z-score is +1.0 (● Table 79.5). Jackson's score of 118 came from a class having a mean of 100 and a standard deviation of 18; thus, his z-score is also +1.0 (see Table 79.5). Originally, it looked as if Jackson did better on his midterm than Jackie. But we now see that relatively speaking, their scores were equivalent. Compared with other students, each was an equal distance above average.

The Normal Curve

When chance events are recorded, we find that some outcomes have a high probability and occur very often, others have a lower probability and occur infrequently, and still others have little probability and occur rarely. As a result, the distribution (or tally) of chance events typically resembles a *normal curve* (● **Figure 79.3**). A **normal curve** is bell-shaped, with a large number of scores in the middle, tapering to very few extremely high and low scores. Most psychological traits or events are determined by the action of a large number of factors. Therefore, like chance events, measures of psychological variables tend to roughly match a normal curve. For example, direct measurement has shown such characteristics as height, memory span, and intelligence to be distributed approximately

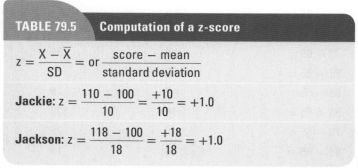

TABLE 79.5	Computation of a z-score

$$z = \frac{X - \bar{X}}{SD} = \text{or} \frac{\text{score} - \text{mean}}{\text{standard deviation}}$$

Jackie: $z = \dfrac{110 - 100}{10} = \dfrac{+10}{10} = +1.0$

Jackson: $z = \dfrac{118 - 100}{18} = \dfrac{+18}{18} = +1.0$

© Cengage Learning

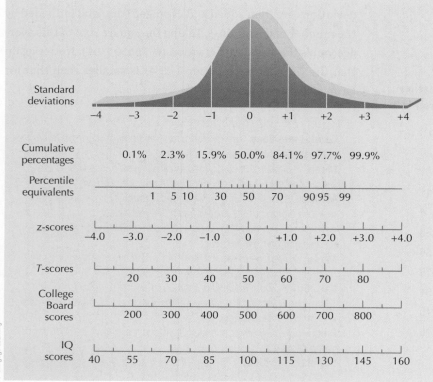

© Cengage Learning

● **Figure 79.3**

The normal curve. The normal curve is an idealized mathematical model. However, many measurements in psychology closely approximate a normal curve. The scales you see here show the relationship of standard deviations, z-scores, and other measures to the curve.

along a normal curve. In other words, many people have average height, memory ability, and intelligence. However, as we move above or below average, fewer and fewer people are found.

It is fortunate that so many psychological variables tend to form a normal curve because much is known about the curve. One valuable property concerns the relationship between the standard deviation and the normal curve. Specifically, the standard deviation measures offset proportions of the curve above and below the mean. For example, in Figure 79.3, notice that roughly 68 percent of all cases (IQ scores, memory scores, heights, or whatever) fall between one standard deviation above and below the mean (± 1 SD); 95 percent of all cases fall between ± 2 SD; and 99 percent of the cases can be found between ± 3 SD from the mean.

● **Table 79.6** gives a more complete account of the relationship between z-scores and the percentage of cases found in a particular area of the normal curve. Notice, for example, that 93.3 percent of all cases fall below a z-score of +1.5. A z-score of 1.5 on a test (no matter what the original, or "raw," score was) would be a good performance, because roughly 93 percent of all scores fall below this mark. Relationships between the standard deviation (or z-scores) and the normal curve do not change. This makes it possible to compare various tests or groups of scores if they come from distributions that are approximately normal.

Correlation—Rating Relationships

SURVEY QUESTION 79.4: How are correlations used in psychology?

As we noted in Module 5, many of the statements that psychologists make about behavior do not result from using experimental methods. Rather, they come from keen observations and measures of existing phenomena. A psychologist might note, for example, that the higher a couple's socioeconomic and educational status, the smaller the number of children they are likely to have. Or that grades in high school are related to how well a person is likely to do in college. Or even, as Jackson found that students who engage in martial arts are also better able to concentrate. In these instances, we are dealing with the fact that two variables are **correlated**—varying together in some orderly fashion.

Relationships

Psychologists are very interested in detecting relationships between events: Are children from single-parent families more likely to misbehave at school? Is wealth related to happiness? Is there a relationship between childhood exposure to the Internet and IQ at age 20? Is the chance of having a heart attack related to having a hostile personality? All of these questions are about correlation (Howell, 2013).

The simplest way of visualizing a correlation is to construct a **scatter diagram**. In a scatter diagram, two measures (grades in high school and grades in college, for instance) are obtained. One measure is indicated by the X axis and the second by the Y axis. The scatter diagram plots the intersection (crossing) of each pair of measurements as a single point. Many such measurement pairs give pictures like those shown in ● **Figure 79.4**.

TABLE 79.6	Computation of a z-score	
z-Score	Percentage of Area to the Left of This Value	Percentage of Area to the Right of This Value
−3.0 SD	00.1	99.9
−2.5 SD	00.6	99.4
−2.0 SD	02.3	97.7
−1.5 SD	06.7	93.3
−1.0 SD	15.9	84.1
−0.5 SD	30.9	69.1
0.0 SD	50.0	50.0
+0.5 SD	69.1	30.9
+1.0 SD	84.1	15.9
+1.5 SD	93.3	06.7
+2.0 SD	97.7	02.3
+2.5 SD	99.4	00.6
+3.0 SD	99.9	00.1

z-score *A number that tells how many standard deviations above or below the mean a score is.*
Normal curve *A bell-shaped distribution, with a large number of scores in the middle, tapering to very few extremely high and low scores.*
Correlation *The existence of a consistent, systematic relationship between two events, measures, or variables.*
Scatter diagram *A graph that plots the intersection of paired measures—that is, the points at which paired X and Y measures cross.*

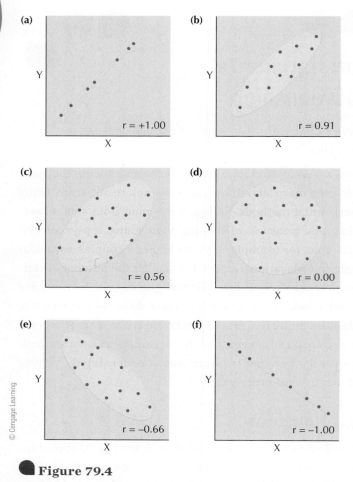

© Cengage Learning

● Figure 79.4

Scatter diagrams showing various degrees of relationship for a positive, zero, and negative correlation.

Figure 79.4 also shows scatter diagrams of three basic kinds of relationships between variables (or measures):

- **Positive relationship:** Graphs a, b, and c show *positive relationships* of varying strength. As you can see, in a **positive correlation**, increases in the X measure (or score) are matched by increases on the Y measure (or score). An example would be finding that higher IQ scores (X) are associated with higher college grades (Y).

- **Zero correlation:** A **zero correlation** suggests that no relationship exists between two measures (see graph d). This might be the result of comparing participants' hat sizes (X) to their college grades (Y).

- **Negative relationship:** Graphs e and f both show a **negative correlation**. Notice that as values of one measure increase, those of the second become smaller. An example might be the relationship between amount of alcohol consumed and scores on a test of coordination: Higher alcohol levels are correlated with lower coordination scores.

The Correlation Coefficient

The strength of a correlation can also be expressed as a **coefficient of correlation**. This coefficient is simply a number falling somewhere between +1.00 and −1.00. If the number is zero or close to zero, it indicates a weak or nonexistent relationship. If the correlation is +1.00, a **perfect positive relationship** exists; if the correlation is −1.00, a **perfect negative relationship** has been discovered. The most commonly used correlation coefficient is called the Pearson r. Calculation of the Pearson r is relatively simple, as shown in ● Table 79.7. (The numbers shown are hypothetical.)

As stated in Module 5, correlations in psychology are rarely perfect. Most fall somewhere between 0 and +/−1. The closer the correlation coefficient is to +1.00 or −1.00, the stronger the relationship. An interesting example of some typical correlations is provided by a study that compared the IQs of adopted children with the IQs of their biological mothers. At age 4, the children's IQs correlated .28 with their biological mothers' IQs. By age 7, the correlation was .35. And by age 13, it had grown to .38. Over time, the IQs of adopted children become more similar to the IQs of their biological mothers.

Correlations often provide highly useful information. For instance, it is valuable to know that there is a correlation between cigarette smoking and lung cancer rates. Another example is the fact that higher consumption of alcohol during pregnancy is correlated with lower birth weight and a higher rate of birth defects. There is a correlation between the number of recent life stresses experienced and the likelihood of emotional disturbance. Many more examples could be cited, but the point is, correlations help us identify relationships that are worth knowing.

Prediction Correlations are particularly valuable for making *predictions*. If we know that two measures are correlated and we know a person's score on one measure, we can predict his or her score on the other. For example, most colleges have formulas that use multiple correlations to decide which applicants have the best chances for success. Usually, the formula includes such predictors as high school GPA, teacher ratings, extracurricular activities, and scores on the *SAT Reasoning Test* or some similar test. Although no single predictor is perfectly correlated with success in college, together the various predictors correlate highly and provide a useful technique for screening applicants.

There is an interesting "trick" you can do with correlations that you may find useful. It works like this: If you *square* the correlation coefficient (multiply r by itself), you will get a number telling the **percent of variance**, or amount of variation in

TABLE 79.7	IQ and Grade Point Average for Computing Pearson r				
Student No.	IQ (X)	Grade Point Average (Y)	X Score Squared (X²)	Y Score Squared (Y²)	X Times Y (XY)
1	110	1.0	12,100	1.00	110.0
2	112	1.6	12,544	2.56	179.2
3	118	1.2	13,924	1.44	141.6
4	119	2.1	14,161	4.41	249.9
5	122	2.6	14,884	6.76	317.2
6	125	1.8	15,625	3.24	225.0
7	127	2.6	16,124	6.76	330.2
8	130	2.0	16,900	4.00	260.0
9	132	3.2	17,424	10.24	422.4
10	134	2.6	17,956	6.76	348.4
11	136	3.0	18,496	9.00	408.0
12	138	3.6	19,044	12.96	496.8
Total	1503	27.3	189,187	69.13	3488.7

$$r = \frac{\Sigma XY - \dfrac{(\Sigma X)(\Sigma Y)}{N}}{\sqrt{\left[\Sigma X^2 - \dfrac{(\Sigma X)^2}{N}\right]\left[\Sigma Y^2 - \dfrac{(\Sigma Y)^2}{N}\right]}}$$

$$= \frac{3488.7 - \dfrac{1503(27.3)}{12}}{\sqrt{\left[189,187 - \dfrac{(1503)^2}{2}\right]\left[69.132 \dfrac{(27.3)^2}{12}\right]}}$$

$$= \frac{69.375}{81.088} = 0.856 = 0.86$$

scores, accounted for by the correlation. For example, the correlation between IQ scores and college grade point average is .5. Multiplying .5 times .5 gives .25, or 25 percent. This means that 25 percent of the variation in college grades is accounted for by knowing IQ scores. In other words, with a correlation of .5, college grades are "squeezed" into an oval like the one shown in graph C, Figure 79.4. IQ scores take away some of the possible variation in corresponding grade point averages. If no correlation existed between IQ and grades, grades would be completely free to vary, as shown in graph d, Figure 79.4.

Along the same line, a correlation of +1.00 or −1.00 means that 100 percent of the variation in the Y measure is accounted for by knowing the X measure: If you know a person's X score, you can tell exactly what the Y score is. An example that comes close to this state of affairs is the high correlation (.86)

Positive correlation *A mathematical relationship in which increases in one measure are matched by increases in the other (or decreases correspond with decreases).*

Zero correlation *The absence of a (linear) mathematical relationship between two measures.*

Negative correlation *A mathematical relationship in which increases in one measure are matched by decreases in the other.*

Coefficient of correlation *A statistical index ranging from −1.00 to +1.00 that indicates the direction and degree of correlation.*

Perfect positive relationship *A mathematical relationship in which the correlation between two measures is +1.00.*

Perfect negative relationship *A mathematical relationship in which the correlation between two measures is −1.00.*

Percent of variance *A portion of the total amount of variation in a group of scores.*

between the IQs of identical twins. In any group of identical twins, 74 percent of the variation in the Y twins' IQs is accounted for by knowing the IQs of their siblings (the X twins).

Squaring correlations to obtain the *percent variance* accounted for is a useful tool for interpreting the correlations encountered in the media and the psychological literature. For example, sweeping pronouncements about relationships are occasionally made on the basis of correlations in the .25 to .30 range even though the values mean that only 6 to 9 percent of the variance is accounted for by the observed correlation. Such correlations may document relationships worth noting, but they are rarely something to get excited about.

Correlation and Causation It is important to reiterate that finding a correlation between two measures does not automatically mean that one causes the other: Correlation does not demonstrate causation. When a correlation exists, the best we can say is that two variables are related. Of course, this does not mean that it is impossible for two correlated variables to have a cause-and-effect relationship. Rather, it means that we cannot *conclude*, solely on the basis of correlation, that a causal link exists. To gain greater confidence that a cause-and-effect relationship exists, an experiment must be performed (see Module 4).

Often, two correlated measures are related as a result of the influence of a third variable. For example, we might observe that the more hours students devote to studying, the better their grades. Although it is tempting to conclude that more studying produces (causes) better grades, it is possible (indeed, it is probable) that grades and the amount of study time are both related to the student's amount of motivation or interest.

The difference between cause-and-effect data and data that reveal a relationship of unknown origin is one that should not be forgotten. Because we rarely run experiments in daily life, the information on which we act is largely correlational. This should make us more humble and more tentative in the confidence with which we make pronouncements about human behavior.

Inferential Statistics— Significant Numbers

SURVEY QUESTION 79.5: What are inferential statistics?

You would like to know whether boys are more aggressive than girls. You observe a group of 5-year-old boys and girls on a playground. After collecting data for a week, you find that the boys committed more aggressive acts than the girls. Could this difference just be a meaningless fluctuation in aggression? Or does it show conclusively that boys are more aggressive than girls? Inferential statistics were created to answer such questions (Heiman, 2014).

Let's say that a researcher studies the effects of a new therapy on a small group of depressed individuals. Is she or he interested only in these particular individuals? Usually not, because except in rare instances, psychologists seek to discover general laws of behavior that apply widely to humans and animals (Babbie, 2013). Undoubtedly, the researcher would like to know whether the therapy holds any promise for all depressed people. As stated earlier, inferential statistics are techniques that allow us to make inferences—that is, they allow us to generalize from the behavior of small groups of participants to that of the larger groups they represent.

Samples and Populations

In any scientific study, we would want to observe the entire set, or **population**, of participants, objects, or events of interest. However, this is usually impossible or impractical. Observing all terrorists, all cancer patients, or all mothers-in-law could be both impractical (because all are large populations) and impossible (because people change political views, may be unaware of having cancer, and change their status as relatives). In such cases, **samples** (smaller cross sections of a population) are selected, and observations of the sample are used to draw conclusions about the entire population.

For any sample to be meaningful, it must be **representative**—that is, the sample group must truly reflect the membership and characteristics of the larger population. In Jackson's study of a concentration drug, it would be essential for the sample of 20 people to be representative of the general population. A very important aspect of representative samples is that their members are chosen at **random**. In other words, each member of the population must have an equal chance of being included in the sample.

Significant Differences

In Jackson's drug experiment, he found that the average concentration score was higher for the group given the drug than it was for persons who didn't take the drug (the placebo group). Certainly this result is interesting, but could it have occurred by chance? If two groups were repeatedly tested (with neither receiving any drug), their average concentration scores would sometimes differ. How much must two means differ before we can consider the difference "real" (not due to chance)?

Tests of **statistical significance** provide an estimate of how often experimental results could have occurred by chance alone. The results of a significance test are stated as a probability. This probability gives the odds that the observed difference was due to chance. In psychology, any experimental result that could have occurred by chance 5 times (or less) out of 100 (in other words, a probability of .05 or less) is considered *significant*. In our concentration experiment, the probability is .025 ($p = .025$) that the group means would differ as much as they do by chance alone. This allows us to conclude with reasonable certainty that the drug actually did improve concentration scores.

Module 79: Summary

79.1 What are descriptive statistics?

- **79.1.1** Descriptive statistics organize and summarize numbers.
- **79.1.2** Summarizing numbers visually, by using various types of graphs such as histograms and frequency polygons, makes it easier to see trends and patterns in the results of psychological investigations.

79.2 How are statistics used to identify an average score?

- **79.2.1** Measures of central tendency define the "typical score" in a group of scores.
- **79.2.2** The mean is found by adding all the scores in a group and then dividing by the total number of scores.
- **79.2.3** The median is found by arranging a group of scores from the highest to the lowest and selecting the middle score.
- **79.2.4** The mode is the score that occurs most frequently in a group of scores.

79.3 What statistics do psychologists use to measure how much scores differ from one another?

- **79.3.1** Measures of variability provide a number that shows how much scores vary.
- **79.3.2** The range is the difference between the highest score and the lowest score in a group of scores.
- **79.3.3** The standard deviation shows how much, on average, all the scores in a group differ from the mean.
- **79.3.4** To express an original score as a standard score (or z-score), you must subtract the mean from the score and then divide the result by the standard deviation. Standard scores (z-scores) tell, in standard deviation units, how far above or below the mean a score is. This allows meaningful comparisons between scores from different groups.
- **79.3.5** Scores that form a normal curve are easy to interpret because the properties of the normal curve are well known.

79.4 How are correlations used in psychology?

- **79.4.1** Pairs of scores that vary together in an orderly fashion are said to be correlated.
- **79.4.2** The relationship between two variables or measures can be positive or negative. Correlation coefficients tell how strongly two groups of scores are related.
- **79.4.3** Knowing a person's score on one measure allows us to predict his or her score on the second measure.
- **79.4.4** Correlation alone does not demonstrate cause-and-effect links between variables or measures.

79.5 What are inferential statistics?

- **79.5.1** Inferential statistics are used to make decisions, to generalize from samples, and to draw conclusions from data.
- **79.5.2** Most studies in psychology are based on samples. Findings from representative samples are assumed to also apply to entire populations.
- **79.5.3** In psychology experiments, differences in the average performance of groups could occur purely by chance. Tests of statistical significance tell us if the observed differences between groups are common or rare. If a difference is large enough to be improbable, it suggests that the results did not occur by chance alone.

Causation *The act of causing some effect.*
Population *An entire group of animals, people, or objects belonging to a particular category (for example, all college students or all married women).*
Sample *A smaller subpart of a population.*
Representative sample *A small, randomly selected part of a larger population that accurately reflects characteristics of the whole population.*
Random selection *Choosing a sample so that each member of the population has an equal chance of being included in the sample.*
Statistical significance *The degree to which an event (such as the results of an experiment) is unlikely to have occurred by chance alone.*

Module 79: Knowledge Builder

Recite

1. Three measures of central tendency are the mean, the median, and the _____.

2. As a measure of variability, the standard deviation is defined as the difference between the highest and lowest scores. *T or F?*

3. A z-score of −1 tells us that a score fell one standard deviation below the mean in a group of scores. *T or F?*

4. A scatter diagram can be used to plot and visualize a _____ between two groups of scores.

5. It is important to remember that correlation does not demonstrate _____.

6. In inferential statistics, observations of a _____ are used to make inferences and draw conclusions about an entire _____.

7. A representative sample can be obtained by selecting members of the sample at _____.

8. If the results of an experiment could have occurred by chance alone fewer than 25 times out of 100, the result is considered statistically significant. *T or F?*

Reflect

Think Critically

9. Suppose it was found that sleeping with your clothes on is correlated with waking up with a headache. Could you conclude that sleeping with your clothes on causes headaches?

Self-Reflect

How would you feel about receiving your scores on classroom tests in the form of z-scores?

Do you think the distribution of scores in Jackson's study of concentration would form a normal curve? Why or why not?

See if you can identify at least one positive relationship and one negative relationship involving human behavior that you have observed. How strong do you think the correlation would be in each case? What correlation coefficient would you expect to see?

If you were trying to test whether a drug causes birth defects, what level of statistical significance would you use? If you were doing a psychology experiment, with what level would you be comfortable?

ANSWERS

1. mode 2. F 3. T 4. correlation 5. causation 6. sample, population 7. random 8. F 9. No. To reiterate, correlation does not prove causality. It is more likely that a third factor is causing *both* the sleeping with the clothes on at night *and* the headaches (too much alcohol, anyone?).

CENGAGE brain.com

Go to **cengagebrain.com** to access **MindTap for Coon/Mitterer** *Psychology Modules for Active Learning* and other online learning tools. MindTap is a fully online learning experience that combines all the tools you need—readings, multimedia, activities, and assessments—into a singular personalized Learning Path that guides you through the course.

Appendix: Life after School

What Her Professor Told Her

She had worried for months. What good was her psychology degree going to be in a tight economy? What kinds of careers would be open to someone with her training? She finally stopped worrying because of what her professor told her.

"Anita," she insisted, "you are young, bright, and energetic. Many careers are open to you, as long as you think about it the right way. While in school, you have learned and practiced many skills: how to read primary research literature, how to find information on your own, how to write about what you found, and how to speak in front of an audience. Think about it more closely and you will see that you have become a skilled young person who would be an asset to many different types of companies."

Let's look into the skills Anita realized she had picked up during her years in school.

aslysun/Shutterstock

SURVEY QUESTIONS

80.1 What skills do psychology students learn?

80.2 What are the career opportunities in the field of psychology?

It's Off to Work We Go— Hi Ho, Hi Ho

SURVEY QUESTION 80.1: What skills do psychology students learn?

To better understand what her professor was trying to tell her, imagine that Anita's first job interview was to become a sales representative with a company selling computer software internationally. Now imagine that she spent her entire interview explaining her interest in hypnosis and her research focus on hypnotizability. If Anita approached her interview by stressing her work in the field of hypnosis it would be entirely understandable if her interviewers failed to see how she could help their company sell software (no hypnotizing potential customers, Anita!). Fortunately, Anita stressed the skills she had acquired throughout her degree and nailed her interview. After her two-week company orientation ended she was off to visit a sales lead in France, a country she had always wanted to visit.

It is entirely fitting that we end this book with some thoughts about your future. What role will psychology play in your life, real or virtual? By far, the most important advice Anita's professor gave her was to focus on the skills she learned throughout her studies. Whether you are just beginning your college career or nearing the end, whether or not you are a psychology major, and whether or not you are planning a career in psychology, you will find it very helpful to take that advice seriously.

A Psychologist's Skill Set

What do you mean by "skills"? Have a look at ● Table 80.1, which lists a few of the career opportunities open to psychology majors.

TABLE 80.1	A Skills-Based List of Some Potential Careers for Psychology Majors	
Addictions counselor		Manager
Administration		Market research analyst
Advertising		Marketing
Career/employment counselor		Mental health worker
Case worker		Motivational researcher
Child care worker		Personnel
Child welfare worker		Population studies researcher
Community worker		Probation or parole officer
Correctional officer		Professional consultant
Counselor		Program coordinator
Cultural diversity consultant		Psychiatric assistant or aide
Customs or immigration agent		Public health statistician
Day care worker, supervisor		Public opinion interviewer
Educational counselor		Public relations
Entrepreneur		Recreation specialist
Fund-raiser or development officer		Research assistant
Gerontology		Sales representative
Government researcher		Social services
Health services		Social worker
Hospice coordinator		Teaching
Human resources		Technical writer
Immigration officer		Travel agent
Labor relations specialist		Youth worker

Source: Adapted from Canadian Psychological Association (2012)

Most college programs in psychology follow the American Psychological Association's (2007) *Guidelines for the Undergraduate Psychology Major*. It is well worth having a look at the full document, which is available online. You can find the URL by looking up "American Psychological Association. (2007)" in the *References* section at the back of this book. It might be helpful if you are more fully aware of what your college psychology program is trying to teach you. For now, ● Table 80.2 lists the major competencies college psychology programs try to teach their students.

Some college students assume that their only goal is to learn "the facts" about psychology. In other words, they think it is all about Goal 1. A student with this mindset will usually complain when given an assignment involving looking up some research articles in the PsycINFO database. "Why am I wasting my time doing this?" he or she might grouse. "Just give me the articles

TABLE 80.2	APA Guidelines for the Undergraduate Psychology Major

I. Knowledge, Skills, and Values Consistent With the Science and Application of Psychology
- Goal 1: Knowledge Base of Psychology
- Goal 2: Research Methods in Psychology
- Goal 3: Critical Thinking Skills in Psychology
- Goal 4: Application of Psychology
- Goal 5: Values in Psychology

II. Knowledge, Skills, and Values Consistent With Liberal Arts Education That Are Further Developed in Psychology
- Goal 6: Information and Technological Literacy
- Goal 7: Communication Skills
- Goal 8: Sociocultural and International Awareness
- Goal 9: Personal Development
- Goal 10: Career Planning and Development

Source: Adapted from American Psychological Association (2007)

so I can get right to reading and learning them." Students who understand that their education also is about acquiring skills appreciate that the process of locating relevant research literature is a set of skills every scholar must learn (Goals 2, 3, and 6?).

Sales representatives, too? Of course. Along with other skills, effective sales representatives need to be able to research the best potential combination of product and service options for their clients, as well as many other bits of relevant information such as what their competitors are likely to offer, relevant government regulations, and any other relevant local circumstances. Granted, the databases being searched likely don't include PsycINFO, but the *skills* involved are very similar. What Anita learned about cross-cultural sensitivity turned out to be *very* helpful in France and the other six countries she visited during her first year on the job. Likewise, Table 80.1 listed fund-raiser, research assistant, consultant, entrepreneur, sales representative, and several other careers that require similar skills.

Don't Be Afraid to Ask If you are not sure *why* you have been asked to do something in a course or if you want to learn more about developing your skill set, ask your instructor. Senior students in your program can often be very helpful as well because they likely already "know the drill." Similarly, counseling services at your department or college also can answer some of those questions. These books might also be of some assistance (If you remember seeing this list at the beginning of this book, good for you.):

"I've got some skills—I'm just not sure they add up to a 'set.'"

Burka, J. B., & Yuen, L. M. (2008). *Procrastination: Why you do it, what to do about it*. Cambridge, MA: Perseus.

Chaffee, J. (2012). *Thinking critically* (10th ed.). Belmont, CA: Cengage Learning/Wadsworth.

Ellis, D. (2013). *Becoming a master student: Concise* (14th ed.). Belmont, CA: Cengage Learning/Wadsworth.

Rosnow, R. L. (2012). *Writing papers in psychology: A student guide to research papers, essays, proposals, posters, and handouts* (9th ed.). Belmont, CA: Cengage Learning/Wadsworth.

Santrock, J. W., & Halonen, J. S. (2013). *Your guide to college success: Strategies for achieving your goals* (7th ed.). Belmont, CA: Cengage Learning/Wadsworth.

Van Blerkom, D. L. (2012). *College study skills: Becoming a strategic learner* (7th ed.). Belmont, CA: Cengage Learning/Wadsworth.

Wong, W. (2012). *Essential study skills* (7th ed.). Belmont, CA: Cengage Learning/Wadsworth.

Skills Introduced in *Psychology: Modules for Active Learning, 13th Edition*

In the meantime, let's close this section with a quick survey of the skills to which you have been exposed throughout this book.

First, what do the study skills covered by the books in the preceding list have to do with my career? The two skill sets actually overlap quite a bit. "Studying" psychology as a student amounts to tackling a new field of knowledge and more or less mastering it. While employers might tolerate new employees who know very little about their new jobs, they won't suffer gladly new employees who have no clue how to "study" their new jobs.

By now, you probably are not surprised to learn that *Psychology: Modules for Active Learning* touches on all the learning guidelines mentioned in Table 80.2 (we're on Goals 9 and 10 right now). Here are some skill highlights:

- **Study skills:** In Module 1, *How to Study Psychology*, we discuss a full set of study skills, from how to read and listen for understanding to how to take tests and overcome procrastination. We introduce the idea of reflective processing and carry it throughout the book. All of those skills are very helpful in many different jobs.

- **Research skills:** We have introduced you to science and psychological research, from the research methods in Modules 2–6 to behavioral statistics in Module 79. This will help you be a more literate consumer of primary literature in your chosen career, especially if it involves applying psychological research in any way.

- **Critical thinking skills:** From the discussion of critical thinking in Modules 2 and 6 to the *Think Critically* questions sprinkled throughout the modules, we stress critical thinking skills. Employers need employees who can think for themselves.

- **Cultural awareness skills:** OK, so we couldn't take you on a field trip to Japan, but throughout the book, such as in the *Human Diversity* highlights, we invited you to reflect on the differences among people of different ethnicities, sexual orientations, ages, and genders. Check out Tables P.3 and P.4 in the *Preface* for more details.

- **Personal skills:** Especially in the *Psychology in Action* modules, we introduced you to a set of helpful personal skills, from how to use the tension-reduction method to how to thrive in a multicultural society, from how to be less shy to how to perceive the world more clearly (Module 45).

Not to put too fine a point on it, but that's a lot of career-relevant skills, no? Once Anita started thinking in terms of her marketable skill set, she began analyzing potential jobs in that light. Imagine her first interviewer's surprise when he met with an applicant who knew exactly what she could bring to his company. Knowing Anita could get up to speed quickly, he had no qualms offering her the job.

Careers in Psychology—Are You Reading My Mind?

SURVEY QUESTION 80.2: What are the career opportunities in the field of psychology?

Just in case you skipped the first part of this module because you are planning a career in psychology, please take our advice and go back and check it out. The *skills orientation* we suggest there will be very helpful to you, too.

Whether you are just beginning your studies or are nearing the end, you are right to wonder about life after an undergraduate degree in psychology. We hope this book has opened you up to the incredible breadth of the psychology field. You might remember looking at Table 3.3 (in Module 3), which lists some of the specialties in psychology, or Figure 3.1, which breaks out where psychologists work and what they do at work. Another way to get a sense of the diversity of psychologists' interests is to browse the American Psychological Association's list of more than 50 specialized divisions and their associated websites. Or you could simply scan the *Table of Contents* of this textbook one more time.

We cannot, in this short section, help you figure out what your specialty should be or what sequence of courses and degrees you should follow to get there. But your professor can help. Your department, division, or college should have career counseling available. Don't be shy about asking for assistance. We especially recommend getting involved in your department by, say, joining your psychology club and attending departmental activities, like colloquia (talks by guest speakers, often from other universities). Try to get connected with senior students; their experience can be invaluable. Also consider becoming a student member of one of the following organizations:

- American Psychological Association (www.apa.org)
- Association for Psychological Science (www.psychologicalscience.org)
- Canadian Psychological Association (www.cpa.ca)

We especially recommend that you acquire (and study) Amira Wegenek and William Buskist's (2010) *The Insider's Guide to the Psychology Major: Everything You Need to Know about the Degree and Profession*, published by the American Psychological Association.

We know that the economy is not as strong as we would all like and that good jobs are harder to come by nowadays. In every event, we hope that your educational journey will be fulfilling and that you will end up in a satisfying career.

The Whole Human: Psychology and You

At the beginning of this book, we described psychology as a journey of self-discovery. It is our sincere hope that you have found enough relevance and value here to spark a lifelong interest in psychology. As your personal journey continues, one thing is certain: Many of your greatest challenges and most treasured moments will involve other people. You would be wise to continue adding to your understanding of human behavior. Psychology's future looks exciting. What role will it play in your life, real or virtual?

Module 80: Summary

80.1 What skills do psychology students learn?

- **80.1.1** Psychology students learn a variety of study skills, research skills, critical thinking skills, cultural awareness skills, and personal skills during their studies.
- **80.1.2** The skills you acquire while studying psychology are important for future career success.

80.2 What are the career opportunities in the field of psychology?

- **80.2.1** A wide range of basic and applied specialties, practiced in a wide range of work settings, provide a rich array of career opportunities.

Module 80: Knowledge Builder

Recite

1. The facts you pick up during your academic studies are the most important aspect of your education. *T or F?*

2. The American Psychological Association has over 50 divisions. *T or F?*

Reflect

Think Critically

3. In this module, we focused on the skills you can learn while studying psychology as opposed to the specific facts comprising your courses. Which memory distinction is this most like?

Self-Reflect

Have you made any career choices yet? From whom are you seeking advice? If you haven't started thinking about this yet, is it time to begin?

Seriously sit down and undertake an inventory of the skills you have learned from your psychology studies and elsewhere.

ANSWERS

1. F 2. T 3. The distinction between declarative and procedural memory (see Module 32). The section of Module 38 on expertise also is relevant here.

References

Aamodt, M. G. (2013). *Industrial/organiza-tional psychology: An applied approach* (7th ed.). Belmont, CA: Cengage Learning/Wadsworth.

Abbott, K. R., & Sherratt, T. N. (2011). The evolution of superstition through optimal use of incomplete informa-tion. *Animal Behaviour, 82*(1), 85–92. doi:10.1016/j.anbehav.2011.04.002

Abel, G. G., Wiegel, M., & Osborn, C. A. (2007). Pedophilia and other paraphilias. In L. VandeCreek, F. L. Peterson, Jr., et al. (Eds.), *Innovations in clinical practice: Focus on sexual health* (pp. 157–175). Sarasota: Professional Resource Press.

Abma, J. C., Martinez, G. M., et al. (2004). Teenagers in the United States: sexual activity, contraceptive use, and child-bearing, 2002. *Vital Health Statistics, 23*(24), 1–48.

Abrahamse, W., Steg, L., et al. (2005). A review of intervention studies aimed at household energy conservation. *Journal of Environmental Psychology, 25*(3), 273–291.

Adachi, P. J., & Willoughby, T. (2011a). The effect of violent video games on aggression: Is it more than just the violence? *Aggression & Violent Behavior, 16*(1), 55–62. doi:10.1016/j. avb.2010.12.002

Adachi, P. J., & Willoughby, T. (2011b). The effect of video game competition and violence on aggressive behavior: Which characteristic has the greatest influence? *Psychology of Violence, 1*(4), 259–274. doi:10.1037/a0024908

Adams, J. (2001). *Conceptual blockbusting* (4th ed.). New York: Basic Books.

Adamson, K. (2004). *Kate's journey: Triumph over adversity*. Redondo Beach, CA: Nosmada Press.

Adan, A., & Serra-Grabulosa, J. P. (2010). Effects of caffeine and glucose, alone and combined, on cognitive performance. *Human Psychopharmacology: Clinical & Experimental, 25*(4), 310–317. doi:10.1002/hup.1115

Addis, K. M., & Kahana, M. J. (2004). Decomposing serial learning: What is missing from the learning curve? *Psychonomic Bulletin & Review, 11*(1), 118–174. doi:10.3758/BF03206470

Adler, S. A., & Orprecio, J. (2006). The eyes have it: Visual pop-out in infants and adults. *Developmental Science, 9*, 189–206. doi:10.1111/j.1467-7687.2006.00479.x

Adolph, K. E., & Berger, S. E. (2011). Physical and motor development. In M. H. Bornstein & M. E. Lamb (Eds.), *Cognitive development: An advanced textbook* (pp. 257–318). New York: Psychology Press.

Adolphs, R. (2008). Fear, faces, and the human amygdala. *Current Opinion in Neurobiology, 18*(2), 166–172. doi:10.1016/j.conb.2008.06.006

Adorno, T. W., Frenkel-Brunswik, E., et al. (1950). *The authoritarian person-ality*. New York: Harper.

Advisory Council on the Misuse of Drugs. (2009). *MDMA ("ecstasy"): A review of its harms and classification under the Misuse of Drugs Act 1971.* Retrieved June 10, 2013, from http://www.drugsandalcohol.ie/13911/

Afifi, T. O., Brownridge, D. A., et al. (2006). Physical punishment, childhood abuse, and psychiatric disorders. *Child Abuse & Neglect, 30*(10), 1093–1103. doi:10.1016/j. chiabu.2006.04.006

Agresti, J. D., & Smith, R. K. (2012). Gun control facts. *Just Facts*. Retrieved July 12, 2013 from http://justfacts .com/guncontrol.asp

Agrigoroaei, S., & Lachman, M. E. (2011). Cognitive functioning in midlife and old age: Combined effects of psychosocial and behavioral factors. *Journals of Gerontology, 66B*, 130–140. doi:10.1093/geronb/gbr017

Ahima. R. S., & Osei, S. Y. (2004). Leptin signaling. *Physiology & Behavior, 81*, 223–241. doi:10.1016/j. physbeh.2004.02.014s

Ahluwalia, M. K., & Pellettiere, L. (2010). Sikh men post-9/11: Misidentification, discrimination, and coping. *Asian American Journal of Psychology, 1*(4), 303–314. doi:10.1037/a0022156

Ai, A. L., Huang, B., et al. (2013). Religious attendance and major depression among Asian Americans from a national database: The mediation of social support. *Psychology of Religion & Spiritualit, 5*(2), 78–89. doi:10.1037/a0030625

Ainsworth, M. D. (1989). Attachments beyond infancy. *American Psychologist, 44*(4), 709–716.

Ajzen, I. (2005). *Attitudes, personality and behaviour* (2nd ed.). New York: McGraw-Hill.

Åkerstedt, T. (2007). Altered sleep/ wake patterns and mental per-formance. *Physiology & Behavior, 90*(2–3), 209–218. doi:10.1016/j. physbeh.2006.09.007

Albarracín, D., Johnson, B. T., & Zanna, M. P. (Eds.) (2005). *The handbook of attitudes*. Mahwah, NJ: Erlbaum.

Albersen, M., Orabi, H., & Lue, T. F. (2012). Evaluation and treatment of erectile dysfunction in the aging male: A mini-review. *Gerontology, 58*(1), 3–14. doi:10.1159/000329598

Alberti, R., & Emmons, M. (2008). *Your perfect right* (9th ed.). San Luis Obispo, CA: Impact.

Alberto, P. A., & Troutman, A. C. (2013). *Applied behavior analysis for teachers* (9th ed.). Englewood Cliffs, NJ: Prentice Hall.

Alberts, H. M., Thewissen, R. R., & Raes, L. L. (2012). Dealing with problematic eating behaviour. The effects of a mindfulness-based intervention on eating behaviour, food cravings, dichotomous thinking and body image concern. *Appetite, 58*(3), 847–851. doi:10.1016/j. appet.2012.01.009

Albrecht, C. M., & Albrecht, D. E. (2011). Social status, adolescent behavior, and educational attainment. *Sociological Spectrum, 31*(1), 114–137. doi:10.1080/ 02732173.2011.525698

Albright, D. L., & Thyer, B. (2010). Does EMDR reduce post-traumatic stress disorder symptomatology in combat veterans? *Behavioral Interventions, 25*(1), 1–19. doi:10.1002/bin.295

Alcock, J. E. (2010). The parapsycholo-gist's lament. In S. Krippner & H. L. Friedman (Eds.), *Mysterious minds: The neurobiology of psychics, mediums, and other extraordinary people* (pp. 35–43). Santa Barbara, CA: Praeger.

Alcock, J. E., Burns, J., & Freeman, A. (2003). *Psi wars: Getting to grips with the paranormal*. Exeter, UK: Imprint Academic Press.

Aldhous, P. (2010, November 11). Is this evi-dence that we can see the future? *New Scientist*. Retrieved June 9, 2013, from http://www.newscientist.com/article /dn19712-is-this-evidence-that-we -can-see-the-future.html

Alegre, A. (2011). Parenting styles and chil-dren's emotional intelligence: What do we know? *The Family Journal, 19*(1), 56–62. doi:10.1177/1066480710387486

Alessandria, M., Vetrugno, R., et al. (2011). Normal body scheme and absent phantom limb experience in amputees while dreaming. *Consciousness & Cognition, 20*(4), 1831–1834. doi:10.1016/j.concog.2011.06.013

Algoe, S. B., Gable, S. L. & Maisel, N. (2010). It's the little things: Gratitude as a booster shot for romantic relationships. *Personal Relationships, 17*(2), 217–233.

Ali, M. M., & Dwyer, D. S. (2010). Social network effects in alcohol consumption among adolescents. *Addictive Behaviors, 35*(4), 337–342. doi:10.1016/j.addbeh.2009.12.002

Allan, R. (2011). Type A behavior pattern. In R. Allan & J. Fisher (Eds.), *Heart and mind: The practice of cardiac psychology* (2nd ed.), pp. 287–290). Washington: American Psychological Association. doi:10.1037/13086-012

Allemand, M., Steiger, A. E., & Hill, P. L. (2013). Stability of personality traits in adulthood: Mechanisms and implications. *Geropsych: The Journal of Gerontopsychology and Geriatric Psychiatry, 26*(1), 5–13. doi:10.1024/1662-9647/a000080

Allen, D., Carlson, D., & Ham, C. (2007). Well-being: New paradigms of wellness-inspiring positive health out-comes and renewing hope. *American Journal of Health Promotion, 21*(3), 1–9.

Allen, J. L., Lavallee, K. L., et al. (2010). DSM-IV criteria for childhood separa-tion anxiety disorder: Informant, age, and sex differences. *Journal of Anxiety Disorders, 24*(8), 946–952. doi:10.1016/j.janxdis.2010.06.022

Allen, J., & Holder, M. D. (2013). Marijuana use and well-being in university students. *Journal of Happiness Studies*. doi:10.1007/s10902-013-9423-1

Allen, K., Blascovich, J., & Mendes, W. B. (2002). Cardiovascular reactivity in the presence of pets, friends, and spouses: The truth about cats and dogs. *Psychosomatic Medicine, 64*(5), 727–739.

Allen, M., Mabry, E., & McKelton, D. (1998). Impact of juror attitudes about the death penalty on juror evaluations of guilt and punishment: A meta-analysis. *Law & Human Behavior, 22*(6), 715–731.

Allen, T. T., & Williams, L. D. (2012). An approach to life skills group work with youth in transition to indepen-dent living: Theoretical, practice, and operational considerations. *Residential Treatment for Children & Youth, 29*(4), 324–342. doi:10.1080/ 0886571X.2012.725375

Alleyne, M. D. (Ed.). (2011). *Anti-racism and multiculturalism: Studies in interna-tional communication*. Piscataway, NJ: Transaction Publishers.

Allport, G. W. (1958). *The nature of preju-dice*. Garden City, NY: Anchor Books, Doubleday.

Allport, G. W. (1961). *Pattern and growth in personality*. New York: Holt, Rinehart, & Winston.

Altemeyer, B. (2004). Highly dominating, highly authoritarian personalities. *Journal of Social Psychology, 144*(4), 421–447. doi:10.3200/ SOCP.144.4.421-448

Alter, A. L., Aronson, J., et al. (2010). Rising to the threat: Reducing stereotype threat by reframing the threat as a challenge. *Journal of Experimental Social Psychology, 46,* 166–171. doi:10.1016/j.jesp.2009.09.014

Altman, L. K. (2002). AIDS threatens to claim 65M more lives by '20. *Arizona Daily Star,* July 3, A7.

Altschuler, G. C. (2001). Battling the cheats. *The New York Times:* Education, January 7, 15.

Alwin, D. F., Cohen, R. L., & Newcomb, T. M. (1991). *Political attitudes over the life span: The Bennington women after fifty years.* Madison, WI: University of Wisconsin Press.

Amabile, T., Hadley, C. N., & Kramer, S. J. (2002). Creativity under the gun. *Harvard Business Review, 80*(8), 52–61.

Amano, T. T., Duvarci, S. S., et al. (2011). The fear circuit revisited: Contributions of the basal amygdala nuclei to conditioned fear. *The Journal of Neuroscience: The Official Journal of the Society for Neuroscience, 31*(43), 15481–15489. doi:10.1523/JNEUROSCI.3410-11.2011

Ambady, N., & R. Rosenthal, R. (1993). Half a minute: Predicting teacher evaluations from thin slices of nonverbal behavior and physical attractiveness. *Journal of Personality & Social Psychology, 64,* 431–441. doi:10.1037/0022-3514.64.3.431

American Academy of Child and Adolescent Psychiatry. (2011a). *Facts for families No. 9: Child sexual abuse.* Retrieved April 11, 2013, from http://www.aacap.org/galleries /FactsForFamilies/09_child_sexual _abuse.pdf

American Academy of Child and Adolescent Psychiatry. (2011b). *Child sexual abuse.* Retrieved April 11, 2013, from http://www.aacap.org/cs/root /facts_for_families/child_sexual_abuse

American Academy of Sleep Medicine. (2013). *CDC data on drowsy driving highlights need to treat sleep illness.* Retrieved March 7, 2013, from http:// www.aasmnet.org/articles .aspx?id=3560

American Lung Association. (2013). *Secondhand smoke.* Retrieved March 5, 2013, from http://www.lungusa.org /stop-smoking/about-smoking/health -effects/secondhand-smoke.html

American Psychiatric Association. (2013). *Diagnostic and statistical manual of mental disorders* (5th ed.). Washington, DC: American Psychiatric Association.

American Psychological Association. (2003a). *Demographic shifts in psychology.* Retrieved January 20, 2013, from http://www.apa.org /workforce/snapshot/2003 /demographic-shifts.aspx

American Psychological Association. (2003b). Guidelines on multicul-tural education, training, research, practice, and organizational change for psychologists. *American Psychologist, 58*(5), 377–402. doi:10.1037/0003-066X.58.5.377

American Psychological Association. (2007a). *APA guidelines for the under-graduate psychology major.* Retrieved May 29, 2013, from http://www.apa .org/ed/precollege/about/psymajor -guidelines.pdf

American Psychological Association. (2007b). *Report of the APA Task Force on the sexualization of girls.* Retrieved April 15, 2013, from http://www.apa.org/pi/women /programs/girls/report.aspx

American Psychological Association. (2008a). *Report of the Task Force on the Implementation of the Multicultural Guidelines.* Retrieved May 11, 2013, from http://www.apa.org/about /policy/multicultural-report.pdf

American Psychological Association. (2008b). *Sexual orientation and homo-sexuality.* Retrieved April 9, 2013, from http://www.apa.org/helpcenter /sexual-orientation.aspx

American Psychological Association. (2010). *Ethical principles of psycholo-gists and code of conduct: 2010 amend-ments.* Retrieved January 20, 2013, from http://www.apa.org/ethics/code /index.aspx

American Psychological Association. (2012). Workplace Survey. Retrieved June 17, 2013, from http://www.apa .org/news/press/releases/phwa /workplace-survey.pdf

Ancis, J. R., Chen, Y., & Schultz, D. (2004). Diagnostic challenges and the so-called culture-bound syndromes. In J. R. Ancis (Ed.), *Culturally responsive interventions: Innovative approaches to working with diverse populations* (pp. 213–222). New York: Brunner-Routledge.

Andersen, M. L., Poyares, D., et al. (2007). Sexsomnia: Abnormal sexual behavior during sleep. *Brain Research Reviews, 56*(2), 271–282. doi:10.1016/j. brainresrev.2007.06.005

Anderson, C. A. (1989). Temperature and aggression. *Psychological Bulletin, 106,* 74–96. doi:10.1037/0033-2909.106.1.74

Anderson, C. A. (2004). An update on the effects of violent video games. *Journal of Adolescence, 27,* 113–122. doi:10.1016/j.adolescence.2003.10.009

Anderson, C. A., & Bushman, B. J. (2002). Human aggression. *Annual Review of Psychology, 53,* 27–51. doi:10.1146/ annurev.psych.53.100901.135231

Anderson, C. A., Anderson, K. B., & Deuser, W. E. (1996). Examining an affective aggression frame-work. *Personality & Social Psychology Bulletin, 22*(4), 366–376. doi:10.1177/0146167296224004

Anderson, C. A., Berkowitz, L., et al. (2003). The influence of media violence on youth. *Psychological Science in the Public Interest, 4,* 81–100. doi:10.1111/j.1529-1006.2003. pspi_1433.x

Anderson, C. A., Gentile, D. A., & Buckley, K. E. (2007). *Violent video game effects on children and adolescents: Theory, research, and public policy.* New York: Oxford University Press.

Anderson, J. R. (2010a). *Cognitive psychology and its implications* (7th ed.). New York: Worth.

Anderson, K. J. (2010b). *Benign bigotry: The psychology of subtle prejudice.* New York: Cambridge University Press.

Anderson, M. C., & Huddleston, E. (2012). Towards a cognitive neurobiological model of moti-vated forgetting. In R. F. Belli (Ed.), *True and false recovered memories: Toward a reconciliation of the debate* (pp. 53–120). New York: Springer. doi:10.1007/978-1-4614-1195-6_3

Anderson, M. C., Reinholz, J., et al. (2011). Intentional suppression of unwanted memories grows more difficult as we age. *Psychology & Aging, 26*(2), 397–405. doi:10.1037/ a0022505

Anderson, S. W., & Booker, M. B. (2006). Cognitive behavioral therapy versus psychosurgery for refractory obsessive-compulsive disorder. *The Journal of Neuropsychiatry & Clinical Neurosciences, 18*(1), 129. doi:10.1176/ appi.neuropsych.18.1.129

Andersson, P., Pluim, J. W., et al. (2013). Navigation of a telepresence robot via covert visuospatial attention and real-time fMRI. *Brain Topography, 26*(1), 177–185. doi:10.1007/ s10548-012-0252-z

André, C., Jaber-Filho, J. A., et al. (2003). Predictors of recovery following invol-untary hospitalization of violent sub-stance abuse patients. *The American Journal on Addictions, 12*(1), 84–89. doi:10.1080/10550490390143394

Andreasen, N. C., Nopoulos, P., et al. (2011). Progressive brain change in schizophrenia: A prospective longitudinal study of first-episode schizophrenia. *Biological Psychiatry, 70*(7), 672–679. doi:10.1016/j. biopsych.2011.05.017

Anekonda, T. S. (2006). Resveratrol: A boon for treating Alzheimer's disease? *Brain Research Reviews, 52*(2), 316–326. doi:10.1016/j. brainresrev.2006.04.004

Anema, H. A., & Dijkerman, H. (2013). Motor and kinesthetic imag-ery. In S. Lacey, & R. Lawson (Eds.). *Multisensory imagery* (pp. 93–113). New York: Springer. doi:10.1007/978-1-4614-5879-1_6

Annesi, J. J., & Marti, C. N. (2011). Path analysis of exercise treatment-induced changes in psychological factors leading to weight loss. *Psychology & Health, 26*(8), 1081–1098. doi:10.1080/ 08870446.2010.534167

Annett, M. (2002). *Handedness and brain asymmetry: The right shift theory.* Hove, UK: Psychology Press.

Annett, M., & Manning, M. (1990). Arithmetic and laterality. *Neuropsychologia, 28*(1), 61–69. doi:10.1016/0028-3932(90)90086-4

Anshel, M. H. (1995). An examination of self-regulatory cognitive-behavioural strategies of Australian elite and non-elite competitive male swim-mers. *Australian Psychologist, 30*(2), 78–83.

Antoni, C. (2005). Management by objectives: An effective tool for teamwork? *International Journal of Human Resource Management, 16*(2), 174–184.

Antony, M. M., & Swinson, R. P. (2008). *The shyness and social anxiety work-book: Proven, step-by-step techniques for overcoming your fear* (2nd ed.). Oakland, CA: New Harbinger.

APA Center for Workforce Studies (2012). *2011 APA member profiles.* Retrieved January 20, 2013, from http://www.apa.org/workforce /publications/11-member/2011 -member-profiles.pdf

Aradillas, E., Libon, D. J., & Schwartzman, R. J. (2011). Acute loss of spatial navigational skills in a case of a right posterior hippocampus stroke. *Journal of the Neurological Sciences, 308*(1–2), 144–146. doi:10.1016/j. jns.2011.06.026

Arch, J. J., Ayers, C. R., et al. (2013). Randomized clinical trial of adapted mindfulness-based stress reduction versus group cognitive behavioral therapy for heteroge-neous anxiety disorders. *Behaviour Research & Therapy, 51*(4–5), 185–196. doi:10.1016/j.brat.2013.01.003

Ariely, D., & Loewenstein, G. (2006). The heat of the moment: The effect of sexual arousal on sexual decision making. *Journal of Behavioral Decision Making, 19*(2), 87–98.

Ariely, D., & Wertenbroch, K. (2002). Procrastination, deadlines, and performance: Self-control by precom-mitment. *Psychological Science, 13*(3), 219–224. doi:10.1111/1467-9280.00441

Arnett, J. J. (2004). *Emerging adulthood: The winding road from late teens through the twenties.* New York: Oxford University Press.

Arnett, J. J. (2010). Oh, grow up! Generational grumbling and the new life stage of emerging adulthood: Commentary on Trzesniewski & Donnellan (2010). *Perspectives on Psychological Science, 5*(1), 89–92. doi:10.1177/1745691609357016

Arnett, J. J. (2011). The cultural psychology of a new life stage. In L. A. Jensen (Ed.),

Emerging adulthood(s): The cultural psychology of a new life stage (pp. 255–275). New York: Oxford University Press.

Arnett, J. J., & Galambos, N. L. (Eds.). (2003). *New directions for child and adolescent development: Exploring cultural conceptions of the transition to adulthood.* San Francisco: Jossey-Bass.

Arnsten, A., Mazure, C. M., & Sinha, R. (2012). This is your brain on meltdown. *Scientific American, April,* 48–53. doi:10.1038/scientificamerican0412-48

Aron, A. (2012). Online dating: The current status—and beyond. *Psychological Science in the Public Interest, 13*(1), 1–2. doi:10.1177/1529100612438173

Aron, A., Fisher, H. E., et al. (2008). Falling in love. In S. Sprecher, A. Wenzel, & J. Harvey (Eds.), *Handbook of relationship initiation* (pp. 315–336). New York: Psychology Press.

Aronow, E., Altman Weiss, K., & Reznikoff, M. (2001). *A practical guide to the Thematic Apperception Test: The TAT in clinical practice.* New York: Brunner-Routledge.

Aronson, E. (2012). *The social animal* (11th ed.). New York: Worth.

Aronson, E., Wilson, T. D., & Akert, R. M. (2013). *Social psychology* (8th ed.). Englewood Cliffs, NJ: Prentice Hall.

Aronson, K. (2003). Alcohol: A recently identified risk factor for breast cancer. Canadian *Medical Association Journal, 168*(9), 1147–1148.

Artz, S. (2005). To die for: Violent adolescent girls' search for male attention. In D. J. Pepler, K. C. Madsen, et al. (Eds.), *The development and treatment of girlhood aggression* (pp. 137–160). Mahwah, NJ: Erlbaum.

Asch, S. E. (1956). Studies of independence and conformity: A minority of one against a unanimous majority. *Psychological Monographs, 70*(9, Whole No. 416). doi:10.1037/h0093718

Aselton, P. (2012). Sources of stress and coping in American college students who have been diagnosed with depression. *Journal of Child & Adolescent Psychiatric Nursing, 25*(3), 119–123. doi:10.1111/j.1744-6171.2012.00341.x

Asgari, S., Dasgupta, N., & Stout, J. G. (2012). When do counterstereotypic ingroup members inspire versus deflate? The effect of successful professional women on young women's leadership self-concept. *Personality & Social Psychology Bulletin, 38*(3), 370–383. doi:10.1177/0146167211431968

Ash, D. W., & Holding, D. H. (1990). Backward versus forward chaining in the acquisition of a keyboard skill. *Human Factors, 32*(2), 139–146. doi:10.1177/001872089003200202

Ashby, F. G., & Maddox, W. T. (2005). Human category learning.

Annual Review of Psychology, 56, 149–178. doi:10.1146/annurev.psych.56.091103.070217

Ashcraft, D. (2012). *Personality theories workbook* (5th ed.). Belmont, CA: Cengage Learning/Wadsworth.

Ashton, M. C. (2007). *Individual differences and personality.* San Diego: Elsevier.

Asmundson, G. J. G., & Taylor, S. (2005). *It's not all in your head.* London: Psychology Press.

Athenasiou, R., Shaver, P., & Tavris, C. (1970). Sex. *Psychology Today, 4*(2), 37–52.

Atkin, D. J., & Lau, T. Y. (2007). Information technology and organizational telework. In C. A. Lin, & D. J. Atkin (Eds.), *Communication technology and social change: Theory and implications* (pp. 79–100). Mahwah, NJ: Erlbaum.

Atkinson, R. C. & Shiffrin, R. M. (1968). Human memory: A proposed system and its control processes. In K. W. Spence & J. T. Spence (Eds.), *The psychology of learning and motivation* (Vol. 2, pp. 742–775). London: Academic Press. doi:10.1016/S0079-7421(08)60422-3

Atwood, J. D. (2006). Mommy's little angel, daddy's little girl: Do you know what your pre-teens are doing? *American Journal of Family Therapy, 34*(5), 447–467.

Au, S., & Stavinoha, P. L. (2008). *Stress-free potty training: A commonsense guide to finding the right approach for your child.* New York, NY: AMACOM.

Aucoin, K. J., Frick, P. J., & Bodin, S. D. (2006). Corporal punishment and child adjustment. *Journal of Applied Developmental Psychology, 27*(6), 527–541.

Ausubel, D. P. (1978). In defense of advance organizers: A reply to the critics. *Review of Educational Research, 48,* 251–257.

Avery, D. H., Eder, D. N., et al. (2001). Dawn simulation and bright light in the treatment of SAD. *Biological Psychiatry, 50*(3), 205–216. doi:10.1016/S0006-3223(01)01200-8

Avolio, B. J., Walumbwa, F. O., & Weber, T. J. (2009). Leadership: Current theories, research, and future directions. *Annual Review of Psychology, 60,* 421–449.

Awadallah, N., Vaughan, A., et al. (2005). Munchausen by proxy: A case, chart series, and literature review of older victims. *Child Abuse & Neglect, 29*(8), 931–941. doi:10.1016/j.chiabu.2004.11.007

Axmacher, N., Do Lam, A. T., et al. (2010). Natural memory beyond the storage model: Repression, trauma, and the construction of a personal past. *Frontiers in Human Neuroscience, 4,* 211. doi:10.3389/fnhum.2010.00211

Ayers, L., Beaton, S., & Hunt, H. (1999). The significance of transpersonal experiences, emotional conflict, and cognitive abilities in creativity. *Empirical Studies of the Arts, 17*(1), 73–82. doi:10.2190/4X8D-XTT4-FKKH-ECJ7

Ayllon, T. (1963). Intensive treatment of psychotic behavior by stimulus satiation and food reinforcement. *Behavior Research & Therapy, 1,* 53–61. doi:10.1016/0005-7967(63)90008-1

Ayman, R., & Korabik, K. (2010). Leadership: Why gender and culture matter. *American Psychologist, 65*(3), 157–170.

Babbie, E. R. (2013). *The practice of social research* (13th ed.). Belmont, CA: Cengage Learning/Wadsworth.

Baddeley, A. (2012). Working memory: Theories, models, and controversies. *Annual Review of Psychology, 63,* 1–29. doi:10.1146/annurev-psych-120710-100422

Baddeley, A., Eysenck, M. W., & Anderson, M. C. (2009). *Memory.* Hove, UK: Psychology Press.

Baer, N., Cialdini, R. B., & Lueth, N. (2012). *Influence: Science and practice: The Comic.* Highland Park, IL: Roundtable.

Bahr, S. J., & Hoffmann, J. P. (2010). Parenting style, religiosity, peers, and adolescent heavy drinking. *Journal of Studies on Alcohol & Drugs, 71*(4), 539–543.

Bailey, C. H., & Kandel, E. R. (2004). Synaptic growth and the persistence of long-term memory: A molecular perspective. In M. S. Gazzaniga (Ed.), *The cognitive neurosciences* (3rd ed., pp. 647–663). Cambridge, MA: MIT Press.

Bailey, L. M., & McKeever, W. F. (2004). A large-scale study of handedness and pregnancy/birth risk events: Implications for genetic theories of handedness. *Laterality: Asymmetries of Body, Brain & Cognition, 9*(2), 175–188.

Baillargeon, R. (1991). Reasoning about the height and location of a hidden object in 4.5- and 6.5-month-old infants. *Cognition, 38*(1), 13–42. doi:10.1016/0010-0277(91)90021-U

Baillargeon, R. (2004). Infants' reasoning about hidden objects: Evidence for event-general and event-specific expectations. *Developmental Science, 7*(4), 391–424. doi:10.1111/j.1467-7604.2004.00357.x

Baillargeon, R., De Vos, J., & Graber, M. (1989). Location memory in 8-month-old infants in a nonsearch AB task. *Cognitive Development, 4,* 345–367. doi:10.1016/S0885-2014(89)90040-3

Baird, A. D., Scheffer, I. E., & Wilson, S. J. (2011). Mirror neuron system involvement in empathy: A critical look at the evidence. *Social Neuroscience, 6*(4), 327–335. doi:10.1080/17470919.2010.547085

Baker, L., & McNulty, J. K. (2010). Shyness and marriage: Does shyness shape even established relationships? *Personality & Social Psychology Bulletin, 36*(5), 665–676. doi:10.1177/0146167210367489

Baker, S. C., & Serdikoff, S. L. (2013). Addressing the role of animal research in psychology. In D. S. Dunn, R. A. R. Gurung, et al. (Eds.), *Controversy in the psychology classroom: Using hot topics to foster critical thinking* (pp. 105–112). Washington, DC: American Psychological Association. doi:10.1037/14038-007

Bakker, G. M. (2009). In defence of thought stopping. *Clinical Psychologist, 13*(2), 59–68. doi:10.1080/13284200902810452

Bales, D., & Bateman, A. W. (2012). Partial hospitalization settings. In A. W. Bateman & P. Fonagy (Eds.), *Handbook of mentalizing in mental health practice,* (pp. 197–226). Arlington, VA: American Psychiatric Publishing.

Balk, D. E., Lampe, S., et al. (1998). TAT results in a longitudinal study of bereaved college students. *Death Studies, 22*(1), 3–21. doi:10.1080/074811898201704

Balsam, K. F., & Mohr, J. J. (2007). Adaptation to sexual orientation stigma: A comparison of bisexual and lesbian/gay adults. *Journal of Counseling Psychology, 54*(3), 306–319.

Baltes, B. B., Briggs, T. E., et al. (1999). Flexible and compressed workweek schedules. *Journal of Applied Psychology, 84*(4), 496–513.

Balthazart, J. (2012). *Biology of homosexuality.* New York: Oxford University Press.

Bandura, A. (1971). *Social learning theory.* New York: General Learning Press.

Bandura, A. (2001). Social cognitive theory: An agentic perspective. *Annual Review of Psychology, 52,* 1–26. doi:10.1146/annurev.psych.52.1.1

Bandura, A., Blanchard, E. B., & Ritter, B. (1969). Relative efficacy of desensitization and modeling approaches for inducing behavioral, affective, and attitudinal changes. *Journal of Personality & Social Psychology, 13*(3), 173–199. doi:10.1037/h0028276

Bandura, A., Ross, D., & Ross, S. A. (1963). Vicarious reinforcement and imitative learning. *Journal of Abnormal & Social Psychology, 67,* 601–607. doi:10.1037/h0045550

Banerjee, D., & Nisbet, A. (2011). Sleepwalking. *Sleep Medicine Clinics, 6*(4), 401–416. doi:10.1016/j.jsmc.2011.07.001

Bangerter, A., König, C. J., et al. (2009). How widespread is graphology in personnel selection practice? A case study of a job market myth. *International Journal Of Selection &*

Assessment, 17(2):219–230. doi:10.1111/j.1468-2389.2009.00464.x

Banich, M. T., & Compton, R. J. (2011). *Cognitive neuroscience* (3rd ed.). Belmont, CA: Cengage Learning/Wadsworth.

Banks, A., & Gartrell, N. K. (1995). Hormones and sexual orientation: A questionable link. *Journal of Homosexuality, 28*(3–4), 247–268.

Barabasz, A., & Watkins, J. G. (2005). *Hypnotherapeutic techniques* (2nd ed.). Washington: Taylor & Francis.

Barber, N. (2010). Applying the concept of adaptation to societal differences in intelligence. *Cross-Cultural Research, 44*(2), 116–150. doi:10.1177/1069397109358041

Bardone-Cone, A. M., Joiner, T. E., Jr., et al. (2008). Examining a psychosocial interactive model of binge eating and vomiting in women with bulimia nervosa and subthreshold bulimia nervosa. *Behaviour Research & Therapy, 46*(7), 887–894. doi:10.1016/j.brat.2008.04.003

Barelds, D. P., & Dijkstra, P. (2009). Positive illusions about a partner's physical attractiveness and relationship quality. *Personal Relationships, 16*(2), 263–283. doi:10.1111/j.1475-6811.2009.01222.x

Barkataki, I., Kumari, V., et al. (2006). Volumetric structural brain abnormalities in men with schizophrenia or antisocial personality disorder. *Behavioural Brain Research, 169*(2), 239–247. doi:10.1016/j.bbr.2006.01.009

Barlow, D. H. (2000). Unraveling the mysteries of anxiety and its disorders from the perspective of emotion theory. *American Psychologist, 55*, 1247–1263. doi:10.1037/0003-066X.55.11.1247

Barlow, D. H., Boswell, J. F., & Thompson-Hollands, J. (2013). Eysenck, Strupp, and 50 years of psychotherapy research: A personal perspective. *Psychotherapy, 50*(1), 77–87. doi:10.1037/a0031096

Barnett, J., Behnke, S. H., et al. (2007). In case of ethical dilemma, break glass: Commentary on ethical decision making in practice. *Professional Psychology: Research & Practice, 38*(1), 7–12. doi:10.1037/0735-7028.38.1.7

Barnier, A. J., McConkey, K. M., & Wright, J. (2004). Posthypnotic amnesia for autobiographical episodes: Influencing memory accessibility and quality. *International Journal of Clinical & Experimental Hypnosis, 52*(3), 260–279. doi:10.1080/0020714049052351

Baron, I. S. (2005). Test review: Wechsler intelligence scale for children (4th ed.). (WISC-IV). *Child Neuropsychology, 11*(5), 471–475. doi:10.1080/09297040590951587

Baron, R. A., Byrne, D., & Branscombe, N. R. (2012). *Mastering social psychology* (13th ed.). Boston: Pearson/Allyn & Bacon.

Barr, M. S., Farzan, F., et al. (2013). Can repetitive magnetic stimulation improve cognition in schizophrenia? Pilot data from a randomized controlled trial. *Biological Psychiatry, 73*(6), 510–517. doi:10.1016/j.biopsych.2012.08.020

Barras, C. (2010, January 9). Microsoft's body-sensing, button-busting controller. *New Scientist, 2742*, 22.

Barratt, B. B. (2013). *What is psychoanalysis? 100 years after Freud's 'secret committee'*. New York: Taylor & Francis.

Barreto, M. L., & Frazier, L. D. (2012). Coping with life events through possible selves. *Journal of Applied Social Psychology, 42*(7), 1785–1810. doi:10.1111/j.1559-1816.2012.00918.x

Barrios, A. A. (2009). *Understanding hypnosis: Theory, scope, and potential.* Hauppauge, NY: Nova Science Publishers.

Barron, F. (1958). The psychology of imagination. *Scientific American, 199*(3), 150–170. doi:10.1038/scientificamerican0958-150

Barrowcliff, A. L., & Haddock, G. (2006). The relationship between command hallucinations and factors of compliance: A critical review of the literature. *Journal of Forensic Psychiatry & Psychology, 17*(2), 266–298. doi:10.1080/14789940500485078

Barry, J. G., Sabisch, B., et al. (2011). Encoding: The keystone to efficient functioning of verbal short-term memory. *Neuropsychologia, 49*(13), 3636–3647. doi:10.1016/j.neuropsychologia.2011.09.018

Barry, S. R., & Sacks, O. (2009). *Fixing my gaze.* New York: Basic Books.

Bartholow, B. D., & Anderson, C. A. (2002). Effects of violent video games on aggressive behavior. *Journal of Experimental Social Psychology, 38*(3), 283–290. doi:10.1006/jesp.2001.1502

Bartholow, B. D., Sestir, M. A., & Davis, E. B. (2005). Correlates and consequences of exposure to video game violence: Hostile personality, empathy, and aggressive behavior. *Personality & Social Psychology Bulletin, 31*(11), 1573–1586. doi:10.1177/0146167205277205

Bartram, B. (2006). An examination of perceptions of parental influence on attitudes to language learning. *Educational Research, 48*(2), 211–222. doi:10.1080/00131880600732298

Basadur, M., Runco, M. A., & Vega, L. A. (2000). Understanding how creative thinking skills, attitudes and behaviors work together. *Journal of Creative Behavior, 34*(2), 77–100. doi:10.1002/j.2162-6057.2000.tb01203.x

Basner, M., & Dinges, D. (2009). Dubious bargain: Trading sleep for Leno and Letterman. *Sleep, 32*(6), 747–752.

Bass, J., & Takahashi, J. S. (2010). Circadian integration of metabolism and energetics. *Science, 330*(6009), 1349–1354. doi:10.1126/science.1195027

Basson, R., & Brotto, L. A. (2009). Disorders of sexual desire and subjective arousal in women. In R. Balon, & R. T. Segraves (Eds.), *Clinical manual of sexual disorders* (pp. 119–159). Arlington, VA: American Psychiatric Publishing.

Batelaan, N. M., de Graaf, R., et al. (2010). The course of panic attacks in individuals with panic disorder and subthreshold panic disorder: A population-based study. *Journal of Affective Disorders, 121*(1–2), 30–38. doi:10.1016/j.jad.2009.05.003

Bateman, A. W., & Fonagy, P. (2012). Antisocial personality disorder. In A. W. Bateman & P. Fonagy (Eds.), *Handbook of mentalizing in mental health practice* (pp. 289–308). Arlington, VA: American Psychiatric Publishing.

Batson, C. D. (2006). "Not all self-interest after all": Economics of empathy-induced altruism. In D. De Cremer, M. Zeelenberg, et al. (Eds.), *Social psychology and economics* (pp. 281–299). Mahwah, NJ: Erlbaum.

Batson, C. D. (2010). Empathy-induced altruistic motivation. In M. Mikulincer & P. R. Shaver (Eds.), *Prosocial motives, emotions, and behavior: The better angels of our nature* (pp. 15–34). Washington: American Psychological Association. doi:10.1037/12061-001

Batson, C. D., & Powell, A. A. (2003). Altruism and prosocial behavior. In T. Millon & M. J. Lerner (Eds.), *Handbook of psychology: Personality and social psychology* (Vol. 5, pp. 463–484). New York: Wiley.

Bauer, J. J., McAdams, D. P., & Pals, J. L. (2008). Narrative identity and eudaimonic well-being. *Journal of Happiness Studies, 9*(1), 81–104. doi:10.1007/s10902-006-9021-6

Bauer, S., Wolf, M., et al. (2011). The effectiveness of Internet chat groups in relapse prevention after inpatient psychotherapy. *Psychotherapy Research, 21*(2), 219–226. doi:10.1080/10503307.2010.547530

Baugh, C. M., Stamm, J. M., et al. (2012). Chronic traumatic encephalopathy: Neurodegeneration following repetitive concussive and subconcussive brain trauma. *Brain Imaging & Behavior, 6*(2), 244–254. doi:10.1007/s11682-012-9164-5

Baum, A., & Davis, G. E. (1980). Reducing the stress of high-density living: An architectural intervention. *Journal of Personality & Social Psychology, 38*, 471–481.

Baum, A., & Valins, S. (1979). Architectural mediation of residential density and control: Crowding and the regulation of social contact. *Advances in Experimental & Social Psychology, 12*, 131–175.

Baum, A., & Valins, S. (Eds.). (1977). *Human response to crowding: Studies of the effects of residential group size.* Mahwah, NJ: Erlbaum.

Bauman, L. J., Karasz, A., & Hamilton, A. (2007). Understanding failure of condom use intention among adolescents: Completing an intensive preventive intervention. *Journal of Adolescent Research, 22*(3), 248–274.

Baumeister, R. F., & Bushman, B. (2014). *Social psychology and human nature* (3rd ed.). Belmont, CA: Cengage Learning/Wadsworth.

Baumeister, R. F., Campbell, J. D., et al. (2003). Does high self-esteem cause better performance, interpersonal success, happiness, or healthier lifestyles? *Psychological Science in the Public Interest, 4*(1), 1–44. doi:10.1111/1529-1006.01431

Baumrind, D. (1991). The influence of parenting style on adolescent competence and substance use. *Journal of Early Adolescence, 11*(1), 56–95. doi:10.1177/0272431691111004

Baumrind, D. (2005). Patterns of parental authority and adolescent autonomy. In J. Smetana (Ed.), *New directions for child development: Changes in parental authority during adolescence* (pp. 61–69). San Francisco: Jossey-Bass.

Beans, D. R. (2009). *Integrative endocrinology:* New York: Routledge.

Bearman, P. S., Moody, J., & Stovel, K. (2004). Chains of affection: The structure of adolescent romantic and sexual networks. *American Journal of Sociology, 110*(1), 44–91.

Beaulieu, C. M. J. (2004). Intercultural study of personal space: A case study. *Journal of Applied Social Psychology, 34*(4), 794–805.

Beck, A. T. (1991). Cognitive therapy. *American Psychologist, 46*(4), 368–375. doi:10.1037/0003-066X.46.4.368

Beck, B. L., Koons, S. R., & Milgrim, D. L. (2000). Correlates and consequences of behavioral procrastination. *Journal of Social Behavior & Personality, 15*(5), 3–13.

Beck, H. P., Levinson, S. & Irons, G. (2009). Finding little Albert: A journey to John B. Watson's infant laboratory. *American Psychologist, 64*(7), 605–614. doi:10.1037/a0017234

Becker, S. W., & Eagly, A. H. (2004). The heroism of women and men. *American Psychologist, 59*(3), 163–178.

Bedny, M., Pascual-Leone, A., et al. (2012). A sensitive period for language in the visual cortex: Distinct patterns of plasticity in congenitally versus late blind adults. *Brain & Language, 122*(3), 162–170. doi:10.1016/j.bandl.2011.10.005

Beeber, L. S., Chazan-Cohen, R., et al. (2007). The Early Promotion and Intervention Research Consortium (E-PIRC): Five approaches to improving infant/toddler mental health in Early Head Start. *Infant Mental Health Journal, 28*(2), 130–150. doi:10.1002/imhj.20126

Beeman, M. J., & Chiarello, C. (1998). Complementary right- and left-hemisphere language comprehension. *Current Directions in Psychological Science, 7*(1), 2–8. doi:10.1111/1467-8721.ep11521805

Begg, D. P., Sinclair, A. J., & Weisinger, R. S. (2012). Thirst deficits in aged rats are reversed by dietary omega-3 fatty acid supplementation. *Neurobiology of Aging, 33*(10), 2422–2430. doi:10.1016/j.neurobiolaging.2011.12.001

Begley, S. (2006). *Train your mind, change your brain*. New York: Ballantine.

Behne, T., Liszkowski, U., et al. (2012). Twelve-month-olds' comprehension and production of pointing. *British Journal Of Developmental Psychology, 30*(3), 359–375. doi:10.1111/j.2044-835X.2011.02043.x

Beirne-Smith, M., Patton, J., & Shannon,K. (2006). *Mental retardation: An introduction to intellectual disability* (7th ed.). Englewood Cliffs, NJ: Prentice Hall.

Bekinschtein, T. A., Shalom, D. E., et al. (2009). Classical conditioning in the vegetative and minimally conscious state. *Nature Neuroscience 12*, 1343–1349. doi:10.1038/nn.2391

Belicki, K., Chambers, E., & Ogilvie, R. (1997). Sleep quality and nightmares. *Sleep Research, 26*, 637.

Bellezza, F. S., Six, L. S., & Phillips, D. S. (1992). A mnemonic for remembering long strings of digits. *Bulletin of the Psychonomic Society, 30*(4), 271–274.

Bem, S. L. (1974). The measurement of psychological androgyny. *Journal of Consulting & Clinical Psychology, 42*(2), 155–162. doi:10.1037/h0036215

Bem, S. L. (1975). Androgyny vs. the tight little lives of fluffy women and chesty men. *Psychology Today*, Sept., 58–62.

Bem, S. L. (1981). Gender schema theory. A cognitive account of sex typing. *Psychological Review, 88*, 354–364.

Ben Abdallah, N. M.-B., Slomianka, L., et al. (2010). Early age-related changes in adult hippocampal neurogenesis in C57 mice. *Neurobiology of Aging, 31*(1), 151–161. doi:10.1016/j.neurobiolaging.2008.03.002

Ben-Itzhak, S., Bluvstein, I., et al. (2012). The effectiveness of brief versus intermediate duration psychodynamic psychotherapy in the treatment of adjustment disorder. *Journal of Contemporary Psychotherapy, 42*(4), 249–256. doi:10.1007/s10879-012-9208-6

Ben-Shakhar, G., & Dolev, K. (1996). Psychophysiological detection through the guilty knowledge technique: Effect of mental countermeasures. *Journal of Applied Psychology, 81*(3), 273–281. doi:10.1037/0021-9010.81.3.273

Benbow, C. P. (1986). Physiological correlates of extreme intellectual precocity. *Neuropsychologia, 24*(5), 719–725. doi:10.1016/0028-3932(86)90011-4

Benedetti, F. (2009). *Placebo effects: Understanding the mechanisms in health and disease*. New York: Oxford University Press.

Benitz, L. (2009). Becoming biliterate: A study of two-way bilingual immersion education. *Journal of Language, Identity, & Education, 8*(1), 54–57. doi:10.1080/15348450802620001

Benjafield, J. G. (2012). *Psychology: A concise history*. New York: Oxford University Press.

Benjafield, J. G., Smilek, D., & Kingstone, A. (2010). *Cognition* (4th ed.). New York: Oxford University Press.

Benjamin, O., & Tlusten, D. (2010). Intimacy and/or degradation: Heterosexual images of togetherness and women's embrace of pornography. *Sexualities, 13*(5), 599–623.

Benloucif, S., Bennett, E. L., & Rosenzweig, M. R. (1995). Norepinephrine and neural plasticity: The effects of xylamine on experience-induced changes in brain weight, memory, and behavior. *Neurobiology of Learning & Memory, 63*(1), 33–42. doi:10.1006/nlme.1995.1003

Bennett, P. (2011). *Abnormal and clinical psychology* (3rd ed.). New York: McGraw-Hill.

Bensafi, M., Zelano, C., et al. (2004). Olfaction: From sniff to percept. In M. S. Gazzaniga (Ed.), *The cognitive neurosciences* (3rd ed., pp. 259–280). Cambridge, MA: MIT Press.

Bensley, L., & Van Eenwyk, J. (2001). Video games and real-life aggression. *Journal of Adolescent Health, 29*(4), 244–257. doi:10.1016/S1054-139X(01)00239-7

Bentley-Condit, V. K., & Smith, E. O. (2010). Animal tool use: Current definitions and an updated comprehensive catalog. *Behaviour, 147*(2), 185–221. doi:10.1163/000579509X12512865686555

Berg, J. (2013). Opposition to pro-immigrant public policy: Symbolic racism and group threat. *Sociological Inquiry, 83*(1), 1–31. doi:10.1111/j.1475-682x.2012.00437.x

Bergeron, S., & Lord, M. J. (2003). The integration of pelvi-perineal reeducation and cognitive-behavioral therapy in the multidisciplinary treatment of the sexual pain disorders. *Sexual & Relationship Therapy, 18*, 135–141.

Berlin, H. A. (2011). The neural basis of the dynamic unconscious. *Neuropsychoanalysis, 13*(1), 5–31.

Berman, S. L., Weems, C. F., & Stickle, T. R. (2006). Existential anxiety in adolescents: Prevalence, structure, association with psychological symptoms and identity development. *Journal of Youth & Adolescence, 35*(3), 303–310. doi:10.1007/s10964-006-9032-y

Berman, S. M., Paz-Filho, G., et al. (2013). Effects of leptin deficiency and replacement on cerebellar response to food-related cues. *Cerebellum, 12*(1), 59–67. doi:10.1007/s12311-012-0360-z

Bermudez-Silva, F. J., Viveros, M. P., et al. (2010). The endocannabinoid system, eating behavior and energy homeostasis: The end or a new beginning? *Pharmacology, Biochemistry & Behavior, 95*(4), 375–382. doi:10.1016/j.pbb.2010.03.012

Bernard, R. S., Cohen, L. L., & Moffett, K. (2009). A token economy for exercise adherence in pediatric cystic fibrosis: A single-subject analysis. *Journal of Pediatric Psychology, 34*(4), 354–365. doi:10.1093/jpepsy/jsn101

Berne, E. (1964). *Games people play*. New York: Grove.

Bernstein H. J., Beale M. D., et al. (1998). Patient attitudes about ECT after treatment. *Psychiatric Annals, 28*(9), 524–527.

Bernstein, D. A., & Lucas, S. G. (2008). *Functional fixedness in problem solving*. In Benjamin L. T. (Ed.), *Favorite activities for the teaching of psychology* (pp.143–144). Washington: American Psychological Association.

Bernstein, D. M., & Loftus, E. F. (2009). How to tell if a particular memory is true or false. *Perspectives on Psychological Science, 4*(4), 370–374. doi:10.1111/j.1745-6924.2009.01140.x

Bernstein, I. H., Rush, A. J., et al. (2008). Symptom features of postpartum depression: Are they distinct? *Depression & Anxiety, 25*(1), 20–26.

Bernthal, M. J. (2003). How viewing professional wrestling may affect children. *The Sport Journal, 6*(3). Retrieved June 9, 2013, from http://www.thesportjournal.org/article/effect-professional-wrestling-viewership-children

Berry, J. W., Phinney, J. S, et al. (2005). *Immigrant youth in cultural transition*. Mahwah, NJ: Erlbaum.

Berscheid, E. (2010). Love in the fourth dimension. *Annual Review of Psychology, 61*, 1–25. doi:10.1146/annurev.psych.093008.100318

Berscheid, E., & Regan, P. (2005). *The psychology of interpersonal relationships*. Englewood Cliffs, NJ: Prentice Hall.

Bersoff, D. M. (1999). Why good people sometimes do bad things: Motivated reasoning and unethical behavior. *Personality & Social Psychology Bulletin, 25*(1), 28–39. doi:10.1177/0146167299025001003

Beseler, C. L., Taylor, L. A., & Leeman, R. F. (2010). An item-response theory analysis of DSM-IV alcohol-use disorder criteria and "binge" drinking in undergraduates. *Journal of Studies on Alcohol & Drugs, 71*(3), 418–423.

Besnard, D., & Cacitti, L. (2005). Interface changes causing accidents: An empirical study of negative transfer. *International Journal of Human-Computer Studies, 62*(1), 105–125.

Best, D. (2002). Cross-cultural gender roles. In J. Worell (Ed.), *Encyclopedia of women and gender* (pp. 279–290). New York: Oxford.

Betancur, C., Velez, A., et al. (1990). Association between left-handedness and allergy: A reappraisal. *Neuropsychologia, 28*(2), 223–227. doi:10.1016/0028-3932(90)90104-V

Beyer, M., Gerlach, F. M., et al. (2003). The development of quality circles/peer review groups as a tool for quality improvement in Europe: Results of a survey in 26 European countries. *Family Practice, 20*, 443–451.

Beyers, W., & Seiffge-Krenke, I. (2010). Does identity precede intimacy? Testing Erikson's theory on romantic development in emerging adults of the 21st century. *Journal of Adolescent Research, 25*(3), 387–415. doi:10.1177/0743558410361370

Bhushan, B., & Khan, S. M. (2006). Laterality and accident proneness: A study of locomotive drivers. *Laterality: Asymmetries of Body, Brain & Cognition, 11*(5), 395–404. doi:10.1080/13576500500457458

Bialystok, E., & Barac, R. R. (2012). Emerging bilingualism: Dissociating advantages for metalinguistic awareness and executive control. *Cognition, 122*(1), 67–73. doi:10.1016/j.cognition.2011.08.003

Bialystok, E., & DePape, A.-M. (2009). Musical expertise, bilingualism, and executive functioning. *Journal of Experimental Psychology: Human Perception & Performance, 35*(2), 565–574. doi:10.1037/a0012735

Biernat, M., & Danaher, K. (2013). Prejudice. In H. Tennen, J. Suls, et al. (Eds.), *Handbook of psychology* (Vol. 5): *Personality and social psychology* (2nd ed.) (pp. 341–367). New York: Wiley.

Binder, J. L. (2004). *Key competencies in brief dynamic psychotherapy: Clinical practice beyond the manual*. New York: Guilford.

Binder, J., Zagefka, H., et al. (2009). Does contact reduce prejudice or does prejudice reduce contact? A longitudinal test of the contact hypothesis among majority and minority groups in three European countries. *Journal of Personality & Social Psychology, 96*(4), 843–856. doi:10.1037/a0013470

Binik, Y. M. (2005). Should dyspareunia be retained as a sexual dysfunction in *DSM-V*? A painful classification decision. *Archives of Sexual Behavior, 34*(1), 11–21.

Binning, K. R., Sherman, D. K., et al. (2010). Seeing the other side: Reducing political partisanship via self-affirmation in the 2008 presidential election. *Analyses of Social Issues & Public Policy,* (1), 276–292. doi:10.1111/j.1530-2415.2010.01210.x

Birgegård, A., Norring, C., & Clinton, D. (2012). DSM-IV versus DSM-5: Implementation of proposed DSM-5 criteria in a large naturalistic database. *International Journal of Eating Disorders, 45*(3), 353–361. doi:10.1002/eat.20968

Biro, F. M., Galvez, M. P., et al. (2010). Pubertal assessment method and baseline characteristics in a mixed longitudinal study of girls. *Pediatrics, 126*(3), e583–e590. doi:10.1542/peds.2009-3079

Bisson, J. I., Ehlers, A., et al. (2007). Psychological treatments for chronic post-traumatic stress disorder: Systematic review and meta-analysis. *British Journal of Psychiatry, 190*(2), 97–104. doi:10.1192/bjp.bp.106.021402

Bizer, G. Y., Hart, J., & Jekogian, A. M. (2012). Belief in a just world and social dominance orientation: Evidence for a mediational pathway predicting negative attitudes and discrimination against individuals with mental illness. *Personality & Individual Differences, 52*(3), 428–432. doi:10.1016/j.paid.2011.11.002

Bjorklund, D. F. (2012). *Children's thinking* (5th ed.). Belmont, CA: Cengage Learning/Wadsworth.

Bjorklund, D. F., & Hernández Blasi. C. (2012). *Child and adolescent development.* Belmont, CA: Cengage Learning/Wadsworth.

Bjornstrom, E. E. (2011). An examination of the relationship between neighborhood income inequality, social resources, and obesity in Los Angeles County. *American Journal of Health Promotion, 26*(2), 109–115. doi:10.4278/ajhp.100326-QUAN-93

Blackmore, S. (2000). First person: Into the unknown. *New Scientist, Nov 4,* 55.

Blackwell, B. (2012). Obituary: Jose Manuel Rodriguez Delgado. *Neuropsychopharmacology, 37*(13), 2883–2884.

Blackwell, D. L., & Lichter, D. T. (2004). Homogamy among dating, cohabiting, and married couples. *Sociological Quarterly, 45*(4), 719–737. doi:10.1111/j.1533-8525.2004.tb02311.x

Blair, K. S., Richell, R. A., et al. (2006). They know the words, but not the music: Affective and semantic priming in individuals with psychopathy. *Biological Psychology, 73*(2), 114–123. doi:10.1016/j.biopsycho.2005.12.006

Blakemore, C., & Cooper, G. (1970). Development of the brain depends on the visual environment. *Nature, 228,* 477–478. doi:10.1038/228477a0

Blanchard, E. B., Kuhn, E., et al. (2004). Studies of the vicarious traumatization of college students by the September 11th attacks: Effects of proximity, exposure and connectedness. *Behaviour Research & Therapy, 42*(2), 191–205.

Blatner, A. (2006). Current trends in psychodrama. *International Journal of Psychotherapy, 10*(3), 43–53.

Blinn-Pike, L., Worthy, S., & Jonkman, J. N. (2010). Adolescent gambling: A review of an emerging field of research. *Journal of Adolescent Health, 47*(3), 223–236. doi:10.1016/j.jadohealth.2010.05.0

Bloom, C. M., & Lamkin, D. M. (2006). The Olympian struggle to remember the cranial nerves: Mnemonics and student success. *Teaching of Psychology, 33*(2), 128–129. doi:1207/s15328023top3302_8

Bloom, J. W. (1998). The ethical practice of WebCounseling. *British Journal of Guidance & Counselling, 26*(1), 53–59. doi:10.1080/03069889800760061

Bloom, L., & Bloom, C. (2012). *What's so special about Fifty Shades of Gray?.* Retrieved April 7, 2013, from http://www.psychologytoday.com/blog/stronger-the-broken-places/201212/whats-so-special-about-fifty-shades-gray

Blumenstein, B., & Orbach, I. (2012). *Mental practice in sport: Twenty case studies.* New York: Novinka/Nova Science Publishers.

Blundon, J. A., & Zakharenko, S. S. (2008). Dissecting the components of long-term potentiation. *The Neuroscientist, 14*(6), 598–608.

Blunt, A., & Pychyl, T. A. (2005). Project systems of procrastinators: A personal project-analytic and action control perspective. *Personality & Individual Differences, 38*(8), 1771–1780. doi:10.1016/j.paid.2004.11.019

Bodner, E. (2009). On the origins of ageism among older and younger adults. *International Psychogeriatrics, 21*(6), 1003–1014. doi:10.1017/S104161020999055X

Boduroglu, A., Shah, P., & Nisbett, R. E. (2009). Cultural differences in allocation of attention in visual information processing. *Journal of Cross-Cultural Psychology, 40*(3), 349–360. doi:10.1177/0022022108331005

Boergers, J., Spirito, A., & Donaldson, D. (1998). Reasons for adolescent suicide attempts. *Journal of the American Academy of Child & Adolescent Psychiatry, 37*(12), 1287–1293. doi:10.1097/00004583-199812000-00012

Boerke, K. W., & Reitman, D. (2011). Token economies. In W. W. Fisher, C. C. Piazza, et al. (Eds.), *Handbook of applied behavior analysis* (pp. 370–382). New York: Guilford.

Bogaert, A. F. (2004). Asexuality: Prevalence and associated factors in a national probability sample. *Journal of Sex Research, 41,* 279–287.

Bogaert, A. F. (2006). Toward a conceptual understanding of asexuality. *Review of General Psychology, 10,* 241–250.

Bogaert, A. F., & Skorska, M. (2011). Sexual orientation, fraternal birth order, and the maternal immune hypothesis: A review. *Frontiers in Neuroendocrinology, 32*(2), 247–254. doi:10.1016/j.yfrne.2011.02.004

Boggio, P. S., Campanhã, C., et al. (2010). Modulation of decision-making in a gambling task in older adults with transcranial direct current stimulation. *European Journal of Neuroscience, 31*(3), 593–597. doi:10.1111/j.1460-9568.2010.07080.x

Bohbot, V., & Corkin, S. (2007). Posterior parahippocampal place learning in H.M. *Hippocampus, 17*(9), 863–872. doi:10.1002/hipo.20313

Bohlin, G., & Hagekull, B. (2009). Socio-emotional development: From infancy to young adulthood. *Scandinavian Journal of Psychology, 50*(6), 592–601. doi:10.1111/j.1467-9450.2009.00787.x

Bohner, G., & Dickel, N. (2010). Attitudes and attitude change. *Annual Review of Psychology, 62,* 391–417. doi:10.1146/annurev.psych.121208.131609

Boiger, M., & Mesquita, B. (2012). The construction of emotion in interactions, relationships, and cultures. *Emotion Review, 4*(3), 221–229. doi:10.1177/1754073912439765

Boivin, D. B., Czeisler, C. A., & Waterhouse, J. W. (1997). Complex interaction of the sleep-wake cycle and circadian phase modulates mood in healthy subjects. *Archives of General Psychiatry, 54*(2), 145–152. doi:10.1001/archpsyc.1997.01830140055010

Boksa, P. (2009). On the neurobiology of hallucinations. *Journal of Psychiatry & Neuroscience, 34*(4), 260–262.

Bolbecker, A. R., Steinmetz, A. B., et al. (2011). Exploration of cerebellar-dependent associative learning in schizophrenia: Effects of varying and shifting interstimulus interval on eyeblink conditioning. *Behavioral Neuroscience, 125*(5), 687–698. doi:10.1037/a0025150

Boldero, J. M., Moretti, M. M., et al. (2005). Self-discrepancies and negative affect: A primer on when to look for specificity and how to find it. *Australian Journal of Psychology, 57*(3), 139–147. doi:10.1080/00049530500048730

Bolt, D. M., Piper, M. E., et al. (2012). Why two smoking cessation agents work better than one: Role of craving suppression. *Journal of Consulting & Clinical Psychology, 80*(1), 54–65. doi:10.1037/a0026366

Bonanno, R. A., & Hymel, S. (2013). Cyber bullying and internalizing difficulties: Above and beyond the impact of traditional forms of bullying. *Journal of Youth & Adolescence.* doi:10.1007/s10964-013-9937-1

Bond, R., & Smith, P. B. (1996). Culture and conformity: A meta-analysis of studies using Asch's (1952, 1956) line judgment task. *Psychological Bulletin, 119*(1), 111–137. doi:10.1037/0033-2909.119.1.111

Bongard, S., al'Absi, M., & Lovallo, W. R. (1998). Interactive effects of trait hostility and anger expression on cardiovascular reactivity in young men. *International Journal of Psychophysiology, 28*(2), 181–191. doi:10.1016/S0167-8760(97)00095-0

Bonham, V., Warshauer-Baker, E., & Collins, F. S. (2005). Race and ethnicity in the genome era: The complexity of the constructs. *American Psychologist, 60*(1), 9–15. doi:10.1037/0003-066X.60.1.9

Boniecki, K. A., & Britt, T. W. (2003). Prejudice and the peacekeeper. In T. W. Britt & A. B. Adler (Eds.), *The psychology of the peacekeeper: Lessons from the field* (pp. 53–70). Westport, CT: Praeger.

Bonk, W. J., & Healy, A. F. (2010). Learning and memory for sequences of pictures, words, and spatial locations: An exploration of serial position effects. *American Journal of Psychology, 123*(2), 137–168.

Bood, S., Sundequist, U., et al. (2006). Eliciting the relaxation response with the help of flotation-REST (Restricted Environmental Stimulation Technique) in patients with stress-related ailments. *International Journal of Stress Management, 13*(2), 154–175. doi:10.1037/1072-5245.13.2.154

Booker, J. M., & Hellekson, C. J. (1992). Prevalence of seasonal affective disorder in Alaska. *American Journal of Psychiatry, 149*(9), 1176–1182.

Bora, E., Fornito, A., et al. (2011). Neuroanatomical abnormalities in schizophrenia: A multimodal voxelwise meta-analysis and meta-regression analysis. *Schizophrenia Research, 127*(1), 46–57. doi:10.1016/j.schres.2010.12.020

Borch-Jacobsen, M., & Shamdasani, S. (2011). *The Freud files: An inquiry into the history of psychoanalysis.* London: Cambridge University Press.

Borg, C., Peters, M. L., et al. (2012). Vaginismus: Heightened harm avoidance and pain catastrophizing cognitions. *Journal of Sexual Medicine, 9*(2), 558–567. doi:10.1111/j.1743-6109.2011.02535.x

Bornstein, R. F. (2012). Rorschach score validation as a model for 21st-century personality assessment. *Journal of Personality Assessment, 94*(1), 26–38. doi:10.1080/00223891.2011.627961

Borod, J. C., Bloom, R. L., et al. (2002). Emotional processing deficits in individuals with unilateral brain damage. *Applied Neuropsychology, 9*(1), 23–36.

Boroditsky, L. (2011). How language shapes thought. *Scientific American, February,* 62–65. doi:10.1038/scientificamerican0211-62

Boroditsky, L., & Gaby, A. (2010). Remembrances of times east: Absolute spatial representations of time in an Australian Aboriginal community. *Psychological Science, 21*(11), 1635–1639. doi:10.1177/0956797610386621

Borst, G., & Kosslyn, S. M. (2010). Fear selectively modulates visual mental imagery and visual perception. *Quarterly Journal of Experimental Psychology, 63*(5), 833–839. doi:10.1080/17470211003602420

Borzekowski, D. L. G., Schenk, S., et al. (2010). e-Ana and e-Mia: A content analysis of pro–eating disorder web sites. *American Journal of Public Health, 100*(8), 1526–1534.

Boskey, E. (2008). *Is oral sex safe sex?* Retrieved June 11, 2013, from http://std.about.com/od /riskfactorsforstds/a/oralsexsafesex .htm

Botes, A. (2000). A comparison between the ethics of justice and the ethics of care. *Journal of Advanced Nursing, 32*(5), 1071–1075.

Botti, S., Orfali, K., & Iyengar, S. S. (2009). Tragic choices: Autonomy and emotional responses to medical decisions. *Journal of Consumer Research, 36*(3), 337–352. doi:10.1086/598969

Bouchard, T. J. Jr. (2004). Genetic influence on human psychological traits: A survey. *Current Directions in Psychological Science, 13*(4), 148–151. doi:10.1111/j.0963-7214.2004.00295.x

Bouchard, T. J., Jr. (1983). Twins: Nature's twice-told tale. In *Yearbook of science and the future* (pp. 66–81). Chicago: Encyclopedia Britannica.

Bourgeois, J. A., Kahn, D., et al. (2009). *Casebook of psychosomatic medicine.* Washington: American Psychiatric Publishing.

Bourne, E. J. (2010). *The anxiety & phobia workbook* (5th ed.). Oakland, CA: New Harbinger.

Bourne, V. J. (2008). Examining the relationship between degree of handedness and degree of cerebral lateralization for processing facial emotion.

Neuropsychology, 22(3), 350–356. doi:10.1037/0894-4105.22.3.350

Bowe, F. (2000). *Universal Design in education: Teaching nontraditional students.* Westport, CT: Bergin & Garvey.

Bowen, N. K., Wegmann, K. M., & Webber, K. C. (2013). Enhancing a brief writing intervention to combat stereotype threat among middle-school students. *Journal of Educational Psychology, 105*(2), 427–435. doi:10.1037/a0031177

Bower, G. H. (1981). Mood and memory. *American Psychologist, 36,* 129–148. doi:10.1037/0003-066X.36.2.129

Bower, G. H., & Springston, F. (1970). Pauses as recoding points in letter series. *Journal of Experimental Psychology, 83,* 421–430. doi:10.1037/h0028863

Bowker, A. (2006). The relationship between sports participation and self-esteem during early adolescence. *Canadian Journal of Behavioural Science, 38*(3), 214–229.

Bowling, N. A. (2010). Effects of job satisfaction and conscientiousness on extra-role behaviors. *Journal of Business & Psychology, 25*(1), 119–130.

Boyd, J., Harris, S., & Knight, J. R. (2012). Screening and brief interventions for the addiction syndrome: Considering the vulnerability of adolescence. In H. Shaffer, D. A. LaPlante, et al. (Eds.). *APA addiction syndrome handbook* (Vol. 2): *Recovery, prevention, and other issues* (pp. 169–194). Washington: American Psychological Association. doi:10.1037/13750-008

Boyle, S. H., Williams, R. B., et al. (2004). Hostility as a predictor of survival in patients with coronary artery disease. *Psychosomatic Medicine, 66*(5), 629–632. doi:10.1097/01. psy.0000138122.93942.4a

Boysen, G. A. (2011). The scientific status of childhood dissociative identity disorder: A review of published research. *Psychotherapy & Psychosomatics, 80*(6), 329–334. doi:10.1159/000323403

Boysen, G. A., & VanBergen, A. (2013). A review of published research on adult dissociative identity disorder: 2000–2010. *Journal of Nervous & Mental Disease, 201*(1), 5–11. doi:10.1097/NMD.0b013e31827aaf81

Brach, T. (2003). *Radical acceptance.* New York: Bantam Books.

Bradbury, J. W., & Vehrencamp, S. L. (2011). *Principles of animal communication* (2nd ed.). Sunderland, MA: Sinauer.

Bradbury, T. N., & Karney, B. R. (2010). *Intimate relationships.* New York: Norton.

Bradley, R. T., McCraty, R., et al. (2010). Emotion self-regulation, psychophysiological coherence, and test anxiety:

Results from an experiment using electrophysiological measures. *Applied Psychophysiology & Biofeedback, 35*(4), 261–283. doi:10.1007/ s10484-010-9134-x

Bradley, R., Greene, J., et al. (2005). A multidimensional meta-analysis of psychotherapy for PTSD. *American Journal of Psychiatry, 162*(2), 214–227. doi:10.1176/appi.ajp.162.2.214

Bradshaw, C., Kahn, A. S., & Saville, B. K. (2010). To hook up or date: Which gender benefits? *Sex Roles, 62*(9–10), 661–669.

Bradshaw, S. D. (2006). Shyness and difficult relationships: Formation is just the beginning. In D. C. Kirkpatrick, D. S. Duck, et al. (Eds.), *Relating difficulty: The processes of constructing and managing difficult interaction* (pp. 15–42). Mahwah, NJ: Erlbaum.

Brainerd, C. J. (2003). Jean Piaget, learning research, and American education. In B. J. Zimmerman & D. H. Schunk (Eds.), *Educational psychology: A century of contributions* (pp. 251–287). Mahwah, NJ: Erlbaum.

Brakel, T. M., Dijkstra, A., et al. (2012). Impact of social comparison on cancer survivors' quality of life: An experimental field study. *Health Psychology, 31*(5), 660–670. doi:10.1037/a0026572

Bramerson, A., Johansson, L., et al. (2004). Prevalence of olfactory dysfunction: The Skovde population-based study. *Laryngoscope, 114*(4), 733–737. doi:10.1097/00005537-200404000-00026

Brammer, R. (2012). *Diversity in counseling* (2nd ed.). Belmont, CA: Cengage Learning/Wadsworth.

Brand, S., Gerber, M., et al. (2010). High exercise levels are related to favorable sleep patterns and psychological functioning in adolescents: A comparison of athletes and controls. *Journal of Adolescent Health, 46*(2), 133–141. doi:10.1016/j.jadohealth.2009.06.018

Brang, D., & Ramachandran, V. S. (2010). Visual field heterogeneity, laterality, and eidetic imagery in synesthesia. *Neurocase, 16*(2), 169–174. doi:10.1080/13554790903339645

Brannon, L. (2011). *Gender: Psychological perspectives.* Boston: Pearson/Allyn & Bacon.

Brannon, L., Feist, J., & Updegraff, J. (2014). *Health psychology: An introduction to behavior and health* (8th ed.). Belmont, CA: Cengage Learning/ Wadsworth.

Braun, K. A., Ellis, R., & Loftus, E. F. (2002). Make my memory: How advertising can change memories of the past. *Psychology & Marketing, 19,* 1–23. doi:10.1002/mar.1000

Breedlove, S. M., Watson, N. V., & Rosenzweig, M. R. (2010). *Biological psychology: An introduction to behavioral and cognitive neuroscience*

(6th ed.). Sunderland, MA: Sinauer Associates.

Brenes, G. A., Ingram, C. W., & Danhauer, S. C. (2011). Benefits and challenges of conducting psychotherapy by telephone. *Professional Psychology: Research & Practice, 42*(6), 543–549. doi:10.1037/a0026135

Brescoll, V. L., Dawson, E., & Uhlmann, E. L. (2010). Hard won and easily lost: The fragile status of leaders in gender-stereotype-incongruent occupations. *Psychological Science, 21*(11), 1640–1642.

Bressan, P., & Pizzighello, S. (2008). The attentional cost of inattentional blindness. *Cognition, 106*(1), 370–383. doi:10.1016/j.cognition.2007.03.001

Bressi, C., Albonetti, S., & Razzoli, E. (1998). "Communication deviance" and schizophrenia. *New Trends in Experimental & Clinical Psychiatry, 14*(1), 33–39.

Bretherton, R., & Orner, R. J. (2004). Positive psychology and psychotherapy: An existential approach. In P. A. Linley & S. Joseph (Eds.), *Positive psychology in practice* (pp. 420–430). New York: Wiley.

Brevers, D., Dan, B., et al. (2011). Sport superstition: Mediation of psychological tension on non-professional sportsmen's superstitious rituals. *Journal of Sport Behavior, 34*(1), 3–24.

Brewer, J. A., Mallik, S., et al. (2011). Mindfulness training for smoking cessation: Results from a randomized controlled trial. *Drug & Alcohol Dependence, 119*(1–2), 72–80. doi:10.1016/j.drugalcdep.2011.05.027

Brewer, N., & Wells, G. L. (2006). The confidence-accuracy relationship in eyewitness identification: Effects of lineup instructions, foil similarity, and target-absent base rates. *Journal of Experimental Psychology: Applied, 12*(1), 11–30. doi:10.1037/1076-898X.12.1.11

Bridges, K. M. B. (1932). Emotional development in early infancy. *Child Development, 3,* 324–341. doi:10.2307/1125359

Bridgett, D. J., Gartstein, M. A., et al. (2009). Maternal and contextual influences and the effect of temperament development during infancy on parenting in toddlerhood. *Infant Behavior & Development, 32*(1), 103–116. doi:10.1016/j.infbeh.2008.10.007

Brief, A. P., & Weiss, H. M. (2002). Organizational behavior. *Annual Review of Psychology, 53,* 279–307.

Bringing Up Baby. (1999). *Sierra,* Jan–Feb, 17.

Britton, P. C., Duberstein, P. R., et al. (2008). Reasons for living, hopelessness, and suicide ideation among depressed adults 50 years or older. *American Journal of Geriatric Psychiatry, 16*(9), 736–741. doi:10.1097/ JGP.0b013e31817b609a

Brodley, B. T. (2006). Nondirectivity in client-centered therapy. *Person-Centered & Experiential Psychotherapies, 5*(1), 36–52.

Brody, S., & Weiss, P. (2011). Simultaneous penile–vaginal intercourse orgasm is associated with satisfaction (sexual, life, partnership, and mental health). *Journal of Sexual Medicine, 8*(3), 734–741. doi:10.1111/j.1743-6109.2010.02149.x

Brondolo, E., ver Halen, N., et al. (2011). Racism as a psychosocial stressor. In R. J. Contrada, & A. Baum (Eds.), *The handbook of stress science: Biology, psychology, and health* (pp. 167–184). New York: Springer.

Brooks, M. (2009). Rise of the robogeeks. *New Scientist, 2697*, 34–36.

Brothen, T., & Wambach, C. (2001). Effective student use of computerized quizzes. *Teaching of Psychology, 28*(4), 292–294. doi:10.1207/S15328023TOP2804_10

Brotto, L.A., Knudson, G., et al. (2010). Asexuality: A mixed-methods approach. *Archives of Sexual Behavior, 39*(3), 599–618.

Brower, A. M. (2002). Are college students alcoholics? *Journal of American College Health, 50*(5), 253–255. doi:10.1080/07448480209595716

Brown, A. S. (2012). *The tip of the tongue state.* New York: Psychology Press.

Brown, A. S., & Marsh, E. J. (2010). Digging into déjà vu: Recent research on possible mechanisms. In B. H. Ross (Ed.), *The psychology of learning and motivation: Advances in research and theory* (Vol. 53, pp. 33–62). San Diego: Elsevier. doi:10.1016/S0079-7421(10)53002-0

Brown, A., Charlwood, A., & Spencer, D. A. (2012). Not all that it might seem: Why job satisfaction is worth studying despite it being a poor summary measure of job quality. *Work, Employment & Society, 26*(6), 1007–1018. doi:10.1177/0950017012461837

Brown, G., & Devlin, A. S. (2003). Vandalism: Environmental and social factors. *Journal of College Student Development, 44*(4), 502–516.

Brown, J. D. (2010). High self-esteem buffers negative feedback: Once more with feeling. *Cognition & Emotion, 24*(8), 1389–1404. doi:10.1080/02699930903504405

Brown, J. D., Cai, H., et al. (2009). Cultural similarities in self-esteem functioning: East is east and west is west, but sometimes the twain do meet. *Journal of Cross-Cultural Psychology, 40*(1), 140–157. doi:10.1177/0022022108326280

Brown, L. M. (2005). *Girlfighting: Betrayal and rejection among girls.* New York: New York University Press.

Brown, M. J., Henriquez, E., & Groscup, J. (2008). The effects of eyeglasses and race on juror decisions involving a violent crime. *American Journal of Forensic Psychology, 26*(2), 25–43.

Brown, P. (1990). The name game. *Journal of Mind and Behavior, 11*, 385–406.

Brown, R., & Kulik, J. (1977). Flashbulb memories. *Cognition, 5*, 73–99. doi:10.1016/0010-0277(77)90018-X

Brown, R., & McNeill, D. (1966). The "tip of the tongue" phenomenon. *Journal of Verbal Learning & Verbal Behavior, 5*, 325–337. doi:10.1016/S0022-5371(66)80040-3

Brown, S. A., Tapert, S. F., et al. (2000). Neurocognitive functioning of adolescents: Effects of protracted alcohol use. *Alcoholism: Clinical & Experimental Research, 24*(2), 164–171. doi:10.1111/j.1530-0277.2000.tb04586.x

Brown, S. D., Lent, R. W., et al. (2011). Social cognitive career theory, conscientiousness, and work performance: A meta-analytic path analysis. *Journal of Vocational Behavior, 79*(1), 81–90. doi:10.1016/j.jvb.2010.11.009

Brown, S. G., Roy, E., Rohr, L., et al. (2006). Using hand performance measures to predict handedness. *Laterality: Asymmetries of Body, Brain & Cognition, 11*(1), 1–14. doi:10.1080/1357650054200000440

Brown, T. A., & Barlow, D. H. (2011). *Casebook in abnormal psychology* (4th. ed.). Belmont, CA: Cengage Learning/Wadsworth.

Browne, N., & Keeley, S. (2010). *Asking the right questions* (9th ed.). Englewood Cliffs, NJ: Prentice Hall.

Brownell, P. (2010). *Gestalt therapy: A guide to contemporary practice.* New York: Springer.

Bruchmüller, K., Margraf, J., & Schneider, S. (2012). Is ADHD diagnosed in accord with diagnostic criteria? Overdiagnosis and influence of client gender on diagnosis. *Journal of Consulting & Clinical Psychology, 80*(1), 128–138. doi:10.1037/a0026582

Bruehl, S. S., Burns, J. W., et al. (2012). What do plasma beta-endorphin levels reveal about endogenous opioid analgesic function? *European Journal of Pain, 16*(3), 370–380. doi:10.1002/j.1532-2149.2011.00021.x

Bruner, J. (1973). *Going beyond the information given.* New York: Norton.

Bruner, J. (1983). *Child's talk.* New York: Norton.

Brunet, P. M., Mondloch, C. J., & Schmidt, L. A. (2010). Shy children are less sensitive to some cues to facial recognition. *Child Psychiatry & Human Development, 41*(1), 1–14. doi:10.1007/s10578-009-0150-0

Bruno, F., & Muzzupappa, M. (2010). Product interface design: A participatory approach based on virtual reality. *International Journal of Human–Computer Studies, 68*(5), 254–269.

Bryan, C. S., & Babelay, A. M. (2009). Building character: A model for reflective practice. *Academic Medicine, 84*(9), 1283–1288. doi:10.1097/ACM.0b013e3181b6a79c

Bryan, L., & Vinchur, A. J. (2013). *Industrial-organizational psychology.* In D. K. Freedheim, & I. B. Weiner (Eds.), *Handbook of psychology* (Vol. 1): *History of psychology* (2nd ed., pp. 407–428). New York: Wiley.

Bryden, P. J., Bruyn, J., & Fletcher, P. (2005). Handedness and health: An examination of the association between different handedness classifications and health disorders. *Laterality: Asymmetries of Body, Brain & Cognition, 10*(5), 429–440. doi:10.1080/13576500442000193

Buchanan, M. (2008). Sin cities: The geometry of crime. *New Scientist, 2654* (April 30), 36–39.

Bucher, S. G. (2011). *344 questions: The creative person's do-it-yourself guide to insight, survival, and artistic fulfillment.* Berkeley, CA: New Riders Publishing.

Buck, J. A., & Warren, A. R. (2010). Expert testimony in recovered memory trials: Effects on mock jurors' opinions, deliberations and verdicts. *Applied Cognitive Psychology, 24*(4), 495–512.

Buckle, P. (2011). 'The perfect is the enemy of the good'—Ergonomics research and practice. *Ergonomics, 54*(1), 2011, 1–11.

Buckner, J. D., Ecker, A. H., & Cohen, A. S. (2010). Mental health problems and interest in marijuana treatment among marijuana-using college students. *Addictive Behaviors, 35*(9), 826–833. doi:10.1016/j.addbeh.2010.04.001

Buckworth, J., Lee, R. E., et al. (2007). Decomposing intrinsic and extrinsic motivation for exercise: Application to stages of motivational readiness. *Psychology of Sport & Exercise, 8*(4), 441–461. doi:10.1016/j.psychsport.2006.06.007

Budney, A. J., & Hughes, J. R. (2006). The cannabis withdrawal syndrome. *Current Opinion in Psychiatry, 19*(3), 233–238. doi:10.1097/01.yco.0000218592.00689.e5

Buehner, M. J., & May, J. (2003). Rethinking temporal contiguity and the judgement of causality: Effects of prior knowledge, experience, and reinforcement procedure. *Quarterly Journal of Experimental Psychology: A Human Experimental Psychology, 56*(5), 865–890. doi:10.1080/02724980244000675

Bukach, C. M., Cottle, J., et al. (2012). Individuation experience predicts other-race effects in holistic processing for both Caucasian and Black participants. *Cognition,* doi:10.1016/j.cognition.2012.02.007

Buller, D. J. (2005). *Adapting minds: Evolutionary psychology and the persistent quest for human nature.* Cambridge, MA: MIT Press.

Bunde, J., & Suls, J. (2006). A quantitative analysis of the relationship between the Cook-Medley hostility scale and traditional coronary artery disease risk factors. *Health Psychology, 25*(4), 493–500. doi:10.1037/0278-6133.25.4.493

Bundy, H., Stahl, D., & MacCabe, J. H. (2011). A systematic review and meta-analysis of the fertility of patients with schizophrenia and their unaffected relatives. *Acta Psychiatrica Scandinavica, 123*(2), 98–106. doi:10.1111/j.1600-0447.2010.01623.x

Bunk, J. A., & Magley, V. J. (2013). The role of appraisals and emotions in understanding experiences of workplace incivility. *Journal of Occupational Health Psychology, 18*(1), 87–105. doi:10.1037/a0030987

Bunn, G. C. (2012). *The truth machine: A social history of the lie detector.* Baltimore, MD: Johns Hopkins University Press.

Burgaleta, M., Head, K., et al. (2012). Sex differences in brain volume are related to specific skills, not to general intelligence. *Intelligence, 40*(1), 60–68. doi:10.1016/j.intell.2011.10.006

Burger, J. M. (2009). Replicating Milgram: Would people still obey today? *American Psychologist, 64*(1), 1–11. doi:10.1037/a0010932

Burger, J. M. (2011). *Personality* (8th ed.). Belmont, CA: Cengage Learning/Wadsworth.

Burgess, C. A., & Kirsch, I. (1999). Expectancy information as a moderator of the effects of hypnosis on memory. *Contemporary Hypnosis, 16*(1), 22–31. doi:10.1002/ch.146

Burgess, K. B., Wojslawowicz, J. C., et al. (2006). Social information processing and coping strategies of shy/withdrawn and aggressive children: Does friendship matter? *Child Development, 77*(2), 371–383. doi:10.1111/j.1467-8624.2006.00876.x

Burka, J. B., & Yuen, L. M. (2008). *Procrastination: Why you do it, what to do about it.* (2008). Cambridge, MA: Perseus.

Burlingame, G. M., Fuhriman, A., & Mosier, J. (2003). The differential effectiveness of group psychotherapy: A meta-analytic perspective. *Group Dynamics: Theory, Research, & Practice, 7*(1), 3–12. doi:10.1037/1089-2699.7.1.3

Burlingame, G. M., McClendon, D. T., & Alonso, J. (2011). Cohesion in group therapy. *Psychotherapy, 48*(1), 34–42. doi:10.1037/a0022063

Burns, G. W. (Ed). (2010). *Happiness, healing, enhancement: Your casebook collection for applying positive psychology in therapy.* New York: Wiley.

Burns, M. S., & Fahy, J. (2010). Broca's area: Rethinking classical concepts from a neuroscience perspective. *Topics in Stroke Rehabilitation, 17*(6), 401–410. doi:10.1310/tsr1706-401

Burstein, M., Ameli-Grillon, L., & Merikangas, K. R. (2011). Shyness versus social phobia in U.S. youth. *Pediatrics, 128*(5), 917–925. doi:10.1542/peds.2011-1434

Burt, S. A., McGue, M., et al. (2007). The different origins of stability and change in antisocial personality disorder symptoms. *Psychological Medicine, 37*(1), 27–38. doi:10.1017/S0033291706009020

Burton, C. M., & King, L. A. (2004). The health benefits of writing about intensely positive experiences. *Journal of Research in Personality, 38*(2), 150–163. doi:10.1016/S0092-6566(03)00058-8

Burton, D. L. (2008). An exploratory evaluation of the contribution of personality and childhood sexual victimization to the development of sexually abusive behavior. *Sexual Abuse: Journal of Research & Treatment, 20*(1), 102–115.

Burtt, H. E. (1941). An experimental study of early childhood memory: Final report. *Journal of General Psychology, 58*, 435–439.

Bushnell, M. C., Villemure, C., & Duncan, G. H. (2004). Psychophysical and neurophysiological studies of pain modulation by attention. In D. D. Price, & M. C. Bushnell (Eds.), *Psychological methods of pain control: Basic science and clinical perspectives* (pp. 99–116). Seattle, WA: IASP Press.

Buss, A. H. (2012). *Pathways to individuality: Evolution and development of personality traits.* Washington: American Psychological Association.

Buss, D. M. (2007). The evolution of human mating. *Acta Psychologica Sinica, 39*(3), 502–512.

Buss, D. M. (2012). *Evolutionary psychology: The new science of the mind* (4th ed.). Boston: Pearson/Allyn & Bacon.

Butcher, J. N. (2011). *A beginner's guide to the MMPI-2* (3rd ed.). Washington: American Psychological Association.

Butcher, J. N., Mineka, S., & Hooley, J. (2010). *Abnormal psychology* (14th ed.). Boston: Allyn & Bacon.

Butler, A. C., Chapman, J. E., et al. (2006). The empirical status of cognitive-behavioral therapy: A review of meta-analyses. *Clinical Psychology Review, 26*(1), 17–31. doi:10.1016/j.cpr.2005.07.003

Butler, B. (2007). The role of death qualification in capital trials involving juvenile defendants. *Journal of Applied Social Psychology, 37*(3), 549–560.

Butler, G. (2008). *Overcoming social anxiety and shyness: A self-help guide using cognitive behavioral techniques.* New York: Basic Books.

Butler, J. C. (2000). Personality and emotional correlates of right-wing authoritarianism. *Social Behavior & Personality, 28*(1), 1–14. doi:10.2224/sbp.2000.28.1.1

Butler, R. (1954). Curiosity in monkeys. *Scientific American, 190*(18), 70–75. doi:10.1038/scientificamerican0254-70

Byrne, S., Barry, D., & Petry, N. M. (2012). Predictors of weight loss success: Exercise vs. dietary self-efficacy and treatment attendance. *Appetite, 58*(2), 695–698. doi:10.1016/j.appet.2012.01.005

Cadet, P. (2011). Androgen insensitivity syndrome with male sex-of-living. *Archives Of Sexual Behavior, 40*(6), 1101–1102. doi:10.1007/s10508-011-9823-4

Cadinu, M., Maass, A., et al. (2005). Why do women underperform under stereotype threat? Evidence for the role of negative thinking. *Psychological Science, 16*(7), 572–578. doi:10.1111/j.0956-7976.2005.01577.x

Caharel, S., Fiori, N., et al. (2006). The effects of inversion and eye displacements of familiar and unknown faces on early and late-stage ERPs. *International Journal of Psychophysiology, 62*(1), 141–151. doi:10.1016/j.ijpsycho.2006.03.002

Cahill, L. (2006). Why sex matters for neuroscience. *Nature Reviews Neuroscience, 7*(6), 477–484. doi:10.1038/nrn1909

Cahn, B. R., & Polich, J. (2006). Meditation states and traits: EEG, ERP, and neuroimaging studies. *Psychological Bulletin, 132*(2), 180–211. doi:10.1037/0033-2909.132.2.180

Cain, S. (2012). *Quiet: The power of introverts in a world that can't stop talking.* New York: Crown Publishers/Random House.

Calabrese, F., Molteni, R., et al. (2009). Neuronal plasticity: A link between stress and mood disorders. *Psychoneuroendocrinology, 34*(Suppl 1), S208–S216. doi:10.1016/j.psyneuen.2009.05.014

Calabria, B., Degenhardt, L., et al. (2010). Systematic review of prospective studies investigating "remission" from amphetamine, cannabis, cocaine, or opioid dependence. *Addictive Behaviors, 35*(8), 741–749. doi:10.1016/j.addbeh.2010.03.019

Calhoun, J. B. (1962). A "behavioral sink." In E. L. Bliss (Ed.), *Roots of behavior* (pp. 295–315). New York: Harper & Row.

Caliari, P. (2008). Enhancing forehand acquisition in table tennis: The role of mental practice. *Journal of Applied Sport Psychology, 20*(1), 88–96.

Callahan, C. M. (2006). Giftedness. In G. G. Bear & K. M. Minke (Eds.), *Children's needs III: Development, prevention, and intervention* (pp. 443–458). Washington: National Association of School Psychologists.

Calzada, E. J., Fernandez, Y., & Cortes, D. E. (2010). Incorporating the cultural value of respeto into a framework of Latino parenting. *Cultural Diversity & Ethnic Minority Psychology, 16*(1), 77–86. doi:10.1037/a0016071

Cambron, M. J., Acitelli, L. K., & Pettit, J. W. (2009). Explaining gender differences in depression: An interpersonal contingent self-esteem perspective. *Sex Roles, 61*(11–12), 751–761. doi:10.1007/s11199-009-9616-6

Cameron, J. A., & Trope, Y. (2004). Stereotype-biased search and processing of information about group members. *Social Cognition, 22*(6), 650–672. doi:10.1521/soco.22.6.650.54818

Cameron, J., & Pierce, W. D. (2002). *Rewards and intrinsic motivation: Resolving the controversy.* Westport, CO: Bergin & Garvey.

Cammaroto, S., D'Aleo, G., et al. (2008). Charles Bonnet syndrome. *Functional Neurology, 23*(3), 123–127.

Campbell, B. (2008). *Handbook of differentiated instruction using the multiple intelligences.* Boston: Pearson/Allyn & Bacon.

Campbell, J. P. (2013). Assessment in industrial and organizational psychology: An overview. In K. F. Geisinger, B. A. Bracken, et al. (Eds.), *APA handbook of testing and assessment in psychology* (Vol. 1): *Test theory and testing and assessment in industrial and organizational psychology* (pp. 355–395). Washington, DC: American Psychological Association. doi:10.1037/14047-022

Campos, A., Camino, E., & Pérez-Fabello, M. (2011). Using the keyword mnemonics method among adult learners. *Educational Gerontology, 37*(4), 327–335. doi:10.1080/03601271003608886

Canales, J. J. (2010). Comparative neuroscience of stimulant-induced memory dysfunction: Role for neurogenesis in the adult hippocampus. *Behavioural Pharmacology, 21*(5–6), 379–398. doi:10.1097/FBP.0b013e32833e16b6

Cannon, W. B. (1932). *The wisdom of the body.* New York: Norton.

Cannon, W. B. (1934). Hunger and thirst. In C. Murchinson (Ed.), *Handbook of general experimental psychology* (pp. 247–263). Worcester, MA: Clark University Press. doi:10.1037/11374-005

Cannon, W. B., & Washburn, A. L. (1912). An explanation of hunger. *American Journal of Physiology, 29*, 441–454.

Caplan, P. J. (1995). *They say you're crazy.* Reading, MA: Addison-Wesley.

Caporro, M., Haneef, Z., et al. (2012). Functional MRI of sleep spindles and K-complexes. *Clinical Neurophysiology, 123*(2), 303–309. doi:10.1016/j.clinph.2011.06.018

Cardeña, E., Winkelman, M., et al. (Eds.). (2011). *Altering consciousness: Multidisciplinary perspectives* (Vol 1): *History, culture and the humanities.* Westport, CT: Praeger.

Carducci, B. J., & Fields, T. H. (2007). *The shyness workbook for teens.* Champaign, IL: Research Press.

Carlbring, P., Gunnarsdóttir, M., et al. (2007). Treatment of social phobia: Randomized trial of internet-delivered cognitive-behavioural therapy with telephone support. *British Journal of Psychiatry, 190*(2), 123–128. doi:10.1192/bjp.bp.105.020107

Carlson, N. R. (2013). *Physiology of behavior* (11th ed.). Boston: Allyn & Bacon.

Carnagey, N. L., & Anderson, C. A. (2004). Violent video game exposure and aggression: A literature review. *Minerva Psichiatrica, 45*(1), 1–18.

Carnagey, N. L., Anderson, C. A., & Bushman, B. J. (2007). The effect of video game violence on physiological desensitization to real-life violence. *Journal of Experimental Social Psychology, 43*(3), 489–496. doi:10.1016/j.jesp.2006.05.003

Carney, R. N., & Levin, J. R. (2001). Remembering the names of unfamiliar animals: Keywords as keys to their kingdom. *Applied Cognitive Psychology, 15*(2), 133–143. doi:10.1002/1099-0720(200103/04)15:2<133::AID-ACP687>3.0.CO;2-P

Carney, R. N., & Levin, J. R. (2003). Promoting higher-order learning benefits by building lower-order mnemonic connections. *Applied Cognitive Psychology, 17*(5), 563–575. doi:10.1002/acp.889

Carr, P. B., & Steele, C. M. (2010). Stereotype threat affects financial decision making. *Psychological Science, 21*(10), 1411–1416. doi:10.1177/0956797610384146

Carrico, A. R., & Riemer, M. (2011). Motivating energy conservation in the workplace: An evaluation of the use of group-level feedback and peer education. *Journal of Environmental Psychology, 31*(1), 1–13. doi:10.1016/j.jenvp.2010.11.004

Carroll, D. W. (2008). *Psychology of language* (5th ed.). Belmont, CA: Cengage Learning/Wadsworth.

Carroll, J. L. (2013). *Sexuality now: Embracing diversity* (4th ed.). Belmont, CA: Cengage Learning/Wadsworth.

Carroll, J. M., & Russell, J. A. (1996). Do facial expressions signal specific emotions? Judging emotion from the face in context. *Journal of Personality &*

Social Psychology, 70(2), 205–218. doi:10.1037/0022-3514.70.2.205

Carroll, R. T. (2011). *The skeptic's dictionary: Superstition.* Retrieved June 10, 2013, from http://www.skepdic.com /superstition.html

Carskadon, M. A., Acebo, C., & Jenni, O. C. (2004). Regulation of adolescent sleep: Implications for behavior. *Annals of the New York Academy of Science, 1021,* 276–291. doi:10.1196/ annals.1308.032

Carter, D. A., Simkins, B. J., & Simpson, W. G. (2003). Corporate governance, board diversity, and firm value. *Financial Review, 38,* 33–53.

Cartwright, D. (2002). The narcissistic exoskeleton: The defensive organization of the rage-type murderer. *Bulletin of the Menninger Clinic, 66*(1), 1–18. doi:10.1521/ bumc.66.1.1.23371

Case, B. G., Bertollo, D. N., et al. (2013). Declining use of electroconvulsive therapy in United States general hospitals. *Biological Psychiatry, 73*(2), 119–126. doi:10.1016/j.biopsych.2012.09.005

Casey-Campbell, M., & Martens, M. L. (2009). Sticking it all together: A critical assessment of the group cohesion–performance literature. *International Journal of Management Reviews, 11*(2), 223–246. doi:10.1111/j.1468-2370.2008.00239.x

Casey, A. A., Elliott, M., et al. (2008). Impact of the food environment and physical activity environment on behaviors and weight status in rural U.S. Communities. *Preventive Medicine, 47*(6), 600–604. doi:10.1016/j.ypmed.2008.10.001

Caspi, A., Roberts, B. W., & Shiner, R. L. (2005). Personality development: Stability and change. *Annual Review of Psychology, 56,* 453–484. doi:10.1146/ annurev.psych.55.090902.141913

Casselle, G. (2009). What is it really like to have electroconvulsive therapy? *Journal of ECT, 25*(4), 289. doi:10.1097/ YCT.0b013e3181a59f97

Cassimatis, N. L. (2012). Artificial intelligence and cognitive modeling have the same problem. In P. Wang, & B. Goertzel (Eds.), *Theoretical foundations of artificial general intelligence* (pp. 11–24). Amsterdam: Atlantis Press. doi:10.2991/978-94-91216-62-6_2

Castañeda, T. R., Tong, J., et al. (2010). Ghrelin in the regulation of body weight and metabolism. *Frontiers in Neuroendocrinology, 31*(1), 44–60. doi:10.1016/j.yfrne.2009.10.008

Castellano, J. A., & Frazier, A. D. (Eds.). (2011). *Special populations in gifted education: Understanding our most able students from diverse backgrounds.* Waco, TX: Prufrock Press.

Castle, D., Murray, R., et al. (Eds.). (2012). *Marijuana and madness* (2nd ed.). London: Cambridge University Press.

Castles, E. E. (2012). *Inventing intelligence: How America came to worship IQ.* Santa Barbara, CA: Praeger.

Castro-Schilo, L., & Kee, D. W. (2010). Gender differences in the relationship between emotional intelligence and right hemisphere lateralization for facial processing. *Brain & Cognition, 73*(1), 62–67. doi:10.1016/j.bandc.2010.03.003

Castro, J., Gila, A., et al. (2004). Perfectionism dimensions in children and adolescents with anorexia nervosa. *Journal of Adolescent Health, 35*(5), 392–398. doi:10.1016/j. jadohealth.2003.11.094

Cattell, R. B. (1965). *The scientific analysis of personality.* Baltimore: Penguin.

Cattell, R. B. (1973). Personality pinned down. *Psychology Today,* July, 40–46.

Cavaco, S., Anderson, S. W., et al. (2004). The scope of preserved procedural memory in amnesia. *Brain: A Journal of Neurology, 127*(8), 1853–1867. doi:10.1093/brain/awh208

Ceci, S. J., & Williams, W. M. (2010). *The mathematics of sex: How biology and society conspire to limit talented women and girls.* New York: Oxford University Press.

Cellard, C., Lefèbvre, A.-A., et al. (2010). An examination of the relative contribution of saturation and selective attention to memory deficits in patients with recent-onset schizophrenia and their unaffected parents. *Journal of Abnormal Psychology, 119*(1), 60–70. doi:10.1037/a0018397

Centers for Disease Control. (2003). *Deaths, percent of total deaths, and death rates for 15 leading causes of death in 5-year age groups, by race and sex: United States, 2000.* Downloaded May 9, 2012, from http://www.cdc.gov/nchs/data/dvs /LCWK1_2000.pdf

Centers for Disease Control. (2011). *National Intimate Partner and Sexual Violence Survey: 2010 summary report.* Retrieved April 11, 2013, from http:// www.cdc.gov/violenceprevention/pdf /nisvs_report2010-a.pdf

Centers for Disease Control. (2012a). *Sexual violence: Facts at a glance.* Retrieved April 11, 2013, from http:// www.cdc.gov/violenceprevention/pdf /sv-datasheet-a.pdf

Centers for Disease Control. (2012b). *2011 Sexually Transmitted Diseases Surveillance.* Downloaded April 16, 2013, from http://www.cdc.gov/std /stats11/default.htm

Centers for Disease Control. (2012c). Smoking & tobacco use. Retrieved May 9, 2013, from http://www.cdc.gov /tobacco/data_statistics/fact_sheets /fast_facts/

Centers for Disease Control. (2012d). *Short sleep duration among workers — United States, 2010.* Retrieved March 7, 2013, from http://www.cdc .gov/mmwr/preview/mmwrhtml /mm6116a2.htm?s_cid=mm6116a2_w

Centers for Disease Control. (2013). *Smoking cessation.* Downloaded March 5, 2013, from http://www.cdc.gov /tobacco/data_statistics/fact_sheets /cessation/quitting/index.htm

Centofanti, A. T., & Reece, J. (2006). The cognitive interview and its effect on misleading postevent information. *Psychology, Crime & Law, 12*(6), 669–683. doi:10.1080/10683160600558394

Centre for Addiction and Mental Health. (2012). *CAMH and harm reduction: a background paper on its meaning and application for substance use issues.* Retrieved March 9, 2013, from http://www.camh.ca/en /hospital/about_camh/influencing _public_policy/public_policy _submissions/harm_reduction/Pages /harmreductionbackground.aspx

Cervone, D., & Pervin, L. A. (2013). *Personality: Theory & research* (12th ed.). New York: Wiley.

Ceylan, M., & Sayin, A. (2012). Neurobiology of repression: A hypothetical interpretation. *Integrative Psychological & Behavioral Science, 46*(3), 395–409. doi:10.1007/ s12124-012-9197-8

Chabas, D., Taheri, S., et al. (2003). The genetics of narcolepsy. *Annual Review of Genomics & Human Genetics, 4,* 459–483. doi:10.1146/annurev.genom. 4.070802.110432

Chaffee, J. (2012). *Thinking critically* (10th ed.). Belmont, CA: Cengage Learning/Wadsworth.

Chakos, M. H., Alvir, J. M. J., et al. (1996). Incidence and correlates of tardive dyskinesia in first episode of schizophrenia. *Archives of General Psychiatry, 53*(4), 313–319. doi:10.1001/ archpsyc.1996.01830040049009

Challacombe, F., Oldfield, V. B., & Salkovskis, P. M. (2011). *Break free from OCD: Overcoming obsessive compulsive disorder using CBT.* London: Vermillion.

Chalmers. D. J. (2010). *The character of consciousness.* New York: Oxford University Press.

Chambers, R. (2012). Adult hippocampal neurogenesis in the pathogenesis of addiction and dual diagnosis disorders. *Drug & Alcohol Dependence.* doi:10.1016/j.drugalcdep.2012.12.005

Chamorro-Premuzic, T., & Furnham, A. (2003). Personality predicts academic performance. *Journal of Research in Personality, 37*(4), 319–338. doi:10.1016/S0092-6566(02)00578-0

Chamorro-Premuzic, T., & Furnham, A. (2010). *The psychology of personnel selection.* New York: Cambridge University Press.

Chance, P. (2014). *Learning and behavior* (7th ed.). Belmont, CA: Cengage Learning/Wadsworth.

Chang, B., Dusek, J. A., & Benson, H. (2011). Psychobiological changes from relaxation response elicitation: Long-term practitioners vs. novices. *Psychosomatics: Journal of Consultation Liaison Psychiatry, 52*(6), 550–559.

Chang, C., Pan, W., et al. (2012). Postural activity and motion sickness during video game play in children and adults. *Experimental Brain Research, 217*(2), 299–309. doi:10.1007/ s00221-011-2993-4

Chang, J.-H. (2009). Chronic pain: Cultural sensitivity to pain. In S. Eshun, & R. A. R. Gurung (Eds.), *Culture and mental health: Sociocultural influences, theory, and practice* (pp. 71–89). New York: Wiley-Blackwell. doi:10.1002/9781444305807.ch5

Chansler, P. A., Swamidass, P. M., & Cammann, C. (2003). Self-managing work teams: An empirical study of group cohesiveness in "natural work groups" at a Harley-Davidson Motor Company plant. *Small Group Research, 34*(1), 101–120.

Chapanis, A., & Lindenbaum, L. E. (1959). A reaction time study of four control-display linkages. *Human Factors, 1,* 1–7.

Chapleau, K. M., & Oswald, D. L. (2010). Power, sex, and rape myth acceptance: Testing two models of rape proclivity. *Journal of Sex Research, 47*(1), 66–78.

Charmaraman, L., & Grossman, J. M. (2010). Importance of race and ethnicity: An exploration of Asian, Black, Latino, and multiracial adolescent identity. *Cultural Diversity & Ethnic Minority Psychology, 16*(2), 144–151. doi:10.1037/a0018668

Charsky, D. (2010). From edutainment to serious games: A change in the use of game characteristics. *Games & Culture, 5*(2), 177–198. doi:10.1177/1555412009354727

Chaves, J. F. (2000). Hypnosis. In A. Kazdin (Ed.), *Encyclopedia of psychology* (Vol. 4, pp. 211–216). Washington: American Psychological Association.

Cheal, M. L., Cooper, S., Jacobsen, et al. (2009). *APA membership: Past, present, and possible futures.* Paper presented to the American Psychological Association annual meeting, August 6–9, Toronto, Ontario.

Check, J. V., & Malamuth, N. M. (1983). Sex role stereotyping and reactions to depictions of stranger versus acquaintance rape. *Journal of Personality & Social Psychology, 45,* 344–356.

Cheek, J., & Buss, A. H. (1979). *Scales of shyness, sociability and self-esteem and correlations among them.* Unpublished research, University of Texas. (Cited by Buss, 1980.)

Chein, J. M., & Fiez, J. A. (2010). Evaluating models of working memory through the effects of concurrent irrelevant information. *Journal of*

Experimental Psychology: General, 139(1), 117–137. doi:10.1037/a0018200

Chen, C., Lin, Y., & Hsiao, C. (2012). Celebrity endorsement for sporting events using classical conditioning. *International Journal of Sports Marketing & Sponsorship, 13*(3), 209–219.

Cheng, C., & Lin, Y. (2012). The effects of aging on lifetime of auditory sensory memory in humans. *Biological Psychology, 89*(2), 306–312. doi:10.1016/j.biopsycho.2011.11.003

Cheng, H., Cao, Y., & Olson, L. (1996). Spinal cord repair in adult paraplegic rats: Partial restoration of hind limb function. *Science, 273*(5274), 510. doi:10.1126/science.273.5274.510

Chess, S., & Thomas, A. (1986). *Know your child*. New York: Basic.

Chessick, R. D. (2010). Returning to Freud. *Journal of the American Academy of Psychoanalysis & Dynamic Psychiatry, 38*(3), 413–440. doi:10.1521/jaap.2010.38.3.413

Cheyne, J. A., & Girard, T. A. (2009). The body unbound: Vestibular-motor hallucinations and out-of-body experiences. *Cortex, 45*(2), 201–215. doi:10.1016/j.cortex.2007.05.002

Chipman, M., & Jin, Y. L. (2009). Drowsy drivers: The effect of light and circadian rhythm on crash occurrence. *Safety Science, 47*(10), 1364–1370. doi:10.1016/j.ssci.2009.03.005

Chisolm, T. H., Willott, J. F., & Lister, J. J. (2003). The aging auditory system: Anatomic and physiologic changes and implications for rehabilitation. *International Journal of Audiology, 42*(Suppl. 2), 2S3–2S10. doi:10.3109/14992020309074637

Choi, H., & Dancy, B. L. (2009). Korean American adolescents' and their parents' perceptions of acculturative stress. *Journal of Child & Adolescent Psychiatric Nursing, 22*(4), 203–210. doi:10.1111/j.1744-6171.2009.00200.x

Chomsky, N. (1975). *Reflections on language*. New York: Pantheon.

Chomsky, N. (1986). *Knowledge of language*. New York: Praeger.

Christakis, N. A., & Fowler, J. H. (2007). The spread of obesity in a large social network over 32 years. *New England Journal of Medicine, 357*(4), 370–379.

Christakis, N. A., & Fowler, J. H. (2008). The collective dynamics of smoking in a large social network. *New England Journal of Medicine, 358*(21), 2249–2258. doi:10.1056/NEJMsa0706154

Christakis, N. A., & Fowler, J. H. (2009). *Connected: The surprising power of our social networks and how they shape our lives*. New York: Little, Brown.

Christian, K. M., & Thompson, R. F. (2005). Long-term storage of an associative memory trace in the cerebellum. *Behavioral*

Neuroscience, 119(2), 526–537. doi:10.1037/0735-7044.119.2.526

Christian, M. S., Edwards, B. D., & Bradley, J. C. (2010). Situational judgment tests: Constructs assessed and a meta-analysis of their criterion-related validities. *Personnel Psychology, 63*(1), 83–117.

Christophersen, E. R., & Mortweet, S. L. (2003). *Parenting that works: Building skills that last a lifetime*. Washington: American Psychological Association.

Chua, H. F., Boland, J. E., & Nisbett, R. E. (2005). Cultural variation in eye movements during scene perception. *Proceedings of the National Academy of Sciences, 102*(35), 12629–12633. doi:10.1073/pnas.0506162102

Cialdini, R. B. (2009). *Influence: Science and practice* (5th ed.). Boston: Allyn & Bacon.

Cialdini, R. B., & Griskevicius, V. (2010). Social influence. In R. F. Baumeister & E. J. Finkel (Eds.), *Advanced social psychology: The state of the science* (pp. 385–417). New York: Oxford University Press.

Cialdini, R. B., Reno, R. R., & Kallgren, C. A. (1990). A focus theory of normative conduct: Recycling the concept of norms to reduce littering in public places. *Journal of Personality & Social Psychology, 58*(6), 1015–1026. doi:10.1037/0022-3514.58.6.1015

Cipani, E., & Schock, K. (2010). *Functional behavioral assessment, diagnosis, and treatment: A complete system for education and mental health settings* (2nd ed.). New York: Springer.

Cisler, J. M., Olatunji, B. O., et al. (2010). Emotion regulation and the anxiety disorders: An integrative review. *Journal of Psychopathology & Behavioral Assessment, 32*(1), 68–82. doi:10.1007/s10862-009-9161-1

Citrome, L. (2011). Neurochemical models of schizophrenia: Transcending dopamine. *Annals of Clinical Psychiatry, 23*(4), S10–S14.

Claessens, M. (2009). Mindfulness and existential therapy. *Existential Analysis, 20*(1), 109–119.

Clayton, A. H., & Hamilton, D. V. (2009). Female orgasmic disorder. In R. Balon, & R. T. Segraves (Eds.), *Clinical manual of sexual disorders* (pp. 251–271). Arlington, VA: American Psychiatric Publishing.

Clayton, N. S., Russell, J., & Dickinson, A. (2009). Are animals stuck in time or are they chronesthetic creatures? *Topics in Cognitive Science, 1*(1), 59–71. doi:10.1111/j.1756-8765.2008.01004.x

Clayton, N. S., Yu, K. S., & Dickinson, A. (2001). Scrub jays (Aphelocoma coerulescens) form integrated memories of the multiple features of caching episodes. *Journal of Experimental Psychology: Animal*

Behavior Processes, 27, 17–29. doi:10.1037/0097-7403.27.1.17

Clearfield, M. W., & Nelson, N. M. (2006). Sex differences in mothers' speech and play behavior with 6-, 9-, and 14-month-old infants. *Sex Roles, 54*(1–2), 127–137.

Clements, A. M., Rimrodt, S. L., et al. (2006). Sex differences in cerebral laterality of language and visuospatial processing. *Brain & Language, 98*(2), 150–158.

Clifford, A., Lang, L., & Chen, R. (2012). Effects of maternal cigarette smoking during pregnancy on cognitive parameters of children and young adults: A literature review. *Neurotoxicology & Teratology, 34*(6), 560–570. doi:10.1016/j.ntt.2012.09.004

Cnattingius, S., Signorello, L. B., et al. (2000). Caffeine intake and the risk of first-trimester spontaneous abortion. *New England Journal of Medicine, 343*(25), 1839–845.

Coates, D. D. (2012). "Cult commitment" from the perspective of former members: Direct rewards of membership versus dependency inducing practices. *Deviant Behavior, 33*(3), 168–184. doi:10.1080/01639625.2010.548302

Cobb, N. K., & Abrams, D. B. (2011). E-cigarette or drug-delivery device? Regulating novel nicotine products. *New England Journal of Medicine, 365*(3), 193–195. doi:10.1056/NEJMp1105249

Cochran, G. M., & Harpending, H. (2009). *The 10,000 year explosion*. New York: Basic Books.

Cochran, S. D. (2001). Emerging issues in research on lesbians' and gay men's mental health. *American Psychologist, 56*(11), 931–947.

Cohen, G. L., Garcia, J., et al. (2009). Recursive processes in self-affirmation: Intervening to close the minority achievement gap. *Science, 324*(5925), 400–403. doi:10.1126/science.1170769

Cohen, K., & Collens, P. (2012). The impact of trauma work on trauma workers: A metasynthesis on vicarious trauma and vicarious posttraumatic growth. *Psychological Trauma*. doi:10.1037/a0030388

Cohen, L. J., Forman, H., et al. (2010). Comparison of childhood sexual histories in subjects with pedophilia or opiate addiction and healthy controls: Is childhood sexual abuse a risk factor for addictions? *Journal of Psychiatric Practice, 16*(6), 394–404. doi:10.1097/01.pra.0000390758.27451.79

Cohen, S., Evans, G. W., et al. (1981). Cardiovascular and behavioral effects of community noise. *American Scientist, 69*, 528–535.

Cohen, S., Tyrrell, D. A., & Smith, A. P. (1993). Negative life events, perceived stress, negative affect,

and susceptibility to the common cold. *Journal of Personality & Social Psychology, 64*(1), 131–140. doi:10.1037/0022-3514.64.1.131

Cohn, E., Bucolo, D., et al. (2009). Reducing white juror bias: The role of race salience and racial attitudes. *Journal of Applied Social Psychology, 39*(8), 1953–1973. doi:10.1111/j.1559-1816.2009.00511.x

Cohn, E., Bucolo, D., et al. (2009). Reducing white juror bias: The role of race salience and racial attitudes. *Journal of Applied Social Psychology, 39*(8), 1953–1973.

Colangelo, J. J. (2007). Recovered memory debate revisited: Practice implications for mental health counselors. *Journal of Mental Health Counseling, 29*(2), 93–120.

Cole, T., Barrett, D. J. K., & Griffiths, M. D. (2011). Social facilitation in online and offline gambling: A pilot study. *International Journal of Mental Health & Addiction, 9*(3), 240–247. doi:10.1007/s11469-010-9281-6

Colin, A. K., & Moore, K., & West, A. N. (1996). Creativity, oversensitivity, and rate of habituation. *EDRA: Environmental Design Research Association, 20*(4), 423–427. doi:10.1016/0191-8869(95)00193-X

Collins, A. M., & Quillian, M. R. (1969). Retrieval time from semantic memory. *Journal of Verbal Learning & Verbal Behavior, 8*, 240–247. doi:10.1016/S0022-5371(69)80069-1

Collins, N. L., Cooper, M. L., et al. (2002). Psychosocial vulnerability from adolescence to adulthood: A prospective study of attachment style differences in relationship functioning and partner choice. *Journal of Personality, 70*(6), 965–1008. doi:10.1111/1467-6494.05029

Collop, N. A. (2005). Obstructive sleep apnea: treatment overview and controversies. In P. R. Carney, J. D. Geyer, & R. B. Berry (Eds.), *Clinical sleep disorders* (pp. 278–289). Philadelphia: Lippincott Williams & Wilkins.

Colucci, E. (2013). Culture, cultural meaning(s), and suicide. In E. Colucci, & D. Lester (Eds.), *Suicide and culture: Understanding the context* (pp. 25–46). Cambridge, MA US: Hogrefe Publishing.

Comer, R. J. (2013). *Abnormal psychology* (8th ed.). New York: Worth.

Compton, W. C., & Hoffman, E. (2013). *Positive psychology: The science of happiness and flourishing* (2nd ed.). Belmont, CA: Cengage Learning/Wadsworth.

Confer, J. C., Easton, J. A., et al. (2010). Evolutionary psychology: Controversies, questions, prospects, and limitations. *American Psychologist, 65*(2), 110–126. doi:10.1037/a0018413

Conley, K. M., & Lehman, B. J. (2012). Test anxiety and cardiovascular responses to daily academic stressors. *Stress & Health, 28*(1), 41–50. doi:10.1002/smi.1399

Conley, T. D., Moors, A. C., et al. (2011). Women, men, and the bedroom: Methodological and conceptual insights that narrow, reframe, and eliminate gender differences in sexuality. *Current Directions in Psychological Science, 20*(5), 296–300. doi:10.1177/0963721411418467

Conlon, K. E., Ehrlinger, J., et al. (2011). Eyes on the prize: The longitudinal benefits of goal focus on progress toward a weight loss goal. *Journal of Experimental Social Psychology, 47*, 853–855. doi:10.1016/j.jesp.2011.02.005

Connolly, T. M., Boyle, E. A., et al. (2012). A systematic literature review of empirical evidence on computer games and serious games. *Computers & Education, 59*(2), 661–686. doi:10.1016/j.compedu.2012.03.004

Conron, K. J., Mimiaga, M. J., & Landers, S. J. (2010). A population-based study of sexual orientation identity and gender differences in adult health. *American Journal of Public Health, 100*(10), 1953–1960. doi:10.2105/AJPH.2009.174169

Conway, M. A., Cohen, G., & Stanhope, N. (1992). Very long-term memory for knowledge acquired at school and university. *Applied Cognitive Psychology, 6*(6), 467–482. doi:10.1002/acp.2350060603

Coolidge, F. L., & Wynn, T. (2009). *The rise of Homo Sapiens: The evolution of modern thinking.* New York: Wiley-Blackwell.

Cooper, J. (2007). *Cognitive dissonance: Fifty years of a classic theory.* Thousand Oaks, CA: Sage.

Cooper, J., Bennett, E. A., & Sukel, H. L. (1996). Complex scientific testimony: How do jurors make decisions? *Law & Human Behavior, 20*(4), 379–394.

Cooper, M. J. (2005). Cognitive theory in anorexia nervosa and bulimia nervosa: Progress, development and future directions. *Clinical Psychology Review, 25*(4), 511–531. doi:10.1016/j.cpr.2005.01.003

Cooper, M., & McLeod, J. (2011). Person-centered therapy: A pluralistic perspective. *Person-Centered & Experiential Psychotherapies, 10*(3), 210–223. doi:10.1080/14779757.2011.599517

Cooper, P. J., & Murray, L. (2001). The treatment and prevention of postpartum depression and associated disturbances in child development. *Archives of Women's Mental Health, 3*(suppl 2), 5.

Cooper, R. P., Abraham, J., et al. (1997). The development of infants' preference for motherese. *Infant Behavior & Development, 20*(4), 477–488. doi:10.1016/S0163-6383(97)90037-0

Cooper, S. J. (2008). From Claude Bernard to Walter Cannon: Emergence of the concept of homeostasis. *Appetite, 51*(3), 419–427. doi:10.1016/j.appet.2008.06.005

Corballis, M. C. (2010a). Handedness and cerebral asymmetry: An evolutionary perspective. In K. Hugdahl & R. Westerhausen (Eds.), *The two halves of the brain: Information processing in the cerebral hemispheres.* Cambridge, MA: MIT Press.

Corballis, M. C. (2010b). Visions of the split brain. *New Zealand Journal of Psychology, 39*(1), 5–7.

Corbin, W. R., & Fromme, K. (2002). Alcohol use and serial monogamy as risks for sexually transmitted diseases in young adults. *Health Psychology, 21*(3), 229–236.

Corcoran, R. (2010). The allusive cognitive deficit in paranoia: The case for mental time travel or cognitive self-projection. *Psychological Medicine, 40*(8), 1233–1237. doi:10.1017/S003329170999211X

Coren, S. (1996). *Sleep thieves.* New York: Free Press.

Corey, G. (2012). *Theory and practice of group counseling* (8th ed.). Belmont, CA: Cengage Learning/Wadsworth.

Corey, G. & Corey, M. S. (2014). *I never knew I had a choice: Explorations in personal growth* (10th ed.). Belmont, CA: Cengage Learning/Wadsworth.

Corr, C. A., Nabe, C. M., & Corr, D. M. (2013). *Death and dying, life and living* (7th ed.). Belmont, CA: Cengage Learning/Wadsworth.

Correa-Chávez, M., Rogoff, B., & Arauz, R. M. (2005). Cultural patterns in attending to two events at once. *Child Development, 76*(3), 664–678. doi:10.1111/j.1467-8624.2005.00870.x

Corrigan, P. W., & Watson, A. C. (2005). Findings from the National Comorbidity Survey on the frequency of violent behavior in individuals with psychiatric disorders. *Psychiatry Research, 136*(2–3), 153–162. doi:10.1016/j.psychres.2005.06.005

Corsini, R. J., & Wedding, D. (2011). *Current psychotherapies* (9th ed.). Belmont, CA: Cengage Learning/Wadsworth.

Costa, M. (2012). Territorial behavior in public settings. *Environment & Behavior, 44*(5), 713–721. doi:10.1177/0013916511403803

Costa, P. T. Jr., & McCrae, R. R. (2006). Trait and factor theories. In J. C. Thomas, D. L. Segal, et al. (Eds.), *Comprehensive handbook of personality & psychopathology: Personality and everyday functioning* (Vol. 1, pp. 96–114). New York: Wiley.

Côté, J. E. (2006). Identity studies: How close are we to developing a social science of identity? An appraisal of the field. *Identity: An International Journal of Theory & Research, 6*, 3–25. doi:10.1207/s1532706xid0601_2

Counotte, D. S., Smit, A. B., et al. (2011). Development of the motivational system during adolescence, and its sensitivity to disruption by nicotine. *Developmental Cognitive Neuroscience, 1*(4), 430–443. doi:10.1016/j.dcn.2011.05.010

Cowan, D. E., & Bromley, D. G. (2008). *Cults and new religions: A brief history.* Malden, MA: Blackwell.

Cowden, C. R. (2005). Worry and its relationship to shyness. *North American Journal of Psychology, 7*(1), 59–69.

Cowles, J. T. (1937). Food tokens as incentives for learning by chimpanzees. *Comparative Psychology,* Monograph, *14*(5, Whole No. 71).

Cox, R. H. (2011). *Sport psychology: Concepts and applications* (6th ed.). New York: McGraw-Hill.

Craig, E. (2012). Human existence (cún zài): What is it? What's in it for us as existential psychotherapists? *The Humanistic Psychologist, 40*(1), 1–22. doi:10.1080/08873267.2012.643680

Craig, L. (2006). Does father care mean fathers share?: A comparison of how mothers and fathers in intact families spend time with children. *Gender & Society, 20*(2), 259–281. doi:10.1177/0891243205285212

Craig, R. J. (2013). Assessing personality and psychopathology with interviews. In J. R. Graham, J. A. Naglieri, et al. (Eds.), *Handbook of psychology* (Vol. 10): *Assessment psychology* (2nd ed., pp. 558–582). Hoboken, NJ: John Wiley & Sons Inc.

Craik, F. I. (1970). The fate of primary items in free recall. *Journal of Verbal Learning & Verbal Behavior, 9*, 143–148. doi:10.1016/S0022-5371(70)80042-1

Crandall, C. S., Bahns, A. J., et al. (2011). Stereotypes as justifications of prejudice. *Personality & Social Psychology Bulletin, 37*(11), 1488–1498. doi:10.1177/0146167211411723

Crane, L., Pring, L., et al. (2010). Executive functions in savant artists with autism. *Research in Autism Spectrum Disorders, 5*(2), 790–797.

Craver-Lemley, C., & Reeves, A. (2013). Is synesthesia a form of mental imagery? In S. Lacey, & R. Lawson (Eds.), *Multisensory imagery* (pp. 185–206). New York: Springer. doi:10.1007/978-1-4614-5879-1_10

Crawford, S. A., & Caltabiano, N. J. (2011). Promoting emotional well-being through the use of humour. *Journal of Positive Psychology, 6*(3), 237–252. doi:10.1080/17439760.2011.577087

Crews, F. T., & Boettiger, C. A. (2009). Impulsivity, frontal lobes and risk for addiction. *Pharmacology, Biochemistry & Behavior, 93*(3), 237–247. doi:10.1016/j.pbb.2009.04.018

Crocker, J., Moeller, S., & Burson, A. (2010). The costly pursuit of self-esteem: Implications for self-regulation. In R. H. Hoyle (Ed.), *Handbook of personality and self-regulation* (pp. 403–429). New York: Wiley-Blackwell. doi:10.1002/9781444318111.ch18

Crooks, R., & Baur, K. (2014). *Our sexuality* (12th ed.). Belmont, CA: Cengage Learning/Wadsworth.

Crowley, M., Tope, D., et al. (2010). Neo-Taylorism at work: Occupational change in the post-Fordist Era. *Social Problems, 57*(3), 421–447.

Crown, C. L., Feldstein, S., et al. (2002). The cross-modal coordination of interpersonal timing. *Journal of Psycholinguistic Research, 31*(1), 1–23. doi:10.1023/A:1014301303616

Crowther, J. H., Sanftner, J., et al. (2001). The role of daily hassles in binge eating. *International Journal of Eating Disorders, 29*, 449–454. doi:10.1002/eat.1041

Cruse, D., Chennu, S., et al. (2011). Bedside detection of awareness in the vegetative state: A cohort study. *The Lancet, 378*(9809), 2088–2094. doi:10.1016/S0140-6736(11)61224-5

Cservenka, A., Herting, M. M., et al. (2013). High and low sensation seeking adolescents show distinct patterns of brain activity during reward processing. *Neuroimage, 66*, 184–193. doi:10.1016/j.neuroimage.2012.11.003

Csikszentmihalyi, M. (1997). *Creativity.* New York: HarperCollins.

Csikszentmihalyi, M., Abuhamdeh, S., Nakamura, J. (2005). Flow. In A. J. Elliot & C. S. Dweck, (Eds.), *Handbook of competence and motivation* (pp. 598–608). New York: Guilford.

Cuijpers, P., Geraedts, A. S., et al. (2011). Interpersonal psychotherapy for depression: A meta-analysis. *The American Journal of Psychiatry, 168*(6), 581–592. doi:10.1176/appi.ajp.2010.10101411

Culver, R., & Ianna, P. (1988). *Astrology: True or false?* Buffalo, NY: Prometheus Books.

Cummings, M. R. (2011) *Human heredity: Principles and issues* (9th ed.). Belmont CA: Cengage Learning/Wadsworth.

Curci, A., & Luminet, O. (2006). Follow-up of a crossnational comparison on flashbulb and event memory for the September 11th attacks. *Memory, 14*(3), 329–344. doi:10.1080/09658210903081827

Curtis, D., Vine, A. E., et al. (2011). Case–case genome-wide association analysis shows markers differentially associated with schizophrenia and bipolar disorder and implicates calcium channel genes. *Psychiatric*

Genetics, 21(1), 1–4. doi:10.1097/YPG.0b013e3283413382

Curtis, J. W. (2013). Faculty salary equity: *Still a gender gap?* Retrieved April 9, 2013, from http://www.aacu.org/ocww/volume39_1/feature.cfm?section=2

Cushen, P. J., & Wiley, J. (2012). Cues to solution, restructuring patterns, and reports of insight in creative problem solving. *Consciousness & Cognition, 21*(3), 1166–1175. doi:10.1016/j.concog.2012.03.013

Cusin, C., Franco, F., et al. (2013). Rapid improvement of depression and psychotic symptoms in Huntington's disease: A retrospective chart review of seven patients treated with electroconvulsive therapy. *General Hospital Psychiatry.* doi:10.1016/j.genhosppsych.2013.01.015

Czeisler, C. A., Duffy, J. F., et al. (1999). Stability, precision, and near-24-hour period of the human circadian pacemaker. *Science, 284*(5423), 2177–2181. doi:10.1126/science.284.5423.2177

Czerniak, E., & Davidson, M. (2012). Placebo, a historical perspective. *European Neuropsychopharmacology, 22*(11), 770–774. doi:10.1016/j.euroneuro.2012.04.003

Dacre Pool, L., & Qualter, P. (2012). Improving emotional intelligence and emotional self-efficacy through a teaching intervention for university students. *Learning & Individual Differences, 23*(3), 306–312. doi:10.1016/j.lindif.2012.01.010

Dadich, A. (2010). Expanding our understanding of self-help support groups for substance use issues. *Journal of Drug Education, 40*(2), 189–202.

Dai, D. Y. (2010). *The nature and nurture of giftedness: A new framework for understanding gifted education.* New York: Teachers College Press.

Dailey, M. N., Joyce, C., et al. (2010). Evidence and a computational explanation of cultural differences in facial expression recognition. *Emotion, 10*(6), 874–893. doi:10.1037/a0020019

Damisch, L., Stoberock, B., & Mussweiler, T. (2010). Keep your fingers crossed! How superstition improves performance. *Psychological Science, 21*(7), 1014–1020. doi:10.1177/0956797610372631

Damman, M., Henkens, K., & Kalmijn, M. (2011). The impact of midlife educational, work, health, and family experiences on men's early retirement. *Journals of Gerontology, 66B*(5), 617–627. doi:10.1093/geronb/gbr092

Danaei, G., Ding, E. L., et al. (2009). The preventable causes of death in the United States: Comparative risk assessment of dietary, lifestyle, and metabolic risk factors. *PLoS Med, 6*(4), e1000058. doi:10.1371/journal.pmed.1000058

Dane, S., & Erzurumluoglu, A. (2003). Sex and handedness differences in eye–hand visual reaction times in handball players. *International Journal of Neuroscience, 113*(7), 923–929. doi:10.1080/00207450390220367

Dang-Vu, T. T., McKinney, S. M., et al. (2010). Spontaneous brain rhythms predict sleep stability in the face of noise. *Current Biology, 20*(15), R626–R627. doi:0.06/j.cub.200.06.032

Dani, J. A., & Balfour, D. J. K. (2011). Historical and current perspective on tobacco use and nicotine addiction. *Trends in Neurosciences, 34*(7), 383–392. doi:10.1016/j.tins.2011.05.001

Daniels, H. (2005). Vygotsky and educational psychology: Some preliminary remarks. *Educational & Child Psychology, 22*(1), 6–17.

Danziger, N., Prkachin, K. M., & Willer, J.-C. (2006). Is pain the price of empathy? The perception of others' pain in patients with congenital insensitivity to pain. *Brain: A Journal of Neurology, 129*(9), 2494–2507. doi:10.1093/brain/awl155

Darcy, A. M. (2011). Eating disorders in adolescent males: A critical examination of five common assumptions. *Adolescent Psychiatry, 1*(4), 307–312. doi:10.2174/2210677411101040307

Darley, J. M. (2000). Bystander phenomenon. In A. E. Kazdin (Ed.), *Encyclopedia of psychology* (Vol. 1, pp. 493–495). Washington: American Psychological Association.

Darley, J. M., & Latané, B. (1968). Bystander intervention in emergencies: Diffusion of responsibility. *Journal of Personality & Social Psychology, 8*, 377–383. doi:10.1037/h0025589

Darou, W. S. (1992). Native Canadians and intelligence testing. *Canadian Journal of Counselling, 26*(2), 96–99.

Daruna, J. H. (2012). *Introduction to psychoneuroimmunology* (2nd ed.). San Diego: Academic Press.

Darwin, C. (1872). *The expression of emotion in man and animals.* Chicago: University of Chicago Press.

Davey, G. (2008). *Clinical psychology: Topics in applied psychology.* New York: Oxford University Press.

Davey, G. (Ed.) (2011). *Applied psychology.* New York: Wiley-Blackwell.

David-Ferdon, C., & Hertz, M. F. (2009). *Electronic media and youth violence: a CDC issue brief for researchers.* Atlanta: Centers for Disease Control. Retrieved July 12, 2013, from http://www.cdc.gov/violenceprevention/pdf/Electronic_Aggression_Researcher_Brief-a.pdf

David, D., & Montgomery, G. H. (2011). The scientific status of psychotherapies: A new evaluative framework for evidence–based psychosocial interventions. *Clinical Psychology:*

Science & Practice, 18(2), 89–99. doi:10.1111/j.1468-2850.2011.01239.x

Davidovitch, N., & Milgram, R. M. (2006). Creative thinking as a predictor of teacher effectiveness in higher education. *Creativity Research Journal, 18*, 385–390. doi:10.1207/s15326934crj1803_12

Davidson, J. E. (2003). Insights about insightful problem solving. In J. E. Davidson & R. J. Sternberg (Eds.), *The psychology of problem solving* (pp. 149–175). New York: Cambridge University Press. doi:10.1017/CBO9780511615771.006

Davidson, L., Shaw, J., et al. (2010). "I don't know how to find my way in the world": Contributions of user-led research to transforming mental health practice. *Psychiatry: Interpersonal and Biological Processes, 73*(2), 101–113. doi:10.1521/psyc.2010.73.2.101

Davidson, R. J., Kabat-Zinn, J., et al. (2003). Alternations in brain and immune function produced by mindfulness meditation. *Psychosomatic Medicine, 65*(4), 564–570. doi:10.1097/01.PSY.0000077505.67574.E3

Davidson, T. L. (2000). Latent learning. In A. E. Kazdin (Ed.), *Encyclopedia of psychology* (Vol. 4, pp. 489–492). Washington: American Psychological Association. doi:10.1037/10519-212

Davidson, W. B., Bromfield, J. M., & Beck, H. P. (2007). Beneficial academic orientations and self-actualization of college students. *Psychological Reports, 100*(2), 604–612. doi:10.2466/PR0.100.2.604-612

Davies, M., & McCartney, S. (2003). Effects of gender and sexuality on judgements of victim blame and rape myth acceptance in a depicted male rape. *Journal of Community & Applied Social Psychology, 13*(5), 391–398.

Davis, C., & Carter, J. C. (2009). Compulsive overeating as an addiction disorder: A review of theory and evidence. *Appetite, 53*(1), 1–8. doi:10.1016/j.appet.2009.05.018

Davis, D. R. (2011). Enhancing graph production skills via programmed instruction: An experimental analysis of the effect of guided-practice on data-based graph production. *Computers in Human Behavior, 27*(5), 1627–1633. doi:10.1016/j.chb.2011.01.013

Davis, D., & Follette, W. C. (2002). Rethinking the probative value of evidence. *Law & Human Behavior, 26*(2), 133–158. doi:10.1023/A:1014693024962

Davis, M. A. (2009). Understanding the relationship between mood and creativity: A meta-analysis. *Organizational Behavior & Human Decision Processes, 108*(1), 25–38. doi:10.1016/j.obhdp.2008.04.001

Davison, G. C., & Neale, J. M. (2006). *Abnormal psychology* (10th ed.). San Francisco: Jossey-Bass.

Day, D. O., & Moseley, R. L. (2010). Munchausen by proxy syndrome. *Journal of Forensic Psychology Practice, 10*(1), 13–36. doi:10.1080/15228930903172981

Dazzi, C., & Pedrabissi, L. (2009). Graphology and personality: An empirical study on validity of handwriting analysis. *Psychological Reports, 105*, 1255–1268. doi:10.2466/pr0.105.F.1255-1268

de Bono, E. (1992). *Serious creativity.* New York: HarperCollins.

De Cuypere, G., Knudson, G., & Bockting, W. (2011). Second response of the world professional association for transgender health to the proposed revision of the diagnosis of gender dysphoria for DSM 5. *International Journal of Transgenderism, 13*(2), 51–53. doi:10.1080/15532739.2011.624047

de Gelder, B. (2013). From body perception to action preparation: A distributed neural system for viewing bodily expressions of emotion. In K. L. Johnson, & M. Shiffrar (Eds.), *People watching: Social, perceptual, and neurophysiological studies of body perception* (pp. 350–368). New York: Oxford University Press.

de Jong, P. J., & Muris, P. (2002). Spider phobia. *Journal of Anxiety Disorders, 16*(1), 51–65. doi:10.1016/S0887-6185(01)00089-5

de Leon, C. F. M. (2005). Social engagement and successful aging. *European Journal of Ageing, 2*(1), 64–66. doi:10.1007/s10433-005-0020-y

Dean, D., Jr., & Kuhn, D. (2007). Direct instruction vs. discovery: The long view. *Science Education, 91*(3), 384–397.

Deardorff, J., Hayward, C., et al. (2007). Puberty and gender interact to predict social anxiety symptoms in early adolescence. *Journal of Adolescent Health, 41*(1), 102–104. doi:10.1016/j.jadohealth.2007.02.013

DeArmond, S., Tye, M., Chen, et al. (2006). Age and gender stereotypes: New challenges in a changing workplace and workforce. *Journal of Applied Social Psychology, 36*(9), 2184–2214.

DeCarolis, N. A., & Eisch, A. J. (2010). Hippocampal neurogenesis as a target for the treatment of mental illness: A critical evaluation. *Neuropharmacology, 58*(6), 884–893. doi:10.1016/j.neuropharm.2009.12.013

Decker, S. L., Brooks, J. H., & Allen, R. A. (2011). Stanford-Binet intelligence scales (5th ed.). In S. L. Decker, J. H. Brooks et al. (Eds.), *Handbook of pediatric neuropsychology* (pp. 389–395). New York: Springer.

Deckers, L. (2010). *Motivation: Biological, psychological, and environmental* (3rd ed.). Boston: Pearson/Allyn & Bacon.

Deckro, G. R., Ballinger, K. M., et al. (2002). The evaluation of a mind/body intervention to reduce psychological distress and perceived stress in college students. *Journal of American College Health, 50*(6), 281–287. doi:10.1080/07448480209603446

Deeb, S. S. (2004). Molecular genetics of color-vision deficiencies. *Visual Neuroscience, 21*(3), 191–196. doi:10.1017/S0952523804213244

Dein, S., & Littlewood, R. (2005). Apocalyptic suicide: From a pathological to an eschatological interpretation. *International Journal of Social Psychiatry, 51*(3), 198–210. doi:10.1177/0020764005056762

del Casale, A., Ferracuti, S., et al. (2012). Neurocognition under hypnosis: Findings from recent functional neuroimaging studies. *International Journal of Clinical and Experimental Hypnosis, 60*(3), 286–317. doi:10.1080/00207144.2012.675295

Delavest, M. M., Even, C. C., et al. (2012). Association of the intronic rs2072621 polymorphism of the X-linked GPR50 gene with affective disorder with seasonal pattern. *European Psychiatry, 27*(5), 369–371. doi:10.1016/j.eurpsy.2011.02.011

Delgado, B. M., & Ford, L. (1998). Parental perceptions of child development among low-income Mexican American families. *Journal of Child & Family Studies, 7*(4), 469–481. doi:10.1023/A:1022958026951

Delhomme, P., Chaurand, N., & Paran, F. (2012). Personality predictors of speeding in young drivers: Anger vs. sensation seeking. *Transportation Research Part F: Traffic Psychology & Behaviour, 15*(6), 654–666. doi:10.1016/j.trf.2012.06.006

Dell, P. F. (2009). The long struggle to diagnose multiple personality disorder (MPD): MPD. In P. F. Dell, & J. A. O'Neil (Eds.), *Dissociation and the dissociative disorders: DSM-V and beyond* (pp. 384–399). New York: Routledge.

Della Sala, S. (Ed.). (2010). *Forgetting*. Hove, UK: Psychology Press.

Demos, J. N. (2005). *Getting started with neurofeedback*. New York: Norton.

Denney, J. T., Rogers, R. G., et al. (2009). Adult suicide mortality in the United States: Marital status, family size, socioeconomic status, and differences by sex. *Social Science Quarterly, 90*(5), 1167–1185. doi:10.1111/j.1540-6237.2009.00652.x

Denollet, J., & Van Heck, G. L. (2001). Psychological risk factors in heart disease. *Journal of Psychosomatic Research, 51*(3), 465–468. doi:10.1016/S0022-3999(01)00230-6

Des Jardins, J. R. (2013). *Environmental ethics* (5th ed.). Belmont, CA: Cengage Learning/Wadsworth.

DeSantis, A. D., & Hane, A. C. (2010). "Adderall is definitely not a drug": Justifications for the illegal use of ADHD stimulants. *Substance Use & Misuse, 45*(1–2), 31–46. doi:10.3109/10826080902858334

Deutsch, M. (1993). Educating for a peaceful world. *American Psychologist, 48*(5), 510–517. doi:10.1037/0003-066X.48.5.510

Deutschendorf, H. (2009). *The other kind of smart: Simple ways to boost your emotional intelligence for greater personal effectiveness and success*. New York: AMACOM.

Devine, D. J., Clayton, L. D., et al. (2001). Jury decision making: 45 years of empirical research on deliberating groups. *Psychology, Public Policy, & Law, 7*(3), 622–727.

Devoto, A., Lucidi, F., et al. (1999). Effects of different sleep reductions on daytime sleepiness. *Sleep, 22*(3), 336–343.

DeWall, C. N., & Anderson, C. A. (2011). The general aggression model. In P. R. Shaver & M. Mikulincer (Eds.), *Human aggression and violence: Causes, manifestations, and consequences* (pp. 15–33). Washington: American Psychological Association. doi:10.1037/12346-001

DeWall, C. N., Lambert, N. M., et al. (2011). So far away from one's partner, yet so close to romantic alternatives: Avoidant attachment, interest in alternatives, and infidelity. *Journal of Personality & Social Psychology, 101*(6), 1302–1316. doi:10.1037/a0025497

Dewar, M., Della Sala, S., et al. (2010). Profound retroactive interference in anterograde amnesia: What interferes? *Neuropsychology, 24*(3), 357–367. doi:10.1037/a0018207

Dewey J. (1910). *How we think*. Lexington, Mass: D.C. Heath.

DeYoung, C. G., Hirsh, J. B., et al. (2010). Testing predictions from personality neuroscience: Brain structure and the big five. *Psychological Science, 21*(6), 820–828. doi:10.1177/0956797610370159

Diamond, M. (2009). Human intersexuality: Difference or disorder? *Archives of Sexual Behavior, 38*(2), 172.

Diano, S., Farr, S. A., et al. (2006). Ghrelin controls hippocampal spine synapse density and memory performance. *Nature Neuroscience, 9*, 381–388. doi:10.1038/nn1656

Dick-Niederhauser, A. & Silverman, W. K. (2006). Separation anxiety disorder. In J. E. Fisher & W. T. O'Donohue (Eds.), *Practitioner's guide to evidence-based psychotherapy* (pp. 627–633). New York: Springer. doi:10.1007/978-0-387-28370-8_62

Dickens, W. T., & Flynn, J. R. (2001). Heritability estimates versus large environmental effects: The IQ paradox resolved. *Psychological Review, 108*, 346–369. doi:10.1037/0033-295X.108.2.346

Diekelmann, S., & Born, J. (2010). The memory function of sleep. *Nature Reviews Neuroscience, 11*(2), 114–126

Diener, E. (Ed.) (2009). *Assessing well-being: The collected works of Ed Diener*. New York, NY: Springer.

Diener, E., & Chan, M. Y. (2011). Happy people live longer: Subjective well-being contributes to health and longevity. *Applied Psychology: Health & Well-Being, 3*(1), 1–43. doi:10.1111/j.1758-0854.2010.01045.x

Diener, E., Ng, W., et al. (2010). Wealth and happiness across the world: Material prosperity predicts life evaluation, whereas psychosocial prosperity predicts positive feeling. *Journal of Personality & Social Psychology, 99*(1), 52–61. doi:10.1037/a0018066

Diener, E., Scollon, C. N., & Lucas, R. E. (2009). In E. Diener (Ed.), *The evolving concept of subjective well-being: The multifaceted nature of happiness* (pp. 67–100). New York: Springer. doi:10.1007/978-90-481-2354-4_4

Diener, E., Tay, L., & Myers, D. G. (2011). The religion paradox: If religion makes people happy, why are so many dropping out? *Journal of Personality and Social Psychology, 101*(6), 1278–1290. doi:10.1037/a0024402

Dieterich, S. E., Assel, M. A., et al. (2006). The impact of early maternal verbal scaffolding and child language abilities on later decoding and reading comprehension skills. *Journal of School Psychology, 43*(6), 481–494. doi:10.1016/j.jsp.2005.10.003

Dietrich, A., & Stoll, O. (2010). Effortless attention, hypofrontality, and perfectionism. In B. Bruya (Eds.), *Effortless attention: A new perspective in the cognitive science of attention and action* (pp. 159–178). Cambridge, MA: MIT Press.

Dijk, D., & Lazar, A. S. (2012). The regulation of human sleep and wakefulness: Sleep homeostasis and circadian rhythmicity. In C. M. Morin, & C. A. Espie (Eds.), *The Oxford handbook of sleep and sleep disorders* (pp. 38–60). New York: Oxford University Press. doi:10.1093/oxfordhb/9780195376203.013.0003

Dik, B. J., Byrne, Z. S., & Steger, M. F. (2013). *Purpose and meaning in the workplace*. Washington, DC: American Psychological Association. doi:10.1037/14183-000

Dikotter, F., Laamann, L., & Xun, Z. (2008). *Narcotic culture: A history of drugs in China*. Chicago: University of Chicago Press.

Dimberg, U., & Söderkvist, S. (2011). The voluntary facial action technique: A method to test the facial feedback hypothesis. *Journal of Nonverbal Behavior, 35*(1), 17–33. doi:10.1007/s10919-010-0098-6

Dimsdale, J. E. (2011). Medically unexplained symptoms: A treacherous foundation for somatoform disorders? *Psychiatric Clinics of North America, 34*(3), 511–513. doi:10.1016/j.psc.2011.05.003

Dinan, T. G. (2001). Stress, depression and cardiovascular disease. *Stress & Health: Journal of the International Society for the Investigation of Stress, 17*(2), 65–66. doi:10.1002/smi.895

Dingus, T. A., Klauer, S. G., Neale, et al. (2006). The 100-car naturalistic driving study: Phase II. Results of the 100-car field experiment. *National Highway Traffic Safety Administration Report No. DOT HS 810 593*. Retrieved June 9, 2013, from http://ntl.bts.gov/lib/jpodocs/repts_te/14302.htm

Distin, K. (2006). *Gifted children: A guide for parents and professionals*. London: Jessica Kingsley Publishers.

Dixon, M. J., Smilek, D., & Merikle, P. M. (2004). Not all synaesthetes are created equal: Projector versus associator synaesthetes. *Cognitive, Affective, & Behavioral Neuroscience, 4*(3), 335–343. doi:10.3758/CABN.4.3.335

Dixon, S. V., Graber, J. A., & Brooks-Gunn, J. (2008). The roles of respect for parental authority and parenting practices in parent-child conflict among African American, Latino, and European American families. *Journal of Family Psychology, 22*(1), 1–10. doi:10.1037/0893-3200.22.1.1

Dobelle, W. H. (2000). Artificial vision for the blind by connecting a television camera to the visual cortex. *American Society of Artificial Internal Organs, 46*, 3–9.

Dobson, K. S., Backs-Dermott, G. J., & Dozois, D. J. A. (2000). Cognitive and cognitive-behavioral therapies. In C. R. Snyder, & R. E. Ingram (Eds.), *Handbook of psychological change: Psychotherapy processes and practices for the 21st century* (pp. 409–428). New York: Wiley.

Dodge, T., Williams, K. J., et al. (2012). Judging cheaters: Is substance misuse viewed similarly in the athletic and academic domains? *Psychology of Addictive Behaviors, 26*(3), 678–682. doi:10.1037/a0027872

Dodson, E. R., & Zee, P. C. (2010). Therapeutics for circadian rhythm sleep disorders. *Sleep Medicine Clinics, 5*(4), 701–715. doi:10.1016/j.jsmc.2010.08.001

Doherty, M. J. (2009). *Theory of mind: How children understand others' thoughts and feelings*. New York: Psychology Press.

Doidge, N. (1997). Empirical evidence for the efficacy of psychoanalytic psychotherapies and psychoanalysis. *Psychoanalytic Inquiry, Suppl.,* 102–150. doi:10.1080/07351699709534161

Dollard, J., & Miller, N. E. (1950). *Personality and psychotherapy: An analysis in terms of learning, thinking and culture.* New York: McGraw-Hill.

Domellöf, E., Johansson, A., & Rönnqvist, L. (2011). Handedness in preterm born children: A systematic review and a meta-analysis. *Neuropsychologia, 49*(9), 2299–2310. doi:10.1016/j.neuropsychologia.2011.04.033

Domhoff, G. W. (2001). A new neurocognitive theory of dreams. *Dreaming, 11,* 13–33. doi:10.1023/A:1009464416649

Domhoff, G. W. (2003). *The scientific study of dreams: Neural networks, cognitive development, and content analysis.* Washington: American Psychological Association.

Domhoff, G. W., & Schneider, A. (2008). Similarities and differences in dream content at the crosscultural, gender, and individual levels. *Consciousness & Cognition, 17*(4), 1257–1265. doi:10.1016/j.concog.2008.08.005

Domingo, R. A., & Goldstein-Alpern, N. (1999). "What dis?" and other toddler-initiated, expressive language-learning strategies. *Infant-Toddler Intervention, 9*(1), 39–60.

Domingos, A. I., Vaynshteyn, J., et al. (2011). Leptin regulates the reward value of nutrient. *Nature Neuroscience, 14*(12), 1562–1568. doi:10.1038/nn.2977

Domjan, M. (2010). *The principles of learning and behavior* (6th ed.). Belmont, CA: Cengage Learning/Wadsworth.

Donnellan, M., Kenny, D. A., et al. (2012). Using trait-state models to evaluate the longitudinal consistency of global self-esteem from adolescence to adulthood. *Journal of Research in Personality, 46*(6), 634–645. doi:10.1016/j.jrp.2012.07.005

Dooling, D. J., & Lachman, R. (1971). Effects of comprehension on retention of prose. *Journal of Experimental Psychology, 88,* 216–222. doi:10.1037/h0030904

Doran, S. M., Van Dongen, H. P., & Dinges, D. F. (2001). Sustained attention performance during sleep deprivation. *Archives of Italian Biology, 139,* 253–267.

Dorfman, J., Shames, J., & Kihlstrom, J. F. (1996). Intuition, incubation, and insight. In G. Underwood (Ed.), *Implicit cognition* (pp. 257–296). New York: Oxford University Press.

Dovidio, J. F., & Gaertner, S. L. (1999). Reducing prejudice: Combating intergroup biases. *Current Directions in Psychological Science, 8*(4), 101–105. doi:10.1111/1467-8721.00024

Dovidio, J. F., & Penner, L. A. (2001). Helping and altruism. In M.Hewstone, & M. Brewer (Eds.), *Handbook of social psychology* (pp. 162–195). London: Blackwell.

Dovidio, J. F., Gaertner, S. L., et al. (2002). Why can't we just get along? *Cultural Diversity & Ethnic Minority Psychology, 8*(2), 88–102. doi:10.1037/1099-9809.8.2.88

Dovidio, J. F., Piliavin, J. A., et al. (2006). *The social psychology of prosocial behavior.* Mahwah, NJ: Erlbaum.

Dow-Edwards, D. (2011). Translational issues for prenatal cocaine studies and the role of environment. *Neurotoxicology & Teratology, 33*(1), 9–16. doi:10.1016/j.ntt.2010.06.007

Dowling, K. W. (2005). The effect of lunar phases on domestic violence incident rates. *Forensic Examiner, 14*(4), 13–18.

Doyle, A. (2013). *Job searching.* Retrieved May 28, 2013, from http://jobsearch.about.com/od/interviewquestionsanswers/a/interviewquest.htm

Dozois, D. J., & Dobson, K. S. (2002). Depression. In M. M. Antony & D. H. Barlow (Eds.), *Handbook of assessment and treatment planning for psychological disorders* (pp. 259–299). New York: Guilford.

Dresler, M., Wehrle, R., et al. (2012). Neural correlates of dream lucidity obtained from contrasting lucid versus non-lucid REM sleep: A combined EEG/fMRI case study. *Sleep, 35*(7), 1017–1020.

Drews, F. A., Yazdani, H., et al. (2009). Text messaging during simulated driving. *Human Factors, 51*(5), 762–770. doi:10.1177/0018720809353319

Drigotas, S. M., Rusbult, C. E., et al. (1999). Close partner as sculptor of the ideal self: Behavioral affirmation and the Michelangelo phenomenon. *Journal of Personality & Social Psychology, 77*(2), 293–323. doi:10.1037/0022-3514.77.2.293

Driver, J. L., & Gottman, J. M. (2004). Daily marital interactions and positive affect during marital conflict among newlywed couples. *Family Process, 43*(3), 301–314.

Drucker, P. (1993). *Post-capitalist society.* New York: HarperCollins.

Druckman, D., & Bjork, R. A. (1994). *Learning, remembering, believing: Enhancing human performance.* Washington: National Academy Press.

Drummond, M., Douglas, J., & Olver, J. (2007). Anosmia after traumatic brain injury: A clinical update. *Brain Impairment, 8*(1), 31–40. doi:10.1375/brim.8.1.31

Drury, S., Hutchens, S. A., et al. (2012). Philip G. Zimbardo on his career and the Stanford Prison Experiment's 40th anniversary. *History of Psychology, 15*(2), 161–170. doi:10.1037/a0025884

Dryden, W. (2011). *Understanding psychological health: The REBT perspective.* New York: Routledge/Taylor & Francis.

Drymalski, W. M., & Washburn, J. J. (2011). Sudden gains in the treatment of depression in a partial hospitalization program. *Journal of Consulting & Clinical Psychology, 79*(3), 364–368. doi:10.1037/a0022973

Duckitt, J., & Sibley, C. G. (2010). Personality, ideology, prejudice, and politics: A dual-process motivational model. *Journal of Personality, 78*(6), 1861–1893. doi:10.1111/j.1467-6494.2010.00672.x

Duckworth, A. L., Peterson, C., et al. (2007). Grit: Perseverance and passion for long-term goals. *Journal of Personality & Social Psychology, 92*(6), 1087–1101. doi:10.1037/0022-3514.92.6.1087

Duclos, S. E., & Laird, J. D. (2001). The deliberate control of emotional experience through control of expressions. *Cognition and Emotion, 15,* 27–56.

Duffy, J. F., & Wright, Jr., K. P. Jr. (2005). Entrainment of the human circadian system by light. *Journal of Biological Rhythms, 20*(4), 326–338. doi:10.1177/0748730405277983

Duffy, S., & Verges, M. (2009). It matters a hole lot: Perceptual affordances of waste containers influence recycling compliance. *Environment & Behavior, 41*(5), 741–749.

Duncan, B. L., & Reese, R. J. (2013). Empirically supported treatments, evidence-based treatments, and evidence-based practice. In G. Stricker, T. A. Widiger, et al. (Eds.), *Handbook of psychology* (Vol. 8): *Clinical psychology* (2nd ed., pp. 489–513). New York: Wiley.

Duncan, J. (2005). Frontal lobe function and general intelligence: Why it matters. *Cortex, 41*(2), 215–217. doi:10.1016/S0010-9452(08)70896-7

Duncker, K. (1945). On problem solving. *Psychological Monographs, 58*(270).

Dunlop, S. M., & Romer, D. (2010). Adolescent and young adult crash risk: Sensation seeking, substance use propensity and substance use behaviors. *Journal of Adolescent Health, 46*(1), 90–92. doi:10.1016/j.jadohealth.2009.06.005

Durán, L. K., Roseth, C. J., Hoffman, P. (2010). An experimental study comparing English-only and Transitional Bilingual Education on Spanish-speaking preschoolers' early literacy development. *Early Childhood Research Quarterly, 25*(2), 207–217. doi:10.1016/j.ecresq.2009.10.002

Durand, V. M., & Barlow, D. H. (2013). *Essentials of abnormal psychology* (6th ed.). Belmont, CA: Cengage Learning/Wadsworth.

Durham, M. G. (2009). *The Lolita effect.* New York: Overlook Press.

Dutta, T., & Mandal, M. K. (2005). The relationship of handedness and accidents: A meta-analytical review of findings. *Psychological Studies, 50*(4), 309–316.

Dutton, D. G., & Aron, A. P. (1974). Some evidence for heightened sexual attraction under conditions of high anxiety. *Journal of Personality & Social Psychology, 30,* 510–517. doi:10.1037/h0037031

Dvash, J., Gilam, G., et al. (2010). The envious brain: The neural basis of social comparison. *Human Brain Mapping, 31*(11), 1741–1750. doi:10.1002/hbm.20972

Dyer, K. A. (2001). *Dealing with death and dying in medical education and practice.* Retrieved June 9, 2013, from http://www.journeyofhearts.org/kirstimd/AMSA/outline.htm

Dyukova, G. M., Glozman, Z. M., et al. (2010). Speech disorders in right-hemisphere stroke. *Neuroscience & Behavioral Physiology, 40*(6), 593–602. doi:10.1007/s11055-010-9301-9

Dywan, J., & Bowers, K. S. (1983). The use of hypnosis to enhance recall. *Science, 222,* 184–185. doi:10.1126/science.6623071

Dzokoto, V. A., & Adams, G. (2005). Understanding genital-shrinking epidemics in West Africa: Koro, juju, or mass psychogenic illness? *Culture, Medicine & Psychiatry, 29*(1), 53–78. doi:10.1007/s11013-005-4623-8

Eagly, A. H. (2009). The his and hers of prosocial behavior: An examination of the social psychology of gender. *American Psychologist, 64*(8), 644–658.

Eagly, A. H. (2013). Women as leaders: Paths through the labyrinth. In M. C. Bligh, & R. E. Riggio (Eds.), *Exploring distance in leader-follower relationships: When near is far and far is near* (pp. 191–214). New York: Routledge/Taylor & Francis.

Eagly, A. H., & Carli, L. L. (2007). *Through the labyrinth: The truth about how women become leaders.* Watertown, MA: HBS Press Book.

Eagly, A. H., Eaton, A., et al. (2012). Feminism and psychology: Analysis of a half-century of research on women and gender. *American Psychologist, 67*(3), 211–230. doi:10.1037/a0027260

Eardley, A. F., & Pring, L. (2007). Spatial processing, mental imagery, and creativity in individuals with and without sight. *European Journal of Cognitive Psychology, 19*(1), 37–58. doi:10.1080/09541440600591965

Earleywine, M. (2011). *Humor 101.* New York: Springer.

Easterbrooks, M., Bartlett, J., et al. (2013). Social and emotional development in infancy. In R. M. Lerner, M. Easterbrooks, et al. (Eds.), *Handbook of psychology* (Vol. 6): *Developmental psychology* (2nd ed.) (pp. 91–120). New York: Wiley.

Eaton, D. K., Kann, L., et al. (2012). *Youth risk behavior surveillance: United States, 2011.* Atlanta, GA: Centers for Disease Control. Retrieved April 17, 2013, from http://www.cdc.gov /mmwr/pdf/ss/ss6104.pdf

Ebben, M. R., & Spielman, A. J. (2009). Non-pharmacological treatments for insomnia. *Journal of Behavioral Medicine, 32*(3), 244–254. doi:10.1007/ s10865-008-9198-8

Ebbinghaus, H. (1885). *Memory: A contribution to experimental psychology.* (H. A. Ruger, & C. E. Bussenius, Trans.) New York: New York Teacher's College, Columbia University.

Eckert, M. J., & Racine, R. J. (2006). Long-term depression and associativity in rat primary motor cortex following thalamic stimulation. *European Journal of Neuroscience, 24*(12), 3553–3560. doi:10.1111/j.1460-9568.2006.05220.x

Eddy, K. T., Dutra, L., et al. (2004). A multidimensional meta-analysis of psychotherapy and pharmacotherapy for obsessive-compulsive disorder. *Clinical Psychology Review, 24*(8), 1011–1030. doi:10.1016/j. cpr.2004.08.004

Edenfield, T. M., & Blumenthal, J. A. (2011). Exercise and stress reduction. In R. J. Contrada, & A. Baum (Eds.), *The handbook of stress science: Biology, psychology, and health* (pp. 301–319). New York: Springer.

Eidelson, R. J., & Eidelson, J. I. (2003). Dangerous ideas. *American Psychologist, 58*(3), 182–192. doi:10.1037/0003-066X.58.3.182

Eifert, G. H., & Lejuez, C. W. (2000). Aversion therapy. In A. E. Kazdin (Ed.), *Encyclopedia of psychology* (Vol. 1, pp. 348–350). Washington: American Psychological Association.

Eigenberg, H., McGuffee, K., et al. (2012). Doing justice: Perceptions of gender neutrality in the jury selection process. *American Journal of Criminal Justice, 37*(2), 258–275. doi:10.1007/ s12103-011-9139-x

Einarsen, S. & Hoel, H. (2008). Bullying and mistreatment at work: How managers may prevent and manage such problems. In A. Kinder, R. Hughes & C. L. Cooper (Eds.), *Employee well-being support: A workplace resource* (pp. 161–173). New York: Wiley.

Eisenberg, N., Valiente, C., et al. (2003). The relations of effortful control and ego control to children's resiliency and social functioning. *Developmental Psychology, 39*(4), 761–776. doi:10.1037/0012-1649.39.4.761

Eisendrath, S., Chartier, M., & McLane, M. (2011). Adapting mindfulness-based cognitive therapy for treatment-resistant depression. *Cognitive & Behavioral Practice, 18*(3), 362–370. doi:10.1016/j.cbpra.2010.05.004

Eisler, I., Simic, M., et al. (2007). A randomized controlled treatment trial of two forms of family therapy in adolescent anorexia nervosa: A five-year follow-up. *Journal of Child Psychology & Psychiatry, 48*(6), 552–560. doi:10.1111/j.1469-7610.2007.01726.x

Ekman, P. (1993). Facial expression and emotion. *American Psychologist, 48*(4), 384–392. doi:10.1037/0003-066X.48.4.384

Ekman, P., & Cordaro, D. (2011). What is meant by calling emotions basic. *Emotion Review, 3*(4), 364–370. doi:10.1177/1754073911410740

Ekman, P., Levenson, R. W., & Friesen, W. V. (1983). Autonomic nervous system activity distinguishes among emotions. *Science, 221*, 1208–1210. doi:10.1126/science.6612338

Ekonomou, A., Ballard, C. G., et al. (2011). Increased neural progenitors in vascular dementia. *Neurobiology of Aging, 32*, 2152–2161. doi:10.1016/j. neurobiolaging.2010.01.007

Elder, P. (2006). *Critical thinking: Learn the tools the best thinkers use.* Englewood Cliffs, NJ: Prentice-Hall.

Eldridge, M., Saltzman, E., & Lahav, A. (2010). Seeing what you hear: Visual feedback improves pitch recognition. *European Journal of Cognitive Psychology, 22*(7), 1078–1091. doi:10.1080/09541440903316136

Eliot, L. (2009). *Pink brain, blue brain.* New York: Houghton Mifflin Harcourt.

Elkington, K. S., Hackler, D., et al. (2012). Perceived mental illness stigma among youth in psychiatric outpatient treatment. *Journal of Adolescent Research, 27*(2), 290–317. doi:10.1177/0743558411409931

Elkins, D. N. (2012). Toward a common focus in psychotherapy research. *Psychotherapy, 49*(4), 450–454. doi:10.1037/a0027797

Elli, K. A., & Nathan, P. J. (2001). The pharmacology of human working memory. *International Journal of Neuropsychopharmacology, 4*(3), 299–313. doi:10.1017/ S1461145701002541

Ellickson, P. L., Martino, S. C., & Collins, R. L. (2004). Marijuana use from adolescence to young adulthood. *Health Psychology, 23*(3), 299–307. doi:10.1037/0278-6133.23.3.299

Elliott, M., & Williams, D. (2003). The client experience of counselling and psychotherapy. *Counselling Psychology Review, 18*(1), 34–38.

Elliott, M., Browne, K., & Kilcoyne, J. (1995). Child sexual abuse prevention: What offenders tell us. *Child Abuse & Neglect, 19*(5), 579–594.

Elliott, R., & Farber, B. A. (2010). Carl Rogers: Idealistic pragmatist and psychotherapy research pioneer. In L. G. Castonguay, J. C. Muran, et al. (Eds.), *Bringing psychotherapy research to life: Understanding change through the work of leading clinical researchers* (pp. 17–27). Washington: American Psychological Association.

Ellis, A. (1979). The practice of rational-emotive therapy. In A. Ellis, & J. Whiteley (Eds.), *Theoretical and empirical foundations of rational-emotive therapy* (pp. 1–6). Monterey, CA: Brooks/Cole.

Ellis, A. (1995). Changing rational-emotive therapy (RET) to rational emotive behavior therapy (REBT). *Journal of Rational-Emotive & Cognitive Behavior Therapy, 13*(2), 85–89. doi:10.1007/ BF02354453

Ellis, A., & Ellis, D. J. (2011). *Rational emotive behavior therapy.* Washington: American Psychological Association.

Ellis, D. (2013). *Becoming a master student: Concise* (14th ed.). Belmont, CA: Cengage Learning/Wadsworth.

Ellison-Wright, I., & Bullmore, E. (2010). Anatomy of bipolar disorder and schizophrenia: A meta-analysis. *Schizophrenia Research, 117*(1), 1–12. doi:10.1016/j.schres.2009.12.022

Emerson, E. (2009). Relative child poverty, income inequality, wealth, and health. *Journal of the American Medical Association, 301*(4), 425–426. doi:10.1001/jama.2009.8

Engelen, E., & Röttger-Rössler, B. (2012). Current disciplinary and interdisciplinary debates on empathy. *Emotion Review, 4*(1), 3–8. doi:10.1177/1754073911422287

Engle, D. E., & Arkowitz, H. (2006). *Ambivalence in psychotherapy: Facilitating readiness to change.* New York: Guilford.

Engler, B. (2014). *Personality theories* (9th ed.). Belmont, CA: Cengage Learning/Wadsworth.

English, T., John, O. P., et al. (2012). Emotion regulation and peer-rated social functioning: A 4-year longitudinal study. *Journal of Research in Personality, 46*(6), 780–784. doi:10.1016/j.jrp.2012.09.006

Enns, M. W., Cox, B. J., & Clara, I. P. (2005). Perfectionism and neuroticism: A longitudinal study of specific vulnerability and diathesis-stress models. *Cognitive Therapy & Research, 29*(4), 463–478. doi:10.1007/ s10608-005-2843-04

Enrici, I., Adenzato, M., et al. (2011). Intention processing in communication: A common brain network for language and gestures. *Journal of Cognitive Neuroscience, 23*(9), 2415–2431. doi:10.1162/jocn.2010.21594

Epstein, S. (2003). Cognitive-experiential self-theory of personality. In T. Millon & M. J. Lerner (Eds.), *Comprehensive handbook of psychology: Personality and social psychology* (Vol. 5, pp. 159–184). New York: Wiley.

Erez, D. L., Levy, J., et al. (2010). Assessment of cognitive and adaptive behaviour among individuals with congenital insensitivity to pain and anhidrosis. *Developmental Medicine & Child Neurology, 52*(6), 559–562. doi:10.1111/j.1469-8749.2009.03567.x

Erickson, C. D., & Al-Timimi, N. R. (2001). Providing mental health services to Arab Americans. *Cultural Diversity & Ethnic Minority Psychology, 7*(4), 308–327. doi:10.1037/1099-9809.7.4.308

Ericsson, K. A. (2000). How experts attain and maintain superior performance. *Journal of Aging & Physical Activity, 8*(4), 366–372.

Ericsson, K. A., & Charness, N. (1994). Expert performance. *American Psychologist, 49*(8), 725–747. doi:10.1037/0003-066X.49.8.725

Ericsson, K. A., & Chase, W. G. (1982). Exceptional memory. *American Scientist, 70*, 607–615.

Ericsson, K. A., Delaney, P. F., et al. (2004). Uncovering the structure of a memorist's superior "basic" memory capacity. *Cognitive Psychology, 49*(3), 191–237. doi:10.1016/j. cogpsych.2004.02.001

Erikson, E. H. (1963). *Childhood and society.* New York: Norton.

Erlacher, D., & Schredl, M. (2004). Dreams reflecting waking sport activities: A comparison of sport and psychology students. *International Journal of Sport Psychology, 35*(4), 301–308.

Ertmer, D. J., & Jung, J. (2012). Prelinguistic vocal development in young cochlear implant recipients and typically developing infants: Year 1 of robust hearing experience. *Journal of Deaf Studies & Deaf Education, 17*(1), 116–132. doi:10.1093/ deafed/enr021

España, R. A., Oleson, E. B., et al. (2010). The hypocretin orexin system regulates cocaine self-administration via actions on the mesolimbic dopamine system. *European Journal of Neuroscience, 31*(2), 336–348. doi:10.1111/j.1460-9568.2009.07065.x

Essien, E. J., Monjok, E., et al. (2010). Correlates of HIV knowledge and sexual risk behaviors among female military personnel. *AIDS & Behavior, 14*(6), 1401–1414.

Ethier, K. A., Kershaw, T., et al. (2003). Adolescent women underestimate their susceptibility to sexually transmitted infections. *Sexually Transmitted Infections, 79*, 408–411.

Evans, G. W. (2006). Child development and the physical environment. *Annual Review of Psychology, 57*, 423–451.

Evans, G. W., & Wener, R. E. (2007). Crowding and personal space invasion on the train: Please don't make me sit in the middle. *Journal of Environmental Psychology, 27*(1), 90–94.

Evans, G. W., Lercher, P., & Kofler, W. W. (2002). Crowding and children's mental health: the role of house type. *Journal of Environmental Psychology, 22*, 221–231.

Evans, G. W., Ricciuti, H. N., et al. (2010). Crowding and cognitive development: The mediating role of maternal responsiveness among 36-month-old children. *Environment & Behavior, 42*(1), 135–148.

Evans, G.W., Lepore, S. J., & Schroeder, A. (1996). The role of interior design elements in human responses to crowding. *Journal of Personality & Social Psychology, 70*(1), 41–46.

Evardone, M., Alexander, G. M., & Morey, L. C. (2007). Hormones and borderline personality features. *Personality & Individual Differences, 44*(1), 278–287. doi:10.1016/j.paid.2007.08.007

Ewen, R. B. (2009). *An introduction to theories of personality* (7th ed.). Hillsdale, NJ: Lawrence Erlbaum.

Eysenck, H. J. (1994). The outcome problem in psychotherapy: What have we learned? *Behaviour Research & Therapy, 32*(5), 477–495. doi:10.1016/0005-7967(94)90135-X

Eysenck, H. J. (Ed.). (1981). *A model for personality.* New York: Springer-Verlag.

Fabrega, H., Jr. (2004). Culture and the origins of psychopathology. In U. P. Gielen, J. M., Fish, et al. (Eds.), *Handbook of culture, therapy, and healing* (pp. 15–35). Mahwah, NJ: Erlbaum.

Fain, G. L. (2003). *Sensory transduction.* Sunderland, MA: Sinauer.

Fandakova, Y., Shing, Y., & Lindenberger, U. (2012). Differences in binding and monitoring mechanisms contribute to lifespan age differences in false memory. *Developmental Psychology,* doi:10.1037/a0031361

Fantz, R. L. (1961). The origin of form perception. *Scientific American*, May, 71.

Farah, M. J. (2004). *Visual agnosia* (2nd ed.). Cambridge, MA: MIT Press.

Farah, M. J. (2006). Prosopagnosia. In M. J. Farah, & T. E. Feinberg (Eds.), *Patient-based approaches to cognitive neuroscience* (2nd ed., pp. 123–125). Cambridge, MA: MIT Press.

Farah, M. J., Haimm, C., et al. (2009). When we enhance cognition with Adderall, do we sacrifice creativity? A preliminary study. *Psychopharmacology, 202*(1–3), 541–547. doi:10.1007/s00213-008-1369-3

Farah, M. J., Illes, J., et al. (2004). Neurocognitive enhancement: What can we do and what should we do?

Nature Reviews Neuroscience, 5, 421–425. doi:10.1038/nrn1390

Faraut, B., Boudjeltia, K. Z., et al. (2011). Benefits of napping and an extended duration of recovery sleep on alertness and immune cells after acute sleep restriction. *Brain, Behavior, & Immunity, 25*(1), 16–24. doi:10.1016/j.bbi.2010.08.001

Farrand, P., Confue, P., et al. (2009). Guided self-help supported by paraprofessional mental health workers: An uncontrolled before-after cohort study. *Health & Social Care in the Community, 17*(1), 9–17. doi:10.1111/j.1365-2524.2008.00792.x

Farroni, T., Massaccesi, S., et al. (2004). Gaze following in newborns. *Infancy, 5*(1), 39–60. doi:10.1207/s15327078in0501_2

Faurie, C., Bonenfant, S., et al. (2008). Socio-economic status and handedness in two large cohorts of French adults. *British Journal of Psychology, 99*(4), 533–554. doi:10.1348/000712608X291563

Fayek, A. (2010). *The crisis in psychoanalysis: In search of a lost doctrine.* Austin, TX: Bridgeway Books.

Federal Bureau of Investigation. (2012). *Crime in the United States, 2011.* Retrieved May 16, 2013, from http://www.fbi.gov/about-us/cjis/ucr/crime-in-the-u.s/2011/crime-in-the-u.s.-2011/violent-crime/violent-crime

Feingold, A. (1992). Gender differences in mate selection preferences. *Psychological Bulletin, 111*, 304–341.

Feldman, S. (2003). Enforcing social conformity: A theory of authoritarianism. *Political Psychology, 24*(1), 41–47. doi:10.1111/0162-895X.00316

Fenigstein, A. (2009). Private and public self-consciousness. In M. R. Leary & R. H. Hoyle (Eds.), *Handbook of individual differences in social behavior* (pp. 495–511). New York: Guilford.

Fenton, M. C., Keyes, K., et al. (2012). Psychiatric comorbidity and the persistence of drug use disorders in the United States. *Addiction, 107*(3), 599–609. doi:10.1111/j.1360-0443.2011.03638.x

Ferguson, C. J., & Dyck, D. (2012). Paradigm change in aggression research: The time has come to retire the General Aggression Model. *Aggression & Violent Behavior, 17*(3), 220–228. doi:10.1016/j.avb.2012.02.007

Ferguson, C. J., & Garza, A. (2011). Call of (civic) Duty: Action games and civic behavior in a large sample of youth. *Computers in Human Behavior, 27,* 770–775. doi:10.1016/j.chb.2010.10.026

Ferguson, C. J., Miguel, C. N., & Hartley, R. D. (2009). A multivariate analysis of youth violence and aggression: The influence of family, peers,

depression, and media violence. *Journal of Pediatrics, 155*(6), 904–908. doi:10.1016/j.jpeds.2009.06.021

Fernald, A. (1989). Intonation and communicative intent in mothers' speech to infants: Is the melody the message? *Child Development, 60*(6), 1497–1510. doi:10.2307/1130938

Fernald, A., Perfors, A., & Marchman, V. A. (2006). Picking up speed in understanding: Speech processing efficiency and vocabulary growth across the 2nd year. *Developmental Psychology, 42*(1), 98–116. doi:10.1037/0012-1649.42.1.98

Fernandez, J., Grizzell, J., & Wecker, L. (2013). The role of estrogen receptor β and nicotinic cholinergic receptors in postpartum depression. *Progress in Neuro-Psychopharmacology & Biological Psychiatry, 40*, 199–206. doi:10.1016/j.pnpbp.2012.10.002

Féron, F., Perry, C., et al. (2005). Autologous olfactory ensheathing cell transplantation in human spinal cord injury. *Brain: A Journal of Neurology, 128*(12), 2951–2960. doi:10.1093/brain/awh657

Ferrari, J. R., & Pychyl, T. A. (2012). 'If I wait, my partner will do it:' The role of conscientiousness as a mediator in the relation of academic procrastination and perceived social loafing. *North American Journal of Psychology, 14*(1), 13–24.

Ferrari, J. R., & Scher, S. J. (2000). Toward an understanding of academic and nonacademic tasks procrastinated by students: The use of daily logs. *Psychology in the Schools, 37*(4), 359–366. doi:10.1002/1520-6807(200007)37:4<367::AID-PITS7>3.0.CO;2-Y

Festinger, L. (1957). *A theory of cognitive dissonance.* Stanford, CA: Stanford University Press.

Festinger, L., & Carlsmith, J. M. (1959). Cognitive consequences of forced compliance. *Journal of Abnormal & Social Psychology, 58*, 203–210. doi:10.1037/h0041593

Ficca, G., & Salzarulo, P. (2004). What in sleep is for memory. *Sleep Medicine, 5*, 225–230. doi:10.1016/j.sleep.2004.01.018

Ficca, G., Axelsson, J., et al. (2010). Naps, cognition and performance. *Sleep Medicine Reviews, 14*(4), 249–258. doi:10.1016/j.smrv.2009.09.005

Field, J. E., Kolbert, J. B., et al. (2009). *Understanding girl bullying and what to do about it: Strategies to help heal the divide.* Thousand Oaks, CA: Corwin Press.

Fields, R. D. (2007). The shark's electric sense. *Scientific American, 297*(8), 74–81.

Fields, R. M., & Margolin, J. (2001). *Coping with trauma.* Washington: American Psychological Association.

Filbey, F. M., Schacht, J. P., et al. (2009). Marijuana craving in the brain. *Proceedings of the National Academy of Sciences, 106*(31), 13016–13021. doi:10.1073/pnas.0903863106

Fine, C. (2010). *Delusions of gender.* New York: Norton.

Fine, L. E. (2011). Minimizing heterosexism and homophobia: Constructing meaning of out campus LGB life. *Journal of Homosexuality, 58*(4), 521–546. doi:10.1080/00918369.2011.555673

Fink, M. (2013). Rediscovering catatonia: The biography of a treatable syndrome. *Acta Psychiatrica Scandinavica, 127*(Suppl 441), 1–47. doi:10.1111/acps.12038

Fink, M., Shorter, E., & Taylor, M. A. (2010). Catatonia is not schizophrenia: Kraepelin's error and the need to recognize catatonia as an independent syndrome in medical nomenclature. *Schizophrenia Bulletin, 36*(2), 314–320. doi:10.1093/schbul/sbp059

Fiore, D., Dimaggio, G., et al. (2008). Metacognitive interpersonal therapy in a case of obsessive-compulsive and avoidant personality disorders. *Journal of Clinical Psychology, 64*(2), 168–180. doi:10.1002/jclp.20450

Fiorina, C. (2006). *Tough choices: A memoir.* New York: Penguin.

Fireman, G., Kose, G., & Solomon, M. J. (2003). Self-observation and learning: The effect of watching oneself on problem solving performance. *Cognitive Development, 18*(3), 339–354. doi:10.1016/S0885-2014(03)00038-8

Firestone, P., Kingston, D. A., et al. (2006). Long-term follow-up of exhibitionists: Psychological, phallometric, and offense characteristics. *Journal of the American Academy of Psychiatry & the Law, 34*(3), 349–359.

Fischer, A. H., Manstead, A. S., et al. (2004). Gender and culture differences in emotion. *Emotion, 4*(1), 87–94. doi:10.1037/1528-3542.4.1.87

Fischer, C., & Kächele, H. (2009). Comparative analysis of patients' dreams in Freudian and Jungian treatment. *International Journal of Psychotherapy, 13*(3), 34–40.

Fischer, P., & Greitemeyer, T. (2013). The positive bystander effect: Passive bystanders increase helping in situations with high expected negative consequences for the helper. *Journal of Social Psychology, 153*(1), 1–5. doi:10.1080/00224545.2012.697931

Fischer, P., Kastenmüller, A., Greitemeyer, T. (2010). Media violence and the self: The impact of personalized gaming characters in aggressive video games on aggressive behavior. *Journal of Experimental Social Psychology, 46*(1), 192–195. doi:10.1016/j.jesp.2009.06.010

Fischer, P., Krueger, J. I., et al. (2011). The bystander-effect: A meta-analytic review on bystander intervention in dangerous and non-dangerous emergencies. *Psychological Bulletin, 137*(4), 517–537. doi:10.1037/a0023304

Fisher, B. S., Cullen, F. T., & Daigle, L. E. (2005). The discovery of acquaintance rape: The salience of methodological innovation and rigor. *Journal of Interpersonal Violence, 20*(4), 493–500.

Fisher, R. P., & Geiselman, R. E. (1987). Enhancing eyewitness memory with the cognitive interview. In M. M. Gruneberg, P. E. Morris, et al. (Eds.), *Practical aspects of memory: Current research and issues* (pp. 34–39). New York: Wiley.

Fiske, S. T., Cuddy, A. J., et al. (2002). A model of (often mixed) stereotype content: Competence and warmth respectively follow from perceived status and competition. *Journal of Personality & Social Psychology, 82*(6), 878–902. doi:10.1037/0022-3514.82.6.878

Flanagan, M. B., May, J. G., & Dobie, T. G. (2004). The role of vection, eye movements and postural instability in the etiology of motion sickness. *Journal of Vestibular Research: Equilibrium & Orientation, 14*(4), 335–346.

Flaskerud, J. H. (2009). What do we need to know about the culture-bound syndromes? *Issues in Mental Health Nursing, 30*(6), 406–407. doi:10.1080/01612840902812947

Flegal, K. M., Carroll, M. D., et al. (2010). Prevalence and trends in obesity among U.S. adults, 1999–2008. *Journal of the American Medical Association, 303*(3), 235–241. doi:10.1001/jama.2009.2014

Fleming, J. (2012). The effectiveness of eye movement desensitization and reprocessing in the treatment of traumatized children and youth. *Journal of EMDR Practice and Research, 6*(1), 16–26. doi:10.1891/1933-3196.6.1.16

Florida Medical Examiners Commission. (2012). *Drugs identified in deceased persons by Florida Medical Examiners: 2011 interim report.* Retrieved March 5, 2013, from http://www.fdle.state.fl.us/Content/getdoc/2f283e2e-a2b5-403b-865e-0a7e8fef6f28/2011-Interim-Drug-Report.aspx

Floridi, L., Taddeo, M., & Turilli, M. (2009). Turing's imitation game: Still an impossible challenge for all machines and some judges: An evaluation of the 2008 Loebner contest. *Minds & Machines, 19*(1), 145–150. doi:10.1007/s11023-008-9130-6

Flowe, H. D., & Ebbese, E. B. (2007). The effect of lineup member similarity on recognition accuracy in simultaneous and sequential lineups. *Law & Human Behavior, 31*(1), 33–52. doi:10.1007/s10979-006-9045-9

Flowers, S. (2011). Mindfully shy. In B. Boyce (Ed.), *The mindfulness revolution: Leading psychologists, scientists,* artists, and meditation teachers on the power of mindfulness in daily life (pp. 166–176). Boston: Shambhala.

Flynn, B. S., Worden, J. K., et al. (2011). Evaluation of smoking prevention television messages based on the elaboration likelihood model. *Health Education Research, 26*(6), 976–987. doi:10.1093/her/cyr082

Flynn, J. R. (2012). *Are we getting smarter? Rising IQ in the twenty-first century.* New York: Cambridge University Press. doi:10.1017/CBO9781139235679

Fochtmann, L. J. (1995). Intractable sneezing as a conversion symptom. *Psychosomatics, 36*(2), 103–112. doi:10.1016/S0033-3182(95)71679-6

Foley, H. J., & Matlin, M. W. (2010). *Sensation and perception* (5th ed.). Boston: Pearson/Allyn & Bacon.

Folkman, S., & Moskowitz, J. T. (2004). Coping: Pitfalls and promise. *Annual Review of Psychology, 55,* 745–774. doi:10.1146/annurev.psych.55.090902.141456

Fontaine, K. R., Redden, D. T., et al. (2003). Years of life lost due to obesity. *Journal of the American Medical Association, 289,* 187–193. doi:10.1001/jama.289.2.187

Foo, P., Warren, W. H., et al. (2005). Do humans integrate routes into a cognitive map? Map- versus landmark-based navigation of novel shortcuts. *Journal of Experimental Psychology: Learning, Memory, & Cognition, 31*(2), 195–215. doi:10.1037/0278-7393.31.2.195

Foot, M., & Koszycki, D. (2004). Gender differences in anxiety-related traits in patients with panic disorder. *Depression & Anxiety, 20*(3), 123–130. doi:10.1002/da.20031

Forbes, G. B., Adams-Curtis, L. E., & White, K. B. (2004). First- and second-generation measures of sexism, rape myths and related beliefs, and hostility toward women: Their interrelationships and association with college students' experiences with dating aggression and sexual coercion. *Violence against Women, 10*(3), 236–261.

Ford, G. G., Gallagher, S. H., et al. (1999). Repositioning the home plate umpire to provide enhanced perceptual cues and more accurate ball-strike judgments. *Journal of Sport Behavior, 22*(1), 28–44.

Ford, J. D. (2012). Ethnoracial and educational differences in victimization history, trauma-related symptoms, and coping style. *Psychological Trauma: Theory, Research, Practice, & Policy, 4*(2), 177–185. doi:10.1037/a0023670

Forgas, J. P., Cooper, J., & Crano, W. D. (Eds.) (2010). *The psychology of attitudes and attitude change.* New York: Psychology Press.

Forney, W. S., Forney, J. C., & Crutsinger, C. (2005). Developmental stages of age and moral reasoning as predictors of juvenile delinquents' behavioral intention to steal clothing. *Family & Consumer Sciences Research Journal, 34*(2), 110–126. doi:10.1177/1077727X05280666

Forsyth, D. R. (2014). *Group dynamics* (6th ed.). Belmont, CA: Cengage Learning/Wadsworth.

Fortunato, L., Young, A. M., et al. (2010). Hook-up sexual experiences and problem behaviors among adolescents. *Journal of Child & Adolescent Substance Abuse, 19*(3), 261–278.

Foster, C. A., Witcher, B. S., et al. (1998). Arousal and attraction: Evidence for automatic and controlled processes. *Journal of Personality & Social Psychology, 74*(1), 86–101. doi:10.1037/0022-3514.74.1.86

Foster, E. A., Franks, D. W., et al. (2012). Social network correlates of food availability in an endangered population of killer whales, Orcinus orca. *Animal Behaviour, 83*(3), 731–736. doi:10.1016/j.anbehav.2011.12.021

Foster, G., & Ysseldyke, J. (1976). Expectancy and halo effects as a result of artificially induced teacher bias. *Contemporary Educational Psychology, 1,* 37–45. doi:10.1016/0361-476X(76)90005-9

Fougnie, D., & Marois, R. (2007). Executive working memory load induces inattentional blindness. *Psychonomic Bulletin & Review, 14*(1), 142–147. doi:10.3758/BF03194041

Fournier, N. M., & Duman, R. S. (2012). Role of vascular endothelial growth factor in adult hippocampal neurogenesis: Implications for the pathophysiology and treatment of depression. *Behavioural Brain Research, 227*(2), 440–449. doi:10.1016/j.bbr.2011.04.022

Fowers, B. J., & Davidov, B. J. (2006). The virtue of multiculturalism: Personal transformation, character, and openness to the other. *American Psychologist, 61*(6), 581–594. doi:10.1037/0003-066X.61.6.581

Fowler, J. H., & Christakis, N. A. (2010). Cooperative behavior cascades in human social networks. *Proceedings of the National Academy of Sciences, 107*(12), 5334–5338. doi:10.1073/pnas.0913149107

Frances, A. (2012). DSM 5 Is guide not bible—Ignore its ten worst changes. *Psychology Today.* Retrieved April 29, 2013, from http://www.psychologytoday.com/blog/dsm5-in-distress/201212/dsm-5-is-guide-not-bible-ignore-its-ten-worst-changes

Frank, J. D., & Frank, J. (2004). Therapeutic components shared by all psychotherapies. In A. Freeman, M. J. Mahoney, et al. (Eds.), *Cognition* and psychotherapy (2nd ed., pp. 45–78). New York: Springer.

Frankl, V. (1955). *The doctor and the soul.* New York: Knopf.

Franzoi, S. L., & Klaiber, J. R. (2007). Body use and reference group impact: With whom do we compare our bodies? *Sex Roles, 56*(3–4), 205–214. doi:10.1007/s11199-006-9162-4

Frazier, A. (2012). The possible selves of high-ability African males attending a residential high school for highly able youth. *Journal for the Education of the Gifted, 35*(4), 366–390. doi:10.1177/0162353212461565

Freberg, L.A. (2010). *Discovering biological psychology* (2nd ed.). Belmont, CA: Cengage Learning/Wadsworth.

Frederickson, N., Petrides, K. V., & Simmonds, E. (2012). Trait emotional intelligence as a predictor of socioemotional outcomes in early adolescence. *Personality & Individual Differences, 52*(3), 323–328. doi:10.1016/j.paid.2011.10.034

Fredrickson, B. L. (2003). The value of positive emotions. *American Scientist, 91,* 330–335. doi:10.1511/2003.4.330

Fredrickson, B. L., & Branigan, C. (2005). Positive emotions broaden the scope of attention and thought-action repertoires. *Cognition & Emotion, 19*(3), 313–332. doi:10.1080/02699930441000238

Freedman, D. H. (2011). How to fix the obesity crisis. *Scientific American, February,* 40–47. doi:10.1038/scientificamerican0211-40

Freeman, D., & Garety, P. A. (2004). *Paranoia: The psychology of persecutory delusions.* New York: Routledge.

Freeman, J. H., & Steinmetz, A. B. (2011). Neural circuitry and plasticity mechanisms underlying delay eyeblink conditioning. *Learning & Memory, 18,* 666–677. doi:10.1101/lm.2023011

French, C. C., Fowler, M., et al. (1991). A test of the Barnum effect. *Skeptical Inquirer, 15*(4), 66–72.

French, S. E., Kim, T. E., & Pillado, O. (2006). Ethnic identity, social group membership, and youth violence. In N. G. Guerra & E. P. Smith (Eds.), *Preventing youth violence in a multicultural society* (pp. 47–73). Washington: American Psychological Association.

Freud, S. (1900). *The interpretation of dreams.* London: Hogarth.

Freud, S. (1949). *An outline of psychoanalysis.* New York: Norton.

Freund, A. M., & Ritter, J. O. (2009). Midlife crisis: A debate. *Gerontology, 55*(5), 582–591. doi:10.1159/000227322

Frew, J. (2013). Gestalt therapy. In J. Frew & M. D. Spiegler (Eds.), *Contemporary psychotherapies for a diverse world* (pp. 215–257). New York: Routledge/Taylor & Francis.

Friedman, H. S. (2002). *Health psychology* (2nd ed.). Englewood Cliffs, NJ: Prentice-Hall.

Friedman, L. J. (2006). What is psychoanalysis? *Psychoanalytic Quarterly, 75*(3), 689–713.

Friedman, L. J. (2004). Erik Erikson on generativity: A biographer's perspective. In E. de St. Aubin, D. P. McAdams, et al. (Eds.), *The generative society: Caring for future generations* (pp. 257–264). Washington: American Psychological Association. doi:10.1037/10622-016

Friedman, M., & Rosenman, R. H. (1983). *Type A behavior and your heart.* New York: Knopf.

Friese, M., Messner, C., & Schaffner, Y. (2012). Mindfulness meditation counteracts self-control depletion. *Consciousness & Cognition, 21*(2), 1016–1022. doi:10.1016/j.concog.2012.01.008.

Fritz, C. O., Morris, P. E., et al. (2007). Comparing and combining retrieval practice and the keyword mnemonic for foreign vocabulary learning. *Applied Cognitive Psychology, 21*(4), 499–526. doi:10.1002/acp.1287

Fry, R. (2012). *Improve your memory* (6th ed.). Belmont, CA: Cengage Learning/Wadsworth.

Fryar, C. D., Hirsch, R., et al. (2007). Drug use and sexual behaviors reported by adults: United States, 1999–2002. *Advance data from vital and health statistics; no. 384.* Retrieved June 5, 2013, from http://www.cdc.gov/nchs/data/ad/ad384.pdf

Frydman, M. (1999). Television, aggressiveness and violence. *International Journal of Adolescent Medicine & Health, 11*(3–4), 335–344. doi:10.1515/IJAMH.1999.11.3-4.335

Fu, J. H., Morris, M. W., et al. (2007). Epistemic motives and cultural conformity: Need for closure, culture, and context as determinants of conflict judgments. *Journal of Personality & Social Psychology, 92*(2), 191–207. doi:10.1037/0022-3514.92.2.191

Fuchs, C., & Obrist, M. (2010). HCI and society: Towards a typology of universal design principles. *International Journal of Human-Computer Interaction, 26*(6), 638–656.

Fukai, S., Akishita, M., et al. (2010). Effects of testosterone in older men with mild-to-moderate cognitive impairment. *Journal of the American Geriatrics Society, 58*(7), 1419–1421.

Fuller-Rowell, T. E., Evans, G. W., & Ong, A. D. (2012). Poverty and health: The mediating role of perceived discrimination. *Psychological Science, 23*(7), 734–739. doi:10.1177/0956797612439720

Fuller, T. E. (2012). *The insanity offense: How America's failure to treat the seriously mentally ill endangers its citizens.* New York: Norton.

Funder, D. C. (2010). *The personality puzzle* (5th ed.). New York: Norton.

Funk, J. B. (2005). Children's exposure to violent video games and desensitization to violence. *Child & Adolescent Psychiatric Clinics of North America, 14*(3), 387–404. doi:10.1016/j.chc.2005.02.009

Fuqua, D. R., & Newman, J. L. (2002). Creating caring organizations. *Consulting Psychology Journal: Practice & Research, 54*(2), 131–140.

Gable, S. L., Reis, H. T., et al. (2004). What do you do when things go right? *Journal of Personality & Social Psychology, 87*(2), 228–245. doi:10.1037/0022-3514.87.2.228

Gadzella, B. M. (1995). Differences in processing information among psychology course grade groups. *Psychological Reports, 77,* 1312–1314.

Gaertner, S. L., Dovidio, J. F., et al. (2000). Reducing intergroup conflict: From superordinate goals to decategorization, recategorization, and mutual differentiation. *Group Dynamics, 4*(1), 98–114. doi:10.1037/1089-2699.4.1.98

Galambos, N. L., Barker, E. T., & Tilton-Weaver, L. C. (2003). Who gets caught at maturity gap? A study of pseudomature, immature and mature adolescents. *International Journal of Behavioral Development, 27*(3), 253–263. doi:10.1080/01650250244000326

Galankin, T., Shekunova, E., & Zvartau, E. (2010). Estradiol lowers intracranial self-stimulation thresholds and enhances cocaine facilitation of intracranial self-stimulation in rats. *Hormones & Behavior, 58*(5), 827–834. doi:10.1016/j.yhbeh.2010.08.006

Galanter, M. (2013). Charismatic groups and cults: A psychological and social analysis. In K. I. Pargament, J. J. Exline, et al. (Eds.), *APA handbook of psychology, religion, and spirituality* (Vol. 1): *Context, theory, and research* (pp. 729–740). Washington, DC: American Psychological Association. doi:10.1037/14045-041

Galanter, M., Hayden, F., et al. (2005). Group therapy, self-help groups, and network therapy. In R. J. Frances, S. I. Miller, et al. (Eds.), *Clinical textbook of addictive disorders* (3rd ed., pp. 502–527). New York: Guilford.

Galati, D., Scherer, K. R., & Ricci-Bitti, P. E. (1997). Voluntary facial expression of emotion: Comparing congenitally blind with normally sighted encoders. *Journal of Personality & Social Psychology, 73*(6), 1363–1379. doi:10.1037/0022-3514.73.6.1363

Galea, S., & Resnick, H. (2005). Posttraumatic stress disorder in the general population after mass terrorist incidents: Considerations about the nature of exposure. *CNS Spectrums, 10*(2), 107–115.

Galea, S., Ahern, J., et al. (2002). Psychological sequelae of the September 11 terrorist attacks in New York City. *New England Journal of Medicine, 346*(13), 982–987. doi:10.1056/NEJMsa013404

Gallagher, S. (2004). Nailing the lie: An interview with Jonathan Cole. *Journal of Consciousness Studies, 11*(2), 3–21.

Gallavan, D. B., & Newman, J. L. (2013). Predictors of burnout among correctional mental health professionals. *Psychological Services, 10*(1), 115–122. doi:10.1037/a0031341

Gallese, V., Rochat, M. J., & Berchio, C. (2013). The mirror mechanism and its potential role in autism spectrum disorder. *Developmental Medicine & Child Neurology, 55*(1), 15–22. doi:10.1111/j.1469-8749.2012.04398.x

Galliher, R. V., Jones, M. D., & Dahl, A. (2011). Concurrent and longitudinal effects of ethnic identity and experiences of discrimination on psychosocial adjustment of Navajo adolescents. *Developmental Psychology, 47*(2), 509–526. doi:10.1037/a0021061

Gallucci, N. T. (2008). *Sport psychology: Performance enhancement, performance inhibition, individuals, and teams.* New York: Psychology Press.

Gamache, G. (2004). *Essentials in human factors.* San Mateo, CA: Usernomics.

Ganis, G. (2013). Visual mental imagery. In S. Lacey, & R. Lawson (Eds.), *Multisensory imagery* (pp. 9–28). New York: Springer. doi:10.1007/978-1-4614-5879-1_2

Ganis, G., Thompson, W. L., & Kosslyn, S. M. (2004). Brain areas underlying visual mental imagery and visual perception: An fMRI study. *Cognitive Brain Research, 20*(2), 226–241. doi:10.1016/j.cogbrainres.2004.02.012

Ganster, D. C., Fox, M. L., & Dwyer, D. J. (2001). Explaining employees' health care costs: A prospective examination of stressful job demands, personal control, and physiological reactivity. *Journal of Applied Psychology, 86,* 954–964. doi:10.1037/0021-9010.86.5.954

Garcia-Barrera, M. A., Direnfeld, E., et al. (2013). Psychological assessment: From interviewing to objective and projective measurement. In C. A. Noggle, & R. S. Dean (Eds.), *The neuropsychology of psychopathology* (pp. 473–493). New York: Springer.

Garcia, E. E. (2008). Bilingual education in the United States. In J. Altarriba & R. R. Heredia (Eds.), *An introduction to bilingualism: Principles and processes* (pp. 321–343). Mahwah, NJ: Erlbaum.

Gardner, H. (2008). Birth and the spreading of a "meme." In J. Q. Chen, S. Moran, et al. (Eds.), *Multiple intelligences around the world* (pp. 3–16). San Francisco: Jossey-Bass.

Gardner, H. (2011). The theory of multiple intelligences. In M. A. Gernsbacher, R. W. Pew, et al. (Eds.), *Psychology and the real world: Essays illustrating fundamental contributions to society* (pp. 122–130). New York: Worth.

Garland, A. F., & Zigler, E. (1999). Emotional and behavioral problems among highly intellectually gifted youth. *Roeper Review, 22*(1), 41–44. doi:10.1080/02783199909553996

Garlow, S. J., Purselle, D. C., & Heninger, M. (2007). Cocaine and alcohol use preceding suicide in African American and white adolescents. *Journal of Psychiatric Research, 41*(6), 530–536. doi:10.1016/j.jpsychires.2005.08.008

Garrosa, E., Moreno-Jiménez, B., et al. (2008). The relationship between socio-demographic variables, job stressors, burnout, and hardy personality in nurses: An exploratory study. *International Journal of Nursing Studies, 45*(3), 418–427. doi:10.1016/j.ijnurstu.2006.09.003

Gass, R. H., & Seiter, J. S. (2014). *Persuasion: Social influence and compliance gaining* (5th ed.). Boston: Allyn & Bacon.

Gastner, M. T., Shalizi, C. R., & Newman, M. E. J. (2005). Maps and cartograms of the 2004 US presidential election results. *Advances in Complex Systems, 8*(1), 117–123. doi:10.1142/S0219525905000397

Gates, A. I. (1917). Recitation as a factor in memorizing. *Archives of Psychology, 40,* 104.

Gatchel, R. J., & Oordt, M. S. (2003). Insomnia. In R. J. Gatchel, & M. S. Oordt (Eds.), *Clinical health psychology and primary care: Practical advice and clinical guidance for successful collaboration* (pp. 135–148). Washington: American Psychological Association. doi:10.1037/10592-008

Gauquelin, M. (1970). *Astrology and science.* London: Peter Davies.

Gawronski, B. (2012). Back to the future of dissonance theory: Cognitive consistency as a core motive. *Social Cognition, 30*(6), 652–668. doi:10.1521/soco.2012.30.6.652

Gayle, H. (2000). An overview of the global HIV/AIDS epidemic, with a focus on the United States. *AIDS, 14*(Suppl 2), S8–S17.

Geddes, L. (2008). Could brain scans ever be safe evidence? *New Scientist, Oct 3,* 8–9.

Gegenfurtner, K. R., & Kiper, D. C. (2003). Color vision. *Annual Review of Neuroscience, 26,* 181–206. doi:10.1146/annurev.neuro.26.041002.131116

Geiselman, R. E., Fisher, R. P., et al. (1986). Enhancement of eyewitness memory with the cognitive interview. *American Journal of Psychology, 99,* 385–401.

Gejman, P. V., Sanders, A. R., & Duan, J. (2010). The role of genetics in the etiology of schizophrenia. *Psychiatric Clinics of North America, 33*(1), 35–66. doi:10.1016/j.psc.2009.12.003

Genty, E., Breuer, T., et al. (2009). Gestural communication of the gorilla (Gorilla gorilla): Repertoire, intentionality, and possible origins. *Animal Cognition, 12*(3), 527–546. doi:10.1007/s10071-009-0213-4

Gerardi, M., Rothbaum, B. O., et al., (2008). Virtual reality exposure therapy using a virtual Iraq: Case report. *Journal of Traumatic Stress, 21*(2), 209–213. doi:10.1002/jts.20331

Gerjets, P., Kammerer, Y., & Werner, B. (2011). Measuring spontaneous and instructed evaluation processes during Web search: Integrating concurrent thinking-aloud protocols and eye-tracking data. *Learning & Instruction, 21*(2), 220–231.

Germain, A., Krakow, B., et al. (2004). Increased mastery elements associated with imagery rehearsal treatment for nightmares in sexual assault survivors with PTSD. *Dreaming, 14*(4), 195–206. doi:10.1037/1053-0797.14.4.195

German, T. P., & Defeyter, M. A. (2000). Immunity to functional fixedness in young children. *Psychonomic Bulletin & Review, 7*(4), 707–712. doi:10.3758/BF03213010

Gershman, S. J., & Niv, Y. (2010). Learning latent structure: Carving nature at its joints. *Current Opinion in Neurobiology, 20*(2), 251–256. doi:10.1016/j.conb.2010.02.008

Gershoff, E. T., & Bitensky, S. H. (2007). The case against corporal punishment of children: Converging evidence from social science research and international human rights law and implications for U.S. public policy. *Psychology, Public Policy, & Law, 13*(4), 231–272. doi:10.1037/1076-8971.13.4.231

Gerstein, E. R. (2002). Manatees, bioacoustics, and boats. *American Scientist, 90*(March–April), 154–163. doi:10.1511/2002.2.154

Geschwind, N. (1979). Specializations of the human brain. *Scientific American, 241,* 180–199. doi:10.1038/scientificamerican0979-180

Ghaemi, S. N. (2010). *The rise and fall of the biopsychosocial model: Reconciling art and science in psychiatry.* Baltimore, MD: Johns Hopkins University Press.

Gheitury, A., Sahraee, A., & Hoseini, M. (2012). Language acquisition in late critical period: A case report. *Deafness & Education International, 14*(3), 122–135. doi:10.1179/1557069X12Y.0000000008

Giancola, P. R., Josephs, R. A., et al. (2010). Alcohol myopia revisited: Clarifying aggression and other acts of disinhibition through a distorted lens. *Perspectives on Psychological Science, 5*(3), 265–278. doi:10.1177/1745691610369467

Giarratano, J. C., & Riley, G. (2004). *Expert systems, principles and programming* (4th ed.). Belmont, CA: Cengage Learning/Wadsworth.

Gibson, E. J., & Walk, R. D. (1960). The "visual cliff." *Scientific American, 202*(4), 67–71. doi:10.1038/scientificamerican0460-64

Gilboa, A., & Tal-Shmotkin, M. (2012). String quartets as self-managed teams: An interdisciplinary perspective. *Psychology of Music, 40*(1), 19–41. doi:10.1177/0305735610377593

Gilchrist, A. L., Cowan, N., & Naveh-Benjamin, M. (2009). Investigating the childhood development of working memory using sentences: New evidence for the growth of chunk capacity. *Journal of Experimental Child Psychology, 104*(2), 252–265. doi:10.1016/j.jecp.2009.05.006

Gilhooly, K. J., Fioratou, E., et al. (2007). Divergent thinking: Strategies and executive involvement in generating novel uses for familiar objects. *British Journal of Psychology, 98,* 611–625. doi:10.1111/j.2044-8295.2007.tb00467.x

Gillespie-Lynch, K., Greenfield, P. M., Lyn, et al. (2011). The role of dialogue in the ontogeny and phylogeny of early symbol combinations: A cross-species comparison of bonobo, chimpanzee, and human learners. *First Language, 31*(4), 442–460. doi:10.1177/0142723711406882

Gillespie, C. F., & Nemeroff, C. B. (2007). Corticotropin-releasing factor and the psychobiology of early-life stress. *Current Directions in Psychological Science, 16*(2), 85–89. doi:10.1111/j.1467-8721.2007.00481.x

Gilligan, C. (1982). *In a different voice.* Cambridge, MA: Harvard University Press.

Gino, F. & Flynn, F. J. (2011). Give them what they want: The benefits of explicitness in gift exchange. *Journal of Experimental Social Psychology, 47,* 915–922. doi:10.1016/j.jesp.2011.03.015

Giummarra, M. J., Gibson, S. J., et al. (2007). Central mechanisms in phantom limb perception: The past, present and future. *Brain Research Reviews, 54*(1), 219–232. doi:10.1016/j.brainresrev.2007.01.009

Gladwell, M. (2005). *Blink: The power of thinking without thinking.* New York: Little, Brown.

Glass, J., & Owen, J. (2010). Latino fathers: The relationship among machismo, acculturation, ethnic identity, and paternal involvement. *Psychology of Men & Masculinity, 11*(4), 251–261. doi:10.1037/a0021477

Glassgold, J. M., Beckstead, L., et al. (2009). *Report of the American Psychological Association Task Force on appropriate therapeutic responses to sexual orientation.* Retrieved June 11, 2013, from http://www.apa.org/pi/lgbt/resources/therapeutic-response.pdf

Gleason, J. B., & Ratner, N. B. (2013). *The development of language* (8th ed.). Boston: Allyn & Bacon.

Glenn, E. N. (Ed.). (2009). *Shades of difference: Why skin color matters.* Palo Alto, CA: Stanford University Press.

Glick, P. (2008). When neighbors blame neighbors: Scapegoating and the breakdown of ethnic relations. In V. M. Esses & R. A. Vernon (Eds.), *Explaining the breakdown of ethnic relations: Why neighbors kill: Social issues and interventions* (pp. 123–146). Malden, MA: Blackwell. doi:10.1002/9781444303056.ch6

Global Footprint Network (2011). *Personal footprint.* Retrieved May 22, 2013, from http://www.footprintnetwork.org/en/index.php/GFN/page/personal_footprint/

Global Footprint Network (2012a). *World footprint: Do we fit on the planet?* Retrieved May 22, 2013, from http://www.footprintnetwork.org/en/index.php/GFN/page/world_footprint/

Global Footprint Network. (2012b). *Footprint basics: Overview.* Retrieved March 14, 2013, from http://www.footprintnetwork.org/en/index.php/GFN/page/footprint_basics_overview

Gloria-Bottini, F., Magrini, A., & Bottini, E. (2009). The effect of genetic and seasonal factors on birth weight. *Early Human Development, 85*(7), 439–441. doi:10.1016/j.earlhumdev.2009.02.004

Glover, R. J. (2001). Discriminators of moral orientation: Gender role or personality? *Journal of Adult Development, 8*(1), 1–7.

Gobet, F. (2005). Chunking models of expertise: Implications for education. *Applied Cognitive Psychology, 19*(2), 183–204. doi:10.1002/acp.1110

Gobet, F., & Simon, H. A. (1996). Recall of random and distorted chess positions: Implications for the theory of expertise. *Memory & Cognition, 24*(4), 493–503. doi:10.3758/BF03200937

Göckeritz, S., Schultz, P. W., et al. (2010). Descriptive normative beliefs and conservation behavior: The moderating roles of personal involvement and injunctive normative beliefs. *European Journal of Social Psychology, 40*(3), 514–523. doi:10.1002/ejsp.643

Godnig, E. C. (2003). Tunnel vision: Its causes & treatment strategies. *Journal of Behavioral Optometry, 14*(4), 95–99.

Goel, N. (2012). Genetics of sleep timing, duration, and homeostasis in humans. *Sleep Medicine Clinics, 7*(3), 443–454. doi:10.1016/j.jsmc.2012.06.013

Gogate, L. J., Bahrick, L. E., & Watson, J. D. (2000). A study of multimodal motherese: The role of temporal synchrony between verbal labels and gestures. *Child Development, 71*(4), 878–894. doi:10.1111/1467-8624.00197

Goldberg, C. (2001). Of prophets, true believers, and terrorists. *The Dana Forum on Brain Science, 3*(3), 21–24.

Goldberg, R. (2010). *Drugs across the spectrum* (6th ed.). Belmont, CA: Cengage Learning/Wadsworth.

Golden, T. D., Veiga, J. F., & Simsek, Z. (2006). Telecommuting's differential impact on work-family conflict: Is there no place like home? *Journal of Applied Psychology, 91*(6), 1340–1350.

Goldenberg, H., & Goldenberg, I. (2013). *Family therapy: An overview* (8th ed.). Pacific Grove, CA: Brooks/Cole.

Goldfried, M. R. (2001). Integrating gay, lesbian, and bisexual issues into mainstream psychology. *American Psychologist,* (Nov.), 977–987.

Golding, J. M., Bradshaw, G. S., et al. (2007). The impact of mock jury gender composition on deliberations and conviction rates in a child sexual assault trial. *Child Maltreatment, 12*(2), 182–190.

Goldschmidt, L., Richardson, G. A., et al. (2011). School achievement in 14-year-old youths prenatally exposed to marijuana. *Neurotoxicology & Teratology,* doi:10.1016/j.ntt.2011.08.009

Goldstein, E. B. (2011). *Cognitive psychology: Connecting mind, research and everyday experience* (3rd ed.). Belmont, CA: Cengage Learning/Wadsworth.

Goldstein, E. B. (2014). *Sensation and perception* (9th ed.). Belmont, CA: Cengage Learning/Wadsworth.

Goldstein, M. H., & Schwade, J. A. (2008). Social feedback to infants babbling facilitates rapid phonological learning. *Psychological Science, 19*(5), 515–523. doi:10.1111/j.1467-9280.2008.02117.x

Goldstein, M., Peters, L., et al. (2011). The effectiveness of a day program for the treatment of adolescent anorexia nervosa. *International Journal of Eating Disorders, 44*(1), 29–38. doi:10.1002/eat.20789

Goldston, D. B., Molock, S. D., et al. (2008). Cultural considerations in adolescent suicide prevention and psychosocial treatment. *American Psychologist, 63*(1), 14–31. doi:10.1037/0003-066X.63.1.14

Goman, C. K. (2008). *The nonverbal advantage: Secrets and science of body language at work.* San Francisco: Berrett-Koehler.

Gomez, R., & McLaren, S. (2007). The inter-relations of mother and father attachment, self-esteem and aggression during late adolescence. *Aggressive Behavior, 33*(2), 160–169. doi:10.1002/ab.20181

González-Vallejo, C., Lassiter, G. D., et al. (2008). "Save angels perhaps": A critical examination of unconscious thought theory and the deliberation-without-attention effect. *Review of General Psychology, 12*(3), 282–296. doi:10.1037/a0013134

Gonzalez, M., Durrant, J. E., et al. (2008). What predicts injury from physical punishment? A test of the typologies of violence hypothesis. *Child Abuse & Neglect, 32*(8), 752–765. doi:10.1016/j.chiabu.2007.12.005

Gonzalez, V. M., Reynolds, B., & Skewes, M. C. (2011). Role of impulsivity in the relationship between depression and alcohol problems among emerging adult college drinkers. *Experimental & Clinical Psychopharmacology, 19*(4), 303–313. doi:10.1037/a0022720

Goode, E. (1996). Gender and courtship entitlement: Responses to personal ads. *Sex Roles, 34*(3–4), 141–169. doi:10.1007/BF01544293

Goodman-Delahunty, J. Greene, E., & Hsiao, W. (1998). Construing motive in videotaped killings: The role of jurors' attitudes toward the death penalty. *Law & Human Behavior, 22*(3), 257–271.

Goodman, G. S., Quas, J. A., Ogle, C. M. (2010). Child maltreatment and memory. *Annual Review of Psychology, 61*, 325–351. doi:10.1146/annurev.psych.093008.100403

Gopie, N., Craik, F. I. M., & Hasher, L. (2011). A double dissociation of implicit and explicit memory in younger and older adults. *Psychological Science, 22*(5), 634–640. doi:10.1177/0956797611403321

Gopnik, A. (2009). *The philosophical baby.* New York: Macmillan.

Gopnik, A., Meltzoff, A. N., & Kuhl, P. K. (2000). *The scientist in the crib: What early learning tells us about the mind.* New York: HarperCollins.

Gordon, A. K., & Kaplar, M. E. (2002). A new technique for demonstrating the actor-observer bias. *Teaching of Psychology, 29*(4), 301–303. doi:10.1207/S15328023TOP2904_10

Gordon, I., Zagoory-Sharon, O., et al. (2010). Oxytocin and the development of parenting in humans. *Biological Psychiatry, 68*(4), 377–382. doi:10.1016/j.biopsych.2010.02.005

Gordon, J. R., Pruchno, R. A., et al. (2012). Balancing caregiving and work: Role conflict and role strain dynamics. *Journal of Family Issues, 33*(5), 662–689. doi:10.1177/0192513X11425322

Gordon, K. A., Wong, D. D. E., et al. (2011). Use it or lose it? Lessons learned from the developing brains of children who are deaf and use cochlear implants to hear. *Brain Topography, 24*(3–4), 204–219. doi:10.1007/s10548-011-0181-2

Gordon, R. M. (2001). MMPI/MMPI-2 changes in long-term psychoanalytic psychotherapy. *Issues in Psychoanalytic Psychology, 23*(1–2), 59–79.

Gorman, A. D., Abernethy, B., & Farrow, D. (2011). Investigating the anticipatory nature of pattern perception in sport. *Memory & Cognition, 39*(5), 894–901. doi:10.3758/s13421-010-0067-7

Goss, S., & Anthony, K. (2009). Developments in the use of technology in counselling and psychotherapy. *British Journal of Guidance & Counselling, 37*(3), 223–230. doi:10.1080/03069880902956967

Gottman, J. M. (1994). *Why marriages succeed or fail.* New York: Simon & Schuster.

Gottman, J. M., & Krokoff, L. J. (1989). Marital interaction and satisfaction: A longitudinal view. *Journal of Consulting & Clinical Psychology, 57*(1), 47–52.

Gourville, J. T., & Soman, D. (2005). Overchoice and assortment type: When and why variety backfires. *Marketing Science, 24*(3), 382–395. doi:10.1287/mksc.1040.0109

Gowensmith, W., Murrie, D. C., & Boccaccini, M. T. (2013). How reliable are forensic evaluations of legal sanity? *Law & Human Behavior, 37*(2), 98–106. doi:10.1037/lhb0000001

Grack, C., & Richman, C. L. (1996). Reducing general and specific heterosexism through cooperative contact. *Journal of Psychology & Human Sexuality, 8*(4), 59–68. doi:10.1300/J056v08n04_04

Grande, T., Rudolf, G., et al. (2003). Progressive changes in patients' lives after psychotherapy. *Psychotherapy Research, 13*(1), 43–58. doi:10.1093/ptr/kpg006

Grandner, M. A., & Kripke, D. F. (2004). Self-reported sleep complaints with long and short sleep: A nationally representative sample. *Psychosomatic Medicine, 66*, 239–241. doi:10.1097/01.PSY.0000107881.53228.4D

Grangeon, M., Guillot, A., & Collet, C. (2011). Postural control during visual and kinesthetic motor imagery. *Applied Psychophysiology & Biofeedback, 36*(1), 47–56. doi:10.1007/s10484-011-9145-2

Granrud, C. E. (2006). Size constancy in infants: 4-month-olds' responses to physical versus retinal image size. *Journal of Experimental Psychology: Human Perception & Performance, 32*(6), 1398–1404. doi:10.1037/0096-1523.32.6.1398

Granrud, C. E. (2009). Development of size constancy in children: A test of the metacognitive theory. *Attention, Perception, & Psychophysics, 71*(3), 644–654. doi:10.3758/APP.71.3.644

Grant, B. (2010). Getting the point: Empathic understanding in nondirective client-centered therapy. *Person-Centered & Experiential Psychotherapies, 9*(3), 220–235. doi:10.1080/14779757.2010.9689068

Grant, B. F., Hasin, D. S., et al. (2006). The epidemiology of *DSM-IV* panic disorder and agoraphobia in the United States: Results from the National Epidemiologic Survey on Alcohol and Related Conditions. *Journal of Clinical Psychiatry, 67*(3), 363–374. doi:10.4088/JCP.v67n0305

Grant, I., Gonzalez, R., & et al. (2001). Long-term neurocognitive consequences of marijuana. In *National Institute on Drug Abuse Workshop on Clinical Consequences of Marijuana,* August 13, 2001, Rockville, MD.

Grant, T. M., Jack, D. C., et al. (2011). Carrying the burdens of poverty, parenting, and addiction: Depression symptoms and self-silencing among ethnically diverse women. *Community Mental Health Journal, 47*(1), 90–98. doi:10.1007/s10597-009-9255-y

Graves, J. L. (2001). *The emperor's new clothes.* Piscataway, NJ: Rutgers University Press.

Gravetter, F. J., & Wallnau, L. B. (2013). *Statistics for the behavioral sciences* (9th ed.). Belmont, CA: Cengage Learning/Wadsworth.

Gredler, M. E. & Shields, C. C. (2008). *Vygotsky's legacy: A foundation for research and practice.* New York: Guilford.

Greene, D. C., & Britton, P. J. (2012). Stage of sexual minority identity formation: The impact of shame, internalized homophobia, ambivalence over emotional expression, and personal mastery. *Journal of Gay & Lesbian Mental Health, 16*(3), 188–214. doi:10.1080/19359705.2012.671126

Greene, D., & Lepper, M. R. (1974). How to turn play into work. *Psychology Today, 8*(4), 49.

Greene, E., & Heilbrun, K. (2014). *Wrightsman's psychology and the legal system* (8th ed.). Belmont, CA: Cengage Learning/Wadsworth.

Greenfield, P. M. (1997). You can't take it with you: Why abilities assessments don't cross cultures. *American Psychologist, 52*, 1115–1124. doi:10.1037/0003-066X.52.10.1115

Greenspan, J. D., Coghill, R. C., et al. (2008). Quantitative somatic sensory testing and functional imaging of the response to painful stimuli before and after cingulotomy for obsessive-compulsive disorder (OCD). *European Journal of Pain, 12*(8), 990–999. doi:10.1016/j.ejpain.2008.01.007

Greenwald, R. (2006). Eye movement desensitization and reprocessing with traumatized youth. In N. B. Webb (Ed.), *Working with traumatized youth in child welfare: Social work practice with children and families* (pp. 246–264). New York: Guilford.

Greenwood, J. G., Greenwood, J. J., et al. (2006). A survey of sidedness in Northern Irish schoolchildren: The interaction of sex, age, and task. *Laterality: Asymmetries of Body, Brain & Cognition, 12*(1), 1–18. doi:10.1080/13576500600886630

Gregory, B. T., Albritton, M. D., & Osmonbekov, T. (2010). The mediating role of psychological empowerment on the relationships between P-O fit, job satisfaction, and in-role performance. *Journal of Business & Psychology, 25*(4), 639–647.

Gregory, R. L. (1990). *Eye and brain: The psychology of seeing.* Princeton, NJ: Princeton University Press.

Gregory, R. L. (2000). Visual illusions. In A. Kazdin (Ed.), *Encyclopedia of psychology* (Vol. 8, pp. 193–200). Washington: American Psychological Association.

Gregory, R. L. (2003). Seeing after blindness. *Nature Neuroscience, 6*(9), 909–910.

Greitemeyer, T. (2010). Effects of reciprocity on attraction: The role of a partner's physical attractiveness. *Personal Relationships, 17*(2), 317–330. doi:10.1111/j.1475-6811.2010.01278.x

Grello, C. M., Welsh, D. P., & Harper, M. S. (2006). No strings attached: The nature of casual sex in college students. *Journal of Sex Research, 43*(3), 255–267.

Grenèche, J., Krieger, J., et al. (2011). Short-term memory performances during sustained wakefulness in patients with obstructive sleep apnea–hypopnea syndrome. *Brain & Cognition, 75*(1), 39–50. doi:10.1016/j.bandc.2010.10.003

Grenier, G., & Byers, E. S. (1995). Rapid ejaculation: A review of conceptual, etiological, and treatment issues. *Archives of Sexual Behavior, 24*(4), 447–472.

Griffin, W. A. (2002). Family therapy. In M. Hersen, & W. H. Sledge (Eds.), *Encyclopedia of psychotherapy* (pp. 787–791). San Diego: Academic Press.

Grigorenko, E. L. (2005). The inherent complexities of gene-environment interactions. *Journals of Gerontology, 60B*(1), 53–64. doi:10.1093/geronb/60.Special_Issue_1.53

Grigorenko, E. L., & Sternberg, R. J. (2003). The nature-nurture issue. In A. Slater & G. Bremner (Eds.), *An introduction to developmental psychology* (pp. 64–91). Malden, MA: Blackwell.

Grilly, D. M., & Salamone, J. (2012). *Drugs, brain, and behavior* (6th ed.). Englewood Cliffs, NJ: Prentice Hall.

Grobstein, P., & Chow, K. L. (1975). Perceptive field development and individual experience. *Science, 190*, 352–358.

Grodzinsky, Y., & Santi, A. (2008). The battle for Broca's region. *Trends in Cognitive Sciences, 12*(12), 474–480. doi:10.1016/j.tics.2008.09.001

Gross, J. J. (2013). Emotion regulation: Taking stock and moving forward. *Emotion.* doi:10.1037/a0032135

Grubin, D., & Madsen, L. (2005). Lie detection and the polygraph: A historical review. *Journal of Forensic Psychiatry & Psychology, 16*(2), 357–369. doi:10.1080/14789940412331337353

Guastello, D. D., & Guastello, S. J. (2003). Androgyny, gender role behavior, and emotional intelligence among college students and their parents. *Sex Roles, 49*(11–12), 663–673.

Guay, R. P. (2013). The relationship between leader fit and transformational leadership. *Journal of Managerial Psychology, 28*(1), 55–73. doi:10.1108/02683941311298869

Guéguen, N., & Lamy, L. (2012). Men's social status and attractiveness: Women's receptivity to men's date requests. *Swiss Journal Of Psychology, 71*(3), 157–160. doi:10.1024/1421-0185/a000083

Guéguen, N., & Pascual, A. (2003). Status and people's tolerance towards an ill-mannered person: A field study. *Journal of Mundane Behavior, 4*(1), 29–36.

Guéguen, N., Jacob, C., & Meineri, S. (2011). Effects of the door-in-the-face technique on restaurant customers' behavior. *International Journal of Hospitality Management, 30*(3), 759–761. doi:10.1016/j.ijhm.2010.12.010

Guéguen, N., Martin, A., & Meineri, S. (2011). Similarity and social interaction: When similarity fosters implicit behavior toward a stranger. *The Journal of Social Psychology, 151*(6), 671–673. doi:10.1080/00224545.2010.522627

Guéguen, N., Pascual, A., & Dagot, L. (2002). Low-ball and compliance to a request: An application in a field setting. *Psychological Reports, 91*(1), 81–84. doi:10.2466/PR0.91.5.81-84

Guerin, S. A., Robbins, C. A., et al. (2012). Retrieval failure contributes to gist-based false recognition. *Journal of Memory & Language, 66*(1), 68–78. doi:10.1016/j.jml.2011.07.002

Guidetti, M., Conner, M., et al. (2012). The transmission of attitudes towards food: Twofold specificity of similarities with parents and friends. *British Journal of Health Psychology, 17*(2), 346–361. doi:10.1111/j.2044-8287.2011.02041.x

Guillot, A., Collet, C., et al. (2009). Brain activity during visual versus kinesthetic imagery: An fMRI study. *Human Brain Mapping, 30*(7), 2157–2172. doi:10.1002/hbm.20658

Gündogan, N. Ü., Durmazlar, N., et al. (2005). Projected color slides as a method for mass screening test for color vision deficiency (a preliminary study). *International Journal of Neuroscience, 115*(8), 1105–1117. doi:10.1080/00207450590914365

Gupta, M. A. (2013). Review of somatic symptoms in post-traumatic stress disorder. *International Review of Psychiatry, 25*(1), 86–99. doi:10.3109/09540261.2012.736367

Gursoy, R., Ziyagil, M., et al. (2012). Handedness, achievement in sport and boxing. In J. Dunham, & T. Davenport (Eds.), *Handedness: Theories, genetics and psychology* (pp. 141–155). Hauppauge, NY: Nova Science Publishers.

Gurung, R. (2014). *Health psychology: A cultural approach* (3rd ed.). Belmont, CA: Cengage Learning/Wadsworth.

Güth, W., Levati, M. V., & Ploner, M. (2009). An experimental analysis of satisficing in saving decisions. *Journal of Mathematical Psychology, 53*(4), 265–272.

Güth, W., Levati, M. V., & von Wangenheim, G. (2010). Mutual interdependence versus repeated interaction: An experiment studying voluntary social exchange. *Rationality & Society, 22*(2), 131–158. doi:10.1177/1043463110366230

Guthrie, R. V. (2004). *Even the rat was white: A historical view of psychology* (2nd ed.). Boston: Allyn & Bacon.

Guttmacher Institute. (2011). *Facts on American teens' sexual and preproductive health.* Retrieved June 11, 2013, from http://www.guttmacher.org/pubs/FB-ATSRH.html

Haaken, J., & Reavey, P. (Eds.). (2010). *Memory matters: Contexts for understanding sexual abuse recollections.* New York: Routledge/Taylor & Francis.

Haas, B. W., Omura, K., et al. (2007). Is automatic emotion regulation associated with agreeableness? A perspective using a social neuroscience approach. *Psychological Science, 18*(2), 130–132.

Haber, R. N. (1970). How we remember what we see. *Scientific American, 222*(5), 104–112. doi:10.1038/scientificamerican0570-104

Haber, R. N., & Haber, L. (2000). Eidetic imagery. In A. E. Kazdin, (Ed.), *Encyclopedia of psychology* (Vol. 3, pp. 147–149). Washington: American Psychological Association.

Hafer, C. L., & Bègue, L. (2005). Experimental research on just-world theory: problems, developments, and future challenges. *Psychological Bulletin, 131*(1), 128–167. doi:10.1037/0033-2909.131.1.128

Haga, S. M., Kraft, P., Corby, E.-K. (2010). Emotion regulation: Antecedents and well-being outcomes of cognitive reappraisal and expressive suppression in crosscultural samples. *Journal of Happiness Studies, 10*(3), 271–291. doi:10.1007/s10902-007-9080-3

Hagger, M., & Chatzisarantis, N. L. D. (2010). Causality orientations moderate the undermining effect of rewards on intrinsic motivation. *Journal of Experimental Social Psychology, 47*(2), 485–489. doi:10.1016/j.jesp.2010.10.010

Haier, R. J., Jung, R. E., et al. (2004). Structural brain variation and general intelligence. *NeuroImage, 23*, 425–433.

Haier, R. J., White, N. S., & Alkire, M. T. (2003). Individual differences in general intelligence correlate with brain function during nonreasoning tasks. *Intelligence, 31*(5), 429–441. doi:10.1016/S0160-2896(03)00025-4

Hakun, J. G., Ruparel, K., et al. (2009). Towards clinical trials of lie detection with fMRI. *Social Neuroscience, 4*(6), 518–527. doi:10.1080/17470910802188370

Hales, D. (2013). *An invitation to health: Choosing to change* (15th ed.). Belmont, CA: Cengage Learning/Wadsworth.

Halim, M., Ruble, D. N., & Amodio, D. M. (2011). From pink frilly dresses to 'one of the boys': A social-cognitive analysis of gender identity development and gender bias. *Social & Personality Psychology Compass, 5*(11), 933–949. doi:10.1111/j.1751-9004.2011.00399.x

Hall, E. T. (1966). *The hidden dimension.* Garden City, NY: Doubleday.

Hall, N. C., Perry, R. P., et al. (2007). Attributional retraining and elaborative learning: Improving academic development through writing-based interventions. *Learning & Individual Differences, 17*(3), 280–290. doi:10.1016/j.lindif.2007.04.002

Hallahan, D. P., Kauffman, J. M., & Pullen, P. C. (2011). *Exceptional learners* (12th ed.). Englewood Cliffs, NJ: Merrill/Prentice Hall.

Halliday, G. (2010). Reflections on the meanings of dreams prompted by reading Stekel. *Dreaming, 20*(4), 219–226. doi:10.1037/a0020880

Halmai, Z., Dome, P., et al. (2013). Associations between depression severity and purinergic receptor p2rx7 gene polymorphisms. *Journal of Affective Disorders.* doi:10.1016/j.jad.2013.02.033

Halonen, J. S., & Santrock, J. W. (2013). *Your guide to college success: Strategies for achieving your goals* (7th ed.). Belmont, CA: Cengage Learning/Wadsworth.

Halpern-Felsher, B. L., Cornell, J., et al. (2005). Oral versus vaginal sex among adolescents: Perceptions, attitudes, and behavior. *Pediatrics, 115*, 845–851.

Halpern, D. F. (2003). *Thought and knowledge: An introduction to critical thinking* (4th ed.). Mahwah, NJ: Erlbaum.

Hamel, M. (2012). Testing aspects of the usability of an online learner dictionary prototype: A product- and process-oriented study. *Computer Assisted Language Learning, 25*(4), 339–365. doi:10.1080/09588221.2011.591805

Hammond, D. C. (2008). Hypnosis as sole anesthesia for major surgeries: Historical & contemporary perspectives. *American Journal of Clinical Hypnosis, 51*(2), 101–121. doi:10.1080/00029157.2008.10401653

Hampson, S. E., Edmonds, G. W., et al. (2013). Childhood conscientiousness relates to objectively measured adult physical health four decades later. *Health Psychology 32*(8), 925–928. doi:10.1037/a0031655

Hancock, J. (2011). *Brilliant memory training: Stop worrying about your memory and start using it—to the full!* Upper Saddle River, NJ: FT Press.

Hancock, P. A., & Ganey, H. C. N. (2003). From the inverted-U to the extended-U: The evolution of a law of psychology. *Journal of Human Performance in Extreme Environments, 7*(1), 5–14.

Handsfield, H. H. (2001). *Resurgent sexually transmitted diseases among men who have sex with men.* Retrieved June 12, 2013 from http://www.medscape.com/viewarticle/408301

Hans, V. P., Kaye, D. H., et al. (2011). Science in the jury box: Jurors' comprehension of mitochondrial DNA evidence. *Law & Human Behavior, 35*(1), 60–71.

Hansen, C. J., Stevens, L. C., & Coast, J. R. (2001). Exercise duration and mood state: How much is enough to feel better? *Health Psychology, 20*(4), 267–275. doi:10.1037/0278-6133.20.4.267

Hansen, N. B., Lambert, M. J., & Forman, E. M. (2002). The psychotherapy dose-response effect and its implications for treatment delivery services. *Clinical Psychology: Science & Practice, 9*(3), 329–334. doi:10.1093/clipsy/9.3.329

Hanton, S., Mellalieu, S. D., & Hall, R. (2004). Self-confidence and anxiety interpretation: A qualitative investigation. *Psychology of Sport & Exercise, 5*(4), 477–495. doi:10.1016/S1469-0292(03)00040-2

Hanyu, H., Sato, T., et al. (2010). The progression of cognitive deterioration and regional cerebral blood flow patterns in Alzheimer's disease: A longitudinal SPECT study. *Journal of the Neurological Sciences, 290*(1–2), 96–101. doi:10.1016/j.jns.2009.10.022

Haq, I. U., Foote, K. D., et al. (2010). Smile and laughter induction and intra-operative predictors of response to deep brain stimulation for obsessive-compulsive disorder. *NeuroImage, (Mar. 10)*, [np].

Harb, G. C., Thompson, R., et al. (2012). Combat-related PTSD nightmares and imagery rehearsal: Nightmare characteristics and relation to treatment outcome. *Journal of Traumatic Stress, 25*(5), 511–518. doi:10.1002/jts.21748

Hardaway, C. A., & Gregory, K. B. (2005). Fatigue and sleep debt in an operational navy squadron. *International Journal of Aviation Psychology, 15*(2), 157–171. doi:10.1207/s15327108ijap1502_3

Harden, K. P., Quinn, P. D., & Tucker-Drob, E. M. (2012). Genetically influenced change in sensation seeking drives the rise of delinquent behavior during adolescence. *Developmental Science, 15*(1), 150–163. doi:10.1111/j.1467-7687.2011.01115.x

Hardin, G. (1968). The tragedy of the commons. *Science, 162*, 1243–1248.

Hardin, M., & Greer, J. D. (2009). The influence of gender-role socialization, media use and sports participation on perceptions of gender-appropriate sports. *Journal of Sport Behavior, 32*(2), 207–226.

Harding, D. J., Fox, C., et al. (2002). Studying rare events through qualitative case studies: Lessons from a study of rampage school shootings. *Sociological Methods & Research, 31*(2), 174–217. doi:10.1177/0049124102031002003

Hardt, O., Einarsson, E. O., & Nader, K. (2010). A bridge over troubled water: Reconsolidation as a link between cognitive and neuroscientific memory research traditions. *Annual Review of Psychology, 61*, 141–167. doi:10.1146/annurev.psych.093008.100455

Hare, R. D. (2006). Psychopathy: A clinical and forensic overview. *Psychiatric Clinics of North America, 29*(3), 709–724. doi:10.1016/j.psc.2006.04.007

Harel, A., Gilaie-Dotan, S., et al. (2010). Top-down engagement modulates the neural expressions of visual expertise. *Cerebral Cortex, 20*(10), 2304–2318. doi:10.1093/cercor/bhp316

Harley, T. A. (2008). *The psychology of language: From data to theory* (3rd. ed.) Hove, UK: Psychology Press.

Harlow, H. F., & Harlow, M. K. (1962). Social deprivation in monkeys. *Scientific American, 207*, 136–146.

Harlow, J. M. (1868). Recovery from the passage of an iron bar through the head. *Publications of the Massachusetts Medical Society, 2*, 327–347.

Harm, D. L. (2002). Motion sickness neurophysiology, physiological correlates, and treatment. In K. M. Stanney (Ed.), *Handbook of virtual environments: Design, implementation, and applications* (pp. 637–661). Hillsdale, NJ: Erlbaum.

Harmison, R. J. (2011). Peak performance in sport: Identifying ideal performance states and developing athletes' psychological skills. *Sport, Exercise, & Performance Psychology, 1*(S), 3–18. doi:10.1037/2157-3905.1.S.3

Harnett, P., O'Donovan, A., & Lambert, M. J. (2010). The dose response relationship in psychotherapy: Implications for social policy. *Clinical Psychologist, 14*(2), 39–44. doi:10.1080/13284207.2010.500309

Harrell, J. P., & Medford, E. (2012). History, prejudice, and the study of social inequities. *Behavioral & Brain Sciences, 35*(6), 433–434. doi:10.1017/S0140525X12001203

Harrigan, J. A. (2005). Proxemics, kinesics, and gaze. In J. A. Harrigan, R. Rosenthal, et al. (Eds.), *The new handbook of methods in nonverbal behavior research*. New York: Oxford University Press.

Harrington, R. (2013). *Stress, health and well-being: Thriving in the 21st century*. Belmont, CA: Cengage Learning/Wadsworth.

Harris, C. (2004). The evolution of jealousy. *American Scientist, 92*, 62–71.

Harris, J. C. (2010). *Intellectual disability: A guide for families and professionals*. New York: Oxford University Press.

Harris, J., Hirsh-Pasek, K., & Newcombe, N. S. (2013). Understanding spatial transformations: Similarities and differences between mental rotation and mental folding. *Cognitive Processing, 14*(2), 105–115. doi:10.1007/s10339-013-0544-6

Harris, L. R., & Jenkin, M. R. M. (Eds.) (2011). *Vision in 3D environments*. New York: Cambridge University Press.

Hart, C. L., Ksir, C. J., & Ray, O. S. (2013). *Drugs, society, and human behavior* (15th ed.). New York: McGraw-Hill.

Hart, D., & Carlo, G. (2005). Moral development in adolescence. *Journal of Research on Adolescence, 15*(3), 223–233. doi:10.1111/j.1532-7795.2005.00094.x

Hart, J. E., Mourot, J. E., & Aros, M. (2012). Children of same-sex parents: In and out of the closet. *Educational Studies, 38*(3), 277–281. doi:10.1080/03055698.2011.598677

Hartlep, K. L., & Forsyth, G. A. (2000). The effect of self-reference on learning and retention. *Teaching of Psychology, 27*(4), 269–271. doi:10.1207/S15328023TOP2704_05

Hartley, S. (2012). *Peak performance every time*. New York: Routledge/Taylor & Francis.

Hartmann, E. (2008). The central image makes "big" dreams big: The central image as the emotional heart of the dream. *Dreaming, 18*(1), 44–57. doi:10.1037/1053-0797.18.1.44

Hartmann, E. (2010). The dream always makes new connections: The dream is a creation, not a replay. *Sleep Medicine Clinics, 5*(2), 241–248. doi:10.1016/j.jsmc.2010.01.009

Hartmann, E. (2011). *The Nature and Functions of Dreaming*. New York: Oxford University Press.

Hartmann, P., Reuter, M., & Nyborg, H. (2006). The relationship between date of birth and individual differences in personality and general intelligence: A large-scale study. *Personality & Individual Differences, 40*(7), 1349–1362. doi:10.1016/j.paid.2005.11.017

Hartung, C. M., Lefler, E. K., et al. (2010). Halo effects in ratings of ADHD and ODD: Identification of susceptible symptoms. *Journal of Psychopathology & Behavioral Assessment, 32*(1), 128–137. doi:10.1007/s10862-009-9135-3

Hashibe, M., Straif, K., et al. (2005). Epidemiologic review of marijuana use and cancer risk. *Alcohol, 35*(3), 265–275. doi:10.1016/j.alcohol.2005.04.008

Hashimoto, I., Suzuki, A., et al. (2004). Is there training-dependent reorganization of digit representations in area 3b of string players? *Clinical Neurophysiology, 115*(2), 435–447. doi:10.1016/S1388-2457(03)00340-7

Hatch, L. (2011). The American Psychological Association Task Force on the Sexualization of Girls: A review, update and commentary. *Sexual Addiction & Compulsivity, 18*(4), 195–211. doi:10.1080/10720162.2011.613326

Hausenblas, H. A., Campbell, A., et al. (2013). Media effects of experimental presentation of the ideal physique on eating disorder symptoms: A meta-analysis of laboratory studies. *Clinical Psychology Review, 33*(1), 168–181. doi:10.1016/j.cpr.2012.10.011

Hawks, J., Wang, E. T., et al. (2007). Recent acceleration of human adaptive evolution. *Proceedings of the National Academy of Sciences, 104*(52), 20753–20758.

Haycraft, E., & Blissett, J. (2010). Eating disorder symptoms and parenting styles. *Appetite, 54*(1), 221–224. doi:10.1016/j.appet.2009.11.009

Hayes, M. R. (2012). Neuronal and intracellular signaling pathways mediating GLP-1 energy balance and glycemic effects. *Physiology & Behavior, 106*(3), 413–416. doi:10.1016/j.physbeh.2012.02.017

Hayes, M. R., De Jonghe, B. C., & Kanoski, S. (2010). Role of the glucagon-like-peptide-1 receptor in the control of energy balance. *Physiology & Behavior, 100*(5), 503–510. doi:10.1016/j.physbeh.2010.02.029

Hayes, S. C., Strosahl, K. D., & Wilson, K. G. (2012). *Acceptance and commitment therapy: The process and practice of mindful change* (2nd ed.). New York: Guilford.

Hayne, H., & Rovee-Collier, C. (1995). The organization of reactivated memory in infancy. *Child Development, 66*(3), 893–906. doi:10.2307/1131957

Hayward, L. C., & Coles, M. E. (2009). Elucidating the relation of hoarding to obsessive compulsive disorder and impulse control disorders. *Journal of Psychopathology & Behavioral Assessment, 31*(3), 220–227. doi:10.1007/s10862-008-9106-0

Head, L. S., & Gross, A. M. (2009). Systematic desensitization. In W. T. O'Donohue, & J. E. Fisher (Eds.), *General principles and empirically supported techniques of cognitive behavior therapy* (pp. 640–647). New York: Wiley.

Healey, C., Morriss, R., et al. (2013). Self-harm in postpartum depression and referrals to a perinatal mental health team: An audit study. *Archives of Women's Mental Health, 16*(3), 237–245. doi:10.1007/s00737-013-0335-1

Heath, R. G. (1963). Electrical self-stimulation of the brain in man. *American Journal of Psychiatry, 120*, 571–577.

Hebb, D.O. (1949). *The organization of behavior*. New York: Wiley & Sons.

Hebblethwaite, S., & Norris, J. (2011). Expressions of generativity through family leisure: Experiences of grandparents and adult grandchildren. *Family Relations, 60*(1), 121–133. doi:10.1111/j.1741-3729.2010.00637.x

Hebl, M. R., King, E. G., & Lin, J. (2004). The swimsuit becomes us all: Ethnicity, gender, and vulnerability to self-objectification. *Personality & Social Psychology Bulletin, 30*, 1322–1331.

Hecht, J. (2007). *The happiness myth: Why what we think is right is wrong*. New York: HarperCollins.

Hedden, T., Ketay, S., et al. (2008) Cultural influences on neural substrates of attentional control. *Psychological Science, 19*(1), 12–17. doi:10.1111/j.1467-9280.2008.02038.x

Heiman, G. W. (2014). *Basic statistics for the behavioral sciences* (7th ed.). Belmont, CA: Cengage Learning/Wadsworth.

Heiman, J. R. (2002). Sexual dysfunction: Overview of prevalence, etiological factors, and treatments. *Journal of Sex Research, 39*(1), 73–78.

Heimann, M., & Meltzoff, A. N. (1996). Deferred imitation in 9- and 14-month-old infants: A longitudinal study of a Swedish sample. *British Journal of Developmental Psychology, 14*(Mar.), 55–64. doi:10.1111/j.2044-835X.1996.tb00693.x

Hein, L. C., & Berger, K. C. (2012). Gender dysphoria in children: Let's think this through. *Journal Of Child & Adolescent Psychiatric Nursing, 25*(4), 237–240. doi:10.1111/jcap.12014

Heinrichs, R. W. (2001). *In search of madness: Schizophrenia and neuroscience*. New York: Oxford University Press.

Heisel, M. J., Flett, G. L., & Hewitt, P. L. (2003). Social hopelessness and college student suicide ideation. *Archives of Suicide Research, 7*(3), 221–235. doi:10.1080/13811110301557

Helenius, D., Munk-Jørgensen, P., & Steinhausen, H. (2012). Family load estimates of schizophrenia and associated risk factors in a nation-wide population study of former child and adolescent patients up to forty years of age. *Schizophrenia Research, 139*(1–3), 183–188. doi:10.1016/j.schres.2012.05.014

Helgeson, V. S. (2012). *The psychology of gender* (4th ed.). Englewood Cliffs, NJ: Prentice Hall.

Hélie, S., & Sun, R. (2010). Incubation, insight, and creative problem solving: A unified theory and a connectionist model. *Psychological Review, 117*(3), 994–1024. doi:10.1037/a0019532

Helle, L., & Säljö, R. (2012). Collaborating with digital tools and peers in medical education: Cases and simulations as interventions in learning. *Instructional Science, 40*(5), 737–744. doi:10.1007/s11251-012-9216-7

Hellige, J. B. (1993). *Hemispheric asymmetry.* Cambridge, MA: Harvard University Press.

Helton, W. S. (2007). Skill in expert dogs. *Journal of Experimental Psychology: Applied, 13*(3), 171–178. doi:10.1037/1076-898X.13.3.171

Helton, W. S. (2009). Exceptional running skill in dogs requires extensive experience. *Journal of General Psychology, 136*(3), 323–332. doi:10.3200/GENP.136.3.323-336

Henderson, N. D. (1982). Human behavior genetics. *Annual Review of Psychology, 33*, 403–440. doi:10.1146/annurev.ps.33.020182.002155

Henderson, T. L., Roberto, K. A., & Kamo, Y. (2010). Older adults' responses to Hurricane Katrina: Daily hassles and coping strategies. *Journal of Applied Gerontology, 29*(1), 48–69. doi:10.1177/0733464809334287

Hennenlotter, A., Dresel, C., et al. (2009). The link between facial feedback and neural activity within central circuitries of emotion: New insights from botulinum toxin-induced denervation of frown muscles. *Cerebral Cortex, 19*(3), 537–542. doi:10.1093/cercor/bhn104

Hennessey, B. A., & Amabile, T. M. (2010). Creativity. *Annual Review of Psychology, 61*, 569–598. doi:10.1146/annurev.psych.093008.100416

Henningsen, D. D., Henningsen, M. L. M., et al. (2006). Examining the symptoms of groupthink and retrospective sensemaking. *Small Group Research, 37*(1), 36–64. doi:10.1177/1046496405281772

Hennink-Kaminski, H., & Reichert, T. (2011). Using sexual appeals in advertising to sell cosmetic surgery: A content analysis from 1986 to 2007. *Sexuality & Culture, 15*(1), 41–55. doi:10.1007/s12119-010-9081-y

Henrich, J., Heine, S. J., & Norenzayan, A. (2010). The weirdest people in the world? *Behavioral & Brain Sciences, 33*, 61–135. doi:10.1017/S0140525X0999152X

Henry, J. F., & Sherwin, B. B. (2012). Hormones and cognitive functioning during late pregnancy and postpartum: A longitudinal study. *Behavioral Neuroscience, 126*(1), 73–85. doi:10.1037/a0025540

Henry, P. K., Murnane, K. S., et al. (2010). Acute brain metabolic effects of cocaine in rhesus monkeys with a history of cocaine use. *Brain Imaging & Behavior, 4*(3–4), 212–219. doi:10.1007/s11682-010-9100-5

Hepper, P. G., Dornan, J. C., & Lynch, C. (2012). Fetal brain function in response to maternal alcohol consumption: Early evidence of damage. *Alcoholism: Clinical & Experimental Research, 36*(12), 2168–2175. doi:10.1111/j.1530-0277.2012.01832.x

Hepper, P. G., Wells, D. L., & Lynch, C. (2005). Prenatal thumb sucking is related to postnatal handedness. *Neuropsychologia, 43*(3), 313–315. doi:10.1016/j.neuropsychologia.2004.08.009

Herbenick, D., Reece, M., et al. (2010a). Sexual behavior in the United States: Results from a national probability sample of men and women ages 14–94. *Journal of Sexual Medicine, 7*(suppl 5), 255–265. doi:10.1111/j.1743-6109.2010.02012.x

Herbenick, D., Reece, M., et al. (2010b). An event-level analysis of the sexual characteristics and composition among adults ages 18–59: Results from a national probability sample in the United States. *Journal of Sexual Medicine, 7*(Suppl. 5), 346–361. doi:10.1111/j.1743-6109.2010.02020.x

Hergenhahn, B. R. (2009). *An introduction to the history of psychology* (6th ed.). Belmont, CA: Cengage Learning/Wadsworth.

Hergenhahn, B. R., & Henry, T. (2014). *An introduction to the history of psychology* (7th ed.). Belmont, CA: Cengage Learning/Wadsworth.

Heriot, S. A., & Pritchard, M. (2004). "Reciprocal Inhibition as the main basis of psychotherapeutic effects" by Joseph Wolpe (1954). *Clinical Child Psychology & Psychiatry, 9*(2), 297–307. doi:10.1177/1359104504041928

Herman, J. L., & Tetrick, L. E. (2009). Problem-focused versus emotion-focused coping strategies and repatriation adjustment. *Human Resource Management, 48*(1), 69–88. doi:10.1002/hrm.20267

Hermanto, N., Moreno, S., & Bialystok, E. (2012). Linguistic and metalinguistic outcomes of intense immersion education: How bilingual? *International Journal of Bilingual Education and Bilingualism, 15*(2), 131–145. doi:10.1080/13670050.2011.652591

Hernstein, R., & Murray, C. (1994). *The bell curve.* New York: Free Press.

Herold, D. K. (2010). Mediating media studies: Stimulating critical awareness in a virtual environment. *Computers & Education, 54*(3), 791–798. doi:10.1016/j.compedu.2009.10.019

Herren, C., In-Albon, T., & Schneider, S. (2013). Beliefs regarding child anxiety and parenting competence in parents of children with separation anxiety disorder. *Journal of Behavior Therapy & Experimental Psychiatry, 44*(1), 53–60. doi:10.1016/j.jbtep.2012.07.005

Hewit, J. K., Cronin, J. B., & Hume, P. A. (2012). Understanding change of direction performance: A technical analysis of a 180° ground-based turn and sprint task. International *Journal of Sports Science & Coaching, 7*(3), 493–501.

Hickling, E. M., & Bowie, J. E. (2013). Applicability of human reliability assessment methods to human–computer interfaces. *Cognition, Technology & Work, 15*(1), 19–27. doi:10.1007/s10111-012-0215-x

Higbee, K. L., Clawson, C., et al. (1990). Using the link mnemonic to remember errands. *Psychological Record, 40*(3), 429–436.

Higgins, S. T., Heil, S. H., & Lussier, J. P. (2004). Clinical implications of reinforcement as a determinant of substance use disorders. *Annual Review of Psychology, 55*, 431–461. doi:10.1146/annurev.psych.55.090902.142033

Higham, P. A., & Gerrard, C. (2005). Not all errors are created equal: Metacognition and changing answers on multiple-choice tests. *Canadian Journal of Experimental Psychology, 59*(1), 28–34. doi:10.1037/h0087457

Hilgard, E. R. (1968). *The experience of hypnosis.* New York: Harcourt Brace Jovanovich.

Hilgard, E. R. (1977). *Divided consciousness* (pp. 32–51). New York: Wiley.

Hilgard, E. R. (1994) Neodissociation theory. In S. J. Lynn, & J. W. Rhue (Eds.), *Dissociation: Clinical, theoretical and research perspectives* (pp. 32–51). New York: Guilford.

Hinrichs, K. T. (2007). Follower propensity to commit crimes of obedience: The role of leadership beliefs. *Journal of Leadership & Organizational Studies, 14*(1), 69–76. doi:10.1177/1071791907304225

Hintzman, D. L. (2005). Memory strength and recency judgments. *Psychonomic Bulletin & Review, 12*(5), 858–864. doi:10.3758/BF03196777

Hinzman, L., & Kelly, S. D. (2013). Effects of emotional body language on rapid out-group judgments. *Journal of Experimental Social Psychology, 49*(1), 152–155. doi:10.1016/j.jesp.2012.07.010

Hirshbein, L., & Sarvananda, S. (2008). History, power, and electricity: American popular magazine accounts of electroconvulsive therapy, 1940–2005. *Journal of the History of the Behavioral Sciences, 44*(1), 1–18. doi:10.1002/jhbs.20283

Hirstein, W. (2005). *Brain fiction: Self-deception and the riddle of confabulation.* Cambridge, MA: MIT Press.

Hobson, A. (2009). The neurobiology of consciousness: Lucid dreaming wakes up. *International Journal Of Dream Research, 2*(2), 41–44.

Hobson, J. A. (2000). Dreams: Physiology. In A. Kazdin (Ed.), *Encyclopedia of psychology* (Vol. 3, pp. 78–81). Washington: American Psychological Association.

Hobson, J. A. (2001). *Consciousness.* New York: Freeman.

Hobson, J. A. (2005). Sleep is of the brain, by the brain and for the brain. *Nature, 437*(7063), 1254–1256. doi:10.1038/nature04283

Hobson, J. A., Pace-Schott, E. F., & Stickgold, R. (2000). Dream science 2000. *Behavioral & Brain Sciences, 23*(6), 1019–1035; 1083–1121. doi:10.1017/S0140525X00954025

Hobson, J. A., & Schredl, M. (2011). The continuity and discontinuity between waking and dreaming: A dialogue between Michael Schredl and Allan Hobson concerning the adequacy and completeness of these notions. *International Journal of Dream Research, 4*(1), 3–7.

Hodges, N., & Williams, M. (Eds.) (2012). *Skill acquisition in sport: Research, theory and practice.* New York: Psychology Press.

Hodgins, H. S., & Adair, K. C. (2010). Attentional processes and meditation. *Consciousness & Cognition, 19*(4), 872–878. doi:10.1016/j.concog.2010.04.002

Hodson, R., & Sullivan, T. A. (2012). *The social organization of work* (5th ed.). Belmont, CA: Cengage Learning/Wadsworth.

Hoerger, M., Chapman, B. P., et al. (2012). Emotional intelligence: A theoretical framework for individual differences in affective forecasting. *Emotion, 12*(4), 716–725. doi:10.1037/a0026724.

Hofer, B. K., & Yu, S. L. (2003). Teaching self-regulated learning through a "Learning to Learn" course. *Teaching of Psychology, 30*(1), 30–33. doi:10.1207/S15328023TOP3001_05

Hoff, E. (2014). *Language development* (5th ed.). Belmont, CA: Cengage Learning/Wadsworth.

Hoff, E., & Tian, C. (2005). Socioeconomic status and cultural influences on language. *Journal of Communication Disorders, 38*(4), 271–278. doi:10.1016/j.jcomdis.2005.02.003

Hoffart, A. (2005). Interpersonal therapy for social phobia: Theoretical model and review of the evidence. In M. E. Abelian (Ed.), *Focus on psychotherapy research* (pp. 121–137). Hauppauge, NY: Nova Science Publishers.

Hoffman, E. (2008). Abraham Maslow: A biographer's reflections. *Journal of Humanistic Psychology, 48*(4), 439–443. doi:10.1177/0022167808320534

Hofman, D. (2008). The frontal laterality of emotion: A historical overview. *Netherlands Journal of Psychology, 64*(3), 112–118. doi:10.1007/BF03076413

Hogan, E. H., Hornick, B. A., & Bouchoux, A. (2002). Focus on communications: Communicating the message: Clarifying the controversies about caffeine. *Nutrition Today, 37*, 28–35.

Hogarth, H., & Ingham, R. (2009). Masturbation among young women and associations with sexual health: An exploratory study. *Journal of Sex Research, 46*(6), 558–567. doi:10.1080/00224490902878993

Hohwy, J., & Fox, E. (2012). Preserved aspects of consciousness in disorders of consciousness: A review and conceptual analysis. *Journal of Consciousness Studies, 19*(3–4), 87–120.

Hohwy, J., & Rosenberg, R. (2005). Unusual experiences, reality testing and delusions of alien control. *Mind & Language, 20*(2), 141–162. doi:10.1111/j.0268-1064.2005.00280.x

Holbrook, T., Moore, C., & Zoss, M. (2010). Equitable intent: Reflections on universal design in education as an ethic of care. *Reflective Practice, 11*(5), 681–692.

Holden, C. (1980). Twins reunited. *Science, 80,* Nov., 55–59.

Holland, J. L. (1997). *Making vocational choices.* Odessa, FL: Psychological Assessment Resources.

Holliday, R. E., Humphries, J. E., et al. (2012). Reducing misinformation effects in older adults with cognitive interview mnemonics. *Psychology and Aging, 27*(4), 1191–1203. doi:10.1037/a002203

Hollins, M. (2010). Somesthetic senses. *Annual Review of Psychology, 61,* 243–271. doi:10.1146/annurev.psych.093008.100419

Hollon, S. D., Stewart, M. O., & Strunk, D. (2006). Enduring effects for cognitive behavior therapy in the treatment of depression and anxiety. *Annual Review of Psychology, 57,* 285–315. doi:10.1146/annurev.psych.57.102904.190044

Holloway, T., Moreno, J. L., et al. (2013). Prenatal stress induces schizophrenia-like alterations of serotonin 2A and metabotropic glutamate 2 receptors in the adult offspring: Role of maternal immune system. *Journal of Neuroscience, 33*(3), 1088–1098. doi:10.1523/JNEUROSCI.2331-12.2013

Holman, A., & Sillars, A. (2012). Talk about "hooking up": The influence of college student social networks on nonrelationship sex. *Health Communication, 27*(2), 205–216. doi:10.1080/10410236.2011.575540

Holman, E. A., Silver, R. C., et al. (2008). Terrorism, acute stress, and cardiovascular health: A 3-year national study following the September 11th attacks. *Archives of General Psychiatry, 65*(1), 73–80. doi:10.1001/archgenpsychiatry.2007.6

Holmes, E. K., & Huston, A. C. (2010). Understanding positive father–child interaction: Children's, father's, and mother's contributions. *Fathering, 8*(2), 203–225. doi:10.3149/fth.1802.203

Holmes, M. (2002). Rethinking the meaning and management of intersexuality. *Sexualities, 5*(2), 159–180.

Holmes, T. H., & Rahe, R. H. (1967). The social readjustment rating scale. *Journal of Psychosomatic Research, 11*(2), 213–218. doi:10.1016/0022-3999(67)90010-4

Holtzen, D. W. (2000). Handedness and professional tennis. *International Journal of Neuroscience, 105*(1–4), 101–119. doi:10.3109/00207450009003270

Holz, J., Piosczyk, H., et al. (2012). EEG sigma and slow-wave activity during NREM sleep correlate with overnight declarative and procedural memory consolidation. *Journal of Sleep Research, 21*(6), 612–619. doi:10.1111/j.1365-2869.2012.01017.x

Hölzel, B. K., Lazar, S. W., et al. (2011). How does mindfulness meditation work? Proposing mechanisms of action from a conceptual and neural perspective. *Perspectives on Psychological Science, 6*(6), 537–559. doi:10.1177/1745691611419671

Hooyman, N. & Kiyak, H. A. (2011). *Social gerontology: A multidisciplinary perspective* (9th ed.). Boston: Pearson/Allyn & Bacon.

Hopwood, C. J., Donnellan, M. B., et al. (2011). Genetic and environmental influences on personality trait stability and growth during the transition to adulthood: A three-wave longitudinal study. *Journal of Personality & Social Psychology, 100*(3), 545–556. doi:10.1037/a0022409

Horgan, J. (2005). The forgotten era of brain chips. *Scientific American, 293*(4), 66–73. doi:10.1038/scientificamerican1005-66

Horn, R. R., Williams, A. M., et al. (2005). Visual search and coordination changes in response to video and point-light demonstrations without KR. *Journal of Motor Behavior, 37*(4), 265–274.

Horsley, R. R., Osborne, M., et al. (2012). High-frequency gamblers show increased resistance to extinction following partial reinforcement. *Behavioural Brain Research, 229*(2), 438–442. doi:10.1016/j.bbr.2012.01.024

Horvath, L. S., Milich, R., et al. (2004) Sensation seeking and substance use: A cross-lagged panel design. *Individual Differences Research, 2*(3), 175–183.

Hosch, H. M., & Cooper, D. S. (1982). Victimization as a determinant of eyewitness accuracy. *Journal of Applied Psychology, 67,* 649–652. doi:10.1037/0021-9010.67.5.649

Hough, L. M., & Connelly, B. S. (2013). Personality measurement and use in industrial and organizational psychology. In K. F. Geisinger, B. A. Bracken, et al. (Eds.), *APA handbook of testing and assessment in psychology* (Vol. 1): *Test theory and testing and assessment in industrial and organizational psychology* (pp. 501–531). Washington, DC: American Psychological Association. doi:10.1037/14047-028

Houghton, D. P. (2008). Invading and occupying Iraq: Some insights from political psychology. *Peace & Conflict: Journal of Peace Psychology, 14*(2), 169–192. doi:10.1080/10781910802017297

Howell, D. C. (2013). *Fundamental statistics for the behavioral sciences* (8th ed.). Belmont, CA: Cengage Learning/Wadsworth.

Howell, R. T., & Howell, C. J. (2008). The relation of economic status to subjective well-being in developing countries: A meta-analysis. *Psychological Bulletin, 134*(4), 536–560. doi:10.1037/0033-2909.134.4.536

Hoyert, D. L., & Xu, J. (2012). *Deaths: Preliminary data for 2011. CDC National Vital Statistics Reports, 61*(6), 1–51. Retrieved April 26, 2013, from http://www.cdc.gov/nchs/data/nvsr/nvsr61/nvsr61_06.pdf

Hsieh, P., Colas, J. T., & Kanwisher, N. (2011). Pop-out without awareness: Unseen feature singletons capture attention only when top-down attention is available. *Psychological Science, 22*(9), 1220–1226. doi:10.1177/0956797611419302

Huang, M.-H., & Rust, R. T. (2011). Sustainability and consumption. *Journal of the Academy of Marketing Science, 39*(1), 40–54.

Hubble, M.A., Duncan, B. L., & Miller, S. D. (Eds.) (1999). *The heart and soul of change: What works in therapy.* Washington: American Psychological Association.

Hubel D. H., & Wiesel, W. N. (2005). *Brain & visual perception: The story of a 25-year collaboration.* New York: Oxford University Press.

Hübner, R., & Volberg, G. (2005). The integration of object levels and their content: A theory of global/local processing and related hemispheric differences. *Journal of Experimental Psychology: Human Perception & Performance, 31*(3), 520–541. doi:10.1037/0096-1523.31.3.520

Huebner, R. B., & Kantor, L. (2011). Advances in alcoholism treatment. *Alcohol Research & Health, 33*(4), 295–299.

Hughes, A. (2008). The use of urban legends to improve critical thinking. In L. T. Benjamin, Jr. (Ed.). *Favorite activities for the teaching of psychology.* Washington: American Psychological Association.

Hughes, J. R., & Callas, P. W. (2011). Is delaying a quit attempt associated with less success? *Nicotine & Tobacco Research, 13*(12), 1228–1232. doi:10.1093/ntr/ntr207

Hughes, M., Brymer, M., et al. (2011). Posttraumatic stress among students after the shootings at Virginia Tech. *Psychological Trauma, 3*(4), 403–411. doi:10.1037/a0024565

Humes, K. R., Jones, N. A., & Ramirez, R. R. (2010). Overview of race and Hispanic origin: 2010. *U. S. Census Bureau News, 2010 Census Brief C2010BR-02.* Retrieved June 9, 2013, from http://www.census.gov/prod/cen2010/briefs/c2010br-02.pdf

Hunter, E. (1998). Adolescent attraction to cults. *Adolescence, 33*(131), 709–714.

Hunter, J. P., Katz, J., & Davis, K. D. (2003). The effect of tactile and visual sensory inputs on phantom limb awareness. *Brain, 126*(3), 579–589. doi:10.1093/brain/awg054

Hurson, T. (2008). *Think better: An innovator's guide to productive thinking.* New York: McGraw-Hill.

Huston, H. C., & Bentley, A. C. (2010). Human development in societal context. *Annual Review of Psychology, 61,* 411–437. doi:10.1146/annurev.psych.093008.100442

Hutchinson, S. R. (2004). Survey research. In K. deMarrais & S. D. Lapan (Eds.), *Foundations for research: Methods of inquiry in education and the social sciences: Inquiry and pedagogy across diverse contexts* (pp. 283–301). Mahwah, NJ: Erlbaum.

Hutchinson, S., Lee, L. H., et al. (2003). Cerebellar volume of musicians. *Cerebral Cortex, 13*(9), 943–949. doi:10.1093/cercor/13.9.943

Hutchison, K. E., McGeary, J., et al. (2002). The DRD4 VNTR polymorphism moderates craving after alcohol consumption. *Health Psychology, 21*(2), 139–146. doi:10.1037/0278-6133.21.2.139

Hyde, J. S. (2013). *Half the human experience* (8th ed.). Boston: Houghton Mifflin.

Hyde, J. S., & DeLamater, J. D. (2011). *Understanding human sexuality* (11th ed.). New York: McGraw-Hill.

Hyde, J. S., & Else-Quest, N. (2013). *Half the human experience* (8th ed.). Cengage Learning/Wadsworth.

Hyman, R. (1996a). Evaluation of the military's twenty-year program on psychic spying. *Skeptical Inquirer, 20*(2), 21–23.

Hyman, R. (1996b). The evidence for psychic functioning: Claims vs. reality. *Skeptical Inquirer, 20*(2), 24–26.

Hyman, R. (2007). Talking with the dead, communicating with the future and other myths created by cold reading. In S. Della Sala (Ed.), *Tall tales about the mind & brain: Separating fact from fiction* (pp. 218–232). New York: Oxford University Press.

Hyman, S. E. (2011). Diagnosis of mental disorders in light of modern genetics. In D. A. Regier, W. E. Narrow, E. A. Kuhl, et al. (Eds.), *The conceptual evolution of DSM-5* (pp. 3–17). Arlington, VA: American Psychiatric Publishing.

Hysenbegasi, A., Hass, S. L., & Rowland, C. R. (2005). The impact of depression on the academic productivity of university students. *Journal of Mental Health Policy & Economics, 8*(3), 145–151.

Iacono, W. G. (2008). Effective policing: Understanding how polygraph tests work and are used. *Criminal Justice & Behavior, 35*(10), 1295–1308. doi:10.1177/0093854808321529

Iannetti, G. D., & Mouraux, A. (2010). From the neuromatrix to the pain matrix (and back). *Experimental Brain Research, 205*(1), 1–12. doi:10.1007/s00221-010-2340-1

Iannone, M., Bulotta, S., et al. (2006). Electrocortical effects of MDMA are potentiated by acoustic stimulation in rats. *BMC Neuroscience, February 16*, 7–13. doi:10.1186/1471-2202-7-13

Ida, Y., & Mandal, M. K. (2003). Cultural differences in side bias: Evidence from Japan and India. *Laterality: Asymmetries of Body, Brain & Cognition, 8*(2), 121–133. doi:10.1080/713754478

Imbimbo, C., Verze, P., et al. (2009). A report from a single institute's 14-year experience in treatment of male-to-female transsexuals. *Journal of Sexual Medicine, 6*(10), 2736–2745.

Immordino-Yang, M. H. (2008). How we can learn from children with half a brain. *New Scientist, 2664*, 44–45.

Impett, E. A. Strachman, A., et al. (2008). Maintaining sexual desire in intimate relationships: The importance of approach goals. *Journal of Personality & Social Psychology, 94*(5), 808–823.

Impett, E. A., Gordon, A. M., et al. (2010). Moving toward more perfect unions: Daily and long-term consequences of approach and avoidance goals in romantic relationships. *Journal of Personality & Social Psychology, 99*(6), 948–963.

Ingham, A. G., Levinger, G., et al. (1974). The Ringelmann effect: Studies of group size and group performance. *Journal of Personality & Social Psychology, 10*, 371–384. doi:10.1016/0022-1031(74)90033-X

Ingravallo, F., Gnucci, V., et al. (2012). The burden of narcolepsy with cataplexy: How disease history and clinical features influence socioeconomic outcomes. *Sleep Medicine, 13*(10), 1293–1300. doi:10.1016/j.sleep.2012.08.002

Innocence Project (2012). *Facts on post-conviction DNA exonerations.* Retrieved February 13, 2013, from http://www.innocenceproject.org/Content/Facts_on_PostConviction_DNA_Exonerations.php

Insel, T. R. (2010). Rethinking schizophrenia. *Nature, 468*(7321), 187–193. doi:10.1038/nature09552

Insel, T. R. (2010). *Spotlight on postpartum depression.* Retrieved May 1, 2013, from http://www.nimh.nih.gov/about/director/2010/spotlight-on-postpartum-depression.shtml

Inta, D., Meyer-Lindenberg, A., & Gass, P. (2011). Alterations in postnatal neurogenesis and dopamine dysregulation in schizophrenia: A hypothesis. *Schizophrenia Bulletin, 37*(4), 674–680. doi:10.1093/schbul/sbq134

Inzlicht, M., & Schmader, T. (Eds.) (2012). *Stereotype threat: Theory, process, and application.* New York: Oxford University Press.

Inzlicht, M., Gutsell, J. N., & Legault, L. (2012). Mimicry reduces racial prejudice. *Journal of Experimental Social Psychology, 48*(1), 361–365. doi:10.1016/j.jesp.2011.06.007

Iosif, A., & Ballon, B. (2005). Bad moon rising: The persistent belief in lunar connections to madness. *Canadian Medical Association Journal, 173*(12), 1498–1500. doi:10.1503/cmaj.051119

Isaacs, D. (2011). Corporal punishment of children: Changing the culture. *Journal of Paediatrics and Child Health, 47*(8), 491–492. doi:10.1111/j.1440-1754.2011.02143.x

Ivanco, T. L., & Racine, R. J. (2000). Long-term potentiation in the pathways between the hippocampus and neocortex in the chronically implanted, freely moving rat. *Hippocampus, 10*, 143–152.

Iverson, R. D., & Zatzick, C. D. (2011). The effects of downsizing on labor productivity: The value of showing consideration for employees' morale and welfare in high-performance work systems. *Human Resource Management, 50*(1), 29–44.

Iyengar, S. S., & Lepper, M. R. (2000). When choice is demotivating: Can one desire too much of a good thing? *Journal of Personality & Social Psychology, 79*(6), 995–1006. doi:10.1037/0022-3514.79.6.995

Izard, C. E. (1990). Facial expressions and the regulation of emotions. *Journal of Personality & Social Psychology, 58*(3), 487–498. doi:10.1037/0022-3514.58.3.487

Izard, C. E. (2011). Forms and functions of emotions: Matters of emotion–cognition interactions. *Emotion Review, 3*(4), 371–378. doi:10.1177/1754073911410737

Izard, C. E., Fantauzzo, C. A., et al. (1995). The ontogeny and significance of infants' facial expressions in the first 9 months of life. *Developmental Psychology, 31*(6), 997–1013. doi:10.1037/0012-1649.31.6.997

Izard, C. E., Woodburn, E. M., & Finlon, K. J. (2010). Extending emotion science to the study of discrete emotions in infants. *Emotion Review, 2*(2), 134–136. doi:10.1177/1754073909355003

Izuma, K. (2013). The neural basis of social influence and attitude change. *Current Opinion in Neurobiology.* doi:10.1016/j.conb.2013.03.009

Jablonski, N.G., & Chaplin, G. (2000). The evolution of human skin coloration. *Journal of Human Evolution, 39*(1), 57–106. doi:10.1006/jhev.2000.0403

Jack, D. C., & Ali, A. (2010). *Silencing the self across cultures: Depression and gender in the social world.* New York: Oxford University Press.

Jackson, D., & Newberry, P. (2012). *Critical thinking: A user's manual.* Belmont, CA: Cengage Learning/Wadsworth.

Jackson, S. L. (2012). *Research methods and statistics: A critical thinking approach* (4th ed.) Belmont, CA: Cengage Learning/Wadsworth.

Jackson, T., Fritch, A., et al. (2002). Towards explaining the association between shyness and loneliness: A path analysis with American college students. *Social Behavior & Personality, 30*(3), 263–270. doi:10.2224/sbp.2002.30.3.263

Jacob, A., Prasad, S., et al. (2004). Charles Bonnet syndrome: Elderly people and visual hallucinations. *British Medical Journal, 328*(7455), 1552–1554. doi:10.1136/bmj.328.7455.1552

Jacobs-Stewart, T. (2010). *Mindfulness and the 12 steps: Living recovery in the present moment.* Center City, MN: Hazelden Foundation.

Jacobs, J., Lega, B., & Anderson, C. (2012). Explaining how brain stimulation can evoke memories. *Journal of Cognitive Neuroscience, 24*(3), 553–563. doi:10.1162/jocn_a_00170

Jacobs, N., van Os, J., et al. (2008). Heritability of intelligence. *Twin Research & Human Genetics, 10*(Suppl), 11–14. doi:10.1375/twin.10.supp.11

Jacobs, S. R., & Dodd, D. K. (2003). Student burnout as a function of personality, social support, and workload. *Journal of College Student Development, 44*(3), 291–303. doi:10.1353/csd.2003.0028

Jacobson, S. W., Stanton, M. E., et al. (2011). Impaired delay and trace eyeblink conditioning in school-age children with fetal alcohol syndrome. *Alcoholism: Clinical & Experimental Research, 35*(2), 250–264. doi:10.1111/j.1530-0277.2010.01341.x

Jaeggi, S. M., Buschkuehl, M., et al. (2008). Improving fluid intelligence with training on working memory. *Proceedings of the National Academy of Sciences, 105*(19), 6829–6833. doi:10.1073/pnas.0801268105

Jaehnig, W., & Miller, M. L. (2007). Feedback types in programmed instruction: A systematic review. *Psychological Record, 57*(2), 219–232.

Jaffe, J., Beatrice, B., et al. (2001). Rhythms of dialogue in infancy. *Monographs of the Society for Research in Child Development, 66*(2), vi–131.

Jahoda, G. (2007). Superstition and belief. *The Psychologist, 20*(10), 594–595.

Jamieson, J. P. (2010). The home field advantage in athletics: A meta-analysis. *Journal of Applied Social Psychology, 40*(7), 1819–1848. doi:10.1111/j.1559-1816.2010.00641.x

Janis, I. L. (1989). *Crucial decisions.* New York: Free Press.

Janis, I. L. (2007). Groupthink. In R. P. Vecchio (Ed.), *Leadership: Understanding the dynamics of power and influence in organizations* (2nd ed., pp. 163–176). Notre Dame, IN: University of Notre Dame Press.

Janowsky, J. S. (2006). Thinking with your gonads: Testosterone and cognition. *Trends in Cognitive Sciences, 10*(2), 77–82.

Janssen, S. A., & Arntz, A. (2001). Real-life stress and opioid-mediated analgesia in novice parachute jumpers. *Journal of Psychophysiology, 15*(2), 106–113. doi:10.1027//0269-8803.15.2.106

Janus, S. S., & Janus, C. L. (1993). *The Janus report.* New York: Wiley.

Janusek, L., Cooper, D., & Mathews, H. L. (2012). Stress, immunity, and health outcomes. In V. Rice (Ed.), *Handbook of stress, coping, and health: Implications for nursing research, theory, and practice* (2nd ed., pp. 43–70). Thousand Oaks, CA: Sage.

Jarvin, L., & Sternberg, R. J. (2003). Alfred Binet's contributions to educational psychology. In B. J. Zimmerman & D. H. Schunk (Eds.), *Educational psychology: A century of contributions* (pp. 65–79). Mahwah, NJ: Erlbaum.

Javitt, D. C., Zukin, S. R., et al. (2012). Has an angel shown the way? Etiological and therapeutic implications of the PCP/NMDA model of schizophrenia. *Schizophrenia Bulletin, 38*(5), 958–966. doi:10.1093/schbul/sbs069

Jawahar, I. M., Stone, T. H., & Kisamore, J. L. (2007). Role conflict and burnout: The direct and moderating effects of political skill and perceived organizational support on burnout dimensions. *International Journal of Stress Management, 14*(2), 142–159.

Jellinger, K. A. (2009). Review of *Interactive atlas of the human brain. European Journal of Neurology, 16*(3), e51. doi:10.1111/j.1468-1331.2008.02456.x

Jenkins, A. C., & Mitchell, J. P. (2011). Medial prefrontal cortex subserves diverse forms of self-reflection. *Social Neuroscience, 6*(3), 211–218. doi:10.1080/17470919.2010.507948

Jenkins, J. G., & Dallenbach, K. M. (1924). Oblivescence during sleep and waking. *American Journal of Psychology, 35*, 605–612.

Jerabek, I., & Standing, L. (1992). Imagined test situations produce contextual memory enhancement. *Perceptual & Motor Skills, 75*(2), 400.

Jiang, L., Bazarova, N. N., & Hancock, J. T. (2013). From perception to behavior: Disclosure reciprocity and the intensification of intimacy in computer-mediated communication. *Communication Research, 40*(1), 125–143. doi:10.1177/0093650211405313

Jin, S.-A A. (2010). Effects of 3D virtual haptics force feedback on brand personality perception: The mediating role of physical presence in advergames. *Cyberpsychology, Behavior, & Social Networking, 13*(3), 307–311.

Joffe, R. T. (2006). Is the thyroid still important in major depression? *Journal of Psychiatry & Neuroscience, 31*(6), 367–368.

Johansen, J. P., Wolff, S. E., et al. (2012). Controlling the elements: An optogenetic approach to understanding the neural circuits of fear. *Biological Psychiatry, 71*(12), 1053–1060. doi:10.1016/j.biopsych.2011.10.023

Johnson, B. T., & Boynton, M. H. (2010). Putting attitudes in their place: Behavioral prediction in the face of competing variables. In J. P. Forgas, J. Cooper, & W. D. Crano (Eds.), *The psychology of attitudes and attitude change* (pp. 19–38). New York: Psychology Press.

Johnson, C. S., & Lammers, J. (2012). The powerful disregard social comparison information. *Journal of Experimental Social Psychology, 48*(1), 329–334. doi:10.1016/j.jesp.2011.10.010

Johnson, C. S., & Stapel, D. A. (2010). It depends on how you look at it: Being versus becoming mindsets determine responses to social comparisons. *British Journal of Social Psychology, 49*(4), 703–723. doi:10.1348/014466609X476827

Johnson, J. J., Hrycaiko, D. W., et al. (2004). Self-talk and female youth soccer performance. *Sport Psychologist, 18*(1), 44–59.

Johnson, K. J., & Fredrickson, B. L. (2005). "We all look the same to me": Positive emotions eliminate the own-race bias in face recognition. *Psychological Science, 16*(11), 875–881. doi:10.1111/j.1467-9280.2005.01631.x

Johnson, M. W., & Griffiths, R. R. (2013). Comparative abuse liability of GHB and ethanol in humans. *Experimental & Clinical Psychopharmacology* doi:10.1037/a0031692

Johnson, R., Nessler, D., & Friedman, D. (2012). Temporally specific divided attention tasks in young adults reveal the temporal dynamics of episodic encoding failures in elderly adults. *Psychology & Aging*, doi:10.1037/a0030967

Johnson, S. (2005). *Everything bad is good for you: How today's popular culture is actually making us smarter.* New York: Riverhead.

Johnson, S. J., Batey, M., & Holdsworth, L. (2009). Personality and health: The mediating role of trait emotional intelligence and work locus of control. *Personality & Individual Differences, 47*(5), 470–475. doi:10.1016/j.paid.2009.04.025

Johnson, T. J. (2002). College students' self-reported reasons for why drinking games end. *Addictive Behaviors, 27*(1), 145–153. doi:10.1016/S0306-4603(00)00168-4

Johnson, W., Jung, R. E., et al. (2008). Cognitive abilities independent of IQ correlate with regional brain structure. *Intelligence, 36*(1), 18–28. doi:10.1016/j.intell.2007.01.005

Johnson, W., Turkheimer, E., et al. (2009). Beyond heritability: Twin studies in behavioral research. *Current Directions in Psychological Science, 18*(4), 217–220. doi:10.1111/j.1467-8721.2009.01639.x

Johnstone, P. M., Nábelek, A. K., & Robertson, V. S. (2010). Sound localization acuity in children with unilateral hearing loss who wear a hearing aid in the impaired ear. *Journal of The American Academy of Audiology, 21*(8), 522–534. doi:10.3766/jaaa.21.8.4

Joiner, T. E., Jr. (2010). *Myths about suicide.* Cambridge, MA: Harvard University Press.

Joinson, C., Heron, J., et al. (2009). A prospective study of age at initiation of toilet training and subsequent daytime bladder control in school-age children. *Journal of Developmental & Behavioral Pediatrics, 30*(5), 385–393. doi:10.1097/DBP.0b013e3181ba0e77

Jones, G. (2012). Why chunking should be considered as an explanation for developmental change before short-term memory capacity and processing speed. *Frontiers in Psychology, 3*, 167. doi:10.3389/fpsyg.2012.00167

Jones, K. L., & Streissguth, A. P. (2010). Fetal alcohol syndrome and fetal alcohol spectrum disorders: A brief history. *Journal of Psychiatry & Law, 38*(4), 373–382.

Jones, M. K., & Menzies, R. G. (1998). Danger ideation reduction therapy (DIRT) for obsessive-compulsive washers. *Behaviour Research & Therapy, 36*(10), 959–970. doi:10.1016/S0005-7967(98)00057-6

Jones, S. E., Mahmoud, S. Y., & Phillips, M. D. (2011). A practical clinical method to quantify language lateralization in fMRI using whole-brain analysis. *NeuroImage, 54*, 2937–2949. doi:10.1016/j.neuroimage.2010.10.052

Jones, S. R., & Fernyhough, C. (2007). A new look at the neural diathesis-stress model of schizophrenia: The primacy of social-evaluative and uncontrollable situations. *Schizophrenia Bulletin, 33*(5), 1171–1177. doi:10.1093/schbul/sbl058

Jones, S. S., & Hong, H.-W. (2001). Onset of voluntary communication: Smiling looks to mother. *Infancy, 2*(3), 353–370. doi:10.1207/S15327078IN0203_4

Jones, W. R., & Morgan, J. F. (2010). Eating disorders in men: A review of the literature. *Journal of Public Mental Health, 9*(2), 23–31. doi:10.5042/jpmh.2010.0326

Jonides, J., Lewis, R. L., et al. (2008). The mind and brain of short-term memory. *Annual Review of Psychology, 59*, 193–224. doi:10.1146/annurev.psych.59.103006.093615

Jonkmann, K., Becker, M., et al. (2012). Personality traits moderate the Big-Fish–Little-Pond effect of academic self-concept. *Learning & Individual Differences, 22*(6), 736–746. doi:10.1016/j.lindif.2012.07.020

Joo, E. Y., Tae, W. K., et al. (2010). Reduced brain gray matter concentration in patients with obstructive sleep apnea syndrome. *Sleep: Journal of Sleep & Sleep Disorders Research, 33*(2), 235–241.

Jordan, K. (2010). Vicarious trauma: Proposed factors that impact clinicians. *Journal of Family Psychotherapy, 21*(4), 225–237. doi:10.1080/08975353.2010.529003

Jorm, A. F. (2012). Mental health literacy: Empowering the community to take action for better mental health. *American Psychologist, 67*(3), 231–243. doi:10.1037/a0025957

Jorm, A. F., Korten, A. E., Rodgers, B., et al. (2002). Sexual orientation and mental health. *British Journal of Psychiatry, 180*(5), 423–427.

Jourard, S. M. (1963). *Personal adjustment.* New York: Macmillan.

Jouvet, M. (1999). *The paradox of sleep.* Boston: MIT Press.

Jowett, G. S. (2006). Brainwashing: The Korean POW controversy and the origins of a myth. In G. S. Jowett, & V. O'Donnell (Eds.), *Readings in propaganda and persuasion: New and classic essays* (pp. 201–211). Thousand Oaks, CA, Sage.

Judson, S. S., Johnson, D. M., & Perez, A. U. (2013). Perceptions of adult sexual coercion as a function of victim gender. *Psychology of Men & Masculinity*, doi:10.1037/a0030448

Juliano, L. M., & Griffiths, R. R. (2004). A critical review of caffeine withdrawal: Empirical validation of symptoms and signs, incidence, severity, and associated features. *Psychopharmacology, 176*(1), 1–29. doi:10.1007/s00213-004-2000-x

Julien, R. M. (2011). *A primer of drug action.* (12th ed.). New York: Worth.

Jun, H. (2010). *Social justice, multicultural counseling, and practice: Beyond a conventional approach.* Thousand Oaks, CA: Sage.

Jurd, R. R. (2011). TiNS special issue: Hippocampus and memory. *Trends in Neurosciences, 34*(10), 499–500. doi:10.1016/j.tins.2011.08.008

Jussim, L., & Harber, K. D. (2005). Teacher expectations and self-fulfilling prophecies: Knowns and unknowns, resolved and unresolved controversies. *Personality & Social Psychology Review, 9*(2), 131–155. doi:10.1207/s15327957pspr0902_3

Justman, S. (2011). From medicine to psychotherapy: The placebo effect. *History of the Human Sciences, 24*(1), 95–107. doi:10.1177/0952695110386655

Kafka, M. P. (2010). Hypersexual disorder: A proposed diagnosis for *DSM-V. Archives of Sexual Behavior, 39*(2), 377–400.

Kahlenberg, S. G., & Hein, M. M. (2010). Progression on Nickelodeon? Gender-role stereotypes in toy commercials. *Sex Roles, 62*(11–12), 830–847. doi:10.1007/s11199-009-9653-1

Kahneman, D. (2011). *Thinking, fast and slow.* New York: Farrar, Straus & Giroux.

Kahneman, D., & Tversky, A. (1972). Subjective probability: A judgment of representativeness. *Cognitive Psychology, 3*, 430–454. doi:10.1016/0010-0285(72)90016-3

Kahneman, D., Slovic, P., & Tversky, A. (1982). *Judgment under uncertainty: Heuristics and biases.* Cambridge, MA: Cambridge University Press.

Kaida, K., Åkerstedt, T., et al. (2008). Performance prediction by sleepiness-related subjective symptoms during 26-hour sleep deprivation. *Sleep & Biological Rhythms, 6*(4), 234–241. doi:10.1111/j.1479-8425.2008.00367.x

Kail, R. V., & Cavanaugh, J. C. (2013). *Human development: A life-span view* (6th ed.). Belmont, CA: Cengage Learning/Wadsworth.

Kalat, J. W. (2013). *Biological psychology* (11th ed.). Belmont, CA: Cengage Learning/Wadsworth.

Kalat, J. W., & Shiota, M. N. (2012). *Emotion* (2nd ed.). Belmont, CA: Wadsworth.

Kallio, S., & Revonsuo, A. (2003). Hypnotic phenomena and altered states of consciousness: A multilevel framework of description and explanation. *Contemporary Hypnosis, 20*(3), 111–164. doi:10.1002/ch.273

Kalmijn, M. (2010). Educational inequality, homogamy, and status exchange in Black-White intermarriage: A comment on Rosenfield. *American Journal of Sociology, 115*(4), 1252–1263.

Kalyuga, S., & Hanham, J. (2011). Instructing in generalized knowledge structures to develop flexible problem solving skills. *Computers in Human Behavior, 27*(1), 63–68. doi:10.1016/j.chb.2010.05.024

Kalyuga, S., Renkl, A., & Paas, F. (2010). Facilitating flexible problem solving: A cognitive load perspective. *Educational Psychology Review, 22*(2), 175–186. doi:10.1007/s10648-010-9132-9

Kamimori, G. H., Johnson, D., et al. (2005). Multiple caffeine doses maintain vigilance during early morning operations. *Aviation, Space, & Environmental Medicine, 76*(11), 1046–1050.

Kamin, L. J. (1981). *The intelligence controversy.* New York: Wiley.

Kammrath, L. K., Mendoza-Denton, R., & Mischel, W. (2005). Incorporating If . . . Then . . . personality signatures in person perception: Beyond the person-situation dichotomy. *Journal of Personality & Social Psychology, 88*(4), 605–618.

Kanas, N., & Manzey, D. (2008). *Space psychology and psychiatry* (2nd ed.). New York: Springer.

Kanayama, G., Kean, J., et al. (2012). Cognitive deficits in long-term anabolic-androgenic steroid users. *Drug & Alcohol Dependence.* doi:10.1016/j.drugalcdep.2012.11.008

Kandler, C. (2012). Knowing your personality is knowing its nature: The role of information accuracy of peer assessments for heritability estimates of temperamental and personality traits. *Personality & Individual Differences, 53*(4), 387–392. doi:10.1016/j.paid.2012.01.004

Kapinos, K. A., & Yakusheva, O. (2011). Environmental influences on young adult weight gain: Evidence from a natural experiment. *Journal of Adolescent Health, 48*(1), 52–58. doi:10.1016/j.jadohealth.2010.05.021

Kaplan, A. (2008). Clarifying metacognition, self-regulation, and self-regulated learning: What's the purpose? *Educational Psychology Review, 20*(4), 477–484. doi:10.1007/s10648-008-9087-2

Kaplan, P. S. (1998). *The human odyssey.* Pacific Grove, CA: Brooks/Cole.

Kaplan, R. M., & Saccuzzo, D. P. (2013). *Psychological testing: Principles, applications, and issues* (8th ed.). Belmont, CA: Cengage Learning/Wadsworth.

Kapleau, P. (1966). *The three pillars of Zen.* New York: Harper & Row.

Kappe, R., & van der Flier, H. (2010). Using multiple and specific criteria to assess the predictive validity of the big five personality factors on academic performance. *Journal of Research in Personality, 44*(1), 142–145. doi:10.1016/j.jrp.2009.11.002

Karageorgis, C. I., & Terry, P. C. (2011). *Inside sport psychology.* Champaign, IL: Human Kinetics.

Kardas, E. P. (2014). *History of psychology: The making of a science.* Belmont, CA: Cengage Learning/Wadsworth.

Kark, R., & Eagly, A. H. (2010). Gender and leadership: Negotiating the labyrinth. In J. C. Chrisler, & D. R. McCreary (Eds.), *Handbook of gender research in psychology* (Vol. 2): *Gender research in social and applied psychology* (pp. 443–470). New York: Springer.

Karpicke, J. D., & Blunt, J. R. (2011). Retrieval practice produces more learning than elaborative studying with concept mapping. *Science, January,* doi:10.1126/science.1199327

Karpicke, J. D., & Smith, M. A. (2012). Separate mnemonic effects of retrieval practice and elaborative encoding. *Journal of Memory and Language, 67*(1), 17–29.

Kasser, T., & Ryan, R. M. (1993). A dark side of the American dream: Correlates of financial success as a central life aspiration. *Journal of Personality & Social Psychology, 65*(2), 410–422. doi:10.1037/0022-3514.65.2.410

Kasser, T., & Ryan, R. M. (1996). Further examining the American dream: Differential correlates of intrinsic and extrinsic goals. *Personality & Social Psychology Bulletin, 22*(3), 280–287. doi:10.1177/0146167296223006

Kassin, S. M. (2005). On the psychology of confessions: Does innocence put innocents at risk? *American Psychologist, 60*(3), 215–228. doi:10.1037/0003-066X.60.3.215

Kassin, S. M., Fein, S., & Markus, H. R. (2014). *Social psychology* (9th ed.). Boston: Houghton Mifflin.

Kataria, S. (2004). A clinical guide to pediatric sleep: Diagnosis and management of sleep problems. *Journal of Developmental & Behavioral Pediatrics, 25*(2), 132–133.

doi:10.1097/00004703-200404000-00012

Katz, P. A. (2003). Racists or tolerant multiculturalists? *American Psychologist, 58*(11), 897–909.

Kaufman, A. S. (2000). Intelligence tests and school psychology: Predicting the future by studying the past. *Psychology in the Schools, 37*(1), 7–16. doi:10.1002/(SICI)1520-6807(200001)37:1<7::AID-PITS2>3.0.CO;2-H

Kaufman, J. C. (2009). *Creativity 101.* New York: Springer.

Kaufman, J. C., & Sternberg, R. J. (Eds.). (2010). *The Cambridge handbook of creativity.* New York: Cambridge University Press.

Kaufmann, J. (2007). Transfiguration: A narrative analysis of male-to-female transsexual. *International Journal of Qualitative Studies in Education, 20*(1), 1–13.

Kawada, R., Yoshizumi, M., et al. (2009). Brain volume and dysexecutive behavior in schizophrenia. *Progress in Neuro-Psychopharmacology & Biological Psychiatry, 33*(7), 1255–1260. doi:10.1016/j.pnpbp.2009.07.014

Kaye, W. H., Wierenga, C. E., et al. (2013). Nothing tastes as good as skinny feels: The neurobiology of anorexia nervosa. *Trends in Neurosciences, 36*(2), 110–120. doi:10.1016/j.tins.2013.01.003

Kearney, A. J. (2006). A primer of covert sensitization. *Cognitive & Behavioral Practice, 13*(2), 167–175. doi:10.1016/j.cbpra.2006.02.002

Kearney, C., & Trull, T. (2012). *Abnormal psychology and life: A dimensional approach.* Belmont, CA: Cengage Learning/Wadsworth.

Keating, C. (2010). Theoretical perspective on anorexia nervosa: The conflict of reward. *Neuroscience & Biobehavioral Reviews, 34*(1), 73–79. doi:10.1016/j.neubiorev.2009.07.004

Keefe, F. J., Huling, D. A., et al. (2012). Virtual reality for persistent pain: A new direction for behavioral pain management. *Pain, 153*(11), 2163–2166.

Keegan, J., Parva, M., et al. (2010). Addiction in pregnancy. *Journal of Addictive Diseases, 29*(2), 175–191. doi:10.1080/10550881003684723

Keel, P. K., & Klump, K. L. (2003). Are eating disorders culture-bound syndromes? Implications for conceptualizing their etiology. *Psychological Bulletin, 129*(5), 747–769. doi:10.1037/0033-2909.129.5.747

Kegel, M., Dam, H., et al. (2009). The prevalence of seasonal affective disorder (SAD) in Greenland is related to latitude. *Nordic Journal of Psychiatry, 63*(4), 331–335. doi:10.1080/08039480902799040

Kell, C. A., Morillon, B., et al. (2011). Lateralization of speech production starts in sensory cortices:

A possible sensory origin of cerebral left dominance for speech. *Cerebral Cortex, 21*(4), 932–937. doi:10.1093/cercor/bhq167

Keller, M. C., & Young, R. K. (1996). Mate assortment in dating and married couples. *Personality & Individual Differences, 21*(2), 217–221.

Kelly, E. (2010). *I always knew I was a girl.* Retrieved June 11, 2013, from http://www.salon.com/life/feature/2010/11/20/how_i_became_a_woman

Kelly, I. W. (1999). "Debunking the debunkers": A response to an astrologer's debunking of skeptics. *Skeptical Inquirer, Nov.–Dec.,* 37–43.

Kelly, M. P., Strassberg, D. S., & Turner, C. M. (2006). Behavioral assessment of couples' communication in female orgasmic disorder. *Journal of Sex & Marital Therapy, 32*(2), 81–95.

Kendall-Tackett, K. (Ed.). (2010). *The psychoneuroimmunology of chronic disease: Exploring the links between inflammation, stress, and illness.* Washington: American Psychological Association.

Kendler, K. S., & Schaffner, K. F. (2011). The dopamine hypothesis of schizophrenia: An historical and philosophical analysis. *Philosophy, Psychiatry, & Psychology, 18*(1), 41–63. doi:10.1353/ppp.2011.0005

Kennedy, S. H., Giacobbe, P., et al. (2011). Deep brain stimulation for treatment-resistant depression: Follow-up after 3 to 6 years. *The American Journal of Psychiatry, 168*(5), 502–510. doi:10.1176/appi.ajp.2010.10081187

Kenny, P. J., & Markou, A. (2006). Nicotine self-administration acutely activates brain reward systems and induces a long-lasting increase in reward sensitivity. *Neuropsychopharmacology, 31*(6), 1203–1211. doi:10.1038/sj.npp.1300905

Kenrick, D.T., Griskevicius, V., et al., (2010). Renovating the pyramid of needs: Contemporary extensions built upon ancient foundations. *Perspectives on Psychological Science, 5,* 292–314. doi:10.1177/1745691610369469

Kern, J. K., Geier, D. A., et al. (2012). Evidence of parallels between mercury intoxication and the brain pathology in autism. *Acta Neurobiologiae Experimentalis, 72*(2), 113–153.

Kernis, M. H., & Goldman, B. M. (2005). Authenticity, social motivation, and psychological adjustment. In J. P. Forgas, K. D. Williams, & S. M. Laham (Eds.), *Social motivation: Conscious and unconscious processes* (pp. 210–227). New York: Cambridge University Press.

Kernis, M. H., & Lakey, C. E. (2010). Fragile versus secure high self-esteem: Implications for defensiveness and insecurity. In R. M. Arkin, K. C. Oleson, et al. (Eds.), *Handbook of the uncertain self* (pp. 360–378). New York: Psychology Press.

Kerns, R. D., Sellinger, J., & Goodin, B. R. (2011). Psychological treatment of chronic pain. *Annual Review of Clinical Psychology, 7*, 411–434. doi:10.1146/annurev-clinpsy-090310-120430

Kessler, D. A. (2009). *The end of overeating: Taking control of the insatiable American appetite.* Emmaus, PA: Rodale Press.

Kessler, R. C. (2010). The prevalence of mental illness. In T. L. Scheid & T. N. Brown (Eds.), *A handbook for the study of mental health: Social contexts, theories, and systems* (2nd ed., pp. 46–63). New York: Cambridge University Press.

Kety, S. S. (1979, Sept.). Disorders of the human brain. *Scientific American, 241*, 202–214. doi:10.1038/scientificamerican0979-202

Keysers, C., Xiao, D.-K., et al. (2005). Out of sight but not out of mind: The neurophysiology of iconic memory in the superior temporal sulcus. *Cognitive Neuropsychology, 22*(3–4), 316–332. doi:10.1080/02643290442000103

Khan, K. M., Thompson, A. M., et al. (2012). Sport and exercise as contributors to the health of nations. *The Lancet, 380*(9836), 59–64. doi:10.1016/S0140-6736(12)60865-4

Khan, O., Tselis, A., & Lisak, R. (2010). Getting to grips with myelin injury in progressive multiple sclerosis. *Brain: A Journal of Neurology, 133*(10), 2845–2851. doi:10.1093/brain/awq271

Kida, T. E. (2006). *Don't believe everything you think.* Buffalo, NY: Prometheus.

Kiecolt-Glaser, J. (2010). Stress, food, and inflammation: Psychoneuroimmunology and nutrition at the cutting edge. *Psychosomatic Medicine, 72*(4), 365–369. doi:10.1097/PSY.0b013e3181dbf489

Kiernan, M., Brown, S. D., et al. (2013). Promoting healthy weight with "stability skills first": A randomized trial. *Journal of Consulting & Clinical Psychology, 81*(2), 336–346. doi:10.1037/a0030544

Kievit, R. A., van Rooijen, H., et al. (2012). Intelligence and the brain: A model-based approach. *Cognitive Neuroscience, 3*, 89–97. doi:10.1080/17588928.2011.628383

Kiff, C. J., Lengua, L. J., & Bush, N. R. (2011). Temperament variation in sensitivity to parenting: Predicting changes in depression and anxiety. *Journal of Abnormal Child Psychology, 39*(8), 1199–1212. doi:10.1007/s10802-011-9539-x

Kim-Cohen, J., Moffitt, T. E., et al. (2004). Genetic and environmental processes in young children's resilience and vulnerability to socioeconomic deprivation. *Child Development, 75*(3), 651–668. doi:10.1111/j.1467-8624.2004.00699.x

Kim, E. H., & Gray, S. H. (2009). Challenges presenting in transference and countertransference in the psychodynamic psychotherapy of a military service member. *Journal of the American Academy of Psychoanalysis & Dynamic Psychiatry, 37*(3), 421–437. doi:10.1521/jaap.2009.37.3.421

Kim, S., Oah, S., & Dickinson, A. M. (2005). The impact of public feedback on three recycling-related behaviors in South Korea. *Environment & Behavior, 37*(2), 258–274. doi:10.1177/0013916504267639

Kimura, R., MacTavish, D., et al. (2012). Beta amyloid-induced depression of hippocampal long-term potentiation is mediated through the amylin receptor. *The Journal of Neuroscience, 32*(48), 17401–17406. doi:10.1523/JNEUROSCI.3028-12.2012

King, B. E. (2012). *Human sexuality today* (7th ed.). Englewood Cliffs, NJ: Prentice Hall.

King, L. A., Richards, J. H., & Stemmerich, E. (1998). Daily goals, life goals, and worst fears: Means, ends, and subjective well-being. *Journal of Personality, 66*(5), 713–744. doi:10.1111/1467-6494.00030

King, N. J., Muris, P., & Ollendick, T. H. (2005). Childhood fears and phobias: Assessment and treatment. *Child & Adolescent Mental Health, 10*(2), 50–56. doi:10.1111/j.1475-3588.2005.00118.x

King, P. M. (2009). Principles of development and developmental change underlying theories of cognitive and moral development. *Journal of College Student Development, 50*(6), 597–620. doi:10.1353/csd.0.0104

Kingsley, C. H. & Lambert, K. G. (2006). The maternal brain. *Scientific American, 294*(1), 72–79.

Kinnunen, L. H., Moltz, H., Metz, J., et al. (2004). Differential brain activation in exclusively homosexual and heterosexual men produced by the selective serotonin reuptake inhibitor, fluoxetine. *Brain Research, 1024*(1–2), 251–254. doi:10.1016/j.brainres.2004.07.070

Kinsey, A., Pomeroy, W., & Martin, C. (1948). *Sexual behavior in the human male.* Philadelphia: Saunders.

Kinsey, A., Pomeroy, W., & Martin, C. (1953). *Sexual behavior in the human female.* Philadelphia: Saunders.

Kirby, D. B. (2008). The impact of abstinence and comprehensive sex and STD/HIV education programs on adolescent sexual behavior. *Sexuality Research & Social Policy, 5*(3), 18–27.

Kirchhoff, B. A. (2009). Individual differences in episodic memory: The role of self-initiated encoding strategies. *The Neuroscientist, 15*(2), 166–179. doi:10.1177/1073858408329507

Kirk, S. A., Gallagher, J. J., et al. (2011). *Educating exceptional children* (13th ed.). Belmont, CA: Cengage Learning/Wadsworth.

Kirsch, I., (2005). The flexible observer and neodissociation theory. *Contemporary Hypnosis, 22*(3), 121–122. doi:10.1002/ch.2

Kirsch, I., & Lynn, S. J. (1995). The altered state of hypnosis. *American Psychologist, 50*(10), 846–858. doi:10.1037/0003-066X.50.10.846

Kirsch, I., & Sapirstein, G. (1998). Listening to Prozac but hearing placebo: A meta-analysis of antidepressant medication. *Prevention & Treatment, 1*, art. 0002a. doi:10.1037/1522-3736.1.1.12a

Kirsh, S. J. (2010). *Children, adolescents, and media violence: A critical look at the research* (2nd ed.). Thousand Oaks, CA: Sage.

Kiser, L. J., Heston, J. D., & Paavola, M. (2006). Day treatment centers/partial hospitalization settings. In T. A. Petti & C. Salguero (Eds.), *Community child & adolescent psychiatry: A manual of clinical practice and consultation* (pp. 189–203). Washington: American Psychiatric Publishing.

Kisilevsky, B. S., & Hains, S. J. (2011). Onset and maturation of fetal heart rate response to the mother's voice over late gestation. *Developmental Science, 14*(2), 214–223.

Kitada, R., Dijkerman, H. C., et al. (2010). Representing human hands haptically or visually from first-person versus third-person perspectives. *Perception, 39*(2), 236–254.

Kitayama, S., Markus, H. R., & Kurokawa, M. (2000). Culture, emotion, and well-being: Good feelings in Japan and the United States. *Cognition & Emotion, 14*, 93–124. doi:10.1080/026999300379003

Kjellgren, A., Buhrkall, H., & Norlander, T. (2011). Preventing sick-leave for sufferers of high stress-load and burnout syndrome: A pilot study combining psychotherapy and the flotation tank. *International Journal of Psychology & Psychological Therapy, 11*(2), 297–306.

Klahr, D., & Nigam, M. (2004). The equivalence of learning paths in early science instruction: Effects of direct instruction and discovery learning. *Psychological Science, 15*, 661–667.

Kleiman, E. M., Miller, A. B., & Riskind, J. H. (2012). Enhancing attributional style as a protective factor in suicide. *Journal of Affective Disorders, 143*(1–3), 236–240. doi:10.1016/j.jad.2012.05.014

Klein, B., Richards, J. C., & Austin, D. W. (2006). Efficacy of internet therapy for panic disorder. *Journal of Behavior Therapy & Experimental Psychiatry, 37*(3), 213–238. doi:10.1016/j.jbtep.2005.07.001

Klein, D. W., & Kihlstrom, J. F. (1986). Elaboration, organization, and the self-reference effect in memory. *Journal of Experimental Psychology: General, 115*, 26–38.

Klein, K., & Boals, A. (2001). Expressive writing can increase working memory capacity. *Journal of Experimental Psychology: General, 130*(3), 520–533. doi:10.1037/0096-3445.130.3.520

Klein, L. A., & Houlihan, D. (2010). Relationship satisfaction, sexual satisfaction, and sexual problems in sexsomnia. *International Journal of Sexual Health, 22*(2), 84–90. doi:10.1080/19317610903510489

Kleinmann, M., & Klehe, U. (2011). Selling oneself: Construct and criterion-related validity of impression management in structured interviews. *Human Performance, 24*(1), 29–46. doi:10.1080/08959285.2010.530634

Klohnen, E. C., & Luo, S. (2003). Interpersonal attraction and personality: What is attractive—self similarity, ideal similarity, complementarity or attachment security? *Journal of Personality & Social Psychology, 85*(4), 709–722. doi:10.1037/0022-3514.85.4.709

Klöppel, S., Mangin, J.-F., et al. (2010). Nurture versus nature: Long-term impact of forced right-handedness on structure of pericentral cortex and basal ganglia. *Journal of Neuroscience, 30*(9), 3271–3275. doi:10.1523/JNEUROSCI.4394-09.2010

Knafo, D. (2009). Freud's memory erased. *Psychoanalytic Psychology, 26*(2), 171–190.

Kneer, J., Glock, S., & Rieger, D. (2012). Fast and not furious? Reduction of cognitive dissonance in smokers. *Social Psychology, 43*(2), 81–91. doi:10.1027/1864-9335/a000086

Knickmeyer, R. C., & Baron-Cohen, S. (2006). Fetal testosterone and sex differences. *Early Human Development, 82*(12), 755–760.

Knoops, K. T., de Groot, L. C., et al. (2004). Mediterranean diet, lifestyle factors, and 10-year mortality in elderly European men and women. *Journal of the American Medical Association, 292*(12), 1433–1439. doi:10.1001/jama.292.12.1433

Koch, I., Lawo, V., et al. (2011). Switching in the cocktail party: Exploring intentional control of auditory selective attention. *Journal of Experimental Psychology: Human Perception & Performance, 37*(4), 1140–1147. doi:10.1037/a0022189

Koda, S., & Sugawara, K. (2009). The influence of diet behavior and stress on binge-eating among female college students. *Japanese Journal of Psychology, 80*(2), 83–89.

Koek, W. (2011). Drug-induced state-dependent learning: Review of an operant procedure in rats. *Behavioural Pharmacology, 22*(5–6), 430–440. doi:10.1097/FBP.0b013e328348ed3b

Kohen, D. P. (2011). Chronic daily headache: Helping adolescents help themselves with self-hypnosis. *American Journal of Clinical Hypnosis, 54*(1), 32–46. doi:10.1080/00029157.2011.566767

Kohlberg, L. (1969). The cognitive-developmental approach to socialization. In A. Goslin (Ed.), *Handbook of socialization theory and research* (pp. 1–134). Chicago: Rand McNally.

Kohlberg, L. (1981). *Essays on moral development* (Vol. I): *The philosophy of moral development*. San Francisco: Harper.

Kohler, P. K., Manhart, L. E., & Lafferty, W. E. (2008). Abstinence-only and comprehensive sex education and the initiation of sexual activity and teen pregnancy. *Journal of Adolescent Health, 42*(4), 344–351.

Kohn, C. S., & Antonuccio, D. O. (2002). Treatment of kleptomania using cognitive and behavioral strategies. *Clinical Case Studies, 1*(1), 25–38. doi:10.1177/1534650102001001003

Köke, A., Schouten, J. S., et al. (2004). Pain reducing effect of three types of transcutaneous electrical nerve stimulation in patients with chronic pain: A randomized crossover trial. *Pain, 108*(1–2), 36–42. doi:10.1016/j.pain.2003.11.013

Kolb, B., & Whishaw, I.Q. (2013). *Introduction to brain and behavior* (4th ed.). New York: Freeman-Worth.

Kolb, B., Gibb, R., & Gorny, G. (2003). Experience-dependent changes in dendritic arbor and spine density in neocortex vary with age and sex. *Neurobiology of Learning & Memory, 79*(1), 1–10. doi:10.1016/S1074-7427(02)00021-7

Kolb, B., Mychasiuk, R., et al. (2011). Brain plasticity and recovery from early cortical injury. *Developmental Medicine & Child Neurology, 53*, 4–8. doi:10.1111/j.1469-8749.2011.04054.x

Komisaruk, B. R., Beyer-Flores, C., & Whipple, B. (2006). *The science of orgasm*. Baltimore, MD: Johns Hopkins University Press.

Kornhaber, M. L., & Gardner, H. (2006). Multiple intelligences: Developments in implementation and theory. In M. A. Constas, & R. J. Sternberg (Eds.), *Translating theory and research into educational practice: Developments in content domains, large-scale reform, and intellectual capacity* (pp. 255–276). Mahwah, NJ: Erlbaum.

Kornilov, S. A., Tan, M., et al. (2012). Gifted identification with aurora: Widening the spotlight. *Journal of Psychoeducational Assessment, 30*(1), 117–133. doi:10.1177/0734282911428199

Koschate, M., & van Dick, R. (2011). A multilevel test of Allport's contact conditions. *Group Processes & Intergroup Relations, 14*(6), 769–787. doi:10.1177/1368430211399602

Kossek, E. E., & Michel, J. S. (2011). Flexible work schedules. In S. Zedeck (Ed.). (2011). *APA handbook of industrial and organizational psychology* (Vol 1): *Building and developing the organization* (pp. 535–572). Washington, DC: American Psychological Association.

Kosslyn, S. M. (1983). *Ghosts in the mind's machine*. New York: Norton.

Kosslyn, S. M. (1985). Stalking the mental image. *Psychology Today, 19*(5), 22–28.

Kosslyn, S. M., Ball, T. M., & Reiser, B. J. (1978). Visual images preserve metric spatial information: Evidence from studies of image scanning. *Journal of Experimental Psychology: Human Perception & Performance, 4*, 47–60. doi:10.1037/0096-1523.4.1.47

Kosson, D. S., Suchy, Y., et al. (2002). Facial affect recognition in criminal psychopaths. *Emotion, 2*(4), 398–411. doi:10.1037/1528-3542.2.4.398

Kost, K., & Henshaw, S. (2013). *U.S. teenage pregnancies, births and abortions, 2008: State trends by age, race and ethnicity*. Retrieved April 11, 2013, from http://www.guttmacher.org/pubs/USTPtrends13.pdf

Kosten, T. R., Wu, G., et al. (2012). Pharmacogenetic randomized trial for cocaine abuse: Disulfiram and dopamine β-hydroxylase. *Biological Psychiatry*. doi:10.1016/j.biopsych.2012.07.011

Kotagal, S. (2012). Hypersomnia in children. *Sleep Medicine Clinics, 7*(2), 379–389. doi:10.1016/j.jsmc.2012.03.010

Kotkin, M., Daviet, C., & Gurin, J. (1996). The *Consumer Reports* mental health survey. *American Psychologist, 51*(10), 1080–1082. doi:10.1037/0003-066X.51.10.1080

Kott, A. A. (2011). Masturbation is associated with partnered sex among adolescent males and females. *Perspectives on Sexual and Reproductive Health, 43*(4), 264. doi:10.1363/4326411_1

Kottler, J. A., & Chen, D. D. (2011). *Stress management and prevention: Applications to daily life* (2nd ed.). New York: Routledge.

Kottler, J. A., & Shepard, D. S. (2011). *Introduction to counseling* (7th ed.). Belmont, CA: Cengage Learning/Wadsworth.

Kovera, M., & Cutler, B. L. (2013). *Jury selection*. New York: Oxford University Press.

Kovrov, G. V., Rusakova, I. M., et al. (2012). Specificity of sleep-wakefulness cycle during a 105-day isolation. *Human Physiology, 38*(7), 695–698. doi:10.1134/S0362119712070109

Kowert, P. A. (2002). *Groupthink or deadlock: When do leaders learn from their advisors? SUNY series on the presidency*. Albany, NY: State University of New York Press.

Kozica, S. L., Deeks, A. A., et al. (2012). Health-related behaviors in women with lifestyle-related diseases. *Behavioral Medicine, 38*(3), 65–73. doi:10.1080/08964289.2012.685498

Krahé, B., & Möller, I. (2010). Longitudinal effects of media violence on aggression and empathy among German adolescents. *Journal of Applied Developmental Psychology, 31*(5). 401–409. doi:10.1016/j.appdev.2010.07.003

Krahé, B., Möller, I., et al. (2011). Desensitization to media violence: Links with habitual media violence exposure, aggressive cognitions, and aggressive behavior. *Journal of Personality & Social Psychology, 100*(4), 630–646. doi:10.1037/a0021711

Krakow, B., & Zadra, A. (2006). Clinical management of chronic nightmares: Imagery rehearsal therapy. *Behavioral Sleep Medicine, 4*(1), 45–70. doi:10.1207/s15402010bsm0401_4

Krall, E. A., Garvey, A. J., & Garcia, R. I. (2002). Smoking relapse after 2 years of abstinence: Findings from the VA Normative Aging Study. *Nicotine & Tobacco Research, 4*(1), 95–100. doi:10.1080/14622200110098428

Kramer, U., Despland, J.-N., et al. (2010). Change in defense mechanisms and coping over the course of short-term dynamic psychotherapy for adjustment disorder. *Journal of Clinical Psychology, 66*(12), 1232–1241. doi:10.1002/jclp.20719

Krantz, M. J., Sabel, A. L., et al. (2012). Factors influencing QT prolongation in patients hospitalized with severe anorexia nervosa. *General Hospital Psychiatry, 34*(2), 173–177. doi:10.1016/j.genhosppsych.2011.08.003

Kreager, D. A., & Staff, J. (2009). The sexual double standard and adolescent peer acceptance. *Social Psychology Quarterly, 72*(2), 143–164.

Kreger Silverman, L. (2013). *Giftedness 101*. New York: Springer.

Krishnan, H. A., & Park, D. (2005). A few good women on top management teams. *Journal of Business Research, 58*, 1712–1720.

Kristof-Brown, A. L., Barrick, M. R., & Franke, M. (2002). Applicant impression management: Dispositional influences and consequences for recruiter perceptions of fit and similarity. *Journal of Management, 28*, 27–46.

Kteily, N. S., Sidanius, J., & Levin, S. (2011). Social dominance orientation: Cause or 'mere effect'? Evidence for SDO as a causal predictor of prejudice and discrimination against ethnic and racial outgroups. *Journal of Experimental Social Psychology,* 47(1), 208–214. doi:10.1016/j.jesp.2010.09.009

Kübler-Ross, E. (1975). *Death: The final stage of growth*. Englewood Cliffs, NJ: Prentice-Hall.

Kuehn, B. M. (2012). Marijuana use starting in youth linked to IQ loss. *Journal of The American Medical Association, 308*(12), doi:10.1001/2012.jama.12205

Kugler, T., & Bornstein, G. (2013). Social dilemmas between individuals and groups. Organizational Behavior & Human Decision Processes, 120(2), 191–205. doi:10.1016/j.obhdp.2012.07.007

Kuhl, P. K. (2004). Early language acquisition: Cracking the speech code. *Nature Reviews Neuroscience, 5*(11), 831–841. doi:10.1038/nrn1533

Kuiper, N. A., & McHale, N. (2009). Humor styles as mediators between self-evaluative standards and psychological well-being. *Journal of Psychology: Interdisciplinary & Applied, 143*(4), 359–376. doi:10.3200/JRLP.143.4.359-376

Kupfersmid, J. (2012). The Oedipus complex: It made no sense then, it makes no sense now. In M. Holowchak (Ed.), *Radical claims in Freudian psychoanalysis: Point/Counterpoint* (pp. 27–40). Lanham, MD: Jason Aronson.

Kuther, T. L., & Morgan, R. D. (2013). *Careers in psychology: Opportunities in a changing world* (4th ed.). Belmont, CA: Cengage Learning/Wadsworth.

Laan, E., Everaerd, W., et al. (1994). Women's sexual and emotional responses to male- and female-produced erotica. *Archives of Sexual Behavior, 23*(2), 153–169.

Laasonen, M., Kauppinen, J., et al. (2012). Project DyAdd: Classical eyeblink conditioning in adults with dyslexia and ADHD. *Experimental Brain Research, 223*(1), 19–32. doi:10.1007/s00221-012-3237-y

LaBar, K. S. (2007). Beyond fear: Emotional memory mechanisms in the human brain. *Current Directions in Psychological Science, 16*(4), 173–177. doi:10.1111/j.1467-8721.2007.00498.x

LaBerge, S. (2000). Lucid dreaming: Evidence and methodology. In F. E. Pace-Schott, M. Solms, et al. (Eds.), *Sleep and dreaming: Scientific advances and reconsiderations* (pp. 1–50). Cambridge, UK: Cambridge University Press.

Laborda, M. A., & Miller, R. R. (2011). S-R associations, their extinction, and recovery in an animal model of anxiety: A new associative account of phobias without recall of original trauma. *Behavior Therapy, 42*(2), 153–169. doi:10.1016/j.beth.2010.06.002

Labov, W. (1973). The boundaries of words and their meanings. In C. J. N. Bailey & R. W. Shuy (Eds.) *New ways of analyzing variation in English* (pp. 340–373).

Washington: Georgetown University Press.

LaBrie, R. A., & Shaffer, H. J. (2007). Gambling with adolescent health. *Journal of Adolescent Health, 40*(5), 387–389. doi:10.1016/j.jadohealth.2007.02.009

Lachman, M. E. (2004). Development in midlife. *Annual Review of Psychology, 55*, 305–331. doi:10.1146/annurev.psych.55.090902.141521

Lachman, M. E., Röcke, C., et al. (2008). Realism and illusion in Americans' temporal views of their life satisfaction: Age differences in reconstructing the past and anticipating the future. *Psychological Science, 19*(9), 889–897. doi:10.1111/j.1467-9280.2008.02173.x

Lackamp, J. M., Osborne, C., & Wise, T. N. (2009). Paraphilic disorders. In R. Balon, & R. T. Segraves (Eds.), *Clinical manual of sexual disorders* (pp. 335–370). Arlington, VA: American Psychiatric Publishing.

Lackner, J. R., & DiZio, P. (2005). Vestibular, proprioceptive, and haptic contributions to spatial orientation. *Annual Review of Psychology, 56*, 115–147. doi:10.1146/annurev.psych.55.090902.142023

Ladouceur, R., Lachance, S., & Fournier, P.-M. (2009). Is control a viable goal in the treatment of pathological gambling? *Behaviour Research & Therapy, 47*(3), 189–197. doi:10.1016/j.brat.2008.11.004

Lagace, D. C. (2011). Does the endogenous neurogenic response alter behavioral recovery following stroke? *Behavioural Brain Research.* doi:10.1016/j.bbr.2011.08.045

Lagos, P., Torterolo, P., et al. (2009). Effects on sleep of melanin-concentrating hormone (MCH) microinjections into the dorsal raphe nucleus. *Brain Research, 1265*, 103–110. doi:10.1016/j.brainres.2009.02.010

Lam, R., & Mok, H. (2008). *Depression.* New York: Oxford.

Lamb, R. J., Kirby, K. C., et al. (2010). Shaping smoking cessation in hard-to-treat smokers. *Journal of Consulting & Clinical Psychology, 78*(1), 62–71. doi:10.1037/a0018323

Lamb, T. D. (2011). Evolution of the eye. *Scientific American, July*, 64–69.

Lambert, E. G., Clarke, A., et al. (2009). Multivariate analysis of reasons for death penalty support between male and female college students: Empirical support for Gilligan's 'ethic of care.' *Criminal Justice Studies: A Critical Journal Of Crime, Law & Society, 22*(3), 239–260. doi:10.1080/14786010903166957

Lambert, M. J., & Ogles, B. M. (2002). The efficacy and effectiveness of psychotherapy. In M. J. Lambert (Ed.), *Handbook of psychotherapy and behavior change* (5th ed., pp. 130–193). New York: Wiley.

Lambert, W. E. (1987). The effects of bilingual and bicultural experiences on children's attitudes and social perspectives. In P. Homel, M. Palij, & D. Aaronson (Eds.), *Childhood bilingualism.* Hillsdale, NJ: Erlbaum.

Lammers, G. J., Bassetti, C., et al. (2010). Sodium oxybate is an effective and safe treatment for narcolepsy. *Sleep Medicine, 11*(1), 105–106. doi:10.1016/j.sleep.2009.08.003

Lamont, K. T., Somers, S., et al. (2011). Is red wine a SAFE sip away from cardioprotection? Mechanisms involved in resveratrol- and melatonin-induced cardioprotection. *Journal of Pineal Research, 50*, 374–380. doi:10.1111/j.1600-079X.2010.00853.x

Lampinen, J. M., Neuschatz, J. S., & Cling, A. D. (2012). The psychology of eyewitness identification. Hove, UK: Psychology Press.

Lamprecht, R., Dracheva, S., et al. (2009). Fear conditioning induces distinct patterns of gene expression in lateral amygdala. *Genes, Brain & Behavior, 8*(8), 735–743. doi:10.1111/j.1601-183X.2009.00515.x

Lamy, L., Fischer-Lokou, J., & Guéguen, N. (2012). Priming emotion concepts and helping behavior: How unlived emotions can influence action. *Social Behavior and Personality, 40*(1), 55–62. doi:10.2224/sbp.2012.40.1.55

Lan Yeung, V. W., & Kashima, Y. (2010). Communicating stereotype-relevant information: How readily can people individuate? *Asian Journal of Social Psychology, 13*(4), 209–220. doi:10.1111/j.1467-839X.2010.01313.x

Lanciano, T., Curci, A., & Semin, G. (2010). The emotional and reconstructive determinants of emotional memories: An experimental approach to flashbulb memory investigation. *Memory, 18*(5), 473–485. doi:10.1080/09658211003762076

Landa, Y., Silverstein, S. M., et al. (2006). Group cognitive behavioral therapy for delusions: Helping patients improve reality testing. *Journal of Contemporary Psychotherapy, 36*(1), 9–17. doi:10.1007/s10879-005-9001-x

Landy, F. J., & Conte, J. M. (2009). *Work in the 21st century: An introduction to industrial and organizational psychology* (3rd ed.). Malden, MA: Blackwell.

Landy, F. J., Shankster, L. J., & Kohler, S. S. (1994). Personnel selection and placement. *Annual Review of Psychology, 45*, 261–296.

Lane, C. (2009). The slippery slope of bitterness disorder and other psychiatric diagnoses. Retrieved June 18, 2013, from http://www.psychologytoday.com/blog/side-effects/200906/the-slippery-slope-bitterness-disorder-and-other-psychiatric-diagnoses

Langer, E. J. (2000). Mindful learning. *Current Directions in Psychological Science, 9*(6), 220–223. doi:10.1111/1467-8721.00099

Langleben, D. D. (2008). Detection of deception with fMRI: Are we there yet? *Legal & Criminological Psychology, 13*(1), 1–9. doi:10.1348/135532507X251641

Langleben, D. D., & Moriarty, J. (2012). Using brain imaging for lie detection: Where science, law, and policy collide. *Psychology, Public Policy, & Law.* doi:10.1037/a0028841

Langleben, D. D., Dattilio, F. M., & Gutheil, T. G. (2006). True lies: Delusions and lie-detection technology. *Journal of Psychiatry & Law, 34*(3), 351–370. doi:10.1037/a0020970

Langleben, D. D., Loughead, J. W., et al. (2005). Telling truth from lie in individual subjects with fast event-related fMRI. *Human Brain Mapping, 26*(4), 262–272. doi:10.1002/hbm.20191

Langone, M. D. (2002). Cults, conversion, science, and harm. *Cultic Studies Review, 1*(2), 178–186.

Larimer, M. E., Neighbors, C., et al. (2011). Descriptive drinking norms: For whom does reference group matter? *Journal of Studies on Alcohol & Drugs, 72*(5), 833–843.

Larsen, R. J., & Buss, D. M. (2010). *Personality psychology* (4th ed.). New York: McGraw-Hill.

Larsen, R. J., & Kasimatis, M. (1990). Individual differences in entrainment of mood to the weekly calendar. *Journal of Personality & Social Psychology, 58*(1), 164–171. doi:10.1037/0022-3514.58.1.164

Larson, M. E., Houlihan, D., & Goernert, P. N. (1995). Effects of informational feedback on aluminum can recycling. *Behavioral Interventions, 10*(2), 111–117.

Larsson, B., Carlsson, J., et al. (2005). Relaxation treatment of adolescent headache sufferers: Results from a school-based replication series. *Headache: The Journal of Head & Face Pain, 45*(6), 692–704. doi:10.1111/j.1526-4610.2005.05138.x

Larsson, J.-O., Larsson, H., & Lichtenstein, P. (2004). Genetic and environmental contributions to stability and change of ADHD symptoms between 8 and 13 years of age: A longitudinal twin study. *Journal of the American Academy of Child & Adolescent Psychiatry, 43*(10), 1267–1275. doi:10.1097/01.chi.0000135622.05219.bf

Latrofa, M., Vaes, J., et al. (2010). The cognitive representation of self-stereotyping. *Personality & Social Psychology Bulletin, 36*(7), 911–922. doi:10.1177/0146167210373907

Lattal, K. A., Reilly, M. P., & Kohn, J. P. (1998). Response persistence under ratio and interval reinforcement schedules. *Journal of the Experimental Analysis of Behavior, 70*(2), 165–183. doi:10.1901/jeab.1998.70-165

Lau, C. Q. (2012). The stability of same-sex cohabitation, different-sex cohabitation, and marriage. *Journal of Marriage & Family, 74*(5), 973–988.

Laub, J. H., & Sampson, R. J. (2003). *Shared beginnings, divergent lives: Delinquent boys to age 70.* Cambridge, MA: Harvard University Press.

Laumann, E., Michael, R., et al. (1994). *The social organization of sexuality.* Chicago: University of Chicago Press.

Laureys, S., & Boly. M. (2007). What is it like to be vegetative or minimally conscious? *Current Opinion in Neurology, 20*, 609–613.

Lautsch, B. A., Kossek, E. E., & Eaton, S. C. (2009). Supervisory approaches and paradoxes in managing telecommuting implementation. *Human Relations, 62*(6), 795–827.

Lavigne, F., Dumercy, L., et al. (2012). Dynamics of the semantic priming shift: Behavioral experiments and cortical network model. *Cognitive Neurodynamics, 6*(6), 467–483. doi:10.1007/s11571-012-9206-0

Lavin, M. (2012). On behalf of free association. In M. Holowchak (Ed.), *Radical claims in Freudian psychoanalysis: Point/Counterpoint* (pp. 153–166). Lanham, MD: Jason Aronson.

Lazarus, R. S. (1991a). Progress on a cognitive–motivational–relational theory of emotion. *American Psychologist, 46*(8), 819–834. doi:10.1037/0003-066X.46.8.819

Lazarus, R. S. (1991b). Cognition and motivation in emotion. *American Psychologist, 46*(4), 352–367. doi:10.1037/0003-066X.46.4.352

Le Berre, A. P., Rauchs, G. G., et al. (2012). Impaired decision-making and brain shrinkage in alcoholism. *European Psychiatry*, doi:10.1016/j.eurpsy.2012.10.002

Le Pelley, M. E., Reimers, S. J., et al. (2010). Stereotype formation: Biased by association. *Journal of Experimental Psychology: General, 139*(1), 138–161. doi:10.1037/a0018210

Le, T. N. (2011). Life satisfaction, openness value, self-transcendence, and wisdom. *Journal of Happiness Studies, 12*(2), 171–182. doi:10.1007/s10902-010-9182-1

Leal, M. C., Shin, Y. J., et al. (2003). Music perception in adult cochlear implant recipients. *Acta Oto-Laryngologica, 123*(7), 826–835. doi:10.1177/8755123312437050

Ledgerwood, A., & Trope, Y. (2010). Attitudes as global and local action guides. In J. P. Forgas, J. Cooper, & W. D. Crano (Eds.), *The psychology of attitudes and attitude change* (pp. 39–58). New York: Psychology Press.

LeDoux, J. E. (2000). Emotion circuits in the brain. *Annual Review of Neuroscience, 23*, 155–184. doi:10.1146/annurev.neuro.23.1.155

LeDoux, J. E. (2012). A neuroscientist's perspective on debates about the nature of emotion. *Emotion Review, 4*(4), 375–379. doi:10.1177/1754073912445822

Lee, M., Zimbardo, P. G., & Bertholf, M. (1977). Shy murderers. *Psychology Today, 11*, 69–70, 76, 148.

Lee, S. W., Clemenson, G. D., & Gage, F. H. (2011). New neurons in an aged brain. *Behavioural Brain Research*. doi:10.1016/j.bbr.2011.10.009.

Leenaars, A. A., Lester, D., & Wenckstern, S. (2005). Coping with suicide: The art and the research. In R. I. Yufit & D. Lester (Eds.), *Assessment, treatment, and prevention of suicidal behavior* (pp. 347–377). New York: Wiley.

Leeper, R. W. (1935). A study of a neglected portion of the field of learning: The development of sensory organization. *Pedagogical Seminary & Journal of Genetic Psychology, 46*, 41–75.

Lefebvre, C. D., Marchand, Y., et al. (2007). Determining eyewitness identification accuracy using event-related brain potentials (ERPs). *Psychophysiology, 44*(6), 894–904.

Lefkowitz, E. S., & Zeldow, P. B. (2006). Masculinity and femininity predict optimal mental health: A belated test of the androgyny hypothesis. *Journal of Personality Assessment, 87*(1), 95–101.

Lefrançois, G. R. (2012). *Theories of human learning: What the professors said* (6th ed.). Belmont, CA: Cengage Learning/Wadsworth.

Leiter, M. P., & Maslach, C. (2005). *Banishing burnout: Six strategies for improving your relationship with work*. San Francisco, CA: Jossey-Bass.

Leiter, M. P., Gascón, S., & Martínez-Jarreta, B. (2010). Making sense of work life: A structural model of burnout. *Journal of Applied Social Psychology, 40*(1), 57–75. doi:10.1111/j.1559-1816.2009.00563.x

Lejuez, C. W., Eifert, G. H., et al. (2000). Preference between onset predictable and unpredictable administrations of 20 carbon-dioxide-enriched air: Implications for better understanding the etiology and treatment of panic disorder. *Journal of Experimental Psychology: Applied, 6*(4), 349–358. doi:10.1037/1076-898X.6.4.349

Lemma, A., Target, M., & Fonagy, P. (2011). The development of a brief psychodynamic intervention (dynamic interpersonal therapy) and its application to depression: A pilot study. *Psychiatry: Interpersonal & Biological Processes, 74*(1), 41–48. doi:10.1521/psyc.2011.74.1.41

Lemogne, C., Nabi, H., et al. (2010). Hostility may explain the association between depressive mood and mortality: Evidence from the French GAZEL cohort study. *Psychotherapy & Psychosomatics, 79*(3), 164–171. doi:10.1159/000286961

Lenzenweger, M. F., & Gottesman, I. I. (1994). Schizophrenia. In V. S. Ramachandran (Ed.), *Encyclopedia of human behavior* (Vol 4, pp. 41–59). San Diego, CA: Academic.

León, I., & Hernández, J. A. (1998). Testing the role of attribution and appraisal in predicting own and other's emotions. *Cognition & Emotion, 12*(1), 27–43. doi:10.1080/026999398379763

Leotti, L. A., Iyengar, S. S., & Ochsner, K. N. (2010). Born to choose: The origins and value of the need for control. *Trends in Cognitive Sciences, 14*(10), 457–463. doi:10.1016/j.tics.2010.08.001

Lepage, J.-F., & Théret, H. (2007). The mirror neuron system: Grasping others' actions from birth? *Developmental Science, 10*(5), 513–523. doi:10.1111/j.1467-7687.2007.00631.x

Lepage, M. M., Sergerie, K. K., et al. (2011). Emotional face processing and flat affect in schizophrenia: Functional and structural neural correlates. *Psychological Medicine, 41*(9), 1833–1844. doi:10.1017/S0033291711000031

Leppänen, J. M. (2011). Neural and developmental bases of the ability to recognize social signals of emotions. *Emotion Review, 3*(2), 179–188. doi:10.1177/1754073910387942

Lerner, D., & Henke, R. M. (2008). What does research tell us about depression, job performance, and work productivity? *Journal of Occupational & Environmental Medicine, 50*(4), 401–410.

Lerum, K., & Dworkin, S. L. (2009). "Bad girls rule": An interdisciplinary feminist commentary on the report of the APA task force on the sexualization of girls. *Journal of Sex Research, 46*(4), 250–263.

Lessow-Hurley, J. (2013). *Foundations of dual language instruction* (6th ed.). Boston: Allyn & Bacon.

Lester, D. (2006). Sexual orientation and suicidal behavior. *Psychological Reports, 99*(3), 923–924.

Lester, D., & Yang, B. (2005). Regional and time-series studies of suicide in nations of the world. *Archives of Suicide Research, 9*(2), 123–133. doi:10.1080/13811110590903972

Lettvin, J. Y. (1961). Two remarks on the visual system of the frog. In W. Rosenblith (Ed.), *Sensory communication* (pp. 757–776). Cambridge, MA: MIT Press.

Leucht, S., Heres, S., et al. (2011). Evidence-based pharmacotherapy of schizophrenia. *International Journal of Neuropsychopharmacology, 14*(2), 269–284. doi:10.1017/S1461145710001380

Leuner, B., & Gould, E. (2010). Structural plasticity and hippocampal function. *Annual Review of Psychology, 61*, 111–140. doi:10.1146/annurev.psych.093008.100359

LeUnes, A. (2008). *Sport psychology* (4th ed.). New York: Psychology Press.

Levant, R. F. (2003). Treating male alexithymia. In L. B. Silverstein, & T. J. Goodrich (Eds.), *Feminist family therapy: Empowerment in social context* (pp. 177–188). Washington: American Psychological Association.

Levant, R. F. (2011). Research in the psychology of men and masculinity using the gender role strain paradigm as a framework. *American Psychologist, 66*(8), 765–776. doi:10.1037/a0025034

Levant, R. F., Good, G. E., et al. (2006). The Normative Male Alexithymia Scale: Measurement of a gender-linked syndrome. *Psychology of Men & Masculinity, 7*(4), 212–224. doi:10.1037/1524-9220.7.4.212

Levant, R. F., Hall, R. J., et al. (2009). Gender differences in alexithymia. *Psychology of Men & Masculinity, 10*(3), 190–203.

LeVay, S. (2011). *Gay, straight, and the reason why*. New York: Oxford University Press.

LeVay, S., & Baldwin, J. (2012). *Human sexuality* (4th ed.). Sunderland, MA: Sinauer Associates.

Levenson, E. A. (2012). Psychoanalysis and the rite of refusal. *Psychoanalytic Dialogues, 22*(1), 2–6. doi:10.1080/10481885.2012.646593

Levenston, G. K., Patrick, C. J., et al. (2000). The psychopathic observer. *Journal of Abnormal Psychology, 109*, 373–385. doi:10.1037/0021-843X.109.3.373

Levesque, M. J., Steciuk, M., & Ledley, C. (2002). Self-disclosure patterns among well-acquainted individuals. *Social Behavior & Personality, 30*(6), 579–592. doi:10.2224/sbp.2002.30.6.579

Levi, A. M. (1998). Are defendants guilty if they were chosen in a lineup? *Law & Human Behavior, 22*(4), 389–407. doi:10.1023/A:1025718909499

Levin, J. (2010). Gestalt therapy: Now and for tomorrow. *Gestalt Review, 14*(2), 147–170.

Levin, R., & Fireman, G. (2002). Nightmare prevalence, nightmare distress, and self-reported psychological disturbance. *Sleep: Journal of Sleep & Sleep Disorders Research, 25*(2), 205–212.

Levin, R., & Nielsen, T. (2009). Nightmares, bad dreams, and emotion dysregulation: A review and new neurocognitive model of dreaming. *Current Directions in Psychological Science, 18*(2), 84–88. doi:10.1111/j.1467-8721.2009.01614.x

Levy, D. A. (2003). *Tools of critical thinking: Metathoughts for psychology*. Long Grove, IL: Waveland Press.

Levy, D. L., Coleman, M. J., et al. (2010). The genetic basis of thought disorder and language and communication disturbances in schizophrenia. *Journal of Neurolinguistics, 23*(3), 176–192. doi:10.1016/j.jneuroling.2009.08.003

Lew, A. R. (2011). Looking beyond the boundaries: Time to put landmarks back on the cognitive map? *Psychological Bulletin, 137*(3), 484–507. doi:10.1037/a0022315

Lewandowski, G. W. Jr., Aron, A., & Gee, J. (2007). Personality goes a long way: The malleability of opposite-sex physical attractiveness. *Personal Relationships, 14*(4), 571–585. doi:10.1111/j.1475-6811.2007.00172.x

Lewis, I., Watson, B., & White, K. M. (2009). Internet versus paper-and-pencil survey methods in psychological experiments: Equivalence testing of participant responses to health-related messages. *Australian Journal of Psychology, 61*(2), 107–116. doi:10.1080/00049530802105865

Lewis, M. B. (1995). Self-conscious emotions. *American Scientist, 83* (Jan–Feb), 68–78.

Lewis, M. B. (2012). Exploring the positive and negative implications of facial feedback. *Emotion, 12*(4), 852–859. doi:10.1037/a0029275

Li, C., Ford, E. S., et al. (2009). Associations of health risk factors and chronic illnesses with life dissatisfaction among U.S. adults: The Behavioral Risk Factor Surveillance System, 2006. *Preventive Medicine, 49*(2–3), 253–259. doi:10.1016/j.ypmed.2009.05.012

Li, W., Farkas, G., et al. (2012). Timing of high-quality child care and cognitive, language, and preacademic development. *Developmental Psychology*. doi:10.1037/a0030613

Lichtman, A. H., & Martin, B. R. (2006). Understanding the pharmacology and physiology of cannabis dependence. In R. Roffman, & R. S. Stephens (Eds.), *Cannabis dependence. Its nature, consequences and treatment* (pp. 37–57). New York: Cambridge University Press.

Liddell, S. K. (2003). *Grammar, gesture and meaning in American Sign Language*. Cambridge, MA: Cambridge University Press.

Lieberman, J. D. (2011). The utility of scientific jury selection: Still murky after 30 years. *Current Directions in Psychological Science, 20*(1), 48–52. doi:10.1177/0963721410396628

Lieberman, J. D., & Sales, B. D. (2007). *Scientific jury selection*. Washington, DC: American Psychological Association.

Lievens, F., & Sackett, P. R. (2006). Video-based versus written situational judgment tests: A comparison in terms of predictive validity. *Journal of Applied Psychology, 91*(5), 1181–1188.

Liles, E. E., & Packman, J. (2009). Play therapy for children with fetal alcohol syndrome. *International Journal of Play Therapy, 18*(4), 192–206. doi:10.1037/a0015664

Lilienfeld, S. O., Ammirati, R., & Landfield, K. (2009). Giving debiasing away: Can psychological research on correcting cognitive errors promote human welfare? *Perspectives on Psychological Science, 4*(4), 390–398. doi:10.1111/j.1745-6924.2009.01144.x

Lilienfeld, S. O., Lynn, S. J., et al. (2010). *50 great myths of popular psychology: Shattering widespread misconceptions about human behavior.* London: Wiley-Blackwell.

Lilienfeld, S. O., Ruscio, J., & Lynn, S. J. (Eds.). (2008). *Navigating the mindfield: A user's guide to distinguishing science from pseudoscience in mental health.* Buffalo, NY: Prometheus Books.

Lin, F. R., Thorpe, R., et al. (2011). Hearing loss prevalence and risk factors among older adults in the United States. *Journals of Gerontology: Series A: Biological Sciences & Medical Sciences, 66A*(5), 582–590. doi:10.1093/gerona/glr002

Lin, T., & Peng, T. K. (2010). From organizational citizenship behaviour to team performance: The mediation of group cohesion and collective efficacy. *Management & Organization Review, 6*(1), 55–75. doi:10.1111/j.1740-8784.2009.00172.x

Lindemann, B. (2001). Receptors and transduction in taste. *Nature, 413,* 219–225. doi:10.1038/35093032

Linderoth, B., & Foreman, R. D. (2006). Mechanisms of spinal cord stimulation in painful syndromes: Role of animal models. *Pain Medicine, 7*(Suppl. 1), S14–S26. doi:10.1111/j.1526-4637.2006.00119.x

Lindsey, B. J., Fabiano, P., & Stark, C. (2009). The prevalence and correlates of depression among college students. *College Student Journal, 43*(4, PtA), 999–1014.

Linting, M., Groeneveld, M. G., et al. (2013). Threshold for noise in daycare: Noise level and noise variability are associated with child wellbeing in home-based childcare. *Early Childhood Research Quarterly.* doi:10.1016/j.ecresq.2013.03.005

Lipka, J., Miltner, W. H. R., & Straube, T. (2011). Vigilance for threat interacts with amygdala responses to subliminal threat cues in specific phobia. *Biological Psychiatry, 70*(5), 472–478. doi:10.1016/j.biopsych.2011.04.005

Lippke, S., Nigg, C. R., & Maddock, J. E. (2012). Health-promoting and health-risk behaviors: Theory-driven analyses of multiple health behavior change in three international samples. *International Journal of Behavioral Medicine, 19*(1), 1–13. doi:10.1007/s12529-010-9135-4

Liu, Y., Gao, J., et al. (2000). The temporal response of the brain after eating revealed by functional MRI. *Nature, 405,* 1058–1062. doi:10.1038/35016590

Livingston, I, Doyle, J., & Mangan, D. (2010, April 25). Stabbed hero dies as more than 20 people stroll past him. *New York Post.* Retrieved July 12, 2013, from http://www.nypost.com/p/news/local/queens/passers_by_let_good_sam_die_5SGkf5XDP5oooudVuEd8fbI

Lobbestael, J., Cima, M., & Arntz, A. (2013). The relationship between adult reactive and proactive aggression, hostile interpretation bias, and antisocial personality disorder. *Journal of Personality Disorders, 27*(1), 53–66. doi:10.1521/pedi.2013.27.1.53

Lodi-Smith, J., Geise, A. C., et al. (2009). Narrating personality change. *Journal of Personality & Social Psychology, 96*(3), 679–689. doi:10.1037/a0014611

Loeber, R., & Hay, D. (1997). Key issues in the development of aggression and violence from childhood to early adulthood. *Annual Review of Psychology, 48,* 371–410. doi:10.1146/annurev.psych.48.1.371

Loftus, E. F. (2003). Make-believe memories. *American Psychologist, 58*(11), 867–873. doi:10.1037/0003-066X.58.11.867

Loftus, E. F., & Palmer, J. C. (1974). Reconstruction of automobile destruction: An example of interaction between language and memory. *Journal of Verbal Learning & Verbal Behavior, 13,* 585–589. doi:10.1016/S0022-5371(74)80011-3

Lokuge, S., Frey, B. N., et al. (2011). Depression in women: Windows of vulnerability and new insights into the link between estrogen and serotonin. *Journal of Clinical Psychiatry, 72*(11), 1563–1569. doi:10.4088/JCP.11com07089

LoLordo, V. M. (2001). Learned helplessness and depression. In M. E. Carroll, & J. B. Overmier (Eds.), *Animal research and human health: Advancing human welfare through behavioral science* (pp. 63–77). Washington: American Psychological Association.

Long, E. C., & Andrews, D. W. (1990). Perspective taking as a predictor of marital adjustment. *Journal of Personality & Social Psychology, 59*(1), 126–131.

Longo, M. R., Long, C., & Haggard, P. (2012). Mapping the invisible hand: A body model of a phantom limb. *Psychological Science, 23*(7), 740–742. doi:10.1177/0956797612441219

López, S. R., & Guarnaccia, P. J. J. (2000). Cultural psychopathology. *Annual Review of Psychology, 51,* 571–598. doi:10.1146/annurev.psych.51.1.571

Lorenzo, G. L., Biesanz, J. C., & Human, L. J. (2010). What is beautiful is good and more accurately understood: Physical attractiveness and accuracy in first impressions of personality. *Psychological Science, 21*(12), 1777–1782. doi:10.1177/0956797610388048

Lounsbury, D. W., & Mitchell, S. G. (2009). Introduction to special issue on social ecological approaches to community health research and action. *American Journal of Community Psychology, 44*(3–4), 213–220. doi:10.1007/s10464-009-9266-4

Lovaas, O., & Simmons, J. (1969). Manipulation of self-destruction in three retarded children. *Journal of Applied Behavior Analysis, 2,* 143–157. doi:10.1901/jaba.1969.2-143

Low, K. G., & Feissner, J. M. (1998). Seasonal affective disorder in college students: Prevalence and latitude. *Journal of American College Health, 47*(3), 135–137.

Lowman, R. L. (Ed.) (2013). *Internationalizing multiculturalism: Expanding professional competencies in a globalized world.* Washington: American Psychological Association.

Lucas, C., & Bayley, R. (2011). Variation in sign languages: Recent research on ASL and beyond. *Language & Linguistics Compass, 5*(9), 677–690. doi:10.1111/j.1749-818X.2011.00304.x

Lucas, R. E., & Diener, E. (2009). In E. Diener (Ed.), *Personality and subjective well-being* (pp. 75–102). New York: Springer.

Lucas, R. E., Clark, A. E., et al. (2003). Reexamining adaptation and the set point model of happiness: Reactions to changes in marital status. *Journal of Personality & Social Psychology, 84*(3), 527–539. doi:10.1037/0022-3514.84.3.527

Lum, D. (2011). *Culturally competent practice: A framework for understanding* (4th ed.). Belmont, CA: Cengage Learning/Wadsworth.

Lum, J. A., & Bleses, D. (2012). Declarative and procedural memory in Danish-speaking children with specific language impairment. *Journal of Communication Disorders, 45*(1), 46–58. doi:10.1016/j.jcomdis.2011.09.001

Lumia, A. R., & McGinnis, M. Y. (2010). Impact of anabolic androgenic steroids on adolescent males. *Physiology & Behavior, 100*(3), 199–204. doi:10.1016/j.physbeh.2010.01.007

Lumley, M. A. (2004). Alexithymia, emotional disclosure, and health: A program of research. *Journal of Personality, 72*(6), 1271–1300. doi:10.1111/j.1467-6494.2004.00297.x

Luppa, M., Heinrich, S., et al. (2007). Cost-of-illness studies of depression: A systematic review. *Journal of Affective Disorders, 98*(1–2), 29–43. doi:10.1016/j.jad.2006.07.017

Luria, A. R. (1968). *The mind of a mnemonist.* New York: Basic.

Lutter, M. (2007). Book review: Winning a lottery brings no happiness! *Journal of Happiness Studies, 8*(1), 155–160. doi:10.1007/s10902-006-9033-2

Luyster, F. S., Strollo, P. R., et al. (2012). Sleep: A health imperative. *Sleep: Journal Of Sleep & Sleep Disorders Research, 35*(6), 727–734.

Luyten, P., & Blatt, S. J. (2011). Integrating theory-driven and empirically-derived models of personality development and psychopathology: A proposal for DSM V. *Clinical Psychology Review, 31*(1), 52–68. doi:10.1016/j.cpr.2010.09.003

Lykken, D. T. (1998). *A tremor in the blood: Uses and abuses of the lie detector.* New York, NY: Plenum.

Lykken, D. T. (2001). Lie detection. In W. E. Craighead, & C. B. Nemeroff (Eds.), *The Corsini encyclopedia of psychology and behavioral science* (3rd ed., pp. 878–880). New York: Wiley.

Lyn, H., Franks, B., & Savage-Rumbaugh, E. S. (2008). Precursors of morality in the use of the symbols "good" and "bad" in two bonobos (*Pan paniscus*) and a chimpanzee (*Pan troglodytes*). *Language & Communication, 28*(3), 213–224. doi:10.1016/j.langcom.2008.01.006

Lynch, K. B., Geller, S. R., & Schmidt, M. G. (2004). Multi-year evaluation of the effectiveness of a resilience-based prevention program for young children. *Journal of Primary Prevention, 24*(3), 335–353. doi:10.1023/B:JOPP.0000018052.12488.d1

Lynn, S. J., & Kirsch, I. (2006). Introduction: Definitions and early history. In S. J. Lynn, & I. Kirsch (Eds.), *Essentials of clinical hypnosis: An evidence-based approach* (pp. 3–15). Washington: American Psychological Association.

Lynn, S. J., & O'Hagen, S. (2009). The sociocognitive and conditioning and inhibition theories of hypnosis. *Contemporary Hypnosis, 26*(2), 121–125. doi:10.1002/ch.378

Lynn, S. J., Kirsch, I., & Rhue, J. W. (2010). An introduction to clinical hypnosis. In S. Lynn, J. W. Rhue & I. Kirsch (Eds.), *Handbook of clinical hypnosis* (2nd ed.) (pp. 3–18). Washington: American Psychological Association.

Lynne-Landsman, S. D., Graber, J. A., et al. (2011). Is sensation seeking a stable trait or does it change over time? *Journal of Youth & Adolescence, 40*(1), 48–58. 10.1007/s10964-010-9529-2

Lyons, H., Manning, W., et al. (2013). Predictors of heterosexual casual sex among young adults. *Archives of Sexual*

Behavior, 42(4), 585–593. doi:10.1007/s10508-012-0051-3

Lyons, R. (2011). The spread of evidence-poor medicine via flawed social-network analysis. *Statistics, Politics, & Policy, 2*(1). doi:10.2202/2151-7509.1024

Lyubomirsky, S., & Tucker, K. L. (1998). Implications of individual differences in subjective happiness for perceiving, interpreting, and thinking about life events. *Motivation & Emotion, 22*(2), 155–186. doi:10.1023/A:1021396422190

MacDuffie, K., & Mashour, G. A. (2010). Dreams and the temporality of consciousness. *American Journal of Psychology, 123*(2), 189–197. doi:10.5406/amerjpsyc.123.2.0189

Macht, M., & Simons, G. (2011). Emotional eating. In I. Nyklicek, A. Vingerhoets, & M. Zeelenberg (Eds,), *Emotion regulation and well-being* (pp. 281–295). New York: Springer.

MacIver, K., Lloyd, D. M., et al. (2008). Phantom limb pain, cortical reorganization and the therapeutic effect of mental imagery. *Brain: A Journal of Neurology, 131*(8), 2181–2191. doi:10.1093/brain/awn124

MacKay, D. G., & Hadley, C. (2009). Supra-normal age-linked retrograde amnesia: Lessons from an older amnesic (H.M.). *Hippocampus, 19*(5), 424–445. doi:10.1002/hipo.20531

Macklin, C. B., & McDaniel, M. A. (2005). The bizarreness effect: Dissociation between item and source memory. *Memory, 13*(7), 662–689. doi:10.1080/09658210444000304

Maddi, S. R. (2006). Hardiness: The courage to grow from stresses. *Journal of Positive Psychology, 1*(3), 160–168. doi:10.1080/17439760600619609

Maddi, S. R., Harvey, R. H., et al. (2009). The personality construct of hardiness, IV: Expressed in positive cognitions and emotions concerning oneself and developmentally relevant activities. *Journal of Humanistic Psychology, 49*(3), 292–305. doi:10.1177/0022167809331860

Maddock, J. E., Laforge, R. G., et al. (2001). The College Alcohol Problems Scale. *Addictive Behaviors, 26*, 385–398. doi:10.1016/S0306-4603(00)00116-7

Maddock, J. E., & Glanz, K. (2005). The relationship of proximal normative beliefs and global subjective norms to college students' alcohol consumption. *Addictive Behaviors, 30*(2), 315–323. doi:10.1016/j.addbeh.2004.05.021

Maddox, K. B. (2004). Perspectives on racial phenotypicality bias. *Personality & Social Psychology Review, 8*(4), 383–401. doi:10.1207/s15327957pspr0804_4

Madon, S., Willard, J., et al. (2011). Self-fulfilling prophecies: Mechanisms, power, and links to

social problems. *Social & Personality Psychology Compass, 5*(8), 578–590. doi:10.1111/j.1751-9004.2011.00375.x

Madras, B. K. (2013). History of the discovery of the antipsychotic dopamine D2 receptor: A basis for the dopamine hypothesis of schizophrenia. *Journal of the History of the Neurosciences, 22*(1), 62–78. doi:10.1080/0964704X.2012.678199

Maggin, D. M., Chafouleas, S. M., et al. (2011). A systematic evaluation of token economies as a classroom management tool for students with challenging behavior. *Journal of School Psychology, 49*(5), 529–554. doi:10.1016/j.jsp.2011.05.001

Maguire-Jack, K., Gromoske, A. N., & Berger, L. M. (2012). Spanking and child development during the first 5 years of life. *Child Development, 83*(6), 1960–1977. doi:10.1111/j.1467-8624.2012.01820.x

Maguire, E. A., Valentine, E. R., et al. (2003). Routes to remembering: The brains behind superior memory. *Nature Neuroscience, 6*(1), 90–95. doi:10.1038/nn988

Mah, K., & Binik, Y. M. (2001). The nature of human orgasm: A critical review of major trends. *Clinical Psychology Review, 21*(6), 823–856.

Mahler, H. I. M., Beckerley, S. E., & Vogel, M. T. (2010). Effects of media images on attitudes toward tanning. *Basic & Applied Social Psychology, 32*(2), 118–127. doi:10.1080/01973531003738296

Mahoney, A. E., & McEvoy, P. M. (2012). Changes in intolerance of uncertainty during cognitive behavior group therapy for social phobia. *Journal of Behavior Therapy & Experimental Psychiatry, 43*(2), 849–854. doi:10.1016/j.jbtep.2011.12.004

Maier, N. R. F. (1949). *Frustration.* New York: McGraw-Hill.

Mailis-Gagnon, A., & Israelson, D. (2005). *Beyond pain: Making the mind–body connection.* Ann Arbor: University of Michigan Press.

Maisto, S. A., Galizio, M., & Connors, G. J. (2011). *Drug use and abuse* (6th ed.). Belmont, CA: Cengage Learning /Wadsworth.

Majka, P., Kublik, E., et al. (2012). Common atlas format and 3D brain atlas reconstructor: Infrastructure for constructing 3D brain atlases. *Neuroinformatics, 10*(2), 181–197. doi:10.1007/s12021-011-9138-6

Malan, L., Hamer, M., et al. (2012). Defensive coping, urbanization, and neuroendocrine function in Black Africans: The THUSA study. *Psychophysiology, 49*(6), 807–814. doi:10.1111/j.1469-8986.2012.01362.x

Malan, L., Malan, N. T., et al. (2008). Coping with urbanization: A cardio-metabolic risk? The THUSA study. *Biological Psychology, 79*(3), 323–328.

Malhi, G. S., Tanious, M., et al. (2012). The science and practice of lithium therapy. *Australian and New Zealand Journal of Psychiatry, 46*(3), 192–211. doi:10.1177/0004867412437346

Malmberg, L., & Flouri, E. (2011). The comparison and interdependence of maternal and paternal influences on young children's behavior and resilience. *Journal Of Clinical Child & Adolescent Psychology, 40*(3), 434–444. doi:10.1080/15374416.2011.563469

Mamen, M. (2004). *Pampered child syndrome: How to recognize it, how to manage it and how to avoid it.* Carp, ON: Creative Bound.

Manber, R., Kraemer, H. C., et al. (2008). Faster remission of chronic depression with combined psychotherapy and medication than with each therapy alone. *Journal of Consulting & Clinical Psychology, 76*(3), 459–467. doi:10.1037/0022-006X.76.3.459

Mancini, M. A., & Wyrick-Waugh, W. (2013). Consumer and practitioner perceptions of the harm reduction approach in a community mental health setting. *Community Mental Health Journal, 49*(1), 14–24. doi:10.1007/s10597-011-9451-4

Manning, R., Levine, M., & Collins, A. (2007). The Kitty Genovese murder and the social psychology of helping: The parable of the 38 witnesses. *American Psychologist, 62*(6), 555–562. doi:10.1037/0003-066X.62.6.555

Mantovani, A., Simpson, H. B., et al. (2010). Randomized sham-controlled trial of repetitive transcranial magnetic stimulation in treatment-resistant obsessive-compulsive disorder. *International Journal of Neuropsychopharmacology, 13*(2), 217–227. doi:10.1017/S1461145709990435

Mantyla, T. (1986). Optimizing cue effectiveness: Recall of 600 incidentally learned words. *Journal of Experimental Psychology: Learning, Memory, & Cognition, 12*(1), 66–71. doi:10.1037/0278-7393.12.1.66

Maran, M. (2010). *My lie: A true story of false memory.* San Francisco: Jossey-Bass/Wiley.

Marazziti, D., & Baroni, S. (2012). Romantic love: The mystery of its biological roots. *Clinical Neuropsychiatry, 9*(1), 14–19.

Marcel, M. (2005). *Freud's traumatic memory: Reclaiming seduction theory and revisiting Oedipus.* Pittsburgh, PA: Duquesne University Press.

Marco, E. M., Romero-Zerbo, S. Y., et al. (2012). The role of the endocannabinoid system in eating disorders: Pharmacological implications. *Behavioural Pharmacology, 23*(5–6), 526–538. doi:10.1097/FBP.0b013e328356c3c9

Marecek, J., & Gavey, N. (2013). DSM-5 and beyond: A critical feminist

engagement with psychodiagnosis. *Feminism & Psychology, 23*(1), 3–9. doi:10.1177/0959353512467962

Margolin, G., & Gordis, E. B. (2000). The effects of family and community violence on children. *Annual Review of Psychology, 51*, 445–479. doi:10.1146/annurev.psych.51.1.445

Marian, D. E., & Shimamura, A. P. (2012). Emotions in context: Pictorial influences on affective attributions. *Emotion, 12*(2), 371–375. doi:10.1037/a0025517

Mariani, R., Mello, C., et al. (2011). Effect of naloxone and morphine on arcaine-induced state-dependent memory in rats. *Psychopharmacology, 215*(3), 483–491. doi:10.1007/s00213-011-2215-6

Mark, G. P., Shabani, S., et al. (2011). Cholinergic modulation of mesolimbic dopamine function and reward. *Physiology & Behavior, 104*(1), 76–81. doi:10.1016/j.physbeh.2011.04.052

Mark, K., Janssen, E., & Milhausen, R. (2011). Infidelity in heterosexual couples: Demographic, interpersonal, and personality-related predictors of extradyadic sex. *Archives of Sexual Behavior, 40*(5), 971–982. doi:10.1007/s10508-011-9771-z

Mark, T., Tomic, K., et al. (2013). Hospital readmission among medicaid patients with an index hospitalization for mental and/or substance use disorder. *Journal of Behavioral Health Services & Research, 40*(2), 207–221. doi:10.1007/s11414-013-9323-5

Markoff, J. (2011). *Computer wins on 'Jeopardy!': Trivial, it's not.* Retrieved June 9, 2013, from http://www.nytimes.com/2011/02/17/science/17jeopardy-watson.html

Markowitz, F. E. (2011). Mental illness, crime, and violence: Risk, context, and social control. *Aggression & Violent Behavior, 16*, 36–44. doi:10.1016/j.avb.2010.10.003

Marks, A., & Baldry, C. (2009). Stuck in the middle with who? The class identity of knowledge workers. *Work, Employment & Society, 23*(1), 49–65.

Marks, D. F. (2000). *The psychology of the psychic.* Buffalo, NY: Prometheus.

Markus H. R., Ryff, C. D., et al. (2004). In their own words: Well-being at midlife among high school and college educated adults. In O. G. Brim, C. D. Ryff, & R. C. Kessler (Eds.), *How healthy are we?: A national study of well-being at midlife* (pp. 273–319). Chicago: University of Chicago Press.

Markus, H. R., Uchida, Y., et al. (2006). Going for the gold: Models of agency in Japanese and American contexts. *Psychological Science, 17*(2), 103–112. doi:10.1111/j.1467-9280.2006.01672.x

Markus, H., & Nurius, P. (1986). Possible selves. *American Psychologist, 41*, 954–969. doi:10.1037/0003-066X.41.9.954

Marsella, A. J. (1998). Urbanization, mental health, and social deviancy. *American Psychologist, 53*(6), 624–634.

Marshall, J. C., & Halligan, P. W. (1995). Seeing the forest but only half the trees? Nature, 373, 521–523. doi:10.1038/373521a0

Marshall, R. D., Bryant, R. A., et al. (2007). The psychology of ongoing threat: Relative risk appraisal, the September 11 attacks, and terrorism-related fears. *American Psychologist, 62*(4), 304–316. doi:10.1037/0003-066X.62.4.304

Marsiglia, F. F., Kulis, S., et al. (2004). Ethnicity and ethnic identity as predictors of drug norms and drug use among preadolescents in the U.S. Southwest. *Substance Use & Misuse, 39*(7), 1061–1094. doi:10.1081/JA-120038030

Martens, R., & Trachet, T. (1998). *Making sense of astrology.* Amherst, MA: Prometheus.

Martin, B. (2011). *Children at play: Learning gender in the early years.* Sterling, VA: Trentham Books.

Martin, C. L., & Ruble, D. N. (2009). Patterns of gender development. *Annual Review of Psychology, 61,* 353–381.

Martin, E. K., Taft, C. T., & Resick, P. A. (2007). A review of marital rape. *Aggression & Violent Behavior, 12*(3), 329–347.

Martin, E., & Weiss, K. J. (2010). Knowing moral and legal wrong in an insanity defense. *Journal of the American Academy of Psychiatry & the Law, 38*(2), 286–288.

Martin, G., & Pear, J. (2011). *Behavior modification: What it is and how to do it* (9th ed.). Upper Saddle River, NJ: Prentice-Hall.

Martin, L. R., Friedman, H. S., & Schwartz, J. E. (2007). Personality and mortality risk across the life span: The importance of conscientiousness as a biopsychosocial attribute. *Health Psychology, 26*(4), 428–436. doi:10.1037/0278-6133.26.4.428

Martin, S. (2007). The labyrinth of leadership. *Monitor on Psychology,* July/August, 90–91.

Martin, W. L. B., & Freitas, M. B. (2002). Mean mortality among Brazilian left- and right-handers: Modification or selective elimination. *Laterality, 7*(1), 31–44. doi:10.1080/13576500143000104

Martinez-Gonzalez, M. A., Gual, P., et al. (2003). Parental factors, mass media influences, and the onset of eating disorders in a prospective population-based cohort. *Pediatrics, 111,* 315–320. doi:10.1542/peds.111.2.315

Martinko, M. J., Douglas, S. C., & Harvey, P. (2006). Understanding and managing workplace aggression. *Organizational Dynamics, 35*(2), 117–130.

Martynhak, B. J., Louzada, F. M., et al. (2010). Does the chronotype classification need to be updated? Preliminary findings. *Chronobiology International, 27*(6), 1329–1334. doi:10.3109/07420528.2010.490314

Maruta, R. (2012). Transforming knowledge workers into innovation workers to improve corporate productivity. *Knowledge-Based Systems, 30,* 35–47. doi:10.1016/j.knosys.2011.06.017

Marx, B. P., Gross, A. M., & Adams, H. E. (1999). The effect of alcohol on the responses of sexually coercive and noncoercive men to an experimental rape analogue. *Sexual Abuse: Journal of Research & Treatment, 11*(2), 131–145.

Mashour, G. A., Walker, E. E., & Martuza, R. L. (2005). Psychosurgery: Past, present, and future. *Brain Research Reviews, 48*(3), 409–419. doi:10.1016/j.brainresrev.2004.09.002

Maslow, A. H. (1954). *Motivation and personality.* New York: Harper.

Maslow, A. H. (1967). Self-actualization and beyond. In J. F. T. Bugental (Ed.), *Challenges of humanistic psychology* (pp. 279–286). New York: McGraw-Hill.

Maslow, A. H. (1969). *The psychology of science.* Chicago: Henry Regnery.

Maslow, A. H. (1970). *Motivation and personality.* New York: Harper & Row.

Maslow, A. H. (1971). *The farther reaches of human nature.* New York: Viking.

Masquelier, G. (2006). *Gestalt therapy: Living creatively today.* Hove, UK: Psychology Press.

Masse, L. C. & Tremblay, R. E. (1997). Behavior of boys in kindergarten and the onset of substance use during adolescence. *Archives of General Psychiatry, 54*(1), 62–68. doi:10.1001/archpsyc.1997.01830130068014

Masters, J. L., & Holley, L. M. (2006). A glimpse of life at 67: The modified future-self worksheet. *Educational Gerontology, 32*(4), 261–269. doi:10.1080/03601270500494022

Masters, W. H., & Johnson, V. E. (1966). *Human sexual response.* Boston: Little, Brown.

Masters, W. H., & Johnson, V. E. (1970). *The pleasure bond: A new look at sexuality and commitment.* Boston: Little, Brown.

Masuda, T., Gonzalez, R., et al. (2008). Culture and aesthetic preference: Comparing the attention to context of East Asians and Americans. *Personality & Social Psychology Bulletin, 34*(9), 1260–1275. doi:10.1177/0146167208320555

Mather, G. (2011). *Foundations of sensation and perception* (3rd ed.). Hove, UK: Psychology Press.

Mathy, F., & Feldman, J. (2012). What's magic about magic numbers? Chunking and data compression in short-term memory. *Cognition, 122*(3), 346–362. doi:10.1016/j.cognition.2011.11.003

Matson, J. L., & Boisjoli, J. A. (2009). The token economy for children with intellectual disability and/or autism: A review. *Research in Developmental Disabilities, 30*(2), 240–248. doi:10.1016/j.ridd.2008.04.001

Matsumoto, D, & Juang, L. (2013). *Culture and psychology* (5th ed.). Belmont, CA: Cengage Learning/Wadsworth.

Mattanah, J. F., Lopez, F. G., & Govern, J. M. (2011). The contributions of parental attachment bonds to college student development and adjustment: A meta-analytic review. Journal of Counseling Psychology, 58, 565–596. doi:10.1037/a0024635

Matthew, C. T., & Sternberg, R. J. (2009). Developing experience-based (tacit) knowledge through reflection. *Learning & Individual Differences, 19,* 530–540.

Matthews, K. A., & Gallo, L. C. (2011). Psychological perspectives on pathways linking socioeconomic status and physical health. *Annual Review of Psychology, 62,* 501–530. doi:10.1146/annurev.psych.031809.130711

Matthews, P. H., & Matthews, M. S. (2004). Heritage language instruction and giftedness in language minority students: Pathways toward success. *Journal of Secondary Gifted Education, 15*(2), 50–55. doi:10.4219/jsge-2004-448

Matthies, E., Selge, S., & Klöckner, C. A. (2012). The role of parental behaviour for the development of behaviour specific environmental norms: The example of recycling and re-use behaviour. *Journal of Environmental Psychology, 32*(3), 277–284. doi:10.1016/j.jenvp.2012.04.003

Mayer, J. D. (2005). A tale of two visions: Can a new view of personality help integrate psychology? *American Psychologist, 60*(4), 294–307. doi:10.1037/0003-066X.60.4.294

Mayer, R. E. (1995). *Thinking, problem solving, and cognition.* New York: Freeman.

Mayer, R. E. (2004). Should there be a three-strikes rule against pure discovery learning? *American Psychologist, 59*(1), 14–19. doi:10.1037/0003-066X.59.1.14

Mayer, R. E. (2011). *Applying the science of learning.* Boston: Allyn & Bacon.

Mazerolle, M., Régner, I., et al. (2012). Stereotype threat strengthens automatic recall and undermines controlled processes in older adults. *Psychological Science, 23*(7), 723–727. doi:10.1177/0956797612437607

Mazzoni, G., Heap, M., & Scoboria, A. (2010). Hypnosis and memory: Theory, laboratory research, and applications. In S. J. Lynn, J. W. Rhue et al. (Eds.), *Handbook of clinical hypnosis* (2nd ed., pp.709–741). Washington: American Psychological Association.

McAdams, D. P., & Pals, J. L. (2006). A new Big Five: Fundamental principles for an integrative science of personality. *American Psychologist, 61*(3), 204–217. doi:10.1037/0003-066X.61.3.204

McAvoy, J. (2012). Exposing the authoritarian personality. In N. Brace, & J. Byford (Eds.), *Investigating psychology: Key concepts, key studies, key approaches* (pp. 16–56). New York: Oxford University Press.

McCabe, C., & Rolls, E. T. (2007). Umami: A delicious flavor formed by convergence of taste and olfactory pathways in the human brain. *European Journal of Neuroscience, 25*(6), 1855–1864.

McCabe, M. P., & Ricciardelli, L. A. (2004). Weight and shape concerns of boys and men. In Thompson, J. K. (Ed.), *Handbook of eating disorders and obesity* (pp. 606–634). New York: Wiley.

McCaffrey, T. (2012). Innovation relies on the obscure: A key to overcoming the classic problem of functional fixedness. *Psychological Science, 23*(3), 215–218. doi:10.1177/0956797611429580

McCall, W. V., Prudic, J., et al. (2006). Health-related quality of life following ECT in a large community sample. *Journal of Affective Disorders, 90*(2–3), 269–274. doi:10.1016/j.jad.2005.12.002

McCall, W. V., Rosenquist, P. B., et al. (2011). Health-related quality of life in a clinical trial of ECT followed by continuation pharmacotherapy: Effects immediately after ECT and at 24 weeks. *The Journal of ECT, 27*(2), 97–102. doi:10.1097/YCT.0b013e318205c7d7

McCalley, L. T., de Vries, P. W., & Midden, C. J. (2011). Consumer response to product-integrated energy feedback: Behavior, goal level shifts, and energy conservation. *Environment and Behavior, 43*(4), 525–545. doi:10.1177/0013916510371053

McCarthy-Jones, S., Barnes, L. J., et al. (2011). When words and pictures come alive: Relating the modality of intrusive thoughts to modalities of hypnagogic/hypnopompic hallucinations. *Personality & Individual Differences, 51*(6), 787–790. doi:10.1016/j.paid.2011.07.003

McCarthy, B. W. (1995). Bridges to sexual desire. *Journal of Sex Education & Therapy, 21*(2), 132–141.

McCarthy, B. W., & Fucito, L. M. (2005). Integrating medication, realistic expectations, and therapeutic interventions in the treatment of male sexual dysfunction. *Journal of Sex & Marital Therapy, 31*(4), 319–328.

McClelland, D. C. (1961). *The achieving society.* New York: Van Nostrand.

McClelland, D. C. (1975). *Power: The inner experience.* New York: Irvington.

McClelland, D. C. (1994). The knowledge-testing-educational complex strikes back. *American Psychologist, 49*(1), 66–69. doi:10.1037/0003-066X.49.1.66

McClelland, D. C., & Pilon, D. A. (1983). Sources of adult motives in patterns of parent behavior in early childhood. *Journal of Personality & Social Psychology, 44,* 564–574. doi:10.1037/0022-3514.44.3.564

McClung, C. A. (2011). Circadian rhythms and mood regulation: Insights from pre-clinical models. *European Neuropsychopharmacology, 21,* S683–S693. doi:10.1016/j.euroneuro.2011.07.008

McCluskey, U. (2002). The dynamics of attachment and systems-centered group psychotherapy. *Group Dynamics, 6*(2), 131–142. doi:10.1037/1089-2699.6.2.131

McCormick, N. B. (2010). Sexual scripts: Social and therapeutic implications. *Sexual & Relationship Therapy, 25*(1), 96–120.

McCrae, R. R., & Costa, P. T. Jr. (2001). A five-factor theory of personality. In L. A. Pervin & O. P. John (Eds.), *Handbook of personality* (pp. 139–153). New York: Guilford.

McDaniel, M. A., Maier, S. F., & Einstein, G. O. (2002). "Brain-specific" nutrients: A memory cure? *Psychological Science in the Public Interest, 3*(1), 12–38. doi:10.1111/1529-1006.00007

McDermott, R., Johnson, D., et al. (2007). Testosterone and aggression in a simulated crisis game. *Annals of the American Academy of Political & Social Science, 614*(1), 15–33. doi:10.1177/0002716207305268

McDonald, S., Edwards, H. M., & Zhao, T. (2012). Exploring think-alouds in usability testing: An international survey. *IEEE Transactions on Professional Communication, 55*(1), 2–19. doi:10.1109/TPC.2011.2182569

McGaugh, J. L., & Roozendaal, B. (2009). Drug enhancement of memory consolidation: Historical perspective and neurobiological implications. *Psychopharmacology, 202*(1–3), 3–14. doi:10.1007/s00213-008-1285-6

McGowan, S., & Behar, E. (2013). A preliminary investigation of stimulus control training for worry: Effects on anxiety and insomnia. *Behavior Modification, 37*(1), 90–112. doi:10.1177/0145445512455661

McGrath, R. E., & Carroll, E. J. (2012). The current status of "projective" "tests." In H. Cooper (Ed.), *APA handbook of research methods in psychology: Foundations, planning, measures, and psychometrics* (Vol. 1, pp. 329–348). Washington: American Psychological Association.

McGrath, R. E., & Moore, B. A. (Eds.). (2010). *Pharmacotherapy for psychologists: Prescribing and collaborative roles.* Washington: American Psychological Association.

McGregor, D. (1960). *The human side of enterprise.* New York: McGraw-Hill.

McGregor, I., McAdams, D. P., & Little, B. R. (2006). Personal projects, life stories, and happiness: On being true to traits. *Journal of Research in Personality, 40*(5), 551–572. doi:10.1016/j.jrp.2005.05.002

McGuinness, T. M., Dyer, J. G., & Wade, E. H. (2012). Gender differences in adolescent depression. *Journal of Psychosocial Nursing & Mental Health Services, 50*(12), 17–20. doi:10.3928/02793695-20121107-04

McGuire, J., & Scott, S. (2002). Universal design for instruction: A promising new paradigm for higher education. *Perspectives, 28,* 27–29.

McIntosh, W. D., Harlow, T. F., & Martin, L. L. (1995). Linkers and nonlinkers: Goal beliefs as a moderator of the effects of everyday hassles on rumination, depression, and physical complaints. *Journal of Applied Social Psychology, 25*(14), 1231–1244. doi:10.1111/j.1559-1816.1995.tb02616.x

McKay, A. (2005). Sexuality and substance use: The impact of tobacco, alcohol, and selected recreational drugs on sexual function. *Canadian Journal of Human Sexuality, 14*(1–2), 47–56.

McKeever, L. (2006). Online plagiarism detection services: Saviour or scourge? *Assessment & Evaluation in Higher Education, 31*(2), 155–165. doi:10.1080/02602930500262460

McKeever, W. F. (2000). A new family handedness sample with findings consistent with X-linked transmission. *British Journal of Psychology, 91*(1), 21–39. doi:10.1348/000712600161655

McKeganey, N. (2012). Harm reduction at the crossroads and the rediscovery of drug user abstinence. *Drugs: Education, Prevention & Policy, 19*(4), 276–283. doi:10.3109/09687637.2012.671867

McKenna, M. W., & Ossoff, E. P. (1998). Age differences in children's comprehension of a popular television program. *Child Study Journal, 28*(1), 52–68.

McKim, W. A. (2013). *Drugs & behavior: Introduction to behaviorial pharmacology* (7th ed.). Englewood Cliffs, NJ: Prentice Hall.

McLay, R. N. (2012). *At war with PTSD: Battling post traumatic stress disorder with virtual reality.* Baltimore, MD: Johns Hopkins University Press.

McLay, R. N., & Spira, J. L. (2009). Use of a portable biofeedback device to improve insomnia in a combat zone, a case report. *Applied Psychophysiology & Biofeedback, 34*(4), 319–321. doi:10.1007/s10484-009-9104-3

McLewin, L. A., & Muller, R. T. (2006). Childhood trauma, imaginary companions, and the development of pathological dissociation. *Aggression & Violent Behavior, 11*(5), 531–545. doi:10.1016/j.avb.2006.02.001

McMahon, C. G., Jannini, E., et al. (2013). Standard operating procedures in the disorders of orgasm and ejaculation. *Journal of Sexual Medicine, 10*(1), 204–229. doi:10.1111/j.1743-6109.2012.02824.x

McMahon, S., & Koltzenburg, M. (2013). *Wall & Melzack's textbook of pain* (6th ed.). San Diego, CA: Elsevier.

McManus, I. C., Moore, J., et al. (2010). Science in the making: Right hand, left hand. III: Estimating historical rates of left-handedness. *Laterality: Asymmetries of Body, Brain & Cognition, 15*(1–2), 186–208. doi:10.1080/13576500802565313

McNally, R. J., & Clancy, S. A. (2005). Sleep paralysis, sexual abuse, and space alien abduction. *Transcultural Psychiatry, 42*(1), 113–122. doi:10.1177/1363461505050715

McNamara, D. S., & Scott, J. L. (2001). Working memory capacity and strategy use. *Memory & Cognition, 29*(1), 10–17. doi:10.3758/BF03195736

McNamara, P. (2011). *Spirit possession and exorcism: History, psychology, and neurobiology* (Vols. 1 & 2). Westport, CT: Praeger.

Mcquaid, N. E., Bibok, M. B., & Carpendale, J. I. M. (2009). Relation between maternal contingent responsiveness and infant social expectations. *Infancy, 14*(3), 390–401. doi:10.1080/15250000902839955

McRobbie, H., & Hajek, P. (2007). Effects of rapid smoking on post-cessation urges to smoke. *Addiction, 102*(3), 483–489. doi:10.1111/j.1360-0443.2006.01730.x

McVea, C. S., Gow, K., & Lowe, R. (2011). Corrective interpersonal experience in psychodrama group therapy: A comprehensive process analysis of significant therapeutic events. *Psychotherapy Research, 21*(4), 416–429. doi:10.1080/10503307.2011.577823

Mead, M. (1935). *Sex and temperament in three primitive societies.* New York: Morrow.

Mecklinger, A. (2010). The control of long-term memory: Brain systems and cognitive processes. *Neuroscience & Biobehavioral Reviews, 34*(7), 1055–1065. doi:10.1016/j.neubiorev.2009.11.020

Medda, P., Perugi, G., et al. (2009). Response to ECT in bipolar I, bipolar II and unipolar depression. *Journal of Affective Disorders, 118*(1–3), 55–59. doi:10.1016/j.jad.2009.01.014

Medhus, E. (2001). *Raising children who think for themselves.* Hillsboro, OR: Beyond Words Publishing.

Meeks, T. W., & Jeste, D. V. (2009). Neurobiology of wisdom: A literature overview. *Archives of General Psychiatry, 66*(4), 355–365. doi:10.1001/archgenpsychiatry.2009.8

Megreya, A. M., White, D., & Burton, A. M. (2011). The other-race effect does not rely on memory: Evidence from a matching task. *The Quarterly Journal of Experimental Psychology, 64*(8), 1473–1483. doi:10.1080/17470218.2011.575228

Mehta, P. J., & Beer, J. (2010). Neural mechanisms of the testosterone-aggression relation: The role of orbitofrontal cortex. *Journal of Cognitive Neuroscience, 22*(10), 2357–2368.

Meichenbaum, D. (2009). Stress inoculation training. In W. T. O'Donohue & J. E. Fisher (Eds.), *General principles and empirically supported techniques of cognitive behavior therapy* (pp. 627–630). Hoboken, NJ: Wiley.

Meier, P. S., Donmall, M. C., et al. (2006). The role of the early therapeutic alliance in predicting drug treatment dropout. *Drug & Alcohol Dependence, 83*(1), 57–64. doi:10.1016/j.drugalcdep.2005.10.010

Meijer, E. H., & Verschuere, B. (2010). The polygraph and the detection of deception. *Journal of Forensic Psychology Practice, 10*(4), 325–338. doi:10.1080/15228932.2010.481237

Meini, C., & Paternoster, A. (2012). Mirror neurons as a conceptual mechanism? *Mind & Society, 11*(2), 183–201. doi:10.1007/s11299-012-0106-0

Mejía, O. L., & McCarthy, C. J. (2010). Acculturative stress, depression, and anxiety in migrant farmwork college students of Mexican heritage. *International Journal of Stress Management, 17*(1), 1–20. doi:10.1037/a0018119

Meltzoff, A. N. (2005). Imitation and other minds: The "Like Me" Hypothesis. In S. Hurley & N. Chater (Eds.), *Perspectives on imitation: From neuroscience to social science: Imitation, human development, and culture* (Vol. 2, pp. 55–77). Cambridge, MA: MIT Press.

Melzack, R. (1999). From the gate to the neuromatrix. *Pain, Aug. Suppl. 6,* S121–S126. doi:10.1016/S0304-3959(99)00145-1

Melzack, R., & Katz, J. (2006). Pain in the 21st century: The neuromatrix and beyond. In G. Young, A. W. Kane, et al. (Eds.), *Psychological knowledge in court: PTSD, pain, and TBI* (pp. 129–148). New York: Springer.

Memon, A., Meissner, C. A., & Fraser, J. (2010). The Cognitive Interview: A meta-analytic review and study space analysis of the past 25 years.

Psychology, Public Policy, & Law, 16(4), 340–372. doi:10.1037/a0020518

Mendelson, D., & Goes, F. S. (2011). A 34-year-old mother with religious delusions, filicidal thoughts. *Psychiatric Annals, 41*(7), 359–362.

Mendolia, M. (2002). An index of self-regulation of emotion and the study of repression in social contexts that threaten or do not threaten self-concept. *Emotion, 2*(3), 215–232. doi:10.1037/1528-3542.2.3.215

Meneses, G. D., & Beerlipalacio, A. (2005). Recycling behavior: A multidimensional approach. *Environment & Behavior, 37*(6), 837–860. doi:10.1177/0013916505276742

Mercer, T., & McKeown, D. (2010). Interference in short-term auditory memory. *Quarterly Journal of Experimental Psychology, 63*(7), 1256–1265. doi:10.1080/17470211003802467

Meyer, G. J., Finn, S. E., et al. (2001). Psychological testing and psychological assessment: A review of evidence and issues. *American Psychologist, 56*(2) 128–165. doi:10.1037/0003-066X.56.2.128

Meyer, I. H., Ouellette, S. C., et al. (2011). "We'd be free": Narratives of life without homophobia, racism, or sexism. *Sexuality Research & Social Policy, 8*(3), 204–214. doi:10.1007/s13178-011-0063-0

Meyerbröker, K., & Emmelkamp, P. M. (2010). Virtual reality exposure therapy in anxiety disorders: A systematic review of process-and-outcome studies. *Depression & Anxiety, 27*(10), 933–944. doi:10.1002/da.20734

Meyers, L. (2006). Behind the scenes of the "Dr. Phil" show. *Monitor on Psychology, 37*(9), 63.

Michaels, J. W., Blommel, J. M., et al. (1982). Social facilitation and inhibition in a natural setting. *Replications in Social Psychology, 2*, 21–24.

Michaliszyn, D., Marchand, A., et al. (2010). A randomized, controlled clinical trial of in virtuo and in vivo exposure for spider phobia. *Cyberpsychology, Behavior, & Social Networking, 13*(6), 689–695. doi:10.1089/cyber.2009.0277

Michalko, M. (1998). *Cracking creativity*. Berkeley, CA: Ten Speed Press.

Michalko, M. (2006). *Thinkertoys: A handbook of creative-thinking techniques* (2nd Ed.). Berkeley, CA: Ten Speed Press.

Mickes, L., Flowe, H. D., & Wixted, J. T. (2012). Receiver operating characteristic analysis of eyewitness memory: Comparing the diagnostic accuracy of simultaneous versus sequential lineups. *Journal of Experimental Psychology: Applied, 18*(4), 361–376. doi:10.1037/a0030609

Middaugh, S. J., & Pawlick, K. (2002). Biofeedback and behavioral treatment of persistent pain in the older adult: A review and a study. *Applied Psychophysiology & Biofeedback, 27*(3), 185–202. doi:10.1023/A:1016208128254

Mikulincer, M. & Shaver, P. R. (Eds.). (2010). *Prosocial motives, emotions, and behavior: The better angels of our nature.* Washington: American Psychological Association.

Miles, L. K., Karpinska, K., Lumsden, J., et al. (2010). The meandering mind: Vection and mental time travel. *PLoS ONE, 5*(5): e10825. doi:10.1371/journal.pone.0010825

Milgram, S. (1963). Behavioral study of obedience. *Journal of Abnormal & Social Psychology, 67*, 371–378. doi:10.1037/h0040525

Milgram, S. (1965). Some conditions of obedience and disobedience to authority. *Human Relations, 18*, 57–76. doi:10.1177/001872676501800105

Milgram, S. (1970). The experience of living in the cities: A psychological analysis. *Science, 167*, 1461–1468.

Milgram, S., Bickman, L., & Berkowitz, L. (1969). Note on the drawing power of crowds of different size. *Journal of Personality & Social Psychology, 13*, 79–82. doi:10.1037/h0028070

Miller, G. A. (1956). The magical number seven, plus or minus two: Some limits on our capacity for processing information. *Psychological Review, 63*, 81–97. doi:10.1037/0033-295X.101.2.343

Miller, G. T., Jr., & Spoolman, S. (2013). *Environmental science* (14th ed.). Belmont, CA: Cengage Learning/Wadsworth.

Miller, J., & Garran, A. M. (2008). *Racism in the United States: Implications for the helping professions.* Belmont, CA: Cengage Learning/Wadsworth.

Miller, L. E., Grabell, A., et al. (2012). The associations between community violence, television violence, intimate partner violence, parent–child aggression, and aggression in sibling relationships of a sample of preschoolers. *Psychology of Violence.* doi:10.1037/a0027254.

Miller, M. A., & Rahe, R. H. (1997). Life changes scaling for the 1990s. *Journal of Psychosomatic Research, 43*(3), 279–292. doi:10.1016/S0022-3999(97)00118-9

Miller, M., Hemenway, D., & Azraela, D. (2007). State-level homicide victimization rates in the US in relation to survey measures of household firearm ownership, 2001–2003. *Social Science & Medicine, 64*(3), 656–664. doi:10.1016/j.socscimed.2006.09.024

Miller, N. E. (1944). Experimental studies of conflict. In J. McV. Hunt (Ed.), *Personality and the behavior disorders* (Vol. 1, pp. 431–465). New York: Ronald Press.

Miller, N. E., & Bugelski. R. (1948). Minor studies of aggression: II. The influence of frustration imposed by the in-group on attitudes expressed toward out-groups. *Journal of Psychology, 25*, 437–442. doi:10.1080/00223980.1948.9917387

Miller, N., Pedersen, W. C., et al. (2003). A theoretical model of triggered displaced aggression. *Personality & Social Psychology Review, 7*(1), 75–97. doi:10.1207/S15327957PSPR0701_5

Miller, P. H. (2011). Piaget's theory: Past, present, and future. In U. Goswami (Ed.), *Piaget's theory: Past, present, and future* (pp. 649–672). Wiley-Blackwell.

Miller, R. (2012). *Intimate relationships* (6th ed.). New York: McGraw-Hill.

Miller, S. R. (2012). I don't want to get involved: Shyness, psychological control, and youth activities. *Journal of Social & Personal Relationships, 29*(7), 908–929. doi:10.1177/0265407512448266

Miller, W. R., & Munoz, R. F. (2005). *Controlling your drinking: Tools to make moderation work for you.* New York: Guilford.

Millet, K., & Dewitte, S. (2007). Digit ratio (2D:4D) moderates the impact of an aggressive music video on aggression. *Personality & Individual Differences, 43*(2), 289–294.

Millman, R. B., & Ross, E. J. (2003). Steroid and nutritional supplement use in professional athletes. *American Journal on Addictions, 12*(Suppl 2), S48–S54. doi:10.1080/713830544

Milne, R., & Bull, R. (2002). Back to basics: A componential analysis of the original cognitive interview mnemonics with three age groups. *Applied Cognitive Psychology, 16*(7), 743–753. doi:10.1002/acp.825

Milner, B. (1965). Memory disturbance after bilateral hippocampal lesions. In P. Milner & S. Glickman (Eds.), *Cognitive processes and the brain* (pp. 97–111). Princeton, NJ: Van Nostrand.

Miltenberger, R. G. (2012). *Behavior modification: Principles and procedures* (5th ed.). Belmont, CA: Cengage Learning/Wadsworth.

Milton, J., & Wiseman, R. (1997). *Guidelines for extrasensory perception research.* Hertfordshire, UK: University of Hertfordshire Press.

Milton, J., & Wiseman, R. (1999). A meta-analysis of mass-media tests of extrasensory perception. *British Journal of Psychology, 90*(2), 235–240. doi:10.1348/000712699161378

Minda, J. P., & Smith, J. D. (2011). Prototype models of categorization: Basic formulation, predictions, and limitations. In E. M. Pothos & A. J. Wills (Eds.), *Formal approaches in categorization* (pp. 40–64). New York: Cambridge University Press.

Minton, H. L. (2000). Psychology and gender at the turn of the century. *American Psychologist, 55*(6), 613–615. doi:10.1037/0003-066X.55.6.613

Mintz, A., DeRouen, K., et al. (2010). *Groupthink versus high-quality decision making in international relations.* New York: Columbia University Press.

Miotto, K., Darakjian, J., et al. (2001). Gamma-hydroxybutyric acid: Patterns of use, effects and withdrawal. *American Journal on Addictions, 10*(3), 232–241. doi:10.1080/105504901750532111

Miranda, R., & Kihlstrom, J. F. (2005). Mood congruence in childhood and recent autobiographical memory. *Cognition & Emotion, 19*(7), 981–998.

Mirsky, A. F., & Duncan, C. C. (2005). Pathophysiology of mental illness: A view from the fourth ventricle. *International Journal of Psychophysiology, 58*(2–3), 162–178. doi:10.1016/j.ijpsycho.2005.06.004

Mirsky, A. F., Bieliauskas, L. M., et al. (2000). A 39-year follow-up of the Genain quadruplets. *Schizophrenia Bulletin, 3*, 5–18.

Mischel, W. (2004). Toward an integrative science of the person. *Annual Review of Psychology, 55*, 1–22. doi:10.1146/annurev.psych.55.042902.130709

Mischel, W., & Shoda, Y. (2010). The situated person. In B. Mesquita, L. F. Barrett, & E. R. Smith (Eds.), *The mind in context* (pp. 149–173). New York: Guilford.

Mischel, W., Shoda, Y., & Smith, R. E. (2008). *Introduction to personality: Toward an integration* (8th ed.). Hoboken, NJ: Wiley.

Mitchell, D. (1987). Firewalking cults: Nothing but hot air. *Laser, Feb.*, 7–8.

Mitchell, L. A., MacDonald, R. A., et al. (2007). A survey investigation of the effects of music listening on chronic pain. *Psychology of Music, 35*(1), 37–57. doi:10.1177/0305735607068887

Mitchell, M. E., Lebow, J. R., et al. (2011). Internet use, happiness, social support and introversion: A more fine-grained analysis of person variables and internet activity. *Computers in Human Behavior, 27*(5), 1857–1861. doi:10.1016/j.chb.2011.04.008

Mitchell, N. S., Dickinson, L. M., et al. (2010). Determining the effectiveness of Take Off Pounds Sensibly (TOPS), a nationally available nonprofit weight loss program. *Obesity, 19*, 568–573. doi:10.1038/oby.2010.202

Mitka, M. (2009). College binge drinking still on the rise. *Journal of the American Medical Association, 302*(8), 836–837. doi:10.1001/jama.2009.1154

Mizock, L., & Harkins, D. (2011). Diagnostic bias and conduct disorder: Improving culturally sensitive diagnosis. *Child & Youth Services, 32*(3), 243–253. doi:10.1080/0145935X.2011.605315

Mock, S. E., & Eibach, R. P. (2012). Stability and change in sexual orientation identity over a 10-year period in adulthood. *Archives of Sexual Behavior, 41*(3), 641–648. doi:10.1007/s10508011-9761-1

Moerman, D. E. (2002). The meaning response and the ethics of avoiding placebos. *Evaluation & the Health Professions, 25*(4), 399–409. doi:10.1177/0163278702238053

Mogg, K., Bradley, B. P., et al. (1998). Selective attention to food-related stimuli in hunger. *Behaviour Research & Therapy, 36*(2), 227–237. doi:10.1016/S0005-7967(97)00062-4

Moghaddam, B. (2002). Stress activation of glutamate neurotransmission in the prefrontal cortex. *Biological Psychiatry, 51*(10), 775–787. doi:10.1016/S0006-3223(01)01362-2

Moghaddam, F. M. (2007). *Multiculturalism and intergroup relations: Psychological implications for democracy in global context.* Washington: American Psychological Association.

Moghaddam, F. M. (2013). *The psychology of dictatorship.* Washington, DC US: American Psychological Association. doi:10.1037/14138-008

Mojtabai, R., Olfson, M., et al. (2011). Barriers to mental health treatment: Results from the national comorbidity survey replication. *Psychological Medicine, 41*(8), 1751–1761. doi:10.1017/S0033291710002291

Mokdad, A. H., Marks, J. S., et al. (2004). Actual causes of death in the United States, 2000. *Journal of the American Medical Association, 291*, 1238–1245. doi:10.1001/jama.291.10.1238

Moksnes, U. K., & Espnes, G. A. (2012). Self-esteem and emotional health in adolescents: Gender and age as potential moderators. *Scandinavian Journal of Psychology, 53*(6), 483–489. doi:10.1111/sjop.12021

Molenberghs, P., Cunnington, R., & Mattingley, J. B. (2012). Brain regions with mirror properties: A meta-analysis of 125 human fMRI studies. *Neuroscience & Biobehavioral Reviews, 36*(1), 341–349. doi:10.1016/j.neubiorev.2011.07.004

Monahan, C. I., Beeber, L. S., & Harden, B. (2012). Finding family strengths in the midst of adversity: Using risk and resilience models to promote mental health. In S. Summers, & R. Chazan-Cohen (Eds.), *Understanding early childhood mental health: A practical guide for professionals* (pp. 59–78). Baltimore, MD: Paul H Brookes.

Monahan, J., Steadman, H. J., et al. (2001). *Rethinking risk assessment: The MacArthur Study of Mental Disorder and Violence.* New York, Oxford University Press.

Monde, K., Ketay, S., et al. (2013). Preliminary physiological evidence for impaired emotion regulation in depersonalization disorder.

Psychiatry Research. doi:10.1016/j.psychres.2013.02.020

Moneta, G. B. (2012). Opportunity for creativity in the job as a moderator of the relation between trait intrinsic motivation and flow in work. *Motivation & Emotion, 36*(4), 491–503. doi:10.1007/s11031-012-9278-5

Mongeau, P. A., Knight, K., et al. (2013). Identifying and explicating variation among friends with benefits relationships. *Journal of Sex Research, 50*(1), 37–47. doi:10.1080/00224499.2011.623797

Monteleone, G. T., Phan, K., et al. (2009). Detection of deception using fMRI: Better than chance, but well below perfection. *Social Neuroscience, 4*(6), 528–538. doi:10.1080/17470910801903530

Montgomery, P., & Dennis, J. (2004). A systematic review of non-pharmacological therapies for sleep problems in later life. *Sleep Medicine Reviews, 8*(1), 47–62. doi:10.1016/S1087-0792(03)00026-1

Monti, M. M., Vanhaudenhuyse, A., et al. (2010). Willful modulation of brain activity in disorders of consciousness. *New England Journal of Medicine, 362*(7), 579–589. doi:10.1056/NEJMoa0905370

Montoya, E. R., Terburg, D., et al. (2012). Testosterone, cortisol, and serotonin as key regulators of social aggression: A review and theoretical perspective. *Motivation & Emotion, 36*(1), 65–73. doi:10.1007/s11031-011-9264-3

Montoya, R. M., & Insko, C. A. (2008). Toward a more complete understanding of the reciprocity of liking effect. *European Journal of Social Psychology, 38*, 477–498. doi:10.1002/ejsp.431

Montoya, R., & Horton, R. S. (2013). A meta-analytic investigation of the processes underlying the similarity-attraction effect. *Journal of Social & Personal Relationships, 30*(1), 64–94. doi:10.1177/0265407512452989

Montreal Declaration on Intellectual Disabilities. (2004). Retrieved June 10, 2013, from http://www.bangkok-id-conference.org/ressources/preparatory-documents/tuesday-november-6-right-to-health/the-montreal-declaration-on-intellectual-disabilities/view

Moore, R. C., Viglione, D. J., et al. (2013). Rorschach measures of cognition relate to everyday and social functioning in schizophrenia. *Psychological Assessment, 25*(1), 253–263. doi:10.1037/a0030546

Moore, S. A., & Zoellner, L. A. (2007). Overgeneral autobiographical memory and traumatic events: An evaluative review. *Psychological Bulletin, 133*(3), 419–437. doi:10.1037/0033-2909.133.3.419

Moore, T. O. (2001). Testosterone and male behavior: Empirical research with hamsters does not support the use of castration to deter human sexual aggression. *North American Journal of Psychology, 3*(3), 503–520.

Moran, E. F. (2010). *Environmental social science: Human–environment interactions and sustainability.* Malden, MA: Wiley-Blackwell.

Moran, F. (2010). *The paradoxical legacy of Sigmund Freud.* London, England: Karnac Books.

Moreno-Cabrera, J. (2011). Speech and gesture: An integrational approach. *Language Sciences, 33*(4), 615–622. doi:10.1016/j.langsci.2011.04.021

Moreno, J. L. (1953). *Who shall survive?* New York: Beacon.

Moreno, M. M., Linster, C., et al. (2009). Olfactory perceptual learning requires adult neurogenesis. *Proceedings of the National Academy of Sciences, 106*(42), 17980–17985. doi:10.1073/pnas.0907063106

Morgan, J. P. (Ed.). (2005). *Psychology of aggression.* Hauppauge, NY: Nova Science Publishers.

Morin, A. (2006). Levels of consciousness and self-awareness: A comparison and integration of various neurocognitive views. *Consciousness & Cognition, 15*(2), 358–371. doi:10.1016/j.concog.2005.09.006

Morisse, D., Batra, L., et al. (1996). A demonstration of a token economy for the real world. *Applied & Preventive Psychology, 5*(1), 41–46. doi:10.1016/S0962-1849(96)80025-4

Morley, T. E., & Moran, G. (2011). The origins of cognitive vulnerability in early childhood: Mechanisms linking early attachment to later depression. *Clinical Psychology Review, 31*(7), 1071–1082. doi:10.1016/j.cpr.2011.06.006

Morrison, M. (2012). *Using humor to maximize living: Connecting with humor* (2nd ed.). Lanham, MD: Rowman & Littlefield Education.

Morrison, R. G., & Wallace, B. (2001). Imagery vividness, creativity and the visual arts. *Journal of Mental Imagery, 25*(3–4), 135–152.

Morrissey, A., & Brown, P. M. (2009). Mother and toddler activity in the zone of proximal development for pretend play as a predictor of higher child IQ. *Gifted Child Quarterly, 53*(2), 106–120. doi:10.1177/0016986208330563

Mosher, W. D., Chandra, C., & Jones, J. (2005). *Sexual behavior and selected health measures: Men and women 15–44 years of age, United States, 2002.* Retrieved June 11, 2013, from http://www.cdc.gov/nchs/data/ad/ad362.pdf

Mosley, M. (2011). *Alien Hand Syndrome sees woman attacked by her own hand.* Retrieved June 9, 2013, from http://www.bbc.co.uk/news/uk-12225163

Most, S. B., Scholl, B. J., et al. (2005). What you see is what you set: Sustained inattentional blindness and the capture of awareness. *Psychological Review, 112*(1), 217–242. doi:10.1037/0033-295X.112.1.217

Motivala, S. J., & Irwin, M. R. (2007). Sleep and immunity: Cytokine pathways linking sleep and health outcomes. *Current Directions in Psychological Science, 16*(1), 21–25. doi:10.1111/j.1467-8721.2007.00468.x

Mõttus, R., Johnson, W., & Deary, I. J. (2012). Personality traits in old age: Measurement and rank-order stability and some mean-level change. *Psychology & Aging, 27*(1), 243–249. doi:10.1037/a0023690

Mowbray, T. (2012). Working memory, test anxiety and effective interventions: A review. *Australian Educational & Developmental Psychologist, 29*(2), 141–156. doi:10.1017/edp.2012.16

Mulavara, A. P., Feiveson, A. H., et al. (2010). Locomotor function after long-duration space flight: Effects and motor learning during recovery. *Experimental Brain Research, 202*(3), 649–659.

Müller, B. H., Kull, S., et al. (2011). One-session computer-based exposure treatment for spider-fearful individuals: Efficacy of a minimal self-help intervention in a randomised controlled trial. *Journal of Behavior Therapy & Experimental Psychiatry, 42*(2), 179–184. doi:10.1016/j.jbtep.2010.12.001

Müller, V. C. (2012). Introduction: Philosophy and theory of artificial intelligence. *Minds & Machines, 22*(2), 67–69. doi:10.1007/s11023-012-9278-y

Mundy, A. (2004). Divided we stand. *American Demographics, 26*(5), 26–31.

Munroe-Chandler, K., Hall, C., & Fishburne, G. (2008). Playing with confidence: The relationship between imagery use and self-confidence and self-efficacy in youth soccer players. *Journal of Sports Sciences, 26*(14), 1539–1546. doi:10.1080/02640410802315419

Munsey, C. (2006). RxP legislation made historic progress in Hawaii. *APA Monitor,* June, 42.

Muran, J. C., & Barber, J. P. (Eds.) (2010). The therapeutic alliance: An evidence-based guide to practice. New York: Guilford.

Murphy, B. C., & Dillon, C. (2011). *Interviewing in action in a multicultural world* (4th ed.). Belmont, CA: Cengage Learning/Wadsworth.

Murphy, D., & Page, I. (2008). Exhibitionism: Psychopathology and theory. In D. Laws & W. O'Donohue (Eds.), *Sexual deviance: Theory, assessment, and treatment* (2nd ed.). New York: Guilford.

Murray, C. D., Pettifer, S., et al. (2007). The treatment of phantom limb pain using immersive virtual reality: Three case studies. *Disability & Rehabilitation, 29*(18), 1465–1469. doi:10.1080/09638280601107385

Murray, S., Holmes, J. G., & Griffin, D. W. (2003). Reflections on the self-fulfilling effects of positive illusions. *Psychological Inquiry, 14*(3–4), 2003, 289–295. doi:10.1080/10478 40X.2003.9682895

Murrell, A. R., Christoff, K. A., & Henning, K. R. (2007). Characteristics of domestic violence offenders: Associations with childhood exposure to violence. *Journal of Family Violence, 22*(7). 523–532. doi:10.1007/s10896-007-9100-4

Music, G. (2011). *Nurturing natures: Attachment and children's emotional, sociocultural and brain development.* Hove, UK: Psychology Press.

Mussen, P. H., Conger, J. J., et al. (1979). *Psychological development: A life span approach.* New York: Harper & Row.

Mustafa, F. (2013). Schizophrenia past clozapine: What works? *Journal Of Clinical Psychopharmacology, 33*(1), 63–68. doi:10.1097/ JCP.0b013e31827a813b

Mustanski, B. S., Chivers, M. L., & Bailey, J. M. (2002). A critical review of recent biological research on human sexual orientation. *Annual Review of Sex Research, 13,* 89–140.

Myers, L. (2007). The problem with DNA. *Monitor on Psychology,* June, 52–53.

Myers, M. W., & Hodges, S. D. (2013). Empathy: Perspective taking and prosocial behavior: Caring for others like we care for the self. In J. J. Froh, & A. C. Parks (Eds.), *Activities for teaching positive psychology: A guide for instructors* (pp. 77–83). Washington, DC: American Psychological Association. doi:10.1037/14042-013

Myrtek, M. (2007). Type A behavior and hostility as independent risk factors for coronary heart disease. In J. Jordan, B. Bardé, et al. (Eds.), *Contributions toward evidence-based psychocardiology: A systematic review of the literature* (pp. 159–183). Washington: American Psychological Association.

Nadel, L. L., Hupbach, A. A., et al. (2012). Memory formation, consolidation and transformation. *Neuroscience & Biobehavioral Reviews, 36*(7), 1640–1645. doi:10.1016/j. neubiorev.2012.03.001

Nahari, G. (2012). Elaborations on credibility judgments by professional lie detectors and laypersons: Strategies of judgment and justification. *Psychology, Crime & Law, 18*(6), 567–577. doi:10.10 80/1068316X.2010.511222

Naitoh, P., Kelly, T. L., & Englund, C. E. (1989). *Health effects of sleep deprivation.* U.S. Naval Health Research Center Report, No. 89–46.

Najdowski, C. J. (2010). Jurors and social loafing: Factors that reduce participation during jury deliberations. *American Journal of Forensic Psychology, 28*(2), 39–64.

Nakamura, J., & Csikszentmihalyi, M. (2003). The motivational sources of creativity as viewed from the paradigm of positive psychology. In L. G. Aspinwall & U. M. Staudinger (Eds.), *A psychology of human strengths: Fundamental questions and future directions for a positive psychology* (pp. 257–269). Washington: American Psychological Association.

Nakamura, Y., Goto, T. K., et al. (2011). Localization of brain activation by umami taste in humans. *Brain Research, 1406,* 18–29. doi:10.1016/j. brainres.2011.06.029

Nakayama, H. (2010). Development of infant crying behavior: A longitudinal case study. *Infant Behavior & Development, 33*(4), 463–471. doi:10.1016/j.infbeh.2010.05.002

National Academy of Sciences. (2003). *The polygraph and lie detection.* Washington: The National Academies Press.

National Center for Chronic Disease Prevention and Health Promotion. (2011). *Tobacco use: Targeting the nation's leading killer.* Retrieved June 17, 2013, from http://www.cdc.gov /nccdphp/publications/aag/osh.htm

National Committee on Pay Equity. (2010). *Women of color in the workplace.* Retrieved April 9, 2013, from http://www.pay-equity.org/info-race .html

National Committee on Pay Equity. (2012). *The wage gap over time: In real dollars, women see a continuing gap.* Retrieved April 9, 2013, from http:// www.pay-equity.org/info-time.html

National Institute of Child Health and Human Development. (2010a). *Link between child care and academic achievement and behavior persists into adolescence.* Retrieved June 9, 2013, from http://www.nichd.nih.gov/news /releases/051410-early-child-care.cfm

National Institute of Child Health and Human Development. (2012). *Sudden infant death syndrome (SIDS) overview.* Retrieved March 7, 2013, from http://www.nichd.nih.gov /health/topics/sids/Pages/default.aspx

National Institute of Mental Health. (2010a). *Suicide in the U.S.: Statistics and prevention.* Retrieved April 26, 2013, from http://www.nimh.nih.gov /health/publications/suicide-in-the -us-statistics-and-prevention/index .shtml

National Institute of Mental Health. (2010b). *Turning the corner, not the key, in treatment of serious mental illness.* Retrieved May 7, 2013, from http://www.nimh.nih.gov/about /director/2010/turning-the-corner -not-the-key-in-treatment-of-serious -mental-illness.shtml

National Institute of Mental Health. (2011). *Warning signs of suicide.* Retrieved April 26, 2013, from http:// www.nimh.nih.gov/health/topics /suicide-prevention/suicide -prevention-studies/warning-signs-of -suicide.shtml

National Institute of Mental Health. (2012a). *Depression.* Retrieved April 16, 2013, from http://www.nimh.nih .gov/health/publications/depression /complete-index.shtml#pub12

National Institute of Mental Health. (2012b). *Help for mental illnesses.* Retrieved June 18, 2013, from http:// www.nimh.nih.gov/health/find-help /index.shtml

National Institute of Mental Health. (2013). *Statistics.* Retrieved April 26, 2013, from http://www.nimh.nih.gov /statistics/index.shtml

National Institute of Neurological Disorders and Stroke. (2007). *Brain basics: Understanding sleep.* NIH Publication No.06-3440-c. Retrieved June 9, 2013, from http://www.ninds .nih.gov/disorders/brain_basics /understanding_sleep.htm

National Institute on Alcohol Abuse and Alcoholism. (2008). *Tips for cutting down drinking.* Retrieved June 10, 2013, from http://rethinkingdrinking .niaaa.nih.gov/strategies/tipstotry.asp

National Institute on Drug Abuse. (2010). *Drugs, brains, and behavior: The science of addiction.* Retrieved March 9, 2013, from https://www.drugabuse .gov/sites/default/files/sciofaddiction .pdf

National Institute on Drug Abuse. (2012a). *DrugFacts: MDMA (Ecstasy).* Retrieved March 9, 2013, from http:// www.drugabuse.gov/publications /infofacts/mdma-ecstasy

National Institute on Drug Abuse. (2012b). *What is tobacco addiction.* Retrieved June 10, 2013, from http:// teens.drugabuse.gov/drug-facts /tobacco

National Institute on Drug Abuse. (2012c). *DrugFacts: Marijuana.* Retrieved March 9, 2013, from http:// www.drugabuse.gov/publications /drugfacts/marijuana

National Institutes of Health (2012). *Hearing loss.* Retrieved February 12, 2013, from http://nihseniorhealth .gov/hearingloss/faq/faq1.html

National Institutes of Health (2013). *Color vision deficiency.* Retrieved February 11, 2013, from http:// ghr.nlm.nih.gov/condition /color-vision-deficiency

Nätti, J., & Häikiö, L. (2012). Flexible work and work–family interaction. *Community, Work & Family, 15*(4), 381–382. doi:10.1080/13668803.2012. 725548

Nau, S. D., & Lichstein, K. L. (2005). Insomnia: Causes and treatments. In P. R. Carney, J. D. Geyer, et al. (Eds.), *Clinical sleep disorders* (pp. 157–190). Philadelphia, PA: Lippincott Williams & Wilkins.

Naveh-Benjamin, M., Guez, J., & Sorek, S. (2007). The effects of divided attention on encoding processes in memory: Mapping the locus of interference. *Canadian Journal of Experimental Psychology, 61*(1), 1–12.

Nawrot, E., Mayo, S. L., & Nawrot, M. (2009). The development of depth perception from motion parallax in infancy. *Attention, Perception, & Psychophysics, 71*(1), 194–199.

Negriff, S., & Trickett, P. K. (2010). The relationship between pubertal timing and delinquent behavior in maltreated male and female adolescents. *Journal of Early Adolescence, 30*(4), 518–542. doi:10.1177/0272431609338180

Nehlig, A. (Ed.). (2004). *Coffee, tea, chocolate, and the brain.* Boca Raton, FL: CRC Press.

Neikrug, A. B., & Ancoli-Israel, S. (2012). Diagnostic tools for REM sleep behavior disorder. *Sleep Medicine Reviews, 16*(5), 415–429. doi:10.1016/j. smrv.2011.08.004

Neitz, J., & Neitz, M. (2011). The genetics of normal and defective color vision. *Vision Research, 51*(7), 633–651. doi:10.1016/j.visres.2010.12.002

Nellis, A., & Savage, J. (2012). Does watching the news affect fear of terrorism? The importance of media exposure on terrorism fear. *Crime & Delinquency, 58*(5), 748–768. doi:10.1177/0011128712452961

Nelson, C. A. (1999). How important are the first 3 years of life? *Applied Developmental Science, 3*(4), 235–238. doi:10.1207/s1532480xads0304_8

Nelson, G., Van Andel, A. K., et al. (2012). Exploring outcomes through narrative: The long-term impacts of better beginnings, better futures on the turning point stories of youth at ages 18–19. *American Journal of Community Psychology, 49*(1–2), 294–306. doi:10.1007/s10464-011-9466-6

Nelson, T. D. (2005). Ageism: Prejudice against our feared future self. *Journal of Social Issues, 61*(2), 207–221. doi:10.1111/j.1540-4560.2005.00402.x

Nelson, T. D. (2006). *The psychology of prejudice* (2nd ed.). Needham Heights, MA: Allyn & Bacon.

Neter, E., & Ben-Shakhar, G. (1989). The predictive validity of graphological inferences: A meta-analytic approach. *Personality & Individual Differences, 10*(7), 737–745. doi:10.1016/0191-8869(89)90120-7

Nettle, D. (2005). An evolutionary perspective on the extraversion continuum. *Evolution & Human Behavior, 26*, 363–373. doi:10.1016/j.evolhumbehav.2004.12.004

Nettle, D. (2006). The evolution of personality variation in humans and other animals. *American Psychologist, 61*(6), 622–631. doi:10.1037/0003-066X.61.6.622

Nettle, D. (2008). The personality factor: What makes you unique? *New Scientist, February 9*, 36–39.

Neubauer, A. C., & Fink, A. (2009). Intelligence and neural efficiency: Measures of brain activation versus measures of functional connectivity in the brain. *Intelligence, 37*(2), 223–229. doi:10.1016/j.intell.2008.10.008

Neufeind, J., Dritschel, B., et al. (2009). The effects of thought suppression on autobiographical memory recall. *Behaviour Research & Therapy, 47*(4), 275–284. doi:10.1016/j.brat.2008.12.010

Neufeld, R. W. J., Carter, J. R., et al. (2003). Schizophrenia. In P. Firestone & W. L. Marshall (Eds.), *Abnormal psychology: Perspectives* (2nd ed., pp. 343–370). Toronto: Prentice Hall.

Neukrug, E. S., & Fawcett, R. C. (2010). *Essentials of testing and assessment: A practical guide for counselors, social workers, and psychologists* (2nd ed.). Belmont, CA: Cengage Learning/Wadsworth.

Nevo, E., & Breznitz, Z. (2013). The development of working memory from kindergarten to first grade in children with different decoding skills. *Journal of Experimental Child Psychology, 114*(2), 217–228. doi:10.1016/j.jecp.2012.09.004

Newell, B. R. (2012). Levels of explanation in category learning. *Australian Journal Of Psychology, 64*(1), 46–51.

Ng, T. H., & Feldman, D. C. (2010). Human capital and objective indicators of career success: The mediating effects of cognitive ability and conscientiousness. *Journal of Occupational & Organizational Psychology, 83*(1), 207–235. doi:10.1348/096317909X414584

Nguyen T. Q., Gwynn R. C., et al. (2008). Population prevalence of reported and unreported HIV and related behaviors among the household adult population in New York City, 2004. *AIDS, 22*(2), 281–287. doi:10.1097/QAD.0b013e3282f2ef58

Nickell, J. (2001). John Edward: Hustling the bereaved. *Skeptical Inquirer, Nov.–Dec.*, 19–22.

Nickerson, C., Diener, E., & Schwarz, N. (2011). Positive affect and college success. *Journal of Happiness Studies, 12*(4), 717–746. doi:10.1007/s10902-010-9224-8

Nickerson, R. S., & Adams, M. J. (1979). Long-term memory for a common object. *Cognitive Psychology, 11*, 287–307. doi:10.1016/0010-0285(79)90013-6

Nicoletti, A. (2009). Teens and drug facilitated sexual assault. *Journal of Pediatric & Adolescent Gynecology, 22*(3), 187.

Niedzwienska, A. (2004). Metamemory knowledge and the accuracy of flashbulb memories. *Memory, 12*(5), 603–613. doi:10.1080/09658210344000134

Niehaus, D. J. H., Stein, D. J., et al. (2005). A case of "Ifufunyane": A Xhosa culture-bound syndrome. *Journal of Psychiatric Practice, 11*(6), 411–413. doi:10.1097/00131746-200511000-00009

Niehaus, J. L., Cruz-Bermúdez, N. D., & Kauer, J. A. (2009). Plasticity of addiction: A mesolimbic dopamine short-circuit? *American Journal on Addictions, 18*(4), 259–271. doi:10.1080/10550490902925946

Niehoff, B. P., Moorman, R. H., et al. (2001). The influence of empowerment and job enrichment on employee loyalty in a downsizing environment. *Group & Organization Management, 26*(1), 93–113.

Nielsen, M., & Dissanayake, C. (2004). Pretend play, mirror self-recognition and imitation: A longitudinal investigation through the second year. *Infant Behavior & Development, 27*(3), 342–365. doi:10.1016/j.infbeh.2003.12.006

Niemiec, C. P., Ryan, R. M., & Deci, E. L. (2009). The path taken: Consequences of attaining intrinsic and extrinsic aspirations in post-college life. *Journal of Research in Personality, 43*(3), 291–306. doi:10.1016/j.jrp.2008.09.001

Nieuwoudt, J. E., Zhou, S., et al. (2012). Muscle dysmorphia: Current research and potential classification as a disorder. *Psychology of Sport & Exercise, 13*(5), 569–577. doi:10.1016/j.psychsport.2012.03.006

Nigbur, D., Lyons, E., & Uzzell, D. (2010). Attitudes, norms, identity and environmental behaviour: Using an expanded theory of planned behaviour to predict participation in a kerbside recycling programme. *British Journal of Social Psychology, 49*(2), 259–284.

Nirenberg, S., & Pandarinath, C. (2012). Retinal prosthetic strategy with the capacity to restore normal vision. *Proceedings of the National Academy of Sciences, 109*(37), 15012–15017. doi:10.1073/pnas.1207035109

Nisbett, R. E. (2005). Heredity, environment, and race differences in IQ: A commentary on Rushton and Jensen (2005). *Psychology, Public Policy, & Law, 11*(2), 302–310. doi:10.1037/1076-8971.11.2.302

Nisbett, R. E. (2009). *Intelligence and how to get it: Why schools and cultures count.* New York: Norton.

Nisbett, R. E., & Miyamoto, Y. (2005). The influence of culture: holistic versus analytic perception. *Trends in Cognitive Sciences, 9*(10), 467–473. doi:10.1016/j.tics.2005.08.004

Nisbett, R. E., Aronson, J., et al. (2012). Intelligence: New findings and theoretical developments. *American Psychologist, 67*(2), 130–159. doi:10.1037/a0026699

Niven, K., Sprigg, C. A., & Armitage, C. J. (2013). Does emotion regulation protect employees from the negative effects of workplace aggression? *European Journal of Work & Organizational Psychology, 22*(1), 88–106. doi:10.1080/13594 32X.2011.626200

Njeri, I. (1991, January 13). Beyond the melting pot. *Los Angeles Times*, E-1, E-8.

Noftle, E. E., & Fleeson, W. (2010). Age differences in big five behavior averages and variabilities across the adult life span: Moving beyond retrospective, global summary accounts of personality. *Psychology & Aging, 25*(1), 95–107. doi:10.1037/a0018199

Noland, J. S., Singer, L. T., et al. (2005). Prenatal drug exposure and selective attention in preschoolers. *Neurotoxicology & Teratology, 27*(3), 429–438. doi:10.1016/j.ntt.2005.02.001

Nolen-Hoeksema, S. (2011). *Abnormal psychology* (5th ed.). New York: McGraw-Hill.

Noltemeyer, A., Bush, K., et al. (2012). The relationship among deficiency needs and growth needs: An empirical investigation of Maslow's theory. *Children & Youth Services Review, 34*(9), 1862–1867. doi:10.1016/j.childyouth.2012.05.021

Norenzayan, A., & Nisbett, R. E. (2000). Culture and causal cognition. *Current Directions in Psychological Science, 9*, 132–135. doi:10.1111/1467-8721.00077

Norlander, T., Bergman, H., & Archer, T. (1998). Effects of flotation rest on creative problem solving and originality. *Journal of Environmental Psychology, 18*(4), 399–408. doi:10.1006/jevp.1998.0112

Norlander, T., Bergman, H., & Archer, T. (1999). Primary process in competitive archery performance: Effects of flotation REST. *Journal of Applied Sport Psychology, 11*(2), 194–209. doi:10.1080/10413209908404200

Norman, D. A. (1994) *Things that make us smart.* Menlo Park, CA: Addison-Wesley.

Norman, P., Conner, M. T., & Stride, C. B. (2012). Reasons for binge drinking among undergraduate students: An application of behavioural reasoning theory. *British Journal of Health Psychology, 17*(4), 682–698. doi:10.1111/j.2044-8287.2012.02065.x

Norman, T. R. (2009). Melatonin: Hormone of the night. *Acta Neuropsychiatrica, 21*(5),

263–265. doi:10.1111/acn.2009.21.issue-510.1111/j.1601-5215.2009.00411.x

Northcutt, R. G. (2004). Taste buds: Development and evolution. *Brain, Behavior & Evolution, 64*(3), 198–206. doi:10.1159/000079747

Nosek, B. A., Greenwald, A. G., & Banaji, M. R. (2005). Understanding and using the implicit association test: II. Method variables and construct validity. *Personality & Social Psychology Bulletin, 31*(2), 166–180. doi:10.1177/0146167204271418

Novella, E. J. (2010). Mental health care in the aftermath of deinstitutionalization: A retrospective and prospective view. *Health Care Analysis, 18*(3), 222–238. doi:10.1007/s10728-009-0138-8

Novelli, D., Drury, J., & Reicher, S. (2010). Come together: Two studies concerning the impact of group relations on 'personal space.' *British Journal of Social Psychology, 49*(2), 223–236.

Nucci, L. P., & Gingo, M. (2011). The development of moral reasoning. In Goswami U. (Ed.), *The development of moral reasoning* (pp. 420–444). London: Wiley-Blackwell.

Nurnberger, J. I., & Zimmerman, J. (1970). Applied analysis of human behaviors: An alternative to conventional motivational inferences and unconscious determination in therapeutic programming. *Behavior Therapy, 1*, 59–69. doi:10.1016/S0005-7894(70)80057-0

O'Conner, T. G., Marvin, R. S., et al. (2003). Child–parent attachment following early institutional deprivation. *Development & Psychopathology, 15*(1), 19–38. doi:10.1017/S0954579403000026

O'Hare, A. E., Bremner, L., et al. (2009). A clinical assessment tool for advanced theory of mind performance in 5 to 12 year olds. *Journal of Autism & Developmental Disorders, 39*(6), 916–928. doi:10.1007/s10803-009-0699-2

O'Keeffe, C., & Wiseman, R. (2005). Testing alleged mediumship: Methods and results. *British Journal of Psychology, 96*(2), 165–179. doi:10.1348/000712605X36361

O'Neill, B. (2003). *Don't believe everything you read online.* Retrieved June 9, 2013, from http://newswww.bbc.net.uk/1/hi/magazine/3151595.stm

O'Neill, P. (2005). The ethics of problem definition. *Canadian Psychology, 46*, 13–20. doi:10.1037/h0085819

Oakley, R. (2004). How the mind hurts and heals the body. *American Psychologist, 59*(1), 29–40. doi:10.1037/0003-066X.59.1.29

Oakley, D. A., & Halligan, P. W. (2010). Psychophysiological foundations of hypnosis and suggestion. In S. J. Lynn, J. W. Rhue, & I. Kirsch (Eds.), *Handbook of clinical hypnosis* (2nd ed., pp. 79–117). Washington: American Psychological Association.

Oakley, D. A., Whitman, L. G., & Halligan, P. W. (2002). Hypnotic imagery as a treatment for phantom limb pain: Two case reports and a review. *Clinical Rehabilitation, 16*(4), 368–377. doi:10.1191/0269215502cr507oa

Oates, J. M., & Reder, L. M. (2011). Memory for pictures: Sometimes a picture is not worth a single word. In A. S. Benjamin (Ed.), *Successful remembering and successful forgetting: A festschrift in honor of Robert A. Bjork* (pp. 447–461). New York: Psychology Press.

Oberauer, K., & Göthe, K. (2006). Dual-task effects in working memory: Interference between two processing tasks, between two memory demands, and between storage and processing. *European Journal of Cognitive Psychology, 18*(4), 493–519. doi:10.1080/09541440500423038

Oberle, E. (2009). The development of Theory of Mind reasoning in Micronesian children. *Journal of Cognition & Culture, 9*(1–2), 39–56. doi:10.1163/156853709X414629

Oestergaard, S., & Møldrup, C. (2011). Optimal duration of combined psychotherapy and pharmacotherapy for patients with moderate and severe depression: A meta-analysis. *Journal of Affective Disorders, 131*(1–3), 24–36. doi:10.1016/j.jad.2010.08.014

Ogden C. L., Carroll M. D., et al. (2010). Prevalence of high body mass index in U.S. children and adolescents, 2007–2008. *Journal of the American Medical Association, 303*(3), 242–249. doi:10.1001/jama.2009.2012

Ogden, C. L., & Carroll, M. D. (2010). *Prevalence of overweight, obesity, and extreme obesity among adults: United States, Trends 1960–1962 through 2007–2008.* Retrieved June 11, 2013, from http://www.cdc.gov/nchs/data/hestat/overweight/overweight_adult.pdf

Ogloff, J. R. (2006). Psychopathy/antisocial personality disorder conundrum. *Australian & New Zealand Journal of Psychiatry, 40*(6), 519–528. doi:10.1111/j.1440-1614.2006.01834.x

Ogrodniczuk, J. S., Piper, W. E., & Joyce, A. S. (2011). Effect of alexithymia on the process and outcome of psychotherapy: A programmatic review. *Psychiatry Research, 190*(1), 43–48. doi:10.1016/j.psychres.2010.04.026

Oishi, S., Kesebir, S., & Diener, E. (2011). Income inequality and happiness. *Psychological Science, 22*(9), 1095–1100. doi:10.1177/0956797611417262

Okiishi, J., Lambert, M. J., Nielsen, et al. (2003). Waiting for supershrink: An empirical analysis of therapist effects. *Clinical Psychology & Psychotherapy, 10*(6), 361–373. doi:10.1002/cpp.383

Olpin, M., & Hesson, M. (2013). *Stress management for life* (3rd ed.). Belmont, CA: Cengage Learning/Wadsworth.

Olson, M., & Hergenhahn, B. (2013). *Introduction to the theories of learning* (9th ed.). Englewood Cliffs, NJ: Prentice Hall.

Olsson, A., Nearing, K., & Phelps, E. A. (2007). Learning fears by observing others: The neural systems of social fear transmission. *Social Cognitive & Affective Neuroscience, 2*(1), 3–11. doi:10.1093/scan/nsm005

Olsson, E. M., El Alaoui, S., et al. (2010). Internet-based biofeedback-assisted relaxation training in the treatment of hypertension: A pilot study. *Applied Psychophysiology & Biofeedback, 35*(2), 163–170. doi:10.1007/s10484-009-9126-x

Ong, A. D., Zautra, A. J., & Reid, M. C. (2010). Psychological resilience predicts decreases in pain catastrophizing through positive emotions. *Psychology & Aging, 25*(3), 516–523. doi:10.1037/a0019384

Onwuegbuzie, A. J. (2000). Academic procrastinators and perfectionistic tendencies among graduate students. *Journal of Social Behavior & Personality, 15*(5), 103–109.

Ooki, S. (2005). Genetic and environmental influences on the handedness and footedness in Japanese twin children. *Twin Research & Human Genetics, 8*(6), 649–656. doi:10.1375/twin.8.6.649

Opland, D. M., Leinninger, G. M., & Myers, M. G., Jr. (2010). Modulation of the mesolimbic dopamine system by leptin. *Brain Research, 1350*, 65–70. doi:10.1016/j.brainres.2010.04.028

Oppliger, P. A. (2007). Effects of gender stereotyping on socialization. In R. W. Preiss, B. M. Gayle, et al. (Eds.), *Mass media effects research: Advances through meta-analysis* (pp. 199–214). Mahwah, NJ: Erlbaum.

Oral Cancer Foundation (2013). *Oral cancer facts.* Retrieved March 5, 2013, from http://oralcancerfoundation.org/facts/index.htm

Oren, E. E., & Solomon, R. R. (2012). EMDR therapy: An overview of its development and mechanisms of action. *European Review of Applied Psychology, 62*(4), 197–203. doi:10.1016/j.erap.2012.08.005

Orenstein, P. (2011). *Cinderella ate my daughter.* New York: HarperCollins.

Orleans, C. T., Gruman, J., & Hollendonner, J. K. (1999). Rating our progress in population health promotion: Report card on six behaviors. *American Journal of Health Promotion, 14*(2), 75–82. doi:10.4278/0890-1171-14.2.75

Ormrod, J. E. (2014). *Educational psychology: Developing learners* (8th ed.). Boston: Allyn & Bacon.

Orr, A. C., & Hammig, S. B. (2009). Inclusive postsecondary strategies for teaching students with learning disabilities: A review of the literature. *Learning Disability Quarterly, 32*(3), 181–196.

Osgood, C. E. (1952). The nature and measurement of meaning. *Psychological Bulletin, 49*, 197–237. doi:10.1037/h0055737

Oskamp, S., & Schultz, P. W. (2005). *Attitudes and opinions* (3rd ed.). Mahwah, NJ: Erlbaum.

Oster, H. (2005). The repertoire of infant facial expressions: An ontogenetic perspective. In J. Nadel & D. Muir (Eds.), *Emotional development: Recent research advances* (pp. 261–292). New York: Oxford University Press.

Otgaar, H., & Smeets, T. (2010). Adaptive memory: Survival processing increases both true and false memory in adults and children. *Journal of Experimental Psychology: Learning, Memory, & Cognition, 36*(4), 1010–1016. doi:10.1037/a0019402

Overmier, J. B., & LoLordo, V. M. (1998). Learned helplessness. In O'Donohue, W. T. (Ed.), *Learning and behavior therapy* (pp. 352–373). Boston, MA: Allyn & Bacon.

Owens, J., & Massey, D. S. (2011). Stereotype threat and college academic performance: A latent variables approach. *Social Science Research, 40*(1), 150–166. doi:10.1016/j.ssresearch.2010.09.010

Oyserman, D., Bybee, D., et al. (2004). Possible selves as roadmaps. *Journal of Research in Personality, 38*(2), 130–149. doi:10.1016/S0092-6566(03)00057-6

Pagel, J. F. (2012). The synchronous electrophysiology of conscious states. *Dreaming, 22*(3), 173–191.

Palmer, S. E., & Beck, D. M. (2007). The repetition discrimination task: An objective method for studying perceptual grouping. *Perception & Psychophysics, 69*(1), 68–78. doi:10.3758/BF03194454

Panksepp, J., & Pasqualini, M. S. (2005). The search for the fundamental brain/mind sources of affective experience. In J. Nadel & D. Muir (Eds.), *Emotional development: Recent research advances* (pp. 5–30). New York: Oxford University Press.

Panksepp, J., & Watt, D. (2011). What is basic about basic emotions? Lasting lessons from affective neuroscience. *Emotion Review, 3*(4), 387–396. doi:10.1177/1754073911410741

Papadatou-Pastou, M., Martin, M., et al. (2008). Sex differences in left-handedness: A meta-analysis of 144 studies. *Psychological Bulletin, 134*(5), 677–699. doi:10.1037/a0012814

Papanicolaou, A. C. (Ed.) (2006). *The amnesias: A clinical textbook of memory disorders.* New York: Oxford University Press.

Paquette, D. (2004). Theorizing the father–child relationship: Mechanisms and developmental outcomes. *Human Development, 47*(4), 193–219. doi:org/10.1159/000078723

Paquette, V., Lévesque, J., et al. (2003). "Change the mind and you change the brain": Effects of cognitive-behavioral therapy on the neural correlates of spider phobia. *NeuroImage, 18*, 401–409. doi:10.1016/S1053-8119(02)00030-7

Paradis, C. M., Solomon, L. Z., et al. (2004). Flashbulb memories of personal events of 9/11 and the day after for a sample of New York City residents. *Psychological Reports, 95*(1), 304–310. doi:10.2466/PR0.95.5.304-310

Park, G., Lubinski, D., & Benbow, C. P. (2008). Ability differences among people who have commensurate degrees matter for scientific creativity. *Psychological Science, 19*(10), 957–961. doi:10.1111/j.1467-9280.2008.02182.x

Park, H. J., Li, R. X., Kim, J., et al. (2009). Neural correlates of winning and losing while watching soccer matches. *International Journal of Neuroscience, 119*(1), 76–87. doi:10.1080/00207450802480069

Park, H., & Lennon, S. J. (2008). Beyond physical attractiveness: Interpersonal attraction as a function of similarities in personal characteristics. *Clothing & Textiles Research Journal, 26*(4), 275–289. doi:10.1177/0887302X07309714

Park, N., Peterson, C., & Seligman, M. E. (2004). Strengths of character and well-being. *Journal of Social & Clinical Psychology, 23*(5), 603–619.

Park, Y. S., Kim, B. K., et al. (2010). Acculturation, enculturation, parental adherence to Asian cultural values, parenting styles, and family conflict among Asian American college students. *Asian American Journal of Psychology, 1*(1), 67–79. doi:10.1037/a0018961

Parke, R. D. (2004). Development in the family. *Annual Review of Psychology, 55*, 365–399. doi:10.1146/annurev.psych.55.090902.141528

Parker, E. S., Cahill, L., & McGaugh, J. L. (2006). A case of unusual autobiographical remembering. *Neurocase, 12*(1), 35–49. doi:10.1080/13554790500473680

Parker, P. D., & Salmela-Aro, K. (2011). Developmental processes in school burnout: A comparison of major developmental models. *Learning & Individual Differences, 21*, 244–248. doi:10.1016/j.lindif.2011.01.005

Parlade, M., Messinger, D. S., et al. (2009). Anticipatory smiling: Linking early affective communication and social outcome. *Infant Behavior &*

Development, 32(1), 33–43. doi:10.1016/j.infbeh.2008.09.007

Pascual, A., Guéguen, N., et al. (2013). Foot-in-the-door and problematic requests: A field experiment. *Social Influence, 8*(1), 46–53. doi:10.1080/15534510.2012.696038

Pasupathi, M., & Staudinger, U. M. (2001). Do advanced moral reasoners also show wisdom? *International Journal of Behavioral Development, 25*(5), 401–415.

Patall, E. A., Cooper, H., & Robinson, J. C. (2008). The effects of choice on intrinsic motivation and related outcomes: A meta-analysis of research findings. *Psychological Bulletin, 134*(2), 270–300. doi:10.1037/0033-2909.134.2.270

Patel, R. B., & Khazeni, N. (2012). Long-term marijuana use and pulmonary function. *Journal of The American Medical Association, 307*(17), 1796–1797.

Paternoster, R., & Pogarsky, G. (2009). Rational choice, agency and thoughtfully reflective decision making: The short and long-term consequences of making good choices. *Journal of Quantitative Criminology, 25*(2), 103–127.

Paton, S. (2013). Introducing Taylor to the knowledge economy. *Employee Relations, 35*(1), 20–38. doi:10.1108/01425451311279393

Paulson, G. W. (2012). *Closing the asylums: Causes and consequences of the deinstitutionalization movement.* Jefferson, NC: McFarland.

Paulsson, T., & Parker, A. (2006). The effects of a two-week reflection-intention training program on lucid dream recall. *Dreaming, 16*(1), 22–35. doi:10.1037/1053-0797.16.1.22

Pavlov, I. P. (1927). *Conditioned reflexes.* Translated by G. V. Anrep. New York: Dover.

Payne, B. K., Krosnick, J. A., et al. (2010). Implicit and explicit prejudice in the 2008 American presidential election. *Journal of Experimental Social Psychology, 46*(2), 367–374.

Payne, K. (2009). Winning the battle of ideas: Propaganda, ideology, and terror. *Studies in Conflict & Terrorism, 32*(2), 109–128. doi:10.1080/10576100802627738

Pearce, C. L., Conger, J. A., & Locke, E. A. (2007). Shared leadership theory. *Leadership Quarterly, 18*(3), 281–288.

Pearce, C. L., Manz, C. C., & Sims, H. P., Jr. (2009). Where do we go from here? Is shared leadership the key to team success? *Organizational Dynamics, 38*(3), 234–238.

Pedersen, A. F., Bovbjerg, D. H., & Zachariae, R. (2011). Stress and susceptibility to infectious disease. In R. J. Contrada & A. Baum (Eds.), *The handbook of stress science: Biology,*

psychology, and health (pp. 425–445). New York: Springer.

Pedraza, C., García, F. B., & Navarro, J. F. (2009). Neurotoxic effects induced by gammahydroxybutyric acid (GHB) in male rats. *International Journal of Neuropsychopharmacology, 12*(9), 1165–1177. doi:10.1017/S1461145709000157

Peek, F., & Hanson, L. L. (2007). *The life and message of the real Rain Man: The journey of a mega-savant.* Port Chester, NY: Dude Publishing.

Pelletier, L. G., Baxter, D., & Huta, V. (2011). Personal autonomy and environmental sustainability. In V. I. Chirkov, R. N. Ryan, et al., (Eds.), *Human autonomy in cross-cultural context: Perspectives on the psychology of agency, freedom, and well-being* (pp. 257–278). New York: Springer.

Pelton, T. (1983). The shootists. *Science, 83*(4), 84–86.

Pemment, J. (2013). The neurobiology of antisocial personality disorder: The quest for rehabilitation and treatment. *Aggression & Violent Behavior, 18*(1), 79–82. doi:10.1016/j.avb.2012.10.004

Penfield, W. (1957). Brain's record of past a continuous movie film. *Science News Letter, April 27,* 265.

Penfield, W. (1958). *The excitable cortex in conscious man.* Springfield, IL: Charles C Thomas.

Pennebaker, J. W. (2004). *Writing to heal: A guided journal for recovering from trauma and emotional upheaval.* Oakland, CA: New Harbinger Press.

Pennebaker, J. W., & Chung, C. K. (2007). Expressive writing, emotional upheavals, and health. In H. S. Friedman & R. C. Silver (Eds.), *Foundations of health psychology* (pp. 263–284). New York: Oxford University Press.

Peoples, C. D., Sigillo, A. E., et al. (2012). Friendship and conformity in group opinions: Juror verdict change in mock juries. *Sociological Spectrum, 32*(2), 178–193. doi:10.1080/02732173.2012.646163

Peplau, L. A. (2003). Human sexuality: How do men and women differ? *Current Directions in Psychological Science, 12*(2), 37–40.

Pereira, M., Estramiana, J., & Gallo, I. (2010). Essentialism and the expression of social stereotypes: A comparative study of Spain, Brazil and England. *Spanish Journal of Psychology, 13*(2), 808–817.

Perlman, D., & Cozby, P. C. (1983). *Social psychology.* New York: Holt, Rinehart & Winston.

Perloff, R. M. (2010). *The dynamics of persuasion: Communication and attitudes in the 21st century.* New York: Psychology Press.

Perls, F. (1969). *Gestalt therapy verbatim.* Lafayette, CA: Real People Press.

Perry, J. L., Joseph, J. E., et al. (2011). Prefrontal cortex and drug abuse vulnerability: Translation to prevention and treatment interventions. *Brain Research Reviews, 65,* 124–149. doi:10.1016/j.brainresrev.2010.09.001

Perry, J., Fowler, J., & Howe, A. (2008). Subject and interviewer determinants of the adequacy of the dynamic interview. *Journal of Nervous & Mental Disease, 196*(8), 612–619. doi:10.1097/NMD.0b013e318181327f

Perry, R. P. (2003). Perceived (academic) control and causal thinking in achievement settings. *Canadian Psychology, 44*(4), 312–331. doi:10.1037/h0086956

Perry, R. P., Hladkyj, S., et al. (2001). Academic control and action control in the achievement of college students: A longitudinal field study. *Journal of Educational Psychology, 93*(4), 776–789.

Pérusse, F., Boucher, S., & Fernet, M. (2012). Observation of couple interactions: Alexithymia and communication behaviors. *Personality & Individual Differences, 53*(8), 1017–1022. doi:10.1016/j.paid.2012.07.022

Pesant, N., & Zadra, A. (2006). Dream content and psychological well-being: A longitudinal study of the continuity hypothesis. *Journal of Clinical Psychology, 62*(1), 111–121. doi:10.1002/jclp.20212

Pescatello, L. S. (2001). Exercising for health. *Western Journal of Medicine, 174*(2), 114–118.

Peters, W. A. (1971). *A class divided.* Garden City, NY: Doubleday.

Peterson, C., & Chang, E. C. (2003). Optimism and flourishing. In C. L. M. Keyes & J. Haidt (Eds.), *Flourishing* (pp. 55–79). Washington: American Psychological Association.

Peterson, C., & Park, N. (2010). What happened to self-actualization? Commentary on Kenrick et al. (2010). *Perspectives on Psychological Science, 5*(3), 320–322. doi:10.1177/1745691610369471

Peterson, C., & Seligman, M. E. (2004). *Character strengths and virtues.* Washington: American Psychological Association.

Peterson, C., & Vaidya, R. S. (2001). Explanatory style, expectations, and depressive symptoms. *Personality & Individual Differences, 31*(7), 1217–1223. doi:10.1016/S0191-8869(00)00221-X

Peterson, L. R., & Peterson, M. J. (1959). Short-term retention of individual verbal items. *Journal of Experimental Psychology, 58,* 193–198. doi:10.1037/h0049234

Petri, H. L., & Govern, J. M. (2013). *Motivation: Theory, research, and application* (6th ed.). Belmont, CA: Cengage Learning/Wadsworth.

Pett, M. A., & Johnson, M. J. M. (2005). Development and psychometric evaluation of the Revised University Student Hassles Scale. *Educational & Psychological Measurement, 65*(6), 984–1010. doi:10.1177/0013164405275661

Peverly, S. T., Brobst, K. E., et al. (2003). College adults are not good at self-regulation. *Journal of Educational Psychology, 95*(2), 335–346. doi:10.1037/0022-0663.95.2.335

Pezdek, K., Avila-Mora, E., & Sperry, K. (2010). Does trial presentation medium matter in jury simulation research? Evaluating the effectiveness of eyewitness expert testimony. *Applied Cognitive Psychology, 24*(5), 673–690.

Philippe, F. L., Koestner, R., & Lekes, N. (2013). On the directive function of episodic memories in people's lives: A look at romantic relationships. *Journal of Personality & Social Psychology, 104*(1), 164–179. doi:10.1037/a0030384

Phillips, D. A., & Lowenstein, A. E. (2011). Early care, education, and child development. *Annual Review of Psychology, 62,* 483–500. doi:10.1146/annurev.psych.031809.130707

Phillips, J., Sharpe, L., et al. (2010). Subtypes of postnatal depression? A comparison of women with recurrent and de novo postnatal depression. *Journal of Affective Disorders, 120*(1–3), 67–75.

Phillips, K. M., Jim, H. L., et al. (2012). Effects of self-directed stress management training and home-based exercise on stress management skills in cancer patients receiving chemotherapy. *Stress & Health, 28*(5), 368–375. doi:10.1002/smi.2450

Phillips, K. W., Rothbard, N. P., & Dumas, T. L. (2009). To disclose or not to disclose? Status distance and self-disclosure in diverse environments. *Academy of Management Review, 34*(4), 710–732.

Piaget, J. (1951, original French, 1945). *The psychology of intelligence.* New York: Norton.

Piaget, J. (1952). *The origins of intelligence in children.* New York: International University Press.

Pickel, K. L., French, T. A., & Betts, J. M. (2003). A cross-modal weapon focus effect: The influence of a weapon's presence on memory for auditory information. *Memory, 11*(3), 277–292. doi:10.1080/09658210244000036

Pierrehumbert, B., Ramstein, T., et al. (2002). Quality of child care in the preschool years. *International Journal of Behavioral Development, 26*(5), 385–396. doi:10.1080/01650250143000265

Pilgrim, D. (2011). The hegemony of cognitive-behaviour therapy in modern mental health care. *Health Sociology Review, 20*(2), 120–132.

Piliavin, I. M., Rodin, J., & Piliavin, J. A. (1969). Good Samaritanism: An underground phenomenon? *Journal of Personality & Social Psychology, 13,* 289–299. doi:10.1037/h0028433

Piliavin, J. A. (2003). Doing well by doing good: Benefits to the benefactor. In C. L. M. Keyes, & J. Haidt (Eds.), *Flourishing,* Washington, DC: American Psychological Association.

Pineda, J. A. (Ed). (2009). *Mirror neuron systems: The role of mirroring processes in social cognition.* New York: Humana Press.

Pinel, J. P., Assanand, S., & Lehman, D. R. (2000). Hunger, eating, and ill health. *American Psychologist, 55*(10), 1105–1116. doi:10.1037//0003-066X.55.10.1105

Pinel, P., & Dehaene, S. (2010). Beyond hemispheric dominance: Brain regions underlying the joint lateralization of language and arithmetic to the left hemisphere. *Journal of Cognitive Neuroscience, 22*(1), 48–66. doi:10.1162/jocn.2009.21184

Pinker, S. (2011). *The better angels of our nature: Why violence has declined.* New York: Viking.

Pinker, S., & Jackendoff, R. (2005). The faculty of language: What's special about it? *Cognition, 95*(2), 201–236. doi:10.1016/j.cognition.2004.08.004

Piper, A., Jr. (2008). Multiple personality disorder: Witchcraft survives in the twentieth century. In S. O. Lilienfeld, J. Ruscio, & S. J. Lynn (Eds.), *Navigating the mindfield: A user's guide to distinguishing science from pseudoscience in mental health* (pp. 249–268). Amherst, NY: Prometheus Books.

Plassmann, H., O'Doherty, J., et al. (2008). Marketing actions can modulate neural representations of experienced pleasantness. *Proceedings of the National Academy of Sciences, 105*(3), 1050–1054. doi:10.1073/pnas.0706929105

Plaze, M., Paillère-Martinot, M., et al. (2011). Where do auditory hallucinations come from?—A brain morphometry study of schizophrenia patients with inner or outer space hallucinations. *Schizophrenia Bulletin, 37*(1), 212–221. doi:10.1093/schbul/sbp081

Plazzi, G., Vetrugno, R., et al. (2005). Sleepwalking and other ambulatory behaviours during sleep. *Neurological Sciences, 26*(Suppl 3), s193–s198. doi:10.1007/s10072-005-0486-6

Pliner, P., & Mann, N. (2004). Influence of social norms and palatability on amount consumed and food choice. *Appetite, 42*(2), 227–237. doi:10.1016/j.appet.2003.12.001

Plous, S. (2003). *Understanding prejudice and discrimination.* New York: McGraw-Hill.

Plutchik, R. (2003). *Emotions and life.* Washington: American Psychological Assocation.

Poland, J., & Caplan, P. J. (2004). The deep structure of bias in psychiatric diagnosis. In P. J. Caplan & L. Cosgrove (Eds.), *Bias in psychiatric diagnosis. A project of the association for women in psychology* (pp. 9–23). Lanham, MD: Jason Aronson.

Polivy, J., & Herman, C. P. (2002). Causes of eating disorders. *Annual Review of Psychology, 53,* 187–213. doi:10.1146/annurev.psych.53.100901.135103

Pollner, M. (1998). The effects of interviewer gender in mental health interviews. *Journal of Nervous & Mental Disease, 186*(6), 369–373. doi:10.1097/00005053-199806000-00008

Polusny, M. A., Ries, B. J., et al. (2011). Effects of parents' experiential avoidance and PTSD on adolescent disaster-related posttraumatic stress symptomatology. *Journal of Family Psychology, 25*(2), 220–229. doi:10.1037/a0022945

Pomaki, G., Supeli, A., & Verhoeven, C. (2007). Role conflict and health behaviors: Moderating effects on psychological distress and somatic complaints. *Psychology & Health, 22*(3), 317–335. doi:10.1080/14768320600774561

Popma, A., Vermeiren, R., et al. (2007). Cortisol moderates the relationship between testosterone and aggression in delinquent male adolescents. *Biological Psychiatry, 61*(3), 405–411. doi:10.1016/j.biopsych.2006.06.006

Post, J. M. (2011). Crimes of obedience: "groupthink" at Abu Ghraib. *International Journal of Group Psychotherapy, 61*(1), 49–66. doi:10.1521/ijgp.2011.61.1.48

Powell, M. D. & Ladd, L. D. (2010). Bullying: A review of the literature and implications for family therapists. *American Journal of Family Therapy, 38*(3), 189–206. doi:10.1080/01926180902961662

Powell, R. A., & Honey, P. L. (2013). *Introduction to learning and behavior* (4th ed.). Belmont, CA: Cengage Learning/Wadsworth.

Power, M. (2010). *Emotion-focused cognitive therapy.* New York: Wiley/Blackwell.

Prat-Sala, M., & Redford, P. (2012). Writing essays: Does self-efficacy matter? The relationship between self-efficacy in reading and in writing and undergraduate students' performance in essay writing. *Educational Psychology, 32*(1), 9–20. doi:10.1080/01443410.2011.621411

Prause, N. (2012). Theoretical, statistical and construct problems perpetuated in the study of female orgasm. *Sexual & Relationship Therapy, 27*(3), 260–271. doi:10.1080/14681994.2012.732262

Preckel, F., Holling, H., & Wiese, M. (2006). Relationship of intelligence and creativity in gifted and non-gifted students: An investigation of threshold theory. *Personality & Individual Differences, 40*(1), 159–170. doi:10.1016/j.paid.2005.06.022

Price, D. D., Finniss, D. G., & Benedetti. F. (2008). A comprehensive review of the placebo effect: Recent advances and current thought. *Annual Review of Psychology, 59,* 565–590. doi:10.1146/annurev.psych.59.113006.095941

Price, J., & Davis, B. (2009). *The woman who can't forget: The extraordinary story of living with the most remarkable memory known to science—A memoir.* New York: Simon & Schuster.

Price, M., Mehta, N., Tone, E. B., et al. (2011). Does engagement with exposure yield better outcomes? Components of presence as a predictor of treatment response for virtual reality exposure therapy for social phobia. *Journal of Anxiety Disorders, 25*(6), 763–770. doi:10.1016/j.janxdis.2011.03.004

Prime, D. J., & Jolicoeur, P. (2010). Mental rotation requires visual short-term memory: Evidence from human electric cortical activity. *Journal of Cognitive Neuroscience, 22*(11), 2437–2446. doi:10.1162/jocn.2009.21337

Prochaska, J. O., & Norcross, J. C. (2010). *Systems of psychotherapy: A transtheoretical analysis* (7th ed.). Belmont, CA: Cengage Learning/Wadsworth.

Prochnow, D. D., Höing, B. B., et al. (2013). The neural correlates of affect reading: An fMRI study on faces and gestures. *Behavioural Brain Research, 237,* 270–277. doi:10.1016/j.bbr.2012.08.050.

Prodan, C. I., Orbelo, D. M., & Ross, E. D. (2007). Processing of facial blends of emotion: Support for right hemisphere cognitive aging. *Cortex, 43*(2), 196–206. doi:10.1016/S0010-9452(08)70475-1

Prokhorov, A. V., Kelder, S. H., et al. (2010). Project aspire: An interactive, multimedia smoking prevention and cessation curriculum for culturally diverse high school students. *Substance Use & Misuse, 45*(6), 983–1006. doi:10.3109/10826080903038050

Przybylski, A. K., Weinstein, N., et al. (2012). The ideal self at play: The appeal of video games that let you be all you can be. *Psychological Science, 23*(1), 69–76. doi:10.1177/0956797611418676

Puente, R., & Anshel, M. H. (2010). Exercisers' perceptions of their fitness instructor's interacting style, perceived competence, and autonomy as a function of self-determined regulation to exercise, enjoyment, affect, and exercise frequency. *Scandinavian Journal of Psychology, 51*(1), 38–45.

Pychyl, T. A., Lee, J. M., et al. (2000). Five days of emotion: An experience sampling study of undergraduate student procrastination. *Journal of Social Behavior & Personality, 15*(5), 239–254.

Quednow, B. B., Jessen, F., et al. (2006). Memory deficits in abstinent MDMA (ecstasy) users: Neuropsychological evidence of frontal dysfunction. *Journal of Psychopharmacology, 20*(3), 373–384. doi:10.1177/0269881106061200

Quinn, P. C., Bhatt, R. S., & Hayden, A. (2008). Young infants readily use proximity to organize visual pattern information. *Acta Psychologica, 127*(2), 289–298. doi:10.1016/j.actpsy.2007.06.002

Raag, T., & Rackliff, C. L. (1998). Preschoolers' awareness of social expectations of gender: Relationships to toy choices. *Sex Roles, 38*(9–10), 685–700.

Rabius, V., Wiatrek, D., & McAlister, A. L. (2012). African American participation and success in telephone counseling for smoking cessation. *Nicotine & Tobacco Research, 14*(2), 240–242. doi:10.1093/ntr/ntr129

Rachman, S. (2013). *Anxiety* (3rd ed.). New York: Routledge.

Radvansky, G. A. (2011). *Human memory* (2nd ed.). Boston: Pearson/Allyn & Bacon.

Raes, E., Decuyper, S., et al. (2013). Facilitating team learning through transformational leadership. *Instructional Science, 41*(2), 287–305. doi:10.1007/s11251-012-9228-3

Raid, G. H., & Tippin, S. M. (2009). Assessment of intellectual strengths and weaknesses with the Stanford-Binet Intelligence Scales (5th ed.) (SB5). In J. A. Naglieri, & S. Goldstein (Eds.), *Practitioner's guide to assessing intelligence and achievement* (pp. 127–152). New York: Wiley.

Ralston, A. (2004). *Between a rock and a hard place.* New York: Atria Books.

Ramachandran, V. S. (1995). 2-D or not 2-D—that is the question. In R. Gregory, J. Harris, P. Heard, & D. Rose (Eds.), *The artful eye* (pp. 249–267). Oxford: Oxford University Press.

Rantanen, J., Metsäpelto, R. L., Feldt, T., et al. (2007). Long-term stability in the Big Five personality traits in adulthood. *Scandinavian Journal of Psychology, 48*(6), 511–518. doi:10.1111/j.1467-9450.2007.00609.x

Raposo, A., Han, S., & Dobbins, I. G. (2009). Ventrolateral prefrontal cortex and self-initiated semantic elaboration during memory retrieval. *Neuropsychologia, 47*(11), 2261–2271. doi:10.1016/j.neuropsychologia.2008.10.024

Rasmussen, S. A., Eisen, J. L., & Greenberg, B. D. (2013). Toward a neuroanatomy of obsessive-compulsive disorder revisited. *Biological Psychiatry, 73*(4), 298–299. doi:10.1016/j.biopsych.2012.12.010

Rathus, R., Nevid, J., & Fichner-Rathus, L. (2013). *Human sexuality in a world of diversity* (9th ed.). Boston: Allyn & Bacon.

Rathus, S. A. (2011). *Childhood and adolescence: Voyages in development* (4th ed.). Belmont, CA: Cengage Learning/Wadsworth.

Rau, W., & Durand, A. (2000). The academic ethic and college grades: Does hard work help students to "make the grade"? *Sociology of Education, 73*(1), 19–38. doi:10.2307/2673197

Ray, J. J. (1983). Half of all authoritarians are left wing: A reply to Eysenck and Stone. *Political Psychology, 4*(1), 139–143. doi:10.2307/3791178

Raymond, D., & Noggle, C. (2013). *Clinical neuropsychology: Biological and cognitive foundations for evaluation and rehabilitation.* New York: Springer.

Reason, J. (2000). The Freudian slip revisited. *The Psychologist, 13*(12), 610–611.

Reed, J. D., & Bruce, D. (1982). Longitudinal tracking of difficult memory retrievals. *Cognitive Psychology, 14*, 280–300. doi:10.1016/0010-0285(82)90011-1

Reed, S. K. (2013). *Cognition: Theory and applications* (9th ed.). Belmont, CA: Cengage Learning/Wadsworth.

Regan, P. C., Levin, L., et al. (2000). Partner preferences: What characteristics do men and women desire in their short-term sexual and long-term romantic partners? *Journal of Psychology & Human Sexuality, 12*(3), 1–21. doi:10.1300/J056v12n03_01

Regev, L. G., Zeiss, A., & Zeiss, R. (2006). Orgasmic disorders. In J. E. Fisher & W. T. O'Donohue (Eds.), *Practitioner's guide to evidence-based psychotherapy* (pp. 469–477). New York: Springer Science.

Regnerus, M., & Uecker, J. (2011). *Premarital sex in America: How young Americans meet, mate, and think about marrying.* New York: Oxford University Press.

Regoeczi, W. C. (2008). Crowding in context: An examination of the differential responses of men and women to high-density living environments. *Journal of Health & Social Behavior, 49*(3), 254–268. doi:10.1177/002214650804900302

Reid, M. R., Mackinnon, L. T., & Drummond, P. D. (2001). The effects of stress management on symptoms of upper respiratory tract infection, secretory immunoglobulin A, and mood in young adults. *Journal of Psychosomatic Research, 51*(6), 721–728. doi:10.1016/S0022-3999(01)00234-3

Reid, R. C., Carpenter, B. N., et al. (2012). Report of findings in a *DSM-5* field trial for hypersexual disorder. *Journal Of Sexual Medicine, 9*(11), 2868–2877. doi:10.1111/j.1743-6109.2012.02936.x

Reiff, S., Katkin, E. S., & Friedman, R. (1999). Classical conditioning of the human blood pressure response. *International Journal of Psychophysiology, 34*(2), 135–145. doi:10.1016/S0167-8760(99)00071-9

Reifman, A. S., Larrick, R. P., & Fein, S. (1991). Temper and temperature on the diamond: The heat-aggression relationship in major league baseball. *Personality & Social Psychology Bulletin, 17*(5), 580–585. doi:10.1177/0146167291175013

Reijntjes, A., Kamphuis, J. H., et al. (2013). Too calloused to care: An experimental examination of factors influencing youths' displaced aggression against their peers. *Journal of Experimental Psychology: General, 142*(1), 28–33. doi:10.1037/a0028619

Reinberg, A., & Ashkenazi, I. (2008). Internal desynchronization of circadian rhythms and tolerance to shift work. *Chronobiology International, 25*(4), 625–643. doi:10.1080/07420520802256101

Reis, H. T., Maniaci, M. R., et al. (2011). Familiarity does indeed promote attraction in live interaction. *Journal of Personality & Social Psychology, Mar 7*, np.

Reis, S. M., & Renzulli, J. S. (2010). Is there still a need for gifted education? An examination of current research. *Learning & Individual Differences, 20*(4), 308–317. doi:10.1016/j.lindif.2009.10.012

Reisner, A. D. (2006). A case of Munchausen syndrome by proxy with subsequent stalking behavior. *International Journal of Offender Therapy & Comparative Criminology, 50*(3), 245–254. doi:10.1177/0306624X05281880

Reiss, M., Tymnik, G., et al. (1999). Laterality of hand, foot, eye, and ear in twins. *Laterality, 4*(3), 287–297. doi:10.1080/135765099396999

Reiss, S., & Havercamp, S. M. (2005). Motivation in developmental context: A new method for studying self-actualization. *Journal of Humanistic Psychology, 45*(1), 41–53. doi:10.1177/0022167804269133

Reissing, E. D., Binik, Y. M., et al. (2003). Etiological correlates of vaginismus: Sexual and physical abuse, sexual knowledge sexual self-schema and relationship adjustment. *Journal of Sex & Marital Therapy, 29*(1), 47–59.

Reissing, E. D., Binik, Y. M., et al. (2004). Vaginal spasm, pain, and behavior: An empirical investigation of the diagnosis of vaginismus. *Archives of Sexual Behavior, 33*(1), 5–17.

Reivich, K., Gillham, J. E., et al. (2013). From helplessness to optimism: The role of resilience in treating and preventing depression in youth. In S. Goldstein, & R. B. Brooks (Eds.), *Handbook of resilience in children* (2nd ed., pp. 201–214). New York: Springer. doi:10.1007/978-1-4614-3661-4_12

Reker, M., Ohrmann, P., et al. (2010). Individual differences in alexithymia and brain response to masked emotion faces. *Cortex, 46*(5), 658–667. doi:10.1016/j.cortex.2009.05.008

Remland, M. S., Jones, T. S., & Brinkman, H. (1991). Proxemic and haptic behavior in three European countries. *Journal of Nonverbal Behavior, 15*(4), 215–232.

Rentfrow, P. J. (2012). The role of music in everyday life: Current directions in the social psychology of music. *Social & Personality Psychology Compass, 6*(5), 402–416. doi:10.1111/j.1751-9004.2012.00434.x

Rentfrow, P. J. & Gosling, S. D. (2003). The do re mi's of everyday life: The structure and personality correlates of music preferences. *Journal of Personality & Social Psychology, 84*(6), 1236–1256. doi:10.1037/0022-3514.84.6.1236

Rentfrow, P. J., Goldberg, L. R., & Levitin, D. J. (2011). The structure of musical preferences: A five-factor model. *Journal of Personality & Social Psychology, 100*(6), 1139–1157. doi:10.1037/a0022406

Rentfrow, P. J., Goldberg, L. R., et al. (2012). The song remains the same: A replication and extension of the music model. *Music Perception, 30*(2), 161–185. doi:10.1525/mp.2012.30.2.161

Rescorla, R. A. (1987). A Pavlovian analysis of goal-directed behavior. *American Psychologist, 42*, 119–129. doi:10.1037/0003-066X.42.2.119

Rescorla, R. A. (2004). Spontaneous recovery. *Learning & Memory, 11*(5), 501–509. doi:10.1101/lm.77504

Restak, R. M. (2001). *The secret life of the brain.* New York: Dana Press.

Revonsuo, A., Kallio, S., & Sikka, P. (2009). What is an altered state of consciousness? *Philosophical Psychology, 22*(2), 187–204. doi:10.1080/09515080902802850

Reynald, D. M., & Elffers, H. (2009). The future of Newman's defensible space theory: Linking defensible space and the routine activities of place. *European Journal of Criminology, 6*(1), 25–46. doi:10.1177/1477370808098103

Rhee, S. H., & Waldman, I. D. (2011). Genetic and environmental influences on aggression. In P. R. Shaver, & M. Mikulincer (Eds.), *Human aggression and violence: Causes, manifestations, and consequences* (pp. 143–163). Washington: American Psychological Association.

Rhine, J. B. (1953). *New world of the mind.* New York: Sloane.

Ribeiro, A. C., LeSauter, J., et al. (2009). Relationship of arousal to circadian anticipatory behavior: Ventromedial hypothalamus: One node in a hunger arousal network. *European Journal of Neuroscience, 30*(9), 1730–1738. doi:10.1111/j.1460-9568.2009.06969.x

Rice, L., & Markey, P. M. (2009). The role of extraversion and neuroticism in influencing anxiety following computer-mediated interactions. *Personality & Individual Differences, 46*(1), 35–39. doi:10.1016/j.paid.2008.08.022

Richardson, K. (2013). The eclipse of heritability and the foundations of intelligence. *New Ideas in Psychology, 31*(2), 122–129. doi:10.1016/j.newideapsych.2012.08.002

Richmond, L. J. (2004). When spirituality goes awry: Students in cults. *Professional School Counseling, 7*(5), 367–375.

Ridenour, T. A., Maldonado-Molina M., et al. (2005). Factors associated with the transition from abuse to dependence among substance abusers: Implications for a measure of addictive liability. *Drug & Alcohol Dependence, 80*(1), 1–14.

Rideout, V., Foehr, U. G., & Roberts, D. F. (2010). *Generation M2: Media in the lives of 8–18-year-olds.* Retrieved June 9, 2013, from http://www.kff.org/entmedia/upload/8010.pdf

Riela, S., Rodriguez, G., et al. (2010). Experiences of falling in love: Investigating culture, ethnicity, gender, and speed. *Journal of Social & Personal Relationships, 27*(4), 473–493. doi:10.1177/0265407510363508

Rigakos, G. S., Davis, R. C., et al. (2009). Soft targets?: A national survey of the preparedness of large retail malls to prevent and respond to terrorist attack after 9/11. *Security Journal, 22*(4), 286–301. doi:10.1057/palgrave.sj.8350084

Riggio, H. R., & Garcia, A. L. (2009). The power of situations: Jonestown and the fundamental attribution error. *Teaching of Psychology, 36*(2), 108–112. doi:10.1080/00986280902739636

Rihmer, Z., Dome, P., et al. (2012). Psychiatry should not become hostage to placebo: An alternative interpretation of antidepressant–placebo differences in the treatment response in depression. *European Neuropsychopharmacology, 22*(11), 782–786. doi:10.1016/j.euroneuro.2012.03.002

Riley, A., & Riley, E. (2009). Male erectile disorder. In R. Balon, & R. T. Segraves (Eds.), *Clinical manual of sexual disorders* (pp. 213–249). Arlington, VA: American Psychiatric Publishing.

Riley, W., Jerome, A., et al. (2002). Feasibility of computerized scheduled gradual reduction for adolescent smoking cessation. *Substance Use & Misuse, 37*(2), 255–263.

Rind, B., Tromovitch, P., & Bauserman, R. (1998). A meta-analytic examination of assumed properties of child sexual abuse using college samples. *Psychological Bulletin, 124*(1), 22–53.

Riquelme, H. (2002). Can people creative in imagery interpret ambiguous figures faster than people less creative in imagery? *Journal of Creative Behavior, 36*(2), 105–116. 10.1002/j.2162-6057.2002.tb01059.x

Ritchie, T. D., Sedikides, C., et al. (2011). Self-concept clarity mediates the relation between stress and subjective well-being. *Self & Identity, 10*(4), 493–508. doi:10.1080/15298868.2010.493066

Ritter, J. (1998). Uniforms changing the culture of the nation's classrooms. *USA Today*, Oct. 15, 1A, 2A.

Ritter, S. M., van Baaren, R. B., & Dijksterhuis, A. (2012). Creativity: The role of unconscious processes in idea generation and idea selection. *Thinking Skills & Creativity, 7*(1), 21–27. doi:10.1016/j.tsc.2011.12.002

Riva, G. (2009). Virtual reality: An experiential tool for clinical psychology. *British Journal of Guidance & Counseling, 37*(3), 337–345. doi:10.1080/03069880902957056

Rizzolatti, G., Fogassi, L., & Gallese V. (2006). Mirrors in the mind. *Scientific American, 295*(5), 54–61.

Roberto, M., & Koob, G. F. (2009). First congress of "Alcoholism and stress: A framework for future treatment strategies": Introduction to the proceeding. *Alcohol, 43*(7), 489–490. doi:10.1016/j.alcohol.2009.10.008

Roberts, B. W., & Mroczek, D. (2008). Personality trait change in adulthood. *Current Directions in Psychological Science, 17*(1), 31–35. doi:10.1111/j.1467-8721.2008.00543.x

Roberts, B. W., Kuncel, N. R., et al. (2007). The power of personality: The comparative validity of personality traits, socioeconomic status, and cognitive ability for predicting important life outcomes. *Perspectives on Psychological Science, 2*(4), 313–345. doi:10.1111/j.1745-6916.2007.00047.x

Roberts, R. D., & Lipnevich, A. A. (2012). From general intelligence to multiple intelligences: Meanings, models, and measures. In K. R. Harris, S. Graham, et al. (Eds.), *APA educational psychology handbook* (Vol 2): *Individual differences and cultural and contextual factors* (pp. 33–57). Washington, DC US: American Psychological Association. doi:10.1037/13274-002

Roberts, R. E., Phinney, J. S., et al. (1999). The structure of ethnic identity of young adolescents from diverse ethnocultural groups. *Journal of Early Adolescence, 19*(3), 301–322. doi:10.1177/027243169901900300

Roberts, T., & Zurbriggen, E. L. (2013). The problem of sexualization: What is it and how does it happen? In E. L. Zurbriggen, & T. Roberts (Eds.), *The sexualization of girls and girlhood: Causes, consequences, and resistance* (pp. 3–21). New York: Oxford University Press.

Roberts, W. A. (2002). Are animals stuck in time? *Psychological Bulletin, 128*(3), 473–489. doi:10.1037/0033-2909.128.3.473

Roberts, W. A., & Roberts, S. (2002). Two tests of the stuck-in-time hypothesis. *Journal of General Psychology, 129*(4), 415–429. doi:10.1080/00221300209602105

Robertson, L. C., & Sagiv, N. (2005). *Synesthesia: Perspectives from cognitive neuroscience.* New York: Oxford.

Robins, R. W., Gosling, S. D., & Craik, K. H. (1998). Psychological science at the crossroads. *American Scientist, 86*, 310–313. doi:10.1511/1998.4.310

Robinson, A. (2010). *Sudden genius? The gradual path to creative breakthroughs.* New York: Oxford University Press.

Robinson, D. N. (2008). *Consciousness and mental life.* New York: Columbia University Press.

Robinson, T. E., & Berridge, K. C. (2003). Addiction. *Annual Review of Psychology, 54*, 25–53. doi:10.1146/annurev.psych.54.101601.145237

Robson, H., Sage, K., & Ralph, M. (2012). Wernicke's aphasia reflects a combination of acoustic-phonological and semantic control deficits: A case-series comparison of Wernicke's aphasia, semantic dementia and semantic aphasia. *Neuropsychologia, 50*(2), 266–275. doi:10.1016/j.neuropsychologia.2011.11.021

Roca, M., Parr, A., et al. (2010). Executive function and fluid intelligence after frontal lobe lesions. *Brain: A Journal of Neurology, 133*(1), 234–247. doi:10.1093/brain/awp269

Rock, A. (2004). *The mind at night: The new science of how and why we dream.* New York: Basic Books.

Rodd, Z. A., Bell, R. L., et al. (2005). Chronic ethanol drinking by alcohol-preferring rats increases the sensitivity of the posterior ventral tegmental area to the reinforcing effects of ethanol. *Alcoholism: Clinical & Experimental Research, 29*(3), 358–366. doi:10.1097/01.ALC.0000156127.30983.9D

Rodríguez-Villagra, O., Göthe, K., et al. (2012). Working memory capacity in a go/no-go task: Age differences in interference, processing speed, and attentional control. *Developmental Psychology.* doi:10.1037/a0030883

Roediger, H. L. III, & McDermott, K. B. (1995). Creating false memories: Remembering words not presented on lists. *Journal of Experimental Psychology: Learning, Memory, and Cognition, 21*(4), 803–814. doi:10.1037/0278-7393.21.4.803

Roese, N. J., Pennington, G. L., et al. (2006). Sex differences in regret: All for love or some for lust? *Personality & Social Psychology Bulletin, 32*(6), 770–780.

Roets, A., & Van Hiel, A. (2011). Allport's prejudiced personality today: Need for closure as the motivated cognitive basis of prejudice. *Current Directions in Psychological Science, 20*(6), 349–354. doi:10.1177/0963721411424894

Roffman, J. L., Brohawn, D. G., et al. (2011). MTHFR 677C>T effects on anterior cingulate structure and function during response monitoring in schizophrenia: A preliminary study. *Brain Imaging & Behavior, 5*(1), 65–75. doi:10.1007/s11682-010-9111-2

Rogers, C. R. (1959). A theory of therapy, personality, and interpersonal relationships, as developed in the client-centered framework. In S. Koch (Ed.), *Psychology: A study of a science* (Vol. 3, pp. 184–256). New York: McGraw-Hill.

Rogers, C. R. (1961). *On becoming a person: A therapist's view of psychotherapy.* Boston: Houghton Mifflin.

Rogers, P., & Soule, J. (2009). Cross-cultural differences in the acceptance of Barnum profiles supposedly derived from Western versus Chinese astrology. *Journal of Cross-Cultural Psychology, 40*(3), 381–399. doi:10.1177/0022022109332843

Roja, I., & Roja, Z. (2010). Use of cognitive hypnotherapy and couples therapy for female patients with psychogenic vaginismus. *Contemporary Hypnosis, 27*(2), 88–94.

Rollero, C., Gattino, S., & De Piccoli, N. (2013). A gender lens on quality of life: The role of sense of community, perceived social support, self-reported health and income. *Social Indicators Research,* doi:10.1007/s11205-013-0316-9

Rollins, A. L., Bond, G. R., et al. (2010). Coping with positive and negative symptoms of schizophrenia. *American Journal of Psychiatric Rehabilitation, 13*(3), 208–223. doi:10.1080/15487768.2010.501297

Rolls, E. T. (2008). Top-down control of visual perception: Attention in natural vision. *Perception, 37*(3), 333–354. doi:10.1068/p5877

Roney, J. R. (2003). Effects of visual exposure to the opposite sex: Cognitive aspects of mate attraction in human males. *Personality & Social Psychology Bulletin, 29*, 393–404.

Roos, P. E., & Cohen, L. H. (1987). Sex roles and social support as moderators of life stress adjustment. *Journal of Personality & Social Psychology, 52*, 576–585.

Rosa, N. M., & Gutchess, A. H. (2011). Source memory for action in young and older adults: Self vs. close or unknown others. *Psychology & Aging, 26*(3), 625–630. doi:10.1037/a0022827

Rosch, E. (1977). Classification of real-world objects: Origins and representations in cognition. In P. N. Johnson-Laird, & P. C. Wason (Eds.), *Thinking: Reading in cognitivescience* (pp. 212–222). Cambridge, MA: Cambridge University Press.

Rosen, R. C., Marx, B. P., et al. (2012). Project VALOR: Design and methods of a longitudinal registry of post-traumatic stress disorder (PTSD) in combat-exposed veterans in the Afghanistan and Iraqi military theaters of operations. *International Journal of Methods In Psychiatric Research, 21*(1), 5–16. doi:10.1002/mpr.355

Rosenhan, D. L. (1973). On being sane in insane places. *Science, 179*(4070), 250–258. doi:10.1126/science.179.4070.250

Rosenkranz, M.A., Jackson, D. C., et al. (2003). Affective style and in vivo immune response: Neurobehavioral mechanisms. *Proceedings of the National Academy of Sciences, 100*, 11148–11152. doi:10.1073/pnas.1534743100

Rosenthal, D., & Quinn, O. W. (1977). Quadruplet hallucinations: Phenotypic variations of a schizophrenic genotype. *Archives of General Psychiatry, 34*(7), 817–827.

Rosenthal, M. (2013). *Human sexuality: From cells to society.* Belmont, CA: Cengage Learning/Wadsworth.

Rosenthal, N. E. (2013). *Winter blues: Everything you need to know to beat seasonal affective disorder* (4th ed.). New York: Guilford.

Rosenthal, R. (1973). The Pygmalion effect lives. *Psychology Today, Sept*, 56–63.

Rosenthal, R. (1994). Science and ethics in conducting, analyzing, and reporting psychological research. *Psychological Science, 5*, 127–134. doi:10.1111/j.1467-9280.1994.tb00644.x

Rosenthal, S. L., Von Ranson, K. M., et al. (2001). Sexual initiation: Predictors and developmental trends. *Sexually Transmitted Diseases, 28*(9), 527–532.

Rosenthal, T. L. (1993). To soothe the savage breast. *Behavior Research & Therapy, 31*(5), 439–462. doi:10.1016/0005-7967(93)90126-F

Rosenthal, T. L., & Rosenthal, R. (1980). *The vicious cycle of stress reaction.* Copyright, Renate & Ted Rosenthal, Stress Management Clinic, Department of Psychiatry, University of Tennessee College of Medicine, Memphis, Tennessee.

Rosner, R. I. (2012). Aaron T. Beck's drawings and the psychoanalytic origin story of cognitive therapy. *History of*

Psychology, 15(1), 1–18. doi:10.1037/a0023892

Rosnow, R. L. (2012). *Writing papers in psychology: A student guide to research papers, essays, proposals, posters, and handouts* (9th ed.). Belmont, CA: Cengage Learning/Wadsworth.

Ross, M., Heine, S. J., et al. (2005). Cross-cultural discrepancies in self-appraisals. *Personality & Social Psychology Bulletin, 31*(9), 1175–1188. doi:10.1177/0146167204274080

Ross, P. E. (2006). The expert mind. *Scientific American, 294*(7), 64–71.

Rossignol, S., & Frigon, A. (2011). Recovery of locomotion after spinal cord injury: Some facts and mechanisms. *Annual Review of Neuroscience, 34*, 413–440. doi:10.1146/annurev-neuro-061010-113746

Rotter, J. B. & Hochreich, D. J. (1975). *Personality*. Glenview, IL: Scott, Foresman.

Rowland, D. L. (2007). Sexual health and problems: Erectile dysfunction, premature ejaculation, and male orgasmic disorder. In J. E. Grant, & M. N. Potenza (Eds.), *Textbook of men's mental health* (pp. 171–203). Washington: American Psychiatric Publishing.

Rowley, S. J., Varner, F., et al. (2012). Toward a model of racial identity and parenting in African Americans. In J. M. Sullivan, & A. M. Esmail (Eds.), *African American identity: Racial and cultural dimensions of the Black experience* (pp. 273–288). Lanham, MD: Lexington Books.

Rozin, P., Kabnick, K., et al. (2003). The ecology of eating: Smaller portion sizes in France than in the United States help explain the French paradox. *Psychological Science, 14*(5), 450–454. doi:10.1111/1467-9280.02452

Rubenstein, C. (2002). What turns you on? *My Generation, July–Aug*, 55–58.

Rubenstein, C., & Tavris, C. (1987). Special survey results: 2600 women reveal the secrets of intimacy. *Redbook, 159*, 147–149.

Runco, M. A. (2012). *Creativity: An interdisciplinary perspective*. New York: Routledge.

Runco, M. A., & Acar, S. (2012). Divergent thinking as an indicator of creative potential. *Creativity Research Journal, 24*(1), 66–75. doi:10.1080/10400419.2012.652929

Rushton, J. P., & Jensen, A. R. (2005). Thirty years of research on race differences in cognitive ability. *Psychology, Public Policy, & Law, 11*, 235–294. doi:10.1037/1076-8971.11.2.235

Russell, S., & Norvig, P. (2010). *Artificial intelligence: A modern approach* (3rd ed.). Englewood Cliffs, NJ: Prentice Hall.

Russo, M. B., Brooks, F. R., et al. (1998). Conversion disorder presenting as multiple sclerosis. *Military Medicine, 163*(10), 709–710.

Rutter, M., Beckett, C., et al. (2009). Effects of profound early institutional deprivation: An overview of findings from a UK longitudinal study of Romanian adoptees. In G. Wrobel, & E. Neil (Eds.), *International advances in adoption research for practice* (pp. 147–167). Wiley-Blackwell.

Rutz, C., Bluff, L. A., Reed, N., et al. (2010). The ecological significance of tool use in New Caledonian crows. *Science, 329*, 1523–1526. doi:10.1126/science.1192053

Rutz, C., Bluff, L. A., Weir, A. A., et al. (2007). Video cameras on wild birds. *Science, 318*, 765. doi:10.1126/science.1146788

Ruva, C., McEvoy, C., & Bryant, J. B. (2007). Effects of pre-trial publicity and jury deliberation on juror bias and source memory errors. *Applied Cognitive Psychology, 21*(1), 45–67. doi:10.1002/acp.1254

Ryan, K. M. (2011). The relationship between rape myths and sexual scripts: The social construction of rape. *Sex Roles, 65*(11–12), 774–782. doi:10.1007/s11199-011-0033-2

Ryan, M. P. (2001). Conceptual models of lecture learning: Guiding metaphors and model-appropriate notetaking practices. *Reading Psychology, 22*(4), 289–312. doi:10.1080/02702710127638

Ryan, R. M., Curren, R. R., & Deci, E. L. (2013). What humans need: Flourishing in Aristotelian philosophy and self-determination theory. In A. S. Waterman (Ed.), *The best within us: Positive psychology perspectives on eudaimonia* (pp. 57–75). Washington, DC: American Psychological Association. doi:10.1037/14092-004

Ryckman, R. M. (2013). *Theories of personality* (10th ed.). Belmont, CA: Cengage Learning/Wadsworth.

Ryff, C. D., & Singer, B. (2009). Understanding healthy aging: Key components and their integration. In V. L. Bengston, D. Gans, D., et al. (Eds.), *Handbook of theories of aging* (2nd ed., pp. 117–144). New York: Springer.

Ryff, C. D., Singer, B. H., & Palmersheim, K. A. (2004). Social inequalities in health and well-being: The role of relational and religious protective factors. In O. G. Brim, C. D. Ryff, et al. (Eds.), *How healthy are we? A national study of well-being at midlife* (pp. 90–123). Chicago: University of Chicago Press.

Saban, K. L., Hogan, T. P., et al. (2013). Burnout and coping strategies of polytrauma team members caring for veterans with traumatic brain injury. *Brain Injury, 27*(3), 301–309. doi:10.3109/02699052.2012.743183

Saber, J. L., & Johnson, R. D. (2008). Don't throw out the baby with the bathwater: Verbal repetition, mnemonics, and active learning. *Journal of Marketing Education, 30*(3), 207–216. doi:10.1177/0273475308324630

Sachdev, P. S., & Chen, X. (2009). Neurosurgical treatment of mood disorders: Traditional psychosurgery and the advent of deep brain stimulation. *Current Opinion in Psychiatry, 22*(1), 25–31. doi:10.1097/YCO.0b013e32831c8475

Sack, R. L. (2010). Jet lag. *The New England Journal of Medicine, 362*(5), 440–447. doi:10.1056/NEJMcp0909838

Sackett, P. R., & Lievens, F. (2008). Personnel selection. *Annual Review of Psychology, 59*, 419–450.

Sackett, P. R., Walmsley, P. T., & Laczo, R. M. (2013). Job and work analysis. In N. W. Schmitt, S. Highhouse, et al. (Eds.), *Handbook of psychology* (Vol 12): *Industrial and organizational psychology* (2nd ed., pp. 61–81). New York: Wiley.

Sacks, O. (2010). *The mind's eye*. New York: Knopf.

Sakaluk, J. K., & Milhausen, R. R. (2012). Factors influencing university students' explicit and implicit sexual double standards. *Journal of Sex Research, 49*(5), 464–476. doi:10.1080/00224499.2011.569976

Saksida, L. M., & Wilkie, D. M. (1994). Time-of-day discrimination by pigeons. *Animal Learning & Behavior, 22*, 143–154. doi:10.3758/BF03199914

Sales, B. D., & Hafemeister, T. L. (1985). Law and psychology. In E. M. Altmeir, & M. E. Meyer (Eds.), *Applied specialties in psychology*. New York: Random House.

Salimpoor, V. N., Benovoy, M. M., et al. (2011). Anatomically distinct dopamine release during anticipation and experience of peak emotion to music. *Nature Neuroscience, 14*(2), 257–262. doi:10.1038/nn.2726

Salisbury, A. G., & Burker, E. J. (2011). Assessment, treatment, and vocational implications of combat related PTSD in veterans. *Journal of Applied Rehabilitation Counseling, 42*(2), 42–49.

Sallinen, M., Holm, A., et al. (2008). Recovery of cognitive performance from sleep debt: Do a short rest pause and a single recovery night help? *Chronobiology International, 25*(2–3), 279–296. doi:10.1080/0742052080210710

Salloum, A., & Overstreet, S. (2012). Grief and trauma intervention for children after disaster: Exploring coping skills versus trauma narration. *Behaviour Research & Therapy, 50*(3), 169–179. doi:10.1016/j.brat.2012.01.001

Salmela, J. H. (1974). An information processing approach to volleyball. *C.V.A. Technical Journal, 1*, 49–62.

Salmela, J. H. (1975). Psycho-motor task demands of artistic gymnastics. In J. H. Salmela (Ed.), *The advanced study of gymnastics: A textbook*. Springfield, IL: Charles C Thomas.

Salovey, P., & Mayer, J. (1997). *Emotional development and emotional intelligence*. New York, NY: Basic.

Salthouse, T. A. (2004). What and when of cognitive aging. *Current Directions in Psychological Science, 13*(4), 140–144. doi:10.1111/j.0963-7214.2004.00293.x

Sam, D. L., & Berry, J. W. (2010). Acculturation: When individuals and groups of different cultural backgrounds meet. *Perspectives on Psychological Science, 5*(4), 472–481. doi:10.1177/1745691610373075

Samson, D., & Apperly, I. A. (2010). There is more to mind reading than having theory of mind concepts: New directions in theory of mind research. *Infant & Child Development, 19*(5), 443–454.

Sánchez, P., García-Calvo, T., et al. (2009). An analysis of home advantage in the top two Spanish professional football leagues. *Perceptual & Motor Skills, 108*(3), 789–797.

Sansone, R. A., & Sansone, L. A. (2010). Road rage: What's driving it? *Psychiatry, 7*(7), 14–18.

Sansone, R. A., Leung, J. S., & Wiederman, M. W. (2013). Self-reported bullying in childhood: Relationships with employment in adulthood. *International Journal of Psychiatry in Clinical Practice, 17*(1), 64–68. doi:10.3109/13651501.2012.709867

Santelices, M. P., Guzmán G. M., et al. (2011). Promoting secure attachment: Evaluation of the effectiveness of an early intervention pilot programme with mother–infant dyads in Santiago, Chile. *Child: Care, Health & Development, 37*(2), 203–210. doi:10.1111/j.1365-2214.2010.01161.x

Santelli, J. S., Abma, J., et al. (2004). Can changes in sexual behaviors among high school students explain the decline in teen pregnancy rates in the 1990s? *Journal of Adolescent Health, 35*(2), 80–90.

Santrock, J. W. (2011). *Child development* (13th ed.). New York: McGraw-Hill.

Santrock, J. W. (2012). *A topical approach to lifespan development* (6th ed.). New York, NY: McGraw-Hill.

Santrock, J. W., & Halonen, J. S. (2013). *Your guide to college success: Strategies for achieving your goals* (7th ed.). Belmont, CA: Cengage Learning/Wadsworth.

Sapolsky, R. (2005). Sick of poverty. *Scientific American, 293*(6), 92–99.

Sarason, I. G., & Sarason, B. R. (2005). *Abnormal psychology* (11th ed.). Mahwah, NJ: Prentice Hall.

Sarkova, M., Bacikova-Sleskova, M., et al. (2013). Associations between assertiveness, psychological well-being, and self-esteem in adolescents. *Journal Of Applied Social Psychology, 43*(1), 147–154. doi:10.1111/j.1559-1816.2012.00988.x

Sartorius, A., Kiening, K. L., et al. (2010). Remission of major depression under deep brain stimulation of the lateral habenula in a therapy-refractory patient. *Biological Psychiatry, 67*(2), e9–e11. doi:10.1016/j.biopsych.2009.08.027

Sateia, M. J., & Nowell, P. D. (2004). Insomnia. *Lancet, 364*(9449), 1959–1973. doi:10.1016/S0140-6736(04)17480-1

Sautter, J. M., Tippett, R. M., & Morgan, S. (2010). The social demography of Internet dating in the United States. *Social Science Quarterly, 91*(2), 554–575. doi:10.1111/j.1540-6237.2010.00707.x

Saxton, M. (2010). *Child language: Acquisition and development.* Thousand Oaks, CA: Sage.

Saxvig, I. W., Lundervold, A. J., et al. (2008). The effect of a REM sleep deprivation procedure on different aspects of memory function in humans. *Psychophysiology, 45*(2), 309–317. doi:10.1111/j.1469-8986.2007.00623.x

Schachter, S., & Wheeler, L. (1962). Epinephrine, chlorpromazine and amusement. *Journal of Abnormal and Social Psychology, 65*, 121–128. doi:10.1037/h0040391

Schacter, D. L. (1996). *Searching for memory: The brain, the mind, and the past.* New York: Basic Books.

Schacter, D. L., & Addis, D. R. (2008). The cognitive neuroscience of constructive memory: Remembering the past and imagining the future. In J. Driver, P. Haggard, et al. (Eds.), *Mental processes in the human brain* (pp. 27–47). New York: Oxford University Press.

Schafer, M., & Crichlow, S. (1996). Antecedents of groupthink: A quantitative study. *Journal of Conflict Resolution, 40*(3), 415–435. doi:10.1177/002200279604000300

Schafer, M., & Crichlow, S. (2010). *Groupthink versus high-quality decision making in international relations.* New York: Columbia University Press.

Schaie, K. W. (1994). The course of adult intellectual development. *American Psychologist, 49*(4), 304–313. doi:10.1037/0003-066X.49.4.304

Schaie, K. W. (2005). *Developmental influences on adult intelligence: The Seattle longitudinal study.* New York: Oxford University Press.

Scharinger, C., Rabl, U., et al. (2010). Imaging genetics of mood disorders. *NeuroImage, 3*(3), 810–821. doi:10.1016/j.neuroimage.2010.02.019

Schechter, E. (2012). Intentions and unified agency: Insights from the split-brain phenomenon. *Mind & Language, 27*(5), 570–594. doi:10.1111/mila.12003

Scheinkman, M. (2008). The multi-level approach: A road map for couples therapy. *Family Process, 47*(2), 197–213.

Schenck, C. H., & Mahowald, M. W. (2005). Rapid eye movement and non-REM sleep parasomnias. *Primary Psychiatry, 12*(8), 67–74.

Scherbaum, C. A., Sabet, J., et al. (2013). Examining faking on personality inventories using unfolding item response theory models. *Journal of Personality Assessment, 95*(2), 207–216. doi:10.1080/00223891.2012.725439

Schetter, C. D. (2011). Psychological science on pregnancy: Stress processes, biopsychosocial models, and emerging research issues. *Annual Review of Psychology, 62*, 531–558. doi:10.1146/annurev.psych.031809.130727

Schick, T., & Vaughn, L. (2014). *How to think about weird things: Critical thinking for a new age* (7th ed.). New York: McGraw-Hill.

Schiller, P. H., Slocum, W. M., et al. (2011). The integration of disparity, shading and motion parallax cues for depth perception in humans and monkeys. *Brain Research, 1377*, 67–77. doi:10.1016/j.brainres.2011.01.003

Schiraldi, G. R., & Brown, S. L. (2001). Primary prevention for mental health: Results of an exploratory cognitive-behavioral college course. *Journal of Primary Prevention, 22*(1), 55–67. doi:10.1023/A:1011040231249

Schlaepfer, T. E., Cohen, M. X., et al. (2008). Deep brain stimulation to reward circuitry alleviates anhedonia in refractory major depression. *Neuropsychopharmacology, 33*(2), 368–377. doi:10.1038/sj.npp.1301408

Schleicher, S. S., & Gilbert, L. A. (2005). Heterosexual dating discourses among college students: Is there still a double standard? *Journal of College Student Psychotherapy, 19*(3), 7–23.

Schlund, M. W. & Cataldo, M. F. (2010). Amygdala involvement in human avoidance, escape and approach behavior. *NeuroImage, 53*(2), 769–776. doi:10.1016/j.neuroimage.2010.06.058

Schmahmann, J. D. (2010). The role of the cerebellum in cognition and emotion: Personal reflections since 1982 on the dysmetria of thought hypothesis, and its historical evolution from theory to therapy. *Neuropsychology Review, 20*(3), 236–260. doi:10.1007/s11065-010-9142-x

Schmalzl, L., Thomke, E., et al. (2011). "Pulling telescoped phantoms out of the stump": Manipulating the perceived position of phantom limbs using a full-body illusion. *Frontiers in Human Neuroscience, 5.* doi:10.3389/fnhum.2011.00121

Schmelz, M. (2010). Itch and pain. *Neuroscience & Biobehavioral Reviews, 34*(2), 171–176. doi:10.1016/j.neubiorev.2008.12.004

Schmidt, F. L., & Hunter, J. E. (1998). The validity and utility of selection methods in personnel psychology. *Psychological Bulletin, 124*(2), 262–274.

Schmitt, D. P., & Allik, J. (2005). Simultaneous administration of the Rosenberg Self-Esteem Scale in 53 nations: Exploring the universal and culture-specific features of global self-esteem. *Journal of Personality & Social Psychology, 89*(4), 623–642. doi:10.1037/0022-3514.89.4.623

Schmitt, N., & Golubovich, J. (2013). Biographical information. In K. F. Geisinger, B. A. Bracken, et al. (Eds.), *APA handbook of testing and assessment in psychology* (Vol. 1): *Test theory and testing and assessment in industrial and organizational psychology* (pp. 437–455). Washington, DC: American Psychological Association. doi:10.1037/14047-025

Schmuck, P., & Vlek, C. (2003). Psychologists can do much to support sustainable development. *European Psychologist, 8*(2), 66–76.

Schnakers, C. C., Perrin, F. F., et al. (2009). Detecting consciousness in a total locked-in syndrome: An active event-related paradigm. *Neurocase, 15*(4), 271–277. doi:10.1080/13554790902724904

Schnakers, C., & Laureys, S. (2012). *Coma and disorders of consciousness.* New York: Springer. doi:10.1007/978-1-4471-2440-5

Schneider, K. J., Bugental, J. F. T., & Pierson, J. F. (2001). *The handbook of humanistic psychology.* Thousand Oaks, CA: Sage.

Schneider, K. J., Galvin, J., & Serlin, I. (2009). Rollo May on existential psychotherapy. *Journal of Humanistic Psychology, 49*(4), 419–434. doi:10.1177/0022167809340241

Schneiderman, N., Antoni, M. H., et al. (2001). Health psychology: Psychological and biobehavioral aspects of chronic disease management. *Annual Review of Psychology, 52*, 555–580. doi:10.1146/annurev.psych.52.1.555

Schramm, D. G., Marshall, J. P., et al. (2012). Religiosity, homogamy, and marital adjustment: An examination of newlyweds in first marriages and remarriages. *Journal of Family Issues, 33*(2), 246–268. doi:10.1177/0192513X11420370

Schreiber, E. H., & Schreiber, D. E. (1999). Use of hypnosis with witnesses of vehicular homicide. *Contemporary Hypnosis, 16*(1), 40–44. doi:10.1002/ch.149

Schreiber, F. R. (1973). *Sybil.* Chicago: Regency.

Schuck, K., Keijsers, G. P. J., & Rinck, M. (2011). The effects of brief cognitive-behaviour therapy for pathological skin picking: A randomized comparison to wait-list control. *Behaviour Research & Therapy, 49*(1), 11–17. doi:10.1016/j.brat.2010.09.005

Schultz, D. H., & Helmstetter, F. J. (2010). Classical conditioning of autonomic fear responses is independent of contingency awareness. *Journal of Experimental Psychology: Animal Behavior Processes, 36*(4), 495–500. doi:10.1037/a0020263

Schultz, D. P., & Schultz, S. E. (2010). *Psychology and work today* (10th ed.). Englewood Cliffs, NJ: Prentice Hall.

Schultz, D. P., & Schultz, S. E. (2012). *A history of modern psychology* (10th ed.). Belmont, CA: Cengage Learning/Wadsworth.

Schultz, D. P., & Schultz, S. E. (2013). *Theories of personality* (10th ed.). Belmont, CA: Cengage Learning/Wadsworth.

Schultz, H. T. (2004). Good and bad movie therapy with good and bad outcomes. *The Amplifier: Official Newsletter of APA Division 46, Media Psychology, Fall/Winter.* Retrieved June 9, 2013, from http://www.apa.org/divisions/div46/Amp%20Winter%2005/for%20Website/ampwinter05.html#outcomes

Schuster, J., Hoertel, N., & Limosin, F. (2011). The man behind Philippe Pinel: Jean-Baptiste Pussin (1746–1811): Psychiatry in pictures. *British Journal of Psychiatry, 198*(3), 198–241. doi:10.1192/bjp.198.3.241a

Schuster, M. A., Stein, B. D., et al. (2001). A national survey of stress reactions after the September 11, 2001, terrorist attacks. *New England Journal of Medicine, 345*(20), 1507–1512. doi:10.1056/NEJM200111153452024

Schwartz, S. J. (2008). Self and identity in early adolescence: Some reflections and an introduction to the special issue. *Journal of Early Adolescence, 28*(1), 5–15. doi:10.1177/0272431607308662

Schweckendiek, J., Klucken, T., et al. (2011). Weaving the (neuronal) web: Fear learning in spider phobia. *NeuroImage, 54*(1), 681–688. doi:10.1016/j.neuroimage.2010.07.049

Schwenzer, M. (2008). Prosocial orientation may sensitize to aggression-related cues. *Social Behavior & Personality, 36*(8), 1009–1010. doi:10.2224/sbp.2008.36.8.1009

Schwitzgebel, E. (2011). *Perplexities of consciousness.* Cambridge, MA: MIT Press.

Sclafani, A., & Springer, D. (1976). Dietary obesity in adult rats: Similarities to hypothalamic and human obesity syndromes. *Psychology & Behavior, 17*, 461–471. doi:10.1016/0031-9384(76)90109-8

Scoboria, A., Mazzoni, G., et al. (2002). Immediate and persisting effects of misleading questions and hypnosis on memory reports. *Journal of Experimental Psychology: Applied, 8*(1), 26–32. doi:10.1037/1076-898X.8.1.26

Scoboria, A., Mazzoni, G., et al. (2012). Personalized and not general suggestion produces false autobiographical memories and suggestion-consistent behavior. *Acta Psychologica, 139*(1), 225–232. doi:10.1016/j.actpsy.2011.10.008

Scollon, C. N., & King, L. A. (2011). In R. Biswas-Diener R. (Ed.), *What people really want in life and why it matters: Contributions from research on folk theories of the good life* (pp. 1–14). New York: Springer.

Scollon, C. N., Koh, S., & Au, E. W. M. (2011). Cultural differences in the subjective experience of emotion: When and why they occur. *Social & Personality Psychology Compass, 5*(11), 853–864. doi:10.1111/j.1751-9004.2011.00391.x

Scott, R. (2012). Amphetamine-induced psychosis and defences to murder. *Psychiatry, Psychology & Law, 19*(5), 615–645. doi:10.1080/13218719.2012.738022

Scruggs, T. E., & Mastropieri, M. A. (2007). Science learning in special education: The case for constructed versus instructed learning. *Exceptionality, 15*(2), 57–74.

Sears, S., & Kraus, S. (2009). I think therefore I om: Cognitive distortions and coping style as mediators for the effects of mindfulness meditation on anxiety, positive and negative affect, and hope. *Journal of Clinical Psychology, 65*(6), 561–573. doi:10.1002/jclp.20543

Seckel, A. (2000). *The art of optical illusions.* London: Carlton Books.

Segal, Z. V., Williams, J. G., & Teasdale, J. D. (2013). *Mindfulness-based cognitive therapy for depression* (2nd ed.). New York: Guilford.

Segerdahl, P., Fields, W., & Savage-Rumbaugh, S. (2005). *Kanzi's primal language: The cultural initiation of primates into language.* New York: Palgrave MacMillan.

Segerstrom, S., & Miller, G. E. (2004). Psychological stress and the human immune system: A meta-analytic study of 30 years of inquiry. *Psychological Bulletin, 130*(4), 601–630. doi:10.1037/0033-2909.130.4.601

Segraves, R., & Woodard, T. (2006). Female hypoactive sexual desire disorder: History and current status. *Journal of Sexual Medicine, 3*(3), 408–418.

Segraves, T., & Althof, S. (2002). Psychotherapy and pharmacotherapy for sexual dysfunctions. In P. E. Nathan, & J. M. Gorman, (Eds.), *A guide to treatments that work* (2nd ed., pp. 497–524). London: Oxford.

Seidman, B. F. (2001). Medicine wars. *Skeptical Inquirer*, Jan.–Feb., 28–35.

Seitz, A., & Watanabe, T. (2005). A unified model for perceptual learning. *Trends in Cognitive Sciences, 9*(7), 329–334. doi:10.1016/j.tics.2005.05.010

Sela, L., & Sobel, N. (2010). Human olfaction: A constant state of change-blindness. *Experimental Brain Research, 205*, 13–29. doi:10.1007/s00221-010-2348-6

Seligman, M. E. (1972). For helplessness: Can we immunize the weak? In *Readings in Psychology Today* (2nd ed.). Del Mar, CA: CRM.

Seligman, M. E. (1989). *Helplessness.* New York: Freeman.

Seligman, M. E. (2003). Positive psychology: Fundamental assumptions. *Source Psychologist, 16*(3), 126–127.

Selye, H. (1978). *The stress of life.* Oxford, England: McGraw-Hill.

Senécal, C., Julien, E., & Guay, F. (2003). Role conflict and academic procrastination: A self-determination perspective. *European Journal of Social Psychology, 33*(1), 135–145. doi:10.1002/ejsp.144

Service, R. F. (1994). Will a new type of drug make memory-making easier? *Science, 266*, 218–219.

Sessa, V. I., & London, M. (2006). *Continuous learning in organizations: Individual, group, and organizational perspectives.* Mahwah, NJ: Erlbaum.

Seto, M. C. (2008). *Pedophilia and sexual offending against children: Theory, assessment, and intervention.* Washington, DC: American Psychological Association.

Seto, M. C. (2009). Pedophilia. *Annual Review of Clinical Psychology, 5,* 391–407.

Seto, M. C., Cantor, J. M., & Blanchard, R. (2006). Child pornography offenses are a valid diagnostic indicator of pedophilia. *Journal of Abnormal Psychology, 115*(3), 610–615.

Seybolt, D. C., & Wagner, M. K. (1997). Self-reinforcement, gender-role, and sex of participant in prediction of life satisfaction. *Psychological Reports, 81*(2) 519–522. doi:10.2466/PR0.81.6.519-522

Seyle, D. C., & Newman, M. L. (2006). A house divided? The psychology of red and blue America. *American Psychologist, 61*(6), 571–580. doi:10.1037/0003-066X.61.6.571

Shaffer, D. R. (2009). *Social and personality development* (6th ed.). Belmont, CA: Cengage Learning/Wadsworth.

Shaffer, D. R., & Kipp, K. (2014). *Developmental psychology: Childhood and adolescence* (9th ed.). Belmont, CA: Cengage Learning/Wadsworth.

Shafton, A. (1995). *Dream reader.* Albany, NY: SUNY Press.

Shamloul, R. (2010). Natural aphrodisiacs. *Journal of Sexual Medicine, 7*(1, Pt 1), 39–49. doi:10.1111/j.1743-6109.2009.01521.x

Shanks, D. R. (2010). Learning: From association to cognition. *Annual Review of Psychology. 61,* 273–301. doi:10.1146/annurev.psych.093008.100519

Shapiro-Mendoza, C. K., Kimball, M., et al. (2009). US infant mortality trends attributable to accidental suffocation and strangulation in bed from 1984 through 2004: are rates increasing? *Pediatrics, 123*(2), 533–539. doi:10.1542/peds.2007-3746

Shapiro, D. A., Barkham, M., et al. (2003). Time is of the essence: A selective review of the fall and rise of brief therapy research. *Psychology & Psychotherapy: Theory, Research & Practice, 76*(3), 211–235. doi:10.1348/147608303322362460

Shapiro, F. (2012). EMDR therapy: An overview of current and future research. *European Review of Applied Psychology, 62*(4), 193–195. doi:10.1016/j.erap.2012.09.005

Shapiro, F., & Forrest, M. S. (2004). *EMDR: The breakthrough therapy for overcoming anxiety, stress, and trauma.* New York: Basic Books.

Shapiro, J. M. (2006). *A "memory-jamming" theory of advertising.* Retrieved June 9, 2013, from http://papers.ssrn.com/sol3/papers.cfm?abstract_id=903474

Shapiro, S. L., & Walsh, R. (2006). The meeting of meditative disciplines and Western psychology: A mutually enriching dialogue. *American Psychologist, 61*(3), 227–239. doi:10.1037/0003-066X.61.3.227

Sharf, R. S. (2012). *Theories of psychotherapy & counseling: Concepts and cases* (5th ed.). Belmont, CA: Cengage Learning/Wadsworth.

Shaver, P. R., & Mikulincer, M. (Eds.). (2011). *Human aggression and violence: Causes, manifestations, and consequences.* Washington: American Psychological Association.

Shaw, E., & Delaporte, Y. (2011). New perspectives on the history of American Sign Language. *Sign Language Studies, 11*(2), 158–204. doi:10.1353/sls.2010.0006

Shaywitz, B. A, Shaywitz, S. E., et al. (1995). Sex differences in the functional organization of the brain for language. *Nature, 373,* 607–609. doi:10.1038/373607a0

Shedler, J. (2010). The efficacy of psychodynamic psychotherapy. *American Psychologist, 65*(2), 98–109. doi:10.1037/a0018378

Shepard, R. N. (1975). Form, formation, and transformation of internal representations. In R. L. Solso (Ed.), *Information processing and cognition: The Loyola Symposium* (pp. 87–122). Hillsdale, NJ: Erlbaum.

Shepherd, G. M. (2006). Smell images and the flavour system in the human brain. *Nature, 444*(7117), 316–321. doi:10.1038/nature05405

Sherif, M., Harvey, O. J., et al. (1961). *Intergroup conflict and cooperation: The Robbers Cave experiment.* University of Oklahoma, Institute of Group Relations. Retrieved July 12, 2013, from http://psychclassics.yorku.ca/Sherif/

Shermer, L. O., Rose, K. C., & Hoffman, A. (2011). Perceptions and credibility: Understanding the nuances of eyewitness testimony. *Journal of Contemporary Criminal Justice, 27*(2), 183–203. doi:10.1177/1043986211405886

Shih, J. J., & Krusienski, D. J. (2012). Signals from intraventricular depth electrodes can control a brain–computer interface. *Journal of Neuroscience Methods, 203*(2), 311–314. doi:10.1016/j.jneumeth.2011.10.012

Shillingsburg, M. A., Kelley, M. E., et al. (2009). Evaluation and training of yes-no responding across verbal operants. *Journal of Applied Behavior Analysis, 42*(2), 209–223. doi:10.1901/jaba.2009.42-209

Shimoda, N., Takeda, K., & Kato, H. (2012). Handedness and mental rotation. In J. Dunham, & T. Davenport (Eds.), *Handedness: Theories, genetics and psychology* (pp. 91–107). Hauppauge, NY: Nova Science Publishers.

Shiner, R. L., Buss, K. A., et al. (2012). What is temperament now? Assessing progress in temperament research on the twenty-fifth anniversary of Goldsmith et al. (1987). *Child Development Perspectives, 6*(4), 436–444. doi:10.1111/j.1750-8606.2012.00254.x

Shins, S. H., Miller, D. P., & Teicher, M. H. (2012). Exposure to childhood neglect and physical abuse and developmental trajectories of heavy episodic drinking from early adolescence into young adulthood. *Drug & Alcohol Dependence, 127*(1–3), 31–38. doi:10.1016/j.drugalcdep.2012.06.005

Shook, J. R. (2013). Social cognition and the problem of other minds. In D. D. Franks & J. H. Turner (Eds.), *Handbook of neurosociology* (pp. 33–46). New York: Springer. doi:10.1007/978-94-007-4473-8_4

Shorrock, S. T., & Isaac, A. (2010). Mental imagery in air traffic control.

International *Journal of Aviation Psychology, 20*(4), 309–324. doi:10.1080/10508414.2010.487008

Short, S. E., Ross-Stewart, L., & Monsma, E. V. (2006). Onwards with the evolution of imagery research in sport psychology. *Athletic Insight: Online Journal of Sport Psychology, 8*(3), 1–15.

Shrira, A., Palgi, Y., et al. (2011). How do subjective well-being and meaning in life interact in the hostile world? *Journal of Positive Psychology, 6*(4), 273–285. doi:10.1080/17439760.2011.577090

Siefert, C. J. (2010). Screening for personality disorders in psychiatric settings: Four recently developed screening measures. In L. Baer, & M. A. Blais (Eds), *Handbook of clinical rating scales and assessment in psychiatry and mental health* (pp. 125–144). Totowa, NJ: Humana Press.

Siegel, D. J. (2007). *The mindful brain: Reflection and attunement in the cultivation of well-being.* New York: Norton.

Siegel, R. D. (2010). *The mindfulness solution: Everyday practices for everyday problems.* New York: Guilford.

Siegel, R. K. (2005). *Intoxication: The universal drive for mind-altering substances.* Rochester, VT: Park Street Press.

Siegler, R. S. (1989). Mechanisms of cognitive development. *Annual Review of Psychology, 40*, 353–379. doi:10.1146/annurev.ps.40.020189.002033

Siegler, R. S. (2005). *Children's thinking* (4th ed.). Mahwah, NJ: Erlbaum.

Siegler, R. S., DeLoache, J. S., & Eisenberg, N. (2011). *How children develop* (3rd ed.). New York: Worth.

Sienaert, P., Vansteelandt, K., et al. (2010). Randomized comparison of ultra-brief bifrontal and unilateral electroconvulsive therapy for major depression: Cognitive side-effects. *Journal of Affective Disorders, 122*(1–2), 60–67. doi:10.1016/j.jad.2009.06.011

Siever, L. J., & Koenigsberg, H. W. (2000). The frustrating no-man's-land of borderline personality disorder. *Cerebrum, 2*(4), 85–99.

Sigelman, C. K., & Rider, E. A. (2012). *Life-span human development* (7th ed.). Belmont, CA: Cengage Learning/Wadsworth.

Silber, B. Y., & Schmitt, J. A. J. (2010). Effects of tryptophan loading on human cognition, mood, and sleep. *Neuroscience & Biobehavioral Reviews, 34*(3), 387–407. doi:10.1016/j.neubiorev.2009.08.005

Silveri, M. C., Ciccarelli, N., & Cappa, A. (2011). Unilateral spatial neglect in degenerative brain pathology. *Neuropsychology, 25*(5), 554–566. doi:10.1037/a0023957

Silverstein, C. (2009). The implications of removing homosexuality from the

DSM as a mental disorder. *Archives of Sexual Behavior, 38*(2), 161–163.

Simister, J., & Cooper, C. (2005). Thermal stress in the U.S.A.: Effects on violence and on employee behaviour. *Stress & Health, 21*, 3–15. doi:10.1002/smi.1029

Simner, M. L., & Goffin, R. D. (2003). A position statement by the international graphonomics society on the use of graphology in personnel selection testing. *International Journal of Testing, 3*(4), 353–364. doi:10.1207/S15327574IJT0304_4

Simon-Thomas, E. R., et al. (2005). Behavioral and electrophysiological evidence of a right hemisphere bias for the influence of negative emotion on higher cognition. *Journal of Cognitive Neuroscience, 17*(3), 518–529. doi:10.1162/0898929053279504

Simons, D. A., & Wurtele, S. K. (2010). Relationships between parents' use of corporal punishment and their children's endorsement of spanking and hitting other children. *Child Abuse & Neglect, 34*(9), 639–646. doi:10.1016/j.chiabu.2010.01.012

Simons, D. J., & Chabris, C. F. (1999). Gorillas in our midst: Sustained inattentional blindness for dynamic events. *Perception, 28*, 1059–1074. doi:10.1068/p2952

Simons, D. J., & Levin, D. T. (1998). Failure to detect changes to people during a real-world interaction. *Psychonomic Bulletin & Review, 5*(4), 644–649. doi:10.3758/BF03208840

Simonton, D. K. (2009). Varieties of (scientific) creativity: A hierarchical model of domain-specific disposition, development, and achievement. *Perspectives on Psychological Science, 4*(5), 441–452. doi:10.1111/j.1745-6924.2009.01152.x

Singer, J. D. (2005). Explaining foreign policy: U.S. decision-making and the Persian Gulf War. *Political Psychology, 26*(5), 831–834.

Singer, M. T. (2003). *Cults in our midst: The continuing fight against their hidden menace.* San Francisco: Jossey-Bass.

Singer, M. T., & Addis, M. E. (1992). Cults, coercion, and contumely. *Cultic Studies Journal, 9*(2), 163–189.

Sinha, R., Garcia, M., et al. (2006). Stress-induced cocaine craving and hypothalamic-pituitary-adrenal responses are predictive of cocaine relapse outcomes. *Archives of General Psychiatry, 63*(3), 324–331. doi:10.1001/archpsyc.63.3.324

Sipos, A., Rasmussen, F., et al. (2004). Paternal age and schizophrenia: A population based cohort study. *British Medical Journal, 329*(7474), 1070. doi:10.1136/bmj.38243.672396.55

Sirois, F. M., & Tosti, N. (2012). Lost in the moment? An investigation of procrastination, mindfulness, and well-being. *Journal Of Rational-Emotive &*

Cognitive Behavior Therapy, 30(4), 237–248.

Sjöqvist, F., Garle, M., & Rane, A. (2008). Use of doping agents, particularly anabolic steroids, in sports and society. *Lancet, 371*(9627), 1872–1882. doi:10.1016/S0140-6736(08)60801-6

Skeels, H. M. (1966). Adult status of children with contrasting early life experiences. *Monograph of the Society for Research in Child Development, 31*(3), 1–56.

Skinner, B. F. (1938). *The behavior of organisms.* Englewood Cliffs, NJ: Prentice-Hall.

Slocombe, K. E., Waller, B. M., & Liebal, K. (2011). The language void: The need for multimodality in primate communication research. *Animal Behaviour, 81*(5), 919–924. doi:10.1016/j.anbehav.2011.02.002

Sloman, A. (2008). The well-designed young mathematician. *Artificial Intelligence, 172*(18), 2015–2034. doi:10.1016/j.artint.2008.09.004

Smedley, A., & Smedley, B. D. (2005). Race as biology is fiction, racism as a social problem is real. *American Psychologist, 60*(1), 16–26. doi:10.1037/0003-066X.60.1.16

Smith, A. P., Christopher, G., & Sutherland, D. (2013). Acute effects of caffeine on attention: A comparison of non-consumers and withdrawn consumers. *Journal of Psychopharmacology, 27*(1), 77–83.

Smith, A. P., Clark, R., & Gallagher, J. (1999). Breakfast cereal and caffeinated coffee: Effects on working memory, attention, mood and cardiovascular function. *Physiology & Behavior, 67*(1), 9–17. doi:10.1016/S0031-9384(99)00025-6

Smith, C. A., & Kirby, L. D. (2011). The role of appraisal and emotion in coping and adaptation. In R. J. Contrada, & A. Baum (Eds.), *The handbook of stress science: Biology, psychology, and health* (pp. 195–208). New York: Springer.

Smith, C. S., Folkard, S., et al. (2011). Work schedules, health, and safety. In J. C. Quick & L. E. Tetrick (Eds.), *Handbook of occupational health psychology* (2nd ed., pp. 185–204). Washington: American Psychological Association.

Smith, H. R., Comella, C. L., & Högl, B. (Eds.) (2008). *Sleep medicine.* New York: Cambridge University Press.

Smith, J. D., Redford, J. S., & Haas, S. M. (2008). Prototype abstraction by monkeys (Macaca mulatta). *Journal of Experimental Psychology: General, 137*(2), 390–401. doi:10.1037/0096-3445.137.2.390

Smith, M. L., Cottrell, G. W., et al. (2005). Transmitting and decoding facial expressions. *Psychological Science, 16*(3), 184–189. doi:10.1111/j.0956-7976.2005.00801.x

Smith, M., Vogler, J., et al. (2009). Electroconvulsive therapy: The struggles in the decision-making process and the aftermath of treatment. *Issues in Mental Health Nursing, 30*(9), 554–559. doi:10.1080/01612840902807947

Smith, S. J., Zanotti, D. C., et al. (2011). Individuals' beliefs about the etiology of same-sex sexual orientation. *Journal of Homosexuality, 58*(8), 1110–1131. doi:10.1080/00918369.2011.598417

Smith, T. W. (2006). *American sexual behavior: Trends, socio-demographic differences, and risk behavior.* University of Chicago National Opinion Research Center GSS Topical Report No. 25. Retrieved June 12, 2013 from http://www.familyindex.net/Categories/Sexuality/Premarital+Sex/06574.htm

Smith, T. W., & Traupman. E. K. (2011). Anger, hostility, and aggressiveness in coronary heart disease: Clinical applications of an interpersonal perspective. In R. Allan & J. Fisher (Eds.), *Heart and mind: The practice of cardiac psychology* (2nd ed., pp. 187–198). Washington: American Psychological Association.

Smith, T. W., Glazer, K., et al. (2004). Hostility, anger, aggressiveness, and coronary heart disease: An interpersonal perspective on personality, emotion, and health. *Journal of Personality, 72*(6), 1217–1270. doi:10.1111/j.1467-6494.2004.00296.x

Smith, T. W., Ruiz, J. M., & Uchino, B. N. (2004). Mental activation of supportive ties, hostility, and cardiovascular reactivity to laboratory stress in young men and women. *Health Psychology, 23*(5), 476–485. doi:10.1037/0278-6133.23.5.476

Smits, R. (2011). The *puzzle of left-handedness.* Chicago, IL: University of Chicago Press.

Smyth, J. D., Dillman, D. A., et al. (2010). Using the Internet to survey small towns and communities: Limitations and possibilities in the early 21st century. *American Behavioral Scientist, 53*(9), 1423–1448. doi:10.1177/0002764210361695

Smyth, J. M., & Pennebaker, J. W. (2008). Exploring the boundary conditions of expressive writing: In search of the right recipe. *British Journal of Health Psychology, 13*(1), 1–7. doi:10.1348/135910707X260117

Smyth, J. M., Pennebaker, J. W., & Arigo, D. (2012). What are the health effects of disclosure? In A. Baum, T. A. Revenson, et al. (Eds.), *Handbook of health psychology* (2nd ed.) (pp. 175–191). New York: Psychology Press.

Smyth, M. M., & Waller, A. (1998). Movement imagery in rock climbing. *Applied Cognitive Psychology, 12*(2), 145–157. doi:10.1002/(SICI)1099-0720(199804)12:2<145::AID-ACP505>3.0.CO;2-Z

Snitz, B. E., O'Meara, E. S., et al. (2009). Ginkgo biloba for preventing cognitive decline in older adults: A randomized trial. *Journal Of The American Medical Association, 302*(24), 2663–2670. doi:10.1001/jama.2009.1913

Snow, C. P. (1961). Either-or. *Progressive, Feb,* 24.

Snowman, J., & McCown, R. (2012). *Psychology applied to teaching* (13th ed.). Belmont, CA: Cengage Learning/Wadsworth.

Snowman, J., & McCown, R. (2013). *Ed psych.* Belmont, CA: Cengage Learning/Wadsworth.

Snyder, A., Bahramali, H., et al. (2006). Savant-like numerosity skills revealed in normal people by magnetic pulses. *Perception, 35*(6), 837–845. doi:10.1068/p5539

Snyder, C. R., Lopez, S. J., & Pedrotti, J. T. (2011). *Positive psychology: The scientific and practical explorations of human strengths* (2nd ed.). Thousand Oaks, CA: Sage.

Sobczak, J. A. (2009). Alcohol use and sexual function in women: A literature review. *Journal of Addictions Nursing, 20*(2), 71–85. doi:10.1080/10884600902850095

Sobel, E., Shine, D., DiPietro, D., et al. (1996). Condom use among HIV/ infected patients in South Bronx, New York. *AIDS, 10*(2), 235–236.

Sobolewski, J. M., & Amato, P. R. (2005). Economic hardship in the family of origin and children's psychological well-being in adulthood. *Journal of Marriage & Family, 67*(1), 141–156. doi:10.1111/j.0022-2445.2005.00011.x

Soderstrom, M. (2007). Beyond babytalk: Re-evaluating the nature and content of speech input to preverbal infants. *Developmental Review, 27*(4), 501–532. doi:10.1016/j.dr.2007.06.002

Soemer, A., & Schwan, S. (2012). Visual mnemonics for language learning: Static pictures versus animated morphs. *Journal of Educational Psychology, 104*(3), 565–579. doi:10.1037/a0029272

Solari, C. D., & Mare, R. D. (2012). Housing crowding effects on children's well-being. *Social Science Research, 41*(2), 464–476. doi:10.1016/j.ssresearch.2011.09.012

Solomon, E. P., Solomon, R. M., & Heide, K. M. (2009). EMDR: An evidence-based treatment for victims of trauma. *Victims & Offenders, 4*(4), 391–397. doi:10.1080/15564880903227495

Solomon, J. L., Marshall, P., & Gardner, H. (2005). Crossing boundaries to generative wisdom: An analysis of professional work. In R. J. Sternberg & J. Jordan (Eds.), *A handbook of wisdom: Psychological perspectives* (pp. 272–296). New York: Cambridge University Press.

Solowij, N., Stephens, R. S., et al. (2002). Cognitive functioning of long-term heavy cannabis users seeking treatment. *Journal of the American Medical Association, 287,* 1123–1131. doi:10-1001/pubs.JAMA-ISSN-0098-7484-287-9-joc11416

Soman, D. (2010). Option overload: How to deal with choice complexity. *Rotman Magazine, Fall,* 42–47.

Sommer, I. E. (2010). Sex differences in handedness, brain asymmetry, and language lateralization. In K. Hugdahl, & R. Westerhausen (Eds.), *The two halves of the brain: Information processing in the cerebral hemispheres.* Cambridge, MA: MIT Press.

Sommer, K. L., Parson, C., et al. (2012). Sex and need for power as predictors of reactions to disobedience. *Social Influence, 7*(1), 1–20. doi:10.1080/15534510.2011.640198

Sorkhabi, N. (2012). Parent socialization effects in difference cultures: Significance of directive parenting. *Psychological Reports, 110*(3), 854–878. doi:10.2466/10.02.17.21.PR0.110.3.854-878

Sörqvist, P. (2010). Effects of aircraft noise and speech on prose memory: What role for working memory capacity? *Journal of Environmental Psychology, 30*(1), 112–118.

Sorrell, J. M. (2009). Aging toward happiness. *Journal of Psychosocial Nursing & Mental Health Services, 47*(3), 23–26. doi:10.3928/02793695-20090301-14

Sousa, K., Orfale, A. G., et al. (2009). Assessment of a biofeedback program to treat chronic low back pain. *Journal of Musculoskeletal Pain, 17*(4), 369–377. doi:10.3109/10582450903284828

Soussignan, R. (2002). Duchenne smile, emotional experience, and autonomic reactivity. *Emotion, 2*(1), 52–74. doi:10.1037/1528-3542.2.1.52

Soyez, V., & Broekaert, E. (2003). How do substance abusers and their significant others experience the re-entry phase of therapeutic community treatment: A qualitative study. *International Journal of Social Welfare, 12*(3), 211–220. doi:10.1111/1468-2397.00454

Spalding, K. L., Arner, E., et al. (2008). Dynamics of f.at cell turnover in humans. *Nature, 453,* 783–787. doi:10.1038/nature06902

Spano, R. (2005). Potential sources of observer bias in police observational data. *Social Science Research, 34*(3), 591–617. doi:10.1016/j.ssresearch.2004.05.003

Sparfeldt, J. R., Rost, D. H., et al. (2013). Test anxiety in written and oral examinations. *Learning & Individual Differences, 24,* 198–203. doi:10.1016/j.lindif.2012.12.010

Special, W. P., & Li-Barber, K. (2012). Self-disclosure and student satisfaction with Facebook. *Computers in Human Behavior, 28*(2), 624–630. doi:10.1016/j.chb.2011.11.008

Spector, P. E. (2012). *Industrial and organizational psychology: Research and practice* (6th ed.). New York: Wiley.

Spence, S. A., Kaylor-Hughes, C., et al. (2009). Toward a cognitive neurobiological account of free association. *Neuropsychoanalysis, 11*(2), 151–163.

Spence, S. A., & David, A. (Eds.). (2004). *Voices in the brain: The cognitive neuropsychiatry of auditory verbal hallucinations.* London: Psychology Press.

Spencer-Thomas, S., & Jahn, D. R. (2012). Tracking a movement: U.S. milestones in suicide prevention. *Suicide & Life-Threatening Behavior, 42*(1), 78–85. doi:10.1111/j.1943-278X.2011.00072.x

Sperry, R. W. (1968). Hemisphere deconnection and unity in conscious awareness. *American Psychologist, 23,* 723–733. doi:10.1037/h0026839

Spiegler, M. D. (2013a). Behavior therapy I: Traditional behavior therapy. In J. Frew, & M. D. Spiegler (Eds.), *Contemporary psychotherapies for a diverse world* (pp. 259–300). New York: Routledge/Taylor & Francis.

Spiegler, M. D. (2013b). Behavior therapy II: Cognitive-behavioral therapy. In J. Frew, & M. D. Spiegler (Eds.), *Contemporary psychotherapies for a diverse world* (301–337). New York: Routledge/Taylor & Francis.

Spiegler, M. D., & Guevremont, D. C. (2010). *Contemporary behavior therapy* (5th ed.). Belmont, CA: Cengage Learning/Wadsworth.

Spiro Wagner, P., & Spiro, C. S. (2005). *Divided minds: Twin sisters and their journey through schizophrenia.* New York, St. Martin's Press.

Sporer, S. L. (2001). Recognizing faces of other ethnic groups. *Psychology, Public Policy, & Law, 7*(1), 36–97. doi:10.1037/1076-8971.7.1.36

Springer, S. P., & Deutsch, G. (1998). *Left brain, right brain.* New York: Freeman.

Squire, L. R. (2004). Memory systems of the brain: A brief history and current perspective. *Neurobiology of Learning & Memory, 82,* 171–177. doi:10.1016/j.nlm.2004.06.005

Squire, L. R., & Wixted, J. T. (2011). The cognitive neuroscience of human memory since H.M. *Annual Review of Neuroscience, 34*(0147-006), 259–288. doi:10.1146/annurev-neuro-061010-113720

Stacks, A. M., Oshio, T., et al. (2009). The moderating effect of parental warmth on the association between spanking and child aggression: A longitudinal approach. *Infant & Child Development, 18*(2), 178–194. doi:10.1002/icd.596

Stall-Meadows, C., & Hebert, P. R. (2011). The sustainable consumer: An insitu study of residential lighting alternatives as influenced by infield education. *International Journal of Consumer Studies, 35*(2), 164–170.

Stallen, M., De Dreu, C. W., et al. (2012). The herding hormone: Oxytocin stimulates in-group conformity. *Psychological Science, 23*(11), 1288–1292. doi:10.1177/0956797612446026

Stanovich, K. E. (2013). *How to think straight about psychology* (10th ed.). Boston: Allyn & Bacon.

Stapel, D. A., & Marx, D. M. (2007). Distinctiveness is key: How different types of self-other similarity moderate social comparison effects. *Personality & Social Psychology Bulletin, 33*(3), 439–448. doi:10.1177/0146167206296105

Starkman, B. G., Sakharkar, A. J., & Pandey, S. C. (2012). Epigenetics: Beyond the genome in alcoholism. *Alcohol Research: Current Reviews, 34*(3), 293–305.

Stawiski, S., Dykema-Engblade, A., & Tindale, R. (2012). The roles of shared stereotypes and shared processing goals on mock jury decision making. *Basic & Applied Social Psychology, 34*(1), 88–97. doi:10.1080/01973533.2011.637467

Steele, C. M. (1997). A threat in the air: How stereotypes shape intellectual identity and performance. *American Psychologist, 52*(6), 613–629. doi:10.1037/0003-066X.52.6.613

Steele, C. M., & Aronson, J. (1995). Stereotype threat and the intellectual test performance of African Americans. *Journal of Personality & Social Psychology, 69*(5), 797–811. doi:10.1037/0022-3514.69.5.797

Stefurak, T., Taylor, C., & Mehta, S. (2010). Gender-specific models of homosexual prejudice: Religiosity, authoritarianism, and gender roles. *Psychology of Religion & Spirituality, 2*(4), 247–261.

Steiger, A. (2007). Neurochemical regulation of sleep. *Journal of Psychiatric Research, 41,* 537–552. doi:10.1016/j.jpsychires.2006.04.007

Stein, L. M., & Memon, A. (2006). Testing the efficacy of the cognitive interview in a developing country. *Applied Cognitive Psychology, 20*(5), 597–605. doi:10.1002/acp.1211

Stein, M. D., & Friedmann, P. D. (2005). Disturbed sleep and its relationship to alcohol use. *Substance Abuse, 26*(1), 1–13. doi:10.1300/J465v26n01_01

Stein, M. I. (1974). *Stimulating creativity* (Vol. 1). New York: Academic.

Stein, M. T., & Ferber, R. (2001). Recent onset of sleepwalking in early adolescence. *Journal of Development, Behavior, & Pediatrics, 22,* S33–S35.

Steinberg, L. (2001). Adolescent development. *Annual Review of Psychology, 52,* 83–110. doi:10.1146/annurev.psych.52.1.83

Steiner, B., & Wooldredge, J. (2009). Rethinking the link between institutional crowding and inmate misconduct. *The Prison Journal, 89*(2), 205–233.

Steinman, S. A., Smyth, F. L., et al. (2013). Anxiety-linked expectancy bias across the adult lifespan. *Cognition & Emotion, 27*(2), 345–355. doi:10.1080/02699931.2012.711743

Steinmayr, R., & Spinath, B. (2009). The importance of motivation as a predictor of school achievement. *Learning & Individual Differences, 19*(1), 80–90. doi:10.1016/j.lindif.2008.05.004

Steketee, G., Frost, R. O., et al. (2010). Waitlist-controlled trial of cognitive behavior therapy for hoarding disorder. *Depression & Anxiety, 27*(5), 476–484. doi:10.1002/da.20673

Stemler, S. E., & Sternberg, R. J. (2006). Using situational judgment tests to measure practical intelligence. In J. A. Weekley & R. E. Ployhart (Eds.), *Situational judgment tests: Theory, measurement, and application* (pp. 107–131). Mahwah, NJ: Erlbaum.

Stephens, D. P. (2012). The influence of mainstream Hip Hop's female sexual scripts on African American women's dating relationship experiences. In M. A. Paludi (Ed.), *The psychology of love* (Vols 1–4, pp. 169–183). Santa Barbara, CA: Praeger.

Stephens, K., Kiger, L., et al. (1999). Use of nonverbal measures of intelligence in identification of culturally diverse gifted students in rural areas. *Perceptual & Motor Skills, 88*(3, Pt 1), 793–796. doi:10.2466/PMS.88.3.793-796

Stern, S. L., Dhanda, R., & Hazuda, H. P. (2001). Hopelessness predicts mortality in older Mexican and European Americans. *Psychosomatic Medicine, 63*(3), 344–351.

Sternberg, E. M. (2009). *Healing spaces: The science of place and well-being.* Cambridge, MA: Harvard University Press.

Sternberg, R. J. (1988). *The triangle of love.* New York: Basic.

Sternberg, R. J. (2004). Culture and intelligence. *American Psychologist, 59*(5), 325–338. doi:10.1037/0003-066X.59.5.325

Sternberg, R. J. (2007). Race and intelligence: Not a case of black and white. *New Scientist, Oct. 27, 16.*

Sternberg, R. J. (2012). *Cognitive psychology* (6th ed.). Belmont, CA: Cengage Learning/Wadsworth.

Sternberg, R. J., & Grigorenko, E. L. (2005). Cultural explorations of the nature of intelligence. In A. F. Healy (Ed.), *Experimental cognitive psychology and its applications* (pp. 225–235). Washington: American Psychological Association.

Sternberg, R. J., & Grigorenko, E. L. (2006). Cultural intelligence and successful intelligence. *Group & Organization Management, 31*(1), 27–39. doi:10.1177/1059601105275255

Sternberg, R. J., & Lubart, T. I. (1995). *Defying the crowd.* New York: The Free Press.

Sternberg, R. J., Grigorenko, E. L., & Kidd, K. K. (2005). Intelligence, race, and genetics. *American Psychologist, 60*(1), 46–59. doi:10.1037/0003-066X.60.1.46

Sternberg, R. J., Grigorenko, E. L., et al. (2011). Intelligence, race, and genetics. In S. Krimsky & K. Sloan (Eds.), *Race and the genetic revolution: Science, myth, and culture* (pp. 195–237). New York: Columbia University Press.

Sterns, H. L., & Huyck, M. H. (2001). The role of work in midlife. In M. Lachman (Ed.), *The handbook of midlife development* (pp. 447–486). New York: Wiley.

Stetz, T., Button, S. B., & Porr, W. B. (2009). New tricks for an old dog: Visualizing job analysis results. *Public Personnel Management, 38*(1), 91–100.

Stickgold, R., & Walker, M. (2004). To sleep, perchance to gain creative insight? *Trends in Cognitive Sciences, 8*(5), 191–192. doi:10.1016/j.tics.2004.03.003

Stinson, F. S., Dawson, D. A., et al. (2007). The epidemiology of DSM-IV specific phobia in the USA: Result from the National Epidemiologic Survey on Alcohol and Related Conditions. *Psychological Medicine, 37*(7), 1047–1059. doi:10.1017/S0033291707000086

Stix, G. (2010). Alzheimer's: Forestalling the darkness. *Scientific American, 302,* 50–57. doi:10.1038/scientificamerican0610-50

Stix, G. (2011). The neuroscience of true grit. *Scientific American, 304,* 28–33. doi:10.1038/scientificamerican0111-29a

Stöber, J. (2004). Dimensions of test anxiety: Relations to ways of coping with pre-exam anxiety and uncertainty. *Anxiety, Stress & Coping, 17*(3), 213–226. doi:10.1080/1061580041233129615

Stokes, D. M. (2001). The shrinking file-drawer. *Skeptical Inquirer, May–June,* 22–25.

Stokes, D., & Lappin, M. (2010). Neurofeedback and biofeedback with 37 migraineurs: A clinical outcome study. *Behavioral & Brain Functions, 6*(Feb 2), ArtID 9. 10 pp. Retrieved June 17, 2013, from http://www.ncbi.nlm.nih.gov/pmc/articles/PMC2826281

Stone, J., Perry, Z. W., & Darley, J.M. (1997). "White men can't jump." *Basic & Applied Social Psychology, 19*(3), 291–306. doi:10.1207/15324839751036977

Stoppard, J. M., & McMullen, L. M. (Eds.). (2003). *Situating sadness: Women and depression in social context.* New York: New York University Press.

Strack, F., & Förster, J. (Eds.). (2009). *Social cognition: The basis of human interaction.* New York: Psychology Press.

Strack. F., Martin, L. L., & Stepper, S. (1988). Inhibiting and facilitating conditions of facial expressions: A non-obtrusive test of the facial feedback hypothesis. *Journal of Personality & Social Psychology, 54,* 768–777. doi:10.1037/0022-3514.54.5.768

Strange, J. R. (1965). *Abnormal psychology.* New York: McGraw-Hill.

Straub, R. (2012). *Health psychology* (3rd ed.). New York: Worth.

Strayer, D. L., Drews, F. A., & Crouch, D. J. (2006). A comparison of the cell phone driver and the drunk driver. *Human Factors, 48*(2), 381–391. doi:10.1518/001872006777724471

Stricker, G. (2011). PsyD programs. In J. C. Norcross, G. R. VandenBos, et al. (Eds.), *History of psychotherapy: Continuity and change* (2nd ed.) (pp. 630–639). Washington, DC: American Psychological Association. doi:10.1037/12353-040

Strickler, E. M., & Verbalis, J. G. (1988). Hormones and behavior: The biology of thirst and sodium appetite. *American Scientist, May–June,* 261–267.

Stroebe, W., Papies, E. K., & Aarts, H. (2008). From homeostatic to hedonic theories of eating: Self-regulatory failure in food-rich environments. *Applied Psychology, 57,* 172–193. doi:10.1111/j.1464-0597.2008.00360.x

Strong, B., DeVault, C., & Cohen, T. C. (2011). *The marriage and family experience: Intimate relationships in a changing society* (11th ed.). Belmont, CA: Cengage Learning/Wadsworth.

Strote, J., Lee, J. E., & Wechsler, H. (2002). Increasing MDMA use among college students: Results of a national survey. *Journal of Adolescent Health, 30*(1), 64–72. doi:10.1016/S1054-139X(01)00315-9

Strubbe, M. J. (2005). What did Triplett really find? A contemporary analysis of the first experiment in social psychology. *American Journal of Psychology, 118,* 271–286.

Stumbrys, T., Erlacher, D., et al. (2012). Induction of lucid dreams: A systematic review of evidence. *Consciousness & Cognition, 21*(3), 1456–1475. doi:10.1016/j.concog.2012.07.003

Stuss, D. T., & Knight, R. T. (2002). *Principles of frontal lobe function.* New York: Oxford University Press.

Suarez, E., & Gadalla, T. M. (2010). Stop blaming the victim: A meta-analysis on rape myths. *Journal of Interpersonal Violence, 25*(11), 2010–2035.

Substance Abuse and Mental Health Services Administration. (2012). *Results from the 2011 National Survey on Drug Use and Health: Summary of national findings and detailed tables.* Retrieved March 5, 2013, from http://www.samhsa.gov/data/NSDUH/2k11Results/NSDUHresults2011.htm

Sue, D., Sue, D. W., et al. (2013). *Understanding abnormal behavior* (10th ed.). Belmont, CA: Cengage Learning/Wadsworth.

Suedfeld, P. & Steel, G. D. (2000). The environmental psychology of capsule habitats. *Annual Review of Psychology, 51,* 227–253.

Suedfeld, P., & Borrie, R. A. (1999). Health and therapeutic applications of chamber and flotation restricted environmental stimulation therapy (REST). *Psychology & Health, 14*(3), 545–566. doi:10.1080/08870449908407346

Sugimoto, K., & Ninomiya, Y. (2005). Introductory remarks on umami research: Candidate receptors and signal transduction mechanisms on umami. *Chemical Senses, 30*(Suppl. 1), i21–i22. doi:10.1093/chemse/bjh093

Suinn, R. M. (1975). *Fundamentals of behavior pathology* (2nd ed.). New York: Wiley.

Suinn, R. M. (1999). Scaling the summit: Valuing ethnicity. *APA Monitor, March,* 2.

Suls, J. M., Luger, T., & Martin, R. (2010). The biopsychosocial model and the use of theory in health psychology. In J. M. Suls, K. W. Davidson, et al. (Eds.), *Handbook of health psychology and behavioral medicine* (pp. 15–27). New York: Guilford.

Summers, A., Hayward, R. D., & Miller, M. K. (2010). Death qualification as systematic exclusion of jurors with certain religious and other characteristics. *Journal of Applied Social Psychology, 40*(12), 3218–3234.

Sunnafrank, M., Ramirez, A., & Metts, S. (2004). At first sight: Persistent relational effects of get-acquainted conversations. *Journal of Social & Personal Relationships, 21*(3), 361–379. doi:10.1177/0265407504042837

Sutin, A. R., & Costa, P. T. Jr. (2010). Reciprocal influences of personality and job characteristics across middle adulthood. *Journal of Personality, 78*(1), 257–288. doi:10.1111/j.1467-6494.2009.00615.x

Suzuki, L., & Aronson, J. (2005). The cultural malleability of intelligence and its impact on the racial/ethnic hierarchy. *Psychology, Public Policy, & Law, 11,* 320–327. doi:10.1037/1076-8971.11.2.320

Sveticic, J., Milner, A., & De Leo, D. (2012). Contacts with mental health services before suicide: A comparison of indigenous with non-indigenous Australians. *General Hospital Psychiatry, 34*(2), 185–191. doi:10.1016/j. genhosppsych.2011.10.009

Swanson, S. A., Crow, S. J., et al. (2011). Prevalence and correlates of eating disorders in adolescents: Results from the national comorbidity survey replication adolescent supplement. *Archives of General Psychiatry, 68*(7), 714–723. doi:10.1001/archgenpsychiatry.2011.22

Synhorst, L. L., Buckley, J. A., et al. (2005). Cross informant agreement of the Behavioral and Emotional Rating Scale: 2nd Edition (BERS-2) parent and youth rating scales. *Child & Family Behavior Therapy, 27*(3), 1–11. doi:10.1300/J019v27n03_01

Szaflarski, J. P., Rajagopal, A., et al. (2011). Left-handedness and language lateralization in children. *Brain Research,* doi:10.1016/j. brainres.2011.11.026

Szollos, A. (2009). Toward a psychology of chronic time pressure: Conceptual and methodological review. *Time & Society, 18*(2–3), 332–350. doi:10.1177/0961463X09337847

Taber, K. H., Black, D. N., et al. (2012). Neuroanatomy of dopamine: Reward and addiction. *Journal of Neuropsychiatry And Clinical Neurosciences, 24*(1), 1–4. doi:10.1176/appi.neuropsych.24.1.1

Tackett, J. L., & Krueger, R. F. (2011). Dispositional influences on human aggression. In P. R. Shaver & M. Mikulincer (Eds.), *Human aggression and violence: Causes, manifestations, and consequences* (pp. 89–104). Washington: American Psychological Association.

Tafarodi, R. W., Shaughnessy, S. C., et al. (2011). The reporting of self-esteem in Japan and Canada. *Journal of Cross-Cultural Psychology, 42*(1), 155–164. doi:10.1177/0022022110386373

Taitz, I. (2011). Learning lucid dreaming and its effect on depression in undergraduates. *International Journal of Dream Research, 4*(2), 117–126.

Tal-Or, N., & Papirman, Y. (2007). The fundamental attribution error in attributing fictional figures' characteristics to the actors. *Media Psychology, 9*(2), 331–345. doi:10.1080/15213260701286049

Talarico, J. M., & Rubin, D. C. (2007). Flashbulb memories are special after all; in phenomenology, not accuracy. *Applied Cognitive Psychology, 21*(5), 557–578. doi:10.1002/acp.1293

Talbot, N. L., & Gamble, S. A. (2008). IPT for women with trauma histories in community mental health care. *Journal of Contemporary Psychotherapy, 38*(1), 35–44. doi:10.1007/s10879-007-9066-9

Tam, H., Jarrold, C., et al. (2010). The development of memory maintenance: Children's use of phonological rehearsal and attentional refreshment in working memory tasks. *Journal of Experimental Child Psychology, 107*(3), 306–324. doi:10.1016/j. jecp.2010.05.006

Tamis-LeMonda, C. S., Bornstein, M. H., & Baumwell, L. (2001). Maternal responsiveness and children's achievement of language milestones. *Child Development, 72,* 748–767. doi:10.1111/1467-8624.00313

Tamis-LeMonda, C. S., Shannon, J. D., et al. (2004). Fathers and mothers at play with their 2- and 3-year-olds: Contributions to language and cognitive development. *Child Development, 75*(6), 1806–1820. doi:10.1111/j.1467-8624.2004.00818.x

Tang, C. Y., Eaves, E. L., et al. (2010). Brain networks for working memory and factors of intelligence assessed in males and females with fMRI and DTI. *Intelligence, 38*(3), 293–303. doi:10.1016/j. intell.2010.03.003

Taraban, R., Rynearson, K., & Kerr, M. (2000). College students' academic performance and self-reports of comprehension strategy use. *Reading Psychology, 21*(4), 283–308. doi:10.1080/027027100750061930

Taris, T. W., Bakker, A. B., et al. (2005). Job control and burnout across occupations. *Psychological Reports, 97*(3), 955–961. doi:10.2466/PR0.97.7.955-961

Tarquinio, C. C., Brennstuhl, M. J., et al. (2012). Eye movement desensitization and reprocessing (EMDR) therapy in the treatment of victims of domestic violence: A pilot study. *European Review of Applied Psychology, 62*(4), 205–212. doi:10.1016/j. erap.2012.08.006

Tatum, J. L., & Foubert, J. D. (2009). Rape myth acceptance, hypermasculinity, and SAT scores as correlates of moral development: Understanding sexually aggressive attitudes in first-year college men. *Journal of College Student Development, 50*(2), 195–209. doi:10.1353/csd.0.0062

Taub, E. (2004). Harnessing brain plasticity through behavioral techniques to produce new treatments in neurorehabilitation. *American Psychologist, 59*(8), 692–704. doi:10.1037/0003-066X.59.8.692

Tauber, A. I. (2010). *Freud, the reluctant philosopher*. Princeton, NJ: Princeton University Press.

Tavakoli, S., Lumley, M. A., et al. (2009). Effects of assertiveness training and expressive writing on acculturative stress in international students: A randomized trial. *Journal of Counseling Psychology, 56*(4), 590–596. doi:10.1037/a0016634

Tavris, C., & Aronson, E. (2007). *Mistakes were made (but not by me): Why we justify foolish beliefs, bad decisions, and hurtful acts*. New York: Harcourt.

Tay, L., & Diener, E. (2011). Needs and subjective well-being around the world. *Journal of Personality and Social Psychology, 101*(2), 354–365. doi:10.1037/a0023779

Taylor, C. A., Manganello, J. A., et al. (2010). Mothers' spanking of 3-year-old children and subsequent risk of children's aggressive behavior. *Pediatrics, 125*(5), e1057–e1065. doi:10.1542/peds.2009-2678

Taylor, D. J., & Roane, B. M. (2010). Treatment of insomnia in adults and children: A practice-friendly review of research. *Journal of Clinical Psychology, 66*(11), 1137–1147. doi:10.1002/jclp.20733

Taylor, G. J., & Taylor-Allan, H. L. (2007). Applying emotional intelligence in understanding and treating physical and psychological disorders: What we have learned from alexithymia. In R. Bar-On, M. J. G. Reuven, et al. (Eds.), *Educating people to be emotionally intelligent* (pp. 211–223). Westport, CT: Praeger.

Taylor, K. (2004). *Brainwashing: The science of thought control*. New York: Oxford University Press.

Taylor, S. E. (2011). The future of social-health psychology: Prospects and predictions. *Social & Personality Psychology Compass, 5,* 275–284. doi:10.1111/j.1751-9004.2011.00360.x

Taylor, S. E. (2012). *Health psychology* (8th ed.). New York: McGraw-Hill

Taylor, S. E., & Master, S. L. (2011). Social responses to stress: The tend-and-befriend model. In R. J. Contrada & A. Baum (Eds.), *The handbook of stress science: Biology, psychology, and health* (pp. 101–109). New York: Springer.

Teglasi, H. (2010). *Essentials of TAT and other storytelling assessments* (2nd ed.). Hoboken, NJ: Wiley.

Tennesen, M. (2007). Gone today, hear tomorrow. *New Scientist, March 10,* 42–45.

Tennie, C., Greve, K., et al. (2010). Two-year-old children copy more reliably and more often than nonhuman great apes in multiple observational learning tasks. *Primates, 51*(4), 337–351. doi:10.1007/s10329-010-0208-4

Teo, A. R., & Gaw, A. C. (2010). Hikikomori, a Japanese culture-bound syndrome of social withdrawal? A proposal for DSM-5. *Journal of Nervous & Mental Disease, 198*(6), 444–449. doi:10.1097/NMD.0b013e3181e086b1

Teresi, L., & Haroutunian, H. (2011). *Hijacking the brain: How drug and alcohol addiction hijacks our brains. The science behind Twelve-Step recovery*. Bloomington, IN: AuthorHouse.

Terkourafi, M., & Petrakis, S. (2010). A critical look at the Desktop Metaphor 30 years on. In G. Low, Z. Todd, A. Deignan, et al. (Eds.), *Researching and applying metaphor in the real world* (pp. 145–164). Amsterdam, Netherlands: John Benjamins.

Terman, L. M., & Merrill, M. A. (1937/1960). *Stanford-Binet Intelligence Scale*. Boston: Houghton Mifflin.

Terman, L. M., & Oden, M. (1959). *The gifted group in mid-life: Genetic studies of genius* (Vol. 5). Stanford, CA: Stanford University Press.

Terry, C. (2006). History of treatment of people with mental illness. In J. R. Matthews, C. E. Walker, et al. (Eds.), *Your practicum in psychology: A guide for maximizing knowledge and competence* (pp. 81–103). Washington: American Psychological Association.

Terry, D. J., & Hogg, M. A. (1996). Group norms and the attitude-behavior relationship. *Personality & Social Psychology Bulletin, 22*(8), 776–793. doi:10.1177/0146167296228002

Tewksbury, R., Higgins, G. E., & Mustaine, E. E. (2008). Binge drinking among college athletes and non-athletes. *Deviant Behavior, 29*(3), 275–293. doi:10.1080/01639620701588040

Teyber, E., & McClure, F. H. (2011). *Interpersonal process in therapy: An integrative model* (6th ed.). Belmont, CA: Cengage Learning/Wadsworth.

Thakral, P. P. (2011). The neural substrates associated with inattentional blindness. *Consciousness & Cognition, 20*(4), 1768–1775. doi:10.1016/j. concog.2011.03.013

Thase, M. E. (2006). Major depressive disorder. In F. Andrasik (Ed.), *Comprehensive handbook of personality and psychopathology: Adult psychopathology* (Vol. 2, pp. 207–230). New York: Wiley.

The Nature Conservancy (2013). *Carbon footprint calculator*. Retrieved July 12, 2013, from http://www.nature.org /greenliving/carboncalculator/

Thiessen, E. D., Hill, E. A., & Saffran, J. R. (2005). Infant-directed speech facilitates word segmentation. *Infancy, 7*(1), 53–71. doi:10.1207/s15327078in0701_5

Thoma, C. A., Bartholomew, C. C., & Scott, L. A. (2009). *Universal design for transition: A roadmap for planning and instruction*. Baltimore, MD: Brookes Publishing.

Thoman, E. (2011). What parents can do about media violence. Malibu, CA: Center for Media Literacy. Retrieved May 16, 2013, from http://www .medialit.org/reading-room/what -parents-can-do-about-media-violence

Thomas, A. K., Bulevich, J. B., & Dubois, S. J. (2011). Context affects feeling-of-knowing accuracy in younger and older adults. *Journal of Experimental Psychology: Learning, Memory, & Cognition, 37*(1), 96–108. doi:10.1037/a0021612

Thomas, E. M. (2004). *Aggressive behaviour outcomes for young children: Change in parenting environment predicts change in behaviour.* Retrieved June 9, 2013, from http://www.statcan.ca/cgi-bin/downpub/listpub.cgi?catno=89-599-MIE2004001

Thompson, A., Boekhoorn, K., et al. (2008). Changes in adult neurogenesis in neurodegenerative diseases: Cause or consequence? *Genes, Brain & Behavior, 7*(Suppl. 1), 28–42.

Thompson, E. R., & Barnes, K. (2012). Meaning of sexual performance among men with and without erectile dysfunction. *Psychology of Men & Masculinity,* doi:10.1037/a0029104

Thompson, R. A., & Nelson, C. A. (2001). Developmental science and the media: Early brain development. *American Psychologist, 56*(1), 5–15. doi:10.1037/0003-066X.56.1.5

Thornton, S. N. (2010). Thirst and hydration: Physiology and consequences of dysfunction. *Physiology & Behavior, 100*(1), 15–21. doi:10.1016/j.physbeh.2010.02.026

Thrift, A. G. (2010). Design and methods of population surveys. *Neuroepidemiology, 34*(4), 267–269. doi:10.1159/000297758

Thyen, U., Richter-Appelt, H., et al. (2005). Deciding on gender in children with intersex conditions: Considerations and controversies. *Treatments in Endocrinology, 4*(1), 1–8.

Tierney, S. (2008). Creating communities in cyberspace: Pro-anorexia web sites and social capital. *Journal of Psychiatric & Mental Health Nursing, 15*(4), 340–343.

Tikotzky, L., Chambers, A. S., et al. (2012). Postpartum maternal sleep and mothers' perceptions of their attachment relationship with the infant among women with a history of depression during pregnancy. *International Journal of Behavioral Development, 36*(6), 440–448.

Till, B. D., & Priluck, R. L. (2000). Stimulus generalization in classical conditioning: An initial investigation and extension. *Psychology & Marketing, 17*(1), 55–72. doi:10.1002/(SICI)1520-6793(200001)17:1<55::AID-MAR4>3.0.CO;2-C

Till, B. D., Stanley, S. M., & Priluck, R. (2008). Classical conditioning and celebrity endorsers: An examination of belongingness and resistance to extinction. *Psychology & Marketing, 25*(2), 179–196. doi:10.1002/mar.20205

Tine, M., & Gotlieb, R. (2013). Gender-, race-, and income-based stereotype threat: The effects of multiple stigmatized aspects of identity on math performance and working memory function. *Social Psychology of Education.* doi:10.1007/s11218-013-9224-8

Tipples, J., Atkinson, A. P., & Young, A. W. (2002). The eyebrow frown: A salient social signal. *Emotion, 2*(3), 288–296. doi:10.1037/1528-3542.2.3.288

Titov, N. (2011). Internet-delivered psychotherapy for depression in adults. *Current Opinion in Psychiatry, 24*(1), 18–23. doi:10.1097/YCO.0b013e32833ed18f

Toates, F. (2011). *Biological psychology* (3rd ed.). Boston: Pearson/Allyn & Bacon.

Tolman, E. C., & Honzik, C. H. (1930). Degrees of hunger, reward and non-reward, and maze performance in rats. *University of California Publications in Psychology, 4,* 241–256.

Tolman, E. C., Ritchie, B. F., & Kalish, D. (1946). Studies in spatial learning: II. Place learning versus response learning. *Journal of Experimental Psychology, 36,* 221–229. doi:10.1037/h0060262

Tom, G., Tong, S., & Hesse, C. (2010). Thick slice and thin slice teaching evaluations. *Social Psychology of Education, 13*(1), 129–136. doi:10.1007/s11218-009-9101-7

Tomasi, D., & Volkow, N. D. (2012). Laterality patterns of brain functional connectivity: Gender effects. *Cerebral Cortex, 22*(6), 1455–1462. doi:10.1093/cercor/bhr230

Toneatto, T. (2002). Cognitive therapy for problem gambling. *Cognitive & Behavioral Practice, 9*(3), 191–199. doi:10.1016/S1077-7229(02)80049-9

Tononi, G., & Cirelli, C. (2003). Sleep and synaptic homeostasis: A hypothesis. *Brain Research Bulletin, 62*(2), 143–150. doi:10.1016/j.brainresbull.2003.09.004

Toro, C. T., & Deakin, J. F. W. (2007). Adult neurogenesis and schizophrenia: A window on abnormal early brain development? *Schizophrenia Research, 90*(1–3), 1–14. doi:10.1016/j.schres.2006.09.030

Torrente, M. P., Gelenberg, A. J., & Vrana, K. E. (2012). Boosting serotonin in the brain: Is it time to revamp the treatment of depression? *Journal of Psychopharmacology, 26*(5), 629–635. doi:10.1177/0269881111430744

Toyota, H., & Kikuchi, Y. (2005). Encoding richness of self-generated elaboration and spacing effects on incidental memory. *Perceptual & Motor Skills, 101*(2), 621–627.

Trainor, L. J., & Desjardins, R. N. (2002). Pitch characteristics of infant-directed speech affect infants' ability to discriminate vowels. *Psychonomic Bulletin & Review, 9*(2), 335–340. doi:10.3758/BF03196290

Travis, F., Arenander, A., & DuBois, D. (2004). Psychological and physiological characteristics of a proposed object-referral/self-referral continuum of self-awareness. *Consciousness & Cognition, 13,* 401–420. doi:10.1016/j.concog.2004.03.001

Traxler, M. J. (2011). *Introduction to psycholinguistics: Understanding language science.* New York: Wiley-Blackwell.

Treffert, D. A. (2010). *Islands of genius: The bountiful mind of the autistic, acquired, and sudden savant.* London, England: Jessica Kingsley Publishers.

Treffert, D. A., & Christensen, C. D. (2005). Inside the mind of a savant. *Scientific American, 293*(6), 108–113. doi:10.1038/scientificamerican1205-108

Tregear, S., Resto, J., et al. (2010). Continuous positive airway pressure reduces risk of motor vehicle crash among drivers with obstructive sleep apnea: Systematic review and meta-analysis. *Sleep: Journal of Sleep & Sleep Disorders Research, 33*(10), 1373–1380.

Trentowska, M., Bender, C., & Tuschen-Caffier, B. (2013). Mirror exposure in women with bulimic symptoms: How do thoughts and emotions change in body image treatment? *Behaviour Research & Therapy, 51*(1), 1–6. doi:10.1016/j.brat.2012.03.012

Treves, T. A., & Korczyn, A. D. (2012). Modeling the dementia epidemic. *CNS Neuroscience & Therapeutics, 18*(2), 175–181. doi:10.1111/j.1755-5949.2011.00242.x

Triandis, H. C., & Suh, E. M. (2002). Cultural influences on personality. *Annual Review of Psychology, 53,* 133–160. doi:10.1146/annurev.psych.53.100901.135200

Tripp, D. A., Stanish, W., et al. (2011). Fear of reinjury, negative affect, and catastrophizing predicting return to sport in recreational athletes with anterior cruciate ligament injuries at 1 year postsurgery. *Sport, Exercise, & Performance Psychology, 1*(S), 38–48. doi:10.1037/2157-3905.1.S.38

Trocmé, N., MacLaurin, B., et al. (2001). *Canadian Incidence Study of Reported Child Abuse and Neglect.* Retrieved June 9, 2013, from http://www.phac-aspc.gc.ca/publicat/cissr-ecirc/

Troll, L. E., & Skaff, M. M. (1997). Perceived continuity of self in very old age. *Psychology & Aging, 12*(1), 162–169. doi:10.1037/0882-7974.12.1.162

Troup, C., & Rose, J. (2012). Working from home: Do formal or informal telework arrangements provide better work–family outcomes? *Community, Work & Family, 15*(4), 471–486. doi:10.1080/13668803.2012.724220

Trujillo, L. T., Kornguth, S., & Schnyer, D. M. (2009). An ERP examination of the different effects of sleep deprivation on exogenously cued and endogenously cued attention. *Sleep, 32*(10), 1285–1297.

Trull, T., & Prinstein, M. (2013). *Clinical psychology* (8th ed.). Belmont, CA: Cengage Learning/Wadsworth.

Tsai, W-C., Chen, C.-C., & Chiu, S-F. (2005). Exploring boundaries of the effects of applicant impression management tactics in job interviews. *Journal of Management, 31*(1), 108–125.

Tulving, E. (1989). Remembering and knowing the past. *American Scientist, 77*(4), 361–367.

Tulving, E. (2002). Episodic memory. *Annual Review of Psychology, 53,* 1–25. doi:10.1146/annurev.psych.53.100901.135114

Tunney, R. J., & Fernie, G. (2012). Episodic and prototype models of category learning. *Cognitive Processing, 13*(1), 41–54.

Turenius, C. I., Htut, M. M., et al. (2009). GABA(A) receptors in the lateral hypothalamus as mediators of satiety and body weight regulation. *Brain Research, 1262,* 16–24. doi:10.1016/j.brainres.2009.01.016

Turiano, N. A., Mroczek, D. K., et al. (2013). Big 5 personality traits and interleukin-6: Evidence for 'healthy neuroticism' in a U.S. population sample. *Brain, Behavior, & Immunity, 28,* 83–89. doi:10.1016/j.bbi.2012.10.020

Turkheimer, E., Haley, A., Waldron, M., et al. (2003). Socioeconomic status modifies heritability of IQ in young children. *Psychological Science, 14,* 623–628. doi:10.1046/j.0956-7976.2003.psci_1475.x

Tversky, A., & Kahneman, D. (1981). The framing of decisions and the psychology of choice. *Science, 211,* 453–458. doi:10.1126/science.7455683

Tversky, A., & Kahneman, D. (1982). Judgments of and by representativeness. In D. Kahneman, P. Slovic, et al. (Eds.), *Judgment under uncertainty: Heuristics and biases* (pp. 84–98). Cambridge, MA: Cambridge University Press.

Twemlow, S. W & Sacco, F. C. (2012). *Preventing bullying and school violence.* Washington, DC: American Psychiatric Publishing.

Twenge, J. M., & Campbell, W. K. (2001). Age and birth cohort differences in self-esteem: A Cross-Temporal Meta-Analysis. *Personality & Social Psychology Review, 5*(4), 321–344. doi:10.1207/S15327957PSPR0504_3

U.S. Census Bureau. (2012). *Poverty: Highlights.* Retrieved February 8, 2013, from http://www.census.gov/hhes/www/poverty/about/overview/index.html

U.S. Department of Energy Office of Science. (2012). *Human Genome*

Project information. Retrieved February 8, 2013, from http://www.ornl.gov/sci/techresources/Human_Genome/home.shtml

U.S. Department of Energy. (2010). *Secretary Chu announces two million smart grid meters installed nationwide.* Retrieved May 23, 2013 from http://www.energy.gov/news/9433.htm

Underwood, B. J. (1957). Interference and forgetting. *Psychological Review, 64,* 49–60. doi:10.1037/h0044616

United Nations (2011). World Population Prospects, the 2010 Revision. Retrieved May 22, 2013, from http://esa.un.org/unpd/wpp/Other-Information/faq.htm

United Nations Programme on HIV/AIDS. (2010). *UNAIDS Report on the global AIDS epidemic 2010.* Retrieved June 11, 2013, from http://www.unaids.org/globalreport/Global_report.htm

Unsworth, G., & Ward, T. (2001). Video games and aggressive behaviour. *Australian Psychologist, 36*(3), 184–192. doi:10.1080/00050060108259654

Uziel, L. (2007). Individual differences in the social facilitation effect: A review and meta-analysis. *Journal of Research in Personality, 41*(3), 579–601. doi:10.1016/j.jrp.2006.06.008

Vago, D. R., & Nakamura, Y. (2011). Selective attentional bias towards pain-related threat in fibromyalgia: Preliminary evidence for effects of mindfulness meditation training. *Cognitive Therapy & Research, 35*(6), 581–594. doi:10.1007/s10608-011-9391-x

Vaillant, G. E. (2002). *Aging well.* Boston: Little, Brown.

Valadez, J. J. & Ferguson, C. J. (2012). Just a game after all: Violent video game exposure and time spent playing effects on hostile feelings, depression, and visuospatial cognition. *Computers in Human Behavior, 28,* 608–616. doi:10.1016/j.chb.2011.11.006

Valentine, S., Godkin, L., & Varca, P. E. (2010). Role conflict, mindfulness, and organizational ethics in an education-based healthcare institution. *Journal of Business Ethics, 94*(3), 455–469. doi:10.1007/s10551-009-0276-9

Valins, S. (1967). Emotionality and information concerning internal reactions. *Journal of Personality & Social Psychology, 6,* 458–463. doi:10.1037/h0024842

Valkenburg, P. M., Sumter, S. R., & Peter, J. (2011). Gender differences in online and offline self-disclosure in pre-adolescence and adolescence. *British Journal of Developmental Psychology, 29*(2), 253–269. doi:10.1348/2044-835X.002001

Vallerand, A. H., Saunders, M. M., & Anthony, M. (2007). Perceptions of control over pain by patients with cancer and their caregivers. *Pain*

Management Nursing, 8(2), 55–63. doi:10.1016/j.pmn.2007.02.001

Vallerand, R. J., Paquet, Y., et al. (2010). On the role of passion for work in burnout: A process model. *Journal of Personality, 78*(1), 289–312. doi:10.1111/j.1467-6494.2009.00616.x

Van Blerkom, D. L. (2012). *College study skills: Becoming a strategic learner* (7th ed.). Belmont, CA: Cengage Learning/Wadsworth.

van de Pol, P. C., & Kavussanu, M. (2012). Achievement motivation across training and competition in individual and team sports. *Sport, Exercise, & Performance Psychology, 1*(2), 91–105. doi:10.1037/a0025967

Van den Bergh, B., & Dewitte, S. (2006). Digit ratio (2D:4D) moderates the impact of sexual cues on men's decisions in ultimatum games. *Proceedings of the Royal Society of London B, 273,* 2091–2095.

van der Hart, O., Lierens, R., & Goodwin, J. (1996). Jeanne Fery: A sixteenth-century case of dissociative identity disorder. *Journal of Psychohistory, 24*(1), 18–35.

van der Kamp, J., & Cañal-Bruland, R. (2011). Kissing right? On the consistency of the head-turning bias in kissing. *Laterality: Asymmetries of Body, Brain & Cognition, 16*(3), 257–267. doi:10.1080/13576500903530778

van Dierendonck, D., & Te Nijenhuis, J. (2005). Flotation restricted environmental stimulation therapy (REST) as a stress-management tool: A meta-analysis. *Psychology & Health, 20*(3), 405–412. doi:10.1080/0887044041231337093

van Dierendonck, D., Díaz, D., et al. (2008). Ryff's six-factor model of psychological well-being, a Spanish exploration. *Social Indicators Research, 87*(3), 473–479. doi:10.1007/s11205-007-9174-7

van Dijk, E., Parks, C. D., & van Lange, P. M. (2013). Social dilemmas: The challenge of human cooperation. *Organizational Behavior & Human Decision Processes, 120*(2), 123–124. doi:10.1016/j.obhdp.2012.12.005

Van Iddekinge, C. H., Putka, D. J., & Campbell, J. P. (2011). Reconsidering vocational interests for personnel selection: The validity of an interest-based selection test in relation to job knowledge, job performance, and continuance intentions. *Journal of Applied Psychology, 96*(1), 13–33.

Van Lange, P. M., Joireman, J., et al. (2013). The psychology of social dilemmas: A review. *Organizational Behavior & Human Decision Processes, 120*(2), 125–141. doi:10.1016/j.obhdp.2012.11.003

Van Lawick-Goodall, J. (1971). *In the shadow of man.* New York: Houghton Mifflin.

Van Volkom, M. (2009). The effects of childhood tomboyism and family experiences on the self-esteem of college females. *College Student Journal, 43*(3), 736–743.

Van Vugt, M. (2009). Averting the tragedy of the commons: Using social psychological science to protect the environment. *Current Directions in Psychological Science, 18*(3), 169–173.

Vandewalle, G., Hébert, M., et al. (2011). Abnormal hypothalamic response to light in seasonal affective disorder. *Biological Psychiatry, 70*(10), 954–961. doi:10.1016/j.biopsych.2011.06.022

Vanheule, S., Vandenbergen, J., et al. (2010). Interpersonal problems in alexithymia: A study in three primary care groups. *Psychology & Psychotherapy: Theory, Research & Practice, 83*(4), 351–362. doi:10.1348/147608309X481829

Vartanian, O., & Suedfeld, P. (2011). The effect of the flotation version of restricted environmental stimulation technique (REST) on jazz improvisation. *Music & Medicine, 3*(4), 234–238. doi:10.1177/1943862111407640

Vasa, R. A., Carlino, A. R., & Pine, D. S. (2006). Pharmacotherapy of depressed children and adolescents: Current issues and potential directions. *Biological Psychiatry, 59*(11), 1021–1028. doi:10.1016/j.biopsych.2005.10.010

Vasquez, E. A., Lickel, B., & Hennigan, K. (2010). Gangs, displaced, and group-based aggression. *Aggression & Violent Behavior, 15*(2), 130–140. doi:10.1016/j.avb.2009.08.001

Veale, J. F., Clarke, D. E., & Lomax, T. C. (2010). Biological and psychosocial correlates of adult gender-variant identities: A review. *Personality & Individual Differences, 48*(4), 357–366.

Velakoulis, D., & Pantelis, C. (1996). What have we learned from functional imaging studies in schizophrenia? The role of frontal, striatal and temporal areas. *Australian & New Zealand Journal of Psychiatry, 30*(2), 195–209. doi:10.3109/00048679609076095

Verma, M. M., & Howard, R. J. (2012). Semantic memory and language dysfunction in early Alzheimer's disease: A review. *International Journal of Geriatric Psychiatry, 27*(12), 1209–1217. doi:10.1002/gps.3766

Vernon-Feagans, L., Garrett-Peters, P., et al. (2011). Chaos, poverty, and parenting: Predictors of early language development. *Early Childhood Research Quarterly,* doi:10.1016/j.ecresq.2011.11.001.

Vi, P. (2006). A field study investigating the effects of a rebar-tying machine on trunk flexion, tool usability and productivity. *Ergonomics, 49*(14), 1437–1455.

Viero, C., Shibuya, I., et al. (2010). Oxytocin: Crossing the bridge between basic science and pharmacotherapy. *CNS Neuroscience & Therapeutics, 16*(5), e138–e156. doi:10.1111/j.1755-5949.2010.00185.x

Vincent, N., Lewycky, S., & Finnegan, H. (2008). Barriers to engagement in sleep restriction and stimulus control in chronic insomnia. *Journal of Consulting & Clinical Psychology, 76*(5). 820–828. doi:10.1037/0022-006X.76.5.820

Visser, B. A., Bay, D., et al. (2010). Psychopathic and antisocial, but not emotionally intelligent. *Personality & Individual Differences, 48*(5), 644–648. doi:10.1016/j.paid.2010.01.003

Vlachou, S., & Markou, A. (2011). Intracranial self-stimulation. In M. C. Olmstead (Ed.), *Animal models of drug addiction* (pp. 3–56). Totowa, NJ: Humana Press.

Vogler, R. E., Weissbach, T. A., et al. (1977). Integrated behavior change techniques for problem drinkers in the community. *Journal of Consulting & Clinical Psychology, 45,* 267–279.

Vojdanoska, M., Cranney, J., & Newell, B. R. (2010). The testing effect: The role of feedback and collaboration in a tertiary classroom setting. *Applied Cognitive Psychology, 24*(8), 1183–1195. doi:10.1002/acp.1630

Volberg, R. A. (2012). Still not on the radar: Adolescent risk and gambling, revisited. *Journal of Adolescent Health, 50*(6), 539–540. doi:10.1016/j.jadohealth.2012.03.009

Volkow, N. D., Gillespie, H., et al. (1996). Brain glucose metabolism in chronic marijuana users at baseline and during marijuana intoxication. *Psychiatry Research: Neuroimaging, 67*(1), 29–38. doi:10.1016/0925-4927(96)02817-X

Volpicelli, J. R., Ulm, R. R., et al. (1983). Learned mastery in the rat. *Learning & Motivation, 14,* 204–222. doi:10.1016/0023-9690(83)90006-1

Vontress, C. E. (2013). Existential therapy. In J. Frew, & M. D. Spiegler (Eds.), *Contemporary psychotherapies for a diverse world* (pp. 131–164). New York: Routledge/Taylor & Francis.

Voss, J. L., Lucas, H. D., & Paller, K. A. (2012). More than a feeling: Pervasive influences of memory processing without awareness of remembering. *Cognitive Neuroscience, 3,* 193–207. doi:org/10.1080/17588928.2012.674935

Vrtička, P., & Vuilleumier, P. (2012). Neuroscience of human social interactions and adult attachment style. *Frontiers in Human Neuroscience, 6.* doi:10.3389/fnhum.2012.00212

Vuillermot, S., Weber, L., et al. (2010). A longitudinal examination of the neurodevelopmental impact of prenatal immune activation in mice reveals primary defects in dopaminergic development relevant to schizo-phrenia. *Journal of Neuroscience, 30*(4), 1270–1287. doi:10.1523/JNEUROSCI.5408-09.2010

Vygotsky, L. S. (1962). *Thought and language.* Cambridge, MA: MIT Press.

Vygotsky, L. S. (1978). *Mind in society.* Cambridge, MA: Harvard University Press.

Wade, K. A., Green, S. L., & Nash, R. A. (2010). Can fabricated evidence induce false eyewitness testimony? *Applied Cognitive Psychology, 24*(7), 899–908. doi:10.1002/acp.1607

Wager, T. D., Rilling, J. K., et al. (2004). Placebo-induced changes in MRI in the anticipation and experience of pain. *Science, 303*(Feb 20), 1162–1166. doi:10.1126/science.1093065

Wagner, R. K. (2011). Practical intelligence. In R. J. Sternberg, & S. Kaufman (Eds.), *The Cambridge handbook of intelligence* (pp. 550–563). New York: Cambridge University Press. doi:10.1017/CBO9780511977244.028

Wakefield, J. C. (1992). The concept of mental disorder. *American Psychologist, 47*(3), 373–388. doi:10.1037/0003-066X.47.3.373

Waldinger, M. D. (2009). Delayed and premature ejaculation. In R. Balon, & R. T. Segraves (Eds.), *Clinical manual of sexual disorders* (pp. 267–292). Arlington, VA: American Psychiatric Publishing.

Walker, E., Kestler, L., et al. (2004). Schizophrenia: Etiology and course. *Annual Review of Psychology, 55,* 401–430. doi:10.1146/annurev.psych.55.090902.141950

Walker, I., & Crogan, M. (1998). Academic performance, prejudice, and the Jigsaw classroom. *Journal of Community & Applied Social Psychology, 8*(6), 381–393. doi:10.1002/(SICI)1099-1298(199811/12)8:6<381::AID-CASP457>3.0.CO;2-6

Walker, M. P., & Stickgold, R. (2006). Sleep, memory, and plasticity. *Annual Review of Psychology, 57,* 139–166. doi:10.1146/annurev.psych.56.091103.070307

Walker, S. P., Wachs, T. D., et al. (2011). Inequality in early childhood: Risk and protective factors for early child development. *The Lancet, 378*(9799), 1325–1338. doi:10.1016/S0140-6736(11)60555-2

Wallach, M. A., & Kogan, N. (1965). *Modes of thinking in young children.* New York: Holt.

Wallis, J., Lipp, O. V., & Vanman, E. J. (2012). Face age and sex modulate the other-race effect in face recognition. *Attention, Perception, & Psychophysics, 74*(8), 1712–1721. doi:10.3758/s13414-012-0359-z

Wampold, B. E., Minami T., et al. (2005). The placebo is powerful: Estimating placebo effects in medicine and psychotherapy from randomized clinical trials. *Journal of Clinical Psychology, 61*(7), 835–854. doi:10.1002/jclp.20129

Wan, C. Y., Demaine, K., et al. (2010). From music making to speaking: Engaging the mirror neuron system in autism. *Brain Research Bulletin, 82*(3–4), 161–168. doi:10.1016/j.brainresbull.2010.04.010

Wandersman, A., & Florin, P. (2003). Community interventions and effective prevention. *American Psychologist, 58*(6/7), 441–448. doi:10.1037/0003-066X

Wang, Q., & Conway, M. A. (2004). The stories we keep: Autobiographical memory in American and Chinese middle-aged adults. *Journal of Personality, 72*(5), 911–938.

Wang, S. S., & Brownell, K. D. (2005). Public policy and obesity: The need to marry science with advocacy. *Psychiatric Clinics of North America, 28*(1), 235–252. doi:10.1016/j.psc.2004.09.001

Wang, S.-H., & Morris, R. G. M. (2010). Hippocampal-neocortical interactions in memory formation, consolidation, and reconsolidation. *Annual Review of Psychology, 61,* 49–79. doi:10.1146/annurev.psych.093008.100523

Ward, L. M. (2004). Wading through the stereotypes: Positive and negative associations between media use and Black adolescents' conceptions of self. *Developmental Psychology, 40,* 284–294.

Ward, L., & Parr, J. M. (2010). Revisiting and reframing use: Implications for the integration of ICT. *Computers & Education, 54*(1), 113–122. doi:10.1016/j.compedu.2009.07.011

Wargo, E. (2008). The many lives of superstition. *APS Observer, 21*(9), 18–24.

Wark, G. R., & Krebs, D. L. (1996). Gender and dilemma differences in real-life moral judgment. *Developmental Psychology, 32*(2), 220–230.

Warren, D. J., & Normann, R. A. (2005). Functional reorganization of primary visual cortex induced by electrical stimulation in the cat. *Vision Research, 45,* 551–565. doi:10.1016/j.visres.2004.09.021

Washton, A. M., & Zweben, J. E. (2009). *Cocaine and methamphetamine addiction: Treatment, recovery, and relapse prevention.* New York, Norton.

Watson, D. L. (2008). The fundamental attribution error. In L. T. Benjamin, Jr. (Ed.). *Favorite activities for the teaching of psychology* (pp. 248–251). Washington, DC US: American Psychological Association.

Watson, D. L., & Tharp, R. G. (2014). *Self-directed behavior: Self-modification for personal adjustment* (10th ed.).

Belmont, CA: Cengage Learning/Wadsworth.

Watson, J. B. (1913/1994). Psychology as the behaviorist views it. *Psychological Review, 101*(2), 248–253. doi:10.1037/0033-295X.101.2.248

Watson, J. M., & Strayer, David L. (2010). Supertaskers: Profiles in extraordinary multitasking ability. *Psychonomic Bulletin & Review, 17*(4), 479–485. doi:10.3758/PBR.17.4.479

Watson, R. A., & Yeung, T. M. (2011). What is the potential of oligodendrocyte progenitor cells to successfully treat human spinal cord injury? *BMC Neurology. 11* doi:10.1186/1471-2377-11-113

Waytz, A., Epley, N., & Cacioppo, J. T. (2010). Social cognition unbound: Insights into anthropomorphism and dehumanization. *Current Directions in Psychological Science, 19*(1), 58–62. doi:10.1177/0963721409359302

Weaver, Y. (2009). Mid-life: A time of crisis or new possibilities? *Existential Analysis, 20*(1), 69–78.

Wechsler, D. (2008). *Wechsler Adult Intelligence Scale* (4th ed.) *(WAIS-IV).* San Antonio, TX: Pearson.

Wedding, D., & Corsini, R. J. (2011). *Case studies in psychotherapy* (6th ed.). Belmont, CA: Cengage Learning/Wadsworth.

Weekley, J. A. & Polyhart, R. E. (Eds.) (2006). *Situational judgment tests: Theory, measurement, and application.* Mahwah, NJ: Erlbaum.

Weeks, G. R., & Gambescia, N. (2009). A systemic approach to sensate focus. In K. M. Hertlein, G. R. Weeks, et al. (Eds.), *Systemic sex therapy* (pp. 341–362). New York: Routledge/Taylor & Francis.

Wegenek, A. R., & Buskist, W. (2010). *The insider's guide to the psychology major: Everything you need to know about the degree and profession.* Washington, DC: American Psychological Association.

Weidenhammer, W., Linde, K., et al. (2007). Acupuncture for chronic low back pain in routine care: A multicenter observational study. *Clinical Journal of Pain, 23*(2), 128–135. doi:10.1097/01.ajp.0000210952.09127.df

Weinberg, R. A. (1989). Intelligence and IQ. *American Psychologist, 44*(2), 98–104. doi:10.1037/0003-066X.44.2.98

Weiner, B. A., & Carton, J. S. (2012). Avoidant coping: A mediator of maladaptive perfectionism and test anxiety. *Personality & Individual Differences, 52*(5), 632–636. doi:10.1016/j.paid.2011.12.009

Weingarten, K. (2010). Reasonable hope: Construct, clinical applications, and supports. *Family Process, 49*(1), 5–25. doi:10.1111/j.1545-5300.2010.01305.x

Weinstein, Y., & Shanks, D. R. (2010). Rapid induction of false memory for pictures. *Memory, 18*(5), 533–542. doi:10.1080/09658211.2010.483232

Weintraub, M. I. (1983). *Hysterical conversion reactions.* New York: SP Medical & Scientific Books.

Weishaar, M. E. (2006). A cognitive-behavioral approach to suicide risk reduction in crisis intervention. In A. R. Roberts & K. R. Yeager, (Eds.), *Foundations of evidence-based social work practice* (pp. 181–193). New York: Oxford University Press.

Weiss, M., Allan, B., & Greenaway, M. (2012). Treatment of catatonia with electroconvulsive therapy in adolescents. *Journal of Child & Adolescent Psychopharmacology, 22*(1), 96–100. doi:10.1089/cap.2010.0052

Weisskirch, R. S. (2005). Ethnicity and perceptions relationship to ethnic identity development. *International Journal of Intercultural Relations, 29*(3), 355–366. doi:10.1016/j.ijintrel.2005.053.008

Weissman, A. M., Jogerst, G. J., & Dawson, J. D. (2003). Community characteristics associated with child abuse in Iowa. *Child Abuse & Neglect, 27*(10), 1145–1159. doi:10.1016/j.chiabu.2003.09.002

Weitzenhoffer, A. M., & Hilgard, E. R. (1959). *Stanford Hypnotic Susceptibility Scales Forms A and B.* Palo Alto, CA: Consulting Psychologists Press.

Welch, R. D., & Houser, M. E. (2010). Extending the four-category model of adult attachment: An interpersonal model of friendship attachment. *Journal of Social & Personal Relationships, 27*(3), 351–366. doi:10.1177/0265407509349632

Wellings, K., Collumbien, M., et al. (2006). Sexual behaviour in context: A global perspective. *Lancet, 368*(9548), 1706–1738.

Wells, B. E., & Twenge, J. M. (2005). Changes in young people's sexual behavior and attitudes, 1943–1999: A cross-temporal meta-analysis. *Review of General Psychology, 9*(3), 249–261.

Wells, G. L., & Olsen, E. A. (2003). Eyewitness testimony. *Annual Review of Psychology, 54,* 277–295. doi:10.1146/annurev.psych.54.101601.145028

Weltzin, T. E., Weisensel, N., et al. (2005). Eating disorders in men: Update. *Journal of Men's Health & Gender, 2*(2), 186–193. doi:10.1016/j.jmhg.2005.04.008

Wentland, J. J., & Reissing, E. D. (2011). Taking casual sex not too casually: Exploring definitions of casual sexual relationships. *Canadian Journal of Human Sexuality, 20*(3), 75–91.

Wenzel, A. J., & Lucas-Thompson, R. G. (2012). Authenticity in college-aged males and females, how close others are perceived, and mental health outcomes. *Sex Roles, 67*(5–6), 334–350. doi:10.1007/s11199-012-0182-y

Wernet, S. P., Follman, C., et al. (2003). Building bridges and improving racial harmony: An evaluation of the Bridges Across Racial Polarization Program. In J. J. Stretch, E. M. Burkemper, et al., (Eds.), *Practicing social justice* (pp. 63–79). New York: Haworth Press.

Wertheimer, M. (1959). *Productive thinking.* New York: Harper & Row.

Werthmann, J., Roefs, A., et al. (2011). Can(not) take my eyes off it: Attention bias for food in overweight participants. *Health Psychology, 30*(5), 561–569. doi:10.1037/a0024291

Wessel, I., & Wright, D. B. (Eds.). (2004). *Emotional memory failures.* Hove, UK: Psychology Press.

West, D., & Sutton-Spence, R. (2012). Shared thinking processes with four deaf poets: A window on 'the creative' in 'creative sign language.' *Sign Language Studies, 12*(2), 188–210. doi:10.1353/sls.2011.0023

Westen, D., & Bradley, R. (2005). Empirically supported complexity: Rethinking evidence-based practice in psychotherapy. *Current Directions in Psychological Science, 14*(5), 266–271. doi:10.1111/j.0963-7214.2005.00378.x

Wester, W., & Hammond, D. (2011). Solving crimes with hypnosis. *American Journal of Clinical Hypnosis, 53*(4), 249–263. doi:10.1080/00029157.2011.10404355

Wethington, E. (2003). Turning points as opportunities for psychological growth. In C. L. M. Keyes, & J. Haidt (Eds.), *Flourishing* (pp. 37–53). Washington: American Psychological Association.

Wethington, E., Kessler, R. C., & Shiner Pixley, J. E. (2004). Turning points in adulthood. In O. G. Brim, C. D. Ryff, et al., (Eds.), *How healthy are we? A national study of well-being at midlife* (pp. 425–450). Chicago: University of Chicago Press.

Wexler, M. N. (1995). Expanding the groupthink explanation to the study of contemporary cults. *Cultic Studies Journal, 12*(1), 49–71.

Wheat, A. L., & Larkin, K. T. (2010). Biofeedback of heart rate variability and related physiology: A critical review. *Applied Psychophysiology & Biofeedback, 35*(3), 229–242. doi:10.1007/s10484-010-9133-y

Whitbourne, S. K., & Halgin, R. P. (2013). *Abnormal psychology: Clinical perspectives on psychological disorders* (7th ed.). New York: McGraw-Hill.

White-Ajmani, M., & Bursik, K. (2011). What lies beneath: Dogmatism, intolerance, and political self-identification. *Individual Differences Research, 9*(3), 153–164.

White, T. L., & McBurney, D. H. (2013). *Research methods* (9th ed.). Belmont, CA: Cengage Learning/Wadsworth.

Whitley, B. E., & Kite, M. E. (2010). *The psychology of prejudice and discrimination,* (2nd ed.). Belmont, CA: Cengage Learning/Wadsworth.

Wickwire, E. M., Whelan, J. P., & Meyers, A. W. (2010). Outcome expectancies and gambling behavior among urban adolescents. *Psychology of Addictive Behaviors, 24*(1), 75–88. doi:10.1037/a0017505

Widner R. L., Otani, H., & Winkelman, S. E. (2005). Tip-of-the-tongue experiences are not merely strong feeling-of-knowing experiences. *Journal of General Psychology, 132*(4), 392–407. doi:10.3200/GENP.132.4.392-407

Wiederhold, B. K., & Wiederhold, M. D. (2005). Acrophobia. In B. K. Wiederhold & M. D. Wiederhold (Eds.), *Virtual reality therapy for anxiety disorders: Advances in evaluation and treatment* (pp. 157–164). Washington: American Psychological Association.

Wiederman, M. W. (2001). Gender differences in sexuality: Perceptions, myths, and realities. *Family Journal-Counseling & Therapy for Couples & Families, 9*(4), 468–471.

Wild, B., Rodden, F. A., et al. (2003). Neural correlates of laughter and humour. *Brain: A Journal Of Neurology, 126*(10), 2121–2138. doi:10.1093/brain/awg226

Wilder, D. A., Simon, A. F., & Faith, M. (1996). Enhancing the impact of counterstereotypic information. *Journal of Personality & Social Psychology, 71*(2), 276–287. doi:10.1037/0022-3514.71.2.276

Wilding, J., & Valentine, E. (1994). Memory champions. *British Journal of Psychology, 85*(2), 231–244. doi:10.1111/j.2044-8295.1994.tb02520.x

Wilkinson, D., & Abraham, C. (2004). Constructing an integrated model of the antecedents of adolescent smoking. *British Journal of Health Psychology, 9*(3), 315–333. doi:10.1348/1359107041557075

Wilkinson, D., Ko, P., et al. (2009). Unilateral damage to the right cerebral hemisphere disrupts the apprehension of whole faces and their component parts. *Neuropsychologia, 47*(7), 1701–1711. doi:10.1016/j.neuropsychologia.2009.02.008

Wilkinson, M. (2006). The dreaming mind-brain: A Jungian perspective. *Journal of Analytical Psychology, 51*(1), 43–59. doi:10.1111/j.0021-8774.2006.00571.x

Wilkinson, R. G., & Pickett, K. E. (2006). Income inequality and population health: A review and explanation of the evidence. *Social Science & Medicine,*

62(7), 1768–1784. doi:10.1016/j.socscimed.2005.08.036

Wilkinson, R. G., & Pickett, K. E. (2007). The problems of relative deprivation: Why some societies do better than others. *Social Science & Medicine, 65*(9), 1965–1978. doi:10.1016/j.socscimed.2007.05.041

Wilkinson, R. G., & Pickett, K. E. (2009). Income inequality and social dysfunction. *Annual Review of Sociology, 35*, 493–511. doi:10.1146/annurev-soc-070308-115926

Willander, J., & Larsson, M. (2006). Smell your way back to childhood: Autobiographical odor memory. *Psychonomic Bulletin & Review, 13*(2), 240–244. doi:10.3758/BF03193837

Williams, D. G., & Morris, G. (1996). Crying, weeping or tearfulness in British and Israeli adults. *British Journal of Psychology, 87*(3), 479–505. doi:10.1111/j.2044-8295.1996.tb02603.x

Williams, J. M. (2010). *Applied sport psychology: Personal growth to peak performance* (6th ed.). New York: McGraw-Hill.

Williams, R. (1989). *The trusting heart: Great news about Type A behavior.* New York: Random House.

Williams, R. B., Barefoot, J. C., & Schneiderman, N. (2003). Psychosocial risk factors for cardiovascular disease: More than one culprit at work. *Journal of the American Medical Association, 290*(16), 2190–2192. doi:10.1001/jama.290.16.2190

Williams, R. L., & Eggert, A. (2002). Note-taking predictors of test performance. *Teaching of Psychology, 29*(3), 234–237.

Wilson, S. B., & Kennedy, J. H. (2006). Helping behavior in a rural and an urban setting: Professional and casual attire. *Psychological Reports, 98*(1), 229–233.

Wilson, S. L. (2003). Post-institutionalization: The effects of early deprivation on development of Romanian adoptees. *Child & Adolescent Social Work Journal, 20*(6), 473–483. doi:10.1023/B:CASW.0000003139.14144.06

Wilson, T. D. (2002). *Strangers to ourselves: Discovering the adaptive unconscious.* Cambridge Harvard University Press.

Wilson, T. D. (2009). Know thyself. *Perspectives on Psychological Science, 4*(4), 384–389.

Wimpenny, J. H., Weir, A. A., et al. (2009). Cognitive processes associated with sequential tool use in New Caledonian crows. *PLoS ONE, 4*(8): e6471. doi:10.1371/journal.pone.0006471.

Winfree, L. T. Jr., & Jiang, S. (2010). Youthful suicide and social support: Exploring the social dynamics of suicide-related behavior and

attitudes within a national sample of U.S. adolescents. *Youth Violence & Juvenile Justice, 8*(1), 19–37. doi:10.1177/1541204009338252

Wingood, G.M., DiClemente, R.J., et al. (2003). A prospective study of exposure to rap music videos and African American female adolescents' health. *American Journal of Public Health, 93*, 437–439. doi:10.2105/AJPH.93.3.437

Winkleby, M., Ahn, D., & Cubbin, C. (2006). Effect of cross-level interaction between individual and neighborhood socioeconomic status on adult mortality rates. *American Journal of Public Health, 96*(12), 2145–2153. doi:10.2105/AJPH.2004.060970

Winner, E. (2003). Creativity and talent. In M. H. Bornstein, L. Davidson, C. L. M. Keyes, & K. Moore (Eds.), *Well-being: Positive development across the life course* (pp. 371–380). Mahwah, NJ: Erlbaum.

Winter, D. D., & Koger, S. M. (2010). *The psychology of environmental problems* (3rd ed.). New York: Psychology Press.

Wise, R. A., & Safer, M. A. (2010). A comparison of what U.S. judges and students know and believe about eyewitness testimony. *Journal of Applied Social Psychology, 40*(6), 1400–1422. doi:10.1111/j.1559-1816.2010.00623.x

Wise, R. A., Gong, X., et al. (2010). A comparison of Chinese judges' and US judges' knowledge and beliefs about eyewitness testimony. *Psychology, Crime & Law, 16*(8), 695–713. doi:10.1080/10683160903153893

Wiseman, M., & Davidson, S. (2012). Problems with binary gender discourse: Using context to promote flexibility and connection in gender identity. *Clinical Child Psychology & Psychiatry, 17*(4), 528–537. doi:10.1177/1359104511424991

Wiseman, R., & Watt, C. (2006). Belief in psychic ability and the misattribution hypothesis: A qualitative review. *British Journal of Psychology, 97*(3), 323–338. doi:10.1348/000712605X72523

Witelson, S. F., Kigar, D. L., & Harvey, T. (1999). The exceptional brain of Albert Einstein. *Lancet, 353*, 2149–2153. doi:10.1016/S0140-6736(98)10327-6

Witherington, D. C., Campos, J. J., et al. (2005). Avoidance of heights on the visual cliff in newly walking infants. *Infancy, 7*(3), 285–298. doi:10.1207/s15327078in0703_4

Witkiewitz, K., Villarroel, N., et al. (2011). Drinking outcomes following drink refusal skills training: Differential effects for African American and non-Hispanic White clients. *Psychology of Addictive Behaviors, 25*(1), 162–167. doi:10.1037/a0022254

Witt, C. M., Schützler, L., et al. (2011). Patient characteristics and variation in treatment outcomes: Which patients benefit most from acupuncture for chronic pain? *The Clinical Journal of Pain, 27*(6), 550–555. doi:10.1097/AJP.0b013e31820dfbf5

Wixted, J. T. (2004). The psychology and neuroscience of forgetting. *Annual Review of Psychology, 55*, 235–269. doi:10.1146/annurev.psych.55.090902.141555

Wohl, M. J. A., Pychyl, T. A., & Bennett, S. H. (2010). I forgive myself, now I can study: How self-forgiveness for procrastinating can reduce future procrastination. *Personality & Individual Differences, 48*(7), 803–808. doi:10.1016/j.paid.2010.01.029

Wolpe, J. (1974). *The practice of behavior therapy* (2nd ed.). New York: Pergamon.

Wong, P. T. (2011). Positive psychology 2.0: Towards a balanced interactive model of the good life. *Canadian Psychology, 52*(2), 69–81. doi:10.1177/0022167811408729

Wong, W. (2012). *Essential study skills* (7th ed.). Belmont, CA: Cengage Learning/Wadsworth.

Wood, E., & Willoughby, T. (1995). Cognitive strategies for test-taking. In E. Wood, V. Woloshyn, et al. (Eds.), *Cognitive strategy instruction for middle and high schools* (pp. 5–17). Cambridge, MA: Brookline Books.

Wood, J. M., Nezworski, M. T., et al. (2003). The Rorschach Inkblot test, fortune tellers, and cold reading. *Skeptical Inquirer, 27*(4), 29–33.

Woodruff-Pak, D. S. (2001). Eyeblink classical conditioning differentiates normal aging from Alzheimer's disease. *Integrative Physiological & Behavioral Science, 36*(2), 87–108. doi:10.1007/BF02734044

Woods, A. M., Racine, S. E., & Klump, K. L. (2010). Examining the relationship between dietary restraint and binge eating: Differential effects of major and minor stressors. *Eating Behaviors, 11*(4), 276–280. Doi:10.1016/j.eatbeh.2010.08.001

Woods, S. & West, M. (2010). *The psychology of work and organizations.* Belmont, CA: Cengage Learning/Wadsworth.

Woods, S. C., & Ramsay, D. S. (2011). Food intake, metabolism and homeostasis. *Physiology & Behavior, 104*(1), 4–7. doi:10.1016/j.physbeh.2011.04.026

Wooldridge, T., & Lytle, P. (2012). An overview of anorexia nervosa in males. *Eating Disorders: The Journal of Treatment & Prevention, 20*(5), 368–378. doi:10.1080/10640266.2012.715515

Woollett, K., & Maguire, E. A. (2011). Acquiring "the Knowledge" of London's layout drives structural brain changes. *Current Biology, 21*(24), 2109–2114. doi:10.1016/j.cub.2011.11.018

Workopolis. (2013). Job interviews. Retrieved May 28, 2013, from http://www.workopolis.com/content/advice/Interviews

World Health Organization (2011). *WHO report on the global tobacco epidemic, 2011: Warning about the dangers of tobacco.* Retrieved June 9, 2013 from http://www.who.int/tobacco/global_report/2011/en/index.html

World Health Organization (2013). *Poverty.* Retrieved April 21, 2013, from http://www.who.int/topics/poverty/en/

Worthen, J. B., & Hunt, R. R. (2010). *Mnemonology: Mnemonics for the 21st century.* Hove, UK: Psychology Press.

Wouters, S., Germeijs, V., et al. (2011). Academic self-concept in high school: Predictors and effects on adjustment in higher education. *Scandinavian Journal Of Psychology, 52*(6), 586–594. doi:10.1111/j.1467-9450.2011.00905.x

Wraga, M. J., Boyle, H. K., & Flynn, C. M. (2010). Role of motor processes in extrinsically encoding mental transformations. *Brain & Cognition, 74*(3), 193–202. doi:10.1016/j.bandc.2010.07.005

Wright, J. P., Dietrich, K. N., et al. (2008). Association of prenatal and childhood blood lead concentrations with criminal arrests in early adulthood. *Proceedings of the National Academy of Sciences, 5*(5), e101. doi:10.1371/journal.pmed.0050101

Wright, K. R., Bogan, R. K., & Wyatt, J. K. (2013). Shift work and the assessment and management of shift work disorder (SWD). *Sleep Medicine Reviews, 17*(1), 41–54. doi:10.1016/j.smrv.2012.02.002

Wright, P. B., & Erdal, K. J. (2008). Sport superstition as a function of skill level and task difficulty. *Journal of Sport Behavior, 31*(2), 187–199.

Wright, T. A., & Bonett, D. G. (2007). Job satisfaction and psychological well-being as nonadditive predictors of workplace turnover. *Journal of Management, 33*(2), 141–160.

Wrightsman, L. S., & Fulero, S. M. (2009). *Forensic psychology* (3rd ed.). Belmont, CA: Cengage Learning/Wadsworth.

Wyatt, J. W., Posey, A., et al. (1984). Natural levels of similarities between identical twins and between unrelated people. *The Skeptical Inquirer, 9*, 62–66.

Xu, T.-X., & Yao, W.-D. (2010). D1 and D2 dopamine receptors in separate circuits cooperate to drive associative long-term potentiation in the prefrontal cortex. Proceedings of the National Academy of Sciences, *107*(37), 16366–16371. doi:10.1073/pnas.1004108107

Yahnke, B. H., Sheikh, A. A., & Beckman, H. T. (2003). Imagery and the treatment of phobic disorders. In A. A. Sheikh (Ed.), *Healing images:*

The role of imagination in health (pp. 312–342). Amityville, NY: Baywood Publishing.

Yamamoto, N., & Philbeck, J. W. (2013). Peripheral vision benefits spatial learning by guiding eye movements. *Memory & Cognition, 41*(1), 109–121. doi:10.3758/s13421-012-0240-2

Yanchar, S. C., Slife, B. D., & Warne, R. (2008). Critical thinking as disciplinary practice. *Review of General Psychology, 12*(3), 265–281. doi:10.1037/1089-2680.12.3.265

Yang, S., & Zheng, L. (2011). The paradox of de-coupling: A study of flexible work program and workers' productivity. *Social Science Research, 40*(1), 299–311.

Yang, Y., Tang, L., et al. (2009). Silkworms culture as a source of protein for humans in space. *Advances in Space Research, 43*(2), 1236–1242. doi:10.1016/j.asr.2008.12.009

Yapko, M. D. (2011). *Mindfulness and hypnosis: The power of suggestion to transform experience.* New York: Norton.

Yarmey, D. (2010). *Eyewitness testimony.* In J. M. Brown, & E. A. Campbell (Eds.), *The Cambridge handbook of forensic psychology* (pp. 177–186). New York: Cambridge University Press.

Yedidia, M. J., & MacGregor, B. (2001). Confronting the prospect of dying. *Journal of Pain & Symptom Management, 22*(4), 807–819. doi:10.1016/S0885-3924(01)00325-6

Yeh, C. J. (2003). Age, acculturation, cultural adjustment, and mental health symptoms of Chinese, Korean, and Japanese immigrant youths. *Cultural Diversity & Ethnic Minority Psychology, 9*(1), 34–48. doi:10.1037/1099-9809.9.1.34

Yi, H., & Qian, X. (2009). A review on neurocognitive research in superior memory. *Psychological Science (China), 32*(3), 643–645.

Yiend, J. (2010). The effects of emotion on attention: A review of attentional processing of emotional information. *Cognition & Emotion, 24*(1), 3–47. doi:10.1080/02699930903205698

Yip, P. S., & Thorburn, J. (2004). Marital status and the risk of suicide: Experience from England and Wales, 1982–1996. *Psychological Reports, 94*(2), 401–407. doi:10.2466/PR0.94.2.401-407

Yokota, F., & Thompson, K. M. (2000). Violence in G-rated animated films. *Journal of the American Medical Association, 283*(20), 2716. doi:10.1001/jama.283.20.2716

Yonas, A., Elieff, C. A., & Arterberry, M. E. (2002). Emergence of sensitivity to pictorial depth cues: Charting development in individual infants. *Infant Behavior & Development, 25*(4), 495–514. doi:10.1016/S0163-6383(02)00147-9

Yontef, G. (2007). The power of the immediate moment in gestalt therapy. *Journal of Contemporary Psychotherapy, 37*(1), 17–23. doi:10.1007/s10879-006-9030-0

Yoon, J., & Bruckner, T. A. (2009). Does deinstitutionalization increase suicide? *Health Services Research, 44*(4), 1385–1405. doi:10.1111/j.1475-6773.2009.00986.x

Yoonessi, A., & Baker, C. L. (2011). Contribution of motion parallax to segmentation and depth perception. *Journal of Vision, 11*(9). doi:10.1167/11.9.13

Young, A. A. (2012). Brainstem sensing of meal-related signals in energy homeostasis. *Neuropharmacology, 63*(1), 31–45. doi:10.1016/j.neuropharm.2012.03.019

Young, R. (2005). Neurobiology of savant syndrome. In C. Stough (Ed.), *Neurobiology of exceptionality* (pp. 199–215). New York: Kluwer Academic Publishers.

Young, S. M., & Pinsky, D. (2006). Narcissism and celebrity. *Journal of Research in Personality, 40*(5), 463–471. doi:10.1016/j.jrp.2006.05.005

Yuille, J. C., & Daylen, J. (1998). The impact of traumatic events on eyewitness memory. In C. Thompson, D. Herrmann, et al. (Eds.), *Eyewitness memory: Theoretical and applied perspectives* (pp. 155–178). Mahwah, NJ: Erlbaum.

Zachariae, R. (2009). Psychoneuroimmunology: A bio-psycho-social approach to health and disease. *Scandinavian Journal of Psychology, 50*(6), 645–651. doi:10.1111/j.1467-9450.2009.00779.x

Zaidi, Z. F. (2010). Gender differences in human brain: A review. *Open Anatomy Journal, 2*, 37–55. doi:10.2174/1877609401002010037

Zampetakis, L. A., & Moustakis, V. (2011). Managers' trait emotional intelligence and group outcomes: The case of group job satisfaction. *Small Group Research, 42*(1), 77–102. doi:10.1177/1046496410373627

Zarcadoolas, C., Pleasant, A., & Greer, D. S. (2006). *Advancing health literacy: A framework for understanding and action.* San Francisco: Jossey-Bass.

Zeidan, F., Johnson, S. K., et al. (2010). Effects of brief and sham mindfulness meditation on mood and cardiovascular variables. *Journal of Alternative & Complementary Medicine, 16*(8), 867–873. doi:10.1089/acm.2009.0321

Zeiler, K., & Wickström, A. (2009). Why do 'we' perform surgery on newborn intersexed children? The phenomenology of the parental experience of having a child with intersex anatomies. *Feminist Theory, 10*(3), 359–377.

Zeisel, J. (2006). *Inquiry by design: Environment/behavior/neuroscience in* architecture, interiors, landscape, and planning. New York: Norton.

Zellner, D. A., Harner, D. E., & Adler, R. L. (1989). Effects of eating abnormalities and gender on perceptions of desirable body shape. *Journal of Abnormal Psychology, 98*(1), 93–96. doi:10.1037/0021-843X.98.1.93

Zemishlany, Z., Aizenberg, D., & Weizman, A. (2001). Subjective effects of MDMA ("Ecstasy") on human sexual function. *European Psychiatry, 16*(2), 127–130. doi:10.1016/S0924-9338(01)00550-8

Zentall, T. R. (2002). A cognitive behaviorist approach to the study of animal behavior. *Journal of General Psychology. Special Issue: Animal Behavior, 129*(4), 328–363.

Zentall, T. R. (2010). Coding of stimuli by animals: Retrospection, prospection, episodic memory and future planning. *Learning & Motivation, 41*(4), 225–240. doi:10.1016/j.lmot.2010.08.001

Zentall, T. R. (2011). Perspectives on observational learning in animals. *Journal of Comparative Psychology, 126*(2), 114–128. doi:10.1037/a0025381

Zhang R. L., Zhang Z. G., & Chopp, M. (2005). Neurogenesis in the adult ischemic brain: generation, migration, survival, and restorative therapy. *Neuroscientist, 11*(5), 408–416. doi:10.1177/1073858405278865

Zhang, B., Hao, Y. L., et al. (2010). Fatal familial insomnia: A middle-age-onset Chinese family kindred. *Sleep Medicine, 11*(5), 498–499. doi:10.1016/j.sleep.2009.11.005

Ziegler, M., Dietl, E., et al. (2011). Predicting training success with general mental ability, specific ability tests, and (un)structured interviews: A meta-analysis with unique samples. *International Journal of Selection & Assessment, 19*(2), 170–182. doi:10.1111/j.1468-2389.2011.00544.x

Zietsch, B. P., Verweij, K. H., et al. (2012). Do shared etiological factors contribute to the relationship between sexual orientation and depression? *Psychological Medicine, 42*(3), 521–532. doi:10.1017/S0033291711001577

Zimbardo, P. G. (2007). *The Lucifer Effect: Understanding how good people turn evil.* New York: Random House.

Zimbardo, P. G., Haney, C., & Banks, W. C. (1973). A Pirandellian prison. *The New York Times Magazine,* April 8.

Zimmer, C. (2010). 100 trillion connections: New efforts probe and map the brain's detailed architecture. *Scientific American, December,* 58–63.

Ziv, I., Leiser, D., & Levine, J. (2011). Social cognition in schizophrenia: Cognitive and affective factors. *Cognitive Neuropsychiatry, 16*(1), 71–91. doi:10.1080/13546805.2010.492693

Zoccola, P. M., Green, M. C., et al. (2011). The embarrassed bystander: Embarrassability and the inhibition of helping. *Personality & Individual Differences, 51*(8), 925–929. doi:10.1016/j.paid.2011.07.026

Name Index

Subject Index/Glossary

Ablation (ab-LAY-shun), 69. Surgical removal of tissue.

Abnormalities, statistical, 512–514

Abscissa, 683

Absolute poverty, 480

Absolute threshold, 138. The minimum amount of physical energy necessary to produce a sensation.

Abuse
of alcohol, 217–218
of amphetamines, 212
of barbiturates, 217
of caffeine, 214
of cocaine, 213
of drugs, 208–211
of GHB, 216
of marijuana, 220
of MDMA, 213
of nicotine, 214
of tranquilizers, 217

Academic ability, 636

Accessibility (in memory), 277. Memories currently stored in memory that can be retrieved when necessary are both available and accessible.

Accommodation, 116, 144, 170. In Piaget's theory, the modification of existing mental patterns to fit new demands (that is, mental schemes are changed to accommodate new information or experiences).

Acculturative stress, 485. Stress caused by the many changes and adaptations required when a person moves to a foreign culture.

Acetylcholine (ah-SEET-ul-KOH-leen), 62

Achieved roles, 600

Achievement, 369

Acquaintance (date) rape, 411–412. Forced intercourse that occurs in the context of a date or other voluntary encounter.

Acquired immune deficiency syndrome (AIDS), 416

Acquired strategies, 320

Acquisition, 238. The period in conditioning during which a response is reinforced.

Acromegaly (AK-row-MEG-uh-lee), 87

Acrophobia, 542

Action potential, 59–61, 63. A nerve impulse.

Activating experience, 573

Activation-synthesis hypothesis, 204. An attempt to explain how dream content is affected by motor commands in the brain that occur during sleep but are not carried out.

Active listening, 5, 594

Actively psychotic, 528

Actor–observer bias, 603. The tendency to attribute the behavior of others to internal causes while attributing one's own behavior to external causes (situations and circumstances).

Actors, 603

Acupuncture, 157–158

Acute stress disorder, 544. A psychological disturbance lasting up to one month

following stresses that would produce anxiety in anyone who experienced them.

Adams, Marilyn, 283

Adamson, Kate, 84

Adaptation/adaptability, 399
dark, 148
sensory, 138–139

Adaptive behaviors, 335, 354, 382. Actions that aid attempts to survive and adapt to changing conditions.

Adderall, 212

Addiction, to nicotine, 214

Additive bilingualism, 312

Adjustment disorder, 544. Emotional disturbance caused by ongoing stressors within the range of common experience.

Adler, Alfred, 28

Adolescence, 126–127. The culturally defined period between childhood and adulthood.
to adulthood, emerging into, 127
developmental milestones during, 124–125
human development during, 126–127
identity formation during, 126–127
puberty and, 126

Adolescents
drugs, use of, 208–209
identity of, 125–127
maturation of, 127
media violence, affect on, 633
sexual intercourse by, 409–410

Adrenal cortex, 88

Adrenal glands, 86–88. Endocrine glands that arouse the body, regulate salt balance, adjust the body to stress, and affect sexual functioning.

Adrenaline, 87, 354. *See also* **Epinephrine** (ep-eh-NEF-rin)

Adrenal medulla, 88

Adults/adulthood
adolescence to, emerging into, 127
aging during, 130–131
challenges of, 129–130
deprivation, affect on, 102
developmental milestones during, 125
emerging, 127
late, 129–131
marriage, criterion for, 126
maturation and, 127
middle, 129–131

Advertising, 605–606

Advice, avoid giving, 594–595

Aerial perspective, 171

Affectional needs, 105. Emotional needs for love and affection.

Affiliation, 621–623

African-Americans, 110, 341

Afterimages, 146

Age
happiness and, 135
hypnosis and regression of, 190
mental, 332
personality trait, of established, 463
suicide, factors affecting rates of, 554

Ageism, 131, 633. Discrimination or prejudice based on a person's age. *See also* **Prejudice**

Agentic leaders, 648

Aggression, 486, 618. Any response made with the intent of causing harm.
antisocial behavior and, 630–633
biological basis for, 631
causes of, 631–633
displaced, 486, 634
electronic, 632
frustration and, 486, 631–632
instincts for, 631
preventing, 633
punishment and, 257–258
social learning and, 632–633
at work, 651

Aging
during adulthood, 130–131
ageism and, 131
conflicts of, 125
sex drive, affect on, 405
sleep and, 196
successful, keys to, 130–131

Agnosia, 79–80

Agoraphobia (ah-go-rah-FOBE-ee-ah), 541–542. The fear that something extremely embarrassing will happen if one leaves the house or enters an unfamiliar situation.

Agreeableness, 440, 444, 445

Ainsworth, Mary, 106

Alarm reaction, 476. First stage of the GAS, during which bodily resources are mobilized to cope with a stressor.

Alcohol, 217–219. *See also* Drinking
abuse of, 217–218
children, risks for, 218
drinking, 218–219
effects of, 217
infants, affects on, 100
sex drive, affect on, 405

Alcoholics Anonymous (AA), 219, 562

Alcohol myopia (my-OH-pea-ah), 217

Alda, Alan, 288

Alexithymia (a-LEXih-THIGH-me-ah), 377. A learned difficulty expressing emotions; more common in men.

Algorithm, 316. A learned set of rules that always leads to the correct solution of a problem.

Alienation, 626

All-or-nothing action potential, 60, 63

All-or-nothing thinking, 310, 572. Classifying objects or events as absolutely right or wrong, good or bad, acceptable or unacceptable, and so forth.

Allport, Gordon, 634

Allport-Vernon Study of Values, 435

Alpha waves, 196. Large, slow brain waves associated with relaxation and falling asleep.

Altered state of consciousness (ASC), 187. A condition of awareness distinctly different in quality or pattern from waking consciousness.

Altering consciousness, 186

Alternative responses, 262

Alzheimer's disease (ALLS-hi-merz), 285, 515, 526. An age-related disease characterized by memory loss, mental confusion, and, in its later stages, a nearly total loss of mental abilities.

Amazing Race, The, 434

Ambady, Nalini, 326

Ambidexterity, 92

Ambiguous stimuli, 166

Ambivalence, 489

Ambivalent attachment, 107

American Association for Marriage and Family Therapy, 596

American Family Therapy Academy, 596

American Idol, 434

American Psychiatric Association, 335, 411, 424, 596

American Psychological Association (APA), 9–10, 22, 33, 596, 694–696

American Sign Language (ASL), 313

Ames room, 162

Amnesia, 190, 289, 544

Amok, 519

Amp, 212

Amphetamine, 212–213, 405, 531

Amphetamine psychosis, 212

Amplitude, 150–151

Amygdala (ah-MIG-duh-la), 85, 375. A part of the limbic system (within the brain) that produces fear responses.

Amyl nitrite, 405

Anagrams test, 323

Anal-expulsive personality, 448. The disorderly, destructive, cruel, or messy person.

Analogies, for problem solving, 346

Anal-retentive personality, 448. A person who is obstinate, stingy, or compulsive and who generally has difficulty "letting go."

Anal stage, 448, 451. The psychosexual stage corresponding roughly to the period of toilet training (ages 1 to 3).

Analysis
in cerebral hemispheres, 76
factor, 442
job, 652
resistance, 569
sensory, 139
task, 672
transference, 569

Analytic intelligence, 341

Anarchia, 521

Androgen, 86, 88, 366, 388. Any of a number of male sex hormones, especially testosterone.

Androgen insensitivity syndrome, 388

Androgyny (an-DROJ-ih-nee), 398–400. The presence of both "masculine" and "feminine" traits in a single person (as masculinity and femininity are defined with one's culture).

Angel dust, 219